1 MONTH OF
FREE
READING

at

www.ForgottenBooks.com

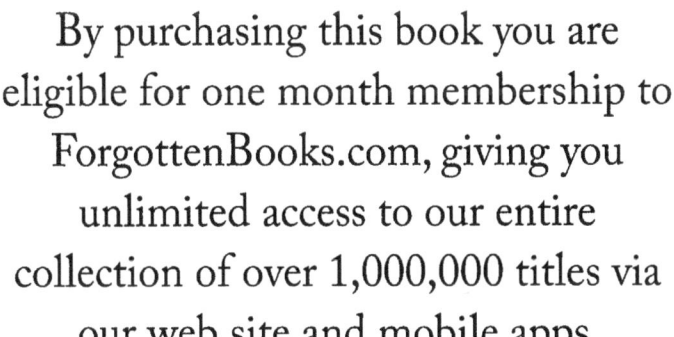

By purchasing this book you are eligible for one month membership to ForgottenBooks.com, giving you unlimited access to our entire collection of over 1,000,000 titles via our web site and mobile apps.

To claim your free month visit:

www.forgottenbooks.com/free933117

ISBN 978-0-260-18679-9
PIBN 10933117

This book is a reproduction of an important historical work. Forgotten Books uses
state-of-the-art technology to digitally reconstruct the work, preserving the original format
whilst repairing imperfections present in the aged copy. In rare cases, an imperfection in
the original, such as a blemish or missing page, may be replicated in our edition. We do,
however, repair the vast majority of imperfections successfully; any imperfections that
remain are intentionally left to preserve the state of such historical works.

OREGON

TEACHERS

MONTHLY

OFFICIAL ORGAN OF STATE TEACHERS' ASSOCIATION

Reorganization of State Teachers' Association
By E. D. RESSLER

Professional Standards
By J. H. ACKERMAN

The High School Library
By E. F. CARLETON

Grade Teachers' Associations
By VIOLA ORTSCHILD

The National Education Association
By L. R. ALDERMAN

Vol. 21   SEPTEMBER 1916   No. 1

CONTENTS

OREGON TEACHERS MONTHLY

The Official Journal of the State Teachers' Association

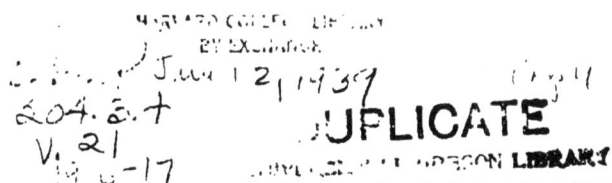

Vol. XXI	SALEM, OREGON, SEPTEMBER, 1916	No. 1

Published Monthly Except July and August by the State Teachers' Association

Entered at the Postoffice at Salem, Oregon, as second-class mail matter, April 1, 1898.

RULES OF PUBLICATION

1. The mailing label on the Oregon Teachers Monthly shows the date to which subscriptions are paid.
2. The Oregon Teachers Monthly will be sent to subscribers until ordered discontinued and all arrearages are paid.
3. Notice of change of address should be given at once, naming both old and new postoffice.
4. When renewing, always state that subscription is a renewal.
5. The subscription price, including membership in State Teachers' Association, is $1.50 a year in advance. Single copy, 20 cents.
6. Advertising rates will be furnished on application.

Address all communications to Oregon Teachers Monthly, Salem, Oregon.

Editorial Notes

The publication of the present issue of the Oregon Teachers Monthly under the direct auspices of the State Teachers' Association means that this journal is going to concentrate its fire on the improvement of the teacher's condition. Better hygienic conditions, better training, better salaries, improved conditions of tenure, these are means by which more effective education for the children of Oregon can be promoted. "As is the teacher, so is the school." Happy, contented, well-trained teachers mean efficiency in education.

† † †

The success of the reorganized teachers' association depends almost entirely on the activity of its local units. We have some vigorous teachers' associations in the city of Portland and among the superintendents and principals of six or eight counties. These are not sufficient as a basis for a vigorous organization. The high school teachers should organize, likewise the rural teachers and the elementary teachers outside of Portland. There should be more principals' clubs. In these local organizations, it will be possible to discuss the questions which are to be before the Representative Council.

Each locality can be intelligently represented in the yearly meeting. Then after the council meeting, the local teachers' bodies can lend all the momentum of their interest to putting through a constructive program.

† † †

"Why are there two hundred applicants for a vacancy worth between $500 and $1000 and only ten or less for one worth from $1500 to $2000?" is a question frequently asked of teachers. You do not find this "positional unrest" among the established professions and probably would not find it among teachers were it not for insecure tenure, low salaries and lack of professional preparation and standards. Referring only to the first of these causes, it is very significant that the National Educational Association at its recent meeting in New York should have considered it of enough national importance to make it the subject of one of its five resolutions. After advocating more thorough supervision and higher and more definite professional qualifications for supervisors, the following resolution was adopted: "(2) The tenure of office of teachers should after a probationary period be permanent. Removal should be possible only for inefficiency, immorality or grievous neglect of duty. Salaries should be fixed so as to insure to teachers a standard of living in keeping with the professional demands made upon them. Retiring allowances or pensions should be provided either by state or local action." Never will the "yearly migratory habit," especially among teachers outside of the larger cities, be broken until a stronger sentiment in favor of continued tenure can be built up among the teachers themselves. They must realize that to profitably stay longer than a year in any place they must grow, and that for the growing teacher the longer she stays the greater opportunity for service. Think this matter over, talk it over with other teachers, with business men, and with parents, and if you believe it, act on it yourself.

† † †

One of the needed reforms which must be brought about by education of teachers and patrons, and one which many consider a delicate one to discuss, is that of increased salaries. This is generally considered a fundamental necessity to the professionalizing of teaching, to the securing of tenure, and to the realizing of teaching's opportunities. Many would say, "Is that not a mercenary basis?" "Where is the satisfaction which comes from service and which figures so strongly in the reward of teachers?" To the first question we answer "No," and to the second, "that satisfaction will ever be one of the principal rewards of teachers, enhanced by better salaries." Most teachers have been reticent about discussing the monetary value of their services, but when buying any marketable product they are accustomed to having the vender set the price—why should not teachers have something to say in placing a price on their services, for not until they value them higher will salaries be increased. Furthermore, the matter need not be embarrassing because the increased salary is not sought in order to upset the markets or bring competitive inconveniences upon any of the moneyed kings of industry, but rather to enable teachers to live better, to buy more books and periodicals, to attend more places of professional advancement, to travel, to have unworried vacations, in short, to teach better and thereby serve better. A general advance in salaries will never be obtained until we unite as a body and professionally outcast the teacher who underbids—regardless of any apparently extenuating circumstances such as boarding at home, etc.; until we unite in advancing the professional requirements and in eliminating the unprepared and the untrained, and until we unite in demanding salaries commensurate with preparation required and services rendered. This is a matter where public sentiment must be created before results can be hoped for and is therefore a matter in which you can help.

† ı ı .

The reorganization of the California Teachers' Association as recorded by A. H. Chamberlain in the June issue of the Sierra Educational News is an interesting example of a movement, felt in our own state a year ago, and which is really nation-wide—a movement toward the closer union of teachers and all organizations of teachers. Present-day conditions, both political and economic, are so highly organized that reforms are obtained, in practically all cases, only by the strength obtained from numbers. Teachers have been about the last people to realize this but now, however, are intelligently interested in it. This interest need not be, should not be, for selfish purposes, but rather for the betterment of education, and effective work can be done in many ways where there is some semblance of unity among the teachers concerned. In one matter of legislation for example, if some special interest (stock raising, fishing, horticulture, lumber, etc.) is involved, everyone expects those immediately affected to be interested, and not only interested but active either in support of or opposition to the proposed law. Is this so with educational legislation or does the brunt of all of that fall upon the very few? How many teachers are "too busy" to inform themselves about the things they are most vitally interested in? How many are thoroughly conversant with the laws pertaining to education passed by the last legislature and those which the State Department desires to have passed at the next? How many have put forth any effort toward having the length of the school year increased, toward securing a wider application of the supervisor law, toward the standardization of high schools and their public support? How many have thoroughly investigated the County Unit Plan of school organization and the advisability of applying it to Oregon? Let us make the closer organization of Oregon's teachers in the new State Teachers' Association stand for something—stand for united effort for progress.

Reorganization of the Western Division Oregon State Teachers' Association

By E. D. RESSLER, Secretary

THE NEW CONSTITUTION

At the 1914 session of the Western Division of the Oregon State Teachers' Association, held at Eugene, December 27-29, a committee was appointed to report on a reorganization of the association at the 1915 meeting. This committee prepared its report and the proposed constitution was printed in the December, 1915, issue of the Oregon Teachers Monthly. The report of the committee was presented to the association on the afternoon of the first day of the 1915 meeting of the association, held at Medford, December 27-29. After full deliberation, in which many points were discussed and a number of changes ordered, the constitution as amended was unanimously adopted. This constitution was printed in full in the February, 1916, number of the Oregon Teachers Monthly.

The purpose of this article is to call attention to a number of the more significant provisions of this new constitution. Article III states that "any person actively engaged in any branch of educational work, including those who are preparing for the same, may become active members of this association upon the payment of annual dues." Article IV enumerates the officers: President, one vice president, a secretary-treasurer, and an executive committee of eight members, including in addition to the above, the retiring president and four elective members, two of whom shall be chosen each year. Any member is eligible to office. Nominations are made by a body styled the Representative Council, but any member of the association is privileged to make other nominations from the floor. The officers of the association are also the officers of the Representative Council.

This council is one of the unique features of the new organization. The constitution vests the active direction of the association in this body and provides for its annual session one day before the general association or any of its departments are convened. Its meetings, however, are open to all members of the association and to the general public. The membership of the council is constituted as follows: (a) One representative from each county, regardless of the number of teachers, but one additional representative for each major fraction of one hundred teachers above the first hundred; (b) one representative from each "regular association of teachers having more than fifteen members and holding at least three meetings each year"; (c) one representative from "each chartered college, university and normal school," and "such other educational institutions, including scientific associations, as the representative council shall see fit to include in the list"; (d) one representative from each county or state organization of school officers, consisting of "not less than fifteen members and having at least one regular meeting each year."

Sections 5 and 6 of Article VIII read as follows: (5) The main functions of the representative council shall be (a) to conduct investigations aiming to promote the general progress of education; (b) to improve the financial condition, the tenure and general conditions of the teacher's work; and (c) such other aims as the council may determine. (6) The representative council shall establish permanent committees on legislation and on investigation of educational problems in addition to special committees on such topics as the administration of rural schools, teachers' pensions, provision for civic education, etc. Any member of the association may be appointed to serve on special or permanent committees without regard to his or her membership in the council, but the chairman of each committee shall be a member of the council.

Article X provides that the annual meeting "shall be held in the city of Portland at a time determined by the executive committee." It is thought that this may lead to an amalgamation of the Eastern and Western Divisions of the State Teachers' Association, as well as insure the largest membership or at least the largest attendance on the annual meetings. Article XII reads: "The annual membership dues of all members shall be one ($1.00) dollar, and in case an official journal is published dues shall not exceed one ($1.50) dollar and fifty cents, which amount shall include subscription to the journal." As will be noted in the minutes of the executive committee, the Oregon Teachers Monthly has been made the "official journal" and the membership fee placed at $1.50.

The foregoing gives the essential features of the new constitution. The establishment of the representative council, sufficiently large and "representative," yet small enough to make membership prized and insure a working body, is the chief achievement of the reorganization. A definite program of investigation, continuous through the permanent committees and flexible through the special committees, makes possible some genuine constructive contributions to the progress of education and the profession of teaching in Oregon. It is hoped that the privilege of representation through associations of teachers and school officers in the counties, towns and cities, will lead to the formation of many such. These organizations will offer a means of expression of the experience of the membership and a splendid training for the delegates sent to the representative council. The effectiveness of this body depends upon its personnel.

A powerful teachers' association means increased power and prestige for each individual teacher. From a purely selfish standpoint, no teacher, even one only temporarily engaged in the work of teaching, can afford to withhold his support. The motto of each county should be, "every teacher in the county a member of the teachers' association." Surely every real teacher, with professional instincts, will wish to add his help and influence in the movement to raise the standard of education in Oregon for the sake of better schools and better opportunities for the boys and girls of the next generation.

MINUTES OF MEETING OF EXECUTIVE COMMITTEE
First Session

Pursuant to the call of the chairman, E. F. Carleton, the Executive Committee of the Western Division of the Oregon State Teachers' Association held its first meeting in the office of the State Superintendent of Public Instruction, in Salem, February 5, 1916. The chairman called the meeting to order at 11:20 a. m. with the following members present: E. F. Carleton, Assistant State Superintendent of Public Instruction, Salem; Geo. A. Briscoe, City Superintendent of Schools, Ashland; Viola Citschild, president Grade Teachers' Association, Portland; H. D. Sheldon, dean School of Education, University of Oregon; O. M. Elliott, City Superintendent of Schools, Salem; J. Percy Wells, County Superintendent of Schools, Jacksonville. H. H. Herdman, principal Washington High School, Portland, was absent. The ex-officio members are Retiring President of the Association, H. H. Herdman; President-Elect, E. F. Carleton; Vice President, Geo. A. Briscoe. J. A. Churchill, State Superintendent of Public Instruction, W. M. Smith, County School Superintendent of Marion county, retiring secretary of the association, and E. D. Ressler, professor of Industrial Education, Oregon Agricultural College, acting secretary of the Association, were also present on invitation of the chairman.

E. D. Ressler was appointed to act as secretary until the election of a secretary-treasurer as provided by the constitution. The chairman stated the object of the meeting to be the election of a secretary-treasurer, the consideration of the matter of an official publication of the Teachers' Association, the appointment of special committees to report at the next annual meeting of the State Association on investigations of certain educational problems, and such other business as would appear. After some discussion, it was agreed to defer the election of a secretary-treasurer until a report had been made on the matter of an official publication. On motion of Mr. Sheldon, the chair was directed to appoint a sub-committee of three members of the Executive Committee, including the chair, to ascertain from the publisher of the Oregon Teachers Monthly upon what terms the Association can acquire the use of the publication as the official organ. The committee will receive instructions from the Executive Committee and is ordered to report the result of the negotiations to the Executive Committee at a meeting to be called by the chairman.

The committee took a recess at 12:15 for luncheon at the Hotel Marion, where discussion of Mr. Sheldon's motion was continued. The following instructions were given the sub-committee: (1) The Association must have editorial control, management of the policy and make-up of the publication, including size, form, number of pages of reading matter, etc. (2) To secure improvement in quality of paper, form of publication, etc., and to include 50c membership fee for the Association, the subscription price may be raised to $1.50. It was the sense of the committee that the membership fee of all subscriptions, including those outside the state, should be paid the Association. The motion to appoint the sub-committee was put and carried. The chair appointed Messrs. Sheldon and Elliott, to act with himself.

In accordance with a provision of the constitution, the chair announced the appointment of Miss V. Ortschild and Messrs. Wells and Elliott to serve as a finance committee. Bill of Medford Printing Company for a four-page folder, ordered by the Medford High School for use at the State Association meeting, was allowed, the amount being $6.25. On motion of Mr. Briscoe, the time of the next annual meeting of the Association was fixed for December 27, 28, 29; the dates are not to be announced until approved by City Superintendent L. R. Alderman of Portland.

After presentation of the votes of about thirty members of the Representative Council at a meeting held in Medford December 28, 1915, in connection with the State Association meeting, on topics for investigation by special committees, on motion of Dr. Sheldon, the chair was directed to appoint a committee of nine, including the chairman, to be designated by the chair, to report to the Representative Council at its next annual meeting on the problem of "Teachers' Retirement Fund and Tenure of Office." On motion of Mr. Elliott, the chair was directed to appoint a similar committee to report on the problem of "Retardation."

The committee returned to the State Superintendent's Office and resumed business. On motion of Dr. Sheldon, the chair was authorized to apportion the sum of $25 for the necessary expenses of the two committees on investigation of educational problems. On motion of Dr. Sheldon, the expenses of the members in attending meetings of the Executive Committee were authorized. Bills were submitted as follows: V. Ortschild, $2.50; Geo. A. Briscoe, $19.65; J. Percy Wells, $21.95. On motion of Dr. Sheldon, the secretary was directed to prepare a summary of the meeting of the Association at Medford, December 27, 28, 29, 1915, including the general sessions and department meetings, for publication in a bulletin to be issued by the State Superintendent.

The Executive Committee adjourned at 3:00 p. m. to meet at the call of the chairman.

Second Session.

Pursuant to the call of the chairman, the Executive Committee of the Oregon Teachers' Association, Western Section, held its second session at the office of State Superintendent Churchill Saturday, April 1. The members present were: J. Percy Wells, Viola Ortschild, H. D. Sheldon, E. F. Carleton and O. M. Elliott. Those absent were: G. A. Briscoe and H. H. Herdman.

The action of President Carleton in securing a protest in the name of this Association to the Congressional Committee against changing the amount of money to be received from the sale of lands under the Oregon-California Land Grant from 40 per cent to 10 per cent was approved.

The proposed contract with the Oregon Teachers Monthly was

the special order of business. The committee expressed a desire to have the contract continue for three years if such arrangement could be made.

The chairman of the Executive Committee was authorized to complete the negotiations with the Oregon Teachers Monthly and to present the contracts to the various members for signatures as soon as all matters had been finally settled and completed.

It was moved by Dr. Sheldon and seconded by Superintendent Wells that the chairman of the Executive Committee be authorized to appoint an editorial board of eleven members representing the various educational interests of the state to control the editorial policy of the Oregon Teachers Monthly as the official paper of the State Teachers' Association, the expenses of members in attending meetings to be paid out of Association funds.

The president and secretary of the Association were authorized to urge a change in the organization of the National Education Association, making it a federated, representative body controlled and directed by the various State Teachers' Associations. The committee was requested especially to propose a reform in the method of selecting the present.

Bills for traveling expenses were submitted as follows: V. Ortschild, $2.50; J. Percy Wells, $22.10.

APPOINTMENTS BY CHAIRMAN OF EXECUTIVE COMMITTEE.

In accordance with the action of the Executive Committee, Chairman Carleton appointed the Editorial Board of the Oregon Teachers Monthly as follows: Dr. H. D. Sheldon, dean of the School of Education, University of Oregon; Prof. E. D. Ressler, head of the Department of Education, Oregon Agicultural College; Prof. E. S. Evenden, head of the Department of Education, Oregon Normal School; Dr. C. G. Doney, president of Willamette University, representing the Independent Colleges; Miss Viola Ortschild, president Grade Teachers' Association, representing the Grade Teachers; Principal Hopkin Jenkins, Jefferson High School, Portland, prepresenting the High School Teachers; City Superintendent George W. Hug, McMinnville, representing the City Superintendents; County Superintendent C. T. Bonney, Wasco County, representing the County Superintendents; Mrs. M. L. Fulkerson, Institute Instructor, Salem, representing the Rural Teachers; Mr. R. E. Chloupek, director of Manual Training, Pendleton, representing the Vocational Teachers; Miss Lillian Tingle, director Domestic Science, Portland, representing the Home Economics Teachers.

The commitee on Teachers' Retirement Fund and Tenure of Office was appointed as follows: Dr. W. T. Foster, president of Reed Institute, chairman; Mrs. A. E. Ivanhoe, superintendent of Union County; Mr. O. C. Brown, superintendent of Douglas County; Mr. J. A. Churchill, State Superintendent of Public Instruction; Mr. E. F Carleton, Assistant State Superintendent; Miss Viola Ortschild, president

Portland Grade Teachers' Association; Dr. J. H. Ackerman, president Oregon Normal School; Mr. J. G. Imel, city superintendent Astoria; Miss Fay Clark, superintendent of Malheur County; Miss Winifred Dennis, teacher Sellwood School, Portland.

The following committee on Retardation was· appointed: Supt. C. W. Boetticher, Albany, chairman; Supt. C. A. Howard, Coquille; Supt.· V. Meldo Hillis, Medford; Supt. F. Thordarson, Bend; Asst. Supt. C. A. Rice, Portland; Supt. I. B. Warner, The Dalles; Asst. Prof. F. L. Stetson, University of Oregon; Prin. C. R. Bowman, Klamath County High School; Supt. H. H. Hoffman, Heppner.

President Foster, chairman of the Committee on Teachers' Retirement Fund and Tenure of Office, submits the following statement of the first meeting of the committee:

"The committee of the Oregon State Teachers' Retirement Fund and Tenure of Office met at the office of the State Department of Education at Salem, on Saturday, July 15th, and made preliminary plans for the work of the committee. President Foster, as chairman - of the committee, reported that he had collected the publications on the subject of all cities and states in the country having retirement funds. He reported further that he had spent some time on two visits to Boston during the year in examining with care the work of the Teachers' Retirement Fund system of Massachusetts.

"The committee discussed the essentials of a Retirement Fund system, and found themselves in substantial agreement upon nearly all points. They requested the chairman of the committee to draw up a tentative plan and to draft a bill to be submitted to the committee for study before the next meeting.

"The committee voted to meet at the business offices of Reed College in the Abington building, Portland, at 1 o'clock on the afternoon of Monday, October 2nd.

"In the meantime, each member of the committee will receive the most valuable recent publications on the subject, in order that all may be prepared to make progress at the next meeting."

MINUTES OF EDITORIAL BOARD.

The Editorial Board of the Oregon State Teachers' Association met for its first meeting at 10:30 a. m., May 20, 1916, in the office of the Superintendent of Public Instruction, Salem, Oregon.

The meeting was called to order by E. F. Carleton, president of the Association. The members present were: H. D. Sheldon, E. S. Evenden, E. D. Ressler, Miss Viola Ortschild, G. W. Hug, R. E. Chloupek, H. Jenkins, C. T. Bonney, Mrs. M. L. Fulkerson. Those absent were: C. G. Doney and Miss Lillian Tingle.

After the reading of the contract with the Statesman Publishing Co., Dr. Sheldon was elected chairman and Mrs. Fulkerson secretary. After an informal discussion concerning the policy to be maintained by the Oregon Teachers Monthly under the new management, the following motions were carried unanimously:

1. To report on events and movements along educational lines of national importance as well as those pertaining to our own state.

2. To commit the policy of the paper to the support of constructive and progressive phases of education.

3. To establish the following news departments: State, Superintendents, Principals, Grade Teachers, High School, Vocational.

4. To allow correspondence from any institution of higher education in the news department.

The chairman was empowered to appoint a sub-committee of five members, himself to be one, this committee to meet once each month and act in the capacity of editors of the magazine. The sub-committee was made up of the following members: Sheldon, Ortschild, Evenden, Ressler, Fulkerson.

Heads of the news departments were chosen as follows: State—E. F. Carleton; Superintendents—C. T. Bonney, School Superintendent Wasco County; Principals—George W. Hug, City Superintendent McMinnville; High School—Hopkin Jenkins, prinicipal Jefferson High School, Portland; Vocational—R. E. Chloupek, Director of Manual Training, Pendleton.

, It was agreed to call two meetings of the entire Editorial Board during the ensuing school year, one at the call of the chaiman, and the second immediately after the close of the annual meeting of the Association in Portland.

Professional Standards

By PRESIDENT J. H. ACKERMAN, Oregon Normal School

The subject assigned indicates that there are standards for different avocations or vocations, and that these standards for the teaching profession are known as professional standards. In order to fully understand the subject, it might be well to have clearly in mind what we understand by the term "professional." The name implies that there is such a thing as a profession, and that there are certain standards that apply peculiarly to that profession. No organization becomes professional until it has certain standards either expressed or implied to which each member must adhere or risk the accusation of being unprofessional. It is conceded that no calling can be called a profession until a certain amount of time, thought and energy is devoted to mastering certain prescribed requisites for such calling. To become a teacher one must make such preparation—hence to that extent we do have the profession of teaching.

There must be certain well developed conventions as to conduct approved by the best thought of the times, the violation of which causes one to lose his professional standing. This standard should be such that a teacher who lives up to it will so impress himself upon the minds and consciences of his patrons that a mother would say to her son or daughter, "I hope you may become as is your teacher." The lives of multitudes of teachers are today living examples that the teaching profession does have such high standards. Another cardinal principle of a profession is that each member jealously guards the professional standing of every other member to the extent that he will not only refuse to speak slightingly or disparagingly of a fellow teacher's work, but on the other hand will defend it as long as possible. That this is coming to be the custom is another proof that there is such a thing as a profession of teaching. The professional teacher is one who neither undermines nor underbids—that is, will not agree to accept less than schedule salary for the sake of securing a position, or will not speak disparagingly of a teacher for the purpose of securing his position. Many teachers absolutely refuse to apply for a position or even make a recommendation for another unless assured that the vacancy exists or is likely to become vacant. In other words, no teacher will attempt to build himself up at the expense of a fellow teacher. These standards are the warp and woof of any profession, especially of the profession of teaching. The professional standards of law, medicine and ministry are all predicated upon the principles enumerated, and the more profesional a members of either is, the more nearly he complies daily with their edicts.

It is firmly believed that enormous strides have been taken during the last decade in outlining, perfecting and establishing definite and permanent educational standards for the teachers of Oregon, and the tendencies are for greater perfection—hence as time passes, these standards will be raised, enriched and perfected so that at the end of another decade, a marked forward movement will be decidedly noted.

It is in order to ask what factors during the last decade and what factors will in the future be potent ones in bringing this about. These will, without doubt, be the State Teachers' Association, advanced legislation, the Oregon Teachers Monthly, the several educational institutions, and last but not least, the public opinion of the teachers themselves. If we as teachers set ourselves resolutely to the task and never say fail, we can and will raise the profession to any heighth we may desire. When such standards have been firmly established, when we see the light and act accordingly, we will be measured as we measure ourselves; then the salary schedule and the tenure of office will be more definite and stable, and we will be respected as members of a noble profession. Then and not until then will all persons who wish to enter the teaching ranks spare no time or effort to train themselves to become worthy members of the same. Then, wherever and whenever a person is receiving such training, he will be admonished in season and out of season that there are such things as professional standards, and that for one to be successful, he must be thoroughly trained in the basic principles underlying them, and to be a professional teacher in the highest sense, he must have ingrained in him the habit of living up to their spirit. Such a teacher will come to know that the professional standards of the teaching profesison do and must necessarily, differ from those of any other profession that many of the conventions that might be tolerated in another profession cannot be in the teaching profession; that the teachers of boys and girls will be held rigidly responsible for living up to those standards, and that all the factors bearing on the training of teachers shall keep an eye single on such standards by thought, word and act to the end that the standards of our beloved professoin shall be raised to the highest and kept there. Surely a most noble work!

The High School Library
By E. F. CARLETON, Assistant Superintendent of Public Instruction

Two years ago the Superintendent of Public Instruction undertook the standardization of the high schools of Oregon. The State Board of Education, upon the suggestion of Superintendent Churchill, adopted rules and regulations defining a standard high school. It was provided that the teachers must be the graduates of standard colleges or universities; there must be suitable laboratory equipment selected from the state list for each science offered; a library of not less than 250 reference books selected from the state list; a dictionary for each twenty pupils; and a standard encyclopedia.

As soon as the requirements were published school boards in all parts of the state ratified the work of the state superintendent by purchasing the necessary equipment. At the opening of the school year 1915-16, 167 school districts had met the requirements for a standard high school. This decisive action on the part of the school boards represents accurately the desire of the people of Oregon to have in every community a free high school, whose efficiency will in no way be hampered by a lack of well trained teachers or by inadequate laboratories.

Now that the school districts have so generously assumed their share of the burden, it remains for the high school teachers to make use of these supplies. The science teachers in nearly every instance are making good use of their material, but many of the libraries show by the accumulation of dust on the bindings that the pupils have not yet been taught the value of reference works. A school superintendent can, by visiting the school library on an average working day, judge to a fairly accurate degree the character of the work of the high school. Bernerd C. Steiner, Librarian Enoch Pratt Free Library, Baltimore, told at the Oakland meeting of the National Education Association of the various ways by which that library makes its volumes attractive to those whom it wishes to serve. Thus in one part of the building are two windows close to the sidewalk. Upon glass cases in these windows are placed collections of books upon topics to which it is desired to call the attention of people, and these are changed every week or so. At one time the librarian sent to each of the four hundred master plumbers in the city a list of the titles of books on plumbing contained in the library. Often a post card is sent to a reader giving a list of books upon a subject in which this person is known to be interested. The speaker mentioned many other little devices the use of which by this library tend to prove that even to those accustomed to using a library, appeals must be made to hold their interest.

The high school teacher should recognize this fact first of all, and use every means of arousing interest in the library. She should follow it up by requiring a certain amount of reference work. The pupil should not be encouraged or even allowed to do a great amount of indiscriminate reading on any topic. Rather he should have clearly in mind the exact assignment, and he should be held for definite results. A lecturer on Physics in Yale once said to his class, "I shall have failed in my teaching, if you will not remember how to find out for yourselves again the facts which you have learned here." This statement illustrates the power which should be acquired by the high school student, if he has been taught how to use properly the high school library.

It is essential also that the student learn to collate and express the results of his reading. To read widely without learning to express concisely the information gained by research is little better than not reading at all. Hence the pupil should not be sent to the library until he knows exactly what is expected of him. In the classroom he should be held for a complete report on every topic assigned to him for collateral reading. Where the teacher simply gives the references without the "follow up" work, the pupils soon lose interest in outside reading, and decide for themselves that it is a waste of time. As a rule only those pupils make intelligent use of the library who know that they are to be held strictly for definite results. Interest again plays its part, for at no other age do boys and girls enjoy so much telling of what they have learned from their reading.

One other caution is necessary. If the reference library is to be effective, it must be kept in working order. It should be properly catalogued according to the rules sent out by the state library. Wherever it is possible, there should be a teacher in the high school who is a trained librarian, and who can devote to the library part or all of the day according to the size of the school. The librarian is needed to teach the students how to find the books from the catalogue, and the references from the index. After these details have been mastered, the librarian can make a small library serve a large number of pupils by doing the detail work for them. For example, if a pupil is studying the Punic Wars and his assignment is on the character and civilization of the Carthaginian people, the librarian should furnish him with the best reference works on hand with book marks indicating the pages where this subject is discussed. The energy of the pupil would thus be devoted entirely to the securing of authoritative material for his next day's recitation. His attention will not be dissipated by seeing other attractive matter in the reference works. He will complete his task in a much less time than if he had searched out the references for himself, and the books will be available for other students.

Our standardization plan has received favorable notice from the United States Commissioner of Education in his annual report; it has attracted the attention of the Eastern Universities interested in the problems of secondary education, especially in those universities that have organized Departments of Education; and the plan is now being studied by the National Education Association Committee on Secondary Education appointed at the New York meeting. We have it in our power to make the high schools of Oregon the most efficient in this country, but no advance can be made unless the teachers use to the very best and most economical advantage all of the equipment, including the dictionaries, the encyclopedias, and the reference works found in the high school libraries.

Grade Teachers' Associations

By VIOLA ORTSCHILD, President of Portland Grade Teachers' Association

For years the one great organization of educators of the United States has had a loosely knit membership of perhaps fifteen to twenty thousand, chiefly women classroom teachers whose half-hearted interest might be attributed to the fact that their chief privileges and duties were to furnish the audiences and to pay the dues which supported this organization.

Within the short space of four years another national organization of educators, also composed largely of women classroom teachers, has attained a membership of at least twenty-five thousand, vitally interested, closely organized, and bound by ties that can at need be greatly strengthened.

The cause of the latter remarkable showing has been evident to some, at least, of those who stand highest in the educational world of America. On the lecture platform and in the public press they have advocated organizations of the elementary teachers. A large number of local teachers' organizations have sprung up in the last decade. It was the combination of the classroom teachers' associations of the United States that formed the League of Teachers' Associations with its thousands of members.

Organizations of classroom teachers have increased so remarkably for several reasons. There has been an ill-concealed unrest among the rank and file of teachers, a long-standing dissatisfaction with the part assigned to them in school systems and state associations. They who are so largely responsible for the ideals and educational progress of the mass of the American people have been entirely ignored when educational policies were being formulated. They have had to struggle to do their best work for their pupils and the community against all sorts of adverse conditions. Their rewards have been few. Their wages have often been less than those paid to unskilled labor.

But, classroom teachers are no longer content to remain in the cloistered school room. They are rapidly taking a new attitude toward their work and toward their co-workers. They are demanding for themselves conditions which will make it possible to render their services effective. There is still one American city in which, during 1915, ten teachers were paid $195 a year. What services can be expected from a teacher who is worth only such a wage? Does not every teacher in that city suffer because of the kind of work done by such poorly paid workers.

Realizing the harm of such a situation organizations of teachers are working for better conditions in their own communities. They are reaching out helping hands across the border lines of their own states to assist others in gaining some of the blessings they themselves are enjoying. "Committees of Correspondence" are spreading the news of what some associations have accomplished to give inspiration to their less fortunate co-workers.

What the individual teacher could not do, organization has done for her. No longer does a grade teacher who is a member of a teachers' association carry herself with a feeling of humility because of her work. She has risen fearlessly to ask for better salaries, tenure-of-office, an adequate pension when her services are no longer of value to her state. She is unashamed and unafraid because she knows the justice of the demand due to the kind of service she renders to the state.

The results of the changed attitude of the classroom teacher toward her vocation, her co-workers, and the community, have been rather remarkable. Thousands of teachers are carrying on or directing teachers' activities. Perhaps it will be best understood what teachers are doing if some late reports from organizations in various parts of the United States are given. No systematic arrangement of these reports will be attempted. They will be tabulated in time to show just what the various organizations composing the League of Teachers' Associations are really doing for themselves and for others.

From Richmond, Virginia, comes this statement of the work accomplished by the Elementary Teachers' Association: "We defeated two bills before the legislature to abolish the Teachers' Retirement Fund and increased the state's contribution $5000. We have an Advisory Council which meets with the superintendent when need arises.

The Winona, Minn., teachers' organization has cultivated the educational and social side of its work this year.

The Walla Walla Grade Teachers' Association is young, but it has discussed local questions and interested the general public in its organization.

The Grade Teachers' Fellowship Society of East St. Louis has announced its purposes in the following statement which appears on its letterhead, "Organized to promote the interest of its members and the cause of education."

Then to keep faith with its promises the East St. Louis Association helped the cause of education as follows: "The laws of Illinois make no provision for the use of the interest on school funds held by the school treasurer. We agitated this question and the school treasurer paid into the school fund the past year interest amounting to $4400." Truly these teachers are serving the "cause of education."

The East St. Louis letter states further: "We have experienced the

joy that comes from working with others. This combined effort has
cultivated closer fellowship among teachers and created in the community at large a deeper sense of the dignity of gradè teachers and
the interests they represent.''

The Topeka, Kansas, Grade Teachers' Club reports as follows:
''We have taken an active part in cultural and educational movements
in the city. Our position in the community has been strengthened. We
have promises of better remuneration dependent on legislative action.''

The Muncie, Indiana, teachers have a peculiar condition in their
city and certainly need to organize strongly to remove the injustice.
They have a day by day contract so that the school board refuses to
pay their salaries on enforced holidays. These teachers have half-day
sessions on Thanksgiving and Memorial Day in order to draw pay. In
spite of this injustice the teachers of Muncie affiliated with the
women's clubs in all community interests, and worked on the legislative, historical, and educational committees.

The Colorado teachers seem to be a wonderful set judging from
what they have done. The Royal Gorge National Teachers' Recreation
Association has acquired forty-five acres at an approximate cost of
$25,000. The project of establishing this home for aged, sick, and
retired teachers promises to be a success. The Denver Association has
secured advances in salaries. It has an advisory council. It is now
working for tenure and a retirement fund. This association has also
stood well in the community, working for civic betterment. At the
meeting of the National Education Association in Oakland last year
the eight delegates sent by the Denver Grade Teachers' Association
laid definite plans to take back to Denver with them everything of
educational interest or value they could find. Thirty-one counties had
representatives at the Oakland gathering. Forty-nine meetings and
500 lecturers were scheduled, but, nothing daunted, the Denver representatives scattred themselves far and wide each day to gain what they
wanted. The Denver Association was thus enabled to reap the benefit
of the accumulated experiences of all its delegates. This is the sort of
thing teachers' associations can do for the individual teacher.

The Minneapolis Grade Teachers' Association carries a satisfactory hospital insurance for its members. It works on the local board of
censorship of moving pictures. It has contributed $50 this summer to
send one of its members to the Columbia Teachers' College in New
York. By co-operation it has secured an Advisory Council and a
Retirement Fund.

The St. Paul teachers have long had a strong, active teachers'
organization which has accomplished striking results. The Advisory
Council is authorized by the city charter. This council recently used
its influence to have two worthless text books abolished and two good
ones chosen. It co-operates with the school board for bettering the
schools and is fearless in its denunciation of whatever is harmful to the
children.

The St. Paul association has published a ''Bulletin'' each month ; it has maintained a Library Service Committee which has co-operated in making the public library more useful to the schools; it has donated $100 to be used for books and pictures destroyed by fire; it donated funds for the municipal Christmas celebration; it has donated $75 to assist a woman student.

The Tacoma, Washington Grade Teachers' Association has worked to establish a feeling of good fellowship among its members. In conjunction with other teachers' organizations of the city it has established a Teachers' Co-operative Insurance which assists teachers in case of illness.

One association states frankly a situation that has also prevailed elsewhere: "Previous to November all employes of the school board were eligible to membership in our organization. With such a personnel, however, the association stood for nothing and accomplished nothing. Accordingly, at the annual meeting in November we adopted a new constitution which limits membership to classroom teachers."

The Los Angeles City Teachers' Club has a membership of almost 1200. It maintains beautiful club rooms. It has a mountain cabin where teachers may enjoy week ends. It has defeated harmful legislation and improved conditions by raising the maximum and minimum salaries.

The Boston and New York teachers' organizations have been too busy with their own problems to co-operate actively with organizations from other cities. The Erie, Pennsylvania, association has been working along cultural and social lines. It is also using its influence for a pension fund and a satisfactory salary schedule.

The Wichita, Kansas, Grade Teachers' Club has had two aims this year—to create an esprit de corps among its members, and to overcome the feeling that the grade teachers are antagonistic to principals and supervisors because they do not admit them to membership in the club. Both objects have been gained.

The Ottumwa, Iowa, correspondent says: "Besides working for teachers' pensions and a benefit fund, we have been interested in and helped in every movement for the betterment of our city."

The South Bend, Indiana, Teachers' Federation reports as follows: "The teachers' associations of our state organized this year and formed a state federation of teachers' clubs. We have a local and a state pension."

The Troy, New York, Teachers' Association reports as follows: "For years we have presented lecture courses of the highest intellectual type, the lectures being among the best which could be obtained. These lectures have always been supported by the social and cultured set among our citizens. Our association has helped largely in organizing and maintaining four play grounds, has helped parent-teacher associations, and assisted in all civic work in charge of women's clubs."

Perhaps it might be well to enumerate here some of the things acomplished by the Portland Grade Teachers' Association during the four years of its existence.

It has been largely instrumental in securing the tenure-of-office law. It helped to establish the Teachers' Retirement Fund, now in active operation. It used its strong influence to assist the Federation of Women's Clubs of Oregon to secure much legislation beneficial to women and children. It has established a Fellowship Fund of its own from which teachers in urgent need may borrow on a low rate of interest. It has organized many classes and given lecture courses. It has assisted actively in civic affairs whenever called upon or needed. It has assisted yearly by a generous donation to the Scholarship Loan Fund of the Portland Women's Club.

The Association has contributed services and funds to local charitable work, and has let its sympathies go to far countries in generous contributions to funds for the starving Jews and the persecuted Armenians. .It contributed $50 to be used for the Third Oregon Infantry on the Mexican border.

It would not be fair to close this enumeration of the activities of teachers' associations (and I could continue indefinitely with the material I have on hand), without mentioning the work accomplished by the Chicago Teachers' Federation which is now being persecuted by the money power of that city. This organization by its own efforts, turned over $600,000 a year into the city's school fund. It caused millions of unpaid taxes to be restored to the city. The following is taken from an editorial in one of our largest Portland papers of July 30, 1916: "The Chicago teachers formed a real trade union some years ago and went on to affiliate with the National Federation of Labor. They took up vital economic issues such as local taxes, teachers' wages, and tenure of position, and effected remarkable results. But finally the Chicago School Board, jealous of its petty prerogatives and egged on by big tax dodgers made war on the teachers' union. What the outcome will be is not yet certain. Teachers need a strong economic union as much as any other class of wage earners. The objection that it would be undignified is 'bunk.' It is a red herring drawn across the trail. In union is strength for teachers and countless benefits for pupils."

The above editorial, especially the last few words, should furnish teachers food for serious thought. Coming from the public press, it is at least significant.

In Medford, Oregon, during December of last year, the State Teachers' Association was re-organized. A constitution "embodying the most modern ideas" was adopted. This constitution provides for a representative council to transact the business of the State Association. In the article apportioning the representatives among the various educational interests and agencies of the state, appears this clause: "A representative from each association of teachers having more than fifteen members and having at least three regular meetings each year."

This clause is the classroom teacher's opportunity. Organization is made easy, because it will·be approved and supported by a great state association. California is a highly organized state. Strong local teachers' associations abound. California has "initiated and secured more advanced educational legislation than any other state in the Union. This is what "The Sierra Educational News" of California has to say of the Oregon educational situation and the new State Teachers' Association: "If the teachers of Oregon use judgment and hang together through their new form of organization, they may accomplish much."

It will be admitted that more can be accomplished if there are many strong local associations to carry on the work initiated by the State Association. Organization is the trend of the times. The classroom teachers have the opportunity to take their full share in the work of the State Association. They can either march abreast of the times in the educational movements going on today, or they can remain isolated individuals doing only the narrowing work of the school room. It remains to be seen what the teachers of Oregon will do. They can see what other teachers have accomplished by their combined efforts in grade teachers' associations.

RURAL TEACHERS.

The best figures available, and, though wholly inadequate they are fairly significant, show that about one-fourth of the teachers in one-room schools are men, that about one-fifth of the whole number, men and women, are married, that two-thirds of the teachers try to hear more than twenty recitations a day, that only an infinitesimal per cent are provided a "home" at public expense, that most teachers live in the district in which they teach, that the average country-teaching life of a teacher is forty-five school months, in an average of three different schools, that but one in twenty-five has had more than an elementary school education.—Journal of Education.

MY CREED.

I would be true, for there are those who trust me,
　I would be pure, for there are those who care;
I would be strong, for there is much to suffer;
　I would be brave, for there is much to dare.

I would be friend of all—the foe—the friendless;
　I would be giving, and forget the gift;
I would be humble, for I know my weakness;
　I would look up—and laugh—and love—and lift.
　　　　　　　　　　　　　　　—H. A. Waters.

What the best and wisest parent wants for his own child, that must the community want for all its children. Any other ideal for our school is unlovely; acted upon it destroys our democracy.—John Dewey.

Hygiene of the Mouth, Nose and Throat as Related to School Progress

By B. W. DEBUSK, University of Oregon

Education must take into account the whole man. And the whole man is built up on what he is physiologically. His education depends upon his ability to profit by the experience of society which the school brings to him. We are just beginning to realize that the inability of many to acquire the full benefit of the education offered them depends on the handicapping influence of some physiological defect. A very interesting group of such defects is found in pathological conditions of the mouth, nose and throat. The retardation caused by the eye and ear is due to the fact that mental processes which depend upon those organs for their stimulation can not function normally on account of the faulty impression. The conditions named above produce a general weakening of the higher mental processes through systemic poisoning.

It is said by a writer on hygiene that a sound tooth is better for a child than a thousand dollars in the savings bank, a statement that is probably not an exaggeration when one considers the relation of defective teeth to the physical ills and to mental retardation of school children. There are in the United States over twenty million school children. It is estimated that from 50 to 90 per cent of these have defective teeth. Supt. Johnson studied 257 boys and 240 girls, varying in ages from 4 to 18 years, and 96.8 per cent had defective teeth. Nine boys and six girls had perfect teeth. Sixty-one per cent of 266,420 children in New York City had defective teeth. The teeth of 2677 Cleveland children revealed 15,061 cavities. Other studies in the United States and abroad confirm the above estimates. The estimate that 90 per cent of the school children have at least one decayed tooth is probably conservative enough. Decay of the tooth begins on the outside and is of outside agency. Bacteria attack the food particles left in the mouth and clinging to the teeth. The resulting acid breaks down the enamel, thus exposing the dentine and opening the way for the invasion of the interior of the tooth. The lime is dissolved out and soft areas are left. The pulp becomes infested, pus appears and the tooth dies. With the appearance of bacteria through the root an abcess develops accompanied by fever. Of course there is marked individual difference in the resistance to the disease and the onset of decay depends upon the character of the enamel. This, at bottom, probably depends on the character of child feeding during the period of the formation of the tooth. Investigation shows a relation between the quality and kind of feeding of the child and the amount of dental caries. Bottle fed children show a higher percentage of defect than breast fed. Also the percentage of good teeth increase with the length of the period of breast feeding. Undoubtedly there is a causal relation between dental caries in children and the malnutrition resulting from improper feeding. The lack of lime and the action of acid forming bacteria work together for the production of the disease.

There is a close relation between this and other diseases found among school children. Among the first is the onset of indigestion resulting from poor mastication. The child tends to protect the sensitive tooth. In the wake of the indigestion comes constipation, auto-intoxication and head-ache. In an advanced stage of tooth decay one must reckon with the effect of pus. It is yet an open question of the effect of pus when taken into the digestive tract. But when absorbed into the blood many toxic effects result. Among other effects one finds the enlargement of the glands, earache, and defect of hearing. Probably 50 per cent of the cases of defective hearing among school children are cases for the dentist. Some forms of epilepsy and chorea may even be traced to defective teeth. There is also a relation between sound teeth and physiological age. Those who have good teeth are on the average a half year more mature than those who have defective teeth.

That there would be a relation between success in school work and sound teeth seems self evident. The work of the child is an expression of its available energy, which in turn is largely a matter of digestion. Ayers found in New York a much larger percentage of defective teeth among dull children. Wallin showed a marked improvement in the quality of work to follow the proper care and treatment of the teeth of a class of retarded children in the Cleveland schools.

Not only the opportunity but the duty of the school is plain. Children should be taught the care of the teeth. The instruction must not stop short of habits of tooth cleanliness. The presentation of a tooth brush to the child may in the long run be worth more than the presentation of a free text-book. The school should also offer treatment. The prevalence of the disease shows that it is useless to expect the parent to deal adequately with the problem. The school dental clinic is the only sure means of securing the necessary treatment.

Health is protected against the invasion of disease germs by the tonsils. These while safeguarding the health when normal lose their protective power when diseased and in turn become the sources of infection through the harboring of disease germs. The normal tonsil appears as a small pink mass of lymphoid tissue. A slight enlargement is normal during the cutting of teeth but a permanent enlargement especially if irregular, containing crypts or white spots is distinctly abnormal. The most commonly listed effects of diseased tonsils are, beside the slight obstruction of breathing that may occur, heart and throat infections, diseases of the ear, chorea, tuberculosis, enlargement and inflamation of the glands of the neck, and a general lowering of vitality and resistance to infection.

The adenoid is a third tonsil situated in the naso-pharynx. When large, adenoids effectively close the nasal passage and force mouth breathing. Adenoids are occasionally found in infants and in adults. There is a tendency to disappear after the age of puberty, but when allowed to disappear by absorption rather than by surgical means the results developed by the early neglect remain. The adenoid may be caused by a lymphatic diathesis, by frequent colds, or exposure to conditions which are unhygienic. The most common symptoms are mouth breathing, the dull inquiring look, irregular teeth, the high arched palate, the nasal voice and occasional speech defect and the flat chest. Nutrition is impaired and growth may not be normal. There is a correlation between tuberculosis and adenoids, since investigation shows a large percentage to be infected with the germs of the disease. It is estimated that there are two million school children in the United States that are victims of this condition. Mentally the adenoid child is characterized by lack of attention and memory. There is difficulty not only of retention but of forming an idea of anything new. Mental processes show a slowness especially in turning from one subject to another. All this is probably due to impaired function of the brain. The adenoid may explain many a case of inattention, nervousness, irritability and misbehavior. The result of an operation is a quick restoration to the normal.

In the defective tooth, in the after effects of tonsilitis, in catarrhal conditions of the upper nasal passages involving the cavities of the bones ordinarily filled with air, one finds frequently buried pus pockets. The mouth and nasal passages are especially open to invasion by bacteria of this type, so that during inflammation of these passages it is surprising the number of pus pockets that can be found. Whenever these are present there is a certain amount of absorption and consequently systemic poison. For a long time there was thought to be a relation between rheumatism and tonsilitis. Later it was observed that many patients suffering with rheumatism also had ulcerated teeth or chronic supperation of the nasal passages or the passages opening into the nose. When such abscesses were treated it was found that the rheumatism improved. It now seems that the buried pus cavity is the prerequisite for the production of rheumatic poison, at least for a number of the varieties of that disease. There can now be no question that the proper treatment of the after effects of colds and tonsilitis and proper dental care would prevent a great deal of child rheumatism.

This group of pathological conditions, adenoids, diseased tonsils, and dental caries together with catarrhal conditions of the nose, colds, and acute tonsilitis is responsible for much temporary mental retardation. The mental effect follows roughly Ribot's law that the last powers to unfold are the first to·be lost. The

powers most affected are just those that the child needs most in adjusting himself to his environment. If these conditions persist for a long time, growth is affected and the rate of physiological maturing slowed down so that a temporary retardation becomes a permanent one.

Reading in the Upper Elementary Grades
By SABRA CONNER, Portland, Oregon.

Reading in the seventh and eighth grades is a subject which needs a chance to take its place in the sun. Every teacher will agree that reading is the foundation of all culture, but in our crowded modern curriculum it is the first subject to° go to the wall on a day of stress. Arithmetic and grammar and history must have full time or the pupils will not make passing marks, but reading does not count.

Arithmetic and grammar, however, do not play as long nor as vital a part in the life of any individual as does a love of reading. That is my text, a love of reading. By the time a boy or girl has reached the seventh grade the mechanics of reading should be mas-tered and the most important thing for the teacher of reading in the last two grades to do is to make certain that every pupil acquires the reading habit, a habit which will mean life-long pleasure and profit.

A study of isolated fragments of stories and poems from a reader will never give eighth grade boys and girls a love of reading. Anything in his reader which is interesting to him has been read by a normal child before the book has been a week in his possession. How then can he be interested in hearing members of his class mumble over a story he already knows by heart? Why should he be expected to enjoy looking up dictionary definitions of lists of words when he knows the meaning of the story?

But suppose he is asked to bring to class a book which he thinks is interesting and read a selection from it. He will bring it and it may be a "pennythriller." Even so, he will not fail to be interested when another boy reads to the class about Tom Sawyer's ingenuity in disposing of his Saturday's chore of white-

washing, and he will want to read all he can find about Tom and his chum, Huck Finn. It will not require much discussion of Treasure Island to show that he finds it as full of thrills as any "thriller." Children know good books and like them when they have a chance, and are guided in their reading. It should be a regular class exercise to bring library books and read selections to the class. The ability to hold attention and arouse interest should be the test of the reading.

Every seventh and eighth grade pupil should be required to read at least one good book every month as a part of the regular course in reading. It may be hard to find books that will interest some of the slow pupils who have found the mechanics of reading so hard to master that they have an active dislike for reading. By carefully choosing for them simple and very interesting short books even these pupils will in six months acquire some facility in silent reading. By giving them frequent "tastes" of interesting books they learn to like reading and form the reading habit.

A well selected class room library from which each child may be helped to find something suited to him, will be a great help in getting children to form the habit of regular reading. In a very short time the general tendency will be to read a book a week rather than one a month. They should be encouraged to reread good books. One Chinese boy in the sixth grade was observed to read and re-read the five volumes of Howard Pyles King Arthur series. He thoroughly saturated himself with the atmosphere of that wonderful court for a period of five months. That isn't a bad way for anyone to study a period.

Besides forming the habit of gen—

eral reading pupils in these grades should learn to know and love literature. Most of the selections from literature should be read to them for few pupils in these grades are capable of appreciative reading. After the reading the selections should be discussed and commented upon. When the bit of literature is a poem it should be memorized, not to be recited once and dropped, but to be given again and again for the pleasure to be derived from giving it and hearing it. Children love poetry and they memorize so easily that their minds should be stored with these bits of literature. Upper grade pupils sometimes seem from disuse to have lost some of this facility, but the giving of memory gems is such valuable training in the use of the voice in enunciation and interpretation that the rather self-conscious older boy and girl should be taught to do it. They need the discipline of it more than the primary pupil does.

Another element of reading which has been largely lost to the upper grades is dramatization. Somewhere in the middle grades as the child has become self-conscious and less imaginative and the teacher crowded for time this use of the child's love of play-acting has been dropped. It is so valuable as a means of gaining force and vividness in reading, as a means of interpretation of literature, as self-expression, that it should be used a great deal in the seventh and eighth grades. Stories and bits of literature and historical incidents should be turned into little plays. They are not too old to enjoy giving the fairy stories and folk-lore. Julius Caesar and the Merchant of Venice are not beyond their powers of appreciation. And how they love it!

A class of seventh grade girls spent weeks of their English time in preparing a play from the Jungle stories. Then they drilled a class of third grade pupils in the parts and presented the play to the other classes, taking throughout the keenest interest though they themselves were not the actors.

A group of eight grade boys wrote a play from the Three Musketeers. They made swords and drilled thoroughly in fencing, then stage-managed their play and presented it to another class.

These seventh and eighth grade classes gave in five months 21 little plays, selecting the plays, managing them and presenting them entirely by themselves. These were all given after school. If they love this work enough to give their play time to it, it is certainly vital enough to them to be valuable as an aid in teaching of reading.

If the upper grammar grade pupils can be taught to love reading and form the reading habit, to love literature and interpret it appreciatively, to express themselves through their reading work, then this will be a stimulating and vital subject and perhaps it will come to be regarded as a major subject.

———

No school board should think of having school open until the school house has been thoroughly cleaned and aired, and all the weeds cut and cleared away from the school grounds. The schoolhouse and the grounds should present a neat, attractive and inviting appearance to the teacher and the pupils when the school opens.—Exchange.

———

A cheerful temper, joined with innocence, will make beauty attractive, knowledge delightful, and wit good-natured. It will lighten sickness, poverty and affliction; convert ignorance into an amiable simplicity, and render deformity itself agreeable.—Addison.

———

Aim at perfection in everything, though in most things it is unattainable; however, they who aim at it, and persevere, will come much nearer to it than those whose laziness and despondency make them give it up as unattainable.—Chesterfield.

———

The human soul is the sun which diffuses light on every side, investing creation with its lovely hues, and calling forth the poetic element that lies hidden in every existing thing.—Mazzini.

———

Mirth is God's medicine. A man without mirth is like a wagon without springs, in which one is caused disagreeably to jolt by every pebble over which it runs.—Beecher.

Oregon Govermental Affairs

By ROBERT CARLTON CLARK, Eugene, Oregon

Supreme Court and Grammar.

Judicial decisions are constantly furnishing examples of the horrifying results of "careless and negligent" speech. The teacher seeking an apt illustration to point a moral and adorn a tale as well as to prod the lagging energies of the pupil who fails to see the value of learning habits of correct expression will find delight in a recent decision of our state supreme court. The illusive "comma", the "dot" over the "i", the cross of the "t", the omission of the inoffensive article "the", all these have brought disaster upon the unwary man who has sought his day in court. Teachers who take care to make a collection of all these horrible examples ought to have no difficulty in arousing an interest in the usually dry subject of grammar among her prospective lawyer pupils. Or is grammar any longer a subject of study in our public schools? Any way one or more Oregon lawyers must repent bitterly their failure to apply themselves more dilligently to the subject since by using "and" instead of "or" they lost their case and failed to secure manifest justice to their client. And this is how it all happened.

A Portland policeman was run over by a truck belonging to a manufacturing company and killed. Against this company his widow brought suit for damages. The company in its answer to the complaint charged that the deceased had been negligent of his safety. In answering this charge the lawyers for the plaintiff entered a denial that the deceased had "carelessly and negligently stepped back directly in the path of the moving wheels of the truck, and that he carelessly and negligently failed to look out for himself and turned his back upon the truck." In this form the supreme court holds that their is no denial of the act itself but only of the manner in which he failed to look after his safety. In other words, there was failure to deny that the deceased policeman stepped back in front of the truck or that he failed to look out for himself and turned his back upon the truck. There was merely denial that these things were done carelessly and negligently. If the conjunction "or" had been used instead of "and" the denial would then have been complete. The circuit court had given a decision favorable to the widow. The supreme court reverses this decision and thus what seems a trifling error causes her to lose all compensation for her loss.

Congress Acts on Land Grant.

Congress has passed a law providing for the survey and sale of the unsold portions of the Oregon and California railway land grant. The secretary of the interior is authorized to classify the grant into power-site lands, timber lands (not less than 300,000 feet to 40 acres), and agricultural lands. Timber off lands will be sold by competitive bidding and after removal of the timber the land will be classed as agricultural. It is estimated that 1,000,000 acres will come under agricultural classification. Entrants may take up 160-acre homesteads, for which they must pay the government $2.50 an acre, 50 cents an acre at time of entry and balance when they obtain patents. Persons who have resided on the land since December 1, 1913 and have improved it for agricultural purposes, shall have preferred right to it. Back taxes unpaid will be paid by the government. Such moneys as remain from the sale of the grant after paying the railroad $2.50 per acre for the land and the unpaid taxes on it is to be divided, 25 per cent for the irreducible state school fund, 25 per cent to the counties in which land is located for schools, roads, etc., 40 per cent to the federal reclamation fund, 10 per cent to general fund of the government.

Initiative Measures.

On July 6, the last day for filing initiative petitions, eight measures had been submitted to the secretary of state with the requisite number of signatures. This year more than 20,-000 names were necessary to validate a petition. With three constitutional amendments submitted by the legislative assembly, the voter will be asked to make a decision in November on only eleven proposals. These measures, if enacted by majority vote of the men and women who take the trouble to vote yes or no on them, will prohibit compulsory vaccination and medical treatment, limit the taxing power of all taxing authorities, repeal and abolish the Sunday closing law, permit the manufacture of beer in Oregon, prohibit importation of liquor for beverage purposes, establish a state normal school at Pendleton, provide for a form of single tax, and establish a system of rural credits. These measures will be described and discussed later.

Candidates' Expenses in Primary Elections.

The expenses of all candidates for state and national nominations at the May election amounted to something near $60,000. The Republican candidates were 75 per cent of the whole number and expended 95 per cent of the total sum. The candidate may not expend for himself in excess of 10 per cent of the first year's salary. He is, however, permitted to expend as much as $100 and space paid for in the state campaign pamphlet does not count against the maximums. A candidate's friends, however, are not limited in their expenditures in his behalf. The successful Republican candidate for president was not obliged to spend one cent to secure the nomination from Oregon while it cost the two unsuccessful candidates some $6,000 each. Expenditures varying from 10 cents to $7,000 were reported in statements filed with the secretary of state. This latest primary election, like its predecessors, seems unnecessary for state offices. It is expensive both for the state and for individual candidates. Not many more than half the qualified voters took the trouble to vote. A single election in November giving the voter an opportunity to exercise two or more choices as between the several candidates for all offices would secure practically the same result now obtained by two expensive elections. There is no good reason for attaching national party names to state candidates but even this might be done and a single election would still be enough.

Rural School Department

Edited by MRS. M. L. FULKERSON, Salem, Oregon

To the rural teachers of Oregon we extend our best wishes for a happy, successful school year. This, the first number of the new Oregon Teachers Monthly, comes to you heralding a new department which is to be devoted solely to the rural school interests. We hope to make it a success but whether we do or not depends upon the assistance you give us. We want to make this magazine the best official state paper in existence. We want your co-operation. May we depend upon every rural teacher in Oregon to do his or her part? If so, success is assured. If not, the attempt will end is disastrous failure.

Here are a few of the things we want you to tell us: Have you worked out some plan in your school that might help other teachers? Do you know of a teacher who is doing something in her school or community that is especially interesting? Is there some subject that you would like to have discussed in this department? In what way can we help you most? This is your department. Please consider it so and everybody boost for the state magazine.

All communications for this department, in order to receive prompt attention, should be in by the fifth of the month previous to publication.

Send directly to the department editor, Mrs. M. L. Fulkerson, R. F. D. 4, Salem, Oregon.

Teachers Exchange.

If you or your pupils would like to correspond with a school in another locality, send us your address and state your preference for location of correspondent and we will publish it in a Teachers Exchange column.

Public School Compositions.

We should like to continue the public school compositions and in order to stimulate interest we will select from those sent us each month, the best one written by a boy and the best one written by a girl and publish them in this department. The names of the winners will be placed on the Composition Honor Roll which will be printed in each issue throughout the year. Compositions should not exceed 300 words and must be in the hands of the editor of this department by the first of the month previous to publication.

Hot Lunches in the Rural School.

Ten or even five years ago, if any one had suggested that something hot be prepared and served to the children who brought their lunches to school, the person making the suggestion would have received but scant attention, if he were not openly ridiculed. Yet today the hot lunch is an established institution in a great many schools where it is proving its right to exist by increasing the efficiency of the pupils and teachers.

Do you belong to the ranks of the skeptics who are yet to be converted to the practice? If so you are probably asking the question, "How can the serving of a hot lunch in a rural school be justified when the teacher is already overworked?" There are a great many arguments for hot lunches among which are the following, which perhaps will serve to answer the above question:

Something warm served with a cold lunch stimulates digestion by starting the flow of the digestive juices. This alone is worth while because until food is digested it cannot be utilized by the body. When children have walked some distance through the cold and rain or snow they use a great deal of the heat and energy supplied by the food eaten at breakfast, which by the way is not always sufficient in quantity or nutriment to carry the child through to noon. Therefore by 12 o'clock he needs the new supply greatly, and the sooner it is available for body building and the furnishing of heat and energy, the sooner the child is ready for work again.

Hot food insures slow eating because it is impossible to bolt it down. This gives opportunity for thorough mastication which in turn assists digestion.

It is more convenient to serve hot cocoa or soup to the children while they are sitting at their desks. This keeps them together which creates sociability and gives an opportunity to teach, by example at least, some of the rudiments of table manners.

Having to display the contents of the lunch pail tends to bring a better lunch. This does not mean a more expensive or elaborate one but a cleaner, neater, better packed one. Many teachers can testify to the need for such an improvement.

The preparation of the food gives opportunity to teach some much needed lessons in simple cookery and cleanliness. This work can all be done by the girls and does not add to the teacher's work at all.

These are only a few of the arguments along this line but should be sufficient to convince anyone that at least it would be well to try serving something hot a few times.

One of the first problems the teacher will have to meet after deciding to try the plan is the one of financing it. This has been accomplished in a number of ways by different teachers to meet local needs. Some find it best to charge the children so much a week so that the materials can be purchased; others ask for volunteer donations and still others assign each pupil a certain day on which he is to suply the material for the hot dish for everyone in the school. Managed in this way, the child can bring something that is most convenient for the mother to send., unless the same food has been served too often already. Since every pupil derives the benefit from the food furnished by the others, this method is quite fair to all. In some school districts there are sufficient school funds to allow the teacher enough money to buy all the materials and in at least one school in the state, a woman was hired to come early and prepare the food. In this case the children were charged enough to cover the cost of the materials.

Of course a rural teacher has too much to do to spend any time cooking for even the hungriest of children but there are always girls who are willing to do the work and even the boys can be taught to help. Two girls can be assigned to work together in preparing the food. On the day on which they are to serve they can prepare the food at the morning recess, putting the soup or cocoa on to cook in the double boiler. (This can be improvised by placing the pan to be used inside of one a little larger. The larger kettle is to contain water to prevent the food from scorching. At noon these same girls can be dismissed five minutes earlier than the rest of the pupils in order to get everything ready. Two other pupils should pass the bowls or cups and spoons and paper napkins, and at 12 the rest of the children can pass out quietly and bring in their lunch. Each child should have two paper napkins, one to use as a tablecloth and the other as a napkin. Then each child should set his own cover neatly and correctly. It takes some time to describe this but the actual work can be accomplished in a very short time.

One difficulty which many teachers have to meet is the lack of cooking utensils. It is really surprising how few articles are really essential after all. One double boiler or its equivalent, which is large enough to contain sufficient food to serve everyone, a knife, large spoon, teaspoon, measuring cup, and a dish pan, and a few dish towels are the essentials. Any teacher who can secure funds for more than this can also find other things that would be useful.

The Oregon Agricultural College has published a bulletin on this subject which gives many more details and also gives recipes. Anyone desiring a copy of this bulletin may have it free of charge by writing to the extension service for bulletin No. 222, School Lunches.—Helen Cowgill, Assistant State Leader Club Work, Corvallis, Oregon.

For the Basket Lunch.

The following suggested menus for the school lunch basket give the child, as nearly as is practicable in such a meal, the proper proportions of the different classes of foods:

1. Sandwiches with sliced tender meat for filling; baked apples, cookies or a few lumps of sugar.

2. Slices of meat loaf or bean loaf; bread-and-butter sandwiches; stewed fruit; small frosted cake.

3. Crisp rolls, hollowed out and filled with chopped meat or fish, moistened and seasoned, or mixed with salad dressing; orange, apple, a mixture of sliced fruits, or berries; cake.

4. Lettuce or celery sandwiches; cup custard; jelly sandwiches.

5. Cottage cheese and chopped green-pepper sandwiches, or a pot of cream cheese with bread-and-butter sandwiches; peanut sandwiches; fruit and cake.

6. Hard-boiled eggs; crisp baking-powder biscuits; celery or radishes; brown-sugar or maplesugar sandwiches.

7. Bottle of milk; thin corn bread and butter; dates; apple.

8. Raisin or nut bread with butter; cheese; orange; maple sugar.

9. Baked bean and lettuce sandwiches; apple sauce; sweet chocolate.
—School News.

The Rural Home and the Farm Woman.

The rural home has much to do with the condition of the rural school. The rural educational problem is wrapped up with the rural home and community problem.

The needs of the rural home have been overlooked and the farm woman has been forgotten in all of the progressive movements for rural betterment until comparatively recent years.

The farm home is the beginning and the end of every day's work. It differs from the town home in this respect. The farm home is an essential part of the farm business. If the farm home and the farm woman are not what they should be, the farm business cannot be what it should be.

If the farm woman's health and strength are conserved by the time-saving and labor-lightening conveniences and she is given the requisite time and training, she can make life in the rural home interesting, wholesome and satisfying, as indeed she has done already in so many instances. She could do much to promote the health, happiness and mental and spiritual well-being of her family, to enrich country life and make it attractive, and thus to free us from farm tenancy, one of the greatest obstacles of the day to farm progress. The country has many natural advantages over the city for making home life what it should be and it only remains for these advantages to be made the most of.

The work is of such magnitude and importance that it can be done thoroughly and satisfactorily only through national agencies and I earnestly hope President Wilson will appoint a national commission to study the problem of the farm home and the farm woman as he has been asked to do by those having this matter very much at heart.

It is not sufficient to give the farm woman all of the conveniences of a model home. Country life must be made socially satisfying.

In order for country life to be financially and socially satisfying the people must have education and own their homes, and must co-operate with each other in rural community activities and must have rural community organization for the promotion and support of an educational, religious, social, business and intellectual community life. Some are of the opinion that the whole rural problem is "practically the problem of the country school." The country school, which is to improve agricultural conditions and keep good citizens on the farm and make good citizens on the farm, must relate its work to the community life of the people served by it, must educate the children for country life instead of away from it, and must relate universal elements of education to the country community needs, must train the children for their future work in the home, on the farm and in the social life around them, must be a "community center of education, instructing both children and adults in terms of country life and pointing the way to community prosperity and welfare," must concern itself with the business and social life of the people, promoting helpful and profitable cooperation and neighborliness. It cannot neglect the health, the recreation nor the social ideals of the people.

Of greater importance than the question of the "high cost of living" is that of the "high cost of wasting," but of greater importance than both of these is that of the "high cost of ignorance." One of the best remedies for the poor home is the teaching of home economics in all of its phases.

Of all the agencies, the neighborhood teacher with agricultural and home economic training and the right spirit of civic service ought to be the most effective. I rejoice that two-thirds at least of our normal schools are contributing effectively to the solution of this farm woman and rural life problem by giving their students training in home economics.

The home economics extension work of normal schools and colleges for rural communities is producing gratifying results. The Smith-Lever bill offers great promise for the development of home betterment work for the country. The Rural Credits Act recently passed by congress will do much to better rural conditions and rural homes. On the whole, I think the outlook or the betterment of rural life conditions is full of hope. Our people are waking up to the vital importance of the rural problem to the welfare of the whole country, as never before in our history, and are girding themselves for a great intelligent and united effort to give help where it is most needed. I think we can thank God and take courage.— David B. Johnson in Journal of Education.

Alphabetic Gem Game.

Being requested by several, who have heard of my "Alphabetic Gem Game," I gladly submit it to the readers of the Oregon Teachers Monthly hoping it will be of assistance to others.

I began by writing with colored crayon the first gem, preceeded by a bold capital A upon the front board and asked the pupils how many would be able to recite it at roll call next morning. Needless to say they all had it by the time mentioned. I then put the second, B, on the board and told them we were going to play part of a game at roll call three times each week and it would possibly take several weeks to win the game, but if they would recall the story of "The Hare and the Tortoise," they could see the value of stick-to-it-iveness and as a reward the two best players would be rewarded with a prize when the final part was played.

When the gems were nearly all learned I asked them how we would decide who were the winners. By a vote they chose the primary teacher to be judge at the contest which we held on a Friday p. m. after recess, the time usually devoted to literary work. The judge considered three points: (1) Correct reproduction, (2) good articulation, (3) declamation.

It is surprising to note the interest caused by this contest. There were over 75 per cent that knew them all and I hear the gems referred to almost daily. The following are the gems used:

(A) An ounce of pluck is worth a pound of luck.

(B) Be a man among men, for your mother's sake.

(C) Conquer your bad habits just as you would conquer a hard problem in arithmetic; one exercise is as good as the other to educate you.

(D) Do what conscience says is right; do what reason says is best; do with willing mind and heart; do your duty and be blest.

(E) Ever learn to live well that thou mayest die so too; to live and die is all we have to do.

(F) Friendship is the cement which really combines mankind.

(G) God is our Creator, our Father and Benefactor, and is such a Creator, Father and Benefactor as deserves our highest love.

(H) Hasty tempers break good resolutions.

(I) I would rather be right than president of the United States.

(J) Join hands with no one who does not love his country and his fellowman.

(K) Keep your pennies and you will never want for dollars.

(L) Love will beget love; a wish to be at peace will keep you in peace; you can overcome evil with good; there is no other way.

(M) Make no promise you cannot keep.

(N) Never strive with your superiors in argument, but submit your judgment with modesty.

(O) Object to being led into doing what you know to be wrong.

(P) Profanity never made a gentleman and has ruined thousands.

(Q) Quarrels are like eggs; they grow worse with age.

(R) Refuse to do a mean action be it ever so small.

(S) Sympathy makes stronger friends than gold, silver, or flattery.

(T) The greatest monument of civilization is the home.

(U) Understand yourself and you will better understand others.

(V) Very poor are they that have no patience; no wound did ever heal but by degrees.

(W) Whatsoever thy hand findeth to do, do it with all your might.

(Y) Yield not to the flattery of one whom you have a reason to suspect.

(Z) Zeal, rightly applied, will make a companion worth knowing.—Floyd D. Moore, Principal of School at Sylvan, Oregon.

Selections for Memorizing.

The following are selections for memorizing prescribed by the Oregon State Course of Study, and are for first, second, third, fourth and fifth grades in the order given:

O Dandelion Yellow As Gold.

O dandelion, yellow as gold,
  What do you do all day?
I just wait here in the tall green grass
Till the children come to play.

O dandelion, yellow as gold,
  What do you do all night?
I wait and wait till the cool dews fall
And my hair grows long and white.

And what do you do when your hair is white,
  And the children come to play?
They take me up in their dimpled hands
And blow my hair away.
  —Anonymous.

A Dutch Lullaby.

Wynken, Blynken, and Nod one night
Sailed off in a wooden shoe—
Sailed on a river of misty light

Into a sea of dew.
"Where are you going and what do you wish?"
The old moon asked the three.
"We have come to fish for the herring-fish
That live in this beautiful sea;
Nets of silver and gold have we,"
    Said Wynken,
      Blynken,
    And Nod.

The old moon laughed and sang a song,
  And they rocked in the wooden shoe,
And the wind that sped them all night long
  Ruffled the waves of dew.
The little stars were the herring-fish
  That lived in the beautiful sea;
"Now cast your nets wherever you wish
  But never afeared are we—"
So cried the stars to the fishermen three,
    Wynken,
      Blynken,
    And Nod.

All night long their nets they threw
  For the fish in the twinkling foam,
Then down from the sky came the wooden shoe,
  Bringing the fishermen home
'Twas all so pretty a sail, it seemed
  As if it could not be;
And some folks thought 'twas a dream they'd dreamed
  Of sailing that beautiful sea.
But I shall name you the fishermen three:
    Wynken,
      Blynken,
    And Nod.

Wynken and Blynken are two little eyes,
  And Nod is a little head,
And the wooden shoe that sailed the skies
  Is a wee one's trundle bed;
So shut your eyes while mother sings
  Of wonderful sights that be,
And you shall see the beautiful things
  As you rock in the misty sea,
Where the old shoe rocked the fishermen three—
    Wynken,
      Blynken,
    And Nod.
        —Eugene Field.

Wishing.

Ring-ting! I wish I were a primrose,
A bright yellow primrose blowing in the spring!
The stooping boughs above me,
The wandering bee to love me,
The fern and moss to creep across,
And the elm tree for our king!

Nay—stay! I wish I were an elm tree,
A great, lofty elm tree, with green leaves gay!
The winds would set them dancing,
The sun and moonshine dance in,
The birds would house among the boughs,
And sweetly sing.

O—no! I wish I were a robin,
A robin or a little wren everywhere to go!
Through forest, field, or garden,
And ask no leave or pardon
Till winter comes with icy thumbs,
To ruffle up our wings!

Well—tell! Where should I fly to,
Where go to sleep in the dark wood or
   dell?
Before a day was over,
Home comes the rover,
For mother's kiss—sweetest this
Than any other thing.
                    William Allingham.

The Year's at the Spring.

The year's at the spring,
   The day's at the morn;
   Morning's at seven;
The hillside's dew pearled;
   The lark's on the wing;
   The snail's on the thorn;
   God's in His heaven—
All's right with the world!
                    —Robert Browning.

Old Ironsides.

Ay, tear her tattered ensign down!
   Long has it waved on high,
And many an eye has danced to see
that banner in the sky;
Beneath it rung the battle shout,
   And burst the cannon's roar;
The meteor of the ocean air
   Shall sweep the clouds no more.

Her deck, once red with heroe's blood,
   Where knelt the vanquished foe,
When winds were hurrying o're the
   flood,
   And waves were white below,
No more shall feel the victor's tread,
   Or know the conquered knee;
The harpies of the shore shall pluck
   The eagle of the sea!

Oh, better that her shattered hulk
   Should sink beneath the wave;
Her thunders shook the mighty deep,
   And there should be her grave;
Nail to the mast her holy flag,
   Set every threadbare sail,
And give her to the god of storms,
   The lightning and the gale!
                    —Oliver W. Holmes.

Oregon State Library

By CORNELIA MARVIN, Librarian, Oregon State Library

Library Literature of Interest.

"Aids in High School Teaching: Pictures and Objects," by J. C. Dana and Blanche Gardner, contains definite information in regard to illustratice material for all the subjects in the high school curriculum—slides, postcards, photographs, etc., being one of the most helpful publications recently received in our library.

The High School Libraries number of the Wilson Bulletin will be of service to anyone who is trying to make a high school library more useful or to organize it more effectively.

Esther M. Davis, librarian of the Broklyn Training School for Teachers, and Agnes Cowie, children's librarian of Pratt Institute Free Library, have issued a pamphlet "Library aids for teachers and school librarians." This gives titles of helpful material for picture study, storytelling, and school literature in general.

The Wisconsin state superintendent has issued a pamphlet on "Lessons on the use of the school library" which will be useful to anyone who is trying to teach children how to use books. The lessons are very definite and helpful, and contain excellent suggestions on the use of ordinary reference books, cyclopaedias, dictionaries, etc.

The National Council of Teachers of English have issued a report of the Committee on Home Reading, which gives a list of books which teachers may recommend for home reading for high school pupils.

The Massachusetts Agricultural College has isued a leaflet recommending the following books for teachers who are to go out to rural schools. Any of these may be borrowed from the state library, as may the pamphlets mentioned above. They are: Benson & Betts, Agriculture; Bryan, Poems of Country Life; Burroughs, Songs of Nature; Carney, Country Life and the Country School; Cubberley, Rural Life and Education; Cutler and Stone, The Rural School; Curtis, Play and Recreation for the Open Country; Eggleston & Bruere, The Work of the Rural School; Field, The Corn Lady; Fiske, Challenge of the Country; Foght, The American Rural School; Kern, Among Country Schools; McKeever, Farm Boys and Girls; Meier, School and Home Gardens; Wray, Jean Mitchell's school.

Cleveland Educational Survey.

The findings of this survey will be issued in a series of twenty-five books which will be bought by the state library. The titles of those already prepared are as follows: Health Work in the Public Schools, Child Accounting in the Public Schools, What the Schools Teach and Might Teach, Financing the Public Schools, Education Through Recreation, Educational Extension, School Buildings and Equipment, Measuring the Work of the Public School. The publications resulting from this survey are as important and useful as any recent educational literature.

New Books on Education.

The following titles, and notes, are taken from the Booklist prepared by the American Library Association. Any of the books may be borrowed from the Oregon State Library:

Bolenius, Teaching Literature in the Grammar Grades and High School, $1.25 net. "A work which is based on a broad conception and on thorough knowledge and experience. It presents literature in practical lessons and yet does not deprive it of its power to please and inspire. It can be used by country as well as city teachers. References to sources are exact and there is a good index."

Bolenius, The Teaching of Oral English, $1 net. An interestingly written, wide awake text for teachers, unique in that it gives so many concrete examples from the author's personal experiences in developing an effective oral English program for the four high-school years. Discusses fundamental principles and gives suggestive exercises which may be adapted for use in any high school.

Dewey, Democracy and Education, $1.40 net. An introduction to the philosophy of education, which endeavors "to detect and state the ideas implied in a democratic society and to apply these ideas to the problems of the enterprise of education." "A notable contribution. . . The book is more than an educational treatise. The student, and especially the teacher, of philosophy will find in it a much-needed statement of the writer's general philosophy, bringing together his views in education, psychology, theory of knowledge, ethics, and social theory."

Espey, Leaders of Girls, 75c net. In a simple manner the author presents the characteristics of girls during the adolescent period, mingling the facts of psychology with the wisdom gained from her own wide experience. Definite help is given on how to solve certain problems of individual girls, and the more general problems of the club life and activities. Useful specially to inexperienced leaders of girls' clubs.

Graves, A Student's History of Education, $1.25 net. Not condensed from the author's History of Education in three volumes but rewritten from a new angle, with stress placed on institutions and practices, rather than on theories, the whole designed to help the teacher understand the origin and significance of current practices. Devotes about a half of the book to the education of modern times and emphasizes American conditions. Helpful features are the outline at the beginning of each chapter and the list of books for supplementary reading at the end.

New York Ethical Culture School; America the Wonderland; A Patriotic Festival, 60c. Describes one of the Patriots' Day festivals, given by the Ethical Culture School, New York, as a part of its school work. Tells in some detail how the sixth and seventh grade children made out their plan, worked out the symbolism and the historic scenes, and prepared for the performance of the play. Gives the text of the play and the music used for the interpretative dances.

Payne, The Child in Human Progress, $2.50 net. A historical survey of the treatment accorded children among primitive people, ancient and modern, of the child's place in the domestic, social and economninc life of ancient society, in the Middle Ages, under the factory system, up to and including the rise of the modern movement for child protection.

Sandwick, How to Study and What to Study, 60c net. The author believes that the "coaching idea" should be applied to studies as it is to athletics. These informal talks to young students give general principles, tell why and how to study various high-school subjects, suggest reasons and requirements for vocational subjects and some of the older professions.

Kraps' Manuals.

Owing to the fact that the price of paper has doubled, J. J. Kraps is compelled to add a few cents each to the price of his manuals. The price of the Students Edition will be 25 cents instead of 20 cents. Teachers manuals for one year paper will remain at the same price, 35 cents, but those for five year papers will be 40 cents and for life papers 50 cents. These prices do not include cost of parcel post which is about 10 cents. These manuals will all be enlarged and brought up to and include the questions for the last June examination, and will be found very useful in the daily work of the school room.

Hight School Teachers' Department
Edited by HOPKIN JENKINS, Portland, Oregon

Printing in the Public Schools.

The introduction of printing in the high schools curiculum has passed the experimental stage and may be classed as a fixture in Eastern cities. but Jefferson High is the pioneer on the Pacific coast.

The correlation between the English, Mathematics, Art and Printing departments in high schools is gratifying and has proved the worth of the latter wherever given a trial. In the English department the work of students electing printing, (for this should be an elective subject) has been, without exception, much improved. It is found greater emphasis can be paced upon errors if the student is compelled to personally correct his mistakes (as he of necessity must do in printing). Like errors are seldom made, once they are corrected in cold type, and a poor speller soon becomes fair, and then good. In punctuation the student's knowledge is emphasized equally with spelling, while in the proper division of words printing fills a long-felt want, for even college graduates are woefully deficient here, that is, those who have not taken up Journalism or Printing. So it is with the four "tions"—punctuation, capitalization, syllabication and indentation (of poetry) the average student's grades are much improved "after-taking."

The subject develops the artistic ability of the student, and enables him to utilize his individuality, which other studies have possibly failed to bring out. The principles of drawing and design are also an issue, as is Mathematics. Wm. B. Kemprath, principal of the public school of printing, Buffalo, N. Y., says: "Typography is an exacting science; its very foundation stone is mathematics."

Superintendent J. P. Brouse of Somerset, Ky., says: "There are six principal values, as I see them, to be gained from the adoption of Printing in the school curriculum, namely: The training in that particular line as a trade or vocation; its value to the student as to his habits, neatness, exactness and initiative, correct use of punctuation marks and spelling, the interest the pupil takes in other school work, through the influence of Printing, design, and ideas of cost."

S. J. Vaughn, of the North Illinois State Normal, says: "Send me a

sleepy-headed, uninterested bad boy from the school, the street or the jail, and I'll put him in the print shop half of each day with a little instruction, and he will wake up, clean up and get busy. He'll at once become absorbed in this real man's work; his pride will grow with his skill and he'll learn more spelling, more arithmetic, more punctuation, more grammar, more patience and more manhood in three months than in the previous three years, if not in all his previous life." These are the views of men who have tried the system and it has not been found wanting.

A few excerpts from the findings of a survey conducted by the Cincinnati Chamber of Commerce are here given, that all may understand how business men consider the subject in the large Eastern cities. They follow: "The public school has a legitimate function which it must perform. It is the duty of the shop to give apprentices full opportunity for that trade training and practical experience which can be secured best in the shop, but to leave to the school supplementary training in technique, theory and citizenship. In other words the school should train for the industries, but not in the industries. This idea is concurred in by the official representatives of the United Typothea of America (employers' association) and by the committee on Industrial Education of the American Federation of Labor.

"On the whole the printing industry offers good opportunity for the boy who wants to learn a trade and is adapted for his work. The work is generally healthful, employment regular and income good.

"Employers in nearly every instance indicate the beginners lack in general intelligence and that they are deficient in reading, writing, grammar, punctuation, capitalization, arithmetic, etc.

"Apprentice instruction now consists of simply turning the boy over to the foreman or some other workman, who does or does not instruct the boy, according to his inclinations or opportunity. The shop is failing in its duty toward the beginner.

"There has appeared no worthy argument in favor of a trade school which is supposed to turn out skilled workmen.

"Printing in the public schools is

highly desirable as manual-training work—but should always be considered as manual-training work strictly and not in any sense the teaching of a trade.

"Schools in which printing is taught as a manual training subject should not commercialize their work. "The teacher of Printing should be selected from the trade and not from the schools."

Another feature may appeal to the school board, and that is the saving which may be effected by a printing plant. By arranging with the instructor for an eight-hour, six-day schedule, working 12 months (that is, with vacation), it will be found that the plant will pay for itself, besides giving students who show an aptitude a chance to learn much regarding the trade which is usually neglected in the shop. These would, of course, eventually find their way into commercial plants, where credit will be given as to time served, according to ability. A plant of this nature soon pays for itself. Only school work, however, is considered legitimate. If outside work is accepted it will be to the detriment of the plant, for any attempt to introduce child labor with the idea of monetary gain for the school district will be taking profit from one of the nation's greatest industries and will not fail to excite righteous indignation among the business interests. But the work for the district should keep the instructor busy.

Comparatively few students who study history become historians; so possibly few who take up Printing will follow the subject as a vocation, but all will leave school much better equipped to meet and master world conditions than those who do not take at least a few terms' work of this new addition to the school curriculum.—Ortley W. Athey, Instructor of Printing, Jefferson High School, Portland.

Grade Teachers' Department

Edited by VIOLA ORTSCHILD, President of Portland Grade Teachers' Association

Elementary teachers and elementary teachers' associations are cordially invited to send news items of their activities which would be of interest or value to other teachers to this department of the The Oregon Teachers Monthly. Address Editor of Grade Teachers' Department, Room 300, Court House, Portland, Oregon.

The Department of the Interior has recently issued a "National Parks Portfolio" which contains beautifully illustrated informational pamphlets of nine of the great "playgrounds" of the American people. These national parks are: Glacier, Mt. Rainier, The Rocky Mountain, The Sequoia, Yosemite, Yellowstone, Mesa Verde, Grand Canyon, and last but not least, our own wonderful Crater Lake. The portfolio does not seem to be designed for general distribution but one may possibly be secured by writing to Oregon congressmen, or directly to the Department of the Interior. Every child in our land should grow up with a knowledge of the beauty and grandeur which is his natural heritage by birthright. Valuable lessons in appreciation and love of his country could be instilled into children through such teaching.

* * *

The Parents' Educational Bureau, Room 551, Court House, Portland, has for distribution some helpful pamphlets which will be sent free and post paid to teachers who may wish to use them in their school work. Among the publications which might be of value to teachers are the following: "The Cigarette Smoking Boy," "Teaching the Boy to Save," "Teaching the Girl to Save." A leaflet issued by the Portland District Dental Society contains much information which children should know. It will also be sent by the Bureau.

* * *

Bulletin, 1915, No. 47, a "Digest of State Laws Relating to Public Education," in force January 1, 1915, is a comprehensive publication of almost 1000 pages. It was issued by the Bureau of Education in 1916. Teachers and teachers' organizations will find a study of this bulletin of value to them if they wish to have an intelligent idea of various phases of education throughout the United States as reflected in school laws. All betterment for teaching conditions must come from teachers themselves.

A study of tenure laws and of teachers' retirement funds would put at the command of members of the teaching profession of Oregon a knowledge of the experiences and experiments of other states as a guide to aid them in legislation which may be enacted in the near future.

* * *

"The Elementary Teacher" is the official organ of the League of Teachers' Associations. It is issued in Baltimore during the school year at a subscription price of 50 cents a year. The aims of this grade teachers' organ are set forth in the following statement: "The Elementary Teacher" is published to promote the welfare of the grade teachers; to cultivate a closer feeling of fellowship; to discuss fairly, freely, and truthfully all questions which may be of interest to teachers and to the community at large; and to use its influence and its columns to bring the general public to a realization of the value—educational, cultural, and moral—of the grade teacher to the community. The teacher is the school."

* * *

During the summer of 1915, Miss Harriet Wood, of the Portland Library, inaugurated a course of talks on children's literature. So enthusiastic were the teachers who attended these talks that the course was repeated during the following winter, and again this summer with an increased attendance, about twenty-five or more coming to each meeting. Beginning with the first Saturday in October the same course will be given in the School Department of the Portland Library at 10:30 o'clock. Teachers may attend one or all of the lectures as they find it convenient. The course is free and is especially designed for those who wish to know how to get their pupils to read good literature. During the past summer those who attended most regularly were: Miss Katherine Cahalin, Miss Olita Cooley, Miss Frances Dowd, Miss Josephine O'Leary, Miss Florence Harris, Miss Lucile Hays, Miss Katherine Padden, Miss Charlotte Reed, Mrs. Lulu D. Scott, Miss Ethel Slusser, Miss Frances Smith, Miss Florence Smith, Miss Anna Sorensen, Miss Matie Train, Miss Teresa Baccrich, Miss Elizabeth Fitz, Miss Ella Anderson, Miss Mary C. Coman of California, and Mrs. C. F. Collier of La Conde, Alberta.

* * *

The School Department of the Portland Library takes the best magazines of value to teachers either for professional reading or for teaching. "The School and Society," a weekly publication, is in advance of its kind. "The National Geographic Magazine," for April, has colored illustrations of Indian life. It is especially interesting. The American Forestry Magazine has, in a late number, some fine pictures of the Columbia Highway. These publications and many others may be taken out for a month on a teacher's card.

* * *

Multnomah county teachers are urged to register in the School Department of the Portland Library immediately. Each teacher may select a library relating to the work of the school. This library will be sent to the school with the library for the home reading of the pupils, just as soon as the school opens. Teachers are asked to make a special effort to interest pupils in books and to keep an accurate record of books taken for home reading. Pictures and books may also be taken on teacher's card for one month or longer. A marked difference is noted in the same schools under different teachers. Some remarkable results have been achieved by several teachers. It is an acknowledged fact that the teacher who is a lover of books is the one who is interesting her pupils in good literature.

* * *

The Tacoma teachers have established a Tacoma Teachers' Co-operative Insurance Fund. Any teacher in the corps may become a member on the payment of an annual premium of two dollars. The benefits are an allowance of $10 for each full week's absence caused by illness of the member, or a payment of $50 to the estate of the teacher in case of death. Those co-operating are: The Tacoma Grade Teachers' Association, the Men Principals' Club, the Tacoma branch of the State Women's Educational League, the High School teachers, and other teachers actively engaged in the instruction department of the Tacoma public schools.

* * *

On May 10, the teachers in the Washington, D. C. high schools organized a union to be affiliated with the American Federation of Labor. A call was issued to 600 high school teachers. The reasons for organizing as follows: "Every class of people the union are enumerated in the call in the country including capital, labor, and the professions have nation-wide organizations for their protection and well being. Teachers alone remain in an unorganized condition."

* * *

In June Superintendent Alderman, of the Portland schools, called together a number of the English teachers to discuss means by which the teaching of correct usage of English might become more effective. The outcome of the discussion led to the formation of a Grammar Club which decided to take up the intensive study of eliminating gross errors of language in the Portland schools. Miss Cartmell, of Shattuck school, was elected president, and Miss Elph Smith of Ladd school, secretary. The club selected ten of the grosser errors for its first efforts. A meeting will probably be called soon after the Portland schools re-open in the fall. All teachers interested are invited to become members.

* * *

The holidays of the Portland schools for the year are ten—three during the first term and seven during the second. They are: November 30 and December 1, January 1, February 22, April 6 and 9, May 30, June 6, 7, 8. The week of Easter holidays is not allowed, but two days are given, Friday, April 6, and Monday, April 9. The Rose Festival days are given as regular holidays instead, June 6, 7, 8.

* * *

Among the Portland teachers who attended the summer school of the University of Washington and distinguished themselves in Journalism were Miss Jessie McGregor, Miss Lillian Porter (Brockton exchange teacher), Miss Estelle J. McIntyre, and Miss Winifred Hawley.

* * *

Miss Alicia Pearl Horner, Miss Anna Johnson, Miss Mathilda Ahrends, Miss Medora Whitfield, Miss Genevieve Ryan, and Miss Ellyn Thelander were appointed by Miss Ortschild, president of the Portland Grade Teachers' Association to represent the Association at the convention of the National League of Teachers' Associations held in New York City, July 3-7. Miss Anna Johnson discussed Portland's tenure law and other legislation favorable to Ore-gon teachers. Intense interest was displayed by the delegates from other states. Miss Ahrends gave a report of the activities of the Association during the past year. Miss Horner was chairman of the Portland delegates.

* * *

The Portland Grade Teachers' Association will hold it regular meetings for 1916-1917 on the second Wednesday of the school month. The meetings are held in Library Hall at half after four o'clock. The change of meeting day was voted at the last meeting in June. The constitution was thus amended because the last of the month, the teacher's busiest time, was inconvenient and because many of the holidays fell on those dates requiring several changes last year. The first meeting this fall will be Wednesday, September 13.

* * *

The Portland Grade Teachers' Association offers to its members a large opportunity for usefulness and self-activity by accepting membership on or co-operating with the Association's commitees appointed to work for the betterment of the community, the teaching profession or the welfare of themselves. These committees are: Civic, Professional, Social, Legislative, Press, Program, Teachers' Affairs, League, "Bulletin," Headquarters, Relief, Out Door, School Garden, and Mailing. There have also been many special committees which arranged classes in aesthetic dancing, swimming, Spanish and other languages, design, etc. The work of the various committees will be resumed with the beginning of the school year on September 4th. The first meeting of the Association will be held Wednesday, September 13.

* * *

The officers of the Portland Grade Teachers' Association for 1916-1917 are as follows: President, Miss Viola Ortschild; Recording Secretary, Miss Lutie Cake; Corresponding Secretary, Miss Eugenia Morse; Treasurer, Mrs. Lucy D. Hoye; Vice-Presidents, First Grade, Mrs Josephine Lisher, Second Grade, Mrs. Cora Fraine, Third Grade, Miss Anna Biesen, Fourth Grade, Miss Anne Cooley, Fifth Grade, Miss Madge Hill, Sixth Grade, Miss Anna Dudley, Seventh Grade, Miss Harriet Monroe, Eighth Grade, Miss Mary Fryer, Ninth Grade, Miss Winifred Dennis. The Association closed the year with a membership of 629. Inquiries concerning the activities of the Association or suggestions for teachers who may desire to form an organization may be addressed to Miss Morse, corresponding secretary at Holladay School, Portland.

Believe with all your heart that you will do what you were made to do. Never for an instant harbor a doubt of this. Drive it out of your mind if it seeks entrance. Entertain only the friend thoughts or ideals of the thing you are bound to achieve. Reject all thought enemies, all discouraging moods—everything which would even suggest failure or unhappiness.—Selected.

Please remember that the price of the Oregon Teachers Monthly is now $1.50 per year and this will include membership in the State Teachers' Association for either the eastern or western division.

Vocational Education Department

Edited by R. E. CHLOUPEK, Pendleton, Oregon

Field Notes.

McMinnville.—A course in concrete work will be offered this year. The manual training department takes care of all the repairs for the school district and has erected the play sheds and wood sheds. Mr. F. H. Buchanan has been re-elected.

Enterprise. — Enterprise offers work in carpentry and forging which is intended to be of immediate, practical value on the farm.

Grants Pass.—Grade equipment is being contemplated as additional. Mr. H. H. Wardrip will again have charge with the assistance of Mr. A. C. Archbold, a newly elected member of the teaching force.

Medford.—Additional equipment of tools and benches to the extent of $600 will be added. The manual training department last year turned out 500 bird houses and 25 rustic seats and benches for the Medford park. Mr. Otto Klum is again at the head of the department with the assistance of Mr. L. H. Blakely, a recent O. A. C. graduate.

Independence.—Mr. Theodore Ellestad has been re-elected and is planning on putting in a cobbling course and forging. A circular saw may be installed.

Forest Grove. — Mr. Randolph Thomas has been re-elected teacher of manual training.

Pendleton.—A course in gas engines and gas tractors will be offered this fall. Mr. R. E. Chloupek will again head the department with the assistance of Mr. Clarence Tubbs (re-elected), who has charge of the

grade woodwork and the forging, and Mr. Virgil Fendall, a last year's O. A. C. graduate in the gas engine work. A short course for farmers is being planned in forging, carpentry, concrete work and gas engine and gas tractor work.

Corvallis.—Mr. A. R. Nichols will again have charge of the manual training.

Wallowa.—Mr. J. C. Hall has been re-elected. Wallowa offers practical courses in carpentry, concrete work and plumbing that are hard to beat.

Astoria.—Emphasis is being placed on the department doing all the repair work possible for the school district. Mr. E. M. Hussong has been re-elected.

Ashland.—New equipment consisting of bench and tool equipment will be installed for the Junior High school. A two year course in' carpentry will be offered. Mr. Delmar Haman has been re-elected and Mr. Heidreich has been added to the faculty.

Baker.—Mr. E. E. Romig will again have charge of the department.

Albany.—Mr. E. A. Hudson and Mr. J. R. Hudson will have charge of the work in Albany.

Newport.—Mr. C. E. Freeland, who has been re-elected, will install the work in the Junior High school.

Manual Training As a Practical Subject.

At the recent N. E. A. meeting one of the topics that gained special attention was Manual Training as a Practical Subject. It would seem that, to be a thoroughly practical subject, manual training must be closely allied with the interests of the community. We teachers of Oregon have practically the same problems to consider in making up our course of study and that is, the giving of work which is directly applicable to farm life. There is not a place in the state perhaps, outside of the city of Portland, which is not dependable on the agricultural interests for its existence. Such being the case why not give the kind of manual training that has an immediate, practical value on the farm. It should mean the giving of carpentry, concrete work, forging, gas engine work, work in leather, and a course in farm mechanics.

From reports from over 65 per cent of the schools in the state in which manual training is given the following figures are noted: Fifty per cent give nothing but joinery, furniture work and mechanical drawing; the remaining 50 per cent offer, besides the above subjects, the following—21 per cent offer carpentry and concrete work, 17 per cent offer carpentry, 11 per cent offer carpentry and forging, one-half per cent offer carpentry, concrete work, forging and gas engine work.

Reports from the remaining schools would probably change these figures slightly but the big point remains that 50 per cent of the schools of the state do not offer the kind of manual training that their communities require. We are as far behind the newer movements in manual training as we were, and still are for that matter, late in adding manual training to our course of study. The majority of schools are giving work which consists of the making of furniture and small models, and nothing but that, to boys, many of whom must make their living on the farm. True, they are being offered handwork which will do them a great amount of good but they are not being offered that type of work which will do them the most amount of good, in that it would be directly applicable in their after life. It is the old theory of offering a subject to the pupil because it is good for them, regardless of the fact that something else might be offered which would give them the same amount of training and at the same time have some practical value which would be of concrete use.

You ask why this state of affairs exists? The answer is this, either superintendents are not so thoroughly in touch with what constitutes real good, live manual training that they will demand that kind, or the manual training teachers are not equipped to teach the practical lines of work and will not take the steps to acquire that knowledge. Some will try to say that they cannot get the money needed to install such courses. Carpentry can be offered with the same equipment that is used for bench work; concrete work calls for a few shovels, a wheelbarrow and some floats; gas engine work for one or two types of engines which can be borrowed from the different implement dealers; forging does call for additional equipment but how many schools there are that are contemplating additional wood working machinery when the call of the community is for agricultural forging. I have in mind a small town in Umatilla county that has a $450 universal saw table, no carpentry, no forging, no concrete work. The teacher is giving the farmer boys the gentle art of making small pieces of furniture and a few models and he is giving it in a community where 95 per cent of the boys will go back to the farm to earn their living.

Many of the schools that are offering carpentry are offering it in a limited way. Why not make the practical courses the strongest courses and do away with the others entirely if there are not enough teachers to handle them? I do not wish to be placed in the position of saying that the teaching of cabinet making is useless. My point is that for this state with its agricultural interests, it is not the course which should receive the most attention as it is at the present time. Make an industrial survey of the community in which you are teaching manual training, find what the industries are, and where the boys go to take up their work, and then give them something that they can use, that will make them better wage earners, and more competent leaders.

A city superintendent, not so very long ago, told me that his community was peculiar in that they wanted manual training for the educational value and did not care to have it placed on a practical commercial basis. Does manual training lose its educational value when we teach it under as nearly the same conditions as we would find in the shop or on some job? Manual training is not a cultural subject and the day when it was given as a fad so that the pupil could do a little arts craft work is long since gone by. If it is not a live subject intimately connected with work that is done by working men and if it has not a practical value in dollars and cents I say it is missing the point that it should make. It should be some: ... for the eight dollar a week boys, something that will make the boy that goes to the farm worth more to the farmer and himself. Will the boy that gets such training have less education than the boy who gets the arts crafts work?

Vocational Education.

As a corollary of the great advancement that has been made in sloyd, manual training, pre-vocational work, vocational education, and industrial education, within the past 30 years, the educational leaders in the United States are confronted with the demand for a more practical study of industrial and vocational conditions.

This demand is nation wide and is being met by the introduction of a new department in our public school system. This late addition to our curriculum is, in its present state of development, commonly known as "Vocational Guidance." Whether this is the term that fully expresses the aim of the departments being organized in many different states, or whether the aim will be more forcefully stated by using the name "Vocational Study," the future will show.

It is self-evident that an education that aims to fit all the children of all the people for an efficient life in the environment where they may be placed must have as a corner stone for the structure, "Universal Education," a broad knowledge of the occupations, industries, vocations, of the world in general and the United States in particular.

Different plans are being tried. Some school people are imbued with the idea that such a study or department must be an off-shoot from the English department. Others claim that only those who have had broad contact with the practical life of the

nation are competent to assume leadership in such a department. Be this as it may, the demand for a "Vocational Guidance" department in our schools is growing apace.

No stronger testimony as to the insistance of the demand for a universal education for the citizens of the United States can be offered than a quotation from the message of President Wilson to the present congress: "A matter which it seems to me we should have very much at heart is the creation of the right instrumentalities by which to mobilize our economic resources in any time of national necessity." Among the recommendations made by the president as suggestive means by which this desired end may be attained is: "We should give intelligent federal aid and stimulation to industrial and vocational education as we have long done in the large field of our agricultural industry."

The great interest that is taken by many of the leaders in congress in behalf of the Smith-Hughes Vocational Education Bill shows that these men are aroused by the demand that is made for an efficient education for all the people.

As an amendment to the Army Bill in the present congress, it was proposed to provide that 70 hours per month of a soldier's time should be given to training in the agricultural and mechanical arts. This amendment was discussed from many different viewpoints and was, after many details were adjusted, included in the army bill as passed in May of this year. (See Industrial-Arts Magazine, August, 1916).

As indications that the demand for the study of vocations will be answered it is useful to note some of the progressive movements along this line. Teachers College, Columbia University, New York City, has been offering a course in vocational education under the direction of Dr. Arthur D. Dean, Director of Industrial Education for the state of New York. Mver Bloomfield of the Vocational Bureau of Boston, Massachusetts, and Dr. David Snedden have been made members of the faculty of the Teachers College to assist in meeting the demand for a broader organization of the study of vocations or vocational guidance.

Commercial clubs and similar civic organizations are showing a commendable interest in vocational study as is shown by the action of Chamber of Commerce of Sacramento, California. F. W. Thomas, chairman of the Vocational Guidance Committee, has charge of the work and subcommittees will investigate or study 16 of the leading industries of Sacramento with a view of recommending the best methods of co-operation between the schools and industries for preparing young people to enter the local industries.,

Many cities are adding vocational guidance or vocational study to their curriculum with the beginning of the school year 1916-17. Among these Seattle, Washington, takes a leading place. They have not completed their organization at this date, but with Supt. Cooper at the head and the co-operation of all concerned it is safe to predict an efficient organization for Seattle.

Report Cards.

The Oregon Teachers Monthly can furnish report cards for one cent each. The cards are well printed on heavy manilla and are arranged for a nine months' term. A sample will be sent free.

City Superintendents' Department

Edited by GEORGE W. HUG, McMinnville, Oregon

School Items of Interest.

Miss Vera Asbury, principal of the Lewisburg high school near Corvallis, has been engaged to teach English in the McMinnville junior high school.

R. W. Kirk, Superintendent of Schools for the last nine years at Corvallis, will be superintendent of Tillamook next year, succeeding Carl Onthank who goes to the University of Oregon to act as private secretary to President Campbell. J. M. Powers of Seattle, formerly superintendent of Salem schools, takes Mr. Kirk's place at Corvallis.

William Scott, instructor in history at Corvallis high school, will be principal of the schools at Monroe this year.

Chester Huggins, famous Oregon athlete who had charge of athletics at Milwaukie high school, this year will coach and teach at Klamath Falls high school.

Burr Tatro, former instructor at Behnke-Walker Business College and last year head of the commercial department at the Oregon City high school, will take charge of the commercial department at the McMinnville high school.

Jesse McCord, principal of schools at Clakskanie, has been re-elected president of the "500 club" at the University of Oregon Summer School.

J. W. Crites of the Coquille high school has been elected principal of the Hood River high school. L. B. Gibson, principal of Hood River high school for the past six years, was appointed county superintendent of Hood River county.

J. H. Pruitt, who secured his M. A. degree from the University of Chicago will teach Physics and Chemistry in the Medford high school. Mr. Pruitt was former instructor of science at Newberg high school.

Superintendent James E. Dunton of Cottage Grove is superintendent of schools at Lebanon this year. Supt. Franklin Thordarson, former superintendent has assumed the superintendency at Bend.

Matrimony seems to have afflicted the Eugene high school. Principal F. A. Schofield was married in California this summer. Miss Mildred Bagley, physical instructor for girls, was married in June to David Graham, a young business man of Eugene. Mable G. Fonda, of the teachers' training department, will wed a business man from New York. Clarence F. Mudge, head of the manual training department, was married to Miss Sylvia Ross in July. Mr. and Mrs. Mudge have gone to Modesto, California, where Mr. Mudge will be head of the manual training of that city.

Carl B. Fenton, famous Oregon athlete and physical director for the Eugene high school is running for assessor of Polk county on the Democratic ticket.

Ray D. Fisher, for seven years head of the English department in the Eugene high school, has resigned and will attend Columbia university next year.

Harvey F. Wilson, after 14 years of efficient service as principal of McMinnville high school, has resigned and is in the automobile business at Forest Grove. G. H. Obertauffer, of Junction City, succeeds him.

Miss Lena Newton, of Springfield high school, has been elected at the Dallas high school next year.

Supt. O. M. Elliott, of the Salem schools, has been appointed president of the Lewiston Normal School, at Lewiston, Idaho. Supt. J. W. Todd, of Auburn, Washington, will succeed him at Salem. The Auburn schools are modeled after the famous Gary, Indiana, schools. The Oregn educational public will watch for some progressive educational developments at Salem.

H. O. Clancy, athletic coach at Salem high school who has been turning out winning teams for that school for the last two years, will not be at Salem this year.

Vernon T. Motchenbaeher, of Klamath Falls high school, will be principal of one of the junior high schools at Medford.

J. O. Russell, for four years principal of the Wasco schools, will be superintendent of schools at Athena.

A. T. Park, principal at Hermiston, is now city superintendent of Pendleton public schools. H. Drill will be principal of the high school.

Supt. John Girdler, of La Grande, was elected superintendent of schools at Ogden, Utah, succeedng J. M. Mill. Mr. Girdler has declined the Ogden offer and will go into business.

Charles E. Olson, principal of La Grande high school will be superintendent at Ilwaco, Washington. Linden McCulloch, superintendent at Roslyn, Washington, will be the new superintendent at LaGrande. A. C. Hampton, of Pendleton, has been offered the high school principalship.

Supt. H. E. Inlow, of Forest Grove, passed the bar examination during July.

Geo. A. Gabriel, history and science teacher at Dayton, is now with Company A of the 3rd Oregon Regiment on the Mexican border. Roy R. Hewitt, principal at Yamhill, and Guy Brace, science teacher at Yamhill, are also in the company.

W. H. Burton, commercial and teacher's training instructor at the McMinnville high school, will attend Teacher's College at Columbia University, New York. Elton C. Loucks, of the same school, will attend the Graduate School of Business of Harvard University next year.

John Mason, of the English and Public Speaking Department of the McMinnville high school, will have similar work at the Oregon City high school next year.

Principal W. L. Arant, of the Newberg high school, will be high school principal at Oregon City.

Miss Grace Henderson, of the McMinnville junior high school, will be principal of the Condon school at Eugene.

Miss Ida Mae Smith, Elementary Supervisor of the Eugene public school, visited schools in California during the month of August.

J. E. McKown, with D. C. Heath and Company, has accepted the principalship of the Bellingham high school.

Luton Ackerson, who has been teaching at Richland, Baker county, has gone to Oxford, England, as the Cecil Rhodes Scholar from Oregon.

Evening on John Day.

Serene, majestic are the hills,
  With meadows gold and green;
The silvery grey of the great John
    Day,
  A winding in between.

The distant low of cattle herd;
  Soft tingling sheep bell sound;
The sun sinks low o'er the mountain
    tops
  And shadows long are on the
    ground.

The greens of sage and Juniper,
  The rim-rock's varied hue,
Of brown and red, of rose and grey;
  And many birds to homeward flew.

O'er all a mighty filmy veil
  Of blues that fade away;
To meet another aery morn,
  'Tis evening on John Day.
  —Rosalie Nicholas, Spray, Ore.

Whoever lives true life will love true love.—Mrs. Browning.

National Education Association Meeting

By L. R. ALDERMAN, Portland, Oregon

The National Education Association for 1916 has gone into history. It met in Greater New York for the first time in many years. The meeting was very well attended, it being estimated that more than 20,000 teachers were there. A most elaborate program had been arranged and it was carried out according to schedule. More eminent men and women, not educators in the sense of being actual teachers, were on the program than have been at any meeting at which I have been present. William H. Taft, Samuel Gomphers, W. J. Bryan and William McAdoo were a few of the speakers of this type.

The general meetings were held in the famous great Madison Square Garden which has a capacity of 20,000 people. In comparison with the tabernacle at Oakland, this meeting place was very satisfactory. The general sessions were well attended. The sectional meetings in some cases were very poorly attended. The teachers in many cases spent this time visiting greater New York to see life as it is lived in this now greatest city in the world.

The school board section was full of interest from the very beginning. The Chicago teacher-school board fight was thoroughly aired. The relation of the school board to administrative officers was taken up by both superintendents and school board members.

The proceedings of this meeting will be extremely valuable and every teacher in Oregon should endeavor to read those that pertain to his or her line of work.

The convention as a whole made me have a stronger liking for the profession of teaching, made me believe more strongly that the average teacher is striving very hard to be a better teacher. But I could not help feeling, too, that many young teachers after attending a great convention such as this was, go home wondering what they ought to do and feeling at a loss as to how to do it, as almost everything we have done and are doing was attacked vigorously.

Throughout the convention there was much discussion of military training in the schools. This provoked the argument of what real preparedness is and caused a general survey of what studies really prepare the student best for life and in consequence, the nation better for defense. I observed a general feeling that we were not doing nearly enough with science and that tradition plays too much of a part in both subject matter and method of teaching.

The convention was free from all signs of politics. This was in great contrast to the meetings of the last few years.

Every teacher ought to plan to attend some meeting of the National Education Association for the satisfaction of soul she would get out of it. The next meeting may possibly come to Portland.

For Making a Hectograph.

Add three ounces of water to one and one-half ounces of white glue. Heat in a water bath (an oatmeal dish answers the purpose very well) until the glue is melted. Then add six ounces of glycerine and pour the mixture into a hollow dish to cool. Place the dish where it will be level, and skim off air bubbles as they rise to the surface with some kind of a straight edge. The pad will be ready for use after standing six or eight hours. Should it prove too hard to copy well, melt it over and add more glycerine, or, if it should prove too soft to wear well, melt it over and add more glue. To use it a bottle of hectograph ink must be obtained. Write the copy and place ink side down on the pad and let it stay a minute or two. Then remove and from that impression let 50 or 100 copies be made. After using, wash the pad off by very gently rubbing it over with a sponge wet with tepid water. As to the cost —the glue can be had for 5 cents, the glycerine for 25 cents, and if a suitable dish is not at hand, a tin 8x10 inches and about half an inch deep can be had for 10 cents. The hectograph ink will cost only 25 cents for the violet and 50 cents for the black, but a bottle will last a long time. A good ink for this purpose may be made by dissolving one dram of purple aniline in one ounce of water.

County Superintendents' Department

Edited by CLYDE T. BONNEY, The Dalles, Oregon

Necessity of Supervision.

The great educational problem be-fore the people of this great commonwealth is "How can we help the rural schools?" The standard of these schools is being raised each year through supervision and the state-wide standardization plan.

About five years ago, when supervision was begun in the rural schools of this state, the standard was very low. At that time the teacher was hired and given a contract to teach the school for a term of from six to nine months. She was expected to take charge of the school and run it the best she could without help. Why should she need any help? She held a teacher's certificate to teach, and knew all about the art of teaching. In a great many of these schools it did not make any difference whether she had any experience, just so she had that certificate.

The school buildings were poorly lighted, heated, and ventilated, had insufficient apparatus, and floors, walls, and cloak rooms were unsanitary. The desks, as a rule, were not adapted to the children, the buildings received very little paint, the grounds were poorly kept, the outbuildings, especially the boys', were in a deplorable condition.

Through the presistent efforts of supervision and the standardization requirements these conditions have been greatly improved. Many have been able to meet all the requirements for a standard school.

These standard schools cannot be had and kept up without supervision. It has caused boards of directors to take a great deal more interest in their schools, and they are now on the alert. They no longer hire a teacher because she holds a certificate, but carefully look up her references, and if she does not measure up to their standard, she is not hired.

If these standards are to grow, we must have the continuity of this supervision. Supervision has been a great factor in bringing about a better co-operation with boards of directors, parents and teachers through social center and parent-teacher organiaztions. All earnest teachers are glad to get help and suggestion, and are glad to be guided by this supervision.—J. E. Calevan, Clackamas County.

Normal Training.

The most important factor in any school system is the teacher and in the smaller districts the teacher is virtually the system. The whole responsibility for the success or failure of the school falls upon her. She does not expect nor get any help in methods of instruction or discipline from her patrons, and even if some of them were able and willing to help her, their work is along different lines which take up all of their spare time, and they are unable to help her. This is also true of the school board, who do not claim to be educators and seldom if ever visit the school. Thus it is that the teacher is left largely to her own resources and succeeds or fails alone.

We congratulate ourselves upon our splendid school system; upon the high qualifications of our teachers but the bare fact remains that our public schools fall far short of the results they should obtain. It is not my intention to discredit in any way the work being done by our public school teacher, but in any enterprise or profession where less than 15 per cent of the number engaged are trained for such work, we cannot expect fair results. I believe, in fact, that the results are beyond what we have a right to expect, considering the opportunities offered by the state for professional training.

Many teachers come to Oregon each year from other states. These teachers are generally well trained. They obtain positions for a year or two in the country schools, then some city superintendent hears of them and takes them into his system. Those teachers whose qualifications city superintendents will not recognize are forced to accept a school for a shorter term at less wages while at the same time the children in the country are given poorer teaching than their more fortunate city cousins. It must be admitted that under present conditions, after all exceptions have been made, that the teaching in the rural districts falls short of the minimum requirements of the village and city schools.

A great majority of our beginning teachers are bright, intelligent, resourceful young men and women, and the only thing to be placed against them is that they lack in education and professional training. It is not enough to say that country teachers are fairly efficient and that under existing conditions they do well. They should be as well trained and the standard of their work should be as high as that required of the city teacher.

Naturally then, we are asked how this defect may be corrected. The question suggests the answer which is, "Better facilities for the educating and training of teachers with especial emphasis on the training for the rural schools." Oregon is far behind her sister states in offering such advantages. In fact only five states in the United States offer as poor accommodations for teacher training as Oregon. There always was and always will be a close relationship between the cost of a school system and its efficiency and while additional advantages for the training of our teachers will mean a little addition to the expense, its value will be returned to the children of the state forty-fold.
—I. E. Young, Umatilla County.

Benton County.

The annual institute for Benton county will be held September 18, 19 and 20.

The School Fair will be held September 14, 15 and 16.

All teachers are hired for the coming year.

Columbia County.

Districts 29, 38, 40 and 44 maintained summer schools this year. Many of the schools open in August and but few later than September 4.

The average salary for men is $100; for women $64. The average district tax voted, 4 mills. With but few exceptions Columbia school districts are free from debt. Only two districts maintained a six-months school during the past year.

The consolidation idea with transportation facilities is growing in this county, the latest consolidation being the Vernonia and Nickerson districts on the Nehalem river with a combined property valuation of over $600,000. Columbia county is using

"kid wagons," autos and launches in effective and satisfactory transportation.

Crook County.

It is the expectation to install military training in the Crook County high school at the opening of the fall term, September 11. Nearly all the boys of the school have voluntarily signed up for it and expect to enlist. At the same time the girls have petitioned for a Red Cross nurses training course and if possible, arrangements will be made for the installation of that course, also.

It now looks as though the three standard high schools in the county, Redmond, Bend and Prineville, would be filled to capacity at the opening of the fall term.

The few boys' and girls' clubs that we have in the county are working with considerable interest on their various problems during the summer months. In the premium list of the county fair this fall, the management has set aside special prizes for club members only, and at the same time is allowing these same club members to participate in the general juvenile prizes.

During the summer months the committee appointed last spring to prepare the course of Bible Study for Crook county, has finished its work and now has the course ready for distribution.

During the summer months several modern school houses were erected.

The annual institute will be held December 18, 19 and 20.

Nearly all the boys in and near Bend, that are old enough, are busily employed in the various saw mills or box factories.

Of the 18 normal graduates in the Crook County high school last May, all have positions for next year with the exception of two, one not desiring a position and the other going away to school.

Hood River County.

Hood River county is nearly the smallest and really the tallest county in the state. It is 11,000 feet up in the air—atop of all other counties. We are also getting up educationally. Every school in the county will be open nine months during the next school year. All the rural schools will open on September 4; the city schools will wait two weeks for the completion of improvements and will open on September 18. This year the boys and girls of our county will be at work and play in 24 buildings; four of these will be splinter new. Wyeth is putting up a neat well-painted two-room building on an improved location. Odell is expending $10,000 on a new high school plant with full cement basement, class rooms, study room, office, library, and auditorium. Hood River is erecting a new grade building, also a new high school annex both of brick and concrete construction and modern in every point. The high school addition will provide rooms for cooking, sewing, drawing and woodwork, an assembly hall and a play room as big as half the outdoors. Come up or down over the Columbia River Highway, visit our schools, meet our hearty energetic people, enjoy our scenery, fish our brooks, lave in our rivers, and stay in Hood River; or if you must go away go with the sublime impression that you have seen the garden of Oregon.

Marion County.

Superintendent John Todd, of Auburn, Washington, has been elected to the superintendency of the Salem schools to succeed Supt. O. M. Elliott who goes to the presidency of the Lewiston (Idaho) Normal School.

The County Educational Board, at its regular meeting in June, elected Jay V. Fike of Hubbard to fill the vacancy caused by the resignation of J. E. Drillette. John W. L. Smith was re-elected.

Burgess F. Ford will be principal of the Jefferson schools next year and Miss Keith Van Winkle will be his assistant.

T. E. Wilson goes to Hubbard next year. He will be succeeded at Turner by J. B. Hatch of Ballston.

Clare G. Morey, of Oswego, will be principal of the North Howell school.

H. C. Seymour, state leader of the Boys' and Girls' Club Work, spent the last week of August visiting clubs and individual members in Marion county.

The Woodburn high school building is nearing completion. When completed, Woodburn will have a building of which the whole county will be proud.

Keizer school district No. 88 has just completed a new four room building. It is one of the neatest buildings in the county.

Polk County.

State Field Worker of Industrial Fairs, Mr. N. C. Maris, accompanied Supt. W. I. Reynolds on a tour of all the districts in which there are members of the Boys' and Girls' Industrial club. They examined all the work done by the club members during the past year, and endeavored to promote more enthusiasm and co-operation among them, as well as instructed them as to the preparation of exhibitions for the coming Eighth Annual School Fair to be held in Polk county, on September 19, 20 and 21. There are a number of valuable prizes offered and every effort is being made to make this fair a success.

Petitions for the abolishment of the office of supervisor were circulated among the directors with a result of only about one-fourth of the petitions being signed, which shows that Polk county is striving for better schools. A new supervisor has been elected.

A great number of Eastern teachers are endeavoring to secure positions in the county, but there are any number of local applicants who are looking for vacancies, some of whom will not be able to secure a position.

German was taught in one of the rural schools during the past year, but much objection has been offered and there is a question as to whether it will be continued.

Two of Polk county's most efficient teachers have been promoted to Portland schools.

Wasco County.

School District No. 29 of Wasco county is building a $10,000 addition to their present school building for the use of the high school grades. Domestic science and manual training will be installed. This will give Dufur an up-to-date school. Dufur has always been a good school town and indications are that the town will keep up its record.

The Dalles is building a three-room addition to the present school building in Thompson's Addition to accommodate the children who live in that district.

Industrial club work seems to be progressing favorably in Wasco county.

The "System Bank Way" has been adopted as an essential part of the club work. This savings bank system secures the co-operation of the home, the school, and the bank, in teaching the school children thrift. Industrial club work teaches the boys and girls how to work and earn the money; the savings bank system installed will teach them how to save and invest their money. The greatness of a nation is measured in terms of thrift and economy. Therefore school children should be taught thrift.

Morrow County.

The school boards of Lexington and Ione are planning to meet the requirements for standardization of their high schools. Lexington will introduce a strong course in domestic science.

The length of school term in the county increased nearly two weeks over the year 1914-15. Very few districts will have less than eight months' school the ensuing year.

A much larger number of pupils have entered the industrial club work this year than heretofore. The outlook for a splendid exhibit at the county fair is very good. There will be a much larger display in the line of handicraft and canning.

Last year the Heppner high school purchased a fine lot of slides for the work in physical geography, botany, and biology. They proved so valuable in the work that a larger number will be added this year. A room was darkened so the slides could be used at the regular class periods. A lantern and a good set of slides should be provided for every high school.

Washington County.

All positions in Washington county are filled for the coming year. Salaries are a shade better than they were last year. A large number of the teachers were re-electd this year, which will insure efficient work from the start.

The McKinley and Bald Peak school districts are building new school houses this year. Miss Frances O'Connor and Miss Margaret Sullivan are the happy teachers.

Wheeler County.

Nine Waterbury heating systems are being installed in country schools this summer.

Paul E. Baker, of Eugene, will be principal of the Wheeler County high school and Fossil public school this year.

School fairs will be held in Fossil, Mitchell, and Spray during the month of September. A joint field meet with Gilliam county is being arranged for the county fair at Fossil.

A 40 feet by 80 feet two-story building is being erected by the Fossil school board. The building will contain a gymnasium on the second floor, with manual training shops for woodwork and ironwork, baths, and swimming pool on the first floor.

Yamhill County.

A circular letter was recently mailed to each club member in the county with the request that each member should reply giving a complete account of what he is doing individually and what the club is doing.

Cove Orchard and Bellevue are erecting modern school buildings which will be ready for the opening of the autumn term.

The Dayton school building is being repainted inside and out. The Dayton people have a splendid eight-room building, and they know how to take care of it, as well as how to conduct a good school.

The building at Fairview, No. 25, is being raised, and a basement will be added, as well as a modern heating plant. This is one of the best kept buildings and grounds in the county.

The new high school law with reference to paying the tuition of a pupil of one county in the high school of another county is working out well and it is doubtless a great convenience to many persons, especially to those who live near the county lines. In this exchange of tuition money, Yamhill county has fared well, as her total bill to outside counties is $326 44, while we have already collected $956 58, and have $320 80 more to collect from Washington county in October, and some small bills from one or two other counties.

Summer Normal School.

The Summer Normal at Salem was one of the most successful in the hitsory of the school. The total enrollment was 130 and the interest was unusually great.

* * *

Never write on a subject until you have read yourself full on it, and never read on a subject until you have first thought yourself hungry on it.—Jean Paul.

The State Schools

University of Oregon.

Dr. B. W. DeBusk, of the university, is in position to put the following series of lectures at the disposal of superintendents or parent-teacher associations which desire them. It is highly desirable that those who plan to have the lectures given should consult Dr. DeBusk at the earliest moment, so that the proper circuits can be arranged. The list of subjects runs as follows: (1) Physical-Mental Examination of the Child; (2) The Retarded Child; (3) The Accelerated Child; (4) Common Physical and Mental Defects of the Child.

The extension department of the university has the following list of film reels at its disposal this coming year: Glacier National Park, 2 reels; Evolution of Writing, Remington Typewriter Co.; Evolution of a Stenographer, Remington Typewriter Co.; Striking a Light, Matches; The Making of Pure Foods in Battle Creek; Breath of Steel, Making of Firearms, 2 reels; Concrete on the Farm; Construction of a Railroad, Grand Trunk; Seventh Annual Junior Week End, University of Oregon; Potash, 2 reels; Home Making in Western Canada, 3 reels; Soil Building, 2 reels; Good Roads, 3 reels; Spinners of Speech, Pacific Telephone & Telegraph Co. Those interested in securing this educational material should correspond with the Director, Extension Division, University of Oregon.

The University of Oregon has secured an option on a number of small empty houses in Eugene. These will be placed at the disposal of students who wish to "batch" at very small cost. This is the beginning of a general plan worked out by President P. L. Campbell. A little later on there will be a series of special two-room cabins built for students who desire to board themselves.

The 70 correspondence courses now offered represent 16 departments of the university, and permit a good deal of freedom in the choice of courses for study. Encouragement is also given frequently to advanced students and to specialists by instructors in their chosen fields who are willing to prepare special courses of study for them and to give them personal attention and assistance. The active registrations of students in these 70 courses numbered 632 at the close of the first quarter of the present year. Of this number, 133 registrations were in educational courses, 115 in English, 71 in literature, 68 in mathematics, 52 in history, 36 in psychology, 39 in economics and sociology, 32 in commerce and the remainder distributed fairly evenly among the other courses. During the past year the course in school administration was completely reorganized and brought up to date. In addition, a new course in secondary education was provided. During the coming year one or two of the older courses, like those in "Child Psychology" and "Teaching How to Study," will be brought up to date. Students who are in doubt as to which courses will best serve their purposes are advised to write to the Department of Education, University of Oregon, Eugene.

The Lane County Survey is now ready for distribution. It may be obtained from the extension department. This thorough and exhaustive survey of 120 pages consists of two parts; the first deals with the conditions of rural churches in Lane county, and leads up to some startling conclusions; the second part, by Dr. F. C. Ayer, deals with the rural and village schools in Lane county from the administrative point of view, closing with a number of conclusions which have great suggestive value.

Dr. Joseph Schafer has revised his "History of the Pacific Northwest" which is expected from the press at the near future. Dr. F. C. Ayer's book on "The Psychology of Drawing," published by the Warwick-York Company, Baltimore, has already appeared.

Mr. P. E. Baker, who completed his course at the university at the last midyear, takes charge of the schools at Fossil during the coming year. Mr. Hedrick succeeds Mr. E. L. Keezel at Monmouth, Oregon.

Oregon Normal School.

The graduating classes of 1916, numbering 43 in February and 126 in June, totaled 169, the largest class ever graduated from a normal school in Oregon. These graduates, with the exception of a few who have decided to continue their work in other institutions, have secured positions in the schools of the state, and we look forward with a good deal of interest to the introduction of normal school standards in these communities.

The summer school session for 1916 made new records in attendance and enthusiasm. The opening day, with an attendance of 680, gave promise of the record-breaking attendance which passed the 800 mark before the close of the third week, and which totaled before the close of the session, 827. People will wonder how this many students could be occommodated with the present equipment, and it is only fair to say that this could not have been done had it not been for the good nature of the students, and their willingness to be crowded and inconvenienced. The assembly hall, in spite of the introduction of benches, 150 camp chairs along the aisles and the walls, the gallery filled, and 165 seated on the rostrum behind the members of the faculty, could not accommodate all of these, so that a number had to stand in the small aisles and outside the doors. The class rooms were many of them crowded to their fullest capacity, and had it not been for the new training school building, the basements of which were utilized for class room purposes, there would not have been room enough for the teachers. The entire work in methods was handled in the training school building, and some of the large classes were held in the training school assembly room.

The dormitory felt, as did all of the rest of the school, this undue crowding, and while it accommodated all possible, it was necessary to fit up the upper floor of the training school building as "The Dormitory Annex," so that it would accommodate 100 girls. Double shifts were installed in the dining room, and a supplementary dining room made out of the old domestic science building.

The student body was organized by counties from which the students came, instead of by classes, as in regular session. The groups and their counties and numbers were as follows: Multnomah, No. 1, with the largest representation; Lane county, No. 2; Polk county, No. 3; Crook, Jefferson, Sherman, Wheeler, Wasco, Morrow and Hood River counties, No. 4; Marion and Clackamas counties, No. 5; Josephine, Douglas, Jackson and Klamath counties, No. 6; Clatsop, Columbia, Coos and Curry coun ties. also students from outside of the state, No. 7; Grant, Gilliam,

Baker, Wallowa, Harney, Malheur, Umatilla and Union counties, No. 8; Lincoln, Benton and Linn counties, No. 9; Tillamook, Yamhill and Washington counties, No. 10. Following the custom of the past, which has practically grown into a tradition, these groups organized for administrative purposes, went on their picnics to the Luckiamute and Rickreall, and were responsible for two of the most successful evenings of the entire summer school when they put on the "Stunt" programs in the grove on the evenings of July 21 and 22. The number of students made the use of the chapel impossible for this program, so the tennis court nearest the gymnasium was fixed with temporary bleachers and other seating arrangements, and the various stunts were performed on the green between that court and the building. The setting among the large maple trees was beautiful, and the strings of overhead lights added to the effectiveness. To go into detail over the individual stunts of the various county groups would take too long. Suffice it to say that state sectional rivalry had every opportunity to manifest itself. The competition was keen; the results gratifying, amusing and decidedly instructive.

Among the attractions furnished by the Lecture Course Committee was a lecture by Dr. Zueblin, of Boston, who spoke upon the subject of "America, Peace Maker and Pace Maker," and those who heard Dr. Zueblin in his Chautauqua work or know of his work throughout the United States will know that this was a profitable evening.

The presence of the Salem band for an open-air concert was the second attraction. This well-organized body of musicians rendered a concert that was thoroughly enjoyed by everybody. As it was held in the grove there was plenty of room for the townspeople of Monmouth and friends from neighboring communities also to enjoy this. One regrettable feature of the size of the summer school is that it mechanically prohibits the attendance of our Monmouth friends from the various school functions.

The next attraction was the entertainment furnished by Mr. John Claire Monteith, baritone soloist of Portland, Mrs. Carmel Sullivan Power. harpist, and Miss Woodbury, reader. The evening's entertainment furnished by these three Portland artists was delightful.

July 15 was the date of the annual summer school excursion to Salem. Over 300 of the students took advantage of this opportunity to visit the capital and the state institutions. The day's itinerary included the supreme court building, the state library, the capitol, the executive offices in the reception room of which they were met by Gov. Withycombe, the house and senate, the county superintendents in session, the state penitentiary and state hospital. The courteous treatment of the state officials was greatly appreciated by all and the day was a decided success. President Ackerman and Mr. Butler were responsible for the plans and efficient management.

On July 26, Gaul's historical cantata "Joan of Arc" was given under the direction of Miss Hoham, head of the music department. The solo parts were taken by a quartet from Portland composed of Mrs. Jane Burns Albert, soprano; Mrs. Lulu Dahl Miller, contralto; Mr. Joseph P. Mulder, tenor; and Mr. Dom J. Zan, baritone. The chorus work was handled by the combined Normal School Glee Clubs. Miss Hoham found many excellent voices among the summer school students, and was able in a short space of time to develop an organization of unusual merit. This was one of the musical treats of the summer session, and much credit should go to Miss Hoham, the director.

The annual meeting of the Board of Regents was held the second week of summer school, which gave them an opportunity to study at first hand the over-crowded conditions. A committee was appointed at that meeting to make a more detailed study of conditions, the training school facilities, the dormitory facilities, and the adequacy of the teaching staff, with a view to limiting the number of students in attendance at the regular session and in the summer school, in order that the work of the normal school might be up to the work of a standard normal school as outlined by the United States Bureau of Education. A report of this committee was put before a called meeting of the entire board on July 21.

July 20 was the day for the surprise of the summer session when Governor James Withycombe marched upon the assembly stage amid spontaneous and enthusiastic applause. His visit had not been announced because of some uncertainties about the date and his reception was a gratifying recognition of his interest in and service for education. His address was inspiring, patriotic and full of praise for Oregon, all of which pleased his audience.

A change in the entrance requirements to the Normal School made necessary various changes in the program which will hold during the years 1916 and 1917, after which, as previously announced, only high school graduates will be admitted. It would be well for prospective students who have completed part of their work to know these changes and be sure, as far as possible, that work which they have not had can be obtained during the semester in which they plan to return.

The State Teachers Association was represented during the summer school by Assistant Superintendent E. F. Carleton, who gave a short talk to the students and teachers on the "Reorganization of the State Teachers Association" and the new plan of editing the "Oregon Teachers Monthly." Visiting with him was Mr. Chas. H. Jones, manager of this paper, who spent some time in the work of securing new subscriptions, and Supt. O. M. Elliott, of Salem, whom we wish to congratulate upon his election to the presidency of the Lewiston Normal School, in Idaho. This comes as a merited recognition of Supt. Elliott's work as an educator.

Supt. J. A. Churchill, representing the State Department of Education, spoke to the students on July 27. Supt. Churchill spoke of the wonderful possibilities for Oregon to have over 800 teachers interested in professional advancement and asked them to use the state department whenever it could be of any service to them.

The last assembly was varied by a special program. Groups sat together and many interesting yells and songs were given. Then musical numbers by Miss Hoham, Mr. David Campbell, Mr. Howard Hanscom were given and also talks by Mr. Floyd Moore, representing the students and by Miss Parrott, Mr. Gentle and Pres. Ackerman representing the faculty. All then sang "My Oregon" and hurried for lunch and the special train provided by courtesy of the S. P. Co.

Oregon Agricultural College.

The summer session this year was the most successful in several par-

ticulars of the last half dozen held on
the O. A. C. campus. The attendance
reached a total of 365, including 50
in the Boys' and Girls' Two Weeks'
Course, 18 Corvallis registrations for
Physical Education only, and eight
faculty folk. One hundred and twenty-five of the net 289 full course registration had never before been on
the college rolls. There were 89 un-
dergraduates of the college and 74
graduates. Forty-four out of the
state students registered from 10
other states and two foreign countries. Washington was represented
by 17, California by 13, no other
state having more than two. Benton
county, in Oregon, led with a registration of 75, Multnomah ranking
second with 43. Lane, Yamhill,
Umatilla, Washington and Marion
in order had from nine to six each.
Eighteen other counties had a representation of one or more each.

The largest registration in any
single department was in Home
Economics, with 150 different students, Industrial Arts coming second
with 81 different students. The gain
over previous registrations in those
two departments was marked, being
about 100 per cent in each. Thirteen
courses were given in Home Economics and 23 in Industrial Arts. The
total registration in other departments, not excluding those registered
in more than one course was as follows: Agriculture, three courses,
22; Natural Sciences, five courses,
62; Commerce, seven courses, 59;
Education, three courses, 108; English, four courses, 36; History, two
courses, 7; Mathematics, two courses,

18; Physical Education, two courses,
49.

The faculty of 60 instructors included several distinguished specialists from other institutions. In Home
Economics, Miss Alice Ravenhill, of
London, England, gave two courses
in the subject of Dietetics; Mrs. L.
W. Robbins, director of Home Economics in Oakland, California, gave a
course in methods of teaching home
economics in the high school. Dr.
Wm. T. Bawden, specialist of the U.
S. Bureau of Education, gave a
course in Industrial Arts and Vocational Guidance. Professor W. L.
Eikenberry, of the University of Chicago gave a course in General Science.
Two very interesting evening stereopticon lectures were given by Prin.
J. B. Garvin of the Denver public
schools, president of the Denver City
Teachers' Association. The Annual
Chautauqua also provided high class
entertainment during one week of
the session.

A high mark was set this year but
the authorities are determined to provide even stronger courses next year,
if possible, and hope that their efforts will meet with the approval and
patronage of the teachers of the
Pacific coast. The high standing of
the teachers' training courses in
Home Economics and Industrial Arts
is gaining wide recognition, the
Bureau of Education's experts ranking the college among the first half
dozen in the country in these departments. A good representation of California and Washington teachers was
in attendance this year and two came
all the way from the middle west.

On August 5, Professor Ressler of
the Appointments Committee, reported 77 teaching positions filled. Forty-
six of these are in Home Economics,
34 being 1916 graduates, the remaining, promotions of previous graduates. Seven are in commercial positions, two in Agriculture, four in
Agriculture and Manual Training and
18 in Manual Training. The supply
of Manual Training teachers is exhausted and the few qualified in
Commerce will doubtless be placed
before these notes are printed.

Returning students in September
will note a number of campus improvements. A fine macadam road-
way on the south and west sides of
the West Quadrangle with a cement
sidewalk will not only improve very
much the appearance of things but
will make for great convenience in
the approach to the Men's Gym, the
new Forestry Building, the Poultry

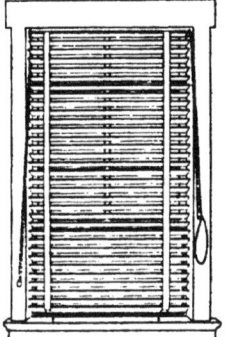

Plant, and Cauthorn Hall. The new Forestry Building is being rushed to completion and is promised for the opening day. The building will not only release Science Hall for more expansion in Chemistry and Pharmacy but will also relieve some of the other overcrowded buildings. Many of the buildings are receiving a new coat of paint and will present quite an improved appearance.

The new school year will begin on September 18, the first two days being devoted to registration and class work beginning on the 20th. The 1916 class of over 300 will leave a big hole but new matriculations of over 600 will fill it and take care of other withdrawals. If the usual increase in enrollment occurs, the long term campus registration should pass 1700 this year. A large number of students are on the Mexican border as members of Corvallis Compank K and other companies of the Third Oregon. War stories will be in order when these veterans return to the campus.

Prospective teachers of the Industrial branches will be interested to learn that California and Washington now recognize the diploma as a valid teaching certificate. Idaho, Montana, Colorado and other states have extended this courtesy for several years. There is practically no barrier in any state for such graduates now, since the Oregon Agricultural College is on the U. S. Bureau of Education's list of "standard colleges."

Oregon Congress of Mothers

By MRS. ELIZABETH HAYHURST, 1070 E. Burnside, Portland

Preparations for the annual meeting will be the first work of the year of the Congress of Mothers and Parent-Teacher Associations. While it is most essential that every Parent-Teacher Circle sends one or more delegates to the annual meeting each year the meeting previous to the legislative session should have full representation in order that every member of every circle be cognizant of the proposed legislation. Hence the executive board urge every circle to do its utmost to be represented this year.

The annual meeting will be held at The Dalles, October 12, 13 and 14. The second day will be occupied with the reports of presidents and a discussion of their problems.

A conference for those interested in the play ground movement will be conducted by Mrs. Wilson McNary, of Pendleton. Mrs. J. G. Kelly and Mrs. H. E. Warks will open the discussion. Mrs. Hattie Vail will preside over the County and State Fairs Conference and Mrs. Edith Tozier Weathered of the state fair board will address the conference.

Mrs. Jennie Kemp, president of the W. C. T. U ; Mrs. C. H. Castner, president of the Oregon Federation of Clubs; and Mr. O. M. Plummer, will speak at the Legislative Conference. Mrs. Millie R. Trumbull, chairman of the Legislative Committee will preside.

Social Service will be discussed at a conference which will be held under the auspices of the Portland Parent-Teacher Association's Social Service Department that has had much practical experience during the last few years.

Supt. J. A. Churchill and representatives of the Extension Department of the University of Oregon and of the Oregon Agricultural College will address the convention, and the city of The Dalles will be hosts at a formal meeting on the opening night.

Delegates will get the usual reduced rates of a fare and one-third and The Dalles P. T. A. will provide rooms for all delegates.

Splendid work has been done by the Playground Committee of the Portland Parent-Teacher Association throughout the summer by the community gatherings in the various parks. These meetings have been the means of taking the work to many a parent who otherwise could not have been reached, and furthermore have made of the parks and play grounds a larger field of usefulness and pleasure, and the transforming of a "dump heap" into a "play ground" has been one of the most constructive movements ever accomplished in the city of Portland, and the "sane" Fourth of July picnics conducted by the various P-T. A.s was another splendid piece of work.

Simplified Spelling

By DE WITT C. CROISSANT, General Field Agent

People who dislike simplified spelling because of an esthetic prejudis against it say that it wil destroy the beauty of the English language. But, in the first place, the language and its spelling ar not synonymus. The language exists as something heard, the spoken word brings a succession of pleasing or displeasing sounds to the ear, and the judgment formd by these spoken sounds is the final criterion of language-beauty. Russian, which seems so harsh to us, is beatiful to those who use it, and even Italian, which is rated everywhere as a melodius language, has combinations like sd and sv which ar not generally felt by us to be especially beautiful, tho to the nativ Italian these ar just as natural and harmonius as any other groups.

Now the visible form of Englis wil be changed, but one must th reason to the winds to say that t change of exterior form wil chan the essentials of speech. This great nonsense. No such calam happend when Spanish, Swedish, a German changed their spelling f the better, and it is not reasonable suppose that the English language wil undergo any break-up either.

It is said that a simplified spelling wil destroy literature. A great many people feel that they could not read the books which they ar accustomed to read in any other spelling. The Simplified Spelling Board has taken this fact into consideration in all of its argument. It points out that no power has been given it to confiscate such books as ar alredy in existence and to force people to read books in simplified spelling. It points out also that, as the new generations arise, new books could wel be printed in a spelling suitable to their training, and those who cling to the old may stil cling. As they die off and new readers arise, the movement wil gradually spred.

It is a sad fact that many people do not kno that English spelling has changed. It was Rider Haggard who committed the egregius blunder of saying that the spelling of Shakspere was good enuf for him. As time has gone on, the language has changed. Chaucer's English is very much different in vocabulary and grammatical structure from the English of today, and his spelling is practically fonetic.

Gradually the fonetic principle has been lost sight of, tho the body of correctly speld words from the past is great—and those who kno about the actual pronunciation of the past kno that it is greater than it seems—but Shakspere and Milton and Pope ar different in spelling, and even the poets of the 19th century hav an almost imperceptibly different spelling from the riters of today. This gradual change givs no one the right to insist on any one spelling out of the past; English spelling is undergoing a slo evolutionary process which historical vision clearly perceives and which the suggestions of the Simplified Spelling Board tend to focus and to concentrate.

But this stil leaves us with those who refuse to look at simplified spelling because of its strange appearance. Such people ar really selfish. They a willing to undergo the discoml of a reform for the sake of the enerations to come. The whole matter becomes ethical. Does English spelling waste time? Does it involv xtra labor? Is it a training in logic? Do the absurd combinations and the useless letters aid in education? Competent observers and investigators like Cook and O'Shea and many others hav proved that English spelling is anti-educational. Therefore to oppose a reform of it because one does not like it is simply unethical. Many a man has told me, while touring for the board, that it was his own children's difficulties with English spelling that converted him to the movement, and it is unfortunately tru that many an opponent is one who has had no practical experience with children and whose general mental attitude is one of esthetic exclusiveness.

The movement is now 10 years old. Like all movements it has gone thru varius stages of opposition. When Nehemiah was rebuilding the walls of Jerusalem, he went thru three of these stages, and they ar fairly typical—abuse, ridicule and a willingness to parley. The Simplified Spelling Board has had the abuse, it has had the ridicule, but it is now pretty wel in the stage where sensible people ar willing to parley and confer. The Board is no infallible group of men with an iron-clad program and an executiv power to put that program

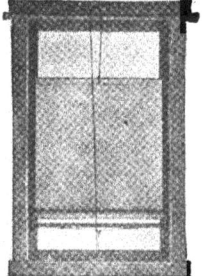

into effect. It is a group of men, eminent in arts and letters and science, who ar earnestly trying to bring about some mesure of the logic and regularity into the caos of our English orthografy. The Board has come to stay; its results ar most encouraging. At this riting over 170 scools and colleges hav gone on record in favor of the movement and some 320 papers hav begun to use simpler forms. When one looks over the clipping files from the past and sees how bitter was the opposition and how confused wer the issues, one cannot help but feel that after all, there is a sound kernel of common sense in us which wil take hold of the obviusly good and carry it on. Every scool teacher can help in the work. Every scool teacher on this coast, which is so favorably inclined toward the movement, can spred information thru her community. Keep in tuch with the Board which has now removed to 18 Old Slip, New York City, and all questions wil be anserd and all circulars cheerfully sent. But above all things, use a few simplifications. Remember that the National Education Association has gone another step forward and at its last meeting agreed to use t in past tense and past participle when the letter is pronounst as "t". Don't be afraid of a little ridicule. Get a rubber stamp for 15 or 20 cents with the words "Simplified Spelling" on it, and print that on your correspondence. Put a leaflet or two in each letter. By doing this you wil be aiding a great work.

Report Booklets.

The Oregon Teachers Monthly has for sale report booklets arranged to fit the school register and can be used for a year's work of school. The arrangement is systematic and convenient. The price is 2½ cents each or 50 for $1. A sample will be sent free on request.

Prohibition in Oregon thus far has done much to improve business conditions in the state. There is a general improvement in every channel of activity as shown by actual figures. The bank deposits have everywhere increased and businessmen report that all goes well with them.

The every cares and duties, which men call drudgery, are the weights and counterpoises of the clock of time; giving its pendulum a true vibration and its hands a regular motion; and when they cease to hang upon its wheels, the pendulum no longer swings, the hands no longer move, the clock stands still.—Longfellow.

Cheering Someone On.

Don't you mind about the triumphs
  Don't you worry after fame;
Don't you grieve about succeeding,
  Let the future guard your name.
All the best in life's the simplest,
  Love will last when wealth is
    gone;
Just be glad that you are living
  And keep cheering someone on.

Let your neighbors have the blossoms,
  Let your comrades wear the crown;
Never mind the little set-backs
  Nor the blows that knock you
    down.
You'll be there when they're forgotten,
  You'll be glad with youth and
    dawn,
If you just forget your troubles
  And keep cheering someone on.

There's a lot of sorrow round you,
  Lots of lonesomeness and tears;
Lots of heartache and of worry
  Through the shadows of the years.
And the world needs more than triumphs;
  More than all the swords we've
    drawn,
It is hungering for the fellow
  Who keeps cheering others on.

Let the wind around you whistle,
  And the storm around you play;
You'll be here with brawn and
    gristle
  When the conquerors decay.
You'll be here in memories sweetened
  In the souls you've saved from
    pawn
If you put aside the victories
  And keep cheering someone on.
        —Baltimore Sun.

How easy it is for one benevolent being to diffuse pleasure all around him; and how truly is a kind heart a fountain of gladness, making every thing in its vicinity to freshen into smiles!

Membership in the State Teachers' Association

The Oregon Teachers Monthly, on July 1, 1916, became the official journal of the State Teachers' Association (both divisions) and the price was raised to $1.50 per year, 50 cents of which goes to the Association. At the end of the first month (July 31) the following teachers had paid $1.50 for their subscription to the Oregon Teachers Monthly, thereby entitling them to membership in the State Teachers' Association:

1 Nellie V. King, Winant
2 Fred Schepman, Waldport
3 John Blough, Toledo
4 Maggie L. Hampton, Toledo
5 M. Lillian Ernest, Denzer
6 Earl Brown, Philomath
7 Chas. Hart, Roselodge
8 S. S. Gosman, Chitwood
9 Borgny Romtvedt, Toledo
10 J. E. Davis, Chitwood
11 R. E. Wood, Orton
12 John Miller, Eddyville
13 Verne Ross, Toledo
14 T. E. Wilson, Turner
15 Paul Wyman, Bay City
16 Chas. Holway, Halsey
17 Laura A. Smith, Cottage Grove
18 H. W. Herron, Portland
19 Mary B. Scollard, Woodburn
20 L. W. Turnbull, Coquille
21 Hazel Henkle, Monkland
22 A. C. Strange, Baker
23 Anna Dunsmore, Orenco
24 Margaret Williams, Portland
25 Adella Chapler, Salem
26 Margaret Boggess, Veneta
27 W. M. Sutton, Burns
28 G. W. Beattie, Eugene
29 Mary E. Slade, Albany
30 Mrs. L. K. Page, Springfield
31 Mrs. A. Alexander, Portland
32 Barbara Hoch, Pendleton
33 Blanche Padley, Bandon
34 Kate Ronde, Clatskanie
35 Edith Harper, Freewater
36 Edith Smith, Banks
37 Alice Rasmussen, Troutdale
38 Della Zimmerman, Troutdale
39 Adda Wright, Warrenton
40 N. A. Frost, Forest Grove
41 Edna Pence, Salem
42 Erica Nordhausen, Aurora
43 Clara Ireland, Portland
44 Julie H. Burch, Oregon City
45 J. P. McGlasson, North Plains
46 Ethel Davis, Myrtle Creek
47 Mrs. E. H. Morrison, Portland
48 Coral Garvin, Corvallis
49 Inez Easton, Sitkum
50 Alethia Chapman, LaGrande
51 May Smith, Mabel
52 Helen Treat, Buell
53 Virginia Nottingham, Carlton
54 Elma Roberts, Sumner
55 Ruby Skinner, Lakeview
56 Frances Potter, Canby
57 Harriet B Horrigan, Hillsboro
58 Grace Egbert, The Dalles
59 Mary B. Underwood, Philomath
60 Ruth Dunbabin, Bourne
61 M. T Means, Philomath
62 Mildred Taylor, Scappoose
63 Marie Senn, Barlow
64 Bessa Lehmann, Sutherlin
65 Anna Bachmann, Clackamas
66 Adeline Buyserie, Hubbard
67 Isa Isaacson, Junction City
68 Anna Weisenborn, Deer Island
69 Myrel A Bond, Irving
70 Rada Antrim, Amity
71 Marvin F Wood, Corvallis
72 Carl E Morrison, Perrydale
73 Waithia Watson, Roseburg
74 H. C. Ostien, Monmouth
75 Eula Campbell, Freewater
76 M. S. Pittman, Monmouth
77 Hazel Goger, Boring
78 Clara Spiekerman, The Dalles
79 Mamie Harper, Wren
80 R. S. Bixby, Nolin
81 Mattie Foster, Klamath Falls
82 Nell G. Lloyd, Klondike
83 Margaret Rice, Shaniko
84 Martha Chase, Portland
85 Myrtle Clayville, Portland
86 C. D. Watkins, Dilley
87 Clara Larson, Toledo
88 Emma Murray, Klamath Falls
89 Marion Ford, Klamath Falls
90 May Wheaton, Coquille
91 Fannie G. Porter, Oregon City
92 Mable F. Johnson, Butte Falls
93 Helene Ogsburg, Eugene
94 Velma Beardslee, Arlington
95 Gladys Sanderson, Clear Lake Ia.
96 Alice Lytle, Bonanza
97 Vara Stewart, Portland
98 Charles Knocke, Mt. Carmel, N. D.
99 Lydia Unden, Winchester
100 Jewell Delk, Drain
101 Matilda Jacobs, Portland
102 Mrs. Gladys Smith, Springfield
103 Helen Anderson, Meda
104 Alma Nichols, Culver
105 Gladys Hatcher, Buell
106 Sylvia Severance, Lexington
107 Dagmar Jeppensen, The Dalles
108 Ora England, Walker
109 Florence E. Howatt, Portland
110 Rachel May, Timber
111 Ellen M. Yocum, Amity
112 Alice Jenkins, Eugene
113 Harry Whitten, Kingsley
114 Violet M. Stolle, Irving
115 Violet McCarl, Portland
116 Maude Largent, Hullt
117 Elnor Sherk, Sutherlin
118 Ruth Peterson, Yoncalla
119 Grace Atkinson, Walton
120 Mrs. Mary Hulin, Carpentaria, Cal.
121 Mary E. Moore, Irving
122 Vera Merchant, Lebanon
123 Emma Kennedy, Coquille
124 Maybelle Wagner, McMinnville
125 Marguerite Freydig, Sutherlin
126 Ruth A. Brown, Eagle Creek
127 Ranie P. Burkhead, Shaniko
128 Mabel McFadden, Halfway
129 Angie Halley, Medford
130 Goldie Groth, Freewater
131 Justina Kildee, Sutherlin
132 May B. Lund, Coquille
133 Mildred Jones, Amity
134 Grace V. Perce, Medford
135 Myrtle Ess, Klamath Falls
136 Sadie Heiberger, Wedderburn

The Boys That Run the Furrow.

You can write it down as gospel,
   With the flags of peace unfurled,
The boys that run the furrow
   Are the boys that rule the world!

It is written on the hilltops,
   In the fields where blossoms blend,
Prosperity is ending
   Where furrow has an end!

The waving banners of the fields
   O'er the broad land unfurled—
The boys that run the furrow
   Are the boys that rule the world!

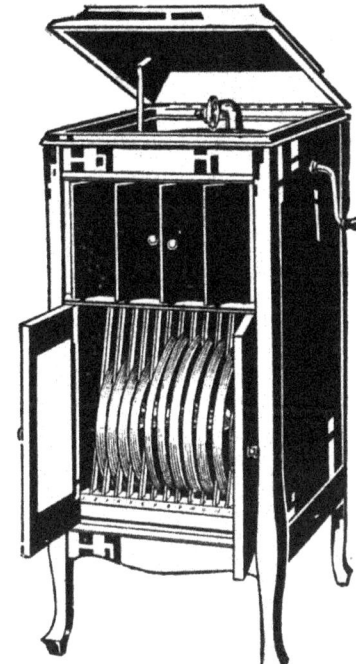

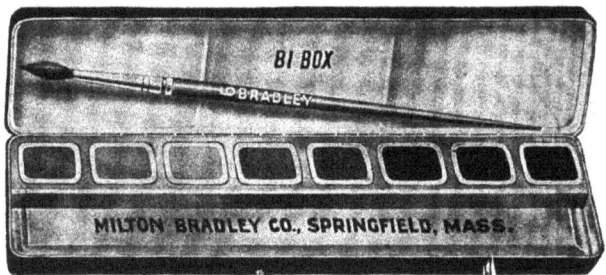

Teachers--Get Big Pay--Government Positions

The Capital Normal School.

The prospect is very bright for the Capital Normal at Salem the coming school year which begins on September 18 and no pains will be spared to make the work successful. Teachers who are desirous of raising their grade at the December or June examination will find it worth while to spend a few months at this school. Tuition and board will be as reasonable as last year.

OREGON TEACHERS MONTHLY

The Official Journal of the State Teachers' Association

Vol. XXI   SALEM, OREGON, OCTOBER, 1916   No. 2

Published Monthly Except July and August by the State
Teachers' Association

Entered at the Postoffice at Salem, Oregon, as second-class mail matter, April 1, 1898.

RULES OF PUBLICATION

1. The mailing label on the Oregon Teachers Monthly shows the date to which subscriptions are paid.
2. The Oregon Teachers Monthly will be sent to subscribers until ordered discontinued and all arrearages are paid.
3. Notice of change of address should be given at once, naming both old and new postoffice.
4. When renewing, always state that subscription is a renewal.
5. The subscription price, including membership in State Teachers' Association, is $1.50 a year in advance. Single copy, 20 cents.
6. Advertising rates will be furnished on application.
Address all communications to Oregon Teachers Monthly, Salem, Oregon.

Editorial Notes

The beginning of a new school year is the time for the teacher's
New Year's resolutions. Experienced teachers can profit by their
former mistakes. New teachers start with a clean slate. A frequent
source of error on the part of both the old and the new teacher is a
"fatal facility of speech." Most of us talk too much, both in the
classroom and outside. Reference in this connection is to that conversation that does not bear directly on school work; inconsiderate
remarks to fellow teachers and to others about one's co-workers, school
policies and the like. Interest in our fellow men and their affairs is
natural and the term gossip is not properly applied to all talk about
one's neighbors. Unfortunately there is a strong tendency in human
nature to start or pass along unkindly comments on one's neighbors.
There is a current sentiment which runs, "Speak kindly of everyone
if you speak of them at all; none of us is so very good." There may
be times when this is not good practice, but it is a pretty safe rule for
the teacher. It is difficult to distinguish between men and measures
and our opposition to the latter too often is attached to the former.

What may often seem innocent comments or playful remarks about a teacher, principal or superintendent may cause annoyance and misunderstanding. Sometimes the silent member in a group of gentle knockers becomes involved and receives credit or discredit for the output. Beat a retreat, if possible, when the hammers start to tapping; if you can't escape, start a new tune or at least refuse to join the chorus, in a positive and kindly manner. The older and more experienced teacher should administer a mild or stern rebuke, as circumstances appear to justify. This little sermon does not mean that a teacher must never have an opinion or must always remain neutral. Courage and independence are admirable qualities, but there are times and places as well as ways and means of asserting them.

†   †   †

The movement for an additional normal school in Eastern Oregon is one which should command the support of every progressive teacher. in the state. Experience has shown that ninety-five per cent of the student body of every normal school is recruited from a territory not more than one hundred miles in radius and immediately adjacent to the school. Students as a rule do not take long journeys to secure this type of training. If Eastern Oregon is to develop its own teachers instead of importing them, a normal school is a necessity. Some years ago when the confusion in the public mind as to the purpose of such schools resulted in the extinction of the existing normals, a careful and cautious policy became necessary. The new State Normal at Monmouth was established with a fixed appropriation and under the control of a real state board. Under wise management it has prospered. Its standards of admission and graduation are high, its efficiency is unquestioned. The time has arrived for the next step, which is to furnish Eastern and Southern Oregon with schools on the same high grade of efficiency.

†   †   †

It has long been the custom among American educators to spend a certain amount of time in Europe studying the educational systems of various countries. Upon their return they inevitably try to graft upon our schools some plan which they observed abroad in successful operation, regardless of the dissimilarity of economic or social conditins. Many such plans have had but brief periods of notoriety and the few which have won the favor of public opinion have been much changed, much Americanized. Now that the unsettled conditions in Europe have made such travel and such studies well nigh impossible, these people are turning their attention more directly to the study of American education, its needs and its efficiency, with the result that some are discovering that we have an educational system of our own, and more, that it is not inferior to those of other countries, as these educational Jasons would have us believe, but in some respects superior. The immediate effect of this discovery has been an increased amount of progressive, adaptive legislation in many of our states. Now of all times in our educational as well as political history is the time for us to be Americans, to have faith in and courage to stand for our ideals, for who dares to say what those ideals may mean to the future civilization of the world. Oregon has been very favorably noticed as a state leading in progressive school laws so let us as the teachers of Oregon evidence our faith, our bigger patriotism, by aiding our system at every opportunity, and particularly in regard to a minimum school term of eight months, to increased standards of professional preparation, and strict certification laws.

† † †

The old idea of a teachers' association included two or three lions from a distance, much hand shaking and at least one banquet, problems were frequently discussed on the basis of individual taste, everybody agreed to differ and nothing of importance ever resulted. Oregon with other progressive states is attempting to establish a state association which discusses questions on the basis of facts and aims to arrive at valid conclusions. Two committees, one on teachers' retirement funds and the other on retardation of pupils, have been appointed and are already at work. An entire session is to be devoted to formulation of policies for teachers. To make this session of value, there must be local support. Why can't we have a principals' club in every county and a local teachers' association in every town? Simply to elect delegates to the representative council is not sufficient; the delegates must know the teachers' wants and be in the truest sense representative. It is only by intelligent combined effort that teaching can be raised to its proper place at the head of the liberal professions. Are you doing your share?

† † †

The remark is often made that a new spirit pervades the institutes of Oregon and now that the institute season is again open it is interesting to see whether that remark is justified. Not many years ago the average teacher in Oregon looked upon the county institute as a three day incarceration in the county seat. The popular instructor then was the entertainer, the story teller, while the instructor who tried to give instruction, classroom devices or every day pedagogy was looked upon as an additional law-imposed punishment to be tolerated by the aid of conversation, pencil sketching and fancy work, and all in order that the district might not lose five dollars. We are glad, however, that this is all changed now and the teachers are showing their desire for practical work at the institutes. These meetings coming as near the beginning of the year as possible are being looked upon by the teachers as means for inspiration, for keeping up with latest movements, for obtaining helpful suggestions for the year's work, for measuring their work with that of others and as such they are taken more seriously, more studiously, more professionally. As a teacher grows in successful experience, in preparation for her work, or in professional ideals, she realizes that there is something positive to be obtained from every speaker at these meetings, even if it is no more than a strengthened conviction that her own method is as good or better than that advocated, or an increased or renewed realization of the worthwhileness of the service she is rendering. At the next institute you attend, see how easy it is to select the teachers who belong to the profession of teaching and who are doing all they can to make it truly a profession, from those who are "just teaching at so and so."

† † †

Granted the opportunity to live in this age when history is being made faster than at any time since man could make permanent records; when political geography has been many times changed and bids fair to undergo many more; when commercial and industrial geography is a constantly varying study as trade, invention, or new war demands make their inroads into established commercial relations; when a new epoch of war-inspired literature is being added to the literary history of every nation; when art and music constantly depict themes of distruction, bloodshed, desolation, desperation, sorrow or exultation; when even the ideals and standards of modern civilization are constantly changing, we as teachers must realize, not only the opportunity but its responsibilities. The teacher will not properly perform her duty to society unless she gives to the "men and women of tomorrow" the ideals, the necessary information to live under these new changed conditions. The traditional subjects taught in the traditional way will not do this. She must know enough about present conditions to leave, if necessary, parts of her texts untouched and teach from living text books—the great periodicals of the day, for from no other source can she secure the desired material. She must not only read extensively but encourage her students to do so as well, and also give them the ability to do so intelligently.

† † †

Times are hard on the Western coast, ancient certificates long since covered with dust are being resurrected, lawyers without clients and physicians with few patients are crowding into teaching, to say nothing of ministers and real estate agents. These recent recruits · desire to remain in the school room only while necessity compels and in many cases are willing to work for salaries which deny the professional teacher the means of growth and successful work. Undoubtedly all the teaching positions in the state of Oregon could be filled by some sort of candidate if the salary was limited to forty dollars a month. The efficiency of the schools would be destroyed and the children would suffer, but nevertheless after a fashion the positions would be filled. What prevents such a state of affairs? Simply the certification laws of the state which provide that every candidate for this important function must produce evidences of good character, respectable general culture and some professional training. These laws are the main support of the professional teacher in periods of financial depression. The influence of every serious minded teacher should be exerted to the limit to create a public opinion favorable to their effective and even-handed enforcement.

Choosing the Teacher

By A. O. STRANGE, Baker City, Oregon

I have selected this subject because it has grown to be the custom of boards of education in districts of the first class and in many others to leave the selection of teachers very largely to the city superintendent or principal, and as the success of his system depends very largely on the care he exercises in performing his duty, the points that he considers, his standards and methods, ought to be of interest to the teachers who constitute the applicants.

In the first place, he must determine the kind of teacher he wants. To do this, he must consider the nature of the work to be done, the character of the community where she is to teach, the character of the people making up that community, and the sort of home training they are giving their children. Not all communities are alike. I have known teachers to have a high measure of success in a certain grade in one part of a city and later in the same grade in another part to fail. Why? Apparently they did not fit into the peculiar conditions prevailing there. Usually the hand-working classes, both foreign and native-born, occupy in large part a separate portion of a district, the wealthy another section, and the professional, constituting largely the more intellectual and better educated, another section. One section of our city, for instance, is given over almost entirely to Mormons and their children make up seventy-five per cent of the attendance of one nine-room school. The reader will readily see that the teacher who lacks adaptability, and some very excellent teachers do, would not fit equally well into all sections. In one section there is little strict parental control (these things often go by fashions, as dress or social customs); hence, the teacher's task is heavier. In another section, parents hold to the old Puritanical idea of "spare the rod and spoil the child" and the children are starved for kindness, patience, sympathy and love, and the teacher must supply these needs. All these things the superintendent must weigh carefully and use his utmost endeavor to select a teacher who fits the environment.

In the second place, he must consider the teacher's preparation to do her work, and it is not enough to choose her because she is a normal or college graduate. Not all normal schools are equally meritorious. The eastern normal may not so adequately prepare the girl to teach in a western environment as the one located in the west. Again, every school of higher education graduates many who do not learn the value of hard work, close application, thoroughness and accuracy, and the teacher who does not possess these qualities cannot teach them. Sometimes these graduates apparently believe their work is done, their preparation is complete when they receive their diplomas, and the superintendent cannot get from them the careful daily preparation, the effort to keep abreast, he holds so important. He must consider more than scholastic training, indispensable as it is, he must form a judgment concerning the measure of thoroughness of her training, her attitude towards her education, and her ideals of future accomplishment.

In the third place, he must know the character of the applicant's experience. Several years of teaching in a small rural school with an average attendance of eight or ten pupils does not well fit the teacher for the city place. Teaching in a small graded school with little supervision is not the best of experience to make the teacher ready for the school where there is much supervision. Not only quantity of experience then must be considered but quality, where gained, under whose direction, and in what environment.

Last and most important of all, he must consider the personality of the applicant and all those things which enter into personality. In the first place, he likes to see a photograph of the applicant or, better still, to see her personally. The teacher who is prepossessing in appearance has an advantage over her who is not; but if the teacher is not personally attractive, she certainly can very largely make up for this lacking by the care with which she dresses. I know excellent teachers who are very far from handsome, in fact, as nearly ugly as a woman ever is, and yet they, by cultivating a pleasant smile and an animation of expression, and by dressing neatly and with taste, overcome very effectively this handicap. In like manner, I know others who have much natural beauty who by dressing in poor taste, in slovenly manner, and by being too obviously pinned together, a fact which seldom escapes the keen eyes of the superintendent, fail to get the promotions which otherwise they have deserved.

Another quality which the superintendent considers may well be expressed in the slang word, "pep." Energy and enthusiasm must be very evident in the applicant. It must be equally obvious that she believes in herself and in her work. This belief must be so strong as to lead her to the most careful of daily preparation, a preparation which will bring her before her classes with a large measure of animation and enthusiasm. She must feel and show ambition to excel in the work whether she expects eventually to drop out or not. These points make up "pep" and the superintendent is exceedingly anxious to ascertain if the applicant possesses these qualities. The applicant must be loyal. No teacher who does not hold loyalty as her first principle of professional ethics is wanted. This loyalty must not be merely a loyalty to her own interests, expressed in standing by her associates and by those in authority over her, but it must be an unswerving loyalty to high ideals of the value and aims of her work.

As the last element of personality, the applicant must be of unobjectionable habits. If a woman, she must be systematic and orderly and of regular habits of eating and sleeping, the latter for hygienic reasons; and if a man, he must be all these and more. It is desirable that he do not smoke or drink or use a flippant, slangy, or profane manner of expressing his thoughts, objectionable qualities which the superintendent ought never to have to consider in connection with the application of a woman, but which he must too often consider in investigating the record of a man. It is true that some of these points are usually investigated only through confidential reports but the superintendent does seek information along these lines and all teachers should know it. We want the applicant to love the society of others and to enjoy social gatherings, but she must hold her work first. The seeking for and attendance at social functions may become a very strong and objectionable habit. She must constantly bear in mind that her work puts on her the responsibility of upholding and even of raising its standard and to do this she must conduct herself with a certain dignity of manner. Flippant conduct is a very objectionable habit. All these are elements of personality the superintendent considers in choosing his teachers.

In concluding this brief article, I would urge the teacher who has failed in securing the desired position not to say, "Well, I have not had a fair deal," but rather, "In which of these various respects am I lacking and what can I do to strengthen myself?" Nothing is truer than that any teacher who knows what is expected of her, who has a reasonable amount of preparation and self confidence, who is determined to succeed and has the spirit of hard work, who practices a little auto-suggestion, and whose ideals are high can much strengthen herself in all these respects and thus fit herself for the desired promotion if she will.

The School Playgrounds of Enterprise

By CHAS. A. MONTANDON, Enterprise, Oregon

. The school playgrounds in Enterprise were started during the summer of 1913. The board then authorized the building of a few pieces of apparatus. Since that time the school has added a little each year, so that now, the playgrounds are covered with a very creditable equipment. This equipment consists principally of the common playground devices with a few original additions. There are swings, traveling rings, Spanish rings, a traveling ladder, climbing poles, climbing ropes, teeter boards, teeter ladders, giant strides, volley ball courts, a basket ball court, hortizontal bars, sliding poles, simple merry-go-rounds made of old wagon wheels, besides facilities for broad jump, high jump, pole vaulting and racing.

The equipment is so far as possible made on the ground, and of native timber, principally of fir. The constructions are all substantially made, but of rather light timber and properly braced. This plan of construction avoids the clumsiness necessarily attaching to articles built of heavy timber. By proper treatment of the parts in the ground, the life of the timber is of considerable duration. The wooden construction is also desirable because it can be erected by various kinds of labor. The equipment as it stands represents labor hired by the board and labor secured from the janitor, from the manual training classes, from the instructor of manual training and even from other teachers interested in the work. Undoubtedly it was secured by "joint effort." The hardware necessary was secured from the local dealers at little more than cost. Building the apparatus of local material, with labor secured from the older boys, also demonstrates the fact that our own resources combined with a little labor and ingenuity may secure for us many of the good things of life.

There is nothing difficult about the construction. Our method of operation, in case the piece to be erected has not been seen, is to work out our plans from cuts found in catalogues and other advertising material. The catalogues show the steel apparatus. But with few exceptions the same articles can be made of wood; and, as before suggested, if the construction be of sound and rather light material, properly braced and neatly painted, it can be made solid, durable and even ornamental. From playground catalogues also, suggestions for the dimensions of the apparatus can be obtained. Wooden construction has other advantages. For instance, it does not get as cold in the winter or as hot in the summer as the steel. But by far the greatest argument in favor of it is its inexpensiveness. Generally speaking, the wooden equipment can be erected for about twenty per cent of the cost of steel apparatus. Of this cost, the material represent, roughly, ten per cent, and the labor ten per cent. So that in cases where the labor cost can be eliminated, as when furnished by manual training classes or others interested, wooden equipment can be secured for about ten per cent of what it would take to buy the steel. For instance, the material in the equipment on our grounds costs about $110.00; the labor to build it would cost about a like sum. But only about fifty per cent of this was hired labor, so that about $165.00 has really equipped our playgrounds.

But the question of equipment is not the only one involved. Proper regulation of playground activities is quite as important. The attempt to make those places self-regulating has been a failure everywhere, in schools as well as in parks. The result of this failure has been the movement for playground supervision. This movement has evolved the "playground director." A few years ago, proper supervision was not easily secured. The teachers appointed to assist in the work could do little more than stand in conspicuous positions, holding their own or somebody else's hands. Many positively did not know how to play or how to help assist or direct play. But with a few suggestions and a few evenings on the playgrounds (by themselves), they soon acquired sufficient skill and interest to make them efficient directors of playground activities. Then, too, the teachers' training schools came to the rescue. Courses in playground work were installed, so that at the present time many teachers make their ability to assist in outdoor exercises a feature of their applications. Most teachers now accept the work as a part of their duties, and a large majority of them find in it recreation and amusement.

As to accident, they have happened, but to no alarming extent. In three years, with a school of from 250 to 400 pupils, only four serious accidents have occurred. Of these, the two most serious, broken legs, did not happen in connection with the use of any of the equipment. Those who objected most when the first apparatus was erected have now become quite reconciled to its safety. To insure safety, however, proper management and supervision are necessary. Certain parts of the grounds are reserved to special grades to avoid congestion; then every section of the grounds is under the eye of a teacher during intermissions.

The strong argument in favor of the playground is the extent of its use. Usually, the grounds are swarming with pupils; even during severe weather large numbers are out exercising on the apparatus. Almost every child uses the playground every day. Some exercise more than others, and many perform real strenuously; but there is no pupil who does not make some use of the playgrounds. The pupil who does not use it every day is the exception. While the grounds are intended primarily for the use of the grades, it is not uncommon to find the high school pupils using it during the evening. Under cover of darkness, even sedate town people make use of it. It would be difficult to point to any other public activity that lends itself to such extensive usage.

The basic idea is through the playground movement to generalize athletics. No doubt, one grave objection to our school athletics as usually conducted is that they neglect the weak and the needy, those to whom physical exercise would be of most value. The playground remedies that. It is for every one. Moreover, it lends itself readily to corrective exercises; that is, a pupil can be instructed to perform especially on the apparatus that will help to re-enforce the weak part of his physique. It is difficult, in the absence of scientific tests, to get the grounds or authority for a valid statement concerning the physical advantages secured. But the feats that our boys and girls perform, the endurance they show, the skill they display when contrasted with "new comers" who are performing for the first time, the especially well developed freshmen who enter high school after three years of spontanous playground work; these, and other facts lead us to believe that our pupils are attaining a physical status far superior to what it would be were it not for their playground exercises.

For about one-half of what it takes to run a football team for a brief season of twelve weeks, 400 pupils can have training for an indefinite number of years. This is not to raise here the question of the merits of inter-school contests. It is simply intended to show what we are getting, or can get, for our money. If physical development be our end, then the playground contributes directly to it. If on the other hand successful high school athletes be the foremost consideration then the product of the playgrounds furnishes a good physique upon which the athletic coach can build. Then, all who are enthusiastic about inter-school athletics, and all who are not, should favor a well equipped playground.

Besides direct physical benefits, the playground activities present other advantages that are worthy of consideration. It facilitates discipline during intermissions. The old difficulties common at recesses are largely eliminated. The teachers are on the grounds, but they are there as directors and helpers, not as policemen. Their work is constructive, not repressive. Moreover, the relations of teachers and pupils on the grounds are usually pleasant and consequently promote more cheerful and helpful relations in the classroom. Teachers who were connected with the school before the playgrounds were equipped and retained their connections after the movement was launched, testify that the difficulties arising during intermissions have been almost extinguished. The pupils have from the first shown the proper attitude toward the equipment. They keep the grounds clean, play as directed, heed suggestions, and not in a single instance have they willfully destroyed or marred any part of the apparatus.

Playground performances lend themselves to competitive exercises. At certain intervals, contests are held. The contests are usually between the different rooms of the grade buildings, with a system of graduated handicaps from the upper to the lower grades. The contests consist of common track events and performances on the equipment. In these events, at least three-fourths of the pupils take part—girls as well as boys. So that all that is generally said in favor of the diciplinary value of athletics can be said for playground contests. These events have been well attended and apparently appreciated by the people of the town.

The playgrounds with us have a salutary effect on tardiness. Instead of loitering on the way to school, seeking fun by the wayside, the pupils hasten to their play center, and consequently are at hand when school calls. Parents have objected that their children did not take time to eat lunch, so anxious were they to resume their fun. In many ways therefore the playgrounds have proved a valuable adjunct to the school.

.Now, even in Enterprise every one is not enthusiastic about playgrounds. Some object that the children work too strenuously, that they are pushing their exercises to a dangerous excess,—though no ailment has ever been traced directly to such excess. One "taxpayer" objected that they were not necessary, since no such luxury adorned the school that he attended. Others object on the ground that the children shirk their chores in the morning, or as suggested, refused to eat at noon. And still others (whom you would least suspect) object that some of the performances for the girls are not "lady like." But the management of the schools from the board to the teachers, favors the movement. Public spirited citizens and friends of the school who have given the matter more than passing attention, have given the playground movement their hearty approval. Conservative men have spoken of it as "a step in the right direction," "a great improvement," "well worth the money," "one of the best improvements that the school has ever put in," etc. So that upon the whole the people are well pleased with their playgrounds and are ready to continue to improve them.

To this end a special playground director has been appointed. The board was fortunate to secure for this position Mr. C. C. Parsell, who is an enthusiastic leader, a lover of athletics and good sport, and a high-class workman. His plan is to improve the playground equipment, and to devise a system of records that will establish the relation between physical and mental development—between proper playground exercises, and success in the classroom . This record, when followed up for some time, may give valuable suggestions to teachers and school authorities, and may well form the basis of another article in this magazine in which the value of a playground to the school may be scientifically demonstrated.

The What and How of Vocational Education

By FRANK H. SHEPHERD, Corvallis, Oregon

There is, at this time, no place for further use of arguments for placing vocational education in our schools as a part of the regular school work. The question that confronts the people of America today is what and how. As a suggestion of WHAT, nothing can be more appropriate than quotations taken from the statements made by different men who are and have been recognized by all as leaders in the educational field.

"All our industries would cease were it not for that information which men begin to acquire as they best may after their education is said to be finished, and were it not for this information which has been from age to age accumulated and spread by unofficial means these industries would never have existed. * * * The vital knowledge, that by which we have grown as a nation to what we are, and which now underlies our whole existence, is a knowledge that has gotten itself taught in nooks and corners, while the ordained agencies for teaching have been mumbling dead formulas." (Herbert Spencer).

"Multitudes of American children take no interest in their school work, or seeing no connection between their studies and the means of later earning a good livelihood, drop out of school far too early of their own accord, or at least offer no effective resistance to the desire of unwise parents that they stop study and go to work. Moreover, they acquire while in school a listless way of working." (Dr. Eliot, N. E. A. Report, 1910).

"But to the great mass of human beings this opportunity is not open. All over the world we have brought these young people, by various types of compulsory legislation, under the influence of the elementary school for, let us say, the years from six or seven to thirteen or fourteen. This great mass of boys and girls get the very admirable and very effective training of the elementary school, but for well known economic reasons they cannot take advantage of what society has to offer beyond that. They are compelled to go out and take hold of life as best they can at that tender age, unadapted, unfitted, with no specific tentacle ready to grip any particular hanging rope on which to climb to economic independence or security.'' (Vocational Education. Dr. N. M. Butler, 1913).

''When but one-third of the children remain to the end of the elementary course, there is something the matter with the schools. When half of the men who are responsible for the business activities, and who are guiding the poltical life of the country, tell us that children from the elementary schools are not able to do definite things required in the world's real affairs, there is something the matter with the schools. When work seeks workers and young men and young women are indifferent to it, there is something the matter with the schools. * * * Our elementary schools train for no industrial employment, they lead to nothing but the secondary school, which in turn leads to the college, the university and the professional school, and so very exclusively to professional and managing occupations. One who goes out of the school system before the end or at the end of the elementary course is not only unprepared for any vocation which will be open to him, but too commonly he is without that intellectual training which should make him eager for opportunity and incite him to the utmost effort to do just as well as he can whatever may be open to him. He goes without respect for manual industries where he might find work if he could do it. He is without the simple preparation necessary to do definite work in an office or a store. He is neither clear about his English nor certain about his figures.'' (American Education, Draper).

These signboards along the way indicate very clearly what should be done. A thinking, reasoning individual, no difference how firmly he may be entrenched behind the breastwork of traditional education, should be able to see the solution of a problem when so forcefully put before him. But the HOW has confronted those who saw the WHAT and for a number of years leaders in the educational, economic, political, and social world have been trying to find the ways and means. Today it seems that the problem will be solved in a great degree by National aid for vocational education.

The bill known as the Smith-Hughes Bill seems to be ready for final action in Congress. February 10, 1916, this bill was introduced in the House of Representatives by Mr. Hughes, was referred to the Committee on Education and ordered printed. On February 12, 1916, it was committed to the Committee of the Whole House on the state of the Union and ordered printed. On July 31, 1916, this bill passed the Senate without a dissenting vote. The title of the bill very clearly explains its intent and purpose as follows: "To provide for the promotion of vocational education; to provide for co-operation with the States in the promotion of such education in agriculture, the trades, industries and home economics; to provide for co-operation with the States in the preparation of teachers of vocational subjects; and to authorize the appropriation of money and to regulate its expenditure."

The bill allows nine years to put the system into full operation, beginning with the year 1916-17 the minimum appropriation is $1,700,-000 and in the year 1924-25 the maximum amount of $7,200,000 is reached. This total appropriation is divided into different parts as follows: for agricultural teachers, for trade and industrial teachers, for training teachers of vocational subjects.

One very significant condition and a condition that should interest every teacher in the United States is: "No State shall receive any appropriation for salaries of teachers, supervisors, or directors of agricultural subjects, until it shall have taken advantage of at least the minimum amount appropriated for the training of teachers, supervisors, or directors of agricultural subjects, as provided for in this act, and that after said date no State shall receive any appropriation for the salaries of teachers of trade, home economics, and industrial subjects until it shall have taken advantage of at least the minimum amount appripriated for the training of teachers of trade, home economics, and industrial subjects, as provided for in this act." This clause shows that the lawmakers of our nation clearly recognize the fundamental principle of trained teachers as essential to the success of any educational movement.

In a letter dated September from Hon. W. C. Hawley he says in part: "In a recent interview with Mr. Hughes' office I learned that it was his opinion that this bill would probably not be reached during the present session of Congress, but he thinks it sure to pass at the session convening next December."

The quotations at the beginning clearly indicate the WHAT. The Smith-Hughes Bill very clearly provides for the HOW, and the social-economic conditions existing in our country show to all thinking, reasoning people, school teachers not excepted, that there has existed and still exists a very forceful why.

————◆————

To speak a kindly word of commendation or encouragement may be a very little thing for you, but a very helpful thing to the one to whom it is spoken. Never a day passes without bringing you opportunities for such service to others. Does a day ever pass without your improving such an opportunity?—Selected.

————◆————

If you would be a man, speak what you think today in words as hard as cannon-balls, and tomorrow speak what tomorrow thinks in hard words again, though it contradicts everything you said today.—Ralph Waldo Emerson.

Financial Problems in Districts of the Third Class

By F. B. HAMLIN, Roseburg, Oregon

The financial problem in districts of the third class is one of the many growing out of that great problem which our State undertook to solve when it assumed responsibility for the education of our succeeding generations, guaranteeing, as nearly as possible, equal opportunities and advantages. Under our laws at the present time the State exercises general direction and control of all school matters, but shifts the responsibility of financial support and immediate control to the counties and districts in which the schools are located.

The State collects and apportions to the counties annually the interest from the irreducible school fund, which amounts to about two dollars per capita of the school enumeration, but contributes nothing from its general fund except to pay the expenses and salaries of the educational department of the State. The State law requires each county to raise annually for school purposes at least eight dollars for each child enumerated between the ages of four and twenty years and leaves each district to provide by special tax for whatever additional sum is necessary to carry on its schools.

It is generally conceded that children living in the cities and towns have better chances for acquiring an education than have those who live in the smaller rural districts. Among the superior advantages which they enjoy are better buildings and equipment, more experienced teachers, longer terms, and more efficient supervision. These conditions are due not only to the ability of the more populous districts to spend more money, but also to the fact that as a rule the urban population appreciates more fully the necessity of superior schools and are willing to tax themselves for the necessary funds.

I have before me a summary of the assessment roll of Douglas county for the year 1915 which shows among other things that of the 144 districts—including joint districts and union districts—132 voted a special school tax, only 12, or eight and one-third per cent, being able or willing to get along with the regular state and county apportionment. The tax rate ranges from .0002 to .0127; the average for the county was .004 while for those districts maintaining high schools the average was .075.

There seems to be a feeling among all classes of our people that even in school matters, it is right to require the strong to help the weak, and this principle has been applied by the Oregon school laws in the affairs of districts of the third class. Let me call your attention to some of the provisions of the law that were intended to be, and are, for their special benefit: (1) In the apportionment of the county fund the county superintendent is required to give each district, without regard to size of school population, the sum of $100. (2) In the matter of voting at school elections, in districts of the third class, the head of a family is permitted to vote without the property qualification required of voters in other districts. (3) Under the supervisory system the law provides for rural supervision. True, the law is optional and is in effect in only a few of the counties. However, in those counties where it has been adopted, where competent supervisors have been employed and where they have received the co-operation and support of the local school officers, their work has been of great value to the schools. (4) The law prescribes for all districts a minimum term of six months and guarantees each the sum of $300 to carry on its school during that time. In other words, there is one provision of the law that requires all districts to have at least six months of school, and another which provides that if any district, which does not receive the required $300 from the regular state and county apportionment, shall fail to levy a special tax of at least five mills to make up the deficiency, then it becomes the duty of the county superintendent to so notify the county court. The county court must then levy a five mill special tax against the property of the district and transfer from the general funds of the county to the special funds of the district whatever sum is necessary to make up any remaining deficiency. The effect upon the receipts of districts of the first and second class is so slight as to be negligible. In the larger districts of the third class, these provisions do not materially affect the total annual receipts, but in the smaller districts of this class the effects are very marked.

In order to show more clearly the practical working of the various provisions of this law let us consider one of our very smallest districts. Take, for example, an imaginary district with an enumeration of ten and an assessed valuation of $10,000. There is at least one district in Douglas county with a smaller assessment and several with fewer pupils. Let us consider first what this district would receive if there were no special provisions in the law.

1. From the State fund, 10 pupils at approximately $2......$ 20
2. From the county fund, 10 pupils at $8................. 80

Total receipts $100

This would provide for not to exceed two months of school and the question of what to do in the matter would be a very serious problem. To raise the additional $200 would require a levy of 20 mills, which, while not illegal, would probably not be voluntarily voted by the taxpayers of the average rural district. One of two things must happen—the people of the district must either burden themselves with a heavy tax or deny their children even the minimum of school privileges. But let us now consider what this same district would receive under our laws as they are:

1. From the State fund, 10 pupils at $2 ....$ 20
2. From the county fund, lump sum 100
3. From the county fund, 10 pupils at $6 per capita........ 60
4. From the county fund for teachers institute attendance.... 5

Total receipts $185

Again it is up to the district to decide what they will do. A special tax of 11½ mills will solve the problem; but if they prefer to vote only the required 5 mills, or to permit the county court to make the levy for them, the balance will be made up as follows:

1. From special district tax, 5 mills on $10,000............$ 50
2. From general fund of the county to special fund of district   65

    Total $115

Thus is the $300 guaranteed and thus is it provided.

In this way is the State of Oregon attempting to improve opportunities for her rural girls and boys. She has made great improvement during the last quarter century in both city and rural schools and it is certainly gratifying to know that we are year by year surely and steadily progressing.

A Plan for Improving Rural Teachers While in Service

By M. S. PITTMAN, Monmouth, Oregon

There are two ways by which the rural school may have trained teachers—first, get them from normal schools already trained, and second, train them while in service. The first method has failed in the rural schools of the United States. Sometimes trained teachers are secured from normals, but in most cases they serve for one year only and then go to town. The second plan will be slow but will likely prove more lasting. A recent survey of the United States shows that 32.3 per cent of the rural teachers in the United States have had no professional training, and a much larger per cent has had but little. In Oregon the situation is equally appalling. To secure teachers who are already trained, for all of our rural schools is yet largely a dream. Let us turn, therefore, with hope to the other possibility.

Outside of the City of Portland there are employed in the State of Oregon at present, approximately 5,000 teachers, which means that for every superintendent and rural supervisor employed in the state there will be from 75 to 100 teachers working in schools of from first to third grades. The majority of these teachers have had little or no professional training. They feel that they must work during the regular school year. Responsibilities and lack of funds render it impossible for them to take off the year for professional training. They can only attend during summer vacations, and train during the regular year. These are the only avenues open to them for professional growth. All of this means that the county superintendents must assume the responsibility of taking their teachers as they are and developing them into well trained teachers by encouraging them to make improvement during their vacation months, and by training them during the regular session. The plan should be comprehensive enough not only to train teachers, but to keep them trained; in other words, to provide continued stimulus for professional growth.

Such a system, I believe, was tried out partially last year in a number of the counties of the state, particularly in Polk and Sherman. I shall present the plan for Polk county in detail, since it was there the plan was given first trial. I shall present the plan as if it had been tried for the entire year, though, in fact, it was not.

The reader at this point of the discussion should cease to think of the superintendent as an administrative officer and should henceforth think of him in this discussion as purely a supervisor of rural schools.

(1) During the first weeks of the school year, the supervisor visited all of the schools of the county to observe the general phases of the school work. He observed the physical side of the school, the general procedure of the teacher's class and school room work, presented to each school the big aims for all of the schools for the year, noted the general points upon which the teacher needed help.

(2) On this first visit, he divided his county into six zones; each zone was to be the unit for a week's work. At the close of his visits to all of the teachers of a zone, he had a meeting of all of the teachers of that zone, at which meeting he discussed with them the work which he had observed in their respective schools. He pointed out the good points which were worthy of imitation, and said little about the weak spots. He was going to eliminate them by the creative plan of presenting that which was worthy of imitation.

(3) He presented to them the plan of the next six meetings which he would have with the teachers of each zone, the average number of each group was twelve. His plan was as follows: 1—Reading, 2—Language, 3—Spelling, 4—Geography, 5—Arithmetic, 6—Music.

(4) At this meeting, he taught two reading classes for demonstration purposes. One was a primary class, the other a grammar grade class. In this he set up special methods and after class discussed the principles involved with the teachers. He set forth the general aims of the subject of reading to be followed by the teachers during the next six weeks till their next class meeting.

(5) He gave references for professional study on the subject of reading to be consulted during those weeks while they were specializing on that subject.

(6) He asked the teachers to take the demonstration which he had put before them, to practice, experiment with it, with the help of the material he had recommended, during the next five weeks. At the end of the five weeks they would send to him their "lesson aims" for all of their classes in reading for the sixth week, which would be the next week he would spend in their zone. With this instruction the first meeting of the class of the first zone ended, and he went on to the succeeding zones to do the same thing with them.

(7) At the beginning of the sixth week, or such time as he may have appointed, he began his second trip. He was armed with the lesson plans, or at least the lesson aims of every teacher in the zone

for every class in the subject of reading, for the entire week. A time was fixed at which he would be at each school. When he arrived, the subject of reading was taken up—the teacher teaching according to her plans which the supervisor had. He made his notes. She had now six advantages: First, two model lessons presented by the supervisor at the last meeting of the class; second, five weeks of practice with those lessons as examples after which to pattern; third, five weeks in which to study on that particular subject; fourth, she knew exactly when the supervisor was coming so she might have lived through the ordeal before it happened; fifth, she had the benefit of hearing this work discussed in class with a number of people who were doing the same kind of work, thus robbing it of the personal elements of individual conference and criticism; sixth, she will see some other teacher of her own class teach a class at the meeting at the end of the week, by whom she may measure her work.

(8) At the close of the week, all of the teachers of the zone will meet for conference. Two teachers will teach classes reproducing and setting forth the methods which the supervisor set up at the last meeting.

(9) At the meeting at the close of the week, two teachers presented the two lessons showing that they had mastered the principles. Then the subject of reading was taken up again for class discussion. All of the teachers had had their practice, their reading, their reflection, and were now in position to ask questions that really were to the point. ' The supervisior had had the same opportunity to study , had observed daily and was in position to direct the discussion with interest and profit.

(10) At the close of the discussion of the subject of reading, the supervisor taught two model lessons in the subject of language, set up principles, demonstrated method, opened it to discussion, and gave assignments and references for the next study period which proceeded as before. This routine was followed throughout the year.

(11) The work which has been described was done in the morning. The afternoon, then, was open to work of a different sort. Two kinds of work were taken up: First, something of an inspirational or aesthetic nature; second, something of an industrial nature such as the Boys and Girls Industrial Club work, or some local industrial problem.

(12) The meetings were held either at the most convenient place or moved to the places where the afternoon meetings would be of most educational benefit. This varied according to the place and circumstances. (Map of Polk county will show the natural centers).

Benefits of the System.

(1) It makes of the supervisor an expert methodologist. He can't help it. He must prepare his lessons carefully before he can present them before a body of teachers. He must study the sources which he gives his teachers as references, else he cannot be sure that they will

be appropriate and that the teacher should have prepared the work which he assigned. He must teach lessons that he prepares for demonstration purposes as many as six times, which makes it possible for him to become artful in his work. He is presenting one subject for observation for six weeks, and observes as a critic at the same time another subject for six weeks. He holds two conferences with his teachers on each subject: One to prepare them for their work, and another to clear up with them any difficulties which they have found in their own practice. Thus, he spends twelve weeks in thinking and studying one subject. This gives him an opportunity also of comparing all of his teachers, thus determining who is strong and who is weak, and it affords him an opportunity not only to use all of his ability in making weak teachers strong, but also that of all of the other teachers in that particular class.

(2) It makes system in the supervisor's work necessary. He must have certain days for certain things. He is saved all the indecision and conflict so easily possible in the supervisor's or superintendent's work.

(3) It makes it possible for teachers to work together in a class large enough to produce enthusiasm and yet not so large that embarrassment is provoked. The classes, too, are of homogeneous nature —all members interested in the same thing. There is no lost motion, no dead weight.

(4) The expense of getting to the meetings is slight and the profit great. The teachers should really be paid for the one day attended and then required to come.

(5) It is possible for school directors and citizens to know that professional work is being done. They will not object to the cost of close supervision.

(6) It makes school meetings of more than local interest possible in the remote rural districts where they are sorely needed.

(7) Work done in this way might be recognized by professional institutions and help toward the graduation of the teachers from college.

There are other reasons, but these will be sufficient to prove the feasibility of training a teacher while in service, if the proper machinery is provided.

———•———

Supt. A. C. Strange of Baker writes in regard to the September number of the Oregon Teachers Monthly as follows: "I have enjoyed very much reading the last issue of the Oregon Teachers Monthly. The taking over of the paper by the State Teachers' Association is a very praise-worthy act which should increase the circulation and the influence of the journal very much."

———•———

What you would find in a people you must first put into its schools.—Humboldt.

Rural School Department

Edited by MRS. M. L. FULKERSON, Salem, Oregon

Teachers Exchange.

If you or your pupils would like to correspond with a school in another locality, send us your address and state your preference for location of correspondent and we will publish it in a Teachers Exchange column.

* * *

Public School Compositions.

We should like to continue the public school compositions and in order to stimulate interest we will select from those sent us each month, the best one written by a boy and the best one written by a girl and publish them in this deparment. The names of the winners will be placed on the Composition Honor Roll which will be printed in each issue throughout the year. Compositions should not exceed 300 words and must be in the hands of the editor of this department by the first of the month previous to publication.

* * *

The Rural School Library.

Much needs to be done toward placing the needs and possibilities of the rural school library before the people. Those who have investigated the rural school problem realize the deplorable condition of the majority of these libraries and are awakening to the fact that something must be done. What organization directs the work matters not so much as that the work be done. In any case the rural teacher plays a most important part in the rural school library and can at least assist in its general supervision. Realizing this, the rural school committee undertook as its chief work the preparation of a bulletin on rural school libraries which should serve as a handbook for the rural teacher. Mr. Claxton, United States Commissioner of Education, has consented to print it and it is now in his office awaiting publication. This bulletin will consist of a general survey of rural school libraries in the United States, an article on the organization of rural school libraries, an article on children's literature, a list of four hundred books for a rural school library and a selected bibliography on the rural school library. To provide something which would be concise and truly a valuable tool for the rural teacher in making her school library a real factor in the life of the people of the rural community has been the aim of the rural school committee.—Orpha M. Peters in Journal of Education.

* * *

Mothers' Day.

In what better way can the mothers' interest be aroused than by inducing them to visit the school? With an exercise arranged with special reference to them their attendance may be confidently expected and the stimulus of their presence made available. Their day should be observed in the early part of the school year, as soon after the opening as may be, in order to make the most of their influence and co-operation.

The manner of observing the day may, I think, be safely left to the teacher, with but a few suggestions: "Omit the military drills so common in most special day exercises, as they are only too sadly suggestive, and the dear loving mothers delight not in the pomp and circumstance of war. Let the exercise be composed of sentiment and suggestions befitting the mother's loving heart." What matter if Grace, who has been carefully drilled, reads the tenderly pathetic old poem, "Rock Me to Sleep," the same poem her mother read when she went to the village school, so feelingly that tears steal down that mother's cheeks! They are happy tears, induced by a mingling of pride in her daughter and a revival of long buried memories of her own happy school days. What matter if some lonely mother, whose birdling has flown from the home nest, feels her loss anew as she hears of "The Little Boy Blue"? The pang is but momentary, for even as she sees a mental picture of her darling and "his pretty toys," there comes to her a feeling of satisfaction as to

> "What has become of our Little Boy Blue
> Since he kissed them and put them there?"

The gleam of mirth that dances over the room after the humorous selection does not detract from the gentle pathos of such selections as I have mentioned. Don't fail to enliven your program with a bit of brightness and humor here and there. Humor is a necessary part of a true mother's makeup. Well she knows that it is just as essential to be what boys call a "jolly mother" as to be a good mother.

At one Mothers' Day that I know of short intermissions in the program gave an opportunity for several of the larger girls to serve a dainty bit of refreshments to the vistors who were mothers, "sisters, cousins and aunts" of the pupils, in fact, all the feminine portion of the district. If refreshments be served they should be light, for you are not feeding a horde of hungry workingmen; you are paying a courteous attention to your visitors. A cup of cocoa and a bit of cake will be a delicious treat to any mother if deftly and quietly served by her own daughter.

Another pretty idea is to decorate your school room with "mother pictures." They cost but a trifle, the beautiful reproductions of famous pictures for sale by the various art companies. First come the Madonnas, and so great is the latitude for choice here that even the most fastidious cannot help being pleased. My own choice of all is the Bodenhausen Madonna with the Sistine for a close second. Next would come the mothers of famous people. For this series your old magazines would prove valuable. It will be easy to find a number of interesting mothers.

Be sure to ask the mothers to remain and spend a few moments visiting each other and the teacher, after the last childish "good-by, teacher," has been said and the whole merry troop is gone. Some friendships which may prove very helpful to the school may be formed in those moments.

Although these gatherings should be informal, it will be found safest to send a few lines of cordial invitation to each one whose presence you desire. One teacher I know of had the pupils themselves write and deliver the invitations.

To what extent the day has been observed I cannot say. I think, however, that nowhere has the idea received the attention it deserves. —Lynn Windall in West Virginia School Journal.

* * *

Parent-Teacher Associations.

In writing this article on the organization of Parent-Teacher Associations I merely wish to give a few plans of organizing the associations and conducting the meetings, also some of the results I have observed, hoping that it may aid some teacher in the organization of an association and thus do some good for her community.

The real purpose of a Parent-Teacher Association is to promote the welfare of the school and the community, to bring the home and school closer together, to form and advance the acquaintance and friendship of the teacher and parent and also to aid each person in the district to, "Become acquainted with your neighbor; you might like him."

Some one in the district will have to take the lead in the organization of the association; if the teacher is wise she will have some person do this under her direction, or if she cannot secure the right person to call the people together for a meeting, she may prepare a short program for some afternoon or evening and invite the parents to attend. Do not forget the fathers. The teacher should explain or have some one explain some of the advantages that may be derived from such an organization; if you can secure your county superintendent or supervisor, have either of them give an address on this subject; then open the meeting for general discussion. Nothing works so well as to have the people present talk, and it aids the teacher in that she will know what her patrons think about this and other subjects pertaining to the school. If possible to form the organization at this meeting, do so. If not, select another date and then ask all to be present; secure some outside speaker, have a light lunch, and then organize by electing a president, vice-president, secretary and treasurer, appointing a committee on constitution and by-laws, one on programs; and right here, let me urge that the membership be not held to only parents or teachers, as some of the best members will not come under either class. The writer well remembers one association where the president was a maiden lady of forty years of age, or over, and another association elected as president a young man of not over 21, and both of these parties were number one officers and led their associations very successfully, accomplishing much for the schools and the communities.

In the forming of the constitution, much aid will be received if the secretary will write to Supt. J. A. Churchill and secure a circular he has published on the organization of associations. This circular will also help in preparing programs from time to time.

Some associations unite with the state association and secure help in this way. The fee for the state association is 10 cents per member. Local fees may be set by the members. I suggest a small membership fee, as this will give money for supplies, expenses of speakers, etc. Meetings should be held at least once per month and always in the school house, unless a grange hall or some other building is used for community gatherings. The school house should be used as much as possible.

Always try and have a good program and change the plan from time to time. Have a luncheon at some of the meetings, as men like to eat, and, as someone has said, "Every time you eat with a person you like him better," so, every time that the people of a community come together and eat, they like each other better and the school reaps the reward.

Many speakers can be secured at no, or very little, expense, such as leading people from adjoining towns or communities, city superintendents, principals, preachers, teachers and others from the near places, also the field workers and members of the State School Superintendent's office, the Extension Workers from the state schools, the University of Oregon, Oregon Agricultural College, Oregon Normal School, and many workers from the other schools of the state.

Every association, in order to reach the greatest number of people in the community, must do something, and in order to do something, it will be necessary to plan some work for the association to do, such as some improvements around the school house, grounds or roads of the community. As long as an association will keep busy it will grow and will not only do much for the school and the community but also for the entire county and even the state. I have in mind one association in a district with a two-room school, which held meetings every month since the time of organization some three years ago. This same association has aided in the following improvements, besides many other matters of interest to the community, secured double or folding doors for the building, thus placing the two rooms in one for general meetings; had make knock-down seats for the rooms, which are stored in the basement when not in use; placed a basement under the building and fitted the same for a community kitchen, with stove, cooking utensils, tables, etc.; built play apparatus for the school grounds; made walks to the school house from the road and to the outbuildings; secured a piano for the school; helped promote better roads in the district; secured many lectures for the meetings, and held each year an annual picnic, which is attended by people from miles around.

The influence of this association has reached over the entire county, has caused the organization of other associations, has used its influence for the betterment of the schools of the county, and has even reached out of the county and helped others to do better work.

The writer could mention many associations where play sheds have been built by their efforts, buildings improved and even new ones built, grounds improved, local school fairs held, and above all else, created a better community.

The tecaher who lends her efforts for the betterment of her school and the future of the children intrusted to her, will be doing her duty, and by the organiztion of a Parent-Teacher Association and carrying it through successfully, will be one of her greatest assets.— H. C. Seymour, Oregon Agricultural College, Corvallis.

* * *

Contentment.

Contentment is submission to your limitations. It is strength, not weakness. Do what you can and fret not. Whatever must be is best for me, is the attitude of the contented mind.

Contentment beautifies character; discontent degrades it. A disagreeable man is both ugly and discontented. Nothing pleases him. The purring of the cat irritates. The joyous laugh of the boy gives him a pain. The stirring music of the Pilgrims' Chorus stirs him to wrath. His grouch is not a habit but a disease. On the other hand a contented person radiates beauty. He speaks in kindly tones. He carries a smiling face and everywhere he goes he scatters sunshine. He transforms a crash into a cushion, a bump into an embrace. Life with him is a matter of shooting the chutes, and bumping the bumps, and he who can take his thumps gracefully, easily, without mental and physical friction is contented.

Contentment makes the indifferent man different. It makes the infirm firm. It will not submit to low ambitions or inferior attainments. The indifferent man who has fine capacity but willing to remain in his ignorance is stupid, not content. He who may be prosperous but satisfied with mere existence and allows his family to suffer is sluggish, not content.

A contented person is not heartless but heartful. His heart may be broken but never rebellious. He sympathizes with him who is in the shadow for he often has had sunless days, yet he is loyal to his better self. He never borrows trouble or loans affliction, but when they come he does not complain or blame fate bitterly. He strives to get what he likes, but he likes what he gets. He is as sensitive to pain as the other man; his muscles quiver and his soul shudders under grief, but with features undisturbed he presses on, knowing that joy cometh in the morning.

Be contented but never satisfied. Be content with what we have but never satisfied to remain on the dead level. Then will the world be a bigger and better place in which to live.—E. J. Klemme, Normal School, Ellensburg, Washington.

* * *

Autumn Leaves Drill.

Seven girls are required. Decorate the stage with autumn leaves. The girls let their hair hang loosely about their shoulders, wear crepe paper dresses of bright autumn leaf colors trimmed with pressed leaves of various kinds and white stockings wound with narrow strips of cloth the same color as the dresses. The Queen of Autumn wears a brown dress with more leaf decorations than the others and carries a wand twined with autumn leaves. The other six girls carry wreaths of autumn leaves. The wreaths should be large enough to slip over their heads easily. We found oak and maple leaves made the prettiest trimming that was available but any kind of leaves could be used. Instead of using regular march music, have pupils who are not in the drill stand behind the scenes and hum, whistle or sing (as directions are given) the song, "Sweet Summer's Gone Away," the music of which is found in "Merry Melodies," published by F. A. Owen Publishing Co. Any march could be used instead, but the song makes a very appropriate accompaniment. The movements of the drill are simple but, with the bright costumes, it is a pretty and effective exercise.

The curtain rises as children are humming softly "Sweet Summer's Gone Away." Enter Queen at center of back of stage waving her wand from right to left. Three girls enter from each side of the back holding wreaths in front of faces. The girls enter with cross step—touching right foot on left side, then left foot on right side, etc., until Queen stands in center of stage and others form circle around her. They kneel about her, holding wreaths towards her and sing to the air of Maryland, My Maryland:

> Hail to the Queen of Autumn Days,
>   Gladdest days of all the year,
> The fruits are gathered, harvest's past,
>   Thanksgiving time will soon be here.
> And on the breath of autumn breeze
> The leaves come fluttering from the trees.
> Oh, soon will come the winter drear,
> But autumn days are full of cheer.

Girls rise. (Pupils hum chorus of "Sweet Summer" twice.) Follow the Queen, single file, the girls on the left side falling in line behind their partners on the right side, to front of stage, to left and around the center back and to center of stage, all with cross-step as before. Now they take position as illustrated in Fig. 1, holding wreaths in front of them and swaying them in time to the music while they sing the first stanza of "Sweet Summer." In the middle of the stanza they change positions, taking the position illustrated in Fig. 2, clasping hands, thus placing the wreaths in a row and still swaying them to the music until stanza is finished. As they sing the chorus, they take the position illustrated in Fig. 3, the Queen standing, the two girls in front kneeling very low, the next two kneeling low enough to hold

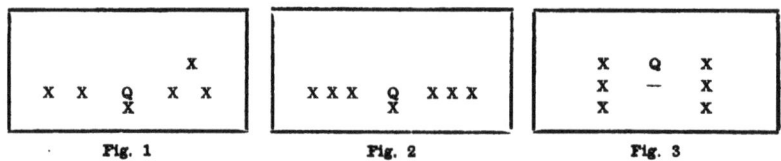

Fig. 1   Fig. 2   Fig. 3

their wreaths just above the heads of the girls ahead of them, and the last two girls standing.

Whistle the tune of the verse. Girls rise. Queen leads to right of stage, girls follow in couples, march around to center back and Queen goes again to center of stage while the girls march three on each side of her until they form a circle around her. Sing the chorus of "Sweet Summer." The girls hold the wreaths out horizontally, above their heads and directly in front of them alternately. Sing second stanza of "Sweet Summer." During first half of this stanza, Queen holds her wand up perpendicularly, and girls hold wreaths up in slanting position, giving sort of umbrella effect with the wand as the handle. During second half of the stanza the Queen remains in the center of the stage. · The girls hold wreaths in their left hands and grasp the right hand of their neighbor, making three couples, and whirl slowly around twice.

Sing chorus. Girls march in circle around Queen, throwing their wreaths over their heads as they march, leaving both hands free. As the verse and chorus is whistled, the girls march around in a circle about the Queen, giving "the right hand to their partner, the left hand to the neighbor, the right hand to the partner, left hand to the neighbor" as in the old singing game of "Pig in the Parlor," but going around the circle, in manner described above, three times, then march around the circle in single file once, removing their wreaths from about their necks. Then they kneel in a circle around the Queen, holding their wreaths up to her while the chorus of "Sweet Summer" is hummed softly.

> There's a purple tint on the woodland leaves,
> And the winds are up all day;
> There's a rustling heard in the yellow sheaves
> And it seems to sadly say:
> "Sweet summer, Sweet summer,
> Sweet summer's gone away;
> Sweet summer, Sweet summer,
> Sweet summer's gone away."

—Written for the Oregon Teachers Monthly by Bertha I. Dunlap, Eugene, Oregon.

Grade Teachers' Department

Edited by SABRA CONNER, 421 West Park Street, Portland, Oregon

Elementary teachers and elementary teachers' associations are cordially invited to send news items of their activities which would be of interest or value to other teachers to this department of the The Oregon Teachers Monthly. Address Editor of Grade Teachers' Department, Room 300, Court House, Portland, Oregon.

Dr. Scott Nearing, formerly of the staff of the University of Panna, and dropped because of his persistent advocating of free speech, and who later became a member of the University of Toledo, stated before the meeting of the League of Teachers' Associations, a department of the N. E. A., that the great question before the teachers of the country was whether the school systems should come under the control of plutocracy or democracy. To have a democracy, to have public control of public affairs, to have equality, liberty and happiness, we must, he said, thrust aside the power of plutocracy by raising the standard of public intelligence to a point where it will no longer tolerate plutocracy, where it will stand for the principles of justice and righteousness. The work of the teachers, he declared, is to make the pupil understand that above all else is needed civic intelligence: Intelligence that will make the boys and girls the kind of Americans that their ancestors were, standing for equality first rather than safety first; for liberty, justice and righteousness, or in other words, standing for the higher things that represent democracy, and not for the lower things that merely characterize the visible fleshpots of existence.

* * *

A Recreation Committee has been appointed by Miss Ortschild, president of the Portland Grade Teachers Association. This committee will take the place of the former Walking Committee. More varied recreations are to be provided than the former "hikes." Teachers interested in some line of recreation can apply to the committee, who will attempt to find others interested in similar activities: thus the committee will be a clearing house for interesting events. Horseback riding, visits to historic places, lecture walks, factory visits, theatre parties, week-end parties in the country, tennis, and other activities have been suggested as the

events to be planned by the Recreation Committee. The fact that nearly every member of the committee is a Mazama promises some interesting things for the members of the association. The members of the committee are: Chairman, Minnie Heath, Irvington school; Pearl Montgomery, Verdi Moore, Bessie Rawson, Pearl Ellis, Alice Banfield, Nelle Crout, Lola Creighton.

* * *

"The Bulletin," the little monthly publication issued by the Portland Grade Teachers' Association, will be sent free to Oregon teachers who are contemplating the formation of a teachers' organization.

* * *

Mr. George H. Himes, of the Historical Society, has contributed some interesting articles to the "Bulletin" of the Portland Grade Teachers' Association. In the September 1916 number the story of the beginning of fruit culture in Oregon is told. The following quotation from the article is interesting: "In 1839 Henderson Luelling disposed of his business in Henry county, Indiana, removed to Henry county, Iowa, and established himself in the nursery business there. A few years afterward the idea of going to Oregon revived, and he began to devise a plan by which young trees might be transported to Oregon without loss. Then he caused to be constructed two especially strong wagons, into the boxes or beds of which he placed a foot of earth intermixed with a certain proportion of charcoal. Into this mixture he planted between 800 and 1000 young trees of vigorous growth, having been grafted a year previous, and in April, 1847, he, with his son, Alfred, with four yoke of oxen attached to each wagon, started across the plains, the father having the first team and the son the second. The young trees were watered from stream to stream along the way, as opportunity offered and the precious loads were brought safely through to what is now the site of Milwaukie, six miles south of Portland, without the loss of a tree, the journey ending on November 20, 1847. A few days later Mr. Luelling secured a tract of land from A. E. Wilson, a pioneer of 1842, already cleared, about a half a mile north of Milwaukie, upon which he and his son set out the trees. This lot of trees was generally known as the "traveling nursery."

* * *

Several Portland teachers were in parties which climbed the snow-clad peaks this summer. Among those who joined the party sent out from the Department of Geology of the University of Washington, July 14, to study the glaciers of Mt. Rainier, were Miss Emma Griebel, Miss Belle Joseph, Miss Winifred Hawley, and Miss Geballe. Miss Geraldine Cartmell and Miss Hallie Bell were members of a party which camped for a week at the timber line on Mt. Adams and ascended to the summit August 10. Miss Alice Joyce ascended Mt. Hood, August 16, accompanied only by a guide. Mrs. Cora D. Fraine was a member of a party which ascended Mt. Hood in August.

* * *

Miss Anna Johnson, of Vernon school, Portland, is chairman of the League Committee of the Portland Grade Teachers' Association. Miss Johnson will be glad to assist by advice or information any group of elementary teachers who wish to form an association. Miss Johnson attended the meetings of the National Educational Association and spoke of "tenure" before the League of Teachers' Association.

* * *

Miss Frances Hardin, of Chicago, president of the League of Teachers' Associations, was unanimously re-elected. Miss Hardin was also elected a vice-president of the National Educational Association. Both honors are a high tribute to Miss Hardin's ability and character.

* * *

A large number of Portland educators attended the summer school sessions of the University of Washington. They were: Emma Barrette, Frances Barnes, Christine Bergsvik, Mabel F. Burghduff, Fuller Combs, Gene Crawford, Grace Crawford, Nellie Dickinson, Edna Doyle, Ruth Dunne, Margaret Ferguson, Edith Forbes, Grace Goodale, Marie Gorman, Marlin Granning, Gertrude Nefzger, Anna Neufeld, Margaret Nugent, Lillian Porter, Louise Quilliam,

Marguerite Reagan, Blanche Ross, Frederick Stauffer, May E. Stephen, Margaret Sutherland, Queenie Swanson, Eunice Townsend, Mrs. Eunice Townsend, Henry Townsend, Mary Townsend, Ruth Turner, Clara Vaughn, Pauline Geballe, Hortense Greffoz, Laura Hallinan, Rachel Hallingly, Winifred Hawley, Estelle Hell, Belle Joseph, Jeanette Kennedy, Katherine Kiemle, Constance King, Marjory Lewis, Ettie Logan, Jessie McGregor, Estelle J. McIntyre, Sadie McInnis, Grace McKenzie, Ida Menzies, William Miller.

* * *

One association states frankly a situation that has also prevailed elsewhere: "Previous to November all employes of the school board were eligible to membership in our organization. With such a personnel, however, the association stood for nothing and accomplished nothing. Accordingly at the annual meeting in November we adopted a new constitution which limits membership to class room teachers."

* * *

The Los Angeles City Teachers' Club has a membership of almost twelve hundred. It maintains beautiful clubrooms. It has a mountain cabin where teachers may enjoy week ends. It has defeated harmful legislation and improved conditions for all Los Angeles teachers by raising the maximum and minimum salaries.

* * *

The Saint Paul Association has published a "bulletin' each month; has maintained a library service committee which has co-operated in making the public library more useful to the schools; it has donated a hundred dollars to be used for books and pictures destroyed by fire; it donated funds for the municipal Christmas celebration; it has donated seventy-five dollars to assist a woman student.

* * *

The Portland teachers are just beginning to realize that they have in Portland one of the finest instructors in Primary Manual Arts, in this country, in Miss Mary F. Ledyard, the kindergartener at St. Helen's Hall. The following teachers have availed themselves during the spring and summer of the opportunity of taking a course of lessons of Miss Ledyard, and are very enthusiastic over the work: Edith Alderson, Miss Adair, Claytie Burrows, Nettie F. Berryman, Mary A. Billings, Lutie Cake, Olita

Cooley, Miss Dalzell, Miss Door, Thenie E. Draper, Ada J. Farmer, Miss Francis, Florence George, Freda Geiger, Miss Harris, Ethelyn Harris, Kate Hickling, Miss Halum, Virginia Hood, Miss Jennings, Joella Johnson, Luella M. Knapp, Ida H. Holmes, Daisy L. Larsen, Mrs. Maxwell, Frances Meyers, Willima Monroe, Eugenia Morse, Jessie Murch, Rozine Epple, Agatha Grondahl, Carrie M. Ogle, Bertha Peaper, Lila Rogers, Cora Sullivan, Paula Schmaltz, Rachel Smith, Naomi Stengel, Maud E. Smart, Crilla Shonkwiler, Selma Norberg.

* * *

Does everybody know that the summer schools of our great universities furnish recreational courses for tired teachers who do not feel equal to the arduous work of educational courses? The folk dancing classes are places of mirth and merriment; one goes in tired and comes away rested. The tennis courts are popular resorts and one need feel no timidity at being a beginner; to a casual on-looker, they are mostly beginners. The domestic science and dressmaking classes give an opportunity for a change of labor, which is really rest, and require very little outside preparation. Then, too, there are the arts and crafts classes where hand work, from basketry to jewelry may be pursued according to one's fancy.

* * *

Now that one vacation is swiftly receding into the past, it is time to begin planning for next year's. Much of the pleasure of a vacation lies in its anticipation; and with the seductive illustrated literature to be obtained concerning the better known playgrounds, not only is the imagination incited to flights of fancy, but much real knowledge is gleaned, as well. Some teachers are enthusiastic over Blue Mountain resorts, others are equally partial to the shore. Many teachers who attended the University of Washington summer school spent the remainder of their vacation in our neighboring state and bring back glowing accounts of its beauty spots, particularly Mt. Rainier, Lake Crescent in the Olympics, and the lovely Lake Chelan. Others who went farther afield, or whose pocketbooks were more plethoric, toured through Yellowstone, or its newer rival, Glacier National Park. It is becoming quite customary to walk through the latter park; the distances between hotels and chalets are not great and

to persons accustomed to walking, the trails are easy and secure. A pamphlet describing these walking tours may be obtained at the railroad offices. No part of the world is so well adapted to out-door life as our great West, and no exercise is so healthful as walking.

* * *

The following Portland teachers attended the summer school at the University of California: C. S. Adchison, Eugenia S. Altman, Arthur H. Babb, Incy A. Baker, Lucile Bracket, Ella Broderick, Sada Brown, Laura Cleland, Sarah E. Conway, G. G. Dewey, Grace Fields, Ray W. Frohman, Chas A. Fry, Anna L. Gatley, Fred Goldman, Delphe Alice Hammond, Marguerite F. Hickey, Anna E. Holman, Gertrude A. James, John L. Kerchen, Ethel L. Lawlor, Mary Florence McCredy, Vivian V. Mickle Elizabeth Miller, Vivian Nelson, Phila Nicoll, Laura H. Northrup, Grace Rodgers, Fina Sagorsky, Cora May Sullivan, Bertha Tuitt Cora I. Wold, Emma Wold, Abbie Wright, Emily C. Young, Kate E. Young.

* * *

The following Oregon teachers were students at the summer school of the University of California: Ruth Evelyn Aiken, Roseburg; Rachel Applegate, Klamath Falls; Harold D. Aten, Bay City; Aldine Bartmess, Hood River; Gladys Barryman, Scio; Frances E. Bragg, Hood River; Kitty Irene Bragg, Hood River; Alice Clement, Albany; Will H. Coghil, Corvallis; Bertha L. Comings, Eugene; Bessie Courtright, Parkrose; Peggy Crim, Hillsboro; Elena L. Crow, Gwendolen; Eva L. Dresser, Marshfield; Pearl M. Eaton, Eugene; Edith E. Elder, Toledo; Frances C. Fitzpatrick, Roseburg; Edna M. Flarida, Corvallis; Myrtle M. Green, Eugene; Olive Hand, Salem; Josephine Kincaid, Beagle; Theresa Kurtenbach, Evensen; John Jacob Landsbury, Eugene; Blanch Landrith, Bandon; Geo. A. Learned, Forest Grove; Cora Ada Lyon, Corvallis; Nellie L. McAndrews, Klamath Falls; Edna C. McNight, Salem; Lois Laughlin McQuaid, Harrisburg; Helen McCall, Manny, Bend; Mabel Claire Mickey, Talent; Nell Brady Harber, Medford; Laura Heist, Lebanon; Mrs. Belle Henney, Hood River; Willard W. Hodge, Albany; Mary A. Hoer, Salem; Ella L. Hogue, Marshfield; Ida Elizabeth Howard, La Grande; Mary Hurst, Jacksonville; Blanch Jeffreys, Milwaukie; Lily Ann Jeffreys, Airlie;

Myrtle J. Jeffreys, Prineville; Bess
D. Kinter, Medford; Georgia Prather,
Crawfordsville; Lottie Lee Penn,
Lebanon; Ethel Ione Rigdon, Salem;
Alvin M. Robertson, Marshfield;
Franc O. Scofield, Eugene; Mary
Helen Smith, Lorane; Sarah Smith,
La Grande; Renel Pembroke Snider,
Cherry Grove; Hazel Martha Stanton,
Hood River; Pearl Adele Tulley,
Klamath Falls; Frank Collins Tay-
lor, Forest Grove; Martin H. Thiels,
Hood River; Grace Margaret Thom-
as, Hillsboro; Herman C. Tschanz,
Medford; Anna Alma Vannet, Hood
River; Norma Lois Venus, Bandon;
Wilma Waggener, Albany; Elizabeth

Wagner, Myrtle Creek; Irma Whittier, The Dalles.

Every progressive and loyal
teacher in the state ought
to be a member of the Oregon
State Teachers' Association.
Membership costs $1.50 and in-
cludes a year's subscription to
the Oregon Teachers Monthly,
which ranks as the best educational paper in the Northwest,
editorially, typographically and
in circulation.

City Superintendents' Department

Edited by GEORGE W. HUG, McMinnville, Oregon

School Items of Interest.

J. H. Pruet is principal of the
Forest Grove high school, succeeding
G. E. Murphy who is teaching in
Portland.

Portland, Ashland, and Baker
opened school on September 4. The
Dalles opened school on September 11.

School systems introducing the
junior high school organization this
year are Ashland, Medford, and Eugene. The junior high school has
been in operation at Salem and
Albany for one year and at McMinnville for two years.

O. M. Plummer, a member of the
Portland school board, is president
of the National Department of School
Boards.

State Supt. J. A. Churchill has
issued a course of study for the commercial departments for high schools
of Oregon. The course has been
planned by Merrit Davis, head of the
commercial department of the Salem
high school.

Royal Niles, famous Whitman college half back, will teach history and
coach athletics in the LaGrande high
school.

August Willman, a graduate of
Reed college this year, will teach
physical training in the Marshfield
high school.

James Dodson, principal of the
Dayton school, is principal of the
Scappoose school. George Gabriel
assumes the principalship at Dayton.

Jesse McCord, for four years principal of the schools at Clatskanie, is
principal of the Terwilliger school in
Portland.

L. L. Summers, the new supervisor of manual training in the Portland public schools, comes from Oak
Park, Illinois, where he has been director of manual training in the Oak
Park high school.

A. A. Sproule, formerly head of
the commercial department of the
state Normal at Salem, Mass., is
principal of the new commercial
high school in Portland located in
the old Shattuck building.

Miss Carolyn Everts is teaching in
the James John high school.

The speakers and instructors at
the Portland Teachers' Institute held
Sepember 1st and 2nd were: Frederick E. Bolton, Dean of the College
of Education, University of Washington; Edward M. Hulme, Department of History, University of
Idaho; Freeman Daughters, Department of Education, University of
Montana; Norman F. Coleman, Professor of English, Reed College; H.
D. Sheldon, Dean of School of Education, University of Oregon; Thos.
H. Gentle, Principal of Training
School, Oregon Normal School; Mary
E. Sutherland, Extension Specialist

in Home Economics, State College of Washington; Ava Milam, Domestic Science Department, Oregon Agriculture College; Grace P. Gillett, Domestic Art Department, Oregon Agriculture College; Mrs. Edna Samson, Supervisor, State Normal, Bellingham, Wash.; E. S. Evenden, Department of Education, Oregon Normal School; Robert Clark, Department of Education, State Normal, Dillon, Mont.; Myrtle Sholty, Primary Supervisor, State Normal, Ellensburg, Wash.; Effie B. McFadden, Supervisor Normal, San Francisco, California.

The city superintendents of the state of California held their annual meeting or convention August 24, 25, and 26, at Lake Tahoe. Lake Tahoe is situated on the Eastern border of the state, and has the reputation of being one of the most beautiful spots in the state of California.

Walter R. Siders, of Pocatello, Idaho, has assumed the superintendency of the schools of Ogden, Utah, to succeed J. M. Mills. Mr. Siders has been an educational leader in state of Idaho for many years. He has been the head of the Pocatello schools since 1899 and was re-elected last spring. He will receive $3600 for the first year and $3800 for the second year.

E. A. Moses is director of the band and orchestra in the Albany high school.

There are nine new instructors in the Corvallis high school. They are Florence Boden, Clarence Thorn, Mina Ferguson, June Philpott, David S. North, E. H. Reichart, Elsie V. Moore, C. C. Ruth, and M. E. Woodcock.

Supt. C. W. Boetticher has worked out a very interesting salary schedule for the Albany schools.

County Superintendents' Department

Edited by CLYDE T. BONNEY, The Dalles, Oregon

Normal School for Eastern Oregon.

Oregon has but one normal school. This is located at Monmouth and most of its students come from Western Oregon, but few of its graduates teach in Eastern Oregon. During the last five years 203 teachers who have graduated from the Monmouth normal have been employed in the Willamette valley as against 39 Monmouth graduates who have been employed in the eastern part of the state. During that same period of time the attendance of students from nine Willamette valley counties was 877 students as against 91 students from the nine leading counties of Eastern Oregon; which shows conclusively that the graduates of our one normal school are secured as teachers in the nearby schools, leaving Eastern Oregon to secure its teachers from other sources and not so well trained.

Of more than 6000 school teachers in the public schools of Oregon, but 13 per cent have been trained in normal schools for their profession of teaching. It is a well established

fact that our one normal school cannot supply the needs of the entire state, as at present Monmouth turns out only about 10 per cent of the additional teachers required in the public schools of Oregon.

Pendleton is ideally located for a standard normal school, as laid down by the government reports from the bureau of education. Geographically it is the most accessible city in Eastern Oregon. Twenty-two passenger trains enter the city each day, giving service from five different directions. It is supplied with an abundance of good pure water from the Blue Mountains, the water system recently constructed at a cost of $300,000. There is a thorough sewerage system. Municipal institutions that will be at the service of normal students include a first class public library, just finished at a cost of $40,000, a beautiful natatorium, costing $10,000 and the largest athletic stadium in the state, with capacity for seating 20,000 people.

One of the most important elements in the construction of a standard normal school, is that there be ample grade students for teaching practice, and Pendleton has to offer to the Eastern Oregon school over a thousand grade pupils for this purpose and the school board of the city of Pendleton have tendered the same to the board of regents of the normal schools of the state. The educators of the state have unanimously endorsed the measure locating the Eastern Oregon normal school at Pendleton, and it should receive the endorsement of every parent in the state, who believes that our children are entitled to instruction under the best trained teachers that we can secure, and these should be from our home state.—J. C. Sturgill, Condon, President County Superintendents' Association.

Benton County.

Twenty seven teachers, not including the teachers in the city schools have been issued professional teacher's certificates, and 111 teachers have completed the reading circle work.

H. C. Seymour, state leader for the boys and girls industrial clubs, has been doing a very effective work among the industrial clubs of Benton county, and Supt. Cannon is expecting good exhibits at the school fair this fall.

All indications are looking forward to a most successful school year, school boards have used precaution in the hiring of teachers, some of the buildings have been remodeled, and school conditions in general have been made better. Three years ago there were 33 improperly lighted buildings in the county, but during the past summer Green Peak school district, Bunker Hill school district, and Wren school district have remodeled their houses, leaving but three buildings in the county with cross lights.

A circular letter has been sent to the school board members of Benton county suggesting fumigation of the building, cleaning of grounds, investigation of water supply, supplying of needed apparatus, the placing of out buildings in first class condition, and urging the loyal support, first, last, and all the time toward the teacher. It is the desire of the Benton county superintendent to make the school the best possible the

coming school year, and teachers, school board members, pupils, and patrons are being solicited to do their part.

Clatsop County.

This year new school houses have been built at Vesper, Waluski, Battle Creek, and Lewis and Clark, and were ready for use by the middle of September. A first class union high school building at Seaside-Gearhart, will soon be completed and school opened therein. A union high school building at Knappa will also be ready for use about October 1.

At Warrenton a 10-acre tract of land has been purchased and a new school building completed at a cost of about $20,000. It contains eight class rooms, a large auditorium, a domestic science room, and manual training room. The grounds are being put in shape for an athletic field, school gardens, and play grounds and when completed will be one of the finest school grounds in Clatsop county. The building is heated with an oil burner hot air furnace, and the air is completely changed every six minutes by an electric fan. Other apparatus is being added which will give Warrenton a finely-equipped school.

An enthusiastic school officers' meeting was held in Astoria on August 25. The subjects under discussion were school district boundaries and special district tax. Addresses were made by Judge T. S. Cornelius, Sheriff J. V. Burns, Supt. O. H. Byland, District Attorney C. W. Mullens, Assessor F. P. Leinenweber, Commissioners John Frye and K. F. Johnson. At the close of the meeting the county school superintendent was instructed to appoint a committee of nine composed of school officers whose duty it was to carefully study conditions with reference to burdensome taxation on the part of some districts, amounting in some cases to 18 and 20 mills, while in others three-tenths mill was sufficient and also to investigate district boundary conditions. In many districts the boundaries are unknown, there being no record of when the districts were formed or what is the extent of their territory.

Crook County.

The manual training building at the Redmond union high school is nearing completion.

The superintendent's óffice has been very busy in getting ready the various outlines for the school year.

Quite a number of Waterbury heaters have been installed in the various school buildings throughout the county during the vacation.

The boys and girls have been very busy the past few weeks assisting their parents and neighbors to harvest Crook county's largest crop, in the history of the county.

Supt. F. Thordarson, the new superintendent of Bend, has established his residence and has been working very vigorously for the successful opening of the school, September 11. The Bend school will install domestic science and manual training departments in the high school. Bend has voted bonds to erect another school building of 12 rooms for the grades.

All schools are supplied with teachers. Wesley G. Anderson, formerly of Jefferson county, will be the new principal at La Pine. Superintendent P. M. Nash, of the Redmond schools, has been re-engaged for another year. Superintendent H. C. Baughman, of the Crook county high school, and Principal Albert Schreder, of the Prineville public schools, will continue in their old positions for the coming year. G. G. Groves, of Terrebonne, and Etta James, of Tumalo, have been re-engaged.

During the month of August a good many personal visits were made to the club members throughout the county. During a part of this time L. J. Allen, state club worker, accompanied the superintendent in these visitations. It was found that in nearly all cases the members were doing most commendable work. However, it was found that the work is much more effectively done when the club leader is active in the good of the cause. The six members of the canning club at Bend will give a demonstration of their work, three days during the county fair. They will confine themselves largely to the canning of such vegetables as grow in this section, and meats. On all lines, the Bend boys' and girls' club has done most commendable work in their various projects, this summer.

Jackson County.

The schools of Jackson will take an active part in the county fair this year. Many cups, medals and other trophies are offered to schools and individuals, as inducements to enter field and athletic contests.

A spelling contest has been conducted in Jackson county during the past year. The final wind-up will take place at the county fair. A list of fifteen hundred words was selected and was used throughout the county in place of the text book. In the final contest, this list will first be used; then the text book. If the contestants prove to be too well prepared for either of these, words will be taken from the Sunday Oregonian of August 20. The winning speller of the county will receive a beautiful silver cup.

Progressive steps are being taken by several schools in Jackson county. District No. 88, Sardine Creek, is erecting a $1200 building. The teachers' training course is being installed in the high schools at Gold Hill and also at Rogue River. Butte Falls, which has heretofore had a two-year course, changes this year to four years. Mr. Leonard M. Buoy is principal, with Miss Elsie Wright as assistant. Eagle Point installs the first year in high school. District No. 65, Laurelhurst, starts off with a four-year course, with Mr. Floris A. Broomfield as principal and Miss Belva Walker as assistant. District No. 3, Ruch, is erecting an addition to the building and will be prepared to do high school work. At present writing a principal has not been secured.

The Medford schools start off with several changes this year. A junior high school will be established in two buildings, the Lincoln and the Washington. Mr. Hanby will continue as principal in the former; Mr. Cramer, a graduate of the University of New Mexico and of the Denver University, will be principal of the grades and junior high school in the Washington building. A course in music will be installed with Miss French at the head. Miss French is a graduate of the University of Washington, in which institution she has given instruction in music. She has also had several years of experience in public schools. A new course in art will be directed by Miss Griffith, who is a graduate of the Newman School of Art; also a graduate of the School of Fine and Applied Arts of New York. She has had several years of experience in her line of work. A course in physical training will be installed, under the dirction of Miss Hunter, a graduate of the University of Oregon. Miss Hunter comes very highly recommended. Superintendent Hillis feels that the biggest step that is being taken by the Medford school system is the installation of the teachers' training course. It is planned to make this one of the best in Oregon. The work will be conducted by Miss Winfrey, a graduate of the Normal School of Missouri; she is also a graduate student of the University of Chicago. She has had several years of experience in directing teachers' training work, and comes well recommended. The manual training department in Medford will be strengthened this year. Mr. Kium, at the head of that department, will be assisted by Mr. Blakely, of the O. A. C. The indications are that the Medford school will take a big step forward this year.

Morrow County.

The graduating class of the Ione school has presented the school with a moving picture machine, and arrangements have been completed for a regular series of educational films.

New schoolhouses will be erected in No. 9 and No. 48 this fall. Owing to some delay in selling the bonds of District No. 29, the new building for this district may not be built until next spring.

Professor L. J. Allen and Miss Helen Cowgill visited several school districts with Superintendent Notson about August 1, in the interest of the club work. They succeeded in arousing much interest. The O. A. C. is certainly doing a splendid work through these workers.

The new town of Boardman, on the main line of the O.-W. R. & N. in the northern part of the county, is growing rapidly, and arrangements are being made to open a school early in October. Boardman is in the territory included in the west extension of the Umatilla Irrigation project.

Dan Cupid has not interfered with the educational interests of this county this year as much as he usually does. Only four of last year's teach-

ers have reported that they have fallen under his unerring aim; these are Misses Mary E. Power, Della Smith, Anna T. Ferm, and Mrs. Harriet Stephens.

Polk County.

Miss Hattie Teats, of Dallas, will run the Ballston schools.

H. H. Lowe, of Carleton, is to be principal of the Falls City schools.

Superintendent W. I. Reynolds is busy with fair and institute programs.

From present indications, the children's part of the Polk County fair will be good.

Floyd D. Moore was elected as supervisor for the coming year. He has the initiative and will make good.

R. G. Dykstra has resigned the high school work at Perrydale. He had a very successful year there.

E. H. Hendrick has been elected principal of the Monmouth high school. He comes highly recommended.

Superintendent W. I. Ford of the Dallas public school is well pleased with his corps of teachers. He has several new teachers as some of the old teachers have married and one is with the troops on the border.

Sherman County.

The Rufus school has two teachers this year and is offering one year of high school work. C. L. McCarthy is principal of the school.

District 21, known as the Fairview school, has built an up-to-date school house since school closed in the district last May. Miss Myrtle Sawyer, who taught in the same district last year, is the teacher this year.

The Kent school has added another teacher this year, making three altogether. This school also has added a year of high school work to its course. This district is building a new $7000 school building, which they hope to have completed before winter.

The Wasco School district, which is the largest district in the county, is erecting a $25,000 school building. When completed, this building will furnish ample room for all pupils who desire to attend the school. This building was made necessary, largely, as a result of the county high school tuition fund law. The outlying districts crowded the school to such an extent last year that more room was absolutely necessary.

The Sherman county schools began the year's work during the month of September. Every school in the county is now in session. There are thirty-one schools employing forty-eight teachers. Five of these schools are in town districts and employ from two to seven teachers each. The other twenty-six districts, employ one teacher each. Of the forty-eight teachers employed for this year, each one has either had special preparation for the kind of work he or she is to do, or has had one or more years of successful experience as a teacher in this state. Eight of the number are graduates of standard colleges or universities; two others are graduates of non-standard colleges or universities containing some provisions for teachers' training courses; seventeen are graduates of standard normal courses; four are graduates of elementary normal school courses; thirteen others have had successful experience in the school rooms of this state previous to this year, and most of these have had one or more years of college or normal school work; the four others are graduates of standard high school teachers' training classes last year. With a trained teacher in every school room in the county, much is expected from our schools this year.

Union County.

November 1, 2, and 3 are the dates set for the big Eastern Oregon meet of teachers and a splendid program is being prepared.

Union County schools in general were in motion on September 4—La Grande, Cove and a few rural districts, however, began on Monday, September 11.

La Grande, Union and Elgin are to have new city superintendents this year. Linden McCullough is the newly elected superintendent of La Grande. E. E. Arant is to be the head of Union school, and A. E. Clawson, of the Elgin schools. All these men are actively engaged in putting everything in shape for a splendid school year.

A. C. Hampton will be La Grande's new high school principal. L. E. Reese, formerly of Oak Grove will be in charge of the Pine Grove school. Mrs. Emma Temple, formerly of Fine

Grove, will be in charge of the Grange Hall school. R. E. Borneman and Miss Bessy Stoddard will conduct the Perry school.

A fine, new, modern, up-to-date school building is nearing completion at North Powder. A new one-roomed school building is being erected in the Hot Lake school district. Kamela expects to have a new building soon, to be used for children's play room during the long deep snow of winter, at the summit of the mountains, and also to be used as a community hall. Hilgard is now an up-to-date standard school, having made substantial and attractive improvements. In fact, the school boards are everywhere cooperating with teachers to make better conditions.

Wasco County.

Nearly all of the schools of Wasco county were in session by Monday, September 11.

The annual institute for Wasco county was held on Monday, Tuesday and Wednesday, September 18, 19, and 20, in the new high school building at The Dalles.

Since March 22, 1914, when the first Industrial Club in Wasco county was organized by Mr. L. P. Harrington, industrial field worker, working from the office of the superintendent of public instruction, industrial club work has been an essential part of the school system of Wasco county. It is estimated that the boys and girls of Wasco county earned in the year 1915 in prizes and otherwise about $2000 in money. According to the best information that the county superintendent is able to obtain, three-fourths of this money was wasted. To teach boys and girls how to earn money and not teach them how to use it wisely, is a sin. Believing extravagance and the unwise spending of money to be our national curse, the "System Bank Way" has been adopted as an essential part of the school system of Wasco county. The object of this savings bank system is to teach thrift to the boys and girls who are growing up. The teachers are required to give one recitation period of each week to the teaching of this most important subject. The lessons for their use are prepared and sent from the office of the county superintendent. Fifteen lessons will be prepared and taught during the first half of the school year and fifteen lessons will be taught during the second half of the school year. This system secures the co-operation of the home, the school and the banks and this co-operation is absolutely necessary in order to make the savings bank system permanently successful and of real educational value. Enough lessons are sent from the office of the superintendent for each teacher and each pupil in the public schools of Wasco county from the youngest to the oldest. The following is the first lesson to be taught in every school room in the county:

"Out of one hundred average healthy young men selected by one of the leading insurance companies years ago, twenty-five years later four were rich, one was wealthy, sixteen were supporting themselves by days labor, sixteen were dead, and sixty-three were dependent for their support upon friends, relatives or charity. The above statistics are furnished from memory and I cannot vouch for their correctness. However, the lesson is the same.

"According to statistics gathered by the United States National Bank of Portland, Oregon, 97 per cent of men meet with reverses between the ages of forty and fifty, and at sixty years of age 95 per cent of men are dependent upon their children or charity because they saved nothing.

"The 'saving habit' leads to happiness and comfort; the 'spending habit' leads to misery and want. Will you practice the self-denial that develops character and results in happiness or comfort, or will you seek the pleasure of the moment and build for yourself a future of wretchedness, misery and poverty?

"The greatness of a nation is measured in terms of efficiency, thrift and economy, and so important is the acquirement of these traits, that a savings bank system has been adopted as an essential part of the public school system of Wasco county. This system is one which secures the co-operation of the home, the bank and the school. The co-operating banks in Wasco county are, French & Company, bankers, The Dalles, Oregon; The First National Bank, The Dalles, Oregon; Johnston Brothers, Bankers, Dufur, Oregon.

"Under this system the pupil has his own little savings bank and does his own business directly with the bank of his choice. Cards of introduction may be secured from either of the three banks mentioned or from the teacher. This card of introduction, after being filled out, must be taken with ten cents to the bank. The pupil will then get a savings bank, into which go the pennies, nickles, dimes and quarters which he wishes to save. As soon as there is one dollar in his savings bank, he takes it to the bank, where it is opened by the cashier and he is given credit for the amount in his savings bank together with the ten cents which he deposited at the start as an evidence of good faith.

"During the coming year one recitation period of each week will be given to teaching the subject of 'thrift.' Material for these lessons will be sent from the office of the county superintendent. It will be determined in an open class how many pupils are savers and how many are depositors, according to the adopted definition of these terms, to-wit: Saver—A pupil who has (1) adopted the plan Systematic Saving; (2) applied for and received a System Bank from the savings bank of his choice; (3) who regularly puts aside in his System Bank one cent or more each week; (4) who reports promptly at the close of each month to his teacher his weekly savings and also his Savings Bank deposits. Depositor—A saver (1) who has attained to the point of having a savings bank account; (2) who adds thereto by further deposits as rapidly as one dollar as accumulated."

Yamhill County.

The new buildings at Cove Orchard and Bellevue will be ready for occupancy at the opening of the autumn term.

A number of new heating plants have been installed during the summer vacation. Those already in use in the county have given splendid satisfaction.

The people of No. 67, Panther Creek district, about six miles west of Carlton, are talking of erecting a new building this fall. The old one was built twenty-six years ago last June.

The annual teachers' institute will be held in McMinnville December 4, 5, and 6. The dates are arranged for the entire state by a committee at the convention of county superintendents, and the schedule is made so that the state superintendent can attend each one as far as he can spare the time; hence some counties must have later dates than others.

James Dodson has resigned the principalship of the Dayton schools, which he has served so long and faithfully, and will have charge of the schools in Scappoose. For more than ten years he has been in control of the work in Dayton, and when he was elected to the city superintendency of the Newport schools 2 years ago, the people of Dayton petitioned him to remain with them. Their regret at his resignation is as great now as it was then, and they will feel his loss keenly.

No. 43 had the honor of ringing the first bell of the season, as school opened in that district Monday, September 4; Miss Marie Vinzellberg is in charge. On Monday, September 11, Miss Ruth Westerman opened her first term at No. 19, Moore's Valley, and Miss Ruby Alexander at No. 82, Deer Creek. Many schools began on September 18, among which was the McMinnville schools. No. 39, Mt. Richmond, northwest of Yamhill, and No. 58, The Beehive, west of Willamina.

The people in No. 21 have just experienced a similar loss, as Miss Lola Kuns has accepted a high school position in Oregon City. Miss Kuns has been in charge of the high school department in No. 21 for four years, and has given excellent satisfaction, and the condition of the school is such that the patrons may well be proud of it. As principal of the school, her control and influence has been everything that could be desired, and the regret at her resignation will be universal. Miss Mildred Bodle, who has during the same length of time had charge of the lower grades, will remain in the school. Her services have also been very satisfactory, as is evidenced by her repeated re-election.

The Annual Teachers' Round Table was held in the county court house in McMinnville during the week beginning August 28, and continued five days. The following teachers were present: Dotsie Reeves, Grace Duran, Ruth Westerman, Helen Milne, Ruby Alexander, Hazel Scott, Frieda Dell, Ethel Ecks, Mary Wilcox, Charles Boosinger, Bernice Deach, Luann Hiatt, Jessie Hadley, S. W. Babcock, Glenn Ladd, Hulda Parr, Margaret McCoskey, Margaret Benfer, Ferris Drill, Ethel Jackman, Eleanor Warner, Icy Bryan, Mabel Curry, Eva Alfrey, Mabel

Bond. Many of these teachers were present at each session, while others attended only part of the time. The first day was given to a discussion of plans for opening school, school management, reports, and many other details connected with the general management of school affairs. The remaining four days were taken up with a discussion of methods for teaching the various branches taught in the grades. Nearly all of one day was devoted to methods in reading in every grade, including instruction in phonics. The importance of this branch was emphasized, as it is indeed the foundation of the entire school curriculum. Nearly one and one-half days were spent on methods in arithmetic, paying special attention to primary work, and the work of teaching fractions. Primary geography, primary spelling, primary language work, history, and physiology received their due share of attention, while the work in the higher grades was gone over carefully also. Methods in grammar intended to teach the pupil from the standpoint of observing the language for himself were given, and plans for allowing the pupils to assist in the work of correcting their own compositions during the recitation period were discussed. Picture study occupied a prominent position on the program, and almost every teacher in the class presented a picture during the class. Opening exercises were quite freely discussed by the class, and the prevailing opinion seemed to be that the teacher should take up a very little of the school time in reading to the pupils. It was held that a small amount of it might be done in order to teach them what to get from the books read, and to interest them in reading, but that it is unwise to devote much time to the exercise. The opening exercise time was thought to be the best time for the presentation of pictures to the pupils, as it was appropriate for that period, and prevented other time from being taken from the regular studies.

Clubbing List.

On another page will be found a clubbing list, and teachers who do not wish to wait until institute time to get subscriptions should send direct to the office of Oregon Teachers Monthly at Salem, so as to get their educational papers started early in the school year.

Getting in Personal Touch with the Big Girl

By EMMA RUSTER, Portland, Oregon

Getting in personal touch with the girls of the upper grades is often not so much a problem as an accident. When I taught by first little school in Eastern Oregon I had no idea that children could not be considered in herds but as actual individuals, just like grown people—each with his own ideas and viewpoint. That the growing girl was an especially peculiarly constructed creature had never occurred to me—possibly because I had so recently emerged from that period myself that I had not yet reached a distance for a perspective. But I did know that poor neglected Mary was lonesome, and since she had no mother and lived with a sister-in-law who "didn't care especially for children," I tried to give her some of the personal attention and affection that she so craved. She had missed so much that it was easy to make her happy, and happy she certainly was.

In the next school the first to arouse my compassion were two sisters who were not "quite right." None of the other boys and girls wanted them at their parties, and the girls were bright enough to feel this. It made one's heart ache to see the wonder and pain in their eyes when they were not bidden to a frolic. One day when the younger girl was in an exceptionally bad mood, her mother called me in to see if I could get her to respond to me. I had "Tom Sawyer" in my hand, and not knowing just what to do, I began to talk about the book and to read to her. At first she gave me the attention due "teacher," but soon she forgot her sulks in the interest of the story. At supper she was full of "Tom," and I had to continue reading so the others could hear it, too. The older girl was struggling with her music, and a little help now and then made her gratitude fairly pathetic. The fidelity and affection these two girls lavished on me would have been irksome, to say the least, but their mother's unspoken gratitude, and the girls' pride in having a "chum", more than repaid me, and when I left, their grief was as sincere as it was noisy.

A family of five children with no mother would arouse any one's interest. The oldest girl was twelve and played housekeeper and mother to the rest. All of their pent-up affection was poured out on their teacher. Who could resist them, especially when the baby, one day just before school closed, climbed up on the rounds of my chair and putting his moist little hand against my face, whispered, "Sweetheart!" and with a crimson face scampered out of the door?

These experiences began to open my eyes to the larger opportunities of a teacher, and it was with regret that I accepted an appointment to the city. I had been told that individuality counted for nothing there, and that the children had so many amusements that the teacher rarely came in personal touch with the children. I should like those people to hear more. Here I came to the knowledge that there were so-called "bad" girls. My first encounter was with Mayme — an over-developed, tempestuous girl of sixteen. At the close of one terrible day she slapped me. I stood speechless, trying to recall what the rules said in regard to such conduct—for I was new, and had studied that little gray book carefully and knew that under no circumstances was I to lay hands on Mayme, but the board had evidently overlooked making a rule forbidding Mayme to lay hands on me. I was still undecided when she suddenly flung herself on her knees and opened her mouth and wailed loud and long until the janitor came to see if I needed help. After that no dog could have been more faithful and obedient, and although some may object to the force of this personal contact with the pupil, it had a lasting effect on Mayme as long as she remained in school.

In the sewing class the appropriateness of dress is so easily discussed, and Millie, who had come to school with the appellation of "bad" firmly tacked to her name, profited thereby. She had a sweet smile but a little demon in her eye that belied the sweetness. She would be as annoying as she dared—and she dared a great deal—but through it all appear perfectly innocent. One day she appeared in an especially daring waist, and gave the girls a look that said, "Now, watch." Of course, neither I nor the sewing teacher admitted Millie's badness, and casually began speaking of an older girl who was very popular and mentioned her neat clothes as one cause of her popularity. Millie became uncomfortably warm and fidgeted in her chair. She did want to be popular and her early efforts had not been very successful. The next day she wore a neat, girlish dress and a much subdued air. When she left school, although she was by no means a model of perfection, she said she "hated" to leave because she had always been treated "white."

The "Cosmopolitan" can hardly be considered suitable reading for girls, and when I saw one on a girl's desk I asked her if I could not have it during the noon hour. In place of it, I gave her "Little Women" from the classroom library. In a few days she returned it and asked for more like it. I casually handed her the borrowed magazine. She flushed and pushed it into the waste basket without even a sigh for the unfinished thriller by Robert Chambers. Later she asked for a library card of her own and after browsing about in the children's room to her heart's content—although she was fifteen—she emerged with Grimm's Fairy Tales under her arm. Her eyes shone like stars and she felt that she had made as big a discovery as Columbus. She was carrying her new ideals home, too, for when a book fell due at the school library one day, she asked to have it renewed so her mother could finish reading it out loud to the children, and a neighbor wanted it after her.

During all this time a real friendship began to develop almost imperceptibly at first, and now it is in the order of the day for one girl to ask how she should have her new dress made, or another to come with a story of her quarrel with her chum, or the numerous other little things that count for friendship, and out of the accidental interest in the girls' affairs has grown something that is worth a great deal more than words

can tell, and I feel that from this personal contact I am gaining much more than the girls who have come to me.

To Young Teachers.

1. Keep a stiff upper lip.
2. Speak in low but firm tones.
3. Do not scold or nag.
4. In determining punishments, consider the home life and training of the child.
5. "Let not the sun go down on your wrath."
6. Hang a thermometer in the schoolroom, and mark the temperature often.
7. Study every lesson you are to teach, and let every step of it from beginning to end be clearly before your mind.
8. If possible—and it should be—teach without a book in your hand.
9. Before you begin the year's work, arrange a course of reading for yourself, and follow it faithfully until you finish. This course should include one or two books on teaching, and several in general literature —prose and poetry.
10. Reserve some time each day for recreation.
11. Make yourself useful in the neighborhood in furthering every work which tends to elevate the people.
12. Write something original, if it be but a paragraph, every day.—Western School Journal.

The Curry county institute was held at Gold Beach, September 7, 8, 9. The instructors were H. C. Seymour of Corvallis and J. Teuscher of Portland. They were assisted by local teachers.

The Model or School Store

By MRS. IRENE SPENCER, Ashland, Oregon

The Model or School Store is practically a new idea. It has been established in some of the eastern states for the past five years. Portland, Oregon, schools are using it and find it of immense value to them. So far as I know the little store that we started in our two room country school, November, 1915, was the only other one in Oregon. To quote from the Educational Foundation Magazine, "like many another institution all its possibilities have not been realized." On first thought we are apt to think of the school store as functioning only in arithmetic, but there its usefulness only begins. In using it in connection with arithmetic we find it of great value in drill on each of the four fundamentals. But as practical as that is the learning to make change quickly and accurately, learning the value of goods, how to make out bills, write orders and even how to go into a store and order a bill of goods which we know so many children and grown people are timid about doing.

In language work the children will be most interested in writing essays on wheat, rice, raisins, and many other things found on the shelves of the store, and in writing letters to friends describing the store. The conversations used between the merchant and the customer is a fine language drill.

Geography and history also come in for their share. The children like to travel from one country to another and get goods from this place or that or trade and study the conditions under which the goods are grown and prepared for market.

Even spelling words are profitably taken from the grocery shelves. These are only a few of the practical values of the school store. I do not think neatness, cleanliness, politeness, and orderliness should be left out.

I am sure that you will agree that it is a good thing, and now the question arises, how can we get it? From our experience the quickest and best way is to go into a grocery store, tell the merchant your business and go to looking on packages of different sorts of goods for the addresses of the factories. We thought it best to confine our stock to our home state, but before we were hardly aware of the fact we were receiving goods from as far away as New York. It will surprise you how willingly the manufacturers send you their dummy packages and cartons. When writing we requested them to be billed to us the same as real goods; the reason will be explained later. Do not overlook the local manufacturers. Teach the value of buying at home. Toy money can be gotten from any school supply house. We bought ours from Milton Bradley company, $300 for 50 cents.

After the goods are ordered it will not take long to fit up the store. We were crowded for room so necessarily our store was small. We used a space 3 feet by 6 feet in the back of the primary room, and put up the shelves using 4 feet 8 inch boards over a 12 inch base and the counter (made out of a 12 inch board 6 feet long and covered with oil cloth) was set about 2 feet in front of the shelves. The children will be anxious to do all the work they can and more. The only expense in our store was for the lumber, scales, and toy money.

By the time our store was ready and we had decided on a cipher word to use in marking the goods, the goods began to arrive. The seventh and eighth grades took charge of the bills, checking and marking the goods so as to make a certain per cent profit. The fifth and sixth grades unpacked the goods, and grades, one, two, three, and four put the cartons together. Grades four, five, six, and seven marked the different lots of goods under the supervision of the eighth grade. Empty grocery cans, boxes, and bottles were brought from home. Use originality in supplying sand for sugar, berries for coffee, leaves for tea, rice, and other things. In this way every child had an interest in the school store and it kept increasing all the time.

Then came the fun that the children were looking forward to with very little patience and a whole lot of interest—to be really keeping store. Every teacher will have to work out her own problem according to her pupils as to how to conduct this. We were inexperienced and consequently took some time and thought to know how to direct the children. We were particular on these points—that the child be the merchant or the customer in talk, manner and actions, and that the bills made out were always correct or corrected as soon as possible (when we had no billheads the children made out their own by ruling their paper), that the correct change was given out as the clerk should do it, and that the customer count her change when she received it. As the customer left she was allowed to take her goods with her or to order them delivered.

Of course the first grade could not play store to any great extent, but they learned to tell the pieces of money and some learned to count it. One interesting game played with the money is to have some one select several pieces of money then say, "I have 32 cents," or whatever the amount, then say, "In how many pieces is it " The one guessing correctly gets to take the leader's place.

The parents became deeply interested in the store, and noticed the interest the children took in the home buying and the increase in interest in the school in general. It is not difficult to secure the co-operation of the parents or board in installing a school store because every one realizes the practical value that the children get from it, especially the ones who live out in the country and seldom get to a store.

The Newspaper in the Home

By RICHARD B. SWENSON, Monmouth, Oregon

All are interested in seeing that the young bride and groom get a right start. The real estate man wants to supply them with a home, the furniture man wants to furnish it, the hardware man would equip the kitchen and pantry; the meat man, the grocer, the dry goods man are all interested. Likewise the newspaper man stands up to assert that one of the first things a young couple, about to set up housekeeping, should do is to subscribe for the newspaper.

The newspaper is an important adjunct in the home. It is one of the things that distinguish the abiding place of man from the residential places of livestock and poultry. All of these must have ministry to the physical body but their lack of ability to assimilate that which feeds the mind and character is what puts the animal on the lower plane of existance.

The newspaper brings you in touch with your neighbor, whether on the next block or on the other side of the world. It brings the people of the earth to your hearthstone. Through its medium you become acquainted with the record of the activities of mankind, the progress of civilization, the achievements and horrors of humanity, its glories and its miseries. You may sit in your easy chair and read of the happenings of a few hours before on the battlefields of Europe, within the halls of congress, the laboratories of science, the courts of law. Or you may read of your neighbors in the more intimate relations you hold with your fellows, the welfare of personal friends and acquaintances, their successes and disappointments; all those activities of fraternal intercourse which mark the difference between a modern home and a hermit's habitation.

When you have finished reading the newspaper it is still useful. It can serve a hundred household purposes, from kindling for fires to covering for cupboard shelves. It is reasonable in price also. Perhaps a thousand men have worked on it from pulp to the time it is delivered to the newsboy, yet sells for the price of an egg that one old hen has manufactured, or a bunch of radishes, or a fraction of a pound of sugar. Of all the food you buy for mind and body the newspaper is the one that returns the most for the money.

The modern newspaper is co-operation worked down to a science. If a similar efficiency and team work obtained in the production of bread and butter you would hear no more of the high cost of living.

The public necessity of the newspaper is recognized and because of this it has obtained important concessions. The newspaper can be sent from here to Chicago for 1 cent a pound while on ordinary merchandise the rate is 3 cents a pound and on human beings from 20 to 50 cents a pound.

I believe the development and evolution of the newspaper has still a long ways to go. Some day the newspapers will be published by the people colletcively, by the government, national, state, county and municipal, and the freeholder will pay his subscription when he pays his taxes. This because accurate information concerning the world's work and play is essential to the development of citizenship.

The newspaper in the home has crowded the political orator off the stump. A few years ago the political spellbinder was an institution. Now he speaks to empty benches and his former audience reads its politics in the newspaper at home. Every one of the political reforms that have enabled the home man to dominate politics have been adopted through the influence of the newspaper.

It is the newspaper that helps in community interest, that relation that connects you with your brothers and neighbors and makes for your convenience. Team work, that faculty of merging the individual for the benefit of the masses finds a ready vehicle in the newspaper.

This is a wonderful world with a wealth of resources put here for the benefit of ordinary mortals. Civilization is slowly pushing it into the dense human intellect how these advantages can be distributed and put within the reach of all. As an educating factor, the newspaper stands supreme. It penetrates where no other educating influence can go.

Its importance in the home, goes without saying. Most of our newspapers are so cleanly edited that children can safely read them. But like everything else he does, the child should be taught to read them in the right way, taught to understand there is something else in the newspaper but the comic picture. The pictures are the pickles and spice of the newspapers and as these are handled at the dining table the pictures should be handled in the newspaper.

Some of the boys will read the baseball reports first and possibly the society doings will interest the girls. These may be the starters but as the mind develops the taste for other columns will expand and grow. Books and magazines should accompany the newspaper and they are all good. Somehow or other I cannot conceive of home life which is indifferent to the outside world and in which the newspaper does not enter.

Multnomah County Institute.

The Multnomah county institute was held at Portland August 31, September 1, 2. The first day the program was held at Library Hall under the supervision of Superintendent A. P. Armstrong. The last two days were held in connection with the Portland teachers' institute, with general sessions at the Lincoln high school. Some of the speakers of the institute were: J. A. Churchill, superintendent of public instruction; Edward M. Hulme, University of Idaho; Freeman Daughters, University of Montana; Norman Coleman, Reed College; H. D. Sheldon, University of Oregon; Thomas H. Gentle, Oregon Normal School; Mary E. Sutherland, Washington State College; Ava Milam, Oregon Agricultural College; Mrs. Edna Samson, Bellingham Normal school; E. S. Evenden, Oregon Normal school; Robert Clark, Montana Normal school; Effie B. McFadden, San Francisco Normal school. This was one of the largest attended institutes in Oregon, with about twelve or thirteen hundred teachers in attendance.

An Outside Opinion.

The following letter has been received from Arthur H. Chamberlain, editor of the Sierra Educational News, the official school journal of the California Teachers' Association: "I want to congratulate you on the progress you are making there in the state in your organization and with the Oregon Teachers Monthly. I always look forward to receiving the journal, and I know of no one who is reaching the rural teacher better than you are doing. I am hoping to strengthen our own organization here and feel sure that you people have taken some forward steps that may be a suggestion to us. I shall want to work in co-operation with you."

Elementary Agriculture

By L. P. GILMORE, Monmouth, Oregon

The Use of the Text.

The fact that agriculture is listed by our state course of study as a reading course, seems to have created a feeling that state requirements are complied with once the pupils have read the text. This is not entirely erroneous, for were the text read in the manner in which the state department desires, the purposes of agriculture in the upper grades in a measure would be attained. The difficulty lies in the construction placed upon the term reading.

If we were to drop into the average rural district using "Burkett, Stevens and Hill's Agriculture for Beginners," we would find something like this: The class reports for recitation, reads the lesson aloud and after little or no discussion is given an assignment and returned to their desks. The children being fairly capable readers complete the book long before the school term is ended, so they review, etc. This is not overdrawn. In fact it is so true to conditions that the author in consultation with an agriculture agent was told that agriculture teaching in the elementary schools is a farce.

What is the cause of this condition? Obviously there are many causes, one of which is the fact that the text is not used properly. Once we realize that reading is taught to enable children to grasp the meaning from the written page, and that the child may grasp it by silent as well as oral reading, we are on a fair road to remedying the condition. Agriculture is a thought subject and so can be taught in part by reading. But some are still laboring under the fallacy that reading can only pass as such when it is oral. They forget that the main reasons for reading aloud, in addition to the above, are to create pleasing habits of expression and correct enunciation. Of course some subjects are better adapted to this form of reading than others. Agriculture happens to be one which is designed to furnish information in a rather undramatic way, hence is admirably adapted to silent reading.

Now what does this have to do with the topic? Simply this. When the teacher bears the above in mind she will use the text as a store house of knowledge instead of as medium for expressive display. She will place a premium on securing the thought instead of upon "calling the words." She will make her assignments, and when the class meets learn by questioning whether the pupils have secured the thought. The remainder of the recitation may then be given over to discussions bearing on the lesson. How different this from the routine fashion so frequently followed of using the recitation period almost entirely for reading the lesson in spite of the fact that the pupils have the thought before they read the lines. Of course there will be times when the pupils fail to grasp the entire thought. At such times indulge in a bit of oral reading during the recitation period. But always bear in mind the prime reason for such reading is to grasp the thought of the context. Then there is another feature. Once a teacher has this point of view she will not hesitate to omit portions of the text or at least to have them studied out of their regular order. Do not misunderstand me. I am not urging that any disregard the author's arrangement of topics. I am merely saying there are times when it is permissible so to do, and that the teacher who uses the text as a store house of facts will do that. For example, this season of the year is practically the only time we can study corn on cob. Then if conditions are such that it is advisable to teach corn in your district the thing for you to do is to study corn no matter in what portion of the text that subject occurs. It happens the assignment in this case would be pages 69-72, and the aim would be, to learn how to select seed corn. To make my application still more explicit, the average teacher would have this lesson read during the recitation period and would stress the manner of expression, and enunciation. The other type of teacher would likely conduct a dogmatic lesson—that is, have one or more pupils reproduce the thought of the lesson, criticise it, and then drill. In all probability she would wind up the topic by taking her school some noon to a nearby corn field and actually select some seed.

There will be times when bulletins, pamphlets, etc., will be used to amplify the text. It will require effort on the part of the teacher to weave in such materials when using the text as indicated in this article. However, the author feels such effort will make agricultural teaching much more effective.

The Examination Problem

By A. R. TOLLEFSON, Corbett, Oregon

This is a day of revolutionary change not alone in the physical world but in the mental world as well. New ideas, new theories, and systems are constantly being promulgated and initiated into practice. This change in the mode of thinking makes it necessary for institutions to make a similar change in their purpose and method in order to conform to the new standards evolved. Nowhere is this fact more evident and important than in the field of education. And here we find our most vital institution. The school trains the mind and the mind shapes things.

Many are the educational problems demanding consideration and solution and one of those questions is that of the examination. Indeed many arguments can and are advanced both for and against the examination. The mistake is generally made in that the merits or demerits are considered as inherent in the problem itself. Whether or not the examination has any value depends almost wholly upon the teacher. Too often it is of a very narrow technical scope, especially if the teacher is disinterested or somewhat incompetent, which is quite often the case, the questions are not framed or worded so as to draw upon the students thinking or reasoning faculties but rather upon the memory and to this end that undesirable cramming is conducive. Then education becomes a stuffing and not a drawing out process as it should be. Oftentimes, too, the student, even after he has entered high school, is regarded as a mere child instead of a reasoning, thinking individual. The truth of the matter is that many times he is a keener, clearer thinker than the teacher and especially so if that faculty is developed through use.

To stimulate the student to think and reason and not memorize should be the aim of the examination question, yet that is not generally the case. Personally, I do not believe the examination should be eliminated until something more substantial and profitable can displace it. To this end I tried a very interesting experiment in my class in high school physics. I asked the class too weeks before the close of the term how many would rather write a paper of not less than a given length upon a subject of their own choice than take an examination. All but one preferred writing the paper so it was agreed upon.

Now it might be argued that here was a chance for the pupil to get out easy but on the contrary they were all very enthusiastic. The next day the subjects were all in and approved and research work in the library began. Each paper was in on time and the results were far better than I had expected. All the papers were very good. They were neatly written and in book arrangement, with introduction and chapters. One of the first subjects handed in and a paper of excellent quality was on "The Molecular Constitution and Vibration of Matter." Note that the subject is of no small dimensions. I shall quote at length from the paper to show that nevertheless it was very ably handled, stimulating depth of thought. This paper was written by F. Murray Smith, a boy of 19 years.

INTRODUCTION.

"We are all familiar with the three most common manifestations of matter, namely gas, liquid and the solid, the last mentioned being the most common to our limited understanding. These three manifestations positively exist and form the basis of all the facts we have on matter.

"As we see these three manifestations on each and every side of us every day we are led to inquire, what is this matter? We know it exists but this very fact makes us all the more curious to find out the cause and the effect. If we did not know that it did exist we would pay no more attention to it than we do to the hundred and one things that exist but of which we are not aware. . . . .

"When we stop and consider that both the solid and the liquid can be transformed into a gas we realize at once that there must be some unseen likeness in their constitution. So also can the gas we breathe commonly called air be changed into a liquid thus showing some great similarity. . . . .

Science never steps backward but is always reaching out for a new field. Knowing that matter does exist in and about us we will take it for granted that the great law of existence is based on these manifestations of matter. As has been said before, science never stands still, so it therefore is quite possible that in years to come we will discover that existance is based not on matter but on some other ground so far away at present that it can not be imagined."

CHAPTER I.

The Smallest Thing in the World.

"Ever since science has discovered the existence of a unit of constitution by the combination of mixtures, the term atom has been used to express this unit. With the single exception of the electron used in the study of electricity the atom is the smallest unit known to exist and still retain any dimensions. . . . ." (The balance of this chapter discusses the molecule and molecular theory).

CHAPTER II.

Exploring the Atom at Home.

"Perhaps the most theoretical and practical consideration in connection with the study of atoms is the possibility of isolating a single atom and actually testing its size. That this has been done is an admitted fact and as to the results there can be no doubt. The apparatus used for this work is the electroscope which consists of two fine gold leaves. This apparatus when charged with electricity, spreads the two leaves apart. The air being a non-conductor causes the leaves to remain in this position until discharged by some foreign body. In order to get the number and secure data on which to base their work, scientists took a known amount of radium which gives off so many particles of good conduction each second. Then by limiting the number of particles given off to two or three a second they recorded the effect on the electroscope. Thus, by the law of proportions, they can tell the number of atoms in radium or any gas simply by the effect of one or two particles on the electroscope. Thus we find an instrument whose delicacy is little less than awe-inspiring and if this small apparatus can detect such a fine thing how can we be so narrow-minded and ignorant of these great laws that we are led to believe only that which we see? . . . . Some idea of the size of the atom is found in taking a picture of it. This is exactly what J. J. Thompson did in 1910. His method was to let the atom transcribe its own record on a plate and then reproduce it for the world. This he did and today we have the positive proof which tells us some of the life of a molecule or atom living undisturbed. Surely this is seeing the invisible and should teach us that all things may be seen if we touch the right key and unlock the hidden power. Just as Sir Thomson gives us a view of the atom so may we see all things if we simply know how to master the law that governs the desired information. . . . . It simply is a question of knowing how and going about that one thing to win."

CHAPTER III.

Vibration.

"The statement has been made I believe that vibration is life. Just how true this is I do not know but surely there is no life without vibration of some kind . . . .vibration is here, there and everywhere and is never out of existence. The only known thing that will stop this motion of the molecules is the extremely low temperature of 273 degrees C., a degree that has never been reached. If it could be reached, as far as the outside world is concerned, existence would cease at least in the form that we see it existing now.

"The art of science has not invented the molecular theory and vibration of matter but merely discovered that such a thing exists. Neither have the terms used to express these things any more bearing on the true law than would the same term were it in Latin or French. The terms are simply the grips with which to pick up things. We may call the vibration of matter the law but that is nothing more than the effect. Some persons think that since the atom is in motion it is motion in itself. If this were so and there were no laws governing motion we should soon be in a sad state of confusion.

"We do know that the vibration of atoms is governed by some law but what it is we know not. What we have termed the law is simply the result of the unknown law. Take for example Newton who is supposed to have discovered the law—gravity. We give him credit and he deserves it, but did he really find the law or merely the effect this law has on matter.

"Personally, I believe there is one law for all matter and that Newton did not find it. If the so-called law of gravity worked on all matter the same it could be called the law-gravity, but it simply refers to the attraction of bodies. In other words gravity is not the law but merely a sidetrack, a pathway to that great law which governs all matter and every known thing. Whether you put this law in the hands of man, God, or the combination of all physical laws, makes no difference as to the working effect of that law. It simply is a study to see where the key is placed with which to unlock the secret, and furthermore if all things are material whether we see them or not, there is bound to be some master law over all existence."

Space will not permit to quote more although there are still, three chapters together with a conclusion. In it are such statements as the following upon which to meditate: "The works of Nature are the result of her laws." "Elias Howe did not make the Singer sewing machine but we have it." How then can we have things if we stop because we do not know how?" "All things are made up of one substance." "In this world we have thousands of things we do not know exist, but just because they do not exist for us we cannot deny that they are material. Such a plan would be folly as proved by the old hen who hid her eyes to escape the Thanksgiving dinner. What she got should be a lesson to us." "If atoms have not intelligence what is the standard of taste with which they judge?" "If you can find a tool with which to work you can find the work for which that tool was made."

Surely it cannot be said that the average set of examination questions can or do stimulate greater depth of thought and more active reasoning and thinking. The ideas here expressed are not those which have been memorized but which have been acquired through research and become an active part of the individual.

It is true that not all papers would measure up to this standard and some would indeed be better, still it seems to me that they would surpass the examination method.

This is but one suggestion which aims at the solution of the examination problem, a field in which a change is bound to come sooner or later. In closing let me quote again from the paper: "If a man wishes for a thing long enough he will need it, if he needs it long enough he will attempt to get it or make it, and if he attempts long enough he will get it or something just as good. Nothing can be more logical than that."

Simplified Spelling

By DE WITT C. CROISSANT, General Field Agent

The Esthetic Argument.

There ar a great many people, who, when they first see a sample of simplified spelling, hav an instinctiv revulsion of feeling against it. They ar accustomed to something else; they do not like that which is strange. For them, the English language seems a sacred possession, like some revered old person, and to see this in what seems to them a new and strange garb hurts their feelings. Now if they object to the reform on these grounds, there is no cause for complaint. They overtly do not like the new spelling and register their honest objections on the basis of a prejudis against such innovations. But when these good people begin to search about for reasons with which to bolster up their dislike, they ar prone to do one of two things. They either bring dishonest arguments to bear, or they wail at the reformers. For instance, a great many of them insist that language is visual as wel as aural. Now this is strictly speaking not tru. Owing to a long course of bad orthografy, lasting down thru generations of readers, we English speaking people hav got the idea that language is visual; but the essence of language is no more visual than the essence of telefoning is. It progresses by constant accretions from the vast number of spoken sounds which subtly permeate the whole linguistic consciusness of the race. We English-speaking peoples, however, ar so provincial in our attitude toward language that what has chanst to seem the case for English during the last century or so, has come to us to represent a principle which applies to all language, especially to English as we kno it.

Such an attitude would be ridiculus—and frequently is—where it is not dishonest. It makes people think that there is something connoting in spelling, whereas it is a denoting process, solely. What givs the word its associations is ultimately the varius sentence settings and ideational groupings which it has. You may think you get a bigger thril or horror from ghost with an h than without, but that is because you hav always seen ghost and not gost, and the h, put there by the early Dutch compositors to represent hard g, has nothing more to do with the horror in the word than the u in catalogue, which was put there in French forms to represent the same hard sound. If we spelt ghost, gueost, or catalog, catalogh, the effect would be lost—which shows clearly that it is not a principle we ar folloing, but a chance, a mere fortutius placing of a letter where it really does not belong.

For instance, a riter in the Baltimore World some years back became very indignant at the spelling challis for chalice. He pointed out how les religius challis lookt, and his reason was that s (for ce) is so hideus a letter. It bears its hed like a snake in the gras, and we, according to this riter, associate it with serpent and sin. How foolish! Do we not also associate it with son, saint, Savior? And how does this serpent letter look in Jesus, which contains it twice? Salvation begins with it as do solem and sweet. So the argument falls to the ground. It is not the letter s which is involvd, but our whole apperception, and in reality the s is just as good as the ce for the sight, and better for the sound.

I could go on multiplying examples like this by the hundreds from the clipping-file of the simplified spelling board, and from arguments which hav been made in my presence. For instance, how one woman wil not spel thru because in that spelling one cannot hear "the full round sound of the gh"; how another person insists that honor is les honourable than honour, forgetting that labor is also les labourius than labour; how another tries to tel you that the c in scythe is there to cut with! But this is all fancy. The Chinese, who hav no real alfabet and therefore cannot spel anything, hav devised a system of indicating spelling, very awkward and cumbersome and inadequate, which they call fan tsieh—and I declare our awkward and cumbersome system might wel be given the same name, fancy! Imagination for facts, almost-indication of the sound where a real indication might be given! These ar the penalties of our present orthografy and the reward of our conservatism: Delay in education, extra expense in printing, and a train of evils which vitiates our scool life and holds our language in the clasp of ded fetters from the past, fetters which retard its development, hinder us in the enjoyment of our poetry, and in general, break down the logical feeling which should gro out of the interaction of the spoken and visible speech.

Hight School Teachers' Department

Edited by HOPKIN JENKINS, Portland, Oregon

High School Teachers Association of Portland.

Out of a movement originating among the teachers of Lincoln high school and tending toward a closer association of all teachers in the secondary schools of the city, there developed during the year of 1914-15 this organization.

To quote from the constitution adopted at time it was formed "It shall be the object of this association to advance the general welfare of the schools, to raise the standard of the profession and to form a representative body able to speak with authority for high school teachers."

The official organization consists of a president, secretary, treasurer, corresponding secretary and a vice-president and a representative from each high school. These officers are elected annually and form the executive board through which most of the routine work is accomplished. In the past, general meetings of the association have been upon call and usually for the purpose of passing upon some specific legislation. There is, however, at this time a considerable sentiment toward regular meetings at stated intervals devoted to programs prepared along professional lines. The membership includes practically all high school teachers.

The activities so far pursued have been largely along the lines of research and investigation into high school conditions in other cities. Growing out of this, there has been one general recommendation for change which has been adopted by the superintendent and principals. This is in changing from the decimal to the literal notation in grading with the consequent wider latitude given teachers in promoting or failing students. This change has met with the approval of a majority of the teaching force. This recommendation is in line with what might be called a definite policy of the association to work toward and further reduction in the clerical duties of teachers. There is a strong feeling that teaching is a teacher's most important work and that those things which interfere with the best teaching just in such measure lower efficiency.

A. F. Bittner of Jefferson high school was the first president of the association and was succeeded by C. Marietta of Lincoln high school. The present president is from Washington high school.—C. P. Holloway, president.

* * *

High school teachers from all sections of Oregon are urged to send material for this department to Principal Hopkin Jenkins, Jefferson high school, Portland, Oregon. Interesting high school news or short articles on high school work will be acceptable.

The State Schools

Oregon Agricultural College.

All available students of horticulture, poultry, dairy and other agricultural courses, secured positions before or immediately after graduation. Since June 8, three graduates of horticulture have been offered and have accepted positions in the Iowa State College at Ames. Another member of the class received an offer from the same institution but did not accept. During the last three years five members of the O. A. C. Horticultural classes have accepted positions at Ames, four of them being now connected with that college. One of the number, Harry Hetzel, has accepted a position in the horticultural work of the United States Department of Agriculture.

Two home economics students, Miss Alice Butler, '14, and Miss Naomi Kirtley, '16, were detailed by Professor Ava B. Milam, head of the domestic science department, to take the work offered by the Mother Chautauqua in the annual summer meet. Both of these young ladies from Oregon won rapid promotion during their brief stay, the former being advanced to buyer and supervisor of one of the tea rooms and supervisor of a kitchen, and the latter being made buyer for and manager of a kitchen. The women were sent east at the instance of Miss Anna Barrows whose marvelous demonstrations at O. A. C. Farmers Week have made her known to thousands of Oregon home-makers and teachers, and Miss Norton, editor of the Chautauqua Home Economics Journal. They gained their promotion in competition with scores of young women from many parts of the United States.

Increased difficulty and cost of operating logging and lumbering machinery, together with the erection of a splendid new forestry building at the college, are doubtless responsible for the rapid growth of interest in the courses in forestry. Pioneer logging operation took the timber most easily and cheaply reached, hauled it but a short distance to small mills, paid low wages for labor and sold the products at considerable profit. The change that has reversed most of these conditions has also enforced scientific and economical manage-

ment, with competent engineering. The demand for trained logging engineers has led to the establishment of a course in logging engineering, with John P. Van Orsdel, an experienced engineer connected with the Portland lumber interests, in charge as professor of logging engineering. This is the first degree course in the branch of logging engineering to be established in the United States, and in connection with the favorable situation of the institution in the center of the greatest timber area in the country, it is bound to draw a large body of young men seeking training in forestry.

The new and vigorous movement for scientific road building has created a demand for trained road engineers far greater than can be met. The good roads committee of the National Automobile Association reports that eighteen state highway commissions say that the greatest drawback to the movement is lack of trained and experienced road builders. A shortage of 1600 highway engineers is reported from these eighteen states and from the same states are wanted 2000 engineers for city and county road units. In recognition of this demand the college has secured the services of C. B. McCullough, who has had eight years' experience as head of the bridge and structural department of the Iowa State Highway Commission, to act as professor of civil engineering. He brings with him one of the most complete private libraries in existence, giving cost data and other items of the greatest values to students of the courses.

A new color scheme for the twenty-five major buildings, black roof and gray trimming lends additional attraction to the well-known beauties of the campus. New decorative and floral designs have been worked out by Professor Peck and Mr. Masterton, and the new fountain, presented by the class of 1916, is ready to minister to both the artistic and physical senses of the returning students. The fountain is at the center of the entrance to Agricultural hall, perhaps the most frequented spot on the campus.

The school of commerce is still further strengthened by the addition of new courses and instructors. H. T. Vance, last year head of com-

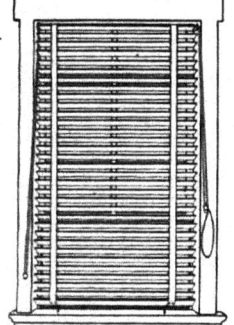

merce in the Jefferson, Portland, high school, has been appointed to take charge of office training, and Dr. Rubener has been selected to fill the vacancy caused by the resignation of Dr. E. J. Brown. Dean J. A. Bexell, head of the school, has just returned from a lecturing tour of the eastern and mid-western sections of the country, and from a series of conferences with leaders of the organization and markets bureaus of the U. S. department of agriculture.

Re-organization of the physical education staff is the most radical of any at the college. Dr. A. D. Browne, of Miami university, is head of the department and will supervise the extensive system of universal physical training in intramural sports, now to be introduced. He will be assisted by Head Coach Joseph A. Pipal, of the University of Southern California, who will handle football and track; Coach May, who will assist in football and coach basketball; Assistant Coach McClung, of Occidental callege, who will assist in coaching the various teams; James Arbuthnot, who will have charge of gymnasium work, wrestling and boxing; and Dr. Wendell J. Philipps, of Philadelphia, who will act as college physician in the new health service just established.

All men students will be divided into three groups—intercollegiate, intra-mural, and non-competitive. Those who are able through physical fitness, training and experience, will represent the institution in intercollegiate sports. The main body of students, those who like to play but do not care to specialize in athletics, will be organized into scores of smaller groups which will be pitted against one another to the extent that all who are able to play any competitive game will have opportunity to play it against those approximately their equals. Soccer, lacrosse, tennis, handball, baseball and field and track events will be the type of sports followed. It is Dr. Browne's belief that in no other way can the proper training of all students be secured, and that this will result in a normal development of the intercollegiate sports. He says that the right order has been reversed and that the beginning was made at the wrong end. For the students not physically fit to compete corrective gymnasium work will be prescribed. In their assignment to

special corrective and developing work students will be in charge of two experts in physical education and medical practice, both Dr. Browne and Dr. Philipps being trained practioners.

Another new feature of work for this year will be the regularly authorized course in news writing conducted by the college news editor, Mr. C. T. McIntosh. The course will be open to students of junior rank. It aims to train students who have a good knowledge and command of English in the special forms of expression and composition required in modern news stories, and give them practice in newspaper and magazine correspondence. Preliminary work carried during the last two years has shown that there is an excellent demand for this work, and a number of stories written by members of the class have been accepted by publications such as the big dailies and Sundays, Orange Judd, Oregon Farmer, Pacific Homestead, Country Gentleman, etc. A number of Oregon weeklies and dailies have found the student contributions available.

The number of appointments of students to teaching positions, has reached 93, as reported by the appointments committee on September 12. A half dozen or more are pending so that the committee is assured that the record of last year, 99, will be equaled if not surpassed. It was estimated that last year's appointees earned about seventy-three thousand dollars. On the basis of average salaries, computed from over eighty students reporting, the 93 appointed at this date will earn seventy-four thousand, four hundred fifty-seven dollars in 1916-17. The average monthly salaries, on the nine months' basis, are eighty-five dollars in Commerce and Home Economics; ninety dollars in Agriculture; one hundred one dollars in Manual Training; and one hundred five dollars in Agriculture combined with Manual Training. Seventy-five of these are first appointments, eleven are second appointments and seven are third or more. Five are under-graduates, four of them in Manual Training. Three hold the M. S. degree. Fifty-seven are from the School of Home Economics, nine from the school of Commerce, nine from the School of Agriculture and eighteen from the School of Engineering (Industrial Arts chiefly). California gets five in Home Economics and one in Agricul-

ture; Colorado, one in Manual Training; Idaho, one in Home Economics, one in Agriculture, and one in Commerce; Illinois, one in Home Economics; Montana, one in Agriculture and Manual Training; Washington, six in Home Economics, two in Manual Training, two in Agriculture and Manual Training and one in Agriculture. Thus, twenty-three of the ninety-three have received appointments outside the state caused almost wholly by larger salaries paid. Many additional calls for teachers of Manual Training and Commerce came from other states and quite a number could not be filled in Oregon. Every available male teacher received a position; those who had athletic prowess as well as pedagogical skill had from two to a half dozen or more offers. The distribution of these ninety-three teachers in Oregon will be of interest. Benton county gets two in Home Economics, one in Manual Training, two in Commerce and two in Agriculture; Clackamas, three in Home Economics, one in Manual Training; Columbia, one in H. E.; Coos, three in H. E., one in M. T.; Crook, two in H E., one in M. T.; Douglas, one in H E., one in Commerce; Grant, one in H. E.; Hood River, one in H. E.; Jackson, three in H. E., two in M. T.; Josephine, one in M. T.; Klamath, one in M. T.; Lane, three in H. E., two in M. T., one in Commerce; Lincoln, one in H. E.; Linn, two in H. E.; Marion, two in H. E., two in M. T., two in Com.; Morrow, one in H. E.; Multnomah, four in H. E.; Polk, three in H. E.; Tillamook, one in H. E., one in M. T., one in Com.; Umatilla, two in H. E., one in M. T., one in Agriculture; Union, two in H. E., one in M. T., one in Com.; Wallowa, one in H. E.; Wasco, two in H. E.; Wheeler, one in H. E.; Yamhill, one in H. E. This makes twenty-five of the thirty-five counties of the state, and six other states in which these appointees will teach.

Oregon Normal School Notes.

As these notes go to press the Oregon Normal School is just opening the sixth year of its work since its re-organization and the enrollment of 383 at the end of the first week is indicative of the steady growth of the school under the able leadership of Pres. Ackerman. The normal school has now reached the place in the educational system of the state which a normal school should occupy

that of being the "standard maker," the "norm setter" for the elementary teachers of Oregon.

During the month past the school has not been in session and the time has been utilized for a thorough renovation of the buildings and for making such minor repairs as were necessary. The most noticeable change was the removal of the old domestic science building which stood west of the main building, and the construction of several new walks.

The six weeks' vacation was variously used by the faculty, some remaining here, others going to distant sections of the country. Pres. Ackerman remained in Monmouth except for motor trips to Hood River and the Columbia Highway and an excursion to the Coos Bay celebration. Mr. Butler also went to Coos Bay and his customary trip to the mountains.

Mr. and Mrs. Ostein and son spent three weeks camping, fishing, and motoring through Central Oregon.

Miss Parrott divided her vacation between Portland and Roseburg.

Miss Butler and Miss West went on an extended auto tour which included the Columbia Highway, the Yellowstone National Park, Glacier National Park, the Canadian Rockies, Banff and other intermediate points of interest.

Mr. and Mrs. Pitman spent their time in Coos county where Mr. Pittman was studying rural schools and also practicing some of his theories.

Mr. Gilmore and his family divided the time between the seashore and remodeling their home in Monmouth.

Miss Arbuthnot visited at Miss Taylor's home in Tacoma for two weeks.

The following teachers returned to their homes: Miss Hoham to Indiana, Miss Todd to Pennsylvania, Miss Taylor to Tacoma, Wash., Miss Kennon to Baker, Ore., Miss Greene to Montana, and Miss Dinuis to Inidana.

Mr. and Mrs. Macy motored through Washington.

The remaining members of the faculty busied themselves about their Monmouth homes.

The faculty for the coming year remains the same as last year with one exception. Mrs. Aultman, critic of the first and second grades, resigned to accept a similar place in her home school, Greeley, Colo. Her place will be filled by Miss Elizabeth Riecker,

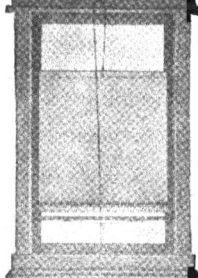

a graduate of Columbia university, N. Y., where she specialized in primary work. For the past four years she has been primary supervisor in the Aberdeen Normal School in South Dakota.

The fall institute season has started, which will demand the entire time of Mr. Pittman and some time from Pres. Ackerman and other members of the faculty.

Supt. Alderman's innovation of holding an institute for Portland teachers was a decided success. The Oregon Normal was represented by Mr. Gentle and Mr. Evenden, each of whom spoke before the three sections of elementary teachers.

A change in the administration of the school was made during the summer when the board of regents created the position of dean of women and elected Miss Jessica Todd to that position. Miss Todd in her new position will have charge of the social life of all women students, and with her thorough knowledge of the school and its social life we feel that the selection was a very wise one. An assistant will be provided to help with the office work of the dormitory.

The annual faculty reception to the students was held in the grove on the afternoon of September 16. The students were received on the tennis court south of the main building, after which a program consisting of remarks by Pres. Ackerman, solos by Miss Hoham and Miss Greene was enjoyed. The general plan of the afternoon was to get acquainted and teachers and students made good use of their time.

At the meeting of the Alumni association in June of this year a plan was adopted to re-organize the association and have county administrative units. The following letter has been sent to the county chairmen:

"At a meeting of the Alumni Association of the Oregon Normal School held at Monmouth on June 17, 1916, a resolution was passed embodying the following:

"The Annual Alumni Reunion including the program shall provide for, and shall be under the supervision of the various classes, rotating in periods of five years, e. g., beginning with the class of 1872, including 1877, 1882, 1887, 1892, 1897, 1902, 1907, 1912, and 1917. These various classes shall provide for all details of this reunion. The idea being

to have these reunions bring together these various classes.

"By this method it is believed that a wider range of interests will be aroused and many warm friends separated by business, distance, years, etc., will thus feel it a duty to return to the 'old school' and strengthen the ties of other days.

"It is suggested that the details of this plan be presented to the members of the association throughout the state. Chairmen were appointed for the various counties and they were requestd to present this in detail at their respective institutes; if possible at a social gathering of all graduates which we hope you will be able to secure.

"Now, that the scope of the work is so rapidly broadening and the members of the association are vitally affecting the school life of the state, and in order that we may more loyally support the president in his efforts to bring the normal school work of the state up to a high point of efficiency, it is urgently requested that all graduates will 'Hear the Call' and lay their plans to attend their respective reunions. All others wishing to come will be as cordially welcome.

"The dues of the association which are 25 cents may be paid to the chairman of his county or direct to Mrs. Alva Craven, Monmouth, Ore.

"Wishing you the best of success in your meeting, and thanking you for helping in this work, I am

"Sincerely yours,
"Lydia Bell, President."

This plan, of course, does not prevent any member of the Alumni returning at any time, but tries to make an added incentive for special classes to return at special times in order that more classmates may be re-united. Will you try and get in touch with your county chairman and give him all the news and assistance you can, especially in notifying him of the names and addresses of any graduates who are not engaged in the work of teaching. A revised directory is very essential.

University of Oregon.

Representatives of the University of Oregon have spoken at the following county teachers' institutes during the month: Dr. B. W. DeBusk, Wasco, Gilliam and Morrow counties; Mr. Earl Kilpatrick, Benton and

An Ideal School Machine

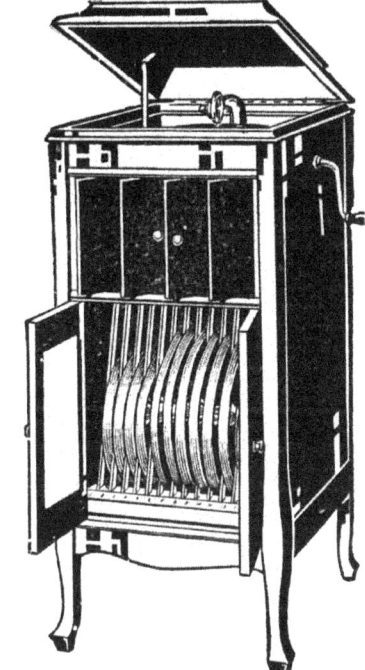

The beautiful $75 Leader Model Grafanola is without doubt the finest machine for school purposes made. Has automatic top life, long running motor, special filing system, equipped with No. 6 Columbia Sound box that will either render the selections with more volume than any other instrument or by a special needle accompanying it will reproduce the same selection so faintly that it can scarcely be heard fifteen feet away Just the instrument for out doors, assembly halls, recitation rooms or the home.

We offer you Special Terms of **ONLY** $5.00 down and $3.50 monthly.

Send for Catalogue.

HYATT
Talking Machine Co.

350 Alder Street,   Portland, Oregon.
Main 6896   A 3277

Linn, Grant and Harney; Dr. H. D. Sheldon, Multnomah, Benton and Linn.

The university is making a collection of text books illustrating the history of method. The present collection numbers more than 1000 volumes and is due mainly to the generosity of various publishing houses. It covers only the most recent periods. The library will appreciate gifts of books in this field. Due recognition will be given the donor. Those interested may correspond with Mr. M. H. Douglas, university librarian.

Those interested in the conditions of entrance to the Moral Codes contest may learn the main items of interest by corresponding with Prof. H. D. Sheldon. Five thousand dollars is to be distributed in prizes by an unknown philanthropist in the East. Methods of instruction will not enter into the discussion; the entire interest in the contest centers on the content of moral instruction.

The following list of elections to teaching positions and re-locations of University of Oregon graduates will interest the alumni. The majority of new positions were received through the efforts of the appointment bureau:

Ralph Allen, 1916, Everett, Wash., history, civics; Louise Bailey, 1916, Pendleton, physical training; P. E. Baker, 1916, Fossil, superintendent; W. G. Beattie, 1901, Cottage Grove, principal; F. A. Beebe, 1915,Vincent, manual training; Verena Black,1913, Lakeview, commercial; Katherine Bridges, 1916, Grants Pass, German and English; Leonard Buoy, 1916, Butte Falls, principal; Prentice Brown, 1916, Centralia; Wm. A. Cass, 1916, Hood River; Esther Campbell, 1916, Springfield, science and Latin; Esther Chalmers, 1916, McMinnville, English; Marie Churchill, 1916, Oregon City; Jacob Cornog, 1916, O. A. C., chemistry; James K. Cossman, 1916, Ione, physical training and history; Helen Crump, 1916, Airlie; Bess L. Cushman, 1916, Sodaville, principal of high school; Lela Cushman, 1917, Riddle, grades; Harry T. Drill, 1916, Pendleton, principal; C. H. Eagy, Coos county, junior high school; Clara Erdman, 1916, Walker, science and mathematics; Mina Ferguson, 1916, Corvallis, mathematics; Clarence Ferguson, 1916, Eugene, Portland principalship; Louis E. Furrow, 1918, Myrtle Point, principal,

grammar school; Roy Glass, 1902, Philomath, superintendent; Emily Griffin, 1917, Salem, physical training; Annie Hales, 1917, Goble, grades; O. C. Hadley, 1916, North Powder, principal; Miss Hamilton, 1915, Roseburg, grades; Hallie Ruth Hart, 1918, Dallas, grades; Fred Hardesty, 1915, Tillamook, oral English; W. H. Hayes, 1916, Astoria; E. H. Hedrick, 1916, Monmouth, superintendent; H. Heidenreich, 1916, Ashland, manual training; G. C. Huggins, 1916, Klamath Falls, physical training and English; Miss Humble, 1911, Elmira; Jennie Hunter, 1916, Medford, physical training; Helen Johnson, 1914, Silverton, Latin and German; Ida Johnson, 1916, Prairie City, history and commerce; Maude Kincaid, 1915, Marcola, German and English; Georgia Kinsey, 1916, Cottage Grove, English and German; Grace Lilly, 1916, Ashland, English; Nellie Lombard, 1916, Bly, principal high school; H. W. Lombard, 1915, Walterville, Wash., commercial and public speaking; Elizabeth Minturn, 1916, Milwaukie, mathematics and physics; V. T. Motschenbacher, 1914, Medford, principal, junior high school; O. B. Needham, 1910, Harrisburg, high school; May Novak, Nyssa, grades (1-8); Lena Newton, 1916, The Dalles, history; C. L. Ogle, 1916, Scappoose, principal; A. T. Park, 1915, Pendelton, superintendent; Hulda Parr, 1916, Fossil; Jessie Purdy, 1916, Metolius, high school; Rex Putnam, 1915, Salem, mathematics and athletics; Alfred Skei, 1914, Cottage Grove, history and science; Mary Stevenson, 1916, Merrill, English, Latin and German; Mabel Stroud, 1916, Walker, principal high school; Jewel Tozier, 1916, La-Grande, physical training; Edward W. Taylor, 1916, Drain, mathematics, physics; J. L. Whitman, 1915, Pendleton, science; Vera Williams, 1916, Springfield, history; Cora E. Ware, Thurston, commercial; Darl Zimmerman, 1916, Sweet Home, high school; Gertrude Buell, 1915, Halsey, history and English; Genevieve Cooper, 1915, Monroe, science and history; Laura Hammer, 1914, Klamath Falls, mathematics; Herman Oberteuffer, 1914, McMinnville, principal high school; Edith Ochs, 1916, Dayton, Wash.; G. W. Schantin, 1912, Sutherlin, principal, high school; Genevieve Shaver, 1916, Sutherlin; Harold Young, 1915, Pendleton, commerce.

Membership in the State Teachers' Association

The Oregon Teachers Monthly, on July 1, 1916, became the official journal of the State Teachers' Association (both divisions) and the price was raised to $1.50 per year, 50 cents of which goes to the Association. At the end of the second month (Aug. 31) the following teachers had paid $1.50 for their subscription to the Oregon Teachers Monthly, thereby entitling them to membership in the State Teachers' Association:

1 Nellie V. King, Winant
2 Fred Schepman, Waldport
3 John Blough, Toledo
4 Maggie L. Hampton, Toledo
5 M. Lillian Ernest, Denzer
6 Earl Brown, Philomath
7 Chas. Hart, Roselodge
8 S. S. Gosman, Chitwood
10 J. E. Davis, Chitwood
11 R. E. Wood, Orton
12 John Miller, Eddyville
13 Verne Ross, Toledo
14 T. E. Wilson, Turner
15 Paul Wyman, Bay City
16 Chas. Holway, Halsey
17 Laura A. Smith, Cottage Grove
18 H. W. Herron, Portland
19 Mary B. Scollard, Woodburn
20 L. W. Turnbull, Coquille
21 Hazel Henkle, Monkland
22 A. C. Strange, Baker
23 Anna Dunsmore, Orenco
24 Margaret Williams, Portland
25 Adella Chapler, Salem
26 Margaret Boggess, Veneta
27 W. M. Sutton, Burns
28 W. G. Beattie, Eugene
29 Mary E. Slade, Albany
30 Mrs. L. K. Page, Springfield
31 Mrs. A. Alexander, Portland
32 Barbara Hoch, Pendleton
33 Blanche Padley, Bandon
34 Kate Ronde, Clatskanie
35 Edith Harper, Freewater
36 Edith Smith, Banks
37 Alice Rasmussen, Troutdale
38 Della Zimmerman, Troutdale
39 Adda Wright, Warrenton
40 N. A. Frost, Forest Grove
41 Edna Pence, Salem
42 Erica Nordhausen, Aurora
43 Clara Ireland, Portland
44 Julie H. Burch, Oregon City
45 J. P. McGlasson, North Plains
46 Ethel Davis, Myrtle Creek
47 Mrs. E. H. Morrison, Portland
48 Coral Garvin, Corvallis
49 Inez Easton, Sitkum
50 Alethia Chapman, LaGrande
51 May Smith, Mabel
52 Helen Treat, Buell
53 Virginia Nottingham, Carlton
54 Elma Roberts, Sumner
55 Ruby Skinner, Lakeview
56 Frances Potter, Canby
57 Harriet B. Horrigan, Hillsboro
58 Grace Egbert, The Dalles
59 Mary B. Underwood, Philomath
60 Ruth Dunbabin, Bourne
61 M. T. Means, Philomath
62 Mildred Taylor, Scappoose
63 Marie Senn, Barlow
64 Bessa Lehmann, Sutherlin
65 Anna Bachmann, Clackamas
66 Adeline Buyserie, Hubbard
67 Isa Isaacson, Junction City
68 Anna Weisenborn, Deer Island
69 Myrel A. Bond, Irving
70 Rada Antrim, Amity
71 Marvin F. Wood, Corvallis
72 Carl E. Morrison, Perrydale
73 Waithia Watson, Roseburg
74 H. C. Ostien, Monmouth
75 Eula Campbell, Freewater
76 M. S. Pittman, Monmouth
77 Hazel Goger, Boring
78 Clara Spiekerman, The Dalles
79 Mamie Harper, Wren
80 R. S. Bixby, Nolin
81 Mattie Foster, Klamath Falls
82 Nell G. Lloyd, Klondike
83 Margaret Rice, Shaniko
84 Martha Chase, Portland
85 Myrtle Clayville, Portland
86 C. D. Watkins, Dilley
87 Clara Larson, Toledo
88 Emma Murray, Klamath Falls
89 Marion Ford, Klamath Falls
90 May Wheaton, Coquille
91 Fannie G. Porter, Oregon City
92 Mable F. Johnson, Butte Falls
93 Helene Ogsburg, Eugene
94 Velma Beardslee, Arlington
95 Gladys Anderson, Clear Lake, Ia.
96 Alice Lytle, Bonanza
97 Vara Stewart, Portland
98 Charles Knocke, Mt. Carmel, N. D.
99 Lydia Unden, Winchester
100 Jewell Delk, Drain
101 Matilda Jacobs, Portland
102 Mrs. Gladys Smith, Springfield
103 Helen Anderson, Meda
104 Alma Nichols, Culver
105 Gladys Hatcher, Buell
106 Sylvia Severance, Lexington
107 Dagmar Jeppesen, Boyd
108 Ora England, Walker
109 Florence E. Howatt, Portland
110 Rachel May, Timber
111 Ellen M. Yocum, Amity
112 Alice Jenkins, Eugene
113 Harry Whitten, Kingsley
114 Violet M. Stolle, Irving
115 Violet McCarl, Portland
116 Maude Largent, Hullt
117 Elnor Sherk, Sutherlin
118 Ruth Peterson, Yoncalla
119 Grace Atkinson, Walton
120 Mrs. Mary Hulin, Carpentaria, Cal.
121 Mary E. Moore, Irving
122 Vera Merchant, Lebanon
123 Emma Kennedy, Coquille
124 Maybelle Wagner, McMinnville
125 Marguerite Freydig, Sutherlin
126 Ruth A. Brown, Eagle Creek
127 Ranie P. Burkhead, Shaniko
128 Mabel McFadden, Halfway
129 Angie Halley, Medford
130 Goldie Groth, Freewater
131 Justina Kildee, Sutherlin
132 May B. Lund, Coquille
133 Mildred Jones, Amity
134 Grace V. Perce, Medford
135 Myrtle Ess, Klamath Falls
136 Sadie Helberger, Wedderburn
137 Marie A. Smith, Buena Vista
138 Carolyn Woods, Cottage Grove
139 Ruth Finlay, Silverton
140 Luella Daniel, Milton
141 Wilbert O. Wilson, Kopiah, Wash.
142 Nettye Moore, Flat River, Mo.
143 Ida Anderson, Early
144 Clara Luther, Halsey
145 Caroline Luther, Redmond
146 Clara Schneider, Gaston
147 Maud Keysaw, Walterville
148 Gladys Burr, Oregon City
149 Emily L. Marshall, Willamette
150 Lapensa Amrine, Oregon City
151 Arabella Davis, Portland
152 Pansy Oswald, Gladstone

153 Pearle Ruegg, Gresham
154 Loney Yoder, Hubbard
155 Mrs. H. L. Hull, Oregon City
156 Ruth F. Hudson, Mulino
157 Elizabeth Roach, Cherryville
158 Brenton Vedder, Gladstone
159 Ruth M. Lingle, Boring
160 John R. Bowland, Oregon City
161 A. C. Thompson, Milwaukie
162 Raymond Boyer, Rickreall
163 L. H. Mallicoat, Boring
164 T. J. Gary, Portland
165 Ellen DeHaven, Salem
166 Jessie Hartley, Portland
167 Amy McDaniel, Weston
168 Rena Roper, Vancouver, Wash.
169 Stella Swift, Junction City
170 Louise Nimmo, Albany
171 Minnie Kulmke, Salem
172 Wm. Westenskow, Imbler
173 D. A. Hoag, Sodaville
174 Laura Moore, Molalla
175 C. Edna Kennedy, Barton
176 Helen M. Hall, Molalla
177 Olga Hanson, Clackamas
178 Margaret Summer, Tigard
179 Mrs. Nannie Thomas, Molalla
180 Mary A. Bickner, Oswego
181 Cora Hasselbrink, Sherwood
182 Chas. H. Jones, Salem
183 Lunah W. Wallace, Rockaway
184 Mabel Wallace, Willamina
185 Anna Nelson, Palmer
186 Adeline Brown, Kingsley
187 Miriam Underwood, Oakland
188 Ozella Anderson, Parkplace
189 Mary E. Sherer, Corvallis
190 Winnifred Roe, Monument
191 Matilda F. Grossen, Hillsboro
192 Vernus Young, Echo
193 Edison Fowler, Riverside
194 Mrs. E. D. Sprague, Lake
195 Lucile J. Lisher, Portland
196 Margaret McDonald, Portland
197 Georgia Smith, Mayville
198 Aver Black, Tygh Valley
199 Viola Ortschild, Portland
200 Margaret Ferguson, Siltscoos
201 Lena Gribble, Aurora
202 Agnes Weatherson, Minerva
203 Benedictine Sisters, Oregon City
204 Myrtle Birtchet, Mt. Angel
205 Viola Nagel, Gaston
206 Gladys Jory, Salem

207 Anna C. Taylor, North Powder
208 C. H. Wilson, Condon
209 May Payne, Mitchell
210 Gladys Denney, Oakland
211 Laura Brenner, Oregon City
212 Pearl Wilson, Milton
213 J. B. Lent, Fairview
214 Mrs. A. E. Watson, Portland
215 Mary Ulen, Portland
216 J. B. Horner, Corvallis
217 Nina Taylor, Portland
218 M. E. V. Hess, Portland
219 Hattiebelle Ogilbee, Portland
220 Helen Dahl, Gresham
211 C. G. Springer, Madras
222 Eva Schneider, Boring
223 Ruth Schmuckli, Portland
224 Marian Robertson, Gresham
225 Nellie Renshaw, Mayville
226 Maude B. Mickel, Grosham
227 P. C. Fulton, Holbrook
228 L. B. Gibson, Hood River
229 Mrs. Ora D. Fleming, Lents
230 Ada Werner, Portland
231 E. Williams, Portland
232 Nellie Washburn, Portland
233 Mrs. Margaret B. West, Portland
234 Minerva Powell, Troutdale
235 Marguerite Miller, Portland
236 Mabel F. Burghduff, Portland
237 Louise Sterling, Corbett
238 Vina Swan, Camas, Wash.
239 Mrs. Jennie Carr, Portland
240 Cornelia J. Spencer, Portland
241 Eva S. Rice, Portland
242 Frances S. Estes, Portland
243 Emma Rueter, Portland
244 Mrs. Minnie Parsons, Portland
245 Nell O. Bevans, Portland
246 Mary E. Hill, Portland
247 Estelle Marias, Portland
248 Lutie E. Cake, Portland
249 Margaret L. Pomeroy, Portland
250 Evlyn Cornutt, Portland
251 C. May Moriarty, Portland
251 Phila Nicoll, Portland
254 Kate E. Wiest, Astoria
254 Jeanette Pound, Salem
255 Mina Magness, Myrtle Point
256 W. F. Cornwell, McEwen
257 Leila Lasley, Toledo
258 Clara Straughan, Pendleton
259 Mary Stein, Union
260 W. M. Smith, Salem

The Independent Colleges

Edited by PRES. CARL G. DONEY, of Willamette University at Salem

Albany College.

Albany College has recently elected to the chair of mathematics and astronomy, to succeed Professor David Torbet, deceased, W. E. Lugenbeel, Ph. D., of Winona Lake, Ind. Dr. Lugenbeel is an experienced teacher of several years standing. He has been at different times president of the Southern Indiana Normal school; president of Borden College, Indiana; president of Austin College, Effingham, Illincis, and professor of mathematics of the Illinois State Normal University at Normal. He is a live worker in teachers' institutes, and a captivating evening lecturer on topics in astronomy and English literature. We welcome to the state so able an educator, and feel sure that Albany College is to be congratulated in his coming.

* * *

Pacific College.

Miss Mary L. Johnson is the head of the new department of commerce. A large enrollment already indicates the demand for this work and is evidence of the strength of the department. Extension lectures are to be widely given during the year by the faculty.

Professors Hawkins and Taggart have been given a year's absence for

graduate work in the University of California. Professors Perisho, Mc-Cracken and Sutton spent the summer in graduate study at the University of Washington. Professor Mark C. Mills is elected to the department of history, and President Levi T. Pennington, who was absent in the East much of last year, will resume his teaching at the head of the department of philosophy. A largely increased enrollment is expected in the college.

* * *

McMinnville College.

Last commencement the honorary degree of Doctor of Laws was conferred upon Hon. Thomas A. Mc-Bride, justice of the Oregon supreme court; and the degree of Doctor of Divinity was given to Rev. Andrew J. Hunsaker, of McMinnville.

President Leonard Riley suffered an operation last June and for three months has been recuperating in Illinois. Ohio and Massachusetts.

Professors Coe and Grover spent the summer in graduate work at the University of Washington.

Four strong courses in education have been added to the curriculum for this year, thereby exceeding the requirements of the state for the certification of graduates.

The campaign for $300,000 endowment is to close October 31, and the prospects are good for its successful completion at that time.

* * *

Pacific University.

The discontinuance of the academy last year has already proven to be wise. Stressing standard college work, the institution increased the Frohman class 75 per cent, a practical system of student self-government has been introduced and the scope of the extension division greatly enlarged. Plans are contemplated for raising considerable sums for improvements and general endowment. The system of student self-help has been re-organized and important extensions of means for such help are under way.

The Conservatory of Music has been strengthened by the addition of the following instructors: William W. Graham, violin and orchestra; Wilma Waggener, piano and organ; Virginia S. Hutchinson, voice and public school music.

Pacific is looking forward this year to a large attendance and an increasing educational work for the Northwest.

Philomath College.

Miss Gulielma George and Mrs. Lizzie DeMoss Davis have been added to the faculty as teachers, respectively, of expression and violin.

Professors Epley and Bennett were engaged in graduate work at the University of Oregon during the summer. The success of Philomath's graduates as teachers is bringing many students to the college and the outlook for a banner attendance is good.

* * *

Willamette University.

Since commencement Willamette has installed a large pipe organ, increased the capacity of the library, added space and equipment to the biological laboratory, and improved the campus.

October 13 is the date for the formal inauguration of President Doney, at which time notable speakers will crowd the day with addresses. A general invitation is extended to every one to attend.

* * *

Conference Scholarships.

The following explanation is made of the conference scholarships annually awarded to standard high schools. The six colleges—Albany, McMinnville, Pacific, Philomath and Reed—offer a scholarship, good in any one of the above institutions to every four-year high school in Oregon. A second scholarship is given a high school that graduates fifty pupils. The student to receive the scholarship is selected by the principal and his teachers on the basis of the pupil's "need of such assistance" and as being "best qualified to benefit by a college education." The latter probably includes a consideration of scholarship, health, character, aim in life and intent to attend college. Scholarship pupils are to be reported by the principals to Professor F. G. Franklin, secretary of the College Conference, Albany, Or., and he also is to be informed of the school which is chosen. Professor Franklin retains a complete list of the scholarship pupils and certifies their names to the various colleges selected by the pupils. The student presents the scholarship to the school of his choice, which accepts it on terms which it makes. Willamette University, though a member of the College Conference, offers a scholarship of its own to all standard high schools.

OREGON TEACHERS MONTHLY
The Official Journal of the State Teachers' Association

Vol. XXI   SALEM, OREGON, NOVEMBER, 1916   No. 3

Published Monthly Except July and August by the State Teachers' Association

Entered at the Postoffice at Salem, Oregon, as second-class mail matter, April 1, 1898.

EDITORIAL BOARD

H. D. SHELDON, School of Education, University of Oregon, Eugene
E. F. CARLETON, Assistant Superintendent of Public Instruction, Salem
C. T. BONNEY, County School Superintendent, The Dalles
R. E. CHLOUPEK, Director Manual Training, Pendleton.
C. G. DONEY, President Willamette University, Salem
E. S. EVENDEN, Department of Education, Oregon Normal, Monmouth
MRS. M. L. FULKERSON, Institute Instructor, Salem
GEORGE W. HUG, City Superintendent, McMinnville
HOFKIN JENKINS, Principal Jefferson High School, Portland.
MISS VIOLA ORTSCHILD, President Grade Teachers' Association, Portland
E. D. RESSLER, Department of Education, Oregon Agricultural College, Corvallis
MISS LILLIAN TINGLE, Supervisor Domestic Science, Portland
CHAS. H. JONES, Business and Managing Editor, Salem

RULES OF PUBLICATION

1. The mailing label on the Oregon Teachers Monthly shows the date to which subscriptions are paid.
2. The Oregon Teachers Monthly will be sent to subscribers until ordered discontinued and all arrearages are paid.
3. Notice of change of address should be given at once, naming both old and new postoffice.
4. When renewing, always state that subscription is a renewal.
5. The subscription price, including membership in State Teachers' Association, is $1.50 a year in advance. Single copy, 20 cents.
6. Advertising rates will be furnished on application.

Address all communications to Oregon Teachers Monthly, Salem, Oregon.

Editorial Notes

In its professional requirement for certificates good in standardized schools, the Oregon state department has hit upon a most fertile and valuable idea. In all professions, efficiency is largely determined by growth. The exhaustive nature of the teacher's work, the necessity for repetition and the isolation of the classroom make it more difficult for a teacher to grow intellectually after the first two or three years of service than for members of other professions. The stimulus of public recognition which the state gives in the form of the professional diploma is most timely and appropriate.

§   §   §

The value of the teachers' institute is a mooted point in the autumn. For many of the smaller and more isolated counties, the gain from a meeting of the present type is a large one. It gathers the discouraged novices together for inspiration, it acquaints them with educational helps and papers, it enlarges their horizon and gives them at least a small stock of new ideas and methods. In the larger centers, the advantages are not so noticeable and a feeling is gaining ground that there should be more actual cooperation and activity on the part of the teachers than is now the case. Why would it not be possible for the county superintendent to appoint permanent committees of the primary teachers, the upper grade, high school and vocational teachers to at least suggest the topics which they desire discussed? The speakers might cooperate by circulating lists of topics or questions, so the teachers might be ready for discussion. At present there are too many cut-and-dried harangues fired like blank cartridges at the teachers' heads. An occasional debate prepared for in advance by the teachers would aid to professionalize the institute. In the course of years the institute should become wholly a voluntary and active meeting of the teachers themselves.

§   §   §

The present constitution of the National Educational Association represents the ideas of organization in vogue during the period of the Civil War. In practice it is close corporation tempered by mass meeting. The teachers of the particular city in which the meeting happens to be held can, if they chose to do so, completely dominate the association. The larger meetings are so huge that the average member considers himself lucky to hear any part of the proceedings, deliberation is impossible. The resolutions adopted deal with every possible topic concerning which the teachers have no control, such as universal peace and simplified spelling. The one element conspicuously lacking is a clear definite policy for the improvement of teaching conditions in the United States. When a committee is appointed to collect data on the economic status of the teacher and submits its findings, they are allowed to remain buried in a complicated report for the association has practically no publicity facilities; the result in most cases is nil. When we compare this loose, amorphous, rhetorical loose-jointed collection of mass meetings with the businesslike efficient organizations of the English and German teachers, the result is not particularly flattering to American pride. As to suggestions, we desire that the members of the old guard answer the following questions: (1) Why cannot the policy and business of the association be placed in the hands of a small body of delegates, representing the different sections of the Union? (2) Why is it not possible to organize a network of teachers' organizations extending from the purely local societies of different types up through the state teachers' associations to a National Association which stands for definite practical policies? (3) Why not concentrate the resources of the organization on a definite plan of campaign involving an improvement in salaries, in teachers' tenure and in teachers' training?

§   §   §

How are you going to vote?—a question which when asked of teachers does not mean for whom or for what are you going to vote but rather what will be the value of your vote in the coming elections. Teachers have always had a grave responsibility in making and maintaining an intelligent electorate; the paramount essential to the permanence of any democracy, and now that Oregon is among the enlightened states which have extended the right of suffrage to women, this responsibility is more than doubled. A teacher by virtue of her position alone is naturally looked upon as a leader by her pupils, by the young people in the community and by many of. the parents, and she should be very jealous of this influence to see that it is not directly or indirectly, consciously or unconsciously, used against the principles of higher citizenship. Any careless, slighting remark, evidenced indifference, gross misinformation or lack of definitely formed opinions will give an undesired color to the attitude of many others toward this great political duty. Probably not since the famous one of 1860 has the national election been of as much significance or held within itself so many balanced potentialities. In addition to this the citizens of Oregon will have to decide on the merits of eleven acts and amendments under Oregon's initiative and referendum policy. Some of these proposed laws have beneath their legal wording radical changes in the method and limitation of raising taxes, in our prohibition status, in our normal school policy, and in the state's subsidy of rural improvements. These are questions which every teacher should thoroughly inform herself upon, for, aside from the vote of lawyers and lawmakers, the vote of teachers should be felt as one of the most intelligent votes of the state.

§ § §

Eliminating, for obvious reasons, the places of scenic beauty in Europe, the teacher who wishes to liberalize her education by the important method of travel, must perforce "see America first." Among the long list of world known natural wonders in this country the latest aspirant for fame is our own Columbia River Highway with its majestic and graceful waterfalls, its wonderful gorges, its towering bluffs of granite, and its sweeping views of mountain peaks and "the river beautiful." Never before in this western world has the conquering mechanical genius of man made it possible for the tourist to see so many interesting things in a single trip. Each turn of the hundreds of graceful ones brings its thrill of delight, its exclamation of surprise, its gasp of wonder and awe, and each wonderful bridge brings you in front of some marvelous waterfall, peaceful dell or rugged canyon. No teacher can make this trip without accumulating a wealth of illustrative material for her work nor without that inspiration which comes only from being in the presence of nature's grandeurs. At such times she teaches the wonderful cumulative effects of small but persistent causes and the teacher realizes that her conscientious toil from day to day may result in the making of a grand man or a beautiful character. Furthermore, no Oregonian can travel that road and

not be proud of his native or adopted state, proud in a way which will make him a better teacher for Oregon boys and girls. Plan for this trip when you are in Portland at the meeting of the State Teachers' Association in December.

§   §   §

The county and state fairs as mediums for bringing people together, for displaying the products and industries of the various sections, for showing new machinery and newer methods of doing things and for educating those who attend and those who participate, have long been recognized. The increasing interest being taken in these fairs by superintendents and teachers shows that they are awake to the opportunities offered by them for motivating much of the practical work of the school and for bringing about a closer co-ordination and a more sympathetic understanding between the school and the community. The exhibits at the fair serve as an incentive for gardening, manual training, domestic science, sewing, accounting and all phases of boys and girls industrial club work, to say nothing of its rebounding reflex upon the regular school subjects. Progressive teachers have seized upon these fairs as valuable aids in solving the problems of local vocational education and guidance and it is with more or less alarm that we observe a growing tendency to turn these meetings over almost exclusively to concession hunters and spectacular speculators. No less than five of the Willamette valley counties this year substituted "Round Ups" for the time-honored county fairs. In the two cases where the substitution was not direct it was nevertheless substituted as far as advertising and public interest was concerned. These shows are interesting reminders of a life that is or was typically Western, but are not particularly appropriate to the Willamette valley. Let's not allow the long-horned Texas steer, the courageous "bull dogger" and the cowboy, who does most of his riding in automobiles, to drive from deserved prominence the boy who has fattened the largest hog with the least expense, or who has helped to develop a true Oregon variety of corn, nor the girl who has reduced the cost of living and prevented a lot of useless waste by canning several hundred cans of fruit and vegetables.

§ § §

Report of the Retirement Fund Committee

By B. F. CARLETON, President State Teachers' Association

The Retirement Fund Committee of the Oregon State Teachers' Association met in the offices of Reed Institute in the Abington Building, Portland, October 2, 1916. The committee agreed upon the following main features for a proposed plan of retirement allowances for Oregon teachers: ·

First: Membership compulsory for all public school teachers beginning serving in Oregon after July 1, 1919; optional for teachers in service previous to July 1, 1919.

Second: Rate of assessment upon teachers to be not less than 3 nor more than 5 per cent of salary in any year; provided that no annual assessment shall be more than $100.

Third: Assessments to be deducted from salaries by local school authorities and forwarded to the secretary of the retirement board at Salem.

Fourth: Each teacher's contribution to be reserved solely for his

own benefit; interest on contributions to be credited on the last day
of each year at the rate of 3 per cent per annum.

Fifth: Teachers allowed to be retired at the age of 60; required to
be retired at the age of 70.

Sixth: Retirement allowance to be of two parts:

(a) The annuity, which is a payment for life, derived, according
to regular life insurance tables, from the members' own contributions and accumulated interest.

(b) The pension, of equal amount, paid by the state.

Seventh: An additional pension to be paid by the state to teachers
who have served 15 years or more in Oregon prior to July 1, 1917, the
amount to be based upon the years of service in Oregon, the minimum
in these cases (annuity plus pension) to be $300 a year.

Eighth: No teacher required to contribute a larger sum than is
necessary to purchase an annuity of $500 at age of 60.

Ninth: Members of the retirement association withdrawing from
the teaching service prior to the time when a pension is due to have all
contributions refunded with interest at 3 per cent per annum.

Tenth: In case of death of member, contributions, with 3 per cent
interest, to be refunded to legal representative.

Eleventh: Management to be vested in board of five members, to
serve without pay, the State Treasurer, the State Superintendent of
Public Instruction, the State Insurance Commissioner and two members of the retirement association in service to be appointed by the
Governor for terms of three years, one of whom shall be a classroom
teacher.

Twelfth: All funds of the retirement system to be in custody and
charge of the Treasurer of the State.

Thirteenth: The cost of administration, exclusive of the payment
of retirement allowances, to be paid from the expense fund, consisting
of appropriations by the Legislature, on estimates submitted by the
retirement board.

The members of the committee are: Mrs. A. E. Ivanhoe, La Grande;
O. C. Brown, Roseburg; J. A. Churchill, Salem; Miss Viola Ortschild,
Portland; J. H. Ackerman, Monmouth; J G. Imel, Astoria; Miss Fay
Clark, Vale; Miss Winnifred Dennis, Portland; Richard W. Montague,
Portland; and E. F. Carleton, Salem.

Again, Thanks.

Should thanks become perfunctory, 'twould scarcely pay to live;
For what's the use of living, if you can't sometimes give
A burst of honest feeling of gratitude to those
Who help and trust and love you through triumphs and through woes.
I feel glad that I'm living and thank the Lord for friends:
For with them joy is living; without them pleasure ends.

—C. R. Scroggie.

Training Teachers of Sex Hygiene

By FRED C. AYER, Professor of Education, University of Oregon, Eugene

The scope of this paper is very necessarily and quite properly limited by the fact that much of the material which might ordinarily be presented has been made available in the literature which has been distributed by the society. The problem of sex instruction from our immediate point of view is not a problem of special teachers of departments, but one of qualifications which any teacher or person should possess before attempting to give sex instruction. For the problems of social hygiene are those which concern education in its broadest meaning, and the whole social organization is involved in furthering the process of this education. I shall, therefore, confine my efforts to a brief statement of three general principles of education which should qualify the work of all teachers of the facts of sex life, and then indicate in outline a number of the specific factors of teaching efficiency which are commonly used in the selection and ranking of teachers, aiming to provoke thoughtful consideration rather than to offer arbitrary opinion.

In the first place, it is well to keep in mind that education starts at birth and that anything which influences future conduct is educative. The education of the individual has not only proceeded far on its way, but has set up extremely persistent habits and fundamentals of conduct before the school is ushered in as an agency of education, or the efforts of special teachers are available. Moreover, once the school period is reached, the formal educative influences of the home, the church, the state, the press, and industrial life do not cease, nor are they, in fact, subordinated to school instruction in any such degree as is commonly assumed by the public mind. These extra-school agencies, combined with such informal educative agencies as social custom and the playground, play the major part in determining the habits and standards of conduct of developing boys and girls. This is particularly true, indeed it is distressingly true of matters pertaining to sex relations. Not only the school, but practically all of the agencies which plan the training of the rising generations, are compelled to combat with all too frequent failure against the moulding influence of group or gang spirit. We are just beginning to realize that the information which we have attempted to suppress from the oncoming generation is regularly taught on the street in its most vulgar form. Unfortunately, it is just this secretive gang-spirit teaching that appeals to child life. The press, the school, the home, the pulpit, have long combined their best efforts to persuade young boys not to smoke cigarets, but as long as Johnnie's social group sanctions

and encourages the habit, the consumption of nicotine "pills" will
continue.

So, too, with habits of sex. Assuming other qualifications to be
equal, the influence of any teacher will affect the conduct of pupils
in exact proportion to the degree he or she gets across the barrier
that separates child and adult life and becomes an actual unit in the
child's social group. It would be a serious mistake to esteem any
teacher qualified to give sex instruction who is held in anything but
a friendly and sympathetic attitude by the pupils. As the teacher's
influence, at best, is but a part of the child's social environment, the
necessity for the correlation of all environmental factors cannot be
emphasized too strongly.

A second general teaching qualification lies in the necessary recognition of the place sex instinct occupies in the development of the
individual. It is a commonly recognized principle of teaching, that it
is much better to change the outlet of the child's instinctive tendencies
and impulses, than to attempt to suppress them arbitrarily. The
emotion or feeling that accompanies an instinct and impells one to
activity may be satisfied by acts notably different from those naturally
associated with the inherited tendency. Thus the individual may learn
to substitute hard words for the use of fists on the rise of anger, or
better still, totally to ignore the offender.

In the utilization of the principle of substituted responses in place
of innate reactions, we are particularly fortunate in the fact that the
sex instinct is a delayed instinct. This makes it possible in normal
cases to train the child to associate other responses to the sex emotion
than the inherited one. Long before the boy or girl is seized in the
grasp of powerful sex emotion, it is possible to set up preferred types
of response which are more acceptable to the standards of Christian
civilization than those impelled by the unlicensed sway of passion.
Thus, the sex feeling may become attached to ideals of protection,
love, or chivalry, or less ideally, to fear of disease, or the penalties
of violated law. This principle must be perfectly clear to the qualified
teacher for not only does it urge the importance and show the way of
early training in sex ideals, but it emphasizes the difference demanded
in sex education before and after puberty.

One other general consideration seems worthy of emphasis just now,
for it is the basis for criticism of an important amount of current
literature and public lecturing on sex hygiene. It is the question of
heredity.

Owing to the possibility of certain diseases or the effects of alcohol
being transmitted directly to the developing embryo, there has arisen
considerable confusion an the part of many as to just what deeds of
parents are likely to affect children by way of direct inheritance. It
seems to me decidedly unfortunate that, while teachers of biology who
are well grounded in the laws of heredity are teaching that characteristics acquired during the life of the parent are not inherited by the
children, at the same time many lecturers on social hygiene are holding

up the ideal of good behavior for the parent, so that his good deeds may be re-echoed directly in the inherited tendencies of his children. By all means we should get together on matters of fact in this question.

I have now suggested that all teachers who are qualified to teach the facts of sex instruction—and the same might well be said of all others—that all such teachers should realize that school instruction plays an indirect although significant part in sex education, that they must grasp the full significance of the late maturing of the sex instinct, and that they should be securely grounded in the laws of heredity. Let us now proceed to the more immediate qualifications of good teaching or instruction.

What is it that makes a good teacher? Most of us who are called upon frequently to describe the good points of this and the other successful teacher will grant that often it seems much easier to recognize a good teacher than it is to mark the separate qualities which constitute his or her particular efficiency. But from the point of view of every one interested in the problem of picking out the best teacher for any given position this is a very real problem. Moreover, numerous attempts have been made to solve it by experts and it is encouraging to be able to state that considerable definite progress has been made and that scales or score-cards for teaching efficiency are rapidly coming into more common use. The following efficiency record is one of the best and most recent. It is taken from the Fourteenth Yearbook of the National Society for the Study of Education, Part II, "Methods For Measuring Teaching Efficiency," by Arthur C. Boyce. The detailed rating on each point may be "very poor," "poor," "medium," "good" or "excellent."

Boyce Efficiency Record.

I. Personal Equipment—
    1. General appearance
    2. Health
    3 Voice
    4. Intellectual capacity
    5. Initiative and self-reliance
    6. Adaptability and resourcefulness
    7. Accuracy
    8. Industry
    9. Enthusiasm and optimism
    10. Integrity and sincerity
    11. Self-control
    12. Promptness
    13. Tact
    14. Sense of justice
II. Social and Professional Equipment—
    15. Academic preparation
    16. Professional preparation
    17. Grasp of subject-matter

18. Understanding of children
19. Interest in the life of the school
20. Interest in the life of the community
21. Ability to meet and interest patrons
22. Interest in lives of pupils
23. Cooperation and loyalty
24. Professional interest and growth
25. Daily preparation
26. Use of English

III. School Management—
27. Care of light, heat, and ventilation
28. Neatness of room
29. Care of routine
30. Discipline (governing skill)

IV. Technique of Teaching—
31. Definiteness and clearness of aim
32. Skill in habit formation
33. Skill in stimulating thought
34. Skill in teaching how to study
35. Skill in questioning
36. Choice of subject-matter
37. Organization of subject-matter
38. Skill and care in assignment
39. Skill in motivating work
40. Attention to individual needs

V. Results—
41. Attention and response of the class
42. Growth of pupils in subject-matter
43. General development of pupils
44. Stimulation of community
45. Moral influence

From our point of view today the most interesting aspect of this outline of teaching efficiency is the relative value of its points. By having a number of superintendents use this card upon teachers of known ability and weakness, Mr. Boyce has been enabled to show that, as far as the teachers measured were concerned, some of the points were more highly correlated with general teaching efficiency than others. All of the 45 factors shown on the score-card are regarded as important but certain of them came first in the estimation of a large number of superintendents. As the teachers who are selected on this basis will ordinarily include those concerned in the problem of sex instruction, it is well worth our pains to give careful attention to the order of merit of points found in this instance, and note how well it agrees with the point of view of this conference. As evidenced by the regard with which certain leading superintendents hold their teachers, the points ranked as follows:

1. General development of pupils
2. Growth of pupils in subject-matter

3. Organization of subject-matter
4. Attention and response of class
5. Skill in habit formation
6. Choice of subject-matter
7. Skill in teaching how to study
8. Skill in stimulating thought
9. Skill and care in assignment
10. Definiteness and clearness of aim
11. Adaptability and resourcefulness
12. Discipline
13. Initiative and self-reliance
14. Attention to individual needs
15. Understanding of children
16. Skill in motivating work
17. Accuracy
18. Professional growth and interest
19. Grasp of subject-matter
20. Skill in questioning
21. Moral influence
22. Euthusiasm and optimism
23. Stimulation of community
24. Industry
25. Tact
26. Interest in lives of pupils
27. Daily preparation
28. Cooperation and loyalty
29. Promptness
30. Self-control
31. Interest in the life of the school
32. Care of routine
33. Integrity and sincerity
34. Intellectual capacity
35. Interest in the life of the community
36. Sense of justice
37. Care of light, heat and ventilation
38. Ability to meet and interest patrons
39. Health
40. Use of English
41. Neatness of room
42. Voice
43. General appearance
44. Academic preparation
45. Professional preparation

It is at once evident that many of these points are of varying importance and that many of us would make material changes in the ranking of the individual factors. On the other hand I assume that it is safe to say that a teacher of biology, domestic science, or physical training whom measured well up to this scale would rank well as a teacher of the facts of sex life. I am equally certain that in picking out the ideal teacher to give sex instruction I should not emphasize the same points of value in the order just given. The peculiar moral and social aspects of sex life necessitate a far different selection. My choice for the first seven factors would be as follows:

1. Moral influence—extent to which the teacher raises the moral tone or life of the school—first instead of twenty-first.

2. Interest in the lives of the pupils—second instead of twenty-sixth; that is, desire to know and help pupils personally outside of school subjects.

3. Understanding of children—insight into child nature, sympathetic, scientific, and practical.

4. Integrity and sincerity—soundness of moral principles and genuineness of character.

5. Choice of subject-matter—skill with which the teacher selects the material of instruction to suit the interests, abilities and needs of the class.

6. Attention to individual needs—teacher's care for individual differences, peculiarities, and difficulties.

7. Grasp of subject-matter—command of the information to be taught.

Many of the other factors are most desirable for acceptable sex instruction but without these fundamental seven, it would be difficult for me to sympathize with a movement to turn instruction in matters of sex life over to any teacher. That there is need for specific selection and preparation in the attainment of such ideal qualifications I am positive, but the discussion of this phase of the problem belongs to others.

Because so much depends upon the attitude of the pupil toward the teacher as to the manner in which sex instruction will be received, permit me to conclude by summarizing very briefly two investigations which have been made to discover what boys and girls have to say about the teachers who have helped them most. The first investigation was made by Kratz. It involved several thousand grade children. It was the purpose of this investigation to learn something of the children's ideas of what constitutes the most helpful teacher. The plan was to ask the pupils of a room to recall all of their teachers, and single out the one who had helped them most. They were then asked questions to bring out the special characteristics of such teachers. In answer to the question, "How did she help you?" the lower grades mentioned such things as, "to be good," "to study," "to like school," "to be polite," and the like, while the higher grades said "to observe," "to control myself," "to strengthen my character." The question about special acts of the teacher which helped the pupils brought out, "a deep sense of appreciation of words of encouragement and commendation." In every grade, except one, more than half of the pupils gave prominence to the teacher's dress and personal appearance. Patience was highly appreciated. Politeness was frequently referred to. Neatness of the teacher's dress and also of her desk was a trait many recalled.

The second investigation had to do with the views of 1,000 high school seniors as to their favorite or their most sympathetic teacher. Among the qualifications described were the following: (1) The favorite teacher understands boys and girls. (2) Another qualification from the point of view of the students is that the teacher be enthusiastic, energetic, young. By young the pupils do not mean so much an age distinction as one of mental attitude. Being **young** means being enthusiastic, full of life, up to date. (3) To be recognized as an ideal teacher one must be **interested in work.** (4) Another essential qualification is scholarship, but one must not be a narrow specialist. (5) No definite **sex qualification** is made. (6) Neither was any **appearance qualification** made. This is in contrast wth Kratz's study of grade children, in which it was found that neatness and appearance were important qualifications. Says Book, "High school pupils seem not only to appreciate but to be accurate judges of a teacher's real worth."

What the favorite teacher does: "Two hundred and eleven teachers were chosen as favorites chiefly because they were always ready and willing to give their pupils the right sort of encouragement." "In all his dealings and intercourse with his pupils the favorite teacher is reasonable, fair, and just. Justice received special emphasis." The teacher allows for individuality. "The pupils' favorite teachers have confidence in their students, put them on their honor, believe in them, and trust them." The pupils like a teacher who "takes an interest" in them outside of school, as well as in.

Finally, I should say above all that the teacher should be possessed of optimism and courage and teach from the viewpoint of health and happiness rather than that of disease and fear, for, as Riley puts it,

"Talk health, this never ending tale
Of mortal malady is worn and stale.
You cannot charm or interest or please
By harping on that minor chord, disease.
'Whatever the weather may be,' says he,
'Whatever the weather may be,
It's the songs ye sing and the smile ye wear
That's making the sunshine everywhere.' "

Give Thanks.

Give thanks for night, give thanks for day;
Give thanks for work, give thanks for play;
Give thanks for sleep, give thanks for food—
Give thanks for all that does us good.   —Selected.

The people who feel, however, that everything is wrong with the schools should take the trouble to visit a few classes. The grudge may be based on outlived conditions which existed in the critic's own school days.—William L. Chenery.

The League of Teachers' Associations

By ANNA K. HALLOCK of Portland before the Conference of Teachers' Clubs at San Francisco

The League of Teachers' Associations is a national organization whose object is "to bring associations of teachers into relations of mutual assistance and cooperation, to improve the social and economic status of teachers and to promote the best interests of education. It gives us courage to know that others are facing the same problems. Their solutions help us. It is inspiring to know that thousands are working for a common aim."

In the four years since its organization the League has increased to more than sixty-two affiliated associations with a membership of some forty thousand classroom teachers. This growth has been slow and quiet, very quiet; but when were classroom teachers known to work otherwise? For years they have been the passive recipients of orders coming down through several subalterns, until this attitude has become characteristic. Their work has been simply the detail and the master head has received the credit and the glory. But those of us who have had the privilege of working with some of these associations and with delegates to their conventions have felt an intensity of interest, a forceful purpose and latent power that will not be curbed.

This slow but sure awakening of the teachers to the sense of their individual responsibility for the impossible conditions that exist in our schools, is to me the most portentous movement in educational circles that has developed for years. Its effects will not be confined alone to improved conditions of the teaching body, nor to the better results in the elementary schools; its effects will be felt throughout the whole educational system. For as long as the lower grade work is not done by free, independent, clear thinking teachers, expert in diagnosing the malady which retards the growth of the whole child, our whole educational system will be like the statue with feet of clay. The work in the higher schools cannot be better nor stronger nor more enduring than the foundation.

The strength of the League lies in the strength of the individual clubs, and the strength of each club is increased by the number with which it is affiliated. Through this association we teachers of the land are beginning to know one another, are finding that by working together we can achieve our highest ideals. The feeling that teachers throughout the state and country are ready to concentrate their forces fills us with a sense of the power which is ours; with the conviction that nothing which hinders the progress of truth, can withstand our united efforts.

The League of Teachers' Associations can do more for the professionalizing of education than can any other movement in this field. We must realize that a profession is self-made, that this requires organized effort, and that organized effort is needed for the protection of great educational interests. One of the greatest needs in education today is a strong organization of teachers for the purpose of conveying to the public the needs of our profession, an organization that will be aggressive and untiring in its endeavor to make society realize the truth. Our Commissioner of Education is continually sending out reports on teachers' salaries and they all reach the same conclusion, leaving no doubt about it, but whose business is it to convince the public that a corrective is needed? Teachers are entrusted with the scholarship and intelligence in the community; they are supposed to know the facts and tell the truth and be the highest authority in their own department of public service. Parents trust them with sublime confidence. And what do we find them doing after school? Going home and staying there, engrossed in other interests. They are not a solid group of people working for social justice or higher standards or better conditions for the boys and girls. Why don't they form platform committees and say to the public some of the things they say to each other in groups at recess about their classroom doors. The public will not fail to respond to an honest appeal in behalf of its own children.

The results accomplished for defective and retarded children suggest what the schools should be for normal minds and bodies; that not more than twenty pupils to a teacher will permit a freedom of movement and a chance for intelligent, initiative, which are impossible in the crowded classroom; that overcrowding must mean suppression and repression of the child's self-activity; must mean subordination of individuality which is so powerful a factor in the progress of civilization. The moment you assemble fifty children in a single room it is not for the purpose of real education but for the purpose of autocratic control. The moment you increase the number of children beyond twenty you have destroyed the chance of that subtle interchange of inspiration which comes from the contact of mind with mind, of soul with soul. You will not find an educational expert who approves of large classes. When asked what is the best number for a class they agree upon from twenty to twenty-five. Statistics of our elementary schools show an average of more than forty per classroom teacher in the larger communities. Every teacher knows she cannot teach forty or forty-five little children in one class. Every day she tries to do so, she participates in the sin of overcrowding the classroom and under-educating the population. It is interesting to notice the increasing number of school officials and officers of Parent-Teachers Associations who are placing their children in ungraded rooms, not because the children are abnormal, but because in these rooms the enrollment is limited to twenty or twenty-two. If the teacher's business is to educate the children, then it is her business to create proper conditions for her work. Alone she can do nothing. The only way this ever will be done is through intelligent group action. She teaches that in union there is strength and fails to apply this in her own efforts. Let the teachers unite in a body representing thousands; let them talk in the newspapers or in public generally, and they can accomplish whatsoever they wish. If each teacher would but give a tithe of her time, one evening in ten, the public would soon be made to realize the truth.

There is still the old inbred feeling among us that it is unseemly and self-seeking for teachers to go before the public and discuss salaries and smaller classes. I tell you it is more unseemly for teachers not to do so. Who knows the inner conditions better than they? Who should be the educational experts if they are not? This would be no more selfish on their part than for the expert in animal husbandry to say to the rancher, "Don't crowd your stock into small, poorly ventilated quarters, nor attempt to raise more stock than you can well care for, if you want the best results," or for the expert in agriculture to say, "Give each plant room to spread and grow, and proper soil conditions." When as much expert attention is given to child welfare as is given to agriculture and animal husbandry this will be a different world. Everywhere the people are asking, "What is the matter with our public schools? Why are the children not more thoroughly grounded in the fundamentals?" Yet who is trying to explain this condition to the public? Who is urging the corrective?

In the struggle for greater democracy in educational systems, more favorable conditions for the work of the teacher and the growth of the child, there may be times when we shall need a fighting fund to organize a flying squadron to come to the aid of teachers who have dared to stand for the right, and with the backing of a large organization they will be sure of success.

By organization we can secure tenure of office laws, so much needed for the freedom and peace of mind of the teacher. But with security of tenure we must have a merit system if we do not wish to encourage and protect incompetency. We must not condemn the principle of merit merely because we have never yet seen a merit system that was fair and just. I believe that this is a corrective that must come from within; that the teachers themselves, under the influence of higher professional ideals will be able to formulate a merit system that will be workable. We ought to be able to enlist a board of membership of such dignity and reputation that its decisions would not be questioned, the purpose of which board would be to examine into teachers' grievances, into the incompetency of teachers, and into the causes of friction between teachers and principals. I believe it would be the greatest preventive of incompetency and friction that could be inaugurated. Something like this is being successfully done in Scotland and on the Continent.

A democratic community has no place for teachers afraid to criticize bad conditions or to suggest reforms, afraid of their superiors in office. Yet as isolated individuals we are helpless, the public will not listen. There must be a unity of purpose backed by united effort. We must prove the solidarity of the teaching body of the state and country. We must boost together if we wish to raise standards and improve conditions.

The citizens of this country are in the midst of a peaceful political revolution whose object is to place more and more power in the hands of the people. As political intelligence grows we are striving to attain greater democracy, more direct control of governmental affairs. In industry also the same revolution is taking place. The concentration of wealth in the hands of the few is showing more and more the necessity for the common man's sharing in the control of great public industries and utilities. A similar problem is arising in the educational world and the teachers must meet it.

We are in the midst of educational surveys which are showing the weak places in our school systems. Broad-minded educators who are seeking the real causes that underlie these weaknesses are awakening to the fact that the school has become one of our great modern machines, a great educational trust under the direction of the modern state; that our schools are governed by a combination of methods derived from other institutions. Now of all great social enterprises that of education requires the highest degree of co-operation; our schools cannot be governed by a system borrowed from the army, all orders coming down from superior officers, nor by a form adapted from the church, nor by methods used in great industrial corporations. They can only be governed as any great cooperative enterprise is governed, by the recognition of the principles of democracy. Every teacher must awaken to a consciousness of her individual responsibility in the final results.

The real school is in the relation between teacher and pupils. Nothing is more conducive to the growth and expansion of the soul than contact with a stronger spirit than one's own. It is the most powerful agency in the uplift of the world today. What a teacher is she teaches. She must have a full stock of vitality, animation and optimism. Now if anything will sap a teacher's store of vitality it is continual fear and worry, nervous anxiety for the future, the anticipation of adverse criticism, ceaseless striving to gain the approval of some person upon whose recommendation she depends for tenure and increase of salary. When every teacher feels free to say, "What I do must be determined by the needs of my pupils," then will her teaching be successful. We need an association which stands for the best instruction, the best moral and ethical influence from its teachers, and that will stand back of those teachers who are fearless in the right.

In England and on the Continent some school authorities and educational committees contain advisory representatives of the teaching corps. They are proving that the introduction of new educational schemes ought never to be undertaken without the help and guidance of the teachers on whom the working out of the new ideas will fall. Much friction is avoided as well as much waste and loss in attempting to apply ideas not sufficiently thought out. In some cities in our own country advisory council plans have been installed, by which the teachers themselves through a representative council from their ranks, are permitted to consult directly with the board of education and superintendents. The powers of these councils are largely advisory, but the possible influence has no limit.

Already throughout the land we can see the results of organization. In many states teachers' association by united efforts have secured pension provision, tenure of office laws, increased salaries, equal pay for equal work, improved institute programs. This is only a beginning. Careful observers are beginning to say that the work in the lower grades with little children in the most plastic period of their lives is more important than the work with more advanced students; a child's habits are fixed in that formative period, his love of knowledge acquired then. That therefore this elementary instruction should command sufficient salary to attract and retain experts, and not be left as now to those who use the elementary grades as stepping stones to other things. The elementary teacher should not wait for others to urge this: no one realizes it more fully than she.

The recognization of the mother-teacher by boards of educations is inducing many women to make teaching a career, with whom it would otherwise have been only the temporary employment of a few years. This will also tend to increase the professional spirit.

Seers in sociology tell us that the two great professions of the future will be agriculture and pedagogy, the nurture of life and the training for life; that law is only palliative and will decline with better sociological conditions; that medicine is only remedial and with our fuller knowledge of the causes of physical ills is already losing ground; that the ministry is in reality identical with education when the highest ideals of both are considered.

I believe that this organizing of classroom teachers all over the land is not the ephemeral movement of a few leading spirits out for temporary tangible rewards. It is rather like the first surface movement of a great tidal wave of conscious responsibility; we may not fathom its meaning nor forsee its future. We can only feel its power and prepare to rise with it.

An economy that would take from any boy or any girl the opportunity to become the best possible man or woman is a false economy and one that must be paid for by the public in some form, either in loss of efficient manhood and womanhood or in taking care of these undevelped or wrecked individuals through penal or other costly and unprofitable institutions.—John H. Francis.

James Whitcomb Riley sang the song of the common folk and sang it into their hearts. Unpractical in early life, judged by the world standard, he later developed his vein of humor until it brought fame and a competence. A century hence people will be weeping and smiling as they read him, as they have done for a generation. He did ot live in vain.—Oregonian.

Our English Problem

By ROSA B. PARROTT, Head of English Department, Oregon Normal School, and Secretary
of the Oregon Council of English Teachers

At the risk of being quoted as discussing a subject, all phases of which have seemingly been exhausted and re-exhausted, I am going to write on "Our English Problem." For, despite the seeming exhaustion of the text, there certainly is something to be said and much to be done in a subject where the results are as unsatisfactory as in English. Why do our pupils emerge from the eighth grade using errors that we attempt to eliminate in the first? There are many different theories advanced to account for this anchronism but ti causes most generally held responsible may be classed under the general heads of social and psychological. To these I am going to add a third and term it pedagogical. These pedagogical causes which are responsible for the use of poor English, I believe are the most important, for both the social and psychological causes would soon cease to exist were the pedagogical removed. Therefore, I shall discuss in this paper what I have termed the pedagogical causes.

1. Our grammars contain many rules and principles that were of benefit to the Latin and Greek scholar but are of no immediate aid to the English student. My first contention is that all rules and principles that do not directly assist the student to use the English language correctly should be omitted from our grammars. My reason for advocating this is, that since our extended study of grammar as it is written has not appreciably improved our defective use of English, therefore the prescription should be changed. The disease is still an epidemic so let us, the physicians, change the medicine. All who have thought about this subject agree that the use of good English is more a matter of ear training than reasoning. Because of this I hold that much of our grammar instruction should give way to language drills in order that the English students' ears may be as keen to detect a false construction as are the musicians' to hear a discordant note. This brings me to my second point which I consider the most vital one in this discussion.

2. There is a popular bit of pedantry that says, "Never allow a pupil to see or hear an incorrect form." In spite of this, children are constantly hearing incorrect forms on the street and in many homes. Because of this constant hearing of the incorrect forms outside of the school, the child should be taught in the school to correct the incorrect form and the stamp of definite disapproval should be placed upon the common blunders made. In order that this may be done effectively, I advocate spending a few minutes each day in quick drill correcting the common errors heard.

3. Another popular pedagogical maxim is, "Do not correct the

child at the time he makes the error. Preserve and drill later.'' The argument used by the advocates of this plan, and they are many, hold that to correct the child at the time embarrasses him and destroys spontaneity of expression. In no other subject do we pursue such an illogical course. In mathematics we work for rapidity but never at the sacrifice of accuracy; so in English, let us work for spontaneity of expression but never at the expense of correctness. And one of the surest helps to correctness is to call attention to the error at the time made.

4. Many of the errors in written work and much of the dislike for it has been because the student knew nothing of the subject assigned. In order to avoid this, oral work should always precede written.

5. Another cause for carelessness in written work has been the length of the themes which inhibited care in detail. To avoid this, have no written work over one page in length.

6. A third cause is, that too much written work has been required. Have pupils write not more than one theme a week. (If you have been accustomed to have pupils write for busy work, let them read instead. If you can train your pupils to use their leisure in reading good books and magazines, you have inculcated a habit that will be invaluable to them and one that will be a pleasure and a profit during their entire lives. The Joint Committee from the National Educational Association and the National Council of Teachers of English, appointed five years ago to investigate the instruction in the vernacular and to formulate some plan for its improvement, have just brought in their report. One of the items says, ''One of the chief aims of the school course in English is to establish the habit of reading good books and magazines. Pupils should be encouraged to read freely during the school period. Time should be allowed for this and credit given.'')

7. Use Type Sentences for Punctuation, Capitalization and Construction. These are emphasized in our State Course of Study so the mere mention of them here is sufficient as you already know their value.

In closing I wish to quote from Lord Chesterfield's ''Letters.'' He says: ''The first thing you should attend to is to speak whatever language you do speak in its greatest purity and according to the rules of grammar.'' These suggestions, if followed conscientiously by the teacher, I believe will assist the child in speaking and writing good English according to the rules of grammar and will be a potent factor in developing that ''English conscience'' so woefully lacking in the average American child.

—————◆—————

''The best kind of information begins at home. The man who knows the history and romance of his own region is a delightful neighbor. He who is familiar with its fields and valleys; knows the value of its flocks and herds, its orchards and waving fields; has a part in its marketplace and its caravans; supports its institutions and loves it all—he is a king—the only monarch in a republic.''—Joseph E. Daniels, Librarian, Riverside, California.

The Junior High School

By W. E. RUTHERFORD, Eugene, Oregon

Not long ago a lady telephoned to me about the school work of her young daughter who was just entering high school. She was very anxious to select the course which would best fit the girl's needs and the future plans for her education. After we had discussed the matter, taking into consideration the girl's plans, likes, dislikes, and aptitudes, and decided upon what we thought to be the proper high school course for her to take, the lady said, "I feel that this is the first time my girl has ever been considered an individual so far as her school work is concerned. I wish we could have had the junior high school two years ago so that we might have considered her an individual then and made her work more closely fit our future plans for her." To my mind this woman came more nearly to the heart of the reason for the junior high school than many learned educators who have written long articles upon the subject.

Many educational writers have expressed surprise at the tremendous growth of the junior high school movement during the past three years. It seems to me that the reason for this rapid growth is the same as that for any movement which provides a solution for a long felt need. The junior high school is the solution for a problem which troubled both parents and teachers for centuries before learned pedagogues had done much writing upon the problems of pre-adolescence, for the boy or girl of twelve and thirteen has been a serious problem in both the home and school. With this age has come new interests, new problems, new difficulties which made it hard to treat the child as in the earlier years of childhood, if either parent or teacher is to avoid serious mistakes and serious misunderstandings. A twelve or thirteen year old boy or girl does not fit in smoothly with home conditions which have seemed to fit the early childhood years, and does not fit in smoothly with the same rigid unvarying treatment that the school affords to pupils of the lower grades. Here is where the parent most often feels the restless boy or girl losing sympathy with home conditions and home restraints unless those conditions are adapted to meet the new needs, and here is where the teacher finds a growing impatience with school requirements. So often is this true that we have come to speak of the "deadly seventh grade" where so many pupils form serious problems for the school, and where only the strict enforcement of the compulsory education law holds many boys and girls in school.

The junior high school is an organization which seeks to take into consideration this problem of pre-adolescent youth—an organization which tries to fit itself to the needs of boys and girls who range from twelve to fifteen years of age, holding the best features of the early grade work and drawing down such features of the high school as are best adapted to pupils of this age. Its organization permits more of liberty than that of the ordinary grade school and less perhaps than that of the high school. Its course of study breaks up the old unvarying line of subjects of the grade school, but it is not quite so freely elective as that of the high school for there are common subjects here which must be adhered to in order that boys and girls may meet the situations in life which every citizen will experience. Its social interests will be those most attractive and best adapted to boys and girls of this age, and its dealing with individuals shall in every way keep in mind the age of its students and the problems common to this period of life.

The course of study of the junior high school should provide for a full development of boys and girls from twelve to fifteen years of age and provide for the varying interests which develop at this time. It should provide for trying out the interests and capabilities of pupils, helping them to find themselves before entrance to the high school. I believe that a great deal of variation in the courses may be worked out within required subjects themselves. The English for instance may be divided into sections, in one of which the oral element may predominate for the benefit of those who have capacity and fondness for this work as well as for those who are in special need of it. In another section of the same subject the written composition may predominate for those with special talent in this line which should be emphasized and for those in particular need of drill in written work. In another English section the literary element may be made the principal feature of the work, and so on. In one section in history, current events may form a leading part; in another, local history may be featured, while in both sections the boys and girls will get the main facts of American history which should be the common possession of all American citizens. In mathematics, elementary science, geography, and other subjects variations may be made in different courses and the pupils grouped according to their interests and needs, thus forming a good deal of variation within the limits of the common subjects required of all. Besides these variations in the common subjects there should be other elective subjects offered to help provide for varying aptitudes and needs. Modern languages are among the best electives for these grades for there is no longer any doubt of the advisability of beginning a study of foreign languages at an early age. Subjects such as printing, typewriting and agriculture should also be provided. My own opinion is that art and music should be elective subjects in the junior high school, for while I believe it advisable for a great majority of boys and girls to continue these subjects, I also believe that students having a decided inability or dislike for either, get little cultured value from it at this age.

The junior high school will soon develop a new type of teacher, for the successful teacher in this work must possess characteristics in addition to those demanded by either grade or high school. The departmental plan of the junior high school will demand that the teacher be well prepared for his or her particular subject, but with pupils of this age it also demands a deeper sympathy with personal problems, a deeper interest in pupils as individuals than is usually found among high school teachers. This teacher should be able to see not only the work of the preceding years which form the pupil's equipment, but should see as well the work of the high school for which this must prepare. The training of the junior high school teacher should be broad and yet it should prepare for the definite problems to be met for the matter of methods must play a greater part in this work than in that of the high school. Perhaps a thorough Normal course with farther work in university or college would be an ideal equipment for the junior high school teacher, although we occasionally find that this same breadth and power to teach may come from varied experience and careful reading on the part of any conscientious teacher. Above all the teacher who will be most successful in the junior high school must be quick to respond to the feelings and interests of pupils of this age. There is no field which offers more attractive work for the teacher especially trained or fitted by personality and experience for success in this work.

The material equipment of the junior high school has much to do with its success. The building and its classrooms need not be so pretentious nor so elaborately equipped as in some of our palatial high schools, but it should be definitely planned for the purpose. The library should be more complete than in the ordinary grammar school for the special teacher of a subject will have the skill and time to make a greater use of books than the teacher of numerous subjects in the ordinary grammar grade. Scientific equipment will be used here to a greater advantage by the teacher well prepared for her work. Facilities for vocational and pre-vocational work of definite kinds must be here if the school is to fulfill the true purpose of testing out its pupils. The assembly room should not be lacking for there must be the cohesion and school spirit, which is promoted by frequent assemblies for opening exercises, literary and musical programs and student body activities.

The problem set before the junior high school and its teachers is a large one if they are to fulfill the true purpose of the organization. They must create an atmosphere specially fitted for boys and girls of this age. They must provide for the new interests and take care of the special problems that develop at this time. They are to take the pupil from the hands of his classroom teacher at the end of his sixth school year, change his methods of work so gradually throughout the next three years that he will not at any time be seriously confused, and at the end of his ninth year turn him over to the high school, a capable, self-reliant high school student. The ideal is a high one, but I confidently believe that well organized junior high schools have already gone a long way toward approximating it.

Autumn Fires.

The maple glows in crimson, and the birch in rarest gold,
And a blaze of amber beauty wraps the beeches in its fold—
Still the mystic torches touch them, in the evening calm and cold;
   And the autumn fires are burning on the hill.

There's a drowsy stillness dwelling within the air at noon;
There's a haze along the valley, beneath the midnight moon;
Strange voices swell the chorus of the rivulet's soft croon;
   And the autumn fires are burning on the hill.

All golden are the daytime hours, and silver is the night;
The harvest hills are teeming, and the harvest stars are bright,
And a pledge of peace and plenty breathes through the glorious light,
   And the autumn fires are burning on the hill.
          —Herbert L. Brewster.

The Better Way.

He serves his country best
Who joins the tide that lifts her nobly on;
For speech has myriad tongues for every day,
And song but one; and law within the breast
Is stronger than that graven on stone;
   There is a better way.

He serves his country best
Who lives pure life and doeth righteous deeds,
And walks straight paths, however others stray,
And leaves his sons, as uttermost bequest,
A stainless record, which all men may read;
   That is the better way.   —Susan Coolidge.

The Plea.

Lord, when the evening closes, and I stand
   With eager, fearful hands toward heaven's far shore,
Bring me no gift of roses, as the sand
   Runs out, to run again for me no more.

But give me one clear hour at close of day,
   And whisper, as the darkling shadows fall,
The names of friends I lost along the way,
   The faithful friends I can no more recall.

And while their names upon my lips are set,
   Oh, speed the silent tides that I must stem,
That ere again I slumber or forget
   I may begin my eager quest of them.
          —Harper's Magazine.

Oregon State Library

By CORNELIA MARVIN, Librarian, Oregon State Library

Several teachers have asked for titles of magazines for the use of children in the grades, and the following suggestions made by the New Jersey Public Library Commission may be of service to others who are interested in this subject: Aeronautics, Bird-lore, Boys' Life, Everyland, Little Folks, Popular Mechanics, St. Nicholas, Scientific American, Something to Do, Wohelo Magazine, Youth's Companion.

* * *

For high schools the few very best magazines, aside from those needed by departments, such as the Manual Training Magazine, The English Journal, etc., are possibly those given in the list below: The National Geographic Magazine is equally as interesting for the grades; The Readers' Guide to Periodical Literature should be in either high school or public library in every town, as it serves as a subject index to all the best magazines. The magazines recommended for high schools are: Atlantic Monthly, Independent, Literary Digest, National Georgaphic Magazine, Outlook, Popular Mechanics, Readers' Guide to Periodical Literature, Review of Reviews, Scientific American, Scientific American Supplement, World's Work. Some of the magazines are offering each month some aids to their use in high schools; the Popular Science Monthly, for instance, advertises a prospectus explaining the principles involved in the inventions described in the issue.

* * *

Teachers of civics and agriculture will find it profitable to add to their libraries certain documents which give material on the resources of Oregon, and others on its government and institutions. Some of the most useful of these are: Labor Commissioner's Report and Labor Laws (apply to Commissioner), Blue Book, Road Laws, Election Laws, etc. (apply to Secretary of State), Fire Prevention Bulletin (apply to Insurance Commissioner), Summary of Industrial Accident Law (apply to Industrial Accident Commission), Proposed Constitutional Amendments, or "Voters' Pamphlet" (apply to Secretary of State), Proceedings of the Horticultural Society and the Report of the Board of Horticulture and the Oregon Almanac may be had from the Oregon State Library upon receipt of necessary postage. State Library will send all the documents to anyone who will refund postage upon receipt.

* * *

The State Library will send to anyone upon request the "Index to Short Stories" and the "Geography Index" which will help to find the library books adapted to the work suggested in the course of study. The "Picture Study Index" for the same purpose is out of print and cannot be distributed, but will be loaned to anyone who wishes to use it. Index to the history material and notes on some of the new books adapted to geography work will appear in the next number of the Oregon Teachers Monthly.

* * *

The request has come for material for the eighth grade on the Federal Reserve Board and Postal Saving's Banks. This will be found in the World Almanac, which should be in every school library and should be consulted for all current material. The American Yearbook which is in the state high school list also gives summary of the important recent legislation.

* * *

The State Library will lend to any high school or to any public library for high school use groups of books for work in history, economics, English, mathematics, science, or any of the studies for which these groups may profitably be used. Loans are made for three months. Application should state the work to be done during the three months and the books available locally. Selections may be made from the state list, or from any other source or bibliography.

* * *

The State Library does not loan to anyone who applies for them the works of Harold Bell Wright for use in high school English. It prefers to refer the applicant to Atlantic Monthly for June, 1915 which contains Mr. Owen Wister's article on "Quack-novels and Democracy," from which the following quotations are taken: "Lastly—like the quack-medicine—the quack-novel is (mostly) harmful; not always because it is poisonous (though this occurs), but because it pretends to be literature and is taken for literature by the millions who swallow it year after year as their chief mental nourishment, and whose brains it saps and dilutes." "The Eyes of the World gathers into its 464 pages all the elements, I think, of the quack-novel; one element appearing rather more conspicuously than in any of Mr. Wright's preceding stories. This is the sensuous suggestion, the carnal pre-occupation, somewhat frequent (but scrupulously pious) reference to illicit sexual relations. The plot concerns eight or nine principal characters, and these are all (except one) taken, without a change in so much as a hair of their heads, from the closet where melodrama keeps its most battered and shop-worn puppets."

* * *

The State Superintendent of California suggests interesting questions for grade debates: (Sixth grade)

Resolved, That drawing is of greater value than music. (Seventh grade) Resolved, That fishery is of more importance than grazing; Resolved, That on the whole the New England colonists treated the Indians fairly; Resolved, That it would have been better for America if the French had won in the French and Indian War; Resolved, That the invention of the cotton gin did more for humanity than the invention of the steamboat. (Eighth grade) Resolved, That the War of 1812 was, in results, an American defeat; Resolved, That the use of the metric system should be made compulsory; Resolved, That Clay was a greater statesman than Webster; Resolved, That Edison is a greater benefactor than Burbank; Resolved, That the Mexican War was unjustifiable; Resolved, That there should be a law against the sale of fireworks (explosives) to inexperienced persons; Resolved, That a vegetable diet is more healthful than a meat diet, (for girls); Resolved, That irrigation produces better fruit than rainfall; Resolved, That simplified spelling should be made compulsory by state law.

* * *

The G. & C. Merriam Company of Springfield, Mass., will send upon request helpful booklets and folders on the use of the dictionary.

Some Boy Problems

By A PORTLAND GRADE TEACHER

Can the old or overgrown backward boy be profitably kept in the grades until he regularly finishes the work? We all find boys who are struggling along, often half heartedly, unable to do satisfactory work in one or all of the major subjects. They are anxious to leave school and go to work, but their parents wish to keep them in school. Sometimes they are there only because they are not quite old enough to quit school. What we can best do for such boys is always a perplexing question. A few terms ago in September we found a group of such boys in an 8A class and they failed to do the required work, some through indolence, some

from lack of ability, and some, unfortunately, from the effects of tobacco. At the end of the term we could not promote them, and, most of them being old enough to leave school, were determined to do so. We had no ungraded class room, but persuaded them to stay with us for another term in a special class (into which we received a couple of boys from other rooms) but working in the same room with the regular 8As. One of the boys would leave school in June, three would enter trade school the next year, while two wished to make up their grades to finish with their class and enter high school. We gave to each, as we could, the things most essential for what they wished to do, and that would make for good and intelligent citizenship.

From such students 'brilliant' results were not to be expected, but the interest and incentive shown were very gratifying, as well as their general attitude toward school-room life. They seemed to realize as never before a real personal interest in them as individuals and that we were working for them, not for "readin', 'ritin' and 'rithmetic." To be sure there were many discouraging days during the five months, but they all proved worth while. The boys carried out their plans, two of those entering the trade school doing a good year's work, and coming back to us occasionally for help. At the beginning of the second term one of the boys came with his algebra, saying, "My professor said this was pretty hard, and he didn't know whether I could get it or not, but I told him I'd take it to my teacher out there and she'd help me. I'd get it all right." It was with the greatest pride that they brought their report cards to us to see how they were doing. They knew us as their friends.

Then there is the boy who comes to school chiefly for the fun and the athletics. School is a very secondary matter, and he will get as much fun and little work out of it as is possible. John was not a good worker in the class room, nor was he a quick student, so his work was poor. In the garden work the teacher discovered a fund of common sense in common things and a helpful spirit which she wished to follow up. She secured work for him for the summer vacation on the home farm, and during the summer they became very good comrades, working, playing, reading, and talking together. The farm life did for him what it will do for any active, growing boy, and he returned to school in September better physically and mentally than he left it in June.

The spirit of comradship continued through the school year to the advantage of scholarship and deportment, and he returned to the farm for another summer. The following February he finished grammar school with the highest rank of any boy in his class, and entered high school. Before another vacation he had a position where he was making

good, and there were a number of applicants for his place on the farm.

A boy who was not very rugged and who had never been on a farm, was chosen and the many new experiences made him in many ways a changed boy. It was an event to him when he could hitch and unhitch the horse and drive it alone, though at first he took no special interest in the horses. The summer wasn't long enough, however, for him to learn to milk a cow, although he tried. His ability to eat and sleep became what it should be for a healthy boy, which was not the case when he came. If every boy could spend at least his vacations in normal farm life what a boon it would be for the boy, and many farm homes can well afford the care of the boy with wage enough to give him a feeling of responsibility and self respect. The regularity of daily life lived out of doors with definite work to do, and a fellowship with the boy and sympathy with his thoughts and doings, bring to the surface all of the best manhood in him.

And the greatest good is not for the boy. Many are the things we may learn of the life and viewpoint of the boy that are very good for us to know, while the joy of receiving his confidence and real companionship are more than recompense for all of the effort expended.

The Portland Parent-Teachers Association has taken unto itself the task of creating public sentiment in favor of municipal garbage gathering, thereby hoping to reduce the city's death rate among the babies of the poor.

It is better only sometimes to be right than at all times to be wrong. Before I resolve to do one thing or the other, I must gain my confidence in my own ability to keep my resolves when they are made.—Lincoln.

A Sixth Grade Reading Class

By MARGARET MONROE, Portland, Oregon

It was the study period for reading in the sixth grade class. They were all sitting in order holding their books but with the exception of about 10 per cent they were not studying. These of the 10 per cent did not need the study; they were excellent readers, ambitious for marks nearing 100 and willing to work hard for them. Why were the 90 per cent so listless? During the arithmetic study period, day after day, they worked hard; they applied themselves with energy to geography and language; even spelling was tackled with more enthusiasm than was given to the reading. And it was the same no matter what hour the reading period came; it could not be that they were tired.

The teacher walked down the aisle and stopped back of Jane's desk. The book was held open to the story of Maggie Tulliver; that story should have interested a bright little youngster like Jane. One hand held her book, the other her stock of pencils and also her interest. The teacher leaned over the desk: "Don't you like Maggie Tulliver?" she asked.

Jane's face glowed: "Oh yes, I read this story last year when I first got the book. I don't like her cousin at all. She always did everything just so." Presto! The whole class were awake.

"Why, Miss ———," said Tom, "Jane is a tomboy just like Maggie was!"

"All the girls in this school are like Maggie," declared Gerald. "The little cousin must have been an old-fashioned girl. I don't know any that are like her."

"How many in the class like Maggie Tulliver?" All hands went up. It developed most of them had read the lesson four or five times. When? Why, the first week they had owned the books.

"For the next month," announced the teacher, "you may choose your own reading lessons. Each may read what he pleases. I advise you to start with the story or book you yourself like best. If the story is long, be ready to tell part of it and, then, read the more interesting part to the class. You may take articles from magazines, St. Nicholas, Current Events, Youth's Companion, or books you have at home, or get from the library. Any who wish to recite poems instead of reading, may do so."

"Don't we have to read out of our readers?" asked a youth who with the persistence of inertia had succeeded in not doing so for several months.

From that time the most enthusiastic and popular hour of the day was the reading period. It was surprising the amount of reading that could be done in half an hour's time; and how they enjoyed it.

One day the daily program was interrupted by a speaker from outside the school. The evident admiration of the boys for the brisk clean-looking business man who addressed them was evidence to the teacher that the visit was of value but it had taken a little time and she announced they would omit the reading for that day. Oh, the disappointment in the children's faces!

"If we get all our lessons and then if there is time can't we have reading?" asked Emil, who usually found a way of getting what he wanted.

"Certainly if you can do it, and I hope you will. I would miss the reading myself," was the teacher's answer. And it was the truth.

There were frequently surprises for the teacher in the choice of the children. The fourth class in the same room begged to be allowed to have the same kind of reading lessons. One morning a very bright little girl, in fact one of the brightest the teacher had ever had the privilege of teaching, came to her.

"Miss ———, I've such a good story to read. It's just the best story!"

The teacher had confidence in this child's discrimination as to what was an interesting story, so she did not look at the book Mary held, but said:

"That's fine! We'll have you read it."

The choice proved to be a senseless, as far as meaning of words was concerned, jingle of words and tones but with rhyme and rhythm. The rhyme and rhythm was all that could have appealed to the child. There was no story in it and hardly a sentence. But Mary read it with joy and with the most perfect confidence that the listeners were also enjoying it. It suggested to the teacher the possibilities that lay in utilizing children's love of rhythm.

A number learned and gave recitations in place of reading. The fourth class gave a play about David that they had written. There was nothing they liked better than humorous stories. The first of this kind was chosen by a bright boy and most entertainingly read. It was a collection of short stories by E. Parker Butler, famous for "Pigs Is Pigs." This was followed by "A Slow Train Through Arkansaw." Abe, who brought this, was afraid I would rule it out for it was in a paper cover. "Helen's Babies" appeared next. We blame adults for having no sense of humor, but do we take the proper steps to develop this highly valuable mental quality in the children?

Of the longer stories that were favorites with them were: Robin Hood, Forest Castaways, Anne of Green Gables, The Lost Prince, The Secret Garden, The Knights of King Arthur, and The Lance of Kanana. Numerous short stories, fairy tales, fables, animal stories and adventure stories were read in a short time.

Histories and information articles were read silently and reported to the class. This was done in connection with geography and language. The assignments were distributed so that every child had a part according to his ability. The report was asked for because we all wanted to know something; for instance, we were studying cotton. Myrtle had lived in Oklahoma; the class asked her a lot of questions about it. She did not know, but she said she would ask her mother that night and tell us the next day.

One day Napoleon was mentioned. One of the boys wanted to tell us about him. We told him to look over his books again that night and to see how much he could tell us in five minutes' time the next day.

After a few weeks the teacher asked them if they did not want a record of the books each child had read kept. Of course they did. So in a big book the pupils' names were entered, each on a page by itself. Under the name was put the names of the books or parts of books he had read during the month. A few skillful questions easily tested the truth of their assertions as to their home reading. Each student kept his own page in the ledger. This was easily managed with a filler notebook, and it gave them practical lessons in spelling, language and penmanship, for they were anxious and ambitious about the appearance of the pages. Then each was given an opportunity to place a review of a book in the ledger. Credits in language for report cards were offered for a good review. This brought up the question of what was a good review. The talking they did to this point was profitable.

Not only were the children enjoying the reading, and doing an immense amout of it, but they were learning to read. They were reading with life, interest, expression. Once in a while, not at a regular reading period, but when they needed a little change, a game was played. The pupils were supplied with a new page. They were given a few minutes to read it silently. The books were closed. A number of questions on this page were on the blackboard. Leaders were appointed; they chose sides. No. 1 on the first side answered the first question. No. 1 on the other side improved the answer if he could; if he could not he took the next question. If No. 1 on the second side had improved the answer No. 1 on the first side gave, then No. 2 on the first side took the same question if he could better the answer. The game never lasted more than 10 or 15 minutes. The test of correctness of the answers was how near they were to the exact idea of the page. Any unfairness, dishonesty, etc., counted them out of the game. As a rule, the boys played a better game than the girls, though the latter answered the questions correctly as often as the boys. But the boys were quicker at making the most of the rules of the game and detecting mistakes.

One day the class was asked if the ability to read was of much value. A short history of writing and the alphabet interested them immensely, especially the part dealing with picture writing. They loved the illustrations of the picture writing of the Indians and the Chinese, and enjoyed making them. The class was given as a problem the task of finding out if our alphabet was taken from pictures. If so, why did we have so few letters when the Chinese had so many? For what did each letter stand? They were asked not to ask anyone but to think out the answer.

Later the Scientific Alphabet used in the Standard Dictionary and "promulgated by the American Philological Association" was explained to the class, but they were not drilled in it or asked to learn it. It was suggested that a better alphabet than the Scientific Alphabet might yet be invented, perhaps by one of them. They cast a unanimous ballot for phonetic spelling. Even Lily, who held the proud record of not having missed a word during the term, thought it a sensible plan. So much simpler are children's views of life than their elders'.

Short, snappy drills in words containing the different vowel and consonant sounds were used occasionally to improve enunciation.

For many years the problem of how to interest a class in the reading lesson had seemed to be without an answer, but at last it was solved.

A Symposium on Speech—A Review

By R. E. STAUFFER, Willamette University, Salem, Oregon

At the request of Prof. Clapp, vice-chairman of the Committee on American Speech, I wish to call attention to a symposium that appeared in the April issue of the Journal of Ophthalmology, Otology, and Laryngology. Every teacher in the state and everyone having to do with public affairs should by all means obtain a copy of this symposium which is now available in reprint. While it was prepared under the supervision of a committee appointed by the National Council of Teachers of English, a glance at the list of contributors immediately discloses that the subject is no mere whim of English teachers and instructors in public speaking. Many men of various callings are deeply concerned about American speaking habits and conditions. Among other contributors are George B. Rice, Professor of Laryngology, Boston University School of Medicine, Frederick B. Noyes, Professor of Orthodontia and History in the Dental College of the University of Illinois, Shirley Gandell, Cosmopolitan School of Music, Chicago, Otis Skinner, actor, Bryn Mawr, Pa., John W. Bradshaw, Division Traffic Supervisor of Chicago Telephone Company, W. B. Towsley, Superintendent of Efficiency and Welfare, Marshall Field and Company, Chicago.

A reform of American speech is being urged for three principal reasons: For the sake of health; for the promotion of greater business and social efficiency; for the pure pleasure that a good speaking voice gives. Most of us realize that our own speech is not perfect; probably few of us have much conception of the enormous problem as it is known to specialists. Dr. D. J. McDonald speaking of New York City says: "A study of speech conditions in our public schools shows that 200,000 of the 800,000 are afflicted with stuttering, mumbling, lisping, or foreign accent."

It may be no news, as Prof. Clapp says, to hear "that the standard of speech among Americans is the worst in the civilized world"; but it is none the less startling. He goes on to say: "American utterance is a slovenly thing, as compared with English, French, German, Italian, Spanish, Russian, and South American. American voices are strident and harsh. We used to regard the fact as a sort of good joke, to regard concern about it as a special mark of the high-brow, the dilettante. Vast numbers of our people view the matter in this light still.

"Many, though, have come to realize that our vicious speech habits are a serious handicap to national efficiency. They impair the speed and accuracy of communication, in business as well as in social life; they increase our liability to disease. Or, to put it the other way round, a general insistence on decent speech—distinct utterance and clear quiet tone—would not only make life more pleasant but would enable us actually to talk faster and be understood more easily, in all our business dealings. It would lessen disease, because it would promote better hygiene of the vocal tract—mouth,

nose, throat, and lungs—among all persons, and because it would lead to the detection and correction of thousands of physical irregularities which now go unhelped and almost unnoticed." But this is sufficient quotation. Let every teacher read the symposium in its entirety and join in giving the movement the widest publicity.

Reprints of the symposium may be had of the Nelson-Schram Company, 14 Devereux St., Utica, New York. Price 25 cents.

City Superintendents' Department

Edited by GEORGE W. HUG, McMinnville, Oregon

Baker schools opened September 4 with an enrollment of 1303, an increase of 131 over the first day of last year. Ella Moulton, Ruth Peters, and Charles W. Frost are the new teachers in the high school. All the principals were re-employed. Systematic physical education with athletics so as to reach all the pupils in the grades has been employed. The Beacon system of primary reading has been adopted.

LaGrande schools began September 11 with an enrollment of 1160 which is practically the same as last year. The late harvest has delayed many pupils from registering the first day. R. A. Wilkerson, formerly at Meacham is principal of the Greenwood school. The new instructors in the high school are A. C. Hampton, principal; Harold Mason, manual training; Naomi Kirtly, domestic science; Jay Fulkerson, mathematics; Royal F. Niles, history, and athletics; Jewell Tozier, mathematics and girl's gymnasium. Some of the new ideas inaugurated are: Physical training for girls, enlarging the manual training work-concrete and carpentry added, competitive tests in the grades.

Ashland schools opened with an enrollment of 903, an increase of 49 over the first day of last year. Among the new instructors in the high school are Henreich Heidenreich, E. T. Hollowell, Grace Lelly and Margaret Anderson. The junior high school has been organized. Hot

lunches at noon are given and a course in Electricity offered.

Marshfield public schools began September 5 with an enrollment of 650. A. C. Morrison is the new principal of the high school. Other new instructors are: August Wilman, physical training; Emily Maud Hooper, Latin; Ruth Hogan, commercial; Bersu Elliott, music; and Marian Mabeer, domestic science. On Friday afternoon 30 minute assemblies are held in the grade buildings. Topical and problem investigation work in history, geography, hygiene with co-operation of all the agencies. French has been added to the high school course.

The Bend schools opened with an increase of 50 per cent over last year. A full four years' commercial course has been installed in the high school. Credits are given in current history. A one-story building is in the course of construction. Stores and churches are being used as schools for the present. F. Thordarson is the new superintendent and Eric C. Bolt the new grade principal.

Salem public schools opened with an enrollment of approximately 2400 pupils. This is a slight decrease over last year, mainly due to the lateness of the season; many pupils did not report until the second or third week. The new instructors in the high schools are: Leland Knox, Elizabeth Macleay, Rex Putnam, Nell Sykes, Ethel K. Hummel, Ermine E. Bushnell.

Eugene schools opened with an enrollment of 1750, a decrease of 122 over last year. Several new high school instructors have been employed this year; they are as follows: E. E. Moining, commercial; Guy E. Dyar, head of English department; W. E. Millikin, mathematics and athletics; Charlotte M. Ballard, physical training; Donald S. Robey, manual training; Willetta Moore, domestic art; A. G. Smith, physics. Miss Ida Patterson and Mrs. Ida O. Sias are the new grade principals. O. H. Jones is principal of the new intermediate school consisting of the seventh and eighth grades. Supt. Rutherford and Elementary Supervisor Ida Mae Smith have worked out a new course of study for the grades. The Washington grade school consisting of six rooms and a covered play ground was opened this fall. The new junior intermediate school is also a new building.

Newberg public schools opened on September 25, with practically the same enrollment as last year. D. L. Cook is the principal of the high school and C. L. Vanwormer is principal of the grade schools. The new high school instructors are: S. W. Arney , Miss Elma Paulsen, Miss Marguerite Barden, Miss Elsie Lee, W. R. McNair, Miss Cora Trumar, Miss Winnie Shields.

The Beacon System of Reading has been adopted at Baker, LaGrande, The Dalles, Ashland, Eugene, and McMinnville.

Vocational Education Department

Edited by R. E. CHLOUPEK, Pendleton, Oregon

Field Notes.

The examination held in June-July for special certificates seemed to find a number unprepared. The state superintendent of public instruction, J. A. Churchill, writes in reply to a letter asking for information: "From the information received in this office not more than 25 per cent of those who presented themselves for the examination turned in their manuscripts. Of those who finished and turned in their manuscripts not more than 25 per cent received certificates."

At last accounts there were still vacancies at the following places in manual training: Enterprise, Lakeview, Heppner. These vacancies were not caused by a failure to pass the examination, but on account of slow action on the part of the administrative body of the school districts.

The following O. A. C. people are employed in Oregon to teach manual training: Paul Amort, Salem; A. C. Archbold, Grants Pass; Lloyd H. Blakley, Medford; Heinreich Heidenreich, Ashland; George O. Leo, Redmond; Zena Mettie, Alsea; O. G. Reeves, Marshfield; Frank H. Struble, Klamath Falls; A. E. Turner, Junction City; Harold W. Turner, Salem; E. F. Underwood, Estacada; Harold Mason, LaGrande; Wm. D. Allingham, Athena; Luther A King, Tillamook.

Donald L. Robey, who has been for the past two years in the Palouse, Washington, high school as teacher of manual training and director of athletics, has secured the position as supervisor of manual training in Eugene. C. T. Mudge, who has been in Eugene for two years has secured a position in California.

J. W. Motley, who was at Heppner last year, has secured a position in Cripple Creek, Colorado, as head of the manual training. As this is a $1200 position Motley made rather a good move.

A few of the O. A. C. men go into other states. Brewer A. Billie teaches manual training and coaches the athletics in Hoquiam, Washington; Ray E. Goble takes charge of the manual training and athletics in a union high school at Fortunia, California; John M. Hamilton will teach manual training and agriculture in Harrington, Washington; Martin A. Schrieber will handle the manual training, German, and some agriculture in the schools at Orifino, Idaho; A. W. Wheeler will have charge of manual training and boys' and girls' club work at Wapato,

Washington; E. W. Heckart will look out for the manual training work and do something in mathematics in Odessa, Washington; Carl W. Morgan gave such satisfaction by his work in manual training for a part of the past year that his work was made less and his salary elevated from $900 to $1200 for the school year.

Harvey Watson, a graduate f'om a Missouri State Normal and from the Stout Institute, has been employed as an assistant for Phillip Parcher in the manual training department of the county high school at The Dalles.

Oregon Agricultural College has placed 22 people as teachers of manual training this year. The minimum salary is $75 paid to Miss Mettie at Alsea. The maximum salary is $1200. The average monthly salary is $100.35.

Manual Training at Pendleton.

The course of manual training for the high school and the eighth grade classes is so planned that during the fall and spring of the year, when the weather permits of outside work, these classes, except the classes in gas engines and forging which run the full semester, do carpentry and concrete work. During the winter months this class is divided into the regular shop work of joinery, cabinet making, woodturning and mechanical drawing.

This year the three eighth grade classes, comprising 41 boys, have the following work outlined: One woodshed 10 feet by 18 feet with a chicken coop in one end; one garage 14 feet by 20 feet; one garage 12 feet by 16 feet; 80 line feet of wood sidewalk; and a block of concrete walk.

Our present enrollment for the high school manual training classes is 85 pupils divided as follows: Forging, 12; gas engine, 15; freshman joinery, 16; carpentry and concrete, 42. The carpentry and concrete class have the following projects completed, under way or to be finished this fall: 300 line feet of concrete curbing, of which 150 feet is curved work; a concrete walk 5 feet by 350 feet; a gas engine building with concrete floor 24 feet by 32 feet; a stone retaining wall 20 inches by 450 feet to be made of sandstone which was left on the completion of the Federal building; this stone had

to be drilled and split to size by the class; a fireproof cage 6 feet by 8 feet by 8 feet, for a moving picture machine in the high school auditorium; a complete set of scenery for the high school stage and a concrete street crossing for the city.

Work starts at 7 a. m. for those boys who get to school at that time. The boys are paid 25 cents an hour for all of the time that they put in, outside of regular school hours. On Saturday the gang works from 7 to 5. Lectures and notes are given every Friday. The class in carpentry and concrete is divided as follows: 12 boys work from 7 to 8:30; 16 boys from 8:40 to 10:15; and 14 boys from 10:15 to 11:40. With this division we have been laying 60 line feet of walk every morning.

For the work of the boys in the gas engine course, which is being taught by Mr. Virgil Fendall a recent O. A. C. graduate, we have two 45 horse-power engines from Holt Caterpillars, which were given to the school by the E. L. Smith Co., and will have four or five different makes of stationary engines as soon as the building is completed. The local Ford agency will send up all the parts needed to complete a Ford engine and the assembling will be taken up as a class project. We have been promised a Holt Caterpillar for demonstration work for the spring work.

The class in forging will complete, besides the regular problems, three 18-foot wheat racks and a hay rack. For the spring work we hope to be allowed to build two concrete tennis courts for the high school and will have one concrete garage and at least one frame garage to erect. At the present time we are working on plans for a farmers' short course of about two weeks to be given in December in forging and gas engine work and possibly a course in farm bookkeeping.

Grade Teachers' Department

Edited by SABRA CONNER, 421 West Park Street, Portland, Oregon

Elementary teachers and elementary teachers' associations are cordially invited to send news items of their activities which would be of interest or value to other teachers to this department of the The Oregon Teachers Monthly. Address Editor of Grade Teachers' Department, Room 300, Court House, Portland, Oregon.

Last year the plan of exchanging teachers with Eastern cities was inaugurated in Portland. This year Miss Fannie Barber from the Washington school, Portland, exchanged with Miss Phila Helt, of Attleboro, Mass.; Miss Cora Sullivan of the Ockley Green School exchanged with Miss Catherine Meagher of Cincinnati; Miss Helen Knowles from the Kerns School with Miss Fannie Kattelle from Melrose, Mass.

* * *

Active members of the National Educational Association a l m o s t unanimously passed the resolution dealing with military training in the public schools, after being assured by the chairman of the committee, reporting the resolution, that it advocated military training in the schools, only so far as such training is educational. The resolution in full, is: "Resolved, That the National Educational Association gives expression again to the consciousness that the school is an institution developed by society to conserve the well-being of humanity, and that on this solid foundation all subordinate aims and uses of the school should be made to rest. Assembled as it is in a time of world wide disturbance, doubt, and uncertainty, and of consequent national concern, the association affirms its unswerving adherence to the unchanging principles of justice between persons and between nations; it affirms its belief that the instruction in the schools should tend to furnish the mind with the knowledge of the arts and sciences on which the prosperity of the nation rests and to incline the will of men and nations toward acts of peace; it declares its devotion to America and American ideals, and recognizes the priority of the claims of our beloved country, our property, our minds, our hearts and our lives. It records its conviction that the true policy to be followed, both by the school and by the nation, which it

serves is to keep the American public school free from sectarian interference, partisan politics, and disputed public policies, that it may remain unimpaired in its power to serve the whole people. While it recognizes that the community, or the state may introduce such elements of military training into the schools, as may seem wise and prudent, yet it believes that such training should be strictly educational in its aims and organization, and that the military ends should not be permitted to pervert the educational purposes and practises of the school."

* * *

The Portland Grade Teachers' Association held its first monthly dinner of the season at the Imperial Hotel, Wednesday, September 13. Superintendent L. R. Alderman, Mrs. Alderman, O. M. Plummer, and Dr. J. Francis Drake, the recently elected member of the school board, were present. After dinner the members adjourned to the parlor where they listened to a few words of greeting from Dr. Drake. The remainder of the evening was spent in becoming acquainted with the mysteries of court proceedings through participating in a mock trial which was conducted by Judge A. E. Gebbardt, J. Hunt Hendrickson, and C. M. Little. The case which was tried before the Honorable Judge and the six ladies of the jury was a suit for $25,000 damages brought by Miss Cynthia Smythe, known as the Singing Swan of Silverton, against the School Bulletin. A poem contributed by Miss Smythe to the Monday Crawfish was copied by the School Bulletin accompanied by such fierce criticism that she was greatly humiliated, her growing reputation was injured, and her health impaired. Polly O'Brien, "a purveyor to the public necessities of the immaculate," in other words a wash lady, and Miss Julia Caramel, alleged head of the candy department in the Owl drug store, testified for the plaintiff. Miss Dew Tell, editor of the School Bulletin, Gertrude Pretzel of the carpet bag and shawl who had testimony to give concerning those who "sat on Nathaniel Hawthorne and Oliver Wendel Holmes," and Mike Sullivan, the courteous office boy, who disdained poetry, were witnesses for the defense. The jury brought in a verdict of 30 cents foi the plaintiff. Miss Lucy D. Hoye, Miss Nettie Richardson, Miss Nugent, Miss Metta Brown, Miss Johanna Cramer and Miss Petch gave excellent delineations of their respective characters. To Judge Gebbardt, J. H. Hendrickson, C. M. Little and Miss Harriet Monroe belong much of the credit for the clever management of the evening's entertainment.

* * *

The special teachers of literature in the Portland grade schools met on September 20 and effected an organization with Miss Sabra Conner of the Shattuck School as president and Miss Roma Stafford of the Brooklyn School as secretary. It is hoped that this organization will be the means of making the subject of literature in the grammar grades a more vital thing.

* * *

The Recreation Committee of the Portland Grade Teachers' Association seems to fill a very real need. They have planned several very pleasant Saturday afternoon walks and a permanent walking club is an outgrowth of these. They made arrangements for the teachers to secure reduced rates to the Tagore lecture and the Elman concert. Saturday and week-end trips are being planned. No teacher need spend a lonely Saturday, just call up the chairman of the Recreation Committee and get your "name in the pot."

* * *

Mrs. Mable Holmes Parsons began the work of the Extension Department of the University of Oregon with her teachers' class in English, which met Saturday, September 30 at 10 a. m. in the central library. This class will study the problems of the presentation of English and literature to the grammar grade pupils. Mrs. Parsons' class in modern drama Saturday evening began with a con-

sideration of Rabindranath Tagore. The second lecture, October 14, was a review of Ibsen, the Conservative. Brand, An Enemy of the People; the Wild Duck; the Doll's House, and Hedda Gabbler, are the works of Ibsen which will be considered.

* * *

The New Jersey public school teachers have a retirement annuity system for disabled teachers, that after 18 years of active operation makes the best financial showing of any teachers' retirement annuity system in the United States. To date 549 annuities have been retired.—Journal of Education.

* * *

Teachers' annuities and retirement allowances, supported wholly or in part by the public, have been extensively developed in European countries during the last quarter of a century. All the states of the German Empire, Austria-Hungary, Switzerland, Denmark, Norway, Sweden, Belgium, France, Italy, and Great Britain pay annuities to teachers.—The Seattle Teacher.

* * *

The advancement of women to responsible places in educational systems is authoritatively revealed by the Federal Bureau of Education's directory for 1915-1916, which discloses the fact that of the 12,000 conspicuous educational positions, largely of an administrative character, 2500 are now held by women. These 2500 prominent educational positions held by women educators include besides several state superintendencies, 24 college and university presidencies, 508 county superintendencies, 1075 library directorships, 14 directorships of industrial schools, 48 of art schools, 10 of state and 16 of private schools for the deaf, and 20 of private institutions for the feebleminded.—Journal of Education.

* * *

The London Teachers' Association was founded in 1872 with a membership of 39. It has now over 17,000 members, a subscription income of over $20,000, and a cash turnover for the year of $100,000. It aims to attract into membership every qualified teacher in every school maintained by the London Education Authority. It seeks to do this by the magnetism of its ideals, the efficiency of its organization, and the attractiveness of the many benefits which it places at the disposal of its members.—The Elementary Teacher.

* * *

A sabbatical year for grade teachers would be of marked value to the community. Teachers who deal year after year with immature minds should have an opportunity to bring to their work renewed enthusiasm and improved scholarship as a result of a year's leave of absence at intervals. At least a dozen American cities recognize the value of a sabbatical year, and after a teacher has given seven years' service in their schools, allow absence on half salary.

* * *

Foreign countries which we consider very conservative and justly so, recognize the value of a teacher's leave of absence for study to the school system and to the community at large. Saxony, Bavaria, Baden, Prussia, Sweden, France, Norway, Austria, and London not only grant such leave on full pay but allow a stipend for foreign study.—School Board Journal.

* * *

The Royal Gorge National Teachers' Recreation Association of Colorado has several features of interest to all women teachers. The association has a two-fold mission, to furnish at a very low cost a summer resort for teachers, and, in time, to build and maintain a home for sick and old teachers. The association has acquired 40 acres at the entrance to the Royal Gorge, and is incorporated under the laws of Colorado. Besides selling blocks of five shares at a dollar a share to those who wish to come to enjoy the low rate living expenses, the association is asking every teacher in the United States to contribute one dollar toward an endowment for the home for old, sick, and needy teachers. Mrs. Lulu W. Granger, of Pueblo, is president of the association.

High School Teachers' Department

Edited by HOPKIN JENKINS, Portland, Oregon

Latin in the Elementary Schools.

The present position of foreign languages in our schools is anomalous. The acquirement of a language is essentially a matter of the memory; and yet the vast majority of our students begin languages when the memory age is coming to a close. The child of 12 takes to Latin derivatives like a duck to water whereas the child of 14 sheds them as a duck does water. The child of 12 yields readily to the drill of any well taught subject, whereas the child of 14, to say nothing of the older student, having begun to develop an interest in social subjects, is not so catholic in his tastes. What presumption then, gratuitously to the subject Latin to the finer competition of the present system and what folly not to begin it at the psychological moment.

The truth of this position is becoming so generally appreciated that many progressive school systems are trying to remedy the situation. Success or failure in the attempt will depend upon whether there is a proper school organization and instruction. In the way of organization it will be necessary to have a principal who is actively in favor of putting Latin into the grades. No less important is it to get the right teacher. First of all she must be a strong grade teacher. She should also be thoroughly versed in the rudiments of the language. The classes should be started with the 6B. Two or three grades may be telescoped for economy in time and effort. The entire curriculum from the 6B to the 8B should be re-organized. It should partake of the elasticity of the present high school course. A few basic studies, such as arithmetic, history, geography, and English should be required of all pupils. To these branches should be added a choice between a language or a vocational subject.

Granted that the conditions are favorable for the introduction of Latin into the grades, the next thing is to arrange the course. First comes the selection of the book. Many schools use Nuttings Primer. The many advantages of this book are largely vitiated by the faulty arrangement, so that I should advise the use of the regularly adopted text. In case the latter course is followed it will be necessary for the teacher to prepare supplementary reading.

The adoption of some such text as Pearson, Scott, or Smith, will help make for thoroughness and thoroughness must be the key note of Latin work in the grades, thoroughness in paradigms, thoroughness in vocabulary, in principal parts, and in parsing.

This drill must be relieved by the use of the direct method. This modern development in the pedagogy of Latin should be used in the presentation of the case idea and in the mastery of the personal endings. From the very first the pupils should become familiar with the Latin words for objects and actions of the school room. By the time they reach the third declension they should learn to parse in Latin. As the uses of the cases arise, the class should learn the question words that fit the corresponding questions; e. g. quare is answered by an ablative of cause. With the development of the principles of the language the teacher will soon find that most of the recitation may be conducted in Latin.

Aside from the advantage to Latin that will come from being started in the grades there is to set down as an added gain the reaction upon our own tongues. If the Latin teacher lives up to her opportunity, she will hammer unceasingly on derivatives and will contiually correlate her subject with English grammar. If so, her English co-adjutor will rise up and call her blessed.

Unless the conditions laid down in this paper pertain it may not be well to put Latin in the grades. If they do, the innovator may feel sure of success and may have the satisfaction of having helped to relieve an intolerable situation.—A. P. McKinlay.

County Superintendents' Department

Edited by CLYDE T. BONNEY, The Dalles, Oregon

A Normal School for Eastern Oregon

The crying need of the rural schools of Eastern Oregon is for better trained teachers. The superiority of normal teachers is very marked. No matter what the natural adaptability of a person may be, special training will render him much more efficient as a teacher. It is impossible to make good schools without trained teachers. The better the teacher's training, the more efficient and successful will be his work. An ideal arrangement is one which will render it possible for teachers to secure their training in that part of the state where they live and then return to their own home county to take up, under conditions that are well known to them, and in an environment which is congenial, the work of training boys and girls for a higher citizenship. This ideal condition cannot be realized for Eastern Oregon until a normal school is established at some central point east of the Cascade mountains. Pendleton is an ideal location for such a normal and will be satisfactory to all of the Eastern Oregon counties. Governor Withycombe of the state of Oregon and such leading educators as Superintendent J. A. Churchill, Superintendent of Public Instruction, President P. L. Campbell of the University of Oregon, President W. J. Kerr of the Oregon Agricultural College, President J. H. Ackerman of the Oregon State Normal at Monmouth, Mr. Robert C. French, former president of the normal school at Weston, Mr. B. F. Mulkey, former president of the normal school of Ashland, have declared in favor of an Eastern Oregon normal school to be located at Pendleton. These men realize fully the educational needs of the state, and their opinion should have great weight. Teachers, parents and all who have at heart the future welfare of the children of Oregon should do all in their power to secure the passage of the measure establishing a normal school at Pendleton. A vote for the Pendleton normal is your part toward bringing to the children of Eastern Oregon the same opportunities for trained teachers now enjoyed by the counties of Western Oregon.—Clyde T. Bonney, Superintendent of Wasco County.

* * *

The Superintendent As a Board Member.

At the June meeting of the county school superintendents the legislative committee recommended that steps be taken toward enacting legislation that would give the superintendent a voice in the selection of teachers. The following article is submitted in behalf of the resolution: Probably at no other point does our school system fail to so great an extent as in the selection and retention of competent teachers. The matter of passing upon the qualifications of teachers requires more experience, more knowledge of school conditions and requirements than is possessed by the great majority of rural school boards. Often extraneous matters, such as kinship, friendship, and residence assume undue importance. Not having definite and dependable standards upon which to base selection, they are at tne mercy of friends with a "pull," or they are forced to accept a mass of "stock-in-trade" testimonials as evidence of fitness. Teachers who make good, teachers who are qualified and make serious efforts to become and remain efficient should have their merits recognized. The task of getting accurate and dependable information concerning such teachers is beyond the facilities of the ordinary school board. At the present time the only person who is in a position to do this for the county as a whole, is the county school superintendent; and the only way in which he can make his knowledge and information available and effective in the selection of teachers is to make the superintendent a member of all boards in districts of the third class when such board meets for the hiring of teachers. As a member of the board he would invariably be consulted to determine the fitness of a teacher, and if there were a difference of opinion

of the regular board members his approval would be necessary to a choice. The superintendent as a board member would be a protection and a source of strength to the efficient teacher. She would feel that her school room work would be the determining factor in gaining or retaining a position. Her selection of a boarding place, or her social proclivities would not assume undue importance. The details of the plan have necessarily been omitted, but it can be worked out, and would, I believe, be a long step toward a more centralized and effective administration of schools.—Fred Peterson, Superintendent of Klamath County.

* * *

Co-operation of County Superintendents.

The semi-annual conventions at Salem do much to promote co-operation among the county superintendents, and in the general discussions which take place, they come to understand one another and the different conditions under which each one labors better; but we might make a few suggestions here as to how this co-operation might be extended: In the matter of recommending teachers from one county to another, each county superintendent should state exactly the conditions surrounding the position before asking the opinion of another county superintendent as to the fitness of the applicant; and in giving this opinion, the other county superintendent should be absolutely frank in stating whether or not the applicant should be elected. County superintendents should be able to place absolute confidence in the recommendations of each other.

Co-operation in the matter of exchange of complete report cards is an important essential to the success of the system and each county superintendent should know perfectly the details of the plan, and carry them out in every particular. We owe it to each other and to the state department to see to it that there is on file in each office a card for each pupil in the county, and that the grades are reported promptly at the end of the year. A card system for a record of the grades made at the eighth grade state examination should be inaugurated, so that a pupil who has grades to his credit in one county, may have them read-ily transferred to another county. One has been installed in this office, and the grades that are made by a pupil at the different examinations that he may take, as well as the date of issuing his diploma, are kept on file, and can be reported to another county without delay.

While the law allows a teacher in a joint district to teach on a permit issued by either county superintendent represented in the district, it is only reasonable to assume that the superintendent that has the school in his county, and therefore supervises it, should issue the permit. In fact, in matters except where the law provides otherwise, the county superintendent in whose county the school house is located should control in all school matters. In the matter of clerks' annual reports, no county superintendent should accept a report until it is exactly correct, and if this is done in a joint district by one superintendent, it brings about an embarrassing condition for the other.

In the matter of registration of certificates, each superintendent should follow the plan provided by the state department for obtaining a reading circle certificate, both because each one should co-operate with the state department, and because a failure to do this will embarrass the county superintendent that wishes to conform to the plan when teachers go from one county to another.

In the matter of exchange of high school tuition money, the closest co-operation is necessary; and it is the duty of each superintendent to secure accurate and complete reports from each high school in the county as to the pupils in attendance from other counties, the number of their resident districts, number of days' attendance, etc. As soon as a county superintendent receives this information, he should, at the earliest moment possible, send a warrant for the tuition of every pupil who is attending high school outside of the county. This exchange will be an easy matter, if all this is done.

In the mater of standardization of schools, each superintendent should hold for exactly what the standardization card calls for, as by allowing schools to become standard when they have not literally complied with the conditions demanded, defeats the real purpose of standardization, and discourages counties that are holding to those conditions.

If one county superintendent has a new idea that is benefitting the schools of his county, he should "pass it along" that other counties may be benefitted also. The state department is doing its part toward this by mailing copies of circular letters received from the various counties.—S. S. Duncan, County School Superintendent for Yamhill County.

* * *

Rural Supervision.

Many states in the Union have tried various forms of supervision in their schools which has recently extended into the rural districts, while others have remained in their puritanical ruts viewing these progressive attempts with skepticism—the result being, nothing attempted, nothing done to alleviate the sad condition among the rural schools. Fortunately Oregon has in its midst many efficient, aggressive, educational men and women who do their work because they love it and love their work because they do it with a pleasing and lasting result. The world is now and will continue to profit by this Oregonian initiative and spirit. Among some things let us refer with pride to the club project work among the schools of our state which is one of the greatest practical trainings a child can get and we observe that the teachers who are enthusiastically engaged in this work are likewise doing enthusiastic and better work in the grade subjects; then the standard school movement which is being adopted by some of our sister states since learning of its advantageous results, and now Oregon is again to be glorified by a new and unquestionably the best form of rural supervision, which has been offered by anyone up to the present time. I refer to M. S. Pittman's plan which was published in the September issue of this magazine. Many teachers as well as patrons in this state have no doubt only heard of rural supervision, but have not been fortunate enough to experience the helpful effect when properly offered. I have recently studied the forms used by various states and from opinions of the best educational men Connecticut seemed to have offered up to this time the most helpful plan, yet those who have studied Mr. Pittman's plan expect more good to be realized from it. A supervisor should be considered a messenger of good who is always ready to aid those who need and desire assistance and there are many such teachers in our rural schools, because of limited training In the city a person in trouble should tell his troubles to a policeman, and a teacher in the rural schools should feel just as free to tell her troubles to the supervisor. In all walks of life people have worked more happily and successfully when they were given assistance when confronted by difficulty. Is not a teacher in the rural school as deserving as anyone? There must be hearty co-operation among teachers and all school officials if we expect to do our duty to our work and our fellow man and we should always accept any suggestion which promises good results. We are anxious to carry out the Pittman plan of supervision in Polk county and with our present staff of teachers we are convinced it will be a record year for accomplishments—Floyd D. Moore, Supervisor for Polk County.

* * *

Benton County.

In the biennial report to the superintendent of public instruction the following were urged: (1) The county unit plan; (2) centers for eighth grade pupils to write on examinations; and (3) a permanent tax in order to increase our state school fund.

Benton county held her county fair September 21, 22 and 23 which was postponed from September 14, 15 and 16. The postponement was made necessary because no covering could be secured for the stock. The school fair was held in connection with the county fair, but several schools had commenced and it was impossible for them to have exhibits.

Out of 61 schools to be in operation in Benton county this year, 36 started September 25, 16 began October 2, and the remainder opened school October 9, that being the latest date set for school to commence in Benton county. All the seasons were late this year, but

school boards conscientiously made an attempt to start school as early as possible.

September 18, 19 and 20 the annual teachers institute of Linn and Benton counties convened in the Presbyterian church in Corvallis. Four hundred and seventeen teachers were present. Superintendent J. A. Churchill, President W. J. Kerr, Edwin T. Read, J. F. Brumbaugh, H. D. Sheldon, Earl Kilpatrick, M. S. Pittman of Monmouth, S. S. Duncan of McMinnville, Jean Parks McCracken of Portland, J. H. Brenneman of Brownsville, H. L. Robe of Tangent, O. V. White of Albany, J. M. Powers of Corvallis, John Teuscher of Portland, and W. L. Finley, completed the list of instructors. Special music was furnished by the Corvallis high school orchestra and Miss Tartar of Corvallis. A public reception was tendered the teachers at the Men's Gym at 8 o'clock Monday night by the Albany and Corvallis commercial clubs. Very fine moving pictures were given Tuesday evening by W. L. Finley, state biologist at the Crystal theatre, which was reserved for the teachers. All the teachers were present, and the institute was a success. M. S. Pittman had charge of the rural school department most of the time and was ably assisted by S. S. Duncan. In the resolutions adopted by the teachers, the Oregon Normal School at Pendleton was strongly indorsed, and all present indicated willingness to support a much needed second normal school in the eastern part of the state.

* * *

Columbia County.

The Columbia county fair closed on Friday, September 22. The schools made a splendid display, filling their building to the limit. The Scappoose schools won the silver cup for the best school exhibit. Second place was won by Warren, St. Helens being third. For best decorated booth, Scappoose won first place; St. Helens second; and Houlton third. Misses Gladys Johnson and Ollie Stoltenberg won a trip to the state fair, having secured the highest number of points on their exhibit at the county fair. Columbia county schools sent an exhibit to the state fair for the first time, in charge of Mrs. J. G. Watts. The St.

Helens Glee Club, under J. H. Mc-
Coy, won the silver cup offered for
best glee club work.

James B. Dodson, late of Dayton,
Ore., has been chosen head of the
Scappoose schools. D. W. Wight is
in charge of the Clatskanie schools.
P. J. Kuntz has enlarged the course
of the Rainier schools considerably,
adding a domestic science course and
a teachers' training course. L. L.
Baker is again in charge of the St.
Helen's schools. C. E. Lake is prin-
cipal of the Houlton school this year
while G. W. Brown is principal at
Yankton, and Lyle B. Chappell at
Quincy. J. P. Claybaugh is principal
at Vernonia. Bertha Stovall, now
Bertha Stovall Fluhrer, remains in
charge at Mayger. The principal at
Goble is Miss Anne J. Ketel; of
Beaver Homes, Miss Anna I. Hales;
of Deer Island, Miss Alice L. Shee-
han. C. J. Russell is in charge at
Warren; Miss Mary McGregor is at
Marshland; while Miss Marguerite
A. Kearns goes to Prescott.

* * *

Douglas County.

Most of the schools of Douglas
county are now in session. The immense prune crop caused many
schools to postpone this opening until the first week in October.

At Roseburg, Prof. Fitzpatrick,
principal of the high school, resigned to accept a position in Montana, and H. Omer Bennett, principal
of the Benson school, was elected to
the position. Roy Dunham, of Medford, is the newly elected principal
of Benson school.

Supervisors H. M. Cross and Geo.
W. Murphy reported to County
Superintendent Brown for duty on
September 1. Mr. Cross makes his
headquarters at Drain and has
charge of the northern section of the
county. Mr. Murphy lives at Riddle
and has charge of the southern section. This is Mr. Cross' third year
of service and Mr. Murphy's second.
The second attempt, within a year,
to do away with the supervisory system by invoking a referendum vote
of the directors was made this summer, with the result that the system
was endorsed by a handsome majority. This victory is due largely to
the efficient work of Supervisors
Cross and Murphy, and their worthy
predecessors.

The Douglas county school industrial fair was held at Roseburg September 13, 14 and 15, in connection
with the annual county fair. Liberal
premiums were offered and exhibits
were entered from practically all
parts of the county. Those winning
free trips to the state fair were Les-
lie Butner, of Fullerton school, Roseburg; Alfred Anderson, of Melrose;
Eva Blackwell, of Riddle; and Leota Wilson, of Yoncalla. Great interest was shown in the canning
team contests. Five teams were entered, including a team of boys from
the Benson school. The Yoncalla
team won first by a small margin
over the Fullerton team. Riddle won
third. The Yoncalla team was trained
by Miss Anna Huntington, who accompanied them to Salem, where
they won first place in the state contest. Two Douglas county boys, Les-
lie Butner, of Roseburg, and John
McMichaels, of Garden Valley, won
scholarships at O. A. C. Douglas
county won third place in the industrial contests at the state fair.

Douglas county has nine standard
four year high schools. They are
Drain, Yoncalla, Oakland, Lutherlin,
Roseburg, Myrtle Creek, Riddle,
Canyonville, and Glendale. Six of
these are under the same superintendents or principals as last year
and changes have been made in three
of them. The new principal at Yoncalla is Emery D. Doane; he succeeds D. W. Wight who goes to Clatskanie. At Sutherlin, Geo. W. Schantin, formerly principal of Oakland
schools, but doing post graduate
work the past year at Harvard, succeeds C. F. Waltman, as principal.
At Myrtle Creek, Prof. E. K. Barnes
is succeeded by Martin D. Coats, of
Klamath Falls. Comparatively few
changes have been made in the
teaching force of these schools.
Those districts making no changes in
the heads of their schools are:
Drain, Watson C. Lea, principal;
Oakland, Alfred Powers, superintendent; Roseburg, F. B. Hamlin,
superintendent; Riddle, H. H. Bronson, principal; Canyonville, J. E.
O'Neel, principal; Glendale, Dr. H.
R. Marsh, superintendent.

* * *

Jefferson County.

Many Waterbury heating plants
have been installed in the rural districts.

The schools of Jefferson county with one exception were in session September 18.

Plans have been approved for two modern school buildings to be erected in the near future.

Two new school districts have been created in this county in the last three months. This raises the number to 40.

Miss Jessie Purdy, a graduate of the Oregon university, has charge of the high school work in Metolius. Miss Purdy is also principal of the grade school.

There are a great many changes in the teaching force in the rural districts but the new force appears to be very enthusiastic and the outlook for a successful school year is very favorable.

The Culver district high school has re-employed Prof. C. K. Overhulse, a graduate of the University of South Dakota. Miss Frances Gittins, a graduate of the Willamette university, is his assistant.

The annual institute for Jefferson county was held September 20, 21 and 22, in the high school building in Madras. Every teacher employed in the county was present throughout the entire three days' session.

The Madras public school is in charge of the very efficient Miss Mary Harrison as principal. Miss Harrison held the same position last year. Her assistants are Raymond Cornwell and the Misses Lela Gard and Flora McWilliams.

The public schools of Culver have an entire new corps of teachers this year, DeWitt Williams having charge of the seventh and eighth grades; S. P. Burgess, the fourth, fifth and sixth grades; and Mrs. Edith Overhulse the primary grades.

Madras Union high school has as principal this year Prof. C. G. Springer, a graduate of Philomath college and of the Oregon State Normal. His assistants are Miss Osee Helena Jewell, a graduate of the University of Michigan, and Mrs. May B. Johnson.

* * *

Morrow County.

The new schoolhouse in district No 48 will be completed soon. This district has been renting a building for more than a year.

The Heppner public school has added a fine grafanola to the equipment of the school. It is to be hoped that other schools in the county will follow the example.

The Morrow county teachers' institute was held at Heppner, September 25-27. Sixty-four teachers were enrolled. The instructors were State Superintendent Churchill, Dr. B. W. DeBusk, M. S. Pittman, Miss Florence Fox, Chas. H. Jones, Dr. D. R. Haylor, and County Superintendent Notson.

The industrial club exhibit from Morrow county at the state fair was awarded second place in the eastern division. The exhibit at the county fair was very commendable, and it was decided to send it to the state fair. Garnett Barratt, Edgar Copenhaver, Vera Cowins, and Elizabeth Brown were the winners of the trip to the state fair camps.

Miss Ruth W. Bowman, the popular teacher in district No. 32, asked to be excused from the institute as soon as she had attended the required time. She informed the superintendent that matters of importance required her to make a long trip into the country. The next day the superintendent received an announcement of her wedding the evening after the close of the institute. Mr. Ralph Adkins is the lucky bridegroom. Mrs. Adkins will continue her work in the school.

* * *

Polk County.

The majority of Polk county schools began either on September 25 or October 2.

The county fair held on September 19, 20 and 21, was a big success and the children answered the call heroically by bringing much club work.

Polk county school children made an excellent showing at the state fair by capturing eight first club project prizes out of 18 that were offered.

Miss Almeda Fuller, who is candidate on Republican ticket for county school superintendent has been assisting with the school exhibits at the fairs.

Superintendent Ford, of Dallas schools reports a slight increase over last year's enrollment. The following teachers have been employed to fill vacancies: High school—Miss Fern Parr of Woodburn who is an O. A. C. graduate and Miss Grant who recently came from the East is a University of Minnesota graduate. Miss Georgia Ellis, of Rickreall, for third grade, Miss Hallie Hart, of Portland, for sixth grade, Miss Helen Gale, of Portland, for fifth grade, and Miss Grace McMinn, of Portland, for seventh grade.

* * *

Wallowa County.

The joint annual institute for Baker, Union, and Wallowa counties, in conjunction with the Eastern Division of the state association, will be held at LaGrande, November 1, 2 and 3. This will be a big meeting and no teacher can afford to miss it. The best educators of the state and some of the best in the United States will be present and will have a lot of good things to say to teachers. Everybody come.

One of the best educational meetings of the year was held at Flora, in the northern part of the county, September 23. Teachers from Joseph, Enterprise, Lostine, and Wallowa went in autos and had a delightful drive of about 40 miles through the timber, enjoyed the beautiful scenery, killed grouse, repaired punctured tires and had the time of their lives. There were about 40 teachers present. Flora has a modern eight room school building, built last year, but are using only four rooms at present. They have a two year high school with Mr. Wilbur Van Pelt at the head.

The school fair, held at Enterprise September 1, 2 and 3, in conjunction with the county fair, was a decided success, Wallowa taking first cash prize of $50, for the best exhibit from the town schools, and Hurricane Creek, district No. 3, a like amount for the best rural exhibit. The exhibits from all were fine and the teachers and pupils are entitled to a great deal of credit for the showing they made. The demonstration work in manual training, sewing, cooking, canning, type-writing, etc., was splendid and was greatly appreciated by all. Wallowa has one of the best manual training departments in the state.

Wasco County.

The following entitled "Wealth in Economy" is Thrift Lesson No. 4 as sent out to the teachers of Wasco county by the school superintendent: (1) Economy is the battle of life.—Spurgeon. (2) Economy is the parent of integrity, of liberty and ease, and the beauteous sister of temperance, of cheerfulness and of health.—Dr. Johnson. (3) Riches amassed in haste will diminish; but those collected by hand and little by little will multiply.—Goethe. (4) No gain is so certain as that which proceeds from the economical use of what you have.—Latin Proverb. (5) Debt is like any other trap, easy enough to get into, but hard enough to get out of.—H. W. Shaw. (6) Economy is the poor man's mint.—Tupper. (7) "We shan't get much here," whispered a lady to her companion, as John Murray blew out one of the two candles by whose light he had been writing, when they asked him to contribute to some benevolent object. He listened to their story and gave $100. "Mr. Murray, I am very agreeably surprised," said the lady quoted, "I did not expect to get a cent from you." The old Quaker asked the reason for her opinion, and, when told, said, "That, ladies is the reason I am able to let you have the hundred dollars. It is by practicing economy that I save up money with which to do charitable actions. One candle is enough to talk by."—From Marden's Architect of Fate.

* * *

Jackson County.

At the joint teachers' institute held in Grants Pass, Ore., October 11, 12, and 13, the teachers of Jackson county presented retiring County Superintendent J. Percy Wells a beautiful gold watch as an appreciation of his work. The committee in charge of the gift selected Prof. Van Scoy to make the presentation. In a few well-chosen words, Mr. Van Scoy traced the growth of Jackson county's schools under the supervision and management of Mr. Wells' term of office saying in part: "Mr. Wells, a Jackson county boy, familiar with the condition of Jackson county schools and their greatest needs had labored faithfully and efficiently for the betterment of the entire school system. That he had succeeded admirably the present status of the schools bore abundant testimony." Mr. Wells, in response, said to the teachers that words failed to express the gratitude he felt for the manifestation of friendship and love that his co-workers had for him. Modestly, he disclaimed any honor or credit for the progress of Jackson county schools, attributing all of it to the loyalty and perseverance of the teachers of the county. Mr. Wells has served as superintendent of Jackson county schools for a number of years and in retiring takes with him the highest appreciation of those who know him best. The schools of the county will long bear the impress of Mr. Wells' work and personality.

Rural School Department

Edited by MRS. M. L. FULKERSON, Salem, Oregon

Club Work.

Club work is the performance of a definite enterprise or enterprises based upon the most economic practices of the farm and home. It is based on sound principles and has come to stay. It is supported by federal and state aid as a definite form of agricultural extension work. Boys and girls on the farm are in this work, and every possible advantage is extended to fit them for a better living "to improve county life," thus bettering our government. Its purpose is to enlist the boys and girls of the state in profitable and interesting activities, which will develop them into economic producers; thus helping these boys and girls to find themselves in useful training in place of allowing them to drift into useless or harmful occupation. It develops leadership and creates co-operation, it inspires the right attitude towards honest toil, and a spirit of sympathy for some calling, however humble. It teaches the child to learn a few basic facts relating to agriculture, animal husbandry, home economics, and relative topics, which he or she will use many times to advantage in future life. It helps to make the whole community more efficient and creates a deeper respect for the school as an educational center. In Oregon club work is carried on by the Oregon Agricultural College, the United States Department of Agriculture, and State Department of Education, all working in co-operation. There were last year 127,822 members enrolled in the club work in the United States, and 11,642 in Oregon, in the following projects: Corn growing, potato growing, vegetable gardening, poultry raising, pork production, dairy herd record keeping, fruit raising, seed grain selection, rural home beautification, farm and home handicraft, baking, canning, and sewing.

The plan of the work is as follows: The child enrolls in the project or projects (and we prefer that not more than one project be carried by a member, as one project well completed is better than several poorly done) with the Oregon Agricultural College, and receives from the college instructions, bulletins circular letters and report blanks, prepared by the members of the faculty of the college and by the department of agriculture of the United States. These all pertain to the particular project the club member may have selected. All help possible is given to the club member throughout the year by the state club leader and his assistants from the college, by the two field workers from the state department of education and by different members of the extension department of the agricultural college, the county agriculturists in counties where these are employed, and the county school superintendent, around whom all club work in his or her county revolves.

The club member is urged to carry his or her project or enterprise to completion, making a report to the state club leader on blanks furnished for the same, and to have an exhibit of the work accomplished at local county and state fairs, if possible. It is urged that local and county fairs be held for the purpose of settling all club awards, also to permit the people of the community or county to examine the work of the members. This will create greater interest in the work and promote a greater community spirit. All who can should exhibit at the state fair, thus helping to promote interest in our state fair which is one of our greatest schools for practical education and also to allow the club members to compete for the state prizes, offered by the state fair board and by public spirited business men of Portland. The later prizes being a trip to the Oregon Agricultural College for the state winner in each project, this trip to cover the two weeks summer school for boys and girls with all their expenses.

Last year 21 boys and girls of Oregon won as many trips and attended the school. This year we have hundreds of boys and girls competing for similar trips.

Last but not least of the club work are the canning teams from the different counties. There is too much waste in Oregon of fruits and vegetables, and a few canning teams will greatly reduce this waste, as well as being profitable to themselves from a money viewpoint. Also the health of those who are thus able to have more fruit and vegetables on the home table, will be benefitted.

Thus club work is in keeping with its motto, "Make the better best," and its emblem of a four-leaf clover, with the four H's representing the head, the heart, the hand, and the health.

* * *

SELECTIONS FOR THANKSGIVING

It should be easy this year to find plenty of material for the decoration of the schoolhouse walls The woods are rich in many-colored leaves. It should be easy, too, to collect many and varied specimens of crops. Let committees be appointed to collect whatever may be necessary.

Betty's Thanksgiving Wish.

She held the wishbone tight with me,
And pulled, and won, exultingly.
"Now Betty, wish," I said, "for when
You get the biggest half, why then
The Wish you wish will come true.
Now wish, dear, as we told you to."
Then Betty looked, with longing eyes

At all the dishes, nuts, and pies,
And, holding up the bit of bone,
She said, with triumph in her tone,
"All right. I wish tomorrow, then,
Would be Thanksgiving day, again!"
    —Mary Carolyn Davies.

If.

If c-a-t spelt dog and cow
And horse and mouse and heaven,
If two plus two made six and nine
And twelve and eighty-seven,
If "see the man" was all there was
To learn inside my reader,
No boy would be as bright as I,
In school I'd be the leader.

If school took up at nine and then
Let out in an hour or less,
If half of this was singing songs
And the other half recess,
If all the days were holidays
'Cept Christmas and Thanksgiving
I'd know what people mean who talk
About the joy of living.
    —St. Nicholas.

On Thanksgiving Day.

Let us give thanks to those who sow
The grain and fruit that make us
    grow.
Thanks for the sun, the rain, the
    snow,
That helped the grain and fruit to
    grow.
Thanks for the turkey and the pie,
Thanks that we live and did not die.
Thanks for the coming of the fall,
Thanks unto God who gives us all.
    —Selected.

Thanksgiving for Harvest.

(Air—The North Wind Doth Blow.)
The harvest is in, the cellar and bin
    Are stored with the fruits of the
    earth;
So let us be gay on Thanksgiving
    Day,
    And keep it with feasting and
    mirth.

For all the good things the rich
    Autumn brings,
For all that the harvest can show,
Most thankful we'd be, dear Father,
    to Thee.
    Whose power and love made them
    grow.
            —Selected.

An Evening Caller.

When the round moon shone so
   bright
On the autumn fields last night,
When the little sleepyheads
All were cuddled in their beds,
Some one came a-calling here,
Though none heard him drawing
   near,
For his footsteps made no clatter,
Not the softest pitter-patter.

All the oaks in purple dressed
To receive their quiet guest;
Maple flamed from root to crown
In a splendid scarlet gown,
And the birch wore wealth untold,
Hung about with wreaths of gold;
Such a grand occasion is it
When this stranger pays a visit.

When the sun rose warm and bright
He slipped softly out of sight,
But beneath the chestnut-tree
He has left you something—see!
Ripe and brown and sound and sweet
Scattered all around your feet;
And we know, when nuts are falling,
That Jack Frost has come a-calling.
     The Youth's Companion.

Thanksgiving Day.

O'er pleasant mead and rugged glen
We keep Thanksgiving Day again,
While bells of joy triumphant ring,
In church and hall the people sing
Their harvest songs, so sweet and
   clear,
Glad anthems of a fruitful year.

From princely home and city street
Come wanderers back with eager feet
To the old farm, where childhood
   hours
Were gaily spent 'mid fragrant flow-
   ers;
Where childhood lessons learned so
   well
It is their joy again to tell.

So long they tarried, but today
They seek the homes where fathers
   pray,
Where sisters and where brothers
   stand
To welcome each with loving hand;
Where mothers with fond smile and
   dear
Serve as of yore, Thanksgiving cheer.
     —Ruth Raymond.

Thanksgiving Story.

The ripe rosy apples are all gathered
   in;
They wait for the winter in barrel
   and bin;
And nuts for the children, a plentiful
   store,
Are spread out to dry on the board
   attic floor;
The great golden pumpkins, that
   grew such a size,
Are ready to make into Thanksgiving pies;
And all the good times that children
   hold dear,
Have come round again with the
   feast of the year.

Now what shall we do in our bright
   happy homes,
To welcome this time of good times
   as it comes?
And what do you say is the very
   best way
To show we are grateful on Thanksgiving Day?
The best thing that hearts that are
   thankful can do
Is this: To make thankful some
   other hearts, too;
For lives that are grateful, and sunny, and glad,
To carry their sunshine to lives that
   are sad;
For children who have all they want
   and to spare
Their good things with poor little
   children to share;
For this will bring blessing, and this
   is the way
To show we are thankful on Thanksgiving Day.
     —Selected.

The Feast-Time of the Year.

This is the feast-time of the year,
When hearts grow warm, and home
   more dear;
When autumn's crimson torch ex-
   pires,
To flash again in winter's fires.
And they who tracked October's
   flight,
Through woods with gorgeous hues
   bedight,
In charmed circle sit and praise
The goodly log's triumphant blaze;
This is the feast-time of the year,
When plenty pours her wine of cheer,
And even humble boards may spare,
To poorer poor a kindly share.
While bursting barns and granaries
   know

A richer fuller overflow,
And they who dwell in golden ease,
Bless without toil, yet toil to please.
This is the feast-time of the year,
The blessed advent draweth near;
Let rich and poor together break
The bread of love, for Christ's sweet
  sake;
Again the time when rich and poor
Must ope for Him a common door
Who comes a guest, yet makes a
  feast,
And bids the greatest and the least.
                        —Selected.

Thanksgiving Joys.

Cartloads of pumpkins, as yellow as
  gold,
Onions in silvery strings,
Shining red apples and clusters of
  grapes,
Nuts and a host of good things,—
Chickens and turkeys and fat little
  pigs—
  These are what Thanksgiving
  brings.

Work is forgotten and play-time be-
  gins,
From office and schoolroom and
  hall,
Fathers and mothers and uncles and
  aunts,
Nieces and nephews and all
Speed away home, as they hear from
  afar,
  The voice of old Thanksgiving call.

Now is the time to forget all your
  cares,
Cast every trouble away,
Think of your blessings, remember
  your joys,
Don't be afraid to be gay!
None are too old, and none are too
  young,
  To frolic on Thanksgiving Day.
                        —Youth's Companion.

That Things Are No Worse, Sire.

From the time of our old Revolution,
  When we threw off the yoke of
  the King,
Has descended this phrase to remem-
  ber—
To remember, to say, and to sing;
'Tis a phrase that is full of a lesson;
  It can comfort and warm like a
  fire;
It can cheer us when days are the
  darkest:
  "That things are no worse, O my
  sire!"

'Twas King George's prime minister
  said it,
  To the King, who had questioned,
  in heat,
What he meant by appointing
  Thanksgiving
In such days of ill-luck and defeat.
"What's the cause of your day of
  Thanksgiving?
  Tell me, pray," cried the King in
  his ire.
Said the minister, "This is the
  reason—
  That things are no worse, O my
  sire!"
                        —Helen Hunt Jackson.

Preserving Time.

Said Mrs. Baldwin Apple
  To Mrs. Bartlett Pear:
"You're growing very plump, madam
And also very fair.

"And there's Mrs. Clingstone Peach,
  So mellowed by the heat,
Upon my word, she really looks
  Quite good enough to eat.

"And all the Misses Crabapple
  Have blushed so rosy red
That very soon the farmer's wife
  To pluck them will be led.

"Just see the Isabellas!
  They're growing so apace
That they really are beginning
  To get purple in the face.

"Our happy time is over,
  For Mrs. Green Gage Plum
Says she knows unto her sorrow
  Preserving time has come."

"Yes," said Mrs. Bartlett Pear,
  "Our day is almost o'er,
And soon we shall be smothering
  In syrup by the score."

And before the month was ended,
  The fruits that looked so fair,
Had vanished from among the leaves
  And the trees were stripped and
  bare.

They were all in jars and bottles
  Or in some dreadful scrape.
"I'm cider," said the apple;
  "I'm jelly," cried the grape.

They were all in jars and bottles
  Upon the shelf arrayed,
And in their midst poor Mrs. Quince
  Was turned to marmalade.
                        —Popular Fashions.

The First Thanksgiving.

"And now," said the Governor,
gazing
Abroad on the piled-up store
Of the sheaves that dotted the clear-
ings,
And covered the meadows o'er,
"'Tis meet that we render praises
Because of this yield of grain,
'Tis meet that the Lord of the harvest
Be thanked for his sun and rain.

"And therefore, I, William Bradford,
(By the grace of God, today,
And the franchise of this people)
Governor of Plymouth, say,
Through virtue of vested power,
Ye shall gather with one accord,
And hold in the month of November
Thanksgiving unto the Lord.

"So, shoulder your match-locks, mas-
ters,
There is hunting of all degrees,
And, fishermen, take your tackle
And scour for the spoils the seas.
And maidens and dames of Plymouth
Your delicate crafts employ
To honor our first Thanksgiving
And make it a feast of joy."

At length came the day appointed;
The snow had begun to fall,
But the clang from the meeting-
house belfry,
Rang merrily over all
And summoned the folks of Plym-
outh,
Who hastened with one accord
To listen to Elder Brewster,
As he fervently thanked the Lord.

In his seat sat Govenor Bradford;
Men, matrons and maidens fair,
Miles Standish and all of his soldiers
With corselet and sword were
there.
And sobbing and tears of gladness
Had each in turn its sway;
For the grave of sweet Rose Stand-
ish,
O'ershadowed Thanksgiving Day.

And when Massasoit, the Sachem,
Sat down with his hundred braves,
And ate of the varied riches
Of gardens and woods and waves,
And looked on the granaried harvest,
With a blow on his brawny chest,
He mutered, "The good Great Spirit
Loves his white children best."
—From Colonial Ballads.

Thanksgiving Program.

The Thanksgiving program can
very easily be the culmination of the
November work. Let the stories and
compositions be of early colony days.
Drawings of the Mayflower, log
houses, block houses, spinning
wheels, turkeys and other things pertaining to those early times will
make good illustrations for the written work. Make a study of written
invitations and then have the children write invitations to their parents to attend the program. Illustrate the invitations with one of the
above suggested drawings. Boys
dressed as Puritans may act as door
keepers and Puritan maids may
usher and give out the programs.

Program:

Song, Thanksgiving song, Jessie
Gaynor.
Composition, Life in Colonial
Days.
Poem, Landing of the Pilgrims,
Mrs. Hemans.
Song, by Little Folks, Over the
River, Music Reader No. 1.
Poem, When the Frost Is On the
Pumpkin, Riley.
Song, Thanksgiving, Music Read-
er No. 2.
Poem, The Pumpkin, Whittier.
Tableau, Pilgrims Going to Church.
Let the children be costumed as are
the figures in the picture seen on
page 128 of the Kimball's Elementary English Book.
Tableau, Church Scene. Let the
people come in and take their seats
and listen attentively while the
preacher from his high pulpit reads
to them. One or two little folks may
fall asleep and the magistrate taps
them with his stick.
Tableau, Thanksgiving Party. Matrons may set a table with all the
fruits of the season and when all is
prepared the families and their
guests, the Indians, may draw
around and partake.
Costumes can be easily made. Pattern after those in pictures. Use
simple settings, but draw on the ingenuity of the children for all the
things needed.—Katherine Arbuthnot, Oregon Normal School, Monmouth.

* * *

The Course of Study in Agriculture.

It is with hesitancy that the auth-
or approaches the task of preparing

an article on a topic so self-explanatory. Certainly the course of study is well prepared, and in the introduction the point of view of its author is clearly stated. In spite of this, however, there are those who fail to catch the significance of its use. For example one teacher writes: "The course of study advises us to 'arrange to have a cow brought to school' when studying dairying but the state board of health orders us to keep the school premises in a sanitary condition. Now, whose orders are we to follow?" Another writes, "You advise us to have live bees for study, what are you going to do if you don't have them and can't get any in the county?" These are merely samples, many others might be cited.

Yes, you are correct; it is sad, but true. And what is more, it comes second nature with some. We can furnish subject matter and method, but we cannot furnish the push or sound judgment necessary to insure proper usage. That remains for the individual. In these two cases both were missing.

It is a simple matter to advise how the course of study may be made to serve. But after the advice is given what will it amount to if the recipient does not possess the initiative to transfer it to his or her problems. Briefly this is the advice: Read the introduction to the course of study until the author's point of view has become yours, then follow directions and proceed.

Most of the faltering questions come from teachers not possessing technical training in agriculture. Of course to handle the subject to best advantage one needs the subject matter himself. When this phase of training has been omitted, the only thing the teacher can do is to make the best of it under the circumstances. Now does it mean that this teacher will fail. The writer has in mind a teacher who by merely following the directions of the course of study so stimulated the pig club boys in that school that all five of the boys did good work, four winning prizes at the county and two at the state fairs. The teacher visited the boys and discussed the situation with the parents and boys, but never offered information more technical than the boys had studied in their class assignments. If one teacher can do this, certainly others can.

Before you question the technicalities of the course of study or discard it as some do, solve this situation. Each year a corps of industrial club organizers, sent from the state office and agricultural college, scour the state offering suggestions, assisting in organizing clubs and everywhere giving unselfish efficient service to all teachers who are willing to use it. Fall rolls around and the unsuccessful teacher is found condoling herself with the thought, "Nobody told me how to organize a club." Whose fault is it, is it a lack of subject matter or method? The wise superintendent knows, but he isn't telling. So it is with the course of study. Once the teacher actually follows directions the bees will take care of themselves. Will you be one of those to follow directions?—L. P. Gilmore, Monmouth, Oregon.

I would rather plant a single acorn that will make an oak of a century and a forest of a thousand years, than sow a thousand morning glories that give joy for a day and are gone tomorrow. For the same reason I would rather plant one living truth in the heart of a child that will multiply through the ages, than scatter a thousand brilliant conceits before a great audience that will flash like sparks for an instant, and like sparks disappear forever.—Edward Leigh Pell.

A Mother's Creed.

I believe in the eternal importance of the home as the fundamental institution of society. I believe in the immeasurable possibilities of every boy and girl. I believe in the imagination, the trust, the hopes, and the ideals that dwell in the hearts of all children. I believe in the beauty of nature, of art, of books and of friendship. I believe in the little homely joys of everyday life. I believe in the goodness of the great design that lies behind our complex world. I believe in the safety and peace which surround us all through the overbrooding love of God.—Mrs. Ozora S. Davis.

There are two ways of being happy—we may either diminish our wants or increase our means; either will do—the result is the same.—Franklin.

Membership in the State Teachers' Association

The Oregon Teachers Monthly, on July 1, 1916, became the official journal of the State Teachers' Association (both divisions) and the price was raised to $1.50 per year, 50 cents of which goes to the Association. At the end of 3½ months (October 15) the following teachers had paid $1.50 for their subscription to the Oregon Teachers Monthly, thereby entitling them to membership in the State Teachers' Association:

1 Nellie V. King, Winant
2 Fred Schepman, Waldport
3 John Blough, Toledo
4 Maggie L. Hampton, Toledo
5 M. Lillian Ernest, Denzer
6 Earl Brown, Philomath
7 Chas. Hart, Roselodge
8 S. S. Gossman, Chitwood
10 J E. Davis, Chitwood
11 R. E. Wood, Orton
12 John Miller, Eddyville
13 Verne Ross, Toledo
14 T. E. Wilson, Turner
15 Paul Wyman, Bay City
16 Chas. Holway, Halsey
17 Laura A. Smith, Cottage Grove
18 H. W. Herron, Portland
19 Mary B. Scollard, Woodburn
20 L. W. Turnbull, Coquille
21 Hazel Henkle, Monkland
22 A. C. Strange, Baker
23 Anna Dunsmore, Orenco
24 Margaret Williams, Portland
25 Adella Chapler, Salem
26 Margaret Boggess, Veneta
27 W. M. Sutton, Burns
28 W. G. Beattie, Eugene
29 Mary E. Slade, Albany
30 Mrs. L. K. Page, Springfield
31 Mrs. A. Alexander, Portland
32 Barbara Hoch, Pendleton
33 Blanche Padley, Bandon
34 Kate Ronde, Clatskanie
35 Edith Harper, Freewater
36 Edith Smith, Banks
37 Alice Rasmussen, Troutdale
38 Della Zimmerman, Troutdale
39 Adda Wright, Warrenton
40 N. A. Frost, Forest Grove
41 Edna Pence, Salem
42 Erica Nordhausen, Aurora
43 Clara Ireland, Portland
44 Julie H. Burch, Oregon City
45 J. P. McGlasson, North Plains
46 Ethel Davis, Myrtle Creek
47 Mrs. E. H. Morrison, Portland
48 Coral Garvin, Corvallis
49 Inez Easton, Sitkum
50 Alethia Chapman, LaGrande
51 May Smith, Mabel
52 Helen Treat, Buell
53 Virginia Nottingham, Carlton
54 Elma Roberts, Sumner
55 Ruby Skinner, Lakeview
56 Frances Potter, Canby
57 Harriet B. Horrigan, Hillsboro
58 Grace Egbert, The Dalles
59 Mary B. Underwood, Philomath
60 Ruth Dunbabin, Bourne
61 M. T. Means, Philomath
62 Mildred Taylor, Scappoose
63 Marie Senn, Barlow
64 Bessa Lehmann, Sutherlin
65 Anna Bachmann, Clackamas
66 Adeline Buyserie, Hubbard
67 Isa Isaacson, Junction City
68 Anna Weisenborn, Deer Island
69 Myrel A. Bond, Irving
70 Rada Antrim, Amity
71 Marvin F. Wood, Corvallis
72 Carl E. Morrison, Perrydale
73 Walthia Watson, Roseburg
74 H. C. Ostien, Monmouth
75 Eula Campbell, Freewater
76 M. S. Pittman, Monmouth
77 Hazel Goger, Boring
78 Clara Spiekerman, The Dalles
79 Mamie Harper, Wren
80 R. S. Bixby, Nolin
81 Mattie Foster, Klamath Falls
82 Nell G. Lloyd, Klondike
83 Margaret Rice, Shaniko
84 Martha Chase, Portland
85 Myrtle Clayville, Portland
86 C. D. Watkins, Dilley
87 Clara Larson, Toledo
88 Emma Murray, Klamath Falls
89 Marion Ford, Klamath Falls
90 May Wheaton, Coquille
91 Fannie G. Porter, Oregon City
92 Mable F. Johnson, Butte Falls
93 Helene Ogsburg, Eugene
94 Velma Beardslee, Arlington
95 Gladys Anderson, Clear Lake, Ia.
96 Alice Lytle, Bonanza
97 Vara Stewart, Portland
98 Charles Knocke, Mt. Carmel, N. D.
99 Lydia Unden, Winchester
100 Jewell Delk, Drain
101 Matilda Jacobs, Portland
102 Mrs. Gladys Smith, Springfield
103 Helen Anderson, Meda
104 Alma Nichols, Culver
105 Gladys Hatcher, Buell
106 Sylvia Severance, Lexington
107 Dagmar Jeppesen, Boyd
108 Ora England, Walker
109 Florence E. Howatt, Portland
110 Rachel May, Timber
111 Ellen M. Yocum, Amity
112 Alice Jenkins, Eugene
113 Harry Whitten, Kingsley
114 Violet M. Stolle, Irving
115 Violet McCarl, Portland
116 Maude Largent, Hulit
117 Elnor Sherk, Sutherlin
118 Ruth Peterson, Yoncalla
119 Grace Atkinson, Walton
120 Mrs. Mary Hulin, Carpentaria, Cal.
121 Mary E. Moore, Irving
122 Vera Merchant, Lebanon
123 Emma Kennedy, Coquille
124 Maybelle Wagner, McMinnville
125 Marguerite Freydig, Sutherlin
126 Ruth A. Brown, Eagle Creek
127 Ranie P. Burkhead, Shaniko
128 Mabel McFadden, Halfway
129 Angie Halley, Medford
130 Goldie Groth, Freewater
131 Justina Kildee, Sutherlin
132 May B. Lund, Coquille
133 Mildred Jones, Amity
134 Grace V. Perce, Medford
135 Myrtle Ess, Klamath Falls
136 Sadie Heiberger, Wedderburn
137 Marie A. Smith, Buena Vista
138 Carolyn Woods, Cottage Grove
139 Ruth Finlay, Silverton
140 Luella Daniel, Milton
141 Wilbert O. Wilson, Kopiah, Wash.
142 Nettye Moore, Flat River, Mo.
143 Ida Anderson, Early
144 Clara Luther, Halsey
145 Caroline Luther, Redmond
146 Clara Schneider, Gaston
147 Maud Keysaw, Walterville
148 Gladys Burr, Oregon City
149 Emily L. Marshall, Willamette
150 Lapensa Amrine, Oregon City
151 Arabella Davis, Portland
152 Pansy Oswald, Gladstone
153 Pearle Ruegg, Gresham

154 Loney Yoder, Hubbard
155 Mrs. H. L. Hull, Oregon City
156 Ruth F. Hudson, Mulino
157 Elizabeth Roach, Cherryville
158 Brenton Vedder, Gladstone
159 Ruth M. Lingle, Boring
160 John R. Bowland, Oregon City
161 A. C. Thompson, Milwaukie
162 Raymond Boyer, Rickreall
163 L. H. Mallicoat, Boring
164 T. J. Gary, Portland
165 Ellen DeHaven, Salem
166 Jessie Hartley, Portland
167 Amy McDaniel, Weston
168 Rena Roper, Vancouver, Wash.
169 Stella Swift, Junction City
170 Louise Nimmo, Albany
171 Minnie Kulmke, Salem
172 Wm. Westenskow, Imbler
173 D. A. Hoag, Sodaville
174 Laura Moore, Molalla
175 C. Edna Kennedy, Barton
176 Helen M. Hall, Molalla
177 Olga Hanson, Clackamas
178 Margaret Summer, Tigard
179 Mrs. Nannie Thomas, Molalla
180 Mary A. Bickner, Oswego
181 Cora Hasselbrink, Sherwood
182 Chas. H. Jones, Salem
183 Lunah W. Wallace, Huntington
184 Mabel Wallace, Willamina
185 Anna Nelson, Palmer
186 Adeline Brown, Kingsley
187 Miriam Underwood, Oakland
188 Ozella Anderson, Parkplace
189 Mary E. Sherer, Corvallis
190 Winnifred Roe, Monument
191 Matilda F. Grossen, Hillsboro
192 Vernus Young, Echo
193 Edison Fowler, Riverside
194 Mrs. E. D. Sprague, Lake
195 Lucile J. Lisher, Portland
196 Margaret McDonald, Portland
197 Georgia Smith, Mayville
198 Aver Black, Tygh Valley
199 Viola Ortschild, Portland
200 Margaret Ferguson, Siltscoos
201 Lena Gribble, Aurora
202 Agnes Weatherson, Minerva
203 Benedictine Sisters, Oregon City
204 Myrtle Birtchet, Mt. Angel
205 Viola Nagel, Gaston
206 Gladys Jory, Salem
207 Anna C. Taylor, North Powder
208 C. H. Wilson, Condon
209 May Payne, Mitchell
210 Gladys Denney, Oakland
211 Laura Brenner, Oregon City
212 Pearl Wilson, Milton
213 J. B. Lent, Fairview
214 Mrs. A. E. Watson, Portland
215 Mary Ulen, Portland
216 J. B. Horner, Corvallis
217 Nina Taylor, Portland
218 M. E. V. Hess, Portland
219 Hattiebelle Ogilbee, Portland
220 Helen Dahl, Gresham
211 C. G. Springer, Madras
222 Eva Schneider, Boring
223 Ruth Schmuckli, Portland
224 Marian Robertson, Gresham
225 Nellie Renshaw, Mayville
226 Maude B. Mickel, Gresham
227 P. C. Fulton, Holbrook
228 L. B. Gibson, Hood River
229 Mrs. Ora D. Fleming, Lents
230 Ada Werner, Portland
231 E. Williams, Portland
232 Nellie Washburn, Portland
233 Mrs. Margaret B. West, Portland
234 Minerva Powell, Troutdale
235 Marguerite Miller, Portland
236 Mabel F. Burghduff, Portland
237 Louise Sterling, Corbett
238 Vina Swan, Camas, Wash.
239 Mrs. Jennie Carr, Portland
240 Cornelia J. Spencer, Portland
241 Eva S. Rice, Portland

242 Frances S. Estes, Portland
243 Emma Rueter, Portland
244 Mrs. Minnie Parsons, Portland
245 Nell O. Bevans, Portland
246 Mary E. Hill, Portland
247 Estelle Marias, Portland
248 Lutie E. Cake, Portland
249 Margaret L. Pomeroy, Portland
250 Evlyn Cornutt, Portland
251 C. May Moriarty, Portland
251 Phila Nicoll, Portland
254 Kate E. Wiest, Astoria
254 Jeanette Pound, Salem
255 Mina Magness, Myrtle Point
256 W. F. Cornwell, McEwen
257 Leila Lasley, Toledo
258 Clara Straughan, Pendleton
259 Mary Stein, Union
260 W. M. Smith, Salem
261 A. R. Nichols, Corvallis
262 Frank W. Weber, Bend
263 Margaret V. Thomas, Gardiner
264 Jessie Wagener, Alsea
265 Edna Burke, Boring
266 Luann Hiatt, Tillamook
267 Mrs. S. E. Barnes, Portland
268 Ivan D. Wood, Union
269 Mabel Saunders, Richland
270 Reta E. Waller, Oakland
271 Marie Wainright, Mayville
272 Ruth H. Ball, Klamath Agency
273 Mrs. Edith Coleman, Lafayette
274 Jessie Armstrong, Astoria
275 Mrs. W. G. Thompson, Nyssa
276 Hugh J. Boyd, Portland
277 Emma Clanton, Portland
278 Merle A. Nimmo, Springfield
279 Blanche Darby, Wilderville
280 Margaret L. Davies, Mt. Vernon
281 Mabel St. Pierre, Salem
282 Ruth E. Hyland, Oakridge
283 G. W. Nash, Bellingham, Wash.
284 Dorothy Waugh, Portland
285 Freda Bohn, Woodburn
286 Delia Rynning, Estacada
287 Ava Owen, Beaver
288 Myrtice Fowler, Nortons
289 Beatrice Buckner, Oak Grove
290 Alice L. Bennett, Mosier
291 Bessie G. Immel, Marshfield
292 Adella Mortensen, Early
293 W. M. Kent, Gold Beach
294 G. P. Harrington, Gold Beach
295 Mrs. Alida Laduron, Brookings
296 W. H. Grant, Cecil
297 Fay Duff, Pendleton
298 Beulah Thorp, Aurora
299 Florence Buell, Oakland
300 Louisa E. Counsell, LaGrande
301 F. A. Bloomfield, Derby
302 E. H. Anderson, Newberg
303 Ethel Ross, Newberg
304 A. R. Tollefson, Corbett
305 Minnie Mascher, Silverton
306 Benedictine Sisters, Woodburn
307 Roy Bower, Lorane
308 Elizabeth Martin, Boyd
309 Minnie Fortna, Athena
310 Neita Lewis, Newberg
311 Lena Wolcott, Peak
312 Winifred King, Corvallis
313 E. Pearl Smith, Corvallis
314 E. H. Castle Philomath
315 G. E. Ross Lebanon
316 Ferd W. Jones, Corvallis
317 Mrs. Earl Miller, Albany
318 Rose Kaldor, Monroe
319 Rhoda Newkirk, Monroe
320 J. V. Kane, Lyons
321 J. E. Dunton, Lebanon
322 Elsie Moore, Corvallis
323 Anna Denman, Lebanon
324 W. L. Jackson, Albany
325 Mrs. Daisy Allen, Shedd
326 J. M. Poe, Berlin
327 Victoria Soderstrom, Harrisburg
328 Nora C. Coleman, Sweet Home
329 Clara Van Matre, Alpine

330	Estella Dooney, Foster	418	Beatrice Runcall, Portland
331	Alice Boyle, Brownsville	419	Ruby Fenwick, Jordan Valley
332	Mary Connet, Foster	420	Laura S. Barry, Plush
333	Engra Benson, Crawfordsville	421	Lulu Maxwell, Banks
334	Smith B. Holt, Thomas	422	F. Irma Coon, Lauree
335	Ruth Simpson, Suver	423	Bess Palmer, Springfield
336	V. B. Higbee, Albany	424	Ethel Mudge, Heceta
337	Jennie Reed, Harrisburg	425	Maude Wakefield, Ione
338	Mrs. Hattie Allen, Hoskins	426	H. O. Nedry, Hardman
339	Sisters of Mercy, Roseburg	427	Sylvia McCarty, Sinnott
340	Jacob Stocker, Foster	428	Catherine J. Doherty, Ione
341	Acie D. McClain, Lebanon	429	H. H. Hoffman, Heppner
342	Ruth A. Wight, Lebanon	430	Sophia Burke, Heppner
343	Mary A. Binns, Monroe	431	Mrs. Blanche Watkins, Heppner
344	Urich S. Burt, Corvallis	432	L. A. Doak, Ione
345	H. B. Brookhardt, Albany	433	S. E. Notson, Heppner
346	Arline Hoerr, Lebanon	434	S. H. Doak, Lexington
347	Helen Myers, Albany	435	E. S. Payne, Heppner
348	Bessie Truelove, Corvallis	436	W. L. Suddarth, Irrigon
349	Joy Extel, Corvallis	437	Orlena Suddarth, Irrigon
350	M. J. Looney, Tangent	438	Edna Carmichael, Lexington
351	Frank Brumbaugh, Lebanon	439	Lera Githens, Morgan
352	G. M. Sprague, Mill City	440	Mrs. Lucy T. Wedding, Heppner
353	Gussie Stadden, Summit	441	Myrtle Miller, Lena
354	O. J. Schroyer, Summit	442	Josephine McDevitt, Lena
355	Helen Metcalf, Scio	443	Olive Moss, Portland
356	Belle Wilson, Harrisburg	444	Metta C. Brown, Portland
357	Alwilda Wilson, Albany	445	Ruby Briggs, Foster
358	C. F. Bigbee, Crabtree	446	Grace Schuebel, Canby
359	B. A. Johnston, Corvallis	447	Alicia Pearl Horner, Portland
360	Helen Rose Plov, Junction City	448	Lena E. May, Sherwood
361	M. E. Arnold, Albany	449	Golda M. Johnson, Crawfordsville
362	Joanna Hislop, Corvallis	450	Bessie M. Hanseth, Monmouth
363	Fred Lockley, Portland	451	R. L. Green, Fossil
364	Esther Gilbertson, Harrisburg	452	Fred Hawes, Winlock
365	Minnie McCourt, Albany	453	Ida Olson, Fossil
366	J. N. Bilyeu, Crabtree	454	Lillian Duff, Fossil
367	D. U. Cochrane, Kings Valley	455	C. R. Deems, Burnt Ranch
368	Marie F. Schrepel, Philomath	456	Eva Boyle Linville, Spray
369	Mabel Hann, Harrisburg	457	Leah Blann, Twickenham
370	Ruth Hacking, Blodgett	458	B. L. Murphy, Spray
371	F. M. Maxwell, Halsey	459	Mrs. Elizabeth Bowerman, Fossil
372	Venia Powers, Payette, Idaho	460	Flora Gilliland, Fossil
373	Blanche Scharmann, Portland	461	Susan E. Prindle, Antone
374	Mrs.Bertha McKinley,Rogue River	462	Rayma Lee Van Horn, Fossil
375	Mary Hostetler, Silverton	463	C. R. Curfman, Kent
376	Mrs. Mary Wight, Beswick, Cal.	464	Kent School, Kent
377	Signa Johnson, Colton	465	Ethel L. Hooper, Hoskins
378	Dale Loftin, Waterloo	466	Edna Hamlin, Brownsville
379	W. J. Patterson, Wamic	467	Oliver Matthews, Boyd
380	Louise Rintoul, The Dalles	468	E. B. Moore, John Day
381	Ica L. Derthick, Wapinitia	469	C. H. Poole, Canyon City
382	Phyllis Fischer, Maupin	470	Bruce Hayes, Prairie City
383	Frankie Allen, The Dalles	471	R. E. Bible, Hamilton
384	Agnes Campbell, The Dalles	472	Margaret Mitchell, Caverhill
385	Enid Bell, Big Eddy	473	Clara B. Carroll, Dayville
386	Ethyl Gibson, Boyd	474	Mabel Thomas, Prairie City
387	Helena Fleck, The Dalles	475	Rachel Ballance, Long Creek
388	Mary U. Michell, The Dalles	476	Mrs. W. W. Slaughter, Ritter
389	Marcia Selleck, Dufur	477	Mrs. C. W. Curtis, Beech Creek
390	Bessie Bonney, Tygh Valley	478	Corwin A. Harvey, Fox
391	Mary Adair, The Dalles	479	C. H. Justice, Cotton Wood
392	Katherine Arbuthnot, Monmouth	480	Mrs. Laura Collins, Hamilton
393	Christine Ketels, The Dalles	481	Wesley Harryman, Long Creek
394	Frances E. Bennett, Dufur	482	Robert Harryman, Monument
395	Elizabeth Leben, Dufur	483	Mrs. L. A. Slaughter, Monument
396	Mary V. Miller, Maupin	484	E. W. Kimberling, Prairie City
397	Rose C. Hassing, Dufur	485	V. E. Danels, Prairie City
398	Ella M. Syron, Maupin	486	Millie Ricco, Austin
399	Margaret Walker, Mosier	487	W. M. Bennett, Dayville
400	J. P. Ross, Mosier	488	Anatta Burch, Enterprise
401	Mrs. G. R. Crofoot, Maupin	489	Wilhemina Hemrich, Albany
402	J. S. Wright, Dufur	490	Amel Moore, Madras
403	Arthur Bonney, Criterion	491	Osie H. Jewell, Madras
404	Ruth VanZandt, Mosier	492	Ethel Klann, Madras
405	Mary Dennis, Boyd	493	Elva J. Smith, Madras
406	Lucy S. Ruggles, Dufur	494	Lelota Horrigan, Gateway
407	Dorothy Passmore, Mosier	494	Christine Ferm, Lexington
408	Clara Lorenzen, The Dalles	496	Hazel Thorson, Bend
409	Hazel Seeley, The Dalles	497	Irene Weekly, Marshfield
410	Ralph Southwick, Wallowa	498	Emma M. Schreiber, McMinnville
411	Virgil Melvin, Ada	499	Bertha King, Corvallis
412	Genevieve Haven, Kent	500	Vera Tipton, Reedsport
413	Hilma Anderson, Portland	501	E. T. Reed, Corvallis
414	H. M. Sherwood, Portland	502	Irene Douglas, Willows
415	Phyllis Purdin, Pendleton	503	Sylvia Hardman, Condon
416	Loretta Harding, Florence	504	Beatrice Snell, Arlington
417	Floyd L. Senter, Acme	505	Enid G. Leeper, Condon

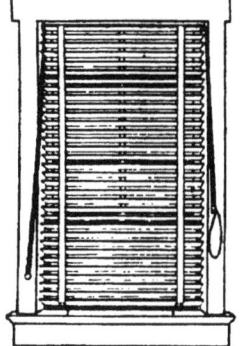

506 Mrs. Lun Searcy, Condon	593 Neita Royer, Salem
507 Eunice Ebbert, Gwendolen	594 Mrs. LaMoine Clark, Salem
508 Phyllis Fate, McDonald	595 Agnes Briggs, Jamieson
509 Clara M. Blais, Condon	596 Frances Chivington, Portland
510 Cora Smith, Condon	597 W. A. Pettys, Portland
511 Lottie Keizur, Condon	598 E. S. Evenden, Monmouth
512 Esther J. Turner, Clem	599 H. D. Sheldon, Eugene
513 Carrie W. Burnham, Arlington	600 Mrs. Marie Stoller, Metolius
514 Bessie C. Lafferty, Condon	601 Emma Agee, Wilsonville
515 Mabel L. Williams, Condon	602 Martina H. Thiele, Hood River
516 Mrs. Ethel Mulkey, Arlington	603 T. J. Skirvin, Wamic
517 P. J. Mulkey, Arlington	604 Amilla Dart, Scio
518 Lydia B. Highlands, Mikkalo	605 Cora Gay, Rickreall
519 Mrs. W. H. Reynolds, Condon	606 Armilda Doughty, Monmouth
520 Maude Grider, Condon	607 Mrs. Chloe Wood, Dallas
521 Lee Byers, Lonerock	608 Lester Gardner, Dallas
522 Mrs. Minnie F. Wilson, Cecil	609 Mrs. Ella Oleman, Hoskins
523 Mildred Force, Arlington	610 Roberta E. Balland, Rickreall
524 Alveda Peterson, Arlington	611 Geneva Sayre, Black Rock
525 Alma Randelin, Condon	612 Mrs. Mattie Neal, Grand Ronde
526 Jessie Hardie, Condon	613 H. H. Matthews, Phoenix
527 Marjory Hardie, Trailfork	614 Rose H. Gay, Gold Hill
528 J. C. Sturgill, Condon	615 W. O. Wheeler, Eagle Point
529 Alice McLean, Mercer	616 Anna Jeffrey, Medford
530 Vida McLean, Eugene	617 Dorothy Hartung, Junction City
531 Ida Foott, Portland	618 Grace L. May, The Dalles
532 Mary E. Thompson, Marshfield	619 Eula Strange, Portland
533 K. W. Onthank, Eugene	620 Neva L. McReynolds, Langells
534 Margaret A. Gray, Thurston	Valley
535 Anne G. Jackson, Knappa	621 Alma Sutherland, Bakeoven
536 Mary Harrison, Madras	622 Ruth Dowd, Weston
537 Albert H. Gillett, Dayton	623 John R. Stuber, Joseph
538 Madge Thomas, Buena Vista	624 Harvey A. Wright, Rickreall
539 Etta Halley, Willamette	625 Nellie Keyt, Independence
540 H. E. Inglow, Forest Grove	626 Willis A. Johnston, McCoy
541 Grace Pryor, White Pine	627 Edith Montgomery, Falls City
542 Clyde L. Knapp, Salem	628 Mrs. E. R. Palmer, Dallas
543 H. C. Todd, Salem	629 Grace Porter, Rickreall
544 Emma C. Brack, Woodburn	630 E. H. Hedrick, Monmouth
545 Ellen Greibenow, Salem	631 W. I. Reynolds, Dallas
546 Emma Walker, Salem	632 Lora Chute, Independence
547 Mattie Neeley, Turner	633 Alice E. Quint, Black Rock
548 Harry Bailie, Silverton	634 Mabel C. Gillette, Independence
549 Henriette Berning, Mt. Angel	635 Elsie L. Taylor, Salem
550 Helen Kefer, Mt. Angel	626 Winona Rowland, Rickreall
551 Josie Thompson, Grants Pass	637 Alice McIntosh, Monmouth
552 Mrs. Harriet Minthorn, Rogue	638 Georgia Curtiss, Dallas
River	639 Effie Cuthbert, Sheridan
553 Lois Sims, Hubbard	640 Gertrude R. Wilson, Monmouth
554 Mabel Van Fleet, Mehama	641 Olive McCready, Suver
555 Hilda M. Nerison, Silverton	642 W. I. Ford, Dallas
556 Flora Grice, Salem	643 Rose Bodayla, Salem
557 F. A. Myers, Aumsville	644 R. W. Tavenner, Independence
558 H. M. James, Silverton	645 Nellie Young, Parkers
559 Mrs. H. H. Paget, Macleay	646 Floyd O. Miller, Dallas
560 J. H. Collins, Woodburn	647 Edna Sweeney, Buell
561 Anna Lindgren, Salem	648 Gladys Stewart, Rickreall
562 Osie Grice, Aumsville	649 Jessie Hunt, Independence
563 W. C. Gauntt, Stayton	650 John Kurtichanov, Chitwood
564 J. G. Noe, Hubbard	651 J. I. Reasoner, Dallas
565 Alta B. Brown, Lyons	652 Gladys Mitchell, Independence
566 Minnie L. Joeckel, Silverton	653 Loraine Goehring, McCoy
567 Margaret West, Oregon City	654 Clara Sampson, Nortons
568 Ellen Currin, Salem	655 June Philpott, Corvallis
569 Kate Willoughby, Arago	656 Sara Huntington, Yoncalla
570 Daisy Carter, Salem	657 Retta M. Allen, Whitney
571 Margaret J. Cosper, Salem	658 Sophia A. Wilson, Portland
572 Mrs. E. H. Belknap, Turner	659 Emma Post, Drain
573 F. P. Sherman, Woodburn	660 Agathe Grondahl, Portland
574 Hilda J Olson, Silverton	661 Dora E. Starke, Amity
575 A. N Arnold, Salem	662 G. W. Milam, Gold Hill
576 E. S. Stultz, Scotts Mills	663 Mrs. W. N. Davis, Rogue River
577 Bertha C. Byrd, Salem	664 Mrs. O. C. Lichens, Kerby
578 B. K. Cook, Salem	665 W. H. Ashcraft, Ashland
579 Julia Iverson, Salem	666 Lillian L. Gammill, Trail
580 Alice E. Estes, Scotts Mills	667 Emily DeVore, Medford
581 Mrs L. R. Stinson, Stayton	668 Elizabeth Elmore, Applegate
582 Elwina E. Schramm, Salem	669 Viola Hogan, Trail
583 Mrs. Marie Ehmer, Salem	670 Chester Cook, Wolf Creek.
584 Greta Phillips, Salem	671 Wessie Griffith, Medford
585 Leota C. Humphrey, Turner	672 H. Howard Grover, Medford
586 Emma F. More, Salem	673 Nellie B. Ross, Ashland
587 R. L. Young, Mt. Angel	674 Annie O'Keefe, Huntington Beach,
588 Abbie S. Davis, Salem	California
589 Mabel Temple, Salem	675 Lela E. Bloom, LaGrande
590 W. J. Mishler, Woodburn	676 Nellie Shelley, Merlin
591 Grace Johnson, Niagara	677 Margaret McQuistion, Grants Pass
592 Ina C. Hubbs, Silverton	678 Susanne Homes, Ashland

679 Gladys Musgrave, Hardman
680 Laura Jackway, Troutdale
681 Mary E. Wilcox, Sheridan
682 Winifred A. Joyce, Portland
683 Sherman Smith, Helix
684 Alice N. Staninger, Waldo
685 Laura E. Hansoln, Ashland
686 Edith R. Fredenburg, Brownsboro
687 Havel Shaver, Ashland
688 Emma Wendt, Jacksonville
689 Roy Brown, Murphy
690 Maude Philbrook, Medford
691 Robert I. Peachey, Jacksonville
692 May Nordoff, Medford
693 Julia Sidley, Eagle Point
694 Vera Kellems, Grants Pass
695 Pearl L. Gould, Butte Falls
696 Blanche Crane, Grants Pass
697 Mary A. Oakes, Hugo
698 G. W. Ager, Talent
699 Anna Potts, Merlin
700 J. A. Churchill, Salem
701 H. C. Seymour, Corvallis
702 C. S. Cramer, Medford
703 E. B. Stanley, Central Point
704 Leonard M. Buoy, Butte Falls
705 A. R. Peterson, Medford
706 Stella M. Paddock, Grants Pass
707 J. C. Banard, Tolo
708 A. E. Humpton, Selma
709 Mrs. Alberta Jones, Beagle
710 D. K. Luthy, Gold Hill
711 Katherine Foley, Gold Hill
712 V. A. Davis, Central Point
713 Mrs. Mollie Belding, Grants Pass
714 H. H. Fox, Lake Creek
715 Florence Querry, Medford
716 Tom L. Ostien, Waldo
717 H. H. Wardrip, Grants Pass
718 Helene Knips, Grants Pass
719 J. A. Bish, Wilderville
720 Marian I. White, Grants Pass
721 Laura C. Atkins, Grants Pass
722 Margaret Gallinger, Jacksonville
723 B. F. Nibert, Applegate
724 Gertrude Engle, Ashland
725 Daisy M. Lewis, Jacksonville
726 P. H. Daley, Medford
727 Kathryn Dunham, Medford
728 Harriet Wilson, Medford
729 Mrs. May Rose, Wonder
730 Lucia C. Chapman, Waldo
731 Pina Benedict, Ashland
732 Clara Skyrman, Trail
733 Lucile Rader, Medford
734 Dewie E. Howe, Trail
735 Hazel Taylor, Central Point
736 Marie Dolan, Hugo
737 Melvina M. Fox, Merlin
738 Aneta M. Chellin, Grants Pass
739 Mrs. Geo. B. Canode, Medford
740 Felix E. Moore, Ashland
741 Elizabeth Neidigh, Knappa
742 Annie Williamson, Fisher
743 Belle M. Yeates, Fossil
744 Minnie Schaller, Salem
745 E. B. Nedry, Nyssa
746 Luther D. Cook, Paradise
747 Walter T. Clay, John Day
748 Sister Mary Amelbergo, St. Paul
749 Carrie B. Livesley, Deschutes
750 Lena Woodward, Medena, Ohio
751 B. H. Calkins, Whiteson
752 A. Devaul, Paisley
753 Gladys Pearson, Hammond

A Good Boost.

A circular sent out by Superintendent J. E. Myers of Crook county to his teachers under date of October 5 contained the following paragraph: "The Oregon Teachers Monthly, beginning with the September number, is entirely under new management.

The State Teachers' Association has entire control of the editorial department. Everything that will be contained in the journal will be of very close interest to the teachers throughout the state. A good many home problems will be discussed in its issues. Since this publication is entirely under the supervision of the teachers, its interests will be the teachers, and we wish to urge every teacher of the county to become a subscriber of our home school paper. The subscription price, including membership in the State Teachers' Association, is $1.50 per year, in advance. Address all communications to Oregon Teachers Monthly, Salem, Oregon."

Washington High School News.

Miss Fannie Barber, of the English Department of Washington high school, Portland, is exchanging places this year with Miss Phila M. Helt, of the North Attleboro, Massachusetts high school. Miss Helt is a member of the 1913 class of Wellesley. Two of the new teachers are graduates of Cornell College, Iowa. Miss Belle Tennant taught last year in Wisner, Nebraska, and Miss Cora Colton comes to us from Cashmore, Washington. The new gymnasium director for boys is Mr. Robert Krohn, Jr., son of the popular city director of athletics. Mr. Krohn recently graduated from Stanford University. Miss Margaret Artingstall has resumed her place in the art department after a year's absence in the East. H. B. Spalding has taken the place in the forge room, left vacant by the resignation of Mr. Granning, who has accepted a similar position at O. A. C.

THE SOLUTION.

When the world seems all distorted,
  And your friends are very few;
When your pocket-book is empty,
  And men frown on all you do;
When ill health seems staring at you,
  And your strength you fear will fail;
When at thought of life's great troubles
  You the fate of men bewail—

Then, my friend, look up! not downward,
  Ope the windows of your soul!
Live above the plain of shadows,
  Keep your eye on distant goal!
For all trouble lies within you,
  Naught but harmony without;
Therefore trust eternal goodness,
  Nevermore give way to doubt!
          —L. S. Foght.

Mirth and cheerfulness are but the reward of innocence of life.—Sir T. Moore.

The State Schools

University of Oregon.

Prof. Earl L. Packard, new this year in the department of geology at the University of Oregon, came here from the University of Washington where he was instructor in geology. Mr. Packard took his A. B. degree at the University of Washington in 1911 and his M. A. there in 1912. His Ph. D. was received from the University of California in 1915. He is doing research work on a group of invertebrates. In May, 1916, he published a paper on "Mezozoic and Cenozoic Mactrinae of the Pacific Coast of North America" and in February of the same year he published "The Faunal Studies in the Cretaceous of the Santa Ana Mountains of Southern California." Just at present he is working on a report in connection with the United States bureau of fisheries.

A new professor in the law department is Ralph S. Hamilton who graduated from the University of Missouri in 1905. He has practiced 11 years, six years in the state of Washington, and five years in Oregon.

Being born in Russia of a German father and a French mother, having traveled for nearly eight years in South America and after that in Africa, H. F. Harthan decided on the Spanish language as a medium to express himself. Mr. Harthan is the new professor of Spanish at the university. When a boy Mr. Harthan went to the same school in Germany where the Prince of Saxonia Meiningen and the son of the chemist, Sresenius, attended. He has traveled all over Europe. He graduated from the University of California in 1912, taught there one year, taught one year in Belmont Military Academy and in 1915 taught at the Missouri State Normal School in the winter and in the following summer session. Mr. Harthan is working on a Spanish reader for high school and university instruction.

George F. Richardson, assistant professor of rhetoric, graduated from Grinnell college, Iowa, in 1904. In 1909 he took his M. A. degree at the University of California and in 1914 his Ph. D. degree there. In 1910-12 he taught at the University of Missouri. He was two years teaching fellow at the University of California and at other times he has taught in public schools. His book, "The Neglected Aspect of the English Romantic Revolt" was published by the University of California in collegiate series. Just at present Mr. Richardson is engaged in a double translation of Beowulf in verse and prose.

A. H. Schroff, the new professor in art at the University of Oregon, is teaching the practical methods which he has actually used in 32 years of experience in making decorative design. His chief interest is in stained glass. At the World's Columbian Exposition in Chicago in 1893, Mr. Schroff took a silver medal for stained glass. Mr. Schroff's first studying was done under his father who was a graduate of the Royal Academy of Berlin. Later he went abroad to study mediaeval 13th century glass in England and France. He painted with and was influenced by Charles H. Woodbury, considered the greatest marine painter in America, who was his chum. Mr. Schroff has devoted himself chiefly to decorative art such as stained glass, mural decoration, designing for various crafts, mosaic, carving and so on.

Albert N. French graduated from the University of Washington with his A. B. degree in 1911 and in 1916 he received his M. A. degree there. He was superintendent of schools at Port Townsend, Wash., for four years. Mr. French has worked out experimentally in public schools the social science corps of instruction for secondary school work. He wrote this thesis on that subject. He is a professor of education at the University of Oregon.

J. Hugh Jackson, who is a professor in the school of commerce, graduated from Simpson college, Indianola, Iowa, in 1912. For one year he was in the Des Moines National Bank and for three years he was an instructor in high schools. While he was teaching in a St. Louis high school he did graduate work one year at Washington university. Mr.

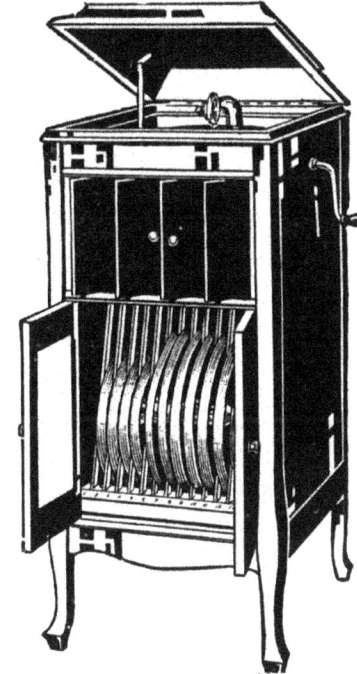

Jackson did graduate work two summers at the University of Wisconsin.

Howard Annett, who was a graduate of Northwestern university in 1914, has studied in the American Conservatory of Music and with private teachers in Chicago. In the summers of 1914-15 he played in Chautauqua. He taught music at Epworth Seminary where he did concert work along with his duties as instructor in music. He is now an instructor at the University of Oregon.

Herman Schwarz was born in Loerrach, Grand Duchy of Baden, in Germany. After attending the gymnasium he went to the universities of Heidelberg and Freiburg where he majored in German and French. He received his doctor degree at Freiburg. Coming to America, Mr. Schwarz was four years in Philadelphia. For one year he was lecturer in the graduate school of the university of Pennsylvania. Following that he was three years instructor in German at the University of California. He is assistant professor in German here.

Allan C. Hopkins was graduated from the Wharton School of Commerce of the University of Pennsylvania in 1914. Following his graduation he was assistant professor in insurance and commerce at that university. This year he is at the University of Oregon as instructor in insurance and commerce, assistant to H. B. Miller.

The new secretary to the president, Karl W. Onthank, took his A. B. degree from the University of Oregon in 1913. One year following he was principal of a high school in Hood River valley. He was superintendent of schools for two years at Tillamook. In 1915 Mr. Onthank got his M. A. degree here. His graduate thesis was "A survey of the Schools in Hood River County." He is very interested in surveys of rural schools. He is secretary in the science and mathematics section of the Oregon State Teachers' Association. In his undergraduate days he was editor of the college paper, the Emerald, and editor of the year book, the Oregana.

With eight years experience as settlement worker in New York and Chicago, librarian, and Y. W. C. A. field secretary, Elizabeth F. Fox comes to the University of Oregon as the new dean of women. After her graduation from Barnard College of Columbia university in 1908 Miss Fox did social work in New York city in connection with Dr. Robert G. Boville. Her chief interest was in the vacation schools, which is a system to get college women to bring joy and fun into tenement youngsters' lives. Following this social work she was substitute librarian on the east side at Chatham square, the largest children's library in the world, where, in her own words: "The place teemed with dirty imps." Later she was associated with an institutional settlement near the navy yard in Brooklyn. As Y. W. C. A. secretary of Northestern university she started an evening school for maids and working girls of which she was superintendent. This was a miniature settlement. While here she conducted college girls in their visits to the settlements of Chicago, to Hull House, Northwestern University Settlement and others. She first came to the Northwest as national field secretary for the Y. W. C. A. Besides her new position at the University of Oregon she also teaches a class in practical ethics for all freshman women and has a class in social agencies, a study in charities and corrections.

E. L. Keezel, who is handling the courses in education by correspondence comes to the University of Oregon with three years' training in elementary grade work and five years of high school principal's experience. Mr. Keezel is president of the principal's club in Polk county. He is specializing in elementary and high schol administration. He was graduated from Philomath college in 1905 and later took his degree at the University of Oregon.

Chester T. Kronenberg graduated from the University of Oregon in 1913 and in the three years since that time has been principal and superintendent in the Elgin, Ore., public schools. He was instructor in mathematics during the last summer session at the University of Oregon and this winter he is here as an instructor in the extension department in charge of mathematics. Mr. Kronenberg is expecting to make a revision of the mathematics extension courses.

Oregon Agricultural College.

A total enrollment of 1901 as compared with 1645 last year was reported to the Oregon Agricultural College board of regents, which met in quarterly session October 6. Since second semester registration usually adds a few hundred to the college roll, the total number of students for the year is sure to exceed 2000, according to Registrar H. M. Tennant. There is an increase of 31 per cent in the freshman class and 25 per cent in all classes. The total enrollment of long course students up to October 6 was 1524, as compared with 1408 last year. An increase of more than 100 per cent is shown in the freshman classes in logging engineering, vocational mechanical engineering, highway engineering and commerce. The classes in highway engineering show an increase of 157 per cent. Electrical engineering shows an increase of 83 per cent in freshmen. Pharmacy freshmen have increased 41 per cent. Industrial art classes gained 24 per cent. In home economics the freshman increase is 46 per cent, and in all classes 14 per cent. Sixty-three students have been transferred from other higher institutions of learning as follows: Thirteen from the University of California, four from the University of Oregon, three from Occidental College, three from Reed, three from Willamette university, four from Stanford university, two from the University of Washington, two from the Colorado Agricultural College and two from Washington State College. Transfers have been received from 29 colleges and six normal schools in 12 different states. A list of attendance by counties shows that Multnomah leads with a total of 266; Benton county has 220; Marion, 72; Polk, 37; Douglas, 26; Umatilla, 35; Lane, 34; Jackson and Yamhill, 32 each, and slightly fewer numbers from the remaining counties of the 34 represented on the rolls. Sixty-nine per cent of the 1901 students are partly or wholly self-supporting, 36 per cent making their way entirely by combining summer work with some form of labor in Corvallis. Another point of interest to the regents was the table comparing the average age of students. The average of men students is 21 years as compared with 21.18 years for women students. Vocational men students average 20.26 years of age as compared with 22.13 for vocational women students. The oldest regular four-year student is 55, the youngest 16. The oldest vocational student is 49 years, the youngest 16.

When the board of regents met in their regular session with President W. J. Kerr, there were present Hon. J. K. Weatherford of Albany, president; N. R. Moore of Corvallis, secretary; and the following members: Hon. J. P. Apperson, Park Place; Walter M. Pierce, LaGrande; H. VonderHellen, Wellerton; George M. Cornwall, Portland, and Clara A. Waldo, Portland. At Convocation on Friday, the board of regents attended in a body. The address of the day was delivered by Mrs. Clara A. Waldo, who spoke on the subject of overcoming difficulties. Mrs. Waldo said that we all can pull ourselves out of the rut and lift ourselves to higher ground. She declared it to be a great handicap to live with a prejudice, and that there is such a thing as really outgrowing ourselves. She then deftly portrayed the lives of a few people who have risen from lower planes to occupy exalted positions in the society and business of the world. Mrs. Waldo is a prime favorite with the students, and spoke before the entire women student body again in the evening.

The Women's League, plans for which were started last spring and more fully developed recently, has been organized at the college. The league has for its main object the bringing together of the women in the college to study questions of interest to the women students. Every girl in the college is taking great interest in the new organization, believing that it means much to her. Regular meetings will be held once a month. The officers are as follows: President, Miss Martha Bechen, of Hillsboro; vice-president, Margaret Patterson, Ashland; secretary, Doris Clark, Portland; treasurer, Jessie Thayer, Rainier.

The annual reception given by President and Mrs. W. J. Kerr in honor of the board of regents was held in the men's gymnasium on the evening of Friday, October 6. The president was assisted in the receiving line by the deans and heads of the departments and their wives and by members of the board of regents.

The hall was beautifully decorated in evergreens and flowers, the decorations being in charge of Prof. A. L. Peck. A program of music and other interesting features concluded the evening's exercise.

When the first meeting of the men's cooking class was held in the home economics building on October 3, 18 young men presented themselves to take the work. This class, in charge of Miss A. Grace Johnson, was organized at the request of several young men who are batching and feel the need for the instruction and training. The first part of the evening is given over to explanations and instructions by Miss Johnson, who tells the members of food values, the importance of a well-balanced diet, the work of different foods in the body and how to plan a well-balanced meal tastefully and economically. The young men then plan their menus which are reviewed and revised by the instructor. The foods are then prepared and cooked for the meal, of which all partake. The menus are then taken into the bachelor homes of the class members where they are utilized in preparing meals for the members of the club.

The college mandolin club, which did some practicing last year but did not formally organize, has now organized with the following officers: H. B. Smith, president; Everett McAllister, secretary-treasurer; Prof. Goetell, director. The Madrigal Club, the women's musical organization, has been re-organized and the 12 vacancies caused by graduation last year have been filled. Twenty-five girls under the direction of Mrs. Genevieve Baum Gaskins tried out for these positions. The club has already begun work on a part-song concert to be given some time before Thanksgiving. Promising material for the cadet band was so plentiful that it has been deemed advisable by Captain Beard, leader, to organize two bands. The first consists now of 45 pieces and the second of 25. Most of the members of the first band have had previous experience here or in other institutions, while the second band is composed almost entirely of freshmen. The aim of the present policy is to have a supply source for musicians in the first band as the ranks are depleted. The freshman band is in charge of J.

B. Yoder of the department of engineering. In the first band are three oriental musicians, the three Ding brothers, Chinese.

Try-outs for the Mask and Dagger Club, the dramatic association of the college, have been held and eleven new members voted in. There were 42 aspirants for these eleven positions, representing a wealth of good material.

In pursuit of the intra-mural athletic policy, Dr. A. D. Browne, head of physical education, has organized the men into divisions for many kinds of intra-mural sports. Dr. Browne has called for volunteers of all members in the faculty who have had experience in coaching high school teams or who have had experience and training on varsity teams, in various educational institutions, to assist in coaching. He expects to have fully 80 per cent of the men engaged in some form of competitive athletics during the college year.

The series of business men's lectures conducted by the school of commerce was opened with an address by Tom Richardson, the noted Portland and Oregon booster. Mr. Richardson told the students of the work now being conducted to develop Oregon's industries rather than seeking new business abroad. "Portland should forget the Alaskan trade and devote her energies to developing the rich resources of the Willamette valley," said he, "and give encouragement to the many small industries which are now springing up everywhere because of local need."

Ninety-six appointments have been made by Prof. Ressler, chairman of the appointment committee, a record approximately equal to all of last years' appointments. These 96 teachers will earn an aggregate salary of $76,652 during the year. In commerce and home economics the average monthly salary is $85.00 for nine months. In manual training the average monthly salary is $101 for a like period.

Miss Louise Schneider, graduate of Toledo University and of Pratt Institute, has arrived at the college to take the place of instructor in domestic art left vacant by the resignation of Miss Anna Castleberry. Miss Schneider has taught at the Pratt Institute, and also in the night schools of New York's social settle-

Sick — and Homesick

What a dismal outlook it would be, if she were not a T. C. U.

But no need for T. C. U. Teachers to worry—T. C. U. checks are coming in to pay the doctor, the nurse and the board bill, or to hire a substitute.

No one can foresee those three dread contingencies that rob so many teachers of their earnings—Accident, Sickness and Quarantine. Out of a clear sky, they come—and how easily one may lose a month's salary and six months' savings. You cannot avoid them. When your turn comes (which it will some day) all you can do is to pay the cost and charge it up to hard luck—unless you are a T. C. U.

But, friends if you take advantage of this opportunity, you don't need to charge it to hard luck—you can charge it to the T. C. U., which makes a business of safeguarding, protecting and guaranteeing you a fixed income any month during the year that you are sick, injured or quarantined, for the small cost to you of less than a nickel a day. Thousands of teachers, by enrolling in the T. C. U. have realized peace of mind and certainty of income.

D. M. Oler, Kimball, S. D., recently wrote: "I appreciate your check very much as I am nearly nine hundred miles from home and among strangers. Will gladly speak a good word for the T. C. U. at any time

Don't hesitate, don't wait, until something happens. At least send the Coupon and find out without obligation, just what the T. C. U. will do for you.

Teachers Casualty Underwriters
201 T. C. U. Building, Lincoln, Nebraska.

Coupon for Free Booklet.   Send Name and Address.

To the T. C. U.
    The National Protective Organization for Teachers,
        201 T. C. U. Building, Lincoln, Nebraska.
    I am a Teacher and I am interested in knowing about your Protective Benefits.
Send me the whole story and booklet of testimonials.

Name ....

Address ....
        (This coupon places the sender under no obligation whatever)

ments, and has interested herself chiefly in the working girls.

The first convocation of the year was the largest ever held at the college. Convocation audiences have so far outgrown the capacity of the hall in the women's gymnasium that President Kerr has announced that convocation meetings will be held hereafter in the men's gymnasium. In a few vigorous sentences the president indicated some intricacies and obstacles in the way of student life at college, and urged all students to be faithful, not alone to their class-room obligations but to the work of broadening their lives and enlarging their usefulness by taking part in student activities. The president also pointed out the futility of offering criticism without indicating means for improvement.

Mrs. Mary E. Fawcett, dean of women, has begun a series of lectures before the Waldo Hall students and such guests as they may invite. Dean Fawcett gave the first of these addresses on Wednesday evening, October 4. She spoke of etiquette in relation to ethics and outlined a history of its development and evolution. She also announced a series of lectures for the closing week in October, to be given by Dr. Mabel Ulrich of Minneapolis, who will speak on the following subjects: The Special and Psychological Evolution of Sex, The Period of Pre-Adolescence, Physical and Mental Changes of Adolescence, Adolescence Ethics, The Unnecessary Evil, Love and Marriage and the Art of Living.

* * *

Oregon Normal School.

The first member of the faculty to use the assembly period was Miss Katherine Arbuthnot, who told the story of "The Transfiguration of Miss Philura", a story delightful in itself and doubly delightful with Miss Arbuthnot's perfect interpretation of the little lady whose faith permitted her to draw on the all-encircling good for all good things.

The last sophomore class to be enrolled in the Oregon Normal School, since after the close of the present year the standards for admission will be raised to eliminate this class, showed its energy and enthusiasm by being the first class to have a "get together" reception and party, which was held at the home of Miss West, the librarian, on the afternoon of

September 23. Miss Kennon read a fairy tale; games and conversation filled up the rest of the afternoon, after which refreshments were served. This small class now feels that it is an acquainted unit.

The societies, Delphian, Vespertine, and Normal, held their first meetings on September 22, and the start-off predicts a prosperous year's work The work of the societies will be conducted much the same as in the past year with the exception of the Normal society which has decided to make debating the big feature of the year's work. A list of topics has been prepared by Mr. Butler, critic of the society, and a well prepared debate will be featured at every meeting.

The normal school has been represented at the county institutes as follows: President Ackerman at Salem, Mr. Pittman at Corvallis, Heppner, Fossil, Condon, Salem, Dallas, and Grants Pass, Miss Arbuthnot at The Dalles and Dallas, and Miss Richter at Salem and Dallas. The county institute to draw most heavily on the Oregon Normal School was Polk, where President Ackerman, Mr. Gentle, Miss McIntosh, Miss Arbuthnot, and Miss Dinuis attended.

The Y. W. C. A. organized for the year with a strong enrollment and held its initial reception in the form of a lawn party at the home of Miss Maggie Butler the afternoon and evening of September 23. An interesting program was rendered and refreshments served. The association will have as its president for this year, Miss Dorothy Bengston.

The plan of introducing an outside speaker every second Friday is to be followed again during the coming year, and the visit of Superintendent John Todd, of Salem, on September 29, was the initial number of this series. Superintendent Todd, who is a newcomer to the educational field in Oregon, chose for his topic, "What a City Superintendent Looks For In An Applicant." Superintendent Todd explained the methods of city superintendents in following up the application blanks and the points noted in personal interviews. This "inside information" was very practical and will be of material help to the students in meeting future superintendents. Superintendent Todd made many friends on his initial visit and

(Cut this out and mail to OREGON TEACHERS MONTHLY)

School Journals and Magazines

Clubbed With Oregon Teachers Monthly, Salem, Oregon

If it is desired to club other journals with the OREGON TEACHERS MONTHLY, you may do so by sending additional amount as shown in the vertical column of prices below. To get the benefit of the prices given below every combination must include the OREGON TEACHERS MONTHLY. Positively no subscriptions to school journals or magazines taken at less than regular prices unless in combination with OREGON TEACHERS MONTHLY. If any journal wanted is not found in the list below, ask about it; it can be furnished at the lowest clubbing price. Check the names of school journals and magazines wanted, carry the price to the right hand margin and give sum of total combination as indicated below. State f journals are new or renewal subscriptions. Sign your name and address plainly and enclose this sheet to us, accompanied by the proper amount.

1	Oregon Teachers Monthly and membership in State Teachers' Association	$1.50	
2	Ladies' World, $1.00	.75	
3	Current Events (weekly), 40c	.35	
4	Normal Instructor and Primary Plans, $1.25	.90	
5	Mothers' Magazine, $1.50	1.00	
6	National Geographic Magazine, $2.50	2.10	
7	Pathfinder (weekly), $1.00	.60	
8	World's Chronicle (weekly), $1.50	.60	
9	Delineator, $1.50	1.10	
11	Something To Do, $1.00	.75	
12	All Outdoors, $1.00	.75	
13	Pictorial Review, $1.50	1.10	
14	Every Week, $1.00	.75	
15	Everybody's Magazine, $1.50	1.10	
16	Primary Education, $1.50	1.25	
17	Popular Educator, $1.50	1.25	
18	Sunset-Pacific Monthly, $1.50	1.00	
19	Woman's Home Companion, $1.50	1.10	
20	American Magazine, $1.50	1.10	
21	Journal of Education (weekly), $2.50	1.50	
22	Review of Reviews, $3.00	2.00	
23	Collier's Weekly, $2.50	1.60	
24	World's Work, $3.00	2.00	
25	McCall's Magazine, 50c	.40	
26	McClure's Magazine, $1.00	.90	
27	Progressive Teacher, $1.00	.60	
28	Scribner's Magazine, $3.00	2.50	
29	St. Nicholas, $3.00	2.50	
30	School News, $1.25	.90	
31	American Penman, $1.00	.60	
32	Etude, $1.50	1.10	
33	Storyteller's Magazine, $1.50	1.00	
34	Outdoor Life, $1.50	1.00	
35	Travel Magazine, $3.00	2.50	
36	Rural Educator, $1.00	.60	
37	Popular Mechanics, $1.50	1.30	
38	School Board Journal, $1.50	1.30	
39	Atlantic Monthly, $4.00	3.60	
40	Scientific American, $3.00	2.60	

Price of Combination Wanted .... $ ....

Date ....191..

OREGON TEACHERS MONTHLY, Salem, Oregon:

You will find herewith $ ....for Journals as shown above.

Name ....

Address ....

NOTE—Please state if journals are new or renewals.

we predict his work in Oregon will be successful.

During the first week of October President Ackerman was called twice to Portland, the first occasion being the meeting of a committee of the State Teachers' Association for the formation of a teachers' retirement fund law to be discussed at the December meeting of the association. The second occasion was in acceptance of a request from the Ad Club of Portland to discuss before them the standardization of normal schools.

The first installment of the new books for the library have arrived and are being read with much interest by students and teachers alike. The definite constructive policy of the library under the direction of Miss West and the supervision of Miss Marvin, secretary of the State Library Commission, add a goodly number of books yearly to the various departments. In this way the library of the school is coming to be a more useful one and a very valuable asset in class-room work.

President Ackerman reports that every graduate of the 1916 classes, both February and June, who desired positions as teachers, are now located. The splendid co-operation of city superintendents and county superintendents throughout the state has made this possible, and the normal school appreciates this step towards the standardization of teaching.

Some temporary inconveniences are being willingly tolerated in Monmouth, due to the introduction of three blocks of paving in the business part of Main street. This step will answer a long-felt need in Monmouth and is indicative of a spirit of progress which has recently been evidenced in a number of ways, and is commendable.

The announcement cards have been received of the wedding of Miss Lucia Campbell to Mr. Elliott Henderson. Many graduates of the normal school will remember Miss Campbell, as the daughter of President Campbell, of the University of Oregon.

The normal school took advantage of the state fair in Salem on Saturday, September 30, when an excursion of nearly 75 visited the grounds. They were very well impressed by the exhibits and the general management of the fair, many of them seeing it for the first time.

The second member to represent the faculty was Mr. Butler, of the history department. He took for his subject "The Teacher's Responsibility in the Economic World" and showed in a clear forceful way the very important work that the elementary teacher has to do in the shaping of character and molding of ideals which will help the citizens of the near future to use wisely the tremenduous financial success of the present day.

The Prohibition Law.

The law has now been in effect eight months. Its benefits are manifest to everybody. The great economic waste is largely stopped. Dunkenness is a rarity. The police and police courts are little concerned with crimes growing out of drunkenness that used to occupy them almost to the exclusion of everything else. People are living better and happier. The merchants are getting a bigger proportion of what used to go over the bars and business has marvelously adapted itself to the new conditions. Public sentiment is emphatically back of the law and the law has justified itself. But the brewers, ill-advised, wanted to get into the game again. They wanted to manufacture for home consumption and then insidiously bring us back to the old ways. Like Mrs. Partington, they were trying to sweep back the ocean with a broom. They did not at first realize that revolutions do not move backward, that people who have got their heads out of a halter are not likely to put them back again. Even Colonel Wood's poetic panacea for breeding a new race of braves on mothers' malted milk has failed to arouse any but ribald comment. As a matter of fact the brewers' amendment is snubbed to the post. It may move from side to side and heave a little, but otherwise, to all intents and purposes it is already too dead to skin.—Evening Telegram.

GENIUS.

He dreamed at night while the wide
    world slept
  And the stars moved ever on;
He rose while the world was still
    asleep
  And wrought in the early dawn;
And his wondering neighbors never
    knew
How he made his exquisite dreams
    come true.
          —Wm. C. Sayrs.

OREGON TEACHERS MONTHLY

The Official Journal of the State Teachers' Association

Vol. XXI   SALEM, OREGON, DECEMBER, 1916   No. 4

Published Monthly Except July and August by the State
Teachers' Association

Entered at the Postoffice at Salem, Oregon, as second-class mail matter, April 1, 1898.

RULES OF PUBLICATION

1. The mailing label on the Oregon Teachers Monthly shows the date to which subscriptions are paid.
2. The Oregon Teachers Monthly will be sent to subscribers until ordered discontinued and all arrearages are paid.
3. Notice of change of address should be given at once, naming both old and new postoffice.
4. When renewing, always state that subscription is a renewal.
5. The subscription price, including membership in State Teachers' Association, is $1.50 a year in advance. Single copy, 20 cents.
6. Advertising rates will be furnished on application.
Address all communications to Oregon Teachers Monthly, Salem, Oregon.

Editorial Notes

The Oregon Teachers Monthly desires articles describing the new and significant departures in Oregon education. As far as the editorial board learn of successful experiments those responsible receive a direct personal invitation to contribute articles. There is much successful experience which the editors, by reason of the vast extent of the state, can know nothing of. If any of these valuable happenings are taking place in your community, write them up and send them in to Salem.

*   *   *

In appointing a special committee on teachers' professional ethics to report at the December meeting of the association, President Carleton has injected a very live issue into the deliberations of the meeting. If current opinion can be accepted, some flagrant violations of any decent code of professional conduct have taken place in Oregon during the past year. While cases should not be prejudiced on hearsay evidence, the prevalence of so much gossip on the subject points to the advisability of some permanent organ of the association to investigate and report on alleged violations. Many interesting questions will doubtless be submitted to the committee by the members of the association. Among others we suggest the following: Is it professional to publicly criticize predecessors? How far may a teacher go in advertising his achievements through write-ups for the newspapers? Is a superintendent justified in bidding for teachers in another system just before the beginning of the school year? Is the practice of writing good recommendations for weak teachers justified?

* * *

At the meeting of the Eastern Division of the Oregon State Teachers' Association in La Grande, November 1, 2, and 3, it was voted unanimously to join with the Western Division in a single State Association. Delegates from each of the three counties, Baker, Union, and Wallowa, were elected to report at the meeting in Portland, December 27, 28, and 29. The tri-county annual meetings will be continued under the name of the Blue Mountain Teachers' Association, next year's session going to Baker. This favorable action was taken on the recommendation of the committee which attended the meeting of the Western Division at Medford last year and which consisted of the three county superintendents, Mr. J. F. Smith, Mrs. A. E. Ivanhoe, and Mr. J. C. Conley. We welcome our sister association most cordially and feel assured that this amalgamation means much to the teaching profession of the state. The constitution was drawn up with the view of a state-wide organization and the elimination of two words in Article I will probably be all the revision necessary. With the hearty co-operation of all the counties, each of which has its representation in the Council, and the prestige of numbers, the Oregon State Teachers' Association will command the recognition and respect of the public.

* * *

To say that the work of teaching is an exemplary one is merely expressing a truism but to say that a large and not very rapidly diminishing number of teachers are not examples in their use of English—if a truism is a deplorable one. The criticism is often voiced now that we are making certain incorrect expressions— American habits, and if this is too broad an accusation, then certainly Western and Northwestern habits, and also that teachers are abbetting in their formation, either thoughtlessly or unknowingly. It is not at all uncommon to hear at a gathering of teachers such expressions as "I done that myself onct." "You can't guess who I seen on my way in this morning." "Hurry up Kid; we ain't got but an hour and a quarter for dinner." There is a possibility that language of this kind will not be used in the school room, but if it isn't it is contrary to all the fundamental laws of habit formation. Teachers must be doubly on their guard in this matter because these and similar expressions are of such a nature that even the fixing stamp of common usage can never make them correct and yet they are so common that teachers are not immune. These English habits are fixed during the early years, in the homes, on the playgrounds, and in some cases even in the schools, and they are not to be easily uprooted—certainly not overnight, and often not in a school epoch. An English crusade is necessary which will take careful planning painstaking effort, ceaseless vigilance, kindly sympathy, and a willingness to receive suggestions. First of all, however, let us be sure that our houses are not of glass.

* * *

There will be determined effort made in the coming session of the legislature to repeal all laws which stand in the way of a return to the old system of electing annually every one in the school system from the superintendent to the janitor. Teachers and superintendents know too well what the annual election means to stand by idly while a blind reaction paralyzes progress. The present law may need changes at important points in order to secure elasticity in the school system, but the essential principle of continuity for those who have proven themselves efficient, should be preserved. An occupation which places its practitioners at the mercy of ward politics and neighborhood gossip once a year can hardly be called a profession. The schools exist for the children, not for the board, the teachers, or the politicians. Incompetent teachers should be discharged, but the machinery for doing this should be of such a character as to preserve the peace of mind of the efficient and not expose them to the silent and insidious workings of political and sectarian animosity. These disastrous results would surely occur under a restored system of annual elections for every one. If the principle of continuity in tenure is to be retained the teachers of the state must realize the importance of the issue at stake, also inform themselves as to the workings of the various systems in vogue throughout the country. The general public should be informed through the press and otherwise of the bearing of tenure on efficiency.

* * *

Pursuant to the call of the chairman, a meeting of the Executive Committee of the Oregon State Teachers' Association (third session) was held at the state capitol in Salem, November 9, 1916. The meeting was called to order at 2:15 p. m., with the following members present: Mr. E. T. Carleton, Miss Viola Ortschild, Mr. Geo. A. Briscoe, Mr. H. D. Sheldon. Absent members were Mr. J. Percy Wells, Mr. H. H. Herdman, Mr. O. M. Elliott. The minutes of the previous sessions of the committee were read and approved. The chairman stated the object of the meeting to be the planning of the program for the annual meeting of the association in Portland, December 27-29 and such other business as may arise. The committee approved the plan of the chairman providing for two general sessions and two sessions for departmental meetings on the two days assigned to the general association: General sessions, Thursday forenoon and Friday afternoon; departmental sessions, Thursday afternoon and Friday forenoon, December 28 and 29. The first day, December 27 is assigned to the meeting of the Representative Council, as required by the constitution. Chairman Carleton reported that he had been in correspondence with a number of educators of national reputation with a view to securing speakers for the annual meeting. The correspondence was considered, other names canvassed and the chairman authorized to secure one or more speakers from the list, and to make local and other arrangements for the annual meeting in Portland. On motion of Mr. Briscoe, it was ordered that the expense of the annual meeting be limited to a maximum of $500, if possible. On motion of Mr. Sheldon, the chairman was authorized to appoint a committee of nine on a "Professional Code for Teachers," to report to the Representative Council at the Portland meeting. Miss Ortschild nominated Mr. William Parker, principal of the Vernon school, Portland, to fill the vacancy on the Executive Committee, caused by the removal of Mr. O. M. Elliott from the state. Mr. Parker was unanimously elected. Mr. Briscoe moved that the chairman and secretary be authorized to procure official stationery; motion was seconded and carried. Chairman Carleton reported the contract with the Salem Statesman Publishing Company for the publication of the Oregon Teachers Monthly as the official organ of the State Teachers' Association. It was ordered inscribed in the minutes of the committee. There being no further business before the committee, the meeting was adjourned, subject to the call of the chairman.

*   *   *

How much have you spent this year to keep alive—professionally? One method of doing this while you are teaching is through your reading. For financial or traditional reasons most teachers select their reading matter for the year during the early months of the term and do so with but little serious thought of the problem involved, which in reality is one of the most important of the entire year and one which has in it many possibilities for growth and success or stagnation and failure. One of the first requisites of a profession is the existence of standards of preparation and of proficiency and in any growing profession the problem of preparation does not extend over a fixed period before graduation but continues year after year. Medical men and lawyers have to spend from $50 to several times that sum each year for periodicals and books in order to keep abreast of the new methods and new discoveries in their work. Surely there is not a field of human endeavor where each succeeding year sees more constructive research, more changed methods, or more new plans with values yet to be determined than that of education, which as surely calls for constant reading and study on the part of the progressive teacher. The statement was recently made by one who has a good opportunity to know that the teachers of Oregon do not average more than $3 a year for professional periodicals. This amount is woefully inadequite to postpone rapid superannuation and is probably caused by the fact that teachers think, financially, in terms of only one month's salary, by which method of calculation a $3 outlay for professional magazines seems a creditable one especially when the salary used for computation is the first one and it, as yet, unpaid. When figured for the year, however, this is merely a start. No Oregon teacher, regardless of her salary, can afford to spend less than $10 a year on her professional reading and those with a keener sense of values and a more far-sighted business sense will invest considerably more in this large dividend-paying concern. This minimum amount will provide a teacher with her state journal, the Oregon Teachers Monthly; an educational magazine, specializing in methods and devices especially for her work; a good weekly or monthly current events magazine, and at least two new books upon some phase of education. While not strictly professional reading, a teacher would do well to have one or more good fiction magazines for recreative reading. In addition it is highly desirable that a teacher have access to a good daily newspaper. Some teachers can not see the advisability of such an investment, but they do not see the value of a mind kept open to new ideas, of a reputation for progressiveness, and of a lengthened period of earning usefulness. It is easy to be "penny wise and pound foolish" in one's mental upkeep.

* * *

The report in this issue shows a membership of about 1400 members in the Oregon State Teachers' Association. All new subscriptions to the Oregon Teachers Monthly and all renewals are taken at the uniform price of $1.50. The publishers remit the 50 cents to the treasurer of the association, thus making every subscriber to the Oregon Teachers Monthly a member of the association. There are approximately 4000 names on the present subscription list but 3000 of these were taken at the former rate and these subscriptions must be renewed at the present rate. We appeal to all old subscribers to renew promptly. The increased cost of all material and the better quality of paper used this year alone justify the increased subscription price. The old membership fee in the State Teachers' Association was $1, so that the combined price of the magazine and the membership is actually less than the former price of both. But the Oregon Teachers Monthly is now OUR official organ. The editorial control is in the hands of a committee duly constituted by the Oregon State Teachers' Association and represents the teachers of the entire state. There is a moral as well as a professional obligation resting upon every teacher to become a member of the State Association and a subscriber to the Oregon Teachers Monthly. At every annual election, both in the choosing of delegates to the Representative Council, and in the selection of officers at this annual meeting, the teachers who are members of the association have it in their power to control the policy of this magazine. The present Board of Editors is undertaking to represent the desires of the teachers as they can be ascertained through information gained in the annual county institutes and through such other sources as are available. Our first annual meeting in Portland, December 27, 28, and 29, under the re-organization, will supply the policies and the program for the association and for the Oregon Teachers Monthly. There are more than 6000 teachers at work in the public schools of Oregon this year. Add those employed in the three state institutions for higher education, in the independent colleges, include school officers and others directly connected with the educational interests of the state, and is it too much to anticipate a membership and a subscription list of 5000 people? What prestige this would give to the teaching profession! The deliberations of such a body would be treated with respect by press and public. The findings of its committees, after thorough and capable investigation, would have great weight. May we urge every old subscriber to renew promptly and every new subscriber and member of the association to boost for the official organ of all the teachers of Oregon.

             *   *   *

The first annual meeting of the re-organized State Teachers' Association will be held in Portland, December 27 to 29, at the Lincoln high school. President Carleton and the Executive Committee, together with the officers of the various departments, are working hard to arrange a strong program. One or more speakers of national reputation will be secured and a number of Oregon's leading educators will be heard at the general sessions. The January number of the Oregon Teachers Monthly will appear about December 18 and will contain the complete program. Make your plans now to attend. Special rates on the railroads and at the hotels will reduce the expense to a minimum. Not the least of the benefits to be derived are the social intercourse with the more ambitious members of the profession and the opportunities for high class entertainment during the holidays in our metropolis. No evening sessions of the association will be scheduled. In accordance with the provision of the constitution, the Representative Council will have two sessions the first day, at which the three important committees on Teachers' Retirement Fund, Retardation, and Professional Code will submit their reports for discussion. Brief summaries of these reports will appear in the next issue of this magazine. The constructive program of the association will be formulated in these sessions and it is desired that every member of the council feel his individual responsibility in making this program worthy of the support of the teachers and the general public. These meetings are open to all members of the Association, although participation in the discussions is limited to council members. General sessions of the association are to be held Thursday forenoon and Friday afternoon, the afternoon of Thursday and the forenoon of Friday being devoted wholly to departmental meetings. To get the most out of these sessions, teachers should study the program with care and plan attendance according to individual need and interest. Come prepared to participate in the discussions both with contributions of your own experience and study and with problems and difficulties you have encountered. Leaders and speakers in the departments should make provision for discussion with the idea of utilizing the wisdom and experience of as large a group as possible and of discovering and developing the talent of the entire body of teachers. Much depends upon the attendance and spirit of the teachers in this first meeting of the re-organized State Teachers' Association. Mark the dates in your calendar, December 27 to 29.

All teachers whose subscriptions to the Oregon Teachers Monthly are in arrears ought to pay up at once so that the magazine can be continued without missing any copies. After the first of the year, those very much in arrears will be discontinued because the price of paper is too great to allow the continuing of the magazine unless payment is made.

Ontario High School Cadets

By E. G. BAILEY, City Superintendent, Ontario, Oregon

Five years ago, or to be a little more exact, about the month of September, 1911, Mr. A. A. Hall, at that time principal of the Ontario high school, decided that the spirit of ruffianism, termed by some the real western spirit, was running too rampant in the high school of Ontario. The wonder to him was how to head it off or lessen it without destroying his prestige as principal.

An inspiration came to him. He could see in the uniform wearer of the eastern college a panacea for his trouble. Mr. Hall was a graduate of Rochester, N. Y., where a different atmosphere pervaded everything, and felt that there was more difference between western and eastern ways than the actual case justified. So, securing permission from Superintendent E. B. Conklin and taking into confidence his co-worker D. C. Petrie, a cadet corps was formed, officers elected and bright blue uniforms ordered. This was the beginning of what has become a permanent organization in the Ontario public schools and one which at the present time is being maintained and sustained under the direct supervision of the superintendent. So our company was not organized with the thought of preparedness as its motive force and it is not being maintained with that in view, and yet it would be a very potent force in case of war, or would be all that any like number of militia would be.

It is a duly organized company with Fred Gramse, Senior, Captain; Joy Husted, Senior, First Lieutenant; Arthur Cockrum, Senior, Second Lieutenant; James Duncan, Senior, First Sergeant; Lee Maddux, Senior, Second Sergeant; Bernard Rader, Junior, Third Sergeant and Right Guide; Arthur Moore, Senior, Fourth Sergeant and Left Guide; Alfred Holland, Senior, Bugler; Paul Van Petten, Senior, Corporal; Edmund Fraser, Junior, Corporal; Darr Dearborn, Senior, Corporal; Claud Christiansen, Junior, Corporal; and Marlin Gramse, Senior, Corporal.

It has become a wonderfully effective force in the matter of general discipline throughout not only the school but the town. It now numbers 70, armed with the old Springfield and clothed in regulation army uniforms of gray. Three periods each week are given for drill. The boys march, counter march, and form various figues, carrying the guns and flag. They are taught in the manual of arms and are really quite a credit to themselves in that respect. An inspection is held each year at the close of the year's work by an army officer and the one ranking highest is given a silver badge. These badges are a great incentive as they are highly prized.

We said in the beginning that this was not organized for military purposes nor is it maintained with that in view. We are a peace-loving people at Ontario having no desire or thought of war, but these uniforms and guns and the flag have changed the entire personnel of the Ontario high school. It teaches respect for government. During drill period they are working under their own officers, doing the work as much alone as if they were among entire strangers in a big field—every outside restraint removed. I do not suggest the principle of self-government but it is here exemplified, and to the good of the school. The officers are extremely sensitive to disorder in the ranks and any second attempt results in quick and meritorious punishment. There are 70 in the corps, 164 in the high school, and its influence is everywhere felt.

Our boys are mighty proud of these uniforms and are taught while wearing them that it is a little short of a crime to do the things that ordinarily boys wink at. They work this out alone also. For instance, just yesterday the captain gave the boys a talk, instructing them that they must always be gentlemen when on the street or in any business house while wearing the uniforms and that it was a real disgrace to the uniforms for one of them to smoke cigarettes while wearing them. These boys are doing remarkably good work in their studies. One of our new teachers, a graduate from one of our prominent colleges and a young man of some experience in teaching, remarked the other day that our upperclassmen averaged much better scholastically than the upper-classmen of his last year's school, which was one of the prominent schools of Western Oregon.

We take semi-annual hikes, at which time a regular camp is organized. A place is selected some time in advance, some place where water is plentiful. The boys have their camp-fires and their sentinels posted. It was here that a new boy filled with fear loaded his gun with a pebble and when strangers attempted to pass the guards, fired. It was also here that an exploding shell penetrated a boy's eye destroying it, both accidents to be deplored, but bespeaking greater care.

Mr. E. D. Ressler, who visited us some time since, pronounced our work really remarkable, and Hon. Bruce Dennis, of La Grande, who called here last spring to deliver a commencement address, spoke of the affair in his paper, the La Grande Daily Observer, in glowing terms. Every citizen in Ontario is justly proud of our cadet corps and the result attempted. Could every school in Oregon have one it would be the greatest step along moral lines that has ever been taken in the state. It includes the big, strong, husky fellow as well as the sickly fellow, and brings out both by bringing them face to face with real patriotism. The boy loves the flag better for marching under its folds. He honors his country more because he feels himself a component element of it. The uniform he wears suggests and teaches this. Out of our 39 Seniors, 18 are boys and 17 of these wear the uniforms. It is not compulsory and some few parents who do not understand the motive back of it, will not permit their children to buy uniforms. We are wanting the new Springfield rifles so tnat in the spring we may take up target practice work. To this end we have written the state government and believe that we will get assistance.

No talent, no self-denial, no brains, no character is required to set up in the grumbling business; but those who are moved by a genuine desire to do good have little time for murmuring or complaint.

Teachers' Organizations and Teachers' Tenure

By H. D. SHELDON, University of Oregon

For many years the leaders in teachers' organizations have devoted themselves to general educational problems and have fought shy of endeavoring to promote what may be frankly called "the trade interests" of their members. By this phrase I mean to cover salaries, pensions, improvement of conditions respecting tenure and the like. This esoteric policy of ignoring in the main those problems which most vitally effect the living conditions of teachers has been a great mistake. It has confined the active interest in the organizations to small groups, mostly composed of highly-paid administrators and has prevented the teachers' organizations from developing any effective machinery for influencing public opinion.

The homopathic attempts which the national educational association has made to influence teachers' salaries have failed of results because of this lack of instrumentalities for agitation and publicity. Referring to the two famous reports of 1904 and 1913 on the economics of teachers' salaries it may fairly be asked, "How largely have the teachers and public been influenced by these reports?" As a matter of fact, with the exception of a few classes in the normal schools and colleges, they have fallen absolutely flat. Until the teachers of this country secure a close organization with trade journals and local chapters in the different towns and cities working along the path of a well-defined policy, teachers' salaries will be the first to fall in periods of depression and the last to rise in good times.

In the matter of teachers' tenure, organization is equally necessary. In the smaller towns and country districts the uncertainty of tenure is probably the most serious obstacle to improvement. For fourteen or fifteen years I have been engaged in training teachers, most of them secondary but some of them going into the ranks of the elementary teaching. I have found that many of the best-trained graduates of our universities go out full of enthusiasm, they take hold of the schools in some outlying district with great ambition to succeed and render social service to the community. After a time such a graduate finds it necessary to do something which antagonizes the editor of the community or an influential member of a woman's club. From that day the teacher or principal is pursued relentlessly with a tomahawk; in an average American community it is surprising what one petty-minded vindictive person can do in this direction. In a majority of cases the principal or teacher goes; after two or three similar experiences he leaves teaching for some other occupation.

I know the pay has something to do with it, but in talking with these men and women I have concluded that the pay is secondary; that an able man or woman in most American communities will be promoted to a living wage in the course of time, but it is this being at the mercy of all the gossips in the community and this continuous effort of combining the wisdom of the serpent with the harmlessness of the dove that gets on the teacher's nerves and causes him to go, whenever possible, into some other line of work. So the teaching profession in this country, if it is to maintain its self-respect, must have a more secure tenure than we have at the present time.

The framing of a tenure law is a difficult proposition. Now, take any system which gives the governing authorities of the school a free hand; should the board get into politics, or a man with more personal ambition than judicial wisdom becomes superintendent of schools, there is nothing to protect the teacher. On the other hand, a law is unjust which compels the governing board to go into court in order to dispossess a teacher. Now, we must strike a happy medium between these two extremes. The solution will be found along the following lines:

1. With larger facilities for training teachers the public should insist that the normal schools and colleges and other institutions for training teachers exercise a much larger degree of selection than they do at the present time. There are admirable citizens who may become good secretaries and bookkeepers, but they are not endowed with the qualities necessary to make them successful teachers. At the outset of their careers they should be kindly but firmly informed of the situation and advised to enter some other calling.

2. The next suggestion is for the establishment of the probationary period of two or three years. If we are to have a fixed tenure for teachers there must be a probationary period and the hands of the authorities must be relatively free during the probationary period. This plan, as it may readily occur to you, opens the door to a certain amount of favoritism and partiality, but I fail to see any plan which would not be open to this objection. It would, however, have this advantage: That after a teacher completed this period it would be possible for her to work quietly and with some respect and with the feeling that her future is secure.

3. After the probationary period is successfully passed, the usual method of the annual election should be abolished and a longer term of service substituted. Perhaps at first teachers should be elected for a definite term of service of three or five years as in colleges, this to be followed by a general appointment on good behavior. Where a question arises as to the qualifications of experienced teachers, the teachers' organizations should be consulted as is done in other professions, notably law and medicine.

At the outset, local teachers' organizations might be disposed to take a narrow and selfish view, supporting all members regardless of qualifications. But in the course of time, combined in a national organization with the necessity of establishing a national policy, they would inevitably grow to take a large and public-spirited position.

The experience of some European teachers' associations along this line confirms me in the opinion that the teachers' associations will have this public-spirited attitude. Take the institute of elementary teachers of Scotland, one of the most successful in the world. Prof. John Adams, now of London, but formerly of Glasgow, told me that while president of the Scottish Elementary

Teachers' Association, the council of that association, through him, passed on cases reported by the inspectors; that is, where the inspectors of schools reported a certain small number of teachers for inefficiency, that the association inquired into these cases and if it seemed to be a case animated by spite of the teacher, the association stood back of the teachers. But where the inspector was right and the teachers had become incapacitated for their work, that the association of Scottish teachers supported the inspectors in their report; and that out of 7000 or 8000 teachers in Scotland there were perhaps seven or eight clear cases of this sort, and in these cases the association co-operated with the educational department.

The point is made in some quarters that the pre-occupation with the material interests of teaching will create a suspicion on the part of the public that teachers are largely mercenary in their aims, seeking a minimum of work for a maximum of pay. This criticism undoubtedly points to a very real danger. The critics must remember, however, that it is only the exclusive pre-occupation with trade interests which is subject to this indictment. There is no reason why the local teachers' associations should not combine the trade protection, so badly needed, with other wider forms of activity.

The most important line of activity may well be the continued growth of the teachers through further study. I think we American teachers can learn a good deal from the German—I do not know that the Germans are very popular just now, but in this field we can learn something from them. They have admirable associations. Take the large cities of Germany like Hamburg and Berlin and Leipzig and you will find the teachers have a building with a gymnasium and even a pyscological testing laboratory in the case of the city of Leipzig. They publish a newspaper and the social activities of the teachers of those cities are centered in this large building, and perhaps one-half or two-thirds of the teachers take part in some organization or other. They have botany clubs and drama clubs and tramping clubs which go into the country and seek the historic spots.

One of the most admirable features of this study activity is the fact that the teachers initiate most of the activities themselves. Once in a while they invite some one in to lecture, but this feature is merely incidental. In our own country it is the weakness of American teachers to listen to highly-spiced lectures by some celebrity rather than to undertake actual study.

In conclusion, I desire to emphasize the truth that such study and self-improvement when voluntarily elected by the teachers themselves than when forced by the edicts of superintendents and boards of education, unless the teacher has a hearty, willing and spontaneous attitude toward the work of professional self-improvement, the energy will be nine-tenths wasted. It is this truth which places so large a responsibility on the local teachers' association or club.

I like a trotting horse that puts all other horses in a gallop; so a teacher that puts all other teachers in a gallop. Take your latitude and longitude frequently and see if someone hasn't passed you; if so, gallop.—David Starr Jordan.

New Life in an Old Community

By JOSEPH K. HART, Reed College, Portland

Theory seems to have become an utterly disreputable creature in these days. Whatever is "theoretical" is questionable; the "practical" alone seems worthy of consideration by the wise. Yet, there was a time when men believed in theory; when they felt sure that theory—a broad, far-reaching view of events, experiences or tasks —was necessary; when, indeed, it was held that by theory alone could life be redeemed from the immediateness of common routine and be made to know freedom. Perhaps that sort of time will come again, in some braver future. At the present, however, theory has no proper standing; practical aims and methods, alone, can claim attention.

Hence, this story shall be practical. It shall be not the wild vaporings of theory in the midst of an otherwise sane world of practical men and women. It shall be the tale of actuality—a real experience, simply told. And though even one who runs may read herein a basic theory of the present task, no moral shall be set forth, no conclusion shall intrude. We shall be wholly practical.

There are many out-of-the-way communities in the Northwest. Some of them were deliberately built in remote regions, where the builders never hoped that the "large world" would come. But others were built in the actual paths of development, where the future seemed secure. They were even once centers of the most pronounced activities, holding their heads high, and boasting of their great futures. Now, they lie defeated, decadent, hopeless. This story shall be of one of these defeated and decadent communities.

"Lone Rock" community lies on the shores of an arm of the Puget Sound region; the salt tides bound its northern reaches; on the east rises the "big hill"; to the south a still-primitive wilderness limits the horizon, and looking westward you are thrilled by one of the most magnificent mountain views in all America. It is a beautiful spot, with its mingling of remoteness, of woods and shore, of mountains and the sea. Nothing seems to happen, there, so the people have been accustomed to say.

Yet, things once happened there. Once great saw-mills gnawed at the mighty forests that covered the hillsides. But in an evil hour the sawmills burned to the ground. They never were rebuilt. Nothing of a similarly large character came to take their place. Industry passed on from the community. The village that had been built up around the mills was gradually deserted. The houses grew old, they fell to ruin and decay. Only a few families remained in the vilage; and along the beach for several miles in each direction a scattering of "ranchers" alone remained to tell the story of the earlier life and hope.

That was nearly thirty years ago. The few families that have remained in the community have struggled, almost hopelessly, to gain a living out of the infertile soils. The energies of the community have been sapped by this long and largely unremunerative toil. Hope seems to beckon them to other places—even to the ends of the earth. Yet it seems impossible for them to go—all that they have is here; and there is little chance for them to realize anything on what they have here; they cannot get away, and there seems to be no reason why they should remain. It is a story often repeated in all the West. Industry passes on, and hope goes with it. What shall be the answer of our calmest intelligence to this striking problem? Can our clear thought bring hope again, and help to renew life in these deserted places? Has such an outcome been secured anywhere? "Lone Rock" offers some practical answers to that question.

From many directions, within the past two years, new life has come to this little community. Of course, the co-operative spirit is in the general atmosphere of our time. It is difficult to say just how it happens upon any particular community at any particular time. But within the past year or two a number of new activities have crept into the life of this one. The day school had been for many years a rather lifeless affair. The school building was a dingy and unattractive affair—big enough, indeed, for the few children who came to it—but singularly repellant both in construction and in decoration. But it is impossible to remake a community school by direct means; it is likely that the dingy little school room and the monotonous school life rather accurately echoed the general lifelessness of the community at large.

But of late, new activities have been inaugurated. Some new members have come into the community. Out of this new membership have come some leaders of new activities. In very simple and quiet ways, these new activities have been inaugurated. A women's club was undertaken, with quite remarkable results. Meeting twice a month at the school house, several results were more or less unconsciously accomplished. For example, the women found that they liked each other; that there were good things in the world to be interested in, which could take the place of the endless gossip and feuds that had been their chief interests; that there were tasks in the community that might be undertaken which would make the common life more worth while. It is likely, too, judging by later events, that these continuous meetings in the school house gradually brought the realization that the school building was an ugly place. not quite fit for the children. At any rate, the women of the community began to move constructively along these lines.

In addition to this, there was a night school for part of one year, made up of the young people of the community, and meeting two evenings each week. Young men and women of the community, long out of school, here met and renewed their interest in intellectual things, for a time. No course of study was followed; each attendant did the work that he thought most worth his while, and usually some general discussion, interesting to all who came, ended the evening's work. Not much in the way of definite education was accomplished, perhaps, but a very great deal in the way of individual awakening was accomplished. Some new books were introduced; and some lasting interests were developed.

Alongside this work, and playing into it, mention must be made of the weekly community meeting, held on Saturday evenings. This was, at first, attended by both men and women; but after the women organized their own club, the Saturday evening meeting fell into the hands of the men, and it became the general debating ground for all community projects. It was called the "Lone Rock Improvement Club," and it lived up to its name. A number of important problems engaged the attention of the members. One of these was the problem of a road over the "big hill" to the east. At the best, farming in the neighborhood was difficult and unremuner-ative. But added to this was the difficulty of marketing. The "big hill" offered an almost insurmountable difficulty. But the Improve-ment Club took up the task. Factions in the community had always prevented a common effort in this direction. Some wanted a road over the hill, some wanted to go round the hill by building a cause-way along the beach. The two parties exactly negatived each other and prevented all progress. Now, however, acting in the new co-operative spirit, the community came together as one indiviaual and asked the proper county officials for the construction of a road, declaring that it was not the business of the local people to decide where the road was to go; that the county engineer was elected for just such services; that it was the duty of the county commissioners to make such decisions acting on the advice of the engineer; and that trusting the proper officials to make proper decisions, the com-munity would accept any road to be decided upon, demanding only that some sort of a road be provided.

Such unusual unanimity of action, coupled with such trust in the elected officials could have but one answer: The road was ordered, surveys were made, and the work of construction has now been completed. It was a practical demonstration of what can be accom-plished by co-operation; and the community will never forget it. The result lies there before their eyes, too plain to be mistaken.

A second task was undertaken by this Saturday evening meeting; at least, the discussion was begun. That was the task of re-creating the industrial life of the community. It is a long and difficult task. It is, of course, just what all communities are doing everywhere, more or less incidentally; and it is what many cities are doing intentionally, and more or less intelligently. But it seemed a rather big task to be undertaken by a little community. Of course, to date not any great progress has been made in this direction. But many interesting ideas are germinating in the fertile social soils of the community. Most of the external leadership of the community is now gone; but the life-forces set at work are still moving. The situ-ation is extremely hopeful. It has taken thirty years to bring the community down from its former industrial strength to its present industrial poverty. It would not be wise to expect to restore or rebuild industrial strength in a few short months. It is a long task, but a real task, and the community will continuously think about it and talk about it, and work at it, until some real progress is achieved.

There are many, many little details of the renewing life of the community that should be told. But one large fact, the most important of all, perhaps, must still be told in order to make this practical tale signify most for the educational movement of today. It has been hinted that out of these various meetings at the school house some of the people began to realize that the school building was not a fit place for the children to spend their plastic days; it was dirty, poorly constructed, disreputable in appearance, and barbarously decorated. The building was large enough for the uses of the school, for the number of the children was small. But these new activities brought home to the people of the community not only that the school building was unattractive, but that it was not really large enough to serve the whole community as a community meeting place; and, perhaps, the most significant result of these new movements in this community life was the definite feeling of the leaders of the community (all of them local leaders) that the community must now have a meeting place, big enough to house the whole community in this new co-operative life, and attractive enough to make these new interests and energies feel quite at home.

Without outside suggestion of any kind, simply as the natural development of the native hopes of the people, stimulated by their own accomplishments, as related above and as unrelated in many details, the people made their plans. The building must be completely rebuilt, enlarged, made modern in construction as nearly as possible, and decorated in such ways as to make it a beautiful home for the new community spirit, as well as a more attractive place for the children in the school. It was a difficult undertaking. The people are poor, and afraid of taxes. Yet so well was the whole plan advertised and promoted, that when election day came not a vote was cast against the project. The expenses were approved, plans were prepared, bids called for, contracts let, the work was done, up to the enthusiastic approval of the whole community; and though there were one or two in the community who felt that the community would be ruined by such extravagance, yet when they came to inspect the finished result, their old fears were stilled and they became willing supporters of the community plan.

The completion of the work was celebrated by a community gathering. Not many of the community were absent. It was the community's own occasion. This new building was not made by others and handed over to the community. Their own hopes had urged it; their own new life had demanded it; their own thinking had conceived it; their own votes had ordered it; their own community members had done the work; their own hands were to pay for it; it was their own. Their children should go to school in it, and be unconsciously molded by it. Their clubs and societies should meet in it, proud of their own new community home. It belonged to all, to every one, to each. And in that community gathering, all old community feuds seemed to fall away, and the new home of the community seemed to shelter a new spirit.

What will come of it? Well, that is theory, and must be here avoided. But the work is going on, both in the school house, and in the community at large. It may pass away; that too is theory. But (this may be theory) the practical lesson of it all seems to be that the way to remake a country school, is to begin on the outskirts of the community, and work in.

A Survey of Oregon High Schools

By WM. M. PROCTOR, Stanford University, Berkeley, California

The study habits of high school pupils and methods employed by high school authorities in administering the school study periods in Pacific Coast high schools, has recently been a subject of investigation by the writer. The school of education of the University of Oregon has very generously co-operated in the work by gathering data from Oregon high school principals and high school pupils. During the month of April, 1916, a questionnaire was sent out to the high school principals by the University of Oregon school of education regarding methods of handling the study periods in their schools. Replies were received from fifty-six of the principals and the papers sent to the writer for tabulation. Following is a summary of the replies received that may be of interest not only to the men who contributed by answering the questionnaire but to all those who are interested in secondary education in Oregon. There were five questions asked, and in giving the summary of replies we will state each question in full, giving the grouping of answers under each in order.

1. METHODS OF HANDLING STUDY PERIODS.

Which of the following methods of handling school study periods are in use in your school? Check the one in use. Where there is more than one method, indicate the number of students handled by each method. (1) Students studying in rear of room where another class is reciting. (2) Separate study rooms presided over by a teacher (assembly room, or class-room). (3) A lengthened or double period, where a portion of the time is used in showing pupils how to study. Indicate length of period. (4) Other methods or plans or any combinations of the above.

1. There were 15 high schools which reported employing the plan of having students study in the rear of rooms where recitations were going on. Most of these were schools having fewer than 100 pupils, but one of them was the Washington high school of Portland which reports satisfactory results with the plan.

2. The assembly room plan was reported by 24 of the high schools. These were for the most part the medium-sized or large high schools.

3. No high school reported using exclusively the double or lengthened period, but there were several schools in which (3) was combined with some other plan.

4. Combinations: (a) Twelve high schools reported using combinations of (1) and (2). That is, some of the pupils studied in assembly rooms and some in classrooms where others were reciting. (b) Two high schools had combinations of (2) and (3) i. e. part assembly room and part double-period. These were the Eugene high school and one other school whose principal neglected to designate his school by name. (c) Two high schools reported a combination of (1) and (3). These were The Dalles high school and another

presided over by an absent-minded principal who forgot to give its name. (d) One high school reported a combination of (1), (2) and (3). The principal of the Silverton high school said he had 20 per cent under (1), 60 per cent under (2), and 20 per cent studying under (3). He hoped soon to eliminate (1) entirely.

2. EFFECTIVENESS OF PLAN USED.

What is your judgment as to the effectiveness of the plan used in your school? (1) Five of the 15 schools using plan (1) reported results as satisfactory; 10 said they were unsatisfactory. (2) Fifteen of those using the assembly plan, (2), said that the plan was effective or fairly so, while nine said it was not satisfactory. (3) This plan not used by any exclusively. (4) Combinations: (a) Seven of the 12 using combinations (1) and (2) said it was satisfactory; five said it was not satisfactory. (b), (c) and (d) Of the five schools reporting some combination of (3) with (1) or (2) or both of them, all reported the results of their experimentation with the double or lengthened period satisfactory so far as they had been able to try it out.

3. HOME STUDY PERIODS.

To what extent do you use home study periods? With what success? Just what was meant by "home study periods" was not exactly clear to a number of the principals, but in compiling the replies all schools which reported that pupils were expected to prepare at least one subject at home, as well as those which reported some definite plan of encouraging or supervising home study, were counted as employing "home study periods."

(a) We found that 39 of the 56 schools reporting make more or less use of home study periods with a measure of success. (b) Nine schools have used such periods with poor results. (c) Eight schools do not use home study periods at all.

4. IMPROVEMENT OF HOME STUDY CONDITIONS.

Have you been able to improve the conditions of home study through conferences with parents or through any other method?

(a) Efforts to improve home study conditions by conferences with parents and through the agency of the parent teacher associations were reported by 41 schools. Of these 11 report very good results; 28 report results that are just fair; while two report no measurable results whatever. (b) Two schools report improving study habits at home by making careful assignment of reference work to be done at home and reported on. (c) There were 13 schools which report making no effort to improve home study by any kind of plan.

5. SUGGESTIONS FOR IMPROVING STUDY HABITS.

What measures would you recommend for the improvement of the study habits of high school pupils?

The answers to this question were difficult to classify because some of the principals gave a number of excellent suggestions and others did not give any at all. In making the classification we selected just one suggestion from each paper, i. e. the one upon which the one who filled out the questionnaire seemed to place most emphasis. These suggestions are grouped below under 12 headings and given in the order of the number subscribing to a given suggestion.

1. Would use the double-period for supervised study, or plan (3) 17
2. Insist that teachers master the technique of study and teach their pupils how to study 14
3. Try to educate parents and teachers to keep week-day evenings, except Friday and Saturday, free from social engagements and religious obligations 5
4. Make lesson assignments more definite and hold pupils to stricter accountability 3
5. Confine work to such as can be prepared during school hours 3
6. Provide an after-school period for those who come up to their recitations unprepared 2
7. Study individual cases and cultivate a more intimate touch between teacher and pupils 2
8. Prepare cards for record of home study on which pupils shall make weekly returns of time spent in home study 2
9. Raise scholarship standards and increase the amount of work necessary for graduation 2
10. Establish an evening study period at school for boys who are backward in their studies 1
11. Single sessions, from 8 a. m. to 12:30 p. m. daily 1
12. No suggestions to offer 4

Total number of principals answering 56

The 56 high schools, whose principals replied to the questionnaire, do not represent a very large portion of the high schools of the state of Oregon, but they constitute the group containing a large proportion of the high school population. All but three or four of the high schools having over 200 students in the state are among the 56 reporting, hence the replies are fairly representative of the secondary schools of the state.

When 10 our of 15 employing Plan One report that the results are unsatisfactory, even though the schools are for the most part small it is a pretty fair indication that one of the most serious problems confronting the principal of a small school is the difficulty of satisfactorily administering the study periods of his pupils. There are so few teachers in these schools, and each teacher has so many teaching periods a day that no time is left for supervision of study or taking charge of a study hall. The best solution of the difficulty both for the high school pupils an the tax-payers is the elimination of the small high schools, wherever possible, by means of consolidation into Union High School Districts, in order that adequate buildings and faculties may be secured to do the work in the most efficient way.

In contrast with the 66.66 per cent of those employing Plan One who said it was unsatisfactory, 62.5 per cent of those reporting the use of Plan Two i. e. the assembly room plan, stated that it was satisfactory, or fairly so. The assembly method of conducting study periods may be said to be the most prevalent type of study administration in the American high schools today. It is the plan employed in most of the schools having over 100 pupils. That it is not the best possible plan is shown by the fact that 37.5 per cent of those using it in Oregon find it unsatisfactory. Its chief weakness, according to the testimony of the principals, lies in the fact that the teacher in charge is not able to properly supervise the study of pupils who are studying subjects with which she is not familiar. Also in the larger schools it happens more often than not that there are so many in the study hall as to make police duty the only function of the study hall supervisor. Several high schools in California have been trying out the plan of securing a "study coach" who devotes her entire time to supervision of the study hall; but in talking with the principals of these high schools the writer has been informed that great difficulty has been experienced in finding a person who combined all around ability in scholarship with the necessary amount of disciplinary force.

The five schools which employ some combination of (1) or (2) with (3), while constituting a very small proportion of the total number of schools reporting, belong to a class of high schools engaged in an interesting experiment with supervised study. None of the five Oregon schools had adopted in its entirety the double-period or lengthened-period plan; but to the extent to which they had tried it out they expressed themselves as satisfied with the results, and as intending to make still further use of the plan in their future work.

At the present time there are 20 to 25 high schools in Oregon, Washington and California employing the double-period plan of supervised study, or Plan Three. The Everett, Washington, high school employs a 90-minute period, divided 45 minutes recitation and 45 minutes supervised study under the teacher of each subject. The Snohomish, Washington, high school, which was the first high school on the Pacific Coast to adopt the double period, has an 80-minute period, divided 40-40. Quite a number of schools have a 60-minute period divided 40-20, 45-15, 35-25, or 30-30. After a careful examination into the experience of these schools with the double period, the writer has failed to find one of them where the results were not more satisfactory than either Plan One or Plan Two.

In the study of the study habits of high school pupils referred to at the beginning of this article the schools having the assembly plan of study administration and those having the double period plan were compared. Pacific Coast high school pupils to the number of 1661 wrote answers to a 10-question questionnaire on their study habits. Nine high schools, from which 1182 replies were received, were of the assembly type, and four, sending 479 replies, were of the double period type.

Answering the question as to how they prepared a history lesson 30 per cent of the pupils from the assembly type of schools said they used "outlines, maps, etc.," while 55 per cent of the pupils from the double period type of schools claimed to have such a method of preparing a lesson in history.

In the matter of having a regular program of study which they aimed to follow every day in preparing their lessons it was found that 55 per cent of the assembly school pupils had such a program, while 83½ per cent of the double period school pupils made the same report.

They were asked the question, "Where do you study best, at home or at school?" Of the assembly school pupils 45 per cent said they could study best at home; 45.70 per cent said at school; and 9.30 per cent had no preference. But only 26½ per cent of the double period pupils said they could study best at home, while 66½ per cent said they could study best at school, leaving 7 per cent who expressed no preference. Improved study facilities and supervised study at school evidently turned the balance of opinion, in the case of the double period pupils, toward study at school.

Again in the matter of the improvement of study habits the replies received are significant. They were asked whether they thought their study habits would be improved if instructed in how to study by their high school teachers. There were 45½ per cent of the assembly school pupils who thought their habits might be so improved; 44 per cent thought they already knew how to study, or doubted the ability of their high school teachers to give worth while instruction in that line; 10½ per cent expressed no opinion. From the double period schools, where they had had some experience with instruction in how to study, 82 per cent of the pupils not only favored such instruction but said their study habits had actually been improved as a result of it; 13 per cent expressed themselves as doubtful of the benefits of instruction in how to study or were opposed to it entirely; and 5 per cent failed to answer the question or did not venture an opinion.

Referring again to the answers given by Oregon high school principals to question No. 2, as to the effectiveness of the plans of administering the study periods in their schools, we find that there were 51 schools out of the 56 which employ Plans One or Two, or some combination of these two plans. Out of that number there are 24 principals who report that these plans are unsatisfactory. That is, there are 47 per cent of the 51 using Plans One and Two who are not satisfied with the results. Taking these figures in connection with the replies of the principals to question No. 5, in which they are asked to make suggestions as to the best means of improving the study habits of high school pupils, we find that 17 of them recommend the double period, or Plan Three; 14 insist that the teachers should master the technique of study and teach their pupils how to study; and three suggest that the work be confined to such as can be accomplished during school hours. These replies would all imply the double period or some other form of supervised study. It would appear, then, that while only five of the 56 principals are now using Plan Three, there are 34, or 60.7 per cent of them, who believe that Plan Three or some kindred plan would do most to improve the study habits of high school pupils.

Returns from the double period type of schools above referred to show that there is a very vital relation between the amount of well directed study time spent in school and the necessary amount of home study time.

The answers of the principals to questions three and four indicate the difficulty of reaching effectively the home study of the pupils. Various means of securing more satisfactory results from home study were reported, but out of the 41 principals making such attempts only 11 report very satisfactory progress; 28 report returns as small; and two indicated that they could get fair returns from assigned readings but not from regular lesson assignments to be prepared at home. The proper line of experimentation would therefore seem to be in the direction of more time spent in school study under some form of supervision superior to Plan One or Two. Plan Three is commending itself to a great many high school principals, not only on the Pacific Coast, but throughout the Middle West and East. It presents difficulties of adjustment, particularly to the small high school with less than six teachers, but if study habits are improved, if discipline is simplified, if elimination is reduced to a minimum, and if standards of scholarship are distinctly raised as a result of the adoption of such a plan of administering the study periods of a high school, the high school principals of Oregon will certainly not be the last to make an effort to try it out. The progressive spirit of their answers to the questionnaire would lead us to believe that they are alive to the seriousness of the problem and have a disposition to try any plan that promises to improve existing conditions.

The River of Dreams.

The river of dreams runs silently down

By a secret way that no one knows;

But the soul lives on while the dream tide flows

Through the gardens bright or the forests brown,

And I think sometimes that our whole life seems

To be more than half made up of dreams;

For its changing sights, and its passing shows,

And its morning hopes, and its midnight fears,

Are left behind with the vanished years.

Onward, with ceaseless motion,

The life stream flows to the ocean,

And we follow the tide, awake or asleep,

Till we see the dawn on love's great deep,

Then the bar at the harbor mouth is crossed,

And the river of dreams in the sea is lost.

—Henry van Dyke.

Rural School Department

Edited by MRS. M. L. FULKERSON, Salem, Oregon

WHAT DOES IT MEAN TO YOU?

What does Christmas mean to you
  As you work and worry away?
Is it   only a break in your slavish tasks,
  A myth, or a holiday?

If you've wept with the sad and shared your crust
  With the needy at your door,
If you've smiled with the glad and shown your trust
  In those who have erred once more,

If each morning bright when the day's begun
You can face the light and no man shun,
  Then Christmas is more than a myth to you,
  For the works of Christ have in you come true,
And all days are the same when done.

—C. R. Scroggie, in Midland Schools.

* * *

IS THE GAME WORTH THE CANDLE?

So you say Industrial Clubs for boys and girls are failures, mere fads, and that the effort expended in this direction is too great for the the returns? Well, if you persist in that opinion, stranger, perhaps you had better accompany me to Monmouth and see whether your sentiments will find backing among the farmers of the community. To make this trip amount to anything, however, let us first inquire into the plan of the work as conducted there. During the spring months of 1916 the seventh and eighth organized a club and the fifth and sixth grade children followed suit. In each case there was nothing unusual in the organization. They availed themselves at Monmouth of the capable assistance offered to all the schools of the state by O. A. C. and Superintendent Churchill. Mr. Seymour and Superintendent Reynolds visited the club once during the school year. On account of the organization of the school itself it was impossible to have more than three club meetings, consequently the work of the advisor became individual in nature. In this capacity the advisor visited each of his club members at least twice, some four times, at his home where the project work was being done. Contrary to your expectation the children live many of them as far as two miles from school. In all, the Ford which the advisor borrowed from an interested party, showed it required 33 miles of traveling to visit all of the club members at their homes. In addition to this, stranger, you must remember the advisor was not the direct teacher of any of the children. So you may well see that it required effort to accomplish whatever the club may have done. Now let us go to Monmouth. This is Monmouth, the home of the Oregon Normal School, which you see over yonder. You wish to interview those interested in the industrial work. Very well, we shall first speak to the teachers who have the children in charge.

"The children take a pride in their achievement and like to discuss their projects in the class." Um—nothing odd about that, all children are that way.

"Yes, but there is such an air of realness and accuracy to their discussion—something that comes only from the actual doing of the thing; the very point emphasized in project work." So? Well, perhaps I have overlooked that feature. Thank you for calling my attention to it. But let me see, who supervises the work?

"The gentleman you see yonder, one of the instructors in the Normal." Sir, I have come to interview you about club work, what have you to say?

"Well, I have a great deal to say, it is nothing for a weakling to attempt, and I may say don't touch it if you are looking for a snap." Why not?

"In the first place it takes as much as three hours a week of the teacher's time, in the second the teacher must be able to meet the parents as well as the children and finally she must have a practical and definite message for patrons and children alike." You mean she must sort 'er educate the community?

"Never, I wish she might, but the teacher who tries it is making a mistake; she should work toward having the parents assist in a definite way the making practical all school lessons. Once the teacher succeeds in getting the parents to the point where they will agree to help 'put Johnnie or Mary through' the project, they have given their tactit consent to have, in many cases at least, new ideas brought into the home. Yes, of course in the end this means a better community." Don't you think this is asking a great deal from the teacher?

"Not as much as it appears so far as my experience in this sort of work goes, I need at least three hours a week of this sort of knocking around out in the open for the exercise if for nothing else. It sharpens the teacher's wits to have to match them with the parent. So I feel my club work has made me keener mentally as well as better physically, and in addition, as I go from home to home I get some valuable sidelights on the successes and failures of the children besides the actual knowledge I pick up for class-room use. I feel I am a much stronger teacher for having taken up club work." I see then you give the time willingly. But will you answer me this, have you any way of knowing whether this work has been of benefit to the children?

"Many ways. Here are a few. One boy raising pigs came to me of his own accord and said, 'I don't see how Mr. A. can afford to keep pigs. He is feeding three times as much grain to his as I feed mine. Now that costs money, I know it because I had to work a day and a half to earn enough to buy a sack of shorts for my pigs.' Get me? The rigid necessity of economy and the value of a dollar were being driven into that boy in a way that class-room exercises could never do. Another boy when told by Mr. Allen that his hogs needed a wallow, acted on the suggestion and dug one in the orchard. He filled it with water, turned the pigs in and then called for his mother. When she came one of the pigs, in its effort to get out, pulled some dirt into the wallow. His mother said, 'Johnnie, why don't you slap that pig, he will fill your wallow if you aren't careful.' Johnnie looked up so innocently and confided, 'I know mamma, but I have to humor them a bit.' And Johnnie did humor his pigs. He never allowed any other to care for them. He had caught a vision no class-room exercise could have driven home with the same force—that pigs must be treated as individuals, not collectively. The breeder puts it this way, feed the individual, not the herd. Another boy kept after his father to get him a pig. The father made promises. Finally after two months of promises, Mr. Allen helped the father make good the promise. To make a long story short, Neal became so infatuated with his pig, Red, that he fed him five times a day. And many a time the parents say, 'Neal would jump up from the table, refusing to eat until he had fed Red.' At the end of the third month Neal's pig had made a gain of 48 pounds for a period of 30 days; the following month Red put on 62 pounds. This brought him to 138 pounds at barely 4 months. The pig was weighed at the town prune dryer where all could see it. Soon the uncle from whom Neal bought the pig was being twitted about the difference in the litter mates. The uncle's would tip barely 70. He replied he 'guessed it didn't pay to force pigs, so he left his to take care of themselves.' Figures show that when Red was putting on two pounds a day it was costing Neal, feed, labor and all, barely 9 cents a day. He was offered 10 cents a pound live weight, so you can figure for yourself whether it paid. Needless to say, Red was the talk of the town. Neal had all the boys come and see Red. I went to see him and found Red delighted to see me. He quite willingly played the different roles Neal had taught him. My story is done. Neal is in the sixth grade this year, and already is planning on a pure-bred sow for next year. I wonder whether it paid. Neal is found at home evenings tending Red. Another boy whom I might mention 'fizzled' his project, never sticks to anything, and spends his time on the streets. With three or four years of such living to base your judgments upon, stranger, which of the two would you pick to succeed?"

Foolish question, you know; but don't you have anything but pigs in Monmouth? "Well, I might tell you how the girls' canning club in the two years it has worked has made so marked an impression that, growing out of a steam pressure canning demonstration held before the parent-teachers' association, at least two different families have been led to purchase canners, while I find it an added pleasure to loan mine for canning beef, fish, etc. I might tell you how Beth Ostrom was so anxious to complete her project well that she refused to go to the hop fields until she had canned everything required in such quantities that she could select a good exhibit from it; how she wrote our her report and put it with the exhibit in my care with the strict injunction that it be exhibited at the town, county, and state fairs. I followed my directions and Beth's spirit of never die together with her general excellence won her the highest honor in the state. There are three other canning girls who did splendid work also. Yet, we had some good gardens, too, some poutlry, some sewing, some baking, some handicraft." Did any fail to complete their work?

"Yes, I see you smile. Don't forget that broken promise of yours, those failures in your work or let us make it more general. Think of the number of failures in the business and professional world. We do not wonder that we have failures, we can only do our best to keep the percentage down. In our club fully 80 per cent did some work worth while, and 50 per cent did considerable work." How about the parents, do they endorse this work?

"We can soon find out. It has been my experience that once the parent undertsands the motive he willingly endorses. Let's take a swing around my club circuit. We will take them all in. The first mother answers the bell. 'Oh, you just must see the excellent work Romaine is doing. I am so glad for the lessons she is using, I find things in them I can use.' Romaine brings her sewing which is excellent and modestly confesses, 'I am working to get the trip to Corvallis.' Down the line a mother steps to the door and says, 'Mr. A., you are just wasting your time coming here, my boys work and they work hard, if you would teach the things up there which you ought to and let us tend to our homes ourselves I would be better satisfied.' Ouch—that stings, but knowing the conditions we reserve our judgment and pass on. 'We are so glad to see you. Mary is having trouble with her report, can't you help us?' Another mother with tears in her eyes, 'Mr. A. I am so glad you are taking an interest in my boys. I appreciate it more than you can realize.' We visit the father in the field and he can't talk enough about how his boy is getting along. 'Worth the trouble, it isn't any trouble to me and besides it is a good thing.' And so we go on, using the camera whenever the children have done anything worth picturing. We arrive at a home where the indulgent mother says, 'I always felt that son had a lot to him but now I know. Visits from you encourage him. His dad just laughs at him.' So we round up the dad and have a talk. Another mother opens the door with a smile on her face— how different from the discouraged look of last year when her children failed to finish their projects—and tells how Johnnie's fly-trap and bird houses are working, how she appreciates our interest. But the farmer at the next field yells out, 'Get out of here, can't you see we are busy; sic 'em Tige! Oh, come back, I didn't know who it was.' and he tries to patch it up for that home appreciates the human interest attached to our work. Now we run out to the J. B. Stump farm and find Mr. Stump a most entertaining host. As we walk around the farm he tells us, 'Now this is the way you should do, come and visit the boys and give them encouragement. There's Mr. Allen, the boys are crazy about him. He is the man Johnnie wants to see. And say, you should have seen how Johnnie dug into his corn after that letter you wrote him. Say, it was just fine; he put in three whole days paying me back with work on the corn. I certainly think a lot of this club work.' And right here let me say Johnnie Stump not only won prizes on his pigs but he took a prize on his corn, too. I wish you could have time to have Johnnie tell the story, how each second day he would take the pony to town and bring out a cart of skim milk, mix it with the barley and feed it, how he dug a wallow for his sows and another for his boars and hauled water from the well, how he washed and handled his pigs; then tell you how after almost giving up his corn he dug in and cultivated three acres twice to pay his father for caring for his eighth acre for two weeks. If any person tells you that Johnnie did not do the work himself, ask him why Johnnie was so concerned about the Burcell pig. Johnnie actually took a string and measured the pigs and compared them with the Burcell pig. He told me a month before fair , 'Burcell can't beat me, why his pig is one and one-half inches shorter than mine and besides he is feeding oil meal.' But enough, stranger, you can see the attitude of the teachers, pupils, and the parents well enough to draw your own conclusions. I leave it with you, is the game worth the candle?"—L. P. Gilmore, Monmouth, Oregon.

*   *   *

CORRESPONDENTS WANTED.

A class of eighth grade boys in a rural school want to correspond with other eighth grade boys who intend to take higher work. Address Miss Nella McCane, R. F. D., Helix, Oregon.

*   *   *

SUGGESTIONS FOR CHRISTMAS.

When you are racking your brain to think of something new for the Christmas program suppose you try staging a good Christmas story. Read and discuss it with your pupils. Let the children make the interpretation and adaption of each part. Let them decide upon the stage setting and the costuming. You will be surprised at the interest they will take in this. The acting will be natural and easy because they will live the scenes they portray. There is a vast amount of language training in this exercise.

*   *   *

The following pictures selected from the list in the Oregon Course of Study are especially fitting to December study: (1) Raphael—Madonna of the Chair; Sistine Madonna. (2) Reynolds—Cherub Choir. (3) Murillo—The Good Shepherd. (4) Lerolle—Arrival of the Shepherd. (5) Breton—Shepherd's Star. Teach the poem, "A Visit from St. Nicholas."

*   *   *

Your older girls will take delight in compiling a cook book as a Christmas gift to mother. Let each one bring her mother's favorite recipe and any others that are available. These may be copied by the pupil and made into booklets having attractive cover designs.

*   *   *

Here are some questions that may be of interest to your pupils in December:

1. How much later does the sun rise December 22 than June 21? How much earlier does it set?

2. What evergreens are much used for Christmas decoration? What Christmas green was held sacred in olden times?

3. How large is Palestine? What other names have been applied to Palestine? What celebrated river flows through it?

4. What is the "Holy City"? How far is it from Bethlehem?

5. Who followed the star to Bethlehem? Why did Joseph take Mary and Jesus to Egypt?

6. What are some of the points of interest to be seen in Egypt?

7. Describe an imaginary journey from your home to the city of Cairo in Egypt.

* * *

For December seat work draw and color the following: Fireplace with stockings suspended; sprays of holly and mistletoe with berries; evergreen trees—pine, fir, hemlock, cedar.

Trace from pattern and color: Reindeer, sleigh, camel, sheep, shepherd's crook.

Cut and color: Stars, bells, stockings. Write "Merry Christmas, 1916" on each. Make Christmas booklets, tying together several leaves of paper with Christmas ribbon. Paste a small Madonna picture on the front cover. Under the picture write, "Merry Christmas, 1916." Write appropriate Christmas poems or quotations on the inside leaves.

Illustrate booklets containing Christmas stories or poems, by using original drawings or pictures cut from magazines.

Make strings of beads from salt and starch: Two tablespoons salt and one tablespoon corn starch, heat thoroughly and add hot water to make a stiff dough. Color may be added to the water before mixing with the dry ingredients. Tube paint, water colors, egg dyes, or even tissue paper may be used for coloring. Measure the dough when cold in a small spoon or thimble so that each bead will be proportionate to the rest. Roll each portion in the palm of the hand until in the desired shape. Place the beads on hat pins or a small wire until dry and then string on strong thread.

* * *

JOINT COMMUNITY FAIR IN KLAMATH COUNTY.

That Klamath county has some live wires among its teachers is evidenced by the following report which has just reached our office. We like to get reports like this. It helps us all to know who is doing things and how things are being done. Here is the report:

The first joint community fair in Klamath county was held at Mt. Laki church, October 20, 1916, by the four adjoining districts: Mt. Laki, C. D. Corpening, teacher; Fairview, R. K. Hannon; Henley, F. S. Sexton, principal, with the Misses Dobry and Rose as assistants; Spring Lake, M. B. Ford. These were the schools that participated in the fair.

Industrial club work was begun in these schools last spring by Messrs. Sexton and Ford and the Misses Selma McReynolds and Neva McKee who were the teachers last year. Mr. Corpening succeeded Miss McReynolds, and Mr. Hannon took up Miss McKee's work this year. At the time of organization the clubs each planned to hold a local school fair, but during the summer Mr. Corpening and Mr. Ford did some planning together and conceived the idea of holding a joint community fair instead. A conference was held with the heads of the two other schools, and then the scheme was laid before the Parent-Teacher Association in each district with the result that all approved. Each association began at once to lay plans to make the fair a success.

Three lines of exhibits were decided upon: (1) Exhibits by pupils who had completed their club projects. (2) Exhibits by pupils of each school in competition with pupils of the same school; exhibits to be products produced by the pupil or selected from the products grown by his parents. (3) A general exhibit by all pupils and club members in competition with all other entries; this division to be subdivided into a section for boys' exhibits and one for girls' exhibits. In this exhibit a boy must show five farm products, two grains and three vegetables, or three grains and two vegetables. A girl must show five articles of home work, two of baking and three of sewing or three of baking and two of sewing.

The plan further provided: That each district should provide a booth in which to exhibit the work from that district; that the forenoon be given to viewing and judging the exhibits, and the rendition of a program consisting of short talks, music, and recitations, all districts participating; that the afternoon be given to sports such as races and a ball game.

The Parent-Teacher Associations of the four districts responded loyally. Each planned and decorated a booth in the most artistic manner possible, using the school colors as a basis. Mt. Laki chose blue and gold, Fairview black and orange, Henley red and gold, and Spring Lake white and gold. Everybody present wore the colors of the district he represented.

The booths were filled to overflowing with exhibits of grain, vegetables, sewing both plain and fancy, baking, jelly, preserves, handicraft and curios. In the yard outside were exhibits of chickens, cattle, and hogs all brought in by the children.

Over 300 exhibits were displayed by 115 pupils. One hundred and thirty dollars were distributed in prizes. This amount was furnished by the county court, which had appropriated $500 to be used in this way throughout the county. About 500 people attended the fair and the day was perfect. A bounteous luncheon was provided by the Parent-Teacher Associations. The afternoon of sports—foot races, egg races, potato races, sack races, and a baseball game—provided a rollicking good time for everybody. People grown old with care forgot it and became young again. Everyone went home happy, voting the fair a complete success.

Plans are being laid for a still bigger event next year. The way has been paved for a much larger and farther reaching social work. The spirit of co-operation has been strengthened by the results shown by this first attempt, and a new view of the teacher's position is being taken by the people in these districts. He is no longer merely a teacher but is looked upon as a representative of the community working for the good of all. Through the efforts of these teachers this group of schools has become the hub—the nucleus of the progressive school work of the county. Such features as student self government, glee clubs for rural pupils, rural school papers, practical rural science and many others are being worked out successfully.   ·

* * *

PUBLIC SCHOOL COMPOSITIONS.

A number of compositions were submitted during the month of October, some of which, while possessing merit, were too long for publication. We are always glad to read the compositions submitted but cannot undertake to make corrections nor return manuscripts unless full postage is sent for mailing purposes.

Before sending a composition to us it should be carefully corrected by the teacher in the presence of the writer and errors pointed out. Then a careful copy should be made by the pupil. If composition writing is to benefit the pupil he must have a hand in correcting his work. The pupil will gain nothing if his composition is corrected in this office, besides we haven't time to make the corrections.

We want only original compositions, on subjects of which the pupils have a personal knowledge. Don't send us reproduction compositions, because we do not consider them of any value in composition work, except in the primary grades.

We should like to receive original compositions and in order to stimulate interest we will select from those sent us each month, the best one written by a boy and the best one written by a girl and publish them in this department. The names of the winners will be placed on the Composition Honor Roll which will be printed in each issue throughout the year. Compositions should not exceed 300 words and must be in the hands of the editor of this department by the first of the month previous to publication.

Grade Teachers' Department

Edited by SABRA CONNER, 421 West Park Street, Portland, Oregon

Elementary teachers and elementary teachers' associations are cordially invited to send news items of their activities which would be of interest or value to other teachers to this department of the The Oregon Teachers Monthly. Address Editor of Grade Teachers' Depart. ment, Room 300, Court House, Portland, Oregon.

A Multnomah County Teachers' Association was organized Saturday, October 14, at Gresham. Superintendent A. P. Armstrong acted as temporary chairman, and after an enthusiastic discussion of the question, the formal organization took place. Mrs. Rhoda Wallace of the Gilbert school was elected president; Miss Marion Robertson of Rockwood, vice-president; Mrs. Grant of Fairview, secretary-treasurer. It was decided to hold the next meeting Saturday, October 28, at 11 a. m., in the office of County School Superintendent A. P. Armstrong. At this meeting the organization was completed and the future work of the association outlined.

* * *

The Recreation Committee of the Portland Grade Teachers' Association has been busy planning outings to industrial plants. The first of this nature was a trip to the Woolen Mills, Paper Mills and Electric plant at Oregon City on November 4. An added attraction was the personally-conducted trip to the McLoughlin Home and other historic points of interest by Mrs. Eva Emery Dye. The recent Columbia Highway trip planned by the recreation committee was especially interesting because of the fact that most of the party were seeing the Columbia scenery for the first time and their enthusiasm was unbounded. In spite of the early morning fog, and the fact that the ladies numbered thirteen, the day was filled with nothing but pleasure, unless it were that the lunch hour at Eagle Creek canyon seemed too short to consume all the good things provided. Many opportunities were given to explore the scenic trails along the highway, the teachers proving themselves good hikers. Altogether it was a day well spent and one to be long remembered.

* * *

Perhaps the grade teachers of Portland hold the record for the size of their theater party at the recent Schumann-Heink concert, as one hundred and sixty-nine of them occupied a block of gallery seats. Many, who were too late to get reservations with the larger group, were scattered in smaller parties throughout the house.

* * *

At the Educational Day meeting of the Federated Clubs, October 21, the members were the guests of the Pendleton Boosters' Club. About twenty-five of the grade teachers of Portland were present. The meeting was addressed by Gov. Withycombe, President Campbell of the University of Oregon, Supt. Churchill, and others in behalf of a Normal School at Pendleton.

* * *

Mrs. Helen Eakin Starrett talked to the teachers of literature in their first regular meeting, October 12, on the subject, How to Cultivate a Love of Literature in Children. "Love of literature as a source of happiness is the view we must take of literature," she said, and gave as the keynote of her talk the old quotation, "A jolly book whereon to look is better to me than gold." She believes that the first crisis in the child's love of literature occurs when he comes from the world of illusion into the

world of realities and first discovers that there is no Santa and no fairies. This period must be carefully bridged by parent and teacher. This is the time to introduce children to the stories of adventure, to animal stories, to literature about pets and nature study. Another critical period is the time of entering the teens. This transition period also must be very carefully handled by teachers of literature. Never tell a child at this period that a book or poem is beyond him or too sentimental for him. Let him have it and get from it what he wishes. Boys and girls at this time are liable to choose such poems as "My Lost Youth" and enjoy its mournful retrospect. Mrs. Starrett recommends as invaluable to the teacher of literature two books by Hiram Corson, The Voice and Spiritual Education and Aims of Literary Education. With these books alone a teacher is well equipped. Add to these Whittier's collection of Child Life in Verse and a teacher has all that is necessary to inculcate a love of literature in children. Mrs. Martha Drury-Scott explained how important freedom of voice is for good interpretation of literature. She illustrated the freedom and simplicity which teachers of literature should seek to cultivate in children by her reading of Over in the Meadow, The Tree, by Joyce Killim, The Yellow Violet, Bryant.

* * *

Ideals.

No body of professional people can wield more influence for good or evil in the developing and moulding of human character than the teaching profession.

The professional aim should be to develop the highest possible moral standard in all that pertains to or will enter into human experience. "Knowledge for knowledge's sake" has its place, but without a standard by which to judge the relative value of this knowledge, the seeker is not prepared to assume the responsibilities which must come to him, nor to handle problems or conditions from the viewpoint of the greatest good to the greatest number.

The teaching profession should occupy the highest place among the professions, but to reach this standard depends entirely upon those within its ranks.

No work is so simple but that some phase ·in this character development can be employed, thus providing one layer in the corner stone for the completed whole.

It is related than an artist upon beholding, for the first time, a masterpiece, exclaimed, "I, too, am an artist." He was conscious of what was within himself and thus was enabled to recognize the same consciousness in the work of the masterpainter.

The consciousness of the power within enabled Lincoln, during the Civil War, to guide the Ship of State to a safe port, in spite of the opposition of those most closely associated with him. The uplifting of humanity was his goal and he stood for his conception of the greatest good to the greatest number.

Disraeli, Lord Beaconsfield, from his study of conditions, during a critical period in England, realized a power within himself which, when put into active use, enabled him to put· through the greatest coup d'etat in English history.

What is it that holds one enrapt before the masterpiece of the sculptor? Is it not that he conveys to the receptivity of the observer the consciousness of his power to express the joys, griefs, beauties or cares of life?

Every masterpice of art or literature, every ennobling deed or act has been possible only through the recognition and development of this power. The highest attenuation of this power is spoken of as a gift, but all are gifted, even if the world does not give recognition.

One educational system may incorporate a line of work in imitation of another system and wonder why the same success does not follow. Why? The new idea was not the result of development; its imitation fell below the ideal; the only remedy for the failure being the acknowledgment and gradual unfolding of the new idea.

Education is defined by Webster as "the systematic training of the moral and intellectual faculties"; character, as "moral excellence." The correlation needs no explanation,

"useless each ,without the other." "Reward?" To know and to see the unfoldment of embryonic thought, in the increased mental force and the understanding of an inward power is the ideal reward of the conscientious and forceful worker.

"With wisdom meet thy brother's need;
Thy thought to worthy effort speed,
Sustained by motives pure as gold—
Thy brother's good thine own must hold."

—Ida Helen Holmes.

The Beacon Method.

Superintendent Fassett has just issued through his publishers, Ginn & Co., an Introductory Second Reader of Animal Folk Tales with illustrations by the famous artist, Charles Copeland. Learning to read by means of The Beacon Method gives the children such a mastery over new words that it is difficult to find enough material properly graded from a phonetic standpoint. The "Beacon Introductory Second Reader" has been carefully compiled to meet this want. Any second grade teacher whose pupils have used The Beacon Method and who is on the lookout for some easy attractive stories properly graded, may have, free of charge for examination, a copy of this book by writing Ginn & Co., the publishers, at 20 Second St., San Francisco, and mentioning Oregon Teachers Monthly.

Mrs. M. L. Fulkerson.

Teachers of the state have missed Mrs. Fulkeerson from the institute this year, but they are all interested in knowing that she has been in Montana this fall spreading the gospel of better rural school methods. Mrs. Fulkerson holds a firm grasp on the hearts of Oregon teachers and they will be glad to welcome her home to Oregon when her work is done in Montana.

Report Cards.

The Oregon Teachers Monthly can furnish report cards for one cent each. The cards are well printed on heavy manilla and are arranged for a nine months' term. A sample will be sent free.

Some Oregon Weeds and Seeds

By A. R. SWEETSER, University of Oregon

It is the plan to describe and illustrate (from month to month) some of the common weeds and their seeds that are to be found in the state.

What is a weed? I have known people who planted in their gardens the seeds of the Bachelor's Button and tended them with great care, but I also know a field wondrously beautiful to look upon because it contains great numbers of this same plant and the owner speaks of them as the troublesome weeds in his pasture. Ruskin says "What is a weed?" "A plant in the wrong place." "It is entirely true that a weed is a plant that has got into the wrong place. But some plants never do. Who ever saw a wood anemone or a heath blossom in the wrong place? Who ever saw a nettle or hemlock in a right one? And yet the difference between flower and weed certainly does not consist merely in the flower being innocent and the weed stinging and venomous. We do not call the nightshade a weed in our hedges, nor the scarlet agaric in our woods. But we do the corn-cockle in our fields." To the agriculturist the weed is a plant which persistently monopolizes the ground desired for other crops. Some one has asked why the weeds thrive while the cultivated plant often languished in spite of the most careful attention. The reply is that the soil is mother of the weed but only stepmother to the other.

For this month we have chosen two of our very common and troublesome inhabitants of the gardens.

The first is the Groundsel or Old Man, known scientifically as Senecio vulgaris, and belonging to the Dandelion family. Figure 1 shows, at the right, a portion of the whole plant, and at the left a single so-called seed, really the fruit, slightly enlarged, with its copious hairs or pappus by which it is parachuted through the air. The middle one is another fruit without its appendage and much enlarged. We say fruit because a careful examination under the microscope would show an outer case, the ripened ovary, with a single seed within, but the whole is commonly spoken of as the seed. The peculiar appearance of the seeds may be made out with any good magnifying glass or one of those three-legged seed testers. The plant is usually clustered, its height and abundance depending upon the richness of the soil but not usually over a foot. The flowers are yellow and inconspicuous and in small heads with an envelope of green bracts. With the ripening of the fruit these bracts turn back, exposing the mass of

Fig. 1.

white hairs, hence the name of Old Man. Since the plant is an annual and grows each year from the seed of the last, the remedy lies in cutting or pulling before the seeds appear.

The second is the Wild Carrot, Queen Ann's Lace, Birds Nest Plant, Daucus carota. This belongs to the large group of plants known as the Umbeliferae because of the sort of flower cluster which occurs in every member and is known as an umbel. It is thought to be the ancestor of the cultivated carrot, but it must have taken a large amount of cultivation and selection to produce the fleshy edible root from the tough one of the wild plant. On the right

Fig. 2.

in Figure 2 is a drawing of a part of a wild carrot plant with its finely-cut leaves and its double-umbel cluster of flowers, with the surrounding bracts finely cut like lace, whence the name queen's lace. As the plant matures the flowers drop and the fruit and lacey bracts roll together, leaving a depression in the center and the whole resembling a bird's nest, or bird's nest weed. To the left is a drawing of an enlarged fruit, also commonly called a seed, with its numerous spines.

This plant is a biennial, that is, it takes two years to mature seed. The first year only a cluster of leaves develops from the seed but the next season flowers and seeds are produced.

The only remedy is to weed them out. As both of these are not native Oregonians but have been introduced with other seeds we see clearly the necessity for protection against undesirable plant immigrants as well as people.

After we have seen the seeds of the common weeds and learned to distinguish them it will be possible to determine the purity of commercial seeds.

City Superintendents' Department

Edited by GEORGE W. HUG, McMinnville, Oregon

Standard Students.

If we have standard grade schools and high schools why not have standard students? We can all see the vast benefit that has been brought about by the policy of the present school administration toward standardization. All common schools have had a measure of their efficiency, a standard to work towards, an ideal to consider and we know what vast improvements have been made to meet these standard requirements. Likewise, with the high schools, equipment has been added where needed, encyclopedias and dictionaries have been supplied by school boards, in fact, the policy of standardization has made its plea to practically every school in the state and

results everywhere in development and improvements.

We know now what a school amounts to if it is on the standard list. We know what to expect of a student entering a standard school, we can estimate the mental ability and preparation of a graduate from standard schools but have we an absolute measure of this ability and preparation? Isn't there a vast range of difference between the brain power of the members of our graduating classes now? A student entering our school coming from a standard school, do we know where to place him or must he pass some sort of an oral or written examination by which we measure his ability? If we judge high schools and classify high schools and grade schools by standardization methods we can apply it still further and judge students and classify students by the same method.

This is not an honor system. The merit of an honor system in high school may be questioned. A standard student is not an honor student. There are certain requirements that one may reasonably expect from students who enjoy the privilege of a modern high school education. It is with this in mind that we have at McMinnville Senior High School worked out a plan of standard students. It is elementary in scope but we feel that it is at least a gentle beginning and, having accepted and entered into zealously by the students, will lead to greater things.

Our requirements for standardization are as follows: A standard student must (1) Have no grades below C or medium; (2) use correct English; (3) spell correctly; (4) write legibly; (5) participate in one student body activity; (6) have no unexcused absense or tardy mark; (7) read one daily newspaper. These requirements are simple and very reasonable but the average high school principal will be surprised at the small number of students who fill all seven.

In our school a faculty commitee of three members have been appointed who have made out the original list and will revise it from time to time. The plan has been put before the students and they are eager and willing to take it up. Competition is keen among boys and girls and among classes, for a place on this standardization list.

The rewards for the standard students will be determined by local conditions. Perhaps, the principal would see fit to exempt standard students from examinations or give them a half day holiday at end of a semester or to allow them some other special privilege of some sort. This may be an aid in securing interest when the plan is first put before the students. About the safest way to insure the success of this plan is to appeal to the pride or school spirit and the interest of the students, and no rewards will be necessary.

What we expect to gain by this is hard to summarize. First, and probably most important, we will have our entire student body working for self-improvement along with the seven reasonable lines of our requirements. Besides this, we will have a measure of the ability of our students that they may know exactly what is expected of them as high school students. Further, other schools may judge our work more closely by our students with which they come in contact if they know that such a student was standard. Furthermore, it shows our community towards what ends we are striving in the development of their children. Lastly, it stimulates each student to do his best to live up to requirements which they realize are not honorary but just, reasonable and proper.—G. H. Oberteuffer, principal of McMinnville High School

The Astoria Schools.

Some of the new ideas and policies inaugurated during the year in the Astoria public schools are the double-periods in the high school, physical training both in the high school and the grades under a physical director, a retardation teacher in one building, and a special departmental teacher, one each of music and of drawing in each building.

The Astoria school board has erected an $80,000 grade building, has completed two portables and three outside play buildings 40 feet by 60 feet.

Superintendent Impel reports that thirty-one of the teachers were in summer school. The school board advanced the salaries $2.50 a month for all teachers who had been with them for three years and would attend some summer term and make six credits. Fifty-one of the fifty-seven teachers have been in school within the past two years.

Night school to teach English and Citizenship to foreigners, has been opened in two buildings during the month of November. An attendance of 138 was recorded the first night and 300 are expected to attend during the winter.

Report Booklets.

The Oregon Teachers Monthly has for sale report booklets arranged to fit the school register and can be used for a year's work of school. The arrangement is systematic and convenient. The price is 2½ cents each or 50 for $1. A sample will be sent free on request.

Oregon Congress of Mothers

By MRS. ELIZABETH HAYHURST, 1070 E. Burnside, Portland

The tenth annual convention of the Oregon Congress of Mothers and Parent Teacher Association that was held at The Dalles October 12, 13 and 14, was more truly a state convention than any previous one as the 100 delegates represented every portion of the state

The self-sacrifice of The Dalles women, together with the untiring efforts of Mayor Anderson, Superintendents Bonney and Andrews, made everyone feel very appreciative of all that was done toward making the convention the splendid success it was.

The speeches were all helpful, and the presence of Mrs. J. Kemp and Mrs. C. H. Castner, the two other state presidents, bespoke a splendid co-operation among the women's organizations.

Supt. Churchill emphatically endorsed the bill for the minimum term of eight months for rural schools and a teacher's pension bill.

A resolution favoring extending the extension courses of the U. of O., the O. A. C., and the state library, was adopted.

The following working plans for the Women's Legislative Council was unanimously adopted, having previously been adopted by the Federated Clubs and the Consumers League:

Representation—Representation in this council shall be extended to state organizations composed of women, and to those state organizations in which the majority membership of both organizations and board of control is composed of women.

Name—The name of this group shall be The Women's Legislative Council of Oregon.

Object—The object of this council shall be to unify, harmonize and co-ordinate the legislative efforts of the state organizations eligible to membership in this council; and to secure connected action on legislative measures. The council shall not initiate any legislation unless directed by a unanimous vote of instruction of the organizations composing its membership.

Membership—Membership in the council shall consist of the chairman of the legislative committees of state organizations eligible to membership, their alternates or appointees. No organization is entitled to more than one vote and no person shall represent more than one organization in this council. The presidents of such organizations shall constitute an advisory committee without vote.

Officers and Rules of Order—(a) There shall be a chairman and secretary, with duties such as pertain to their respective offices. (b) These officers shall be elected by the council at a time not later than the month of February of the year immediately preceding the state legislative session. (c) The council shall have the power to make rules for its own conduct. Robert's Rules of Order shall govern parliamentary procedure. (d) As to any matter, other than that of business conduct of council, no action shall be taken without a full attendance of its membership, their alternates, or their appointees; provided, that in case in failure or representation of an organization for two consecutive meetings for which not less than twenty-four hours notice shall have been given, formal notice shall be served by the secretary upon the president of the delinquent organization, that membership will be declared forfeited unless an accredited representative shall appear at the next session of the council. (e) Any endorsement of proposed legislation shall have the unanimous vote of the council. (f) The council shall provide each member of the state legislature with a list of the measures bearing the endorsement of the council. (g) Before taking the final vote on any measure, each member of the council shall submit the question under consideration to her legislative committee (or authority) and her vote in the council shall be under direction of her committee (or authority); such consideration in her committee shall be governed by the rules of her organization.

Divisions—There shall be four divisions in this council, the chairman to be appointed by the chairman of the council subject to the approval of its members: (a) Economic, (b) hygienic welfare, (c) educational, (d) civic.

The LaGrande Meeting.

The sixteenth annual convention of the Eastern Division of the Oregon State Teachers' Association at La-Grande, November 1, 2, and 3, was up to the usual high standard and reflected credit on the officers and executive committee. The president, Superintendent Linden McCullough, of La Grande, has a fine presence, a good voice and grace of manner and kept matters well in hand at all times. Superintendent Mrs. A. E. Ivanhoe, of Union County, was secretary and Mrs. N. G. Neill, of La-Grande, was treasurer. These officers and State Superintendent J. A. Churchill, Superintendent J. C. Conley, of Wallowa County, Superintendent J. F. Smith, of Baker County, Superintendent Roy Conklin of Wallowa, and Mr. A. F. Gay, of Baker, constituted the executive committee.

Representatives of the La Grande Commercial Club met all incoming trains with autos the opening day and extended a cordial greeting to visiting teachers. Principal A. C. Hampton and Mr. A. H. Prince, of the La Grande High School, went to Wallowa and Baker counties to accompany the teachers and work out entertainment assignments en route. In these and many other ways true "Eastern Oregon Hospitality" was dispensed, to the great pleasure and comfort of the visitors. Music was provided by the pupils of the La Grande schools in various organizations, under the capable direction of the music supervisor, Miss Cecile Hindman. A very delightful feature of the convention was the banquet Wednesday evening, served by the students of the Home Economics department. Plates were laid for about 400 people and the dinner served in courses. The instructor, Miss Naomi Kirtley, and her pupils deserve great credit for the admirable manner in which the affair was conducted. The Neighborhood Club gave a delightful reception Thursday evening. The educational program was strong and well balanced. Speakers from without state were Mr. E. O. Sisson, commissioner of education in Idaho, Miss Florence Fox, specialist in the U. S. Bureau of Education, Washington, D. C., and Professor W. R. Davis, of Whitman College. Among Oregon instructors were Supt. Churchill, Asst. Supt. Carleton, and Mr. N. C. Maris of the state department, President Carl G. Doney of Willamette University, Dean Joseph Schafer and Prof. DeBusk of the University of Oregon, Prof. Ressler of the Oregon Agricultural College, Mr. H. C. Seymour, state leader of boys' and girls' clubs, President Ackerman and Prof. Pittman of the Oregon Normal School, and Miss Hindman of the La Grande schools. The convention accepted the report of its committee, sent to the Medford meeting of the Western Division of the State Teachers' Association last year, and composed of the three county superintendents, which report recommended that the Eastern Division merge with the Western in the formation of a State Association. Representatives were appointed to attend the meeting in Portland, December 27-29. The tri-county meeting will be continued under the name "Blue Mountain Teachers' Association" and will be held in Baker next year, with Principal A. C. Voelker, of the Baker high school as president.

For the first time the school at Willamette, Oregon, has a four-year high school course. At the opening of the school the enrollment was 20, but at present this number has been doubled. The high school course includes a Teachers' Training class. D. F. Romig is the principal of the school.

FAIR WARNING.

Please remember that at the beginning of 1917, all subscribers of the Oregon Teachers Monthly whose subscriptions are one year or more in arrears will be dropped from the list. The exceedingly high price of paper makes it impossible to carry subscribers who do not pay. The mailing label tells the date to which your subscription is paid.

Oregon State Library

By CORNELIA MARVIN, Librarian, Oregon State Library

Interesting Books for Teachers to Read.—I suggest the following titles of books which are really interesting and worth reading: A group of fiction, Cather's "Song of the Lark," Conrad's "Victory," Fisher's "The Bent Twig," Parker's "The Money Master," Tarkington's "The Turmoil," Tarkington's "Seventeen." Of non- fiction, the most interesting and fascinating of the recent books which I have seen are John Hay's "Autobiography," Osborn's "Men of the Old Stone Age," Aldrich's "The Hilltop on the Marne,' Stewart's "Letters of a Woman Homesteader" and "Letters of an Elk Hunt," Rhibany's "A Far Journey," Wald's "House at Henry Street."

The Best English Novels.—"That ancient and altogether unsolvable problem as to which is the best English novel has been exhumed again by the New York Times," said the Publisher's Weekly not long since, "and the vote of twenty-eight modern authors awards "Vanity Fair" first place, "Tom Jones" second, "David Copperfield" third, "Scarlet Letter fourth, and "Robinson Crusoe" fifth. Sixth place was a quadruple tie among "Ivanhoe," "Lorna Doone," "Tess of the D'Urbervilles," and "Tristam Shandy."

Good Book Week of the Boy Scouts.—The week beginning December 4 has been set aside by the Boy Scouts' organization as Good Book Week for the whole country and booksellers and libraries will do all they can to encourage the buying and reading of better works. The organization suggests that teachers give their pupils names of books to ask for for Christmas, that they interest the Parent-Teachers's Associations and co-operate with the library in all possible ways to get better books into the homes. The State Library has for free distribution a list of children's books suggested for Christmas gifts, also two bookmarks which serve the same purpose—one called "When Mother Reads Aloud," and the other, "The Golden Stair-

case." Any teacher may have these for asking and may have them to distribute to parents.

Books to Give Away.—The State Library has a few primers and readers to give away to some country school. They have been used, but are in fairly good condition. Please don't ask for them if you have any of these books in your school library. We want to send them to the place which needs them most.

Best Books of 1915.—The New York State Library has compiled a list of books—which were published during the year 1915—and generally considered best for libraries. This is an interesting list with notes on the books. You may have a copy if you will write to the State Library for it.

Educational Pedlodicals.—It is probable that the very best of the educational periodicals are those which are indexed in the Readers' Guide to Periodical Literature. These are the titles selected by that index: Education, Educational Review, Manual Training and Vocational Education, School and Society, School Review, United States Bureau of Education, Bulletin. Those which are indexed in the Supplement which are a little more highly specialized, but considered among the best periodicals are as follows: American Physical Education, English Journal, Geographical Review, Journal of Education, Kindergarten Primary Magazine, Nature Study Review, Pedagogical Seminary, School Science and Mathematics, Teachers College Record. Teachers may borrow sample copies of any of these from the State Library if they wish to look them over before making subscription, or if they are interested in keeping up with the best of the current literature.

Some Things the State Library Has for You.—You may have some groups of twenty good books on the Revolutionary period for your sixth and seventh grades and may keep them for three months. You may have an interesting collection on the same period for the use of high schools. You may have the standard bill on "Health Insurance" upon payment of 10 cents. This will be needed by members of the debate league. You may have traveling libraries for your schools. Do you have all the books you need in your community this year, and if not why do you not register for service with the State Library? The library does not loan the state texts which teachers need to prepare for the examination; it does not loan sets of textbooks or supplementary readers all of one kind.

Supplementary Readers for Seventh and Eighth Grades.—The following titles have been suggested as interesting and worth reading: Parkman's "Rivals for America," compiled from his works, Irving's "Fur Traders," Muir's "Stickeen," Antin's "The Promised Land," Shakespeare's "Julius Ceasar" and "Midsummer Night's Dream," Buxton's "Stories of Persian Heroes."

A New High School List is in Preparation.—The list now in use in Oregon has been checked by the best school librarians of the country who have offered their suggestions. The list being prepared by the Bureau of Education has been compared with ours. We have checked carefully the Publishers Weekly which gives a weekly record of all books published in the country, as well as the American Library Association Booklet, which gives a monthly annotated list of the best books published each month, and we have asked the cooperation of all Oregon school teachers. Have you sent your suggestions? Please let us know what books you would like to have in your high school library which are not in the list. This is the time to help to make the list adequate.

Modern Fiction for High Schools. —A teacher has asked for a list of contemporary fiction suitable and desirable for high school use. Please send suggestions to the State Library naming only those books which you have read. We will try to publish the list next month.

Christmas Plays.—The State Library has a large collection of Christmas Plays which will be loaned to teachers on application.

Binding.—If the books in your school library need binding or recasing or mending write to the State Library for information, prices and a manual which will help you to collect material and do the work.

Umpqua, Beautiful Waters.

I stood where thy glad, rippling waters
Cast bright, shining waves at my feet;
Where ever thy swift foaming rapids
Sing lullabies, gladsome and sweet.
Beyond them the gold of the Maples,
Fringed by the Firs, tall and green,
Hiding the bare bluffs behind them
With their sweet-scented, emerald screen.

Umpqua, thou beautiful waters,
Pride of our great, sunshine state;
Robed in thy rich, shining garments,
Like a bride who in beauty doth wait;
Yet soon will thy water, so icy,
Flow from the Great Cascade Land,
And all who wait near thee may gather
A glimpse of thy wonders so grand

Yet ever thy waters press onward,
Nearer to Winchester Bay
Who waits near the deep, briny ocean
Fretting at all thy delay.
Far out from his home shore he'll meet you,
Coming with arms open wide;
Then safe in his bosom he'll bear you,
Out on the swift moving tide.
—Mable M. Rader, Tyee, Oregon.

The State Teachers' Association

The State Teachers' Association will hold its next meeting in Portland, December 27, 28, and 29. Are you planning to attend? Look for the program in the January Oregon Teachers Monthly. Have you paid your registration fee? You will find the names of those who have paid on another page of this number. Please help swell the list by sending $1.50 for membership in the State Teachers' Association and subscription to Oregon Teachers Monthly.

Florence O. Fox.

"Perfectly splendid" is what the teachers say of the primary work of Miss Fox who has come all the way from the department of education at Washington, D. C., to atend institutes in Oregon Her kind, genial manner and helpful attitude has won the friendship and high regard of everyone she has met. Her work in the institutes will have a good influence on educational matters in the state.

County Superintendents' Department

Edited by CLYDE T. BONNEY, The Dalles, Oregon

The good people of Mosier have had their first annual Improvement Day of the grounds of the public school; I say annual because there is a feeling among us that it will be an annual event hereafter. The willingness to help has been apparent on every hand, and we all feel that the day has been a success both socially and economically. The steep approach to the building from the road has been terraced in steps, and will now afford a safe and easy way to reach the front entrance. The general appearance of the grounds was very much improved by the school children who cut down the dead weeds and raked them together in piles and burned them. Several loads of broken granite, the screenings from the rock crusher here, were hauled by one of our public-spirited citizens, and spread over the play areas so that the rainy season will not now render such places useless. Another of our many good citizens donated the raw material for a line of traveling rings, and a giant stride, which will be erected very soon by our larger boys. Provision has also been made for the little ones on their side of the grounds for the means of amusing themselves in a safe and delightful fashion. The ladies of the neighborhood deserve the highest praise for the part they acted in today's program. Several days ago a committee canvassed the community for donations to the bill of fare at noon on Improvement Day; everybody responded. There was enough, after feeding about seventy-five, to feed them again in the evening; but as the work that had been planned was finished early, the surplus food was otherwise disposed of. The girls in the newly-established department of domestic science in the high school assisted in preparing and serving the meal which consisted of soup, macaroni and cheese, baked beans, scalloped potatoes, salad, coffee and apple pie. We feel that the day has been a success. Everybody went home happy and satisfied. The school grounds look better, and the respect with which we all regard our school plant has been heightened by the civic pride of our splendid community acting together in the common cause. When we have moved into a new, modern building here in Mosier and had several annual events like this one and made our building and grounds conform to our ideal, we hope still to look forward to Improvement Day. If our picks, shovels and axes are not then needed in improving the surface of the earth, there will be no lack of willing hands and hearts in the work of social service. Every school in Oregon could have an Improvement Day.—B. A. Berry.

Coos County.

Coos county now has six consolidated schools—Bridge, Eastside, Riverton, Coos River, Catching Inlet, and Herman. Besides these, Englewood, at the last annual meeting, consolidated with the Marshfield city schools.

The Herman and Dement schools, on the south fork of the Coquille river, were the last two to consolidate, and are progressing nicely in their remodeled building, under the principalship of E. R. Jones. They have added a modern heating and ventilating system and have converted the old system of windows on both sides of the room into the unilateral system. They will add upper grades until the school has a full four-year high school course.

The Catching Inlet school formed from consolidations effected a year ago last June are nearly ready to enter their fine new building. This is an imposing structure on an elevated bench and affords a splendid view of the surrounding country. There are four large class rooms, two of which may be thrown into a large assembly room by means of a rolling partition, besides the library, office, etc. There is a full cement basement with play rooms, furnace room, toilets, etc. The building is steam heated and has all modern conveniences. It is hoped that the building will be ready for occupancy by the first of next month. Preparations are being made for dedicatory exercises on quite an elaborate scale, on which occasion it is hoped to have speakers from some of the educational centers.

A large number of the schools of the county are striving hard for standardization and several have nearly attained the goal.

Pennants have just been sent out to the Ocean View school, standard A, and to Glenn Junction, standard B..

Three schools, Herman, McKinley and Dora have put in modern heating and ventilating systems within the last few weeks.

Jefferson County.

The average per cent of attendance for the county for the month ending October 6 is 94.5. Districts 13, 16, 19, and 26 each report 100 per cent attendance.

Miss Llota Horigan is working wonders in the educational line with her small pupils in the Cross Keys district, No. 13. Miss Horigan is bending her efforts toward standardizing.

In Pony Butte school, district 33, Miss Opal Carnes and her enthusiastic little band were found doing excellent work. Miss Carnes is a very efficient teacher and great progress is expected in this school.

The Donnybrook school, district 19, was the second school visited. Mrs. J. C. Grater is very enthusiastic in the work here. She declares her intention of serving warm lunches to her pupils. While the enrollment at present is small it is safe to predict that the warm lunches will be the cause of an increase.

The first school visited by the county superintendent this school year was the Ashwood school, district 8. Mr. Roy Lowther is in charge here and this means a successful term. Mr. Lowther aims to bring the school up to the standardization mark before spring and with the co-operation of the parents and school board he will do this.

A very enjoyable evening was spent at the Gateway school, district 17, Friday, October 13. Mrs. Harriett Woolsey and her pupils deserve great praise for the manner in which the excellent program was carried out. The dramatization of Hiawatha was especially good. After the program a number of boxes well filled with delicious cookery were auctioned off and the neat little sum of $26 was realized. The money is to be used in meeting the few requirements which will bring the school up to the standardization mark.

Morrow County.

The proposition to add a strong domestic science department to the Heppner high school will be submitted to the voters of the district. There is no doubt as to its approval by the people.

A new school house has just been completed in district No. 48. This is a small district, but the school house is a very creditable building. A box social was held to raise money for library books. The proceeds will add a nice lot of books.

County Superintendent Notson has been elected district attorney for Morrow county. Mrs. Lena Snell Shurte will succeed him as county superintendent. Mrs. Shurte will be the second lady to fill the office. Several years ago, Miss Anna Balsiger held the office one term.

Polk County.

The library books have been received and partly distributed.

The schools are in excellent condition, and they are starting out with a successful year's work.

The first local institute will be held December 2. Supt. Churchill, of the state office, and Prof. Ressler, of O. A. C., have promised to be present.

Three zone meetings have been held under the new plan of supervision. One was at Fern, Oregon, and there were twelve teachers present; the second was at Bethel, with fourteen teachers present; and the third was at Greenwood with fifteen teachers present. All the teachers in each zone were present with one or two exceptions. In these zone meetings, Mr. Moore took up Reading in the second and eighth grades, and illustrated the present method of teaching. This usually occupied the morning session, and the afternoon session was devoted to round table discussions on subjects that pertain to the school work. Much interest has been aroused among the teachers in regard to these zone meetings, and they will accomplish good results. Supt. Reynolds has been present at two of these meetings, lending help with discussions.

Sherman County.

The new Wasco school building will be ready for occupancy about January 1. As the old building is much too small for the school at present, both teachers and pupils are very anxious to see the completion of the new building.

The Kent school will probably be able to occupy the new building, being erected, by January 1. The Kent people are justly proud of this school building, which when completed, will be one of the best arranged and furnished school buildings in the state.

The Kent and Grass Valley high schools have both ordered the necessary apparatus and library books for standardization. It is expected that both these schools will become standard high schools before January 1. Both these schools are doing excellent high school work, and there is a real demand for a standard high school in each place.

Sherman County Annual Teachers' Institute was held in Wasco, November 20, 21, and 22. The following were the instructors for the institute: Supt. J. A. Churchill, Salem; Mrs. M. L. Fulkerson, Salem; Mr. Earl Kilpatrick, Eugene; Mr. H. C. Seymour, Corvallis; J. Teuscher, Jr., Portland; Chas. H. Jones, Salem; W. A. Terral, Wasco; and F. E. Dunton, Moro.

Four local industrial fairs were held in Sherman county during the week, October 2-7, at the following places: Wasco, Moro, Grass Valley, and Kent. All these fairs were very successful and they did much to make the county fair, held the following week, a success. Between $300 and $400 in cash was distributed as premiums at these fairs, to the school children of the county.

Tillamook County.

The first meeting for the year of the Parent Teachers' Association was held in the assembly room on November 13.

The Tillamook county annual institute was held in Tillamook City, October 23, 24, and 25. Among the instructors were Supt. J. A. Churchill, Miss Florence Fox of Washington, D. C., Mrs. Harriett Hickox Heiler, M. S. Pittman, H. C. Seymour, F. C. Ayer and R. W. Kirk.

During the institute a School-Mistress' club was organized, with Miss Clara Lorpabel of Beaver as president. The first regular meeting of the club was held in Tillamook, November 11. The School-Masters' club held its first meeting of the year at Bay City on November 18.

School district No. 21, of Sandlake, has made a fine showing in club work. Out of the twelve members who enrolled, eleven of them completed all of the work required in the club projects undertaken. Miss Claudia Brown, teacher and adviser, certainly deserves a great deal of credit for her work.

Tillamook is fortunate in securing the services of R. W. Kirk. who. for the past seven years has been superintendent at Corvallis. The following teachers are employed in Tillamook: High school—Mrs. Bertha Hanson, Mr. George Sanders, Mr. Fred Hardesty, Mr. Wm. King, Miss Mauryce Currey, Miss Margaret Hanson, Miss Hazel McKown, and Miss Julia Miller; grades—Miss Clara Pruehs, Miss Edith Snere, Miss Lillian Crapson, Miss Beatrice Chaeney, Miss Stella Goyne, Miss Retta Smith, Mrs. Frances Wiley, and Mrs. Clara Burge.

Washington County.

A number of schools in Washington county are preparing to serve hot lunches this winter. Serving and table etiquette will receive special instruction.

The annual teachers' institute held last month in Washington county was one of the best ever held in the county. There were more than 200 teachers in attendance. The lectures were attended by school officers and patrons.

Mr. C. N. Maris will be in this

county for a period of two weeks working on the industrial club movement. It is hoped to do more and better work along this line than has previously been done.

Union County.

Hot Lake is putting the finishing touches on a new modern school house.

Hallowe'en exercises were given in nearly all of the schools and it is a joy to see the flag flying from school houses this year all over the valley.

Rural schools are rapidly promoting the standardization work. Since Mr. L. E. Reese has taken charge of the Pine Grove school he has about succeeded in having the board place his school on the list of the standard schools.

North Powder schools have just moved into one of the most complete and up-to-date school buildings in the county. The citizens of North Powder will find that increased and improved facilities will bring an interest on all they are doing for the youth of their city. North Powder's high school will now become standard.

The Eastern Division of the State Teachers' Association held a splendid meeting in La Grande, November 1, 2, and 3. About four hundred and twenty teachers were registered. Speakers from state institutions were Dr. De Busk, and Dr. Schafer of the University of Oregon, Messrs. E. D. Ressler and H. C. Seymour from O. A. C., and Pres. Ackerman and M. S. Pittman of the Monmouth Normal. Other speakers were Dr. Carl Doney of Willamette University, Prof. W. R. Davis of Whitman College, Dr. Edward O. Sisson of Idaho, and Florence Fox of Washington, D. C., and from Supt. Churchill's office were J. A. Churchill, E. T. Carleton, N. C. Maris. Mr. A. C. Strange of Baker, Miss Murphy of the A. N. Palmer Co., and Mr. A. C. Hampton of La Grande also assisted in the sectional work. The music was entirely in the hands of Miss Cecile Hindman, musical director of La Grande schools and the music presented was very enjoyable. Mr. Linden McCullough, the newly-elected superintendent of La Grande schools, made an excellent presiding officer, showing rare tact and ability

in moving the "Big Institute." The detail work of the association in the hands of all the committees appointed, moved like clockwork and all went away feeling the institute would give a new impetus to the school work. The citizens of the community took an active part in the entertainment of the teachers and also largely attended the institute. One pleasant feature was to see Postmaster Bragg, who also presided at the first meeting of the Eastern Division of the State Teachers' Association, the first to appear on the program and introduce in a happy manner the presiding officer, Supt. McCullough. Among the business features of the association was a unanimous vote to dissolve the Eastern Division of the State Teachers' Association and unite with the Western Division of the Association. Supts. A. C. Strange, J. C. Conley and Mrs. A. E. Ivanhoe were chosen to represent the body in the council.

Yamhill County.

Cove Orchard school now has a modern building in every way. The district was recently enlarged, and the enrollment is much greater than it was last year.

The Sheridan schools are continuing the hot lunch idea. Every one is well pleased with it so far. The parent-teacher circle is assisting very materially in carrying out the idea.

The Waddell school has been given a new coat of paint, and certainly presents a fine appearance. Miss Icy Bryan is in charge of the school and her work is in keeping with her surroundings.

The Carlton school is trying out the department plan in part of the elementary grades. Principal E. M. Haley is well satisfied with results. The Carlton school has also something new in the way of fire escapes.

Bellevue has one of the finest country school houses in the state. It is much like the Ewing Young school house in the Chehalem valley, with a few changes that the Bellevue people chose to make. The old building has been moved back and is used for a playshed. J. W. Lorett, of McMinnville, has charge of this school.

The annual institute will be held in the high school building in Mc-

Minnville, December 4, 5, and 6. A good program is being arranged, and the time will be pleasantly and profitably spent. The ladies of the Civic Improvement Club of McMinnville will have charge of the reception to teachers on the evening of December 5. This insures a pleasant evening. The Ewing Young School, and several other Chehalem Valley schools gave a local fair not long ago. Every one was well pleased with the venture. The local fair idea is gaining ground, and should be encouraged, as many exhibit there that can not conveniently take part in the county fair ,and those that do take part in the county fair can quite easily exhibit at both. Each fair has its own work to do, and one is really a help to the other. ,Prof. Anderson and Miss Hevland are still in charge of the Ewing Young school, and did much to make the local fair a success. The teachers of the adjoining schools that took part deserve credit for the intrest they took in the work.

FAIR WARNING.

Please remember that at the beginning of 1917, all subscribers of the Oregon Teachers Monthly whose subscriptions are one year or more in arrears will be dropped from the list. The exceedingly high price of paper makes it impossible to carry subscribers who do not pay. The mailing label tells the date to which your subscription is paid.

The State Schools

Oregon Normal School.

The first member of the faculty to take the chapel period for this month was Mr. Butler, head of the History department, who took for his subject "The Teachers' Economic Responsibility," and outlined in a general way the immense responsibilities which are falling to the teachers of the present age while history and economic conditions are changing so rapidly.

The institute series throughout the state has drawn upon the faculty as follows: President Ackerman at Grants Pass, Hillsboro, La Grande, and Pendleton; Mr. Pittman, at Tillamook, Marshfield, Madras, Rainier, La Grande, and Pendleton; Mr. Evenden at Roseburg and Hood River; and Mr. Gentle at Hillsboro.

The second member to represent the faculty in chapel was Miss Hoham, who explained the new Oregon Course of Study in Music for rural schools. and showed the student body how this could be carried out. Through the courtesy of Sherman Clay Company, Miss Hoham has several Victor machines with which to demonstrate the method of teaching musical appreciation. The talk was very helpful and the series of which this was the first is being looked forward to with much pleasure.

Saturday, October 14, was the first and main feature of the Lyceum course for the semester. This consisted of the presenting of Israel Zangwill's "The Melting Pot" by a company of eight actors, some of whom were in the original caste when this play was first produced in America. The presentation made this wonderful story of American patriotism very vivid and its lessons of Americanism more forceful.

The crowning social event of the semester was the reception of President and Mrs. Ackerman to the citizens of Monmouth, the faculty and students of the Oregon Normal school in the parlors of Normal hall, Saturday, October 21. President and Mrs. Ackerman were assisted in the receiving line by Miss Marvin of Salem, Mr. and Mrs. Butler, Mr. and Mrs. Gentle, Miss Todd, Miss McIntosh, Miss Arbuthnot, Miss Dinius and Miss Riocker. Other members of the faculty presided at the serving table and assisted about the rooms in entertaining the guests. Special musical numbers which contributed greatly to the pleasure of the evening were vocal solos by Miss Dagmar Inez Kelly, and harp solos by Mrs. Carmel Sullivan Powers, both of Portland. The whole affair was delightful in its cordial hospitality and afforded a delightful opportunity for students, faculty and townspeople to gather in a social way.

An extra number of the Lyceum course and one which afforded pleasure to the faculty and students was the concert of Mr. Hartridge Whipp, assisted by Mrs. Leonora Fisher Whipp at the piano. Mr. Whipp's lecture recital was delightfully given, full of rare musical treats and instructive comments on the songs and the composers. Mr. Whipp thoroughly captivated his audience and in turn expressed himself as highly pleased with the Normal School and with the work that is being done here.

The third member of the faculty to appear during the month was Miss Myra Butler, who told in a most interesting way of the trip which she and Miss West took during last summer to the Yellowstone National Park, Glacier Park, through the Canadian country about Banff and the return through Vancouver and western Washington. Miss Butler traced the trip on a blackboard map and brought in so many points of interest that a number of converts to the "Ford method" of spending the vacation was won throughout the audience.

Miss Todd, matron of the dormitory, has started the plan of being at home to the girls of the different classes. This furnishes an occasion for the students to meet socially and also to become better acquainted with Miss Todd, who in her capacity as Dean of Women, has such a vital interest in the social life of the school.

The great Ince production, "Civilization," came to Monmouth October 27, and because of lack of room in the moving picture show and through the courtesy of President Ackerman, the film was presented in the Normal chapel. A matinee production was given in the afternoon for the benefit of the Training School children and for any who could not get seats for the evening performance. This picture was very effective in driving home its lessons on the horrors of warfare and the blessings of peace.

Rev. W. A. Elkins, pastor of the Christian church, at Monmouth, was the outside speaker on October 27. Rev. Elkins took for his topic "The Overcoming of Difficulties," which he illustrated by a crayon drawing of the Matterhorn. Rev. Elkins' talk was full of practical and helpful suggestions to the teachers in showing

that true progress comes through the meeting and overcoming of life's difficulties.

Saturday, October 28, was the occasion for the Junior and Senior class parties commemorative of the Hallowe'en season. The Seniors held their party in the gymnasium and the Juniors in the basement of the training school. Both buildings were appropriately decorated in autumnal browns and the evening was replete with entertaining reminders of the days of witchcraft. Dainty refreshments, also in keeping with the occasion, were served.

The first Senior to represent the class in chapel for the year was Miss Frances Gardiner, of Baker, Oregon. Miss Gardiner took for her topic "The Influence of a Strong Personality," and showed the many ways in which a teacher's personality goes over into the school work, with its opportunities as well as its responsibilities.

C. L. Starr, attorney at law, of Portland, and member of the board of regents of the Oregon Normal School, was the special speaker at chapel on November 3. Mr. Starr in his concise and logical way showed the student body the reasons for and the possible results of the pending 6 per cent limitation amendment. Mr. Starr's thorough knowledge of the taxation problem of Oregon, from his years of service as secretary of the State Tax Commission, made his especially fitted to talk on the subject. Their interest in his remarks was evident by the way he was received and the close attention given him by the students.

The Normal School orchestra made its initial appearance at the joint musical program of the three literary societies on the night of October 20. The membership for the year is unusually large with the addition of several skillful musicians among the students which presages an exceptional year for the orchestra under the direction of Miss Hoham. This organization plays a very important part in the school activities.

The first joint session of the literary societies was held Friday, November 3. The program was of unusual merit and showed the conscientious work of the committees of the three societies. The Normal Society contributed for its part a debate on the question of the Value of

Labor Unions. The Delphians presented Longfellow's "Pandora" and the Vespertines the "Frolic of the Witches." These principal numbers were interspersed with readings and musical numbers by members of the different societies.

Mr. Pittman has spent a week visiting the rural school departments of the normal schools at Lewiston, Ida., and Cheeney, Wash., before returning to Monmouth to take up his regular classes in the rural school department.

Oregon Agricultural College.

A special department of the military organization at the college has been organized to teach students how to command, organize, and control a company of recruits in case of war. In this new course the individual cadets are given instructions in raising regiments, enlisting recruits, equiping them, and organizing and training a company of 150 men. The work includes such procedure as enrollment, examinations, physical, mental and moral, and providing suitable equipment. This equipment includes clothes, tents, signal apparatus, engineering apparatus and must be requisioned through proper channels from the different departments with the least possible delay. The amount of food, suitable rations and other necessary supplies are also subject to study.

The Third Annual Hort show given by the faculty and students of the Horticultural division was held at the college November 3 and 4. It was said by good judges that it has been the most artistic expedition of horticultural products ever assembled in the Northwest. The show was both educational and historical. In a historical way it was staged in a replica of the early English "Tudor" garden. The garden was re-constructed with all the features that distinguished the charming gardens of early England. The court was inclosed in walls of living hedge with vistas for viewing the exhibits and for the entrance to walks. All decorations and other elements of the garden were composed of Oregon native ornamentals. The exhibit was staged in three divisions, floriculture in the center, with pomology on one side, and vegetable gardening on the other side. The special feature of floral section was the chrysanthemum display. This queen of fall flowers was grown in the college green house and was displayed in great profusions and variety of color, size, and general type. One of the most prominent features of the pomology display was the floor map of the United States laid out in moss. On each state was given a characteristic display of its horticultural products. Another feature of this section excited a great deal of interest was the competitive display of fruits grown by O. A. C. graduates, another competitive exhibits was fruits grown by students at the present time. Perhaps the most artistic feature was 60 baskets decorated by members of the Home Economics section. There were also comprehensive displays of sub-tropical fruits and of Oregon by-products. On one of the tables was a housewife's exhibit showing the varieties of apples best adapted to each month of the year. The possibilities of decoration with Oregon native plants also were demonstrated. In the vegetable gardening section one of the most notable features was for the model green house in which was seen growing under glass some of the leading varieties of vegetables that lend themselves to this form of production. A cauliflower display, and market packs of celery and other vegetables are owned by Prof. Bouquet and his assistants, showed points of preparing vegetables for market. There were many splendid groups of Oregon vegetables, fruit crops, and such products produce as tomatoes, peppers, etc. The exhibits were raised largely at the expense of the faculty and students and was free to all residents of Oregon.

A tryout of the freshman was held to select representatives in inter-class debate. W. L. Cusick, Walter Stone, and Glenn Beagle were successful. A large number turned out for the preliminary contest and those who did not succeed in making the team will be given an opportunity to make another tryout for inter-freshman debate. It has also been pointed out that freshman are eligible to the extension team and also to a position on the team that debates with the University of Oregon.

President W. J. Kerr went to Washington, D. C., on November 8 to attend the meetings of the Associations of American Agricultural Colleges and Experiment Stations. It was also President Kerr's purpose to meet with the officials of the Department of Agriculture to adjust matters relating to co-operative work in Oregon. He gave an address before the meeting of the general Agricultural Societies of Maryland, which were in convention in Baltimore. He is expected to return to Oregon about the 20th of this month.

R. D. Hetzel, extension director, and Paul V. Maris, state leader of county agricultural agents, went to Washington, D. C., early in November to attend the National Associations of County Agricultural Leaders. Prof. Hetzel will deliver one of the principal addresses and in conjunction with Mr. Maris will prepare a report of discussions, and policies of the association for the County Agricultural Agents section of Farmers' Week, January 28 to February 2. Prof. Hetzel will also consult with the offices of the States Relation Service on co-operative work in Oregon.

The campus chapter of Kappa Psi Fraternity sent A. R. Woodcock, of Corvallis, Ore., as delegate to the national convention which met at Atlanta, Ga., November 13 to 15. In connection with the convention of the fraternity the southern Medical Association met at Atlanta. All Kappa Psi delegates have received invitations to attend the various meetings and reecptions tendered the physicians. Other delegates from the Pacific coast include one from the North Pacific Dental School at Portland and one from the University of California. These members co-operated in a movement to present the claims of the Pacific Coast schools of pharmacy to the recognition which their standing seems to deserve.

Ex-Senator Charles W. Fulton delivered a political address at the men's gymnasium on the evening of Thursday, November 2. Senator George E. Chamberlain also presented a political address on the Wednesday preceding. More than a thousand students turned out to hear these addresses.

Reading Circle Books.

The reading circle list for 1916-1917 has just been issued by J. A. Churchill, superintendent of public instruction. Under the laws of Oregon each teacher is required to read one professional work each year chosen from a list prepared by the state superintendent.

The University of Oregon and the Oregon Agricultural college, through their extension departments, offer to the teachers free courses in the adopted reading circle books. A certificate to the effect that the applicant has read one of the required works from either of these institutions is accepted by the county superintendent when he registers the teacher's certificate.

In order to simulate professional reading, Superintendent Churchill offers a special certificate of merit to each teacher who reads two of these books under the direction of one of the schools mentioned and meets certain other conditions. During the past year 487 teachers met the requirements for these professional certificates.

During the past year 5600 certificates for reading circle work were issued by the extension departments of the two colleges. Following are the books adopted for the year 1916-1917:

Bagley, "School of Discipline"; Cubberley, "Public School Administration"; Dewey, "School of Tomorrow"; Earhart, "Types of Teaching"; Foster, "The Social Emergency"; Gesel, "The Normal Child and Primary Education"; Hart, "Educational Resources of Village and Rural Communities"; Johnston, "The Modern High School"; Judd, "Psychology of High School Subjects"; Kendall and Mirick, "How to Teach the Fundamental Subjects"; Moore, "What is Education"; Morgan, "The Backward Child"; Parker, "Methods of Teaching in High Schools"; Pickard, "Rural Education"; Spencer, "Education," (Everyman's library); Swift, "Learning and Doing"; Terman, "The Hygiene of the School Child"; Carney, "Country Life and the Country School"; Kahn and Klein, "Principls and Methods in Commercial Education."

When a person is so far engaged in a dispute as to wish to get the victory he ought ever to desist. The idea of conquest will so dazzle him that it is hardly possible he should discern the truth.—Shenstone.

Give the children the best and you will not have to worry about evil tendencies.—Florence Holbrook.

Membership in the State Teachers' Association

The Oregon Teachers Monthly, on July 1, 1916, became the official journal of the State Teachers' Association (both divisions) and the price was raised to $1.50 per year, 50 cents of which goes to the Association. At the end of 4½ months (November 17) the following teachers had paid $1.50 for their subscription to the Oregon Teachers Monthly, thereby entitling them to membership in the State Teachers' Association:

1 Nellie V. King, Winant
2 Fred Schepman, Waldport
3 John Blough, Toledo
4 Maggie L. Hampton, Toledo
5 M. Lillian Ernest, Denzer
6 Earl Brown, Philomath
7 Chas. Hart, Roselodge
8 S. S. Gossman, Chitwood
10 J. E. Davis, Chitwood
11 R. E. Wood, Orton
12 John Miller, Eddyville
13 Verne Ross, Toledo
14 T. E. Wilson, Turner
15 Paul Wyman, Bay City
16 Chas. Holway, Halsey
17 Laura A. Smith, Cottage Grove
18 H. W. Herron, Portland
19 Mary B. Scollard, Woodburn
20 L. W. Turnbull, Coquille
21 Hazel Henkle, Monkland
22 A. C. Strange, Baker
23 Anna Dunsmore, Orenco
24 Margaret Williams, Portland
25 Adella Chapler, Salem
26 Margaret Boggess, Veneta
27 W. M. Sutton, Burns
28 W. G. Beattie, Eugene
29 Mary E. Slade, Albany
30 Mrs. L. K. Page, Springfield
31 Mrs. A. Alexander, Portland
32 Barbara Hoch, Pendleton
33 Blanche Padley, Bandon
34 Kate Ronde, Clatskanie
35 Edith Harper, Freewater
36 Edith Smith, Banks
37 Alice Rasmussen, Troutdale
38 Della Zimmerman, Troutdale
39 Adda Wright, Warrenton
40 N. A. Frost, Forest Grove
41 Edna Pence, Salem
42 Erica Nordhausen, Aurora
43 Clara Ireland, Portland
44 H. Burch, Oregon City
45 J. P. McGlasson, North Plains
46 Ethel Davis, Myrtle Creek
47 Mrs. E. H. Morrison, Portland
48
49
50 Alethia Chapman, LaGrande
51 May Smith, Mabel
52 Helen Treat, Buell
53 Virginia Nottingham, Carlton
54 Elma Roberts, Sumner
55 Ruby Skinner, Lakeview
56 Frances Potter, Canby
57 Harriet B. Horrigan, Hillsboro
58 Grace Egbert, The Dalles
59 Mary B. Underwood, Philomath
60 Ruth Dunbabin, Bourne
61
62
63
64 Bessa Lehmann, Sutherlin
65 Anna Bachman, Clackamas
66 Adeline Buyserie, Hubbard
67 Isa Isaacson, Junction City
68 Anna Weisenborn, Deer Island
69 Myrel A. Bond, Irving
70 Rada Antrim, Amity
71 Marvin F. Wood, Corvallis

72 Carl E. Morrison, Perrydale
73 Waithia Watson, Roseburg
74 H. C. Ostien, Monmouth
75 Eula Campbell, Freewater
76 M. S. Pittman, Monmouth
77 Hazel Goger, Boring
78 Clara Spiekerman, The Dalles
79 Mamie Harper, Wren
80 R. S. Bixby, Nolin
81 Mattie Foster, Klamath Falls
82 Nell G. Lloyd, Klondike
83 Margaret Rice, Shaniko
84 Martha Chase, Portland
85 Myrtle Clayville, Portland
86 C. D. Watkins, Dilley
87 Clara Larson, Toledo
88 Emma Murray, Klamath Falls
89 Marion Ford, Klamath Falls
90 May Wheaton, Coquille
91 Fannie G. Porter, Oregon City
92 Mable F. Johnson, Butte Falls
93 Helene Ogsburg, Eugene
94 Velma Beardslee, Arlington
95 Gladys Anderson, Clear Lake, Ia.
96 Alice Lytle, Bonanza
97 Vara Stewart, Portland
98 Charles Knocke, Mt. Carmel, N. D.
99 Lydia Unden, Winchester
100 Jewell Delk, Drain
101 Matilda Jacobs, Portland
102 Mrs. Gladys Smith, Springfield
103 Helen Anderson, Meda
104 Alma Nichols, Culver
105 Gladys Hatcher, Buell
106 Sylvia Severance, Lexington
107 Dagmar Jeppesen, Boyd
108 Ora England, Walker
109 Florence E. Howatt, Portland
110 Rachel May, Timber
111 Ellen M. Yocum, Amity
112 Alice Jenkins, Eugene
113 Harry Whitten, Kingsley
114 Violet M. Stolle, Irving
115 Violet McCarl, Portland
116 Maude Largent, Hullt
117 Elnor Sherk, Sutherlin
118 Ruth Peterson, Yoncalla
119 Grace Atkinson, Walton
120 Mrs. Mary Hulin, Carpentaria, Cal.
121 Mary E. Moore, Irving
122 Vera Merchant, Lebanon
123 Emma Kennedy, Coquille
124 Maybelle Wagner, McMinnville
125 Marguerite Freydig, Sutherlin
126 Ruth A. Brown, Eagle Creek
127 Ranie P. Burkhead, Shaniko
128 Mabel McFadden, Halfway
129 Angie Halley, Medford
130 Goldie Groth, Freewater
131 Justina Kildee, Sutherlin
132 May B. Lund, Coquille
133 Mildred Jones, Amity
134 Grace V. Perce, Medford
135 Myrtle Ess, Klamath Falls
136 Sadie Helberger, Wedderburn
137 Marie A. Smith, Buena Vista
138 Carolyn Woods, Cottage Grove
139 Ruth Finlay, Silverton
140 Luella Daniel, Milton
141 Wilbert O. Wilson, Kopiah, Wash.
142 Nettye Moore, Flat River, Mo.
143 Ida Anderson, Early
144 Clara Luther, Halsey
145 Caroline Luther, Redmond
146 Clara Schneider, Gaston
147 Maud Keysaw, Walterville
148 Gladys Burr, Oregon City
149 Emily L. Marshall, Willamette
150 Lapensa Amrine, Oregon City
151 Arabella Davis, Portland
152 Pansy Oswald, Gladstone
153 Pearle Ruegg, Gresham

154 Loney Yoder, Hubbard	240 Cornelia J. Spencer, Portland
155 Mrs. H. L. Hull, Oregon City	241 Eva S. Rice, Portland
156 Ruth F. Hudson, Mulino	242 Frances S. Estes, Portland
157 Elizabeth Roach, Cherryville	243 Emma Rueter, Portland
158 Brenton Vedder, Gladstone	244 Mrs. Minnie Parsons, Portland
159 Ruth M. Lingle, Boring	245 Nell O. Bevans, Portland
160 John R. Bowland, Oregon City	246 Mary E. Hill, Portland
161 A. C.' Thompson, Milwaukie	247 Estelle Marias, Portland
162 Raymond Boyer, Rickreall	248 Lutie E. Cake, Portland
163 L. H. Mallicoat, Boring	249 Margaret L. Pomeroy, Portland
164 T. J. Gary, Portland	250 Evlyn Cornutt, Portland
165 Ellen DeHaven, Salem	251 C. May Moriarty, Portland
166 Jessie Hartley, Portland	251 Phila Nicoll, Portland
167 Amy McDaniel, Weston	254. Kate E. Wiest, Astoria
168 Rena Roper, Vancouver, Wash.	254 Jeanette Pound, Salem
169 Stella Swift, Junction City	255 Mina Magness, Myrtle Point
170 Louise Nimmo, Albany	256 W. F. Cornwell, McEwen
171 Minnie Kulmke, Salem	257 Leila Lasley, Toledo
172 Wm. Westenskow, Imbler	258 Clara Straughan, Pendleton
173 D. A. Hoag, Sodaville	259 Mary Stein, Union
174 Laura Moore, Molalla	260 W. M. Smith, Salem
175 C. Edna Kennedy, Barton	261 A. R. Nichols, Corvallis
176 Helen M. Hall, Molalla	262 Frank W. Weber, Bend
177 Olga Hanson, Clackamas	263 Margaret V. Thomas, Gardiner
178 Margaret Summer, Tigard	264 Jessie Wagener, Alsea
179 Mrs. Nannie Thomas, Molalla	265 Edna Burke, Boring
180 Mary A. Bickner, Oswego	266 Luann Hiatt, Tillamook
181 Cora Hasselbrink, Sherwood	267 Mrs. S. E. Barnes, Portland
182 Chas. H. Jones, Salem	268 Ivan D. Wood, Union
183 Lunah W. Wallace, Huntington	269 Mabel Saunders, Richland
184 Mabel Wallace, Willamina	270 Reta E. Waller, Oakland
185 Anna Nelson, Palmer	271 Marie Wainright, Mayville
186 Adeline Brown, Kingsley	272 Ruth H. Ball, Klamath Agency
187 Miriam Underwood, Oakland	273 Mrs. Edith Coleman, Lafayette
188 Ozella Anderson, Parkplace	274 Jessie Armstrong, Astoria
189 Mary E. Sherer, Corvallis	275 Mrs. W. G. Thompson, Nyssa
190 Winnifred Roe, Monument	276 Hugh J. Boyd, Portland
191 Matilda F. Grossen, Hillsboro	277 Emma Clanton, Portland
192 Vernus Young, Echo	278 Merle A. Nimmo, Springfield
193 Edison Fowler, Riverside	279 Blanche Darby, Wilderville
194 Mrs. E. D. Sprague, Lake	280 Margaret L. Davies, Mt. Vernon
195 Lucile J. Lisher, Portland	281 Mabel St. Pierre, Salem
196 Margaret McDonald, Portland	282 Ruth E. Hyland, Oakridge
197 Georgia Smith, Mayville	283 G. W. Nash, Bellingham, Wash.
198 Aver Black, Tygh Valley	284 Dorothy Waugh, Portland
199 Viola Ortschild, Portland	285 Freda Bohn, Woodburn
200 Margaret Ferguson, Siltscoos	286 Delia Rynning, Estacada
201 Lena Gribble, Aurora	287 Ava Owen, Beaver
202 Agnes Weatherson, Minerva	288 Myrtice Fowler, Nortons
203 Benedictine Sisters, Oregon City	289 Beatrice Buckner, Oak Grove
204 Myrtle Birtchet, Mt. Angel	290 Alice L. Bennett, Mosier
205 Viola Nagel, Gaston	291 Bessie G. Immel, Marshfield
206 Gladys Jory, Salem	292 Adella Mortensen, Early
207 Anna C. Taylor, North Powder	293 W. M. Kent, Gold Beach
208 C. H. Wilson, Condon	294 G. P. Harrington, Gold Beach
209 May Payne, Mitchell	295 Mrs. Alida Laduron, Brookings
210 Gladys Denney, Oakland	296 W. H. Grant, Cecil
211 Laura Brenner, Oregon City	297 Fay Duff, Pendleton
212 Pearl Wilson, Milton	298 Beulah Thorp, Aurora
213 J. B. Lent, Fairview	299 Florence Buell, Oakland
214 Mrs. A. E. Watson, Portland	300 Louisa E. Counsell, LaGrande
215 Mary Ulen, Portland	301 F. A. Bloomfield, Derby
216 J. B. Horner, Corvallis	302 E. H. Anderson, Newberg
217 Nina Taylor, Portland	303 Ethel Ross, Newberg
218 M. E. V. Hess, Portland	304 A. R. Tollefson, Corbett
219 Hattiebelle Ogilbee, Portland	305 Minnie Mascher, Silverton
220 Helen Dahl, Gresham	306 Benedictine Sisters, Woodburn
211 C. G. Springer, Madras	307 Roy Bower, Lorane
222 Eva Schneider, Boring	308 Elizabeth Martin, Boyd
223 Ruth Schmuckli, Portland	309 Minnie Fortna, Athena
224 Marian Robertson, Gresham	310 Neita Lewis, Newberg
225 Nellie Renshaw, Mayville	311 Lena Wolcott, Peak
226 Maude B. Mickel, Gresham	312 Winifred King, Corvallis
227 P. C. Fulton, Holbrook	313 E. Pearl Smith, Corvallis
228 L. B. Gibson, Hood River	314 E. H. Castle Philomath
229 Mrs. Ora D. Fleming, Lents	315 G. E. Ross Lebanon
230 Ada Werner, Portland	316 Ferd W. Jones, Corvallis
231 E. Williams, Portland	317 Mrs. Earl Miller, Albany
232 Nellie Washburn, Portland	318 Rose Kaldor, Monroe
233 Mrs. Margaret B. West, Portland	319 Rhoda Newkirk, Monroe
234 Minerva Powell, Troutdale	320 J. V. Kane, Lyons
235 Marguerite Miller, Portland	321 J. E. Dunton, Lebanon
236 Mabel F. Burghduff, Portland	322 Elsie Moore, Corvallis
	323 Anna Denman, Lebanon
237 Louise Sterling, Corbett	324 W. L. Jackson, Albany
	325 Mrs. Daisy Allen, Shedd
238 Vina Swan, Camas, Wash.	
	326 J. M. Poe, Berlin
239 Mrs. Jennie Carr, Portland	

327 Victoria Soderstrom, Harrisburg	414 H. M. Sherwood, Portland
328 Nora C. Coleman, Sweet Home	415 Phyllis Purdin, Pendleton
329 Clara Van Matre, Alpine	416 Loretta Harding, Florence
330 Estella Dooney, Foster	417 Floyd L. Senter, Acme
331 Alice Boyle, Brownsville	418 Beatrice Runcall, Portland
332 Mary Connet, Foster	419 Ruby Fenwick, Jordan Valley
333 Engra Benson, Crawfordsville	420 Laura S. Barry, Plush
334 Smith B. Holt, Thomas	421 Lulu Maxwell, Banks
335 Ruth Simpson, Suver	422 F. Irma Coon, Lauree
336 V. B. Higbee, Albany	423 Bess Palmer, Springfield
337 Jennie Reed, Harrisburg	424 Ethel Mudge, Heceta
338 Mrs. Hattie Allen, Hoskins	425 Maude Wakefield, Ione
339 Sisters of Mercy, Roseburg	426 H. O. Nedry, Hardman
340 Jacob Stocker, Foster	427 Sylvia McCarty, Sinnott
341 Acie D. McClain, Lebanon	428 Catherine J. Doherty, Ione
342 Ruth A. Wight, Lebanon	429 H. H. Hoffman, Heppner
343 Mary A. Binns, Monroe	430 Sophia Burke, Heppner
344 Urich S. Burt, Corvallis	431 Mrs. Blanche Watkins, Heppner
345 H. B. Brookhardt, Albany	432 L. A. Doak, Ione
346 Arline Hoerr, Lebanon	433 S. E. Notson, Heppner
347 Helen Myers, Albany	434 S. H. Doak, Lexington
348 Bessie Truelove, Corvallis	435 E. S. Payne, Heppner
349 Joy Extel, Corvallis	436 W. L. Suddarth, Irrigon
350 M. J. Looney, Tangent	437 Orlena Suddarth, Irrigon
351 Frank Brumbaugh, Lebanon	438 Edna Carmichael, Lexington
352 G. M. Sprague, Mill City	439 Lera Githens, Morgan
353 Gussie Stadden, Summit	440 Mrs. Lucy T. Wedding, Heppner
354 O. J. Schroyer, Summit	441 Myrtle Miller, Lena
355 Helen Metcalf, Scio	442 Josephine McDevitt, Lena
356 Belle Wilson, Harrisburg	443 Olive Moss, Portland
357 Alwilda Wilson, Albany	· 444 Metta C. Brown, Portland
358 C. F. Bigbee, Crabtree	445 Ruby Briggs, Foster
359 B. A. Johnston, Corvallis	446 Grace Schuebel, Canby
360 Helen Rose Plov, Junction City	447 Alicia Pearl Horner, Portland
361 M. E. Arnold, Albany	448 Lena E. May, Sherwood
362 Joanna Hislop, Corvallis	449 Golda M. Johnson, Crawfordsville
363 Fred Lockley, Portland	450 Bessie M. Hanseth, Monmouth
364 Esther Gilbertson, Harrisburg	451 R. L. Green, Fossil
365 Minnie McCourt, Albany	452 Fred Hawes, Winlock
366 J. N. Bilyeu, Crabtree	453 Ida Olson, Fossil
367 D. U. Cochrane, Kings Valley	454 Lillian Duff, Fossil
368 Marie F. Schrepel, Philomath	455 C. R. Deems, Burnt Ranch
369 Mabel Hann, Harrisburg	456 Eva Boyle Linville, Spray
370 Ruth Hacking, Blodgett	457 Leah Blann, Twickenham
371 F. M. Maxwell, Halsey	458 B. L. Murphy, Spray
372 Venia Powers, Payette, Idaho	459 Mrs. Elizabeth Bowerman, Fossil
373 Blanche Scharmann, Portland	460 Flora Gilliland, Fossil
374 Mrs.Bertha McKinley,Rogue River	461 Susan E. Prindle, Antone
375 ·Mary Hostetler, Silverton	462 Rayma Lee Van Horn, Fossil
376 Mrs. Mary Wight, Beswick, Cal.	463 C. R. Curfman, Kent
377 Signa Johnson, Colton	464 Kent School, Kent
378 Dale Loftin, Waterloo	465 Ethel L. Hooper, Hoskins
379 W. J. Patterson, Wamic	466 Edna Hamlin, Brownsville
380 Louise Rintoul, The Dalles	467 Oliver Matthews, Boyd
381 Ica L. Derthick, Wapinitia	468 E. B. Moore, John Day
382 Phyllis Fischer, Maupin	469 C. H. Poole, Canyon City
383 Frankie Allen, The Dalles	470 Bruce Hayes, Prairie City
384 Agnes Campbell, The Dalles	471 R. E. Bible, Hamilton
385 Enid Bell, Big Eddy	472 Margaret Mitchell, Caverhill
386 Ethyl Gibson, Boyd	473 Clara B. Carroll, Dayville
387 Helena Fleck, The Dalles	474 Mabel Thomas, Prairie City
388 Mary U. Michell, The Dalles	475 Rachel Ballance, Long Creek
389 Marcia Selleck, Dufur	476 Mrs. W. W. Slaughter, Ritter
390 Bessie Bonney, Tygh Valley	477 Mrs. C. W. Curtis, Beech Creek
391 Mary Adair, The Dalles	478 Corwin A. Harvey, Fox
392 Katherine Arbuthnot, Monmouth	479 C. H. Justice, Cotton Wood
393 Christine Ketels, The Dalles	480 Mrs. Laura Collins, Hamilton
394 Frances E. Bennett, Dufur	481 Wesley Harryman, Long Creek
395 Elizabeth Leben, Dufur	482 Robert Harryman, Monument
396 Mary V. Miller, Maupin	483 Mrs. L. A. Slaughter, Monument
397 Rose C. Hassing, Dufur	484 E. W. Kimberling, Prairie City
398 Ella M. Syron, Maupin	485 V. E. Danels, Prairie City
399 Margaret Walker, Mosier	486 Millie Ricco, Austin
400 J. P. Ross, Mosier	487 W. M. Bennett, Dayville
401 Mrs. G. R. Crofoot, Maupin	488 Anatta Burch, Enterprise
402 J. S. Wright, Dufur	489 Wilhemina Hemrich, Albany
403 Arthur Bonney, Criterion	490 Amel Moore, Madras
404 Ruth VanZandt, Mosier	491 Osie H. Jewell, Madras
405 Mary Dennis, Boyd	492 Ethel Klann, Madras
406 Lucy S. Ruggles, Dufur	493 Elva J. Smith, Madras
407 Dorothy Passmore, Mosier	494 Lelota Horrigan, Gateway
408 Clara Lorenzen, The Dalles	494 Christine Ferm, Lexington
409 Hazel Seeley, The Dalles	496 Hazel Thorson, Bend
410 Ralph Southwick, Wallowa	497 Irene Weekly, Marshfield
411 Virgil Melvin, Ada	498 Emma M. Schreiber, McMinnville
412 Genevieve Haven, Kent	499 Bertha King, Corvallis
413 Hilma Anderson, Portland	500 Vera Tipton, Reedsport

501 E. T. Reed, Corvallis	588 Abbie S. Davis, Salem
502 Irene Douglas, Willows	589 Mabel Temple, Salem
503 Sylvia Hardman, Condon	590 W. J. Mishler, Woodburn
504 Beatrice Snell, Arlington	591 Grace Johnson, Niagara
505 Enid G. Leeper, Condon	592 Ina C. Hubbs, Silverton
506 Mrs. Lun Searcy, Condon	593 Nelta Royer, Salem
507 Eunice Ebbert, Gwendolen	594 Mrs. LaMoine Clark, Salem
508 Phyllis Fate, McDonald	595 Agnes Briggs, Jamieson
509 Clara M. Blais, Condon	596 Frances Chivington, Portland
510 Cora Smith, Condon	597 W. A. Pettys, Portland
511 Lottie Keizur, Condon	598 E. S. Evenden, Monmouth
512 Esther J. Turner, Clem	599 H. D. Sheldon, Eugene
513 Carrie W. Burnham, Arlington	600 Mrs. Marie Stoller, Metolius
514 Bessie C. Lafferty, Condon	601 Emma Agee, Wilsonville
515 Mabel L. Williams, Condon	602 Martina H. Thiele, Hood River
516 Mrs. Ethel Mulkey, Arlington	603 T. J. Skirvin, Wamic
517 P. J. Mulkey, Arlington	604 Amilla Dart, Scio
518 Lydia B. Highlands, Mikkalo	605 Cora Gay, Rickreall
519 Mrs. W. H. Reynolds, Condon	606 Armilda Doughty, Monmouth
520 Maude Grider, Condon	607 Mrs. Chloe Wood, Dallas
521 Lee Byers, Lonerock	608 Lester Gardner, Dallas
522 Mrs. Minnie F. Wilson, Cecil	609 Mrs. Ella Oleman, Hoskins
523 Mildred Force, Arlington	610 Roberta E. Balland, Rickreall
524 Alveda Peterson, Arlington	611 Geneva Sayre, Black Rock
525 Alma Randelin, Condon	612 Mrs. Mattie Neal, Grand Ronde
526 Jessie Hardie, Condon	613 H. H. Matthews, Phoenix
527 Marjory Hardie, Trailfork	614 Rose H. Gay, Gold Hill
528 J. C. Sturgill, Condon	615 W. O. Wheeler, Eagle Point
529 Alice McLean, Mercer	616 Anna Jeffrey, Medford
530 Vida McLean, Eugene	617 Dorothy Hartung, Junction City
531 Ida Foott, Portland	618 Grace L. May, The Dalles
532 Mary E. Thompson, Marshfield	619 Eula Strange, Portland
533 K. W. Onthank, Eugene.	620 Neva McReynolds, Langells Val.
534 Margaret A. Gray, Thurston	621 Alma Sutherland, Bakeoven
535 Anne G. Jackson, Knappa	622 Ruth Dowd, Weston
536 Mary Harrison, Madras	623 John R. Stuber, Joseph
537 Albert H. Gillett, Dayton	624 Harvey A. Wright, Rickreall
538 Madge Thomas, Buena Vista	625 Nellie Keyt, Independence
539 Etta Halley, Willamette	626 Willis A. Johnston, McCoy
540 H. E. Inglow, Forest Grove	627 Edith Montgomery, Falls City
541 Grace Pryor, White Pine	628 Mrs. E. R. Palmer, Dallas
542 Clyde L. Knapp, Salem	629 Grace Porter, Rickreall
543 H. C. Todd, Salem	630 E. H. Hedrick, Monmouth
544 Emma C. Brack, Woodburn	631 W. I. Reynolds, Dallas
545 Ellen Greibenow, Salem	632 Lora Chute, Independence
546 Emma Walker, Salem	633 Alice E. Quint, Black Rock
547 Mattie Neeley, Turner	634 Mabel C. Gillette, Independence
548 Harry Bailie, Silverton	635 Elsie L. Taylor, Salem
549 Henriette Berning, Mt. Angel	636 Winona Rowland, Rickreall·
550 Helen Kefer, Mt. Angel	637 Alice McIntosh, Monmouth
551 Josie Thompson, Grants Pass	638 Georgia Curtiss, Dallas
552 Harriet Minthorn, Rogue River	639 Effie Cuthbert, Sheridan
553 Lois Sims, Hubbard	640 Gertrude R. Wilson, Monmouth
554 Mabel Van Fleet, Mehama	641 Olive McCready, Suver
555 Hilda M. Nerison, Silverton	642 W. I. Ford, Dallas
556 Flora Grice, Salem	643 Rose Bodayla, Salem
557 F. A. Myers, Aumsville	644 R. W. Tavenner, Independence
558 H. M. James, Silverton	645 Nellie Young, Parkers
559 Mrs. H. H. Paget, Macleay	646 Floyd O. Miller, Dallas
560 J. H. Collins, Woodburn	647 Edna Sweeney, Buell
561 Anna Lindgren, Salem	648 Gladys Stewart, Rickreall
562 Osie Grice, Aumsville	649 Jessie Hunt, Independence
563 W. C. Gauntt, Stayton	650 John Kurtichanov, Chitwood
564 J. G. Noe, Hubbard	651 J. I. Reasoner, Dallas
565 Alta B. Brown, Lyons	652 Gladys Mitchell, Independence
566 Minnie L. Joeckel, Silverton	653 Loraine Goehring, McCoy
567 Margaret West, Oregon City	654 Clara Sampson, Nortons
568 Ellen Currin, Salem	655 June Philpott, Corvallis
569 Kate Willoughby, Arago	656 Sara Huntington, Yoncalla
570 Daisy Carter, Salem	657 Retta M. Allen, Whitney
571 Margaret J. Cosper, Salem	658 Sophia A. Wilson, Portland
572 Mrs. E. H. Belknap, Turner	659 Emma Post, Drain
573 F. P. Sherman, Woodburn	660 Agathe Grondahl, Portland
574 Hilda J. Olson, Silverton	661 Dora E. Starke, Amity
575 A. N. Arnold, Salem	662 G. W. Milam, Gold Hill
576 E. S. Stultz, Scotts Mills	663 Mrs. W. N. Davis, Rogue River
577 Bertha C. Byrd, Salem	664 Mrs. O. C. Lichens, Kerby
578 B. K. Cook, Salem	665 W. H. Ashcraft, Ashland
579 Julia Iverson, Salem	666 Lillian L. Gammill, Trail
580 Alice E. Estes, Scotts Mills	667 Emily DeVore, Medford
581 Mrs. L. R. Stinson, Stayton	668 Elizabeth Elmore, Applegate
582 Elwina E. Schramm, Salem	669 Viola Hogan, Trail
583 Mrs. Marie Ehmer, Salem	670 Chester Cook, Wolf Creek.
584 Greta Phillips, Salem	671 Wessie Griffith, Medford
585 Leota C. Humphrey, Turner	672 H. Howard Grover, Medford
586 Emma F. More, Salem	673 Nellie B. Ross, Ashland
587 R. L. Young, Mt. Angel	674 Annie O'Keefe, Huntington Beach

675	Lela E. Bloom, LaGrande
676	Nellie Shelley, Merlin
677	Margaret McQuistion, Grants Pass
678	Susanne Homes, Ashland
679	Gladys Musgrave, Hardman
680	Laura Jackway, Troutdale
681	Mary E. Wilcox, Sheridan
682	Winifred A. Joyce, Portland
683	Sherman Smith, Helix
684	Alice N. Staninger, Waldo
685	Laura E. Hansoln, Ashland
686	Edith R. Fredenburg, Brownsboro
687	Havel Shaver, Ashland
688	Emma Wendt, Jacksonville
689	Roy Brown, Murphy
690	Maude Philbrook, Medford
691	Robert I. Peachey, Jacksonville
692	May Nordoff, Medford
693	Julia Sidley, Eagle Point
694	Vera Kellems, Grants Pass
695	Pearl L. Gould, Butte Falls
696	Blanche Crane, Grants Pass
697	Mary A. Oakes, Hugo
698	G. W. Ager, Talent
699	Anna Potts, Merlin
700	J. A. Churchill, Salem
701	H. C. Seymour, Corvallis
702	C. S. Cramer, Medford
703	E. B. Stanley, Central Point
704	Leonard M. Buoy, Butte Falls
705	A. R. Peterson, Medford
706	Stella M. Paddock, Grants Pass
707	J. C. Banard, Tolo
708	A. E. Humpton, Selma
709	Mrs. Alberta Jones, Beagle
710	D. K. Luthy, Gold Hill
711	Katherine Foley, Gold Hill
712	V. A. Davis, Central Point
713	Mrs. Mollie Belding, Grants Pass
714	H. H. Fox, Lake Creek
715	Florence Querry, Medford
716	Tom L. Ostien, Waldo
717	H. H. Wardrip, Grants Pass
718	Helene Knips, Grants Pass
719	J. A. Bish, Wilderville
720	Marian I. White, Grants Pass
721	Laura C. Atkins, Grants Pass
722	Margaret Gallinger, Jacksonville
723	B. F. Nibert, Applegate
724	Gertrude Engle, Ashland
725	Daisy M. Lewis, Jacksonville
726	P. H. Daley, Medford
727	Kathryn Dunham, Medford
728	Harriet Wilson, Medford
729	Mrs. May Rose, Wonder
730	Lucia C. Chapman, Waldo
731	Pina Benedict, Ashland
732	Clara Skyrman, Trail
733	Lucile Rader, Medford
734	Dewie E. Howe, Trail
735	Hazel Taylor, Central Point
736	Marie Dolan, Hugo
737	Melvina M. Fox, Merlin
738	Aneta M. Chellin, Grants Pass
739	Mrs. Geo. B. Canode, Medford
740	Felix E. Moore, Ashland
741	Elizabeth Neidigh, Knappa
742	Annie Williamson, Fisher
743	Belle M. Yeates, Fossil
744	Minnie Schalier, Salem
745	E. B. Nedry, Nyssa
746	Luther D. Cook, Paradise
747	Walter T. Clay, John Day
748	Sister Mary Amelbergo, St. Paul
749	Carrie B. Livesley, Deschutes
750	Lena Woodward, Medena, Ohio
751	B. H. Calkins, Whiteson
752	A. Devaul, Paisley
753	Gladys Pearson, Hammond
754	Mary Hoham, Monmouth
755	Guy L. Lee, Dallas
756	Mamie Longworth, Perdue
757	J. H. Bosard, Roseburg
758	Oscar Gorrell, Oakland
759	Sybil Farnsworth, Millwood
760	J. E. O'Neel, Canyonville
761	Irma L. Vance, Winchester

762	Mrs. Aura D. Jackson, Dillard
763	Mary M. Whipple, Myrtle Creek
764	Walter E. Hercher, Myrtle Creek
765	Mattie I. Carr, Yoncalla
766	Emery D. Doane, Yoncalla
767	Mrs. C. W. Hartley, Sutherlin
768	Myrtle Powell, Sutherlin
769	Mary Edgerton, Roseburg
770	Elizabeth Northcraft, Camas Val.
771	A. J. Flurry, Days Creek
772	Myrtelle Gross, Oakland
773	Gladys Price, Myrtle Creek
774	Nellie M. Wood, Days Creek
775	Lillie Duncan, Perdue
776	Mildred Waite, Sutherlin
777	Mrs. Emma Leeper, Oakland
778	Addie M. Wilson, Yoncalla
779	John Kernan, Roseburg
780	Kathryn Agee, Roseburg
781	Mrs. Myrtle Bradford, Roseburg
782	Mary Aitken, Edenbower
783	Hannah Ruden, Kellogg
784	Ruth Swinney, Roseburg
785	Elizabeth Parrott, Roseburg
786	Watson C. Lea, Drain
787	Alice Ueland, Roseburg
788	Jennie Cook, Roseburg
789	Mrs. E. S. Ackert, Myrtle Creek
790	Harl H. Bronson, Riddle
791	Myrtle L. George, Canyonville
792	Florence P. Allen, Drew
793	Adeline Stewart, Roseburg
794	F. B. Hamlin, Roseburg
795	Fred A. Goff, Roseburg
796	W. Alice Goff, Roseburg
797	Ellen Millikin, Drain
798	Floy McCormack, Dillard
799	Floyd Watson, Oakland
800	Lora B. Pummill, Riddle
801	Mamie Langdon, Yoncalla
802	Margaret Bremmer, Brockway
803	H. Omer Bennett, Roseburg
804	Wilfred Brown, Camas Valley
805	A. E. Street, Camas Valley
806	Burt A. Adams, Lakeview
807	Stella Curtis, Burns
808	Frances Kirsch, Berdugo
809	Lacy B. Copenhaver, Springfield
810	Emma Haroun, Wamic
811	Anna Taylor, Mapleton
812	Lola B. Thompson, Grants Pass
813	Mabel McLean, Oregon City
814	A. C. Stanbrough, Newberg
815	Jene Mallory, Spray
816	Lelah McGee, Burns
817	Orisa Hurd, Harper
818	Martha Peters, Holbrook
819	Edith O. Messenger, Disston
820	LaVilla Buell, Cottage Grove
821	Ivy J. Ten Eyck, Boring
822	Mrs. C. W. Shurte, Heppner
823	Esther Hughet, Narrows
824	M. N. Bonham, Hillsboro
825	Mrs. Minnie Gates, Hillsboro
826	Sue Berg, Portland
827	Jessie B. Greer, Forest Grove
828	Lenore Isaacson, Portland
829	Grace M. Thomas, Hillsboro
830	Maude Brennan, Beaverton
831	R. L. Wann, Orenco
832	C. C. Ailor, Banks
833	Mary Yoder, Beaverton
834	Pearl R. Reed, Oswego
835	Sisters of St. Mary, Verboort
836	Marion Crawford, Timber
837	Daphne Henderson, Hillsdale
838	Mrs. Emma Frazelle, Multnomah
839	S. M. Ramsay, Tualatin
840	Elsie Lathrop, Forest Grove
841	H. T. Evans, Garden Home
842	Cleo Rector, Hillsboro
843	Susie Scott, Sheridan
844	G. A. W. Russell, Buxton
845	Mary L. Criteser, Yoncalla
846	Lura H. Grout, Koler
847	R. G. Hall, Roseburg

848	Lillie MacIver, Roseburg		934	Mrs. Emma E. Easton, Empire
849	Purl Patrick, Oakland		935	B. S. Gannvell, Powers
850	John E. Flurry, Canyonville		936	Ernest Root, Myrtle Point
851	O. C. Brown, Roseburg		937	Anne Wickman, Marshfield
852	Mrs. O. C. Brown, Roseburg		938	Nettie Belloni, Prosper
853	B. W. Barnes, Hillsboro		939	Hazel I. Matthews, Powers
854	Mrs. Minnie Conant, Banks		940	Grace Delmore, Sumner
855	Martha Dillon, Beaverton		941	Ellen E. Kelley, Marshfield
856	Winifred Bondy, North Plains		942	Helen Robbins, Broadbent
857	E. E. Amsden, Hillsboro		943	Anna M. Thomas, Bridge
858	Lowell C. Bradford, Hillsboro		944	Metta E. Hansen, Arago
859	Jessie M. Cypher, North Plains		945	Margaret Stambuck, North Bend
860	L. C. Mooberry, Cornelius		946	Anna Clinkinbeard, North Bend
861	Mrs. L. L. Trayler, Hillsboro		947	Selma Thomas, Marshfield
862	S. W. Babcock, Tigard		948	Ernest C. Lloyd, Marshfield
863	Linda B. Koch, Cornelius		949	Mrs. Ella M. Rea, Bandon
864	Mrs. M. C. Saltus, Sherwood		950	Della L. Bryant, Bandon
865	Myrtle Strickler, Sherwood		951	Etta E. Darnell, Myrtle Point
866	R. L. Wildman, Timber		952	Ida E. Gamble, Bandon
867	Roy C. Bierly, Beaverton		953	Ruth Peebley, North Bend
868	Mrs. Harriet H. Heller, Portland		954	Helen E. Mende, North Bend
869	Ellie M. Sage, Dilley		955	Helen M. Sprague, Marshfield
870	Lottie Cole, Sherwood		956	Lola Greene, Myrtle Point
871	Laura J. Bell, Forest Grove		957	May N. Allen, Coquille
872	J. W. Peabody, Forest Grove		958	Lila A. Smith, Bridge
873	Helen E. Weed, Dilley		959	Hilda Mcnson, Sulphur Springs
874	Jennie Beamish, Portland		960	Muriel Watkins, Myrtle Point
875	Lillian Troedson, Morgan		961	Edith R. McLeod, Marshfield
876	R. H. Harris, Shedd		962	Phina Anderson, Marshfield
877	James H. Bohle, Orton		963	Elsie G. Philpott, Riverton
878	Ada M. Peebles, Portland		964	C. A. Howard, Coquille
879	Grace Wiltshire, Bonita		965	Agnes McCracken, Myrtle Point
880	Georgia Bell, Portland		966	Anna Sollie, Bandon
881	Florence Bollam, Portland		967	W. E. Moses, Marshfield
882	Florence Caldwell, Portland		968	Ellen Knudsen, Empire
883	Margaret McCabe, Portland		969	Clara Moser, Gravelford
884	Sarah Beattie, Portland		970	Ivy Bryan, McMinnville
885	Martha Irwin, Portland		971	Bessie E. Jones, Cascadia
886	Florence Blumenaeur, Portland		972	Floyd Bridges, Kellogg
887	Alice Ormandy, Portland		973	Juanita Porter, Wheeler
888	Evangeline Van Horne, Portland		974	Nora A. Kellow, Hemlock
889	Charlotte Lucas, Portland		975	Mrs. J. H. Dustan, Tillamook
890	Mrs. Laura Black, Portland		976	Alice M. Phillips, Tillamook
891	Mrs. Clara Pratt, Stayton		977	Mabel R. Terry, Tillamook
892	Crystal H. West, Mt. Vernon		978	C. S. Armold, Blain
893	Dorothy Litscher, Sheridan		
894	Myrtle Byers, Clarno		979	Mary L. White, Tillamook
895	E. May Moore, Laurel		980	Gertrude Schlappi, Tillamook
896	Anna M. Schwall, Cornelius		981	H. S. Brimhall, Garibaldi
897	Mrs. Effie R. Arns, Portland		982	Myrtle Wallin, Tillamook
898	Stella M. Hinman, Cherry Grove		983	Ethel R. Glines, Tillamook
899	Clara M. Walker, Gales Creek		984	Katherine Loerpabel, Barnesdale
900	Frances M. O'Connor, Laurel		985	Helen L. Clair, Woodburn
901	Wm. Irle, Portland		986	Evelyn Walker, Gold Hill
902	Mrs. Minerva T. Brown, Hillsboro		987	Clara A. Nelson, Grass Valley
903	J. M. Stretcher, Beaverton		988	Justus A. Miller, Lexington
904	J. R. Chapman, Metzger		989	Bertha McCallister, Grants Pass
905	Cora E. Stephens, Laurel		990	Cordelia Stiles, Salesville, Mont.
906	Ruth J. Frost, Gaston		991	Ethel Notter, Mulino
907	Ruth Johnston, Beaverton		992	Virginia V. Worsham, Portland
908	Gladys O. Willard, Gaston		993	Ruby V. Hazlett, Salem
909	C. L. Nelson, Mountaindale		994	G. B. Lamb, Tillamook
910	Floy A. Norton, Forest Grove		995	Ella R. Sperry, Beaver
911	Florence Enschede, Forest Grove		996	Harriet M. Ford, Tillamook
912	E. W. Luecke, Cornelius		997	Mrs. H. C. Hanson, Tillamook
913	Jessie L. Smith, Gales Creek		998	C. E. English, Nehalem
914	Edith Mensing, Hillsboro		999	Sarah Donohue, Oreton
915	Mrs. H. A. Ball, Hillsboro		1000	Eleanor Spall, Rockaway
916	Naomi Billeter, Orenco		1001	Fred C. Peusser, Hebo
917	Ruth Canright, Kent		1002	Effie Williamson, Fossil
918	Gladys K. Asher, Mt. Vernon		1003	H. F. Pfingsten, The Dalles
919	Mrs. Cecil Porter, Metolius		1004	Alah A. Hunt, Fossil
920	Nella M. Van Horn, Madras		1005	Lela M. Forest, Three Pines
921	Iva Cox, Lapine		1006	Varena M. Puntenney, Albany
922	A. J. Prideaux, Portland		1007	George R. Schreiber, Shedd
923	Grace Mann, Portland		1008	Mrs. Eva Scott, Oregon City
924	Artie Nichols, Bonanza		1009	Elva Austin, Salem
925	Mrs. L. M. Gilbert, Salem		1010	Emma Kirkpatrick, Newberg
926	Orvill G. Reeves, Marshfield		1011	Ruth C. Warren, Harney
927	Louis E. Furrow, Myrtle Point		1012	Ethel I. Bowers, Mist
928	S. C. Sherrill, Riverton		1013	A. M. Winn, Vernonia
929	Nina Dano, Bandon		1014	Mrs. E. Colvin, Clatskanie
930	J. F. Croft, Bridge		1015	Alice Sheehan, Deer Island
931	Kate Chatburn, Bandon		1016	Lloyd W. Shisler, St. Helens
932	Rose E. Grossop, Marshfield		1017	K. R. Blakeslee, Rainier
933	Mrs. P. M. Wilbur, Marshfield		1018	May Novak, Yankton

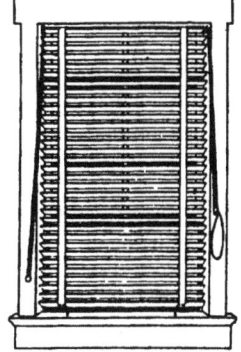

1019 Mrs. M. W. Hatfield, Scappoose	1105 Margaret McNamara, Parkdale
1020 Gertrude McCarty, Vernonia	1106 N. E. Fertig, Hood River
1021 W. W. Patterson, Scappoose	1107 V. M. Vose, Hood River
1022 Florence L. Bennett, Westport	1108 Regina Cash, Wyeth
1023 Frederick I. Knight, St. Helens	1109 Marion Howe, Hood River
1024 Mary Dahlgren, Warren	1110 Harriet Alexander, Hood River
1025 Ethel B. Lawpaugh, Yankton	1111 Edith Baker, Hood River
1026 Mary R. Thomas, Warren	1112 C. R. McCoy, Hood River
1027 Mrs. Bird B. Clark, Chapman	1113 Mrs. Elizabeth Curtis, Mt. Hood
1028 Mrs. Gladys L. Smith, Vernonia	1114 Mrs. J. H. Crenshaw, Dee
1029 Bertha Lewison, Clatskanie	1115 J. O. McLaughlin, Hood River
1030 David L. Cook, Newberg	1116 Selma E. Lahti, Prairie City
1031 W. E. Buell, Buena Vista	1117 Echo Githens, Morgan
1032 W. Hurley, Keasey	1118 Dora G. Jackson, Gooseberry
1033 Gladys Richey, Rainier	1119 Raymond L. Cornwell, Madras
1034 Mary McGregor, Marshland	1120 Mrs. B. Jorgensen, Hillsboro
1035 Clarence Phillips, Clatskanie	1121 Ruth Howard, Jefferson
1036 James Dodson, Scappoose	1122 L. A. Wright, Eugene
1037 Agnes Brown, Trenholm	1123 Lucile Risch, Catlow
1038 Florence Taylor, Goble	1124 Hazel Bevans, Burns
1039 Madeline Slotboom, St. Helens	1125 Henrietta Hoyser, Salem
1040 Velma Snider, Mist	1126 Mrs. E. K. Mitchell, Tillamook
1041 Mrs. E. E. Mallaber, Goble	1127 Ila Knox, Spray
1042 Jessie H. McDonald, Scappoose	1128 Roy W. Glass, Philomath
1043 Lillie M. Leith, St. Helens	1129 Estella Phiester, Medford
1044 Ethel A. Allen, Rainier	1130 Ora Cox, Medford
1045 G. W. Brown, Houlton	1131 Murl Coffeen, Medford
1046 Mrs. Ada Holaday, Scappoose	1132 Sue Hoffman, Medford
1047 Lyle B. Chappell, Quincy	1133 G. W. Godward, Jacksonville
1048 Lillian Cooper, Goble	1134 Elizabeth Ferguson, Medford
1049 Hilda Muhr, Warren	1135 Heloise Phillips, Echo
1050 Madelina Thomas, Warren	1136 Fern Hoisington, Pilot Rock
1051 C. C. Cassatt, St. Helens	1137 Mrs. Paralee Hailey, Pendleton
1052 C. E. Lake, St. Helens	1138 Alice Hudson, Hermiston
1053 O. T. Tabler, Rainier	1139 Ada Earl, Stanfield
1054 J. W. Allen, St. Helens	1140 Anice Barnes, Stanfield
1055 Mabel Molin, Bacona	1141 J. O. Russell, Athena
1056 Bessie Kennard, Falls City	1142 Lillian D. Dobson, Athena
1057 Mamie E. Ayres, Beaverton	1143 Mrs. Ora A. Powell, Freewater
1058 Marie Groves, Carlton	1144 Clara Partridge, Athena
1059 Agatha DeCarle, Gales Creek	1145 A. T. Parks, Pendleton
1060 Margaret Davis, Mt. Vernon	1146 Nellie McCane, Helix
1061 Angeline Adoradio, Dundee	1147 J. W. Smith, Milton
1062 Julia C. Harrison, Narrows	1148 H. M. Allen, Pendleton
1063 Effie M. Lovegren, Cherry Grove	1149 Lucy Coffey, Freewater
1064 Elizabeth C. Riecker, Monmouth	1150 J. A. Hawks, Nolin
1065 Anna Gallup, Mist	1151 F. W. Beatty, McKay
1066 Mrs. Effie Wilson, St. Helens	1152 H. C. Fetter, Weston
1067 Roberta Smith, Drewsey	1153 Gilbert C. Woods, Freewater
1068 Glennie McBane, Culver	1154 Bessie Hatch, Nye
1069 J. Victoria Huston, Tumalo	1155 Mabel Montgomery, Weston
1070 A. L. Stephens, Taft	1156 Violet Kendig, Adams
1071 Edith Witzel, Monmouth	1157 Anne L. Saling, Nye
1072 Nellie Springer, Colton	1158 Mrs. M. L. Fulkerson, Salem
1073 Henry H. Dirksen, Hubbard	1159 Mrs. Orpha K. Sevey, Stanfield
1074 Norma Holman, Airlie	1160 Metta Johnson, Milton
1075 J. Y. Bethune, Salem	1161 Vesta Cutsforth, Pendleton
1076 Victor Boyd, Leona	1162 L. B. Kicker, Milton
1077 Marjorie Whipple, Gunter	1163 Edith May Richardson, Helix
1078 Mrs. Mamie J. Rafferty, Banks	1164 W. S. Mayberry, Milton
1079 Mamie Cachelin, Dixonville	1165 Luella B. Pinkerton, Weston
1080 Kathryn Dougherty, Silverton	1166 Mrs. H. W. Drew, Helix
1081 Harriet Chambers, Silverton	1167 H. W. Drew, Helix
1082 Mary E. Frazier, Hood River	1168 Pauline Heacock, Pilot Rock
1083 Cheo Shoup, Parkdale	1169 Mrs. L. B. Cordery, Adams
1084 W. H. Alwin, Cascade Locks	1170 Mrs. Florence Kelley, Milton
1085 Charlotte Kinnaird, Hood River	1171 Irma Belles, Wallula, Wash.
1086 Antonia A. Bauer, Hood River	1172 J. S. Danforth, Freewater
1087 Mrs. Mary Millard, Sheridan	1173 Rose Monterastelli, Helix
1088 Ray R. Canterbury, Tumalo	1174 Myrtle Sneve, Freewater
1089 J. F. Santee, Connell, Wash.	1175 Hattie E. Pulliam, Pilot Rock
1090 Isolda B. Roper, Antelope	1176 C. E. Graham, Pendleton
1091 Anna C. Godbersen, Hood River	1177 Kate Christensen, Freewater
1092 Gertrude Jones, Hood River	1178 Alice Butler, Pendleton
1093 Mrs. W. E. Blashfield, Hood River	1179 Glee Wharton, Freewater
1094 Eleanor Coe, Hood River	1180 Hazel Adams, Pendleton
1095 Elizabeth Grant, Cascade Locks	1181 Eunice Smith, Helix
1096 Elizabeth McDonald, Hood River	1182 Frank R. Doble, Pine Grove
1097 Sylvia Elder, Mosier	1183 Mrs. L. D. Idleman, Pendleton
1098 Clara E. Rand, Hood River	1184 Erma D. Heacock, Pendleton
1099 Wm. A. Cass, Hood River	1185 E. E. Geiss, Pendleton
1100 Mrs. W. W. Rodwell, Hood River	1186 W. C. Howard, Stanfield
1101 Sadie McKenzie, Cascade Locks	1187 Mrs. Margaret Cramer, Holdman
1102 Elizabeth Swanson, Hood River	1188 Camille Dolson, Pendleton
1103 Mary E. Sheppard, Hood River	1189 H. T. Drill, Pendleton
1104 Nellie Crocker, Hood River	1190 Paul M. Reed, Freewater

1191	Sarah E. Wilson, Adams
1192	Mae W. Chrisholm, Pendleton
1193	Ethel Freeman, Pendleton
1194	Walton J. Roork, Adams
1195	Agnes Carlson, Touchet, Wash
1196	Jessie B. Brierly, Athena
1197	Inez Wagner, Umapine
1198	Leota Wagner, Athena
1199	Juanita Friedly, Adams
1200	Daisy McPherson, Pendleton
1201	Edith M. Fraker, Pendleton
1202	Frances M. Simmons, Adams
1203	Nell Savely, Adams
1204	Louise A. Deute, Pendleton
1205	Ethel E. Haw, Pendleton
1206	Olive Bovee, Pendleton
1207	Elsa Strever, Pilot Rock
1208	Grace Frost, Pilot Rock
1209	Esther F. Compton, Milton
1210	Bessie Swain, Burns
1211	E. G. Bailey, Ontario
1212	Hazel Harris, Silverton
1213	Juanita Randall, Crawfordsville
1214	Nina M. Conlee, Marshfield.
1215	Arma Keen, Halsey
1216	Nora Ward, Dorena
1217	E. R. Jones, Broadbent
1218	Julia Sears, Portland
1219	Anna DeLin, Portland
1220	Mathilda Ahrends, Portland
1221	Lillian J. Goodspeed, Portland
1222	R. R. Steele, Portland.
1223	P. N. Plamondon, Seattle, Wash.
1224	Mrs. W. W. Wiley, Tillamook
1225	Stella G. Goyne, Tillamook
1226	E. K. Barnes, Perrydale
1227	Estelle McClure, Prineville
1228	Geo. F. Thompson, Willamette
1229	Claire G. Morey, Gervais
1230	E. R. Houck, Alvadore
1231	Mrs. Amy Campbell, Winant
1232	Martha Hinkle, Sutherlin
1233	Mary Elliott, Monkland
1234	Laura Waggoner, Independence
1235	Curtis Christy, Sisters
1236	Eva Alfrey, McMinnville
1237	Martha Jensen, Silverton
1238	Mrs. Clara Vickers, Seaside
1239	John L. Ashton, Derby
1240	Enid Elliott, The Dalles
1241	L. L. Baker, St. Helens
1242	Susie M. Barton, Devils Lake
1243	Marie O. Glaze, Gaston
1244	Marie Reese, Salem
1245	Edith Bork, La Grande
1246	Grace Van Winkle, Suplee
1247	Laura Edgerton, Ft. Bidwell, Cal.
1248	Paul Wiser, Carlton
1249	Mabel E. Orcutt, Payette, Ida.
1250	James R. Forsythe, Monmouth
1251	Betha Graham, Rolyat
1252	Alma E. Riley, Beaver
1253	Marion Z. Clarke, Medford
1254	Eileen Tompkins, Cascade Locks
1255	Lelia Drew, Tillamook
1256	A. Dawkins, Grants Pass
1257	I. D. Serfling, Thomas
1258	W. W. Hewitt, Umpqua
1259	Susie Mahan, Baker
1260	Vera Storie, Durkee
1261	Eleanor Storie, Gypsum
1262	J. C. Hall, Wallowa
1263	Wilfred Davies, Troy
1264	J. F. Engle, Halfway
1265	Mrs. Emmett Temple, La Grande
1266	Jessie F. Hindman, Baker
1267	Erma Hawley, Baker
1268	Edna M. Bennett, Baker
1269	Roy Conklin, Wallowa
1270	Elizabeth Bond, La Grande
1271	Isabelle Miller, La Grande
1272	Janette Willgerodt, Flora
1273	Myrtle Schuman, Promise
1274	Mildred Yantis, Baker
1275	Nettie Murray, Flora
1276	Ellen Long, Haines
1277	E. Leota Holmes, Wallowa
1278	Minnie Brown, Baker
1279	Julia Coleman, Sparta
1280	Edna A. Dammon, Sumpter
1281	Reba Williamson, La Grande
1282	Esther Harris, Unity
1283	Alice McCurdy, Granite
1284	Fred G. Potter, Promise
1285	Gene W. Hall, North Powder
1286	Nellie Rush, Elgin
1287	Stella Mayfield, Elgin
1288	Mrs. May Hodson, Enterprise
1289	Mrs. Nettie C. Bussard, Halfway
1290	Bessie M. Conley, Enterprise
1291	Nina Kane, La Grande
1292	E. May Barton, Minam
1293	Mary Braughton, Enterprise
1294	Lenora Huff, Baker
1295	Cora Barnes, Durkee
1296	Vincent N. Patterson, Chico
1297	Alpha Busick, Union
1298	M. Elma Cusick, North Powder
1299	Esther Koplin, Enterprise
1300	Lewis E. Reese, Elgin
1301	Mrs. Rose Clawson, Elgin
1302	J. I. Sturgill, Durkee
1303	G. W. Sammons, Imnah
1304	Teresa Castle, La Grande
1305	Dora Caton, Durkee
1306	Frances O. Lees, Baker
1307	Retta B. Mercer, North Powder
1308	Mae A. Gilliam, Baker
1309	Frieda M. Euberg, Baker
1310	D. Chesley Bones, Halfway
1311	R. A. Wilkerson, La Grande
1312	Anna Meyer, Baker
1313	Martha Miller, Elgin
1314	Royal J. Allen, Cove
1315	B. Southwick, Promise
1316	Edith Welch, Alicel
1317	Grace Fine, Elgin
1318	Ruth A. Ghormley, La Grande
1319	Helen Huff, Baker
1320	Hulda Anderson, La Grande
1321	Nellie G. Neill, La Grande
1322	Ethel L. Davis, Baker
1323	Erma F. Cole, Audrey
1324	Manuel Snider, La Grande
1325	Beatrice Pugh, Kamela
1326	Isabelle Gray, Philomath
1327	Estelle J. McIntyre, Portland
1328	Emily C. Roberts, Portland
1329	Isabelle Chalmers, Portland
1330	Josephine Lisher, Portland
1331	A. M. Cannon, Portland
1332	Grace Sweeney, Taft
1333	Eleanor Warren, Dundee
1334	Vida A. Dunlop, Halsey
1335	F. Silsbee, Aurora
1336	Raymond E. Baker, Coquille
1337	Dorothea McCauley, Terrebonne
1338	Dorothea Pike, Birkenfeld
1339	Mrs. Enos M. Fluhrer, Mayger
1340	Dorothy Zinser, Oswego
1341	Margaret Horton, North Powder
1342	Stella M. Denzer, Summer Lake
1343	F. E. Dunton, Moro
1344	Roy Bowman, Moro
1345	Cecil Lutey, Toledo
1346	Grace M. Tyler, Heppner
1347	Lula E. Peterson, Suver
1348	Nina M. Ross, Clover Flat
1349	Cora D. Fraine, Portland
1350	E. D. Ressler, Corvallis
1351	Hettie Powers, Joseph
1352	Frances Bartshe, Payette, Ida.
1353	J. E. Calavan, Oregon City
1354	Ada Ross, Lexington
1355	Mattie Knottingham, Skullspring
1356	Lena Ulen, Portland
1357	Blanche Wilson, Terrebonne
1358	Emma Weaver, Vincent
1359	Ina B. Graham, Falls City
1360	Central School, Klamath Falls
1361	Riverside School, Klamath Falls
1362	Mills School, Klamath Falls

1363 Pelican School, Klamath Falls
1364 R. H. Dunbar, Klamath Falls
1365 W. S. Buel, Tillamook
1366 A. B. Haverly, Woodburn
1367 B. G. Harding, Rogue River
1368 Albert Schreder, Prineville
1369 Howard S. Miller, Yamhill
1370 Hazel Fawcett, Coquille
1371 Lincoln Savage, Grants Pass
1372 J. E. Drillette, Marion
1373 Violet Rush, Elgin
1374 Evaline Falconer, Enterprise
1375 Effie McDaniel, Portland
1376 Elizabeth Robinson, Medford
1377 Altha Chandler, Devil's Lake
1378 Margaret Reilly, Hood River
1379 H. O. Pearson, Eugene
1380 Florence Pifer, Parkdale
1381 Opal C. Rice, Helix
1382 Edith M. Clark, Astoria
1383 B. T. Youel, Eugene
1384 E. F. Carleton, Salem
1385 Gertrude A. Orth, Portland
1386 Owena Crow, Scappoose
1387 Mrs. Janet M. Grant, Fairview
1388 C. E. Barker, Beaverton
1389 Amy E. Whipple, Monmouth
1390 Mrs. J. A. Bohannon, Toledo
1391 D. W. Hammock, Condon
1392 Callie B. Shelton, Beulah
1393 Mrs. J. C. Grater, Ashwood

1394 Lenora Armstrong, Baker
1395 Nellie A. Pugh, Molalla
1396 Mrs. G. L. Whitels, Prineville
1397 A. C. Crews, Hood River
1398 Mrs. A. F. Beardsley, Salem
1399 Elina Thorsteinson, Salem
1400 Hettie A. Thomas, Roy
1401 Emma Wilson, Aloha
1402 Mrs. Agnes Roberts, Yamhill
1403 Frank K. Welles, Salem
1404 John W. Anderson, Maupin
1405 Esther Evans, Banks
1406 Mary D. Schlegel, Pilot Rock
1407 Jennie Hunter, Medford
1408 Grace M. Wilson, Newberg
1409 Sarah M. Parr, Timber
1410 Merl E. Dimick, Hubbard.

If we fondle and pamper our griefs they grow to an unwieldy size and become unmanageable.—Landor.

Government Positions for Teachers

All teachers should try the U. S. Government examinations soon to be held throughout the entire country. The positions to be filled pay from $1200 to $1800; have short hours and annual vacations, with full pay.

Those interested should write immediately to Franklin Institute, Dept. S 240, Rochester, N. Y., for schedule showing all examination dates and places and large descriptive book, showing the positions obtainable and giving many sample examination questions, which will be sent free of charge.

Selections for Christmas

Arranged by MRS. M. L. FULKERSON, Salem

Christmas in the Primary Grades.

Contrast Thanksgiving, the "gathering-in-time," with Christmas, the "giving-out-time." Tell the story of the first Christmas, reading first, to catch the true spirit yourself, the Gospel account. Tell the legend of St. Nicholas. Let the children talk freely of Santa Claus, getting in this way their ideas of when he comes, why he comes, how he comes; how they prepare for him in the homes; who are Santa's helpers; where he goes when his work is done, etc., etc.

This will lead to the spiritual significance—so much done for love of them and to make them happy. Question as to who works all the time for them to make them happy, then lead them to feel a desire to be like Santa Claus, in secretly working for others. Plan with them to make this a happy Christmas for someone, father, mother, and for those who have not anyone to work for them. Be sure that the child's belief in Santa Claus has helped to emphasize what he can give to others beyond what he may expect to receive.

In questioning about the Christmas tree, the children will speak of the cedar and pine, the trees commonly used in the South. Tell them of the trees used elsewhere, the spruce, the fir, and hemlock. In the cities the florists will supply twigs of some of these that the children may enjoy seeing what others use.

Christmas in other lands will charm the children—Belgium's little people filling their shoes with hay or oats, placing them outside in the window ledge for Santa Claus' pony to eat. In many European countries special cakes are baked for Christmas, as we have our fruit-cake.

For decoration, if without any talent for drawing, send for stencils of Christmas bells, Santa Claus, and other Christmas emblems, and your boards will soon delight the little folks. When the pattern is transferred to the board, the children will be happy to trace, saving your energy for other work.

If you have carried out the idea of giving, you must certainly help the children to prepare their gifts. For older people, out of card board, with baby ribbon, many useful and attractive articles can be made: Postal card cases; sachet envelopes; blotting pads; telephone cards; Christmas bags of card board or raffia; booklets for clippings; needle books; shaving paper pads.

In the idea of decoration and of preparing presents, do not forget appropriate pictures—Madonna, one of Raphael, or other famous artists, large enough to be seen from any point in the room. The small Perry pictures framed in passepartout, make beautiful gifts.—Educational Exchange.

What They Want for Christmas.

First Child—

I want a little dolly
.With eyes that shut up tight,
So she can sleep whenever
    She goes to bed at night.
And I want a dolly buggy
    And a bed to put her in,
And a book of fairy stories
    And a pretty little ring.

Second Child—

I mostly want a little stove
    With an oven that will bake,
So I can cook my dinner
    And bake a really cake.
And I'd like a set of dishes
    And a little rocking chair,
And perhaps a woolly doggy
    Or a pretty teddy bear.

Third Child—

I want a lot of story books
    And some ribbons for my hair,
And I'd like a little bracelet
    And a pretty dress to wear.
Also a pair of roller skates
    And a game or two,
Then with the nuts and candy,
    I think that they might do.

Fourth Child—

I want a brand new wheel
    That I can ride to school,
So I never will be late
    And break the teacher's rule.
And I'd like a football also,
    With a baseball, mit and bat,
And I want a gun, but mama
    Says no use to wish for that.

Fifth Child—

I would like a train of cars
    On a really little track,
You wind them up and start them
    And they'll go around and back.
And a knife just like my daddy's,
    That will cut just anything,
And a big, big buzzing top
    That you wind up with a string.

Sixth Child—

They left me for the very last
    Because I am so small,
And I don't see's there's anything
    For me to take at all.
So the best that I can do
    Is to leave it to St. Nick,
Perhaps he'll give me all that's left
    When they have took their pick.
        —Progressive Teacher.

The Two Little Stockings.

Two little stockings hung side by side
Close to the fireside broad and wide.
"Two?" said Saint Nick, as down he
    came,
Loaded with toys and many a game.
"Ho, no!" said he, with a laugh of fun,
"I'll have no cheating, my pretty one.

"I know who dwells in this house, my
    dear.
There's only one little girl lives here."

So he crept up close to the chimney
    place,
And measured a sock with a sober face.
Just then a wee little note fell out
And fluttered low like a bird about.

"Aha! what's this?" said he, in surprise,
As he pushed his specs up close to his
    eyes,
And read the address in a child's rough
    plan.
"Dear Saint Nicholas," so it began;
"The other stocking you see on the
    wall
I have hung up for a child named Clara
Hall.

"She's a poor little girl, but very good,
So I thought perhaps you kindly would
Fill up her stocking, too, tonight,
And help to make her Christmas bright.
If you've not enough for both stockings
    there,
Please put all in Clara's, I shall not
    care."

Saint Nicholas brushed a tear from his
    eye,
And, "God bless you darling," he said
    with a sigh,
Then, softly he blew through the chim-
    ney high
A note like a bird's, as it soars on high,
When down came two of the funniest
    mortals
That ever was seen this side earth's
    portals.

"Hurry up," said Saint Nick, "and nicely
    prepare
All a little girl wants where money is
    rare."
Then, oh! what a scene there was in
    that room!
Away went the elves, but down from
    the gloom
Of the sooty old chimney comes tum-
    bling low,
A child's whole wardrobe from head to
    toe.

How Santa Claus laughed, as he gath-
    ered them in,
And fastened each one to the sock with
    a pin.
Right to the toe he hung a blue dress,
"She'll think it come from the sky, I
    guess,"
Said Saint Nicholas, smoothing the
    folds of blue
And tying the hood to the stocking, too.

When all the warm clothes were fast-
    ened on,
And both little socks were filled and
    done,
Then Santa Claus tucked a toy here
    and there,
And hurried away to the frosty air,
Saying "God pity the poor and bless the
    dear child
Who pities them, too, on this night so
    wild."

The wind caught the words and bore
    them on high
Till they died away in the midnight
    sky;
While Saint Nicholas flew through the
    icy air,
Bringing "peace and good will" with
    him everywhere.
                        —Sara K. Hunt.

Round 'Bout Christmas Time.

Aunt Nan she says I'm always good,
    An' Pa says, "Yes—asleep"—
An' Ma she don't say nothing, but
    Her eyes they says a heap;
An' I—well, I keep sorter quiet,
    An' try to look sublime—
But you jus' bet, I'm good as gold,
    Round 'bout Chris'mus time.

At other times it's hard as fun
    To do jus' w'at you're told,
An' like to get up early, an'
    Be thankful when they scold;
But somehow when December comes,
    An' hazel-nuts is prime,
I get so good I nearly die,
    Round 'bout Chris'mus time.

I once played hookey, yes, I did,
    An' went a-fishin', too,
An' wished next day I hadn't 'fore
    The principal got through;
But that was way last May that I
    Committed of that crime—
I wouldn't do it now, no sir,
    Round 'bout Chris'mus time.
                        —N. Y. Herald.

Santa Claus and the Mouse.

One Christmas eve, when Santa Claus
    Come to a certain house,
To fill the children's stockings there,
    He found a little mouse.

"A merry Christmas, little friend,"
    Said Santa, good and kind.
"The same to you, sir," said the mouse;
    "I thought you wouldn't mind

"If I should stay awake tonight
    And watch you for a while."
"You're very welcome little mouse,"
    Said Santa, with a smile.

And then he filled the stockings up
    Before the mouse could wink—
From toe to top, from top to toe,
    There wasn't left a chink.

"Now they won't hold another thing,"
    Said Santa Claus, with pride,
A twinkle came to the mouse's eyes
    But humbly he replied:

"It's not polite to contradict—
    Your pardon I implore—
But in the fullest stocking there
    I could put one thing more."

"Oh, ho!" laughed Santa, "silly mouse.
    Don't I know how to pack?
By filling stockings all these years,
    I should have learned the knack."

And then he took the stocking down
    From where it hung so high,
And said: "Now put in one thing more,
    I give you leave to try."

The mousie chuckled to himself,
    And then he softly stole
Right to the stocking's crowded toe
    And gnawed a little hole.

"Now, if you please, good Santa Claus,
    I've put in one thing more;
For you will own that little hole
    Was not in there before."

How Santa Claus did laugh and laugh!
    And then he gayly spoke:
"Well! You shall have a Christmas
    cheese
For that nice little joke."

If you don't think this story true,
    Why! I can show to you
The very stocking with the hole
    The little mouse gnawed through.
                        —Emilie Poulsson.

Playing Santa Claus.

Once Peter and Patty and Polly
Went out for a ride on the trolley.
   A quarter and dime
   Each had at the time
To spend on some sweet Christmas
   folly.

Polly and Patty said "candy,"
While Peter, a bit of a dandy,
   Decided to buy
   A dainty necktie
To make himself look spick and spandy.

And, then—on the corner stood Molly,
Thin, ragged, and quite melancholy
   And sobbing aloud
   In the hurrying crowd,
For she'd fallen and broken her dolly.

Such a poor little midget they thought
   her,
That right up between them they
   caught her;
   To a toy shop they went,
   Every penny they spent,
And a lovely new dolly they bought
   her.

What a Christmas thing! and so jolly,
That Peter and Patty and Polly,
   All out for good times
   With their quarters and dimes,
Should have chosen to spend them on
   Molly!

—St. Nicholas.

A Plan That Failed.

Characters—Jack Lee, a boy of seven.
Santa Claus, a boy of eight. Scene—
Jack is seated on an ottoman pulling
off stockings. He is dressed in gown
and cap ready for bed. A small bed is
at the back of stage.

Jack—
Whoever saw such slim legs as these!
Here's a hole in one toe and look at
   the knees;
Such a lot of things I 'xpect Santa to
   bring; .
These socks are too small for anything.
A pair of skates, a football suit,
A knife like Ned's, O say, it's a beaut!
A book or so, and a nice little gun,
A truly watch that will really run,
Some nuts and apples and lots of
   candy,
Such stuff as that is always handy.
Such legs as these must cause lots of
   worry
For poor Kris Kringle when he's in a
   hurry.
Why, those golf socks of Tom's (He's
   my cousin)
Are 10 times bigger'n these, or a dozen.
I b'lieve one would reach clear down to
   the floor
And I know it would hold a bushel or
   more.
Why, gee whiz! I'll tell you what 'tis,
Why couldn't I borrow that old one of
   his!
It's of no use to him, at any rate,
He can't wear it; he's lost the mate,
And then old Santa would think it was
   mine.

(Goes out and returns with very big
stocking in very gay colors, which he
pins up near the front of the stage.)

My, how it looms up! What a dandy,
It'll hold everything and a peck of
   candy,

Hark! Isn't that Santa? That's surely
   his sled,
Guess I'd better hop, real spry, into bed.

(Gets into bed and kicks a few times,
then lies still and begins to snore softly at first, then quite loudly. A racket
is heard outside. Enter Santa sneezing
and coughing.)

Santa—
It's enough to make a goblin sneeze,
These stove-pipes are such a killing
   squeeze. (Drops pack.)
Ah, the days of my youth I remember
   with pain,
I never shall see such chimneys again.
They built them so low and so thick
   and so wide,
No trouble at all down one to slide,
But now I must struggle and twist and
   squirm,
And force myself through like an angle
   worm.
Ah, then I was fat and hearty and
   round,
And weighed, I should say, nigh three
   hundred pound,
But now, just look, 'tis easy to see,
What a wreck these improvements
   have made of me.
In trying to squeeze through without
   making a noise,
I've kept reducing my avoirdupois,
Till I've so little left of frame and
   muscle,
That lifting my pack is quite a tussle.
And I've seen the time when a single
   toy
Would drive a child nearly wild with
   joy.
But now, if I bring less than seven or
   eight
They think that their's is a joyless
   fate.
Then the elbows and dampers, too,
And a horrible stove for me to crawl
   through,
Such a trial to me. If good folks only
   knew
In pity they'd build an old-fashioned
   flue.
My friends have oft urged me this busi-
   ness to leave
But think how the dear little children
   would grieve
If Santa should fail them some sad
   Christmas Eve,
I never could bear the dark desolation
That would fall on the wee ones all
   over creation.
That reminds me, I must make haste.
If I get clear round there's no time to
   waste.
Let's see, this is the home of Jack Lee,
   I believe,
I've some very fine gimcracks at this
   place to leave. (Takes out Jack's
   bundle.)
Some new fangled skates and a foot-
   ball suit,
This dangerous gun for him to shoot,
A truly watch that will really go,
A ten-bladed knife and a book or so,
Candy enough to cause much woe.
This is his bed-room, too, I see,
Now where can that boy's stocking be?
There's only that one hanging there.
   (Goes up and examines stocking.)
It belongs to a giant, I declare.
It surely can't be that this one I see
Is the one that is worn by little Jack
   Lee.
But since there's no other it really
   must be.

When tillage begins, other arts follow. The farmers, therefore, are the founders of human civilization.—Daniel Webster.

In thy affairs do thou only what is right, the rest will follow of itself.—Goethe.

I never expected to find such a stocking!
The way these boys grow is certainly shocking.
Why, a fellow who wears such a stocking as this
Won't care for little boys' things, I wis.
A boy of seven would have thought them a prize. (Searches in pack.)
But they're no good at all for a chap of this size.
I'll put them all into my pack again,
And find something else, more adapted to men. (Puts cup, razor and book in stocking.)
Here's a mustache cup, a razor, too,
A small dictionary, and that must do.
It looks pretty lank, but then, O my,
I never could fill it, it's no use to try.
But I'll just pin a note here to Jack to say: (Writes, reads and pins note on stocking.)
"If you keep on growing this wonderful way,
Next year I shall find you toothless and gray
Your stocking won't need to be so big,
I'll bring you false teeth and a wig."
(Puts Jack's thing back into pack.)
Now I must go and Oh, how I dread
The toilsome climb to my team and sled,
How much it would add to St. Nicholas' joys
If chimneys would grow as fast as boys. (Exit.) (Jack wakes up, rubs eyes and looks about.)

Jack—
Hello, Hurrah! 'Tis morning, I see,
(Goes to stocking.)
I wonder what Kris Kringle left for me.
This leg, I think, looks mighty thin;
Guess I'll take a peep within. (Takes out cup.)
A horrible cup, for a mustache, too,
Guess I'll save it for a year or so;
A razor, that I can use at any rate.
Just the thing to carve fish-bait.
Here's a book—a dictionary. Why, old St. Nick
Has played me just an awful trick,
There's not a thing I wanted at all,
Not a skate nor a knife, not even a ball,
Oh, here's a note pinned to the toe.
Santa left it for me, I know,
It's all because of my wonderful plan.
(Reads note aloud.)
St. Nicholas thinks I've grown a man.
I'll never get nice presents again,
Next year he'll bring specs and cane.
Boo hoo! That's my pay for being a pig,
I'm 'fraid that stocking was most too big.

—Luella M. Huff.

Along the Columbia Highway

By ALMA H. ARNOLD, Albany, Oregon

Oregon has beautiful scenery, but man is not content and tries to improve it; thus wonderful things are wrought. The Columbia River Highway is a wonderful monument of man's achievement and is grand with natural beauty. Along the one side is the Columbia river, while on the other rise the fir-covered hills, mountains, peaks, falls, etc.

The Highway is paved for miles and miles east from Portland and winds in and out, ever adding some new beauty for the eye to feast upon. There are seventeen concrete bridges. Shepperd's Dell is one of the most picturesque spots. Eleven acres at this point was given to Portland by George Shepperd for a public park. Here there is a 24-foot road which was cut out of solid rock. The Shepperd Dell bridge is 140 feet above the stream. Wah-Kee-Na Falls are very beautiful. To the south is a mountain towering up 3000 feet into the clouds. From its base rushes a stream with water as cold as ice.

Multnomah Falls is called the "Queen of All American Cataracts." There are really two falls; the first one falls 600 feet and the waters dash into a circular basin with a noise like thunder, then it rushes under a slenderly arched bridge and drops almost 70 feet where it joins the Columbia river. It is a sight never to be forgotten.

Another grand view is the Bridge of the Gods which can be seen in the distance. At Crown Point the highway encircles the top of a rock and here you can view the shining Columbia river for 35 miles in either direction. At the highest point reached by the road is Vista House, constructed of concrete, steel, copper, and glass. It is used as a rest-house by the thousands of tourists who travel the highway. The sights that can be viewed from this house are beyond words. The government fish hatchery at Bonneville is said to be one of the largest in the world. Here every year millions of tiny trout and salmon are propagated to re-populate the streams. At this place a large tract of government land is free for the public to use for recreation.

Only a faint idea is received by reading this or any other description. I have only mentioned a few of the sights which can be seen. The only way to fully appreciate this highway is to see it with one's own eyes. A woman who had traveled in Europe stated that nothing she saw there could compare with the grandeur of the beauty viewed from the Columbia River Highway.

OREGON TEACHERS MONTHLY
The Official Journal of the State Teachers' Association

| Vol. XXI | SALEM, OREGON, JANUARY, 1917 | No. 5 |

Published Monthly Except July and August by the State Teachers' Association

Entered at the Postoffice at Salem, Oregon, as second-class mail matter, April 1, 1898.

EDITORIAL BOARD

H. D. SHELDON, School of Education, University of Oregon, Eugene
E. F. CARLETON, Assistant Superintendent of Public Instruction, Salem
C. T. BONNEY, County School Superintendent, The Dalles
R. E. OHLOUPEK, Director Manual Training, Pendleton.
C. G. DONEY, President Willamette University, Salem
E. S. EVENDEN, Department of Education, Oregon Normal, Monmouth
MRS. M. L. FULKERSON, Institute Instructor, Salem
GEORGE W. HUG, City Superintendent, McMinnville
HOFKIN JENKINS, Principal Jefferson High School, Portland.
MISS VIOLA ORTSCHILD, President Grade Teachers' Association, Portland
E. D. RESSLER, Department of Education, Oregon Agricultural College, Corvallis
MISS LILLIAN TINGLE, Supervisor Domestic Science, Portland
CHAS. H. JONES, Business and Managing Editor, Salem

RULES OF PUBLICATION

1. The mailing label on the Oregon Teachers Monthly shows the date to which subscriptions are paid.
2. The Oregon Teachers Monthly will be sent to subscribers until ordered discontinued and all arrearages are paid.
3. Notice of change of address should be given at once, naming both old and new postoffice.
4. When renewing, always state that subscription is a renewal.
5. The subscription price, including membership in State Teachers' Association, is $1.50 a year in advance. Single copy, 20 cents.
6. Advertising rates will be furnished on application.
Address all communications to Oregon Teachers Monthly, Salem, Oregon.

Editorial Notes

Chairman Ackerman of the committee on Teachers' Code of Ethics has been addressing the annual teachers' institutes on that theme. His severe arraignment of unprofessional conduct has been heartily endorsed as shown by the applause and resolutions. If the State Association adopts a fairly complete program and decides to enforce the observance of a code by punishing offenders, it will be comparatively easy to bring members into line. Many, if not most of the unethical acts are the result of thoughtlessness and ignorance of what professional conduct should be. If the association succeeds in enlisting in its membership a substantial majority of the representative teachers, the code which will result from the careful deliberations of the Representative Council in the annual meeting, December 27-29, will set a standard not only for the membership but for all teachers in the state. The fact that associations of physicians, lawyers and other professions have a Grievance Committee and actually pass judgment on offenders against their codes is a strong factor in their high standing with the public. It will probably be deemed inadvisable to set up too drastic standards at first because teachers must be given time to re-adjust their thinking and to develop a sort of class consciousness. Strict enforcement of a moderate and generally approved code against intentional violators will do much in the way of strengthening the State Association with its members and in gaining the respect of the public. The machinery of enforcement may be the appointment of a state committee with a representative in each county or independent county committees subject to review by a state committee.—R.

*   *   *

What is the difference between "He's an old fogy" or "he's a young fogy," and "he's up to date," "he's progressive"? It is a difference which all teachers are very interested in knowing and in having made in regard to their educational status. It is a difference which cannot be maintained without constant growth and into which no petrified ideas may enter. With the ranking of education as a science and the application of scientific methods to its study, there is perhaps no work which is progressing faster or which calls for a more constant effort to keep up the pace. This may be done in many ways, both in service and by periodic intervals of fresh preparation, but to many teachers, especially to those upon whom others are dependent for support or assistance or who have children to educate, this recurring demand for additional preparation seems unfair, and some times is an unjust hardship. On the other hand, the work of teaching is that of giving the ideas which will serve as the foundation for the life work of all men and women and these ideas must, therefore, be true, distinct, and up-to-date. For the purpose of keeping the sources of knowledge fresh and of avoiding Dr. Arnold's "stagnant pools" the accepted standard is the traditional sabbatical year of rest, travel and study, or the more frequent attendance of summer schools and institute courses. In cases where the salary is none too large and expenses heavy this frequently means a period of conscientious saving in order to do some further work and thereby become prepared for the next period of conscientious saving. To complain at this demand is to confess a failure to fully appreciate the responsibilities of a teacher and to comply with it means in many cases being dependent in old age. To many underpaid teachers the "bugaboo" of that "rainy day" in the future is the influence which comes in conflict with the demand for more preparation, more travel, more study and more research. If the demands of professional efficiency are so heavy that they make adequate saving unusually hard, destroy recreative summers and cause worry over the future, is not this condition an argument in favor of an intelligent teachers' retirment fund which will at least enable the teacher to meet these professional requirements more cheerfully?—E.

*   *   *

Speed the day when prospective teachers will have to pass health examinations and when these examinations will be the most rigid of any to be passed. A great many people feel that teaching has too long been the vocational asylum for financial incompetents, industrial misfits, and the physically and nervously debilitated. This feeling, based upon a conspicuous minority, casts an unjust reflection upon the thousands of worthy men and women teachers. It does, however, make it rather imperative for teachers to guard their health and conserve their strength, for teaching stands notably low in the number of years of service and correspondingly high in mortality during service. It is hard to convince the person who is not a teacher that the six or seven hours spent in the school, which is all he sees to it, is extremely enervating, to say nothing of the hours spent in preparation for the following day or the ever-increasing number of demands upon her time and energy for social and community obligations, the phase of the teaching work which is perhaps most fatiguing is the incessant rapid change of attention, from question to answer, from discipline to temperature of room, from distribution of questions to devices of instruction, from class requirements to needs of individuals, all and more of which use nervous force very rapidly. In addition even to this a teacher must be an inspiring example of enthusiasm which it is almost impossible to maintain under the handicap of physical weakness. Isn't it very significant that certain pulmonary troubles and neurasthenia are now being called teacher diseases? Surely teaching is a work which deserves the best you can give and this best is largely conditioned by your health. You should then make your preparation for this part of your work, if anything, more thoughtful, more regular than for any other part or parts, for what will be the use of having your arithmetic or geography lesson outlined and prepared if you are not able to get it properly before the class? Increase your teaching efficiency by starting a systematic campaign for personal health, and as three essential parts of that campaign initiate a regular daily program, cheerful recreation and regular exercise. During the short days of winter the last of these is the hardest to follow but is also more necessary than at any other season. Be especially careful of the hours between four and six in the afternoon; that is the time when the fatigue curve for the day is at its lowest and is not the time to remain in school rooms, full of vitiated air, to prepare the work for the next day, but rather a time for exercise and fresh air, even if it is necessary to obtain them in front of an open window. Look well to your health and you will not need as much attention to your work, or your happiness, and you'll be none the less a teacher.—E.

Some men make you feel as though the warm sun had just broken through the clouds, while others make you feel as though a sudden east wind, with its arms full of cold fog, had caught you with too thin clothing.—Selected.

Memory is the cabinet of imagination, the treasury of reason, the registry of conscience, and the council chamber of thought.—Basil.

Retardation in the Public Schools

By G. A. BRISCOE, Superintendent of Ashland Schools

For the purposes of this discussion the term retardation is used in the commonly accepted meaning of "lagging" behind an established grade normal for the age of the child. The year between the age of 6 and 7 is considered the normal one for the first grade, 7 to 8 for the second grade, 8 to 9 for the third, and 13 to 14 for the eighth. The age given for the first grade is an arbitrary one, probably finding its best reason, if one be needed, in the large numbers of children of this age in the first grade. When the age for first grade is determined for any investigation each succeeding grade necessarily finds its related age.

A pupil progressing regularly, beginning school at six would complete the elementary school course of eight years before he had passed his fourteenth birthday. Such a child would make a normal record. If he, for any reason, should get on in school faster than the age for grade indicates he would be an accelerate, or below age for grade, and should he lag behind grade for age he would be a retard or above age for grade.

The causes of retardation are many. Among the most productive ones are the following: Late entrance, irregular attendance, sickness, inability to use and to understand the English language, physical defects such as poor sense organs, adenoids, diseased teeth, tonsils, etc. Of course it goes without saying that to effect a cure for retardation the cause or causes must be diagnosed and treatment administered in an intelligent manner.

* * *

The full meaning of over-age does not lie wholly in the fact that children may leave the elementary school before completing the course but in the fact that while they are in school the instruction may not be well adapted to their abilities. Therefore, they do not receive the full benefit of the instructions given on the one hand and on the other being improperly classified they are a burden to the teacher, preventing her from giving the proper attention to the other members of her class. In addition to all this, the number of over-age pupils in the grade affects the number of children going to the high school and the number that remain therein to complete the course; for it is well known that few over-age pupils have the courage to remain in high school to complete the full course.

During the year 1913-14, the teachers in the Ashland schools made a preliminary study of retardation in the schools of that city. When the data was tabulated it was found there were enrolled in the grammar schools for the year, 801 pupils, divided as follows: 381 boys and 420 girls. Of these 275 were below age for grade (accelerates),

113 boys and 162 girls. There were 272 pupils of normal age for grade, 136 boys and 136 girls. The group above age for grade contained 254 pupils, 134 boys and 120 girls.

The equality of the number of pupils in each group was surprising and can be shown more definitely by the following: (a) Below age for grade, 275; normal age for grade, 272; above age for grade, 254. (b) Below age for grade, 113 boys and 162 girls; normal age for grade, 136 boys and 136 girls; above age for grade, 134 boys and 120 girls.

Some time was devoted to a study of the causes operating to produce retards. These were grouped into a few general terms such as (1) did not enter school till late, (2) moved frequently and was often put back a grade, (3) protracted illness, (4) physical disabilities, (5) slow development, and (6) lack of parental control.

In the writer's opinion, one very large factor in non-promotion, consequently in retardation, does not show in any data that may be collected. This factor is so intangible that to name it is as difficult as to collect it. It is traditional, all but personal and very pervasive. For lack of a better name we will call it not revenge, not retaliation by way of the law of compensation, not self-defense, but a fear upon the part of the teacher of criticism by the teacher in the next grade above her, and this fear reinforced by the conviction that the pupil did not do his best or the result would have been different. Probably no teacher would be quite willing to admit that she is influenced by such conditions, yet the fact remains that pupils are held in grades when the odds are greatly in their favor that they could go on with the work of the next division just as satisfactorily as they are at the present standing.

During the school years 1914-15 and 1915-16 the teachers in the same system have worked with the hope of increasing the efficiency of the system in order to reduce the amount of retardation. At the end of each semester data was collected which showed that some gain was made at each tabulation. However, figures collected November 1, 1916, will be given for comparison with those of May, 1914. These figures are used because they serve a double purpose—they show the exact standing of each pupil in the schools at that date as to retardation and as to the results of the conditional promotion in the schools: Below age for grade, 302; normal age for grade, 243; above age for grade, 178.

Reducing the figures of May, 1914, to per cent we find at the end of the school year, 34.4 per cent of the entire enrollment to be accelerates or above grade for their age, 33.7 per cent at grade for age or normal, and 31.7 per cent retarded or below grade for age. Reducing the figures of November, 1916, on basis of actual attendance, we get the following: 41.7 per cent of the pupils are accelerated. 33.4 per cent of the actual attendance is normal, and 24.6 per cent of the actual attendance is retarded. It is well to notice here that the 9 B grade is included in the figures of 1916 and that a larger number in that class shows retardation than any of the others. If that class were taken from the report the per cents would read 42.9 per cent accelerates, 33.3 per cent normal, and 23.7 per cent retards.

These figures show that there are more accelerated pupils in the Ashland schools in 1916 than 1913, that the number of normal children for their grades is the same and that the number of retarded children is fewer. It seems fair to conclude that progress is being made in reducing the number of retarded pupils as well as to increase the number of accelerates.

Mr. Strayer, in "Some Problems of City School Administration," gives as the results of the study of the Butte, Montana, schools the following facts: "7.4 per cent of the total number of pupils in the schools are under age for grade. 41.1 per cent of the pupils are of normal age for grade, and 51 per cent are over age for grade."

Therefore it may be quite interesting to continue the study in order that we may find what has led to such a result in a small city school system. Ashland has a population between 5,000 and 6,000. Its people are thoroughly American and deeply interested in educational affairs. The question of dealing with foreigners must be eliminated to begin with. Ashland is also a typical western town, its population being subject to the fluctuation common to all western towns. A large part of the retardation is due, possibly, to those who enter school at over age because of residence in districts where no school privileges are provided or because the children have had poor school accommodations before moving to Ashland. Other than these questions the conditions for no retardation are favorable in Ashland.

* * *

There are two regular periods of promotion in the Ashland schools: One at the middle of January, the other at the close of the school year in May. However, any pupil may be promoted or demoted at any time during the school year if it is the judgment of the principal and the teacher that better work can be done by that pupil in some other grade than the one to which he has been regularly assigned. At the regular promotion period, there are two kinds of transfers or promotions given; one does not bear the word "conditional" and the other does, stating the subjects in which the pupil is conditioned.

Pupils receive eight report cards during the school year. Excepting the six weeks at the beginning of each term a report card is sent home regularly every four weeks. The grades on these cards are made up by the teacher's estimate, records of daily work and monthly tests given by the teacher. Any pupil in the grades having an average standing of 90 per cent in any study and 95 per cent in deportment may, if he cares to, escape the examinations given by the principal when he sees fit to give them. At the end of each semester the superintendent of schools gives an examination in each of the subjects. Any pupil, however, who has maintained an average of 90 per cent in any subject and 95 per cent in deportment may be excused from the superintendent's examination. If any student fails to secure a grade of 75 per cent upon the superintendent's written examination he is conditioned in that subject. If more than two subjects are unsatisfactory he is retained. At the January promotion he must show satisfactory progress in his new grade at the end of the sixth week or be returned to a grade where he can do satisfactory work. For the May promotion period he must, during the summer, make up the conditions marked upon his grade. This may be done by home study, by private tutor or attendance at a summer school. However, a satisfactory examination, given by the superintendent of schools must be passe 1 before these conditions are removed.

The question now arises, what is the effect of such a system? Does it lead to confusion? Does it tend to place pupils in higher grades when they should be repeating work, or does it enable pupils to go on into the next grade and there do satisfactory work when, upon the face of the teacher's records, the pupil is unable to earn a regular transfer? To get at these facts the transfer of May, 1916, will be used.

In May, 1916, the following illustrates the situation at that time: Number retained, 54; number conditioned, 107; number promoted, 440. After the school had been in operation for two months this year there were in school in the grammar grades 668 pupils, which makes 67 more pupils than there were at closing time in May, 1916. This means that the losses, while great, were overbalanced by the gain in moving into the city, the effect of which is to increase the amount of retardation. The pupils that this part of the article cares to deal with are the 107 pupils that were conditionally promoted. We find, by examining the figures that 17.8 per cent of the pupils in school in May received a conditional promotion and 8.8 per cent of the pupils in school were retained in the same grades as they were the preceding semester. In other words, not over 73 per cent of the pupils received a straight transfer to the next grade, few, if any, of whom are ever returned to the grades below. About 9 per cent of the pupils remaining in school are left in the grades for another semester. Occasionally, one passes to the next grade through summer work, but not often.

Lying between these two groups—those regularly transferred and those retained in grade—is another including about 15 per cent of the number of students in school at the promotion period. The teachers are not willing to give them a regular transfer upon basis of work done, yet feel there is a possibility that some, it may be many, could do as well in next grade as they have done in the grade below. To these should be given a conditional transfer, naming in red ink the subjects in which the pupil is weak. There is no opportunity out of school for the removal of these conditions at the beginning of the second semester. So the conditioned pupil is put in next grade on trial for six weeks. If his work is satisfactory to the teacher in charge at the end of the trial period he is permitted to remain. But the pupil and the parent both understand that poor work upon the part of the pupil will reurn him to a lower grade.

Those conditioned at the end of the school year have the vacation period to remove the condition. This they may do by home study, summer school or private tutor. However, each pupil must take a written examination, given by the superintendent of schools for the removal of all conditions. It seems that a large advantage of this condition and trial period comes from it putting the pupil to his best efforts and enlisting the parents' support in the child's welfare. As evidence of the results obtained a few reports upon pupils conditionally promoted will be inserted.

"Retained in 6 B grade, but on account of Miss ——'s room being so much larger than mine, I have been giving him a chance to try 6 A work; he has succeeded in doing good work in all but two subjects and I am working to strengthen him in these; he has done better work than some who were given straight promotions. I believe he will make his grade."

"Conditioned in arithmetic and physiology; removed same by examination; is doing fair work in all his studies."

"Straight promoted, but put back in 6 B on account of poor work; is babied too much by parents who allow him to stay out of school for least sign of cold, etc."

"Four conditioned in 7 A arithmetic; all have removed conditions and are doing satisfactory work in 8 B."

"Ten conditioned in 8 B arithmetic. One has moved away, one failed to remove condition and was returned to 7 A; the other eight are now doing good work in 8 A."

"There were three retained in 3 B; one does excellent work, the other two are still poor in their work. One promoted conditionally into 3 A, by reading in both classes, does fairly good work."

"In 1 B, two retained; two promoted conditionally—one moved away, the other doing satisfactory work."

"In 4 A, one retained. Two conditioned—one removed condition by summer school, the other by home study. Both doing good work."

"The three conditioned are doing fair to good work in 5 B."

"Did 8 B and 8 A work last semester, now doing good work in 9 B."

Of the 107 pupils who were conditionally transferred the reports of November 1, 1916, show that ten of them were returned to the grades below. The reasons assigned for these failures are sickness, laziness, lack of ability. In the end, then, 537 separate pupils earned single promotions and 17 earned a double promotion, making in all 554 promotions out of a possible 601, or nearly 91 per cent of the possible single promotions.

Mr. Ayers, in "Laggards in Our Schools," gives the following per cents of transfers for some of the larger cities of the United States: New York City, 81 per cent; Chicago, 84 per cent; Cincinnati, 83 per cent; Columbus, 78 per cent; Kansas City, 71 per cent. He says, "From

these figures it appears that we shall not greatly err if we estimate
that about 80 per cent of the pupils in a system may be reasonably
expected to advance at each regular time of promotion, and that 20
per cent will fail to be so advanced." Mr. Ayers says further in his
study and survey of the Springfield, Illinois, schools: "In general,
the promotion rates are well up, ranging from 85 to 90 per cent. The
promotion rate for the entire city at the end of June, 1913, was 90
per cent, while at the end of January, 1914, it was 87 per cent. For
the individual schools the rate varied from 79 per cent to 97 per cent.
* * * In connection with the study of promotion rates it is noteworthy
that the schools having the higher promotion rates have fully as good
showings in the quality of their class room work in writing, spelling,
and arithmetic as do those having lower promotion rates. In the
opinion of the members of the survey staff the promotion rates in
Springfield are not too high and it is believed that more general satisfactory progress is being made with these relatively high promotion
rates than would be the case if a smaller proportion of the children
were promoted at the end of each term."

In the 1914 annual report of Supt. C. I. Collins, Eugene, we find:
"At the close of the first semester, 89 per cent of our pupils in all
departments received promotion. At the close of the second semester,
93 per cent were promoted."

The survey staff in Butte, Montana, found that 18 per cent of
pupils remaining at the end of the semester failed to receive promotion.

In May, 1914, the per cent of promotion in the Ashland schools was
93. In the same schools in May, 1916, the per cent of promotions was
nearly 91.

* * *

The findings of the Butte, Montana, survey board, the conclusion of
Mr. Ayers, after the Springfield, Illinois, survey, the experience of the
Eugene schools, and the Ashland schools—all point to 90 per cent of
the pupils remaining in school at the end of any term, as a reasonable
number for a somewhat efficient system to pass from grade to grade.
It seems that such a number might be established as a standard or
measuring stick for a system of schools. If the number of promotions
greatly exceed that mark, it might be well to investigate the reasons
therefor and if a system of schools fails to approximate 90 per cent of
number belonging at transfer time, it may be well to conclude that too
many pupils are being held in grade. In other words, the course of
study somewhere does not fit the abilities of the children. To ward
off the suggestion that the application of the State Course of Study in
the Ashland schools is administered with an easy hand, the results of
the state examinations given in Oregon to eighth grade pupils may
be taken as evidence.

In the Ashland schools in 1914, 96 per cent of the pupils writing
received their promotions to high school. In 1916, 94 per cent of the
pupils received their promotions to the high school. The questions for

these examinations are made out by the State Superintendent and the manuscripts are graded by a county examining board. All those writing from any county being graded by a group of school men familiar with the wishes and ideals of the state office and concerned about the best interests of the schools are not likely to err repeatedly by passing a large number of unprepared pupils into the secondary schools of any community. The largest number of failures is in the first grade and decreases, not regularly but irregularly, until the eighth grade is reached. Since the amount of retardation is not great in the Ashland schools as compared with some other systems, being less than 25 per cent, and the number passing the eighth grade state examinations being large, does it not seem that the rate of promotion in any school can be large without destroying the efficiency of the school?

A large promotion rate accomplished in the following ways: (1) Semi-annual promotion periods enabling the teacher to re-adjust her classes frequently; (2) a trial promotion giving every pupil who has at least a possibility of doing the work an opportunity; (3) the chance of any child being promoted at any time in the year when he demonstrates ability to do work in an advanced grade, or being demoted when it seems that the best work can be done in a lower grade; (4) extra help given by the teacher to the brightest and the slowest pupils to help one make an advanced grade and to assist the other to keep in grade; tends toward keeping the pupils in any system from being highly retarded.

When a system is free from a large amount of retardation for a few years or several years, it is far more economical, efficient and satisfying. It is more economical because one-half or one-third of the pupils of a system repeating the work already done requires more teachers than would otherwise be necessary. It is more efficient, because pupils of the same age, likes and dislikes are grouped together. The teacher devotes her time to teaching pupils of the same age and ability instead of having to adapt her work to many ages and abilities. Satisfying, because the pupils who annoy by lack of attention and effort are gone and the teacher is able to devote her time to the instruction of a class of children whose ages cause them to have like interests and response. It seems that in thus measuring any system of schools, the amount of retardation, when taken into consideration with other modifying conditions, should determine the effectiveness of that system of schools.

Like flakes of snow that fall unperceived upon the earth, the seemingly unimportant events of life succeed one another. As the snow gathers together, so are our habits formed. No single flake that is added to the pile produces a sensible change; no single action creates, however it may exhibit, a man's character.—Jeremy Taylor.

A Teacher's Code of Professional Ethics

Suggestions by PRES J. H. ACKERMAN and MARION COUNTY COMMITTEE

Much interest in school circles is manifested concerning the adoption of a code of ethics for teachers; so much so that many institutes have passed resolutions favoring such a code and also requesting the State Association to take favorable action on such resolutions. So insistent has the demand been made that a committee has been appointed by Mr. E. F. Carleton, president of the State Teachers' Association, to consider the matter and report its recommendations at the forthcoming meeting of the association. Some of the proposed articles of the code are:

1. Loyalty to all movements looking towards raising the standards of the teaching profession, to the principal or superintendent and to his fellow workers.

2. Never to make an application for a position until a vacancy has actually occurred.

3. Never to underbid.

4. Never to undermine.

5. To immediately withdraw all applications when a position has been secured.

6. To immediately notify all persons who may be actually assisting him in securing a position.

7. When a contract has once been signed not to ask a release from the same without the willing and written consent of the contracting school board.

8. To support the State Teachers' Association to the extent of subscribing for the Oregon Teachers Monthly.

* * *

Teachers' Code of Ethics.

To establish profession ideals, to dignify the profession, to standardize professional conduct, to elevate the professional spirit, and to create in the minds of others a deeper respect for the profession, this code is devised.

1. The teacher should have a single standard of conduct, both in, and out of the school room; this standard should be governed by the highest principles of courage, justice, purity, and unimpeachable morality.

2. All who teach should cultivate the cardinal virtues of discretion, economy, honesty, temperance, engaging in only such avocations or pursuits as will bring the profession into the highest respect.

3. Teachers must remain loyal to the profession at all times.

4. The practice of using the teaching profession as a stepping-stone to other, so-called, higher professions is hereby deprecated and con-

demned; persons engaged in teaching avowedly under such conditions are unprofessional and are not entitled to be classed as professional teachers.

5. No teacher should in the slightest degree encourage aspirants for the profession unless the parties be known to be especially fitted for the arduous duties and responsibilities thereof.

6. Teachers should strive at all times to honor, dignify, and professionalize their work. They should fearlessly expose immoral, corrupt, or dishonest conduct in the profession, and there should be no hesitancy on the part of teachers in exercising utmost diligence to disqualify and disbar the teacher whose conduct at any time becomes a reproach to the profession.

7. The indiscriminate giving and receiving of recommendations is hereby condemned. Teachers should refrain from asking for testimonials, but rather ask for the privilege of referring to those who can and will give accurate, intelligent information concerning their qualifications.

8. It is perfectly proper for teachers to seek preferment and promotion by legitiment means; but, any sort of endeavor to establish reputation, or to obtain position by inuendo, exploitation, complimentary press notices, or advertisements, is undignified and unprofessional.

9. It is undignified and unprofessional for teachers to bid for positions. A teacher should know the salary attached to a given position before applying for the same. All other things being equal, it is undignified for a teacher to succeed to a position at a lower salary than that paid the preceding teacher. Teachers should constantly strive to create a public opinion favorable to remuneration commensurate with their work.

10. It is unprofessional, undignified, and dishonorable for any teacher to apply for a position not avowedly vacant, or to under bid another teacher, or to attempt to secure a position which another holds or has a fairly good chance of holding.

11. Teachers should refrain from and discourage the indiscriminate applying for different positions at the same time. It is unjust, undignified, unprofessional, and dishonest to accept one position without withdrawing all applications for other positions.

12. Self-respecting teachers will, in their several relations, endeavor to exemplify the "golden rule."

13. A letter from one teacher to another, inclosing return postage, should always receive a reply. If the information cannot be given or the desire granted, professional courtesy requires that the author of the original communication be so informed.

14. Confidential communications of any kind between teachers must not be violated at any time thereafter. The daily transaction of business in the school room should be free from discussion outside. Teachers' **gossip is unpardonable.**

15. It is undignified, unprofessional, and dishonorable for a teacher desiring to succeed to a given position to use any influence whatever whereby the incumbent may be handicapped or vacancy created.

16. In a contest for position, none but strictly fair and honorable means should be used.

17. Adverse criticism of a predecessor or of a co-worker, either in or out of school is unethical, unless made to the proper officials and with the intent of serving professionally.

18. A retiring teacher should leave full reports for the guidance of his successor.

19. A superintendent or other official to whom is intrusted the power to employ teachers should not knowingly employ a teacher under contract without the knowledge and consent of the employers of said teacher.

20. Families of deceased teachers are commended to the special care and favor of surviving teachers, particularly to those in authority. All the courtesies common to members of the older professions should be observed by members of the teaching profession. Surviving teachers are especially enjoined to attend carefully to the education and employment of the children of deceased teachers.

21. Bad opinion of the members of a board of education, of a superintendent or other superior school official, no matter what the cause for such opinion, can never justify a teacher or other inferior school official in publicly expressing such opinion as long as such official relation exists. Those in authority are, in turn, duty bound to withhold from the public information and opinions as to the personal qualities or the professional attainments of teachers so long as said teachers are under contract.

22. It is the duty of teachers to aid in every honorable way in establishing and maintaining the dignity, good name, and usefulness of boards of education, superintendents, and others in authority. Boards of education, superintendents, and others in authority are, in turn, bound to recognize and maintain all the rights, privileges, and amenities justly accruing to teachers.

23. Teachers owe it to their employers and supervisors to attend punctually, regularly, and faithfully to all duties assigned them, and at all times to show good cause for failure to do so.

24. The practice of violating contracts with boards of education, at unseasonable times, is hereby deprecated. The mere release of a board of education is not sufficient to justify a teacher in terminating a contract in a shorter time than that allowed by law. In general, teachers moved by the highest consideration for the profession will terminate contracts only for the gravest and most important causes.

25. In communicating with parents or guardians, teachers should exercise the utmost candor. They should hold inviolable all information as to the financial limitations of children or wards, their physical

or mental defects, their geneologies, and any information the public discussion or the mention of which would tend to prove humiliating, discouraging or displeasing to said parents, guardians, children, or wards.

26. It is the duty of any teacher coming into a community to surrender or forego such of his or her pleasures as may conflict with the best influence in that community even though he or she may be strongly of the opinion that such pleasures are harmless.

27. The very best services of which a teacher is capable must be given the community where employed.

28. The true teacher will strive to place whatever educational facilities the state can afford within reach of the humblest of her citizens.

29. Every teacher owes it to himself, to the profession, and to the state to secure the most efficient training and to strive for professional growth in service.

30. Every unit of organization shall maintain a committee to investigate, and pass upon all cases coming within the provisions of this code.—Marion County Committee.

A SONG THERE WAS

A song there was that quelled the fears
  Of they who ancient pastures trod,
Back through the length'ning stretch of years
  When came the infant son of God.

And through the years that self-same song
  Has journeyed with life's caravan,
Until today, sweet, clear and strong
  It cheers the hungering heart of man.

A light there was, a light ablaze
  And wise men knelt them down to pray,
Then hurried on in great amaze
  To where the new-born Christ Child lay.

And through the years that self-same light
  That hung o'er Bethlehem of old,
Has shown for mankind clear and bright,
  A guide unto the Shepherd's fold.
                              —Lewis Allen.

He only is great who has the habits of greatness; who, after performing what none in ten thousand could accomplish, passes on like Samson, and "tells neither father nor mother of it."—Lavater.

Adolescence and School

By E. S. EVENDEN, Department of Education, Oregon Normal School

One of the most important periods in the development of boys and girls, and one of the most important problems for teachers to solve is the "storm and stress" period of adolescence. After the monumental work of Pres. G. Stanley Hall had so forcibly called this period to the attention of the educational world there was a lull in the interest in this subject, which is now giving way to a new realization of the significance of adolescence in school work. This awakening has caused such recent changes in our organization of schools as the junior high school, which claims as one of its chief advantages a better adjustment to the adolescent and the ever-increasing, not-to-be-denied demands of capitalists, labor unions and industrial leaders, for more vocational education. If this new interest is to be effective in bringing about any real reforms it must be based upon a thorough understanding of this stage of development by every teacher and not merely by a few superintendents, college presidents and judges of juvenile courts. This is too tempestuous a period to brook delays and indecision, for as the iron must be struck when it is at the right heat to make the truest steel, just so must the ideal be given when the demand comes—not after other and undesirable ones have been substituted. Above all else the knowledge of this period must be tempered with sympathy.

In this time of many changes the most noticeable are the physical ones. There now begins rapid growth, during which the body reaches practically its full height, the chest capacity increases, not always in proportion to the weight and height, and the larger muscles increase so rapidly that a period of awkwardness follows before these new arms and legs can be brought under control. This change is made more pronounced by the high degree of muscular coordination which characterizes the period before adolescence. The heart increases in size and strength faster than the arteries, making it a period of varying blood pressures, with resultant physical restlessness. The brain and nervous system attain their mature size and development, the sexual instinct appears, the sexual organs function, and in the case of the boy the voice changes. These are all normal changes, but are new and not understood by the adolescent, consequently they should not occasion mirth or slighting comment, as the last mentioned change is very prone to do. This is the time when the boy or girl needs exercise and out-of-door recreation, the constructive kind, which will recognize the physical differences and strengthen where new strength is needed. This period is characterized by active athletics, especially in high schools, and very frequently they are too active. It is so easy now for the boy with his man's body to overtax his unknown strength in such a way that interest is paid on his ignorance or over-enthusiasm for the remainder of his life. Here is a time when some of John Locke's "Hardening Process" may profitably be initiated, such as plain, but nourishing food, plenty of fresh air in sleeping rooms, cold baths and regular exercise. There is a tendency, especially with girls at this period, toward pampering, which is not conducive to future happiness. Mortality is low during this time but the resistance to disease is offset by a very high morbidity, which is yearly becoming more of a problem as our young people are forced to enter the economic struggle of life unprepared.

Adolescence is characterized by mental and moral changes as pronounced as the physical changes, even though not so apparent. Justice has never been done in describing this mental upheaval started by the sudden realization by the individual that he or she is a member of society with all the duties and responsibilities which this entails. Without much warning the boy or girl is flooded with introspections and observations largely concerned with himself. These introspections concern the fundamental laws of nature, society, the family and religion, the "whys" and "wherefores" of facts which he had simply taken unquestioningly up until then. Now he is prone to set up standards of efficiency, appearance, accomplishments, social, athletic and scholastic, and apply these to himself. Generalizations of any kind are at a premium because of the increased power they give him in his abstract problems.

Adolescence is also a period of social transformations, starting many times in the home where parents fail to understand and make allowance for these many changes. This frequently causes a drifting from intimate family relationships previously maintained, because with all these bewildering changes the boy or girl needs some one to advise with him, to sympathize with his wild schemes, to admire him, to love him, and parents do not find it easy to make the transition, but rather try to hold to the old order for a while longer, and resist the first pair of long trousers or the "doing-up" of the hair. Social groupings are very common now, based on the wealth, education or occupation of the parents. Within these groups is liable to be the special confidant in matters which should go to the parents or teacher. Consciousness of the opposite sex is one of the first social changes, manifested in its earlier appearance by excessive shyness and a certain amount of aloofness, to give way soon after to the many studied attempts to please and attract attention. To the unsympathetic this is the time of annoying giggles and "he saids" on the part of the girls, and of crude braggadocio and roughness on the part of the boys. Out of these grow the adolescent love affairs, many transient and a very few life-long.

In addition to these physical, mental and social changes there is another point of paramount importance to be remembered by the teacher, and this is the idealistic nature of this period. Life's governing ideals are formed now and are made into the habits which comprise character. History is replete with instances of great men and women from all walks of life, whose life work started from adolescent ideals, and moreover, who accomplished some notable piece of work along their chosen line before the completion of later adolescence. Relatively few successful changes of occupation occur after the close of this period.

The boy or girl is full of wild schemes to make money or plans for establishing his financial and social independence. Problems of moral import are now prominent and much self-analysis results. Matters of religion are of utmost importance as testified to by the large number of conversions during adolescence. The negative side of this influence is also operative in that by far the greatest number of criminal careers have their foreshadowing in the juvenile courts. Emotional states are frequently in the ascendency here and the consequences of their first few manifestations upon the individual and their reception by others will largely determine the controlling emotions of subsequent years.

A brief mention of some of the ways these characteristics make themselves felt in the school room may be of interest to teachers. First, what kind of teacher is most successful in dealing with adolescents and is it wholly a gift? Sanford Bell in a study of 543 men and 488 women in regard to the characteristics of their well-liked teachers, enumerates the following qualities in order of preference: Giving of purpose, arousing of ideals, kindling of ambition to do or to be something, encouragement to overcome circumstances, inspiring self-confidence, being understood, timely and kindly advice, stability and poise of character, purity, absence of hypocrisy, independence, personal beauty, athleticism and vigor. It is hopefully noteworthy that all with the exception of the last three are characteristics which any teacher may inculcate into her character, with the added incentive of knowing that they belong there anyway. All discussion of the subject of adolescence in school is useless if the teacher cannot secure the respect, admiration and confidence of her students, consequently this first point, the personality of the teacher, is perhaps the most important point for starting any constructive reform in the educational handling of this problem.

Second, adolescence heralds a new attitude toward language, grammar and literature. By means of the new interest in abstractions more can be done now in half a year with formal grammar than in the preceding seven or eight. Language as a medium of thought expression is newly motivated. Literature as the greatest source of information about those phases of life which are so problematic at this age becomes in many cases a consuming interest which is easily directed if taken in time. Boys and girls are now more sensitive than at any other time of the fact that they are no longer children. They want stories of men and women, of love, of war, of adventure, of society, and it is far better that teachers and parents recommend the better stories than to allow them through ignorance to read that which is liable to be trash. It seems unwise now to risk this liking for literature by too much literary dissection and word-analysis, but better to instill a habit of reading for the love of reading. Poetry has increased popularity, especially the poetry of romance and sentiment. Poems on more abstract themes have their place here, also, such as Thanatopsis or Gray's Elegy.

"Many a flower is born to blush unseen
And waste its sweetness on the desert air"

is literally a single flower blooming on the desert to the child of ten or twelve, but to the adolescent it is the expression of one of life's great tragic truths. The teacher faces a grave responsibility during this time, that of recommending reading and following it up. She must realize also that she cannot make mistakes and suggest the wrong book. She must show her interest in the story and be able to converse with the student about the plot and the characters. If this is skillfully and honestly done, it will open the way for questions from the boy or girl on matters other than the story. Many helpful talks along various lines, even on sex problems, have been thus introduced. Opportunities for such work come easily from stories like "Ivanhoe," "Lorna Doone" and countless others. A list of books, with brief synopses and suggestions as to the ages for which the stories are appropriate, such as that published by the Oregon Library Commission, will aid the teacher in selecting books, but should not act as a substitute for reading them.

The third apparent line of endeavor in school work is to reform the work in mathematics and science, to make the former less formal, and both more practical. These subjects offer answers to many of their questions, could they but be made to realize it, and especially is this true of the biological sciences. Mathematics on the other hand has relied too long upon its traditional advantages and in many instances has failed to make itself felt in every-day problems. The adolescent boy or girl is introduced to the subject of interest in arithmetic, but regardless of the "method" used he has not a true conception of interest until he either has it coming or going. To have the more desirable of these situations true he must have been encouraged in a saving habit either through the teacher and the school bank or at home, and also should have some means of earning, not merely asking for a certain amount of money to spend as he sees fit. When the courses in mathematics and science are so handled that the boys and girls of this age will bring their own or a home problem for solution, then the teachers are making the most of their opportunities.

The fourth obvious change of attitude is toward the subjects of history and civics, which deal with society, government and economic conditions. These are not merely memory subjects, but should be thought-producers, and yet how few teachers know enough about them to utilize this phase. History must be made to live, to deal with real men, real panics, real situations and to do this best it must deal with present situations, present strikes, present presidential elections, present foreign relations and do so in the light of past instances. Then and then only will the student realize the immense importance of these subjects in the new life of citizenship opening before him. The one necessity for all this is a broad thorough up-to-date knowledge of these subjects by the teacher, broad enough to make the men of ideals in history live again and pass on ideals of Americanism to the next civic generation. What an opportunity for implanting dynamic ideals of citizenship!

The fifth and perhaps the most promising of these changes is that toward vocational education, the most pronounced tendency of present day education. Upon the solution of this problem depends all the other plans and amibitions of the boy or girl, for success in his chosen work is always a prerequisite to all his other plans. A popular slogan among educators is to the effect that schools must fit children to live and do a part of the world's productive work. This certainly is one of the chief functions of education, but for a long while, at least, the schools will be unable to do this very completely, handicapped as they are by lack of funds, large classes and insufficient time. Furthermore, in this age of specialization it takes a longer and longer time to become vocationally trained and professionally educated, longer than the school has at its disposal, so that its chief function must needs be largely that of guidance until some of the obstacles are removed by public demand. This guidance must be intelligently based on a knowledge of the individual's own powers and abilities. Many a boy has faced the problem of choosing a life work with no better basis for his choice than that he liked to work with electricity or mother wanted him to be a minister. Teachers must thoroughly inform themselves about occupations and professions, the amount of time they take in preparation and the possible returns. Many a boy would like to be a doctor, but is unwilling to pay the price in time and money required. The recognition of individuality and the giving of intelligent advice is at least a long step toward vocational education, provided it can be found in every school. As fast as possible the schools must prepare to do more than this in actual vocational training, but if they can only do this much now it will save many a misspent life and society from industrial misfits and miscontents.

In conclusion, the school has these many opportunities to serve the adolescent, provided he remains there to be served, which suggests that the problem of elimination from schools is a serious one, but its solution is closely linked with the solution of this other problem. When teachers understand the physical, mental, moral, social and idealistic changes of adolescence and when they are able to meet the needs of these changes in their own personalities as teachers, in litera-ture, mathematics, science, history, vocational subjects and in fact, in all the school subjects, then will school work be attractive enough to hold the boys and girls and solve the problem of elimination. An easier, happier basis for school relationships between teacher and student is established as soon as the latter realize that the school can help them, when it is worth dollars and cents to them, when they feel they are sympathetically understood and the teachers are the only ones who can make these real schools that real boys and real girls will know are real.

The Hour Period and Supervised Study

By F. A. SCOFIELD, Principal of Eugene High School

This article does not presume to be an argument for the hour-period in high school work in preference to all other plans, but is an attempt to describe the system which has been used in the Eugene high school since September, 1915, when a schedule of five hour-periods and a closing period of 40 minutes was put into effect. This makes the day longer, as school opens at 8:45 and closes at 3:40, with a noon intermission of an hour and five minutes, but about 100 pupils are excused at 3 o'clock upon written consent of parents and upon the condition that all class standings be above the average. It was hoped five periods of 70 minutes could be introduced this year, but such a program demanded additional teaching force.

One of the first arguments in favor of the plan was the belief that home study would be decreased, not only because of the longer day, but because an opportunity would be afforded for individual instruc-tion and supervised study during school time by subject teachers in all except one period of the day. The first 40 minutes of each period, except the last, is devoted to recitation and the last 15 minutes to study. In this time the student goes over the lesson for the next day, begins reports, looks up references or definitions and gets any help needed upon work just recited, or upon new assign-ments. It is not possible to compare the amount of home study done under this plan with the amount under the 45-minute schedule, but two sets of records were taken last year to determine the amount of time used.

Mr. Proctor, of Stanford University, and Dr. H. D. Sheldon, of the University of Oregon, conducted an investigation of the home study habits of pupils in 12 high schools selected from Oregon, Washington and California and in the tabulated results Eugene ranked fifth in home study. Each student was asked to record the amount of study each day for a week and in this way a fairly accurate schedule was received, but since this information was secured from less than one-fifth of the school, it was not deemed sufficient for the school authorities to estimate the average time for every one.

The writer attempted to check these results by asking each student to state the average amount of time spent in home study and found that the time was much greater than the amount found in the first study. This is probably due to the fact that one is more apt to give larger figures for what he thinks he has done in the past, than he will when accurate account is kept each day for a week.

Recently the writer asked the teachers to express their opinions of the hour-period and to state what use they were making of the 15-minute study period. The practice teachers from the university, and the teachers of art, music, manual training, cooking, typewriting, physics physical geography, and biology were not included, since they devoted no time to supervised study, but used the entire period, and additional time, for laboratory work. The work of these departments is given under "Special Subjects," but the following quotations indicate quite clearly what is being done in history, language, English, and mathematics.

1. I think the 60-minute period with time for supervised study is an improvement over the old plan. I find the pupils having a few minutes of supervision do better work as a rule than those in the last period class (40 minutes of recitation, with no study). I try to teach concentration and speed in studying.

2. The poor, but conscientious students receive the most help from the 15 minutes of supervised study. During this time the class work at their seats for the first five minutes, without assistance. In the next 10 minutes the instructor passes through the aisles, helping the students in order. Each member of the class must be prepared to ask all the questions necessary while the teacher is in his part of the room.

3. I can give suggestions for economizing time, help slow students discover and help to overcome difficulties of weak students and give directions to entire class.

4. If any of the class has had trouble with the day's lesson, I give help to them.

5. During that time I can help the students in learning how to study their history and also have them make a beginning of looking up outside topics and reports in my little library.

6. I am in favor of but 15 minutes each period if the student can be led to follow the "Study Help" hint which suggests reading over the lesson quickly first in order to get principal points.

7. The study period is used to good advantage by about 90 per cent of the class. The opportunity to spend even 15 minutes on a subect with which the mind is already occupied is beneficial.

8. Supervised study ought to teach the pupil to begin studying without waste of time and ought to teach him to concentrate.

9. I plan my work for the average student and then by means of supervised study and conferences it is possible to properly care for the slow and fast types of students. Requesting pupils to come after school for conferences usually meets with failure.

10. I nearly always use the time for helping each pupil at his seat, explaining individual difficulties and assisting with prepara-

tion of advance lesson. Many students are too timid about asking for explanations in class, while in the study period they will tell me what seems difficult.

11. The supervised study period is a fine idea, I think, but a special problem in "Oral English." It takes the study period for criticisms and suggestions, assignments, and sometimes to help in methods of reading, committing, etc.

12. There are many lessons left unstudied because pupils have no time for conference with the teachers and the 15 minutes is the logical questioning time.

13. Sometimes I spend the entire period helping the backward ones. When circumstances demand, I spend a part of the period explaining some of the problems in the next day's lesson. At other times I run the recitation over into the period when I intend making no advance assignment for the next day.

14. From the standpoint of the teacher I think it works very well as it gives the teacher a chance, if only a few minutes, to help the student get started in his preparation of the lesson. He knows how to proceed and there is no question as to what the lesson is. From the standpoint of the student I have found that as a rule he feels he has studied his lesson sufficiently when he has worked during the 15 minutes, and consequently that is all the studying he does. A longer period with less time in the study hall is better, I think.

15. In the cookery work the one-hour period is too short. The sewing work can be handled nicely in the one-hour period.

16. I do not like the hour plan for history classes unless they can be much smaller than ours are. The hour plan forces the use of the text every day and hence often the use of inadequate or inferior material by students.

The first week in October of this year was known as "study week" and an attempt was made to interest the pupils in learning how to study. They were given a list of "study helps," most of them taken from the ones prepared in the Chicago University high school, and the English classes were allowed to use the subject of "Study Difficulties and Study Helps" as the topic for the next theme. Nearly everyone took the assignment seriously and wrote quite freely about their troubles and their use of the 15-minute study period, and as they were only writing what they regarded as their usual composition, their remarks may be taken as representing the reactions of the student body toward the problem of supervised study. No attempt was made to secure percentage of total number mentioning certain points, but a summary was made of all the papers handed in and some of these points are given here.

Fifteen-Minute Study Period.—(1) Prepared part of next day's lesson (practically everyone). (2) Read lesson over for main points and then reviewed at home or in study hall. (3) Asked questions about difficult points. (4) Secured help on lesson just recited. (5) Asked questions about work to be made up when absent. (6) Preferred to study there rather than in study halls, because assignments had just been made and if not understood individual help could be secured (only three pupils preferred to remain in study hall for work). (7) Could work faster and concentrate better in quiet class room.

Objections and Criticisms.—(1) Teacher talked too much. (2) Wanted to be allowed to study or review lesson for next period rather than spend time on lesson just recited. (Not very many made this statement. Teachers often allow the quicker students, or those who work well without supervision and find few difficulties in the preparation of the subject, to review other work). (3) Conversation between pupil and teacher. (This criticism refers to questions asked by the pupil without permission or without going to the teacher's desk. Some teachers reply to these questions for the benefit of the class in order to meet a similar difficulty from other students, but most teachers refuse to do this, preferring to answer the same difficulty for several individuals rather than disturb the entire group.

Study Difficulties.—(1) Inability to get to work. (2) Inability to stick to a subject which is not interesting. (3) Outside disturbances—(a) Whispering, (b) Visitors, (c) Music (glee clubs and orchestra practice during school hours and if the doors are open some of the nearby rooms are disturbed).

Study Helps Most Useful.—(1) Make definite study program. (2) Have materials and books ready before beginning work. (3) Take notes on assignments and important points of lesson.

The teachers in cooking and manual training objected to the plan last year, but arrangements were finally made which removed these objections. Students in manual training, and typewriting also, must schedule for at least two extra periods per week, so that the maximum time is often greater than two 45-minute periods for the slow pupils. Those who work only seven hours per week have learned to get down to business quickly and accomplish just as much as under the former schedule. The instructor in manual training this year has worked out a chart showing the exact amount of time spent in the shops by each boy, the projects made, and time spent on school furniture and other work, and is more than satisfied with the arrangement.

The household arts department has arranged a very admirable plan of securing additional work by co-operating with the home. Every girl must bring a statement from her parents certifying that a certain amount of home work has been done and full credit is not allowed without this. The teacher in cooking makes out a list of these duties so that the pupil is required to do in the home the things she has been taught in the school room, and thus she is sure that her work is put on a practical basis and that her pupils are not "cooked to death" in the school kitchens. It seems much better to have more girls in this work and to allow them to connect the school and the home with less laboratory instruction than to teach fewer girls a longer time with less home co-operation. Under the hour-period the enrollment in cooking and sewing, manual training and typewriting has increased 20 per cent in each department over the classes two years ago, with the same number of teachers and a student body of about the same size, the total enrollment this year being 10 per cent less than last year's figures due to the University high school taking care of one section of 9th grade pupils, and the unusually large senior class of last year.

From the standpoint of administration the hour-period has several advantages of the the 45-minute schedule. In addition to the increased enrollment in special subjects, particularly the household arts courses for girls and the manual training for boys, it has made possible larger classes in the academic subjects. Notwithstanding the objection raised by one of the teachers, one of the administrative points in favor of the Batavia system of instruction was the larger classes which the regular teachers were able to control. The six-period day has decreased the number in the study halls and thus decreased the discipline problem and increased the possibility of uninterrupted work for those who are there, but it makes necessary a careful arrangement of individual schedules and a program of study for each student in order that laboratory work may be taken care of. It has been responsible for the raising of the standard of work because attention can be given to the slower pupil, who has heretofore been a serious problem in large classes. An attempt was made last semester to separate the slow and fast pupils in some of the language and mathematics classes, but it made the slower sections a drudgery for the teacher besides depriving those students of the inspiration of the quicker ones. Much better is it to have mixed sections and by individual instruction to care for the one who is not keeping up with the class.

A longer study period is undoubtedly better but it is not certain that this would answer the objection that some students feel they do not need to spend more time on some of their lessons. There is a group of students in every school, probably, willing to skim through the work with the lowest passing grades and 15 minutes would be enough study for this group under any circumstances. If there is objection to the pupils studying from their history text, reference books can be taken to the room from the library, or some of the pupils might be allowed to go there to work during the 15 minutes. Such an objection is a minor matter which can be cared for by co-operation with the library staff.

Briefly summarized, we offer the following: The hour-period (1) Allows time for supervision of the slow pupil, as well as attention to the fast. (2) Gives opportunity for questions concerning points in the advance lessons to be answered by the teacher in that subject rather than by anyone who happens to have charge of the study hall. (3) Allows the student to get more work done in school and hence less home work is needed. (4) Allows teacher an opportunity to relax for a few moments before another class begins. (5) Increases enrollment in special subjects because regular program is not broken into by double periods. (6) Gives opportunity to raise standard of work by bringing up the laggards. (7) Enables teachers to handle larger groups in the academic subjects because the problem of the weak students is not so apt to hold back the group and make the bright pupil restive.

The disadvantages: (1) Give some students idea that 15 minutes' study is sufficient. (2) Necessitates extreme care in arranging individual schedules. (3) Some teachers are apt to disregard the 40-minute bells when discussing an interesting topic and thus deprive the students of the study period.

Rural School Department

Edited by MRS. M. L. FULKERSON, Salem, Oregon

Life is a leaf of paper white
Whereon each one of us may write
His word or two and then comes night.
Greatly begin! Though thou have time
But for a line, be that sublime,—
Not failure, but low aim is crime.   —Lowell.

* * *

Good-bye 1916! Hail, 1917! Turn over a new leaf; forget the blots and blurs on the old one. Do your best every day and maybe **your** teacher will place a golden star on this new page in 1917.

* * *

Suggestions for the Month.

(1) Teach the children how to care for the birds who remain with us for the winter. (2) Study the habits of hibernating animals. Tell the story of the Three Bears, and let the primary pupils make posters of free hand cuttings to illustrate it. (3) Study the different forms of water-clouds, fog, mist, rain, dew, frost, snow, ice. (4) Study life and customs in Eskimo land. Build Eskimo scenes on the sand table, using salt, or cotton, or cotton with salt sprinkled over it to represent snow; snow scenes in broad chalk work on the blackboard; imaginary journeys in Eskimo land. (5) Plant bulbs for early spring blooming in window boxes. Put the boxes away in a dark place where there is no danger of frost and give the bulbs a chance to form good roots before bringing them into the strong light of the window. (6) Teach such pictures and poems suggested in the State Course of Study as pertain to winter. (7) Try to have something of special interest in the school work to create enthusiasm after the "dissipation" of the annual holiday season.

* * *

A New Year's Party.

"This year," said Winter to herself, "I must give all my birds a party—a New Year's party." So the winds swept the floor of her big parlor, and the snow fairies put down a soft white carpet. Then Winter sent tiny notes on snowflake paper to all the little birds, asking them to come to the party. And a great many came, for I saw them from my window.

First came the chick-a-dees, dressed in soft gray suits, with black caps. They greeted Winter with a sweet "day-day-day." Close behind them were some fat, jolly little wrens, all in brown. So happy were they and so full of song Winter smiled to see them. Next came some cheery snowbirds and saucy sparrows, and soon after a crowd of dainty little birds so white that they were called snowflakes. There may have been more, but I did not see them, for Winter at once said, "Dinner."

They all sat on the white carpet and ate. What? Why, the queerest things—grubs and moths' eggs and dried seeds of chickweed and ragweed. I was glad to see that Nellie had scattered some bread crumbs outside the window. And someone had told Fred to tie some pieces of fat pork along the clothes-line. These were the dainties and were kept until last.

After dinner the north wind whistled, and the snowflake birds danced with the real snowflakes. Then the wrens sang beautifully and all the others joined in the chorus. Each bird sang different words: The chick-a-dees their own sweet "chick-adee-dee-dee;" the snowbirds something like "tsip;" the snowflakes "cheep-cheep," and the sparrows thrilled away all by themselves, using no words at all. And, strange to say, the whole was very sweet.

When they went home, as happy as only little birds can be, Winter was so pleased that she said she would give them a party each New Year's day. Will you all help her?—Primary School.

*   *   *

How to Get the Most Out of a Community Meeting.

How to get the most out of a community meeting is a problem that naturally confronts every teacher. This is particularly true of the rural teacher because the only kind of meetings ever held in some communities are those held at the school house, those that are prepared by the teacher and the children. Since this is true, let us consider a few principles that should be taken into consideration by the teacher as she prepares for the meeting and also after it is gone.

First, the meeting should be opportune as to time and purpose. Not long ago it was the privilege of the writer to be invited to a parent-teacher meeting. I went but when I arrived I found that a meeting of the same nature had been held just two weeks before. While I had been invited to a parent-teacher meeting, the teacher had advertised it on that evening by letter to the parents as a "box party," one of those affairs where you pay several times what a thing is worth to get what you do not want simply not to appear a "piker." Well, since one of these same meetings was held just two weeks before and since the meeting was advertised so late, nobody came. Do you blame them? Meetings to be a success must be in keeping with community need and community sense of justice and desire for pleasure.

Second, the program should be an outgrowth of regular school work. Every day, humdrum work should be motivated with the prospect of future use. There is no motive, perhaps, which will make such an appeal to the child as that of the possibility of presenting that same matter to the public later. I have seen community meetings delightfully entertained with exhibitions of reading, writing, spelling, dramatization, anything and everything that is a part of the regular school work.

Third, the approaching meeting should be properly introduced, by the right person, whoever that is, at the right time, with the right setting, etc.

Fourth, the appreciation of the meeting must be cultivated. The meetings must not be too close together nor too far apart. Time must be given for living through the event with happy anticipation, for, remember, "anticipation is greater than realization," but we must also remember that "hope deferred maketh the heart sad." Therefore we must start preparation for an entertainment or a community event just long enough before to get the most pleasure out of preparation for it.

Fifth, three phases of work should be attended to with great interest in this preparation and cultivation. The first is to make intellectual preparation, make intellectual use of the event in the way of writing invitations that are the very best possible, touching up and toning up the work that is to be exhibited. The second is to improve the physical side of the school now while the spirit of interest is keen. Everybody will work now with great zeal and much pleasure but after the meeting is over the motive will be gone. The school house and yard can now be put in beautiful condition but not later with the same good effects. The third is to make social use of the event. Now is the time to train ushers, train children to make introductions, develop the spirit of the host and the hostess in the children.

Sixth, after the event is over it should be used for a day or two in whatever way it can to get the most out of it in intellectual, social, and moral growth. Many opportunities for this can be found if the teacher will look for them. *

*   *   *

The Farmer's Picket Fence.

Aim: To interest primary children in direction of movement in penmanship.

Farmer Brown had many nice chickens of which he was very fond. He took the very best care of all of them but there was one little White Leghorn hen that he liked best of all. He named her Peggy and she always came when he called until one morning in early spring, when Farmer Brown came to the poultry yard with a plate of scraps from the breakfast table. He saved the choicest morsels for her, but he called Peggy in vain. For a long time he searched for her and then he gave her up as lost. But she came back three weeks later and she didn't come alone. She had ten fluffy white chicks with her.

Farmer Brown was so proud of her then that he made a nice little coop for her and put it in his own door yard near the garden. Peggy could not get out of the coop to scratch and the chicks were too little, so everything went well for a time. By and by the little wing feathers grew and grew and grew and the little chicks flew and flew and flew and soon made trouble in the garden.

Farmer Brown tried to teach old Sport, the dog, to drive them out when they got into mischief, but Sport was too rough. The farmer built a fence that looked like this: (See "push and pull" movement exercise in Palmer Writing Lessons for Primary Grades). The chickens had to stay out of the garden then. Can you make a fence like that?—M. L. Fulkerson.

* * *

The Rural School Outlook in Marion County.

Rural school work in Marion county has gone forward by leaps and bounds since the beginning of the new school year. Rural Supervisors John W. L. Smith and J. V. Fike report the organization of several new Parent-Teacher Associations, showing that the various communities are taking an interest in the cause of education. Marion county people are making it manifest that their interest does not center entirely in prunes, potatoes, and pigs. They are showing the world that they have faith in the human race by providing the best for their school children. For more than a year Macleay has served hot lunches regularly to the pupils in the school. New wells have been drilled at Looney, Cloverdale and Illihee. New woodsheds have been built at Union Hill, McAlpine and Sunnyside. Salem Heights and Illihee have repainted their buildings. Liberty has put in a fine new circular swing. Stayton has planned a new thousand-dollar gymnasium with equipment. Turner is to have a new one also. Shaw has built a large playshed and furnished it with play apparatus, and Donald, Hullt and Silver Falls are followng suit. Belle Passi and Greasy Pond have standardized. Industrial clubs and debating societies are being organized for the young people, and rural life is being made a thing to be desired because of the fact that the people, the rural supervisors and the teachers are all putting their shoulders to the wheel and when County Superintendent Smith says, "One, two, three,—Boost!" things move.—F. F. S.

* * *

Trouble Column.

In this column questions pertaining to rural school problems will be promptly and cheerfully answered if sent in to the office by the first of each month.

1. "Can you tell me of something that will create an interest in fourth grade geography work?" If you can arrange to do so, have copies of the Tarr-McMurry First Book in Geography for supplementary reading. In this book you will find "Suggestions to Pupils" scattered throughout the text. These suggestions are very helpful and interesting because they lead the pupil to gather knowledge independently.

2. "I am having trouble in getting my pupils in the third grade to read with expression. Is there anything that will help?" Try using some of the dramatic readers recommended in the State Library List. A number of these books have been added recently for this specific purpose.

3. "Where can I get a book on seat work for rural schools?" Look through the catalogues of the various school supply houses for suggestions. The best thing, however, is for you to make a scrap-book for yourself. Put in every suggestion you can find anywhere and everywhere, whether you want to use it just now or not. Look through all your old school magazines and institute notebooks. If hand work is suggested make a sample and paste it in the scrap book. In a surprisingly short time you will have a book that will be a veritable gold mine to you as a rural teacher.

4. "My patrons do not seem to take much interest in the school. Do you think a Parent-Teacher Association would help?" Yes, but first you must create a demand for the Parent-Teacher organization. Arrange a public school program that will get the people out. Let them have a social hour after it. Perhaps a few meetings like that will make them want to meet regularly. Do not try to organize unless there is an interest in it. A dead Parent-Teacher Association is worse than none. Work slowly and carefully and your efforts will be rewarded in due time.

* * *

Assignment in Agriculture.

The Good Book says it takes the simple things to confound the mighty, and it speaks wisely. How often we hear of people who undergo endless torture of mind simply because they are too proud to acknowledge to some friend, who could be of assistance, that they do not know some simple fact concerning their work. We are all more or less guilty of this in the teaching profession, and as a consequence we refrain from discussing the fundamentals of our work. In their stead we generally find teachers' meetings turning their attention to some abstraction with which only the few is acquainted. If the rank and file attempt to discuss, their contributions are often glittering generalities, largely because they are not certain of the fundamentals upon which the abstraction depends. For this reason the articles which appear from time to time under this department will deal with fundamentals.

It is worth our while to discuss briefly what constitutes an assignment. Very frequently our teaching of agriculture, or any other subject for that matter, is attended with indifferent success simply because we have not made a good assignment. If that be true, then what constitutes a good assignment? Mefore answering this let us examine the usual type of assignment. The untrained teacher as the period draws to a close says something like this, "Children, for tomorrow we will begin with 200 and take to 204.'' The teacher's reason for making such an assignment is that the State Course of Study requires her to cover so many pages in a given time. We shall not dwell on this kind of assignment longer than to say that in time the children will become as much bored by it as the teacher. Neither feels satisfied. Yet were the teacher to be asked how her work is progressing, she will blandly reply, ''Nicely.'' Obviously the first essential to the assignment to make it worth the time is this: The teacher must have some reason other than covering the course of study for assigning these pages. It happens that pages 200-204 take up the subject swine. She must have a motive, a purpose, an aim else the work of the class will begin nowhere in particular and end nowhere. In the outside world we do not need to look long for the difference between the successful man and the shiftless tramp. The one always has a reason for whatever he does. But the tramp starts from nowhere in particular and not even he knows where he is going. Leaving the reader to figure out the anology, we pass on to say that the teacher who has a remote as well as an immediate purpose or aim in making the assignment adds a certain exactness to the course which the children enjoy, and which makes them feel at the close of each recitation or the end of the course that they have achieved. What may be the teacher's remote aim for asking her children to study swine? If they live in the country, that they may learn something that will make them better farmers; if in the city, that they may have a broader vision of life. The immediate aim for the country child so far as the teacher is concerned, is to have the children learn how to tell a good hog when they see one, how to care for hogs and to understand why the hog is a profitable animal for the farm, etc. The city child may study to learn how the present-day hog has developed from his ancestors, how hogs should be cared for so as to make wholesome, sanitary eating, what kind of hogs make the best food, etc. Of course if the teacher sets out with such an aim in view she will naturally have to organize her subject matter before making the assignment. She will do this by reading over the assignment, in advance, checking off what she thinks important, what should be enlarged upon, which points are unimportant, and what should be explained before in her work the teacher must have a grip on the to have purpose in her work the teacher must have a grip on the subject matter she expects to teach.

The children are assembled before the teacher at the close of a recitation and she is about to make the assignment. Before doing this, . however, she will build up an approach to the subject, either by discussing the subject herself, or by what is better, drawing the points from the children. In the approach the teacher always holds before herself her reasons for asking the children to study the subject. If she can make her pupils feel the subject is important and that it will help in making a livelihood, she has given them a motive for studying. She may have the class give expression to their several reasons for studying swine. Various reasons will be given, depending upon the interests of the class, for instance, study swine to learn why they are called "mortgage lifters," to learn how to raise a pig, to learn how to tell a good pig, to see where pigs came from, etc. All of these are good aims and the text has something either directly or inferentially on each of these aims. The teacher may have the class decide which aim is desired for the basis of their study. Once this has been decided upon, she will say something like this, "Children, you may study pages 200-204 in the text and note the points bearing on this problem, why swine are called mortgage lifters. John, what is it we are to learn for tomorrow's lesson?" (Why pigs are called mortgage lifters.) "Very well. I have looked over the text and find no difficult words or expressions which you do not understand, so unless there are some questions on the assignment the class will be dismissed." A pause, the class is dismissed.

There are some facts given in these pages the children will not use in the solving of the above problem. To glean these, set up another aim in like manner for a later lesson.—L. P. Gilmore, Monmouth.

* * *

Card Games as Incentive to Study.

"Playing cards in school!" Do I see hands held aloft in horror? Please wait until I explain. The cards to which I refer are "educational cards" and may cover almost any subject. Those which I have used in my teaching which I have considered of especial value, being historical, geographical, grammatical and arithmetical. Of the historical there is the "White House" game, dealing with each president's administration, giving the time, important events, political party, etc.; the game of "American Battles," dealing with the six wars in which our country has been engaged, and "Historical Question," being miscellaneous question and answers. Then there are Bible games which are really historical.

Of the geographical games there are the "Produce Game," giving three sources of each of fourteen of the most useful products, "Geographical Questions" and "Flags of the Nations." A little girl became so interested in the different countries from playing these games, she spent so much time in poring over maps that before she was eight years old she could locate almost any country in the world more definitely than many eighth grade graduates, and could tell you, unhesitatingly, the capitals and principal cities, the larger rivers and the principal products; and would sometimes bewilder her elders by asking such questions as which is the greater nation, Holland or Switzerland? Peru or Bolivia? Brazil or the United States?

These historical and geographical cards I bought, but not finding anything which just suited in the grammatical and arithmetical line, I proceeded to make cards having for the "Language Game" 26 books of four cards each. (This can easily be divided into two games by using only those covered by the end of the seventh grade for one and the remainder for another.) The complete game covers practically every definition in Kimball's English, Book 2.

The different books have titles as nouns, mode, sentence, parsing, verbals, drama, dictionary, classification, independents, parts of speech, etc. Verbs required two books, so I named them Verbs A and Verbs B. There was also sentence, according to meaning and sentence form. The cards are played like authors, as: Someone calls for nouns, the person holding a card whose title is nouns asks for the underscored word as, ''What is a collective noun?'' If the one who called is able to give the definition he wins the card, if not, the call passes to the next. I have found that the English book has a new interest for the pupils who play the game.

The Arithmetic game is on the same plan except that I gave the different books alphabetical titles, as Book A, Book B, etc. It is played the same as the Language game. I made a Game of Measures, in which the title of the books are, lengths, volume, money, liquid, etc., and finally a game of number combinations and tables for the little folks.

The busy teacher will find that the children will become much interested and incidentally ''pick up'' a lot of facts and definitions if allowed to help make these games. Some of the children even copied my games in making games to play at home, and be assured I did not discourage them in that, as I believe more knowledge lodged in their minds from that than there did from ''studying lessons'' for a month.

I believe I have dealt somewhat at length with this article, but if some wish to ask any questions I will gladly answer them if they write me, inclosing a self-addressed stamped envelope.—Mrs. Laura Trachsel, Summit, Oregon.

* * *

The man of genius dwells with men and with nature; the man of talent in his study; but the clever man dances here, there, and everywhere, like a butterfly in a hurricane, striking everything and enjoying nothing, but too light to be dashed to pieces.—Hazlitt.

* * *

Mirth is like the flash of lightning that breaks through the gloom of the clouds and glitters for a moment; cheerfulness keeps up a daylight in the soul, filling it with steady and perpetual serenity.—Selected.

* * *

Who shoots at the mid-day sun, though he be sure he shall never hit the mark, yet as sure he is that he shall shoot higher than he who aims but at a bush.—Sir P. Sidney.

* * *

It is better to be the builder of our own name than to be indebted by descent for the proudest gifts known to the books of heraldy.—Ballou.

The Teacher of Our Public Schools

By O. P. HOFF, Labor Commissioner, Salem

There is no more honorable, responsible or onerous calling or profession than that of the teacher in the public schools. To the teacher of the public school falls the arduous duty and responsibility of moulding the character and fundamental principles of good citizenship of the average child. In point of fact the destiny of a nation is, to a great measure, chargeable and credited to the teacher of the public school. Much of the future of the child depends upon the "building abilities" of the teacher. Therefore, all possible encouragement should be given them by the public in order that none but those of the highest standard of manhood and womanhood and the best of mental qualities need aspire to that grave responsibility and trust and be induced to enter the field of teaching as a life work. A high standard of training should be required and those who are entrusted with the management and conduct of a public school should exercise the greatest care to ascertain the qualifications of a new teacher, to the end that the incompetent and immoral may at once learn that they have entered the wrong field.

It is a source of much gratification to note that, within the past few years, there has been a decided tendency to recognize the real worth and function of a public school teacher and to place him or her upon the rightful plane of equality with the highest of professions. Having been subjected to a reasonable period of probation and, having demonstrated their competency to fulfill the high mission of their calling, it is no more than right that they should be placed upon a substantial basis of sustenance and material appreciation of their worth be manifested. Once their status is established their remuneration should be sufficient to enable them to live according to American standards and also to provide against want and misery during their declining years.

In response to a query sent out to all of the prinicpals of the public schools of Portland, under the guarantee of strict confidence, a largely representative number of answers has been received upon the following leading questions involving the success or failure of the "Tenure of office" law, enacted by the legislative assembly of 1913 and placed in application to the public school system of Portland during the past three years: Its benefits; its drawbacks, and suggestions for its improvements. With but a solitary exception, all of the principals pronounced the act far-reaching in its benefits and particularly from the fact that it effectually removed the element of doubt and uncertainty of re-election which preyed upon the minds—and efficiency—of the teaching staff, as a whole, attendant upon the period of a few weeks or months previous to the election of the teaching staff for the ensuing school year. While a comparatively few complain that the requirements incident to the removal, transfer or discharge of a teacher are objectionable, in that they subject the complainant to the alleged disquieting position of being placed upon the defensive in the substantiation before the public of charges preferred against a teacher, the great majority is inclined to view the measure, in its essential features, with approval. However, teachers having fitted themselves for the work certainly ought to be guaranteed a public hearing before being placed on the "non-desirable list" by any authority. Some suggestions were offered for the amendment of the act, chiefly designed to eliminate the element of alleged antagonism, or, suspicion of personal preference, as it were, from the operation of the law, but practically all agreed that the law is still in the stage of experimentation and is undergoing the time-trying process of interpretation and that it should be allowed to stand upon its merits until proven inadequate.

As to the efficacy of the adoption of such a law and the application of its principles to school districts of a lesser magnitude than the city of Portland to which the present law exclusively applies, or the enlargement of its scope to incorporate the entire commonwealth, this department deems itself unqualified to recommend, inasmuch as the law is still in the experimental stage. But, whatever the cost, it does not hesitate to say, without equivocation, that any law, which has for its purpose the amelioration and edification of the status of the public school teacher, the lifting of it from the slime of petty politics and factional dissention, is a forward step toward the uplift of humanity and the realization of a higher and better plane of American citizenship and should have the unstinted moral and active support and encouragement of all loyal citizens of the commonwealth and the nation.

Grade Teachers' Department

Edited by SABRA CONNER, 421 West Park Street, Portland, Oregon

Elementary teachers and elementary teachers' associations are cordially invited to send news items of their activities which would be of interest or value to other teachers to this department of the The Oregon Teachers Monthly. Address Editor of Grade Teachers' Department, Room 300, Court House, Portland, Oregon.

A Dramatic Club has been formed by the members of the Grade Teachers' Association with 25 members. A play has been selected and is being rehearsed for public performance in December in interest of the Fellowship Fund.

* * *

A chorus of 21 members has been formed among the Portland Grade Teachers directed by Prof. Boyer. Fine things will be expected from this organization.

* * *

About 200 members of the Portland Grade Teachers' Association dined at Hotel Multnomah, after the regular business meeting at Library Hall, November 8. Interesting five minute talks were given by several guests of the association, Mr. O. M. Clark, president of the Chamber of Commerce; Mr. W. F. Woodard, vice-president of the Chamber of Commerce; Mr. N. C. Pike, president of the Rotary Club; and Mr. F. E. Taylor, president of the Realty Board. During the dinner Miss Metta Brown, accompanied by Miss Edith Kelly, sang several delightful old ballads. Miss Viola Ortschild, president of the association, introduced the speakers and made an urgent plea for co-operation between the teachers and the various business organizations of the city. There were a number of invited guests entertained and the evening was a very pleasant one.

* * *

From the report of the delegate to the state convention of the Oregon Congress of Mothers and Parent-Teacher Associations held at The Dalles, October 12, 13, 14, 1916: "On Friday the school board of The Dalles dismissed school to permit the teachers to attend. I met several of these teachers and I was glad to hear that they had resently formed an association among themselves. As was the case in the convention of the O. F. W. Clubs held at Seaside, no teachers (except those in higher institutions) were on the programs. As class room teachers hold a large membership in the Parent-Teacher Circles, this fact is significant, and the condition will remain unless the convention is held at a time when teachers are not excluded from any part of the sessions. Since many topics of vital interest are discussed and acted upon, it seems only fair that their membership shall be fully recognized, and conceded the same privileges and duties as other members."

* * *

The 'Colonial Party" planned for February 22 at Hotel Multnomah promises to be a very attractive affair. The program will be patriotic and, also, typical of colonial times. The object is to secure funds for the Fellowship Board's work. It is hoped to give a delightful evening to all who attend. Miss Whitfield, chairman of the program committee, is working out details.

* * *

The Recreation Committee has planned a series of visits to Industrial plants. The first visit was taken to Doernbecher Furniture factory. The teachers were conducted over the entire plant by Mr. Frank S. Doernbecher, president of the company, who explained in detail the workings of the plant and the evolution of a piece of timber from the time it entered the factory until it left a perfected piece of furniture. There are 300 men employed in the factory and the normal output is 300 pieces of furniture, or one piece to each man. The making of plate glass mirrors is one of the interesting lines carried on by this concern. The day was one of great pleasure and profit and was arranged by Miss Nelle Crout, Miss Alice Banfield and Miss Minnie Heath.

* * *

The Trip to Oregon City.

Lowering skies, chilly temperature, gusty winds and occasional splashes of rain could not keep 40 enthusiastic members of the Grade Teachers' Association from truly enjoying a wonderful day at Oregon City on November 4. A 14 mile ride in a comfortable electric car brought us to the heart of the Mill City as it may well be called. The forenoon was spent in visiting the mills and electric plant under the leadership of efficient guides. The woolen mill, said to be the largest west of the Mississippi, a solid structure of red brick with innumerable windows, stands on the principal thoroughfare. The three great paper mills that supply the coast with paper stand like massive forts at the rivers' edge. These great mills produce annually 75,000 tons of paper, or 235 tons daily. They employ more than a thousand people and distribute $300,000 in wages annually. The largest mill has started many reforms and the men are given a percentage of the profits. Passing over the suspension bridge which links the town to the west side we came, at the end of a 20-minute walk along ivy and fern-clad bluffs, to the electric plant which supplies the whole region, including Portland, with light and power. Here the waterfalls harnessed and subdued, pour decorously over the big dam built to give more power, thus sacrificing beauty to progress. The building trembles with the mighty rush of waters in the great turbines far underground. The various processes by which the electricity thus generated is poured along the wires, stored and distributed, and the almost uncanny intelligence of the instruments by which the social and industrial activities in the area supplied with light and power as indicated in the demand for them are recorded, were explained by a courteous official. We must confess that while some of the methods are incomprehensible to the uninitiated, electricity is the most fascinating of industries. Back again to Main street we take the municipal elevator, a new convenience, by which we are lifted to the top of the 80-foot bluff on which are most of the residences. A moment's walk brings us into McLoughlin Park, donated, half a century ago, to the city by its generous founder, Dr. John McLoughlin. The old McLoughlin house, which originally stood at the end of Main street, was recently brought up to the park, by the Women's Club. It was a ruin, but the club has it restored, painted, papered and furnished as it was in the 40's. A residence housekeeper assures its being kept in good order. It is a substantial square white frame building set in harmonious surroundings of well-kept lawns, rose-beds and shrubbery, made and kept beautiful by the Women's Club. In this house, in Mrs. McLoughlin's sitting room, in fact, we had two delightful hours with Mrs. Eva Emery Dye, author of The Conquest, McLoughlin and Old Oregon and other books on the Pacific Northwest, in the romantic style. Mrs. Dye founded the Chautauqua of Oregon City, the grounds for which are at Gladstone, a mile or so below the town. Here hundreds get pleasure, inspiration and new ideas every summer. Mrs. Dye's account of life in the early days, with its chief figure John McLoughlin, head factor of the Hudson Bay Company, whose kindness in welcoming and feeding the horde of weary sick and destitute emigrants of the early 40's, lost him his position with the company and led him to cast in his lot with the Americans, held us spell bound until late in the afternoon. Mrs. Dye then conducted us personally to the graves of McLoughlin and his wife. Down a skeleton flight of easy steps, over the rock-ribbed bluff through beautiful greenery we made our way to the church under whose walls rest the body of the founder and his wife. It was the unanimous feeling of the party that the day's experience had brought us into touch with things that are vital, reaching out of the past into present conditions of social and industrial activity and all were kindled with the desire to learn more about our wonderful state.—Mathilda Ahrends.

Oregon Govermental Affairs

By ROBERT CARLTON CLARK, Eugene, Oregon

Results of the Election.

Of the 11 measures submitted to vote of the people at the November election six received majorities and have been proclaimed law by act of the governor. The measures that have become effective are the so-called "bone-dry," single-item veto, ship taxation exemption, repealing Sunday law, rural credits, and state-wide tax proposals. The effect of these measures, except single-item veto discussed below, will be to prohibit the bringing into Oregon of all kinds of alcoholic liquors and thus put an end to the use of such beverages in the state except for medicinal purposes and church observances; by repeal of the Sunday closing law Oregon is left without state legislation on this subject; the state is to undertake to sell its bonds to the amount of $18,000,000, and loan the money to farmers at a rate not higher than 1 per cent above the interest it has to pay for the money; and henceforth no governing body authorized to collect taxes in the state may collect more money than a 6 per cent increase over the amount raised during previous year. The last-named measure threatens to place state, counties, municipalities, and many school districts in serious embarassment for funds and makes impossible any very great expansion of expenditure in any direction because the property valuations generally all through the state, as shown by this year's assessments, have greatly declined With less property from which to collect taxes there has been a very generous increase in the rate of taxation for state, county, city, and school district. Some of the smaller cities that have been most progressive in their school systems, erecting most modern buildings and adding all the other branches of learning now demanded by advanced school men and that have undertaken other expensive municipal enterprises are finding themselves facing a total tax levy this year approaching five mills. The Portland rate advances by only a few mills and remains under three mills total tax.

The Intelligence of the Vote.

The intelligence of the voters at the recent election has been called in question because of the erratic character of one or two of the votes. One of the measures proposed to repeal a clause of the state constitution that prohibited negro and mulatto suffrage. This measure was defeated by less than 600 votes. It would seem that every citizen that has reached his majority ought to know that negroes may vote and presumably do vote in Oregon. Familiarity with the federal constitution, such information as comes from the study of elementary civil government or United States history, ought to have acquainted voters, who for the most part have come of age since the Civil War, with the fact that the fifteenth amendment declares that the right of citizens of the United States to vote shall not be denied or abridged on account of race, etc. It ought also to be a matter of common information that the federal constitution supersedes and annuls all parts of a state constitution that may violate its provisions. The legislature had the laudable desire to strike out of the constitution a section that is no longer operative and so proposed an amendment that would accomplish this object. The large vote against the measure, a small majority at that, seems to indicate an unwillingness to permit the negro to vote in

Oregon. The ballot title for this measure did not clearly indicate its purpose and the average voter seems not to read the full copy of the proposals as they appear in the voter's pamphlet sent out weeks before the election. A straw ballot taken at the university just before the election resulted in an adverse majority for this measure. Loyal defenders of our Oregon system of initiative and referendum must feel chagrined at such unintelligent voting whatever the explanation made for it. Every citizen ought to know the more important results of the Civil War. Teachers of government and history should take a lesson from this vote and insist on a somewhat more thorough knowledge of their subjects. Newspaper editors speak of a flood of letters from correspondents wishing to know what is meant by the electoral college and showing a manifest lack of acquaintance with the method of electing a president. Interest in the presidential election and some agitation arising from it for election by direct popular vote should be taken advantage of to explain the present method and its origin.

Another measure that failed of passing by only a few hundred votes was one making illegal compulsory vacination. Such a vote seems also hard to explain since vacination as a preventative to the spread of smallpox seems long since to have vindicated itself. It must be due to the feeling that there is no longer danger from this disease or else to a repugnance to anything compulsory. Yet at the same election a majority decided that liquor may not be received into the home for individual consumption.

Shall We Have a New Constitution?

After almost every election at which the voter is asked to pass upon a large number of complicated legislative measures or constitutional amendments there is discussion of the need of establishing safe-guards against the misuse of the initiative and referendum. Fictious signatures to initiative petitions make it seem desirable that some other method than one that puts a premium on fraud by permitting payment for circulation at a fixed rate per name. Then, too, the Oregon constitution has lost much of the sacred character that is supposed to

attach to such documents, that of fundamental and basic law, something not easily changed. Under our system it is as easy to amend the constitution as it is to make a law by initiative petition. The result is that the constitution seems subject to every whim of popular fancy. A bare majority of one vote may modify some fundamental provision of it. Under such conditions there is nothing in the way of governmental organization or sacred individual privelege to which one may pin faith or count as stable and certain. "If we are to have constitutional government it is necessary that we hold sacred the cardinal principles upon which personal welfare and ownership of property depends." Such is the argument of those who see great danger in too popular government. The result of this reaction against the too democratic machinery of Oregon government has been the organization of a "Constitutional Revision Association of Oregon." Its headquarters are in Portland. The character of the personnel of this organization is indicated by the statement of a journal. the "Oregon Voter," which stands for the ideals of the "fathers." "An association with such substantial men in charge is certain to be an effective force in a field that needs attention. Heretofore the field has been too much occupied by talkers, writers, dreamers and demagogues." A "Statement of Principles" has been put out by the association and a petition to the legislature to undertake a revision of the constitution is being circulated. There can be no objection to a movement that has for its object to clarify, simplify, and harmonize conflicting clauses of the constitution, in order to bring the constitution out of its present more or less chaotic condition and present it in such form that it may once more be printed in school texts on civil government. However, any movement that has for its object to make the constitution difficult of amendment, any less easy to amend than at present, is foredoomed to defeat. Popular government as embraced in the so-called "Oregon System" seems to have come to stay and reactionaries are wasting effort and time in attempting its overthrow. For the information of those citizens of Oregon who believe that constitutions are something to be guarded with jealous care it is well to call to mind that England has no constitution that may not be changed by simple legislative enactment. Her government may and has been from time to time modified by act of parliament, notably in recent years by the abolition of the veto power of the house of lords, fixing the life of parliament at five years, and the payment of members of parliament. France since 1875 has had no constitution except such as has been established and changed from time to time by act of the legislature. No one argues that these states are in danger of going on the rocks because their constitutions are "not protected from amendments which are written in the form of laws."

The Single Item Veto.

The only change in the organization of the Oregon government, or rather in the functions of one of the departments of government, and the only change that needs to be incorporated into formal texts descriptive of our state government as the result of the recent election is the constitutional amendment confering upon the governor the power to veto single items of bills appropriating money as passed by the legislature. The governor may now single out from a bill carrying a large number of appropriations for distinctive purposes a single item and veto it. Some states give the governor the additional authority to reduce the amount of a single item. This would have been a wise provision to add to the amendment and it seems unfortunate that it was overlooked in its formulation. The veto of the governor may of course be overcome by a two-thirds vote of both legislative houses. This amendment adds greatly to the governor's power and his control of legislation. It also makes it possible to place responsibility for legislative extravagance upon him or to give him credit for economy.

Oregon Congress of Mothers

By MRS. ELIZABETH HAYHURST, 1070 E. Burnside, Portland

Legislative measures have been uppermost in the minds of the women the last month. The Oregon Congress of Mothers and Parent-Teachers' Association will mother the eight months' school bill; a bill that will provide for the removal of property qualifications at school elections so that all parents may vote; an act that will empower school boards of the first class districts to establish parental schools and amendments that will strengthen the widow's pension law.

* * *

As an outgrowth of the inspiration given at the convention, the counties are being formed into county councils. Multnomah county (outside of Portland) completed its organization December 9 at Troutdale with Superintendent A. P. Armstrong and Superintendent-elect Alderson present. A bounteous dinner was served by the Troutdale Parent-Teachers' Association to the assembled delegates and all augurs well for a very helpful council. Clackamas, Jackson, and Lane are forming councils, and Marion and Polk are contemplating joining the state organization.

* * *

The president, Mrs. Geo. McMath, has been appointed chairman of a committee to investigate the State Training School for Boys, and the State Industrial School for Girls and report to the legislature.

* * *

A committee from the Oregon Congress of Mothers and Parent-Teachers' Associations will censor the films that are sent to the various state institutions from the Portland Exchanges.

* * *

The Social Service Committee of the Portland Council of Parent-Teachers' Association reports that over 1000 bundles of clothing were received in response to Bundle Day appeal. One hundred baskets were filled with provisions and sent to the needy at Thanksgiving time.

Preliminary Program of State Teachers' Association

Held at Portland, Oregon, December 27, 28, 29, 1916

THE REPRESENTATIVE COUNCIL.
Hotel Portland.

WEDNESDAY, December 27, 9:30 a. m.

The entire day will be spent in transacting the business of the association. The president will make a general report of the work of the association. Reports of standing committees will then be considered in the following order: (1) A Retirement Fund for Teachers by President Wm. T. Foster; (2) A Code of Ethics for Teachers by President J. H. Ackerman; (3) The Retardation Problem by Supt. C. W. Boetticher; (4) Other business which may be presented by any of the delegates.

Former students of the University of Oregon, the Oregon Agricultural College and the Oregon Normal School are planning to hold their annual dinner and reunion Wednesday evening. The official program will contain information as to the hours and places for the respective institutions. A dinner or banquet is planned for Thursday evening in honor of the distinguished visiting educators, concerning which announcement will also appear in the official program.

GENERAL ASSEMBLY.
Lincoln High School Auditorium.

The sessions of the General Assembly will occupy all of Thursday forenoon, December 28, 1916, and all of Friday afternoon, December 29, 1916.

THURSDAY, December 28, 9 a. m.

Music; Report of Representative Council, Pres. E. F. Carleton.

Address, Pres. Henry Suzzallo, University of Washington.

The Relationship of Industrial and Commercial Development in the State of Oregon, W. H. Dobson, Secretary Chamber of Commerce, Portland.

"That Thy Days May Be Long in the Land," Pres. Carroll G. Pearse, Milwaukee, Wisconsin State Normal School.

FRIDAY, December 29, 1:30 p. m.

Music; Business meeting.

School Dividends, Pres. Carroll G. Pearse.

Address, Pres. Henry Suzzallo.

DEPARTMENT OF CITY SUPERINTENDENTS.

V. Melde Hillis, Medford, Chairman.

THURSDAY, December 28, 1:30 p. m.

Medical Inspection in the Public Schools, Supt. R. H. Dumbar, Klamath Falls.

Laggards in the Schools; Some Causes; Some Methods of Cure, Pres. Carroll G. Pearse.

Teaching Practice in the Teachers' Training Course, Supt. I. B. Warner, The Dalles.

FRIDAY, December 29, 9 a. m.

The Mentally Defective in the Public Schools, Dr. J. N. Smith, Superintendent School for Feeble Minded.

State Publication of Textbooks, a representative of the Portland Telegram; discussion led by Supt. F. A. Tiedgen, Marshfield.

The Oregon System of Textbook Adoption, Supt. John G. Imel, Astoria; discussion led by Supt. Walter I. Ford, Dallas.

DEPARTMENT OF HIGHER EDUCATION.

F. G. Franklin, Albany, Chairman.

THURSDAY, December 29, 1:30 p. m.

The Possibility of Scientific Training of Teachers, Prof. J. K. Hart, of Reed College; discussion led by Prof. H. D. Sheldon of University of Oregon.

Academic Freedom, Pres. W. T. Foster, of Reed College; discussion led by Pres. L. T. Pennington, of Pacific College.

FRIDAY, December 29, 9:30 a. m.

The Real Purpose of the Privately Supported College, Pres. C. G. Doney, of Willamette University; discussion led by Prof. C. P. Coe, McMinnville College.

Relation of the College to the Rural Communities, Prof. M. J. Fenenga, of Pacific University; discussion led by Prof. Hector Macpherson, of Oregon Agricultural College.

DEPARTMENT OF SECONDARY SCHOOLS.

E. L. Keesel, Eugene, Chairman.

THURSDAY, December 28, 1:30 p. m.

Address, Dr. Henry Suzzallo.

DIVISION OF SCIENCE AND MATHEMATICS.

L. P. Gilmore, Monmouth, Chairman.

THURSDAY, December 28, 2 p. m.

The Mathematical Responsibility of the High School, F. L. Griffin, of Reed College. At the close of each paper the chairman will conduct a round table discussion.

Mathematical Deficiencies of Students Entering College, R. M. Winger, of University of Oregon.

FRIDAY, December 29, 9 a. m.

The Why of General Science, L. P. Gilmore, of Oregon Normal School.

The How of General Science, Francis D. Curtis, James John High School.

The Project Method of Teaching Physics, G. W. Wilder, Benson Polytechnic School; discussion led by Geo. W. Shantin, Sutherlin.

DIVISION OF HISTORY.

Miss Elizabeth Bain, Portland, Chairman.

THURSDAY, December 28, 1:30 p. m.

The Teaching of Recent American History, Mr. J. P. O'Hara, University of Oregon.

Shall We Extend Our First Year's

Work to the Year 1600? May Darling, Washington High School.

Community Civics as a Pre-requisite to the Social Studies, A. N. French, University of Oregon.

Elementary Sociology in the High School, H. H. Moore.

FRIDAY, December 29, 9 a. m.

The Selection and Management of Collateral Reading, Jessie U. Cox, Salem High School.

Methods of Handling Current Events, F. E. Moore, Ashland High School.

The Use of Magazines in History and Civics Classes, Marian Culver, Lincoln High School.

Vitalizing the History Recitation, Jeanette Paddock, Jefferson High School.

OREGON COUNCIL OF ENGLISH TEACHERS.

Ernest S. Bates, Eugene, Chairman; Rosa B. Parrott, Monmouth, Secretary.

THURSDAY, December 28, 1:30 p. m.

The Periodical in the English Course of the High School, Frederick Berchtold, O. A. C.

Dramatization in the High Schools, Rosa B. Parrott, Oregon Normal School.

English With English Left Out, Julia Burgess, University of Oregon.

FRIDAY, December 29, 9 a. m.

The Correlation of Latin and English, A. P. McKinley, Lincoln High School, Portland.

The Vital versus the Conventional in the Teaching of English, Guy E. Dyar, Eugene High School.

"Mehr Licht," Ernest S. Bates, University of Oregon.

ADVANCED DIVISION ELEMENTARY SCHOOLS.

Edward D. Curtis, Portland, Chairman.

THURSDAY, December 28, 1:30 p. m.

Reading, L. R. Alderman.

The Seven Lamps, D. A. Grout.

FRIDAY, December 29, 9 a. m.

Demonstration of the Stereopticon as an Aid in Teaching, L. A. Wiley.

Some Home Made Tests of the Teachers' Efficiency, Carroll G. Pearce.

Moving Pictures, Earl Kilpatrick, University of Oregon.

Supervised Study, I. B. Warner.

Ungraded Work, Mrs. Grace McCord.

INTERMEDIATE DIVISION ELEMENTARY SCHOOLS.

THURSDAY, December 28, 1:30 p. m.

Some Home Made Tests of the Teachers' Efficiency, C. G. Pearse.

Efficiency Tests, Charles A. Rice.

FRIDAY, December 29, 9 a. n..

Demonstration of the Stereopticon as an Aid in Teaching, L. A. Wiley.

Moving Pictures in Connection With the School and the Community, A. T. Park.

Address, Brenton Vedder.

PRIMARY DIVISION ELEMENTARY SCHOOLS.

THURSDAY, December 28, 1:30 p. m.

Some Home Made Tests of the Teachers' Efficiency, Carroll G. Pearse.

Interpretative Reading in Primary Grades, Mrs. Josephine Lisher.

FRIDAY, December 29, 9 a. m..

During the first and second periods advanced, intermediate, and primary divisions will meet in joint session in the Shattuck school.

Demonstration of the Stereopticon as an Aid in Teaching, L. A. Wiley.

Primary Manual Arts, Mrs. Ada J. Farmer.

A Character Sketch, Mrs. M. L. Fulkerson.

The Retail Grocery Store, Fannie G. Porter.

DEPARTMENT OF VOCATIONAL EDUCATION.

H. H. Wardrip, Grants Pass, Chairman.

THURSDAY, December 28, 1:30 p. m.

Oregon's Interest in National Aid for Industrial Education in Secondary Schools, E. D. Ressler, O. A. C.

Importance of Design in Drawing and Woodworking, H. C. Brandon, Oregon Agricultural College.

Manual Training Adapted to the Community, R. E. Chloupek, Pendleton.

Manual Training versus Prevocational Training, Donald L. Robey, Eugene.

Continuation Schools of the City of Munich, L. L. Summers, Portland Schools.

FRIDAY, December 29, 1916.

Manual Training and Its Relation to Industrial Efficiency, F. H. Shepherd, Oregon Agricultural College.

Mechanical Drawing in the High Schools, A. K. Trenholme, Washington High School.

The Relation of High School Drawing to College Drawing and Commercial Drawing, F. E. Mangold, Jefferson High School.

Some Sociological Phases of Industrial Education, Joseph K. Hart, Reed College.

HOME ECONOMICS DIVISION.

Sarah L. Lewis, Corvallis, Chairman.

THURSDAY, December 28, 1:30 p. m.

Address, E. D. Ressler, Oregon Agricultural College.

The Domestic Science Teacher and the School Luncheon, Alice Butler, Pendleton; discussion led by Lucile Chase, Eugene.

Industrial Art Education in Relation to the Home, Grace Gillett, Oregon Agricultural College; general discussion led by Myra Butler, Oregon Normal School.

FRIDAY, December 29, 9 a. m.

Domestic Science in the Schools and Its Relation to the Home, Edna Groves, Portland; general discussion.

Domestic Art in the High School, Mrs. A. A. Sanborn, Portland; general discussion.

Household Education in Some Foreign Schools, Lillian E. Tingle, Portland; general discussion.

Address, Joseph K. Hart, Reed College.

COMMERCIAL DIVISION.

A. C. Crews, Hood River, Chairman; Mrs. G. Holmes Lawrence, Portland, Secretary.

THURSDAY, December 28, 1:30 p. m.

Address, E. D. Ressler, Oregon Agricultural College.

The Importance of Commercial Education in the School Curriculum and What Oregon Is Doing, Hon. H. D. Miller.

Teaching Bookkeeping in High Schools, A. H. Sproul, High School of Commerce.

Some Fallicies in Teaching Bookkeeping, I. M. Walker, Behnke-Walker Business College.

Adjusting the Bookkeeping Course to Local Industrial Conditions, Dean D. Walter Morton, University of Oregon.

Correlation Between the Commercial Course in High School and the Higher Schools of Commerce, Dean J. A. Bexell, Oregon Agricultural College.

FRIDAY, December 29, 9 a. m.

Co-operation Between the Business Man and Commercial Teachers, W. F. Woodard, Woodard-Clark Drug Company.

The Office Training Course, H. T. Vance, Oregon Agricultural College.

The Management of a Typewriting Department, Miss Etha Mabel Maginnis, Oregon Agricultural College.

How to Teach Retail Selling in High Schools, G. Robert McAuston, Ulnversity of Oregon.

Method of Teaching Commercial Geography, Dr. L. A. Rufener, Oregon Agricultural College.

Address, Joseph K. Hart, Reed College.

ART DIVISION.

Mr. Ellis F. Lawrence, Portland, Chairman.

THURSDAY, December 28, 1:30 p. m.

Report of chairman and appointment of committees.

School Beautifying with Special Reference to Pictures for School Room Walls, Mrs. J. Elliott King, Portland.

Psychology of Drawing, Prof. Frederick C. Ayer, University of Oregon.

The Purpose of Art Education in the Oregon Agricultural College, Farley D. McLouth, Oregon Agricultural College.

FRIDAY, December 29, 9 a. m.

Report of committees and election of officers.

Art Training in the Portland Public Schools, illustrated by exhibition of student work.

Aims and Ideals, Miss Esther Wuest.

Primary Division, Miss Phyllis Muirden.

Grammar Grade Division, Miss Helen Worth.

High School Division, Mrs. Mae Gay.

., Discussion of Methods, Prof. A. H. Schroff, University of Oregon; Miss Alberta Green, State Normal School; Miss Edna M. Flarida, Oregon Agricultural College.

DEPARTMENT OF LIBRARIANS.

Harriet E. Weed, Portland, Chairman.

THURSDAY, December 28, 1:30 p. m.

Grade Schools.—Miss Bailey, East Portland; Miss Blood, Vernon Branch; Miss Metz, The Dalles; Miss Connor, Shattuck; Miss Slusser, Ockley Green; Miss Stacy, Ladd.

High Schools.—Miss Drew, Jefferson High; Miss Case, Salem High; Mr. Linnehan, Washington High; Miss Griebel, Lincoln High;.

Normal Schools.—Miss West, Monmouth; Miss Blood, Washington High.

Colleges. — Miss Kidder, Corvallis; Mr. Douglas, Eugene.

General State Work.—Miss Marvin, Salem.

Throughout the convention an exhibit will be held in the Lincoln Library of books and other helps for all grades. At the close of the program on Friday afternoon a demonstration of book mending will be given.

DEPARTMENT OF PHYSICAL TRAINING.

Mabel L. Cummings, Eugene, Chairman.

THURSDAY, December 28, 1:30 p. m.

The Hygienic Significance of the Erect Posture, Dr. Bertha S. Stuart, Reed College.

Methods of Posture Training Adapted to Elementary Schools, Laura J. Taylor, Oregon Normal School.

Posture Grading and the Bancroft Posture Test, Frieda Goldsmith, University of Oregon, and Robert Krohn, Portland.

FRIDAY, December 29, 9 a. m..

Adolescent Characteristics of Particular Interest to the Teacher of Physical Training, Dr. B. W. DeBusk, University of Oregon.

Methods and Organization of Physical Training for Adolescent Girls, Dr. Mary V. Madigan, Franklin High School.

Methods and Organization for Adolescent Boys, A. J. Grilley, Y. M. C. A., Portland.

DEPARTMENT OF RURAL SCHOOLS.

E. R. Peterson, Medford, Chairman.

THURSDAY, December 28, 1:30 p. m.

The State Library as a Factor in Rural Education, Miss Cornelia Marvin, Salem.

Round Table Discussion, led by J. A. Churchill, Salem.

Conservation vs. Consolidation, C. W. Tenney, Helena, Mont.

FRIDAY, December 29, 9 a. m.

Business session.

Indoor Games Demonstrated, Miss Emily Devore, Medford.

What Can I As a Teacher Do for the Betterment of My Community? Pres. J. H. Ackerman, Oregon Normal School.

Demonstration of Hot Lunches in the Rural School, Miss Florence Jennings, Coos County.

As a part of this place in the program, a hot lunch will be served to a limited number. A charge of 10 cents will be made to cover the cost of materials.

The Modern Language Department will have a program, also the Music Supervisors.

The Foreign Language Department will hold its program in conjunction with the Classical Association of the Pacific States.

Shrew (contemptuously): What would you have been if it weren't for my money?

Shrewd: A bachelor.—Chaparral.

Membership in the State Teachers' Association

The Oregon Teachers Monthly is the official organ of the State Teachers' Association, and all subscribers who pay $1.50 for a year's advance subscription become active members of the association. Below are the names of those who are entitled to membership:

1 Nellie V. King, Winant
2 Fred Schepman, Florence
3 John Blough, Toledo
4 Maggie L. Hampton, Toledo
5 M. Lillian Ernest, Denzer
6 Earl Brown, Philomath
7 Chas. Hart, Roselodge
8 S. S. Gossman, Chitwood
10 J. E. Davis, Chitwood
11 R. E. Wood, Orton
12 John Miller, Eddyville
13 Verne Ross, Toledo
14 T. E. Wilson, Turner
15 Paul Wyman, Bay City
16 Chas. Holway, Gervais
17 Laura A. Smith, Cottage Grove
18 H. W. Herron, Portland
19 Mary B. Scollard, Woodburn
20 L. W. Turnbull, Coquille
21 Hazel Henkle, Monkland
22 A. C. Strange, Baker
23 Anna Dunsmore, Orenco
24 Margaret Williams, Portland
25 Adella Chapler, Salem
26 Margaret Boggess, Veneta
27 W. M. Sutton, Burns
28 W. G. Beattie, Eugene
29 Mary E. Slade, Albany
30 Mrs. L. K. Page, Springfield
31 Mrs. A. Alexander, Portland
32 Barbara Hoch, Pendleton
33 Blanche Padley, Bandon
34 Kate Ronde, Clatskanie
35 Edith Harper, Freewater
36 Edith Smith, Banks
37 Alice Rasmussen, Troutdale
38 Della Zimmerman, Troutdale
39 Adda Wright, Warrenton
40 N. A. Frost, Forest Grove
41 Edna Pence, Salem
42 Erica Nordhausen, Aurora
43 Clara Ireland, Portland
44 Julie H. Burch, Oregon City
45 J. P. McGlasson, North Plains
46 Ethel Davis, Myrtle Creek
47 Mrs. E. H. Morrison, Portland
48 Coral Garvin, Corvallis
49 Inez Easton, Sitkum
50 Alethia Chapman, LaGrande
51 May Smith, Mabel
52 Helen Treat, Buell
53 Virginia Nottingham, Carlton
54 Elma Roberts, Sumner
55 Ruby Skinner, Lakeview
56 Frances Potter, Canby
57 Harriet B. Horrigan, Hillsboro
58 Grace Egbert, The Dalles
59 Mary B. Underwood, Philomath
60 Ruth Dunbabin, Bourne
61 M. T. Means, Philomath
62 Mildred Taylor, Scappoose
63 Marie Senn, Barlow
64 Bessa Lehmann, Sutherlin
65 Anna Bachmann, Clackamas
66 Adeline Buyserie, Hubbard
67 Isa Isaacson, Junction City
68 Anna Weisenborn, Deer Island
69 Myrel A. Bond, Irving
70 Rada Antrim, Amity
71 Marvin F. Wood, Corvallis
72 Carl E. Morrison, Perrydale
73 Waithia Watson, Roseburg
74 H. C. Ostien, Monmouth
75 Eula Campbell, Freewater
76 M. S. Pittman, Monmouth
77 Hazel Goger, Boring
78 Clara Spiekerman, The Dalles
79 Mamie Harper, Wren
80 R. S. Bixby, Nolin
81 Mattie Foster, Klamath Falls
82 Nell G. Lloyd, Klondike
83 Margaret Rice, Shaniko
84 Martha Chase, Portland
85 Myrtle Clayville, Portland
86 C. D. Watkins, Dilley
87 Clara Larson, Toledo
88 Emma Murray, Klamath Falls
89 Marion Ford, Klamath Falls
90 May Wheaton, Coquille
91 Fannie G. Porter, Oregon City
92 Mable F. Johnson, Butte Falls
93 Helene Ogsburg, Eugene
94 Velma Beardslee, Arlington
95 Gladys Anderson, Clear Lake, Ia.
96 Alice Lytle, Bonanza
97 Vara Stewart, Portland
98 Charles Knocke, Mt. Carmel, N. D.
99 Lydia Unden, Winchester
100 Jewell Delk, Drain
101 Matilda Jacobs, Portland
102 Mrs. Gladys Smith, Springfield
103 Helen Anderson, Meda
104 Alma Nichols, Culver
105 Gladys Hatcher, Buell
106 Sylvia Severance, Lexington
107 Dagmar Jeppesen, Boyd
108 Ora England, Walker
109 Florence E. Howatt, Portland
110 Rachel May, Timber
111 Ellen M. Yocum, Amity
112 Alice Jenkins, Eugene
113 Harry Whitten, Kingsley
114 Violet M. Stolle, Irving
115 Violet McCarl, Portland
116 Maude Largent, Hulit
117 Elnor Sherk, Sutherlin
118 Ruth Peterson, Yoncalla
119 Grace Atkinson, Walton
120 Mrs. Mary Hulin, Carpentaria, Cal.
121 Mary E. Moore, Irving
122 Vera Merchant, Lebanon
123 Emma Kennedy, Coquille
124 Maybelle Wagner, McMinnville
125 Marguerite Freydig, Sutherlin
126 Ruth A. Brown, Eagle Creek
127 Ranie P. Burkhead, Shaniko
128 Mabel McFadden, Halfway
129 Angie Halley, Medford
130 Goldie Groth, Freewater
131 Justina Kildee, Sutherlin
132 May B. Lund, Coquille
133 Mildred Jones, Amity
134 Grace V. Perce, Medford
135 Myrtle Ess, Klamath Falls
136 Sadie Heiberger, Wedderburn
137 Marie A. Smith, Buena Vista
138 Carolyn Woods, Cottage Grove
139 Ruth Finlay, Silverton
140 Luella Daniel, Milton
141 Wilbert O. Wilson, Kopiah, Wash.
142 Nettye Moore, Flat River, Mo.
143 Ida Anderson, Early
144 Clara Luther, Halsey
145 Caroline Luther, Redmond
146 Clara Schneider, Gaston
147 Maud Keysaw, Walterville
148 Gladys Burr, Oregon City
149 Emily L. Marshall, Willamette
150 Lapensa Amrine, Oregon City
151 Arabella Davis, Portland
152 Pansy Oswald, Gladstone
153 Pearle Ruegg, Gresham
154 Loney Yoder, Hubbard
155 Mrs. H. L. Hull, Oregon City
156 Ruth F. Hudson, Mulino

157 Elizabeth Roach, Cherryville
158 Brenton Vedder, Gladstone
159 Ruth M. Lingle, Boring
160 John R. Bowland, Oregon City
161 A. C. Thompson, Milwaukie
162 Raymond Boyer, Rickreall
163 L. H. Mallicoat, Boring
164 T. J. Gary, Portland
165 Ellen DeHaven, Salem
166 Jessie Hartley, Portland
167 Amy McDaniel, Weston
168 Rena Roper, Vancouver, Wash.
169 Stella Swift, Junction City
170 Louise Nimmo, Albany
171 Minnie Kulmke, Salem
172 Wm. Westenskow, Imbler
173 D. A. Hoag, Sodaville
174 Laura Moore, Molalla
175 C. Edna Kennedy, Barton
176 Helen M. Hall, Molalla
177 Olga Hanson, Clackamas
178 Margaret Summer, Tigard
179 Mrs. Nannie Thomas, Molalla
180 Mary A. Bickner, Oswego
181 Cora Hasselbrink, Sherwood
182 Chas. H. Jones, Salem
183 Lunah W. Wallace, Huntington
184 Mabel Wallace, Willamina
185 Anna Nelson, Palmer
186 Adeline Brown, Kingsley
187 Miriam Underwood, Oakland
188 Ozella Anderson, Parkplace
189 Mary E. Sherer, Corvallis
190 Winnifred Roe, Monument
191 Matilda F. Grossen, Hillsboro
192 Vernus Young, Echo
193 Edison Fowler, Riverside
194 Mrs. E. D. Sprague, Lake
195 Lucile J. Lisher, Portland
196 Margaret McDonald, Portland
197 Georgia Smith, Mayville
198 Aver Black, Tygh Valley
199 Viola Ortschild, Portland
200 Margaret Ferguson, Siltscoos
201 Lena Gribble, Aurora
202 Agnes Weatherson, Minerva
203 Benedictine Sisters, Oregon City
204 Myrtle Birtchet, Mt. Angel
205 Viola Nagel, Gaston
206 Gladys Jory, Salem
207 Anna C. Taylor, North Powder
208 C. H. Wilson, Condon
209 May Payne, Mitchell
210 Gladys Denney, Oakland
211 Laura Brenner, Oregon City
212 Pearl Wilson, Milton
213 J. B. Lent, Fairview
214 Mrs. A. E. Watson, Portland
215 Mary Ulen, Portland
216 J. B. Horner, Corvallis
217 Nina Taylor, Portland
218 M. E. V. Hess, Portland
219 Hattiebelle Ogilbee, Portland
220 Helen Dahl, Gresham
221 C. G. Springer, Madras
222 Eva Schneider, Boring
223 Ruth Schmuckll, Portland
224 Marian Robertson, Gresham
225 Nellie Renshaw, Mayville
226 Maude B. Mickel, Gresham
227 P. C. Fulton, Holbrook
228 L. B. Gibson, Hood River
229 Mrs. Ora D. Fleming, Lents
230 Ada Werner, Portland
231 E. Williams, Portland
232 Nellie Washburn, Portland
233 Mrs. Margaret B. West, Portland
234 Minerva Powell, Troutdale
235 Marguerite Miller, Portland
236 Mabel F. Burghduff, Portland
237 Louise Sterling, Corbett
238 Vina Swan, Camas, Wash.
239 Mrs. Jennie Carr, Portland
240 Cornelia J. Spencer, Portland
241 Eva S. Rice, Portland
242 Frances S. Estes, Portland

243 Emma Rueter, Portland
244 Mrs. Minnie Parsons, Portland
245 Nell O. Bevans, Portland
246 Mary E. Hill, Portland
247 Estelle Marias, Portland
248 Lutie E. Cake, Portland
249 Margaret L. Pomeroy, Portland
250 Evlyn Cornutt, Portland
251 C. May Moriarty, Portland
252 Phila Nicoll, Portland
253 Kate E. Wiest, Astoria
254 Jeanette Pound, Salem
255 Mina Magness, Myrtle Point
256 W. F. Cornwell, McEwen
257 Leila Lasley, Toledo
258 Clara Straughan, Pendleton
259 Mary Stein, Union
260 W. M. Smith, Salem
261 A. R. Nichols, Corvallis
262 Frank W. Weber, Bend
263 Margaret V. Thomas, Gardiner
264 Jessie Wagener, Alsea
265 Edna Burke, Boring
266 Luann Hiatt, Tillamook
267 Mrs. S. E. Barnes, Portland
268 Ivan D. Wood, Union
269 Mabel Saunders, Richland
270 Reta E. Waller, Oakland
271 Marie Wainright, Mayville
272 Ruth H. Ball, Klamath Agency
273 Mrs. Edith Coleman, Lafayette
274 Jessie Armstrong, Astoria
275 Mrs. W. G. Thompson, Nyssa
276 Hugh J. Boyd, Portland
277 Emma Clanton, Portland
278 Merle A. Nimmo, Springfield
279 Blanche Darby, Wilderville
280 Margaret L. Davies, Mt. Vernon
281 Mabel St. Pierre, Salem
282 Ruth E. Hyland, Oakridge
283 G. W. Nash, Bellingham, Wash.
284 Dorothy Waugh, Portland
285 Freda Bohn, Woodburn
286 Della Rynning, Estacada
287 Ava Owen, Beaver
288 Myrtice Fowler, Nortons
289 Beatrice Buckner, Oak Grove
290 Alice L. Bennett, Mosier
291 Bessie G. Immel, Marshfield
292 Adella Mortensen, Early
293 W. M. Kent, Gold Beach
294 G. P. Harrington, Gold Beach
295 Mrs. Alida Laduron, Brookings
296 W. H. Grant, Cecil
297 Fay Duff, Pendleton
298 Beulah Thorp, Aurora
299 Florence Buell, Oakland
300 Louisa E. Counsell, LaGrande
301 F. A. Bloomfield, Derby
302 E. H. Anderson, Newberg
303 Ethel Ross, Newberg
304 A. R. Tollefson, Corbett
305 Minnie Mascher, Silverton
306 Benedictine Sisters, Woodburn
307 Roy Bower, Lorane
308 Elizabeth Martin, Boyd
309 Minnie Fortna, Athena
310 Neita Lewis, Newberg
311 Lena Wolcott, Peak
312 Winifred King, Corvallis
313 E. Pearl Smith, Corvallis
314 E. H. Castle, Philomath
315 G. E. Ross, Lebanon
316 Ferd W. Jones, Corvallis
317 Mrs. Earl Miller, Albany
318 Rose Kaldor, Monroe
319 Rhoda Newkirk, Monroe
320 J. V. Kane, Lyons
321 J. E. Dunton, Lebanon
322 Elsie Moore, Corvallis
323 Anna Denman, Lebanon
324 W. L. Jackson, Albany
325 Mrs. Daisy Allen, Shedd
326 J. M. Poe, Berlin
327 Victoria Soderstrom, Harrisburg
328 Nora C. Coleman, Sweet Home

329 Clara Van Matre, Alpine	415 Phyllis Purdin, Pendleton
330 Estella Dooney, Foster	416 Loretta Harding, Florence
331 Alice Boyle, Brownsville	417 Floyd L. Senter, Acme
332 Mary Connet, Foster	418 Beatrice Runcall, Portland
333 Engra Benson, Crawfordsville	419 Ruby Fenwick, Jordan Valley
334 Smith B. Holt, Thomas	420 Laura S. Barry, Plush
335 Ruth Simpson, Suver	421 Lulu Maxwell, Banks
336 V. B. Higbee, Albany	422 F. Irma Coon, Laurel
337 Jennie Reed, Harrisburg	423 Bess Palmer, Springfield
338 Mrs. Hattie Allen, Hoskins	424 Ethel Mudge, Heceta
339 Sisters of Mercy, Roseburg	425 Maude Wakefield, Ione
340 Jacob Stocker, Foster	426 H. O. Nedry, Hardman
341 Acie D. McClain, Lebanon	427 Sylvia McCarty, Sinnott
342 Ruth A. Wight, Lebanon	428 Catherine J. Doherty, Ione
343 Mary A. Binns, Monroe	429 H. H. Hoffman, Heppner
344 Urich S. Burt, Corvallis	430 Sophia Burke, Heppner
345 H. B. Brookhardt, Albany	431 Mrs. Blanche Watkins, Heppner
346 Arline Hoerr, Lebanon	432 L. A. Doak, Ione
347 Helen Myers, Albany	433 S. E. Notson, Heppner
348 Bessie Truelove, Corvallis	434 S. H. Doak, Lexington
349 Joy Extel, Corvallis	435 E. S. Payne, Heppner
350 M. J. Looney, Tangent	436 W. L. Suddarth, Irrigon
351 Frank Brumbaugh, Lebanon	437 Orlena Suddarth, Irrigon
352 G. M. Sprague, Mill City	438 Edna Carmichael, Lexington
353 Gussie Stadden, Summit	439 Lera Githens, Morgan
354 O. J. Schroyer, Summit	440 Mrs. Lucy T. Wedding, Heppner
355 Helen Metcalf, Scio	441 Myrtle Miller, Lena
356 Belle Wilson, Harrisburg	442 Josephine McDevitt, Lena
357 Alwilda Wilson, Albany	443 Olive Moss, Portland
358 C. F. Bigbee, Crabtree	444 Metta C. Brown, Portland
359 B. A. Johnston, Corvallis	445 Ruby Briggs, Foster
360 Helen Rose Plov, Junction City	446 Grace Schuebel, Canby
361 M. E. Arnold, Albany	447 Alicia Pearl Horner, Portland
362 Joanna Hislop, Corvallis	448 Lena E. May, Sherwood
363 Fred Lockley, Portland	449 Golda M. Johnson, Crawfordsville
364 Esther Gilbertson, Harrisburg	450 Bessie M. Hanseth, Monmouth
365 Minnie McCourt, Albany	451 R. L. Green, Fossil
366 J. N. Bilyeu, Crabtree	452 Fred Hawes, Winlock
367 D. U. Cochrane, Kings Valley	453 Ida Olson, Fossil
368 Marie F. Schrepel, Philomath	454 Lillian Duff, Fossil
369 Mabel Hann, Harrisburg	455 C. R. Deems, Burnt Ranch
370 Ruth Hacking, Blodgett	456 Eva Boyle Linville, Spray
371 F. M. Maxwell, Halsey	457 Leah Blann, Twickenham
372 Venia Powers, Payette, Idaho	458 B. L. Murphy, Spray
373 Blanche Scharmann, Portland	459 Mrs. Elizabeth Bowerman, Fossil
374 Mrs. Bertha McKinley, Rogue River	460 Flora Gilliland, Fossil
375 Mary Hostetler, Silverton	461 Susan E. Prindle, Antone
376 Mrs. Mary Wight, Beswick, Cal.	462 Rayma Lee Van Horn, Fossil
377 Sigra Johnson, Colton	463 C. R. Curfman, Kent
378 Dale Loftin, Waterloo	464 Jessie Hill, Kent
379 W. J. Patterson, Wamic	465 Ethel L. Hooper, Hoskins
380 Louise Rintoul, The Dalles	466 Edna Hamlin, Brownsville
381 Ica L. Derthick, Wapinitia	467 Oliver Matthews, Boyd
382 Phyllis Fischer, Maupin	468 E. B. Moore, John Day
383 Frankie Allen, The Dalles	469 C. H. Poole, Canyon City
384 Agnes Campbell, The Dalles	470 Bruce Hayes, Prairie City
385 Enid Bell, Big Eddy	471 R. E. Bible, Hamilton
386 Ethyl Gibson, Boyd	472 Margaret Mitchell, Caverhill
387 Helena Fleck, The Dalles	473 Clara B. Carroll, Dayville
388 Mary U. Michell, The Dalles	474 Mabel Thomas, Prairie City
389 Marcia Selleck, Dufur	475 Rachel Ballance, Long Creek
390 Bessie Bonney, Tygh Valley	476 Mrs. W. W. Slaughter, Ritter
391 Mary Adair, The Dalles	477 Mrs. C. W. Curtis, Beech Creek
392 Katherine Arbuthnot, Monmouth	478 Corwin A. Harvey, Fox
393 Christine Ketels, The Dalles	479 C. H. Justice, Cotton Wood
394 Frances E. Bennett, Dufur	480 Mrs. Laura Collins, Hamilton
395 Elizabeth Leben, Dufur	481 Wesley Harryman, Long Creek
396 Mary V. Miller, Maupin	482 Robert Harryman, Monument
397 Rose C. Hassing, Dufur	483 Mrs. L. A. Slaughter, Monument
398 Ella M. Syron, Maupin	484 E. W. Kimberling, Prairie City
399 Margaret Walker, Mosier	485 V. E. Danels, Prairie City
400 J. P. Ross, Mosier	486 Millie Ricco, Austin
401 Mrs. G. R. Crofoot, Maupin	487 W. M. Bennett, Dayville
402 J. S. Wright, Dufur	488 Anatta Burch, Enterprise
403 Arthur Bonney, Criterion	489 Wilhemina Hemrich, Albany
404 Ruth VanZandt, Mosier	490 Amel Moore, Madras
405 Mary Dennis, Boyd	491 Osie H. Jewell, Madras
406 Lucy S. Ruggles, Dufur	492 Ethel Klann, Madras
407 Dorothy Passmore, Mosier	493 Elva J. Smith, Madras
408 Clara Lorenzen, The Dalles	494 Lelota Horrigan, Gateway
409 Hazel Seeley, The Dalles	494 Christine Ferm, Lexington
410 Ralph Southwick, Wallowa	496 Hazel Thorson, Bend
411 Virgil Melvin, Ada	497 Irene Weekly, Marshfield
412 Genevieve Haven, Kent	498 Emma M. Schreiber, McMinnville
413 Hilma Anderson, Portland	499 Bertha King, Corvallis
414 H. M. Sherwood, Portland	500 Vera Tipton, Reedsport

501	E. T. Reed, Corvallis	587	R. L. Young, Mt. Angel
502	Irene Douglas, Willows	588	Abbie S. Davis, Salem
503	Sylvia Hardman, Condon	589	Mabel Temple, Salem
504	Beatrice Snell, Arlington	590	W. J. Mishler, Woodburn
505	Enid G. Leeper, Condon	591	Grace Johnson, Niagara
506	Mrs. Lun Searcy, Condon	592	Ina C. Hubbs, Silverton
507	Eunice Ebbert, Gwendolen	593	Neita Royer, Salem
508	Phyllis Fate, McDonald	594	Mrs. LaMoine Clark, Salem
509	Clara M. Blais, Condon	595	Agnes Briggs, Jamieson
510	Cora Smith, Condon	596	Frances Chivington, Portland
511	Lottie Keizur, Condon	597	W. A. Pettys, Portland
512	Esther J. Turner, Clem	598	E. S. Evenden, Monmouth
513	Carrie W. Burnham, Arlington	599	H. D. Sheldon, Eugene
514	Bessie C. Lafferty, Condon	600	Mrs. Marie Stoller, Metolius
515	Mabel L. Williams, Condon	601	Emma Agee, Wilsonville
516	Mrs. Ethel Mulkey, Arlington	602	Martina H. Thiele, Hood River
517	P. J. Mulkey, Arlington	603	T. J. Skirvin, Wamic
518	Lydia B. Highlands, Mikkalo	604	Amilla Dart, Scio
519	Mrs. W. H. Reynolds, Condou	605	Cora Gay, Rickreall
520	Maude Grider, Condon	606	Armilda Doughty, Monmouth
521	Lee Byers, Lonerock	607	Mrs. Chloe Wood, Dallas
522	Mrs. Minnie F. Wilson, Cecil	608	Lester Gardner, Dallas
523	Mildred Force, Arlington	609	Mrs. Ella Oleman, Hoskins
524	Alveda Peterson, Arlington	610	Roberta E. Balland, Rickreall
525	Alma Randelin, Condon	611	Geneva Sayre, Black Rock
526	Jessie Hardie, Condon	612	Mrs. Mattie Neal, Grand Ronde
527	Marjory Hardie, Trailfork	613	H. H. Matthews, Phoenix
528	J. C. Sturgill, Condon	614	Rose H. Gay, Gold Hill
529	Alice McLean, Mercer	615	W. O. Wheeler, Eagle Point
530	Vida McLean, Eugene	616	Anna Jeffrey, Medford
531	Ida Foott, Portland	617	Dorothy Hartung, Junction City
532	Mary E. Thompson, Marshfield	618	Grace L. May, The Dalles
533	K. W. Onthank, Eugene.	619	Eula Strange, Portland
534	Margaret A. Gray, Thurston	620	Neva McReynolds, Langelis Val.
535	Anne G. Jackson, Knappa	621	Alma Sutherland, Bakeoven
536	Mary Harrison, Madras	622	Ruth Dowd, Weston
537	Albert H. Gillett, Dayton	623	John R. Stuber, Joseph
538	Madge Thomas, Buena Vista	624	Harvey A. Wright, Rickreall
539	Etta Halley, Willamette	625	Nellie Keyt, Independence
540	H. E. Inglow, Forest Grove	626	Willis A. Johnston, McCoy
541	Grace Pryor, White Pine	627	Edith Montgomery, Falls City
542	Clyde L. Knapp, Salem	628	Mrs. E. R. Palmer, Dallas
543	H. C. Todd, Salem	629	Grace Porter, Rickreall
544	Emma C. Brack, Woodburn	630	E. H. Hedrick, Monmouth
545	Ellen Greibenow, Salem	631	W. I. Reynolds, Dallas
546	Emma Walker, Salem	632	Lora Chute, Independence
547	Mattie Neeley, Turner	633	Alice E. Quint, Black Rock
548	Harry Baillie, Silverton	634	Mabel C. Gillette, Independence
549	Henriette Berning, Mt. Angel	635	Elsie L. Taylor, Salem
550	Helen Kefer, Mt. Angel	626	Winona Rowland, Rickreall
551	Josie Thompson, Grants Pass	637	Alice McIntosh, Monmouth
552	Harriet Minthorn, Rogue River	638	Georgia Curtiss, Dallas
553	Lois Sims, Hubbard	639	Effie Cuthbert, Sheridan
554	Mabel Van Fleet, Mehama	640	Gertrude R. Wilson, Monmouth
555	Hilda M. Nerison, Silverton	641	Olive McCready, Suver
556	Flora Grice, Salem	642	W. I. Ford, Dallas
557	F. A. Myers, Aumsville	643	Rose Bodayla, Salem
558	H. M. James, Silverton	644	R. W. Tavenner, Independence
559	Mrs. H. H. Paget, Macleay	645	Nellie Young, Parkers
560	J. H. Collins, Woodburn	646	Floyd O. Miller, Dallas
561	Anna Lindgren, Salem	647	Edna Sweeney, Buell
562	Osie Grice, Aumsville	648	Gladys Stewart, Rickreall
563	W. C. Gauntt, Stayton	649	Jessie Hunt, Independence
564	J. G. Noe, Hubbard	650	John Kurtichanov, Chitwood
565	Alta B. Brown, Lyons	651	J. I. Reasoner, Dallas
566	Minnie L. Joeckel, Silverton	652	Gladys Mitchell, Independence
567	Margaret West, Oregon City	653	Loraine Goehring, McCoy
568	Ellen Currin, Salem	654	Clara Sampson, Nortons
569	Kate Willoughby, Arago	655	June Philpott, Corvallis
570	Daisy Carter, Salem	656	Sara Huntington, Yoncalla
571	Margaret J. Cosper, Salem	657	Retta M. Allen, Whitney
572	Mrs. E. H. Belknap, Turner	658	Sophia A. Wilson, Portland
573	F. P. Sherman, Woodburn	659	Emma Post, Drain
574	Hilda J. Olson, Silverton	660	Agathe Grondahl, Portland
575	A. N. Arnold, Salem	661	Dora E. Starke, Amity
576	E. S. Stultz, Scotts Mills	662	G. W. Milam, Gold Hill
577	Bertha C. Byrd, Salem	663	Mrs. W. N. Davis, Rogue River
578	B. K. Cook, Salem	664	Mrs. O. C. Lichens, Kerby
579	Julia Iverson, Salem	665	W. H. Ashcraft, Ashland
580	Alice E. Estes, Scotts Mills	666	Lillian L. Gammill, Trail
581	Mrs. L. R. Stinson, Stayton	667	Emily DeVore, Medford
582	Elwina E. Schramm, Salem	668	Elizabeth Elmore, Applegate
583	Mrs. Marie Ehmer, Salem	669	Viola Hogan, Trail
584	Greta Phillips, Salem	670	Chester Cook, Wolf Creek.
585	Leota C. Humphrey, Turner	671	Wessie Griffith, Medford
586	Emma F. More, Salem	672	H. Howard Grover, Medford

673 Nellie B. Ross, Ashland	759 Sybil Farnsworth, Millwood
674 Annie O'Keefe, Huntington Beach	760 J. E. O'Neel, Canyonville
675 Lela E. Bloom, LaGrande	761 Irma L. Vance, Winchester
676 Nellie Shelley, Merlin	762 Mrs. Aura D. Jackson, Dillard
677 Margaret McQuiston, Grants Pass	763 Mary M. Whipple, Myrtle Creek
678 Susanne Homes, Ashland	764 Walter E. Hercher, Myrtle Creek
679 Gladys Musgrave, Hardman	765 Mattie I. Carr, Yoncalla
680 Laura Jackway, Troutdale	766 Emery D. Doane, Yoncalla
681 Mary E. Wilcox, Sheridan	767 Mrs. C. W. Hartley, Sutherlin
682 Winifred A. Joyce, Portland	768 Myrtle Powell, Sutherlin
683 Sherman Smith, Helix	769 Mary Edgerton, Roseburg
684 Alice N. Staniger, Waldo	770 Elizabeth Northcraft, Camas Val.
685 Laura E. Hansoln, Ashland	771 A. J. Flurry, Days Creek
686 Edith R. Fredenburg, Brownsboro	772 Myrtelle Gross, Oakland
687 Havel Shaver, Ashland	773 Gladys Price, Myrtle Creek
688 Emma Wendt, Jacksonville	774 Nellie M. Wood, Days Creek
689 Roy Brown, Murphy	775 Lillie Duncan, Perdue
690 Maude Philbrook, Medford	776 Mildred Waite, Sutherlin
691 Robert I. Peachey, Jacksonville	777 Mrs. Emma Leeper, Oakland
692 May Nordoff, Medford	778 Addie M. Wilson, Yoncalla
693 Julia Sidley, Eagle Point	779 John Kernan, Roseburg
694 Vera Kellems, Grants Pass	780 Kathryn Agee, Roseburg
695 Pearl L. Gould, Butte Falls	781 Mrs. Myrtle Bradford, Roseburg
696 Blanche Crane, Grants Pass	782 Mary Aitken, Edenbower
697 Mary A. Oakes, Hugo	783 Hannah Ruden, Kellogg
698 G. W. Ager, Talent	784 Ruth Swinney, Roseburg
699 Anna Potts, Merlin	785 Elizabeth Parrott, Roseburg
700 J. A. Churchill, Salem	786 Watson C. Lea, Drain
701 H. C. Seymour, Corvallis	787 Alice Ueland, Roseburg
702 C. S. Cramer, Medford	788 Jennie Cook, Roseburg
703 E. B. Stanley, Central Point	789 Mrs. E. S. Ackert, Myrtle Creek
704 Leonard M. Buoy, Butte Falls	790 Harl H. Bronson, Riddle
705 A. R. Peterson, Medford	791 Myrtle L. George, Canyonville
706 Stella M. Paddock, Grants Pass	792 Florence P. Allen, Drew
707 J. C. Banard, Tolo	793 Adeline Stewart, Roseburg
708 A. E. Humpton, Selma	794 F. B. Hamlin, Roseburg
709 Mrs. Alberta Jones, Beagle	795 Fred A. Goff, Roseburg
710 D. K. Luthy, Gold Hill	796 W. Alice Goff, Roseburg
711 Katherine Foley, Gold Hill	797 Ellen Millikin, Drain
712 V. A. Davis, Central Point	798 Floy McCormack, Dillard
713 Mrs. Mollie Belding, Grants Pass	799 Floyd Watson, Oakland
714 H. H. Fox, Lake Creek	800 Lora B. Pummill, Riddle
715 Florence Querry, Medford	801 Mamie Langdon, Yoncalla
716 Tom L. Ostien, Waldo	802 Margaret Bremmer, Brockway
717 H. H. Wardrip, Grants Pass	803 H. Omer Bennett, Roseburg
718 Helene Knips, Grants Pass	804 Wilfred Brown, Camas Valley
719 J. A. Bish, Wilderville	805 A. E. Street, Camas Valley
720 Marian I. White, Grants Pass	806 Burt A. Adams, Lakeview
721 Laura C. Atkins, Grants Pass	807 Stella Curtis, Burns
722 Margaret Gallinger, Jacksonville	808 Frances Kirsch, Berdugo
723 B. F. Nibert, Applegate	809 Lacy B. Copenhaver, Springfield
724 Gertrude Engle, Ashland	810 Emma Haroun, Wamic
725 Daisy M. Lewis, Jacksonville	811 Anna Taylor, Mapleton
726 P. H. Daley, Medford	812 Lola B. Thompson, Grants Pass
727 Kathryn Dunham, Medford	813 Mabel McLean, Oregon City
728 Harriet Wilson, Medford	814 A. C. Stanbrough, Newberg
729 Mrs. May Rose, Wonder	815 Jene Mallory, Spray
730 Lucia C. Chapman, Waldo	816 Lelah McGee, Burns
731 Pina Benedict, Ashland	817 Orisa Hurd, Harper
732 Clara Skyrman, Trail	818 Martha Peters, Holbrook
733 Lucile Rader, Medford	819 Edith O. Messenger, Disston
734 Dewie E. Howe, Trail	820 LaVilla Buell, Cottage Grove
735 Hazel Taylor, Central Point	821 Ivy J. Ten Eyck, Boring
736 Marie Dolan, Hugo	822 Mrs. C. W. Shurte, Heppner
737 Melvina M. Fox, Merlin	823 Esther Hughet, Narrows
738 Aneta M. Chellin, Grants Pass	824 M. N. Bonham, Hillsboro
739 Mrs. Geo. B. Canode, Medford	825 Mrs. Minnie Gates, Hillsboro
740 Felix E. Moore, Ashland	826 Sue Berg, Portland
741 Elizabeth Neidigh, Knappa	827 Jessie B. Greer, Forest Grove
742 Annie Williamson, Fisher	828 Lenore Isaacson, Portland
743 Belle M. Yeates, Fossil	829 Grace M. Thomas, Hillsboro
744 Minnie Schaller, Salem	830 Maude Brennan, Beaverton
745 E. B. Nedry, Nyssa	831 R. L. Wann, Orenco
746 Luther D. Cook, Paradise	832 C. C. Ailor, Banks
747 Walter T. Clay, John Day	833 Mary Yoder, Beaverton
748 Sister Mary Amelbergo, St. Paul	834 Pearl R. Reed, Oswego
749 Carrie B. Livesley, Deschutes	835 Sisters of St. Mary, Verboort
750 Lena Woodward, Medena, Ohio	836 Marion Crawford, Timber
751 B. H. Calkins, Whiteson	837 Daphne Henderson, Hillsdale
752 A. Devaul, Paisley	838 Mrs. Emma Frazelle, Multnomah
753 Gladys Pearson, Hammond	839 S. M. Ramsay, Tualatin
754 Mary Hoham, Monmouth	840 Elsie Lathrop, Forest Grove
755 Guy L. Lee, Dallas	841 H. T. Evans, Garden Home
756 Mamie Longworth, Perdue	842 Cleo Rector, Hillsboro
757 J. H. Bosard, Roseburg	843 Susie Scott, Sheridan
758 Oscar Gorrell, Oakland	

844 G. A. W. Russell, Buxton
845 Mary L. Criteser, Yoncalla
846 Lura H. Grout, Koler
847 R. G. Hall, Roseburg
848 Lillie MacIver, Roseburg
849 Purl Patrick, Oakland
850 John E. Flurry, Canyonville
851 O. C. Brown, Roseburg
852 Mrs. O. C. Brown, Roseburg
853 B. W. Barnes, Hillsboro
854 Mrs. Minnie Conant, Banks
855 Martha Dillon, Beaverton
856 Winifred Bondy, North Plains
857 E. E. Amsden, Hillsboro
858 Lowell C. Bradford, Hillsboro
859 Jessie M. Cypher, North Plains
860 L. C. Mooberry, Cornelius
861 Mrs. L. L. Trayler, Hillsboro
862 S. W. Babcock, Tigard
863 Linda B. Koch, Cornelius
864 Mrs. M. C. Saltus, Sherwood
865 Myrtle Strickler, Sherwood
866 R. L. Wildman, Timber
867 Roy C. Bierly, Beaverton
868 Mrs. Harriet H. Heller, Portland
869 Ellie M. Sage, Dilley
870 Lottie Cole, Sherwood
871 Laura J. Bell, Forest Grove
872 J. W. Peabody, Forest Grove
873 Helen E. Weed, Dilley
874 Jennie Beamish, Portland
875 Lillian Troedson, Morgan
876 R. H. Harris, Shedd
877 James H. Bohle, Orton
878 Ada M. Peebles, Portland
879 Grace Wiltshire, Bonita
880 Georgia Bell, Portland
881 Florence Bollam, Portland
882 Florence Caldwell, Portland
883 Margaret McCabe, Portland
884 Sarah Beattie, Portland
885 Martha Irwin, Portland
886 Florence Blumenaeur, Portland
887 Alice Ormandy, Portland
888 Evangeline Van Horne, Portland
889 Charlotte Lucas, Portland
890 Mrs. Laura Black, Portland
891 Mrs. Clara Pratt, Stayton
892 Crystal H. West, Mt. Vernon
893 Dorothy Litscher, Sheridan
894 Myrtle Byers, Clarno
895 E. May Moore, Laurel
896 Anna M. Schwall, Cornelius
897 Mrs. Effie R. Arns, Portland
898 Stella M. Hinman, Cherry Grove
899 Clara M. Walker, Gales Creek
900 Frances M. O'Connor, Laurel
901 Wm. Irle, Portland
902 Mrs. Minerva T. Brown, Hillsboro
903 J. M. Stretcher, Beaverton
904 J. R. Chapman, Metzger
905 Cora E. Stephens, Laurel
906 Ruth J. Frost, Gaston
907 Ruth Johnston, Beaverton
908 Gladys O. Willard, Gaston
909 C. L. Nelson, Mountaindale
910 Floy A. Norton, Forest Grove
911 Florence Enschede, Forest Grove
912 E. W. Luecke, Cornelius
913 Jessie L. Smith, Gales Creek
914 Edith Mensing, Hillsboro
915 Mrs. H. A. Ball, Hillsboro
916 Naomi Billeter, Orenco
917 Ruth Canright, Kent
918 Gladys K. Asher, Mt. Vernon
919 Mrs. Cecil Porter, Metolius
920 Nella M. Van Horn, Madras
921 Iva Cox, Lapine
922 A. J. Prideaux, Portland
923 Grace Mann, Portland
924 Artie Nichols, Bonanza
925 Mrs. L. M. Gilbert, Salem
926 Orvill G. Reeves, Marshfield
927 Louis E. Furrow, Myrtle Point
928 S. C. Sherrill, Riverton

929 Nina Dano, Bandon
930 J. F. Croft, Bridge
931 Kate Chatburn, Bandon
932 Rose E. Grossop, Marshfield
933 Mrs. P. M. Wilbur, Marshfield
934 Mrs. Emma E. Easton, Empire
935 B. S. Gannvell, Powers
936 Ernest Root, Myrtle Point
937 Anne Wickman, Marshfield
938 Nettie Belloni, Prosper
939 Hazel I. Matthews, Powers
940 Grace Delmore, Sumner
941 Ellen E. Kelley, Marshfield
942 Helen Robbins, Broadbent
943 Anna M. Thomas, Bridge
944 Metta E. Hansen, Arago
945 Margaret Stambuck, North Bend
946 Anna Clinkinbeard, North Bend
947 Selma Thomas, Marshfield
948 Ernest C. Lloyd, Marshfield
949 Mrs. Ella M. Rea, Bandon
950 Della L. Bryant, Bandon
951 Etta E. Darnell, Myrtle Point
952 Ida E. Gamble, Bandon
953 Ruth Peebley, North Bend
954 Helen E. Mende, North Bend
955 Helen M. Sprague, Marshfield
956 Lola Greene, Myrtle Point
957 May N. Allen, Coquille
958 Lila A. Smith, Bridge
959 Hilda Mcnson, Sulphur Springs
960 Muriel Watkins, Myrtle Point
961 Edith R. McLeod, Marshfield
962 Phina Anderson, Marshfield
963 Elsie G. Philpott, Riverton
964 C. A. Howard, Coquille
965 Agnes McCracken, Myrtle Point
966 Anna Sollie, Bandon
967 W. E. Moses, Marshfield
968 Ellen Knudsen, Empire
969 Clara Moser, Gravelford
970 Ivy Bryan, McMinnville
971 Bessie E. Jones, Cascadia
972 Floyd Bridges, Kellogg
973 Juanita Porter, Wheeler
974 Nora A. Kellow, Hemlock
975 Mrs. J. H. Dustan, Tillamook
976 Alice M. Phillips, Tillamook
977 Mabel R. Terry, Tillamook
978 C. S. Armold, Blaine
979 Mary L. White, Tillamook
980 Gertrude Schlappi, Tillamook
981 H. S. Brimhall, Garibaldi
982 Myrtle Wallin, Tillamook
983 Ethel R. Glines, Tillamook
984 Katherine Loerpabel, Barnesdale
985 Helen L. Clair, Woodburn
986 Evelyn Walker, Gold Hill
987 Clara A. Nelson, Grass Valley
988 Justus A. Miller, Lexington
989 Bertha McCallister, Grants Pass
990 Cordelia Stiles, Salesville, Mont.
991 Ethel Notter, Mulino
992 Virginia V. Worsham, Portland
993 Ruby V. Hazlett, Salem
994 G. B. Lamb, Tillamook
995 Ella R. Sperry, Beaver
996 Harriet M. Ford, Tillamook
997 Mrs. H. C. Hanson, Tillamook
998 C. E. English, Nehalem
999 Sarah Donohue, Oreton
1000 Eleanor Spall, Rockaway
1001 Fred C. Peusser, Hebo
1002 Effie Williamson, Fossil
1003 H. F. Pfingsten, The Dalles
1004 Alah A. Hunt, Fossil
1005 Lela M. Forest, Three Pines
1006 Varena M. Puntenney, Albany
1007 George R. Schreiber, Shedd
1008 Mrs. Eva Scott, Oregon City
1009 Elva Austin, Salem
1010 Emma Kirkpatrick, Newberg
1011 Ruth C. Warren, Harney
1012 Ethel I. Bowers, Mist
1013 A. M. Winn, Vernonia

1014	Mrs. E. Colvin, Clatskanie	1099	Wm. A. Cass, Hood River
1015	Alice Sheehan, Deer Island	1100	Mrs. W. W. Rodwell, Hood River
1016	Lloyd W. Shisler, St. Helens	1101	Sadie McKenzie, Cascade Locks
1017	K. R. Blakeslee, Rainier	1102	Elizabeth Swanson, Hood River
1018	May Novak, Yankton	1103	Mary E. Sheppard, Hood River
1019	Mrs. M. W. Hatfield, Scappoose	1104	Nellie Crocker, Hood River
1020	Gertrude McCarty, Vernonia	1105	Margaret McNamara, Parkdale
1021	W. W. Patterson, Scappoose	1106	N. E. Fertig, Hood River
1022	Florence L. Bennett, Westport	1107	V. M. Vose, Hood River
1023	Frederick I. Knight, St. Helens	1108	Regina Cash, Wyeth
1024	Mary Dahlgren, Warren	1109	Marion Howe, Hood River
1025	Ethel B. Lawpaugh, Yankton	1110	Harriet Alexander, Hood River
1026	Mary R. Thomas, Warren	1111	Edith Baker, Hood River
1027	Mrs. Bird B. Clark, Chapman	1112	C. R. McCoy, Hood River
1028	Mrs. Gladys L. Smith, Vernonia	1113	Mrs. Elizabeth Curtis, Mt. Hood
1029	Bertha Lewison, Clatskanie	1114	Mrs. J. H. Crenshaw, Dee
1030	David L. Cook, Newberg	1115	J. O. McLaughlin, Hood River
1031	W. E. Buell, Buena Vista	1116	Selma E. Lahti, Prairie City
1032	W. Hurley, Keasey	1117	Echo Githens, Morgan
1033	Gladys Richey, Rainier	1118	Dora G. Jackson, Gooseberry
1034	Mary McGregor, Marshland	1119	Raymond L. Cornwell, Madras
1035	Clarence Phillips, Clatskanie	1120	Mrs. B. Jorgensen, Hillsboro
1036	James Dodson, Scappoose	1121	Ruth Howard, Jefferson
1037	Agnes Brown, Trenholm	1122	L. A. Wright, Eugene
1038	Florence Taylor, Goble	1123	Lucile Risch, Catlow
1039	Madeline Slotboom, St. Helens	1124	Hazel Bevans, Burns
1040	Velma Snider, Mist	1125	Henrietta Hoyser, Salem
1041	Mrs. E. E. Mallaber, Goble	1126	Mrs. E. K. Mitchell, Tillamook
1042	Jessie H. McDonald, Scappoose	1127	Ila Knox, Spray
1043	Lillie M. Leith, St. Helens	1128	Roy W. Glass, Philomath
1044	Ethel A. Allen, Rainier	1129	Estella Phiester, Medford
1045	G. W. Brown, Houlton	1130	Ora Cox, Medford
1046	Mrs. Ada Holaday, Scappoose	1131	Murl Coffeen, Medford
1047	Lyle B. Chappell, Quincy	1132	Sue Hoffman, Medford
1048	Lillian Cooper, Goble	1133	G. W. Godward, Jacksonville
1049	Hilda Muhr, Warren	1134	Elizabeth Ferguson, Medford
1050	Madelina Thomas, Warren	1135	Heloise Phillips, Echo
1051	C. C. Cassatt, St. Helens	1136	Fern Hoisington, Pilot Rock
1052	C. E. Lake, St. Helens	1137	Mrs. Paralee Hailey, Pendleton
1053	O. T. Tabler, Rainier	1138	Alice Hudson, Hermiston
1054	J. W. Allen, St. Helens	1139	Ada Earl, Stanfield
1055	Mabel Molin, Bacona	1140	Anice Barnes, Stanfield
1056	Bessie Kennard, Falls City	1141	J. O. Russell, Athena
1057	Mamie E. Ayres, Beaverton	1142	Lillian D. Dobson, Athena
1058	Marie Groves, Carlton	1143	Mrs. Ora A. Powell, Freewater
1059	Agatha DeCarle, Gales Creek	1144	Clara Partridge, Athena
1060	Margaret Davis, Mt. Vernon	1145	A. T. Parks, Pendleton
1061	Angeline Adoradio, Dundee	1146	Nellie McCane, Helix
1062	Julia C. Harrison, Narrows	1147	J. W. Smith, Milton
1063	Effie M. Lovegren, Cherry Grove	1148	H. M. Allen, Pendleton
1064	Elizabeth C. Riecker, Monmouth	1149	Lucy Coffey, Freewater
1065	Anna Gallup, Mist	1150	J. A. Hawks, Nolin
1066	Mrs. Effie Wilson, St. Helens	1151	F. W. Beatty, McKay
1067	Roberta Smith, Drewsey	1152	H. C. Fetter, Weston
1068	Glennie McBane, Culver	1153	Gilbert C. Woods, Freewater
1069	J. Victoria Huston, Tumalo	1154	Bessie Hatch, Nye
1070	A. L. Stephens, Taft	1155	Mabel Montgomery, Weston
1071	Edith Witzel, Monmouth	1156	Violet Kendig, Adams
1072	Nellie Springer, Colton	1157	Anne L. Saling, Nye
1073	Henry H. Dirksen, Hubbard	1158	Mrs. M. L. Fulkerson, Salem
1074	Norma Holman, Airlie	1159	Mrs. Orpha K. Sevey, Stanfield
1075	J. Y. Bethune, Salem	1160	Metta Johnson, Milton
1076	Victor Boyd, Leona	1161	Vesta Cutsforth, Pendleton
1077	Marjorie Whipple, Gunter	1162	L. B. Kicker, Milton
1078	Mrs. Mamie J. Rafferty, Banks	1163	Edith May Richardson, Helix
1079	Mamie Cachelin, Dixonville	1164	W. S. Mayberry, Milton
1080	Kathryn Dougherty, Silverton	1165	Luella B. Pinkerton, Weston
1081	Harriet Chambers, Silverton	1166	Mrs. H. W. Drew, Helix
1082	Mary E. Frazier, Hood River	1167	H. W. Drew, Helix
1083	Cleo Shoup, Parkdale	1168	Pauline Heacock, Pilot Rock
1084	W. H. Alwin, Cascade Locks	1169	Mrs. L. B. Cordery, Adams
1085	Charlotte Kinnaird, Hood River	1170	Mrs. Florence Kelley, Milton
1086	Antonia A. Bauer, Hood River	1171	Irma Belles, Wallula, Wash
1087	Mrs. Mary Millard, Sheridan	1172	J. S. Danforth, Freewater
1088	Ray R. Canterbury, Tumalo	1173	Rose Monterastelli, Helix
1089	J. F. Santee, Connell, Wash.	1174	Myrtle Sneve, Freewater
1090	Isolda B. Roper, Antelope	1175	Hattie E. Pulliam, Pilot Rock
1091	Anna C. Godbersen, Hood River	1176	C. E. Graham, Pendleton
1092	Gertrude Jones, Hood River	1177	Kate Christensen, Freewater
1093	Mrs. W. E. Blashfield, Hood River	1178	Alice Butler, Pendleton
1094	Eleanor Coe, Hood River	1179	Glee Wharton, Freewater
1095	Elizabeth Grant, Cascade Locks	1180	Hazel Adams, Pendleton
1096	Etheljane McDonald, Hood River	1181	Eunice Smith, Helix
1097	Sylvia Elder, Mosier	1182	Frank R. Doble, Pine Grove
1098	Clara E. Rand, Hood River	1183	Mrs. L. D. Idleman, Pendleton

1184	Erma D. Heacock, Pendleton	1269	Roy Conklin, Wallowa
1185	E. E. Geiss, Pendleton	1270	Elizabeth Bond, La Grande
1186	W. C. Howard, Stanfield	1271	Isabelle Miller, La Grande
1187	Mrs. Margaret Cramer, Holdman	1272	Janette Willgerodt, Flora
1188	Camille Dolson, Pendleton	1273	Myrtle Schuman, Promise
1189	H. T. Drill, Pendleton	1274	Mildred Yantis, Baker
1190	Paul M. Reed, Freewater	1275	Nettie Murray, Flora
1191	Sarah E. Wilson, Adams	1276	Ellen Long, Haines
1192	Mae W. Chrisholm, Pendleton	1277	E. Leota Holmes, Wallowa
1193	Ethel Freeman, Pendleton	1278	Minnie Brown, Baker
1194	Walton J. Roork, Adams	1279	Julia Coleman, Sparta
1195	Agnes Carlson, Touchet, Wash	1280	Edna A. Dammon, Sumpter
1196	Jessie B. Brierly, Athena	1281	Reba Williamson, La Grande
1197	Inez Wagner, Umapine	1282	Esther Harris, Unity
1198	Leota Wagner, Athena	1283	Alice McCurdy, Granite
1199	Juanita Fridly, Adams	1284	Fred G. Potter, Promise
1200	Daisy McPherson, Pendleton	1285	Gene W. Hall, North Powder
1201	Edith M. Fraker, Pendleton	1286	Nellie Rush, Elgin
1202	Frances M. Simmons, Adams	1287	Stella Mayfield, Elgin
1203	Nell Savely, Adams	1288	Mrs. May Hodson, Enterprise
1204	Louise A. Deute, Pendleton	1289	Mrs. Nettie C. Bussard, Halfway
1205	Ethel E. Haw, Pendleton	1290	Bessie M. Conley, Enterprise
1206	Olive Bovee, Pendleton	1291	Nina Kane, La Grande
1207	Elsa Strever, Pilot Rock	1292	E. May Barton, Minam
1208	Grace Frost, Pilot Rock	1293	Mary Braughton, Enterprise
1209	Esther F. Compton, Milton	1294	Lenora Huff, Baker
1210	Bessie Swain, Burns	1295	Cora Barnes, Durkee
1211	E. G. Bailey, Ontario	1296	Vincent N. Patterson, Chico
1212	Hazel Harris, Silverton	1297	Alpha Busick, Union
1213	Juanita Randall, Crawfordsville	1298	M. Elma Cusick, North Powder
1214	Nina M. Conlee, Marshfield.	1299	Esther Koplin, Enterprise
1215	Arma Keen, Halsey	1300	Lewis E. Reese, Elgin
1216	Nora Ward, Dorena	1301	Mrs. Rose Clawson, Elgin
1217	E. R. Jones, Broadbent	1302	J. I. Sturgill, Durkee
1218	Julia Sears, Portland	1303	G. W. Sammons, Imnah
1219	Anna DeLin, Portland	1304	Teresa Castle, La Grande
1220	Mathilda Ahrends, Portland	1305	Dora Caton, Durkee
1221	Lillian J. Goodspeed, Portland	1306	Frances O. Lees, Baker
1222	R. R. Steele, Portland.	1307	Retta B. Mercer, North Powder
1223	P. N. Plamondon, Seattle, Wash.	1308	Mae A. Gilliam, Baker
1224	Mrs. W. W. Wiley, Tillamook	1309	Frieda M. Euberg, Baker
1225	Stella G. Goyne, Tillamook	1310	D. Chesley Bones, Halfway
1226	E. K. Barnes, Perrydale	1311	R. A. Wilkerson, La Grande
1227	Estelle McClure, Prineville	1312	Anna Meyer, Baker
1228	Geo. F. Thompson, Willamette	1313	Martha Miller, Elgin
1229	Claire G. Morey, Gervais	1314	Royal J. Allen, Cove
1230	E. R. Houck, Alvadore	1315	B. Southwick, Promise
1231	Mrs. Amy Campbell, Winant	1316	Edith Welch, Alicel
1232	Martha Hinkle, Sutherlin	1317	Grace Fine, Elgin
1233	Mary Elliott, Monkland	1318	Ruth A. Ghormley, La Grande
1234	Laura Waggoner, Independence	1319	Helen Huff, Baker
1235	Curtis Christy, Sisters	1320	Hulda Anderson, La Grande
1236	Eva Alfrey, McMinnville	1321	Nellie G. Neill, La Grande
1237	Martha Jensen, Silverton	1322	Ethel L. Davis, Baker
1238	Mrs. Clara Vickers, Seaside	1323	Erma F. Cole, Audrey
1239	John L. Ashton, Derby	1324	Manuel Snider, La Grande
1240	Enid Elliott, The Dalles	1325	Beatrice Pugh, Kamela
1241	L. L. Baker, St. Helens	1326	Isabelle Gray, Philomath
1242	Susie M. Barton, Devils Lake	1327	Estelle J. McIntyre, Portland
1243	Marie O. Glaze, Gaston	1328	Emily C. Roberts, Portland
1244	Marie Reese, Salem	1329	Isabelle Chalmers, Portland
1245	Edith Bork, La Grande	1330	Josephine Lisher, Portland
1246	Grace Van Winkle, Suplee	1331	A. M. Cannon, Portland
1247	Laura Edgerton, Ft. Bidwell, Cal.	1332	Grace Sweeney, Taft
1248	Paul Wiser, Carlton	1333	Eleanor Warren, Dundee
1249	Mabel E. Orcutt, Payette, Ida.	1334	Vida A. Dunlop, Halsey
1250	James R. Forsythe, Monmouth	1335	F. Silsbee, Aurora
1251	Betha Graham, Rolyat	1336	Raymond E. Baker, Coquille
1252	Alma E. Riley, Beaver	1337	Dorothea McCauley, Terrebonne
1253	Marion Z. Clarke, Medford	1338	Dorothea Pike, Birkenfeld
1254	Eileen Tompkins, Cascade Locks	1339	Mrs. Enos M. Fluhrer, Mayger
1255	Lelia Drew, Tillamook	1340	Dorothy Zinser, Oswego
1256	A. Dawkins, Grants Pass	1341	Margaret Horton, North Powder
1257	I. D. Serfling, Thomas	1342	Stella M. Denzer, Summer Lake
1258	W. W. Hewitt, Umpqua	1343	F. E. Dunton, Moro
1259	Susie Mahan, Baker	1344	Roy Bowman, Moro
1260	Vera Storie, Durkee	1345	Cecil Lutey, Toledo
1261	Eleanor Storie, Gypsum	1346	Grace M. Tyler, Heppner
1262	J. C. Hall, Wallowa	1347	Lula E. Peterson, Suver
1263	Wilfred Davies, Troy	1348	Nina M. Ross, Clover Flat
1264	J. F. Engle, Halfway	1349	Cora D. Fraine, Portland
1265	Mrs. Emmett Temple, La Grande	1350	E. D. Ressler, Corvallis
1266	Jessie F. Hindman, Baker	1351	Hettie Powers, Joseph
1267	Erma Hawley, Baker	1352	Frances Bartshe, Payette, Ida.
1268	Edna M. Bennett, Baker	1353	J. E. Calavan, Oregon City

1354 Ada Ross, Lexington	1439 Edith E. Smith, Powell Buttes
1355 Mattie Knottingham, Skullspring	1440 H. K. Shirk, Burns
1356 Lena Ulen, Portland	1441 Gertrude Imus, Dundee
1357 Blanche Wilson, Terrebonne	1442 Wm. Ray McNair, Newberg
1358 Emma Weaver, Vincent	1443 Margaret Riley, Albany
1359 Ina B. Graham, Falls City	1444 O. M. Washburn, Fairview
1360 Augusta Parker, Klamath Falls	1445 Ruth A. Gray, Nehalem
1361 Mary Stewart, Klamath Falls	1446 Anna Riebhoff, Prineville
1362 Nellie McAndrews, Klamath Falls	1447 Olive L. Dawson, Lents
1363 Nett D. Peterson, Klamath Falls	1448 John D. Taylor, Narrows
1364 R. H. Dunbar, Klamath Falls	1449 Grade Teachers' Ass'n., Portland
1365 W. S. Buel, Tillamook	1450 Cornelia Marvin, Salem
1366 A. B. Haverly, Woodburn	1451 Bonnie Olson, Waconda
1367 B. G. Harding, Rogue River	1452 S. I. Pratt, Corvallis
1368 Albert Schreder, Prineville	1453 M. E. Hay, Redmond
1369 Howard S. Miller, Yamhill	1454 Etta Lamson, Monmouth
1370 Hazel Fawcett, Coquille	1455 Chas. H. McKnight, Junction City
1371 Lincoln Savage, Grants Pass	1456 Mrs. J. A. Flanigan, Junction City
1372 J. E. Drillette, Marion	1457 Ray G. Penney, Springfield
1373 Violet Rush, Elgin	1458 Aubrey G. Smith, Eugene
1374 Evaline Falconer, Enterprise	1459 P. M. Stroud, Springfield
1375 Effie McDaniel, Portland	1460 Minnie Morris, Marcola
1376 Elizabeth Robinson, Medford	1461 H. W. Gustin, Mohawk
1377 Altha Chandler, Devil's Lake	1462 G. T. Beck, Elmira
1378 Margaret Reilly, Hood River	1463 Elizabeth Wilson, Eugene
1379 H. O. Pearson, Eugene	1464 O. H. Jones, Eugene
1380 Florence Pifer, Parkdale	1465 Irene Holdredge, Junction City
1381 Opal C. Rice, Helix	1466 Margaret McCulloch, Eugene
1382 Edith M. Clark, Astoria	1467 Grace Henderson, Eugene
1383 B. T. Youel, Beulah	1468 Frances E. Cox, Cottage Grove
1384 E. F. Carleton, Salem	1469 Marion Harper, Springfield
1385 Gertrude A. Orth, Portland	1470 A. I. O'Reilly, Marcola
1386 Owena Crow, Scappoose	1471 Henry W. Chezem, Florence
1387 Mrs. Janet M. Grant, Fairview	1472 Nora Queen, Trent
1388 C. E. Barker, Beaverton	1473 Orpha Benson, Cottage Grove
1389 Amy E. Whipple, Monmouth	1474 Ambrosine Murphy, Portland
1390 Mrs. J. A. Bohannon, Toledo	1475 Elba Huston, Elmira
1391 D. W. Hammock, Condon	1476 Jane Gilcrist, Crow
1392 Callie B. Shelton, Beulah	1477 G. E. Jacoby, Pleasant Hill
1393 Mrs. J. C. Grater, Ashwood	1478 F. F. Cooper, Pleasant Hill
1394 Lenora Armstrong, Baker	1479 Ona V. Liles, Lorane
1395 Nellie A. Pugh, Molalla	1480 Ernest Purvance, Cottage Grave
1396 Mrs. G. L. Whiteis, Prineville	1481 W. P. Sheridan, Eugene
1397 A. C. Crews, Hood River	1482 Dell Bown, Elmira
1398 Mrs. A. F. Beardsley, Salem	1483 Mrs. Grace Paslay, Eugene
1399 Elina Thorsteinson, Salem	1484 Angie V. Hall, Noti
1400 Hettie A. Thomas, Roy	1485 Esther Wilkins, Eugene
1401 Emma Wilson, Aloha	1486 Ethol McFarland, Eugene
1402 Mrs. Agnes Roberts, Yamhill	1487 Emma Chase, Eugene
1403 Frank K. Welles, Salem	1488 Lottie Van Scholack, Dorena
1404 John W. Anderson, Maupin	1489 Lawrence Ryan, Paris
1405 Esther Evans, Banks	1490 Mrs. F. F. Cooper, Pleasant Hill
1406 Mary D. Schlegel, Pilot Rock	1491 Ida Patterson, Eugene
1407 Jennie Hunter, Medford	1492 Mary Rouse, Springfield
1408 Grace M. Wilson, Newberg	1493 Anna McCormick, Springfield
1409 Sarah M. Parr, Timber	1494 Hazel Loynes, Springfield
1410 Merl E. Dimick, Hubbard.	1495 F. A. Scofield, Eugene
1411 Dora Fridley, Wasco	1496 Carrie A. Mathers, Eugene
1412 Salome Sias, Grass Valley	1497 G. A. Burkhead, Wendling
1413 Mrs. M. Milstead, Kent	1498 Chas. L. Weaver, Earl
1414 Floyd E. Clodfelter, Wasco	1499 Lola Howe, Eugene
1415 Lillian Schassen, Grass Valley	1500 Ida Mae Smith, Eugene
1416 Lola Messinger, Moro	1501 Ida O. Sias, Eugene
1417 Hazel Sneve, Wasco	1502 Echo Drury Spores, Eugene
1418 Myrtle Sawyer, Monkland	1503 Lida Garrett, Creswell
1419 Frank E. Fagan, Moro	1504 Lucy Ely, Eugene
1420 R. J. Baldwin, Grass Valley	1505 Jessie Fagerstrom, Eugene
1421 W. A. Terrall, Wasco	1506 Maude M. Drury, Springfield
1422 Isabelle McGregor, Rufus	1507 Bess Van Matre, Crow
1423 Irene Barnes, Wasco	1508 Maude Gerald, Eugene
1424 Vera G. Knotts, Moody	1509 Anna T. Buck, Eugene
1425 Nina Searcy, Moro	1510 W. R. Rutherford, Eugene
1426 Alta Odell, Wasco	1511 W. P. Boynton, Eugene
1427 Edna Prieve, Grass Valley	1512 Mary Powell, Anlauf
1428 Blanche DeArmond, Moro	1513 Mrs. Ella A. Fisher, Eugene
1429 Evelyn Grebe, Grebe	1514 Ruth E. Ellis, Goshen
1430 Catherine Fleck, Biggs	1515 Jennie Bossen, Eugene
1431 Lula Mobley, Mikkalo	1516 Mrs. Otto Gilstrap, Eugene
1432 Lucy D. Hoye, Portland	1517 Ella M. Deyoe, Eugene
1433 Lucie M. George, Portland	1518 E. L. Keezel, Eugene
1434 Martha Loretz, Mitchell	1519 R. S. Goff, Goshen
1435 E. A. Brown, Gold Beach	1520 Sara Van Meter, Medford
1436 Hazel M. Stanton, The Dalles	1521 Agnes Meyer, Yoncalla
1437 Myrtle Albright, Marquam	1522 Myrtle S. Freeman, Junction City
1138 W. L. Smith, Riddle	1523 Elsa R. Berner, Portland

1524	Margaret Monroe, Portland	1609	J. W. Lorett, McMinnville
1525	V. B. Goin, Portland	1610	Elma Poulsen, Newberg
1526	Mary E. Daugherty, Grandview	1611	Zadie Hartman, McMinnville
1527	Winifred Ingraham, Astoria	1612	A. C. Arehart, Lafayette
1528	J. T. Lee, Warrenton	1613	Carlotta Crowley, McMinnville
1529	Gladys Palmer, Vesper	1614	Mrs. Carrie Ogle, Portland
1530	Cynthia H. Roberts, Astoria	1615	R. G. Dykstra, Independence
1531	Florence R. Sale, Astoria	1616	Benedictine Sisters, Mt. Angel
1532	James F. Elton, Astoria	1617	Etta E. Wrenn, The Dalles
1533	Bert P. Lovett, Seaside	1618	Mrs. Stella Ingle, LaGrande
1534	F. E. Burns, Knappa	1619	Frances U'Ren, Madras
1535	Isabel L. Snider, Hamlet	1620	Jessie W. Hineline, Hermiston
1536	Anna Lewis, Astoria	1621	Bessie Strebin, Troutdale
1537	Lillie Lewis, Astoria	1622	Ruth Alder, LaGrande
1538	Edna I. Lamar, Astoria	1623	J. N. Shainwald, Portland
1539	Mrs. E. H. Smith, Jewell	1624	Gladys Bradley, Beaver
1540	May Utzinger, Astoria	1625	R. W. Kirk, Tillamook
1541	Gertrude Couillard, Svensen	1626	Nannie Bagby, McMinnville
1542	M. E. Grace, Astoria	1627	Cordelia Murphy, Portland
1543	Mrs. Mabel Washbond, Gearhart	1628	Lucina Richardson, Springfield
1544	Mrs. A. L. Fulton, Astoria	1629	Franklin B. Launer, Canby
1545	Myron O. Gaston, Astoria	1630	E. A. Miller, Salem
1547	Roy C. Andrews, Astoria	1631	Cora Darr, Portland
1548	Nelle M. Bonney, Estacada	1632	Blanche E. Delury, Portland
1549	Mae McCann, Gales Creek	1633	T. C. Young, Marshfield
1550	Laura A. Simmons, Fossil	1634	Henrietta Stermer, Dayton
1551	Electa Chapman, Haines	1635	Inez Miller, Wilbur
1552	Anna Fischer, Salem	1636	Enid Cawlfield, Burns
1553	L. W. Grimm, Shaw	1637	Lena Benson, Huntington
1554	Guy E. Dyar, Eugene	1638	U. S. Dotson, Salem.
1555	Mrs. Emma Keen, Beaverton	1639	Dr. Henry Suzzallo, Seattle
1556	Alma Babcock, Molalla.	1640	R. L. Kirk, Springfield
1557	Kate M. Moore, Yankton	1641	T. C. Brown, Roseburg
1558	Anna Kelley, Kent	1642	Myrtle Thornburg, Dermitt, Nev.
1559	Jeanette G. Leggett, Wilbur	1643	Margaret G. Barry, Astoria
1560	R. U. Moore, McMinnville	1644	Lelia Eaton, Talent
1561	F. L. Strait, Newberg	1645	Mabel F. Goyne, Pacific City
1562	Mrs. Grace Duren, Sheridan	1646	Isabelle T. Mann, Rainier
1563	Olive Ramsey, Springbrook	1647	Bessie M. Gayette, Hood River
1564	Ella S. Thomas, Amity	1648	Henriette Cornelius, Hood River
1565	Laura Judy, Springbrook	1649	W. E. Keplinger, Pendleton
1566	Mrs. Elizabeth Meyer, Newberg	1650	J. G. Imel, Astoria
1567	F. H. Buchanan, McMinnville	1651	Opal E. Bretz, Heppner
1568	Geo. A. Briscoe, Ashland	1652	Mrs. Ida Kidder, Corvallis
1569	E. J. Hadley, Portland	1653	C. H. Eagy, Hubbard
1570	Minnie Davis, Gresham	1654	Elizabeth Matthews, Oak Grove
1571	Ruth E. Crouch, Portland	1655	Jean M. Byers, Macleay
1572	Elsie A. Coe, Hamlet	1656	L. M. McCullough, LaGrande
1573	Geo. A. Gabriel, Dayton	1657	A. J. Hanby, Medford
1574	Maude Williamson, Amity	1658	Ella Carpenter, Portland
1575	Ada Farmer, Rickreall	1659	L. A. Wiley, Portland
1576	Charles Boosinger, Sheridan	1660	Agnes Matlock, Portland
1577	Mrs. Leota Leever, McMinnville	1661	Vida Hammond, Portland
1578	Flora Clement, Salem	1662	Grace McCord, Portland
1579	D. Lynn Gubser, Dayton	1663	Nellie Beckett, Portland
1580	S. David Titus, Amity	1664	Mrs. Sadie Griffith, Portland
1581	Lilly Hagman, Willamina	1665	Annette Duthie, Portland
1582	Mrs. J. R. Whitcomb, Sheridan	1666	Edith Costello, Portland
1583	Mrs. Celinda Deford, Laurel	1667	Mildred Greenman, Portland
1584	Mildred Pope, Amity	1668	Rhea Benson, Portland
1585	Marie Vinzelberg, McMninville	1669	Hulda Scheel, Portland
1586	Lena Stilwell, Dayton	1670	Helen Peery, Portland
1587	Mrs. Grace Hollister, Amity	1671	Mrs. Mamie Rosenburg, Portland
1588	Ethel Bolen, Carlton	1672	Jemima Bell, Portland
1589	Nellie F. McNeill, Dundee	1673	Harriet Thayer, Portland
1590	Ella Anderson, Amity	1674	Adeline Hammond, Portland
1591	Julia Huss, McMinnville	1675	Mrs. J. C. Taggart, Woods
1592	Laura Beckwith, Sheridan	1676	Florence M. Goodman, Prosper
1593	Julia Lewis, Dayton	1677	Minnie M. Herman, Myrtle Point
1594	Alma E. Stone, Newberg		
1595	Gertrude K. Brown, McMinnville		
1596	Maggie A. Triplett, Lafayette		
1597	Laura C. Morris, Newberg		
1598	Mabel E. Rush, Newberg		
1599	J. A. Nagel, Sheridan		
1600	Ellen Jackson, McMinnville		
1601	Frank J. Deach, Newberg		
1602	Pauline Alderman, McMinnville		
1603	M. Esther Miles, Dundee		
1604	Geo. W. Hug, McMinnville		
1605	Earl Kilpatrick, Eugene		
1606	Kate L. Knox, McMinnville		
1607	Amy Johnson, McMinnville		
1608	C. L. Van Wormer, Newberg		

Opportunities are very sensitive; if you slight their first visit you seldom see them again.

When buying your ticket to the meeting of the State Teachers' Association, be sure to take a receipt from the station agent so that you may secure the return fare at one-third.

County Superintendents' Department

Edited by CLYDE T. BONNEY, The Dalles, Oregon

The Oregon Trinity.

The Department of Agriculture at Washington, D. C., the Oregon Agricultural College at Corvallis, and the State Department of Education at Salem constitute this trinity. Therein abideth education, organization and cooperation and the greatest of these is co-operation, because through it, the best of good things is made possible.

Industrial club work is here, and here to stay. It has been adopted as a permanent part of the Oregon school system. It is vital to the success of the work in Oregon that it remain a part of the school system. This is possible only by having at least two field workers under the direct supervision of the superintendent of public instruction.

Industrial club work is more than worthy. It is fundamental. No county that has it established would think of laying it aside and the counties which have done only a little will the sooner come into their own through a continuation of the splendid trinity which we now have. A continuing appropriation providing for two field workers from the state superintendent's office should be passed by the coming legislature in order that industrial club work in Oregon may not suffer.—Editor.

The Importance of Field Workers.

The school and the home must be brought closer together. Club work is designed to make the school work apply to the farm, the home and the practical things in life. It must be correlated with the school system. Its effect should be to help in the teaching of arithmetic, language and all the common branches. A boy who has grown a patch of corn and kept a careful project report, should be and is better able to apply every subject in school. This has actually been the effect. Boys and girls with little interest in school have, through club work, done better school work. Many of our club winners have excelled in school work also.

Now this is where the state department of education functions in its relation to industrial club work. If school and club work are closely associated and correlated then the department of education must have a live interest and direction in this club education as well as in all other forms of education. The state department maintains this direct connection through its field workers.

Men, young in enthusiasm, spirit and vision and old in judgment and experience like Mr. Maris and Mr. Harrington, carry the gospel of club work to every county that is willing to receive it. Smiling at untold hardships, conducting campaigns through vicissitudes that would stop the German army and fired with the irresistible gospel of industrial education like a modern Marquette, these men are pioneering the way for a more efficient citizenship and a greater Oregon.

We of the younger generation like to work side by side with the men trained in the University of Hard Knocks, men who first caught the vision of the relation of efficiency in education and the idealizing of home life, and organizers of a future industrial Oregon.—A. R. Chase, County Agent for Wasco County.

Method of Hiring Teachers.

Every county superintendent realizes the need for a change in the method of hiring teachers for the rural schools. The least that can be done along this line is to make the county superintendent a member of the school board for the purpose of hiring teachers in districts of the third class. The following is a bill proposed by the legislative committee of the county superintendents: "The board at a general or special meeting called for that purpose, shall hire teachers, and shall make contracts with such teachers which specify the wages, number of months to be taught, and time employment is to begin, as agreed upon by the parties and shall file such contracts in the office of the district clerk. No contract shall be made with any teacher who is related by blood or marriage within the third degree to any member of the school board without the concurrence of all the members of the board, by a vote duly entered on the clerk's records of proceedings. In districts of the third class the county superintendent shall be a member, ex-officio, of each such board when it meets for the purpose of hiring teachers, and it shall require the concurrence of three members of such board to hire a teacher. When not present in person, the vote of the county superintendent may be transmitted by mail or otherwise to be filed with the district clerk, copies of which vote may be filed with members of the school board, and such vote shall be counted for the teacher designated therein. The district clerk shall give the county superintendent at least 10 days' notice of the exact time and place of any such meeting to hire teachers, and if after receiving such notice the superintendent is not present, and has no vote filed with the clerk or with any member of the board, then a majority of those present may proceed to elect teachers. Duplicates of all applications for teaching positions in third class districts shall be filed with the superintendent. The superintendent may from time to time suggest suitable dates for meetings at which to hire teachers. Unless otherwise provided in the teachers' contract, it shall be understood that the branches to be taught are those provided in the state course for the first eight grades, except school law and theory and practice of teaching."

Clackamas County.

A very interesting local teachers' meeting was held at Estacada, October 28. Assistant State Superintendent Frank K. Welles and Superintendent Fred J. Tooze, of Oregon City school, were the principal speakers.

The state-wide standardization requirements for elementary schools are being stressed in most the the schools by boards of directors, teachers, parents and pupils. They are no longer looked upon as an experiment, but they are recognized as a potent factor in making more efficient schools.

Mt. Pleasant, Barlow, and Sandy schools have just met the requirements and have been added to the standard list. Several other schools will soon meet them. Clackamas county now has 52 standard schools.

The Willamette High School was added to the high school standard list in October. This makes a total of eight in this county. The location of these high schools is such that it places a high school in reach of every boy and girl.

The necessity for play sheds has not been overlooked. Oswego and Willamette schools have added magnificent big playsheds to their school plants. The Clackamas school has one under construction. These sheds are 80 feet long, 40 feet wide, and 14 feet to 16 feet high, except the one at Clackamas which is to be 94 feet long. They are sufficiently large for basketball and all other play apparatus. They cost about $1000 each.

Haxilla and Echo Dell school districts have built and equipped modern one-room buildings. The Milwaukie school district has just put the finishing touches on their strictly modern eight-room building on one floor. This building is occupied by the elementary schools.

Clarks school gave a very interesting entertainment at the Clarks Hall Friday evening, November 24. It was well patronized, even though the rain was pouring and a small admission fee was charged. The teachers and pupils are to be commended on their splendid program. L. P. Harrington and Superintendent J. E. Calavan were present and made short talks. The proceeds are to help defray the standardization expense.

Malheur County.

Enrollment in the three standard high schools of the county has increased very materially this year. Ontario now has 161 pupils, Vale 60, and Nyssa 56. Doubtless much of this increase is due to the fact that the law now requires the county to pay the tuition of boys and girls from the rural and village districts who attend these schools.

The school children of the county respond well to the call of Supt. Arne of the Boys' and Girls' Aid Society of Portland for donations of money and supplies. It is impossible, at this time, to make a report of what was done by all of the schools. Supt. Bailey of Ontario reports the splendid contribution of $26.50 and Supt. Brainard's

school in Nyssa has ready for shipment some 200 pounds of potatoes, about 200 pounds of assorted vegetables, 30 quarts of fruit, and some clothing. As the society feels the need of more extra help this year and the railroads ship contributions of food and clothing to them free of charge from November 15 to December 31, any school that did not assist at Thanksgiving time may do so at Christmas. No more worthy object of charity than the Aid Society exists in Oregon.

Creston is the only school in the county making an allowance in their budget for hot lunches. This is the third year that Creston has furnished hot lunches for their children and they certainly deserve much credit. Other rural districts would do well to adopt the plan. Mrs. Delva St. Clair Wall is teaching in this school.

Miss George Hodgson and Miss Mary Fikan are teaching their third year in Juntura. They are doing the same splendid grade of work that has characterized the Juntura schools for the past few years.

The Jamieson people are justly proud of one of the most up-to-date two room schools in Eastern Oregon. The building is nicely furnished and is fitted with sanitary toilets, drinking fountains and other modern conveniences. The teachers and pupils felt that since the people of the district had given them the beautiful new building they should show their appreciation by adding something useful. By their own efforts they have given the school a new range on which the girls will learn to cook and some manual training equipment with which the boys can work. Under the direction of Mr. Zevely and Miss Baird, teachers, and Mrs. Cox, a good friend of the school, the boys and girls have taken up Industrial Club work with great enthusiasm. Excellent class room work is being done in the Jamieson school. This is the second year that Mr. Zevely and Miss Baird have had the work in charge.

School work in Malheur county is progressing nicely. There are now 66 school districts with 115 teachers employed. Parents and patrons are co-operating with the teachers in their efforts to build up the schools and good results are being obtained. Special mention should be made of the two splendid Basque schools in the southern part of Malheur county where teachers are employed for a term of 10 months at $100 a month. Both schools are small but the parents of the boys and girls, most of whom know very little of American school work, wish to make well educated citizens of their children. They certainly deserve great credit for their efforts along this line.

Industrial clubs are being organized throughout the county as a result of a visit from Mr. Seymour last month. More than the usual amount of interest is being shown.

Columbia County.

The county superintendent visited the 15 Nehalem school recently, and as a general thing, found pupils and teachers doing splendid work. The only drawback was a lack of numbers for which neither teachers nor pupils were to blame. About one-half of Columbia county is owned by the timber interests which prohibit access to home builders. The Nehalem valley is practically an immense body of standing green timber which must be removed before the country can settle up. School consolidation is the vital question in the Nehalem valley, and as a splendid system of roads is being built, consolidation is now becoming prevalent. Vernonia has consolidated several districts already, and will consolidate further. Mist is a natural community center, and several schools should consolidate at this center. The Mist school is already overcrowded and a new building is badly needed; the people are fully aware of this, and in the course of a short time, much improvement in school facilities may be expected at Mist.

The rural schools in Columbia county, as a rule, are not what they should be. Many buildings are poor, anything but modern, and equipment is lacking. However, many districts have built modern schools and are leading the way; others will follow. The country boys and girls are entitled to the same school privileges as the city pupils. The country school districts are more than able to provide school facilities for their children. The country school districts do not have to levy 8 or 10 mills for city purposes, are not worried about street improvements, sewers, etc.; even a 5 mill levy for school purposes would ordinarily be more than sufficient for them to run a most up-to-date school, fully equal to the best.

District No. 28, South Scappoose; District No. 45, West of Yankton; District No. 43, adjoining the last named district; No. 12, near Rainier; No. 29, near Mayger; No. 18, Keasey; and No. 34, near Deer Island, have already led the way with modern buildings, and most of them are well equipped. No. 43, Trenholm, is in the lead of all rural schools, and is still making improvements such as beautification of school grounds, permanent walks, and electric lights. It is the only rural school in the county that has electric lights. Play sheds and play apparatus are becoming more and more prevalent. District No. 33 is to erect a new school building very soon. District No. 55 will erect a neat, modern play shed this fall. Columbia county has a better teaching force than ever before.

Marion County.

The regular meeting of the Marion County Parent-Teacher Association was held in Salem, Saturday, November 11. Reports were made by the delegates of the progress in various parts of the county. Mrs. D. C. Thoms, vice-president of the State Parent-Teacher Association was present and gave an interesting address, as did the county president, Mrs. M. L. Fulkerson. Prof. Seymour told of his experience and the success of such organizations in Polk county and Prof. F. K. Welles gave many good suggestions on what to do at the local meetings.

Nearly 100 teachers gathered at the local institute at Silverton on Saturday, November 18. At the morning session many important problems were discussed by the teachers and principals. In the afternoon a splendid program was given by the pupils of the Silverton schools. This was followed with addresses by State Superintendent Churchill and Prof. Arthur D. Carpenter of Seattle.

A School Board Convention convened at Salem, Saturday, December 2. Eighty districts sent delegates to this meeting. Practically all of the delegates took part in the discussions. The principal addresses were given by Governor Withycombe, Prof. M. S. Pittman, and Mrs. M. L. Fulkerson.

Marion county will have the following representatives at the State Teachers' Association in Portland, December 27-29: J. H. Collins, Woodburn, Or., Principals' Association; Mrs. M. L. Fulkerson, Salem, Or., School Board Convention; W. C. Gauntt, Stayton, Or., the County Institute; T. E. Wilson, Hubbard, Or., County Institute; Burgess F. Ford, Jefferson, Or., County Institute; Jean M. Byers, Macleay, Or., County Institute.

Polk County.

Local institute was held on December 2 at Dallas, at which session Prof. Ressler, of O. A. C., and Supt. J. A. Churchill were the principal speakers. The meeting being held so near Thanksgiving was poorly attended, only about one-third of the teachers were in attendance.

Superintendent Reynolds and Supervisor Moore have visited at all schools in the county, and are now on their second circuit, reporting noticeable improvement in nearly every district.

Several schools in the county have reported sickness; Liberty school is being interferred with by hooping cough; Monmouth by scarlet fever; Independence and Dallas have a measles scare.

Miss Martha Skersies, teacher of Antioch, reports having a successful basket social, clearing nearly $45 which will be spent toward new seats for the school room.

Miss Norma Holman, teacher at Pedee, has equipped her school with a new teacher's desk and several smaller articles, the money for the same being obtained at a basket social.

Supt. W. I. Reynolds and Prof. W. I. Ford, of Dallas schools, are to be Polk county's representatives at the state Teachers' Association meeting in Portland, December 27, 28, and 29.

Hood River.

In Hood River valley this year the apple harvesting situation became acute, due to the late season and lack of adequate preparations, and on Tuesday, October 17, an emergency call was sent to the town. The high school was closed for the rest of the week and the 200 students and dozen teachers scattered to the orchards. The desire to help out the serious situation pervaded the groups, the weather was fine, and all worked hard. Besides, a prize of $10 had been offered to the one who picked the most. Robert Newton, of the freshman class, won the prize, picking whole trees to a total of 311 boxes in the three days. The 103 pupils who kept account of their pick gathered an aggregate of 19,603 boxes. School work suffered somewhat from the interruption but on the whole, the experiment was quite satisfactory, and may lead to a solution of the economic problem through the expedient of opening the Hood River schools about August 1 and dropping out the month of October for the apple harvest.

Klamath County.

The county high school board plan to build a gymnasium in the near future. The building will be built 70 by 130 feet, with large stage 50 by 30. The plan is to make the building a community center as well as a school gymnasium.

Besides the Klamath Fall and Merrill high school cafeterias, six other schools are serving hot lunches. The results are encouraging as it tends to better health, better children and better work.

Miss Pearl Stevens of Eugene has been elected to a position in the Merrill high school.

The county school tax of Klamath county has been fixed at $66,000. This will yield about $24 per pupil. The county high school budget calls for $28,600. The average district tax is about one-half mill for maintainance.

Of the 2200 children attending school in Klamath county all but 16 attend school in buildings that are new, modern, properly lighted, and as good as money can buy.

Union County.

The Summerville school district, No. 13, has just become standard. Principal and Mrs. W. L. Starr are on their second term in this district and are to be congratulated on their splendid efforts to place this school among the standard schools of the county and state.

Union City schools are in splendid condition this year under the capable supervision of Mr. E. E. Arant. System is everywhere apparent and he is introducing among many other excellent things, a high school orchestra, high school choral society, and is using a high school study program, leading to better methods in preparing work. The grades have reached the standard requirements and a big mid-year entertainment is in process of preparation.

District 44 gave a fine Thanksgiving entertainment under the direction of Miss Alice Watts and netted $39 for play apparatus.

Elgin city schools are in fine shape. The high school has the largest attendance in the history and all seem to have the spirit of good hard work. Superintendent A. E. Clamon and his teachers are all enthusiastic and happy. Miss Metzger of the domestic science department, co-operating with Parent-Teacher Association, is serving a hot lunch for children who live out of town.

Wasco County.

The opening of the fall term marks the beginning of a new epoch in the history of the Dufur schools. With the new and modern building the board has increased the teaching staff and equipment to meet the requirements for a standard four-year high school. They were fortunate in securing the services of Prof. J. S. Wright who has shown great judgment in the work of re-organizing the school and equipping the domestic science, manual training, and science departments. He has insisted that only essentials be purchased so that the students learn to do their work under the same conditions in school as will confront them in actual life. Then, while insisting that the standard of school work be maintained at the highest place, the principal and his able staff of teachers have won the loyal support of a greatly increased student body by a rational co-operation in all student activities. Prof Wright has organized and acts as coach for a football team, a boys' and girls' basketball team, and has organized and is instructor of a school band. A new piano has been purchased and chorus singing has become a wholesome pastime, and a glee club has been organized. This is essentially a well-organized, well-balanced school with the emphasis properly placed on the essentials, but with a sympathetic interest in all that pertains to the physical, mental and moral development of the student body.

Washington County.

There are 103 school buildings in Washington county; 81 of these have an approved system of heating and ventilating; 21 have stoves with jackets; one has stove and no jacket.

The county spelling contest will begin January 1 and close April 20. There were 1800 pupils last year in the contest.

The county school superintendent is arranging with the pupils and teacher of each district to put up at least two road signs in the district this winter. It is proposed to have the sign boards made by the manual training schools of the county. The signs will be uniform in appearance.

Yamhill County.

The Parent-Teacher Circle of White Cloud gave an entertainment and banquet on the afternoon of November 29. Almost the entire district attended, and the afternoon was pleasantly and profitably spent. The White Cloud circle is one of the most active in the county.

The Parent-Teacher Circle of Chehalem Center gave an entertainment on the evening of December 2. The people of this district are very much alive to the interests of their school. A new piano is the latest indication of their desire to increase its efficiency.

The Carlton school recently had a "gala day" consisting of club talks and a trip to the farm of Ed Cary, the noted breeder of Jerseys..

Miss Maude Williamson is trying an interesting experiment in the Hopewell school. Having determined to "try out" the oft repeated statement, that languages should be taught in the lower grades if taught at all, she has a seventh grade Latin class. Her experiment will be watched with interest.

The people of No. 69, the Coast Creek school, are planning to erect a new building and to install a water system. They have recently purchased a new flag, a dictionary, and erected a new porch.

Whiteson reports a social that netted $29.5v. They have purchased microscope, and will secure some material for basketry weaving. Miss Martin will teach the basketry work and Prof. Calkins will teach manual training to the boys.

The annual teachers' institute was held December 4, 5, 6. A splendid corps of instructors made the three days' session pleasant and profitable to every teacher present, and the entertainment by the Civic Improvement Club, the college, and the orchestras of Carlton and McMinnville high schools, added much to the pleasure of the occasion.

Supt. A. P. Armstrong.

Superintendent A. P. Armstrong, of Multnomah county, will lose no time in going from his present work to a school position, at the expiration of his term of office. He will cease to be school superintendent of

Government Positions for Teachers

All teachers should try the U. S. Government examinations soon to be held throughout the entire country. The positions to be filled pay from $1200 to $1800; have short hours and annual vacations, with full pay.

Those interested should write immediately to Franklin Institute, Dept. S 240, Rochester, N. Y., for schedule showing all examination dates and places and large descriptive book, showing the positions obtainable and giving many sample examination questions, which will be sent free of charge.

Multnomah county at noon January 1, 1917. At 9 o'clock on the following morning he will enter on his duties at the Holmes Business College of Portland, of which he will become part owner and associate principal.

The work and teachers of the commercial department will be under his supervision. Professor Armstrong is a specialist in commercial school work, and is widely and favorably known as a successful educator in general. He served as school superintendent of Multnomah county from 1896 until 1900, and will soon complete a second term of four years in that office. He will return to his old-time work with an abundance of his characteristic enthusiasm. Incidentally, it is no secret that he will offer a text on bookkeeping, at the next state adoption, intended for use in the seventh and eighth grades, and another for high school pupils. He will offer, also, a manual on the use of capital letters and punctuation marks, intended for all grades.

He Loveth Most.

We'll banish envy, strife, and hate,
　And welcome love and labor;
He loveth most who serveth best
　His brother and his neighbor.

If thou desire to be held wise, be so wise as to hold thy tongue.—Quarles.

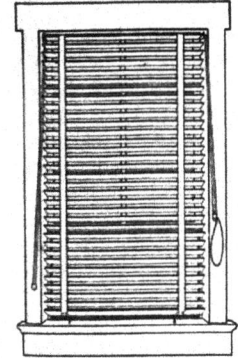

Oregon State Library

By CORNELIA MARVIN, Librarian, Oregon State Library

New Books on Education.

Atwood, Theory and Practice of the Kindergarten. Price 60c. A simple, interesting treatment, planned to "help the young kindergartner to refresh her memory, and to gather together some essentials in relation to kindergarten practice."

Bolenius—Teaching Literature in the Grammar Grades and the High School. Price $1.25. "A work which is based on a broad conception and on thorough knowledge and experience. It presents literature in practical lessons and yet does not deprive it of its power to please and inspire."

Cubberley, Pupblic School Administration. Price $1.75. The aim is three fold, " to state the fundamental principles underlying the proper organization and administration of public education in the United States; to state briefly the historical evolution of the principal administrative officers and problems; and to point out what seem to be the most probable lines of future evolution." Devotes most space to city school systems, but the results of the experience of cities are applied to county and state administration.

Dewey, Democracy and Education. Price $1.40. An introduction to the philosophy of education, which endeavors "to detect and state the ideas to the problems of the enterprise of education."

Dooley, The Education of the Ne'er-Do-Well. Price 60 cents. Analyzes, both from the social and economic and the personal side, the problem of the child who, with no aptitude for literary studies, leaves school to drift into "blind alley" occupations and ultimately into the army of the inefficient. Cites both American and foreign experience in handling the problem, and suggests concrete programs involving pre-vocational education and continuation schools.

Kendall, How to Teach the Fundamental Subjects. Price $1.25. Practical, definitely helpful book. Gives the guiding principles for selecting material in the "fundamental sub-jects" for the various grades of the elementary schools, and methods of dealing with the material selected.

Payne, The Child in Human Progress. Price $2.50. A historical survey of the treatment accorded the children among primitive people, ancient and modern, of the child's place in the domestic, social and economic life of ancient society, in the Middle Ages, under the factory system, up to and including the rise of the modern movement for child protection.

Sandwick, How to Study and What to Study. Price 60 cents. The author believes that the "coaching idea" should be applied to studies as it is to athletics. These informal talks to young students give general principles, tell why and how to study various high-school subjects, suggest reasons and requirements for vocational subjects and some of the older professions.

Starr, The Adolescent Period, Its Features and Management. Price $1. A book for the parent or teacher, surveying in brief and untechnical chapters the physical, mental and emotional phases of the adolescent boy and girl. It is fuller on the disorders, faults and criminal tendencies of the period than on its normal development, and will meet the average teacher's need for aid in the subjects for which Hall's Adolescence and Moll's Sexual Life of the Child are recommended in most reading lists.

Titchener, A Beginner's Psychology. Price $1. A clear, readable account, which the author has tried to make the kind of book which he would have found useful when he began his own study of psychology. Unlike most writers of elementary texts he has omitted the customary chapter on physiology. Not a revision of his Primer, for not only has the material been rewritten, but the attitude changed, less stress laid upon knowledge, more on point of view.

The State Schools

Oregon Normal School.

The first member of the faculty to take the assembly period this month was Miss Lillian Dinius, the critic teacher of the third and fourth grades, who had her grades present a Riley program. Miss Dinius explained that the program had been selected by the children, and also the songs, and how the expressions and interpretations were those of the children, making the occasion an example of what any teacher can do in preparing school programs. The children carried it out very creditably.

Tuesday, November 7, was the birthday of President Ackerman, and was the occasion for an impromptu assembly program by the students. Special songs were sung and short talks given by Mr. Benjamin, Miss Cowgill, Mr. Baker and Mr. Gentle, on the subjects, Mr. Ackerman the Man, the Friend, the Educator, and the Co-Worker. At the close of the program Mr. Ingram, president of the student body, in the attire of a baker, presented the president with a huge birthday cake, the gift of the student body. The entire occasion was a surprise to President Ackerman, having been prepared in his absence. Tuesday evening the members of the faculty and their wives, together with Miss Marvin, a member of the board of regents, gathered at a dinner given by the domestic science department under the direction of Miss Butler, in honor of the day. The table was beautifully decorated with chrysanthemums and autumn leaves, and the places were marked by cards designed and painted for the occasion by members of Miss Greene's art classes. After the splendidly served dinner with Mr. Butler as toastmaster, toasts were responded to by Miss Marvin, Miss West, Mr. Gentle, Miss Parrott, Miss McIntosh and Mr. Evenden.

Mrs. H. H. Heller, who is field representative for the Boys and Girls Aid Society of Portland, was the special speaker for the assembly period of November 10. Mrs. Heller took for her topic "What Makes 'em Behave So" and gave a very splendid talk on the motives for the conduct of boys and girls, and applied it very practically to the work of teaching.

At a joint meeting of the finance and executive committees of the board of regents it was unanimously agreed to ask the forthcoming legislature for the following needed improvements at the Normal school: For addition to the main building which will provide sufficient chapel room, and lockers for the gymnasium, $25,000; for necessary addition to the girls' dormitory, $50,000; for paving of street adjoining the Normal grounds, and other general improvements of the Normal school campus, $5000; for taking over a school or schools which may be used for practice teaching purposes for the Normal, $6000; total, $86,000. Also, to ask for $420 for needed repairs to the Normal school buildings at the Southern Oregon Normal school.

The senior class was represented during the month by Miss Margaret Parrott, who took for her topic Camp Fire Girls, Miss Myrtle Copenhaver whose paper was on The Value of a School Library, Miss Lena Foster who spoke on Working in a Rural Community, and Mr. Ingram, on Vocational Training as an Aim in Education. These papers were all strong, interesting and practical.

The large number of students enrolling in Mr. Pittman's rural school courses, rural school problems, rural school methods, rural sociology and rural school administration, is a flattering indication of the effectiveness of Mr. Pittman's work in this departent, as well as a hopeful sign for the increased interest in the rural school work throughout the state. It is the purpose of the Normal school to feature the rural school side as strongly as possible and this increasing interest is very gratifying.

The second member of the faculty to take the assembly period for the month was Mr. Evenden who took as his topic "What are you going to do with the Adolescent in your school?" in which he tried to show the application of this problem to the everyday work of the school, and its possibilities in the various subjects.

During the month the faculty have participated in institutes as follows: President Ackerman at Eugene and McMinnville, Mr. Gentle at Astoria and McMinnville, Mr. Pittman at Eugene and McMinnville, Miss Riecker at Eugene. Besides this Mr. Pittman attended a school board conference at Salem, and Mr. Evenden spoke before the parent-teacher meeting at Arleta.

During the Thanksgiving holidays Miss Mary Hoham, head of the department of music, spoke before the State Music Teachers association in Portland, at which time she brought very forcibly to the attention of this body the work being done by the Normal school in elementary school music and the need of more work along this line.

During the month on two separate occasions Miss Todd was hostess at teas to the women of the junior and senior classes. These social gatherings have proved very delightful in promoting a closer ecquaintance between the members of the class and the dean of women, and are social innovations which are well worth perpetuating.

Miss West has on exhibition in the library a very fine collection of illustrated books suitable for Christmas gifts. This loan collection from the state library has been the center of interest for lovers of beautiful books.

The Thanksgiving vacation furnished an opportunity for a large percentage of the student body to return to their homes, which was facilitated through the courtesy of the Southern Pacific special train which left Monmouth early on Wednesday morning. A number of the teachers used this opportunity also for various forms of rest and opportunities to visit Portland for purposes of Christmas shopping.

A good many of the Normal school faculty intend to be in Portland at the time of the meeting of the State Teachers' Association during the Christmas holidays. A number of them have been asked to participate in the discussions of the various department meetings. This meeting, as a source of inspiration and an opportunity to meet educational workers from other fields as well as former students in the school, is always enjoyed by the faculty.

Oregon Agricultural College.

Professor R. D. Hetzel returned about Thanksgiving time from an extended Eastern visit, during which he investigated extension work in various states, conferred with the states relation service of the United States Department of Agriculture on matters related to extension work in Oregon, attended some of the agricultural society meetings of the government, and delivered an address before the association of county agriculturists, held at the national capital.

A dinner for all teachers who are graduates or former students of the college has been scheduled during the State Teachers Association meeting in Portland for Wednesday, December 27, at 6:15. All arrangements will be made by a committee appointed for that purpose. Special notice of the place of the dinner will be sent to all guests whose addresses are known. It is expected that all details will have been arranged by the time this issue of Oregon Teachers Monthly reaches the readers. Any one failing to receive notice should write Prof. E. D. Ressler, Corvallis, for information. Those failing to receive notice prior to their arrival in Portland can easily see Mr. Ressler, since he is secretary of the convention. He will be at the Hotel Portland on and after Tuesday, December 26. The committee desires to know the approximate number of plates by noon of December 27. All who are reasonably certain to attend the banquet are kindly requested to send their names to Professor Ressler. Guests of former students will be welcome.

"The Business Side of Government" was the subject of an address by Ben W. Olcott, secretary of state, before the School of Commerce in the business men's series. He took his own office as a type, and said that it is like a county clerk's office enlarged 35 times. The secretary serves on many boards and commissions, in addition to doing the office work.

A series of extension debates has been arranged by Prof. Sigurd H. Peterson, of the public speaking department. The system provides that a team of four men, two affirmative

and two negative, shall go out to any town co-operating in expenses, and debate the question selected by the school securing the debate, from a list of two or three questions submitted. The questions to date are on the proposed government ownership of railways, the state ownership and operation of lime factories, using convict labor and selling lime to the farmers at cost, and possibly the single tax question. The men selected by competition for this debate are as follows: Phillip Parrish, Corvallis; Robert Reichart, Corvallis; Bernard Mainwarring, Newberg; Vernon I. Basler and Theo. Cramer, Grants Pass; E. W. McMindes, Lenora; I. H. Forrey, Kuna, Idaho; and Jas. L. Sprague, Portland. It is expected that each team will visit five or six towns, most of the debates coming during the Christmas recess.

Which high schools of Oregon are using their own printing plant on which the school periodical is issued? Prof. F. H. Shepherd, of the industrial education department, is in search of this information to use in the "Teachers Exchange," and any high school instructor or principal who is solving the high cost of issuing the junior annuals by the home-print periodical substitute will confer a favor by reporting the same to Prof. Shepherd, at Corvallis.

Prof. Edwin T. Reed, college editor, delivered a series of six addresses in southern Oregon the second week in December. He spoke before the high schools of Medford and Central Point, before the local grange and the Southern Oregon Masters' club.

Prof. E. D. Ressler was a speaker before the Dallas Parent-Teacher circle, the McMinnville Teachers' institute, and the Clackamas Teachers' association which met at Milwaukie the second week in December. His subject at Milwaukie was "Social Recreation for High School Students."

Excellent progress in organizing the girls' and boys' industrial club work for the coming year is reported by Prof. H. C. Seymour and his assistants in club work. The plan is co-operative, the state department of education co-operating with the college and the United States Department of Agriculture in conducting the work in Oregon.

The Hillsboro Schools.

The Hillsboro high school has an enrollment this year of 192 which is 27 above the high mark of last year. E. E. Amsden is the new superintendent of schools, coming to Hillsboro from Mosier. Because of the increased attendance this year and the prospects of a much larger increase next year it will be necessary to vote bonds at once to enlarge the high school building. Something rather new is being worked out by the high school this year along the literary line, and is proving very successful. As part of the regular English work, each student is required during the year to participate in one or more of the extra-curricular activities. For this work 15 credits are given on the second semester's grade in English. If a student earns 10 credits, his grade remains the same as the classroom average; if less than 10 his grade will be as much less the class average as his credits are less than 10; if more than 10 and up to a maximum of 15, his grade will be as much more than the class average as his credits are more than 10.

Hot soup is served to the pupils every day in District No. 47 of Coos county. The boys and girls take turns in providing the soup and each brings what he needs when his turn comes to furnish the soup. A pan of water is heated on the stove and every pupil washes his own dish after he has eaten the soup. The school room seating has been re-arranged and new book shelves have been added. Classes in sewing and mechanical drawing have been organized and are proving interesting. Several of the pupils are preparing for the January eighth grade examinations.

At the November meeting of the Washington County Teachers Association the following officers were elected: President, H. C. Cochran; first vice president, A. P. Patten; second vice president, Mrs. C. E. Barker; third vice president, Martha Dillon; reporter, Hettie A. Thomas. The principal address was given by Dr. Sheldon of the University of Oregon.

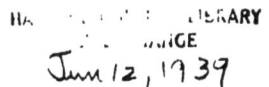

OREGON TEACHERS MONTHLY
The Official Journal of the State Teachers' Association

Vol. XXI	SALEM, OREGON, FEBRUARY, 1917	No. 6

Published Monthly Except July and August by the State Teachers' Association

Entered at the Postoffice at Salem, Oregon, as second-class mail matter, April 1, 1898.

EDITORIAL BOARD

H. D. SHELDON, School of Education, University of Oregon, Eugene
E. F. CARLETON, Assistant Superintendent of Public Instruction, Salem
C. T. BONNEY, County School Superintendent, The Dalles
R. E. CHLOUPEK, Director Manual Training, Pendleton.
C. G. DONEY, President Willamette University, Salem
E. S. EVENDEN, Department of Education, Oregon Normal, Monmouth
MRS. M. L. FULKERSON, Institute Instructor,.Salem
GEORGE W. HUG, City Superintendent, McMinnville
HOFKIN JENKINS, Principal Jefferson High School, Portland
MISS VIOLA ORTSCHILD, President Grade Teachers' Association, Portland
E. D. RESSLER, Department of Education, Oregon Agricultural College, Corvallis
MISS LILLIAN TINGLE, Supervisor Domestic Science, Portland
CHAS. H. JONES, Business and Managing Editor, Salem

RULES OF PUBLICATION

1. The mailing label on the Oregon Teachers Monthly shows the date to which subscriptions are paid.
2. The Oregon Teachers Monthly will be sent to subscribers until ordered discontinued and all arrearages are paid.
3. Notice of change of address should be given at once, naming both old and new postoffice.
4. When renewing, always state that subscription is a renewal.
5. The subscription price, including membership in State Teachers' Association, is $1.50 a year in advance. Single copy, 20 cents.
6. Advertising rates will be furnished on application.
Address all communications to Oregon Teachers Monthly, Salem, Oregon.

Editorial Notes

The greater part of this issue is devoted to the proceedings and addresses of the State Teachers' Association. The board made an effort to secure the manuscripts of all addresses and is publishing all that were available for this issue. It happens that they represent various sections of the Secondary Department. The March issue will be almost entirely devoted to additional addresses, which will doubtless represent all other departments. The leading articles include the three reports presented to the Representative Council and should prove very interesting reading, as each was the subject of prolonged consideration and discussion in the council.—R.

* * *

The first meeting of the reorganized State Teachers' Association was an unqualified success. Only two counties were unrepresented so far as the records show, Curry and Grant. It is estimated that fifteen hundred teachers were in attendance. Unfortunately no provision was made for registration. Announcement from the platform was made at one session but only about five hundred names were secured. A card index of these was made as a permanent record for the association. All who read this who did not report names are kindly requested to send names with address and teaching position to the secretary. Not alone in attendance, which was absolutely voluntary, but in the professional spirit and enthusiasm as shown in the regularity of attendance and earnest attention to the program, did this first meeting set a standard. The council meeting was particularly successful, over one hundred delegates being present, representing every section of the state. The principal speakers at the general sessions, President Pearse of Wisconsin and President Suzzallo of Washington, represent quite distinct types of educational leadership and both were features of the program. Reports from the different departments indicate most satisfactory results. Some of the new officers are already formulating plans for the next year's meeting. Topics are being selected, speakers and committees assigned and studies begun based on actual school problems.—R.

* * *

The membership of the State Association has reached the fine total of 2112. This represents a gain of 367 secured at the state meeting and up to January 1. The campaign has been made chiefly at the annual county teachers' institutes. In addition, the principals in the Portland schools presented the matter in teachers' meetings and several reported that every teacher in the building enrolled. Some county and city superintendents have also been active. If all or even a majority will take enough interest to present the association membership to the teachers, we can reach the goal of four thousand, necessary to conduct an aggressive program in building up the profession of teaching in Oregon.—R.

* * *

In years to come and the not too distant ones at that, teachers in Oregon will look back at the meeting of the State Teachers' Association of 1916 with a grateful realization that it took a long decisive step toward professionalizing teaching when its representative council passed, almost without discussion, the code of ethics for teachers. That there is need of such a code for teachers demands no better proof than the fact that every county institute where the matter was presented went on record as unanimously favoring the adopting of a state code. Some violations of all points in the adopted code and many violations of some of the points have become so noticeable in the last few years as to make teachers and superintendents keenly conscious of the reality of this problem. These violations have been by the uninformed, the unthinking, the unprepared, the unprofessional and the unprincipled, but would any other profession allow such individuals to interfere with its efficiency, decrease its opportunity of service and lessen its claim for being a profession? At present the only provision for enforcing this code is the powerful one of public opinion—powerful however in this case only when guided by a thorough knowledge of the standards set forth in the code and of the conditions which actually exist. Add to this an enthusiastic desire on the part of every true teacher to see teaching recognized as a profession and also the individual willingness to accept the responsibility of enforcing directly or indirectly the provisions of the code and Oregon may demonstrate that it can create a sentiment strong enough to rid itself of the unethical without the aid of a "Grievance Committee." Six thousand Oregon teachers, earnest in their support of, and scrupulous in their practice of this code will unify and dignify teaching to a degree which will reflect deserved honor upon themselves, their profession and their state.—E.

* * *

One of the pieces of progressive and constructive legislation which it is hoped the legislature now in session at Salem will pass, is the increase of the minimum school term to eight months. This has long been recognized by students of educational problems as one of Oregon's most needed reforms. Only three states in the Union outside of a few in the South have a shorter average school term than Oregon and this is not compatible with the progressive stand we have taken in matters of education. In practically all cities, towns and villages the school term has been increased to eight and more frequently nine months so that our present law places a handicap only upon the country boy or girl—a handicap which is based much more upon tradition than necessity. What county in Oregon is going to plead for the shorter term and base its plea upon lack of school organization, impassable roads or too scattered population—three self-refuting arguments? Furthermore, Oregon's wealth is very largely composed of its natural and agricultural resources and these must be conserved and increased not by city trained boys and girls but rather by country boys and girls who are educated to appreciate the opportunities of the country. This cannot be done by a schooling too short even for the fundamentals of elementary instruction, let alone the kind of work which will vocationally prepare him for the work he is to do. Inefficiency and discontent are the results of the poor economy or blind allegiance to custom which spends so much in the education of the rural children and then allows most of that expenditure to be wasted because the little additional, necessary to complete the work thoroughly, is not available. Our legislators, pledged to economy, have never managed the business affairs of the state upon any such near-sighted business policy as this and there is no reason to suppose that this matter will be an exception if they see it in this light. What can you do toward the creation of a public sentiment in favor of at least eight months of educational opportunity for the boys and girls of Oregon?—E.

* * *

The annual meeting of the National Education Association in Portland the second week in July will be a great event in Oregon educational history. The state is to be host for the first time to the greatest educational organization in existence. As loyal members of the profession in Oregon, it should be our ambition to equal or surpass the best record in percentage of attendance of any state that has been honored by this body. Only an insurmountable obstacle will prevent the presence of those who have attended before and any other who permit this rare opportunity to pass will be their own worst enemies in a professional sense. The National Education Association is fifty-five years old and has established a noteworthy record in its influence on educational progress in the United States. Most of the great educators of the nation, particularly in an administrative capacity, have been associated with its management and direction. Our ablest teachers, city and state superintendents, college and university professors and presidents have contributed through the years to the substantial achievements of the N. E. A. It is expected that the entertaining state guarantee an associate membership of the large percentage of its teachers. This associate membership costs two dollars and entitles the holder to the large bound volume of the proceedings, including the valuable committee reports and most of the addresses. The State Director for Oregon this year is Mr. O. M. Plummer of the Portland Board of Education. He is proposing the unique scheme of having every school district in Oregon take a membership for each school building, volume to be placed in the school library. Portland and a number of first-class districts in the state have already done so. This is in addition to the individual memberships of the teachers. In the near future, membership blanks will be distributed through the county superintendents and here is our first duty and opportunity to help Oregon make good its pledges in securing this great meeting. We believe the teachers of Oregon will respond promptly and unanimously. Many will desire to become active members with voting and all other privileges. The same blank makes provision for this, the process calling for the recommendation by an active member to vouch for the applicant and a fee of two dollars. Our second duty is to begin laying plans at once to attend the Portland meeting. All Northwest summer schools will adjourn during the convention and transportation companies will make special rates. Each teacher is a committee of one, first to become a member of the National Education Association, second to secure the membership of his school district, third to attend the meeting next July.—R.

Minutes of Executive Committee

By E. D. RESSLER, Acting Secretary

Pursuant to the call of the chairman, a meeting of the Executive Committee of the Oregon State Teachers' Association (fourth session) was held in Parlor G of the Hotel Portland, Portland, Tuesday evening, December 26, 1916. The meeting was called to order at 7:30 o'clock with the following members present: Mr. E. T. Carleton, Miss Viola Ortschild, Mr. H. D. Sheldon, Mr. G. A. Briscoe, Mr. J. Percy Wells, Mr. W. D. Parker. Absent, Mr. H. H. Herdman. Messrs. W. R. Rutherford, acting treasurer, and E. D. Ressler, acting secretary, were also in attendance.

Chairman Carleton reported a communication from the Portland Grade Teachers' Association, requesting permission to hold a meeting as a branch of the National League of Teachers, at some hour on Friday. After informal discussion, it was agreed that the president of the State Association confer with the officers of the Portland Association and appoint a suitable time not in conflict with any existing schedule.

A communication was read from Director O. M. Plummer of the Portland Board of Education and Oregon Director of the National Education Association, requesting an appropriation by the Oregon State Teachers' Association of at least two hundred and fifty ($250.00) dollars for the maintenance of State Headquarters at the annual convention of the National Education Association to be held in Portland in July next. Mr. Sheldon moved that Mr. Plummer be invited to address the general assembly of the State Teachers' Associaion for ten minutes on the convention of the N. E. A. It was so ordered.

A bill for telephoning was presented by Mr. H. H. Wardrip, chairman of the Department of Vocational Education, incurred in his preparation of the program of the state meeting. Mr. Sheldon stated that he knew of other similar bills. On motion of Mr. Briscoe, this bill and all others submitted by department and other officers in connection with the meeting of the State Teachers' Association were referred to the Finance Committee with power to act.

Chairman Sheldon of the Editorial Board of the Oregon Teachers Monthly, official journal of the convention, made a brief report of the work of that body in explanation of the plan of organization, assignments, appointment of sub-committee and meetings of the sub-committee and of the general board.

Professor H. B. Torrey, representing the Oregon Social Hygiene Society, presented the matter of the importance of instruction in sex hygiene. He recommended the appointment of a special commission of the State Teachers' Association to investigate and report on the present status of sex instruction in the United States. On motion of Mr. Briscoe, the matter was referred to the incoming Executive Commitee for consideration at the same time as other proposed investigations.

Mr. Plummer was then invited to address the committee in reference to the convention of the National Education Association. After some discussion, Mr. Parker moved that the Executive Committee recommend that the Representative Council approve Mr. Plummer's plan of working up institutional memberships in the N. E. A., including every public school in Oregon. The motion prevailed.

Mr. Parker presented at length the merits of the Portland tenure of office law for teachers and requested the endorsement of the State Teachers' Association. After prolonged discussion, no formal action was taken but it was agreed the Mr. Parker, as a regular member of the Representative Council, present the matter to the council on its merits.

The meeting adjourned at 10 p. m.

Minutes of Representative Council

By E. D. RESSLER, Secretary

At 9:30 a. m., December 27, 1916, in the assembly room of the Portland Hotel, President Carleton called to order the first session of the first Representative Council of the Oregon State Teachers' Association. The first order of business was the report of the committee on credentials. Chairman E. D. Ressler reported that the committee had held a two-hour session on the afternoon of December 26 and a three-hour session on the evening of the date. While the majority of credentials were in regular form, there were a large number that departed in one way or another from the form prescribed, making technical violations of the regulations, which the committee thought advisable to ignore. There was but one delegate whose credentials were not favorably acted upon by the committee, that of Mr. R. L. Kirk of Springfield, who came as a representative of the Lane County Parent-Teachers' Association. The committee ruled that the constitution did not recognize such an organization and the matter was referred to the council, which sustained the committee. The names of two delegates were submitted from Multnomah county outside the city of Portland and the committee ruled that the number of teachers justified only one delegate. The council sustained the committee and Mr. E. L. Goodwin was selected as the delegate. The council also seated Miss Fay Clark as the representative of Malheur county, who was present, but with no credentials for the reason that the county had held no institute since the provisions of the constitution became effective. The council also seated Mr. J. A. Nagel of Yamhill county, for whom no credentials had been presented, but whose regular appointment had been witnessed by President Carleton and Mrs. M. L. Fulkerson in the Yamhill county institute. H. H. Wardrip was seated as a delegate from Josephine county, vice Lincoln Savage, who had been chosen as delegate but nominated Mr. Wardrip in his stead. The president of the Portland High School Teachers' Association was present and informed the council that his association had appointed as delegates Messrs. A. F. Bittner and C. R. Hallowell, who were duly seated by the council. On motion of Mr. E. H. Sheldon, Mr. R. L. Kirk was seated as a delegate from the Education Club of the University of Oregon, vice Mr. Fred

Ayer. The roll of delegates to the Representative Council as completed was
as follows: (The names appear in alphabetical order by counties, including
representatives of the county teachers' associations, the various educational
organizations of the county not being indicated on account of lack of space.
The only names not given in the county lists are those of representatives of
the colleges and the universities.)

Baker county, A. C. Strange; Benton, D. S. North; Clackamas, J. E.
Calavan, Lena Ulen, Brenton Vedder; Clatsop, Mrs. M. J. Barry, J. F. Elton,
J. G. Imel; Columbia, J. W. Allen; Coos, R. E. Baker, C. A. Howard, L. W.
Turnbull, Muriel Watkins; Douglas, H. O. Bennett, H. H. Bronson, O. C.
Brown, F. B. Hamlin, Mrs. B. Harley, Alfred Powers, A. E. Street; Gilliam,
J. C. Sturgill; Harney, Mrs. Frances Clark; Hood River, J. W. Crites, L. B.
Gibson; Jackson, P. H. Daily, Emily Devore, Gertrude Engle, M. O. Wheeler;
Jefferson, Mrs. Lillian Watts; Josephine, H. H. Wardrip; Klamath, R. H.
Dunbar, Edna Wells; Lake, Burt A. Adams, C. E. Oliver; Lane, W. G. Beattie,
Jennie Bossen, Maude Hooper, W. R. Rutherford, L. A. Wilson, Mary B.
Wright; Lincoln, R. P. Goin; Linn, C. W. Boettichner, G. E. Dunton, F. M.
Maxwell, Jessie Wilde; Malheur, Fay Clarke; Marion, Jean M. Byers, J. H.
Collins, Burgess Ford, Mrs. M. L. Fulkerson, W. C. Gauntt, J. W. Todd, T.
E. Wilson; Morrow, Mrs. Lena S. Shute; Multnomah, Emma Barrette, A. F.
Bittner, Lutie Cake, Alice Collier, A. R. Draper, E. F. Goodwin, Gertrude
Greathouse, Emma Griebel, C. R. Hallowell, Madge Hill, I. A. Melendy,
Harriet Monroe, Viola Ortschild, Wm. Parker; Polk, H. J. Elliott, W. I.
Ford, Mrs. F. H. Morrison, W. I. Reynolds; Sherman, F. E. Fagan; Tillamook,
Lilly Crapson, Ethel R. Glines, Mrs. Bertha Hanson, R. W. Kirk; Umatilla,
R. E. Chloupek, A. T. Park, G. R. Robinson, J. O. Russell, Gilbert Woods,
I. E. Young; Union, Mrs. A. E. Ivanhoe, Linden McCullough; Wallowa,
J. C. Conley, C. A. Montandon; Wasco, Wilhemina Koerth, I. B. Warner;
Washington, C. E. Barker, Elsie K. Lathrop, Nan Miller, J. M. Stretcher;
Wheeler, H. J. Simmons; Yamhill, E. H. Anderson, S. S. Duncan, G. W.
Hug, Ellen Jackson, J. A. Nagel. Colleges and Universities—Albany, W. H.
Lee; McMinnville, C. P. Coe; Pacific University, H. L. Bates; Oregon Agri-
cultural College, E. D. Ressler; O. A. C. Industrial Education Club, F. H.
Shepherd; Oregon Normal School, J. H. Ackerman; Reed College, J. K. Hart;
University of Oregon, H. D. Sheldon; University of Oregon Education Club,
R. L. Kirk.

President Carleton as chairman of the Executive Committee made a
report of the meetings held during the year. He stated that a full transcript
of the minutes had appeared in issues of the Oregon Teachers Monthly and
he would not go into detail with regard to the business transacted. The
president announced the appointment of the committees on resolutions,
credentials and nominations as follows: Resolutions, F. A. Tiedgen, Marshfield, Madge Hill, Portland, W. G. Beattie, Cottage Grove, Burt A. Adams,
Lakeview, William Parker, Portland; Credentials, A. R. Draper, Portland,
Linden McCullough, La Grande, L. W. Turnbull, Bandon, Harriet Monroe,
Portland, Alfred Powers, Oakland, A. T. Park, Pendleton, H. L. Bates, Forest
Grove; Nominations, W. R. Rutherford, Eugene, Edna Wells, Klamath Falls,
J. C. Imel, Astoria, Viola Ortschild, Portland, Geo. W. Hug, McMinnville.
He deferred the appointment of the Committee on Finance for the action
of the new Executive Committee.

At 10:10, Mr. J. A. Churchill took the floor to present the report of the
Committee on a Retirement Fund for Teachers. He explained that the
chairman of the committee, Mr. W. T. Foster, was unavoidably absent,
having been called out of the state on urgent business. Mr. Churchill took
twenty minutes to explain in some detail the provisions of the bill, copies
of which were in the hands of members of the council. Because of the fact
that members of the council had not had opportunity to read the bill carefully, it was voted that further consideration of the question should be postponed until 2:00 p. m., when the report would become a special order. With
the consent of the chair and the house, Miss Ortschild gave a brief argument
in opposition to certain features of the bill. A brief response was made by
Mr. Churchill.

At 10:43, Chairman J. H. Ackerman of the Committee on a Code of
Ethics for Teachers took the floor. After reading the entire record, it was
moved that the council take up the provisions, principle by principle, and

after discussion take a vote on adoption or rejection. A lively discussion ensued an continued until the adjournment at 11:50 a. m., at which time the entire report had been adopted with amendments. The report as finally accepted by the council appears in this issue of the Oregon Teachers Monthly. A motion for adjournment until 2:00 p. m. was carried.

The second session of the 1916 Representative Council met in the assembly room of the Portland Hotel promptly at 2:00 p. m. Chairman Carleton called to order. President Foster, chairman of the Committee on a Retirement Fund for Teachers had returned to the city and was present. He took charge of the report and made a presentation of its origin and history, showing how the present draft was agreed upon after prolonged discussion of the members and advice from experts, not members of the committee. He answered questions and conducted the debate on the report until 2:50, when on motion the report of the committee was adopted, with only three dissenting votes. (Some further changes in the wording of the different sections have been made since the adjournment of the State Teachers' Association and the bill, as it will be presented to the legislature, appears on other pages of this issue of the Oregon Teachers Monthly.) On motion the committee was continued and authorized to represent the association as a Legislative Committee in presenting the matter to the members of the legislature to convene in Salem in January. The council took a recess of five minutes at 3:45 and resumed at 3:50 with E. T. Carleton in the chair. The chairman of the Committee on Retardation, Mr. C. W. Boetticher, made an introductory statement in regard to the report, giving a history of the appointment of the committee, an account of its meetings and plans of investigation and then introduced Prof. F. L. Stetson, who presented the statistical findings of the committee with an interpretation and brief discussion. At 4:25, on motion, the report of the committee as presented was adopted and the committee continued to pursue its investigations the coming year. A report of the Committee on Resolutions was called for, but on request of the committee it was postponed to a called meeting at 11:00 a. m. Friday, December 29. The Committee on Nominations made the following report, which was unanimously adopted: For president, Supt. G. A. Briscoe, City Public Schools, Ashland; for vice president, Dean H. D. Sheldon, School of Education, University of Oregon; Executive Committee for the two-years' term, Mrs. A. E. Ivanhoe of La Grande, Superintendent Union County Schools; Mr. W. T. Fletcher, principal of St. Johns High School, Portland. To succeed Dr. Sheldon on the Executive Committee for the remainder of his two-years' term, Mr. E. H. Whitney, principal of the Ockley-Green School, Portlan.d

Notice was given of the following amendments to the constitution, which would be presented for adoption at the next session of the council Friday morning at 11:00 a. m. by E. D. Ressler: To amend Article 1 by cutting off the last two words, "Western Division," so that Article 1 would read: "This society shall be known as the Oregon State Teachers' Association." By F. H. Shepherd to substitute the following for Section 5 of Article 8 and change the numbering of the present sections 5, 6, 7, 8, 9 to 6, 7, 8, 9, and 10. "The officers of the General Association and the chairman of each department and each section of each department of the Oregon State Teachers' Association shall be ex officio members of the Representative Council with full power." By H. D. Sheldon to amend Article 4 by changing 8 to 9 and adding after the words "Retiring President," "State Superintendent of Public Instruction," so that the amended article would read: "The officers of this association shall be a President, one Vice President, a Secretary-treasurer, and an Executive Committee of nine members of which committee, the President, Vice President, Secretary-treasurer, Retiring President, and State Superintendent of Public Instruction shall be ex officio members."

Mr. Henry B. Hazard, representing the United States Naturalization Service of the Department of Labor was introduced and made a brief address, setting forth the work of the Bureau of Naturalization and its importance in the work of education. He urged the council and the educators of Oregon to make a study of the work and assist in all possible ways in advancing the interests of this important undertaking of the general government. On motion, a vote of thanks was extended the speaker and his suggestions referred to the Resolutions Committee. On motion, the council adjourned at 4:30 p. m. to meet in the Lincoln High School at 11 a. m. Friday, December 29.

The third session of the 1916 Representative Council was called to order by Chairman Carleton at 11:15 in Room 311, Lincoln High School. The first order of business was the vote on the amendments proposed at the previous session. The amendment offered to Article 1 was unanimously adopted. The amendment offered to Article 4 was unanimously adopted. After some discussion the, amendment offered to Article 8 was changed to read as follows: "to substitute for Section 5 and to renumber sections 5, 6, 7, 8 and 9 to 6, 7, 8, 9 and 10." Section 5. "The officers of the General Association shall be ex officio members of the Representative Council with full power."

The Committee on Resolutions made its report. On motion, the resolution to advise the Executive Committee to call the annual meeting at the Thanksgiving holidays was stricken out. The rest of the report was adopted as read. (The resolutions in full appear in this issue of the Oregon Teachers Monthly.)

Mr. Wm. Parker, President of the Portland Principles' Association, was granted the floor to present an argument in favor of the retention of the present tenure of office as applied to Portland. There was no discussion. On motion, the Representative Council of 1916 adjourned sine die at 11:59.

Minutes of the General Sessions

By E. D. RESSLER, Acting Secretary

President E. T. Carleton called the first general session of the re-organized Oregon State Teachers' Association to order in the Lincoln High School auditorium, Portland, at 9:25 a. m., Thursday, December 28. 1916. Director Will H. Boyer of the Portland City Schools led the assembly in singing "America" and several familiar songs. The President announced that it had been decided to omit addresses of welcome and responses, since the association had made Portland the annual meeting place in its constitution and that the welcome and appreciation would be taken for granted. After brief introductory remarks in reference to the significance of this first session under the re-organization, the conscientious work of the new Representative Council the preceding day, and the state-wide attendance, the President introduced the first speaker, President Henry Suzzallo of the University of Washington, with a complimentary reference to the notable educational career of the distinguished guest of the association. Dr. Suzzallo delivered a scholarly and inspiring address on "Standards of the Teaching Profession."

A recess of ten minutes was taken at 10:30, after which Mr. Claire Monteith, President of the Oregon State Association of Music Teachers, delightfully entertained the assembly with a baritone solo, "On the Road to Mandelay," by Oley Speaks. Mrs. Warren H. Thomas was at the piano. Secretary W. H. Dodson of the Portland Chamber of Commerce was introduced at 10:50 and gave a brief and informing address on "The Relationship of Industrial and Commercial Development in the State of Oregon." President Carroll G. Pearse of the State Normal School at Milwaukee, Wis., ex-President of the National Education Association and chairman of its Board of Trustees, was introduced at 11:15 and spoke on the subject, "That Thy Days May be Long in the Land," a wise and illuminating presentation of the teacher's relation to his profession and the community. The session adjourned at 12:15.

The afternoon was devoted to departmental and divisional programs as follows: Department of City Superintendents; Department of Higher Education; Department of Secondary Education, with division meetings in Science and Methematics, History, and Modern Languages; Department of Foreign Languages, which met with the Classical Association of the Pacific States, an organization holding its session during the same dates as the Teachers' Association; the Oregon Council of English Teachers; Department of Elementary Schools, with division meetings, Advanced, Intermediate and Primary; Department of Rural Schools; Department of Vocational Education, with division meetings in Manual Training, Home Economics, and Commerce; Art Division; Department of Music; Department of Librarians; Department of Physical Training. The same departments, divisions, associations, etc., held session during Friday morning, December 29.

The second and last general session of the association was called to order by President Carleton at 1:30 p. m., Friday, December 29, in the Lincoln High School auditorium. After assembly singing, led by Director Boyer, the report of the Committee on Resolutions was read by the chairman, Supt. F. A. Tiedgen of Marshfield, and adopted without division. Supt. W. R. Rutherford of Eugene presented the report of the Committee on Nominations, which was also adopted unanimously. The newly elected officers are Superintendent G. A. Briscoe of Ashland, President; Dean H. D. Sheldon of the University of Oregon, Vice President; Executive Committee, two-year term: Mrs. A. E. Ivanhoe, County School Superintendent, Union County; Principal W. T. Fletcher, James John High School, Portland; successor to Dean Sheldon, one year, Principal E. H. Whitney, Ockley-Green School, Portland. The hold-over elective member is Mr. J. Percy Wells of Jacksonville. Ex officio members of the Executive Committee are the Retiring President, E. T. Carleton, Assistant State Superintendent of Public Instruction, Salem; President G. A. Briscoe; Vice President H. D. Sheldon, Eugene; State Superintendent of Public Instruction J. A. Churchill, Salem; and the Secretary-treasurer, to be elected by the Executive Committee.

President Pease was introduced at 2:10 p. m. and gave his second assembly address on the subject, "School Dividends," again demonstrating the value of his wide experience and helpful counsel. After acknowlgments of the valuable service of his colleagues, the untiring efforts of the several standing committees, the capable performance of the various chairmen and other officers of the departments, the hospitality of the Portland teachers and school officers, the excellence of the newspaper accounts of the annual meeting, the courtesy of the pupils of the Manual Training Department of the Pendleton Schools in presenting the presiding officer with a handsome gavel made in their shops, and congratulations to all who attended the sessions, President Carleton introduced the last speaker, Dr. Suzzallo, who spoke fluently and eloquently on "Standards of Culture." With Mrs. Thomas at the piano, Mrs. Jane Burns Albert, soprano, and Mrs. Lula Dahl Miller, gave a brilliant rendition of a duet from Puccini's "Butterfly," concluding the program and sixteenth annual session of the "Western Division," or the first session of the State Teachers' Association.

Resolutions of the State Teachers' Association

To the President and members of the Oregon Teachers' Association, in the sixteenth annual session assembled, at Portland, Oregon, December 27, 28 and 29, 1916; We, your Committee on Resolutions, beg leave to submit the following which we recommend to your favorable consideration and adoption: Be it resolved:

1. That this association most heartily endorses and commends the efforts of those influences which secured for Portland and the Northwest, the 1917 convention of the National Education Association and that this association pledges the exertion of every effort and influence toward making of the 1917 National Education Association convention the most successful in the history of its existence, and that boards of education be urged to take out individual memberships in the National Association.

2. That a committee on Social Service be appointed with full power in the exercise of its function during the ensuing year and report the results at the next annual meeting of this association.

3. That this association endorses and recommends the enactment of a law making eight months the minimum of a school year and a minimum salary law based upon certification and experience.

4. That the work of the United States Bureau of Naturalization, in its efforts to improve the educational status of the alien in preparing him for

the necessary qualifications for citizenship, be endorsed by this association and that it pledges its support and assistance in the carrying out of the purposes of the work.

5. That, in recognition of the rural educational problem as one of the most important before the educators of the state today, and, inasmuch as the rural schools derive the least direct benefit from the influence of this association, it is the sense of this body that a committee of seven be appointed to make a constructive investigation of the conditions surrounding such rural schools to the end that the cooperation of this organization be extended for the improvement of such conditions.

6. That the Legislative Assembly of 1917 enact such operative legislation as will immediately put into force and effect the letter and spirit of the so-called "Bone-Dry" prohibition amendment·to the constitution of the state, as adopted by initiative petition at the general election, held on November 7, 1916, and that this association pledges its support to the enforcement of the provisions of such enactment.

7. That, inasmuch as there is no question that the use of cigarettes is a menace to the youth of our state and that their use and sale should be absolutely prohibited, the law already upon the statutes prohibiting the sale of cigarettes to minors be strictly enforced, and that, if the present law is not adequate to meet the needs, the Legislative Assembly of 1917 be urged to enact such legislation as will cure such defects and render the use of cigarettes by minors impossible within the state.

8. That a committee of five be appointed, with power to act and with authority to confer with the county superintendents of the state and the State Superintendent to prescribe a set of standard requirements for music teachers wishing their work credited; prescribe a form of application blank and report blank to be used and request the state department to print the same for the use of the schools.

9. That the thanks of the association be extended to the Board of Editors of this association in appreciation of the labor and efforts put forth by said board and the success attained in the promotion of the best interests of the organization through the medium of the Oregon Teachers Monthly, the official publication of this association; that a vote of thanks be extended to the press of the city of Portland for the full and complete reports of the proceedings of the association and other courtesies extended its membership, individually and collectively; to the management of the Portland Hotel for courtesies extended and services rendered; to the Oregon Congress of Mothers; to the teachers of Portland; to the Fine Arts Museum and to the Board of Education of Portland and the Multnomah County Library for courtesies shown and accommodations provided in the matter of spacious and comfortable places of meeting, and to the people of Portland, generally, for their kind consideration and thoughtful solicitation in ministering to the comfort and pleasures of the membership and to all other influences which contributed in a greater or less degree toward the unqualified success of the 1916 convention of this association.

Salute to the Flag.—"We give our heads and our hearts to our country. One country, one language, one flag." Directions—(1) The children rise and direct attention to the flag by extending right arm, pointing to it. (2) Touch foreheads with tips of fingers, repeating the words, "We give our heads." (3) Hands placed over heart, repeating, "and our hearts." (4) Both hands wave up, repeating, "to our country." (5) Weight forward, hands at side, repeating, "One country." (6) Still standing, repeating, "one language." (7) Right hand pointing to the flag, repeating with emphasis, "one flag."—Selected.

What education is, and how the young should be educated, are questions that require discussion. At present there is a difference of opinion as to the subjects to be taught; for men are by no means in accord as to what the young should learn, whether they aim at virtue or at getting the best out of life. Neither is it clear whether education is more concerned with intellect or with character.—Aristotle.

Proposed Retirement and Pension System Bill for the Public School Teachers of Oregon

By W. T. FOSTER, President Reed College, Chairman of Committee

Section 1. The following words and phrases as used in this act, unless a different meaning is plainly required by the context, shall have the following meanings:

1. "Retirement system" shall mean the arrangement provided in this act for payment of annuities and pensions to teachers, and for the retirement of teachers from service.

2. "Anuities" shall mean payments for life derived from contributions from teachers.

3. "Pensions" shall mean payments for life derived from contributions from the state.

4. "Teacher" shall mean any teacher, principal or superintendent employed by the board of directors of a school district or a county in a public school within the state.

5. "Public school" shall mean any school conducted within the state under the order and superintendence of a board of school directors elected by authority of the laws of the state.

6. "Regular interest" shall mean interest at three per cent per annum, compounded annually on the last day of December of each year.

7. "Retirement board" shall mean the teachers' retirement board, as provided in Section 4 of this act.

8. "Retirement association" shall mean the teachers' retirement association, as provided in Section 3 of this act.

9. "Expense fund" shall mean the fund provided for in paragraph numbered one in Section 5 of this act.

10. "Annuity fund" shall mean the fund provided for in paragraph numbered two in Section 5 of this act.

11. "Pension fund" shall mean the fund provided for in paragraph numbered three in Section 5 of this act.

12. "School year" shall mean the twelve months from the first day of July of any year to the thirtieth day of June next succeeding, inclusive.

13. "Assessments" shall mean the annual payments to the annuity fund by members of the association.

Section 2. A teachers' retirement system shall be established on the first day of July, nineteen hundred and seventeen.

Section 3. A teachers' retirement association shall be organized among the teachers in the public schools as follows:

1. All teachers, except those specified in paragraph 3 of this section, not in the service of the public schools during the term immediately prior to July first, nineteen hundred and seventeen, who enter such service on or after July first, nineteen hundred and seventeen, shall become thereby members of the association.

2. All teachers, except those specified in paragraph 3 of this section, who shall have entered the service of the public schools before June thirtieth, nineteen hundred and seventeen, may at any time between July first, nineteen hundred and seventeen, and Septembr thirtieth nineteen hundred and seventeen, upon applictation in writing to the retirement board, become members of the retirement association. Any teacher failing so to do may thereafter become a member of the retirement association by paying in instalments as the retirement board may direct an amount equal to the total assessments, together with regular interest thereon, that he would have paid if he had joined the retirement association on September thirtieth, nineteen hundred and seventeen.

3. Any teacher hereafter employed in any school district in this state

wherein a teachers' retirement fund association, under the provisions of Chapter 280 of the Acts of the Legislature of the State of. Oregon for the year 1911, is in existence, shall not be subject to the provisions of this act.

Section 4.   1.   The management of the retirement system is hereby vested in the teachers' retirement board, consisting of five members, the State Insurance Commissioner, the State Superintendent of Banking, the State Superintendent of Public Instruction, who shall be ex officio members, and two members of the retirement association.   Upon organization of the retirement association, the members thereof shall elect from among their number, in a manner to be approved by the ex officio members of the retirement board, two persons to serve upon the retirement board, one member to serve for one year, and one for two years; and on the expiration of their respective terms the members of the retirement association shall elect annually from among their number, in a manner to be approved by the retirement board, one person to serve upon the retirement board for a term of two years.   Vacancies occurring among other than the ex officio members of the board shall be filled by the board for the unexpired portion of the elective term.   Until the organization of the retirement association and the election of two representatives therefrom, the ex officio members of the retirement board shall perform the duties thereof.   The office of the retirement board shall be with the State Superintendent of Public Instruction until it shall otherwise direct.

2.   The members of the retirement board shall serve without compensation, but they shall be reimbursed from the expense fund of the retirement association for any expenditures which they may incur through serving on the board.   All claims for reimbursement on this account shall be subject to the approval of the Governor, Secretary of State, and State Treasurer.

3.   The retirement board shall have power to make by-laws and regulations not inconsistent with the provisions of this act; to employ a secretary who shall give a bond in such amount as the board shall approve; and to employ clerical and other assistance as may be necessary.   The compensation of the secretary and other assistants shall be fixed by the board, with the approval of the Governor, Secretary of State, and State Treasurer.

4.   The retirement board shall provide for the payment of retirement allowances and such other expenditures as are required by the provisions of this act.

5.   The retirement board shall adopt for the retirement system one or more mortality tables ,after consultation with an actuary, and shall determine what rates of interest shall be established in connection with such tables, and may later modify such tables or prescribe other tables to represent more accurately the expense of the retirement system or may change such rates of interest, and may determine the application of the changes made.

6.   The retirement board shall perform such other functions as are required for the execution of the provisions of this act.

Section 5.   The funds of the retirement system shall consist of an expense fund, an annuity fund, and a pension fund.

1.   The expense fund shall consist of such amounts as may be appropriated by the legislature to defray the expenses of the administration of the act until July first, nineteen hundred and nineteen.   Thereafter there shall be set apart for the expense fund such portion of the interest on the invested funds of the association as the retirement board may appropriate for that purpose.

2.   The annuity fund shall consist of assessments paid by members of the retirement association, and interest derived from investments of the annuity fund.   Each member of the retirement association shall pay into the annuity fund, by deduction from his salary in the manner provided in Section 9, paragraph five, of this act, such assessments upon his salary as may be determined by the retirement board.   The rate of assessments shall be established by the retirement board on the first day of July of each year to take effect after a prior notice of at least three months, and shall at any given time, be uniform for all members of the retirement association, and shall not be less than three per cent nor more than five per cent of the member's salary; provided, however, that when the total sum of assessments on the salary of any member at the rate established by the retirement board would

amount to more than one hundred dollars or less than thirty-five dollars for any school year, such member shall in lieu of assessments at the regular rate be assessed one hundred dollars a year or thirty-five dollars a year as the case may be, payable in equal instalments to be assessed for the number of months during which the schools of the community in which such member is employed are commonly in session. Any member of the retirement association who shall for thirty years have paid regular assessments to the annuity fund as provided herein, shall be exempt from further assessments; but such member may thereafter, if he so elects, continue to pay his assessments to the fund. No member so electing shall pay further assessments after the total sum of assessments paid by him shall at any time have amounted, with regular interest, to a sum sufficient to purchase an annuity of five hundred dollars at age sixty under the tables then in use by the retirement board; and interest thereafter accruing on such member's assessments shall be paid to the member at the time of his retirement.

3. The pension fund shall consist of such amounts as shall be appropriated by the Legislative Assembly from time to time on estimates submitted by the retirement board or otherwise for the purpose of paying the pensions provided for in this act.

Section 6. 1. Any member of the retirement association may retire from service in the public schools on attaining the age of sixty years, or after twenty-five years of service in the public schools, of which not less than fifteen, including five years immediately preceding retirement, have been in the public schools of this state; or at any time thereafter, if incapable of rendering satisfactory service as a teacher, may, with the approval of the retirement board, be retired by the employing board of school directors.

2. Any member of the retirement association, on attaining the age of seventy years, shall be retired from service in the public schools.

3. A member of the retirement association after his retirement under the provisions of paragraphs numbered 1 or 2 of this section, shall be entitled to receive from the annuity fund, as he shall elect at the time of his retirement, on the basis of tables adopted by the retirement board and then applicable under their rules: (a) an annuity, payable in quarterly payments, to which the sum of his assessments under Section 5, paragraph 2, with regular interest thereon, shall entitle him; or, (b) an annuity of less amount, as determined by the retirement board for the annuitants electing such option, payable in quarterly payments, with the provision that if the annuitant dies before receiving payments equal to the sum of his assessments under Section 5, paragraph 2, with regular interest, at the time of his retirement, the difference between the total amount of said payments and the amount of his contributions with regular interest shall be paid to his legal representatives; but exercising this option (b) shall not operate to reduce the pension payable in accordance with paragraph numbered 5 of this section if he had elected option (a) of this paragraph.

4. Any member of the retirement association receiving payments of an annuity as provided in paragraph numbered 3 of this section shall, if not rendered ineligible therefor by the provisions of Section 5 of this act, receive with each quarterly payment of his annuity an equal amount to be paid from the pension fund as directed by the retirement board.

5. Any teacher who shall have become a member of the retirement association under the provisions of paragraph numbered 2 of Section 3, and who shall have served fifteen years or more in the public schools of the state, not less than five of which shall immediately precede retirement, shall, on retiring as provided in paragraphs 1 and 2 of this section, be entitled to receive a retirement allowance as follows: (a) such annuity and pension as may be due under the provisions of paragraphs numbered 3 and 4 of this section; (b) an additional pension to such an amount that the sum of this additional pension and the pension provided in paragraph 4 of this section shall equal the pension to which he would have been entitled under the provisions of this act if he had paid thirty assessments on his average yearly wage for the fifteen years preceding his retirement and at the rate in effect at the time of his retirement; provided, (1), that if his term of service in the state shall have been over thirty years, the thirty assessments shall be reckoned as having begun at the time of his entering service and as drawing

regular interest until the time of retirement; and further provided, (2), that if the sum of such additional pension, together with the annuity and pension provided for by paragraphs numbered 3 and 4 of this section, is less than three hundred dollars in any one year, an additional sum sufficient to make an annual retirement allowance of three hundred dollars shall be paid from the pension fund.

6.   If at any time it is impossible or impracticable to consult the original records as to wages received by a member during any period, the retirement board shall determine the pension to be paid under paragraphs numbered 5 (b) of this section in accordance with the evidence they may be able to obtain.

7.   In determining the retiring allowances of a member of the teachers' retirement association, who, prior to the first day of June, nineteen hundred and nineteen, had been regularly employed in any school district within the state, credit shall be given in the manner provided for by paragraph 5 of this section, for all such periods of employment rendered prior to the first day of June, nineteen hundred and nineteen; except, however, that this paragraph shall not apply to teachers becoming members of the teachers' retirement association who were at the time of entering the service of the public schools members of the teachers' retirement fund association provided by Chapter 280, Laws of 1911.

Section 7.   1.   Any member of the retirement association withdrawing from service in the public schools, before becoming eligible to retirement shall be entitled to receive from the annuity fund all amounts contributed as assessments (together with regular interest thereon), in the manner hereinafter provided.

2.   If such withdrawal shall take place before six annual assessments have been paid, the total amount to which such member is entitled as determined by the retirement board under the provisions of this act may be paid to him in one sum or in instalments as the board may direct.

3.   If such withdrawal shall take place after six annual assessments have been paid, the amount so refunded shall be in the form of such annuity for life based on the contributions of such member (together with regular interest thereon), as may be determined by the retirement board according to its annuity tables, or in four annual instalments, as such member may elect.

4.   If a member of the association withdrawing and receiving payments in accordance with either paragraph numbered 2 or 3 of this section, shall die before the amount of such payments equals the amount of his contributions to the annuity fund with regular interest, the difference between the amount of such payments and the amount of his contributions (with regular interest), shall be paid to his legal representatives.

5.   Any member of the retirement association who shall have withdrawn from service in the public schools shall, on being re-employed in the public schools, be reinstated in the retirement association in accordance with such plans for reinstatement as the retirement board shall adopt.

6.   If a member of the retirement association shall die before retirement, the full amount of his contributions to the annuity fund with regular interest to the day of his death shall be paid to his legal representatives.

Section 8.   That portion of the salary or wages of a member deducted or to be deducted under this act, the right of a member to an annuity or pension, and all his rights in the funds of the retirement system shall be exempt from taxation, and from the operation of any laws relating to bankruptcy or insolvency, and shall not be attached or taken upon execution or other process of any court.   No assignment of any right in, or to, said funds shall be valid as against the state nor between the assignor and assignee, but shall be wholly void to all intents.   The funds of the retirement system, so far as invested in personal property, shall be exempt from taxation.

Section 9.   1.   The school board of every district in the state shall, before employing in any teaching position any person to whom this act may apply, notify such person of his duties and obligations under this act as a condition of his employment.

2.   On or before October first of each year the school board of every district in the state shall certify to the retirement board the names of all. teachers to whom this act shall apply.

3. The school board of every district in the state shall, on the first day of each calendar month, notify the retirement board of the employment of new teachers, removals, withdrawals, changes in salary of teachers, that shall have occurred during the month preceding.

4. Under the direction of the retirement board the school board of every district in the state shall furnish such other information as the board may require relevant to the discharge of the duties of the board.

5. The school board of every district in the state shall, as directed by the retirement board, deduct from the amount of the salary due each teacher employed in the public schools of such districts such amounts as are due as contributions to the annuity fund as prescribed in this act, shall send to the clerk of said district a statement as voucher for such deductions, and shall send a duplicate statement to the secretary of the retirement board.

6. The school board of every district in the state shall keep such records as the retirement board may require.

Section 10. 1. The school clerk of every district in the state, on receipt from the school directors of the vouchers for deductions from the teachers' salaries provided for in Section 9, shall transmit monthly the amount specified in such voucher to the secretary of the retirement board.

2. The secretary of the retirement board shall monthly pay to the State Treasurer all sums collected by him under the provisions of paragraph 1 of Section 10.

3. All funds of the retirement system shall be in the custody and care of the State Treasurer, and the Treasurer shall invest such funds as are not required for current disbursements. All funds of the retirement association shall be invested by the State Treasurer in the class of securities authorized for the investment by banks of savings deposits under the laws of this state. He may, wherever he sells securities, deliver the securities so sold upon receiving the proceeds thereof, and may execute any or all documents necessary to transfer the title thereto.

4. The State Treasurer shall make such payments to members of the retirement association from the annuity fund and pension fund as the retirement board shall order to be paid in accordance with Sections 6 and 7 of this act.

5. On or before the third Wednesday in January, the State Treasurer shall file with the State Insurance Commissioner and with the secretary of the retirement board, a sworn statement exhibiting the financial condition of the retirement system on the thirty-first day of the preceding December and its financial transactions for the year ending at such date. Such statement shall be in the form prescribed by the retirement board and approved by the Insurance Commissioner.

Section 11. The district court of Marion county, or of the county in which the district concerned may be situated, shall have jurisdiction in equity upon petition of the Insurance Commissioner or of any interested party to compel the observance and restrain the violation of this act, and of the rules and regulations established by the retirement board hereunder.

Section 12. Biennially, beginning December first, nineteen hundred and eighteen, the retirement board shall present to the Governor, to be transmitted to the legislature, a statement of the amount expended and a full report of all proceedings of the retirement board and association prior to the preceding first day of July.

Section 13. Provisions of this act shall not apply in any way to teachers employed in school districts having 100,000 or more inhabitants.

---•---

God gives us always strength enough and sense enough for what he wants us to do. If we either tire ourselves or puzzle ourselves, it is our own fault. And we may always be sure, whatever we are doing, that we cannot be pleasing Him if we are not happy ourselves.—John Ruskin.

---•---

Any coward can fight a battle when he's sure of winning; but give me the man who has the pluck to fight when he's sure of losing.—George Eliot.

The Teacher's Code of Professional Ethics

By Pres. J. H. ACKERMAN, Chairman of Committee

The following code of profession ethics was adopted by the Representative Council of the State Teachers' Association at its meeting December 27, 1916:

1. To govern one's conduct in public and private life by the highest principles of courage, justice, morality, and truth.

2. To be loyal to all movements looking toward the raising of the standards of the teaching profession with a reciprocal loyalty between teachers, superintendents and principals.

3. Not to make application for an administrative position until a vacancy has occurred, nor to apply for other positions until every effort has been made to determine whether a vacancy exists.

4. Never underbid. Never undermine.

5. To withdraw immediately all applications when a contract has been signed and to notify immediately all persons who may be actually assisting in securing a position.

6. To have a high regard for the sacredness of a contract, while in turn employers should have every regard for the advancement of a teacher.

7. To take active part in all community activities of an educational nature.

8. To refuse to give or accept open recommendations.

9. To support the State Teachers' Association to the extent of subscribing to the Oregon Teachers Monthly.

Report of the Committee on Retardation

By F. L. STETSON, Secretary, Eugene, Oregon

Report.—This report represents the work of the committee up to the time of the December meeting of the Association. The work is not complete in that the data from Eugene are not included, and that the answers to the question on the causes for repetition have not been fully tabulated.

The Problem.—As the committee was not definitely organized for work until after the opening of the schools in September, and a report was desired in December, it was decided to limit the investigation to a study of the actual conditions regarding the progress of children through the elementary schools of Oregon, with particular attention to the extent and seriousness of retardation and to the probable causes of retardation.

The Methods.—The brief time in which to work made it inexpedient to attempt to collect information regarding all of the schools of the state, or even regarding all of the schools of a certain size or class. The schools in which the various members of the committee were working, however, seemed to be fairly representative, both of various sections of the state and of village or small city districts, so the investigation was again limited to the following schools: Albany, Bend, The Dalles, Coquille, Heppner, Klamath Falls, Medford, and one school in Portland. The report then is based upon the study of the records of 4703 pupils found in the first eight grades of the above cities. Each member of the committee distributed blanks to the various teachers in his city, asking them to give the following information regarding each pupil enrolled in their respective rooms on November 6: Name, grade, sex, date of birth, date of entering school (first grade), grades repeated or skipped, and probable causes for retardation or repetition. This information was not all available for all pupils, and information given upon the last point especially would frequently be only the teacher's estimate, instead of a definitely established fact, yet it was felt that it was as reliable as any that could be secured, and would at least be of value in indicating the problem of retardation as the teachers see it.

The data were worked over according to the general method of Doctor Strayer in the Butte Survey of 1914. The age of each pupil was computed for September 1, 1916, and a chart constructed for each city, and one for all cities together, to show the placement of all the pupils by age and grade, using half year and half grade groups. Then, assuming, as Doctor Strayer does, and as has been done in other recent surveys, that the latest normal age for completing the elementary school is up to 15, the following were taken as the normal age limits for entering each grade: 1B, 6 up to 7; 1A, 6½ up to 7½; 2B, 7 up to 8; 2A, 7½ up to 8½, and so on to grade 8A, which should be entered from 13½ up to 14½.

The number of pupils who were entering each grade at the normal age, under the normal age, and over age was then determined (Table 3), as well as the extent of over-ageness or under-ageness in years (Table 4). This material was taken as the answer to the question on the extent and seriousness of retardation. The attempt was then made to answer, as far as time permitted, the question on the causes of retardation by segregating the retarded or repeating pupils and tabulating the information given regarding them.

Conditions.—The following tabular summaries give in concise form the more important facts regarding the actual placement and progress of pupils as indicated by the study, the initials representing cities mentioned above:

Table 1. Enrollment by Grades.

Grades	A	B	C	D	H	K	M	F	Totals
1	117	88	40	137	38	114	94	22	622
2	93	82	56	105	32	81	90	89	628
3	92	105	32	131	26	72	99	106	663
4	64	97	48	109	19	59	111	95	602
5	58	86	32	123	30	69	70	93	570
6	92	65	86	113	24	69	114	104	617
7	94	61	33	72	33	58	98	88	537
8	94	45	30	77	17	64	65	72	464
	704	629	307	867	181	586	750	670	4703
No age given	49	30	8	9	71	8	14	4	193
Net total	655	599	299	858	110	578	736	675	4510

In this table we note especially the general similarity in the sizes of grades 1 to 7 in a number of the cities. Instead of the definite decrease in the size of successive grades that is often described, there is a strong tendency in these cities toward an upper grade enrollment that is relatively quite large. This becomes more apparent in the column showing total enrollment for each grade, indicating that there are approximately as many pupils in each grade up through the sixth as in the first, with a drop of nearly twelve per cent between the sixth and seventh and a drop of about thirteen per cent between the seventh and eighth. Evidently, then, practically all the pupils remain through the sixth grade with a small decrease in number in the last two grades. The second fact is that the enrollment in the upper two grades is 1001, or 21 per cent of the entire enrollment. This is a high percentage as compared with the average for the United States, 14 per cent, but Doctor Ayer found 23 per cent of the Lane county pupils enrolled in these grades. From these facts, it is seen that the holding power of the Oregon schools is probably very good, but we get a suggestion also that there must be a considerable number of over-age or retarded pupils in the upper grades.

Table 2. Enrollment by Ages and Grades.

Grade	5	6	7	8	9	10	11	12	13	14	15	16	17	Totals
1B....	119	256	86	23	4	5	..	..	..	..	..	..	..	493
A....	8	48	41	17	2	1	1	..	..	..	..	1	..	109
2B....	..	68	187	86	28	7	2	..	..	..	..	..	..	378
A....	..	18	92	84	31	5	3	2	1	..	..	..	..	236
3B....	1	7	61	180	94	29	15	4	1	1	..	..	..	393
A....	..	..	16	89	88	29	7	2	3	..	..	..	..	234
4B....	..	2	9	65	141	92	38	12	5	2	..	..	..	366
A....	..	..	4	22	65	75	34	9	4	..	2	..	..	215
5B....	..	..	..	8	58	138	102	33	15	9	2	..	..	365
A....	..	..	..	4	16	60	64	32	13	4	4	..	..	198
6B....	..	..	..	..	11	61	130	97	46	24	5	2	..	376
A....	..	..	..	..	1	8	41	57	47	18	4	2	1	179
7B....	..	..	..	..	1	3	53	117	90	49	17	4	1	335
A....	..	..	..	..	..	..	10	47	57	37	18	4	5	178
8B....	..	..	..	..	..	1	6	35	105	83	54	18	3	306
A....	..	..	..	..	..	1	3	9	37	52	25	16	7	150
Totals..	128	394	496	578	540	515	509	456	423	279	131	47	17	4510

In this table, the half-year groups have been combined, for economy of space, thus making it impossible to designate accurately the number of pupils entering under age, at age, or above age, but several other significant points should be noted. The number of pupils under six is quite large, numbering nearly 3 per cent of the whole. In the 6-year group are 394, or 8.7 per cent, and in the 7-year group are 496, or 11 per cent, a total of 22.7 per cent in the three age groups. Lane county had slightly over 13 per cent in the same groups. The number of pupils who, at the beginning of the year are 15 or over is 199, or 4 per cent, about the average for the United States, and less than in Lane county, which had 13 per cent in 1916

A third point is found in the wide variation in ages of pupils who are supposedly doing the same grade of work. In each grade, at least six different ages are represented, and in some as high as ten. The conditions in the individual cities are very similar, indicating that many pupils are probably not receiving the proper type of subject matter or instruction. In the Portland Survey (p. 141) it is suggested that for children of from 6 to 14 years, a range of more than three years is not desirable in any grade, yet practically all of the schools studied have a greater range in each grade.

Table 8.   Number of Pupils Under-age, Normal-age, and Over-age.

	Under-age		Normal-age		Over-age		
	Number	Per cent	Number	Per cent	Number	Per-cent	Totals
A	107	16.3	282	43.0	266	40.6	655
B	90	15.0	238	39.7	271	45.2	599
C	40	15.3	119	39.4	140	46.8	299
D	135	15.7	371	43.2	352	41.0	858
H	20	18.1	39	35.0	51	46.0	110
K	106	18.3	241	41.7	231	40.0	578
M	173	23.5	311	42.8	252	34.2	736
P	178	26.3	254	37.6	243	34.0	675
	849	18.8	1855	41.1	1806	40.0	4510

This table shows the number and per cent of pupils found in each of the three groups in each system studied. The under-age pupils vary from 13 per cent to 26 per cent, the normal-age from 35 per cent to 43 per cent, and the over-age from 34 per cent to 46 per cent. However, the total number of under-age pupils (18.8 per cent) is rather large, and the number of over-age (40 per cent) is decided so, being above the median for the United States as given in Strayer's study of 1911. The following figures enable comparisons: In "Laggards in our Schools," Doctor Ayres estimated that thirty-three per cent of the elementary school population of this country was over-age. A study of 227 cities of over 1000 population in Michigan in 1915 showed 6.5 per cent under age, 65.5 per cent at age, and 24 per cent over-age; Portland in 1913 had 24.4 per cent over-age; Port Towsend, Wash., in 1915 had 13 per cent over-age; Blaine, Wash., 39 percent; and Ashland, Oregon, in 1914 had 31 per cent over-age and 34 per cent under-age.

Table 4.   Extent of Variation from Normal Age.

A.—Under Age.

	Less than 1 yr.		1 yr. and less than 2		Over 2 years		Totals		
	Boys	Girls	Boys	Girls	Boys	Girls	Boys	Girls	
A	52	49	5	1	..	..	57	50	107
B	38	45	2	5	..	..	40	50	90
C	12	27	..	1	..	..	12	28	40
D	59	65	1	3	1	..	61	68	135
H	6	5	1	..	..	..	7	5	20
K F	56	43	1	4	..	..	57	47	106
M	62	67	12	7	3	1	77	75	173
P	53	75	13	9	1	1	67	85	178
Totals	338 (52)	376	35 (10)	30	5 (1)	2	378 (63)	403	849
	766		75		8				

Numbers in ( ) indicate pupils whose sex was not given.

B.—Over Age.

	Less than 1 year		1 year and under 2		2 years and under 3		3 years and under 4		4 years and under 5		Totals	
	Boys	Girls	Boys	Girls	Boys	Girls	Boys	Girls	Boys	Girls	Boys	Girls
A	89	72	27	32	14	19	6	3	3	*	139	127
B	87	74	43	33	12	11	6	2	2	1	150	121
C	38	42	21	12	10	7	3	5	2	..	74	66
D	121	100	37	34	17	11	6	4	1	‖1	183	150
H	7	9	4	9	5	..	..	..	..	..	17	18
K	63	65	30	34	11	10	6	4	2	..	112	113
M	72	54	36	20	9	8	2	1	..	..	119	83
P	70	71	31	20	8	4	3	4	4	¶2	116	101
	547	487	229	194	86	70	32	23	15	4	910	779
	(73)		(33)		(9)		(1)				(117)	
	1107		456		165		56		19		1806	

*Add 1 girl at 10.   ‖Add 1 boy at 5.   ¶Add 1 pupil at 8.

In Part A is shown the extent of under-ageness. The significant fact disclosed by this table is that the 766 pupils in the first group, continuing normally, can complete the eight grades by 14½ or slightly earlier; the 75 continuing normally, can finish the work between 13 and 14; while 8 will finish under the age of 13. In Part B, it is seen that 1107 pupils, continuing normally, cannot complete the elementary school under 15 or 15½; 456 cannot finish under the age of 16; 165 under 17; while 75 cannot finish under 18. Needless to say the chances for the last two groups to continue in school past the compulsory attendance age limit are small, and prabably many of the 456 will also drop out.

Table 5. Number and Per Cent of Pupils Under-age, Normal-age, and Over-age, by Grades.

Grade	Under-age		Normal-age		Over-age		
	Number	Per cent	Number	Per cent	Number	Per cent	Totals
1	128	21.0	330	54.8	144	23.9	602
2	112	18.2	296	48.2	206	33.2	614
3	121	19.8	283	45.2	222	35.4	626
4	124	21.3	227	39.0	230	39.5	581
5	119	21.1	201	35.7	243	43.1	563
6	94	16.9	186	33.5	275	39.5	555
7	85	16.5	175	34.1	253	49.3	513
8	66	14.4	157	34.4	233	51.0	456
	849	18.8	1855	41.1	1806	40.0	4510

The chief points to be noted in this table are the drop in the number of under-age and normal-age pupils in the upper grades, and the steady increase in the number of over-age, up to 51 per cent, in the eighth grade. It is certainly a rather startling fact to find that one-half of all the pupils in the upper grades of these systems are over-age, a situation that can only exist through some decidedly unwholesome conditions at some earlier point.

The Causes.—Retardation or over-ageness is due to late entrance or slow progress or to a combination of both. In attempting to discover why the Oregon schools have such a large number of retarded pupils, the late entrance factor must first be considered. Lacking the opportunity to tabulate all information, the question was answered in this manner: Selecting one city as fairly typical of all, it was found that of 98 1B pupils who entered school last fall, 47, or 48 per cent, were at the normal age; 33, or 33.6 per cent, at an early age; and 18, or 18.3 per cent, late in entering. While this is insufficient evidence upon which to base a final statement, at least it indicates that late entrance, while a factor, is not the only or main one. This is further borne out by the fact that in this same system 53.5 per cent of the eighth graders are over-age.

Considering next the question of slow progress, 305 pupils in the system had repeated one or more half grades; 81 had skipped one or more; and 46 had both repeated and skipped grades. There were 759 pupils who had been in the school long enough to repeat work. In all, 351, a total of 46.2 per cent had done so at some time. Evidently, then, slow progress or slow progress after late entrance is chiefly responsible for the 40 per cent of retarded pupils.

The lack of complete records made it difficult to determine accurately the cause for repetition, but 255 cases were selected for which the teachers gave a reason, secured from records, personal acquaintance, or inquiry of pupil or parent.

Absence was held accountable for 86 cases, illness being specified as a cause for 69, and irregular attendance due to work, distance from school, etc., for 17. Moving or changing schools was given as a reason for 33 more; and physical condition, including poor vision 5, malnutrition 2, adenoids and tonsils 14, goiter 2, and bad habits 3, was thought responsible for 26. Some factor connected with mental development or mental condition was given for 99 cases. These included such statements as slow development, slow thinkers, immature, defective, no application, nervous, listless, or difficulties with special subjects. Scattering reasons, as the desire of a parent for thoroughness or the difficulty of new work after skipping a grade, etc., accounted for the remaining 11.

Combining groups, mental condition was a suggested cause for 99 cases, illness or poor physical condition for 95, irregular attendance due to other causes for 50, and scattering reasons for 11. Doubtless some physical factor not discovered by the teacher was responsible for many cases of poor mental condition, and also the tendency to enter pupils at an early age may account for many others, but clearly attention must be called to the need for more health work in the schools as well as to more effective placing of pupils if the large amount of retardation and repetition be decreased.

Tentative Conclusions.—From the present status of the study, the following points seem evident: (1) Oregon schools, while not showing as high a percentage of retardation as has been disclosed in surveys of some large city systems, still have a much larger number of over-age pupils than is warranted under existing conditions. The situation becomes serious in the upper grades, where every other pupil is over-age. (2) The number of pupils who remain in school after reaching the age of 15 is fairly large, although there is a marked decrease in the number of pupils at age 14. The holding power of the schools seems, on the whole, to be good. (3) A large number of pupils enter under the normal age, but afterward are quite apt to make slow, rather than rapid or even normal, progress. Quite a few who enter early and repeat work are yet able to finish at the normal time, but the situation is still unsatisfactory. (4) Repetition of work, a most potent cause for retardation, is altogether too prevalent. While a certain amount of retardation must be expected on account of the number of families who shift from place to place, according to the economic demands, it is hardly a defensible proposition that nearly every other child should be obliged to repeat work at some time in his school career. (5) A large problem for administrators and supervisors is found in the early entering, slow-moving group. Immaturity and poor physical health are very significant causes for much repetition, while late entrance and irregular attendance are also contributory to retardation.

Recommendations.—(1) That a committee be appointed to continue the investigation of retardation, working on a broader and more systematic plan, and especially asking the cooperation of county superintendents in securing information regarding typical rural or small village communities. (2) That the reduction of retardation be made a special problem in the state of Oregon, involving: (a) Adoption and use, in all schools, of a permanent record system which will give for each child such data as birth, age of entrance, complete attendance record, health, physical defects, school progress (promotion, repetition and skipping), record on school subjects, and causes for repetition. (b) More health work in schools. (c) Special attention to slow-moving pupils. (d) More careful grading of pupils in regard to mental age. (3) That entrance at the normal age, rather than earlier be encouraged, and that rapid progress or flexible promotion be allowed whenever a pupil is distinctly able to do the work of an advanced grade.

The Teaching of Recent American History

Summary of a paper read before the History Division of the Oregon State Teachers' Association, December 29, 1916, by J. P. O'HARA, of the University of Oregon

Mr. O'Hara dealt with certain economic phases of recent American history, confining his attention chiefly to a consideration of the passing of the era of free lands. He referred briefly to some of the more important influences which the frontier has exercised on American history and pointed out that these influences may be expected to become weaker as the West passes further and further from frontier conditions. In particular he described how the free lands of the West long aided in maintaining a high level of wages in the eastern parts of the country by offering an opportunity for eastern laborers and immigrants to escape from untoward city conditions. The passing of the era of free lands, he said, showed the American people the necessity of conserving their natural resources and especially of bettering their methods of agricultural production. The passing of free lands is intimately associated with the high cost of living and a score of other practical problems which face the American people. Consequently, the speaker suggested, this phase of American economic development offers an excellent basis for the study of recent American history in the schools because it touches at so many points the social and political interests of the people during the past forty years.

The speaker distributed copies of an interesting chart prepared by Dr. Schafer of the University of Oregon which exhibited in a striking manner some of the results already observable from the passing of free lands.

	Total number of farms.	Average size of farms.	Total value of farms and buildings.	Value of the average farm.	Average value per acre.	Per cent improved land.
1850	1,449,078	202.6	$ 8,271,575,426	$2,257.84	$11.20	38.5
1860	2,044,070	199.2	6,645,045,007	3,250.88	16.30	40.1
1870	2,650,985	158.3	7,444,054,492	2,808.03	17.80	46.8
1880	4,008,907	133.7	10,197,006,776	2,543.58	18.25	53.1
1890	4,564,641	136.5	13,279,252,649	2,909.15	21.83	57.4
1900	5,737,372	146.2	16,614,647,485	2,896.00	19.33	49.4
1910	6,361,592	138.1	34,791,125,697	5,471.00	39.50	54.4

Community Civics as a Prerequisite to the Social Studies

By A. N. FRENCH, Department of Education, University of Oregon

Our age is striving to make finer adjustments than those demanded by our fathers. Democracy, as a type of civilization, is being pragmatically tested.

Four recent tendencies since 1900 may be taken as illustrative of our efforts to readjust ourselves to social changes. First, the tendency to emphasize industrial and prevocational courses in secondary instruction. Second, making provision for the study of retardation and elimination, or in other words, the necessary treatment of individual differences. Third, the tendency to measure instruction by accurate, objective scientific scales and standards. Fourth, an endeavor to define and organize moral, civic and social instruction.

Being in sympathy with the view that moral instruction may be realized largely through social intelligence, we shall confine our efforts to the civic and social phases of instruction. Our field is that of the 7th, 8th and 9th grades recently defined by the junior high school. As the title of this paper suggests, our purpose is to emphasize the values of community civics as a prerequisite to the social studies providing it has in its organization the elements basic to all efficient socialization.

The natural limits of this paper will not permit of invoicing our current and social needs. It is enough to point to the fact that the secondary school teachers of the social studies have an enviable opportunity to instruct and train in the rudiments of community welfare a million and a half of pupils, pupils at an impressionable stage, the high school age. Likewise, an adequate pen sketch of the recent development of community civics and its relationship to the rise and growth of the social sciences as a whole is impossible. We must assume all this, as well as the appreciation of the fact of social change and evolution, and content ourselves with the statement that a social view of education presents a permanent problem which, like the poor, we have always with us; namely, the problem of living together as democratic citizens. This social problem is usually defined as good citizenship.

The relation between doing and thinking is implied in the following, "Learn to do something worth while better by giving thought to the doing." Generally speaking, education is accepted as worth doing but not as worth thinking about.

"Education, variously called moral, ethical, civic or social education, and appropriate to the demands of a democratic civilization inspired with a scientific attitude toward life has not yet found conscious development anywhere"—such is the statement found in "The Modern High School," edited by Chas. H. Johnston, from the pen of none other than David Snedden of Columbia. "It is true," he says, "that the secondary school, the college, and even the elementary school constantly assert that one of their chief purposes, not their controlling purpose, is education for citizenship. An examination of the means and methods employed, however, will disclose the fact that nowhere are programs or processes consciously and purposefully adjusted to this alleged end. In other words, insofar as social education as a name is held by our educational institutions, it operates usually as a vision or hope or article of faith and almost nowhere as a conscious purpose controlled by scientific methods."

Recent mail has brought to my desk Bulletin 1916, No. 28 (U. S. Bureau of Education) on "The Social Studies of Secondary Education—a six year program adapted both to the 6-3-3 and the 8-4 plans of organization," by Arthur W. Dunn. This is the long looked for report on Social Studies promised in 1913 by the chairman, Clarence D. Kingsley, of the commission of the National Education Association on the re-organization of secondary education.

The above bulletin contains a program "consciously and purposefully adjusted" to training for citizenship which it is the purpose of this paper to criticize constructively. The theory involved in the comments on the proposed educational procedure will be tempered with practical first-hand experiences of the writer with a course similar to Dunn's proposed program taught for three years in a school of 600 pupils organized on the 8-4 plan in Washington. Also the discussions will be influenced by experiences which are now being received from experimental work in the University High School of the University of Oregon, organized along junior high school lines.

The problem to be faced is as follows: Can our educational effort be so unified in junior high school; can the training function of the teacher be so understood; can the subject matter be so chosen, so organized about a given core and so presented as to realize first, those general, and second, those special efficiencies basic to secondary education? Can we consciously and purposefully train a democratic type of citizen? An examination of the content and organization involved in Bulletin 1916, No. 28, will help us to answer these questions.

The content recommended by the committee on social studies as stated in the general plan, page 12, includes such studies as might be made to contribute most effectively to the purpose of secondary education, namely, geography, history, European and American, and civics for years seven, eight and nine, with history and problems of democracy as the content for years ten, eleven and twelve. The arrangement of these subjects implies the organization into cycles which it is deemed wise they should possess. The course as outlined is intended to be flexible and possible of a high degree of differentiation that may be necessary to meet the practical needs of typical groups of pupils in country or city, east, west, north or south.

The organization of subject matter is adaptable to the 6-3-3 or to the traditional 8-4 plan of secondary school administration. A choice of three plans is given: First, the three subjects may run parallel with more or less dependence upon each other; second, these social studies may be taken up in sequence in the following order: geography, history, civics; third, a plan providing for the introduction of civics one or two days each week along with geography and history. Independent of the plan followed, the committee has committed itself to about a year and a half of civics in the first three years of junior high school (7th, 8th and 9th grades).

The committee suggests that the following elements of welfare be studied as topics (p. 23): (1) Health, (2) Protection, (3) Recreation, (4) Education, (5) Civic beauty, (6) Wealth, (7) Communication, (8) Transportation, (9) Migration, (10) Charities, (11) Correction. In addition the course may well include the topics dealing with the mechanism of community agencies, inclusive of how governmental and voluntary agencies are conducted and financed.

The aim of such civics is to lead the pupil to see (1) the importance and significance of the elements of community welfare; (2) to know the social agencies that aid in securing these elements; (3) to recognize and respond to civic obligations.

Some of the social facts upon which the method recommended by the committee is based are: (1) The pupil is now a citizen with real present interests, hence a factor in his group life; (2) having an interest in community affairs and a more or less acute sense of responsibility, he will want to know how to act, how to respond to obligations; (3) knowing that right action depends upon information, social intelligence naturally follows; (4) intelligence implies training and judgment.

As to method, three steps in teaching the elements of welfare are suggested: (1) The approach to the topic which is largely inductive; (2) Given the topic like health well developed, the agencies are next investigated for securing this element of welfare: (3) The recognition of definite and well placed responsibility concludes the class treatment of the subject or topic at hand. Patriotism, nationalism and world interests are amplified. Vocational enlightment is recommended because of its bearing upon vocational guidance. Civics is correlated with history. This relation is seen when community civics is studied in connection with local history. Primitive history, because of its simplicity, aids in clarifying communty concepts.

Summarizing, the report says (p. 34), "Community civics is a course of training in citizenship, organized with reference to the pupil's immediate needs, rich in its historical, sociological, economic and political relations, and affording a logical and pedagogically sound avenue of approach to the later social studies."

Brevity demands that we omit the treatment that the report gives to the administrative features concerning geography and history in grades 7, 8 and 9, also all of part three dealing with the "Social Studies for Years 10-12."

It is in part III where standards—preparation of teachers—and availibility of material are discussed that we find our chief difficulties to conscious and purposeful effort towards matters of re-organization of high school instruction. We repeat the questions asked or implied by the committee. "Can standards be formulated so that we may have a common basis for comparison, an...so that any teacher may put her work to the test from day to day, or from week to week, and see, not whether it conforms to the opinions of some one, but whether it measures up to clearly recognized criteria?" Can teachers be adequately trained in the technique of method and can they come to their work with a broad view of the social studies rather than with a narrow view of history, or geography, or civil government? Can teachers be trained in service? Can suitable textbooks be secured along the lines of this report? The committee has faith that all these questions can be answered in the affirmative.

We have clearly before us at this stage of our theme: (1) The problem of educational expert, what the criteria by which the social science content is to be evaluated? (2) The problem of teacher training institutions, how improve the teacher's efficiency along lines of scientific method? (3) To meet real needs, what principles are to characterize our new textbooks for use in the junior high school?

In the spirit of constructive criticism may we ask, is not the report of the committee deficient: (1) In not giving an adequate conception and definition of the field of the social studies? (2) In not pointing out the elements basic to the organization of community civics and all social studies? (3) In not contending for a socialized curriculum through the unity of organization which the group of the social studies gives to the humanities, on the one hand, and the natural science group of studies on the other? How long are we going on advocating the socialization of separate and now more or less isolated subjects, i. e. English, history, mathematics, etc. Why a piecemeal program? Vision is essential to the team work of a high school teacher. Point of view is vital to well organized text material. Unity, coherence and directness are as important to curriculum building as to paragraph structure.

You ask how would you clarify the conception of the social sciences? How would the definition of this field aid in the teaching of civics, assuming that community civics is a core of instruction in grades 7, 8 and 9? The teacher's viewpoint must be enlarged: (1) By tracing the development of social sciences in their relation to the exact sciences (physics, chemistry, etc.); to the earth sciences (physical and mathematical geography, geology, etc.); to the biological sciences (zoology, botany and physiology) according to Comte's reasoning in his heirarchy of sciences. (2) By tracing the relationships existing between the social studies and their empirical beginnings as found in the arts and humanities. This being done, the next step is to show that at least three elements are basic to civics and the social sciences. These elements of necessity reveal two aspects which are complements of each other. One is objective and reflects society's interest in its own preservation. The other is subjective and is composed of data of individual experience, i. e. of human wants and human desires. Dewey has expressed these two aspects in the following, "What the best and wisest parent wants for his own child, that must the community want for all its children. Any other ideal for our schools is narrow and unlovely: acted upon, it destroys our democracy." (School and Society, p. 1).

We can classify the facts and factors—elements in social welfare as follows: (1) Physical and geographical influences; (2) Biological influences; and (3) Human institutional influences, in other words, the influences of the non-living and the living worlds. The reason for this is found in the fact that the child as a growing organism is environmentally situated in the world of nature and in the world of man.

Prominent writers have classified social influences or interests as follows: physical, biological, economic, spiritual and ideal influences. The above three-fold division which we have made of our elements, basic to the social studies suggests an analogy to the growth of the natural, biological and social sciences. To the latter social science, Bogardus gives a division of seven parts: (1) Hygienic and eugenic—those influences of health; (2) Economic—those interests of food and wealth getting; (3) Political and legal—those interests working for protection against the anti social; (4) Ethical and religious—the influences of right thinking and doing or life in its spiritual phases; (5) Aesthetic—the interests of the artistic, ornate, etc., briefly a recognition of beauty; (6) Intellectual—the influences which arise from the development of mind; (7) Associational—those influences which are the resultants from the action and interaction of mind upon mind.

Our thought is well defined when we point that social science is largely concerned with associational influences and their embodiment in human institutions. The activities of a people—human doings however are unthinkable apart from their natural environment. It is quite as essential that man be taught to recognize his partnership with nature as to be taught the mechanics of government. Why? Because "one set of social influences seldom operates without assistance from many others." (Suzzallo).

Frances Gulick Jewett has made the biological influences of heredity, environment and personal development clear in her little book, "The Next Generation."

The home can profitably be studied in all grades as typical of the five simpler forms of institutional life, their nature and scope, since "the family is not a product, so far as we can see, of other forms of association, but rather it itself produces these other forms of association. The family, in other words, is not a result of social organization in general, but seems rather to antedate both historically and logically the forms of social life. It is not a produce of society, but it itself produces society." (Elwood, Sociology and Modern Social Problems).

The field of the social sciences, dealing with the organization and development of human society and with man as a member of social groups may, as Dunn's report suggests, include simply geography, history and civics for junior high schools, but whether the content be civics or civil government, industrial or political history, commercial or poltical geography, domestic or political economy all must bear the pragmatic test of efficiency. We are of the opinion that the term social problems rightly understood is adequate for high school use. Academic terms are well enough in the mind of the teacher, provided, the essential viewpoint is not clouded thereby.

"Our schools are troubled with a multiplication of studies each in turn having its own multiplication of materials and principles....some clue of unity, some principle of simplification, must be found." (Dewey). Team work—cooperation among teachers must begin in high school if educational effort is to be unified. All teachers, whatever their specialty, must possess a comprehensive view of the curriculum as a whole, inclusive of the place and function of the social science group.

One cannot always be a hero, but one can always be a man.—Goethe.

A Plea for Common Vital Aims and Functioning Results in the English Work

By GUY E. DYAR, Eugene, Oregon

Without thinking much about it we who are conducting the work of the English departments in the high schools have accepted the place assigned to us in the curriculum as a traditional inheritance, and have pursued the methods of teaching with which we became familiar when we were in high school ourselves. But let us pause to inquire: "What is this that we are doing? Is it the best thing to do? What do we hope to accomplish by it?" Our problem is concerned with two subjects—literature and composition.

The study of English literature in American high schools is a development of the last thirty years. It had its origin in a discussion, which became current following the publication of an essay by Charles W. Eliot wherein he pointed out that a few high schools were then giving a very little training in the reading of literature, and that many high school were giving no such training, and which led to the introduction of a prescribed list of books to be read in high school as a requirement for entrance to a group of New England colleges. Originating in this manner the first methods of teaching received the impress of the classic learning of the colleges of a generation ago, and an impulsion in the direction of formal treatment which became perpetuated in formal habits of literary criticism, in the habitual choice for study of a formal body of subject matter, and in a formal code of procedure, the validity of which has until recently remained unquestioned. These formalities have consisted in the conduct of dissecting clinics and autopsic investigations upon the body of certain "classics" chosen because of their superior qualities, or because of their importance in the history of English and American literature. The analysis has been upon style, structure, metre, figure of speech, allusion, and the like, accompanied, more often preceded, by a biographical study of authors under the guidance of a textbook in the history of literature. Classic texts in literature have been prepared by classic scholars who have contributed learned commentaries for the front pages wherein the student's thinking has been done for him, and copious annotations for the back pages in the minute analysis of thought, line, phrase, and word, wherein every obscurity is sought to be disclosed, every allusion painstakingly traced to its sources, and every irregularity exposed with extreme nicety and care. Following the study of these texts with the work all done for us we invariably require the student to write a nice little "essay" or "composition" purporting to be in original analysis of the subject matter, or in original estimation and contrast of human character, but which always come up to us in phrases and terms "conned" from the commentator.

In the work in composition we have also unfortunately placed the emphasis upon the formal, as distinguished from the vital. Books and methods still widely in use are framed about the notion that the major concern of high school "composition work" is the rhetorical, that of turning the student's attention to his mental processes in composition, as distinguished from the content about which those processes are concerned; that is, he is started off with definitions of "unity," "coherence," and "emphasis," sought to be encouraged by having his attention drawn to distinguished examples of unity, coherence and emphasis, and then assigned to the work of producing a paragraph or composition which gives evidence of unity, coherence, and emphasis. In like manner do we require the student to begin with a topic sentence and then develop his paragraph from that topic sentence by way of "repetition," "specific instances," "comparison," "contrast," and the like. The student does not naturally think "rhetorical forms;" neither do we when we are doing our writing, but they are our standards of judgment for him. The student is absorbed in things, in people and their doings. He is not likely to be primarily concerned with forms of thought. On the other hand we teachers are absorbed in the manner in which the student expresses himself and we are inclined to overlook the vital subject matter.

This is what we have been doing with literature and composition in the high school. Is it the best thing to do? Most teachers are prepared to admit that it is not the best thing to do, and that the conventional methods have been a good deal of a failure. Responsible as the colleges have been for giving these characteristics to our teaching, they now fortunately, are no longer satisfied with what we seem able to do in the high schools, and the "freshman and his English" subjects us to much caustic criticism and ridicule. Business and professional men to whom we are sending our graduates as stenographers, typists, and office assistants are far from being satisfied with what our product is able to do. The pupils themselves have never been satisfied and have persistently, wantonly, it has seemed to us, regarded English courses as dry, uninteresting, and unprofitable. In the past few years teachers, individually, have sought to "do something about it," and under the alluring doctrine of "creating interest" have introduced this and that innovation in this and that manner, seeking to put "life" into the English work. Current issues of educational publications abound in description of devices for giving zest and variation to the English work. Many, perhaps all of these, offer valuable and helpful suggestions, and the teacher in whose breast this, that, and the other innovation strike a responsive thrill, adopts one or more of them; but we have not all adopted the best of these devices; there are as many different opinions as there are different devices; and we ourselves lack unity, coherence, and proper emphasis in common aim and method. Shall we say that "It all depends upon the individuality, or personality, of the teacher," or shall we seek some more satisfactory and comprehensive solution? Can we not find a basic, rational, definitely acknowledged, common aim and commonly recognized functioning value for our work in the common-sense processes of the socializing, adjustment-making secondary education of today and tomorrow?

Let us first answer the question, "What do we reasonably hope to accomplish in our work?" with the further question, "Who is this whom we are preparing for graduation from high school?" Is he a literary critic-to-be? Is he a writer-to-be of literature? Is he a poet-to-be? Is he an essayist-to-be? Is he even a good editor or newspaper reporter-to-be? He is no one of these! If he hopes to be any one of these he will find a way to go to college or the specializing school to prepare to be it! But as the high school graduate he is Tom, Dick, and Harry, Mary, May, and Myrtle, two out of every hundred of whom will be professional writers doing newspaper or hack work, and considerably less than one of whom will be writers or critics of literature! Perhaps ten or fifteen in a hundred will have occasion sometime in their lives to write for publication; about forty in a hundred will write papers for missionary meetings or women's clubs, or reports for stockholders' meetings or governing bodies; the rest of the hundred, practically half of the whole number, will be writing business correspondence under dictation or upon their own initiative concerning the shipment of goods, offering merchandise for sale, or fixing a price, or arranging a contract. Let us not then assume that we are making writers or critics of literature out of any considerable portion of our high school pupils. Our student is one who is going out into business and the professions to become an articulating unit in the work-a-day world, and the recognition of him as such must constitute the common viewpoint which must form the basis for our common aim.

How then shall we prepare him for this presumably inconspicuous, yet important function? How shall we make our English teaching "go to the mark" in the sense that it will be of real service to him in real life? These are questions involving considerations of both aim and method, hence the discussion that follows will correlate aim and method. They have to do with both subjects with which our problem is concerned, namely, literature and composition; and since aims and methods in literature are radically different from the aims and methods in composition, and should have separate places in the administration of the curriculum, the two subjects will be considered separately in the discussion that follows:

In the past few years constructive criticism solidly grounded upon sound reasoning has built out into the current of conventional theory and practice in secondary education jetty structures that have served to swerve it from the traditional channel of "mental discipline" as a primary aim to the new and deeper pathways of "socialization," or those aims and methods whereby the individual is adjusted to those elements of his environment that are of concern to him in modern life. The result of this constructive work has, in a constantly increasing measure, served to bring a larger part of that great "inland empire" of individual native abilities and possibilities into closer contact with the great "world's work" without, so that we are now beginning to see moving out upon the better directed current of the new channel individual students who, by reason of the new vocational and socializing aims and methods, have had their powers so developed and rationally trained that they are able to make proper and efficient use of them in business life, in the vocations, and to some extent in the professions. The constructive criticism mentioned has been that of conceiving education as being the process of adjusting the individual boys and girls to a working relationship with their environment, and that of finding such values in the subjects in the curriculum that pursued will result in the acquirement of "knowledge that will function," and habits of thought and action that will "get to the mark" in life employments. Aims and methods must stand or fall under the exacting demands of these requirements.

Our subject of literature, then, must have adjustment-making values. What are they? They must have to do with things that are of concern to us in modern life, but any things that are of concern to us in modern life are more than ways and means whereby we make a living or a "mark" in the world. We are concerned also with our avocations, our habits of harmless enjoyment, and personal culture, and these come through the development of intellectual and aesthetic appreciations, tastes, ideals, and interests. We are concerned with gettting on pleasantly with our fellows, and this becomes possible through the development of sympathy and toleration, reliability and integrity. It is at the invitation of these demands that the study of literature has its "inning." No longer does anyone not hopelessly moored to the barnacled and rejected doctrine of mental discipline as a primary aim insist that literature must be read with an encyclopedia at the reader's elbow, or that parsing exercises must be made of the classics. "Literature is the body of written truth about life"; "Literature reveals the ideals, patriotic, social, domestic, religious, which the race has cherished in the past, and which democracy needs now more than ever before." If so, why not teach it as such? Most of us now do, but now and then there bobs up from the conscientious mind the annoying suggestion that we may have broken too completely from the past, and that we ought to "make" the students do this, that, or the other sanctioned by historic precedent of the kind heretofore described. But let us not be troubled! Do we not want the student to enjoy his work in literature now, so that when he passes out from us he will retain a lasting liking for, at least a predisposition in favor of, things literary. When a Shakespearean drama comes to his town we want him to go and see it, do we not, prompted by the pleasant memories he retains of the work he did in high school classes in the study of the production? We want him to want to have and use a set of the Harvard Classics in his home, do we not? We want him to acquire the habit of picking up a bit of good poetry or prose in current literature as it appears in the magazines and reading it for enjoyment, do we not? We want him to be sympathetically familiar with the leading essayists, story-writers, and dramatists of the day, do we not, as well as have a conversational familiarity with the classic authors? In short, we are agreed that we want his appreciations of good literature to be a vital part of his every-day living. Then in the class room we shall see to it that the pupil learns of the truth about life through literature, that he thinks and talks of human strifes and emotions as presented there, of the relation of these strifes and these emotions as seen in the characters of literature to his own individual experiences and his probable future experience, in a manner that emphasizes the fundamental moral and spiritual values, rather than that "Shakespear's later plays have more light endings than his earlier plays," or that Macaulay was fond of hyperbole and antithesis. We shall induce him to analyze and discuss faulty motives and perverted ambitions, rather than how to detect every faulty accent or to memorize the rhyme scheme of a sonnet by combinations of the letters of the alphabet. These are the values and aims that should give a vital place to literature in our curriculum.

But we can go too far in prescribing exact method for the teaching of literature in high schools. The treatment appropriate to one piece of literature is unsuited to another. If we are seeking to give stimulus to the appreciation of literature we find that we have several forms of natural reactions which have to do with appreciations; namely, reactions to content, reactions to form, reactions to rythym, and to some extent, perhaps, in the high school, such reactions as correspond to an appreciation of style. No teaching of literature in the secondary school can be all of one type. Any method which reduces the study of the classics to rule and formula is the very thing that we are trying to get away from, but we should have the common, leading aim which we should keep before us, whereto we may adjust relative interests, and whereby we may evaluate the things in any particular piece of literature with a view to getting the best results with a given group of pupils. What we must remember is that we are studying and reading literature, not so much about literature; that we are training the mind of youth to the appreciation of literature, not to memorize facts in biography or the history of literature, except to the extent that knowledge of an author's career or personality, or the conditions of the time in which he lived aids to the understanding of the particular selection given for reading. Texts in the history of literature should be used in the background for reference work and oral report in class. They should not have the leading place we are wont to give them. Nothing should be allowed to obscure the idea that it is the work, and not the worker that is essentially vital.

Now as to our aims in composition, better called expression. This subject again takes us back to our answer to the question, "Who is this whom we are preparing for graduation from high school," the answer to which we are obliged to admit is, "He is one who is going out into business and the professions to become an articulating unit in the work-a-day world." Here, then, our aims are intensely practical. Our student must acquire a correct, vigorous, efficient use of the vernacular. Let us further inquire into the need for this aim, with some discussion of methods.

A question directed to any business or professional man who employs office assistants as to what is the matter with high school graduates will get the response that they do not know how to use the English language, that they cannot spell and punctuate correctly, and that they cannot be trusted alone with a business letter. They leave the high school unprepared to do the things that they will most likely be called upon to do. The few apparently simple things they ought to be able to do they cannot do. It is a good deal the fault of the student himself, no doubt, and yet it must be our fault to a considerable contributory extent. The situation is not necessarily discouraging, but, first having a definite, practical aim, we must have a more rational and definite method. This demands that our study of expression be separated from the study of literature—as is now recommended in the course of study recently published by the National Council of English Teachers. The time-endorsed method of three days a week for literature, and two days a week for composition has no valid sanction. The "composition days" disturb the continuity of the studies in literature, and the "piecemeal" methods so obnoxious can hardly be avoided. This time division also prevents that continuity and persistency in the composition work which permits sustained and progressive attention to a particular aim. which results in sought-for habits of thought and action. The alternate semester method endorsed by the National Council no doubt will be found to be the most satisfactory, but it may be done by way of alternating six-week periods with good results. Any shorter period than the latter invites "lost motion" and denies permanent results.

More particularly as to the administration of the course of study, the next step in standardization in Oregon should be a standard course in the vernacular from the first grade through to the twelfth, wherein definite continuities and correlations are provided for, with repetitions of intensive drill upon the essentials at definite intervals. Under such a system the child who removes from one district to another in the state would not suffer dis_ turbance in the essential continuity of his work in grammar and composition. In the high school division of this twelve-year course the first semester of the Freshman year should be devoted to a review of the essentials of grammatical form presented inductively; that is, the pupils should be given practice sentences with blanks calling for the insertion of the nominative or objective case of pronouns, the singular or plural of verbs, the use of shall or will, and the like, leading to a recognition and statement of the reason for the proper use. Analysis or diagraming of sentences should be done insofar as it leads to a proper understanding of the relationship of words that determines case and the need for punctuation, enables the student to visualize the sentence, and gives him a standard whereby to judge the grammatical correctness of new word combinations with which he will be from time to time confronted. Similar work should be definitely and comprehensively repeated in the first semester of the Junior year, and again briefly in the last part of the Senior year.

In the work of written expression we should no doubt give attention to matters of paragraph structure in a considerable degree, but the study of the paragraph should not begin with definitions of what constitutes unity, coherence, and emphasis, but just as the newer science texts are beginning with practical references to, and explanations of, the phenomena of the immediate environment of the pupil, leading thence to a recognition and statement of rule, law, and definition, so the work in written expression should begin with the subject matter that interests the student in his immediate environment and lead to a recognition of form. We must first give the student something to express, and an opportunity to express himself, and then be interested with him in the subject matter to which he gives expression. Let him write upon vocational topics, industrial topics, how-to-make-and-do-things topics, topics from leisure interests and student activities, topics in other school studies, current biography of successful men, news of business and science, and such other things as he may find of interest in the literary publications. Give him subjects that require investigation and report, not accounts of his vacation and his camping trip, for upon the latter the teacher cannot check for truth. Let us give attention to form, style, and structure so far as it is necessary to the statement of truth, to the statement of accurate observation, to the statement of narration that is clear in its sequences, to the judicious choice of the important, and the careful elimination of the unimportant, concerning some subject preferably with which the student is not familiar at the time of the assignment, but that requires investigation calling for the exercise and development of his power of accurate observation, his power of judicious selection, and his power of seeing truth, with the emphasis upon truth and accuracy.

A great help to written expression is a much neglected form of English work, namely, that of oral expression. Most people employ oral expression much more frequently than they do written expression. Examples of the need for the training in oral expression are found in many forms of vocational activity, conspicuously in all forms of salesmanship, and particularly in the dictation of letters. The young man in business should be able to approach another man in business and in an alert, straightforward and direct manner "say something" adequately and to the point. One full semester of this work conducted under the direction of an enthusiastic and competent teacher for every student in high school would go far in the direction of the results we are seeking. The work overcomes self-consciousness and embarrassment, develops self-control and poise, and "tones up" the whole demeanor and bearing. It is exceedingly valuable in the "appreciative study" of the classics by way of directing the mind of the student to a recognition of the necessity for, and the value of, vigorous and interpretative reading. Conducted in connection with the work in written composition it is of great value in bringing to the attention of the student the correlation between the written and spoken vocabulary. A very good way to do is to make the investigation assignment for oral report first, insisting upon an extemporaneous report made from a carefully prepared, brief outline. It will be found that the ability to make logical and climactic arrangement of thoughts can be developed. Follow this with written work upon the same subject matter, and it will appear, if the outline for the extemporaneous speech has been logically prepared and developed, that the transfer of the thought to written expression will give sufficient evidence of unity, coherence, and emphasis, concerning which latter three things so much time is now being consumed from the approach of definitions.

But complete success cannot be had in the work with the vernacular until we get the cooperation of other teachers for the discouragement and intolerance of the garbage, scrap-can English so commonly employed by the pupils in their recitations. The requirement that pupils make answer to questions in complete sentences is one which is beyond our control as English teachers outside of our own classes. This responsibility is the principal's, a part of whose business should be to see in visiting class rooms that the proper standards are maintained.

An employer of office help recently said to me that his greatest difficulty with employes of the high school graduate's age is to find those who are not continually waiting to be told what to do, but who have initiative enough to seek out or think up work to do. Perhaps our high school methods of the past, now being gradually discarded for better, have contributed to this unfortunate typical situation.

May not we English-teachers, therefore, recognize a common aim in our work, and to a large extent a common method? May we not so evaluate our work that we may more successfully do our part in "adjusting the individual high school student to those elements of his environment that are of concern to him in modern life, and developing and training his powers so that he may make proper and efficient use of them?" In short, let us give him knowledge that will function, and habits of thought and action that will get to the mark in life employments!

The Oregon Council of English Proceedings

By ROSA B. PARROTT, Secretary

The 1917 meeting of the Oregon Council of English, held in conjunction with the State Association, was the most successful in its history and much credit is due to President Ernest S. Bates who prepared the program. Many excellent papers were read and the discussions showed that all were interested in English in a constructive way. The meeting augured well for the future of English instruction in Oregon.

The papers given will appear in full in this magazine, so I shall not discuss them but shall mention only the English problems brought up by these papers which were referred to a committee consisting of Dr. A. P. McKinley, Lincoln High, Portland; Miss Viola Ortschild, President Grade Teachers' Association, Portland; and Miss Rosa B. Parrott, head of English Department, Oregon Normal School. This committee is to investigate the following problems and report at the next meeting: The advisability of separate teachers for literature and composition; the practicability of separate semesters for literature and composition; the advisability of a definite cumulative course in English for the grades; a plan for making the grade examinations in English more stringent. They were also to investigate and report on a resolution submitted that all candidates for a teacher's certificate be required: (1) To master the rudiments of a foreign language; (2) To have a working familiarity with prefixes, suffixes and one hundred roots from the Latin; (3) To master the sentences by daily work, both analytical and constructive, covering the period of a year and based upon some text of a difficulty equivalent to Caesar.

The council hopes by investigations and reports such as these to raise the standard of English instruction and to make it more practical.

The Local Council instructed the secretary to invite the National Council to meet at Portland in conjunction with the N. E. A. The secretary is happy to announce that the invitation was extended and has been accepted by the National Council.

The 1917 meeting closed with the election of the following officers: President, Miss Mary Perkins, University of Oregon; First Vice President, Miss Viola Ortschild, Portland; Second Vice President, Miss Brunquist, Hood River; Secretary-treasurer, Miss Rosa B. Parrott, Oregon Normal School; Member at Large, E. F. Carleton, Assistant State Superintendent; Executive Members, M. G. Merriam, Reed, and Professor Berchtold, O. A. C.

Dramatization in the High School

By ROSA B. PARROTT, Oregon Normal School; Demonstrated by a /Group of Students from Oregon Normal School

Dramatics in the high school have been the subject of much discussion recently and, because of its popularity and practicability, I am going to discuss a phase of it which I have found most helpful in my work and designate it as "Dramatization in the High School." Dramatics, as previously stated, have been long advocated for high school work as has dramatization for the primary grades; but I believe there is a type of dramatization that can be used most advantageously in the upper grades and high school as well as in the lower grades. This is book dramatization. By book dramatization, I mean the reading of the lines from the book instead of memorizing them. The advantage of this is that it allows more dramatization than could possibly be done if the lines were memorized. I advocate the production of, at least, one play each year staged, costumed and memorized. This is about all that can be done if you do memorize the parts. One play, however, is not enough to get results. Students must appear before their mates many times before that "wigglesome self-consciousness" is eliminated and poise gained. Pupils should also impersonate many different types of characters. These things cannot be done if only one play a year is given, but they can be done if you dramatize several productions wholly or in parts.

I am not going to discuss the many values of dramatization, for, if I did, I fear you would get the impression that I find it a panacea for all the ills that beset the overworked English instructor. I am going to mention one, however, in addition to those already suggested. It creates a love for good literature. This alone should recommend it to all English instructors. You will recall that the committee appointed from the National English Council and the N. E. A. to investigate the "Condition of English Instruction," emphatically reported that the greatest work of the English instructor was to create a love for good literature; tacitly implying that we were not accomplishing this work. Did you ever hear a student say, "I hate that! We dramatized it in high school." But have you not often heard students say, "I hate that! We studied it in high school."

All selections studied cannot be dramatized, as many of them have no dramatic qualities; but select, at least, two each semester that can be dramatized wholly or in parts. There are many methods used in dramatizing, all of which bring results more or less satisfactory. I shall, however, briefly outline the method I have found to be the most practical.

The production should be taught first, so the student has a knowledge of it as a whole. Here, as in dramatizing it, many different methods may be used, so shall leave it to the individual teacher to select her own method of procedure. After it has been taught, select the chapter, act, stanza or part you wish to dramatize. Caste it and have the students read the lines at their desks. If you think it necessary, let some one read the narrative and descriptive parts, as these often give the setting, costumes and action. (This is not always necessary, however, as the students get this from their study of the selection as a whole.) After the parts have been read, discuss the staging, costumes and action. The students should be familiar with the location of the scene, the apparatus necessary and the costumes and customs of the age in which the scene is laid, in order to get the atmosphere of the production. We, however, in this type of dramatics use only the simplest apparatus and no costumes, but lay particular stress only upon the acting and speaking. Because of its importance bits of the action are frequently worked out by individuals in the class before the caste appears for its performance. For example, the bowing of the attendants before King Arthur and the kneeling of the suppliants should be demonstrated. Even after this has been carefully done and all parts fully discussed, don't expect a perfect performance at the first presentation. I would suggest, however, that after it has been given once, you either recaste it, or let the same actors present it again, after you have discussed with the class where the acting might be improved. Then, if time permits, let a third group give it. This presentation should be fairly satisfactory, but remember we are not working to develop stars but for a better understanding and a greater appreciation of the selections studied and poise for the student before an audience. I, have no hesitancy in asserting that these results are attained if dramatization is engaged in systematically.

As I have suggested, many of the selections read cannot be dramatized at all, others only in parts and a few as a whole. The program, as the story-teller who gives the connecting links between the scenes is frequently called, is of great assistance in those productions which can be dramatized only in parts. It is a modernized Greek chorus. She is invaluable if you wish to dramatize for exhibition work, as she can give the parts of the story that do not lend themselves easily to dramatic interpretation. In the class room she is not so indispensable, as the students know the parts omitted from their previous study.

In closing I wish to say that the productions given in the State Course for High Schools that I should advocate for dramatization are: "Gareth and Lynette," which we are going to use this afternoon to demonstrate this work; scenes from "The House of Seven Gables," selections from the "Iliad," parts of the "Gold Bug," Peabody's "Piper," parts of "Beowulf," "Robin Hood," parts, if not all, of the Shakespeare plays studied; parts of "Pilgrim's Progress," scenes from "Robinson Crusoe," scenes from the "Vicar of Wakefield," parts of "Marmion," scenes from "Ivanhoe," "The Pied Piper of Hamelin," parts of "Silas Marner," "selections from "A Tale of Two Cities," parts of "Treasure Island." This is a splendid list to select from and I hope every high school teacher in Oregon, who has not, will take advantage of the opportunity to present, at least, one during the spring semester.

(At the close of the talk two scenes from Tennyson's Idyll "Gareth and Lynette" were given by the Normal students.)

English with English Left Out

By JULIA BURGESS, University of Oregon

The challenging phrase of our title may arouse question and doubt. Is English left out? What is this English, which, we aver, is left out? In answer we inquire: What is French? What is German? What are Greek and Latin? Languages, all of them. So with English; it too is a language, not primarily a body of thoughts expressed in literature.

It is as a language that we wish to consider it. May there be a course in so-called English in which the language receives far less than its share of attention? What would a course in Latin be without a discipline in Latin grammar? What would a course in German be without study of the construction of a German sentence? What would a course in any foreign language be without a technical foundation?

The ultimate purpose of a language course may be to enable the student to read the literature of that language understandingly, or it may be to qualify him to converse and write fluently. The purpose of English is to accomplish both these ends. Neither aim can be satisfactorily attained without technical training; and this is especially true of the latter—the power to converse and write. The power of expression is a fine art. Like every other art it has its technique. Unlike every other, it is often regarded as easy of acquisition, requiring no basis of scientific information, no tools ,and no drill in using them. That this universally needed but difficult art requires laborious, long-continued language drill, and that it should receive more of such drill than it now does, it is the purpose of this paper to bring out. "By their fruits ye shall know them." Is English—the mastery of the English language—left out in so-called English courses? The fruits seem to indicate that in considerable degree it is.

Among the ninety freshmen whom I attempt to instruct in English composition, and who are quite representative, about thirty, or one-third, are commonly guilty of what is known as the sentence error. They write, with entire statisfaction, to themselves, the following as sentences:

1. Participial phrases as: "The music being furnished at first by a victrola"; "Not even attempting to delve deeply into the subject;" "The belts being double"; "One of these medals coming from France."

2. Relative clauses, as: "Which looked more like a devil than a ghost."

3. Clauses beginning with while: "While Washington was well acquainted with the Indians."

4. Part of a compound predicate: "And forced her to stop warfare against merchant ships."

Several students are likely to write five or six such incomplete sentences in a paper of three hundred words. These thirty students run jauntily on over the barriers of independent clauses and sentence division, as in the following, written without any punctuation whatever: "It's very easy to do that anybody can but offering something better in place of that is not so easy." "At last they were to the O he started to paint it." "About 2 per cent is direct interest the rest goes toward lowering the principal." "I knew there was no getting out of it so I ceased."

Often a comma is made to serve the purpose of the necessary semicolon or period, as: "Bill assured them that the team was in good condition, in fact he said—" etc. "We hear people say 'Pres. Wilson kept us out of war,' is this true?"

Instances of the "comma fault" are the most usual of all the errors in sentence structure, and arise from a failure on the part of someone to realize the imperative need of imparting a knowledge of fundamental principles of punctuation, especially the use of the semicolon to mark off independent clauses in the same sentence.

Other mistakes in punctuation are rife. One would say that the use of the interrogation point is nearly unknown, from the infrequency of it after such a question as, "What is it to study." "Wilsons Internal Policy," or like expression, is rarely accompanied by apostrophe to denote possession. Restrictive and non-restrictive ideas are seldom distinguished. From a desire to be thorough, a student will write: "Thus, only those, unfit for labor; children and decrepit old people—."

Too much punctuation is as bad as too little; just enough is of incalculable value. It is my full belief that two reasons account for the hopeless chaos or the great void in students' papers in the matter of punctuation.

One reason is that there is abroad a notion that punctuation is a small matter, that much attention to it is "sissified." Teachers even are heard to say that they do not like a page "peppered with punctuation." Neither does any one of the strongest advocates of the study of punctuation, if by such a remark allusion is made to an indiscriminate, unmeaning use of points. Yet any page of dialogue in the Saturday Evening Post will exhibit a liberal and yet wholly correct and inevitable peppering of commas and quotation marks. If the teachers and students who believe that punctuation is going out of fashion, would take the trouble to read with critical eye ten pages of any book put out by one of the best publishing houses, they would find that their belief was error. Certain changes of usage are taking place, but they are minor changes.

The other reason for poor punctuation is very different. It is ignorance of the principles of construction of the English sentence. Punctuation serves to indicate structure. How can the student indicate something which he does not know? The average student has a very vague idea of the difference between a dependent and an independent clause, does not know a noun clause beginning with "that" from a relative clause, and cannot distinguish restrictive from non-restrictive clauses or phrases.

Punctuation can be taught, if students have a knowledge or are given a knowledge of grammar, and if teachers believe it worth while to have them taught this art.

That students do not, however, have a satisfactory working knowledge of grammar, so far as clauses are concerned, has been shown by examples already given. There is equal ignorance of usage in matters not affecting punctuation. Pronoun reference is very generally bad: "Charles E. Hughes, republican nominee for president of the U. S., which expires in 1920." "Every one, before they see fit to go into business—."

Pronouns shift from first person to second, and to the impersonal "one," within a paragraph. Misrelated participles are thick as blackberries: "Knowing that narcotics are injurious, laws have been passed."

Verbs fail to agree with subjects, and verbal forms are often a hodgepodge, as: "If this teacher had have taken time to have washed the windows—" which is often varied to "had of taken time."

Connectives are misused: "It looked like O. A. C. had a fine team." The student blithely writes: "Most all of us"; "quite a ways"; "Being that this is the case." Even his reading is inaccurate, for in reproducing it he says, "Bengal is a providence of British India"; and speaks of "Wilson's policy of meditation" (mediation) "in Mexico." One would naturally form the conclusion that the student, to use his own words, "never got to go to school, but very little." And one quite agrees with the girl who complains that "These people are too illiterate for health."

What is the cause for this illiteracy? It would be hard to say, but certain it is, the illiteracy exists. A report on preparation in English was called for from the students recently. One student diagnoses her case as follows:

1. I attended ———— High School, before entering the University.

2. English was my major subject. I had four years of Composition and Literature in the above mentioned preparitory school: (a) The Freshmen year was devoted to composition, with the exception of one or two poems. (b) The Sophomore year was a study of principles of style in Composition and Literature. (c) The Junior and Senior years were all devoted to literature; all English courses were five hours.

3. Nature of work in Composition: (a) In composition classes: As I remember a theme was required every two weeks, with a choice of subject being given. My themes were descriptive, as I can remember. Of our vacations, and the like. These themes were read before the class and criticized in the class period. If they were good nothing was said, and very little if they were not, we were given a grade and never thought anything more about our papers. There was no revision of papers required and that is why I am having such a disgraceful time now.

4. In Composition, Literature classes—(a) When we were studying such books as Dickens' "Christmas Carol," a character sketch was usually required. We only wrote one theme for a book like this. Our grade was the most important criticism we could receive. These papers were usually handed back, but nothing was ever marked so the pupil could find his mistake. There was no revision required. My last year of High School English was entirely "Literature." A certain number of books had to be read and a book review of a certain number of words was required for a passing grade.

As I look back and see how little we knew of the fundamentals of composition and how much we need this kind of work in our everyday life it seems almost unbelievable.

Another student says: "Criticism was poor and indefinite. Never revised anything—merely looked over criticisms if I happened to have time." Another says: "The themes would sometimes be handed back with corrections, and other times not even returned. I never had revised a paper until coming to the university." Another: "The themes we wrote were not corrected, if I remember rightly, except when they were read in class. I do not remember of revising or rewriting a single theme, no matter how poor." Another says: "Through the whole course no especial emphasis was laid on English composition; it was neglected more than anything else."

About one-half the students whose reports were examined, stated that they had never made revisions on papers in high school work. Many said that class discussions were all the criticism given; some expressed opinion that drill in sentence structure was insufficient. One student said that papers were marked with following general terms: "Good," "Could be better," "Be more careful," etc.

From the alarming ignorance of correct usage exhibited by the students' work, and from the testimony offered by various students, it would appear that greater efforts should be made somewhere to secure correctness of expression among entering university classes. The university should not be compelled to teach elementary grammar. Unless these efforts are made and made successfully, it may be necessary, however, for the university to institute classes in sub-freshman work which shall be required of all students failing to pass a thorough entrance examination in grammar, but for which no credit shall be given.

But this is the suggestion of a palliative only. Better preparation should certainly be shown by entering classes. How can it be attained? And how can the university be assured of it?

The answer to the first question is, it can be attained through separate instruction in English composition under teachers who are specially prepared to do the work, who care for the work sufficiently to give patient toil to it, and who are allowed time for the examination of papers and for conferences with the students—with the poorer students at least. I believe that approximately one-half the time of the four years in English should be given strictly to composition, whether in the combined composition-literature classes or in special courses. It might be well for one of these courses, if given separately, to be required in the Junor or Senior year. Subjects for themes should not be exclusively taken from literature, but should often require the organization of material derived from observation or experience.

Above all, teachers of English composition need special fitness for their work, and should not be chosen without special recommendation for that work. It does not follow that a lover or interpreter of good literature is a safe quide in composition. Composition requires a painstaking attention to detail, as well as an appreciation of literary effect. One must care a great deal for the ideal of correct expression and for the students' good, to see any reward for the hours of toil involved.

And here I wish to say that the correction of papers is, to my mind, an absolute essential. Criticism of oral English is most helpful to the student in regard to his thought, his organization of material, his qualities of interest and force, his use of illustrations, his general choice of words. But the kind of error shown in the examples quoted, cannot be combatted in that way. It is impossible to stop the student every time he is guilty of wrong pronoun references, and require him to correct his mistake. He cannot recall, probably, his exact words, even a moment after he has spoken them. The teacher also finds it difficult to recall them. The recitation must not lose unity by frequent interruptions. Detailed criticisms at the end are practically impossible. And yet these minute criticisms are exactly those needed, and the minute excellences are those that mark the master of style. Careful correction of many papers, and revision of many, if not all, are, I believe, necessary.

I would not leave this point of the subject without making acknowledgment of the genuinely excellent work done by many of the English teachers of the state. In speaking of university freshmen I have deplored the submerged one-third—the illiterates. It is true that there is a superior one-third—the well-trained—who testify to well-planned, thorough courses of instruction. It is also true that the way of the composition teacher in the high school is beset with difficulties, and that the accomplishment of admirable results under the conditions that prevail, merits the warmest encomium.

How can better preparation in English composition be attained? we have been asking. And now, how can the university be assured of this better preparation? By the complete segregation of composition from literature in the matter of grading—we would answer. The study of composition is the study of an art, with some basis of science. The study of literature is a study of content, of substance, of thought and feeling, with attempt also at appreciation of literary form. Literature, it is true, may serve as a model for the art, but one cannot become an artist simply by looking at masterpieces. Excellence in appreciation does not presuppose excellence in execution. A grade, therefore, given in literature is no evidence of the proper grade in composition. No matter whether the course is a combined composition-literature course—two hours of one and three hours of the other—separate grades should be given for the composition. And separate grades of passing rank in composition should be made a requisite for entrance at the university. At present there is no guarantee that a student accredited in English with a high grade, has earned that grade through composition Good grades in English are offered by some of our illiterate students. It is impossible to account for these, except on the supposition of extreme laxity of standards in bestowing such credit, or on the assumption that the grade presented for entrance to one department of university instruction was earned in work so distinctly different as to be reckoned that of another department.

Separate grades in literature and composition would go far toward remedying the evils and solving the problems presented in this paper. Such separate accrediting of work done in English would enable the university to admit or reject candidates intelligently; would greatly simplify the work of the Freshman year by obviating the necessity for a lengthy review of first principles; would afford a means for just valuation of the composition work done in each high school; and, finally, would vastly stimulate the work of composition in these high schools and promote its excellence, and by so doing would bring about a condition in which there could be no such thing as English with its most important element—training in English language—left out.

Rural School Department

Edited by MRS. M. L. FULKERSON, Salem, Oregon

ROUND TABLE DISCUSSION.

The following are some of the questions asked in the Rural School Department of the Oregon State Teachers' Association, together with a synopsis of Superintendent Churchill's answers:

1. Would the course of study in grammar be covered if composition only, with no technical grammar, be taught through the first six grades? Yes. Begin technical grammar in the seventh grade as outlined in the revised course of study. If possible have two periods for language in the seventh and eighth grades, one period for composition and one for technical grammar. The composition work may be correlated with the work in history, geography, etc., and thus save time.

2. Has any definite step been taken to procure lantern slides to illustrate stories, poems, etc., for the use of the rural schools of the state? The legislature of 1915 was asked to appropriate a sum for this purpose but the bill failed to pass. Some county courts furnish machines for this purpose. Lane, Clackamas, Douglas, and Klamath counties have equipment to meet this demand.

3. What are some of the advantages of a school becoming standardized? In many cases the length of the school term is extended because an eight months' term is a requirement for standardization. Proper lighting is encouraged; one county has twenty-two schools in which lights have been changed because of standardization. The pride of the district is stimulated. People wake up to the fact that their school must be as good as any other. It unites the community to one purpose.

4. Should the light in a school room all come from one side? Yes, if sufficient light can be obtained.

5. Which is better, a large or a small jacket on a school room stove? The large jacket is better. It should be nine or ten inches from the stove rather than a less distance. The patent heating plant is preferable to the jacketed stove.

Mr. Churchill also suggested that a committee be appointed by the association to investigate the rural schools of the state—that this committee consist of such people as really know rural schools, who will give us not statistics only, but a constructive criticism such as will help to better rural conditions in Oregon.

* * *

CONSERVATION VERSUS CONSOLIDATION.

The hope of the rural school situation is the tendency that is leading toward a larger administrative unit, whether that unit be obtained by consolidation of small and weak districts, the conservation of larger areas, or legislation that will give a similar result.

It must be kept in mind, however, that the Northwest, with its mountains, its hills and its valleys will, for a long time at least, have as many one-room schools as it now has and that these smaller buildings should have just as good teachers and should be made and kept as clean, neat and inspirational as the larger plants. Again, it must be remembered that the best way to get the larger school is to do the best possible with the one on hand, but with all of this the ideal must be kept in mind. With all of this, it must be remembered that the one-room rural school cannot do the work, and give the country boys and girls the preparation that they are entitled to and ought to have.

You can standardize it, teacherage it, Parent-Teacher it, and even supervise it, but the one-room school will still be a twenty-two caliber short weapon, while the hills and valleys are abounding with opportunities for the big game of preparing boys and girls for actual life.

The one-room school is behind the times. It is as far behind the times as the turkey-wing cradle is behind the combined harvester; as far behind the times as the day when grandmother carded the wool, spun the yarn, wove the cloth and manufactured the garments for the entire family is behind the age of the suffragette, the woman's club, and the Ladies' Home Journal. It is as ancient as the dinky engine when compared with a modern locomotive or electric motor. It should have no important place in this day and age, when efficiency is the watchword of the hour and when the Ford, the electric light, the telephone and the fireless cooker are invading even the smallest and most remote farm homes.

Of course, there will long be pockets, invaded by the homeseeker, where it will be difficult to get pupils together in sufficient numbers to justify a larger school, just as there will always be little isolated patches of grain that cannot be handled by the reaper or the header, but the bulk of the work in rural schools must be done by districts large enough to provide funds for adequate supervision, suitable buildings, equipment for domestic science, manual training, agriculture, and teachers with stability as well as ability that will enable them to put the educational work of their community on a constructive and permanent basis.

Where the districts have already been created in too great numbers and with too little valuation, consolidation will help to do this. It will provide better buildings, better equipment for less money, larger play grounds, a working library and good janitor service. Consolidation will increase the attendance and diminish the number of cases of tardiness. It will give the inspiration of larger classes and the special courses, furnish a home high school and hold the boys on the farm. It will keep the money now spent in boarding schools at home, increase the valuation of local property and build up the home community.

Consolidation will equalize taxation, encourage other progressive movements, provide an auditorium large enough for community gatherings and afford modern methods of heating, lighting and ventilation that will make the schools more efficient and save the lives of our boys and girls. It will reduce the cost of instruction per pupil for the same grade of work, hasten the day when good roads will be the rule rather than the exception, hold pupils in school from two to four years longer, secure a larger percentage of promotions from grade to grade, eliminate many petty neighborhood strifes and jealousies, give teachers a chance to improve themselves by associating with other teachers, keep feet and clothing dry, cause fewer colds and stop quarreling, improper language and improper conduct on the road to and from school. It will save shoe bills, medicine bills and doctor bills, start children in school a little older and graduate them a little younger than the one-room school, and will work equally well wherever the superintendents, trustees, teachers, and patrons have the vision, the energy and persistence that will enable them to effect it, maintain it and make it succeed.

Consolidation is not a cure-all and should not be tried in a settlement so sparsely settled that the one-room buildings are already widely separated. On the other hand, if a drive of about one hour will bring the pupils from any given neighborhood to a school of two or more rooms that is already established and is not overcrowded, the expense of transportation will, as a general rule, be less than that required for the maintenance of a good one-room school, while the instruction will or should be of a much better grade. That is, when a good school has been established it should have the support, the encouragement and the cooperation of every patron within five miles of it, and the pupils living within that distance of a good school, well equipped and well conducted, should not be compelled to attend a school of the one-room type, with its one-pupil classes, its many recitations per teacher and its general lack of inspiration or hope for a better day or for better things.

Again, when a community finds its schools, none of which give the pupils the advantage of special primary work, practical courses or high school subjects, within easy distance of each other, it should be remembered that one good school, centrally located, with transportation provided at district expense, is worth more than any number of schools that lose from five out of six of their pupils before they finish even the elementary work.

When an investigation of the territory has shown that consolidation is feasible, the first thing to do is to create the sentiment in favor of one school that will prepare the boys and girls for actual work in actual life instead of three or four of the kind that lead them in far too many instances to the land of nowhere. This can best be done by personal work, followed by a general program, given mostly by the pupils, the concluding number of which is a round table discussion of the question, "Would consolidation and transportation give a better education to a greater number of pupils than the system now employed?" At this round table those in favor of the central school should remember that sentiment for a good school is more desirable than a larger school, erected in opposition to the desires of many of the people. No angry words should be spoken, the fullest explanations given and the best literature bearing on the question that it is possible to obtain, distributed.

The law dealing with the question should be studied and the process outlined followed to the letter. If the consolidation is effected and transportation is to be used, the different routes must be selected, always with the thought of the greatest good to the greatest number in mind. Only in rare cases should the majority of the pupils be on the road more than one hour. The wagons should be first class and should be furnished with lap-robes and heaters arranged in such a way that there will be absolutely no danger of fire. The team should be both safe and able, while the man in charge of the team should be selected with the same care that is exercised in the employment of a teacher. This is especially important, for the team-ster must see to it that no improper conduct is allowed on the road to and from school and as a usual thing a man who has children of his own will be best suited to the work. Organized in this way and carried on in a systematic business-like manner, consolidation can and will do for many other districts in the Northwest what it has already done and is doing for those places that have adopted it.

One thing about consolidation does not look so favorable. While during the past five years many schools have consolidated and provided the transportation that has meant a better school and more of it, during this same time about ten times that number of new districts have been created and had every appeal been granted that number would have been greatly increased. Many of these new districts do not have valuation or finances enough back of them to finance a poor pop-corn wagon, much less a good school. Most of them, it is safe to say, have no vision of anything more than a one-teacher school and have no dream of a plant that will adequately care for the future. Many of the people in these districts have never stopped to think that schools, after all, are a good deal like eggs, and that one good one will do more for a community and furnish more real satisfaction than any number of those of doubtful flavor and quality that can be provided.

Consolidation has proven to be a good thing. It has done much to improve the condition of rural schools, but without any thought of making that good less than it really is, the conservation of school territory and educational opportunity has meant more, yes, much more for the real educational progress of the Northwest than all of the examples of consolidation combined. The worker for consolidation has been in the lime light. He has been honored and his praises have been sung by Federal bulletin, farm journal, educational journal, and the popular magazine, while those county superintendents, or other educational workers "who have stood behind the guns, who have fought, first, last and all the time against the creation of new districts, that meant poorer instead of better schools, who spent hour after hour and even day after day in listening to long pleadings and still more lengthy hearings, who have received the blame, and who have even been kicked out of office, because they worked unselfishly for the best interests of their boys and girls, have only the unnamed and unlettered monument of good schools as their monuments.

The consolidation laws of most states are too bunglesome. They require too much red tape. Even where most of the people have been willing to consolidate, the technicalities of the laws in many cases have allowed the will of the community to prevail. Even a good law in regard to consolidation would not avail much because local interest, and the prejudice of some people in favor of the school that was good enough for grandfather, good enough for father, good enough for me, etc., would still be in the way of the right kind of progress and the proper amount of it. What the Northwest needs is a larger unit. It needs a district large enough to finance an efficient superintendent and special supervisors of primary work, agriculture, manual training, domestic science, etc., with buildings and equipment suitable and adequate for efficient and thorough work.

If the educators and legislators cannot agree upon a county plan, they could at least help much by increasing the minimum size of the third class district, or by making the second class district the smallest unit for administrative purposes. This would give the smaller towns and centers the same individuality and freedom that the larger ones now have and thus place a premium upon local pride and initiative, while state aid or an icreased county tax, with an equitable basis of apportionment would tend to equalize the educational opportunity. The units would be compact and small, instead of the size of the larger counties, with holes here and there, such as would be occasioned by the dropping out of the cities or the first and second class districts as is usually provided in the county unit plan. Without change of law or constitution, the county superintendent would have the same relation to all districts that he now has and the school houses could be located where they would serve the greatest possible number of pupils, while local men would still be retained to look after the interests of local property. The advantage of this larger unit would be to bring at once what it would take years to get by the consolidation plan.

The best is none too good for the boys and girls of the Northwest, and those boys and girls forty miles from the railroad are entitled to just as good a teacher, just as good a building, just as good equipment, just as good an education and just as much of it as their city cousins in Portland, Spokane, Boise or Butte. To get it for them emphasis must be placed upon the thought that there is a greater need for better teachers than there is for more teachers, a greater need for better buildings than for more buildings, a greater need for better managed and more able districts than for more districts, and a greater need for practical thorough work than there is for many fads, fancies, subjects and courses, with a smattering knowledge of them all.—(A portion of the address given by C. W. Tenney, State Inspector of Rural Schools, Helena, Montana, in the Rural Department of the Oregon State Teachers' Association, Portland, Oregon, Dec. 29, 1916).

● ● ●

MOTION PICTURES IN THE SCHOOL.

Considerable interest is evident among the school men of Oregon on the question, "What use should we make and what use can we make of the motion picture for educational purposes?"

Thomas Edison is said to have declared that ten years hence motion pictures will have supplanted textbooks in the public school. Of course, Mr. Edison, however great his achievements in mechanical invention, can hardly qualify as an educational expert. We can be quite certain that no such sweeping change will come about. Study of the educational possibilities of the motion picture does convince a person, however, that unless we are even more conservative than school people are wont to be, the motion picture will have made a place for itself in our regular school work long before the expiration of ten years.

The development of the motion picture as a nation-wide force has been rapid. The Boston Transcript ranks the motion picture industry as the second largest in the United States with a gross earning of three hundred million dollars per year. There are in the United States by conservative estimate fifteen thousand motion picture theaters with an average daily attendance of six million people. Consider these facts and then remember that the first reference in standard American magazines to motion pictures under that name was not made until 1905 or 1906. It is true that the Scientific American between 1900 and 1904 published several articles discussing motion pictures as scientific curiosities and referring to them as kinematographs. No one discussed the general educational possibilities of the "movies" in the public prints previous to discussion on this topic at the N. E. A. in 1912. It is true that the Scientific American in 1909 mentioned the "movies" as possible aid in teaching trades.

The moving picture, notable mainly as a curiosity even ten years ago, has now spread all over the world. Developed first in France and later in Germany, it seems to have been most successfully promoted in the United States. The Esquimaux enjoy Wild West films. The Chinaman goes to the moving picture house at five in the afternoon and stays until midnight, protected by an oblique screen at the door to keep off the devils and wiping the perspiration from his face at intervals with hot towels furnished by the usher. The picture on the screen shows him cowboys with queues acting in a cattle ranch scene located by the Japanese producer in Kansas City, Missouri. After the "animated weeklies" have run their course in this county, they become news to the Chinaman. The Maharajah Gaikwar of Baroda, whom a native admirer insists is "the only most sensible Prince India has today," has been a factor in establishing the traveling motion picture show in his vicinity and it is said that "to educate the people is the only ultimate object."

If it is true that the motion picture has gone to the ends of the earth, it is even more true that it has permeated every section of our own country. There can be no doubt that the motion picture is an integral part of the experience of practically every high school boy and girl in America and of the greater number of grade school children. It is therefore an educational force, whether we like it or not.

For the very reason that motion picture production is a business and that producers are anxious above all things to make money, the development of educational film is coming about rather slowly. No one has yet written a standard textbook to be illustrated with moving pictures rather than with half tones; no state school system has as yet recognized the motion picture machine as a part of the necessary equipment of an up-to-date school. It is true that Orange, New Jersey, and Los Angeles, both of them centers of the motion picture industry, have equipped their schools and that many cities throughout the country have followed them at a distance.

In general, the school men seem theoretically convinced that the motion picture must be used in education. David Snedden, former Commissioner of Education for Massachusetts, says, "It is now clear beyond any question that the motion picture is destined to be an educational agency of first rate importance." President Emeritus Eliot of Harvard says, "The moving picture is a valuable means of instruction and all of our school systems ought to seize upon it." Superintendent Hyatt of California writes, "The time is at hand when moving pictures will be as much of an adjunct of any properly equipped school as textbooks." Henry W. Lanier expresses a very common opinion when he says, "Indeed the educator must use it, for at the present time film manufacturers are educating five million children a day along more or less undesirable lines." Commissioner Claxton of the United States Bureau predicts that "The future use of the educational cinematograph bids fair to surpass the predictions of its most sanguine advocates within the next decade and moving pictures will be an indispensable adjunct to every teacher and educational lecturer."

Common sense tells us that as soon as we have taken the necessary steps to make motion pictures available in the schools, many subjects even in the lower grades will be made more interesting, more valuable and more vital. Compare the relative value of the statement in an American geography book that "The Alps are covered with snow the year round" with the following outline of a motion picture lesson on the Alps taken from a German educational magazine: (a) Views along Eiger and Monch peaks, Interlaken, (b) Glaciers on the Grundewald, (c) Trip from Lauterbrunnen to the station Eismeer, (d) Mountain climbing, (e) Rocks of Saxon Switzerland, (f) Avalanche of a Cliff.

Why indeed should not pupils actually see this region and its customs through the medium of the motion picture, and be held for recitation upon what they have seen? Is there any doubt as to the comparative value of the statement that leaves everything to the child's imagination and the medium that brings enough of the actual scenery and life of the region under his observation to give him an adequate basis for ideas concerning the phenomena discussed?

In this, as in other movements, we are going to have to pray to be delivered from our friends—our too enthusiastic friends, who would supplant the printed page of literature with the motion picture film and who would limit the sweep of the child's imagination by portraying to him more or less crudely ideas which can be adequately pictured only by the inward eye. Guarding against all such perversions, we still can rest in the conviction that the school work in certain subjects can be immensely broadened through the use of the motion picture. Just as we have noticed that the showing of motion pictures is now a common event in every corner of the globe, so it is true that every part of the world and many phases of human experience can be brought to us through this medium. Professor Starr might be talking for any one of us when he says, "I have seen Niagara thunder over her gorge in the noblest frenzy ever beheld by man; I have watched a Queensland river under the white light of an Australasian moon go whirling and swirling through strange islands lurking with bandicoot and kangaroo; I have watched an English railroad train draw into a station, take on its passengers and then chug away with its stubby little engine through the Yorkshire Dells, past old Norman Abbeys silhouetted against the skyline, while a cluster of century-aged cottages loomed up in the valley below, through which a yokel drove his flocks of Southdowns; I have beheld fat old Rajahs with the price of a thousand lives bejeweled in their monster turbans and the price of a thousand deaths sewn in their royal nightshirts as they indolently swayed in golden howdahs, borne upon the backs of grunting elephants; I saw a runaway horse play battledoor and shuttlecock with the citizens and traffic of a little Italian village, whose street had not known such commotion since the sailing of Columbus; I know how the Chinaman lives and I have been through the homes of the Japanese; I have marveled at the daring of the Alpine tobogganists and admired the wonderful skill of the Norwegian ski jumpers; I have seen armies upon the battlefield and their return in triumph; I have looked upon weird dances and outlandish frolics in every quarter of the globe, and I didn't have to leave Chicago for a moment."

In spite of our theoretical agreement as to the value of the motion picture in educational work, we are progressing rather slowly in making use of it. Meanwhile the business of film production continues to grow, a conservative estimate being that one and a half million feet of film are being produced every week in the United States alone.

Gregory Mason, writing in the Outlook for August 24, 1914, states the present situation pretty well when he says, "When it comes to the use of moving pictures as an integral part of the curricula of the schools, colleges and educational boards of the country, we find an extremely chaotic condition. . . . Schools and colleges are using moving pictures to teach, but for the most part they are going ahead blindly and alone. The result is that the demand for educational films is unorganized, fluctating and sporadic and as yet but few manufacturers consider it worth while to turn out films directly aimed to meet class work."

Mr. Mason makes a very adequate statement of the present situation when he says in the same article: "The trouble is that educators and film manufacturers do not get together. The teachers are waiting for film men to come to them with tentative programs of moving picture textbooks for all school courses; the manufacturers on the other hand are making so much money in the theatrical field that they prefer to wait for a definite and large-sized order from the schools."

It is not at all certain that the educational field will continue to be unnoticed by film producers. Several companies have made efforts which seem quite sincere, to make a beginning in the production of educational and scientific films in the United States. Many others have established so-called educational departments, the function of which seems to be to gather together in lists such title as seem to have educational possibilities. The efforts of these cataloguers at their best are limited by the fact that practically every foot of film is produced primarily for purposes of amusement and consequently does not lend itself to class room use to the best advantage. At their worst, the efforts of these people are pathetic, as witness lists recently sent to the University of Oregon by certain film exchanges in which such titles as "Three Weeks," "His Crooked Career," "Mabel's Beau," "Old Maid's Love," and "Toodles" were recommended as having distinctly educational value. It is very evident that as this matter is one that concerns the curricula of the schools, the school people will be obliged to take an interest in determining the nature of the educational film that is produced. The motion picture producers are carrying the technique of their art to a high point but they are not competent to outline textbooks to be illustrated with motion pictures. Neither, perhaps, as the school men until they have set themselves patiently to work to learn the possibilities of this new agency.

Such slight investigation as we have been able to make among manufacturers and exchanges leads us to believe that these people will welcome any steps looking toward the development of an educational market. Educational institutions are invariably good pay and motion picture theaters are not always safe financial risks. Furthermore, the development of the strictly educational motion picture is not likely, at the outset at least, to interfere seriously with the commercial use of film or with the business of the theaters.

In spite of the interest of film producers in a possible educational market, we are expecting the impossible if we suppose that they are going to turn their activities into what at present is a relatively unremunerative phase of the work out of any interest in education in the abstract, or in the interest of the future welfare of the boys and girls of America. Only such impractical people as school masters and preachers ever do anything of that sort. Since, then, it is clearly our task as school people, how shall we set about it to make use of this new educational agency?

Clearly we must recognize the fact that, if we are to depend on commercial producers, only with the development of an adequate market will come the real educational motion picture of the future. In this same connection we must realize that beginnings are often more or less unsatisfactory, but that they are very necessary. We should then put ourselves in position to furnish at least the suggestion of an adequate educational market. Resolving to make use of the great amount of fairly usable material now available for educational purposes we should equip our schools quite generally with motion picture projection apparatus, and while making use of the best that is to be had, should not cease to demand more suitable film. Fortunately, much of the socalled industrial film, produced of late for great manufacturing concerns to familiarize people with the operations in their plants, has great educational value. Furthermore, it is usually to be had for the asking, and thus fits the situation in which most school superintendents find themselves of having little or no budget with which to pay rental on film. The University of Oregon is in position to furnish almost any quantity of interesting and valuable motion picture film of this character, provided a sufficient number of organizations in the state are equipped with projection apparatus to make it worth while to bring the film to the coast. Among four hundred or more reels thus available, many have evident educational value. Some of the titles are: Good Roads, Saftey First, Evolution of Writing, Pure Food, Glacier National Park, City Sanitation, Carpet Weaving, The Gathering of News, Book Binding, Photography, Locomotive Building, The Chocolate Industry, Beef Packing, Irrigation, The Building of Automobiles, The Making of Shoes, Immigration, Ceylon Tea, Mining in British Columbia, Electricity on the Farm, Workman's Compensation, Modern Banking, Character and Habits of American Indians, Yosemite National Park, Yellowstone National Park, Mount Rainier National Park, Crater Lake National Park, The Fly Pest, Bird Life, and Preparation of Condensed Milk. While making use of such film as is available, we must do some hard thinking, some conscientious studying, and some constructive planning toward the development of the motion picture for use in the class room. Without allowing our imaginations to carry us away, yet with due appreciation of the wonderful educational possibilities that we are neglecting in this field, we must realize our obligation to make use of these possibilities and must set to work to learn how to utilize this tremendous educational force now so often badly used and so inevitably part of the experience of our pupils.—(Earl Kilpatrick, Assistant Dean, Extension Division University of Oregon, given in the Elementary Department of the State Teachers' Association).

Vocational Education Department

Edited by R. E. OHLOUPEK, Pendleton, Oregon

HOME ECONOMICS WORK AT PENDLETON.

By Alice Butler, Pendleton

In the "Ethics of the Dust," Ruskins says: "Cooking means the knowledge of Medea, and of Circe and of Helen, and of Rebekah and of the Queen of Sheba. It means the knowledge of all herbs and fruits and balms and spices and of all that is healing and sweet in the fields and groves and savory in eats. It means the carefulness and radiness of appliance; it means the economy of your great-grandmothers and the science of modern chemists; it means much tasting and no wasting; it means English thoroughness and French art and Arabian hospitality, and it means in fine that girls are to be perfectly and always, ladies loaf givers."

These words from the lips of one who devoted his life to the correlation to the beautiful and useful, show that he considered cookery no homely art. Indeed, it is an art which calls for much knowledge and skill and is worthy of one's best efforts.

It s not enough to follow directions of recipes. One must infuse into cooking one's own thoughts and ingenuity and individuality. Many are the things every girl needs to know concerning food before preparing it.

In purchasing she should know what foods to select, whence they came, and how prepared for market and the means of transportation. Since intelligent expenditure of the income is necessary for thrifty living, she must know how to get the best value in foods. In order to do this she must know the composition and nutritive value of foods. Today we have a great variety of foods. Some have little food value and are expensive. Often cheaper foods are very nourishing and can be made very palatable.

After the foods have been purchased the student must know how to prepare them. If she obtains the art of cookery she must think; that is, she must have the fundamental principles plus brains. She needs to learn to read a cook book—see the large things. Every girl must know the laws which govern fire and water; if she is alert she will observe all results and make a careful note of them. There is no such thing as "good luck." There is a cause for every failure and it should not occur the second time.

Since science is classified knowledge in applying science to the preparation of foods ,one principle of cookery is related to another. The methods of preparing one cooked cereal can be applied to all cooked cereals. If the girl has prepared one cream soup she can prepare all. She soon learns the fundamental principles.

In fruit and vegetable cookery the first thing to master is the classification. They are classified as to nature, cooking, composition and characteristics. Our foods must be cooked according to the foods and not the recipe. One should separate garnish from flavor. Never garnish with something one can not eat. The girl must learn the difference between essentials and variations. "Beware of tawdery." All through the work the student must apply the principles.

The ability to observe and reason while working is the most valuable asset for success in any kind of work. Hand work guided by an active mind is always prized. Skill in cookery may mean the acquisition of characteristics which make for success in any field of activity. In cooking one must use addition, subtraction, multiplication and division.

In addition to being a good cook, one must combine for the most perfect nutrition and flavor. She must know how foods are served and how they are digested. This brings in the mastery of physics, chemistry, ethics, history, and English.

Whatever path a girl may choose there will be a need of giving the mind the power of control over the body. Also the need of order, system, cleanliness and neatness. These are all gained in the laboratory while she is learning to cook. Not only has the study of food offered years of work to men and women but the art of home making has opened a large field for many.

No nation can rise higher than the highest type of home in the nation. In order to place every home of our land on a high plane, our girls are being taught the practical application of the theory which is taught at school. If the girl takes a music lesson she is required to practice an hour to an hour and a half a day in order to master these principles. Many schools are realizing that the principles of cookery alone do not prepare the girl for her real life work, "a home maker."

The city of Pendleton has realized this. The board has gone so far as to rent a house furnished completely.

Here the home economics teachers and the physical education instructor live. They pay rent and their grocery bills. The students in the housewifery class are divided into groups of four. Each group is given one hour daily in which to put the house in order. They study the makes of stoves, and all equipment of the house. The best methods of caring for a home are also studied. This same class in groups take turns in cooking in the cafeteria, planning the menus and doing the buying. The advanced class in domestic science cook, buy, plan and serve all special dinners and luncheons in the Practice House. The class in laundry take entire care of the table linen and each girl must wash a sweater, master the art of doing fine laundry work. The class in home management is also divided into groups. These groups do planning and buying of food for three meals a day for the instructors who live in the practice house. This class is planning and furnishing a home for $2000. They make excursions to the stores, studying linoleum, carpets, furnishings and equipment.

There are 112 girls taking domestic science and are in the high school and 115 girls from the grades. The domestic art girls have furnished a bed, making three comforters, the sheet and pillow cases. They have used the machine attachments and are learning hand and machine sewing. They are taught the use and application of the commercial pattern. It is interesting to note the change in a short time in the ideals of dress, after studying this work under the able direction of Miss Wilson and Miss Cavender. This department has ten machines, dress forms, good lockers, tables and a triple mirror. Just before the holidays they were given time to make Christmas gifts in yarn and thread crochet, also basketry and cretonnes. The thought of cast and appropriateness was held before them. A high standard is set and exactness is demanded. The girls are taught to be ever ready to serve the public.

A class outside of school in catering has been formed. There are nine girls doing this work. They find it a pleasure and of value. They go into homes, prepare luncheons, dinners and afternoon teas. The girls are well paid for their time.

If the practice house proves successful the classes in manual arts under the supervision of Professor Chloupek will erect a bungalow and build all of the furniture. This will offer the boys in agriculture a good opportunity to beautify and care for the lawn. This work in the West is rong but it is a goal for home economics instructors to work toward.

Vocational Department for 1917.

Officers for 1917—Pres. J. A. Bexel (commercial), Corvallis; vice president, Myra Butler (home economics), Monmouth; secretary, Alice Joyce (agriculture), Portland; delegate to the N. E. A. convention, H. H. Wardrip (manual training), Grants Pass.

Manual Training Division—Chairman, Phillip Parcher, The Dalles; vice chairman, F. M. Groshong, St. Johns High School, Portland; secretary, A. R. Nichols, Corvallis; delegate, L. L. Sommers, Portland.

Agricultural Division—Chairman, H. C. Seymour, Corvallis; vice chairman, N. C. Maris, Salem; secretary, Fay Clarke, Vale; delegate, Alice Joyce, Portland.

Commerce Division—Chairman, C. D. Lazenby, Portland; vice chairman, E. E. Evans, Prineville; secretary, Mrs. G. Holmes Lawrence, Portland; delegate, J. A. Bexell, Corvallis.

Home Economics Department—Chairman, Edna Groves, Portland; vice chairman, Sarah L. Lewis, Corvallis; secretary, Edna Mills, Forest Grove; delegate, Grace Gillett, Corvallis.

City Superintendents' Department

Edited by GEORGE W. HUG, McMinnville, Oregon

The City Superintendents' Association of the State of Oregon met in Portland December 28 and 29. Practically every city superintendent in the state attended the meetings and expressed themselves as having fully enjoyed them all.

Many excellent papers were read, some of which are as follows: Supt. Dunbar of Klamath Falls gave a paper on the "Medical Inspection in the Public Schools." The paper was very practical and of great help to those present. Supt. E. N. Mc. Donnell of Hoquiam, Wash., gave an address on "The Two Period Plan of Recitation and Study." A paper was given by Supt. J. O. McLaughlin of Hood River upon a greatly discussed school problem of the present time which presented many good ideas, "A Scheme for Granting Credit for Music in the Public Schools."

The meeting called at 9:15 of Friday, December 29, was not in any way lacking of good addresses, for Dr. J. N. Smith opened the meeting with a very interesting topic, "The Mentally Defective in the Public Schools." The subject of State Publication of Textbooks was very ably

dealt with by Supt. F. A. Tiedgen of Marshfield and was fully discussed by him from all angles. Following this paper was given one similar in substance by Supt. J. G. Imel of Astoria on "The Oregon System of Textbook Adoption."

Prior to these addresses the officers of the association were elected and Supt. L. W. Turnbull of Bandon was elected president, while C. A. Howard was re-elected secretary-treasurer.

Meeting of the Oregon High School Debating League.

The annual meeting of the Oregon High School Debating League was called to order by President Kirk in room 115, Lincoln high school building at 9 o'clock on Friday, December 29, 1916. The minutes of the meeting of 1915 were read and approved.

The secretary announced the following actions of the executive committee during the school year: The creation of the 10th district consisting of Klamath and Lake counties; the transfer of Tillamook county from the Lower Columbia district to the North Willamette district upon petition of the Tillamook high school; the transfer from the South-

ern Willamette district to the Southern Oregon district of that portion of
Douglas county south of the 43d parallel of latitude.

The constitution of the league was
amended changing the date for issuing the annual bulletin from "before
December 1" to "before October 1."
The constitution was amended providing that in preliminary debates
within districts the number of the
debaters on the team shall be two

unless a definite number is agreed
upon by the schools participating.

The question of assisting the state
library to obtain sufficient material
to provide for the needs of all the
participating schools was referred to
the executive committee.

Charles H. Boyd, of Portland, was
elected president of the league by
an unanimous vote, and Earl Kilpatrick, of the University of Oregon, was
re-elected as secretary-treasurer.

Grade Teachers' Department

Edited by SABRA CONNER, 421 West Park Street, Portland, Oregon

Elementary teachers and elementary teachers' associations are cordially invited to send
news items of their activities which would be of interest or value to other teachers to this
department of the The Oregon Teachers Monthly. Address Editor of Grade Teachers' Department, Room 300, Court House, Portland, Oregon.

The coming summer already looms
large upon our threshold. Every
Portland, every Oregon teacher must
realize how incalculable a privilege
it is to have the National Educational Association in our very midst. The
inspiration of the master minds who
gather at this great concourse, the
glorious comradeship with thousands
of eager enthusiasts who throng this
mighty conference, and the realization of the altruism, the high ideals,
the desire for service of this vast
army of peace is an uplift, an exalta-
tion that no one can afford to miss.
Every teacher in the Northwest
should honor herself and her profession by so planning her summer that
she may be in attendance at the
N. E. A.

* * *

I have attended every session of
the Oregon Teachers' Association for
a number of years and the present
session is the largest and by far the
most representative gathering ever
known in the history of the association. The most pleasing and encouraging feature of the convention, to
my mind, aside from the splendid
attendance, is the spirit of good will
and earnestness everywhere manifest
and the large amount of good, progressive work that is being accomplished. Heretofore, sessions of the
convention have been marked to a
greater or lesser degree by apathy.
This year, however, the delegates,
present from all parts of the state,
have been devoted to sober and seri-

ous discussions of the subjects in
hand, and I feel that a tremendous
amount of genuine progress is being
made. The association is certainly
doing itself proud and there is much
of encouragement in the present advancement and the prospect for general educational development in this
state.—J. A. Churchill, State Superintendent of Public Instruction.

* * *

The six educational associations
of the city combined Thursday to
entertain informally the several hundred visiting teachers attending the
convention of the State Teachers' Association. The reception was held in
the gymnasium of the Lincoln high
school from 4 until 6 o'clock. Tea
and wafers were served and an orchestra provided sweet music and a
good chance for Portland teachers
to become acquainted with those
teaching in all parts of the state
was offered. Miss Viola Ortschild,
president of the Portland Grade
Teachers' Association, was general
chairman of the committee that planned the reception The other educational organizations and their representatives who served on the general committee were: Portland Principals' Association, W. T. Fletcher;
High Teachers Association, Miss Vera
Darling; Manual Training Teachers'
Association, William Hood; Portland
Educational Association, Fred Gro-

shong; Home Economics' Association, Miss Lora Hendershott.

* * *

"The most delightful feature of the entire convention"; thus did the visiting teachers characterize the reception given at the chamber of commerce in their honor by the Oregon Congress of Mothers. Over 1000 people crowded the chamber between the hours of 8 and 11. The first hour was given over to an informal reception, giving the people an opportunity to meet each other, then came a musical program of unusually high character. Mrs. Ralph Walker gave a group of her own piano compositions Madam Lucie Valair gave a number of songs in her most finished and delightful manner. Franck G. Eichenlaub was heard in violin numbers and John Claire Monteith sang. These musical numbers were interspersed with short speeches by Governor Withycombe, Dr. Carrol Pearse, president of the Milwaukee Normal, Milwaukee, Wis. Dr. Pearse is a member of the committee that voted the N. E. A. meet next year in Portland and he spoke concerning this gathering. O. M. Plummer and L. R. Alderman also spoke briefly on the great convention which is to come to Portland next year. Mrs. George W. McMath, president of the congress, acted as mistress of ceremonies The rooms were suitably decorated in holly and mistletoe. During the evening delicious iced fruto was served.

* * *

Two of the best known educators of the United States, the president of a great university, and the president of a state normal school, offered an intellectual treat and gave advice from their experience to the teachers of Oregon Thursday at the convention. The university president was Dr. Henry Suzzallo of the University of Washington; the normal school president was Dr. Carrol G. Pearse (pronounced Perce) of the Milwaukee, Wisconsin, normal. Dr. Suzzallo said: "The teaching occupation is not a business but a profession, on equally as high a plane as the ministry, law or medicine. The lawyer and physician, however, are out in the hurly-burly of the world. They know something of life. The teacher and minister fall into a natural group of themselves. They live and work sheltered from the world. The teacher in the class room is far from the busy marts of trade, from the arena of politics, from contact with those who make the wheels of the world go around. The teacher lives an academic life, which is an intellectual way of saying monastic. The great defect of the profession is that the point of view is not social but academic, not worldly in the best sense of the word, but intellectual in its most narrow sense. Teachers must make a social study of the world in which we live, for today the practice of classroom does not check up with the practice of the world. Temptation is not placed before the teaching profession as in law or the practice of medicine, for the teacher is paid on a flat salary and does not have to depend on fees. There should be no danger of the teaching profession becoming commercialized. The merchant who keeps thinking of the dollar will be a better merchant, but the teacher's thoughts must be of service, a social service that must be practiced under the highest idealism."

* * *

Following a spirited discussion, the teachers' retirement fund plan, drawn up by a committee of the state teachers' association headed by President Foster of Reed College, was adopted by the representative council of the organization with only three dissenting votes. The committee will lay the plan before the legislature. Principal objections were voiced against the proposal to allow pensions in proportion to the salary received by the teacher. "Such a plan is the extreme of unfairness," said S. S. Duncan, superintendent of Yamhill county. "Any pension system is unfair that will give one man more than another. When the state gives, it should give as much to one man as to another."

* * *

To arouse interest in the coming convention of the National Educational Association in Portland an effort is to be made among the visiting teachers to have every school teacher in Oregon to take out an institutional membership in the nation-wide organization.

County Superintendents' Department

Edited by CLYDE T. BONNEY, The Dalles, Oregon

Proposed Distribution of School Fund Law.

Section 1.—The county school superintendent shall make an apportionment of the entire school fund then in the county treasury on the first Monday in October of each year, and at such other times as he may deem advisable. The county school fund collected in pursuance of the school tax levied by the county court, shall be apportioned as follows: (a) He shall apportion one-half of the said fund to the districts of his county in proportion to the number of teachers employed during the preceding school year; provided, that where a teacher was employed for a less term than eight months, then such districts shall receive one-eighth of an apportionment for each teacher for each month actually employed; provided that for each additional teacher, where a teacher was not employed for the preceding school year, a district shall be apportioned funds on the basis of a teacher for a term of seven months; provided, that no district shall receive apportionments on a greater number of teachers than are employed for the current year. (b) The remainder of the county school funds shall be apportioned to the districts of his county in proportion to the aggregate daily attendance in such districts during the preceding school year; provided, that each district shall be credited with a constructive attendance, in addition to actual attendance, of three hundred days for each month for each regularly established school in operation during the preceding school year; provided that for each school in operation at the time of an apportionment, which was not in operation during the preceding school year, a district shall be apportioned funds on a constructive attendance of two thousand days.

Section 2.—In joint districts each county shall apportion one-half a teacher's apportionment and attendance monies on one-half the construction attendance; provided that on actual attendance each county shall apportion funds on the attendance coming from each county.

Section 3.—Non-resident pupils shall be admitted to a school by the consent of the school board and the approval of the county superintendent.

Section 4.—The consent of the district boundary board of the county must be secured for the establishment of additional schools in districts of the third class if such schools are to be considered in the distribution of county funds.

Section 5.—The basis of all apportionments under this act shall be the teachers annual reports, and other records in the office of the county school superintendent.

Section 6.—The provisions of this act shall apply to public schools only.

Section 7.—In lieu of the establishment of new schools or the maintenance of established schools, the district boundary board of the county may, when conditions seem to warrant, fix such a rate for the board or transportation of public school pupils as it may deem fit and proper, and thereafter any expense incurred in boarding or transporting such pupil up to the rate fixed by said board, shall be a charge upon the common school fund of the county; provided, that where provision is made by the boundary board for the board or transportation of any pupil, the provisions of the compulsory education law shall be enforced at the option of said boundary board, even if such pupils reside more than three miles from an established school.

Left-over Articles.

Some material that should have been used in this number of the Oregon Teachers Monthly was unavoidably crowded out because space was not available. The authors of this material will have to be patient; the articles will be published as soon as they have been passed upon by the editorial board.—C. H. J.

If Men Cared Less.

If men cared less for wealth and fame,
 And less for battlefields and glory;
If writ in human hearts a name
 Seemed better than in song and story;
If men instead of nursing pride,
 Would learn to hate it and abhor it;
If more relied on Love to guide,
 The world would be the better for it.
 —M. H. Cobb.

The State Schools

OREGON AGRICULTURAL COLLEGE.

The Viewpoint of a Country Editor was the theme of an address given by Mr. Ben Kuppenbender, editor of the Nehalem Times, to the news writing class recently. He impressed upon the students the necessity for having a definite aim in writing a news article. That the occupation and interest of the people expected to read the article would partial'y determine its content was made plain.

The expression and public speaking courses offered at Oregon. Agricultural College afford students an opportunity to become adept in facing audiences. Such courses are necessary to those who expect to teach or to assist O. A. C. in the desire to spread information. Supported by the various English classes which give foundation, these courses are particularly attractive. They are taken advantage of by those who know good things and want others to know them also.

The Educational Club of the Oregon Agricultural College, which was organized in 1914, is composed of those students who are taking industrial educational subjects, and who will teach agriculture, home economics, commerce, or manual training. The club meets twice each month, and addresses are given by visiting educators, by members of the college faculty, and by the students. Among the subjects discussed the present semester were "The Parent-Teachers' Association," "New School Laws," "Playground Work," "The Gary School System," and "Physical Education." At each meeting reports on the various magazines relating to teaching, are given by different members of the club. The officers, who are elected yearly, are: Claude Sanders, Ashland, president; Fred C. Pewers, Oakland, vice president; Eva Yates, Corvallis, secretary; Albert Shankland, Corvallis, treasurer.

C. C. Ruth, E. O. Ferguson and J. E. Currey, graduates of O. A. C., have been notified that they successfully passed the civil service examination for assistant grain samplers.

Mr. Ruth, who hails from Umatilla county, the banner wheat county of Oregon, was second on the list throughout the United States, while Mr. Currey was eighth and Mr. Ferguson fourteenth. Mr. Currey is from Olympia, Washington; Mr. Ferguson from Helix, Oregon.

Members of the faculty who were in attendance on annual convention of the Oregon State Teachers' Association included E. D. Ressler, secretary of the association; Sarah L. Lewis, chairman of the Home Economics division; J. A. Rexell, elected. president of the Vocational department; H. C. Seymour, elected chairman of the Agricultural division; F. Berchtold, F. H. Shepherd, J. B. Horner, H. C. Brandon, Dean Fawcett, Grace Gillett, Laura Cheney, F. D. McLouth, Edna Flarida, Mabel Maginnis, H. T. Vance, L. A. Rufener, E. B. Lemon, D. G. Thayer, and President Kerr.

Exactly 643 women from various parts of the state, besides 76 women, students, registered for the Home-Makers' Conference held during-farmers' week, January 2-6. The program included lectures, discussions, and demonstrations on social life; community welfare; club leadership; civics; literature; art; religion; thrift; household management and accounts; household furnishing and decoration; markets; care, preparation, and service of food; and child development. The series of lectures on child development by the well-known English specialist, Miss Alice Ravenhill of British Columbia, emphasized, as she remarked, the object of all the others — a higher type of human being.

The winner of the first prize in the state for junior sewing is Marian Lowe of Owyhee, Malheur county. She is 15 years old and in 1915 won the first prize for canning. Thinking it unfair to the other girls, she refused to enter the canning contest in 1916 and turned her attention to sewing. Marian's ambition is not confined to her own achievements alone, but she is very anxious to promote enthusiasm among her mates and it was largely through her efforts that 19 of the 21 members of the industrial club in her school were induced to complete their work. The prize won by Marian is a two weeks' summer course at the Oregon Agricultural College, where special classses are conducted for the boys and the girls who are prize winners along the various lines of industrial arts and agriculture.

An innovation at the recent farmers' week conventions was the day nursery in charge of some half dozen Y. W. C. A. girls, who entertained small children with story telling and games while their mothers attended home-makers' conference. Proceeds were turned over to the association. Many students in the state high schools of Oregon now graduate at the end of the first semester, instead of at the regular June commencement. Recognizing this fact, the Oregon Agricultural College has made it as convenient for students to register at the college at the beginning of the second semester as at the beginning of the first semester. Students who are so fortunate as to be graduating from high school this mid-year, may be interested (not only in the circular, "Schools and Departments," which is being mailed to you just now), but also on the following facts regarding second semester registrations. Dates of second semester registration are February 5 and 6, 1917. The class schedule is arranged to accommodate a large number of entering students each year at the opening of the second semester. First semester courses will be repeated for new students entering in February. Students entering in February may, by taking summer school work, graduate one year earlier than by waiting until September to register. Further detailed information may be secured by addressing the Registrar, Corvallis, Oregon. The College Catalogue for 1916-17 which will be sent on request, will give information concerning the Courses of Study and entrance requirements.

OREGON NORMAL SCHOOL.

During the month the faculty has been represented at a number of public gatherings and parent-teacher meetings. Miss Mabel West, librarian, addressed the parent-teacher association at Newberg on the subject of Children's Books. Mr. Pittman

spoke before a similar association at Corvallis and also before the general assembly at Corvallis during farmers' week, and Mr. Evenden addressed the Monmouth parent-teacher association on the subject of Child Development.

One of the pleasant social events during the month was the party given by the boys of the Normal Society to some of the young ladies in the student body and to the members of the faculty. The gymnasium was artistically decorated in evergreens, making attractive backgrounds for the charades and other parts of the very novel entertainment furnished by the boys during the evening. One of the features which gave, perhaps, the most enjoyment was the plan of providing the guests with 20 cents with which to purchase from the town stores a lunch which had to pass the inspection of competent judges upon the return to the gymnasium.

The faculty has been represented during the month by Mr. Gentle, who read a paper entitled "A Man Who Made Good." This paper, written and delivered in Mr. Gentle's inimitable way, made a lasting impression upon the student body. It traced the life work and professional growth of a young man in facing the problems of instruction and discipline which might befall any teacher at the present time.

Shortly before the holidays the Normal School was visited by a part of the legislative investigating committee appointed at the last session of the legislature to investigate the needs of the state educational institutions. The only members present were Senator Strayer, of Baker, and Representative Childs, of Brownsville. The two gentlemen made a thorough two-day study of the situation at Monmouth, and appeared before the assembly on Wednesday morning. The remarks made by Representative Childs in regard to the applications of teachers, and the attitude toward contracts were very timely and helpful. The theme of Senator Strayer's talk was Sympathy, and his way of expressing the sympathy which he felt for the students for having various speakers inflicted upon them was highly entertaining and instructive. These men made many friends during their brief stay here and we would be glad to have a repetition of the visit.

At a city election of Monmouth held during December Prof. H. C. Ostien, of the mathematics department, was unanimously elected as mayor. This comes after Mr. Ostien has served the city in the capacity of councilman for three years, and is a flattering recognition of his interest and efficiency in civic affairs.

Under the direction of Miss Laura Kennon, of the English department, the two divisions of the class in advanced literature dramatized Silas Marner ,adapting the story for dramatization, selecting the characters, and arranging the setting. Try-outs were held between the two sections, and the winning section presented it for the student body on Thursday evening, December 14.

Friday morning, December 15, R. A. Booth of Eugene was the speaker in one of the finest chapel exercises of the year. Senator Booth chose for his subject "Success in Life." Success in life is not to be measured by what a man possesses but by the sum of his life, by what his character actually is. By countless illustrations and with keen desire to show his audience the real touchstone of success, Senator Booth drove home his splendid address to every person in his audience. It was a real pleasure to have as the guest of the Oregon Normal such a speaker as Senator Booth, who has long been a friend of education in Oregon.

The feature of the meeting of the societies on the night of the 22d, the evening before the Christmas holidays, was the presentation by the three societies of the Birds' Christmas Carol. This was presented under the direction of Miss Kennon, and the cast had been so well selected that the presentation was of almost professional merit. To make individual mention of the characters would be to mention the entire cast, since all the parts were so adequately portrayed. Special music during the evening was furnished by Miss Randall and Mr. Clark.

Thursday evening, December 21, was the date for the annual dormitory Christmas party given by the matron, Miss Todd, and the girls of the dormitory. The invited guests were the members of the faculty. After dinner a very interesting program was carried out by the girls, representing an old English Christmas with its various delightful customs of hanging the mistletoe, wishing on the Yule log, and the burning of evergreens. Readings were given by students, and costumed dances, all of which appropriately led up to the presentation of a Victrola to the dormitory, the Christmas present of the year. One delightful feature of the program was the serenade of old English carols by members of the glee club. Each year the party seems to demand superlative adjectives in its description, and each one seems to be better than the preceding one.

Miss Todd finished her pre-vacation entertaining by being at home to all the students on the afternoon of Friday, the 22d, when each guest was given a beautiful poinsetta—a Christmas greeting from the dean of women.

The Christmas vacation for the students was lengthened and made much more comfortable by the kindness of the Southern Pacific in furnishing two special trains, one to take the northbound students to Portland early Saturday morning, December 23, and the other leaving Portland at 6 o'clock Sunday, January 7. The amount of extra work which these specials imposed upon the Southern Pacific Company is appreciated, and their kindness in looking after the comfort and welfare of their patrons has won them the loyal support of the Normal student body.

The Oregon Normal School faculty was very largely represented at the State Teachers' Association held in Portland. Those present were President and Mrs. Ackerman, Miss Parrott, Miss Kennon, Miss Greene, Miss McIntosh, Miss Todd, Miss Arbuthnot, Miss Hoham, Miss Riecker, Mr. Pittman, Mr. Evenden, Mr. Ostien and Mr. Gilmore. A number of these were represented on the department programs, or had other work to do in connection with the business of the association. One of the pleasant features of the meeting was the opportunity which the association afforded for members of the faculty to see and visit with the graduates and former students of the school, and the big reunion of one hundred and fifty held at the Portland Hotel Thursday noon was an event long to be remembered. So successful was this that the slogan for Normal School people for the coming year is to be, "Meet me at the banquet table at the state association," and it is confidently expected that the number present will be doubled by the meeting next year. The state association has been universally voted as perhaps the most successful association held in Oregon, and much deserved praise is due to Mr. Carleton, the president of the association, and the members of the executive committee.

The first speaker for 1917 was Supt. Clyde T. Bonney, of The Dalles. Supt. Bonney addressed the assembly on January 9 and in his happy, inspiring way told a number of stories on Normal School graduates working in his county. These stories told of the good work actually being accomplished by graduates of this school, and acted as a stimulus to further endeavor in school work here with the determination on the part of many that what has been done by others could be duplicated in many districts throughout the state. Supt. Bonney can not visit us with a message like this too frequently, and especially is this true since the particular mission which brought him to Monmouth was to secure twenty-five or thirty Normal trained teachers for Wasco county.

Oregon Govermental Affairs

By ROBERT CARLTON CLARK, Eugene, Oregon

Industrial Accident Commission.

Since the establishment of the state industrial accident commission in 1913 to end of last year its receipts, coming from employers, workmen, and state, with interest on invested funds, have reached almost $1,800,000. In that period more than one half million dollars have been paid out to injured workmen and to widows and children of those killed. There have been 17,459 non-fatal accidents and 186 fatal ones reported to the commission. These figures are significant in showing what a large amount of distress has been relieved under the operation of the workmen's compensation act.

Expense of Elections.

Our democratic government is costly. The addition of primary nominating elections to general elections has added greatly to the expense. Much of this expense is borne by candidates for office, their friends, or the party organizations to which they belong. It cost almost a year's salary for the office to elect the successful candidate in the Multnomah county congressional district. It is estimated that the presidential election cost the various party organizations something like $25,000,000. The state and county governments have to bear the actual expense of conducting an election. The cost of the November election to the state alone was $30,000. The expense to the counties for election judges, ballot boxes, etc., for 1200 precincts would bring the total above $100,000. A bill before the present legislative assembly claims to reduce the cost of such election by $25,000 in abolishing one election judge, and by providing that ballot boxes may be sent by parcel post and left in custody of the chairman of the election board. Another effective way to reduce the cost of elections would be to have only one. Abolish the primary election and provide for the exercise of first, second, and third choices at the general election and essentially the same result would be secured as now under our dual system.

"Petticoat Government."

One city in Oregon enjoys the unique distinction of having elected none but women officers at the last election. Mayor, recorder, treasurer, and four new councilmen (or should I say "councilwomen"?) are all women. Two men hold over as councilmen but they are sadly in the minority. Umatilla is the city that is to enjoy this beneficient rule. The new mayor has announced a policy of economy and expresses entire confidence in the ability of the women to administer the affairs of the city wisely. Who can doubt it? The experience of Umatilla will be watched with interest by other communities that have vainly sought efficient government by man directed means.

The Socialist Vote in Oregon.

Although only about 7000 voters registered as Socialists last year, or only 2.4 per cent of the total registration, 27,000, or more than 10 per cent of the total number voting, voted for state or local Socialist party candidates at the last election. Benson, the Socialist party presidential candidate, received less than 10,000 votes. At the preceding presidential election the party candidate received 13,000 votes. Throughout t h e country the socialist vote has fallen off by 150,000 in 1916 as compared with 1912. It has been suggested that President Wilson because of his labor and idealistic foreign policies was able to win about a half million Socialist votes, perhaps enough to elect him. In Oregon it has been found that the Socialists are stronger in counties in which there is a considerable logging, mill, mining, fishing, or railroad population.

A Legislative Year.

The legislature began its forty day session on January 8. The measure adopted at the last election limiting appropriations to amounts not to exceed 6 per cent of expenditures for the previous two years has committed the assembly perforce to a policy of economy. Some ingenuity will be needed to make the appropriations come within the limit prescribed because the taxable property of the state has decreased in value. The governor in his message to the assembly urges the abolition of useless boards and commissions and points out that one of the greatest weaknesses of our state government is its decentralization. He recommends the concentration of greater power in the hands of the governor alone.

Law Questions Answered

By ELMO S. WHITE, Salem, Oregon

Under this head Elmo S. White, of the Marion County Bar, will endeavor to answer such questions of law as our readers may care to ask. Conformably with the established policy of this magazine to be of the greatest usefulness possible, there will be no charge for this service. Questions will be answered in the next issue after receipt whenever possible. Every question must be accompanied by the name and address of the inquirer, but these will not be published unless the person so desires. Questions accompanied by a fee of one dollar will be answered by mail as quickly as possible and will not be published unless requested by sender. Address all communications to Attorney Elmo S. White, Masonic Temple, Salem, Oregon.

"Mr. White: Can an Oregon real estate agent collect a commission for selling a parcel of a school's real property located in this state, where no written agreement was ever made with him to that effect?"

Answer: No; (Section 808 Lord's Oregon Laws). Our supreme court, in a recent case holds thus: "Under the statute of frauds of this state an unwritten authority to sell real estate is absolutely void; such an authority, in order to entitle the broker to compensation must be signed by the party to be charged and state what the compensation is to be."— (Taggart v. Hunter, 78 Or. 139; 152 Pac. 871).

"Dear Mr. White: A friend of mine has had exceptionally bad luck lately and can not pay his debts now, though later on he probably can. His home is paid for. Can those whom he owes take his little home away from him and his family and turn them into the highway?"

Answer: No; not if it is paid for and the family lives in the home owned by some member of the family and claim it as their abode, giving to the officer of the law the legal description thereof (if he serves them with papers) any time before a judicial sale thereof is held; and provided it does not "exceed $1500 in value nor 160 acres in extent if not located in town or city laid off into blocks and lots; if located in any such town or city, then it shall not exceed one block; but in no instance shall it be reduced to less than twenty acres nor one lot, regardless of value."— (Lord's Oregon Laws, Sections 221 and 222). It must be understood that this right is one which is meant for the protection of the family, and only if they choose to take advantage if it. It therefore can be waived. Thus, if your friend and his wife should have mortgaged the home, and fail to pay the mortgage off, upon foreclosure of the mortgage the home could be sold away from the family; likewise, if they should move away, so that the place would no longer be their home. Even though death should remove the member of the family owing the debt, e. g., the father, the property would continue exempt, and, if not devised or conveyed, would, exempt from his previous debts, descend to his heirs. If the home were not paid for, of course it would not be exempt from a claim for money due and unpaid upon its purchase price.

"Attorney Elmo S. White: I hold a note given in this state to me eight years ago, due one year after its date. Nothing has been paid me upon it. Is it collectible?"

Answer: Not if its signer takes advantage of the Oregon Statute of Limitations (Lord's Oregon Laws, Section 6), which permits a note to "outlaw" six years from the date when due. If any payment has been made on the note, or, if you can get your debtor to make a payment, no matter how small, any time, the note will be "renewed" for another period of six years from the date of the payment. The Oregon law does not cancel the debt if not paid within six years from the date when due, but says, in effect, that if the unpaid creditor does not protect his own interests by bringing action at law to enforce collection within six years after due, or after the latest payment if same has been made after the due date, he will not be permitted by law to bring action after that length of time to recover his money, for such old matters can not be allowed to be continuously coming up to disturb the even tenor of the community's way, at a time when, perhaps, witnesses have died or removed from the state, and when it would be difficult for impartial minds to discover the real truth.

Studies of Famous Pictures

A complete list of other famous pictures will be mailed free on application to Parker Estate, Taylorvilie, Illinois.

LINCOLN—SAINT GAUDENS.

By L. Eveline Merritt

In 1887 there was unveiled in Lincoln Park, Chicago, a statue which was conceded at that time to be great. It stands near the entrance of the park today and as one approaches it he realizes that the feeling for it has not abated. It is still considered a great statue; in fact, it seems to grow in appeal rather than diminish. The question that arises is—how does this particular statue have such a universal appeal? The answer to the query will explain the greatnesss in all works of arts, and is of course due largely to the artist himself.

We know from that that Saint Gaudens was an artist who valued individual character, personality, above mere beauty of form. It was the beauty of the inner life that appealed to him rather than that of the outward expression. He was a man who entered intimately and sympathetically into any theme upon which he was working. His imagination aided him to see relationships, to understand character. He, too, was quick to see what gesture or attitude would best express that character. The essentials for telling the story were emphasized by him while unimportant details were either ignored or subordinated to the whole. The essentials, too, were put together according to the best known rules of composition. When a master mind and master hand deal with a great theme the result inevitably stirs men's souls.

It is unnecessary here to recall the facts in Lincoln's life or of the times during which he so successfully led our nation. His was a wonderfully versatile spirit. That awkward, gaunt, homely figure was the home of one of the finest, at the same time strongest, natures. His intellect was unsurpassed. He had wonderful executive ability and yet was of such a sympathetic nature that he was well beloved of the common people. He was a great orator and yet unassuming in attitude. He felt keenly the burden laid upon him and was saddened by the inevitable conflict. His was a personality of power; power of intellect, power of leadership, power of oratory, power of sympathy, power of moral purity and purpose.

What a problem must have confronted Saint Gaudens to represent in a single statue all those qualities!

but all time and all activities are suggested in the moment and attitude selected. So, although this statue is purely American in conception, it is classic in ideal.

As one approaches the park, he is impressed by the wonderful harmony of the whole group in its setting. This was obtained through the joint work of Saint Gaudens and the architect Stanford White. They tested the effect from all points of view and from all distances and stopped only when

In solving that problem Saint Gaudens acted upon the lesson taught through the highest classic sculpture. The Greek always chose to represent that moment which just preceded the crucial moment. Action was thus represented symbolically rather than actually. Dramatic effect was obtained through the very repose of the figure. Thus Saint Gaudens did not choose any particularly eventful period in Lincoln's life, neither did he choose any especial phase of his various activities,

they felt that the general effect was the best.

There is a slightly raised platform 60 feet wide by 30 feet in depth, around three sides of which curves a stone seat. From this platform rises the pedestal. On this is a massive chair, in front of which, as though he had just risen, stands the tall, slim figure with bowed head. All this is seen at the first glance and is most satisfying to the eye, just as any fine design gives a feeling of satisfaction. On nearer approach one detail after another disappears from view till one stands gazing into that fine, sad, thoughtful face of greatness. All this surely shows consummate skill on the part of the artist.

Let us now stand there and force ourselves to study the group in detail and try to understand what the artist has done and how and why. In the first place, why is a chair introduced? If a chair must be present, why is Lincoln not seated in it? That is part of the symbolism to which reference has been made. The large chair with its American eagle in low relief on the back is very evidently the "chair of state." Had Lincoln been seated it would have represented the executive leader only. Since he has just risen, both the executive leader and the active worker are suggested at one and the same time.

Lincoln stands firmly and calmly with the left foot slightly advanced, his left hand holding the lapel of his coat while the right hand is behind his back. This produces a perfect balance of the figure and is at the same time a characteristic gesture of the man. The head is bent forward slightly, although the figure itself is erect. In the face is depicted all the pathos of the times, the kindly, sympathetic feeling for all. It seems almost lost in thought, yet there is depicted a courage to dare and to do and the intellect to know what to do and how. He is probably about to address an audience. Behind that quiet, calm dignity is felt an energy to remove all obstacles. That man would first find out what was right and do it whatever the cost. Saint Gaudens has understood the real Lincoln and given it to the world for all time.

Printing was often used by Saint Gaudens as a part of the general effect. The inscriptions here have been placed on the back of the stone seat which curves around three sides of the platform. In the center is Lincoln's name with the dates of his birth and death. On either side is a quotation from the address made by Lincoln at Cooper Union in New York City in 1860. At one end is, "With malice toward none, with charity for all, with firmness in the right as God gives us to know the right, let us strive on"; and on the opposite side, "Let us have faith that right makes might, and in the faith let us to the

end dare to do our duty as we understand it." The figure itself is bronze and is 11½ feet high.

There are three things which make this a great statue and will assure its living with other works of art: (1) The idea behind the conception is universal in its appeal; (2) the creation has been worked out in accordance with the laws of composition; (3) the technical skill of the artist is of a high order. In studying the statue closely the details come out more clearly. In fact, all details are brought out carefully and accurately, yet in such a way that they are subordinate to the whole and enhance the effect of the whole. Saint Gaudens is probably the only sculptor who has succeeded in producing grace in the modern costume. He seemed to hesitate at nothing provided that thing could be made to express individual character.

So the Lincoln stands there at the entrance of a public park in a hustling, bustling city where all may linger and think of the life of this great man as depicted by a great artist.

WASHINGTON—STUART.

By William C. Casey

In the sunny meadows of old Virginia, over a hundred and sixty years ago a bright-eyed little boy played in the clear waters of the brook. He might have been the sun-kissed barefoot lad of Whittier's poem or the gay, rollicking prince of the artist's painting for he was such a boy as they have pictured—merry and true hearted!

What school lad has not romped with George Washington, if only in fancy, over those same Virginia acres? Who has not followed him in the soldier drills of the schoolground or watched with breathless interest his mad dash on the high spirited colt? Who of us has not heard, too, his honest words by the fallen cherry tree or read with interest his rules of politeness in the bold, round writing of his copy book?

We have seen him as a dauntless youth hurrying through miles of trackless forests in the service of his native state. As the hero of many Indian battles and the greatest soldier in Virginia, we know him in his early manhood. When the merry making of the Boston Tea Party was hushed in the echoing hoof beats of Paul Revere's famous steed we have seen him called to lead the patriot hosts of the nation.

General Washington! What American boy or girl is not thrilled by a hundred daring charges of that great war. Fresh in our memory is that journey on the ice-blocked water of the Delaware. We, too, have bowed in reverence in that sacred hour when the general of a great army knelt in prayer on the snow of Valley Forge. How we rejoiced as did the

native land, a new ambition, greater than he had ever known, thrilled the painter. One character above all others he wished to paint. The heroic Washington, man among men, impressed him as no other had ever done. When news of the election of Washington as president of his native country reached England, the artist waited no longer. Wealth and fame were given up as he left for America.

What pleasant memories must cluster about a picturesque little stone building oh the outskirts of

patriots of old when the Yorktown victory was heralded everywhere!

Far away in England an artist heard of the same glorious victory He, too, was a patriot whose boyhood days had been spent amid these same stirring scenes. But when the sounds of battle startled the Americans they no longer bought his paintings and he had gone to England where his fame had grown rapidly. Kings in their jewel robes, great generals in their glittering uniforms, nobles and princes were flocking to his studio.

When peace was restored to his

Philadelphia. There it was within those vine covered walls, that balmy spring breezes found Washington in black velvet uniform, lace and ruffles sitting for his portrait. At his side might have been seen, from time to time, the president's wife in quaint lace cap and kerchief, busily knitting. Occasionally his favorite generals, Knox and Lee, would accompany him and pass the hours with conversation "elegant and refined." Rapidly sped the days and weeks in such pleasant companionship as this and the portrait was finished at last.

One critic's greatest objection to the portrait is a certain feebleness about the lines of the mouth. But the difficulty under which the artist labored when painting the lines of the mouth has become of historic interest. Nothing less than an ill-fitting set of false teeth proved the real difficulty. Said the artist, "When I painted Washington he had just had a set of false teeth inserted, which accounts for the constrained expression so noticeable about the mouth and lower part of the face." In spite of this the artist has so skillfully passed over the defect, that the straight, firmly-set lips and broad, rounded chin detract very little if any from the strength and dignity of the entire head. Again some critics regret that the artist did not chance to meet Washington when the latter was in the full bloom of youth. Some would welcome with greater interest a portrait of a more youthful Washington mounted on prancing steed in all the glory of a general's uniform.

Since its exhibition in 1795 it has come to be the standard portrait of Washington. So pleased with the work was the artist that he purposely neglected to finish the background in order to keep it with him. Several months passed and at last he asked Washington's consent to keep the original provided he would make him a copy. To this the president kindly consented and the portrait remained with the painter. Happily for him, when in need of money, he had only to make a copy or two and sell them. Little wonder that in his delight he called it his "Hundred Dollar Bill or Nest Egg." At his death it was purchased by the Washington Association and presented in 1831 to the Boston Athaenaeum. Since that time it has been called the Athaenaeum portrait of Washington. Today it hangs with a similar portrait of Martha Washington in the Allston Room at the Boston Museum of Fine Arts.

Few portaits in the history of art are more widely known. From it comes the world's impression of Washington's appearance. Over two hundred times engraved it is seen in the school rooms and homes of many nations, while postage stamps and bank notes carry it to all parts of the country. Years will remove farther and farther those scenes in which Washington lived and talked among men. But the nation's children for centuries to come need only to pause before the serious noble face of this great painting to share with those patriots of old, the wise counsel and the blessing of the nation's father.

Other School Papers.

During the institute season, thousands of subscriptions were taken of other school papers clubbed with the Oregon Teachers Monthly. Some mistakes have undoubtedly been made, in fact it would be strange if many mistakes were not made in handling such a large business. We hope that any one who had subscribed for a magazine and is not getting it will notify us promptly. Every effort will be made to rectify all mistakes that may be called to our attention.—C. H. J.

Subscriptions in December.

Such a very large number of subscriptions to the Oregon Teachers Monthly were taken in December, and in handling all of these it will not be strange if some mistakes may have occurred. It is hoped that teachers will be patient and if any mistakes have been made, they will write to us as soon as possible and ask for corrections.—C. H. J.

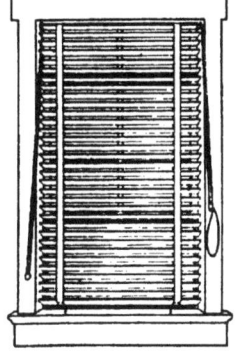

Membership in the State Teachers' Association

The following are the names of teachers who became members of the State Teachers' Association by subscribing for the Oregon Teachers Monthly, in addition to those published in the January number, for the year ending December 31, 1916:

1677 C. Pearl Yoder, Hubbard
1678 Minnie M. Herman, Myrtle Point
1679 Lulu Miller, Empire
1680 Lucile Brackett, Portland
1681 Myrtle McNeill, Lents
1682 H. W. Ager, Lents
1683 Frederick L. Rice, Bend
1684 Ethel Craig, Silverton
1685 J. G. French, Salem
1686 V. V. Willis, Turner
1687 B. P. Alexander, Merrill
1688 Winifred Dennis, Portland
1689 Mattie Leehmann, Lakeview
1690 Ina V. Johnson, Heppner
1691 N. W. Bowland, Oregon City
1692 J. F. Axley, Salem
1693 Maude Hooper, Cottage Grove
1694 Geo. W. Murphy, Riddle
1695 Hallie Thomas, Portland
1696 Incy Baker, Portland
1697 Frances Barnes, Portland
1698 Grace DeGraff, Portland
1699 Hopkin Jenkins, Portland
1700 J. H. Ackerman, Monmouth
1701 Ella Thacker, Albany
1702 Nellie J. Parrish, Merrill
1703 N. Isa Hoskins, Oregon City
1704 Burgess F. Ford, Jefferson
1705 J. B. V. Butler, Monmouth
1706 L. L. Gooding, Harrisburg
1707 Marjorie Speed, Halfway
1708 P. J. Kuntz, Rainier
1709 Elmer F. Goodwin, Greshan.
1710 H. L. Bates, Forest Grove
1711 I. B. Warner, The Dalles
1712 Anne B. Swezey, Salem
1713 O. D. Byers, Albany
1714 Fay Clark, Vale
1715 Letitia Shewey, Lexington
1716 R. P. Goin, Toledo
1717 Mrs. A. E. Ivanhoe, LaGrande
1718 A. P. Armstrong, Portland
1719 H. C. Baghman, Prineville
1720 Alfred Powers, Oakland
1721 P. H. Berg, Dallas
1722 C. F. Grover, Orenco
1723 Frances Clark, Burns
1724 Leota Sloan, Newberg
1725 Lellah Foster, Antelope
1726 Ada Grimes, Prineville
1727 Louie Russell, Redmond
1728 Mrs. May Wigle, Prineville
1729 Hatta F. Carden, Bend
1730 Mrs. M. B. Grant, Sisters
1731 Rose Lillie, Tumalo
1732 Effie Newman, Alfalfa
1733 Etta James, Tumalo
1734 Elizabeth Beier, Prineville
1735 Mary H. Prieshoff, Brothers
1736 J. W. Crites, Hood River
1737 Mrs. Lillian Watts, Culver
1738 I. E. Young, Pendleton
1739 H. J. Simmons, Fossil
1740 Lela C. Erickson, McMinnville
1741 Mrs. F. H. Morrison, Dallas
1742 J. C. Conley, Enterprise
1743 J. C. Nelson, Salem
1744 C. E. Oliver, Lakeview
1745 Lilly Crapson, Tillamook
1746 Mrs. M. C. Case, Hillsboro
1747 Edna Metcalf, Portland
1748 E. M. Hussong, Astoria
1749 A. R. Draper, Portland

1750 R. E. Chloupek, Pendleton
1751 F. A. Tiedgen, Marshfield
1752 A. D. Hulburd, Astoria
1753 Gertrude Greathouse, Portland
1754 Madge Hill, Portland
1755 I. A. Melendy, Portland
1756 G. R. Robinson, Weston
1757 Alice H. Collier, Portland
1758 David S. North, Corvallis
1759 C. W. Beotticher, Albany
1760 F. H. Shepherd, Corvallis
1761 J. K. Hart, Portland
1762 Maude MacPherson, Portland
1763 Marie Falb, Portland
1764 Wilhelmine Koerth, The Dalles
1765 Nan Miller, Forest Grove
1766 J. F. Grubbs, Portland
1767 H. J. Elliott, Perrydale
1768 C. A. Davidson, Myrtle Point
1769 F. G. Franklin, Albany
1770 V. Meldo Hillis, Medford
1771 Ida V. Turney, Eugene
1772 Bess Owens, Dallas
1773 S. S. Duncan, McMinnville
1774 W. T. Foster, Portland
1775 H. R. Marsh, Glendale
1776 J. E. Myers, Prineville
1777 E. T. Moores, Salem
1778 John W. L. Smith, Salem
1779 M. M. Sampson, Portland
1780 Verdi Monroe, Portland
1781 Jennie Richardson, Portland
1782 Frances Myers, Forest Grove
1783 Esther Kane, Portland
1784 Kate Protzman, Portland
1785 C. M. Kiggins, Portland
1786 Nort B. Green, Portland
1787 Johanna Cramer, Portland
1788 John W. Todd, Salem
1789 Ray W. Logan, LaGrande
1790 A. H. Sprolue, Portland
1791 Chas. A. Rice, Portland
1792 C. R. Bowman, Klaamth Falls
1793 A. C. Hampton, LaGrande
1794 L. R. Alderman, Portland
1795 Jesse McCord, Portland
1796 Laura H. Kennon, Monmouth
1797 A. E. Shumate, Portland
1798 H. L. Hussong, Astoria
1799 R. W. Broecker, Eugene
1800 Janette N. Elliott, Portland
1801 Lucy E. Humphreys, Portland
1802 Ethel M. Smith, Portland
1803 Floyd D. Moore, Dallas
1804 J. Wesley Smith, Prineville
1805 R. W. Rose, Molalla
1806 V. Myrtle Copenhaver, Warrenton
1807 C. P. Coe, McMinnville
1808 Frances Dewar, Portland
1809 Wm. Parker, Portland
1810 Anna Johnson, Portland
1811 Helen Bennett, Portland
1812 Belle Eade, Portland
1813 Rosa E. Smith, Portland
1814 Edith Nordeen, Portland
1815 Mrs. Georgia Swafford, Portland
1816 Queen Lynn, Portland
1817 Evelyn Cormack, Portland
1818 Maude Laman, Portland
1819 Lucy Parker, Portland
1820 Gertrude Ost, Portland
1821 Matilda Leverman, Portland
1822 Sada V. Brown, Portland
1823 Imo Clifton, Portland
1824 Juanita V. Parker, Grants Pass
1825 H. Angenette Crissey, Portland
1826 Maude Cooke, Portland
1827 Minerva Thiessen, Clatskanie
1828 Nellie M. Stevens, Portland
1829 Kate Casto, Milwaukie

1830 B. W. DeBusk, Eugene	1915 Irene Rippley, Portland
1831 Jessie Wilde, Lebanon	1916 Mrs. Laura Mack, Sanda
1832 Clara A. Hettinger, Portland	1917 Vivian Young, Moscow, Idahu
1833 L. P. Gilmore, Monmouth	1918 Lilli Schmidli, Portland
1834 D. A. Thornburg, Seattle, Wn.	1919 Rosa B. Parrott, Monmouth
1835 J. A. Bexell, Corvallis	1920 F. N. Haroun, Portland
1836 E. J. Moore, Eugene	1921 Lena Ayers, Portland
1837 W. A. Dickson, Portland	1922 Emily O'Malley, Portland
1838 E. T. Falting, Portland	1923 Alda Overstreet, Portland
1839 W. E. Dolde, Phoenix	1924 Myrtle A. Weeks, Portland
1840 M. L. Cummings, Eugene	1925 Marcia Romig, Portland
1841 Caroline A. Barnes, Portland	1926 Mrs. Meta G. Watson, Portland
1842 Robert Goetz, Milwaukie	1927 Vava Burns, Portland
1842 Alice Hughes, Portland	1928 Helen Petsch, Portland
1844 F. L. Stetson, Eugene	1929 Crilla Shonkwiler, Portland
1845 Ben H. Williams, Eugene	1930 Elizabeth Keber, Portland
1846 Lauis Barzee, Lents	1931 Violet Johnson, Portland
1847 W. C. Alderson, Portland	1932 Mabel Peterson, Portland
1848 Susan B. Dinsmore, Eugene	1933 Nelie Crout, Portland
1849 Estella B. Parker, Portland	1934 L. A. Read, Gladstone
1850 Edith Alderosn, Portland	1935 Frances E. Smith, Portland
1851 Mabel Albee, Mill City	1936 Maude K. Darnall, Lents
1852 Nellie Albee, Mill City	1937 Marie Meagher, Portland
1853 Elsie Pruner, Gates	1938 Marion Dickey, Portland
1854 C. W. Tenney, Helena, Mont.	1939 Lulu George, Portland
1855 Alberta M. Greene, Monmoutn	1940 Pansy Tull, Milwaukie
1856 Lucile Chase, Eugene	1941 Ethel Evarts, Lents
1857 H. W. Turner, Salem	1942 A. F. Hershner, Lents
1858 A. E. Turner, Junction City	1943 Grace MacKinzie, Portland
1859 Jessie V. Miller, Salem	1944 Christine Bergsvik, Portland
1860 Luella M. Knapp, Portland	1945 Charlotte Ballin, Portland
1861 Lena Nealond, Portland	1946 Edith Lewis, Portland
1862 Ella Thompson, Portland	1947 Anne Donovan, Portland
1863 Vieva Walker, Lents	1948 Margaret Seiple, Portland
1864 Matie B. Train, Lents	1949 Ruble Goulet, Portland
1865 Mrs. H. Lee aGrden, Bandon	1950 Pearl Ellis, Portland
1866 Elsie Calkins, Ft. Klamath	1951 Nellie Workman, Weston
1867 Evelyn Fatland, Ft. Klamath	1952 Maybelle Lloyd, Lents
1868 R. G. Stafford, Portland	1953 Gertrude Hanks, Bend
1869 Anna Sorensen, Portland	1954 Inez Penn, Bend
1870 Lillie D. Thomas, Portland	1955 Elmer Brown, Portland
1871 George F. Sanders, Tillamook	1956 J. C. Ryan, Troutdale
1872 Leida H. Mills, Portland	1957 L. K. Epley, Philomath
1873 Mrs. Emilie Shaw, Milwaukie	1958 Mrs. Mina Epley, Philomath
1874 Alice Joyce, Portland	1959 B. A. Thoster, Portland
1875 C. V. Kilgore, Portland	1960 Mrs. L. W. Ausmus, Portland
1876 Mrs. Anna Read, Portland	1961 Della P. Sharpless, Portland
1877 Sarah E. Tousey, Portland	1962 Delpha Hammond, Portland
1878 Nellie Lee Jones, Portland	1963 Olive Hallingby, Portland
1879 Alverta Kraeft, Portland	1964 Marian Bolin, Portland
1880 E. H. Whitney, Portland	1965 Mrs. Carrie Moreland, Portland
1881 Emma L. Bircher, Portland	1966 Winifred Hawley, Portland
1882 S. F. Ball, Portland	1967 Virlena Ambrose, Portland
1883 Adele Lovell, Oswego	1968 Edith Corrillson, Portland
1884 Mrs. Helen Workman, Portland	1969 Flake Howard, Portland
1885 Lula Parmely, Portland	1970 Anna Davies, Portland
1886 Eric P. Bolt, Bend	1971 May Jefferson, Portalnd
1887 J. W. Shantin, Sutherlin	1972 Louise Hoefer, Portland
1888 Maybelle· E. Ross, Portland	1973 Addie Clark, Portland
1889 J. W. Noblet, Coquille	1974 Margaret Conway, Portland
1890 J. J. Kraps, Salem	1975 May Pike, Portland
1891 Nellie Fawcett, Portland	1976 Chas. H. Boyd, Portland
1892 D. T. VanTine, Portland	1977 Mrs. E. H. Wilkins, Portland
1893 Bess Shepherd, McMinnville	1978 Mrs. E. B. Parker, Portland
1894 Anna Dudley, Portland	1979 Ruth Turner, Portland
1895 I. N. Garman, Portland	1980 Mary Gene Smith, Portland
1896 A. P. Patten, Hillsboro	1981 Mrs. A. E. Myers, Portland
1897 P. H. White, Portland	1982 Grace Davis, Portland
1898 C. M. Stafford, Portland	1983 Mae Ziegler, Portland
1899 G. E. Jamison, Portland	1984 Catherine Graves, Portland
1900 N. C. Maris, Salem	1985 Lillie Hendrickson, Portland
1901 Carol M. Hoge, Lents	1986 Winifred Winnard, Portland
1902 Mrs. M. B. Hogue, Lents	1987 R. L. Edwards, Portland
1903 L. H. Baker, Portland	1988 E. E. DeCou, Eugene
1904 Mary Mancur, Portland	1989 Mrs. A. A. Sanborn, Portland
1905 J. Percy Wells, Jacksonville	1990 Lyla Ransom, Portland
1906 Emma H. Richards, Portland	1991 Genevieve Shaver, Sutherlin
1907 Ruth Richards, Springwater	1992 Mrs. L. Marshall, Portland
1908 A. O. Freel, Portland	1993 Katherine McMillan, Portland
1909 Annie J. Young, Milwaukie	1994 Anna Gately, Portland
1910 Mrs. W. A. Barnum, Oregon City	1995 R. E. Winger, Gaston
1911 Ada C. McLaughlin, Milwaukie	1996 Effie Carlson Smith, Portland
1912 Ilma L. Beager, Cottage Grove	1997 A. F. Bittner, Portland
1913 Helen Woodring, Portland	1998 C. R. Holloway, Portland
1914 Vida Evans, Shaniko	1999 Robert Krohn, Portland

2000 Warren D. Smith, Eugene
2001 Lucile Hayes, Rainier
2002 Edna L. Mills, Forest Grove
2003 Lillian Tingle, Portland
2004 Grace P. Gillett, Corvallis
2005 Sarah L. Lewis, Corvallis
2006 Gertrude Conroy, Portland
2007 Eva Jackson, Prineville
2008 Anna Bergman, Astoria
2009 A. N. French, Egenue
2010 S. S. Chambers, Milwaukie
2011 L. H. Strong, Portland
2012 Ragnhild, Stromberg, Portland
2013 Perle Leibo, Bend
2014
2015 Mary Peery, Portland
2016 Estella A. Hell, Portland
2017 Mary E. Lemon, Portland
2018 Alma Harris, Portland
2019 Florence R. Harris, Portland
2020 Mary A. Harris, Portland
2021 Arthur K. Trenhold, Portland
2022 H. C. Brandon, Corvallis
2023 L. L. Summers, Portland
2024 J. L. Whitman, Pendleton
2025 Leona Larrabee, Portland
2026 Naomi Stengel, Portland
2027 P. B. Arant, Cove
2028 A. P. McKinley, Portland
2029 L. D. Roberts, Portland
2030 Ella McDonough, Portland
2031 H. E Monroe, Portland
2032 Vivian Mikle, Portland
2033 Mary F. Hamilton, Portland
2034 C. C. Thomason, Portland
2035 Carolyn Evarts, Portland
2036 Maud Chollar, Portland
2037 W. T. Fletcher, Portland
2038 Ruth Anunsen, Portland
2039 Rosealma Thibert, Portland
2040 Anna G. Moore, Portland
2041 Paulina Rossner, Portland
2042 Emma O. Pickler, Portland
2043 Marie Luders, Portland
2044 Mrs. Blanche Macaulay, Portland
2045 H. B. Blough, Portland
2046 Irene Carter, Portland
2047 Georgia C. Barry, Astoria
2048 Mae Blayney, Portland
2049 Medora Whitfield, Portland
2050 Blanche Comstock, Portland
2051 Evangeline Roche, Portland
2052 Emerol A. Stacy, Portland
2053 P. E. Schwabe, Portland
2054 F. J. Spangle, Dufur
2055 Vera Hughes, Fossil
2056 Myrtle M. Baker, Portland
2057 Jennie Darnall, The Dalles
2058 Zella Dimmock, Newberg
2059 Edna B. Gray, Clackamas
2060 Guy Powell, Hay Creek
2061 J. P. Tyrell, Medford
2062 J. J. Mills, Canby
2063 M. J. Clapp, Vancouver, Wn.
2064 Mrs. J. R. Harrison, Lebanon
2065 Golda E. Mumma, Vernonia
2066 J. R. Landers, Boulder, Colo.
2067 Fanchon Elliott, Pendleton
2068 Ethel Hoffman, LaGrande
2069 Gertrude S. Grahame, Portland
2070 Emma Aplegate, The Dalles
2071 Mrs. Florence Root, Marshfield
2072 O. V. White, Scio
2073 Mrs. J. W. Wroten, Jordan Valley
2074 Georgia Wright, Union
2075 Public Library, LaGrande
2076 Belle Slate, Tangent
2077 Zelia Hazelton, Portland
2078 C. Keturah Likely, Portland
2079 Mrs. Jean P. McCracken, Portland
2080 Josephine M Roche, Portland
2081 Anna B. Neuman, Pleasant Home
2082 Edna B. Allen, Portland
2083 Mrs. Chas. A. King, Corvallis
2084 J. H. McDonald, Salem

2085 Daisy Newhouse, Newberg
2086 Lovina Spalding, Lonerock
2087 Emma E. Barette, Portland
2088 Elizabeth Fits, Portland
2089 Bertha Palmer, Portland
2090 Elsa Ohle, Portland
2091 Nettie Richardson, Portland
2092 Alma Wickander, Portland
2093 Septima Ansley, Portland
2094 Myrtle Chandler, LaGrande
2095 E. E. Arant, Union
2096 C. E. Fergson, Portland
2097 Ellen Nelson, Portland
2098 Mrs. Harriet S. Shields, Portland
2099 Benedictine Sisters, Portland
2100 Margaret Percefull, Portland
2101 Helen Gould, Pendleton
2102 Ruth Westerman, Yamhill
2103 Maude E. Leadsworth, LaGrande
2104 Intha Irvine, Salem
2105 Louise Wyvel, Milwaukie
2106 Crystal M. Pratt, Wapinitia
2107 F. E. Bornemann, LaGrande
2108 Alice M. Lund, Flora
2109 J. W. Branstator, Seaside
2110 P. E. Christensen, Alicel
2111 R. D. Taylor, Portland
2112 Elsie VonWintzinglrode, Portland

Certificate No. 2014.

During the State Teachers' Meeting in Portland, certificate of membership 2014 was given to some teacher; unfortunately the stub to this certificate was not filled out so we do not have the name of the teacher. If this matter comes to the attention of the teacher who holds this number or to any one else who might know of it, it is hoped that she will send us her name and address, otherwise we will not be able to send the Oregon Teachers Monthly to her.—C. H. J.

He's armed without that's innocent within.—Pope.

An honest man's the noblest work of God.—Pope.

Give the Boys a Chance.

People who claim that schools are costing too much do not see that when they stop or curtail education they attack the very factors upon which their property values rest. The time to save a boy is before, not after. There are some six thousand now under the jurisdiction of the juvenile court where there would not be sixty if every boy and girl were given their chance. It pays to invest in your boys and girls. This nation is facing the greatest danger in its history. Not the ships of foreign fleets, nor internal labor troubles, nor even the liquor question are to be feared as much as the hosts in the coming generations with too much unoccupied time. The greatest contribution that you can make to the future of any boy and girl is to give him a chance for his own self-discovery and self-development.— John H. Francis.

Home Nursing

By ALICE MARKS DOLAN, Oregon Agricultural College

The earliest notion of the cause of disease was the belief than an evil spirit or demon entered the body and took possession of it. This belief is still held among many of the lower tribes and it becomes the ruling spirit towards well doing, for they believe that so long as they do as their gods wish them to do they will be kept free from the demon of disease. Granting that a spirit or a demon is the cause of disease, then the next thing to be done was to get the demon out of the body. This was done by sacrifice of a child, by fair promise, by the wearing of so-called charms, by the beating of tom-toms, or in many cases it meant that the patient himself was subjected to agonizing torture.

With the advance of knowledge of the human body, its structure, and its functions, there arose a new theory of disease known as the Hippocratic theory. According to this celebrated theory the body was composed of four humors — blood, phlegn, yellow bile, and black bile and just as long as these four humors were in the proper proportions the person remained in health, but if they became unbalanced or of unequal proportions disease was sure to follow. The work of the physician of those days was to keep these humor in proper balance and if the person became sick the physician was blamed for not having performed his duty. This theory held undisputed sway until the seventeenth century when it was superceded by the theory of homeopathy—this in turn was followed by the theory of fermentation, and out of this grew the present day germ theory.

The belief now is firmly established that the infectious diseases are caused by definite small plants and animals that are so tiny they can not be seen except by the aid of the microscope. Disease germs may enter the body through a break in the skin, through the mouth, the nose, or through any cavity of the body that has an external opening. Disease germs are always destructive. They tear down and destroy the living tissues of the body and their excretions are poisonous substances to the body. Disease may be spread by dust, by flies, by mosquitoes, by unclean clothes or unclean vessels, by public drinking cups, by animals or by direct contact in handling. The sick room should always be protected from flies as a safeguard not only to the sick people but to the well people also.

To be able to detect signs of illness often times means being able to prevent illness. One of the first signs is a loss of appetite. In many diseases the first symptoms are alike, that is, there is a rise of temperature and the skin loses its moistness and becomes hot and dry. There may be excessive thirst or more or less pain in the back and limbs and usually there is pronounced digestive disorder. When several of these symptoms exist together it is time for the mother or home nurse to be up and doing. Many diseases are ushered in with a chill if the patient is an adult and with convulsions if the patient is a child. This is true with many of the so-called "breaking-out diseases". Convulsions in a child are oftentimes relieved by placing the child in a hot bath and increase the heat by the addition of hot water up to a temperature of 112 degrees F., taking care to keep the head cool by using an ice bag.

The average normal temperature of the human body is 98.6 degrees F., although there are variations. Age has an appreciable influence upon the body temperature—the child's being somewhat higher while the temperature of an old person is lower. The time of day will make a slight variation in the body temperature. In sickness the change of a degree of temperature from the normal does not mean so much to a child as it does if the patient is an elderly person.

It must be remembered that a child's digestive apparatus is easily thrown out of order and is often followed by a rise of temperature out of all proportion to the cause. In a case of this kind after the bowels have been unloaded the fever will often subside as quickly as it arose.

Mouth breathing is an indication

that something is wrong. It may be that the nose is stopped up because of secretions or because of enlarged tonsils or because of adenoids. The tonsils may become so enlarged that they produce a pressure upon the inner ear and cause deafness. Adenoids may and do become so large that the space back of the nasal passages is completely closed. A mouth breather does not sleep as well as the ordinary child; he usually snores, the voice becomes unsound in tone and clear pronunciation is difficult. In time the face takes on a dull, apathetic look and he gets a name of being stupid in his studies, and unless the conditions are removed he is both physically and mentally handicapped.

The writer wishes that something might be said to arouse mothers to a realization of the wrong and harm done to the child by the use of the baby pacifier, or of thumb sucking for that matter. The soft bones of the mouth are pushed out of shape causing often times a protruding upper jaw and a misshapen mouth, but the real harm comes from the narrowing of the air passages of the nose—this in turn causing mouth breathing. A mouth breather is at all times more susceptible to disease than the one that breathes through the nose. A bad breath is another indication that something is wrong. It may be from dirty or decayed teeth or from decaying food stuff in the intestinal tract.

Many people do not take care of a child's first teeth because they think, "Oh, he will lose those teeth, so what's the use of having the tooth filled or taken care of." Many do not stop to think that the beginnings of the second teeth are already started and getting their nourishment and protection from the first little teeth and that if a tooth decays or is pulled before it really is ready, that the teeth above it suffer, the jaw bone contracts and does not leave enough room, so when the permanent or second teeth do come they most often are crowded and crooked. A child should early be taught that it is even more necessary to keep the mouth and teeth clean than it is to keep the face clean.

Whatever the threatened or actual disorder may be there are two important things to be done at the beginning. First, to have absolute rest and quietness for the patient. Second, to keep the skin clean, to keep the room clean and to have plenty of good, clean, fresh air for the patient to breathe, for every time we inhale or take a breath we take air into the lungs. This air if it is pure will contain with other things about 20 per cent of oxygen; then when we exhale or give out this air it has lost a part of its oxygen and has taken up various waste materials from our body. When the oxygen gets as low as 13 per cent we suffer and if it gets as low as 8 per cent death may result. Realizing how much we need fresh air and that without it we soon become sluggish, then it is easy to realize how vitally important fresh air is to the sick person. If a room is so arranged that it is impossible to have the window open wide, then put a board under the window. This will let the air in between the windows; or you may tack muslin over the window. This will let in fresh air and will not cause a draft; or an umbrella may be raised and placed at the side of a patient.

———————

Truth is the highest thing that man may keep.—Chaucer.

Summer Session 1917

Oregon Agricultural College

JUNE 11 to JULY 21

1. Courses for Teachers.
2. Courses for College Entrance and College Credit.
3. Boys and Girls Short Courses.
4. Preparation for Teachers Examinations.
5. Vocal and Instrumental Music.

SPECIAL INSTRUCTORS

Miss Alice Ravenhill, London, England
Mrs. Mary Schouck Woolman, Boston
Both in Home Economics.
Additional Specialists will be secured in Manual Training,
Agriculture, etc.

REGULAR COLLEGE FACULTY

Instructors from the regular staff include specialists in
Home Economics, Manual Training, Commerce, Agriculture, Art,
Biology, Chemistry, Physics, Education, Economics, Political
Science, Psychology, etc. In all, about one hundred courses
will be offered.

CUT OUT AND MAIL COUPON BELOW

E. D. RESSLER, Director
O. A. C. Summer School,
Corvallis, Oregon.
Please send copy of 1917 Summer School Bulletin to my address.

....

....

....

OREGON TEACHERS MONTHLY

The Official Journal of the State Teachers' Association

Vol. XXI   SALEM, OREGON, MARCH, 1917   No. 7

Published Monthly Except July and August by the State Teachers' Association

Entered at the Postoffice at Salem, Oregon, as second-class mail matter, April 1, 1898.

EDITORIAL BOARD

H. D. SHELDON, School of Education, University of Oregon, Eugene
E. F. CARLETON, Assistant Superintendent of Public Instruction, Salem
C. T. BONNEY, County School Superintendent, The Dalles
R. E. CHLOUPEK, Director Manual Training, Pendleton.
C. G. DONEY, President Willamette University, Salem
E. S. EVENDEN, Department of Education, Oregon Normal, Monmouth
MRS. M. L. FULKERSON, Institute Instructor, Salem
GEORGE W. HUG, City Superintendent, McMinnville
HOFKIN JENKINS, Principal Jefferson High School, Portland.
MISS VIOLA ORTSCHILD, President Grade Teachers' Association, Portland
E. D. RESSLER, Department of Education, Oregon Agricultural College, Corvallis
MISS LILLIAN TINGLE, Supervisor Domestic Science, Portland
CHAS. H. JONES, Business and Managing Editor, Salem

RULES OF PUBLICATION

1. The mailing label on the Oregon Teachers Monthly shows the date to which subscriptions are paid.
2. The Oregon Teachers Monthly will be sent to subscribers until ordered discontinued and all arrearages are paid.
3. Notice of change of address should be given at once, naming both old and new postoffice.
4. When renewing, always state that subscription is a renewal.
5. The subscription price, including membership in State Teachers' Association, is $1.50 a year in advance. Single copy, 20 cents.
6. Advertising rates will be furnished on application.
Address all communications to Oregon Teachers Monthly, Salem, Oregon.

Editorial Notes

It is the duty of every loyal teacher to stand solidly behind the state and national governments in their attempts to protect the country. Some of these attempts in the direction of drilling the boys in the schools may not yield the military results hoped for, yet we must remember that every serious effort to promote the common welfare, either in school or out, will have the effect of unifying national sentiment and of developing steadfastness in the hour of danger.—S.

† † †

In accordance with the plan announced in the February issue, the articles in this number, with few exceptions, are addresses made in the various departments and divisions of the State Teachers' Association, held December 27-29. The editorial board has endeavored to secure material representing every department and has succeeded in getting from some more than can be used. Everything submitted from the Elementary and Rural departments is printed and more was desired because they represent the majority of our membership. It may be possible to use in succeeding issues some of the manuscripts

remaining. The suggestion has been made that a better plan another
year would be to confine to one issue all the proceedings and addresses
of the annual meeting, by doubling or trebling the number of pages.
Doubtless next year's editorial board will welcome suggestions on
this point. Communications on this or other matters relating to the
conduct of the official organ are invited. Address Oregon Teachers
Monthly, Salem, Oregon.—R.

† † †

College professors as a class have no great reputation for either
team work or business capacity, yet the work of the Association of
University Professors shows both of these necessary qualities. In
every case where the freedom of teacher has been attacked the association has appointed committees of investigation, consisting of men
of national reputation. The able and unbiased and yet courageous
reports submitted on conditions in such institutions as Utah, Colorado,
Wesleyan and Pennsylvania have done much to clear the atmosphere
and place the work of the college teacher on a satisfactory basis, yet
the only weapon used has been publicity, letting the public know the
actual facts. Why cannot strong national and state associations extend
the same protection to all the teachers of the country?—S.

† † †

A mistaken and narrow-minded notion of economy is today the
worst enemy of educational efficiency in Oregon. Salaries are being
cut, superintendents are being hectored, school boards are being
frightened, and as a result school work is becoming more formal and
less effective. Neither the teachers nor children were responsible for
the last big real estate boom, yet they are being punished for the
financial reaction. Oregon is situated between two unusually vigorous
and well organized commonwealths. In the last two years many of
the most capable vocational and high school teachers have left the
state; let the present movement of parsimony and stupidity continue
and many of the most wide-awake teachers in other fields will follow
their example. The notion popular among a certain school of frontier
politicians that all public employees, including teachers, are merely
incipient grafters, parasites and public burdens, rendering no real
service, is likely to carry its Nemesis with it.—S.

† † †

Does it seem out of place in an educational magazine to ask, "Are
you a good roads booster?" Think about it for a moment and any
apparent incongruity will rapidly disappear. The state-wide improvement of the roads in Oregon during the last ten years and the resulting
increase in the number of automobiles (perhaps it would be better
put, the increase in automobiles and the resulting improvement in
roads) has been one of the biggest factors in the betterment of Oregon's
rural schools. Better roads shorten the distance to the city and bring
a consequent modernizing of living conditions in the country, which
in turn call for more modern school houses, and better teachers. All

this has been accomplished but the future holds yet more promise, for better roads are the first essential to the consolidation of schools—a movement barely begun in this state and yet one which is, without much question, going to be the ultimate solution of our rural school problem. Interest yourself, then, in the plan of congress to establish great trunk highways across the continent with a net-work of lateral roads erected by the various states. Interest yourself in the road problem and road legislation in Oregon where many of the counties are making starts with permanent hard surface roads. But above all do not forget to show that interest. Talk good roads in your home, when you visit at parent-teacher's meetings, in the geography class, in the artithmetic recitation, in the language lesson and do it knowing that you are talking for the improvement of your profession.—E.

† † †

"Oregon products for the Oregon people" does not evidently apply to the election of city school superintendents, if the experience of the last few years may be taken as representative. A man from most any other section of the country, backed by a private teachers' agency and supported by testimonials from notables never before heard of west of the Rocky Mountains, is frequently preferred to individuals long identified with the progress of the state. The result of this preference for the unknown and the distant over the known and the tried, on the younger men and women of the state who are attempting to win recognition for themselves may easily be imagined. The Oregon teachers should assert themselves and demand a fair field and no favor, school boards should realize that local record which can be examined is more likely to yield results than the echoes of distant record embalmed in highly imaginative testimonials. This protest should not be interpreted as opposition to the assimulation of a certain number of eastern teachers and principals in our school systems, adding variety of outlook and thus avoiding provincialism. Cosmopolitanism, however, may be purchased at too dear a price if it means the turning over the management of half the important school systems in the state to men who are ignorant of the traditions of the state and out of sympathy with people with whom they work.—S.

† † †

The school savings bank is being organized in various sections of the state, in response to the activities of national and state banking associations and as one form of expression of the thrift idea, now assuming national significance. About seventeen years ago several school banks were started in Oregon and conducted two or three years. The present revival of interest is promising for several reasons: a wider interest, including several sections of the state; the mode of operation, which makes the local banks directly responsible for the conduct of the savings bank; and the fostering care of several national organizations, with state and local representatives. The National Education Association appointed a Thrift Committee two years ago, which conducted one or more prize essay contests, one calling for a plan of teaching thrift in the public schools. The seven prize essays, with a synopsis of the essays presented by other contestants, have been printed as a monograph, which may be secured of Secretary D. W. Springer, Ann Arbor, Michigan. This Thrift Committee is continuing its investigations and conducting another prize contest this year for public school pupils, concerning which all county superintendents have had directions. Dean J. A. Bexell of Corvallis, Oregon, is a member of the committee and will be pleased to receive suggestions for the meeting to be held at this annual National Education Association convention in Portland in July. As stated in the first sentence of this editorial, the savings bank with its saving of money is but one of a number of phases of thrift. At least one county superintendent in Oregon, Mr. C. T. Bonney, has launched a campaign on this broader basis. The matter of appointment of a committee of the Representative Council of the Oregon State Teachers' Association to study this problem will be presented at the next meeting of the Executive Committee. Suggestions by those interested as to the scope of this investigation, other related problems that may be assigned to the same committee, etc., should be sent at once to the chairman of the Executive Committee, J. Percy Wells, Jacksonville, Oregon.—R.

† † †

The teachers of Oregon are depending upon a forceful and enlightened public sentiment to make their recently adopted code of ethics effective. What have you done during the last month to make forceful that sentiment? The next few months will be a particularly good time to keep in mind the third and fourth points of the code, for in the spring a migratory teacher's fancy strongly turns to thoughts of moving. This is the season of the year when it is the unprofessional practice of some teachers to cast their eyes over the map of the state, select the location which they think desirable and then send a deluge of applications with the faint hope that some one of them may arrive at some place at the opportune time for favorable consideration. This method of applying weakens the teacher, reduces salaries, shortens tenure and lowers standards. It weakens the teacher in that it accustoms her to scattered, "happy-go-lucky," or "take-a-chance" ways of doing things rather than knowing definitely what she wants, and setting out with determination to secure it. It reduces salaries because it gives a false idea of the supply of teachers in relation to the demand, since each different application from the same teacher stands in the market for an additional teacher. School boards will be slow to financially recognize the value of a good teacher when other teachers constantly create in their minds the idea that there are large numbers of teachers, probably just as competent, who are anxious for the position. It shortens tenure because it puts practically every teacher everywhere on the defensive, so far as her position is concerned, against the swarm of people who apply for it. This consequently makes it easier for petty things to cause her removal. It also stamps with the approval of common practice a tendency to change schools almost annually for very slight excuses and many times for none whatever. It lowers standards by making both teacher and school board feel that the contract is a form of trial which may be for two years and sometimes more, but probably for only one, and as an inevitable result the teacher does not put forth the effort to please and succeed nor does the school board demand as high qualifications as would be true if the "teacher tramp" with her promiscuous appli- cations were not so common.—E.

† † †

In the January number of the National Education Association Bulletin, on page 9, the editor makes some comments on the campaign in the Northwest for advance memberships, account of the annual convention in Portland July 7 to 14. Referring to the Oregon di- rector's plan of having every school district become an associate member, he says: "Those of us who have watched Mr. Plummer at work in connection with one of the dinners or meetings of the Depart- ment of School Administration can readily see what the school is up against in that section of the country that does not take out a member- ship on the first invitation." The great honor of Portland's selection for the annual convention of the National Education Association is due in large measure to assurances given the national officers by Director Plummer, State Superintendent Churchill, City Superintend- ent Alderman and other Oregon leaders, of loyal support by the teachers of Oregon and the other northwestern states. Naturally the Oregon teachers must lead. Our early, hearty response to the call for membership will encourage our neighbors in Idaho, Washington and California. Our leaders have aroused great expectations and it will require most unusual effort on our part to justify their confidence and live up to the reputation they have given us abroad. If possible, we must rise to the heights attained by Utah in 1913 at the annual convention held in Salt Lake City, when the state actually took out more memberships than there were teachers, better than a hundred per cent record. No other record has been better than fifty per cent, and there have been only two or three of those. We have about seven thousand teachers and twenty-five hundred school districts. There are a sufficient number of districts with two or more buildings to raise the total to twenty-seven hundred. Now we really should get five thousand memberships out of these nearly ten thousand prospects. If Oregon can provide five thousand, Washington, twenty-five hundred, Idaho, five hundred and California, one thousand, other states, near and remote, should supply as many more, giving a grand total of eighteen thousand and ranking us among the four largest conventions in the fifty-five years' history of the National Education Association. Five times the annual convention has met in California, the registra- tion reaching over seventeen thousand twice, both times the visitors from east of the Rocky mountains numbering more than ten thousand. Visitors this summer will doubtless be given such rates that they may include California with the Northwest in their trip, and with the National Parks as an added attraction en route there should be even more than ten thousand. Let's go after that attendance record, both in total memberships and in percentage of Oregon teachers enrolling. Send names at once to the County Superintendent, so that he may send you the membership blank immediately on its receipt from Director Plummer. Also line up the school board. Let's make our slogan, "Five thousand memberships in Oregon before June first!"—R.

Financial Report of the State Association

By W. R. RUTHERFORD, Acting Treasurer

This statement of the receipts and expenses of the Oregon State Teachers' Association includes all transactions under the re-organization, which took effect at the close of the Medford meeting, December 29, 1915. All bills presented to the proper officer and duly audited have been paid. No other accounts are payable, so far as known. In addition to the amount receivable from the state of Oregon through the office of the State Superintendent of Public Instruction, as noted in the receipts, Manager Chas. H. Jones of the Oregon Teachers Monthly, the official Association organ, will remit each month fifty cents on each membership paid since previous report. Receipts from this source have totaled $1056 to February 1.

Receipts to February 10, 1917.

1916 Balance on hand after closing expense of 1915 session . . . $	175.51
Aug. 11—From Oregon Teachers Monthly	68.00
Sept. 7—From Oregon Teachers Monthly	62.00
Oct. 7—From Oregon Teachers Monthly	120.00
Nov. 15—From Oregon Teachers Monthly	310.00
Dec. 2—From Oregon Teachers Monthly	215.00
Dec. 14—From Oregon Teachers Monthly	62.00
Feb. 1, 1917—From Oregon Teachers Monthly	219.00
From State Department (available but not yet on hand) .	125.00
Total Receipts	$1,356.51
Total disbursements to date	878.12
Balance in treasury . . . . $	478.39

1916   Disbursements to February 10, 1917.

Feb. 19—G. A. Briscoe (traveling expense—Executive Committee) . $	19.65
Feb. 19—J. Percy Wells (traveling expense—Executive Committee)	21.95
Feb. 19—Viola Ortschild (traveling expense—Executive Committee)	2.50
May 18—Viola Ortschild (traveling expense—Executive Committee)	2.50
May 18—J. Percy Wells (traveling expense—Executive Committee)	22.10
June 30—J. A. Churchill (Oregon Headquarters at N. E. A.)	50.00
July 13—Viola Ortschild (Editorial Board traveling expense)	3.25
July 13—Hopkins Jenkins (Editorial Board traveling expense)	3.25
July 13—George W. Hug (Editorial Board traveling expense)	3.90
July 13—R. E. Chloupek (Editorial Board traveling expense)	22.00
Dec. 16—E. S. Evenden (Editorial Board traveling expense)	8.35
Dec. 16—Western Union Telegraph Co. (Tolls to Nov. 21)	8.11
Dec. 16—H. D. Sheldon (traveling expense—Editorial Board)	5.40
Dec. 16—G. A. Briscoe (traveling expense—Executive Committee)	21.15

Dec. 16—Viola Ortschild (traveling expense—Executive Committee) ... 7.50
Dec. 16—Pacific Telephone & Telegraph Co. 10.30
Dec. 29—Merle Wadsworth (ushering State Association convention) ... 3.00
Dec. 29—Raymond Koessel (ushering State Association convention) ... 3.00
Dec. 29—Alexander Brown (ushering State Association convention) ... 3.00
Dec. 29—William Brandt (ushering State Association convention) ... 3.00
Dec. 29—Carroll G. Pearse (lecturer State Association convention) ... 350.00
Dec. 29—Henry Suzzallo (lecturer State Association convention) ... 125.00
Jan. 2, 1917—Elliott Printing Co. (printing programs) 40.00
Jan. 6—F. L. Stetson (expense—Committee on Retardation).... 23.47
Jan. 6—M. L. Fulkerson (expense—Editorial Board) 2.75
Jan. 6—E. R. Peterson (expense—Hot Lunch Demonstration).... 1.45
Jan. 6—Lester B. Davis (service as Official Reporter).......... 38.75
Jan. 9—H. H. Wardrip (telephone—Industrial Section Program) ... 5.20
Jan. 23—H. H. Wardrip (postage—Industrial Section Program).. 1.00
Jan. 23—Portland Hotel Co. (expense of Lester B. Davis)........ 12.95
Feb. 5—State Printing Board (printing Pension Law, etc.)...... 45.64
Feb. 9—Pacific Telephone & Telegraph Co. (Tolls—E. F. Carleton) 5.05
Feb. 9—E. D. Ressler (expense—Rubber Stamps, etc.).......... 2.95

Total .. ..$ 878.12

Classified Disbursement Statement.

Meetings of Executive Committee (three meetings) ....$ 97.35
Meetings of Editorial Board 48.90
Oregon N. E. A. Headquarters, New York, 1916........ 50.00
Expenses of Council Committees 69.11
Telegraph and Telephone (chiefly Annual Meeting).... 28.66
Annual Meeting, Portland, Dec. 27-29.............. 584.10

Officers of Departments State Teachers' Association

An effort was made to secure a report from every department and division of the State Association of the officers elected. At the time for reporting copy to the printer the following result was obtained. It is also desired to secure copies of the minutes or proceedings of each subdivision for permanent record in the secretary's office; these should be sent to E. D. Ressler, Corvallis, Oregon. List of officers of the general association was published in the February issue in the minutes of the General Session, page 333; of the Department of Vocational Education, with four divisions, in the Vocational Education Department, page 369; of the Oregon Council of English Teachers in Miss Parrott's account of the proceedings, page 354.

Other 1917 officers are—Department of City Superintendents (no report). Former President, V. Meldo Hillis, city superintendent, Medford. Department of Higher Education: President, W. T. Foster, president of Reed College; Secretary, F. Von Eschen of Willamette University. Department of Secondary Education: (no election). Former officers, President, E. L. Keezel, Extension Division University of Oregon; Secretary, H. F. Wilson, McMinnville. Division of Science and Mathematics: Chairman, L. P. Gilmore, Department of Science Oregon Normal School; Secretary, E. L. Keezel, University of Oregon. Executive Committee: A. F. Bittner, Jefferson High School, Portland; E. D. Curtis, James John High School, Portland; J. L. Whitman, High School, Pendleton. Special Committee on correlation of high school courses in mathematics: Professor F. L. Griffin of Reed College, chairman, who will appoint four associates. Special Committee on content and method in high school science course: Professor W. P. Boynton of the University of Oregon, chairman, who will appoint four associates. Division of History: (no report). Former chairman, Elizabeth Bain, Washington High School, Portland. Division of Modern Languages: Chairman, Professor F. E. Dunn of the University of Oregon; Secretary, Professor R. W. Broecker of the University of Oregon. High School Debating League:

President, Charles H. Boyd, principal of Highland School, Portland; Secretary, Earl Kilpatrick, assistant dean Extension Division University of Oregon. Department of Elementary Schools: President, Jesse McCord, principal of ———— School, Portland; Secretary, A. J. Prideaux, principal of Woodstock School, Portland.   Advanced, Intermediate and Primary Divisions: Chairmen to be appointed by president of the department.   Department of Rural Schools: President, Mrs. M. L. Fulkerson, Institute Instructor, Salem. Art Division: Chairman, Dean Ellis F. Lawrence, School of Architecture and Arts, University of Oregon; Vice-chairman, Miss Alberta Greene, Oregon Normal School; Secretary, Miss Helen M. Worth, Portland.   Department of Music: President, Miss Jessie V. Miller, Salem; Secretary, Miss Lyla Rancorn, Portland. Department of Librarians: (no report).   Former President, Miss Harriet A. Wood, Portland.   Department of Physical Training: (no report).   Former President, Miss Mabel Cummings, University of Oregon.

Business Tests of School Products

By WILLIAM F. WOODWARD, Portland, Oregon

For over three decades the speaker has been engaged in active business, having directly to do with the employment of young men and women, students and graduates of our public schools.   He is a parent and has watched his children, five in number, through the educational courses provided by our public schools; has three in attendance at the present time, therefore, what he has to say upon the correlation of our public schools and business conditions of today, he may honestly state is born of personal experience and observation.   He has no use for the senseless scolding and criticism to which our schools are constantly subjected by unthinking people; his wife, a graduate and former teacher in the public schools of Portland, has always shared with him his sympathetic interest in the great service which the teachers are called upon to perform—the practical rearing of our children—and his remarks today spring wholly from this feeling.

I recently submitted the following questionaire to a number of the leading bankers and business men of Portland, those who have to do with the employment of hundreds of young men and women.   The questions follow:

1.   Do you consider graduates from our high schools or commercial courses sufficiently prepared for work in office or store?   Reply—No, 4; Yes, 5; qualified, 4.

2.   Do you find that in the majority of cases there has been a sufficient degree of proficiency in the elementary branches, namely—quickness in figures, legible hand-writing, correct spelling, expressive reading?   Reply—No, 13.

3.   Do you consider our present common and high school courses would be improved by lessening the number of studies and accentuating the elementary studies mentioned above?   Reply—Yes, 13.

4.   In your office, is preference given to graduates from business colleges or our public schools?   Reply—No distinction.

The replies indicate clearly that our schools today fail to accomplish what cannot but be regarded as an elementary task—the equipping of our children with the four essentials of a practical education—quickness and accuracy in figures, correct spelling, legible hand-writing, expressive reading.   No boy or girl—no young man or woman, entering a business house today, lacking in all or any one of these essentials, can hope to attain a full measure of material success without suffering an unnecessary handicap by reason of any shortcoming as to these studies or branches.

I would call to your attention the weekly educational menu of a child in one of the grammar grades of our public schools, a little girl of thirteen: Grammar, history, arithmetic, reading and German every day; spelling and current events three times a week; drawing, music and gymnasium two times a week; writing once a week; sewing and cooking once every other week.

I submit in all humility, based on personal observation, that there is too much work in this for the average, immature mind; that it produces a form of mental indigestion; the memory becomes blunted; the retentiveness of the mind impaired; the child's intellect is struggling in a chaos of facts, figures, problems, rules, exceptions, conditions, all too complex and involved. High school is finally reached. Here emphasis is given to what are termed "higher" branches; there are selective courses. It is but natural that a child will bend every effort to select those studies toward which natural aptitude or training may lead him.

The writer has carefully scrutinized the hand-writing of many high school students. He believes he is correct in stating that there is insufficient attention given to this very essential accomplishment. These are days of mechanical appliances in the office as well as factory. Typewriters, adding machines and a myriad of devices have relieved the office worker of many mental processes; a clear, legible hand, however, is still essential. In our own experience we find that young ladies seeking positions, as a rule, are better penmen than the boys.

Our tongue is fearfully and wonderfully made. There can be no criticism made of an occasional slip in the spelling of unusual words, but even so, there should not be necessary the constant reference to the dictionary.

Arithmetical problems as given in the schools, seem to be in many instances, of complicated nature. My children frequently call my attention to problems which seem to be more in the nature of conundrums and rather supersede the drilling in figures as they are met in the counting-house.

Correspondence is necessarily an elementary feature in almost every business or manufacturing industry. Construction of a letter is based upon good reading, the use of correct grammar and familiarity with our forms of speech. It is self-evident that expressive reading and familiarity with standard authors is an essential in this work. In these days of so-called "cheap" reading (and withal it is the most expensive to be thought of), it is difficult to fix the mind of the growing child upon what may be termed "literature of standard or permanent value." The table at home is apt to be too well supplied with so-called "current literature," much of which is but rubbish.

In all that has been said thus far, let it be clearly understood that it is not intended as a criticism of the teacher so much as the system which has grown up with the years by greater accretions; a system today overloaded, where it is impossible to give sufficient attention to the essentials of the child's education, and this becomes painfully apparent when the graduate enters the world of business and the daily struggle for bread and material advancement.

Our public schools and particularly our commercial courses, are not in touch with the business office today. In thirty-five years of the writer's experience, there has been but one occasion when a class in accounting has entered our office for the purpose of inspecting the methods pursued by a concern employing over two hundred people and transacting a diversified business running into seven figures. How can the teacher expect to keep in touch with present day methods if his activities and observation are confined to books and the school room? What can he know of the thousand and one short-cuts which the practical accountant in charge of a score or more of workers finds it necessary to adopt? How can the teacher or class advance when no time or·opportunity is given them to grasp the advances which are made by a thousand fertile minds engaged in active business, honestly endeavoring to simplify and improve present day methods? Is it strange that the children who come from our schools into the office are painfully lacking? It can be safely said that every business man in our city would welcome the opportunity of assisting our schools along these lines; every accountant would take pride in showing the progress which he has made in his own particular office, in efficient methods and labor-saving devices.

We have thrown the Bible out of our public schools, and along with it, practically all moral teaching, even of the most elementary character.

Parents today are delegating to various agencies the bringing up of their children, reserving merely for themselves the fundamental steps necessary for bringing them into the world. In the great world of commerce today, is it not essential that there should be something said in our schools in behalf of moral training as well as merely figures? Why should not high ideals in business be illustrated? Why should we make of our school system, a great unmoral machine? Cannot Jew, Gentile, Roman Catholic, Presbyterian and Unitarian work out a plan whereby the day's task in our schools will begin at least with a simple statement of mankind's dependence upon a power higher than mere human agencies?

The Ungraded Work

By MRS. GRACE McCORD, Montavilla School, Portland

The ungraded work in Portland has been largely experimental. We have no set system nor do I think it would be practical to outline any one specific course for all teachers to follow; for, each school in Portland has had its own particular problems to solve and each principal has had the ungraded room conducted to suit his own local situation.

Before I go farther, I want to get before you what I deem to be a more fitting name than the "ungraded room." It has never seemed to me a fitting name for the so-called room. Let me refer to it as the adjustment work or adjustment room. I can see how the term "ungraded room" might fit a situation where a teacher has the sub-normal children of the building and she instructs them in just the subjects and as far in those subjects as they are mentally capable of going, not trying to reach any certain grade by the end of a term. Such children should not be in our graded schools, however, for we have a separate school for them. Where no such provision is made, however, an ungraded room, as the name implies, would be of greatest benefit. It would give sub-normal children a chance to get much more of the work they are capable of doing and not drag along in grades being passed year after year just to get rid of them. In most schools in our larger towns enough sub-normal pupils could be found to form such a room.

Our so-called "ungraded room" in the Montavilla, and in the greater number of the schools of Portland, has not been used as a place for sub-normals; our school has never had a sufficient number of such pupils to warrant us making a room especially for them. It has been an adjustment room, a place where normal-minded children who, having been retarded for various causes in their grade, may go and by special attention given them be enabled to catch up in their work. Pupils who are unusually bright or super-normal pupils are allowed to go as fast as they are capable of doing. This plan has resulted in many children completing one and one-half to two terms' work in one, and I have in mind one boy who completed two and one-half years' work in one. Other adjustment rooms have had like experiences, especially where they have had the foreign element.

As I have said before, the problems are not all alike in this adjustment work. Our problem where we have practically no children of foreign parentage is a vastly different one from the Failing school where the greater percentage of the pupils are of foreign parentage and even foreign birth. So, in some schools, the adjustment room has been of the greatest value as a place where the foreign speaking children can learn to speak the English language. You all know how difficult it is to give adequate help to a foreign child when you have from thirty to thirty-five other pupils needing your attention. In some schools the work has been almost entirely with sub-normal children whose parents could not be induced to send them to the school provided especially for them.

The idea has been quite prevalent, I find, to have the children recite singly. In all the ungraded rooms that I have visited in the city, and I've visited nearly all of them, the children do very little single recitation. I have had all the way from two to nine pupils in a class and the classes represented from three to six different grades—not unlike a country school. We try so far as possible not to exceed twenty pupils in a room; fifteen is preferable, thus giving time for individual help. One of the strong attributes of this special room is the small classes with few children to discipline.

I have in mind several schools in the city where the pupils go to the adjustment room only for recitation in the subjects in which they are retarded, but they are registered in their regular class. During some periods the teacher has but one child in the room, who gets her undivided attention. Personally, I have never tried this method though I can see its strong points. I prefer to oversee the study periods of the pupils who recite to me, for I believe that properly used study periods mean everything to the retarded pupil, especially those retarded on account of application. When you come right down to the point on the question of what causes children to drop behind in their work, I believe that fully three-fourths are retarded on account of lack of application.

I want you to see the purpose of the work aside from the mere convenience. How often we pity the boys and girls in our classes who have lost out and just can't seem to keep up in spite of all they may do in and out of school hours. Can't you see what it means to such pupils to be placed where they can go back a little and review—not be demoted—just brush up, then made able to go ahead and make the grade for which they are striving? Such pupils in large classes get disheartened and drop out of school, especially in the eighth grade; or if they are not ashamed of continual failure, become a drag and a nuisance.

I like the term that our Superintendent Alderman uses so often when referring to these special rooms, "The Room of Opportunity"—opportunity not only for the children but for the teacher also. What a chance to mother the discouraged boys and girls! So often we find them needing sympathy and encouragement along with personal attention. What an opportunity for the bright child to go ahead, for the retarded child to catch up in his work, for the foreign child to get more help in mastering the English!

Our work in Portland so far has been an experiment, yet we believe it is a practical work and if established as a permanent institution, a much larger field could be covered than I have briefly outlined to you.

School Credit for Private Music Study

By J. O. McLAUGHLIN, Hood River, Oregon

In presenting this subject of giving credit for music work pursued outside of school, it is presumed that the giving of credit for outside work is well established in our state and that no active opposition now exists. This is the third year we have given credit in our high school for such work; sixteen per cent of the high school students are taking music for credit; the school is well pleased with the working of the system; the music teachers are happy relative to the arrangement and the parents feel that the school is getting closer to actual life. This year we are offering credit for Bible study pursued in the churches and Sunday schools; it has been well received and about forty per cent of the students are taking this work. We plan to extend this form of credit to any legitimate form of development which is directed and supervised by a competent teacher.

The most serious problem confronted in giving credits for music is establishing a system of accrediting the teachers with definite requirements. This has been left by the State Department of Education to the individual school. When we first offered this credit two years ago, an informal meeting was held of some of the music teachers whom we knew to be qualified. A standard was set requiring that all teachers wishing their work to be

accredited must have had three years of training under competent instructors, this training to be above elementary instruction in the subject to
be taught.

As the work developed we realized that our requirements for teaching
were too lax and last year a more formal meeting of all of the music
teachers was held and the entire plan revised. It is this plan that I have
been asked to present to you.

Music teachers, wishing their instruction work accredited, must have
had five years of training under competent teachers, this training to be
above elementary instruction in the subject to be taught; or be a graduate
of an accredited and recognized musical conservatory; and shall file with
the principal such data as to their qualifications as is required on blanks
furnished by the school. These blanks are made with the typewriter, since
only a few of them are needed. At first a letter sized sheet was used, then
we tried a 4x6 card, but that proved too small, and now we are using the
letter sized sheet again.

Every application is considered carefully. Eighteen teachers are now
accredited in our school; we have refused to accredit some and in every
instance without any animosity on their part because we showed them that
their qualifications were not up to the standard of our school.

A bill has been prepared by Mr. Goodrich of the State Association of
Music Teachers which is to be introduced at the coming session of the legislature. This bill aims to make music teachers declare what their preparation
is and to protect the public against those who charge for instruction and
have no adequate preparation for teaching. While it does not include very
much, it seems to be all that can be done at this time and is a step in the
right direction and should be supported by the school men. While it will
simplify obtaining the qualifications of a teacher, it does not relieve the
school of passing on whether a teacher's work shall be accredited in the
school or not. From the amount of agitation among the schools and music
teachers, it seems that something should be done to standardize our requirements; this would assist the State Association of Music Teachers in their
work of raising the standard of musical instruction and would assist our
schools in maintaining standards of accredited work.

Under such a standard system the music teacher who did not render
satisfactory service in one community could hardly expect to move to a
new place and subject that community to her ignorant and unsatisfactory
methods until she had time to seek another location. The superintendent
of the town into which she had moved could write to the brother superintendent as he does now relative to other teachers; the correspondence would
reveal that the teacher was incompetent and the second school would be
saved the embarrassment and misfortune of accrediting an unsuccessful
teacher. But this arrangement would be unfair to the music teacher unless
the schools have standard requirements.

In our school as many as three credits toward graduation may be earned
in either vocal or instrumental music; Provided that it must be certified to
the school that the pupil has spent at least eighty minutes a day, five days
in the week for thirty-six weeks; that the pupil must appear in a public
recital held by the school or sanctioned by the school; and all pupils earning
their second and third credits must appear in two other musical performances during the year. We will add next year that instruction lessons shall
be given by the teacher at least once each week.

We have not attempted to dictate to the music teachers anything as to
their methods of instruction and shall not do so as long as the present
arrangement exists. The speaker does not understand the methods of the
various schools of music well enough to tell the music teacher, who has
studied abroad or is the graduate of a great conservatory, how she should
present the lessons; in the second place, music is art and cannot be outlined
in certain fixed and mechanical routes. Our teachers realize that it is up
to them to maintain the standard of the work, and I have no doubt as to
the quality of their instruction. The recitals at the close of the year in
which the pupils of the various teachers will appear helps much to tone up
the work and weed out the inefficient teacher. The poor teacher will lose

patronage and she knows it. The law of competition and elimination works much better among the music teachers than it does in our public school systems.

Two other appearances are required of pupils pursuing their second and third years' work. Pupils taking music for the first year are not required to appear in other than the recital at the close of school. Many of these pupils are just beginning in music and are not skilled sufficiently to appear and such a requirement would keep some from choosing music who need it and are timid about the public appearance.

To keep a record of the pupil's work we have outlined a system of reports, each covering a six weeks' period. The pupil is given one card at a time and must finish the work for that six weeks before another card can be obtained; a grade is given each six weeks. This requires them to be prompt, helps the music teachers and gives organization to all of the work. When the present supply is exhausted, we shall possibly make a slight change in them. On the other side we will have printed blank spaces in which the music teacher will record the dates when instruction lessons were given and the length of each lesson. There is a tendency on the part of some teachers with few pupils to want to go away for a week, telling the pupils to keep practicing, and that they will make up the lesson next week. This is not fair to the pupil or the school.

I am so well pleased with this form of giving credit that I wish to continue it and I trust the day will soon come when such work can be carried on in the seventh and eighth grades as it may be in the junior high school, and that the work in music may be substituted for such subjects as physiology, history, geography, or agriculture.

Real Purpose of a Privately Supported College

By PRESIDENT CARL GREGG DONEY, Willamette University

The discussion of this subject never ends for the very reason that no one can define a college and every person's judgment of what a college is for is based on a different set of facts or opinions. There are as many kinds of colleges as there are colleges, each with an individuality and, consequently, with differing programs. However, there are certain indices of a college and for our purposes we shall consider that institution to be a college which offers four years of work beyond that of the standard high school, which has not fewer than six professors, a hundred students, proper library and laboratory facilities and an income which allows the school to secure good instructors and material equipment. With less than this, the institution is something else; much more than this, it may be a university.

Colleges are organized and maintained for the purpose of serving the people in some particular not met by any other institution. It makes little direct contribution to society; its service must pass from its students to the larger organism. It increases the power of individuals and through them sends enrichment to others.

The point of contact between education and life is represented by a moving dial. The varying conditions of business, society, politics and morals make corresponding demands on education. The changed conditions, however, demand adaptations in the practical application of education, rather than in the substance of education itself. As an illustration, we note that in early times when the American colonies were seeking national unity while preserving liberty, the task of the teacher was to discover the way and to enlighten the public mind therein. Later, the question was that of developing the resources of the nation, and education responded by stressing the natural sciences and technical training while it relaxed attention in other directions. In both instances the demand was for an appropriate kind of truth; and this is the demand always; but the truth may come from different spheres and find application in changing forms of interest.

The difficulty lies in discovering what truth is. This is the cross upon which reformers have met their crucifixion, where also some teachers have paid a last penalty. They have felt that it was right to adhere to a belief that was sustained by reason rather than to follow a belief that had no such sustaining evidence; they have stood for rational demonstration instead of the formulations of prejudice and self-interest.

We have fondly thought that the time was forever gone when the scholar did not have full freedom to teach the truth. It is gone from educational institutions so far as open restraint is concerned, except in rare instances where the dead hand or the living demagogue has interfered. But I cannot join in the happy conviction that all educators are free from influences which impel them to teach much which does not wholly commend itself. The insistent clamor of an unthinking public has tended to disturb the mental poise of the scholar and by oft reiteration has impressed his mind with doubts and misgivings.

One can see what I mean when he considers the effect of a demonstrative and contending public on the attitude of a popular government. Wise and conscientious statesmen are compelled to compromise and to stand for what they know is less than the best. The church has likewise been tempted to conform to doctrines and teachings to meet the demands of masses of people. And it is clearly too much to say that teachers have escaped from a like influence. It is one of the dangers arising from a democracy and a consequent development of excessive individualism. Do not understand me as saying that democracy and individualism are anything less than priceless; but I do say they have their dangers, and one of the dangers is that which arises from unthinking or uninformed individualism. A person may easily overestimate the value of his opinions and it often happens that the more ignorant one is the more he contends for his views. When this person is multiplied by thousands the effect is searching and powerful.

It is proper to ask what influence this condition has upon the program of education, and whether the scholar and teacher should resist the influence. One expression of public opinion, represented by a considerable portion of the people, demands a popularization of education. This is a highly taking term; and we are told that education is valuable only to the degree that it helps one in the struggle of life, only to the degree that it is practical, which usually means making money. In the face of this claim, what should be the attitude of the schools? One is tempted to say immediately that people should have what they pay for and what they want. To do otherwise would be to destroy the rule of the people and to set up an aristocracy. I am not certain that this would be a safe and sound conclusion. History will sustain the statement that the minority has as often expressed the voice God as the majority has. We well know that the voice of the people does not direct in the discovery and use of the principles of science, that it does not control in the matters of medical hygiene, that it does not establish the laws of art, that it is not dominant in determining the highest methods in any interest or vocation. The judgment of the expert whose study and experience have been given to a particular subject is required and respected.

The mind of the many should always control if it were well instructed in the matter which is at issue; but until it has attained an analytic judgment, there must be those whose special ability entitles them to lead. If there are those who, because of superior knowledge, can be wise in law and medicine, in science and art, in invention and commerce, there should be those who are wise educationally. And there are; and my plea is that their judgment should not be founded in anything except the truth evidenced by clear facts. The physician who does not use the typhoid serum or vaccine because there is a sentiment against it is no less culpable than the educator who defines the purposes of education according to sentiment. To popularize education for no other reason than that an uninstructed class wish it to be so, is to devitalize it and ultimately to find it a corpse.

I will say then that in determining the purpose of a college, the educator should not take his standards from the inexpert and uncritical, for you can no more make concessions in education than you can in science and religion. Therefore, the question of the educator is not what some people want, but what is the education that is best for them to have. In replying to that question, we shall move toward the answer by picturing ourselves the ideal man, the person like whom we would wish all other persons to be; and then determining what contribution the college can make toward him.

The ideal person would have a perfect moral character. The basal importance of this is apparent, but however necessary it is, I do not think the chief purpose of a college is moral and religious instruction. The college shares this function with the church and the home. Every college should be definitely religious. It should not tolerate an unreligious teacher and much less one who is irreligious. It should strongly encourage its students to be religious and should always demand of them a high standard of moral conduct; and while one of the purposes of a college is to deepen and strengthen religious character, this is not its peculiar function. Neither do I think that the principal purpose of the college is to afford mental discipline, however essential that is. Assuredly there will be regularity of habits both in conduct and in methods of thought, but these have often been acquired beyond college walls. Nor is a college the place where chief attention is given to the acquisition of facts. This attainment also can be secured outside the class room and laboratory. The principal service of the college should be to do for the student that which no other institution can do; it should have some outstanding purpose peculiar to itself and to which it is committed in its major efforts.

Irrespective of location, the purpose of a college, I am constrained to believe, is to train students to think. The college must make its own contribution to society and, if one were asked what it is from the educational standpoint that society needs most of all, the answer would be immediately given that we need thinkers. As a people we have many virtues, but the thing most lacking is downright, constructive thinking. A moment's reflection will convince us of that. Interpreted positively, the great impacts which have pushed the race forward have come from the thinkers. Whether they had been Puritans deliberating over their relations to God, or Continental Fathers devising a new system of government; whether they have been scientists wresting secrets from reluctant nature or inventors laboriously contriving methods to use discovered forces; whether they have been statesmen preparing the laws of a nation or sociologists investigating the phenomena of society; whether they have been artist, author, preacher, teacher, farmer, merchant—whoever he has been, if he gave men light for darkness, he has first of all been a man of thought. Interpreted negatively, the great obstacle to advancement has come from the unthinking. Whether he has been the demagog misleading by vociferous rhetoric or the dull follower of credulity and tradition; whether he has been the simple plodder who blunders with his hands or the enthusiast who deceives himself by undetected sophisms—whoever he has been, if he has stood in the way of possible gains, he has been a man who did not think.

I know that morals is a surpassingly vital consideration in all these matters; but we are to remind ourselves again that we are trying to determine what the chief and especial function of the college is and that we believe it to be to train students to be thinkers. Every problem, every interest and activity, every dream and plan of man involves thought, thought to create and thought to direct. If we are to get an inch farther forward in any field, the mind of man must tell us where and how to go.

I fear that few colleges have, with avowed decision and clearness, set themselves to this task. We have been tempted and confused by the demand of the uninformed for a popular education, an education that is easy and practical; and this has sometimes led to the emasculation of teaching in the hope of making it acceptable to the multitude. The college should be the highest organized opportunity for producing the thinking man; and it is a demonstrated truth that in order to become a thinker one must think. Increased strength comes to an organ or faculty only by use, use prolonged and heavy enough to approach the breaking point. The occasional or dilettante toying with brain problems has never produced an Edison or a Webster.

Most of the colleges offer the subjects which will afford the training needed to produce the thinker. What is needed further are common sense as a basis, right methods and the sufficient application. In the study of the sciences, one observes phenomena, then compares, infers and reaches conclusions. Mathematics is the science of absolute truths, and forces the mind to reason. The study of languages is essentially scientific; the student observes, discriminates and deduces the general principle. The historian must be a reasoner and a gatherer of data for the further exercise of reason. He traces the great law of cause and effect in human society. Likewise the study of sociology and economics presents a myriad of human elements for classification and evaluation; and enlists the best powers of the reasoning faculties. The content of philosophy, rooted in life itself, is the most rationally awakening of studies. It demands the interpretation of human phenomena, complex, unseen, fugitive; and no mind can be exercised therein without feeling the inflow of power. English may be studied philogically, as literature, or in its creative relations. In the first instance, it has the scientific value of Latin or Greek. As literature, it has the worth of history in its relation to the law of cause and effect. And creatively it is proper to demand of all who write that they put into words only that which reflects studious thought. Incidentally, it is to be observed that the argumentative theme has been too much replaced by floods of merely descriptive writing.

A college curriculum which includes all these subjects properly balanced and valiantly pursued, in which the student actually works for four faithful years, will go far towards fitting him to solve the questions which will confront him in his vocation and home and society. It may not make him fruitful in original research, it may not make him a great leader, but he will be in possession of his resources. And this purpose of the college to train a man to think may reveal him as a leader, as an uncommon man. And if one uncommon man can be discovered in a generation, the race is secure in its progress and the college has rendered society an immeasurable service.

We have said, however, that in order to produce a thinking man, he must for a long period exercise himself in thinking. College men fail in their vocations because they are lazy or self-important or immoral or from a lack of common sense. No college can supply the last quality. If a person is born with his mind cut on the bias he will always see things out of their true perspective. Should he have the saving wit to know that he is thus deficient, the college can help him to avoid some of the more obtrusive examples of sheer foolishness.

Should a student be lacking in moral character, the college should represent to him a code of conduct so clearly fixed and defined that the youth will either leave the institution or conform to the established precepts. If he is willing to change his point of view, four years of honest agreement with high ideals should permanently transform him; and a school that allows a person to graduate who has, throughout his course of study, been dodging and trickily evading the moral life is criminally guilty of malfeasance.

The conceited student is more difficult to deal with than the immoral one, for frequently his excessive self-estimate is rooted in a lack of common sense. The fine confidence to be expected of the freshman is, however, usually toned down by his fellows who are particularly sensitive in such matters. What with the help of older students, the college should be able to so acquaint a student with the great world of wisdom that he will see himself in proper relation to it. Again, we hold a college to be derelict which graduates a bumptious nuisance.

I am constrained to believe that most failures of college men are due to a lack of industry. An enthusiasm for hard work not only accomplishes positive results, but negatively it saves from much of badness, conceit and assininity. Clever terms are devised to caricature the hardworking student: He is a "grind," a "shark," a "bone," a "faculty pet," and the like; but he is also the one who usually leads when he gets out of college. Most students do not work enough while in college. They are tremendously busy, but a vast deal of their busyness is about things which add nothing to their gray matter. As the school system is now organized, seven hundred days of college attendance leads to a degree, a little more than two years extended over four years. Unless the seven hundred days be days of real work, there will be engendered habits which are loose, evasive and destructive. The marvel is that some colleges produce any truly industrious men. The clear duty for all of them is to be so exacting that tasks constantly invite and drive, and sometimes demand the last ounce of mental power. Only thus will the college do its duty toward producing the real thinker.

The question naturally arises concerning the function of the college to fit men for their particular life work. I do not undervalue technical training, but I contend that it should follow the college course and not be a substitute for it. It would seem reasonable to believe that the farmer has as great need for constructive thinking as the lawyer or doctor or preacher has. Why should the learned professors require two or more years of graduate work while the farmer, the engineer, the journalist think they can get on with undergraduate technical training?

It is true that the schools face the issue raised by those who are positively unable to devote more than four years to preparing for their vocation. Should this class pursue the ordinary college course or should they follow a technical course? There are two answers to this inquiry. For those who refuse the hard drill of the mentally stimulating subjects and whose native abilities suggest that they must be content with slight success in their vocations, I would prescribe a course of study which includes much of the purely technical. But for the strong-minded, ambitious youth who will not cease to be a student when he leaves college, I would prescribe a thorough course in the college of liberal arts.

Aside from the conclusions of reason, I base this judgment upon observation. I am rather intimately acquainted with the careers of a company of men who were graduated from a university twenty to thirty years ago. The school then had from two hundred to five hundred students and its laboratory equipment was that of a fairly good present day college. Almost all of the students followed a rigidly prescribed course which included the time-worn and established subjects. Their technical opportunities were small, and they simply studied and studied. Were I permitted to name these persons you would find them on the United States Board of Defense, captains of industry with the Edison, Westinghouse and General Electric companies, the Niagara Falls and the Zambesi Falls engineers, the leading physicists of Harvard and Yale, notable authors, manufacturers, educators—an amazing percentage of highly successful men. It is my belief that they have succeeded largely because they were schooled in the old-fashioned courses, were obliged to work until their brains whirled and made to become independent thinkers. A few did graduate work, but most of them entered upon their vocations with only the four years of undergratuate study. It was, however, a real training in thinking and not in how to fill out a dance program or to applaud an opera.

Allow me to mention another example. I have a friend who is a considerable manufacturer of electrical machinery. He seeks original and inventive skill as well as the ability to direct the enterprises of a large industry. He has a standing request to have the opportunity to engage any of our college graduates whom I will recommend. He knows that we can offer the most limited technical training. He says that he does not care for that; he wants men who can think, who are industrious and moral, who have capacity to grow.

The man who thinks at once becomes the master of all who do not think. If the power of the thinker be so controlled by a social conscience that he will not use his ability to exploit these of less power, he is the world's benefactor. The college which produces such men shares in the praise of those who rise up to call them blessed.

Patience and gravity of bearing are an essential part of justice; and an overspeaking judge is no well-tuned cymbal.—Bacon.

The ablest pilots are willing to receive advice from passengers in tempestuous weather.—Cicero.

Every absurdity has a champion to defend it, for error is always talkative.—Goldsmith.

Sewing in the High School

By MRS. A. A. SANBORN, Portland, Oregon

The subject of sewing in the schools is so far reaching that to attempt to select just the one branch, the sewing in the high schools seems like a subject without a beginning or an end.

Woodrow Wilson says: "Education has this useful effect—that it narrows of necessity the circle of one's egotism. No student knows his subject. The most he knows is where and how to find out the things he does not know in regard to it, and in dealing with complex affairs to find where to get the information necessary to understand at least a part of it at a time. What we need is a universal revival of Common Council." These remarks it would seem fittingly applies to the several activities comprised under the head of Home Economics. The division of the sewing in the different schools and colleges seems not very well defined by a large number of people interested in education.

The elementary work in sewing as in all other subjects must be foundational; it should be simple and practical so it may apply at once with home problems. The first term of high school sewing must of a necessity over-lap the elementary work and serve as a review as well as to introduce much that is new.

The trade school, as we understand, is designed to prepare the apprentice for a particular trade. The technical school aims to help those who already know something of a certain class of work and wish a more scientific and theoretical knowledge of it. It does not propose to take the place of apprenticeship but to develop the foreman. Hand work is given to explain the science rather than to fit a student for a trade worker. The normal and agricultural college deal mostly with the one problem of training teachers and professionals, and with more mature minds, therefore the large range of subjects touched upon in high schools should be carried to the highest point of efficiency.

It is generally conceded that to successfully teach any of the manual arts, one must have a thorough working knowledge of all phases of activity to be employed in the presentation and results to be attained in the subject.

To be a successful teacher of sewing one should possess much native ability coupled with the desire to investigate and grasp the subject from a broad viewpoint, to utilize that which is of practical use, as well as to discard the useless. Many teachers reach out for the graduate work when it is the more elementary work she needs. The successful and resourceful teacher is one who is able to work out her problems satisfactorily to herself and pupils. No set rule or course should hamper the work or prevent the girl from receiving the lesson that is of the greatest practical value. The teacher's characteristics may differ to the extent that one teacher may get good results by one method, another equally as good by a different method. The teachers' personality also exerts a great influence over the pupil, therefore it should be of the best. There is possibly no line of work taught in the schools of today that contribute so directly to the upbuilding of the character of the girl as the home economics subjects.

The introduction of manual training as a necessary part of education has raised sewing to an art of great importance. Outside of the practical advantage of being able to use the needle, the mental training through hand and eye has been proved to have a permanent effect on the character of the child. The training of hand makes it dexterous in other employments as well as to inculcate in the child habits of thrift, cleanliness, patience, accuracy and economy, and to develop the inventive faculty. The enthusiastic and progressive teacher can, through sewing, make freer and more capable beings of her pupils and help round out their characters. All methods of presentation of a subject should be thoroughly studied; to be successful she must know her subject from all sides.

The course in sewing is correlated with many phases of activity, besides stitches, seams and the making of garments. As the growth, manufacture and use of the different textile fibers, the commercial aspect of all matters pertaining to materials and making of garments, intelligence in buying, art in dress and many allied subjects. The specific aim should be to develop the girl along lines of right thinking so she may view her responsibilities as a social factor in a broad and intelligent manner, and that she may become a more useful member of society as well as to fit herself for a practical home life.

Points to be considered in outlining a course in sewing are many, as each city or each school is a law unto itself. Conditions differ so greatly that much thought must be given to the subject and the testing of different methods is the only solution. In the high schools we have girls with various degrees of knowledge. Some have no understanding of sewing, some a very little, others have some knowledge of stitches, seams and garment-making but lack much of the technical knowledge. So in the high schools as in the grades much detail work is necessary, as the younger and less experienced the pupil, the more detail work is required.

We also have the exceptional girl who must have special attention and methods to meet her particular needs. Therefore the Domestic Art course should be so flexible that each teacher may adapt some part of it to meet individual needs.

Some of the definite problems that each pupil must understand before she can hope to advance to any considerable degree, is to become familiar with the names of stitches and seams and their application to the different garments, name of materials and methods of handling.

The intelligent use of patterns is most essential; the use of the drafting in schools has undergone a great revolution of late years. Once it was thought to be of great importance as a pattern making necessity. Now with the many splendid patterns its use is only essential as it applies to an intelligent interpretation of the patterns. Therefore the importance of thoroughly understanding measurement and changing and manipulation of patterns cannot be over-estimated. The study and testing of materials is of great importance in the life of the girl, if she hopes to select materials intelligently, and in this connection she will need to make use of many mathematical problems related to buying and making of garments, also in the keeping of accounts and the making of the budget. All these subjects and many more of like nature are of necessity made use of in a high school course of sewing.

There is no formula by which the knowledge of sewing can be gained except by the doing. Because of the complications arising in ever-changing styles and complexity of the work, there should be a course outlined and made optional, extending over a period of three years at least, so the girl who has not the time or means of entering college can get more advanced practice, as many girls, on leaving high school, are expected to make all their own garments and those of the family, thereby reducing the cost of clothing about one-half. We hear much about teaching the pupil in school that which will be of the most value to him in the line of work he wishes to pursue. Would not this apply to the home economic subjects as well?

In Portland we have one ninety-minute period of sewing every day of the five days in the week, making seven and one-half hours per week, a little over eighteen days of eight hours a term, or about two and one-half months of sewing in two years. Can you conceive of any one, much less a young girl of high school age, being able to fit herself for independent work in that length of time? Examinations, holidays and other interruptions coming out of the time would leave about two months in the two years' course given to the actual practical work. We think Portland is fortunate in having so much time where many places have much less, but should not every high school course be so arranged that if the girl felt she needed more of a particular subject she would be able to obtain it?

He that is taught only by himself had a fool for a master.—Johnson.

To be angry is to revenge the faults of others upon ourselves.—Pope.

Character is the diamond that scratches every other stone.—Bartol.

How Can the Higher Schools of Commerce Best Serve the High Schools?

By J. A. BEXELL, Oregon Agricultural College

In attempting to answer this important question, I shall emphasize the idea of service at the outset. I take it for granted that there can be no division of the opinion that the highest aim of education is public service and the elevation of the general citizenship of the state. There are three parties interested in the high schools who may be served by the higher schools of commerce: Namely, the administrative authorities, the commercial teachers, and the pupils; how may these be served most effectively?

The question of finance, of teaching force, of courses of study, equipment and facilities for doing work, are uppermost in the minds of the school authorities. These questions affect the school permanently, regardless of the teacher. The instructors come and go but these fundamental questions remain the same from year to year. The large correspondence of the O. A. C. School of Commerce with school authorities relating to these questions convinces me that these are practical and not theoretical problems.

Courses of Study.—One of the most effective aids the higher schools of commerce can render the high schools is undoubtedly in the preparation of standard courses of study. The colleges and universities are usually equipped with large libraries and their faculties usually have had an opportunity to observe more widely than the average instructor in the small high school, hence the higher institutions should be clearing-houses for information regarding the most advanced thought in every field of education, and they should be in a position to extend this knowledge to high school authorities. It is often objected, and too often on good grounds, that the college instructor is impractical and knows less of the needs of the outside world the longer he remains at college. But while this criticism may be fair respecting the old time college man, I do not admit that it is true to the same extent at present and it should be still less true in the future.

Two methods have been suggested as finishing courses for practical pursuits: One is suggested in the Oregon Course of Study, namely, a semester or two of apprentice work for which credit is given, and the second has been suggested by many thoughtful educators, namely, to insist on at least one year intervening at practical work between the high school and college. It is claimed that this would be a great aid for the student in selecting the proper course of study. I am one of those who doubt seriously the advisability of the latter plan. The first would, doubtless, be a greater stimulus to continued studies, while the latter plan would be a more effective method of elimination from advanced studies altogether.

Some work has already been done toward standardizing commercial courses of study in Oregon. Though laying no claim to finality, the courses of study for departments of commerce by the superintendent of public instruction last year was a move in the right direction.

Room and Equipment.—The next field of service of the more advanced institutions is in the study and dissemination of information regarding room and equipment. One of the first questions for consideration in the development of a new department is the facilities for work. Since a well equipped commercial department is one of the most expensive in the average high school and since an unwise selection of equipment and planning of room will retard the progress of the work for many years, it is of the utmost importance that reliable information be obtained from disinterested sources before costly mistakes are made. This relates to desks, chairs, typewriters, copy holders, office equipment and material of great variety. Too little attention is paid to standardization of this equipment with the result that a lot of hit-and-miss material is accumulated only to find its way to the scrap heap after the costly experiment. The higher schools of commerce should co-operate with the department of public instruction in a thorough study of these problems and give the high schools the benefit of their research.

It should be emphasized, however, that too great importance is often laid on elegance of equipment rather than on serviceability. Very satisfactory desks, filing cabinets, shelves and so forth may be made in the high school manual training department, or by some of the most enterprising boys, at exceedingly low cost to the school. Besides, elegance and extravagance in equipment is apt to lead to wasteful habits which must be overcome before the student has proceeded far in his business career. And everyone knows that there is often a compensating advantage in working against and overcoming difficulties.

Text Books, Library, and Material.—Another most fruitful field of co-operation lies in the selection of text books and laboratory material. What a fearful waste in our educational system by the careless selection of the sources of information. True, the state maintains a very efficient text book commission and on the whole the interests of the schools are well guarded, but there is room for thorough investigation by the normal school and higher schools of commerce before the text book should be considered by the commission.

That the preparation of text books and laboratory material is a fundamental need is shown by the efforts of such agencies as the Harvard University Bureau of Business Research, the U. S. Office of Markets and Rural Organization and the Federal Trade Commission. Every teacher should be on the mailing list of these organizations. Every high school commercial department should develop a business men's library which should be selected with great care. It is unreasonable to expect that the instructor in the small high school should be able wisely to lay the foundation for such a library. The combined experience of the higher schools of commerce and the collected information and experience of the more advanced high schools should be placed at his disposal.

Commercial geography and local industries are subjects receiving increasing attention in the large high schools in every part of the country. To teach these subjects properly and to inspire enthusiastic interest in local and state depelopment, requires a great variety of illustrative material. Such collections are commonly dignified by the name of Commercial Museum. The great Commercial Museum of Philadelphia offers a variety of collections to illustrate different subjects at very reasonable prices. Manufacturers are always glad to furnish such material to schools which make proper use of it. A miscellaneous collection of material, however, is worse than useless if it is not properly classified and studied in connection with lessons it is intended to ilustrate. The higher schools of commerce should be active in assisting the high schools, both in securing the material and in standardizing its use.

Training of Teachers.—Perhaps the most important service the higher schools of commerce can render the high school authorities is in training teachers who shall be, not only competent instructors, but who shall thoroughly understand the conditions of the state and be in hearty sympathy with every movement which makes for industrial development and social uplift. Few people realize the fact that of the entire enrollment of considerably over a million high school pupils, at least one-fourth of all high school teachers must be trained for their profession by the higher school of commerce. To be exact, the commissioner of education reports 52,491 high school teachers in 1913, of which Oregon is credited with 679. Then allowing for rapid increase during the last two years, there should be at least 200 teachers interested in business courses.

The importance of the summer schools at the state institutions is often overlooked by both the authorities and the teacher. Equipment of great value and a large teaching staff are devoted to a comparatively insignificant attendance when the halls of learning should be crowded to the limit. High school authorities should offer inducement to the ambitious teacher to avail himself of these opportunities. This would probably have to take the form of indirect recognition and advancement rather than direct financial aid.

Preparation of the Teacher.—How can the higher schools of commerce best serve the teacher? Obviously, the first assistance the advanced school can render the teacher is in adequate preparation. The large excess over the supply for competent commercial teachers leads me to believe that this is a field which may well be cultivated. This is especially true regarding applications for men who have chosen teaching as their life work and not merely as a stepping stone to other vocations. My observation has been that the average applicant for a high school position is deficient in one or more of three fundamental requisites: (1) Intensive training in specialty, such as accounting, office training, stenography, commercial law, or economics; (2) insufficient fundamental training in English, mathematics and science; (3) insufficient training in student activities and leadership. It is the duty of the higher schools of commerce to watch the progress of prospective teachers with a view to correcting these defects.

Reading Courses.—The college or university can be of great service in conducting reading courses for the benefit of the commercial teacher. A start in the right direction has already been made by the state department of public instruction and most of you are familiar with the reading courses which were started last year. O. A. C. instructors have found the conducting of such courses a real pleasure because it puts them in touch with various conditions in the entire state. Some of the most lasting and profitable friendships are formed in the courses of this co-operative work.

Correspondence Courses.—What is true of the reading courses is equally true of the more formal correspondence courses. This method of instruction lends itself peculiarly to the teacher because in the course of his daily work his shortcomings and difficulties are discovered and emphasized. And the instructor is obviously better fitted to pursue self study than any other class of students. A multitude of correspondence courses are offered by a variety of individuals and schools, but in many cases the courses are too expensive and ill suited to the needs of the student. No institution should be better fitted to furnish the assistance to the high school teacher than the state colleges and universities. Both O. A. C. and the University of Oregon are rapidly developing correspondence courses in commerce within their respective fields. These courses are offered at practically no cost to the student beyond the necessary books and material. Many of these courses are offered as part of the requirements for a degree under suitable restrictions.

Educational and Vocational Guidance.—The services which the higher school of commerce can render the pupil is less definite but no less important. Among the most difficult and vital problems in education, especially beyond the high school, is educational and vocational guidance. Who should be encouraged to pursue a college course? Who discouraged? Who should pursue law? Who, agriculture? Who, commerce? These questions are of tremendous importance to the commonwealth as well as to the individual. I am not ready or competent to lay down specific rules to be followed, but I am here to say that as careful methods should be used in determining fitness for position as in the selection of proper equipment for our factories, or stock for our dairy farms. If the colleges and universities gave more serious attention to the study of the prospective candidate before he leaves the high school rather than during the college course, there would be far less educational and vocational misfits. This cannot be done without serious, painstaking investigation any more than important results can be achieved without research in scientific investigation. This slow and often costly investigation should be performed by the local authorities in co-operation with the colleges and universities.

Correlation of Commercial Courses.—This discussion would not be complete if I did not say a word regarding the correlation of the courses of study of the higher schools of commerce and the commercial departments of the high schools. What should constitute the end of the high school course and the beginning of the college course? Under what circumstances may college credit be granted for high school work? What is the distinction between higher and elementary work in commerce? These are questions which press for answer in the minds of both the college and the high school authorities, as well as by the pupil preparing for college. The quantity of work required for graduation from the high school is measured by fifteen units and may be readily equated with college credits. If all high school graduates knew exactly what course to pursue and all college preparatory courses were standardized in high schools of equal facilities, the problem would be easily solved. But neither of these suppositions are true or will likely ever be true. A classical high school student often decides to enter the college commerce course and a commerce high school graduate as often chooses the university course in liberal arts. Under either circumstance, the college or university generally offers beginning courses which are just as elementary as courses offered in the best high school, junior and senior years. The only difference lies in the measure of the work spent on the course.

Lest I be misunderstood, I must make the practice of O. A. C. perfectly clear by two examples: Take, for instance, the department of mechanical engineering. The first semester of the freshman year requires a two credit course in mechanical drawing. This means six hours of work per week for eighteen weeks. Many of the Portland high school graduates come with a year's credit in the subject and it has been found that this work, usually given in the last two years of high school, is fully equivalent to the college courses of half a year. Hence, mechanical drawing is credited in the freshman year, but the student becomes deficient in an equal number of elective credits. These may be made up by taking any work for which the student is prepared during the college course, usually in English, modern languages, mathematics, science, or commerce. It is generally conceded that a very good elementary course can be given in the high school in both stenography and accounting, but that advanced courses in both subjects are out of the question in high schools, due for the most part to the immaturity of the student. Hence, if a student has finished two years of either stenography or accounting in high school, he may register in the sophomore year in either subject, deficiencies being noted in elective credits. This correlation is typical of all other departments. In other words, a total of fifteen units of high school work, plus 136 credits of college work must be completed before a student can obtain a degree in any course at O. A. C.

In my judgment, there is no reason why this principle should not be established for all high schools reaching a certain standard set by first-class colleges and universities. Here, obviously, is an opportunity for real constructive work on the part of the higher schools of commerce. The distinction between higher and elementary commerce lies both in the kind of work and in the intensity and extent of the work. Latin may be begun either in high school or in college and advanced work may be pursued both in the college and the university, and yet Latin is Latin. The same is true of accounting, of economics, of commercial law or of English.

Conclusion.—In conclusion, I venture the hope that by the continued co-operation of the state department of education, the several higher schools of commerce, and the rapidly developing high school commercial departments, Oregon will be able to assume leadership in commercial education on the Pacific coast. Speaking for the higher schools of commerce in Oregon, we welcome every request for any assistance we may render in the development of commercial education throughout the state.

Manual Training and Its Relation to Industrial Efficiency

By FRANK H. SHEPHERD, Oregon Agricultural College

The value of manual training to the industries is best studied along two lines: First, its cultural value in developing individual ability; second, vocational preparation, in laying foundations for future activities.

Let us define the terms of our subject; the dictionary is our authority. Culture is the training, development, or strengthening of the powers, mental or physical, or the conditions thus produced; improvement or refinement of mind, morals or taste; enlightenment or civilization. Efficiency is the power that accomplishes a desired or designed work; the quality that produces the best results or the most effective service. Industrial denotes the processes or products of manufacture, or commercial production in general. Manual training is a system of education whereby pupils are instructed in handicrafts as carpentry, blacksmithing, etc., for boys, and sewing, cooking and household duties for girls.

The history of manual training as developed in the United States may serve to guide us to an understanding of its relation to industry. Go back to the days when John Runkle, Col. Parker, Charles Ham, and that grand old pioneer of manual training, Dr. C. M. Woodward, of St. Louis, Mo., and a few others were dreaming, studying, experimenting, working toward the expression of a new ideal in a course of study for public schools in the United States. A progressive, democratic people were more and more insistent in demanding a system of education that should offer equal opportunities for an education to all the children of all the people. There were trials and errors, hopes, doubts and fears, adverse criticism and lofty indifference. But in 1879, on the sixth day of June, the St. Louis Manual Training School was established.

A very similar course of study, written by Philip Parcher, is now used under his direction in the schools of The Dalles, Oregon. There is this difference; long experience since 1879 has shown it advisable to offer such work to boys of even less age than fourteen. The course has been arranged accordingly to cover five or six years. The last year is devoted to specialization, with courses adapted to meet modern conditions in the industrial world.

Now from the doors of that manual training school in the city of St. Louis, let us follow the trail that proceeds with many twists and turns, but ever widening and improving, until it has almost developed into a national highway of industrial education. As we pass along over this trail, we see a side track or spur that leads off to the Russian system of joint construction in woodwork. You may be surprised to know that there are still tickets sold for stations along that trail, but here is a letter dated December 7, 1916, signed by the principal of a vocational high school in a middle western state. He says:

"There is no question in my mind but that the best work was obtained and the very best workmen made in the days when we used the old Russian system of joints. I have seen so much useless trash made of late years with no other idea than to keep boys busy or because they liked to do that thing.

So many of these things did not teach one new idea, so I frankly say I have lost faith in the work. So a system of exercises that will bring out some desirable principle or teach the use of some new tool or a new form of construction is, I think, the proper course to give."

After pausing at the Russian System Junction we move on and very soon come to a broad and well marked road known as Swedish Sloyd. For a short time this road was in the hands of a company known as practical sloyders but it soon went into the hands of a receiver and the stock was taken over by the traditional school men who changed the name to Educational Sloyd and closely followed the fifty sloyd models for their educational values. To show you that this method still prevails in many of our schools I will tell you in general of a statement made in a letter from a teacher in a school in Oregon who recited in detail the work done by his 7th grade pupils in making a rule from soft pine. The said rule was to be 3-8 inch by 1 inch by 12 inches with the various details found on rules of this kind. This teacher showed me that after 20 hours work the boys of the 7th grade had nearly finished their rules. Soon after the educational sloyd people had their line in active operation, two rival companies were formed. "Our Schools for Culture Only" club cast covetous eyes on the Arts-Craft movement, and the controlling interest in that company soon passed into the hands of the educational conservatives. They still do a deal of press agent work in the interest of their holdings. The rival company was known as the Industrial Movement and their policy is shown by the following short synopsis of an address made by a strong supporter and a large stock holder in the industrial organization. He says, in part: "In the past it has been claimed that the making of pieces of household furniture was actually connecting the school with the home, but the fact is, the furniture of a home does not make up the home life, and without the co-operation of the other departments of the school, pieces of furniture are all the manual training teacher has to realize the home life with." He follows this with a description of what should be done by manual training teachers by illustrating a study of an industry in the school he represented. The industry of which the study was made happened to be a foundry. A demonstration was given in the school room with soft metal to illustrate molding and casting. The boys then made a flask, a rammer, a slicker and a vent wire. To furnish power for the building of a model of a foundry, water wheels were made and the best water wheel was selected to run the blower. "These boys made the foundry, including the building, cupola, elevator for fuel and metal, blower and the crane." There is no reason for going into greater detail to show you the trend of the industrial movement other than to say that courses of study in schools where the industrial movement prevailed were arranged covering the chief industries such as transportation, mining, fishing, etc.

For the past five years the tendency has been strongly toward the vocational movement, and while there are a few so called manual training men who are still clinging to their shares of stock in one or more of the rival organizations it seems that about 97 per cent of those who are interested in an educational system that offers equal opportunities to all the children of all the people are now in or heading for the main line that had its origin in the St. Louis manual training school thirty-seven years ago. As the problem for solution now stands it is not the method or the movement that you follow that counts for efficiency. Each of these movements has its good points, and it is quite within the range of human possibility that any progressive, up-to-date manual training man of today is using the good points from each of them.

All manual training work to deserve the name of manual training must lead to industrial efficiency. In the first grade the paper folding and cutting, the furnishing of the home of "The Three Bears" should lay the foundation for future study of house furnishing and construction. In the third grade work with raffia should be the nucleus around which a vast fund of related matter should be woven. Time will not permit a detailed outline of all such work, but the matter may be summed up by saying that whatever the media of construction, or the name of the lesson, unless the teacher makes each step in the lesson an opportunity to fasten a bit of valuable truth that will afterward function in the life of the child as a member of society, the work is worse than worthless.

In illustrating the relation of manual training to industrial efficiency let us use the subject of carpentry in a high school course. Here are a number of enlarged photographs of a garage that was built by the high school boys of the Corvallis school under the direction of their teacher, A. R. Nichols. Let us assume that this garage was built by Mr. Nichols and one boy, Mr. Nichols as a contractor working for pay, doing the job for so many dollars and the boy working as an apprentice to learn the trade of a carpenter and also earn one dollar a day for his wage. It follows, in my opinion, that Mr. Nichols will try to do the job in as little time as possible for the purpose of making as much profit as he can. It also follows that Mr. Nichols if he is an efficient contractor and builder will keep his boy on such work as the boy can do the greatest amount of in any given time. Mr. Nichols will, perhaps, do all the laying out and keep the boy busy sawing. Now it follows that while the boy may become very expert in sawing he is surely having no opportunity to become efficient if we measure efficiency by the definition as quoted in the beginning. But Mr. Nichols and the high school boys built this garage not as contractors and builders but as a teacher and pupils. They made a study of garages; they looked at different garages; they measured cars; they drew the plan and made the specifications; they talked of materials, lumber, nails, hardware, etc.; they studied costs and made estimates; they learned the cost in the open market for such materials as were to be used in such a building. They made out bills in proper form and thus, in the planning and constructing of this garage, added vastly to their store of practical as well as cultural education. Now I am sure they did not, but let us go farther and see what more could have been done to increase their industrial efficiency while working with this garage as their project. Suppose they had been using that wonderful text book "Occupations," by Gowin and Wheatley, published by Ginn & Company; they would have taken up chapter IX, The Building Trades, and made a study of the following: The Carpenter, The Mason, The Structural Ironworker, The Plumber, The Practical Electrician, The Painter and Decorator, The Janitor. Under the general head, The Carpenter, they would have found the following sub-heads: Rank of carpentry as a trade, Nature and remuneration, Natural qualifications, Facts concerning this trade by a prominent carpenter, Fine carpentering or cabinet making. Each of these steps would add to their general knowledge, broaden their view and thus bring them nearer to industrial efficiency.

That industrial efficiency may be attained through the manual training work in our public schools, the teacher must realize that he must ever have his lamps trimmed and burning. There is no place in manual training for dead ones or for those who sleep on the job. Success depends upon your ability to readjust yourself and your work to the ever changing economic and industrial conditions of the rapidly changing industrial world. Inventions are so frequent that manufacturers are hardly able to meet the expense necessary to keep abreast of the times. The one who was industrially efficient a few years since, measured by the standard of that day, may be a back number today. As a specific illustration of this statement you have only to go over in your minds the wonderful progress made in the industrial world in the past few years. Electric constructions and applications, the automobile, the airships, the wireless telegraphy, the automatic telephone, the under-sea crafts, the uses of concrete and other building materials than wood. This mental retrospection will convince the most skeptical that to preserve a balanced relation between manaul training and industrial efficiency the teacher must keep in touch with the workings of the industrial world. I have a letter asking about a certain book on carpentry. The writer had heard the book mentioned and wished to know if it should be adopted as a text book on carpentry in his school. I secured a copy of the book and after examining it very carefully I found that for modern construction it was obsolete. There were a number of splendid plates to show the different steps from the time the location was chosen until the building was completed, but the entire frame was made with mortise and tenon construction. The specifications for plumbing called for wooden bath tubs, lined with tin and painted with, not enamel paint, but common white lead.

When Dr. Woodward of St. Louis wrote that ordinance by which the St. Louis manual training school was established I am sure that he had a vision of the many advancements in the industrial world that have taken place since the year 1879 and in response to that mental stimulation brought about by the shadow of events to come, he wrote into that ordinance: "And such other instruction of a similar character, as it may be deemed advisable to add to the foregoing from time to time." In the Portland school survey which was made some five years ago, I find that Dr. Cubberly or another has set forth therein three principles, in the way of advice or suggestion to the teachers and principals in the Portland schools. If these suggestions are made part of the working creed of any teacher, whether he be in the Portland schools or a rural school, on Greenland's icy mountains or India's coral strand, the relation of manual training to industrial efficiency will be well taken care of. These three principles exactly state the relation that should exist between manual training and industrial efficiency: (1) The children and the youth of the community must be constantly and sympathetically studied by teachers and principals, in order that these may understand at all times the condition, the capacity, the interests, and the educational needs of each child or youth; (2) the various present and prospective opportunities and needs of the community for worthy service must also be studied, constantly and appreciatively, particularly by those immediately responsible for the education of youth soon to be called upon to take effective part in the occupations and life of the community; (3) the instruction of each child and youth—the content, method, and the immediate purpose of that instruction —must be constantly adapted to the needs of that child or youth, in the light of the needs of the community."

If school boards will only employ men as teachers of manual training who truly square up to this standard; if teachers will test themselves by these principles and, if they fall short of the required O. K., refuse to continue to take money under false pretenses there will never be cause to intimate that manual training falls short of developing thoroughly efficient boys to enter the industrial walks of life. If manual training is taught as it should be, the relation of manual training to industrial efficiency is, (1) its cultural relation as shown in the training, developing and strengthening of the powers, mental and physical; and (2) the same relation that exists between reading and so-called liberal education, that is, the foundation. Reading is fundamental as a foundation for a liberal education. Manual training, properly taught, is as necessary to industrial efficiency as is reading to the liberal education.

Manual Training and Its Relation to the Community

By R. E. CHLOUPEK, Pendleton, Oregon

If one were to talk on adapting manual training to the community in many states one would have to give an abstract talk because the conditions in one locality would not be the same as in some other locality, due to the fact that many of the states have large manufacturing interests. We teachers of Oregon are not met with such a situation. Practically every manual training teacher of the state meets, or should meet, the need of adapting his manual training to a community which is largely dependent on agriculture pursuits. Many of us, in fact the greater per cent of us, are not meeting these needs. From reports gathered this fall the following figures are noted: Fifty per cent of the schools, in which manual training is taught, give nothing but cabinet making, joinery, mechanical drawing and some woodturning and patternmaking. The remaining 50 per cent offer besides the above subjects, 21 per cent, carpentry and concrete, and many of these said their courses in these subjects were limited; 17 per cent carpentry only; 11 per cent carpentry and forging but no concrete work; ½ per cent carpentry, concrete, forging and gas engine work.

This means that half of the schools of the state are trying to make cabinet makers and draughtsmen out of the boys who will eventually work back to some form of farm work. Any manual training is good for the boy but is your manual training doing your boys the greatest amount of good? His cabinet work and woodturning do give him a splendid training, but my point is that these subjects should not be the ones upon which the emphasis is laid. Give him the fine hand training that goes with these subjects, but do not stop until you have given him something that he can apply directly on his leaving school. We have only one city in the state of any size and in which we find any manufacturing interests to speak of. The rest of the cities and towns draw their boys from the farm or from localities in which the farming interests predominate. Why then start the boy out with joinery? Have him make a small piece of furniture, then another piece of furniture and then some more furniture.

I'll grant you it is a fine feeling to have some fond parent come to you at the time of the annual exhibit and tell you how much you've done for his boy, because he had made a footstool or a table for the home, but it isn't in it with the feeling of pride that you would have if that same parent came up to you and told you that his boy had done all the blacksmithing of the farm or that he had built a cement walk or a shed of some kind.

You may say that if the boy has cabinet making that he can readily take up carpentry, concrete, or forging because his hands are trained. If that were to hold true many of us would make wonderful carpenters or blacksmiths. My experience, in working for contractors for two summers and in a general mill one other summer, has been that the $3 a day I was paid was about $2 a day more than I was worth, and I know positively that I can do better hand work than any man that was on the job with me.

May I illustrate by telling you how we are trying to adapt manual training in Pendleton. When the department was installed about four and one-half years our strong point was furniture work and mechanical drawing, and some very creditable work was done. The course in carpentry was added two and one-half years ago. Concrete work was added the following fall and the manual training classes started work on a forge shop 24 feet by 38 feet with concrete floor and foundation. That fall we built some 120 feet of low retaining wall and a couple of 10-foot ornamental light posts. The forging class started the second semester and a class in concrete work built a walk between the forge shop and the main building. The work in forging is deigned to meet the class of work which would be called for by the farmer, different forms of welding, clevices, pinch bars, S wrenches, chain and hooks, and as a class project the class built two 16-foot wheat racks and an 18-foot rack. Each boy in the class was required to study wheat racks and talk with the farmers with the idea in mind of finding out where the racks could be improved, and each boy was supposed to put some improvement into the rack. Two of the boys worked on the brake parts, another two on improving the bulk head, some of them on working out the way to fix the sides so they wouldn't wear out the sacks in the hauling, and two of the boys worked in the truss rods. The racks were sold for the cost of the material and the men that got them were so well pleased that this year we have had requests for eight more. The class will only turn out three racks, as they will work on two bulk wheat wagons, the design of which have been worked out by one of the freshmen in high school who has made three for his brother, working nights after school. Another boy is now at work making a stump puller out of a caterpillar part, and one of the boys is working on a stacker. Last summer four of the boys got jobs at $4.00 a day doing blacksmithing and repair work on the farm.

The gas engine or farm mechanics course takes up stationary gas engines and tractors. We have installed two 45-horsepower Aurora engines from Holt Combines, and four stationary engines ranging from one and one-half to three horsepower. The Holt Caterpillar Company is sending us a 75 Caterpillar which will remain at the high school and which they will replace whenever they put out a new type of engine. This machine will be used to demonstrate operations, upkeep, and repair. This course also takes up belt lacing, rope splicing, knots and hitches.

This fall we have built 350 feet of concrete walk, a 350-foot curbing around one of the driveways in the school block, a cross walk for the city, and an addition to the forge shop 24 feet by 32 feet which is used for the gas engine work. This work is in addition to the work inside of the building such as two sets of scenery for the stage, footlights, a house for the moving picture machine, lockers for the Domestic Art department and all the repairing and alterations that are done in the building.

The work in the high school is offered in the following manner: First semester boys are required to take joinery, and all of the rest, excepting those taking gas engine and forging work, are given concrete and carpentry as long as the good outside weather lasts in the fall. When the winter sets in the classes are taken into the shops and divided into cabinet making, wood turning, mechanical drawing, and the more advanced boys in carpentry are given textbook work. For the boys that we know will follow agriculture pursuits we require one semester of joinery, three semesters of carpentry and concrete, one semester of forging, two semesters of gas engine work and one semester of mechanical drawing. Those that do not fall into this class, and they are a very small class, are permitted to substitute mechanical drawing, cabinet making and wood turning for the farm subjects. The cabinet work does appeal to the average boy and the shops are open to those who desire to take up this work at any time that they have vacant periods.

We are drawing 87 per cent of the boys of the high school into the manual training work and the enrollment of boys in the high school has increased by about forty-five boys in the last two years. We make it a point to find out, if possible, how long a boy is going to remain in school and what line of work he intends to follow when he finishes his schooling. If we find that he will probably only be with us one year we give him a little joinery and the carpentry and concrete course; if two years we add a semester of forging. We do not attempt to outline a rigid four year course and make every boy take it in the regular order on the assumption that he will be with us for four years, because we find that only about 45 per cent of the boys that enter our high school, graduate. Of that 45 per cent about one-half got to college, making about one-fourth of the boys who enter the high school that get a college education. Of the 55 per cent that stop their schooling before they graduate from high school, the greater per cent drop out in the freshman and sophomore years. This means that we have to give

as much practical work as possible in the seventh and eighth grades and
the first two years of the high school, and by practical, I mean some form of
hand work that the boy can apply around Pendleton, not Massachusetts or
some other far-off place.

One hears different reasons for not giving work such as this. One
teacher told me that Pendleton was different than many places. Why different? We are an agricultural community like all the other cities of the
state. Our school board doesn't spend money any easier than yours, but
like yours it will spend it if we give them a run for it. Carpentry does not
call for additional equipment; concrete work means the purchase of half a
dozen shovels, some trowels, two wheelbarrows, a mixing board and a couple
of markers. If I couldn't get the forging equipment I'd sell some of the
cabinet-making machinery and put in a couple of forges. Your local dealers
will probably put in the gas engines as an advertisement. It isn't a matter
of the time element because you would simply be cutting down on the other
lines of work. You know the real reason that many of us are not giving
this work is because we don't know very much about it and are afraid to
tackle it.

A course along these lines has been outlined by Mr. Shepherd of the
Oregon Agricultural College and every teacher in the state has or should
have this course. When the course in carpentery was first added to our
course my fund of knowledge along this line was very limited. I spent all
of my spare time for weeks studying the different kinds of construction
that was being carried on in the town and my evenings were spent with a
contractor who told me the different steps in the construction of the forge
shop. Whenever I was stuck I'd have him come up and straighten us up.
Our work is not of the highest grade, but it is fair work for boys and we
are trying to improve right along.

Please understand that I do not claim that we are the only city in the
state doing this type of work. Of the towns with which I am acquainted
in Eastern Oregon, The Dalles is doing some very fine manual training along
these lines; La Grande this year has added the work in concrete. Both of
these cities have wonderful opportunities to develop the additional courses
in machine shop practice and steam engine work with thorough courses in
shop mathematics, due to the fact that they both have large railroad shops.
Wallowa, a little town of some 1500, is giving strong courses in carpentry,
concrete, plumbing, plastering, paper-hanging, and Mr. Hall, who has charge
of the work there, takes a class of boys during the summer and puts up
houses.

In closing may I leave with you the idea of making your manual training
fill the needs of your community. We are too willing to follow the course
of study laid out by the school from which we are graduated regardless of
the fact that, good as that course might be, it might be entirely inadequate
for our community. This applies mostly to men that graduated before these
practical courses were offered in school. Give the ten dollar a week boy
something that will mean his advancement and be giving him some form of
work that will be of use in his community.

Rural School Department

Edited by MRS. M. L. FULKERSON, Salem, Oregon

ART IN THE SCHOOL ROOM.

The little log school house of pioneer days, with its rude benches,
stove, and tin bucket, made as little pretense at decoration as at ventilation
or sanitation. Wild flowers from the fields provided the one, and open
door and windows afforded the other.

Now that our civilization has progressed to the stage of automobiles,
victrolas and other luxuries for the home, we are not content with ugly

school buildings and unadorned rooms, but demand model school rooms for our children. This is partly due to the fact that we have learned something of the value of unconscious influences in the child's education. The surroundings of home, school, and social companions,—dress, manners and casual speeches—all make more lasting imprint than does direct teaching. Especially should we concern ourselves with the environment of school children when we consider that the school furnishes the only cultural influence in many of the narrow little lives.

A neat artistic structure with suitable rooms is needed, and this will not cost any more than an architectural monstrosity. Ignorance is the chief excuse for so many ugly things, but this can no longer be offered as excuse, for the State Superintendent of Oregon has issued a most valuable book of designs for country school houses, fitting varied needs. The hardest part is to arouse a strong public sentiment which will encourage the school directors to build when necessary. I believe that any wide-awake teacher, seconded by the Parent-Teacher Association, can accomplish this.

Within, windows and seats should be arranged so that the light shall come over the pupil's left shoulder. The walls must be tinted in some soft neutral color, buff or light tan is best in our climate; for a sunny room pale gray is good. Natural fir finished in oil is good for the woodwork, while the window shades should be of a harmonizing shade. There should be a bulletin board for the diplay of pupils' work, of cork if possible, though burlap will serve the purpose if neatly arranged. A cupboard for books and supplies should have glazed doors, or, the glass doors may be lined with a wallpaper of ingrain or small figured pattern. Drapery curtains either for cupboard or windows are not advisable because they are difficult to keep in order. The school room is first of all a work room, and all attempts at furnishing and decoration must take this into consideration. Window boxes and growing plants are valuable, but must be properly cared for.

The flowers which children are sure to bring present a serious problem. They are most desirable but hard to manage, being usually a miscellaneous collection, while the teacher's supply of vases is quite inadequate. Pupils can be taught to select only a few of the largest and choicest flowers, of one variety each day, and fitted for the vase the teacher has. Different kinds of receptacles are required—low, flat dishes for violets and daises, tall ones for dahlias and crysanthemums. Very good glass, or brown and green pottery jars may be had cheaply by a little shopping. There should be no gaudy decoration on the vase itself, and the colors should be low in tone, harmonizing with the flowers and foliage. In rural communities, or where purchases are impossible, vases might be borrowed from school patrons for a week or a month at a time. If the teacher recognizes the importance of this side of her work, she will be impelled to take the necessary thought, or direct someone else in the doing.

The American flag is a popular article for school room decoration and it is too often sadly misused. Nothing is more pathetic and less patriotic than the sight of two small, dusty, faded emblems of our country's glory draped limply over the school room clock. They have hung there so long that the children scarcely even see them, and as for any moral uplift furnished, that is long past. The school room flag should be held always in utmost reverence; it should be as large and as fine as can be afforded, and must be cared for religiously, being brought forth with honor on appropriate occasions. It must be used with ceremony to inspire patriotism, not ignored and forgotten. Above all, the teacher must remember that her own attitude and feeling towards flag and flowers and pictures is what will form the children's minds, far more than any words she may speak about them.

It seems needless to emphasize the importance of perfect neatness and simplicity in the teacher's dress. Chalk dust makes this difficult. I do not think that aprons or worsted jackets are appropriate in the school room. There are dress materials that shed dust fairly well, and cloths (cheesecloth) used for erasers will lessen this difficulty. The teacher is well and becomingly dressed, in simple, good-looking, practical gowns which are up to date in a moderate degree, never extreme. If the teacher permits herself frills and furbelows during work hours, the young girls under her will be only too quick to imitate.

I have more than once been shocked at the disorder apparent on the teacher's desk—even principals' rooms are not always above criticism in this respect. Books can be neatly arranged in a rack, papers kept in a drawer, or piled carefully with a weight, rulers and pencils laid on a tray, inkwell and blotters clean. The waste basket must be of good size and of solid variety, open ones lined with cloth are not practical.

Many teachers like to have a cabinet or shelf for a "beauty corner," to which the children bring curious or beautiful objects from day to day. This is a splendid practice, teaching children to observe the wonders of nature, and often serving to bring out latent qualities in pupils who may be dull in books. But the collection needs careful watching and artistic arrangement, articles being promptly discarded on losing their beauty or other value.

Why do we need pictures on the school room walls? If the school is a work room are they not out of place? A party of visitors in a factory were surprised to see around each wall of the spacious work room a broad, exquisitely painted frieze. The figures upon it were a dainty, dancing company, beautiful in color as well as in form, and fit to grace the walls of a dwelling rather than a mill. Finally an outspoken dame asked the owner why he made beauty such an object. He smiled, "Well, come to think of it, it's a very practical reason," he said, "I find that it makes better thread." The writer from whom I quote this story continues: "Will not the contemplation of the beautiful make better human thread? The more we teach children to love and admire the beautiful productions of man, the more we open their eyes to the glories of nature, the more we teach them of the joys of form and color, the more richly stored will be their minds with sources of happiness and maturity."

So far has the pendulum swung toward the practical and utilitarian in educational circles that one hesitates to speak the words "artistic," "esthetic" and "beautiful;" they seem to almost require an apology, certainly an explanation—so far removed do they seem from the "practical." Is it then true that we are training our children only to make them efficient in earning their daily bread? We educate the body by carefully chosen physical exercises, we stuff the mind with facts, dates, and rules—is this the full meaning and proper extent of education? Does our educational scheme contemplate to any degree the making of a good citizen, the training of a sane man and woman who can live a full and well balanced life? Are we teaching our boys and girls how to get the most out of life and to put the most into life? With this ethical side of education the teaching of art and music appreciation has to do. Most children are born with a love of beauty, a sense of rhythm and color harmony. Why have the mature men and women lost it? "Trailing clouds of glory do we come—Heaven lies about us in our infancy— At length the man perceives it die away, and fade into the light of common day."

"But," you say, "we have an excellent course in drawing—a flourishing school art department." The mere teaching of a child to draw and color does not train him to know and love the best in art. It may even antagonise him, for all children have not technical ability while practically every child can be encouraged in a love of the beautiful. Just as the Victrola has done much to familiarize the public with good music, making it possible to have the best artists play and sing in our homes; so the modern reprints in colors of hundreds of classic masterpieces makes it easy to place before children pictures that will influence them to love the best in art, and be to them a constant joy as well.

It is a mistake to pay too much attention to the subject matter of a picture; illustrations for a book are one thing, and pictures as high ideals of the painter's art are quite another. The illustrations may or may not be good from an artistic standpoint, the pictures shown to encourage art appreciation must reach the highest standard. Do not misunderstand me as meaning that children should be shown masterpieces which are beyond their comprehension; that is by no means necessary, for from among many good things it is easy to make choice of material that will interest any grade of pupils. The simple themes of animal and child pictures appeal to the little ones, landscape and general subjects to the middle grades, while architectural and classic works are suitable for upper and high school classes. But always good compositions must be selected with fine line and color.

The hanging and framing of a picture are quite as important as the choice of the print, for a picture hung on the wall must form a harmonious part of that wall—must fit into its setting as a permanent decoration. Blackboards are of course a serious though necessary obstacle to the proper hanging of pictures. The pictures cannot be hung on a level with the eyes, as they must be above the blackboard, but they can be hung only a couple of inches above the moulding, not resting upon it however. Two picture hooks should be used, the wire running through the screw eyes on the frame, the picture hanging flat against the wall. The frame must suit the picture; a plain moulding of oak from four to six inches in width, according to the size of the print, and toned to harmonize with the darkest tones in the picture, is a safe choice. Carvings or other decorations are out of place and hard to keep clean, while gilt frames do not suit the plain walls and furniture of a school room.

The pictures must be of fairly large size to look well on the large wall spaces. Occasionally small pictures may be grouped together but this is difficult as frames, subjects and lights are hard to harmonize in a group The lighting for a picture is very important as a good picture is easily spoiled in the hanging, the light should come if possible from the same direction in which it appears in the picture. Size is not the only consideration, the picture must be one that carries well, that is, it must not have too fine details but rather strong masses which will be effective at the distance from which it must be seen; and also it should have decorative value.

Pictures are painted in color, so the colored reproductions are to be preferred when good, as more nearly like the original and as being more attractive to the children. Very fair prints in color can be obtained at reasonable prices. In Germany large numbers of reproductions of modern paintings are made for use in the schools, and we are able in normal times to buy these for from $1.00 to $2.50. Now of course the supply is nearly exhausted. There are many prints of old masters carelessly made with in correct coloring; sometimes hand colored prints are bad even if expensive. For this reason it is impossible to select from a catalogue without risk, it is necessary to see the individual print. If carbons are chosen, care must be taken to secure those which are good in values, and which will not fade. Copies of the same picture vary decidedly in these respects.

As to the cost of good pictures, it is true they cannot be had for two or three dollars. It is far better to have one good than half a dozen poor pictures; and it is better to work and save to buy a picture which will always be a delight and of which the school will be proud, than to hastily buy a cheap print which has not artistic merit. There are, however, certain pictures which, though fine, have become so commonplace by reason of frequent selection and many poor copies, as to be undesirable. Among these I would class the "Angelus," Watt's "Sir Galahad," and the "Song of the Lark." It is not advisable to select for a school pictures which may be seen anywhere when there is an almost infinite variety to choose from. Pictures of poets, statesmen and other notables are popular subjects, but they are not decorative nor interesting to the children except for a time when new. I advise keeping all such in a portfolio to be brought out as occasion demands. An exception might be made in case of Washington and Lincoln, as good photographs of the Stuart portrait of the former, and of St. Gaudens Statue of the latter can be obtained. These are real works of art and will prove an ornament to the room.

Plaster casts furnish ideal decoration for corridors and assembly halls as well as class rooms. They are used largely in eastern schools. In the west the freight charges (from Caproni's Boston) almost double the cost; but the beautiful bas reliefs of Della Robbia's Cantoria, the Victory of Samothrace, Mercury, and the Parthenon Frieze casts are well worth the effort made to get them.

The requirement for pictures in standardized schools is an excellent step in the right direction, but it would be better if the pictures could be chosen or passed upon by some committee which would guarantee a fixed standard.

I will colse with a quotation from Montaigne: "Were it left to my ordering, I should paint the school with the pictures of joy and gladness, Flora and the Graces, as the philosopher Speusippus did his. Where their profit is there let them have their pleasure also."—(Read before the Art Section of Oregon State Teachers' Association at Lincoln High School, December 28, 1916, by Mrs. J. C. Elliott King).

* * *

WHAT CAN I AS A TEACHER DO FOR THE BETTERMENT OF MY COMMUNITY?

A man once hoped that he might commit one sin so that the experience would enable him to sympathize more fully with all sinners. So it is well for a principal or a superintendent to teach at some time in each and every grade so that he may know, understand and sympathize in the true sense.

The teacher should have her heart attuned to her community. She should sympathize with the country people if she is teaching in a rural district; rural is a relative term. The New Yorker is apt to look upon Chicago as a village; Chicago takes the same view of Portland; Portland speaks of Salem as "the little town on the Willamette;" people in Salem look upon Monmouth in a similar manner; Monmouth in turn thinks of Airlie as being out in the rural district; Airlie has a like sentiment towards the little mount community. Become attuned to your community whatever its size or location.

Too often the teacher looks townward; perhaps, that is because she has not been trained for rural life. If she can be persuaded to remain in the same school for two or three years she may begin to feel at home there. Generally speaking, the town bred teacher is apt to teach the boys and girls, unconsciously perhaps, along lines that lead away from the farm. For this reason it is well to take a teacher who has been brought up in a rural community, train her for her work, and then send her back to teach in the land from which she came.

The Normal School has a plan, inaugurated by Mr. Pittman, whereby the members of the training class will be sent out into the country schools for one week in February. Each student is to live and work with the teacher in the district to which she goes. It is hoped that this little experience will enable the students to better apply the principles taught them when they go out into schools of their own letter.

The teacher should relate herself to the community and be a part of it while she is in it. This means that she should not leave every week end and come back just in time for school on Monday. The rural teacher must be tactful. She should not educate away from the farm but for the betterment of farm life; strive to make the community active but remain neutral in all factional quarrels and disputes; develop team work; do not expect to make friends of all in the community. While he is not absolutely necessary, sometimes a good live enemy is valuable. He spurs one on to do one's best and causes one to guard one's actions carefully. To win an enemy, ask a favor of him; borrow of him as Franklin did.

In community meetings work for the social betterment of the community. Work for better health of body, better health of mind, better outbuildings and better literature for study and recreation. Study the community and tactfully guide its aspirations and hopes. Study its finances and its social life, its music and modes of entertainment. Join some of its organizations, Grange, etc. Visit the patrons of the school, Mrs. Smith as well as Mrs. Jones. Finally, do not fail to take recreation so that you may put new life and energy into your work.—(Outline of address of Pres. J. H. Ackerman before the Rural School Section of the State Teachers' Association).

* * *

GAMES FOR THE SCHOOL ROOM.

Indoor Drop the Handkerchief.—One child is chosen as "It." The other children fold arms on desks and rest the head on them with eyes closed. "It" drops the handkerchief at a desk he chooses and tries to get around the room and back to the handkerchief before it is discovered. The game is played very much on the plan of the outdoor game of the same name.

Nut Race.—"It" holds a nut or other small article in his hand. The other pupils sit at their seats with one hand over eyes and the other stretched out, palm up. "It" drops the nut into an outstretched hand and runs on. The one receiving the nut runs in the opposite direction and tries to reach the seat he left before "It" does. If he fails he is "It."

Slide.—Children sit up at attention. The teacher or some chosen pupil says, "Slide right," when all pupils slide out of their seats into the seats directly opposite at their right. Should there be no row of seats at the right then the pupils in that part of the room remain standing until the command "Slide left" is given. The change should be made swiftly and as silently as possible. This is a restful exercise.

Good Morning.—"It" has a bandage over the eyes. The teacher points to some pupil but says nothing to indicate who is chosen. The pupil designated says, "Good Morning." "It" must tell who has spoken. If he fails to recognize the voice, the teacher designates another pupil, and the process is repeated. If he guesses correctly the pupil named takes his place. This is excellent ear-training when pupils are well acquainted with one another.

Touch.—The first pupil goes to the front of the room, touches an object and after naming it takes his seat. The next pupil touches the same article and one other and goes back to his place. The next one follows in like manner, etc. Illustration: The first pupil says, "I touched an eraser." Second pupil, "I touched an eraser and the desk." Third pupil, "I touched an eraser, the desk and the bell." Fourth pupil, "I touched an eraser, the desk, the bell and the box," etc. This game develops attention and concentration.

Clap.—Pupils stand at attention. The teacher claps her hands once and the girls stoop. Two claps, the boys stoop. Three claps, all stoop. If a pupil stoops at the wrong signal he is "caught."

Charlie Over the Water.—Pupils stand in a ring with "It" in the center. All repeat or sing: "Charlie over the water, Charlie over the sea. Charlie catch a black bird, can't catch me." At the words, "Can't catch me," all stoop while "It" tries to touch one before he can stoop. If successful, the one caught is "It" and the game begins again.

Buzz.—Pupils count in turn, giving the numbers in regular order until a multiple of seven, or some other chosen number is reached, when the pupil whose turn it is, says, "buzz" instead of the name of the number. Thus, 1, 2, 3, 4, 5, 6, buzz, 8, 9, 10, 11, 12, 13, buzz, etc. This game is a good drill in multiplication.

Bean Bag Relay Race.—Pupils are supplied with small cloth bags filled with beans. They sit or stand in two rows an equal number in each row. The pupil at the head of each row holds a bean bag. At a given signal the bag is quickly passed to the pupil next to the leader who faces front passing the bag over his head. The second pupil passes it to the third and so on down the line. The row which succeeds in getting the bag to the end of the row first wins.

Relay Ball.—The pupils choose sides. The leader on each side holds a ball in his hand and at a given signal, bounces the ball, catches it and passes it to the pupil next in his line, who does likewise. The side which succeeds in getting the ball to the rear of its line first, wins.

All Up Relay.—Pupils choose sides. Four circles are drawn on the floor at the front of the room, two for each team. In one of the circles belonging to each side three Indian clubs stand on end. At a given signal, each leader changes the clubs to his other circle and takes his seat. The next member of the team changes them back to the first circle, etc. No player can be seated until he has succeeded in making the clubs stand upright in the circle. The side whose last member changes the clubs first, wins. (The above games were demonstrated by Miss Emily DeVore of Medford in the Rural Section of the State Teachers' Association).

*   *   *

RESPONSIBILITY OF THE HOME.

Our State Superintendent announces his intention to prepare a course of instruction in morals, a much needed step forward educationally. Moral education is so comprehensive, covering as it does so many activities of the child's life, that we must do more than give formal or even incidental instruction.

Probably the most important step, and a difficult one, is to get the home (I mean in the aggregate, not the individual home) to assume a heavier responsibility. Our investigators tell us that home discipline was once over-severe, that it was based on the doctrine of "spare the rod and spoil the child" and that the whole policy was one of strict repression. Since that time, however, as the consequence of a somewhat superficial study of child nature, we have arrived at the conclusion that such a policy is psychologically harmful and have swung to the other extreme of allowing the child a high degree of freedom with the delusion that we are following the natural method of development. What are the results? We find children on the streets unguarded and often unwarned as to the perils of such environment at all hours of the day and of the early night. Why should this be? What is the matter with the latter-day parent? And when his child becomes wayward, does he admit his fault? Seldom; on the contrary we too frequently hear him condemning the school and its teachers.

. This incident was told the writer last summer: A certain teacher was once employed in a mining town in Northern Michigan, a place of somewhat low moral standards. It was a custom among many young people and children of the town to gather at the railway station before the coming in of a passenger train which was due there at eleven o'clock at night. One night the teacher alighted from this train and found the usual large group of boys and girls. She boarded a street car to go to her home and found a seat behind two middle-aged matronly appearing women. She soon discovered by their conversation, which she could not help over-hearing, that they were mothers and that they were discussing the lamentable condition mentioned above. In this discussion she was astonished by this startling statement or question: "Where are their teachers?" Here we have exemplified a too common attitude among parents. The father who cannot control three or four children in his home is very free to condemn the teacher for the resulting waywardness of his children. If the children are on the streets until five or six o'clock after school, the mother is likely to say, "I must speak to the teacher." If the young people go to a dance and stay out too late or participate in suggestive dances, the teachers are at fault for not having chaperoned the dance or assumed the responsibility for it. As a matter of fact the teacher had neither legal nor moral responsibility for this condition and probably was not even informed of the dance. Young people who love to "rag" until late at night seldom go out of their ways to invite their teachers to attend the function. What is the matter with the American home? Isn't the parent willing to carry his God-given responsibility of controlling and training his own children?

Then again we find parents who defend this leniency. The mother will say when her child is impudent or disrespectful to her in the presence of visitors, "I am raising him scientifically. I am allowing him to learn self control by practicing it." It is well that we have gotten away from the old severe repressive home and school discipline, but it is not well to allow our children to do as they please. There is certainly nothing scientific about it. No psychology will tell us that the child is able to control himself. He is rather the creature of very powerful natural impulses and instincts, and he is governed by them, unless he is governed by an authority from without, until he learned self control, which is learned effectively only through the learning of implicit obedience. He seldom becomes master of self before sixteen or eighteen and often not even then. If firmly controlled at home and in school, he learns control of self earlier, but if allowed too much liberty, he is likely to reach physical maturity without that mastery of his powers which is the greatest indication of real manhood. God gave the parent a responsibility when he gave him children and if he does not expect, even, if necessary, compel, his children "to honor their father and mother," he is guilty in greater measure of sinning against God's law than his children. Cannot we as teachers do something to bring about a more effective performance of this greatest work in moral training?—(By A. C. Strange, Superintendent of Baker Schools).

RECIPE FOR HEKTOGRAPH.

Take gelatine, four and one-half ounces; glycerine, one pint; water, one pint. Dissolve the gelatine in the water, add the glycerine and boil hard in a double boiler for one hour. Pour in shallow pan to set. (Given by Mrs. Ada Farmer in Primary Section of State Teachers' Association).

* * *

SCHOOL HOUSEKEEPING.

One day while in Wasco county it was my good fortune to see an example of good school housekeeping that I believe other teachers throughout the state will be interested in.

It was a little shack of a building very forlorn looking on the outside but the little teacher was ingenious enough to transform the interior of the building until you would not believe that the inside could belong to the outside. She had very little money to spend but she had the home makers' instinct, which is of more value than money. She bought enough gray blue building paper to cover the walls and ceiling and she put it on carefully herself. Then she took a piece of building paper and neatly covered her desk around three sides to the floor and over the top to cover the unsightly rough boards of which the table was made. She had no bookcase or shelf so she procured an apple box, knocked off one side and covered this box with building paper, too. Can you visualize the room? Every child was clean, happy and busy. The floor and stove were clean and the childrens' desks were neat. Needless to say they all unconsciously were living up to the teacher's desk and the walls.

It takes so little after all to make even a very poor little school room more attractive and I hope this little story will inspire others to make their school rooms more homelike.—(By Helen Cowgill, Assistant State Leader of Club Work).

* * *

THE TUMBLE WEED.

(Aim: To interest the child in the "extended oval" exercise in penmanship).

Out in the garden a little weed grew. It was so tiny at first that the farmer's boy missed it when he was hoeing, and the little weed grew bigger every day. When fall came it had spread over the ground like mother's big, round rug.

One day the West Wind came. He saw the weed who thought himself so very fine. The West Wind cried, "Ho, ho! Come and race with me, Tumble Weed."

"No, no. I am very happy here. By next year I think I shall be big enough to cover the whole garden."

"You foolish Tumble Weed! You cannot grow any more. Can you not see that you are as dry as an old dead stock?" said the West Wind. "I shall take you with me."

Then the West Wind puffed his cheeks and blew hard. The weed felt itself lifted just a little. The West Wind blew harder and soon the weed found itself rolling just like this: (Extended oval exercise in Palmer Writing Lessons for Primary Grades).—Mrs. M. L. Fulkerson.

* * *

SUGGESTIONS FOR MARCH.

1. Study Holland, using the imaginary journey plan. Study canals, dykes, windmills, Dutch houses and customs; Dutch children—their dress, amusements, schools, pets, etc.

2. The wind as a force in transportation, mills, etc.

3. The story of Robert Fulton and the first steam boat; Story of Aelous and the Bag of Winds.

4. Logging camps will re-open this month. Make a study of the different phases of lumbering in connection with the subject of shelter.

5. Begin the spring window gardens. Bring in twigs with buds, place them in jars of water in the sunny windows and watch the awakening of the buds. Who will find the first "Spring Beauty?" The first "Lamb's Tongue?"

6. Make a special study of the robin, the blue bird, and the wood-pecker. Encourage the pupils to watch for the return of the birds. As soon as a bird has been reported as seen by a pupil, post a picture of it in the school room with the name of the pupil who reported it.

7. Make kites, windmills, and sail boats from paper, as occupation work.

8. Teach two or three short, catchy spring songs.

9. From the Oregon Course of Study list, teach these poems: Who Has Seen the Wind? The Wind, If I Were a Sunbeam, Hiawatha's Chickens, The Sandpiper, The Daffodils.

10. Teach these stories: The Sun and the Wind, The Hare and the Tortoise, The Frog King, Latona and the Frogs, The Legend of the Narcissus, Legend of the Dandelion, Why the Robin's Breast is Red, Why the Wood-pecker's Head is Red; Legend of the Pussy Willow.

NEW COUNTY SCHOOL SUPERINTENDENTS.

County.	Name.	Postoffice.
Baker	Miss Elmetta Bailey	Baker
Benton	R. E. Cannon	Corvallis
Clackamas	J. E. Calavan	Oregon City
Clatsop	O. H. Byland	Astoria
Columbia	J. W. Allen	St. Helens
Coos	R. E. Baker	Coquille
Crook	J. E. Myers	Prineville
Curry	W. M. Kent	Gold Beach
Deschutes	J. Alton Thompson	Bend
Douglas	O. C. Brown	Roseburg
Gilliam	J. C. Sturgill	Condon
Grant	W. W. Austen	Hamilton
Harney	Frances Clark	Buchanan
Hood River	L. B. Gibson	Hood River
Jackson	G. W. Ager	Jacksonville
Jefferson	Lillian Watts	Culver
Josephine	Alice M. Bacon	Grants Pass
Klamath	Edna I. Wells	Klamath Falls
Lake	C. E. Oliver	Lakeview
Lane	E. J. Moore	Eugene
Lincoln	R. P. Goin	Toledo
Linn	Ida M. Cummings	Albany
Malheur	Fay Clark	Vale
Marion	W. M. Smith	Salem
Morrow	Lena S. Shurte	Heppner
Multnomah	W. C. Alderson	Portland
Polk	Fred S. Crowley	Dallas
Sherman	F. E. Fagan	Moro
Tillamook	G. B. Lamb	Tillamook
Umatilla	I. E. Young	Pendleton
Union	Mrs. A. E. Ivanhoe	La Grande
Wallowa	J. C. Conley	Enterprise
Wasco	C. T. Bonney	The Dalles
Washington	B. W. Barnes	Hillsboro
Wheeler	H. J. Simmons	Fossil
Yamhill	S. S. Duncan	McMinnville

The torture of a bad conscience is the hell of the living.—Calvin.

There never was a good war or a bad peace.—Franklin.

City Superintendents' Department

Edited by GEORGE W. HUG, McMinnville, Oregon

Supt. Thordarson and Principal Bolt of the Bend schools have been re-elected for next year at an increase in salary. The Bend school board has just completed a new school building. The school population of Bend has practically doubled in the past year.

Principal Hampton of the La Grande high school and secretary-treasurer of the Oregon High School Athletic Association makes the following financial statement: Receipts, balance from last year, $14.60; fees 1916-1917, $46; total of $60.60; expenditures, $5.65; balance on hand, $54.95.

The Aberdeen high school, Washington, will adopt the 70-minute recitation-study period system, and as far as known is the first high school to adopt this plan. Principal Holmquist believes it will prove superior to the 60 and 90-minute recitation-study system now in vogue in many high schools. He says: "It will give us plenty of time for laboratory work and will give us five periods a day so that students may take five subjects without causing irregularities."

There are about 175 standard four-year schools in Oregon. Last year there were 2400 graduates. The enrollment this year in standard high schools is about 24,000.

Principal R. U. Moore has this to say about printing in the McMinnville Junior High School: "The boys of the seventh, eighth, and ninth grades may select printing in their course. Seventh and eighth grade boys may earn one-fourth of a credit, while ninth grade boys may earn one-half of a credit. A small paper entitled 'The Junior High School Journal' is printed by this class under the direction of the principal. The paper is edited by a member of the student body who is responsible for news and stories. The boys of the class set up the articles, proof-read them, and then arrange them in proper space in the paper. Some job work is done for the school in the way of printing excuse slips, attendance records, and order blanks, but the policy of the department has been not to enter into competition with the printers of the town. The work is more nearly correlated with the English and spelling departments. Boys who fail in eighth grade spelling examinations are required to take the work in the ninth grade. These boys are given sets of spelling words which they are to set up and proof-read correctly. The department has for its object not the turning out of commercial printers but the training of the motor type of individual. The school paper has a valuable function in keeping alive school spirit."

Lester M. Ellis, physical director of the Astoria public schools, has worked out a system of athletics known as "Rational Athletics." This plan provides some form of athletic for every boy in school. Its object is to provide for all healthful recreation, usually enjoyed only by a selected few who comprise the team. Many other schools in the state are working out this same problem. Mr. Ellis has this to say about the system: "This system allows a maximum of health co-ordination and physical development, combined with qualities that tell for good sportsmanship, teamwork and voluntary self-improvement. In addition it eliminates to a great extent the overdose of response work usually found in systems designed for physical development and results in self-confidence and originality instead of grudging response to uncomprehended orders. Upon investigation of the athletic situation here, I found that only about 8 per cent of the pupils of each school had ever taken an active part. We hold to three standards in our work: (1) Athletics are for the benefit of the pupils; (2) the work is democratic; (3) no other form of athletics is discouraged. The scoring system is so arranged that the poor athlete receives equal encouragement with the first class athlete. In scoring an event the score made by the entire school is divided by the number in the school to obtain the school standing. The events used last year were chinning the bar, potato race, combination dip, high jump, and standing broad jump. These events are chosen also for the all around development that continued practice of each event will give.

For instance, the muscular type of boy soon finds that by practice he can attain the maximum points allowed for the combination dip and the bar chinning. He wishes to go on and make more points, but as we do not encourage over development along any line and are looking for symetrical development we tell him that though he made fifty points he would receive credit for only fifteen in the contest. So there is no incentive to over-do. He has done for his school and himself all that he can do in this event. It is possible to make fifteen points in each of the five events, making a grade of seventy-five possible. All boys making fifty-five points or more are presented with a first-class athlete's badge. Those making thirty-five points or better receive a grade of second-class athlete, while the third class athlete must make twenty-five points or better. Anyone making less is considered an athletic failure. A contest is later held between first class athletes to decide who is the champion of the city. After conducting work along this line for about a year and a half, I am sure that the improvement made in the health and athletic ability of the children has paid me in full for my time. I figure that each aenemic, sissified boy that has been rounded up by this system and made self-confident and athletic is worth more to me and society in general than if I had worked with best athletes only and discouraged those not so good."

Grade Teachers' Department

Edited by SABRA CONNER, 421 West Park Street, Portland, Oregon

Elementary teachers and elementary teachers' associations are cordially invited to send news items of their activities which would be of interest or value to other teachers to this department of the The Oregon Teachers Monthly. Address Editor of Grade Teachers' Department, Room 300, Court House, Portland, Oregon.

The teachers of the public schools of Portland were the honor guests at a reception given Monday, January 22, at the Neighborhood House by the Council of Jewish Women. Mrs. Isaac Sweet, president of the council, and Mrs. S. M. Blumauer, chairman of the Neighborhood House committee, were in charge of the affair.

At the Little Theatre Friday evening a delightful program of three one act plays was given to a large audience of friends by the Dramatic Club of the Grade Teachers' Association. These plays were presented under the direction of Miss Nina Greathouse, Miss Medora Whitfield announcing them. Lady Gregory's "Spreading of the News" was the first number on the program. Mrs. Josephine Lisher played the role of the deaf apple woman, and won the audience in her interpretation of the part. The imposing magistrate, Anna Chalmers, and the humble policeman, Maud Ragon, did clever work. Bartley Fallon, the man always expecting misfortune, was sympathetically portrayed by Lora Foster, while the role of Mrs. Fallon, given by Emma Doble, called for a variety of emotions which were well expressed. Jack Smith, the man to be waked, was given a natural and hearty interpretation by Helen Nesbit. The four gossips, Tim Casey, Jeanette Doble; Shawn Early, Lulu Simmons; James Ryan, Elizabeth Shoemaker; and Mrs. Tully, Gertrude Greathouse, added fun to the scene. In the second play, "Petticoat Perfidy," a satire on fashionable London society, Louise Kelly, as Mrs. Montrevor, and Vinson Gorman as Mrs. Norwood Jones, did a finished piece of work, while Charlotte Ballin, as the French maid was extremely clever and one of the most admired of the evening. In the last play, "Op-Q' Me Thumb," made famous by Maude Adams, Olga Hallingby as Celeste, Miss McNevin as Rose, and Mrs. McCaulay as Clem, were extremely good. Mrs. Jennie Richardson, as the irrascible French shopkeeper, did excellent work, while Miss Tettleson, as the pathetic laundry drudge, and Miss Petch as the man about whom she has woven a romance, moved the audience alternately to laughter and tears.

January 31, at a special meeting, the G. T. A. voted to sustain the

Orton Bill which provides that when charges are made against a teacher or when proceedings for removal or transfer are instituted, a teacher may be given a hearing before a non-partisan committee of three citizens to be named by the presiding judge of the circuit court. The commission shall serve one school year. The teacher is given a choice as to whether the hearing shall be public or private, with or without counsel.

A class in shorthand, three nights a week, at Commercial High School, has been organized; one class a week in penmanship at the Night School, Mr. Wesco, instructor.

In place of the usual monthly dinner, the Grade Teachers' Association was host at a co-operative luncheon given at the Multnomah hotel on January 13. To this luncheon were invited the members of the various educational organizations of the city, the board members and wives, and the superintendents. That the spirit of helpful co-operation and the desire to "get together" on a common level —for as Mr. Alderman aptly expressed it, there is only one level, after all—are making themselves manifest in our ranks was clearly shown by the splendid attendance at the luncheon, there being over 400 teachers present. Miss Viola Ortschild, president of the Grade Teachers' Association, presided over the luncheon and introduced the speakers. Mr. W. T. Olds and Mr. J. E. Werlein, both of whom have given so generously of their time to serve on the Teachers' Retirement Fund Board, were the special guests of the association, as was also Miss Nettie Spencer. The speeches which followed the luncheon were received with much appreciation. Mr. Olds dwelt on the subjects which, from the standpoint of a business man, should receive special attention in the schools. A short talk by Mr. Werlein followed. Mr. Herdman, of Washington High, who has just returned from a trip to California where he visited high schools, told of the problems engaging the attention of the educational world down there, especially those pertaining to the high school field. Mr. Parker, president of the Principals' Association, spoke on the value of co-operation. Mr. Alderman in his remarks, voiced his appreciation of the spirit of the luncheon and expressed the hope that this would be followed by others—one a month, at least. Mr.

Cannon, principal of Couch school, in his remarks expressed himself as preferring a teacher with initiative, rather than one who always does as she is told. He thinks the teacher should have a place in the community, not as teachers alone, but as citizens, in every sense of the word. Mr. Melendy, president of the Portland Educational Association, spoke of the work that association has been doing along the line of bringing able lecturers to the city. Miss Lutie Cake made some apt remarks on the necessity of harmony and co-operation. Mr. O. M. Plummer spoke of the coming N. E. A. which, we all know, convenes in Portland on July 7, and of his part in it—the unenviable role of money raiser. Mr. Plummer expects to persuade all the teachers of Oregon that it is their privilege to contribute two dollars, each, toward the entertainment fund of the N. E. A. We predict his entire success. The luncheon was arranged for by the social committee of the Grade Teachers' Association.—Anne W. Biesen, chairman social committee.

Duties of Rural Teachers.

1. Visit all homes and get acquainted with the patrons.

2. Study conditions from all angles so as to adapt the school work to the needs of the community.

3. Live in the district seven days in the week during the school term.

4. Keep a school contract unless honorably released by trustees.

5. Be loyal to pupils and patrons.

6. Conduct yourself outside of school so as to win respect for yourself and your profession.

7. Stay more than one year in a district unless a change means decided professional and financial advancement.

8. Arouse an interest in the school and do your part to educate patrons to the need of a better school to meet the demands of the present day by: (a) Urging them to visit schools; (b) loaning them literature to show what is being done all over the country for rural regeneration; (c) getting them acquainted with the modern methods of teaching.—Selected.

Give today to laziness and laziness will steal tomorrow from you.—Selected.

Oregon State Library

By CORNELIA MARVIN, Librarian, Oregon State Library

A teacher who is using Perry's Discipline As a School Problem, published by Houghton, says that it is the best and one of the most practical books on the subject ever published.

* * *

The Bookman for January, 1917, gives the following list of the best novels of the year 1916 selected by Mr. H. W. Boynton who reviews the fiction for that magazine. Mr. Boynton is a skilled literary critic and a good guide in the selection of fiction: The Dark Forest, by Hugh Walpole; Mr. Britling Sees It Through, by H. G. Wells; Fondie, by Edward C. Booth; These Lynnekers, by J. D. Beresford; Love and Lucy, by Maurice Hewlitt; The Spinster, by Sarah M. Cleghorn; The Conquest, by Sidney L. Nyberg; Windy McPherson's Son, by Sherwood Anderson; The Rising Tide, by Margaret Deland; El Supremo, by Edward Lucas White.

* * *

Interesting new books, not fiction, but among the best sellers of recent date are: A Diplomat's Wife in Tramping Through Mexico, Guatemala and Honduras, by Harry A. Franck; The First Hundred Thousand, by Ian Hay; The Wrack of the Storm, by Maurice Maeterlinck; My Home in the Field of Honor, by Frances Wilson Huard; The Advance of the English Novel, by William Lyon Phelps; Rhymes of a Red Cross Man, by Robert W. Service; Told in a French Garden, by Mildred Aldrich; Years of My Youth, by William Dean Howells; O. Henry Biography, by C. Alphonso Smith; The Melancholy Tale of "Me," by E. H. Sothern.

* * *

An article in the English Journal for March, 1916, recommends the following plays which have been successfully given in the Stadium High School, Tacoma: As You Like It; The Rivals; She Stoops to Conquer; Quality Street; The Piper; A Scrap of Paper; A Rose of Plymouth Town; Twelfth Night; The Cricket on the Hearth; and Mice and Men.

* * *

Monmouth Normal School teachers send the following list of most desirable periodicals: Teacher's College Record and Monographs, The Elementary School Journal, N. E. A. Proceedings (Magazine form), Popular Educator, Primary Education, Primary Plans and Normal Instructor, Industrial Arts, School Arts, Educational School Journal, Playground Magazine, Story Teller's Magazine, Nature Study Review, Bird Lore, National Geographic Magazine.

* * *

The new edition of the High School Library List to be used for 1917 orders has been prepared and will be printed some time before March 1. Large high schools should postpone making their orders until they receive this list as numbers and prices are changed throughout. Supplementary sheets for part I will soon be issued. Many publishers have changed all prices beginning with January 1, 1917, and it is necessary to wait until the schedules of changes are available before issuing correction sheet, supplementary list and new edition of the high school list.

Truth is tough. It will not break, like a bubble, at a touch; nay, you may kick it about all day, like a football, and it will be round and full in the evening.—Oliver Wendell Holmes.

The telling of a falsehood is like the cut of a saber; for though the wound may heal, the scar of it will remain.—Sadi.

Let us, then, be what we are, and speak what we think, and in all things keep ourselves loyal to truth.—Longfellow.

Every war, even to the nation that conquers, is nothing less than a misfortune.—Von Moltke.

It is easier to see the faults of others than to correct our own.—Selected.

I will study, and get ready and maybe my chance will come.—Lincoln.

Studies of Famous Pictures

A complete list of other famous pictures will be mailed free on application to the C. M. Parker Estate, Taylorville, Illinois.

RETURN TO THE FARM—TROYON

By L. Eveline Merritt

Sevres, France, the home of the famous porcelain manufactory, has been the birthplace of many an artist. Constant Troyon (pronounced trwa-yon) was born there in 1810, his father being connected with the manufactory. The father died when Constant was a young boy. We are told that the mother kept the family together by making pictures, using feathers to form the different flowers. Constant entered the porcelain works early and became a master

others of the Barbizon painters. Young as he was, he instantly recognized their aim and purpose. He was one with them in spirit and joined them in their work. He was known and honored as a landscape painter long before he began to study animals seriously. "Before he reached the age of forty he had created a name for himself, and this too before he had taken up the study of or had painted a single work showing animal life as a motive." This is probably the reason why his landscapes are always such an essen-

decorator. However, the breadth of his nature refused to be hampered within such narrow confines. The time outside the work hours was spent in the fields with a sketch book. At twenty years of age he started out for himself, painting landscapes as he went till his money gave out, when he would stop at the first china manufactory he came to and work at his trade till his finances once more warranted travel.

Troyon seems to have studied under the artist Roquelan, who introduced him to Rousseau, Dupre, and

tial part of his animal pictures— never a mere background.

It was in 1849 that Troyon went to the Hague, where he came under the influence, through their pictures, of Paul Potter, Cuyp, and Rembrandt. The study of the painstaking "Young Bull," the wonderful animals of Cuyp and the light and shade of Rembrandt had a marvelous effect upon him, although, strange as it may seem, rather than any copying of the old masters, his own individuality burst forth. These men seemed to open a gateway through which Troyon gained entrance to his own best endeavors. He found himself. From now on it was animals which he studied with deep intimacy and love; it was animals which he painted with intimate knowledge and truth. He developed rapidly and success followed him.

The Return to the Farm is one of Troyon's best, painted in 1859, in the very height of his power. The original is in the Louvre in Paris, but let us look at the reproduction.

What do you see? In the first place a most charming home-like landscape is spread before us. What an interesting sky with those lovely summer afternoon clouds! They form a background for the dark mass of trees with their beautiful silhouettes. Did you ever notice particularly the shapes of trees as they are silhouetted against the sky? If never before, do it now. That is one of the infinite pleasure sensations this world has in store for those who have eyes to see. After you have done that, you will be interested to see how artists have shown that in their pictures. You will be astonished to find how few there were before Barbizon painters who depicted the truth of nature in that line. And yet the shapes are not haphazard. An artist is true to nature, yet designs the whole to bring his pictures into harmony.

But to go back to our picture. There is a quiet pool at the left in which two of the cows are drinking, and the road, that peaceful country road, winds around it. See how well that road goes back into the picture, not only because it diminishes according to the laws of perspective, but the values are such as to make the ground level and recede. A beautiful landscape, and yet how perfectly simplified! Hardly a thing is brought out in detail, even in the foreground. Why not? Because no point in the landscape is the focal point. What is then the center of interest? There can be no question. It is that wonderful group of animals which the setting sun lights up as in a glory as they come along the road toward the spectator on their way to the farm for the night.

Have you ever lived in the country? Do you know cows and sheep and dogs? If so you must appreciate Troyon's animals. He seems to bring out their very character without in the least sentimentalizing

them as Landseer sometimes does. Someone has said that he painted sheep with a "bleating truth." Look at this little group of sheep and you will understand what is meant by the expression. We cannot look very long before we actually seem to see one after another look up as that one a little in the back is doing, and stretch his nose out and bleat his joy or fear. The timidity, the gentleness of the sheep is all there.

Then look at those two cows. Those can stand as types of all the cows the world over. The heaviness, the awkwardness, the clumsiness, the gentleness, how could a painter get all the qualities!

Then the nervous running, barking dog!. Can't you hear those sharp little barks as he faithfully does his duty as he sees it? Two of the cows have wandered off as cows always do, to drink at the quiet pool. Others are lazily returning. It is all just a bit of nature depicted with the consummate skill of an artist. And what do we mean when we say that?

When one looks at the picture he feels the breadth of it, yet the simplicity of it, the sub-ordination of all non-essentials yet the vigorous handling of the essentials; he feels the truth in the interpretation of the character of the animals, the technical skill in drawing, and handling of materials, and an intelligent use of light and shade.

Hamerton speaks of Troyon as "the most synthetic painter of the century." What does he mean by that? He means that Troyon chose from the infinite of nature those few essentials that were needed to tell the story as a whole. This could be done only after a great deal of careful study and an intimate knowledge of details which make up the whole. Troyon's early years were spent in careful study. In fact, it was long before he could rid himself of the limitation thrust upon him by his early work as a decorator of china, the beauty of which lay in the fine, careful, exact workmanship. More than all else, too, Troyon continued all his life to make many sketches in which he studiously analyzed all details. His studies were for accuracy and intimate knowledge. After that preparation his great intellect looked for the few important features which would tell the thought in the quickest, surest way; he cast aside all else, giving to the world the broad treatment seen in the picture. Thus were his sketches analytic, while his finished pictures were synthetic, and we have nature and animals in their very essence.

As has been said before, Troyon's animals seem to be an inherent part of the landscape which is as essential as the animals themselves. There is a feeling of atmosphere in front, behind, all around. It envelops everything and brings all into harmony. To quote Stranahan, "But he made the sunshine play upon and around his cattle, he endued them with a sentiment that expresses the story of vigorous creatures patiently serving a weaker being, he placed them in such perfect relation to the atmosphere and field that, if his animals are not always of an obviously accurate anatomy, his pictures are most charming, and he an artist of the highest rank." We are told that Troyon was a kindly, happy man with the same largeness of heart that his pictures show of largeness of spirit. Of course, he was in consequence surrounded by loyal friends. Unlike many artists, he amassed quite a fortune.

SHEEP-SPRING—ANTON MAUVE

By L Eveline Merritt

Anton Mauve (pronounced Mov) was born in Zaandam, in the north of Holland, in 1838. He was the son of a Baptist minister, and entered the field of art against the wishes of his parents. His early training in the studio of Van Os was along the old academic line. Its hard, dry manner did not appeal to him. His friends probably helped him more than his studio training. Among the latter was Josef Israels, the pioneer and leader of the modern tendency in Dutch painting, and who was Mauve's senior by fourteen years. Through this influence Mauve found himself in a freer handling and a broader conception.

Mauve won medals in Vienna, Philadelphia, Antwerp, Amsterdam, and received a gold medal in Paris in 1888, the very year in which he suddenly died when he was only fifty years of age. We are told that he was beloved by his fellow artists.

The truth of the following quotation will be apparent if it be read in the light of our picture: "He excelled in rendering the soft, hazy atmosphere that lingers over the green meadows of Holland and devoted himself almost exclusively to depicting the peaceful rural life of the fields and country lands of Holland. A little sad and melancholy, his pastoral scenes are nevertheless conceived in a peaceful, soothing, lyric mood, which is in marked contrast to the epic power and almost tragic intensity of J. T. Millet." For color, Mauve usually used the delicate greens, grays and light blue—the colors of poetic fancy.

We have spoken of Mauve as a landscape painter, and this he was, although the landscape was ever a setting for animals or toilers who were an intimate part of their surroundings. "Though far from being an animal painter in the limited sense of the term, it is undeniable that Mauve found in beast rather than man his happiest inspiration." Judging from his pictures, his appeal seemed to be divided between sheep, cattle and horses. He seems, however, to have set the standard for all time for a certain horse—the working, toiling horse. Study in this connection such pictures of his as "Carting Sand," "The Sand Cart," "Homewards," "Watering Horses," and many others. Many are his pictures of cows. It was not till he went to live in Laren, which is distinctly a sheep section of the country, that sheep began to appeal to him. There he knew intimately the sheep and their shepherds; he understood them and loved them. Many, many pictures are the result of this intimacy.

Of all the portrayals of sheep, the companion pictures of "Spring" and "Autumn" are most interesting to us. To a casual observer of their reproductions they may seem one and the same picture, and yet they are very different in composition, grouping, coloring, which is shown in values in the reproductions, and more than in all else they differ in message.

In the "Autumn," the colors show the autumnal tints, darker in value than those of "Spring"; the sheep are going away from the observer, they are going homeward, for it is the end of the day as well as of the year. A distant harbor is seen on the horizon. The shepherd is an old man in the autumn time of life. It is a most natural, characteristic scene in the life of any shepherd, and yet it all seems symbolic of a beautiful, harmonious life coming to a peaceful close. Sad? Some think so, but not to us. Isn't it rather a deep, abiding peace—yea, even joy, in quiet contemplation of a life well spent?

Compare with "Autumn" our picture of "Spring," the original of which is in the Metropolitan Museum of New York. Here the coloring is in the lighter values of Spring. There is the same broad expanse of landscape, with the distant village on the horizon, and a suggestion of the ever-present water of Holland. In this picture, however, contrasting with the flatness of the land, are the vertical lines shown in the row of young trees that are just leafing out with their spring foliage. This contrast gives a freshness and a vigor that would be out of harmony in the

quietly and stolidly contemplating his flock, or of his alert little dog at his side, whose head is up and who is just beginning to wag his tail. The faithful little dog is watching every movement of the sheep, and is ready to dash instantly if one should venture ever so short a distance from its companions.

Look again at the shepherd. His thoughtful, contemplative nature is accentuated by the crook which he holds in a horizontal position, thus echoing the line made by the backs of the sheep and the level horizon. That very thing makes the shepherd one with the land rather than with the young trees, which echo the direction of his body. It has been suggested that he, being an old man, is

"Autumn." The sheep in this picture have just come out to the field in the morning. They are still facing the spectator and are still eager for the fresh, green grass. They have not yet begun to wander about, for they are hungry and the feeding is good. They can't even stop to look up. Have you ever seen a flock of sheep start out in the morning? If not, you cannot half appreciate the naturalness of the picture. As we look at it we seem to see the noses move along the ground, the heads bob up and down, and the ears move. It is a marvel of naturalness, but it is far more.

Not a word has been said thus far of the patient shepherd as he stands

out of harmony with the idea of spring. We cannot think that Mauve who was a very master in harmonious relationships, could have done that thoughtlessly. What would be the effect had he been a young man? Wouldn't the message be a different one? As the picture stands now it gives the message of joy in the new life of spring and more—the joy together with a deeper knowledge of the meaning of spring, which is ever followed by the later ripening season. That deeper knowledge brings us into truer relation with life, but does not in any way detract from the joy in life. So let us not quarrel with Mauve for putting into his picture of "Spring" an old shepherd.

No beginnings are intelligible without an older spirit to interpret the meaning. This shepherd loves his flock dearly; he will tend them faithfully, aided by his dog; and at the end of the day he will drive them slowly homeward. Not one will be lost. Not one will be left behind, even if he should have to carry a lame or sick one in his arms. We know that is all true, although in this picture the freshness of the morning is most apparent. Which do we like the better, the "Spring" or "Autumn"? Who can tell? Is it necessary to tell? Isn't it rather a matter of temperament if not of mood? Both are fine interpretations of peaceful homelife. In one is emphasizing the beginning, whereas in the other life is nearing the close.

As we compare modern pictures with those of a century or two back we are struck almost dumb with the strides that have been made along certain lines. One great difference is in atmospheric perspective. This is well shown in all of Mauve's paintings. See how those trees go off into the distance! See how the land itself grows less and less distant till the things on the horizon are merely suggested. In addition to the diminution of size, the massing of details, the blurring of outlines, the dulling of colors, there is a subtle gradation of values of which the older artists knew absolutely nothing. Notice, too, how Mauve has represented a flock of sheep. Those in the immediate foreground are quite distinct in detail. The character of the individual is shown in those. Fewer and fewer details are given till those farthest away are a mere mass of light backs. If it were not for those in the foreground those in the distance could never be recognized as sheep. Yet the flock as a whole is perfect. That shows the hand of a master painter. It is another phase of aerial or atmospheric perspective. One cannot fail to feel the truth to nature in all of Mauve's pictures. There is a sincerity which bespeaks truth; but there is more. This truth is told in exquisite poetry. There is a serious note to all, but the seriousness is of calm, quiet, peaceful contentment. The message, too, is told simply.

The State Schools

Oregon Agricultural College.

Fifty-nine members of the Oregon legislature visited and inspected the college on Saturday, January 20. Upon reaching the campus at 11 o'clock in the forenoon, the delegates and a number of their friends inspected the O. A. C. cadet regiment, reviewed some of their military exercises and proceeded to the men's gymnasium for convocation. After being welcomed by President Kerr, a short musical program was carried out, after which the address of the day was delivered by Rev. W. W. Youngson, of Portland. The subject of his address was "The American Spirit." Upon adjournment the delegates were taken to Waldo Hall for their noon luncheon. Following this, they were divided into groups of half dozen each and taken over the campus by special student guides appointed for the purpose. A great deal of time was spent in the library building investigating the need for a new building. It was shown that the excellent college library is very inconveniently housed in small offices and one auditorium on three floors of the administration building. A banquet was served the delegates and their friends in the evening by the students of the home economics department. The menu was prepared and served by the students of domestic science.

George Fred Buxton, one of the authors of the elementary text book, "Paper and Cardboard Construction Work," used in the Oregon schools, has been secured for manual training work in the summer school which will be held at the agricultural college June 11 to July 26. "An introduction of Mr. Buxton to any progressive manual training man is something like carrying coals to New Castle," says Prof. Frank H. Shepherd in making the announcement. Mr. Buxton has been connected with Stout Institute of Menomonie, Wisconsin, as director of manual training and of summer sessions since 1905.

His active interest in national educational association work and the western drawing and manual training associations has been supplemented by numerous writings.

The annual short course of the college for farmers and others engaged in practical industries of Oregon, closed Friday, February 2. At the conclusion of the short course students passed resolutions thanking the faculty members for the care with which they carried out the work of the course, declaring their belief in the efficiency of the work and pledging themselves to assist in carrying out the high ideal of the institution.

The sum of $36.65 was subscribed by the students of the annual short course and turned over to the librarian to be invested in additional books for the college library. This money is expended by the college librarian, Mrs. Ida A. Kidder, for a special short course library. The fund for this section of the general library was founded in 1910, under the auspices of Homer Rogers, of Hood River. While the books secured by this library fund are technical in character and highly scientific they are written in the popular vein well adapted to the needs of short course students. The section now numbers several hundred volumes.

A campaign of considerable interest to school boys is being conducted in the counties of Tillamook, Lane, and Yamhill. This campaign deals with the control of rodents, especially the gopher and mole. Because of the high price of furs it has been found that the mole skin has a commercial value of from 15 to 25 cents and that there is a large demand for it. Under the auspices of the extension service of the United States biological survey and the county agents in charge of the work of scientific agriculture in the various counties, a campaign of extermination by trapping is being carried on. Meetings are held with granges and other farmers organizations and at school houses. Many of the farmers are deeply interested in the control measures that they add a bonus of a 5-cent bounty, and also buy traps to lend the boys for carrying on the work. The campaign in Oregon is directly in charge of Prof. Theo. Scheffer, of the United States biological survey. Prof Scheffer says that the boy would far rather earn a dollar by exercising his skill as a trapper than by working for it by any of the ordinary means. "Boys like to put their skill against other members of the animal kingdom," says Prof. Scheffer, "and this is especially true of those boys whose boy scout interests have led them to adopt the outdoor life."

In the final tryouts for the intercollegiate debates the following men won the right to represent O. A. C.: R. R. Richart, Corvallis; V. I. Basler, of Grants Pass; Bertram Mainwaring, Portland; and E. W. McMindes, Loraine. Ted Cramer of Grants Pass was elected alternate. This team will meet the State University on March 9. It is quite likely that they will also debate the Washington State College later. Following this, the team will travel over the state in carrying on extension debates. All of these men have had previous experiences on the team. Mr. Richart has been on the varsity debating team during the last three years. The other three men have represented their classes in debates for the last two years.

The regular class work of the first semester of the present school year came to a close on Friday, January 26. Examinations occupied most of the time the following week. Following this, a brief mid-year vacation was granted extending to Monday, Febraury 5, when registration for the second semester began. Reports from the registrar's office show that the number enrolled in regular college work for the semester closed was 1771. It is estimated that the number matriculating for the second semester will lift the enrollment for the year to the 2000 mark or better.

Glenn S. Strome, of Eugene, won first prize in the first annual state cereal judging contest held at the college this winter. Second place went to Claude C. Calkins, of Airlie, and Alexander Galbraith, of Corvallis. The students were required to identify and judge a number of various samples of many kinds of grain. The contest was held under the auspices of Prof. G. R. Hyslop, who announces that it will be a regular event.

The average grades of all men students at the college for the last three semesters is 85 This is also the average grade of the nine fraternities for the same period. The clubs, too, have reached the same. The grade of the women is somewhat higher and the average of all women of the three sororities for the three last semesters is almost 88. Only two fraternities in the entire twenty-seven reports fell more than 2 per cent below the average for the student body and this for only one each. Each fraternity has a faculty advisor who is held responsible for the progress of the organization. The fraternities are governed by a code of regulations adopted by themselves, and it is one of the duties of the faculty advisors for each house to see that the rules are properly enforced. Most of these rules are very exacting and the very general observance of them tends to promote a high grade.

Horace Kerr, son of President W. J. Kerr, has been made head of the Colorado state bureau of markets and organization in the United States bureau of organization and markets. His headquarters are at Denver. He expects to take up his new duties at once.

E. R. Jory, a junior in the school of pharmacy, is not terrified by the high cost of living. Last year he lived on eight dollars a month which he earned doing janitorial work. He lived in a tent with another boy and the two did their own cooking. During the last semester Mr. Jory has lived alone in his tent which is situated in the back of the armory. During the summer he earned money to pay his expenses (by careful management) this year, so that he may be able to carry on the four years' work in the pharmacy department. He is now living on from $7 to $7.50 a month including $1 a month rent on the ground for his tent. Since this room is too cold to use as a study room, he spends his evenings largely in the library. This room is so much crowded that it is frequently necessary for a number of the boys to stand while doing their studying.

The 1917 summer session will begin June 11 and continue until July 28, with a week's recess the second week in July on account of the N. E. A. meeting in Portland. It is possible that only a three day recess will be declared, during which time students not attending the meeting may continue work in the laboratories, library, etc. Should this plan be followed, any who desire to spend the entire week in Portland will have an opportunity to make up work missed. Students are expected again this year, as in previous years, from the East and Middle West. In addition to "seeing America first," they will be able to attend the N. E. A. Among the special instructors supplementing the regular faculty are Mr. George Fred Buxton of Stout Institute, in manual training; Miss Alice Ravenhill of London, England, in domestic science; and Mrs. Mary Schevick Woolman of Boston, in domestic art. Each of these enjoys a national reputation in his or her specialty, having published books and articles recognized as authoritative. Each will give two or more courses daily throughout the entire session. Additional instructors may be announced later. The regular summer school bulletin will be ready for mailing by March 1st and will contain full details in regard to instructors, courses, etc.

University of Oregon.

In co-operation with the Portland committee on the National Educational Association, the university has decided to establish an intermission of one week between the two halves of the summer school. This will be the second week in July—July 8 to 14. This will enable the teachers and principals to secure a full summer semester's work, as well as affording them the opportunity of hearing the world-famous speakers in the association meeting in Portland.

Among the famous men who have been secured for lectures during the summer session, the best known perhaps to Oregon teachers is Dr. G. Stanley Hall, president of Clark University and author of books on "Adolescence," "Educational Problems," etc. This is Doctor Hall's second visit to the university's summer school. The second speaker of prominence is President King, of Oberlin, one of the best-known speakers on ethical lines in the country. Dr. J. Duncan Spaeth, of Princeton, well known for his researches and studies in English literature, will again have charge of this important department.

The university is making a special effort to extend its usefulness by including a number of new courses and departments. There will be work in the pedagogy of music, of art, and on high school commercial teaching. There will be additional courses in Spanish, Latin, psychology, civics, and economics. There will be a new course in education, dealing with methods in civics teaching, by Mr. A. N. French, of the university high school. Dr. B. W. DeBusk will conduct a special advanced course for those who are interested in securing special training in diagnosing cases of defective children. Superintendent Frazier, of Everett, Washington, will give two courses dealing with different aspects of school administration.

Dr. Fred C. Ayer, of the chair of school administration, will exchange places with Prof. C. A. Gregory, of the University of Iowa, during the second semester of the present year. This is the first case of regularly planned exchange of instructors between the East and West. Doctor Ayer will have charge of twenty-five graduate students in the University of Iowa, and will train them in the methods of conducting school surveys.

Miss Nellie Cox, who completed her work at the university the first semester, goes to the English department of the Medford high school. Miss Myra McFarland takes up the work in general science and physical geography in the Eugene high school. Mr. George Turnbull succeeds Prof. Colin V. Dyment in the department of journalism. Mr. Turnbull will have charge of the University Press Bulletin.

Dr. B. W. DeBusk has completed his course of instruction in Portland dealing with the nutrition and treatment of defective children. Dr. DeBusk expects to visit different sections of the state in the next few months where there is an interest in the problem of defectives and backward children. Any superintendent or club interested in this matter should correspond directly with him at the university.

Statistics for the first semester show an enrollment of 1421 students in the departments of the university located on the campus at Eugene. This shows a gain of 27 per cent over the enrollment of last year, which was 1113. In addition to the departments on the campus, there are 73 students in the university school of medicine in Portland; there are 675 students, mostly teachers, registered for correspondence-study work; and there are 1694 persons taking regular courses for credit in extension courses given at a distance from the university.

For some time some of the departments of the university have been endeavoring to secure a much higher grade of work for the ablest students in the junior and senior years. A system of honor courses has been devised open only to students who have made a brilliant record during the first two years of their course. During the first semester there were eighteen such students in the university. On January 19 the members of the university faculty gave the honor students a banquet at the Osburn Hotel. The following speeches were made: (1) "We Are Only Starting: A Look Ahead," by Herbert C. Howe, toastmaster; (2) "A Scale of Values in a University," P. L. Campbell; (3) "Looking Back On An Honor Course From Not Very Far Ahead," Grace Edgington; (4) "We Are All Different, Seeking Different Ends," Frank Beach; (5) "We Are All Alike, Seeking the Same End," Frances Shoemaker; (6) "How We Did It in Michigan," Mable Holmes Parsons; (7) "How They Do It in the British Universities," C. V. Dyment; (8) "The European Student As a Dynamic in Society," George Rebec.

The Lane county survey has been made the basis of an article in the February number of the Review of Reviews. This survey has been attracting favorable attention from many parts of the United States.

The Philosophy Club of the university held its regular monthly meeting on January 23. The paper of the university was given by Prof. H. C. Howe, of the English department, and dealt with the logic of John Dewey. An animated discussion followed. The paper for February will be by Dr. E. S. Bates, and will deal with Betrand Russell and the new school of realism. This organization is open to both students and members of the faculty.

Oregon Normal School.

Mr. L. P. Gilmore, head of the science department, represented the faculty in the chapel exercises of January 12. Mr. Gilmore took as his subject, "Boys' and Girls' Club Work," and by a number of slides which he had prepared from the club work around Monmouth during the past two years presented this phase of Oregon's industrial education in such a way that the students derived many practical suggestions from it. Enough details of the week and its management were given so that the address will undoubtedly instigate the introduction of this work in many schools. The value of club work, not only for the work itself, but for its reflection on the regular school work, was shown in a number of concrete cases.

The combined Oregon Normal School Glee Clubs, with Mrs. Jane Burns Albert. soprano; Mrs. Lulu Dahl Miller, contralto; Mr. Norman A. Hoose, tenor; and Mr. Hartridge Whipp, baritone; as soloists and Mrs. Leonora Fisher Whipp and Miss Olga Wikberg, accompanists, presented under Miss Mary Hoham's direction the very lovely cantata, "Rose Maiden," by Frederic H. Cowen. This unusually finished and artistic performance made the program one long to be treasured as a rare musical treat. The chorus ensemble was perfect in its fine numbers, the solo work was of high worth and the general effect of the entire cantata in interpretation of tone and feeling was indicative of understanding and art on the part of the director, Miss Hoham. The story of the cantata is a charming one which was adequately and artistically interpreted by the sympathetic voices of the soloists, particuarly by Mr. Whipp and Mrs. Albert, who had the heavier parts. Mrs. Miller and Mr. Hoose were heard to good advantage both in solo work and in quartet numbers. The Oregon Normal School orchestra appeared splendidly in the prelude to the program. Three numbers from the "Nut Cracker Suite" of Tschaikowski—"Danse Trepak," "Danse de la Dragee" and "Pas des Fleurs"— were given with wonderful skill and spirit and showed a discriminating taste in program making. The artistic success of the complete performance is due to the good musical taste and magical talent for direction which Miss Hoham always displays in her annual programs.

The Oregon Normal School was extremely fortunate in having as its honored guest and chapel speaker, Mrs. Eva Emery Dye, who needs no further introduction to Oregon residents, for her books are widely read and appreciated everywhere the name of pioneer is known. Mrs. Dye was happy in her choice of subject for she has such wealth of illustration and incident concerning pioneer times and spirit. Mrs. Dye, who is a very entertaining speaker, held her audience perfectly through a splen-

did talk which emphasized both the old and the new pioneer spirit which is necessary wherever progress is to be made. It is sincerely the wish of the Oregon Normal audience who heard Mrs. Dye that she may again speak so inspiringly in some later chapel exercises.

A week-end guest of the Oregon Normal School was Mrs. Alexander Thompson of The Dalles, a member of the Oregon House of Representatives, who remained over until Monday morning to address the faculty and students at chapel time. Mrs. Thompson's subject was the most interesting one of "Women in Politics." She touched upon the big issues of the present time and showed by her forceful manner of speaking and her fine arguments that politics needed women; that the force of women in politics is for betterment of all conditions; that reform in politics would be accomplished by women. Mrs. Thompson's ready wit and her ability to use apt illustrations held her audience in an apreciative mood through her splendid speech. Mrs. Thompson will be accorded a hearty welcome on any future visit to the Oregon Normal School.

Wednesday, the 24th of January, was given over to an excursion to Salem to visit the legislature in session and the state institutions, President Ackerman and Mr. Butler having charge of the trip. This excursion afforded the opportunity for many students coming from distant parts of the state to see the state capital and for many other students the opportunity to visit the legislative houses in session. This was a practical lesson in civics and economics which was thoroughly enjoyed by 250 students who availed themselves of the opportunity and the information gained will enliven many future class-room recitations and discussions.

The first semester closed January 26 and was marked by special chapel exercises. The songs by the classes, the presentation of the basketball trophy cups to the winning teams and closing remarks by President Ackerman were the special chapel features of this assembly. The regent trophy cups were this year won by the junior men and the senior women. In addition the class numerals were presented to the members of the various teams and pennants to the student coaches. After closing

remarks by President Ackerman apropos of the work done during the past semester and the prospect for work in the second semester, the remaining number of the assembly programme was given by Miss Greene, representing the faculty on that occasion. Miss Greene took for her subject for this address the "Appreciation of the Beautiful in Nature." In presenting this Miss Greene showed how every student could at least have an artistic appreciation of the beauties which would everywhere surround her in Oregon, and by numerous concrete examples taken from the neighborhood of Monmouth showed how nature, with her everchanging beauties could be a source of daily inspiration.

The close of the first semester found a good many of the fifty-five mid-year graduates already located in schools over the state, with openings for practically all of the remaining members of the class.

The second semester opened January 29 with practically all of the old students programmed and matriculated on the preceding Saturday. Work began with the first period. The new students entering at this time brought the total registration by the end of the first week to 507. This is the first time in the history of the school that the regular attendance during any semester has passed the five hundred mark, indicating an increase of nearly 25 per cent in attendance over last year, all of which is an encouraging indication of the work that the Normal School is doing in the training of elementary teachers for Oregon.

The senior class was represented during the month by Miss Olive Valck, who took as her subject, "What the N. E. A. Can Do for the Professional Uplift of Teachers." Miss Valck's paper explaining the nature and method of work of the N. E. A. was most opportune and profitable in the light of the coming of the N. E. A. to Portland in July.

One of the biggest progressive steps taken by the Normal School since its reorganization was culminated January 26 when a contract was entered into with the Independence school board to use the common school of that city for training purposes for the Oregon Normal School. The addition of the 350 pupils from Independence to the present enrollment of the Monmouth training school will give the largest training school enrollment in proportion to the enrollment of the normal school of any in the Northwest. In addition to this a contract has been entered into with the directors of the Mountainview school, a conveniently located two-room rural school, which is to be used as a model practice school for the rural school department. As the size of the graduating classes has steadily increased the providing of adequate practice facilities has been the greatest problem confronting the administration of the school. With the acquisition of these additional facilities this problem is practically solved. It has been definitely determined that this new training arrangement will begin operation in September, 1917.

Professional Certificates.

Supt. J. A. Churchill has sent out the following letter to the school officers of the state:

"This department is interested in having the teachers throughout the state meet the requirements for the professional teacher's certificate. The certificate is issued without cost to those applicants who meet the requirements established by this department. We believe that much professional growth will come to the teachers through the efforts put forth to earn this certificate.

"We have today in Oregon some teachers who go from county to county after but a year's residence in each, and who fail to give the right service in every district where they go.

"The profesional certificate is a guarantee that a teacher is interested in her work, and that she is progressive. Other things being equal school boards should give preference to the teacher holding this certificate. This action on the part of the school board would tend to eliminate those teachers who are not interested in their work and who do not care to make additional preparation from year to year for the benefit of the districts and the children whom they are to serve."

Truth will always be the chief power of honest men.—Madame de Stael.

There is nothing so powerful as truth.—Daniel Webster.

Some Oregon Weeds and Seeds

By A. R. SWEETSER, University of Oregon

For our consideration this month we have two immigrant pests that readily adapt themselves to any soil and to all conditions, make them perfectly at home, and proceed to crowd out native born plants; and are only hindered by a constant warfare.

The first (Fig. 1) is known as mon adulterant of clover and grass seed. The leaves and flower clusters all come from the roots which are stout and persistent and store up abundant nourishment for the continuous existence of the plant. The leaves have several pronounced ribs which are more or less parallel; but if examined closely it will be seen that these are connected by a network of fine cross veins. The long slender flower stalk bears at its top a cluster of flowers known as a spike. If this is examined closely, especially with the aid of a magnifying glass, it will be seen that it is made up of many small but complete flowers. These have a four-parted calyx and four-parted corolla, usually four stamens, which protrude when the flower opens, and a single pistil.

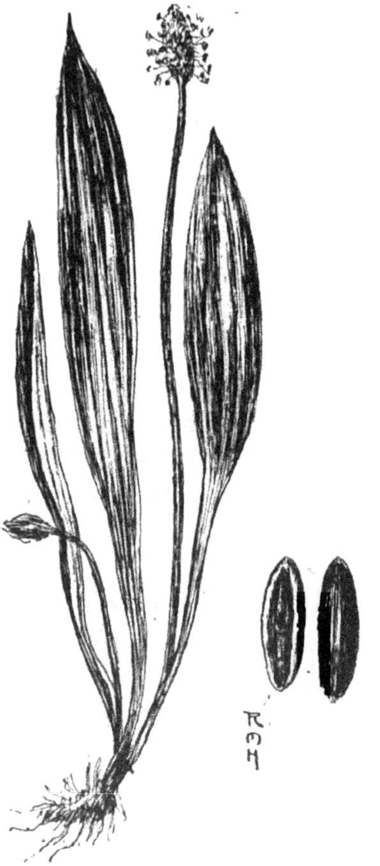

Fig. 1.—Buckhorn; Rib Grass; Nigger Head. Seed much enlarged.

Fig. 2.—Bread-leaf Plantain. Seed enlarged.

English Rib Grass, Buckhorn or Nigger Head, or in scientific language Plantago lanceolata. It is readily started by its seed, which is a com-

It will also be noticed that all the flowers are not in bloom at the same time, the earliest appearing at the base of the cluster and progressing

Summer Session 1917

JUNE 11 to JULY 28

Oregon Agricultural College

1. Courses for Teachers.
2. Courses for College Entrance and College Credit.
3. Boys and Girls Short Courses.
4. Preparation for Teachers Examinations.
5. Vocal and Instrumental Music.

SPECIAL INSTRUCTORS

1. Home Economics
   Miss Alice Ravenhill, London, England
   Mrs. Mary Schenck Woolman, Boston
2. Manual Training
   Mr. Geo. Fred Buxton, Stout Institute
3. Additional Specialists
   Will be announced in bulletin and subsequent advertisements.

REGULAR COLLEGE FACULTY

Instructors from the regular staff include specialists in Home Economics, Manual Training, Commerce, Agriculture, Art, Biology, Chemistry, Physics, Education, Economics, Political Science, Psychology, etc. In all, about one hundred courses will be offered.

CUT OUT AND MAIL COUPON BELOW

E. D. RESSLER, Director
  O. A. C. Summer School,
    Corvallis, Oregon.
  Please send copy of 1917 Summer School Bulletin to my address.

....

....

upwards. In a short time after flowering the pods will ripen, producing a couple of seeds which if examined under the microscope will appear, as in the accompanying drawing, somewhat resembilng brown date stones.

The other (Fig. 2) is also an introduced weed and is known as the Broad-leaf Plantain or Plantago major. It belongs to the same family and has the same general structure, but the spike is very much longer and each pod contains several seeds. This spike is often gathered and fed to canaries. Its seeds also are found quite frequently in impure grass seed.

Both of these plants may be eaten more or less by the stock, but they are said to impart a bitter flavor to milk. The remedy is found in the use of cleaned and certified seed and in everlasting cultivation.

Oregon Govermental Affairs

By ROBERT CARLTON CLARK, Eugene, Oregon

The Legislative Assembly.

The present session of the legislative assembly, like all its predecessors and its duplicate in other states, seems chiefly useful as an exhibition of how law-making ought not to be done. In the first place there are two legislative chambers in every essential way of identical character. No one claims that a state senator is any wiser, any more experienced, or any better trained for the work of making laws than a state representative. One chamber is merely a replica of another. Originally bicameral legislatures were a device to prevent hasty legislation. One was to serve as a check on the other. It was a device of men suspicious of democracy, distrustful of popular government. I dare anybody to show how the two houses of the Oregon legislature serve to restrain each other in any essential or useful way. One evil of the two house plan is that it breeds timidity in individual legislaltors. They vote for an unwise measure in the hope that the other house will kill it. Any way with the referendum "as a weapon behind the door" with which to head off seriously injurious legislation a single chambered assembly, small in numbers, could not imperil the safety of the state by too hastily considered laws. The most ardent champion of the present system would scarcely claim that any great number of the bills passed receive any real consideration by the legislature as a whole. One of the characteristics of the present session has been the absence of any real debate on the floor of the two houses. The very fact that the most important measures that ultimately become law are those that have been carefully worked out in committee or by their friends outside of the legislature seems to be a further point in favor of a single house sitting through a period sufficiently long to give every bill most careful consideration.

Consolidation of State and City Elections.

Few of the proposals that have come before the legislative assembly will change the actual machinery of government even if they have the good fortune to become law. Some of the numerous commissions are threatened with extinction or consolidation but it seems unlikely that there will be anything very sweeping accomplished in this direction. The passion for consolidation has led to a proposed constitutional amendment to consolidate city and state elections. This measure may also be due to a passion for economy. It is claimed that the holding of state and municipal elections on different days costs an additional $50,000. Such a proposal shows how short is the human memory. The reason these elections were separated in the first place was the very good one that state and national elections ought not to come simultaneously with city elections because of the different kinds of interests involved. National politics have generally been driven from city elections because of this difference in dates. City elections might not receive the attention they

The door opened suddenly and a lady rushed in.

"Oh, doctor," she cried, "the baby has swallowed some ink and he's now looking blue. What shall I do?"

"Give him a dose of blotter," said the doctor. "This is certainly an absorbing case."—The Widow.

deserve. Still it must be admitted that a single election every two years might make a demand upon the voter's sense of duty not too excessive. Too many elections is one of the vices of our present system of government.

The "Third House."

Extra constitutional devices have come to play a very important part in the business of government. The motive power behind the enactment of bills into law scarcely resides in the legislative assembly at all. It is furnished by various and sundry kinds of "lobbies" sometimes called the "third house." The measures that have the most certain hope of being enacted into laws are those that have behind them the most vigorous and persistent "lobby." When the champions of an anti-cigarette or good-roads law swoop down upon the legislature its valiant members surrender with scarcely more than the pretense of resistance. Good and worthy causes, not to mention those that can not claim such merit, would not have the ghost of a show if they were not thus championed by devoted men and women who fear not to waylay a legislator and to whisper into his ear until a promise is exacted to vote for their darling bill. The "third house" has become a potent not to say an essential instrument of legislation.

A Longer Session Needed.

This session of the legislature as all others before has shown that forty days are not enough for the serious business of making laws. All the appropriation bills and the greater number of other measures must be jammed through during the last days of the session. There can be but the merest pretense of discussion and no opportunity for amendment on the floor of the house. Representative government was devised on the principle that there is wisdom in numbers. Deliberation and discussion are fundamental in really representative government. These cannot be secured in a session of forty days. A session of the legislature costs all of $50,000 or more. A small body of men might be well paid to act as legislators for a period of six months

or more and have ample time to consider well all bills presented. There must be some real merit in such a bungling legislative system as we now possess but in this day when we are seeking to improve all other sorts of machinery and have little confidence in the tools and machines that our fathers used why put up with an antiquated legislative machine?

Voting in School Elections.

A measure long past due to become a law has already passed the assembly under the terms of which all legal voters may hereafter vote for school officials. Heretofore only tax-payers could vote in school elections. Elections on school bonds are confined to tax-payers as before. There is no good reason to keep this latter provision. Every man is indirectly a tax-payer if he is a renter of property in any way. Still it is a step in the right direction to make school elections open to all tax-payers to this extent. Every parent surely ought to have a voice in the election of the men who act as school directors.

Requirements for Professional Certificate.

The requirements for securing the professional certificate include the following:

Teachers who are successful in their work for at least eight months during the years of 1915 and 1916.

Teachers who meet all the requirements for a teacher in a standard school and comply strictly with all the laws relating to fire dangers and fire drills.

Teachers who send promptly to the county superintendents all reports requested by him or required by law.

Teachers who attend the annual institutes or training school and at least one local institute.

Teachers who read during the year under the direction of the University of Oregon or Agricultural college two books on the teachers' reading list.

The requirement that a teacher shall meet the requirements of a teacher of a standard school means that she must maintain good order at all times; supervise playground; have her work well prepared; follow state course of study; take at least one educational journal; have program posted in room; keep register

in good condition; be neat in attire.

When a teacher feels that she has met the requirements for a professional certificate, she makes application to the county school superintendent on the proper blank, giving necessary information, and if the county superintendent is satisfied with the report and the work done. he makes recommendation to the state superintendent, who issues the certificate.

Law Questions Answered

By ELMO S. WHITE, Salem, Oregon

Under this head Elmo S. White, of the Marion County Bar, will endeavor to answer such questions of law as our readers may care to ask. Conformably with the established policy of this magazine to be of the greatest usefulness possible, there will be no charge for this service. Questions will be answered in the next issue after receipt whenever possible. Every question must be accompanied by the name and address of the inquirer, but these will not be published unless the person so desires. Questions accompanied by a fee of one dollar will be answered by mail as quickly as possible and will not be published unless requested by sender. Address all communications to Attorney Elmo S. White, Masonic Temple, Salem, Oregon.

"Attorney White: Is a school district a public corporation?" Yes.

* * *

"Elmo S. White, Attorney: If the clerk of a school district in meeting assembled fails or refuses to act, what is the proper and legal procedure?" When the clerk of a school district fails or refuses to act the meeting has the power to appoint a secretary pro tem, whose acts as such are authentic; and the appointment of a clerk, made by the chairman, who acts without objection, is the act of the meeting.

"thi·   * * *

not "Mr. White: How long does it legake before the right to bring an action at law for an assault and battery will 'outlaw' in Oregon?" Two years from the time the act was committed.

* * *

"Attorney White: Can an unlawful act of a school district clerk be imputed to the district so as to make the district responsible?" No.

* * *

"Mr. White: What is the U. S. government's fees for a patent?" Fifteen dollars when the patent is applied for, and twenty dollars when the patent is issued.

* * *

"Attorney Elmo S. White: I am over eighteen years of age. Can I make a will?" You can make a will disposing of your personal property; but cannot so dispose of your real property until you have reached the age of twenty-one.

"Dear Mr. White: Has a school board any powers other than such as are expressly granted it by the legislature?" A board of school directors can exercise only powers expressly granted to it by statute, and such powers as may be necessary to carry into effect a granted power.

* * *

"Attorney Elmo S. White: Is there any way in which one who is the father of school children can compel a school board to admit them to the school?" A father, being the natural guardian of his minor children, charged by law with the duty of attending to their education and guilty of a misdemeanor if he fails to send them to the public schools according to law, has the right to maintain mandamus proceedings to compel the school board to permit his children to attend and be instructed in the public schools.

Truth is the mightiest thing that man can keep.—Chaucer.

In all things keep yourself loyal to truth.—Selected.

New School Legislation

The legislative assembly of 1917 enacted a number of good laws for the benefit of the public schools, and passed a resolution introduced by Sheldon of Jackson county, placing on the ballot for the next general election the proposition of establishing a state normal school at Ashland, and one in Eastern Oregon to be located by the Normal Board of Regents.

* * *

The Thompson bill, introduced by Mrs. Alexander Thompson of Wasco county, requires every school district in Oregon to have at least eight months of school each year. To the school children of this state, the law authorizing this is the most important one enacted by the 1917 legislature. There were only five votes against the bill in the House, and it passed the Senate without a dissenting vote. The demand for the law giving each district eight months of school has come from the rural districts, and it is entirely in the interests of the children who attend the one-room rural schools.

According to the provisions of this bill, each school must have at least eight months of school each year. The apportionment law was not changed. In order to understand this new law, it is necessary to be familiar with the apportionment law. Each county levies a tax sufficient to produce a sum equal to $8 for each child of school age. This fund is apportioned by first giving to each district $5 for each teacher employed therein. The balance of the money is apportioned to the school districts according to the number of children of school age.

Now, under the present law, if the money received by any district does not amount to $300 the district must levy a tax not to exceed 5 mills. If the 5 mill tax does not bring the amount up to $300, then the balance must be appropriated by the county court from the general fund of the county (not the school fund).

The new law provides that each district must have $400 instead of $300, and eight months of school instead of six months. The present law is not otherwise changed, and the law does not affect the amount received in any other district. The additional money will be supplied by local tax in the districts not now having eight months of school, and by small appropriations from the general county fund. About 700 districts now have less than eight months of school. Of these only 157 will need help from the county, according to statistics secured by State Superintendent J. A. Churchill. The following counties will not have to make any appropriations: Clatsop, Curry, Gilliam, Hood River, Jefferson, Klamath, Lake, Marion, Sherman, Tillamook, Umatilla, and Yamhill. Eleven others will have to appropriate less than $600 each. Many of the districts in the counties named above will have to levy only 1 or 2 mills of tax in order to have a fund of $400. For example, in Umatilla county sixteen districts have less than eight months of school, eight of these will have to levy only 1 mill, and the others from 2 to 4 mills.

In making the estimate required by this bill, the state fund is not considered. Each district receives in addition to the amount apportioned from the county school fund, its share of the interest on the irreducible state school fund, which is apportioned according to the number of children of school age.

* * *

Under the provisions of Senate Bill 270, by Senator Cusick, a teacher, after signing a contract, cannot resign within thirty days before the term of school begins, or at any time during the school year without the unanimous consent of the school board.

* * *

Additional professional training for teachers who are not graduates of a normal school or college was provided by a bill introduced by the house committee on education. This act changes the law requiring at least six weeks of professional training as a pre-requisite for securing a teachers' certificate by examination to twelve weeks. The law takes effect September, 1919. This will mean that in order to secure by examination a certifiacte to teach, one must be the graduate of a standard four-year high school, and must have had at least 12 weeks of professional training. This may be secured at any

chartered educational institution, or in a standard four-year high school. In the high school it will mean that the course will extend over the last two years instead of only the last year.

* * *

Senate Bill 195, introduced by Senator Orton, makes certain changes in the school tenure law applicable only to the city of Portland. It classifies the teachers as follows: First, supervisors; second, high school principals; third, grade school principals; forth, assistant supervisors; fifth, heads of departments in high schools; sixth, high school instructors; seventh, grade school teachers; eighth, special teachers. The bill further provides that a teacher may, before being transferred to a branch of the service which position is of a lower rank or before being dismissed, demand a hearing. This shall be before a commission. The members of the commission are to be three disinterested persons appointed on the first Tuesday after the first Monday in January of each year by the presiding judge of the circuit court. The bill is considered by the teachers of Portland as strengthening the tenure of office law. It was endorsed by the Teachers' Co-operative Committee representing six organizations of teachers. Active in the support of the bill were Mr. Wm. Parker, chairman of the general committee, and Miss Viola Ortschild, president of the Grade Teachers' Association.

* * *

Senate Bill 41, by Senator Hawley, atuhorizes the district school board to use all or any part of the public schools under its jurisdiction for training school purposes. Under this bill the school board of Independence will have authoirty to permit its schools to be used as a training school for the Oregon State Normal School at Monmouth.

* * *

Senate Bill 90, introduced by Senator Cusick, changes the time for closing the polls for the annual school meeting in districts of the first class from 6 p. m. to 7 p. m.

* * *

Senate Bill 95, by Senator Eddy, provides for recall of school directors in districts of the first class. The recall now applies to all elective officers excepting school officers, and this bill makes it applicable for school directors in districts of the first class. There must be a petition first signed by the legal voters of such district equal in number to 15 per cent of the number of children of school age in said district as shown by the last preceding school census.

* * *

The Sheldon bill provides that the property qualifications for school voters shall not apply in the election of a school director or of a school clerk. This will mean that women as well as men may vote at all school elections for the purpose of electing school directors or school clerks.

* * *

House Bill 20, by Jones of Lane, changes the time for taking the school census from November 25 to October 25, and House Bill 39, by the same author, changes the time for making the apportionment of school money from the first Monday in October to the second Monday in November. Under this plan the apportionment will follow immediately after the census. This will cause the districts to wait for some time after the opening of school for the fall apportions, but it will probably be an advantage to have the apportionment based on the census of the same year.

* * *

Senate Bill 81, by Senate Vinton, changes the time for Arbor Day. Hereafter the second Friday in February will be known as Arbor Day for Western Oregon, and the second Friday in April as Arbor Day for Eastern Oregon.

* * *

House Bill 249, by Dr. Anderson of Wasco county, designates the fourth Friday in October of each year as Frances E. Willard Day and provides that a portion of the afternoon of such day shall be set apart for exercises commemorating the life work and achievement of Frances E. Willard.

* * *

Senate Bill 2, by Senator Olson, authorizes the school board of Portland to establish kindergartens. It limits the number and the amount of money which may be expended for this purpose.

OREGON TEACHERS MONTHLY
The Official Journal of the State Teachers' Association

Vol. XXI	SALEM, OREGON, APRIL, 1917	No. 8

Published Monthly Except July and August by the State
Teachers' Association

Entered at the Postoffice at Salem, Oregon, as second-class mail matter, April 1, 1898.

RULES OF PUBLICATION

1. The mailing label on the Oregon Teachers Monthly shows the date to which subscriptions are paid.
2. The Oregon Teachers Monthly will be sent to subscribers until ordered discontinued and all arrearages are paid.
3. Notice of change of address should be given at once, naming both old and new postoffice.
4. When renewing, always state that subscription is a renewal.
5. The subscription price, including membership in State Teachers' Association, is $1.50 a year in advance. Single copy, 20 cents.
6. Advertising rates will be furnished on application.
Address all communications to Oregon Teachers Monthly, Salem, Oregon.

Editorial Notes

One-third or more of this issue is devoted to material relating to the rural schools. Other contributions will doubtless have interest also for the rural teacher. It is hoped that this matter will be of value as well to teachers engaged in other divisions of the school system. It is well for all of us to do some professional reading outside our special fields. Several of the articles were prepared for the late meeting of the State Association. While there is never a dearth of material, it is always a problem for the editorial board to decide what to select. Sometimes a lack of variety and the failure of some contributors make a particular issue seem one-sided. The board endeavors to conduct the Oregon Teachers Monthly in the interest of the Association membership.—R.

* * *

Entertaining the annual convention of the National Education Association is a large undertaking. The general committee was appointed early in January. Offices were established with adequate clerical force, sub-committees appointed and a systematic campaign begun. Six months of strenuous work will be required, involving the time and thought of many busy people and the expenditure of thousands of dollars. We can trust Portland and the educational leadership of the state to see that the city and state prove worthy hosts to the great association. Every teacher also has a part and a most important one in making a success of the convention. The National Education Association requires a large annual income and its chief source is the annual membership fees. The region of the country where the annual convention is held is relied upon to supply at least one-half the memberships. If the Northwest falls below five thousand, the general officers will be disappointed in us and our reputation will be damaged. The brunt of the burden rests upon Oregon, which receives the chief honor. Idaho, Washington and California are cooperating but they naturally expect us to take the lead. Early action on our part in the way of reporting memberships is highly desirable. We must not disappoint our friends by failing to rise to the occasion. Read the article on the N. E. A. in this issue of the Oregon Teachers Monthly.—R.

*   *   *

State Superintendent Churchill's plan of teaching morals in the schools is meeting with criticism both favorable and unfavorable. A recent announcement of the ten foremost virtues, as determined by a vote of teachers, calls forth the ridicule of the editor of the Statesman in the following words: "This sissy list will make mollycoddles, but it will not produce men and women fit to live and work in a real world. Hang up this roll of pretty, conventional virtues beside the womanish face of the paper-doll Sir Galahad and the future of the school-room is assured." The list thus characterized is composed of honesty, truthfulness, cleanliness, obedience, respect, courtesy, patriotism, kindness, industry, punctuality. The editor does not supply a list of virile virtues which he would substitute, although he concedes that kindness, industry and patriotism in the order named represent moral qualities. One wonders why love of country should be placed last in these critical days in our national affairs. It may be a question whether the "school-ma'am" list, as contemptuously charactrized by the editor, is inclusive of all the desirable virtues, but there should be no question as to the desirability of those included. Has the editor never heard of Honest Abe or Truthful George? Is the philosophy of Poor Richard good only for weaklings and milk-sops? Is there not a hygienic as well as a moral value in cleanliness? Is there no need of respect for and obedience to the law of the land to say nothing of filial duty, the lack of which is so much deplored? The implied suggestion that the State Superintendent seek opinions also from people in other occupations is good. It is to be expected that some editors will object to giving first place to honesty and truthfulness, but we believe they will be included in most lists of ten virtues in a referendum vote of the members of any reputable calling, including editors. It is probably indelicate for a teachers' magazine to resent unduly the references to the narrow-minded, bigoted, petty tyrants in the schoolroom who have suggested this "sissy list," but we beg to assure the gentleman that we are tolerant and broad-minded enough to charge up his peevish diatribe to a case of indigestion. It is altogether probable that the general public prefers teachers to editors as moral instructors of the youth.—R.

* * *

The last session of the legislature, memorable in many respects, will long be referred to because of the laws it enacted on educational matters, and these references will in most cases be favorable ones. In this connection it is fitting that the teachers of Oregon express their appreciation of the work of their educational leader, State Superintendent of Public Instruction J. A. Churchill. The laws especially fostered by the State Department, viz: the Eight Months Minimum School term, the Additional Professional training for teachers, the Restrictions on Breaking Contracts, and others are of such a nature as to bring Oregon much favorable notice for its educational progressiveness. Throughout the entire session, Superintendent Churchill stood courageously, sometimes in the face of adverse criticism, for what he believed to be for the best interest of the schools of the state, and this best interest was well served by his long experience and clear insight into Oregon's needs and future developments. The teachers of Oregon, who realize that professional standards have been raised and that the boys and girls of the rural communities have been given a more equal opportunity, congratulate the Twenty-Ninth Legislative Assembly, Superintendent Churchill and his able assistants E. F. Carleton and F. K. Welles for their good work of 1917.—E.

* * *

Point five of our teachers' Code of Professional Ethics reads as follows: "To withdraw immediately all applications when a contract has been signed, and to notify immediately all persons who may be actually assisting in securing a position." This is one of the points in the code which has its foundation principle in the idea of "fair play." Some teachers apply for three or four positions and then try to delay answering notifications of election or signing of proffered contracts until they hear from the other places. This delay is unbusinesslike and unprofessional besides being grossly unfair to other teachers. To thus "dog-in-the-manger" several positions will undoubtedly cause other applicants to take other and less desirable places, only to have these places of their first choice thrown open later in the season and filled by teachers unable to secure positions before that time. Is this practice not just as unfair from the point of view of the school board? Oftentimes their meetings are separated by weeks so that this delay sometimes becomes a space of two or three months which makes a difference in the number and quality of teachers available. Notification of those persons assisting in securing any positions, which is the second part of this point of the code, is the only courteous thing to do. It also bears directly upon the above mentioned bad results since failure to do so prevents them from placing other teachers in positions where they are uselessly trying to place a teacher who is already elected to another position. The spirit of giving a "square deal," not to mention the Golden Rule, will tend to rapidly eliminate this unprofessional practice.—E.

* * *

What promises to be a far reaching educational inovation was successfully carried out by M. S. Pittman, head of the Rural School Department of the Oregon Normal School, in what is now known as "Rural School Week," February 19 to 24. During that week 150 students who are taking work in the Rural Department visited seventy-five rural schools of Marion, Benton, Polk and Washington counties. The plan was to have two students go to each of these schools and live in the community for the week. The first day was to be spent in observation, after which they were to be allowed to do as much teaching or assist in as many ways as the teacher thought profitable. After the week of observation and practice the students and teachers held community rallies in each county where round table discussions over the week's work were conducted by the county superintendents, in the morning, and special programs by the Normal students and a member of the Normal School faculty were given in the afternoon. Another practical feature of the week was the opportunity for the students in the class in Rural Supervision to make the actual rounds of visits with the superintendents and supervisors. The week was made possible and much of its success was due to the enthusiasm and cooperation of County Superintendents Smith, Cannon, Crowley, Barnes and Duncan and the teachers in their counties. The rural schools of Oregon have long been the practice schools for teachers whose sole interest in them was a step ladder over the fence of required experience into the city schools. This condition has made the majority (used advisedly) of rural school teachers an ever-changing unsympathetic and in a few cases unscrupulous body, which has kept salaries low, interfered with progress by lack of community interest and effort, and educated the boys and girls away from the country. In spite of these conditions the people in many of the rural districts in Oregon are among our most progressive citizens and they are demanding the same standards in the management of their schools, which they insist on in all their other interests. This demand will in a short time change the economic and professional status of the rural school teacher, and "Rural School Week" is a move by the Oregon Normal School toward meeting that demand and an evidence of its avowed interest in rural schools. The net result of the week were: (1) It enabled the class to accumulate a wealth of concrete information about rural schools and conditions; (2) It gave the opportunity to test their theories and methods by actual conditions; (3) It proved the point that preparation for rural school work must be done in rural schools; (4) It furthered the realization in these rural communities that the work of a normal school bears directly upon their problems and is not merely a training school for city teachers.—E.

Educational Movies

By W. H. HURLEY, Vernonia, Oregon

This article is a description of the moving picture apparatus now in use in the Upper Nehalem valley, including a few remarks on the methods used to introduce this phase of education into a remote mountain community. In presenting this article the writer hopes that it may be of assistance to those who are endeavoring to operate motion picture outfits where the commercial electric current is not available, or are interested in portable outfits.

The teachers of Nehalem valley were first to realize the possibilities of motion pictures in their community, and through their efforts and the encouragement of a large number of residents of the community, the project was begun. A portable outfit, flexible enough to permit use under varying conditions provided with as good light as is used in theatres was considered essential. Such an outfit has been developed and in successful operation the past two years.

A Baby Grand Chevrolet automobile supplies power to operate the dynamo. A Ford has been used and operates the apparatus equally well and has the advantage of being lighter. A small wooden frame made from fir pieces 2 inches by 4 inches rests on the ground. To this are secured the dynamo, a counter-shaft and two V supports. In these V supports rests the rear axle of the automobile, the wheels being thereby raised from the ground. Three-inch belts are run over each of the tires of the rear wheels to two 6-inch steel pulleys placed at opposite ends of the counter-shaft which is 1 3-16 inches in diameter. Near the center of the counter shaft is fastened a 13-inch wooden pulley from which a 4-inch belt runs to a 5-inch steel pulley on the dynamo. All pulleys have 4-inch crowned faces and 4-ply rubber belts are used throughout. The counter-shaft turns in two dolly boxes mounted at one end of the wooden frame. The V supports are fastened at the other end and hold the rear axle high enough to prevent placing the dynamo under the axle. This gives as long belt as possible from counter shaft to dynamo, which is essential when driving from a large to a small pulley.

As the dynamo makes 1800 revolutions per minute the counter shaft runs at 692 revolutions per minute, and the rear wheels of the auto, being 32 inches in diameter, make 130 revolutions per minute. Hence the engine will be running at the same speed necessary to make 12½ miles per hour on the road.

The dynamo, a Fairbanks-Morse 2 K. W. 67½ Volt D. C. machine, is compound wound. It delivers about 30 amperes, but will carry 25 per cent overload without overheating. A field-rheostat, adjustable series resistance, voltmeter and ammeter complete the electrical equipment. These are all controlled by the operator handling the projecting machine.

A second attendant cares for the power plant while in operation. It is necessary to sprinkle the radiator with water occasionally. The evaporation cools the water in the tank and keeps the engine cool. With a water circulator sprinkling is unnecessary. After the arc is lighted the gas throttle is set so that the dynamo operates at proper speed under full load. The current is then about 30-35 amperes with 48 volts pressure across the arc, with enough resistance in series so that when it is removed the current increases to 35-40 amperes. This increase in load causes the engine to slow down a little which automatically decreases the voltage. The dynamo then operates at about 50 volts and allowing 2 volts for line drop there is still a pressure of 48 volts across the arc. No governor is needed on the engine as the load varies but slightly. The wooden frame, with dynamo and shafting attached can be hung on two iron suppors on the rear of the auto and transported from one place to another. As the supports are fastened to the underneath side of the auto, it is not necessary to deface the body of the car.

No. 8 D. R. C. flexible copper cable is used to carry the main current while No. 12 D. R. C. flexible cable carries current from the field rheostat to the shunt field winding of the dynamo. Metal hinge-joint belt lace, secured by means of rivets has been found most satisfactory for use on the short belts and small pulleys at high speeds. No trouble has ever been experienced with belts coming off tires. They work equally well over plain or nobby tread tires.

The projecting apparatus is an Edison exhibition model machine. It throws a steady picture, is substantially made light in weight, simple in construction and operation and has the advantage of being quite compact, making it a practical portable machine. A Gundlach lens, which is standard among theatres, is used. Its equivalent focus is $3\frac{1}{2}$ inches. This allows the projecting of regular size pictures at short throws, as found in the average school room. A stereopticon attachment is also provided for showing lantern slides.

The rewind is a simple apparatus and is fastened to a table or shelf by means of a thumbscrew, making it readily detachable for moving, during which process the generating plant is fastened to the rear of the auto, as previously mentioned, while the projecting apparatus is placed in the rear compartment, leaving the front seat for two operators.

The pictures are shown on a white cloth screen made from ordinary sheeting. The whole outfit works O. K., the pictures being equal in every way to those shown in theatres about the country. As it is necessary that the entertainments pay their own expenses, it is necessary to charge a small admission fee. This pays operating costs, such as film rental, express, cost of carbons and running auto. During the two years the outfit has been in use it has paid all expenses, but no charge has been made by the operators.

The Nehalem people demand high-class pictures. Bluebirds are the only dramas in demand. "Gloriana" and "End of the Rainbow" are of the type mostly desired. The educational side of the program is made up of the "Animated Weekly," travelogues and industrial subjects. The two last-named are frequently obtained from the University of Oregon. Too many of these are so badly worn as to make them useless. The weakest part of their service at present is the lack of suitable dramas and comedies. On lists published, no titles of such pictures are to be found. A program consisting entirely of educational pictures of the travelogue and industrial types is as badly crippled as a program containing neither of these. The educational value of the drama is recognized in other forms, so why not recognize it in the movies and develop it? A clean comedy to loosen the tenseness caused by dramatic action is then all that is required to balance the program.

If the University would supply complete balanced programs on the same basis as the present supply of films is sent out, the most remote community could be included in the shipping circuit and the poorest school district would be well able to enjoy the benefits of the service. Many very valuable lessons could thus be brought to farmers in districts where lecturers from the Agricultural College are practically unknown.

It is essential to the success of the educational movies, directed by educational institutions, that no admission be charged. It is a fact that here in the Nehalem valley many people are denied the education and entertainment they might otherwise profitably enjoy merely because they haven't the money, though it is but a small amount.

In closing, the writer wishes to state that he feels a more than pecuniary interest in the development of the educational movies among our schools and will gladly give any further information concerning his own experience to interested parties.

If you see an editor who pleases everybody, there will be a glass over his face and he will not be standing up.—Exchange.

Play is God's method of teaching children how to work.—Francis W. Parker.

Beauty in Nature

By ALBERTA M. GREENE, Oregon Normal School

Spring is the season in which nature revives itself with new energy and new coloring, and because of the surroundings it is the best time to teach the appreciation of the beauties in nature. Very few of us fully appreciate the things we see about us, and very few of us make any effort to develop ourselves in this appreciation. Therefore, I think that it is a timely subject to call your attention to.

Edward Howard Griggs in one of his books has said that four things are really necessary to make a happy life: Love, the love of our friends, the love of family, the love of our work; wisdom, the wisdom that comes from training and experience; faith, the faith in our fellow-beings, faith that good will dominate, faith in ourselves; and, lastly, the appreciation of beauty.

If, then, it is one of the necessary things in life we each need to make an effort to appreciate more. It is a great thing to paint a picture—it also is great to be able to appreciate what others have painted. One need not be a sculptor to appreciate sculpture, or a composer to enjoy music. Neither is it necessary to be a literary critic to understand literature. Then why must we feel that we must be artists to appreciate beauty?

Oregon abounds with the wonders of nature, so let us awaken ourselves and see them. If you live near a snow-capped mountain have you watched it when dressed in its rosy garb, when it threw a cold blue veil across its face? Have you noticed that at times it seems to be crushing down upon you with its gigantic force, and at other times towers high above you, majestic in its beauty? The mountains are wonders of beauty, ever-changing, yet changeless.

If you live near a group of fir trees watch for the difference in shadows, of moonlight and sunlight; walk in the grove on a misty morning when it is all but hidden from your view. Learn to see the distant hills in their changing colors from black to indigo, and from indigo to violet. Then the flowers offer an abundance of beauty in colors and in form. Do you know the blueness of a field of camas or the rosy glow of a roadside banked with rose brier?

The birds are as varied and beautiful as the flowers. Watch for the orange lining of a flicker's wing, or the curves and slants of a swallow's flight. Even so common a thing as a spider's web filled with dew reminds us of a diadem beset with jewels. So, then, let us make some effort to cultivate our appreciation of the beautiful. A poem that has meant much to me in just that appreciation of the beauty of the fields is this one of Elizabeth Barrett Browning's:

> The little cares that fretted me,
> I lost them yesterday
> Among the fields above the sea,
> Among the winds at play,
> Among the lowing of the herds,
> The rustling of the trees,
> Among the singing of the birds,
> The humming of the bees;
> The foolish fears of what might happen,
> I cast them all away
> Among the clover-scented grass,
> Among the new-mown hay,
> Among the hushing of the corn
> Where drowsy poppies nod,
> Where ill thoughts die and good are born,
> Out in the fields with God.

We need not feel that the sights with which we are most familiar are not beautiful. Usually it is because we have not seen the beauty. If one will give the attention to it he will find that it is the recurrence of familiar things that grow most upon us. Watch the same tree that you pass each morning, see it in its lights or shadows, notice the same hills and broad fields each day and see the varied beauties that they offer.

The story is told of Erasmus, a friend of Martin Luther's, that as he traveled across the Alps into Italy he saw none of the beauties of the Alps, for in writing home to a friend of his trip he mentioned only the dirty lodging that he found, the smoky stoves and the sour wine. Yet many of us would pay a big price and travel far to see the Alps. The story only goes to prove that the sun shines only to the eye that can see it.

So at this season when we have found the many beauties for ourselves let us help the children in our charge to see them. The following is an outline of suggested lessons for the months of April and May. If these lessons are systematically taught and thoughtfully carried out I am sure that the children and the teacher alike will enjoy the beauties of nature more.

The first week would necessarily be given over to the special subject of Easter cards for primary grades and intermediate grades, made of white paper and simply decorated with water colors or crayons. Use for the motif in this decoration the symbols of the Easter season, such as chickens, ducks, lilies, any early flower, pussy-willows, birds, rabbits and eggs. Suitable envelopes may be made to fit the cards so that they may be used for mailing purposes.

Place cards should be made by the intermediate and upper grade children, using practically the same suggestions for decoration as we did for cards, paying particular attention to the space that should be left for the name. These may be made with folded paper so that they will stand, or with an extra base that is pasted on the back of the card, or may be made more decorative by having the upper portion of the card cut out around the design.

The Easter poster is an excellent medium through which the Easter thought may be brought out. Individual posters may be made where each child works out the entire picture for himself, or if you have not tried the community poster, to which each child in the room contributes something, try it this Easter. For instance, the first grade might cut from paper, egg shapes, and color them in delicate colors with water colors or very softly with crayons. The teacher will make the nest to be fastened on the side of the blackboard of yarn or raffia, or it may be drawn on a piece of bristol board with the back half of the ellipse of the nest cut so that the eggs may be slipped in and pasted. A rabbit or hen may be cut or drawn by the teacher to add to the interest of the nest, or if one doesn't feel that she has the ability to do this let the children cut out flowers such as tulips, tall grass leaves and paste them around the nest.

The children are intensely interested in anything that requires community spirit, and this gives the child who has the least ability or does the poorest work in the class an equal opportunity with any of his classmates.

A suitable poster for second grade children would be the hen, a chicken coop and chickens. These parts may be cut from paper, colored and mounted upon a piece of bristol board or may be pinned or pasted upon the blackboard. If you have some one or two children in the room who do especially good cutting let one of these cut the mother hen, another cut the coop, another may cut the dish in which the feed is placed, the other children each cutting a chick. Pains should be taken in the mounting of these posters, showing some little background such as a distant tree or a fence, or a portion of a house or a barn. This can best be done with crayon or charcoal. The proper perspective should be kept in mind, the small chicks put in the distance.

A suitable poster for third grade may be worked out in this way: Someone cuts and colors the flower pot, another cuts the green stem and leaves of the Easter lily, all the others cutting from white paper the flowers, some in front view, some side view, some buds. These flowers may be cut from the common white drawing paper or they may be made from white tissue paper or even crepe paper. If the pot, stem and leaves are colored on both sides and you have a suitable window these parts may be pasted against the window pane and will look much like living flowers from indoors and out. If this is not practical it can be pasted against a background of soft tan or gray-blue or even fastened against the blackboard.

Another pleasing poster for fourth and fifth grades would be a window display of Easter hats. This is the most effective when pasted against the window pane, but also may be mounted on bristol board where a few black lines have been used to represent the show window. Hats of all kinds may be cut by the children and colored. They will be interested in watching the store windows down town and the styles of hats that they see on the street, coming in to cut and color what they have seen. Special attention should be given in this problem to training the tastes of the children. This poster lends an excellent opportunity to teach good color combinations.

The upper grade children would probably not be interested in community or individual posters. They might care more to make an Easter booklet in which some suitable poem is written, or possibly they would enjoy lettering a text, coloring it carefully and decorating it with some simple design.

Other things that are specially interesting to lower grades in the Easter season are the many amusing objects that may be made from the egg shapes. Let each child bring a shell from which the egg has been blown and help him to make a tumbling doll. Place the egg large end down and put a few pebbles or a few grains of shot—anything that will add weight—in the egg, letting run over that a few drops of melted wax from a candle. The egg will stand. Then the front of the egg may be decorated to represent a face, a boy's face, a lady's face, the face of a Chinaman, etc., with suitable coloring and hats. The hats may be made of thin paper, and even colored paper, and pasted over the opening at the top. The face is easiest made by merely drawing black lines for eyebrows, spots for the eyes, two tiny dots for the nose and an irregular line curved down or up for the mouth. The orange color used thinly may be applied for the cheeks. If desired brown, yellow or black may be painted on the egg in a very effective way to represent hair, for the Chinaman's face use some black yarn pasting it at the top of the egg, enough to cover the end of the egg all the way around, then braiding it into a cue.

The second week of April you can study birds—the robin, the meadow lark, the bluebird—any bird that is familiar to your children. The lower grades cut bird forms, then color them. The upper grades draw with pencil for form, then draw with crayons and color. Three lessons may follow where you use the paints. The best models possible for this kind of lessons are the colored pictures of birds. The coming of birds may be illustrated by a little picture that shows only sky, tops of trees, tops of telephone poles and telephone wires, flocks of birds shown in the air or alighted on the wires. Another picture might be made of a bird house cut from paper and placed upon the branch of a tree or upon a pole, with possibly three birds cut out, colored and mounted around the bird-house. This is a good season of the year also to study chickens, ducks, any of the familiar barnyard fowls.

The little people may make a frog pond. Paste some blue tissue paper across the lower part of the window pane, cutting and coloring some dark green rushes, pasting these in front of the tissue paper. Let the children cut frogs and color them. These may be mounted in suitable positions around the pond. Ducks may be cut and put in the pond.

Another window poster that the smaller children enjoy is the fish bowl. Cut from two pieces of paper the shape of the fish bowl, paste over each, one thickness of very transparent white tissue paper. Cut two or three fishes the size of gold fish, color these on both sides, paste them using very little paste against one of the pieces of tissue paper. A tiny little castle, shells or pebbles and a spray of greenplant—anything suitable for a fish bowl—may be cut and colored in like manner, pasted on the piece of paper with the fish and then the two pieces of the bowl put together. The little poster needs to be pasted in the window to be most effective.

Upper grade children throughout the spring months should give special attention to design. In the teaching of design we should attempt to develop in the child a fine distinction of color, a feeling for pleasing space relations and harmonious forms. To do this design can best be taught by paper cutting. From a folded piece of paper, cutting always from the folded side, one may cut a leaf form, a tree form or other simple familiar forms. When this is unfolded both halves of your space are alike. This can be used then as a unit in a border design, placing the paper on a background of some neutral color, as gray or brown, tracing around the pattern and using as many repetitions as your space requires. When you wish to color this use a flat tone of dull green, brown, gray, yellow, any of the neutralized colors. This border may be used as a decorative front for a booklet cover for language or history, a cover in fact for any purpose that you may care to use it for.

There should always be a definite purpose in teaching design.' Designs may be made that you can apply to book covers, color decorations for writing pads, designs that will fit the side of a cardboard waste-paper basket. Border designs in cross-stitch for the girls to use in their sewing classes, simple geometric figures designed by the boys to use in their sloyd work, or where you have neither sewing or manual training taught, the upper grade children should be doing some construction work. Candle shades are easily made and need simple thoughtful designs. The most practical material to use in the schoolroom for candle shades is the regular construction paper, cutting out your design and lining the shade with the Dennison crepe paper of a suitable color. Construction paper also makes practical corners for writing pads.

Throughout the third week in April or at any time when the flowers may be had study the spring flowers. First, second and third grade children —any class in fact that does not see form readily—should cut the form of the flower before they attempt to color it. Pretty window decorations may be made from the daffodil, cutting, coloring on both sides and pasted across the window or mounted on long, slender panels and used above the blackboard. A very effective border of daffodils may be made in this manner: Cut the saucer part of the flower showing the six points from a square of paper folded, color this yellow on both sides, or better still colored yellow paper may be used, then using some thin paper and coloring it or using yellow paper make the trumpet part of the flower. Paste this into the saucer, cutting and coloring stem and leaves, mounting all on a brown or gray background, each child making his flower and mounting it on a separate piece of background. If all the background papers are the same size they will make a pleasing border when hung above the background. Tulips, hyacinths or any of the spring flowers may be worked out in like manner. When using the early flowers for drawing models do not forget the use of the common blackboard chalk on gray or colored paper. This may be combined with crayon or with water colors. Sometime during the spring make careful study of buds, pussy-willows, and young leaves. Especially should this done in the upper grades where pencil is used.

As the May basket is an incentive to the more careful and painstaking effort along construction lines it is well to give the last week in April over to the making of May baskets. The first grade children may save some of his woven mats from the early spring to be fastened in cornacopia style with a handle attached to be used as a basket. Baskets may be constructed from the square or from the large circle. There are numerous styles of baskets that can be made from common drawing paper. They may be made a little more effective if the paper is first stained a soft green or brown or a very soft dull yellow, the color used so thinly that you really have straw color. But the natural color of the paper will be much better than to let the children daub on brilliant spots of yellow and blue and red. This same delicate coloring can be done with crayons as well as with water colors. The construction paper, of course, may be used in the same way if one has this material. The intermediate grades may make baskets from the paper or they may take small boxes, covering them with softly colored tissue paper or making a cover of the common drawing paper decorated with an all-over design, or this coloring may be put upon the box itself. If one cares to trouble with Japalac or even common carriage paint of soft neutral colors, children can make beautiful boxes by using the common cracker box, or candy boxes. Care must be taken if you wish to use this that you have good colors.

The upper grade children may not care to make May baskets. They possibly would like to make cards better. These cards may be decorated with flowers, pussy-willows or tiny landscapes. Some suitable greeting should be printed upon the card. Here is a chance for excellent application of design they have made previously, also the knowledge they have gained from the painting of spring flowers.

May offers a little different subject matter for our consideration. Flowers should be carefully studied both for form and color. Trees should have some attention, especially the trees with which the children are most familiar. They may be worked out with scissors or pencil for form from gray paper and then the coloring done with crayons or water colors. If the trees have been carefully studied they should be used in their natural position in landscapes, making your landscapes like the country the children know.

If you live where mountains can be seen have mountains in your landscapes. If you live near the ocean make pictures of the ocean. The spring colors should be brought out in the foliage and the grass. The landscape needs to be studied first in crayons and then in water colors.

The upper grade children may make more designs, using for their motifs birds, buds, butterflies, bugs; familiar animal forms squared and used for borders. If you can have peg printing sets make a suitable all-over pattern for a book cover or better still, if you can give as much time as is necessary let the seventh and eighth grades make stenciling patterns. These can best be made by folding the paper and cutting your pattern. If you do not care to use oil paints or stenciling dye, excellent effects can be gotten by the use of common wax crayons on cloth or paper.

Children from the fifth grade to the eighth should be taught to do good lettering. Letters given in regular sequence are somewhat difficult, but if given in groups of easier letters first, followed by the more difficult groups, children can be taught to do excellent lettering. For the first group take the straight letters, I, L, T, H, E, F. Practice all these, then study the oblique line letters, A, V, W, M, N, K, X, Y, Z. Follow these with the half-curved letters, P, R, B, D, U, and J, then last of all give the curved letters, O, Q, C, G, and S. The simplest letter form is to place all letters within a block three measures tall and two measures wide or in the proportion of three to two.

The spring of the year is the time to do appreciation work, especially landscape pictures. Copies of Innes or Corot, or any of the better landscape painters may be used.

The latter part of May you may wish to emphasize Memorial Day in some way. If you are having programs let the children make a suitable program cover, making the decoration simple enought to be well worked out by your grade of children. The flag or the shield may be used, or the laurel wreath cut and colored. Gray paper should be used for the front page and margin of the program. Be careful not to over-decorate.

No one needs to feel that he cannot carry out much of this that is suggested because of lack of material. If you have not the construction paper or the water colors or any other material named here find something else that will answer. Common oatmeal wall paper makes an excellent background for mounts for children's pictures. The common drawing paper will answer for any or all of these suggested lessons. If one cannot use water colors the five-cent wax crayons will answer very well and a pair of scissors can always be had.

Should it be impossible for you to have the flowers or the birds or other named subjects needed at the time stated, use them some other time when you can get the materials. The big thought behind all spring work is to make a careful study of nature, and it can be done to good purpose even in the schools where little material is furnished.

Qualifications for Teachers.

Do you possess sympathy, self-control and forbearance?

Do you have piety, courtesy, prudence and gentleness?

Do you practice frugality, punctuality, generosity, forgiveness and toleration?

Are you a paragon of patience, patriotism, justice, gratitude, liberality and uprightness?

Are you filled to the brim with enthusiasm, honor, truthfulness, faith, hope, charity, honesty and courage?

Are you sure of your virtue, chastity, fidelity, self-government, devoutedness, disinterestedness and sobriety?

Are you satisfied with your knowledge, principle, confidence, ideality, morality, unselfishness, temperance, humility, probity, amiability and veneration?

How about your intelligence, preparation, scholarship, thriftiness, economy, reverence, frankness, unostentatiousness, ministration, elaboration, instruction, energy, heroism, nobility, trustworthiness, leadership and conscientiousness?—North Carolina Education.

The Mathematical Responsibility of the High School

By F. L. GRIFFIN, Reed College

Very severe criticism has been and is being directed at the mathematical courses of the high school. Commissioner Snedden of Massachusetts asserts that the disciplinary value of mathematical studies is questioned by most students of education, that their utility is greatly exaggerated, especially as regards the needs of girls, and that the cultural aims of these studies are not realized—that the majority of students gain neither in comprehension of the world nor in appreciation of their social inheritance. Again Dr. Abraham Flexner declares that what mathematics should be taught depends upon what is needed, when it is needed and the form in which it is needed; and he intimates that a proper balance of the curriculum would greatly reduce the prominence given to mathematics. Again the superintendent of schools in a large city seems to regard it as inadvisable for girls to study algebra at all. Such illustrations can easily be multiplied. Even college teachers of mathematics and other sciences add to the criticism by declaring that the students get a sure grasp neither of the technique of algebra nor of the facts of geometry; and various efficiency tests tend to substantiate this judgment.

How shall we meet this storm of criticism? We might return it with interest, and ask whether students actually get what they are supposed to gain from other studies. Does the average student get from his four years of English either the ability to write and speak effectively, or a wide familiarity with and intelligent appreciation of the best literature? Does he get from his study of a foreign language a real command of the language, comprehension of its choicest literature and knowledge of its relations to his mother tongue? Does he get from history an all-embracing world-view and understanding of the origins of our present complex civilization? Does he even in his scientific courses achieve as much as you teachers might desire? Possibly we could answer the indictment of our mathematical teaching somewhat in this vein; but we prefer not to do so. We prefer to face the issue on its own merits. So much criticism means that something is wrong. We, more than anyone else, are eager to find the trouble and put our house in order.

We face the question confident that the fault is not with the science of mathematics itself. Why, mathematics is indispensable in the construction of our houses, bridges, railroads, water-mains and sewers, in our electric lighting, phones, maps, our very lot-lines, time-service, etc.—even in the grinding of the lenses used in making and exhibiting our moving pictures! Calculations of one sort or another, and the determination of geometric spatial relations, are the most basic and the most common of all human problems. Scientific men and women know that mathematics, while the servant of all other sciences, is itself a vast and wonderful science which has opened to human thought other universes far transcending that of our physical senses.

Prof. R. E. Moritz, in a recent address before the Mathematics and Science Section of the Washington Educational Association, showed clearly that "Mathematics provides the most effective training of (1) the power of undivided attention and prolonged concentration of mind; (2) the power of exact definition, of clear statement and of critical analysis; (3) the power of deductive reasoning, of drawing logical conclusions from given premises. I am aware that there are some who believe these powers to be developable quite as well through any and all studies of any ultimate worth. But I commend to all such persons a careful perusal of Dr. Moritz' address. Indeed, it is my humble opinion that unprejudiced reflection will convince anyone of the unrivalled adaptability of mathematical studies to the development of the powers just mentioned.

Mathematical studies will develop a student's originality and his reasoning faculty, only if we make him think for himself. If we let his algebra degenerate into rules and routine processes, and if we use the very pernicious type of text in geometry, which has most of the proofs worked out for him, so that he merely runs over the reasoning of other people, how can we expect his reasoning power to be greatly enhanced? Geometry will help him to appreciate the dependence of conclusion upon hypothesis only in case we frequently direct his attention to this matter. It is surprising how many "educated" people suppose that in geometry we have absolute proofs; whereas, of course, not a single proposition is certainly known to be true. If students really grasp the dependence of conclusion upon hypothesis, why do they not see that all the proofs rest ultimately upon the original assumptions —axioms and postulates? And what could be a more wholesome antidote for dogmatism of all sorts than the realization that nowhere is there certain knowledge—neither in philosophy nor in religion nor in science?

Mathematical studies will help a student to interpret the world about him, whether material, spiritual or social, only if we show him how his studies are connected with the world. He may say, "Yes, I have no doubt that mathematics is very essential in daily life, in the providing of modern conveniences, etc., but what has that to do with this factoring?" And of course, as far as utility is concerned, a topic has none for those students who will never actually use it —though the pointing out of its usefulness to humanity as a whole may give it a legitimate interest for all. In this latter direction of vitalizing the topics, great advances have been made in the texts of recent years, and doubtless still further improvements are coming.

It seems to me that the worst faults of the present courses can be remedied only by a very radical revision of the order of topics. To see this clearly, picture to yourselves the great throng of students who enter the high schools every year. Out of each one hundred, about sixty-three will reach the second year, forty-four the third year, thirty the fourth year and ten will go to college. The 90 per cent who do not enter college have no chance to become familiar with analytic geometry and the calculus; analytic geometry which has revolutionized modern scientific thought; and the calculus, that marvelous tool without which we could not have the modern sciences of astronomy and physics, nor physical chemistry with its applications to biology and medicine, nor the theory of probability with its many uses in biology and sociology. The 70 per cent who do not reach the fourth year, see nothing of these subjects, nor even of trigonometry, whose applications occur in nearly every line of human activity, nor of logarithms, the most wonderful means ever devised for making numerical calculations. The 56 per cent who do not reach the third year see nothing of these subjects, nor even any solid geometry, nor even progressions, with their manifold applications to the theory of investments, sinking funds, amortization of debts, etc.

The 37 per cent who do not reach the second year see nothing of all this, nor do they even get any plane geometry whatever; its logical aspects and utility are alike lost to them. They get merely some elementary algebra —rather formal at that. In fact, in spite of all that we can do, much of the algebra is bound to be rather abstract if presented at this time, since it finds its applications only in connection with more advanced mathematical tools such as in calculus.

The traditional courses seem to have been planned primarily for the few who are going on. But unfortunately they are not well adapted even to the needs of that group, since algebra learned in the first year of high school to be used in the second year of college is generally forgotten in the meantime. Thus the courses do not discharge the obligation of the high school to this group much better than they discharge the far larger obligation to the larger number who do not go on to college. What ought to be done? Should we, as Commissioner Sneddon recommends, establish separate courses for those who are expecting to use mathematics as a tool, and for those who would study it simply for cultural reasons? Not too early in the curriculum; for students usually do not know until pretty late what their life work will be; indeed, many are still undecided when about to graduate from college. The introductory course at least can be so planned as to be of more value to all students than any specialized course could be. May I suggest a tentative plan for such a course?

1. Practical Uses of Graphs.—Not plotting equations nor using the idea of co-ordinates, but simply such a representation of varying quantities as is used in business, in engineering, and in pure science. Given a table of values, say the cost of oil tanks of various capacities, students can easily be taught to lay out a horizontal scale of capacities, erect vertical lines whose lengths shall represent the given costs, and draw a smooth curve through

their ends—also to use the resulting graph to read off intermediate values, find rates of increases, etc. Well chosen examples will make students see what a remarkably useful "ready computer" a graph is. Incidentally they will get the very fundamental idea of one quantity changing with another in a definite way, i. e., the function idea.

2. Formulas.—From elementary arithmetic students are familiar with various mensuration formulas (somehow expressed.) They can now be shown the convenience of using letters and exponents to secure brevity. (Only positive integral exponents, and no rules for their combination, as yet.) Practice substituting values in formulas.

2. Simple Equations With Positive Roots.—Show how much easier problems in arithmetic now become. Also give problems on solving simple formulas for some unknown.

4. Simple Fractions and Parentheses. —Show the convenience of combining coefficients of a common factor before multiplying, also of combining fractions, etc. Check literal work constantly by numerical substitutions.

5. Numerical Short-cuts. —Those most frequently useful, such as squaring numbers, and multiplying numbers nearly equal, dividing by 25, etc. Algebraic proofs of the methods.

6. Experimental Geometry.—Constructional work will familiarize students with the use of the instruments, with the terms most commonly used, and with the idea of a geometrical theorem. This work will also reveal its own inadequacy; some students' figures will show that the medians of a triangle are concurrent, some will not. The inconvenience of making many constructions with figures of different shapes to see whether the same result would always be obtained, and the uncertainty of the conclusion even then, will make students welcome the suggestion of proving the statement once for all by a brief argument.

7. Elementary rational geometry of lines and triangles, informal at first, then giving more attention to the logical side, and finally pointing out the element of uncertainty even here, viz., in the bare possibility that our axioms are untrue.

8. Elementary Trigonometry, Introduced by Graphical Work.—Any surveying problem can be solved roughly by drawing to some chosen scale and measuring the required distance or angle. Similarly for problems in statics, such as finding the forces acting along the members of a bridge or framed structure. The trigonometry proper should be limited to the definition of sine and tangent (possibly adding the cosine and cotangent) and the use of tables to solve triangles—a few oblique triangles by dissection. No formulas should come in here.

9. Negative numbers, introduced in connection with temperatures below zero, directed line segments, etc. Show the big gain in generality of operation. Negative roots of simple equations interpreted. Graphical solution of higher equations. (Nothing is easier than to make a table showing the value of the polynomial for different values of X, plot the graph, and see where the polynomial becomes zero.)

10. Powers of Ten, Logarithms.—Laws of combining exponents; meaning of negative exponents. Expressing numbers in the very brief and convenient. Expressing numbers completely as powers of 10: Any number between 1 and 10 equals 10 to some fractional power, given by logarithmic tables. Computing by combining such powers of 10. Show the wonderful calculations which can be made in a jiffy. Calculations with scientific formulas, compound interest, trigonometry, etc.

This course would give students in their first year those mathematical tools which are most widely used in practical affairs, and a good idea of the power and variety of mathematical methods. Also it would have close connections with elementary arithmetic and would ensure to all high school students some training in geometrical reasoning. The subject matter is no more difficult than the more abstract topics commonly included in first-year algebra. Indeed, though differing in important respects from the excellent course worked out by Mr. E. R. Breslich, and others, at the University High School in Chicago, it is not so very different in general plan or spirit; and the latter course has been taught successfully for years. The course outlined above is not so very different from those given in various European schools; so that this plan is not a wildly fanciful and untried scheme. Indeed, I am much less interested in saying something novel than in suggesting what seems to me the most valuable course, and in inviting you to consider it seriously.

For the work of the second year, I would suggest a more advanced combination course in algebra, geometry and trigonometry, but including little if any trigonometric analysis. In the junior year, there might be a term of algebra and a term of geometry finishing the work usually given in those subjects, with a good systematic review of each, designed to organize the subject as a whole.

This plan of carrying algebra and geometry along side by side for three years should not only permit better correlation of the two subjects but also insure a better final grasp of each and the ability to use the technique of algebra and the theorems of geometry at any later time. This plan again is nothing novel; it is the regular thing in France, Germany and various other countries noted for able mathematicians and scientists.

In the senior year there should be a combination course in the elements of analytic geometry, calculus, trigonometry analysis and some topics of higher algebra —not a formal abstract course, but one dealing with the remarkable practical applications of these subjects. This would result in a tremendous gain in the power of high school graduates to deal with scientific problems either in business or early in their college course. To be sure this course would require teachers who are fully prepared for their work. In fact, that is the greatest single need of the average high school even now. We can not hope for the best results from courses in secondary mathematics until school authorities awake to the need of teachers who have a broad grasp of mathematics beyond that which they must teach.

Rural School Department

Edited by MRS. M. L. FULKERSON, Salem, Oregon

THE OREGON NORMAL'S RURAL WEEK.

Over at the Normal School at Monmouth, Mr. Pittman, head of the rural school department, has been trying for three years to train teachers for rural school work. For three years he has talked to his classes and urged them to read all books and magazines available, concerning rural schools. The results were good, of course, but he felt that they might be better. Other sciences require laboratories, why should the science of education be an exception? Mr. Pittman believed in a laboratory for rural teachers and broached the subject to President Ackerman. Together they persuaded the rest of the faculty to fall into line and the Rural Week was planned for February 18-24. The weather man did his part by sending the very worst weather possible for the occasion in order that the student-teachers might have a taste of the pleasure of wading through mud and snow in a Western Oregon winter. Arrangements were made with the county superintendents of Benton, Marion, Polk, and Washington counties and schools selected to which students were to be sent. On Friday preceding Rural Week, Mr. Pittman led his class out of chapel and sent them out to the rural communities. On Monday after the week of visiting, the county superintendents and rural supervisors returned, each with his consignment of teachers, each group trying to outdo the others in enthusiasm. The scheme was hailed everywhere with delight and was more successful than the most optimistic dared hope.

We are planning to have a statement of the results as reported by Mr. Pittman and his class in another number of the magazine, but with the thought that the letters, etc., sent to the resident teachers and those given the students on their departure from the Normal would be of interest to all rural teachers, we are giving them space in this issue. Perhaps some of the questions will enable us to "see ourselves as others see us." Under date of February 12, the following letter was sent to the resident teacher in each district chosen for visitation:

"On behalf of the Oregon Normal I wish to thank you in advance for co-operating with us to make our Rural School Week a success. We are pleased that you are willing to take two or three of our young people into your school and into your community for a week. They will arrive on Sunday, the 18th. I trust someone can meet them at the station. They are coming to you to study the rural school with a view to fitting themselves to teach in the country. They most likely are entirely without experience and probably will have never seen a rural school until they visit yours. They come, therefore, as students, not as critics. They come anxious to learn and to do all they can to help you, for, in doing so, they will help themselves. I trust and know that you will give them a glad welcome, make them feel at home in your school, on the play ground with the children, and in the community with the people. They probably are from the town and know nothing of the country—its life, its problems, its advantages and disadvantages. They may not know a silo from a sausage mill, a Jersey cow from a Plymouth Rock chicken; so, be patient with their ignorance, sympathetic with their hopes, permit them to work all you can and all they will just so it does not disturb your school work. Advise them as to how to get on with people and assist them in any other way that you know will be of assistance to a poor beginning rural teacher. Remember your own beginning and be kind.

"These students are very limited in means. Many of them in the class are working their way through school by their own effort. Naturally, therefore, they want to live just as cheaply as possible during the week that they are with you. Any kindness that may be shown them, therefore, that will reduce their expense to a minimum will be greatly appreciated by me and by them. With the hope that they each might be able to work some while with you I have had them make a bit of preparation to teach certain phases of the work. After the first day, if you think these young people are safe and can be trusted to try their hand a bit, you might let them teach, increasing the amount during the week as they show themselves able to measure up to the responsibility. This will be lots of fun for you and very profitable to them and I think even the children will enjoy it. They might also assist you by writing your assignments on the board, cleaning the boards, putting on the blackboard borders, assisting any slow child with his work, drilling pupils on any work that requires drill, assisting with school housekeeping, teaching games, etc.

"I trust that it will be possible to have a community meeting at your school on Friday afternoon or night, the 23d, so that these young people may know what a community is and so they may have the experience of meeting the people. With this in mind, I have had them collect material suitable for a Washington birthday program. They may be able to assist you with it. On Saturday, the 24th, there will be a meeting of all of these student teachers to which I trust you can go. Your county superintendent will conduct this as he sees best. Some one from the Normal School faculty will participate in the program of the day.—M. S. Pittman, Head of of Rural School Department, Oregon Normal School."

The list of questions following were sent to the resident teachers as a guide in reporting their visitors:

1. Did the student meet you with good spirit? Was it easy to get acquainted? Did your friendship improve on acquaintance? If not, why not?

2. Did she get acquainted with the pupils easily? What ability did she show in playing with them?

3. What teaching was done by her? With what success did she teach? Did her work improve rapidly?

4. In her work where did she seem strongest? Where weakest? Did she seem to be strong in subject matter? With what grade was she the most successful?

5. Was she watchful and alert to be of assistance to you? Was she too anxious?

6. Did you see any signs of bad temper? Discourtesy? If so, explain.

7. Did the student show good ability to discipline a room? What in your opinion was her strongest quality? Weakest quality?

8. Did she meet any of the people of the community? If so, was she at ease? Did she make them feel at ease?

9. Did the student show ability to appraise people at their real worth or did appearance go a long way? What do the people say of her where she stayed?

10. What are some of the things the children have said of her since she left?

11. Did the student seem prone to use slang? Were there any signs or affectation? What? Was the student on time for all duties?

12. Do you recommend this person as a rural school teacher? What sort of place will she suit best?

The letter and questions printed below were given to each student on leaving the Normal for the week in the rural community:

You are now starting on a week of observation in the rural schools of Washington, Polk, Marion and Benton counties. I trust that you are going with joyous hearts, willing hands, open eyes, and thoughtful minds to see, to think, to help, to learn, to serve, to get, to give and that throughout all the rest of your lives you may remember with pleasure and profit the observations and experiences of this week. You are going as students, not critics, as one who earnestly desires to leave all with whom you meet happy and thankful that they met you. You carry with you the good wishes and the good name of the Oregon Normal School. It will rejoice with you in all that you accomplish, be proud of you for your fine effort and be measured by what you say and do. That you may have some help in your observations the following suggestions are given you. You will seek the information that is herein asked for and will make a report in writing to the department when you return. Be tactful, happy and earnest in securing and reporting your findings.

1. What is the size in acres of the school district in which you are visiting?

2. What is its valuation? What is the tax rate for school purposes alone? What is the amount of school funds thus raised?

3. What is the length of the school term and what is the salary of the teacher?

4. What is the entire school budget of the district and from what sources did it come and for what purpose is it being spent this year?

5. Name the occupations of the people of this district. Report fully on the most important one: (a) Of what does it consist? (b) How many families of the district are engaged in it? (c) How many in other industries? (d) What is the average gross annual product of the district measured in value? (e) How is it marketed, by individuals or by an organization? (f) Where is it marketed and what is the present price per unit? (g) Visit the best example of this industry in the district so that you may tell of this in detail.

6. In your judgment are the people of this district engaged in the best business for their territory?

7. To what extent do they use the Agricultural College? How many people in the district have attended the Farmers' Week within the last three years?

8. What county agencies are being used for the improvement of rural industries?

9. What nationalities are represented in the school district? Have they united into Americans or are the racial tendencies still distinct? Do they still have any social or religious organizations that are peculiar to their former nationality?

10.   How many churches and of what faith are there in the district? Are they thriving or decadent?   Do they work harmoniously or is there denominational discord?   Is the church providing for social needs of the young people?   Is there a Sunday school in the district?   If so, how well attended?

11.   What organizations are there in the district that have for their purpose the industrial improvement of the community?

12.   What organizations are there for the entertainment and growth of the women?   For the young?

13.   If the organizations are succeeding to whom does the community give credit?   If organizations have been organized and died, why did they die?

14.   What is the character of entertainments most common?   In your opinion what does the community most need along social lines?

15.   What is the size of the school ground?

16.   Is the house properly located to give the maximum service?   Beauty? Protection of property?

17.   Is the building properly lighted as to amount?   Direction?

18.   Is it properly heated?   What system of heating is used?   What did it cost?   Where was it purchased?

19.   What provision is made for the water supply?

20.   Where are the toilets located?   Are they sanitary?   How are they kept so?

21.   What other buildings are located on the grounds?   If there is a play shed, how was it secured?

22.   What has been done by the school board to make the interior of the school room beautiful?   By the teacher and the children?   By parent-teachers association?

23.   What has been done by school board to make the school grounds beautiful?   By the children and the teacher?   By the parent-teacher association?   What did you do to make the school more beautiful?

24.   What system was used for getting children into school building and into their seats?   How were the seats arranged as to size and grade?

25.   Name the type of morning exercises for the five mornings you were present.

26.   Copy the daily program in use in this school and place it as a supplement to this report.

27.   What three games did you teach the children during the week?

28.   How are the little children kept employed?   What assistance were you able to render in this particular?

29.   To what extent are monitors used in the school?

30.   Are there any retarded children in the school?   What was responsible for this retardation?

31.   When are the small children excused for the day?   Why at that hour?

32.   What subject do the children of the school enjoy most?   Why?

33.   Make out the last monthly report of the teacher to the county superintendent and attach it to this report as a supplement.   Be sure that you understand every detail of it.

34.   What organizations are there in the school for the stimulation of the children?   Write a brief report of the best one and attach as a supplement.

35.   Is there a Parent-Teacher Association?   What is it doing?

36.   What organizations exist in the community as a result of the effort of the school?

37.   To what extent is the teacher entertained in the homes of the community?

38.   Does the school situation in this community favor consolidation of schools?   What is the sentiment on the subject among the patrons of the community.

39.   What is the attitude of the people toward the county unit of school administration and supervision?

40. To what extent is the school used as an industrial center? As a social center?

41. What in your judgment are the five best points of the school? What in your judgment does the school most need?

If the information that is called for in the foregoing questions is carefully worked out by you by reference to your note book and your text, I think you will find it exceedingly helpful to you. I believe you will find it a piece of work of which you will always be proud. You may have some hardships this week. If so, know that they are but samples of real life. Life all depends upon how we take it. "Two men looked through prison bars, one saw mud, the other saw stars." Who will see the mud this week? Who will see the stars? Those who look for them. Let me remind you of three things. (1) Take care of your health; it is your bank account. (2) Take care of your reputation; it is your passport to good society and honorable position. (3) Take care of the reputation of the Oregon Normal School; it is your best professional friend. Good luck! God bless you! I am expecting YOU to make good!—M. S. Pittman.

* * *

OTHER PHASES OF MORAL EDUCATION.

The most important activity of the child is his play. Several theories, with all of which the reader no doubt is familiar, have been advanced to explain this fact. I shall not discuss all of these theories but rather lay emphasis on but one, and that is, that the child's play is a preparation, a rehearsal, for the later activities of his life. Different from most adults, he gets the keenest pleasure out of a vigorous activity of his muscular and nervous systems. As his principal business at this period of his life is to grow and growth can come only through vigorous activity, this is perfectly natural and he should be given the opportunities for this activity. His second most important business is to learn; this he does normally through imitation. Therefore, it is entirely natural that he do those things which others about him are doing, the activities or games which he sees others engaging in. In these two facts are contained the principal reasons for the child's playful life and the reason why we should study how to utilize his play.

God put in the child's nature the instinct to play that he might learn the lessons of life, physical, moral, and intellectual. Schools do not make up a part of nature's scheme for child training; on the contrary, play is nature's school. Through the natural play activities, every moral virtue or fault can be learned. Children in their play are enacting selfishness or unselfishness, honesty or dishonesty, truth or falsehood, and every other in the category. The play supervisor, the teacher, the parent, can direct play into channels where the good alone is taught, but if the play be unguarded, no one knows what will be played, what lessons will be learned.

Allow me to give an instance of a wise use of the instinct. I know a mother who has two girls and a boy between the ages of ten and fourteen. For the girls she has fitted up an extra room in her house, a play home. With low partitions made of beaver board, she has divided this room into four parts. One is the little girls' play kitchen, another their dining room, another a bed room and fourth a sitting room. Each room is furnished with miniature furniture. The kitchen contains a stove and kitchen utensils, the dining room a dining table, buffet, etc., the bed room a doll's bed and the sitting room the furniture belonging to the room. Here the little girls bring their dolls and play home-making. Here they learn home-mindedness and mother-mindedness; here they learn self sacrifice, consideration for others, devotion to duty, love for children, and a deep appreciation of the responsibilities of the housewife and mother and all out of their play.

For the boy who is the oldest, she has fitted up in the basement a workshop with tools of all kinds and a small gymnasium with simple apparatus, boxing gloves, a punching bag, etc. In the shop, the boy plays at working, plays he is supporting himself and learns self reliance, initiative, responsibility and courage to face the obligations of life. In the plays in his gymnasium, in his boxing and contests of skill with other boys, he is learning quickness of thought and judgment, fair play, consideration for others' rights, and the necessity of clean living to build up his body and make it strong and hard.

This instance is typical of a wise use of play. I could give many similar uses being made of the instinct in the school. The fact that I wish to emphasize is that in the child's play there is far more of moral growth than in any talks or stories which we may use in the school room. The parent who is wise will go so far as he can afford it do as did the mother of whom I spoke and provide for his children opportunities to rehearse at home life's activities. Groups of parents, too, will, by collective action, provide play grounds near their homes where their children may romp and play and strive against each other in their game life and gain in such manner all the moral growth which naturally arises from such activities. And in like manner, the teacher who is wise will encourage parents to do this and will utilize and promote play at the school.

By social life I have reference particularly to the association in parties and in keeping company together of adolescent boys and girls. Before adolescence, the sexes as a rule play apart, boys with boys and girls with girls. With the passage of puberty, however, we find the boy seeking the society of the girl and vice versa. This is as it should be and, properly safe-guarded, such association may, probably will, result in great good to both. Mary, though, in choosing her beau is in danger of finding the wrong kind. Bear in mind that the girl matures earlier than the boy and, consequently, when she reaches sixteen, probably the most critical year of the boy-struck age, she is much more of a woman physically than John is a man at the same age. Hence, she is very likely to find her male company with some young fellow who is from nineteen to twenty-one years of age. This young fellow may be the blase, the sophisticated type, that is, he has seen something of life, he has drunk a little, he smokes freely, and believes that because of these experiences, he is very much of a man. He boasts a good deal about what he has done in college, of his athletic career, of his social life, and of what he is going to do when he gets out into the world. Mary is at the age when the romantic appeals to her and she is naturally strongly influenced by him. If the youth is clean minded and of high ideals, it is all right; if, on the contrary, he believes it manly to tempt the girl, Mary had better be in other company. The father who says to her, "Mary, you must not go with this young fellow; I forbid it," is making a grave mistake. Mary has read of maidens who were shut up in dark dungeons to keep them from marrying the objectionable knights, of young Lochinvars who came in the night and carried away the beautiful ladies, and the romance of a clandestine love affair appeals to her. She pictures herself as the locked-up maiden and her lover as the brave knight, and she will move heaven and earth to meet the young fellow. If, however, the father appeals to her pride and shows her that she can do better, that the young fellow because of his habits and life is her inferior, he has reached her at her most sensitive point, her self respect, and he will probably very soon find Mary searching for excuses to keep from going out with the youth. Control of the adolescents' love affairs is not a matter for authority but for psychology. Young people must have parties and very probably will have love affairs. These are natural and normal needs, both of which are matters for tactful advice and guidance rather than absolute control. No wise parent forbids parties; he takes this normal desire as he finds it and sees that such life is furnished in ample quantity, no more, and in wholesome surroundings.

I shall not discuss in this article the moral value of the party but taking it for granted that this value will not be doubted, ask in conclusion a question. Ought not the school and the home to take steps to furnish social life in correct environment, in places under the control of the home? We too much allow these things to go unguarded and this is just as much true in the country as it is in the town. Let us consider these matters carefully and by proper utilization of the instincts which manifest themselves in the desire to play or to seek social life, take one of the greatest of steps in moral education.—A. C. Strange, Superintendent of Baker Schools.

* * *

SPELLING.

In the early days of modern elementary education, the three "R's"— reading, 'riting, and 'rithmetic—were considered the only fundamentals of an education. Spelling was merely an adjunct to each of these until after the art of printing was well developed and printed books began to appear. The need of an accepted standard for the arrangement (spelling) of the letters of each word soon became apparent. Out of this need grew our first so-called readers which were nothing more nor less than spellers with a few pages of real reading material in short sentences in the back part of the book. The method at first was wholly synthetic—a vowel and consonant were combined into syllables and the syllables into words. Then followed a time when such great stress was laid upon the pronunciation of each syllable in the word as it was spelled that it became an absurdity and in due course, syllabication was almost wholly ignored. Syllabication has its place in spelling as an aid to correct pronunciation and in writing, that the word may be divided correctly if it occurs at the end of a line.

In the days of our parents, spelling was considered quite an art and the "spelling bee" that was held at the little district school house was the most popular form of entertainment during the long winter evenings. But, unfortunately, spelling began to lose much of its prestige when the wave of a "fuller curriculum" began to sweep over our educational world. It was crowded on one side by science, jostled on the other by music, halted in front by art, and pushed in the rear by industrial work. So is it any wonder that the business world has complained of the "poor speller" product our schools have sent them?

Spelling was long considered a merely formal subject and until quite recent years was so taught. In fact, one will find it thus taught even today in many rural school where the teacher has not had the advantage of some instruction in present day methods. The mere pronunciation of the word and naming the letters in their proper relation to each other and the whole is not sufficient in this utilitarian age. We want no "lumber" in our store-room— the brain. Use is the keynote of the words we are learning to spell today. And if the learner is to be able to use the word it must be related to his experience, that is, there must be some word he already knows that he can use to interpret the new—a synonym if you please. When the new word is put before the child—in the lower grades it should be written on the board— the first thing he wants to know is what it says, otherwise it remains an unknown symbol to him. If it is an "ear" word, he can get the pronunciation through his knowledge of phonics; but it should not be diacritically marked— only the syllables and accent should be indicated; the former by underlining and not by separation. (Nothing but the essentials should enter into the child's mental image of the word.) If it is an unfamiliar sight word, the teacher should pronounce it for the child. It must be borne in mind that children know many, many words by sound that they do not know by sight— written or printed. If the word is new to him, he naturally wants to know what it means and the meaning therefore is naturally the second step in the process of learning the new word. Here the teacher's skill comes in in calling up—suggesting the right thing in the child's experience that will help him take possession of this new word and make it a part of his working vocabulary. If the new word is so wholly outside of his experience that it cannot be made understandable to him, what is the sense in teaching him to memorize the form of it? We sinned grievously in this respect in the past. How many learned to spell words, the meaning of which they had not the faintest idea? "Lumber," nothing but "lumber"! When the child knows the meaning of the word, he is ready to name and memorize the letters in it in their proper sequence, i. e., spell it. After much study and experimentation on this point, I am fully convinced there is no means so successful and at the same time economical of energy as visualization. From the moment the child's attention is first directed to the word written on the board, he is getting a visual image of it. This image is of the word as a whole until his mind is directed to the component parts by the teacher and he is asked to close his eyes and spell it. Closing the eyes helps the child to concentrate his mind on the mental picture of the word. If he can not "see" it he is asked to look again at the word on the board spelling it to himself as he does so. Then he tries to spell it with his eyes closed or writes it on the board or in the air. I like this much oral spelling at this point as it helps the auditory child to link the two. However, more children are visual-minded than auditory and the latter can be trained to acquire the ability to "see" mental images to a greater extent than one would suppose. And it is an acquisition decidedly worth while. Tests have proven conclusively that the fluent readers and good spellers are invariable visual minded.

The next step is to have the child use the word in an intelligent sentence. I use the word "intelligent" to mean that the context of the sentence must reveal the meaning of the word.

Each word should be taken through these four steps. Then a few minutes drill should follow to thoroughly fix the words in the pupils' memory. These drills may take the form of games such as "I'm thinking of a word that means——." The guesser says, "It is" and spells out the word he guesses. Then the It says "Yes, it is ——" or "No, it is not ——," pronouncing the word the child spelled. Or, instead of giving the synonym, the It may say "I'm thinking of a word that begins with ——," naming the first letter of it. The game proceeds as in the other. A visual drill is to have words on board—pupils close eyes—teacher erases a word—pupil spells word erased or writes it on board or paper, etc. Many similar devices will suggest themselves to the wide awake teacher.

After a little skill has been acquired, a teacher can teach a lesson of ten words to a class successfully in a twenty-minute recitation. One requisite for successful work in visualization is that the pupil must be responsive and alert. If his interest is keen he gives attention instinctively and his mind is in the most favorable state to get lasting impressions. Games and devices that have some play element thus appeal to the younger children through interest to which they owe their effectiveness.

If the teacher can not give more than ten minutes to the spelling class, then by all means let that time be given to the four steps outlined, after which the pupils can do the drill-part as seat work either by writing sentences using the word or writing the words with their synonyms. In this study work train the children to take pride in being able to write the word correctly after taking a careful look at it in the book. Do not permit mere copy work. After pupils know how to use the dictionary intelligently, all but the first step can be done by them at the study period. It is quite essential that the correct pronunciation be given so it is wise to have this much preparation given under the direction of the teacher. Since spelling is used only in writing, every lesson should properly end with a witten test; but, where this is not possible, because of lack of time, there should be such a test at least once a week over all the work covered in that time.—Lillian Dinius, Critic Teacher, Oregon Normal School.

* * *

A DOZEN NUMBER GAMES.

After the combinations have been developed daily drills are necessary to make them automatic. Games relieve the monotony of these drills. The following are games used in the primary department:

1. Climbing Ladders or Stairs.—Draw a ladder or steps on the blackboard. Write combinations, without answers on each rung or each step. Children take turns running up and down the ladder or stairs by giving the answers to the combinations. A miss means a fall.

2. Picking Fruit.—Draw a tree on the board with fruit on it. Write the combinations without answers, on the fruit. The game is to pick the fruit by giving the answers to these combinations. The fruit may be put into baskets drawn on the board and counted to show how many "apples" each child picked or how many fell to the ground thus keeping the combinations that require more drill.

3. Fishing.—Draw a fish on the board. Write combinations on the fish. The game is to catch fish by giving the answers to these combinations. Draw a circle for the pail into which these fish are put. The child having the most fish has won the game.

4. Stepping Stones.—Draw stones on the board, write the combinations on these stones. The game is to cross the river and keep the feet dry. A child that misses a combination has fallen into the water.

5. Race.—Write two rows of numbers on the board. Two children write the answers. The one writing them first has won the race.

6. Relay Race.—Write two rows of numbers. Divide the class into two teams. The leaders take the chalk and write one answer. Then they give the chalk to the next child in line who writes one answer and gives the chalk to the next in line who also writes an answer. The team which has all the answers written first has won.

7. The Ark.—Appoint a door keeper. One child leaves the class. The child raps and says, "May I come into the Ark." The door keeper answers, "Yes, if you know your name." Child asks, "What is my name?" Door keeper answers, 5 plus 3, or any combination you are drilling on. Child answers, "My name is eight." Door keeper says, "Can you write your name"? Child writes 5 plus 3 equals 8. Another child leaves the room and the game continues.

8. Number Class With Flash Cards.—Arrange the children in a line, call one end head and the other foot. Hold up the card with a combination written on it. The child at the head gives the answer. If he misses, the next child in line gives the answer and goes up. The honor is to reach the head and stay there. Always put the poorest one at the head to give him a chance.

9. Mail Carrier.—Save old envelopes and write the combinations on them. Appoint a mail carrier and several postmasters, station the postmasters in different parts of the room, name the stations 7, 8, 9, 10. The mail carrier delivers all the letters whose combinations make 7, to 7, all those that make 8, to 8, etc.

10. Railroad.—Draw ties and an engine on the board. Write the combinations on the ties. Name one end of the track your nearest town. The other end a city farther away. A child takes the pointer, gives the answers and travels from one city to the other. If he goes rapidly he is fast train, if slowly he is a freight. A talk on traveling is necessary before playing this game.

11. Stage Coach.—Number the children. Have the children sitting opposite numbered so their sum will be some combination you are drilling on. The leader tells a story using the answers to these combinations. When he says seven, 3 and 4 change places or they are caught. The first one caught becomes the leader and the game continues the story.

12. Baseball.—Have two rows of combinations written on the board. (1) Divide the class into two teams; (2) write the names of the teams on the board, the leaders' names first; (3) appoint a score keeper; (4) children alternate one from each side giving answers; (5) teacher time them with her watch, a mistake adds one second to the score; (6) write the score after each name on the board; (7) add the score. The team having the smaller score has won. The leader of each team will coach the poor ones in his team.—Elizabeth C. Riecker, Critic Teacher, Oregon Normal School.

* * *

HOW TO TEACH BUDDING.

During the present month orchard men are turning their attention from pruning to grafting and in some cases budding. It is therefore timely to teach Chapter 4 of Burkett, Stevens and Hill. It is a simple matter to work out lessons which demonstrate planting, pruning, grafting and budding. To illustrate this I have had Miss Agnes Carter, one of the student teachers at the Normal, prepare a type plan for presenting budding. With a few changes this plan can be substituted for grafting. I may say that if rose bushes be handy and the conditions favorable, nothing could be better than to bud the rose bush.

Lesson Plans on Budding.

1. What Is to Be Known: (a) Select a stock that is two or three years old; (b) cut a T-shaped incision in the bark; (c) pull the bark back from the wood; (d) select a strong bud from last year's growth; (e) make the cut for the bud directly above the bud; (f) insert the bud in the T-shaped incision; (g) tighten the bark over the bud; (h) take some raffia and twist it around the bud and incision, very tightly; (i) raffia should be left until the buds set.

2. What Is Known: Pupils will probably not know anything about making a bud.

3. What Is to Be Taught: (See a, b, c, d, e, f, g, h, i.)

4. What Is to Be Done: (a) Have pupils reproduce the lesson assigned from the text; (b) have the pupils do a piece of budding at their seats; (c) buds, wood, knife, and raffia should be on the desk.

---

1. Model of Method.—Children read the method of budding in the text or "Country Gentleman." The difficult words and expressions were cleared up in the assignment, the day previous.

2. Imitation.—What is our aim today, Alfred? (How to Bud.) You may all tell me what we are going to learn. (How to bud.) You may tell us how to bud, Bernie. (Bernie reproduces as follows from he text: In order to bud we will first select a stock that is two or three years old. Then you cut a T-shaped incision in the bark. The bark should then be pulled back and the bud put in the incision.)

3. Criticism.—Is the bud all finished now, Bernie, (Yes, I think so.) Is there any danger that the bud will fall out? (Oh, yes, I forgot to say that raffia should be twisted around the bud and incision.) Did Bernie leave anything out, John? (He didn't tighten the bark over the bud.) Can you add anything, Alfred? (The bud should be cut directly above the bud.)

4. Drill.—You may give all the steps in their order, Alfred. I will write them on the board as you give them: (a) Select a stock that is two or three years old; (b) make a T-shaped incision in the stock, and pull the bark back; (c) select a strong bud; (d) cut the bud directly above the bud; (e) insert the bud in the incision; (f) tighten the bark over the bud; (g) take some raffia and twist it around the bud and incision.

---

1. Model.—Now, children, I am going to do a piece of budding according to the points on the blackboard. You watch me closely so you will be able to do it when I have finished. (The teacher need not do the whole piece, before she asks the children to do it. She may only do a part of it and have the children imitate a small portion at a time. This will depend on the ability of your class.)

2. Imitation.—Children, you may select your stock and do the budding according to the points on the board.

3. Criticism.—(Teacher will move about freely, watching the pupils and helping them as they work.)

4. Drill.—Tonight you may all make two buds at home and bring them to school tomorrow.—L. P. Gilmore, Oregon Normal School.

＊   ＊   ＊

PUBLIC SCHOOL COMPOSITIONS.

In the public school composition contest, the winners for March were Dorothy Winters, Riverview, Lane county, and Teddy Ray Roberts, Reith, Umatilla county.

Getting a Fortune.

The best way to make money is to keep right at a thing. If you are not making very much money and a man comes along and says that he made a fortune there, do not run wherever it is to make a fortune. You may lose the little you have. Everybody will go and if everybody does one thing, all of them will not make anything. Keep getting little by little. Always tend to your own business. If you hear of some one who found a lump of gold by a white house, don't go by every white house you see looking for gold. You will not be apt to find it. It just happens that some one has lost it there. Never stop your work to try to find gold. Keep at what you are doing and you will win.—Dorothy Winters, age 10 years.

The Little Brook.

"You happy, merrily skipping brook,"
Said the maiden and the cook,
"You ripple, ripple all day through,
And at night when you should lie to rest
You ripple, ripple to do your best.
I think I hear your little song
Rippling, rippling all day long.
You murmur, murmur all the day,
With the pebbles and sand you play."
                    —Teddy Ray Roberts, age 10 years.

*   *   *

ARBOR DAY IN OREGON.

After this year, Western Oregon will observe Arbor Day on the second Friday in February and in the counties east of the Cascade mountains the present date—second Friday in April—will be observed. In many places the planting of trees is superfluous, there being already more than enough in the school yard. In such a case the pupils may be taught to choose the best and the undesirable ones may be taken out, thus giving the others a chance to make the most of themselves. In other places the soil is such that many trees will not thrive even if planted and cared for during the school term. When the school has closed and the pupils can not conveniently care for them, they dry up in the hot summer sun and wind, and the children come back in the fall, look sadly at their dead hope, and decide that planting trees is a useless task. A county superintendent in Central Oregon suggests that in such cases the pupils may well study trees and forests even if they can not have them at the door just now. Perhaps in a few years the situation will be different, and the little trees, chosen from a variety adapted to such conditions, will be planted and cared for properly. The object is a worthy one, so let us observe the day by honoring Nature in some manner wherever we are.

*   *   *

ARBOR DAY AND ITS PURPOSES.

On the rolling prairies of the great middle west, where but a scant natural tree growth meets the eye of the traveler, the idea of Arbor Day originated. The people felt the need of the groves denied them by nature, and they soon found that this need could be easily supplied.

True to the prevailing modern idea that new movements are most readily received by the younger persons, and that the best way of reaching this class is through the schools, one day each year was set apart for tree planting and tree study, and appropriate exercises were arranged to interest the boys and girls in this very important work.

Perhaps the necessity for interesting the older persons through the children was not so great as was at first seemingly apparent, for any one who is familiar with the prairie states knows that tree planting about the homes has far out-stripped tree planting on the school grounds, and that it would be difficult to trace the beginning of any of the splendid groves that are so common in the middle west to the influence of the schools; therefore one might be excused for being somewhat skeptical as to whether the inauguration of Arbor Day has accomplished its original purpose, which was to interest the people through the children in supplying the omissions of nature, and in training a new generation of men and women who would relieve the barrenness of some other new country by dotting its surface with trees.

If Arbor Day has not accomplished in full its original purpose, what then has it accomplished? In the prairie states, the chief result has been to interest the boys and girls in providing for the school grounds the shade trees that are so necessary to the comfort of the pupils, and that add so much to the beauty of the grounds; to train them to plant and cultivate flowers and shrubbery of all kinds, and last but not least, to lead them to appreciate beautiful surroundings. This training school will be reflected in their home life, both during their youth, and in later life, and many a well arranged ground may be traced to the training the boy or girl received during Arbor Day exercises.

The point upon which we are somewhat skeptical is as to whether we have reached the parents to any great extent through the children by the Arbor Day idea, and as to whether the children themselves have been interested in an extended growing of trees, and indeed, as to whether they should be. Our observation in the prairie states would lead us to know that the people do not care to have the country forested, but prefer to have the ground clear for farming operations; while their lack of timber is easily supplied by substitutes that answer quite as well, both for fuel and for other purposes; and in timbered countries, such as the Willamette valley, where pupils often see their fathers endeavoring to rid themselves of the trees so that they may grow necessary crops, they can not be expected to be interested in the growing of trees, except those which bear fruit, or useful products of some kind; therefore, we must conclude that the only utilitarian benefit we have derived from the celebration of Arbor Day is the knowledge they have acquired of beautifying both school and home grounds, and we might add, the desire to do so.

We believe, however, that the greatest result of the celebration of Arbor Day is not utilitarian, in the commonly accepted use of the word, but that the result that is of supreme importance is character building. If the boy who is rough and rude by nature can be interested in growing and observing a beautiful flower, his character will be modified, and he will think oftener of better things. If he is careless in his habits, and cares little for the arrangement and placing of his belongings in either home or school, helping to plan a flower bed, or to arrange a bit of shrubbery will lead him to see how much can be added to the appearance of anything by just a little care, and to love order and to dislike confusion. He will be a better farmer, a better business man because of this, and what is of extreme importance, he will get a greater joy out of his life's work because he has learned to be systematic and to love the beautiful.

A love for nature undoubtedly brings one nearer to nature's God, and the boy or girl who is taught to love and care for flowers, and to beautify his or her surroundings in every way possible, will grow to be a better man or woman because of this training; therefore, while we should not forget in arranging our Arbor Day programs that we wish to train the boys and girls to cultivate flowers and shrubs for the purpose of beautifying both the school and home grounds, we must remember that the primary purpose is to develop in them a love for the beautiful in character as well as in nature, to the end that they may enjoy to the fullest extent the world in which God has placed them, and do their share towards helping others to attain the same results.—S. S. Duncan, Superintendent of Yamhill County.

*   *   *

ARBOR DAY IN DISTRICT TWENTY-NINE.

"The planting of trees should have a special significance to every child in our beloved state. Let no school fail to observe Arbor Day in a proper manner this year."

Thus ended the circular letter sent out by the superintendent of schools to every teacher in his territory. The Slip-of-a-girl trying to keep up the dignity of the office of teacher in District Twenty-nine had just received the communication, though it had been mailed from the office ten days previously. A passing neighbor had hailed the "school ma'am" just as she was mounting the stile at the entrance to the school grounds on this particular April afternoon, and handed her a bundle of letters from the outside world. Getting the mail once a week was a luxury in District Twenty-nine, but it sometimes happened. This was one of the times when there had been no letters for two weeks and the Slip-of-a-girl sat right down on top of the stile to read her treasures. The sun had dropped behind the fir trees when she replaced the Arbor Day circular in its envelope picked up her lunch basket and continued her walk to the place she called home for the week.

"Arbor Day next Friday," she said to herself. "I wonder if the superintendent really thinks another tree or two planted in this wilderness would mean anything to my boys and girls. Trees to the right of them, trees to the left of them, and brush in between. It would seem more like doing things if we cut out some of this thicket and let the sunlight in. Why not? I'm going to ask the trustee this very evening."

The school house had stood for two generations in a tangle of sweet-briar, hazel-brush, hard hack and vines of various kinds over which towered tall firs and spreading maples. A narrow path led to the door in front of which there was really cleared space enough to permit a group of twenty children to stand without much crowding.

"Mr. Jones," began the Slip-of-a-girl, as the school trustee settled him-self for his after supper smoke that evening. "Next Friday is Arbor Day and I have a letter from the county superintendent requesting that we observe it in a proper manner."

"Well just what does he mean by that?" drawled Mr. Jones, taking his pipe from his mouth and blowing a cloud of smoke into the room.

"He means that he wants trees planted on the school grounds in the county and the state has set aside Friday afternoon for that purpose. I've been thinking that it might be better to trim out the underbrush and give the trees we already have a chance. Couldn't you see some of the men in the district and get them to come over for an hour or two Friday afternoon? We could do wonders in that time if everybody would help. The children are too small to do much cutting but they could pile the brush and burn it."

The trustee looked steadily at the Slip-of-a-girl for a full minute and then he said, "Hump! It seems to me you're taking a pretty high swing at things, bein' as you've only been here five weeks. Think us farmers ain't got nothin' to do in the spring o' the year? The superintendent is goin' a little too far when he talks about tree plantin', and the like. We elected him to run the schools and nothin' else. We're payin' you twenty-three and a third dollars a month and boardin' you around and we can't afford to have you awastin' time on trees and brush, and I'm agoin' to tell him so next time I go into town."

"But, Mr. Jones, it's a state law and—"

"Hang the state law! No teacher we've ever had before has paid any attention to it as I know on."

The Slip-of-a-girl wanted to say, "That's very evident," but she didn't. Her chin tilted a little, that's all.

The next morning she had a confidential talk with the children concern-ing the significance of Arbor Day. She told them of her desire to let the sunshine in at the windows, of the beauty of the grounds if only a little clearing could be done, but she concluded by saying, "Of course, we shall have to give it up because we cannot cut the brush ourselves and the men are all busy."

"Oh, gee! Teacher don't give it up. It would be such fun. Please let us try," said twelve-year-old Harry Black.

"We'll bring axes. We're big enough to chop and the little kids can carry the brush," chimed in Henry who was Harry's twin.

Everybody was so delighted over what they considered a frolic that the Slip-of-a-girl took heart and agreed to make the trial.

Excitement ran high on Arbor Day in District Twenty-nine. The twins had smuggled their big brothers' axes to school in the morning. The other children brought hatchets and hoes and rakes, while little Jack Mitchell timidly approached the teacher's desk and lisped, "Teacher, I brought thum matcheth 'cauthe maybe we'll want to make thum bon-fireth."

As soon as lunch had been eaten everybody began to work under the leadership of the Slip-of-a-girl. The twins wielded the big axes with all the power available in their willing arms and the smaller boys tugged at the tangled vines, tearing them out root and branch. They played they were pioneers fighting Indians and building homes with Daniel Boone in Kentucky.

Over at the Black farm consternation reigned for had not Sam and Joe hunted for their axes for a solid hour after dinner? Had they not planned to fell the big fir in the barn lot on this fine April afternoon? Kathleen, the baby and family pet, stoutly denied all their accusations and stuck to her first statement:

"Harry 'n Henry took 'em."

"Nonsense!" said Sam. "What would they want with axes at school? Your four-year-old head is muddled, Kathleen."

"Harry 'n Henry took 'em, I say," and she stamped her little foot by way of emphasis.

Joe looked at her meditatively for a moment and then said, "Well, Sam, we may save time by going over to the school and asking the twins. They may know where the axes are. Anyway we can't do anything here."

"Just as well, boys, said their father. "I think Kathleen knows what she is talking about. The twins may have had the axes and left them somewhere." So Sam and Joe hurried over the half mile of woodland to the school premises. There they stopped short and looked at each other in amazement.

"Well, if that isn't the limit!" said Joe. "Kathleen was right. Look at the twins."

The twins were endeavoring to trim the low bows from a fir tree that stood at the corner of the schoolhouse. They found it hard work to reach as high as they desired but were manifesting an unusual amount of perseverance in their efforts. Henry spied the big boys first.

"Here, you fellows!" he shouted. "Come and help. I'm Daniel Boone and this is in Kentucky."

"Harry give me the ax. What do you mean by running off with it?" demanded Sam.

The Slip-of-a-girl came up just then with her arms full of hazel-brush and explained the meaning of the unusual proceedings.

"That's a bright idea all right," said Sam when she had finished. "I wonder why no one ever thought of it before. Joe, why didn't we do it when we were going to school?"

"It isn't too late yet," put in Harry. "And it will look a whole lot better than standing there watching the rest of us."

"Right you are, kid. Come on, Joe," and Sam taking his ax from the smaller boy soon finished the trimming of the big fir.

With two sturdy young men to wield the axes "Daniel Boone" and his comrades made short work of the thicket that had hitherto hidden the beauty of the spot. Little Jack Mitchell danced about in glee when the Slip-of-a-girl used his "matcheth" to light a brush fire. By four o'clock the oldest inhabitant would have believed himself in another world, had he happened along, for the schoolhouse could actually be seen from the county road.

In less than a week every man and woman in the community had heard of the wonderful change and most of them made it a point to call at the school and see for themselves. Many wondered how those beautiful maple trees could have been there all these years and no one know it. Then it suddenly dawned upon some one that if the schoolhouse had two or three coats of white paint it would look more in keeping with its surroundings. It was not long before the paint was a reality and District Twenty-nine began to be known as a wide-awake community.

The trustee, however, was much concerned over the awakening, and when he had occasion to go to the county seat he called at the superintendent's office, and said he: "That Slip-of-a-girl you sent out to teach our school is a disturbin' element. She's got the whole neighborhood stirred up over the school. They've gone ahead ag'in my orders and painted the buildin', and now they're wantin' to buy factory desks to put inside. The Lord only knows where it'll end up at. Now, didn't you say to plant trees on Arbor Day?"

"Yes, that is what I said." replied the superintendent.

"Well, that Slip-of-a-girl went contrary to your orders, for she and her scholars grubbed up trees and brush all afternoon. What do you say to that?"

"What do I say? Just this: I have been out there and seen the wonderful change and I say, it is a poor rule that won't work both ways. That Slip-of-a-girl has let the sun shine into your district in more ways than one."— Mrs. M. L. Fulkerson in American Primary Teacher.

*   *   *

BIRD GAMES.

One of the best ways to teach birds to the children is through "games." They make such a cheerful happy time in the day's work, and how readily the children learn the names of the various birds. Do have some "bird games" for through them the child's vocabulary is much increased. The "bird" composition is not a hard task at all after the children have played some of the games.

Let five or six children who do the best tracing and crayon work, take big colored pictures (Perry Pictures are very clear) of birds to the window and trace them on the manila drawing paper. Then color them, making the colors just as bright as in the Perry Picture. Mount these on stiff cards 8x18 (the 18-inch side is the top.)

Print descriptive adjectives, suitable for the bird on the card. For example, paste a crow on the card at the right end; print in front of it, "bold, robber crow." Have ten or fifteen such cards, "If I Were." Place these cards along the chalk tray. Teacher asks: . "Earl, if you were a bird what bird would you like to be?"

Earl (with card held by both hands so that each child in the room may see it) answers: "If I were a bird, I'd be the bold, robber crow."

Each child takes the card to his desk as his turn comes. To replace cards on chalk tray when all have been taken off, the teacher says: "Earl, what bird are you?" and Earl (placing card on chalk tray) answers: "I am a bold, robber crow."

At first have the game with only a few cards, then increase the number slowly so that later there will be enough cards to make a pleasing game for some "Mother's Day"—perhaps. This pleases parents.

Prepare charts 9x24 (9-inch side for top.) Paste at top, picture of a bird (Audubon Picture), perhaps of a chickadee. Below print his menu—grasshoppers, beetles, caterpillars, moths, ants, wasps, bugs, flies and spiders (found in Farmers Bulletin, Washington, D. C.) Have ten such charts. Show one or two at a time—just as the birds are studied. Teach the length of the bird and at least one important fact about it.

Now we are ready for the game, "The Farmer's Friends." At intervals across top of front blackboard, drive fine wire nails eight inches apart. At four inches to left and right of center of the charts, punch holes. Hang the ten charts up.

Teacher—"If you were a farmer which bird would you like best, James?"

James (with pointer in hand and standing near the chickadee chart)—"I would like the chickadee best. He is 5¼ inches long. He likes suet and bread crumbs. He helps the farmer because he eats grasshoppers, beetles, caterpillars, etc." (pointing to each word on the chart as he names it.)

Use charts 24x18. Use 18-inch side for the top. Let apt child color a purple gallinule, a black-necked stilt, and a blue heron (Perry Pictures.) Cut them out. Mount in a vertical row on left side of chart. Opposite the purple gallinule print "tall"; opposite the black-necked stilt print "taller"; and opposite the blue heron print "tallest."

"Comparison of Adjectives" or "Adjective Game."—Ask a child to read the chart. He says, "The purple gallinule is tall; the black-necked stilt is taller; but the blue heron is tallest. Teacher covers the black-necked stilt, child says, "The purple gallinule is tall but the blue heron is taller," etc.

Let three children stand. Ask another child to tell about the heights of the children, etc.

Have six or eight such charts. Easy way to teach comparison of adjectives and the child acquires a long list of bird names. Hang these charts on the nails across front of board.

Mount fifty bird pictures (Perry, or Audubon) on neat gray mats. Cut off the margin, paste only the two upper corners, then paste name of bird on back of picture. In various ways, during the weeks given to bird study, draw attention of the children to the names of the birds. For some program or when a mother is visiting the school, let the children see what child can name all the birds with no help. It is a surprise to parents to see how many birds a child can name. These cards may be hooked to a wire stretched across front of room.

Cards 6x12. Use 12-inch side for top. Print, "I saw a ——" "I saw an ——" "I have seen a ——" etc. on them, using various form of "see" and the articles "a" and "an." Place some mounted pictures and these cards in a chalk tray. Let child make a sentence with "I see a ——" with the card and picture to read "I see a hawk," etc. I know that pupils often learn the use of "see" and "saw" from this game. The teacher may ask: "Jane, what bird do you see?" Jane says: "I see an American goldfinch."

Here is a good little game for sense training: Child steps to front of room and says, "Whoo, Whoo!" Next child stands by his side and says, "Whoo, Whoo!"—adding, "chickadee-dee-dee." The third child in line says, "Whoo, Whoo!"—"Chickadee-dee-dee" and adds the call, "Teacher, teacher, teacher, teacher," etc.

Continue the game until there are as many songs imitated as the children can make; the fifteenth child giving the fourteen sounds made before his turn, also adding one for himself.—Indianola Willcuts, Holyoke, Minn.

The National Education Association

By E. D. RESSLER, Corvallis

The fifty-fifth annual convention of the National Education Association will be held in Portland this summer, July 7 to 14. This will be the first session in the Northwest and the seventh west of the Rocky Mountains. San Francisco has had the honor in 1888 and 1911; Los Angeles in 1899 and 1907; Salt Lake City in 1913 and Oakland in 1915. The largest membership of these six meetings west of the Rockies was at San Francisco in 1911, reaching a total of 18,587, of which California furnished 6961, Oregon 255, Washington 241, Idaho 123. It exceeded 13,000 at Oakland, 17,000 at Los Angeles in 1907 and as far back as 1899 at Los Angeles it reached 13,656. It was 11,573 at Salt Lake City. Well informed officers of the association estimate a minimum of 10,000 visitors this year at Portland from east of the Rockies. The largest membership in the history of the Association was at Boston in 1903, reaching 34,983. Last year at New York it exceeded 27,000.

Why do so many teachers travel thousands of miles annually to attend this convention? There are many reasons, among others (a) the pleasure and profit of travel and sight-seeing; (b) the value of the general and departmental programs; (c) the opportunity of seeing, hearing and meeting the leaders in their profession; (d) the informal interchange of experiences and professional opinions with their fellow teachers from many states; (e) the professional inspiration and enthusiasm always characteristic of national conventions of any organization. State headquarters are maintained, receptions given and other experiences had which make these conventions epochs in the lives of the teachers who attend.

The National Teachers' Association was organized in 1857 at Philadelphia, annual sessions being held except in 1861, 1862 and 1867. In 1871 at the St. Louis meeting the name was changed to National Educational Association. No sessions were held in 1878 and 1906. In 1907 at the Los Angeles meeting the name was again changed to National Education Association of the United States. The present organization comprises twenty-one departments covering all phases of education, such as superintendence, kindergarten, elementary, secondary, higher, normal, vocational, music, business, rural and agricultural, library, physical, etc. The general association and all departments meet in annual convention in July except the Department of Superintendence, which meets in February. A number of other departments are also represented at the February meeting. Each department has its separate organization. The officers of the general association are a president, twelve vice-presidents, secretary, treasurer, board of directors, executive committee and board of trustees. The board of directors is composed of one representative from each state, elected by the active members of the state; there are also a few ex-officio members but the large majority are state directors. There is a permanent fund of about $200,000, the income of which together with direct appropriations from annual income from memberships, is used in making exhaustive, expert investigations of professional matters through committees.

The annual meeting continues for a week, general sessions occurring in the evenings except two half day sessions, and the departmental programs occupying the day time. The topics and speakers are carefully chosen with the purpose of presenting the latest and most authoritative discussions of the many general and special problems in education. The reports of special committees, some of which have been at work for years, are always a feature of the program. Among the committees to report at the Portland meeting are Salaries, Tenure and Pensions; Health Problems in Education; Vocational Education and Vocational Guidance; Economy of Time in Elementary Education; Culture Element and Economy of Time in Education; Re-organization of Secondary Education; and Military Training in Schools.

Naturally, many meetings are held simultaneously, but the printed volume of proceedings contains all the formal papers and part of the discussion. All members are entitled to these proceedings, issued in a bound volume of about 1000 pages or in magazine form issued in ten monthly numbers. The membership fee is $2 per year. No pedagogical library is complete without the N. E. A. volumes, which really constitute an encyclopedia of American education.

What sort of a showing will Oregon make as host to this great association. The city of Portland can be trusted to take care of its part, which is a highly important one. It involves months of organization, scores of hard-working committeemen and thousands of dollars of expense. Just two things are asked of the teachers, namely: (a) The taking of advance memberships at $2 each and (b) the securing of advance membership of each school district at $2. For this money there is sufficient reward in the volume of proceedings, a valuable addition to the school library as well as to the teacher's library. But in addition to this our state reputation and honor are at stake. The success of this great convention will be determined in great part by the membership. The business of the association requires a large annual revenue, which is derived chiefly from the region of the annual convention. Because of the comparatively small number of teachers in the Northwest, a heroic effort must be made, and the brunt must be borne by the entertaining state. The greatest record ever made was by Utah in 1913 when 108 per cent of her teachers enrolled. The next best record was made by California in 1888 with 86 per cent. There are over 6000 public school teachers in Oregon and enough additional in the private schools and higher institutions to swell the number above 7000. With over 2500 school districts, which are to be called on, a new departure invented by our Oregon representative on the board of directors, O. M. Plummer of Portland, we have a chance to go after these records of California and Utah.

By the time this April number of the Oregon Teachers Monthly is in the hands of its readers, the campaign for advance memberships will have been begun. More than 4000 Oregon teachers are readers of the Oregon Teachers Monthly, which means that one third of our force must be reached by the remaining. Tell your neighbor that you are sending your $2 to the county superintendent or whoever is the authorized person to receive memberships and invite him to go and do likewise. Then make an appointment to present the matter to your school board and have the clerk send that membership in. While this appeal is made to our state pride and professional loyalty, let us not overlook the fact that thousands of teachers from all sections of the country will pay this membership fee and in addition spend many times that amount in traveling to the meeting and attending the convention, because they want to for the values cited above.

The Why of General Science

By L. P. GILMORE, Oregon Normal School

I shall treat the subject along three distinct lines: Reasons for any form of science instruction, the content of general science, and what the advocates of general science claim for it.

To discuss fully the reasons for teaching science is to strike at the very roots of education in search for an aim. Hardly a science or mathematics teacher who has been in the profession ten years or more, who does not realize that we are right now in a period of transition and that during the past decade content and method have been constantly shifting to meet the changing conditions. The days of using the catch problem as a test of ones mathematical ability are past. Likewise we no longer measure ones scientific aptitude in terms of the wonderful; instead nowadays we draw as far as possible from the individual environment the topics for study, and search for principles which may be used later in solving difficult phenomena; in other words it is more of a crime today not to be able to make a plant grow well than it is not to know its genus and species.

Later the aim shifted so as to include only such things as were of practical value to the man or child. Hardly an educator past fifty but recalls how the students of the so-called humanities looked upon this type of practicalism as narrow and illiberal. The standards by which subjects were measured a quarter of a century ago were distinctly cultural. Hence the idea of the useful was relegated to the background and science and mathematics became secondary to the dead languages and kindred subjects. These were days when educators believed in formal discipline so it is but natural that science try to justify its right to a place in the course of study in terms of mental discipline. Consequently looking beyond the question of utility, teachers began inquiring into the habits of thought which science studies should foster. As a result today we use as one of our strongest arguments for the studying of science, the notion that conscientious study of science quickens the senses in making accurate observations, in analyzing phenomena logically.

We have since learned that the more successful peoples of the world owe their commercial supremacy to applied science and that, broadly speaking, the keystone of their educational structure is the fitting of the individual to his environment for better service to society. Science instruction serves this aim by "giving such an insight into nature as would stimulate the proper adjustment to ones environment." Our educational pulse has been quickened by the examples of these peoples and we too are coming to use science as such a tool. So to express it differently, we are in an era where science teachers are attempting more than ever to make their courses practical and usable. How this is being accomplished will be more fully explained later. To summarize, science aims have gradually evolved from the use of the wonderful as the central idea, to the practical with emphasis on the disciplinary and finally to the practical with emphasis on its application to living conditions. If general science is to be entitled to a place among sciences, it must be proven that the topics studied and the ends sought are coincident with those of science. It must further be shown that it serves these ends better than any other science that might be offered in the upper grammar and freshman year of the high school. Accordingly it is necessary that we spend a brief time on the content of general science.

As chairman of a committee appointed three years ago to study the possibilities of general science, i had the pleasure of reviewing the general science texts, six in all, then on the market. I distinctly remember how different were the points of view of the different authors. One of the first texts published had no illustrations, but sprinkled at intervals through the book were carefully prepared bibliographies. The subject matter was not attractive. In happy contrast I was carried away with the simplicity and excellence of the subject matter of some of the texts. My training has been more or less technical but I can say candidly that the presentation of some of the technical topics such as the making of soaps, etc., gave me a clearer understanding than I had ever had before. The subject matter covers all phases of science. Some of the texts go so far as to include a smattering of all sciences. Then we have other texts which have as their central ideas the explaining of the simplest phenomena. The first chapters of such texts usually deal with the air or water. From such common and simple material they lead as logically as permitted to the more intricate. I have in mind a successful text patterned after this outline. It is perhaps the most interesting of all, and leads by degrees from the simpler things about the air and water into more complex until towards the close of the text the pupil seems to have been led naturally to a discussion of breeding. Then follows the record of an experiment carried on in Texas when Zebus and Herfords were crossed. It is well illustrated and amply explained. I may be confessing ignorance when I say the few pages thus used in this text have meant more to me than hours of lectures. I can think of no better text so far as my personal choice is concerned for first year science. I have in mind another text which my class is using, which is also good. It, too, works from the simpler to the more difficult with marked ease. The one big objection is that more chemistry is employed than some schools will be equipped to handle effectively. This text's treatment of baking powders, soaps, paints, removing of stains, etc., is admirable. Where the teacher has sufficient technical training, I feel this text is well worth while. I am using this text in preference to the other because it fits my class better. Some of the students of the class I am instructing are high school graduates. As general science is at its best when taught in terms of the community environment, we can hardly expect to find any text that will be uniformly pleasing to the teachers. Accordingly do not misunderstand the recommendations made above.

After a brief survey of the content of general science I hear the physical geography teacher saying, "By your own token general science is something like physical geography." Yes and no. I do not wish to contrast courses. I feel physical geography has its place and that in many cases it is filling it acceptably. But I also feel that it is out of place in the smaller and especially rural high schools. It happens that I have taught both physical geography and general science. Regardless as to what some people say, it takes an excellent teacher to fathom the possibilities of physiography. I cannot say that I was ever satisfied with the work I did in this subject. In analyzing my failures I feel they were due in part at least to the lack of suitable apparatus and to the complex nature of what I did have. Then, too, whenever we used apparatus instead of the real thing, we throw an air of artificiality about our work. In other words what the pupil sees in the class-room is so far different from the way he will see it in the big world, that he does not always make the correct application. I believe that general science, in part at least, eliminates this difficulty, in that the apparatus is that of the shop, the store, the mill, etc. General science can best be taught with real things instead of toys are studied. This seems to be a hazy dream for a high school. However, when one thinks seriously about it he realizes that in a large high school there is a number of very excellent things right at ones very door for study. To illustrate: How many of us know how the school room is ventilated, how the heat is furnished, how the furnace is regulated, how the classes are called, how the lighting and tinting are planned, how the walls are made, how electricity is used in the school, how the water supply is kept pure, how the sewage is disposed of, etc? How many of us can see in finishing of the wood-work of our rooms, texts for botany lessons, in the portable sawmill, a lesson on power, or can teach climate in terms of the dew? To be definite, suppose a child were to ask, after you had taught a lesson on humidity, "Teacher, will we have dew tonight," could you answer in terms of science and make yourself understood? Would you be willing to back your judgment? Can you explain so children can understand why some soaps are harder on the skin than others? Can you explain why the creaminess of sea-foam and some other candies is secured through beating, etc? Can you make clear to young people so that there can be no shadow of a doubt and yet none can take offense, the necessity of clean living? Can you see in the blacksmith shop, the print shop, the bakery, the industries of your community,

materials for class work? If you can, and possess the ability to enlist the
good will of those operating these plants, you have two of the qualifications
for teaching general science If I can not apply my teaching to living conditions, I either do not teach that bit of subject matter, or I study it in practice
before presenting it. A few years ago I was told to take charge of a bell
system and electric clock along with my other duties. It came home to me
pointedly then, though I had seen service in electric railroading and had
studied electricity under a noted inventor, I had not been fitted to solve that
problem. I immediately mailed a letter to my Alma Mater. Imagine my
surprise when this great inventor, head of a department of physics which
was turning out electrical engineers, replied that while they taught wiring,
his time and that of his assistants was so occupied that whenever they had
wire trouble they invited in an electrician. He advised me to do the same.
That was four years ago. I turned my face from the university to an humble
youth who had "just picked up" what he knew. I learned from him what a
college education had failed to give. I went to an electric supply house, to
an Oregon Electric sub-station, phone exchange, wiremen; with the result
that the electric clock is no longer a problem. Another example of how I
pick up information, making it real to myself first and to the class later:
With so many kodak enthusiasts in school, I felt I owed them more than a
paragraph of fine print. Accordingly I build a dark-room for the school and
then set about improving my own ability to take and develop pictures. I
visited and became an understudy to the local photographer. I visited different studios, observing and questioning. I visited in other words, men who
were in the business, not those who talked about it. Now when I teach this
portion of general science I have a camera before the class, and demonstrate
how to take a picture. Sometimes we visit the local photographer. When we
study meters we have a dogmatic lesson on how to read a meter and as a
drill step the class reads the electric meters of the vicinity. I even go so far
as to take my class to the blacksmith and print shops, etc. One trip which
we all enjoyed and which was novel, was on a local locomotive. The engineer
demonstrated the machine and then took the class for a short ride. Understand, of course, all such lessons are either accompanied by discussion right
on the spot if time permits, or at the class-room the following day. In order
to make sure the class observes things I desire, I sometimes place in their
hands mimeographed copies of questions designated to bring out the desired
points.   •

     To return to the contrast between physical geography and general
science: Do you not see from the above a fundamental difference between
the uses of the subject matter as used in these courses? In the former we
study more for the cultural aspects and take the practical as incidental; in
the latter this order is reversed. This does not mean that mental discipline
is not sought in general science. While forced into the background it is
nevertheless sought. However, it is sought through the study of things in
which the child is interested because of some future use. Not to enlarge, I
believe this is one of the big factors favoring general science.

     Finally we have discussed reasons for teaching any science, the content
of general science: Now to the last point, why teach general science. I
believe from the foregoing you have already inferred the reasons. The big
aim for teaching any science is that science gives an insight into nature which
stimulates the individual to properly adjust himself to his environment. Do
you recall how, after you had considered the different professions in turn,
you finally chose teaching as a makeshift? Can you imagine how much better
a teacher you might have become had you made that decision two years
earlier and then bent every effort toward preparing for your present work?
If you can think in these terms, you will better understand why Benjamin
Franklin's father took the young son along with him to call upon the business
houses in Boston. You remember the results. A sufficient number of
similar examples can be sighted to establish the premise that such observation
is worth while. Need we say, that coming as it does in the upper grammar
grades or lower high school general science helps to point the pupil toward a
definite life aim. If this be true do we not have a strong argument for
general science? In order to attain the larger aim for science instruction it

is necessary that the subject matter offered be in accord with the times. There is no denying that the present unsettled conditions in Europe are seriously affecting our own commercial structure. If we are to aspire to industrial supremacy, we must meet the changes brought on by these conditions. We must produce our dye-stuffs, chemicals, etc. I know of no science which covers the ground more clearly or more opportunely than general science. I shall not enlarge. There is another feature which is selfish; since the increased freedom in electing subjects, you have doubtless noticed smaller science classes. In spite of this the demands upon our graduates call for increased scientific training. What better can we do than to offer a course at the outset that is interesting and not full of scientific abstractions? It may awaken the desire on the part of some pupil to further pursuance of science. It may help some future Edison to uncover a new ambition. It can certainly stimulate respect for the different crafts.

It would be misrepresenting the facts were I to leave you with the impression that I think general science has no faults; it has. It really is not a science, it is too unorganized, too shallow, too smattering. It covers so large a scope that it requires a teacher of deeds, not words. These are hard to find, when accurate, first hand knowledge is desired. Then too, being based upon local conditions it is difficult to secure a satisfactory text. This perhaps is an advantage.

Self-Examination Today.

Have I been cowardly and evaded issues I should have squarely met?

Have I been vacillating and weak, where I should have been firm and decided?

Have I kept the good resolutions I have made, or broken them?

Have I indulged in self-pity?

Have I indulged in morbid or gloomy thoughts?

Have I worried?

Have I been petulant, fretful, or irritable?

Have I spoken sharp, fretful, or ill-tempered words?

Have I been deceitful, pretending affection I did not feel?

Have I been disloyal, saying in anyone's absence what I would have been ashamed or afraid to say in his presence?

Have I stored this day as a pleasant spot in the memory of anyone?

Have I taken proper physical exercise?

Have I studied, done any hard, mental concentration?

Have I had one hour of quiet, by myself?

Have I eaten or drunk too much?

Have I done my work with sincerity and earnestness, the best I could?

Have I been entirely honest in everything I did?

Have I kept anyone waiting? Have I been punctual in every engagement?

Have I done anything the memory of which may soil another person's life?

Have I lost self-control at any time?

Have I failed in consideration toward children, aged persons, servants, or others, inferior in any way to myself, either in capacity or station?

Have I done anything really worth while?

Have I taken myself too seriously, and failed to see the humor and enjoy the pleasures that came my way?

Have I read anything useful?

Have I done a good deed for anybody, and if so, was I anxious to get credit and appreciation for it, or did I conceal it the best I could, and avoid the reward?—Dr. Frank Crane.

Make the most of yourself, for that is all there is of you.—Emerson.

Selections for Arbor Day

Arranged by MRS. M. L. FULKERSON, Salem, Oregon

Stand In Thy Place and Smile.

Out in Dame Nature's school room,
　As I wandered there one day,
I chanced on a bed of orchids
　In the dark woods hid away.
Dressed in their silken beauty,
　Lovingly, side by side,
They grew where the lofty fir trees
　Cast needles far and wide.

I said, "Your lives are wasted
　So far from the haunts of men,
Only some weary hunter
　May chance on you now and then."
Listen! A soft, glad answer
　Weighted with sweet perfume,
Came from the smiling beauties,
　Lighting the forest gloom:

"Our mission is not in choosing,
　But to stand in our place and smile,
And perhaps some weary hunter,
　By our beauty, sweet, beguiled,
May find what long he's sought for,
　In the crowded city street,
Faith in the God above us,
　And peace surpassingly sweet."

There in the deep, dark forest
　I lifted my heart in prayer;
My life need not be wasted
　Far back from the city's glare.
Never a life so lonely
　But a lonelier one may cheer;
Never a heart so hungry
　But succor waiteth near.

"Help me, O gracious Father,
　To stand in my place and smile
Help me o'er some dark pathway
　The shadows to lighten awhile."

　　　　—Mabel M. Rader.

Who Loves the Trees.

First child—
　Who loves the trees best?
　"I," said the Spring
　"Their leaves so beautiful
　　To them I bring."

Second child—
　Who loves the trees best?
　"I," Summer said,
　"I give them blossoms,
　　White, yellow, red."

Third child—
　Who loves the trees best?
　"I," said the Fall.
　"I give luscious fruits,
　　Bright tints to all."

Fourth child—
　Who loves the trees best?
　"I love them best,"
　Harsh Winter answered,
　"I give them rest."

　　　　—Alice M. Douglas.

We Love the Trees.

First child—
　I love a tree in spring,
　　When the first green leaves come
　　　out,
　And the birds build their nests and
　　　carol
　　Their sweet songs about.

Second child—
　I love a tree in summer,
　　When, in the noon-tide heat,
　The reapers lie in its shadow,
　　On the greensward, cool and sweet.

Third child —
　I love a tree in autumn,
　　When Frost, the painter old,
　Has touched with his brush its
　　　blanches,
　And left them all crimson and gold.

Fourth child—
　I love a tree in winter,
　　Mid snow and ice and cloud,
　Waving its long, bare branches
　　In the north wind, wailing loud.

All—
　Let us plant a tree by the wayside,
　　Plant it with smiles and with tears.
　A shade for some weary wanderer,
　　A hope for the coming years.
　　　　—Luela M. Mooney.

A Prayer.

Teach me, Father, how to go
Softly as the grasses grow;
Teach me, Father, how to be
Kind and patient as a tree.
Let me, also, cheer a spot,
Hidden field or garden grot—
Place where passing souls can rest
On the way and be their best.
　　　　—Edwin Markham.

More Than All

O Painter of the fruits and flowers,
　We thank thee for thy wise design,
Whereby these human hands of ours.
　In Nature's garden work with thine.

Give fools their gold; give knaves their
　　power;
　Let fortune's bubbles rise and fall;
Who sows a field, or trains a flower,
　Or plants a tree, is more than all.
　　　　—Whittier.

Pine-Needles.

If Mother Nature patches
　The leaves of trees and vines,
I'm sure she does her darning
　With needles of the pines!

They are so long and slender;
　And sometimes in full view,
They have their thread of cobwebs
　And thimbles made of dew.
　　　　—William H. Payne.

The Overall Boys.

All recite—
We are the overall boys,
Surely you don't mind our noise.
Tools we have brought everyone,
Planting a tree is just fun.

First boy—
First with this spade I'll dig deep,
Throw up a jolly big heap.
Tender roots then we'll put down
Where soil is soft, rich, and brown.

Second boy—
With this nice, new rake of mine
I'll make some dirt nice and fine.
Then I will sift it with care
O'er the small roots waiting there.

Third boy—
I'll put the dirt in its place.
Bobby and I'll have a race,
Filling that hole deep and wide,
Making it smooth on each side.

Fourth boy—
I have brought water to pour.
When weather's dry I'll bring more.
Through the warm summer I say
It may need water each day.

Fifth boy—
I'll make a fence round about.
All of you fellows stay out!
Trees that are pulled here and there
Surely can't live anywhere.
—American Primary Teacher.

The Bird School.

First pupil—
The sparrows in the primary class
sat down beneath the trees,
Their little faces were upturned to
listen to the breeze.

Second pupil—
The wind stooped low to tell them
the big earth's history;
A bee was their bright teacher in
field geography.

Third pupil—
A butterfly taught numbers; a lily
showed them grace;
A shower gave them tests in health
and washed each birdie's face.

Fourth pupil—
So apt the little pupils! But the les-
son they learned best
Was cheerfulness—a robin, good, lec-
tured from his nest!
—E. A. Stewart.

Birds and Trees.

First pupil—Birds love trees and oft-
en make their homes in them.
Second pupil—Trees love birds, because the birds do such a lot to protect
them.
Third pupil—Some of the birds that
love to make their nests in trees are
the robins, bluebirds, martins, titmice,
nuthatchers, flickers, and woodpeckers.
Fourth pupil—The woodpeckers are
great friends of trees, for they eat the
little insects which harm the trees.
Fifth pupil—Robins choose big strong
trees in which to build their nests.

Sixth pupil—The bluebirds like scattered trees in pastures or in orchards.
Seventh pupil—The modest wren and
the lively catbird like to go where the
trees are thick.
Eighth pupil—The birds are friends
of the trees, and without them, our
woods would be very lonely.
—American Primary Teacher.

A Little Planter.

Down by the wall where the lilacs
grow,
Digging away with a garden hoe,
Toiling as busily as he can—
Eager and earnest, dear little man!
Spoon and shingle are lying by,
With a bit of evergreen, long since dry.
"What are you doing, dear?" I ask.
Ted for an instant stops his task,
Glances up with a sunny smile,
Dimpling his rosy cheeks the while;
"Why, it's Arbor Day, you see,
And I'm planting a next year's Christ-
mas tree;
For last year, auntie, Johnny Dunn
Didn't have even the smallest one,
And I almost cried, he felt so bad,
When I told him 'bout the splendid
one we had;
And I though if I planted this one here,
And watered it every day this year,
It would grow real fast—I think it
might;
(His blue eyes filled with eager light;)
And I'm sure 'twill be, though very
small,
A great deal better than none at all."
Then something suddenly comes be-
tween
My eyes and the bit of withered green,
As I kiss the face of our Teddy boy,
Bright and glowing with giving's joy,
And Johnny Dunn it is plain to see,
Will have his next year's Christmas
tree.
—Selected.

The Mulberry Tree.

O, it's many the scenes which are dear
to my mind
As I think of my childhood so long left
behind;
The home of my birth, with its old
puncheon-floor,
And the bright morning-glory that
glowed round the door;
The warped clab-board roof where the
rain it run off
Into streams of sweet dreams as I laid
in the loft,
Countin' all the joys that was dearest
to me,
And a-thinkin' the most of the mulberry tree.

And today as a dream, with both eyes
wide-awake,
I can see the old tree, and its limbs as
they shake,
And the long purple berries that rained
on the ground
Whare the pastur' was bald whare we
trommpt it around.
And again, peekin' up through the
thick leafy shade,
I can see the glad smiles of the friends
when I strayed
With my little bare feet from my own
mother's knee
To foller them off to the mulberry
tree.
—Riley.

The Elm Tree.

The farmer stood by the carriage-house
 door,
Surveying with pride his homestead
 o'er.
"I wish I had planted one more tree,
Just here on this side, by the vines,"
 thought he.

Then he brought to the spot that sweet
 spring day,
A young, strong elm, from over the
 way,
And placed it there by the carriage-
 house door,
Just where it was needed so much before.

Lo, the years went by, till ninety were
 told—
One sows, nor reaps, 'tis the story old—
When a farmer, young stood by the
 door,
Surveying with pride his domain o'er.

Said he, "The most beautiful thing I see
Is this grand, o'er-arching, old elm tree.
Who planted it, boy? His name we
 must read
In the loving thought, the loving deed."
　　　　　　　—S. B. B. Merrifield.

Dear Little Trees.

Tune—Old Black Joe.
Dear little trees, who have found new
 homes today,
Love brought you here, may you happy
 be alway.
Green be the banners that to the breeze
 you fling,
And may you shelter happy birds that
 nest and sing.

Chorus—
We greet you, we greet you, trees who
 stand in homes so new,
Take root, grow tall, and lift your
 green leaves toward the blue.

Wand'rers will rest 'neath your cool
 and grateful shade,
Song birds will come to your arms
 from woodland glade.
Children will play round your feet with
 laughter gay,
Dear trees, who've been transplanted
 on this Arbor day.

Thousands of new homes for small
 trees everywhere,
Homes all alone, on the prairies broad
 and bare,
Homes in the school yard and on the
 village green.
From north to south, from east to
 west, new trees are seen.
　　　　　　—American Primary Teacher.

A Song of the Trees.

Characters—Arbor Queen; Spirits of
the Trees—Oak, Maple, Elm, Pine,
Palmetto, Olive, Orange; Children;
Lovers; Aged Couple; Woodmen.

Costumes—Arbor Queen wears a
gown of gauzy white, trimmed with
leaves and flowers, and a wreath upon
head. Spirits of Trees wears white or
other colors suggestive of the trees
represented, with appropriate decorations. Woodmen may wear frocks,
overalls, etc. Children and others wear
ordinary costumes suited to the age
represented.

Scene—A village green, or any out-
of-door scene in spring. (Enter Arbor
Queen.)

Arbor Queen—
I am the joyful Arbor Queen,
 The Queen of the Arbor Day;
I bring the foliage rich and rare,
 And the flowers so fresh and gay.

And now upon this gladsome morn,
 I'll do my best to please,
By calling forth my woodland folk—
 The Spirits of the trees.
(Blows horn at side of stage.)

From northern forests deep, they
 come,
From the sunny southern clime,
From woodlands by the eastern seas,
 And from western hills sublime.
(Points to left.)

Oh, see! they come, the fairy folk!
 From mountain crest and dell,
Each with a message of the spring,
 Sweet greetings now to tell.
(Enter Spirit of the Trees.)

Oak—
I am the oak, the grand old oak,
 For a century I have stood;
From a tiny acorn I have grown
 To be monarch of the wood.

Maple—
I am the Maple with spreading
 boughs;
Folks love me for my shade,
And hosts of children in years gone
 by
Beneath by boughs have played.

Elm—
I am the noble and graceful elm,
 My branches wide I spread
Like a mighty parasol of green
 Above your dainty head.

Pine—
I am the Pine so straight and tall,
 In the breeze I softly sigh;
The product of all the trees am I
 As I lift my head to the sky.

Palmetto—
The famed Palmetto tree am I,
 From the south that blooms so gay,
And maidens sit beneath my boughs
 And pickaninnies play.

Olive—
I am the peaceful Olive tree
 From the valleys of the West;
By the fruit and the oil I freely give
 The people know me best.

Orange—
I am the Orange tree that blooms
 So fair and fresh and sweet;
I offer my golden fruit to you
 As a most delicious treat.

(All join in singing "A Song of the
Trees," to tune of "Auld Lang Syne.")
O, sing a song of mighty woods,
 Oh, sing a song of the trees;
We'll sing of leaves so fresh and
 green
 That flutter in the breeze;

We'll sing of trees on mountain tops,
Of those by raging seas;
Oh, sing a song of mighty woods,
O, sing a song of trees.

All—

Now here are the children, full of fun,
A lover and his maid,
And some old, old people coming, too,
To sit beneath our shade.

Arbor Queen—

Then hie away, my fairy folk,
With the swiftness of the breeze,
For mortal eyes shall not behold
The Spirits of the Trees.
(Enter children, right. Fairies vanish at left or rear.)

First Child—

Oh, here is the place for us to play,
Right under this big old tree;
We'll play "I Spy" or "Mulberry Bush,"
Whichever it may be.

(One or two call "I Spy"; others call "Mulberry Bush." All form in circle playing "Here We Go Round the Mulberry Bush." Enter Lovers, right. They sing stanza of some love song as they take seats on bench beneath the tree.)

(Enter aged couple, right, arm in arm. They sing stanza of some old-time song, such as "When You and I Were Young" or "Darby and Joan." They sit on bench at opposite side from lovers, while children continue to play at center. Enter Woodmen, right, with axes.)

First Man—

Ah, here it is! Let's haste to work,
We've a mighty task, 'tis true.
There's timber enough in that old tree
To build a house or two.

(They remove coats and prepare to chop tree.)

Children—Don't let them do it, Grandpa.
Just see the men with axes sharp!
Don't let them cut the tree,
For then we'd have no splendid shade
And sorry we should be.

Grandpa (reciting to Woodmen)—

"Woodman, spare that tree!
Touch not a single bough;
In youth it sheltered me,
And I'll protect it now;
'Twas my forefather's hand
That placed it near his cot,
There, Woodman, let it stand,
Thy axe shall harm it not!"

Second Man (to companion)—

Come, Jerry, we must give it up,
We'll heed what he has said;
I haven't the heart to cut it down,
We'll use concrete instead.

Grandpa (laying hand upon Woodman's shoulder)—

Well done, my man; I thank you, Sir,
It does my old heart good;
I have no doubt the trees themselves
Would thank you if they could.

(All group themselves as follows for the closing stanza of song: Aged

Couple, right; Lovers, left; Woodmen, center; Children at front. Spirits of Trees may appear in background if desired.)

Here's to the fair palmetto tree,
Here's to the northern pine,
Here's to the monarch of the woods,
And here's to the orange fine—
Oh, here's to the trees on the mountain top,
And those by the raging sea;
We'll sing a song of mighty woods,
We'll sing a song of the trees.
—Willis N. Bugbee, in The School Century.

School of Primary Methods.

So many teachers have sent requests to Mrs. Ruby Shearer Brennan that she has finally decided to hold her summer school of primary methods again this year. It will be held in Portland and begin June 23 and continue ten days, for which a tuition of $10 will be charged. The building for holding the school has not yet been selected but as soon as Mrs. Brennan knows about how many will attend, she will announce the place where it will be held. The course of study will include methods in reading, arithmetic, language, spelling, story-telling, hand work, music, calisthenics, and folk dancing. All school room classes will be demonstrated with pupils. The sessions will begin at nine o'clock a. m. and continue until 3:30 in the afternoon. More than 700 teachers have had Mrs. Brennan's work in primary methods. Mrs. Brennan is well known to teachers under the name of Miss Ruby Shearer. You can attend the primary methods school and then remain over for the National Education Association. If you are a primary teacher and have not had Mrs. Brennan's work, you should plan to attend. Write her a card at 460 E. Burnside Street, Portland, Oregon, telling her that you are thinking of attending.

National Education Association.

Mrs. Ruby Shearer Brennan will hold her primary methods school just before the National Education Association. If you are planning to attend the association and are a primary teacher, make arrangements to go two weeks earlier and take in Mrs. Brennan's school. She would like to hear from you and you had better send her a card at 460 E. Burnside Street, Portland, Oregon, telling her about your plans.

Oregon State Library

By CORNELIA MARVIN, Librarian, Oregon State Library

Plays for high school production are still in demand. Aside from the list, issued by the Drama League we have just received two very interesting lists of plays—one, those which have been successfully given in the high schools in Iowa, another, a list of college plays successfully produced throughout the country. These lists tell whether royalty must be paid, the number of acts, the number of stage settings, the number of male and female characters and the grade of satisfaction the play gave the community. We shall be pleased to loan these to anyone who is searching for good plays for schools. We have ordered all the best plays on the list.

* * *

The Sons of the Amercan Revoluton have given the state library money for four more sets of the little grade libraries on the Revolutionary period. These are the most attractive twenty-volume collections we can buy, selected for the purpose of interesting seventh grade pupils in Revolutionary times. There are books of biography, fiction and history. These sets will be loaned for three months to any school in the state.

* * *

The state library has been collecting books on tests and has also ordered all the standard tests which were described in the Elementary School Journal for September, 1916, and in the Wisconsin Educational News Bulletin for the 1st of November, 1916. Anyone who is interested in these tests may borrow the books about them and copies of the tests for study before ordering. The collection includes all the standard tests for reading, arithmetic, writing, spelling, composition and grammar, geography, drawing, algebra, free hand lettering—a very interesting collection. Special instruction in the use of tests in schools was given in Wisconsin in a week's institute entirely devoted to this subject.

* * *

The Pratt Institute Free Library of Brooklyn, N. Y., established "An Alcove Collection" for the purpose of bringing into inviting prominence certain of the outstanding books of the English language in order that everyone using the library might become acquainted with the books that have gained pre-eminence in literature. A list of these carefully chosen books has just been published with notes for each title. Copy of it may be borrowed from the state library or bought from the Pratt Institute for 10 cents. It is one of the most fascinating lists we have received and anyone who is interested in good books would enjoy checking it over. Those who are planning courses of reading will find it an attractive guide. It is similar to the lists of books for general reading published by the English department of the University of Wisconsin and loaned by the state library. The contest conducted by E. P. Dutton & Co. for list of best ten titles in Everyman's Library resulted in the following choice: Shakespeare's Works, the Bible, Dicken's David Copperfield, Hugo's Les Miserables, Everyman's Encyclopaedia, Scott's Ivanhoe, Bunyan's Pilgrim Progress, Thackeray's Vanity Fair, Dante's Divine Comedy, Homer's Iliad.

* * *

Lafcadio Hearn's "Appreciation of Poetry," recently published, are recommended in The Dial for use in high school English classes. These appreciations were in the form of lectures delivered to Japanese students in the attempt to arouse their interest in English literature. The book is said to lack the charm of Hearn's other works, but to be "a rare and precious aid" to the young student of poetry.

* * *

"Greek photoplays" by Effie Seachrest will help teachers to prepare plays based on Greek myth and story. The plays are simple and contain careful directions for costuming and preparation.

* * *

A summary of the "Smith-Hughes Act" providing Federal aid for vocational education has been issued by the Board of Education. This may be borrowed from the state library.

* * *

New Books on Education.

Atwood, Theory and Practice of the Kindergarten.—A simple, interesting treatment, planned to help the young kindergartner to refresh her memory, and to gather together some essentials in relation to kindergarten practice. Discusses the conduct of the kindergarten, the accessories, program, gifts, and has a good chapter on story-telling. No index, but outline of chapters.

Bigelow, Sex-education. — The most important contribution yet made to the subject of sex instruction, adapted from lectures delivered at Columbia University and elsewhere. Takes up in a clear and comprehensive way the problems and organization of sex education, the selection of teachers, the use of books, and the adaptation of sex instruction to different stages in development.

Dearborn, How to Learn Early.— Under such headings as Economy in study, Observation and the taking of notes, Educative imagination, Examination-preparedness, the writer gives sensible, easily understood suggestions to students and teachers and something of the psychology underlying the suggestions.

Dooley, The Education of the Ne'er-do-well.—Analyzes, both from the social and economic and the personal side, the problem of the child who, with no aptitude for literary studies, leaves school to drift into "blind alley" occupations and ultimately into the army of the inefficient. Cites both American and foreign experience in handling the problem, and suggests concrete programs involving pre-vocational education and continuation schools.

Freeman, Experimental Education. —A laboratory book dealing with the great processes of learning and with some experiments on the special school subjects. The book will be very useful as a textbook in normal schools and college departments of education and will serve to introduce students of education to the technique of laboratory work in educational fields.

Hall, The Question As a Factor in Teaching.—Concrete, practical chapters on the teaching of stories and other subjects, made up mainly of model questions that are suggestive and could be used directly in lower-grade class-room teaching. The method is not absolutely novel, but in its presentation it is impressively in advance of the unstudied and unfruitful questioning which very frequently appears in routine school work.

Hazlitt, Thinking as a Science.— Clear, as untechnical as possible, and helpful to people who are sincere in wishing to continue their own mental development. The same information can be obtained in any good psychology.

Paxson, A Handbook for Latin Clubs.—Part 1 consists of thirty-six well worked out programs, with specific references to books and periodicals where material can be found; part 2 contains selections from modern and Latin authors; part 3, a number of Latin songs with music.

Sargent, How Children Learn to Draw.—A clear, definite exposition of the methods and results of an experiment conducted for the last few years in the Elementary School of the School of Education in the University of Chicago. "Presents some of these records, selected to show representative series of lessons, accompanied by explanatory notes and illustrations from the work of the children" and follows with a statement of the conclusions reached.

Wilson, The Motivation of School Work.—Suggestive as a fresh attack on an old problem of the teacher's, that of making the work in the various school studies significant and purposeful to each child. Based on twenty years of experience in teaching and supervision, it contains many concrete and helpful plans and hints for putting new life into the old subjects.

President Wilson's Cabinet.

Secretary of State, Robert Lansing; Treasurer, William Gibbs McAdoo; War, William Diehl Baker; Attorney-General, Thomas Watt Gregory; Postmaster-General, Albert Sidney Burleson; Secretary of Navy, Josephus Daniels; Interior, Franklin Knight Lane; Agriculture, David Franklin Houston; Commerce, William C. Redfield; Labor, William Bauchof Wilson.

Learning is wealth to the poor, an honor to the rich, an aid to the young and a support and comfort to the aged.—Lavater.

Grade Teachers' Department

Edited by SABRA CONNER, 421 West Park Street, Portland, Oregon

Elementary teachers and elementary teachers' associations are cordially invited to send news items of their activities which would be of interest or value to other teachers to this department of the The Oregon Teachers Monthly. Address Editor of Grade Teachers' Department, Room 300, Court House, Portland, Oregon.

The February meeting of the Special Teachers of Literature was a very interesting one. A report was made of the management of classroom library in a building remote from even a branch library. A talk was given on dramatization in the reading recitation and selections in the Elson Readers suitable for dramatization. Another topic discussed was how to manage reports on outside reading. The talks and the round table following were full of helpful suggestions for reading teachers. At the March meeting Mrs. Mable Holmes Parsons gave a talk on Poems That Are Worth Teaching. She said that the poetry of the reader has been too long under the influence of the schoolman. That children do not need and certainly do not want the abstract poems, the dull sermon in verse. They need and will easily learn to love the poem that shows them an objective world. The appreciation and love for objective poetry will and must lead to a desire for creation. The newer poets, she said, in many cases are writing better poetry than many of our earlier poets to whose verse we cling. Since we teach children current history and current science why cling too conservatively to the earlier poets. She gave a list of poems new and old which children love. This list will be printed in the Portland School Bulletin. It will be a valuable supplement to the reader in every grade.

* * *

Grade teachers should show their interest in the coming meeting of the National Education Association by an early membership enrollment. A large local enrollment is one of the best means of insuring a large number of teachers from all over the state to attend the convention. Nothing will take the place of local enthusiasm in making a convention a success.

* * *

Mr. Puffer's lectures on Vocational Training were full of very definite and practical help to the teacher who wishes to give personal advice and guidance to the boys and girls who are seeking help in deciding what they should become. In a day and age where people have come to regard manual labor as unsuited to the individual who has even a little book learning, his appeal for a realization of the dignity and the vital need of the skilled tradesman is most timely. The ideals formed by children during their school days are the determining factor in deciding their life work, and anything which will help a teacher to instil a respect for the creative ability—for the man and woman who produces something of value to the community will be of permanent civic value. The mistaken idea of the purpose of education is the cause of the great number of misfits in life.

* * *

The Colonial Entertainment was an immense success both socially and artistically. Rarely has the public attended so numerously or appreciated so enthusiastically a grade teacher affair, and this in spite of a night that produced all too realistically the atmosphere of that winter in Valley Forge. The dramatic skit, directed by Miss Greathouse, portrayed General Washington's winter headquarters with Washington himself skillfully enacted by Mr. E. Whitney. The cast, all of whom did excellent work, was as follows: George Washington, Mr. Whitney; Martha Washington, Miss Whitfield; Mary, niece of Washington, Miss Ballin; Colonel Fitzgerald, Mr. Thomas; Baron Fairfax, Mr. Hugh Boyd; Mrs. Green, Miss Humason; Mrs. Knox, Miss Kelly; Dr. Craik, Mr. Purcell; Billie, Mr. Webber; Two soldiers, Messrs. Martin and Trowbridge. At the conclusion of the playlet, music was furnished by the Grade Teachers' chorus under the direction of Mr. Boyer. This was their first public appearance and the delightful blending of voices as well as the perfection of rendition was a happy surprise to the charmed audience, as was the double quartet of Jefferson high school boys whose work was also distinctly good. Miss Metta Brown sang two charming old-time ballads in her usual happy manner and had hard work to satisfy an audience who continually demanded "more." Little Miss Marian Farrell danced exquisitely the Blue Danube waltzes and gave a delightful encore. Perhaps the most effective of the various events on the program was the minuet danced by ten couples in beautiful Colonial costumes. The gay costumes of both men and maidens, the powdered coiffures, the coquettish patches and the stately figures of the dance formed so enchanting a picture that it was repeated several times at the request of the delighted audience. The proceeds of the entertainment, $213, are to be given to that most worthy cause, the Fellowship Fund, a fund set apart for the use of teachers who through sickness or misfortune are in need of financial assistance.

High School Teachers' Department

Edited by HOPKIN JENKINS, Portland, Oregon

The Teaching of Biology.

Biology has furnished us the highest interpretation of educational endeavor in the idea of evolution. It has given us the wonderful and inspiring conception of a teacher as a conscious instrument in the process of remaking society according to a more perfect pattern. Interpreting, further, the idea of social evolution in terms of the thought of today, we may say that it involves the increasing of the efficiency of the individual in his social and economic relations. In other words, in this evolution of society which we seek to bring about, we aim at increased social efficiency and increased vocational efficiency. Our slogan is "Efficiency, Social and Vocational."

It is apparent that the science of biology dominates our educational philosophy, but the subject of biology has failed to find a commensurate place in the schools. Surely, if we were to exploit this subject to the full it would take the place it deserves.

I have heard pupils ask, "What is biology? Is it 'bugology'?" Worse than that I have known pupils who after taking the subject still thought that it was "bugoolgy." The emphasis must have been on the bug. Where should the emphasis have been? This brings us back to our statement of the aim of education, social and vocational efficiency. If we were to analyze out the most important factors of social and voca-tional efficiency and see that our teaching emphasizes these factors, perhaps biology would come into its own. I shall attempt to do this from my point of view.

Health, co-operation, leadership, a high and rational standard of morals, together with an appreciation of known and latent economic values in plants and animals; at these things I intend to aim in choosing for myself what to teach, what to emphasize, and how to present the work.

The health of the individual and of the community depends in a large measure on two things, (a) a knowledge of metabolism, and (b) an appreciation of the relation of several plant and animal families to themselves and to man, (such families as the bacteria, diptera, etc.) The ability to co-operation and its correlate the ability to lead are best developed by actual practice. The experimental work in biology readily lends itself to a method of treatment (group work and reports), which furnishes this practice. Furthermore, the subject matter of biology builds a firm and rational basis for the development of these abilities. The ants, bees, wasps, tent caterpillars, crows, geese, chickens, seals, beavers, wolves, elk, cattle, horses, monkeys, and many other genera furnish almost innumerable opportunities to study co-operation and leadership in simplified form. Above all, even the most superficial study of evolution and the so-called "survival characters" will demonstrate to the pupil that the "ability to co-operate" far exceeds in value any of the other "characters." Biology enables the student to understand the intricate nature of man by comparing its elements with the less intricate but homologous elements in the nature of other living things. An understanding of the behavior and instincts of other living things is a wonderful asset in working with and leading men.

The last factor of social efficiency which I have chosen to emphasize is the "moral standard." Almost all of the methods of teaching ethics in the schools, which have been advocated attempt to strengthen our old "custom morality," simply by giving it more emphasis. What we need is to rationalize our moral standard and then exercise it in actual school work. There are two courses eminently fitted for this task: Biology can rationalize our moral standard and athletics can exercise it. Of course it is apparent that all school activities may contribute. If the pupil in studying evolution and the behavior of animals comes to understand that the most important survival characteristic of the animals is the ability to co-operate, he can scarcely escape the conclusion that it is right to work with others and wrong to work against them. Such a conclusion is strengthened by the study of the lives and work of great plant and animal breeders, Burbank for example, all of whose work has been done for the benefit of the race.

Our morals of sex relations and parenthood are rationalized in the study of reproduction, plant and animal breeding, and heredity, as well as incidentally, in the study of bacteria, etc., under the head of the interrelation of living things. Biology teaches that the dominant object of every race of living things is to perpetuate its kind but that is not all— to perpetuate a stronger and fitter race of its kind. These two rational principles from biology, "to work with each other and not against each other" and "to perpetuate an improved race," support our highest moral standards as expressed in such phrases, "The greatest good to the greatest number," "The brotherhood of man," and even in the word "service."

Before taking up the last factor which is strictly vocational, I wish to make the idea of vocational efficiency, as aimed at by the school, clear. We do not mean efficiency in making a living. The pupil who attempts to get from the school what information and tricks of the trade he can and then go out and obtain by means of this equipment a living and perhaps more, for himself, deserves nothing at our hands. We have but one duty with regard to him and that is to reform his morals. What we do mean by vocational efficiency is effeciency in the production of economic values. We wish to train pupils so that when they become workers they will to their highest possibilities produce values for society as a whole. This aim is vastly different and it holds true with the student who is destined to a "white collar job" as well as with the student who looks forward to a "soft shirt job."

The contribution which biology can make to vocational efficiency is an appreciation of the known and latent economic values in living things. These values readily fall under two heads, negative and positive. Some of the negative values are found in insect pests, the fungi and the predatory animals. Among the positive values are those embodied in the living things which are used for food, building and structural work, clothing, and labor. These values are: Known and latent. The known values must be handed down from one generation to the next as a part of our social inheritance. The latent values are to be searched for and discovered with the work of our famous plant and animal breeders as an inspiration.

With this discussion as a basis I have made a tentative outline of work for two terms of biology as follows:

First Term.—(1) Structure of living things; (2) metabolism (to be summarized in the circulation of carbon); (3) the interrelation of living things including disease, sanitation, economic values of the several plant and animal families necessitating a study of plant and animal classification.

Second Term.—(1) Reproduction including propagation, dispersal, etc.; (2) plant and animal breeding and other related processes of evolution; (3) heredity including application to eugenics; (4) the tropisms, senses, and behavior of living things, including a short study of instincts.

Besides the question of content and emphasis there is the additional question of method of presentation. Since we are not concerned so much with the development of the subject as with the development of the pupil we ought to feel free to begin the subject of metabolism, for example, with the lower animals, the subject of reproduction with the plants and the subject of structure with either or both. We should never feel obliged to complete the application of any principle to plants before applying it to animals or vice versa. In fact we wish to keep the unity of living things in the foreground and not their divisibility. We are teaching biology, not a combination of botany, zoology and physiology. It is also possible that there will be some things which we learned at college that will not be able to pass on to our students either from lack of time or suitable opportunity, but that should not give us undue pain if we accomplish our own object in teaching the subject.

As far as possible the work should be presented to the pupils in the form of problems which they are to solve. For example, the introductory work in structure can be accomplished by giving the pupils a section of epidermis from the bases of the leaves in the onion bulb after first giving thorough instructions as to the use of microscopes. Ask them to draw the tissue as they see it and describe its structure, but in the meanwhile answer any questions as to the names of the parts which they observe. If plenty of time is taken, the work done in groups of two, or, perhaps three, if there are not sufficient microscopes, and if the teacher encourages questions the whole class will soon realize, at least the simpler facts of structure. A repetition of this exercise with amoeba, diatoms, desmids, spirogyra, paramoecium, vorticelli, thread worms, rotifers, chara, tissues of higher animals, sections of stems, roots, etc., sometimes stained, would within two or three weeks time, at most, give students a working knowledge of structure and an interest in the work if not too much drawing and writing is required but the emphasis placed on solving the problem of structure. Work of this study-recitation type requires a period of more than an hour (two periods) in order to accomplish anything worth mentioning.

This sort of work punctuated with review recitations in which the experimentation is talked over, summarized and the results systematized should make the backbone of the course. Then there ought to be a written report from each pupil on some subject of interest once each term if possible. These reports may also take the problem form, especially in the discussion of the economic value of certain families as the diptera, or two winged insects, the fish, the gramina or grass family, etc.

Most of the details of the course must, for the present, be determined by the individuality of the teacher and the materials which the teacher can secure, but it should never be forgotten that aimless teaching is worthless teaching and that our aim is social and vocational.—Elbert Hoskin. (Paper read to the teachers of Franklin high school, Portland.)

Portland's Awakening.

It is a great deal to say that Portland will break all records by way of entertainments, but it is true, literally true. Some things will be done that have never before been possible. The Mazamas will conduct as many thousand teachers as wish to engage in a mountain climbing expedition, the event to either be staged just prior to the opening of the convention or immediately afterward. The swimming clubs are all preparing for the entertainment of teachers who wish to indulge such sports; clam bakes and salmon dinners will be spotted along the side lines, while always there are the splendidly interesting drives over the wonderful Columbia River highway and the boulevards, the completion of which has cost Portland $4,000,000. On Sunday afternoon, July 8, an afternoon meeting will be held at the auditorium at which Governor Ernest Lister of Washington, Governor James Withycombe of Oregon, and prominent educators of the world will be heard. The meeting will dedicate the municipal auditorium, on which $600,000 has been expended. —Journal of Education.

I hope I shall always possess firmness and virtue enough to maintain what I consider the most enviable of all titles, the character of an honest man.— Washington.

Oregon Tree Studies

By WM. E. LAWRENCE, Department of Botany and Plant Pathology, O. A. C.

XI—Western Larch.

Of the four larches found in North America only two occur in Oregon—the western larch extensively and the woolly larch in the Mt. Hood regions. Since larches lose their leaves in autumn, as the broad leafed trees, and yet produce cones in common with all conifers, it is not at all difficult to recognize Oregon larches by the association of absence of leaves with presence of cones.

The western larch, Larix occidentalis Nutt., is also called the red American larch, great western larch, and western tamarack, although commonly spoken of as larch or tamarack. It occurs within the Columbia river drainage basin, at elevations of 2000 to 6000 feet. Its range lies between the western slope of the continental divide in Montana from Southern British Columbia to Southern Oregon and the eastern slope of the Cascade mountains in Oregon. In Oregon it is found mainly in the Blue and Wallowa mountains of Eastern Oregon and on the east side of the Cascades, crossing the divide only for short distances at various places.

The western larch is the largest known species of larch in the world. It produces tapering trunks three to four feet in diameter, clear of branches for 60 to 100 feet or more, which together with short, narrow crowns of comparatively few short, horizontal branches, gradually taper to slender points at from 100 to 180 feet. (Fig. 1.) Trees 200 feet high are usually five to eight feet in diameter. In the open, the branches often reach almost to the ground. It attains its largest size in the Bitterroot mountains of Northern Idaho.

It requires from 250 to 300 years to produce a trunk sixteen to twenty inches in diameter. Merchantable timber of twelve inches in diameter is attained in about 100 years in the Priest River drainage basin of Northern Idaho. The larch as a tree is a rather slow but persistent grower. The larch is long-lived, living between 300 and 500 years, as a rule, while the largest trees reach 600 and 700 years of age.

The bark is very thick near the base of the trees—three to six inches—and deeply furrowed, gradually be-

(Fig. 1).

coming less deeply furrowed and thinner at twenty or more feet above the ground. The thickness of the bark seems to vary with the locality, being about two inches in the Blue mountains of Washington and Oregon and nearly a foot thick in the Bitterroot mountains of Northern Idaho. The thick bark offers a very excellent protection to the tree against fire, and many of the large trees show that they have successfully passed through several forest fires. The bark of younger trees and branches is thin, scaly, and dark or grayish-brown; while that of middle-aged and old trees is a reddish-cinnamon brown.

The branches are rather slender, but not graceful, owing to the presence of short, stumpy branches, which support the clusters of leaves. Pine and larch are alike in having two kinds of branches—long branches becoming limbs and short foliar branches upon which may be found, in the spring and summer, from fourteen to about thirty stiff, sharp-pointed, flat, triangular leaves from one to two inches long. (Fig. 2.) The larch is one of the earliest deciduous trees to display new growth in the spring, the leaves appearing towards the last of April. The leaves are a pale yellowish-green and needle-like, becoming a bright yellow lemon late in the fall, and falling during October. This marked difference in the color of the leaves enables the traveler to distinguish the larch from other conifers readily. It may be picked out while passing by on the train; as, for example, along the O-W. R. & N. railroad at the top of the Blue Mountain grade near Meacham. They may be seen also along the Sumpter Valley and other mountain railroad lines.

The cones are small (1 to 1½ inches long), stand erect, mature in one season and ripen in August. (Fig. 2.) The presence of excerted three-pointed bracts is a feature in common with the Douglas fir and the true or balsam firs. They open soon after maturity and fall from the trees by the end of October or November. Larches rarely produce seed before twenty-five years, but become prolific seeders at forty to fifty years. The light chestnut brown seeds are small and scarcely more than half the length of their thin, frail wings. Like many other conifers, such as pines and firs, the seeds bear wings which materially assist in dissemination. Falling from the top of such tall trees they are rapidly scattered, often falling upon the snow over which they are sometimes blown for considerable distances.

The cones ripen in August and September. The cone scales open very readily in dry weather but close during rains so that the duration of the period of the seeds' dispersion varies to some extent with local cli-

(Fig. 2).

matic conditions. The seeds of the western larch are rather exacting as to moisture requirements. They require considerable moisture for germination which accounts for their occurrence in high mountain valleys and slopes and their predominance on many of the northern slopes. Although western larch demands considerable water, the soil on which it grows must be well-drained. In relatively dry regions, like the Blue mountains of Eastern Oregon, the larch attains its best development in moist draws or in fertile valleys not parallel with the direction of the prevailing winds. The larch will grow well in the mineral soils of burned-over areas where it is likely to compete only with lodgepole pines for dominance and where the dominance depends upon which tree started first. If both lodgepole pine and western larch have an equal start, the more rapid growth of the larch assures its etsablishment, while the light color of the foliage and sparsely scattered leaves of the larch do not injure the development of the lodgepole pine. If the lodgepole pine has the earlier start, its denser shade is likely to crowd out the more intolerant larch.

Western larch sometimes grows in pure stands, but usually in mixed stands. Its best growth is in northeastern Washington, northern Idaho, and in northwestern Montana, where it often occurs in open forests, in valleys and on slopes. In the Blue mountains of Washington and Oregon it occurs on typical flats. Here, also, the areas of this larch and lodgepole pine are interspersed with Engelmann spruce, white and lowland firs and Douglas firs; the silvical characteristics of larch and lodgepole pine appear very similar in view of the common associations.

The western larch is seriously damaged by the larch mistletoe (Fig. 1), a flowering plant which sends its suckers into the living wood of the limbs and branches of the trees, thus deriving all of its source of water from the larch. The larch mistletoe is so abundant in the Blue mountains of Oregon and the injurious effect so marked that it results in considerable suppression of the larch as a source of valuable timber.

At present the western larch is but little used, although it compares favorable in strength with the wood of the western hemlock and Douglas fir. Western larch and western yellow pine are practically the only woods used for building purposes in some parts of northern Idaho and western Montana and eastern Washington. However, the wood of the western larch is not found upon the market to any great extent outside of its geographical range. Its use is therefore largely confined to the states of Oregon, Washington, Montana and Idaho. There is considerable wastage in lumbering so that the western larch yields an average of about 10 per cent of clear lumber. Western larch is used for making railroad cross ties, flooring, siding, ceiling, and molding, lath, inside finishing, veneer. It takes a high polish and stains well. It is especially valuable for round and pole timbers.

The wood of the western larch should not be confused with the wood of the noble fir. Lumbermen frequently refer to the wood of noble fir (Oregon Tree Studies 9, published in the Oregon Teachers Monthly February, 1916) as "larch." This is an erroneous application of the term and its use should not be continued, on account of its correct application to the western larch and eastern larch.

He is the best artist who feels a thing most nobly and most beautifully. He is the best technician, whether with the brush of the painter, the shuttle of the weaver, the chisel of the carver in wood, or the hammer of the worker in metal, whose tool most readily and most vitally expresses the thought of his brain, who feels least the limitations of an artificial ideal of finish.—Theodore C. Steele.

New County School Superintendents.

Baker, Miss Elmetta Bailey, Baker
Benton, R. E. Cannon, Corvallis
Clackamas, J. E. Calavan, Oregon City
Clatsop, O. H. Byland, Astoria
Columbia, J. W. Allen, St. Helens
Coos, R. E. Baker, Coquille
Crook, J. E. Myers, Prineville
Curry, W. M. Kent, Gold Beach
Deschutes, J. Alton Thompson, Bend
Douglas, O. C. Brown, Roseburg
Gilliam, J. C. Sturgill, Condon
Grant, W. W. Austen, Hamilton
Harney, Frances Clark, Burns
Hood River, L. B. Gibson, Hood River
Jackson, G. W. Ager, Jacksonville
Jefferson, Lillian Watts, Culver
Josephine, Alice M. Bacon, Grants Pass
Klamath, Edna I. Wells, Klamath Falls
Lake, C. E. Oliver, Lakeview
Lane, E. J. Moore, Eugene
Lincoln, R. P. Goin, Toledo
Linn, Ida M. Cummings, Albany
Malheur, Fay Clark, Vale
Marion, W. M. Smith, Salem
Morrow, Lena S. Shurte, Heppner
Multnomah, W. C. Alderson, Portland
Polk, Fred S. Crowley, Dallas
Sherman, F. E. Fagan, Moro
Tillamook, G. B. Lamb, Tillamook
Umatilla, I. E. Young, Pendleton
Union, Mrs. A. E. Ivanhoe, LaGrande
Wallowa, J. C. Conley, Enterprise
Wasco, C. T. Bonney, The Dalles
Washington, B. W. Barnes, Hillsboro
Wheeler, H. J. Simmons, Fossil
Yamhill, S. S. Duncan, McMinnville

Summer School.

Mr. J. J. Kraps will begin his summer school at Salem on March 26, and it will continue thirteen weeks. Classes in all branches for all kinds of certificates will be organized. While it is always best to enter at the first of the term, yet teachers may enter at any time.

True liberty consists only in the power of doing what we ought to will, and in not being constrained to do what we ought not to will.—Jonathan Edwards.

Some Oregon Weeds and Seeds

By A. R. SWEETSER, University of Oregon

The Dandelion.

The artist and the aesthete may soar into rhapsodies over the golden dandelion, but the owner of a lawn into which this dandelion army is swarming and taking possession to the exclusion of the grass feels no such exultation.

This is a stemless plant with a large tap root and much-cut leaves. The common name may be a corruption of the old Latin specific name

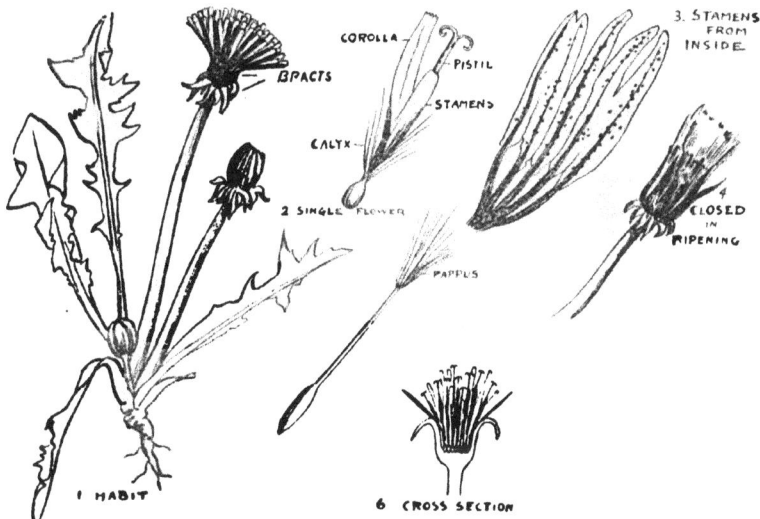

1 HABIT

CROSS SECTION

wards. Fig. 3 shows this stamen tube split down and seen from within. On the lower end of the flower is the ovary or egg case containing a single little egg. On the top of the egg case is a style which at its upper end separates into two pollen-receptive portions or stigmas. While still in the bud the style is included in the stamen tube and the stigmas are closed so that it is impossible for them to receive any of their own pollen, but as they emerge they un-

which was dens-leonis, or tooth of the lion. This may possibly have referred to the shape of the root.

The flower stalk springs from the root and carries on its upper end a cluster of flowers called a head. On the outside of this head are numerous, green, leaf-like bracts. Within this fringe of bracts are many complete flowers. This is clearly shown in the section of the head.

Fig. 2 is a drawing of one of these single flowers with the parts labelled. The corolla forms a tube below, spreading out on one side into a sort of a blade with five small points on the end. Within the corolla are the stamens united into a tube around the pistil and shedding the pollen in-

roll and are ready to receive the pollen brought by the insect from another flower. The calyx is united to the ovary and consists of numerous soft, hair-like bristles, also called a pappus.

Linaeus used the dandelion as one of the flowers in his floral clock, as it opens early in the morning and closes in the evening. When maturing it closes as in Fig. 4, the corolla stamens, and pistil are dropped off, and the neck of the egg case elongates, carrying up the pappus which spreads out into the form of the familiar parachute by which this ripened fruit is widely wafted by the wind. This shows how futile is the fight unless waged before the plant has gone to seed.

The leaves are much relished by many people as a spring green, although the bitter flavor is disagreeable to some. Near various eastern cities the dandelion is cultivated as a garden crop.

The dandelion root is used in medicine as a spring tonic, also as an addition to coffee in the same manner as chicory. Heretofore dandelion

Fig. 7.—Batchelor Button.

root has been largely imported but the home product is every bit as good and there is no reason why we should not supply our own demand. The methods of raising and curing are fully explained in the Scientific American Supplement Number 81.

But we of Oregon are more particularly interested in the extermination of this pest. The plant is perennial, the root thickening and tak-

ing hold more firmly each year. It is claimed that spraying with a 5 per cent solution of copper sulphate or a 15 per cent solution of sulphate of iron will destroy the dandelion. But the value of this treatment is yet to be proven. The best method is to use a weed puller which removes the roots, but this is practical only in small areas of ground. The lawn should be frequently mowed and every effort used to prevent the flowering and going to seed. It is also claimed that cutting the roots of the plant and applying salt will kill them off, but this appears to be about as much work as the proverbial application of salt to a bird's tail.

The bachelor's button (Fig. 7) is designated by several other names, such as bluebottle, ragged robin, corn flower, etc., and is scientifically known as Centaurea cyanus. It belongs to the same family as the dandelion and will show the same general arrangement of parts. Its pappus, however, is made up of but a few, short, rusty-brown hairs and it does not form a parachute as in the case of the dandelion.

It is often planted in the flower garden for its beauty, but in many places has escaped and become a pest in the fields. It has a wide range of color and were it not for the economic loss would adorn the country landscape.

It is an annual, springing each year from seed, so may be held in check by cultivation of the ground although the vitality of the seed may persist for several years. The best protection in all cases is to be found in the use of high grade seed which is as free as possible from the admixture of weed seed.

Farmers Bulletin No. 660 gives an interesting account of some of our common weeds and how to control them. These and other bulletins may be obtained free upon application to the Department of Agriculture at Washington, D. C.

I can think of no more pleasant way of being remembered than by the planting of a tree. Birds will rest in it and fly hence with messages of good cheer. It will be growing while we are sleeping, and will survive us to make others happier.—Lowell.

The State Schools

University of Oregon.

More than usually brilliant is the array of lecturers obtained for the 1917 summer school of the university. Most prominent among these are President G. Stanley Hall of Clark University; President Henry Churchill King of Oberlin College; Dr. John Timothy Stone of the Fourth Presbyterian Church of Chicago; and perhaps Dr. Carl A. Kraus of Columbia University. Dr. J. Duncan Spaeth of Princeton will also return.

Prof. Robert P. Reeder of the Law School has just issued a book on the Validity of Rate Regulations, State and Federal, which is attracting a great deal of attention in legal and legislative circles. The California Law Review speaks of it as a scholarly, concise, practical and comprehensive treatise.

The university was represented at the recent meeting of the Society of the Society of College Teachers of Education at Kansas by Dean Sheldon of the School of Education. Dr. Sheldon discussed the work of the colleges in the preparing of their graduates for socialization work in the schools.

A History of the Pacific Northwest, by Joseph Schafer, professor of history in the University of Oregon is announced by Macmillans for publication in the spring. This is a revised and rewritten edition of the author's History of the Pacific Northwest brought out in 1905 by the Macmillan Company. The new edition will show the results of more than

ten years' additional research, particularly that which the author conducted in the archives of the British government at London, where he had access to all of the manuscript material relating to the history of the boundary dispute — the so-called "Oregon Question." Other portions of the earlier book have been recast, expanded, reconstructed, as the case may be, and all statements tested by the results of the latest investigations. The book contains three chapters which are entirely new and in which Dr. Schafer attempts to make a distinct contribution to our knowledge of Northwestern affairs of the recent past. These chapters are entitled: The Progress of Agriculture, Industry and Commerce, and Social and Political Development. In this book, therefore, the reader traverses the long bridge from the past of this section, and takes a good look about him upon the life that is going on today.

The Extension Division of the University of Oregon is publishing a series of botany leaflets prepared by A. R. Sweetser, professor of botany. These leaflets describe common Oregon wild flowers in a semi-technical way and are planned to be of use to teachers of botany and of general nature study courses. A leaflet that is just off the press describes two early bloomers: The spring queen and sweet coltsfoot. Another leaflet that is in preparation describes the Oregon grape and Indian plum. These leaflets may be secured upon request from the Extension Division.

Oregon Agricultural College.

The entire school of forestry of O. A. C. will make their annual trip into the Cascade mountains during the latter part of April and the first of May. They have planned to go into what is known as the "Blow-Out" country, near Detroit and cruise a large area of timber land and prepare a topographical map of the region. The work will be carried on in co-operation with the Federal Forest Service and will be under the direct supervision of Mr. Hall, supervisor of the Santiam Forest Reserve. The purpose of the trip is to give the men practical woods experience in the most upto date methods of cruising and map making.

The Commercial Print, put out by the students of the commercial department of O. A. C. is off the press, and reports from Dean Bexell's office indicate that it is well up to the high standard set by the editor, Robert Reichert, a senior in commerce. The publication contains many articles on timely subjects of commercial interest, besides a revised student directory and a directory of all faculty members, fraternities, sororities and clubs.

Rodger W. Simpson, son of the Episcopal Rector at Corvallis, and a freshman at O. A. C., has been appointed as candidate to West Point, as the result of the preliminary examination for the U. S. Military Academy held in Corvallis, February 24. Merril D. Richmond, of Salem, is named as first alternate, and Robert W. Montague, a freshman in the University of Oregon, as second alternate.

Teachers who may be thinking of adding fruit to the school grounds may be interested in the three bulletins just published by the Extension Service of O. A. C. on the general subject of small fruits. The bulletins are: "The Strawberry," Extension Bulletin No. 146; "The Loganberry," Extension Bulletin No. 165; and "The Brambles," Extension Bulletin No. 192. Such subjects as soils, propagation, cultivation etc. are covered in these publications, as well as insects and diseases, harvesting, cost, and marketing.

Miss Carrie Pimm, graduate of O. A. C. in 1911, has received an appointment as extension lecturer on Home Economics in the New Jersey State College, at an initial salary of $1500 per year. Miss Pimm was formerly head of Home Economics in the Eugene high school, resigning in 1915 to attend Teachers' College at Columbia University. After being there a year and a half she received her present appointment.

Miss Minnie Price, graduate of 1911, is now on the extension staff of the Massachusetts State College, at a salary of $2100 per year. Miss Price taught two years in the Salem high school and attended Teachers' College for two years.

Faculty members at the Oregon Agricultural College most closely in touch with the growth and development of Greek Letter fraternities are quite unanimously agreed that scholastic pride, general student democracy, and qualities of leadership characterize these organizations.

During the school year of 1913 the fraternities made a request of college authorities to be granted the privilege of monthly grade reports from each instructor for every fraternity member and pledge. Since that time there has been keen and wholesome rivalry between the various houses for first place in scholarship. Each of the nine fraternities has strict house rules to be enforced against low grade members. Typical among these are week end social privileges withheld; underclassmen assign to upper classmen as proctors and tutors. Definite semester averages in all subjects must be obtained by every pledge before initiation into full membership. In some houses the average requires is as much as five per cent higher than the official average required by the faculty Student Affairs Committee. The general effect of this has been most wholesome as shown by the fact that last semester (typical of conditions for the past three or four years) the weighted average of fraternity members was 84.5 as compared with an average of 80.3 for men not in fraternities. The democratic spirit of O. A. C. fraternity men is evidenced by the fact that, according to reports taken from the registrar's records, 17 per cent of fraternity men here are entirely self supporting, 25 per cent are one-half self supporting, 34 per cent are partly (less than half) self supporting or a total of 76 per cent of fraternity men partially or entirely self supporting as compared with 24 per cent who receive all of their financial support from parents or guardians. Sixty-nine per cent of all students in college, both fraternity and non-fraternity are reported as being partially or wholly dependent upon their own resources for financial support. It is this type of self supporting, progressive students who can be relied upon by college officials to support the best in student conduct and government. In spite of the fact that the fraternity membership constitutes only about 20 per cent of the male student body more than 50 per cent of the men in student activities such as athletics, student publications, musical organizations, dramatics, oratory and debate, etc., are members of one or other of the nine fraternities on the campus.

Twenty students of the school of commerce of O. A. C. under the direction of Professors Dubach and Maxey, of the political science department, recently spent two days in Salem studying the government of our state at first hand. Calls were made on Governor Withycombe, the legislature, the offices of the secretary of state, the industrial accident commissioner, and the insurance commissioner, and a few of the party inspected the penitentiary and the hospital for the insane.

The class in Institutional Management, with Miss Hadwen as instructor, is planning the meals for Waldo Hall. Each girl plans the meals and does the ordering for two weeks, and during this time she is responsible to the instructor for everything in the kitchen and dining room, and must report any deficiency. Later the class will make an inventory of the kitchen and dining room equipment. The course is a one-semester elective for junior and senior girls in the domestic science department.

The scope of the work of the catering class of the domestic science department has been enlarged this semester to include a limited number of small banquets, teas, luncheons and dinners. Special orders will be taken for fancy cookery once or twice a month.

The latest figures from the registrar's office show the total enrollment at O. A. C. to be 1803, exclusive of the short course students. Of this number, 857 are new students this year, of whom 101 are transfers from other colleges or universities. There are 56 post-graduates from 17 different institutions, including Purdue, Pennsylvania State College, Ohio State College and Stanford.

Twenty-four boys of the college have registered for the one semester course in camp cookery, given under the direction of Miss Grace Johnson, of the domestic science department. Attired in aprons and armed with kitchen utensils, the boys work from 7 o'clock until 10 on Monday nights, learning the scientific construction of flapjacks and mulligans. During the second semester work will be taken up in the field, and meals will be prepared in the open as in actual camp life.

Ben Rush, of Elgin, a senior in irrigation engineering, has accepted a position at Bremerton, Wash., in the mold loft of the United States navy. Mr. Rush, who has been a leader in the student activities of the college, was this year manager of the Barom-

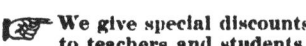

eter, the student newspaper, and is a member of the Alpha Tau Omega fraternity. He takes up his new work immediately.

Oregon Normal School.

All connected with the Normal School were delighted that the last legislature found it possible to grant us the money necessary for taking over the Independence schools for training school facilities, and also for extending the chapel. These two factors of the Normal School work have long since been over-crowded, and both additional opportunities will be thoroughly appreciated.

Dean Alden, of the Department of History at Willamette University, was the assembly speaker for February 2, taking for his topic, "Historical Lies." Dean Alden's presentation of the method of historical research and the inaccuracies which creep into it was a very interesting and scholarly presentation of his subject.

On the 2nd of February the Lyceum Course provided for the entertainment of the school the motion picture film, "King Lear." This was also made use of by the Department of English.

February 10 was the date of the Polk county institute at Monmouth. The plan, which is becoming almost an annual one, of holding one of the local Polk county institutes at Monmouth on a Saturday, when the regular school work in the Normal and training department is held, is a delightful way of bringing the teachers of Polk and other neighboring counties into closer relationship with the Normal School, giving them an opportunity to know the actual work of the various departments. Lunch was served by the domestic science class, under the direction of Miss Butler, and the 125 teachers were adequately provided for. Miss Laura Taylor, of the Department of Physical Education, gave her chapel talk in the afternoon for the benefit of the school and the visiting teachers. Miss Taylor took as her subject, "The Use of the Victor in Rhythmic Exercises," and by drills, folk dances, songs and other exercises by the children of all grades in the training department gave a very pleasing and instructive demonstration of how extremely use-

ful the Victor can be made in school work.

The Normal School held a special program for Lincoln's birthday, with Rev. C. E. Cline, of Portland, as the principal speaker. Rev. Cline's intimate knowledge of that part of the country where Lincoln lived, and his personal recollection of many of the stories and incidents of Lincoln's career enabled him to speak about the life of this greatest of Americans in a way that was a revelation to his hearers. For nearly two hours Rev. Cline held the large, appreciative audience at perfect attention.

Mrs. George McMath, president of the Oregon Congress of Mothers and Parent-Teacher Associations, was the assembly speaker for February 16. Mrs. McMath spoke on the work of the parent-teacher associations, and gave the assembled teachers many very practical suggestions as to the organization and management of parent-teacher associations, showing them with a number of concrete illustrations how these associations can be made of very great value in the school work of the community.

"Rural School Week," an expression which has long been heard around the Normal School, and which actually materialized between February 18 and 24, was a very noteworthy event in the history of the school. During this week 150 Normal School students of the Rural Department visited, observed and taught in the rural schools of Marion, Benton, Yamhill, Washington and Polk counties. (The arranged-for work could not be carried out in Yamhill County, as a good many of the schools were closed on account of contagious diseases.) This gave them an insight into actual rural school conditions and a grasp of the actual teaching situations which no amount of class room work could equal. At the close of the week county meetings were held at Hillsboro, South Salem, Mountain View and Elkins. These county meetings were attended by the regular teachers and the Normal School students of that county and the experiences of the week were given in round table discussions, under the guidance of County Superintendents Barnes, Smith, Cannon and Crowley. In the afternoon programs were given by the Normal School students of each county, and addresses by some member of the Normal School faculty. President

Ackerman attended the Hillsboro meeting, Mr. Ostien the Marion county meeting, Mr. Pittman and Mr. Butler the Benton county meeting, and Mr. Evenden the Polk county meeting. The outline of the plan and some of the details will be found in another part of the paper. Suffice it to say, that in meeting the rural school problem of Oregon which the Oregon Normal School has always tried to do, this week will mark a great progressive step.

The History Department, under the direction of Mr. Butler, head of that department, gave a program for Washington's birthday. This program was of the type which can be given by the students in their respective schools, and as such was very helpful. It was also well done, and a very pleasing presentation of some of the scenes of Washington's life.

February 26, following the rural school week, County Superintendents Barnes, Smith, Cannon and Crowley were visitors at the Normal School, where they witnessed the return celebration of the rural school people and participated with their county groups. These men were enthusiastic over the work which had been accomplished and much credit for the success of the previous week can rightly be given to their hearty cooperation. They spent the remainder of the day visiting classes in the Normal School.

Prof. F. S. Dunn, of the University of Oregon, spoke to an appreciative audience on the "Holy Land," using stereoptican slides to illustrate his lecture. Prof. Dunn's intimate knowledge of this subject, his extensive research into it, and his power of description, made this lecture extremely worth while to the students and towns-people who heard it. The lecture was given under the auspices of the Y. W. C. A.

The Normal School was especially favored when the Lyceum Course Committee was able to secure a lecture by Miss Ida M. Tarbell. Miss Tarbell lectured on "Industrial Idealism," a topic which perhaps no one in this country can speak upon with more authority. Her presentation of the brighter sides of industrialism, and the many ways in which the large industries are benefiting and revolutionizing society was a revelation to most of her audience. Miss Tarbell explained the motives back of such work, showing that it was a typically American desire for efficiency, and not necessarily any feeling of philanthropy which prompted this. Underneath, however, Miss Tarbell found reason to hope for a brighter day and an equal ability to share in the result of labor for the great mass of people of this country. Miss Tarbell's visit to the Oregon Normal School will be long remembered and will bear fruit in many school rooms over the state.

Much interest is being manifested in the Normal School over the coming inter-collegiate oratorical contest at Corvallis. In the final tryout Miss Mamie Radabuagh, of Oakland, Oregon, was selected to represent the Oregon Normal School, and the student body are enthusiastic in their support, and plan to send a large delegation to Corvallis.

During the month the senior class was represented by Mary Randall, who took for her subject, "The Use of the Victrola in the School," and Mr. R. W. Dobell, who spoke on the attitude of teachers toward crippled children. Both of these papers were splendid presentations of their subjects.

Law Questions Answered.

Attorney Elmo S. White: "What is the maximum interest which I can get upon school warrants now held by me?" Six per cent.

* * *

Attorney Elmo S. White: "How long after a mortgage is foreclosed in this state does one have in which to redeem the property?" One year.

* * *

Attorney Elmo S. White: "When are taxes payable?" The first half of all taxes legally levied and charged to be paid on or before the fifth day of April following, and the second half on or before the fifth day of the next October.

* * *

Mr. White: "What provision of law is there in Oregon for military training in the public schools?" The session of the legislature just closed passed a bill which will be the law on and after May 21, 1917, providing for establishing military training in the high schools of the state subject to direction, supervision and inspection directed by the governor. Graduation credit is to be given, the amount to be determined by the state board of education.

County Superintendents' Department

Edited by CLYDE T. BONNEY, The Dalles, Oregon

Benton County.

During the week of February 19 to 23, thirty teachers from the Oregon Normal School visited in the county in twelve different districts.

Supt. S. S. Duncan of Yamhill was in Benton county during the week of March 12 to 17, visiting. The visit is in exchange for one to be made by Supt. Cannon in Yamhill county.

Local teachers institutes have been held at Monroe and Philomath. At these institutes the teachers take part in round-table discussions, waich proves very interesting. Local conditions are discussed and phases of school work regarding individual districts where the teachers are teaching are talked over.

Spelling contests are being entered into enthusiastically by the schools in Benton county. Last year in the annual spelling contest no more than 125 were expected to be on hand to spell, but when the date of May 20 rolled around there were 325 enthusiastic boys and girls ready to spell. The successful spellers had competition to the very finish. One girl spelled 2238 words correctly. This year the annual spelling contest occurs May 19.

The Luckiamute Club, which has a charter signed by Supt. Cannon, has been organized in the Hoskins school. The club gave a social entertainment in November at which $17.40 was raised, to be used for purchasing of school supplies. The Hoskins school has been second highest in attendance in the county during one month and had no tardiness for four months. There are 24 pupils enrolled. The school building is new and fully equipped. It was built on the grounds of the historic old Fort Hoskins.

Coos County.

The Parent-Teachers' Association of Bridge school gave a basket social on the evening of January 27. It was a great success and, althougn a stormy evening, the people turned out in full force. Fifty dollars was raised from the sale of baskets and this will be used for the purchasing of apparatus. The entertainment was held in the new gymnasium building.

On February 10, a program was given by the Sumner school children in the Sumner Hall. It was followed by a basketball game between Sumner and Marshfield Independents in which Marshfield won, the score being 38 to 12. The baskets were auctioned, and luch served in the dining room to them without baskets. Mrs. Grace Delmore, the teacher, received many compliments on the program rendered and the good time following. Forty-five dollars was the returns and it will bo used for school house improvements, another $45 being on hand for playground apparatus.

Crook County.

The superintendent's office has recently sent out complete sets of flash cards for primary reading and the fundamentals of arithmetic.

School work in Crook county has been greatly interfered with by an epidemic of measles and the heavy snows and severe weather has kept some of our young people out of school.

Miss Cowgill, one of the state club workers, accompanied Supt. Myers to a number of schools spreading the gospel of club work. A number of young people have shown quite an enterprising spirit in the work.

It is proposed to have the Annal Track Meet and Declamatory Contest in May, but the participants now will consist of the pupils from Jefferson, Deschutes and Crook Counties. This is a continuation of the old Crook county field day. This year the event will be held at Bend. In times past this spirited school day has attracted larger crowds than any other holiday or celebration during the year and it is hoped that the combination of the three counties may, if anything, increase the popularity of the day.

The most active work in the reading circle work is being done that we have seen since the scheme was introduced. The plan of having a number of books in the superintendent's office, to be loaned to the teachers, has encouraged this more than any other one thing. Supt. Myers keeps on hand at least one of all of these books and of some he has three or four copies. They are loaned to the teachers for two weeks and in some cases longer. He reports that the books are in use all the time and some of the teachers in Crook county have read three or four of them. The money expended for these books, Supt. Myers claims is money well spent.

Red Cross drills for the girls in the Crook County high school are being tried this year. Up to the severe weather the experiment has worked out very satisfactorily. The girls are under the charge of two lady teachers who understand this class of work. It has been particularly efficient in bringing a reasonable amount of systematized exercise to those girls who would otherwise not receive any at all. The boys have organized a military squad (guns and ammunition furnished by Uncle Sam) and have done very efficient work in their various drills. In connection with this a military band was organized which is developing into quite a musical organization and can now play a number of good musical selections. Now since the boys have their military suits, the three drill days each week have become quite an important feature. Many of the townspeople have been visitors on the campus during these drill periods and have given the boys much encouragement, not only by their presence ebut by their commendation of the work, which has been done in an orderly way.

Jackson County.

Unless the landlady is compelled to make another raise on the board bill, Jackson county will be well represented at the National Education Association in Portland this summer.

County Judge F. L. Tou Velle proclaimed Friday, February 22 Arbor Day for Jackson county. Severe storms made it impossible to plant trees, shrubbery, etc. on that day, but in many cases appropriate exercises were held and the yards will be made more beautiful later by the addition of desirable planting.

A writing contest has been under way in Jackson county for some time. Papers showing the best skill of each student are sent each month to the superintendent's office and at the close of the contest prizes will be awarded students making the greatest improvement during the year. Mr. A. N. Palmer, author of the state text will aid in judging the papers. Much interest is being shown by both teachers and pupils. Many teachers who had not previously completed the course or who did not take it, are now enrolling for the free course being offered by the A. N. Palmer Company. Spelling and composition are receiving attention by means of contests also.

An effort is being made to bring a large per cent of the schools up to the requirements for an Oregon standard school. A series of illustrated talks will be given in different parts of the county in which slides of some standard schools of remote parts of Oregon also a few from Jackson county will be shown. All but a few of the schools of the county should be able to meet these requirements. Schools meeting the requirements since the first of the year are: Galls Creek, Maude Miller, teacher; Valley View, W. H. Ashcraft, Ashland; Pine Grove, Mrs. Harriet Minthorn, Rogue River; Foots Creek, Mrs. Bertha McKinney, Rogue River; North Phoenix, Alice Cromar, Medford; Little Applegate, Mrs. E. E. Sams, Buncom; Crater Lake, Pearl Gould, Butte Falls.

Lincoln County.

The new law requiring the eight month term will give the pupils in thirty-four districts in this county a much better chance to get the schooling they are entitled to, for of that number, twenty-nine now give a six months' term while the other five get but seven.

Of the sixty-nine school districts in Lincoln county, that are in good standing, ten will have summer schools. Just a few years back, at least one-half of the schools in the county held summer terms. In the near future when all districts have the eight months' term there will be but few if any truly summer sessions.

There are three standard high schools in the county and the attendance in them is much better than in former years. The schools at Newport and Toledo have each a daily attendance of about one-fourth above last year. The junior high school at Newport is holding the pupils in the school that might otherwise tire of the grammar grades.

On Saturday, February 17, a local institute was held at Newport with about thirty-five teachers in attendance. ~A good program was carried out, the main theme of which was "Little Things." During the noon hour the domestic science class served lunch in the dining room of the high school building.

Multnomah County.

The first unit of the Multnomah county teachers institute was held in the Lincoln high school, Saturday, March 10, 1917. Reading was the principal theme of this session. Miss Sabra Conner of Shattuck school, Mrs. Jean McCracken and Mrs. Josephine Lisher of Couch school illustrated different phases of eighth, fourth and primary reading with their respective classes. Miss Conner's eighth grade class first read from the Agricultural Readers, new to the class, to show that the boy or girl should be able to read intelligently at sight any ordinary page; then what may be done to form habits of reading was proven when pupils gave lists of library books read in a month and selected readings from Tom Sawyer, The Long Trail, Autobiography of Franklin, Oliver Twist and Rebecca of Sunny Brook Farm. The third part of the lesson taught a love and appreciation of poetry, selections being recited from Longfellow, Lowell, Riley, and Tagore. The lesson concluded with an illustration of the use of dramatization in the reading recitation, to teach expressive reading by selections from The King of the Golden River, and Oliver Twist. The fourth grade reading demonstrated by pupils under the direction of Mrs. Jean Park McCracken dealt first with a study recitation to illustrate the intensive mode of dealing with reading. "The Brook" by Tennyson was selected and the children prepared for it by a short biographical and geographical setting. The story found in the first part of the poem

was informally told accompanied by illustrative pictures drawn by Miss Esther Hawkins of Couch school. The second period developed a prose selection read at sight. The pupils read fluently in a pleasant natural voice with a nicety of pronunciation and that expression which is the result of a sympathetic understanding of the text. Mrs. Lisher amplified the teaching of interpretation in reading. She claims that the teaching of true interpretation is quite as important in the first grade as it is in the fourth. A part of the time of each period was given to a detailed dissection of H. C. Bunner's poem "One, Two, Three," in Wheeler's Third Reader. This explicit interpretation illustrated the value of the use of simple, standard rules by which any teacher can be guided in her preparatory work on the interpretation of a new lesson. It was shown also that an observance of these rules might prove the means of correcting prevalent faults in oral reading. The last half of each period was given to class work demonstration of the value of the art of questioning by the teacher for the purpose of getting from pupils interested response and correct expression. At the assembly in the afternoon the teachers were given a musical treat by the Chemawa Indian Orchestra in native costume. Then Robert Krohn director of physical culture in the Portland public schools instructed teachers in games and plays which may be used with value in the rural schools. Marked interest was shown by visiting teachers and many expressions of pleasure and approval were heard. The next unit will be held Saturday, April 7, 1917.

Polk County.

The zone meetings have been held through the month as usual and have been well attended in spite of the bad weather.

Supt. Crowley addressed the Woman's Club of Independence February 27, on the subject of Industrial Work in the Schools.

The week of February 19-23 was Rural Week at the Oregon Normal and Polk county had twenty-eight of these student teachers in the rural schools during that week. The first of the week the visiting teachers observed the work of the schools but later in the week in most of the

schools they did some of the teaching. It was a time of inspiration for both visitors and local teachers as it called forth the very best efforts of all. During the week the various schools were visited by Superintendent Crowley, Supervisor Moore, Prof. M. S. Pittman of the Normal, and Normal students who are taking the Supervisor's Course. On Saturday, February 24, a rally was held at the Elkins school which was attended by the local teachers and their visitors. The work of the week was reviewed, each visiting teacher giving a short talk on the things observed during the week. A delicious luncheon was served by the patrons of the Elkins school and in the afternoon a program was given. This consisted of music, readings, addresses by the county superintendent and supervisor and a drill and playlet by the Normal students. All voted the experiment a success and hope for a longer period of such work next year.

Union County.

A local institute was held at La-Grande, February 24, which was in every way a profitable meeting. About seventy-five teachers were present and all went away feeling it was good to have been there.

It is hoped that every teacher in Union County will be able to attend the National Education Association in Portland, July 7-14 and enroll as an associate member. It is surely the coming event in educational circles.

Supt. E. E. Arant of Union has been unanimously re-elected and for a term of three years. Supt. A. E. Clawson of Elgin has been unanimously re-elected and has signed a contract for two years. Both gentlemen have had an advance in salary.

North Powder students are enjoying the splendid new school house and Supt. Churchill on a recent visit there checked up the high school and pronounced it standard. The school attendance throughout the county has been lowered by the deep and almost impassable snow storms and drifts.

Umatilla County.

A. T. Park has been re-elected city superintendent of the Pendleton school for another year. Mr. Park has built up the Pendleton school giving special attention to the grades, and has now reached a point where the excellence of the course has demonstrated itself. Particular attention has been paid to the proper division of time between regular and special subjects. Departmental instruction has been introduced in the upper grades. The Pendleton plan carries departmental or junior high school methods into the fifth, sixth, seventh and eighth grades.

Wasco County.

An illustration of harmony in a school district and appreciation of truly good work on the part of a thoroughly competent and very conscientious teacher, was recently exemplified in the "Rail Hollow" school, District No. 36 of Wasco county. The occasion was the sixtieth birthday anniversary of Mrs. Lucy S. Ruggles, the teacher of the district. Mrs. Ruggles has raised her own family and is giving the closing years of her life to improve the citizenship of the world, through the medium of teaching. Mrs. Ruggles is a graduate of Monmouth Normal and a teacher of wide-spread experience. The county superintendent insists that the best supervising a superintendent can do is in the matter of assisting school boards to secure thoroughly competent teachers. He insists further, that some of Wasco county's best teachers are in the rural schools. They have been serving hot lunches in this school and on this particular day, one of the good ladies of the district notified Mrs. Ruggles that the lunch for this day would be sent up just at 12 o'clock. Nearly every man and woman appeared at the school house laden with the baskets and boxes containing all kinds of good things to eat as only farmers' wives know how to prepare them. Two tables were prepared reaching entirely across the school room and the visitors, including Supt. C. T. Bonney and the children, stood around these tables and did full justice to the splendid lunch. After the dinner, which was a complete surprise to Mrs. Ruggles, there was an hour of speech-making in which the county superintendent, members of the school board and a few of the patrons took part. The meeting was unanimous in favor of hiring Mrs. Ruggles on a three-year

contract and at substantial increase in salary.

Yamhill County.

The Parent-Teacher Circle of Springbrook, recently held a bazaar, at which they cleared $109.27, which will be used for the benefit of the school.

Mrs. Grace Duren, who has charge of Lower Gopher Valley school, finds the new heating plant a great improvement over the stove they used last year. The plant is giving perfect satisfaction.

Miss Meda Goodrich, the teacher in Dupee Valley, is rejoicing with her pupils over a supply of new and modern seats. The people contemplate several improvements in this building in the near future.

Miss Lula Mae Long, Rock Creek school, reports that a new water system has been installed. This district has a modern building and now needs only a heating and ventilating plant to make it a standard school.

Whiteson, the Waddell school, and the Durham school met in Whiteson on Friday, March 2, and gave a splendid program by the pupils, while the patrons and teachers discussed many matters of interest to the schools. The manual training department of the Whiteson school had some splendid work on exhibition, and the basketry by the girls and some by the boys was certainly a credit to both pupils and teacher. Dinner was served in the primary room, and the social hour, as well as the luncheon was thoroughly enjoyed by every one present.

Miss Ruby Alexander, of Deer Creek is teaching in one of the least expensive and yet one of the most modern school buildings in the county. A recent fire deprived the district of the building they were using, but the Gopher Valley Lumber Co. furnished the logs and mill free, and the men gave their labor, with the result that in a comparatively few days the pupils were better housed than ever in a modern building, lighted as it should be and seated as well as the best. The total cost to the district was about $100 for furniture, nails, and windows, and they are now provided with a building that will amply serve their purpose for years.

The first rally for the year was held in Masonville, District No. 13, Tuesday, February 27. Muddy Valley school and No. 47 joined with Masonville in the meeting and did their part to make the day a success. The Masonville school gave the welcome song, after which the remainder of the morning session was given to discussions by various patrons and teachers, and an address by Earl Kilpatrick, a member of the faculty of the U. of O. The more serious parts of the program were interspersed with recitations and songs by the pupils of the various schools, which were thoroughly enjoyed by all present. After the noon luncheon, which certainly gave no hint of the high cost of living, the afternoon program was opened by the rally song by all the schools, and this was followed by other numbers by the pupils. Mr. Kilpatrick's second address closed the meeting, and every one present felt that the day had been well spent. Mr. Kilpatrick has worked in the rallies in this county for the past three years, but he always has something new for his audience, so the announcement that he is to address the meetings is always received with delight.

Membership in the State Teachers' Association

Membership in the State Teachers' Association for 1917 began with January 1. Already a number of teachers have enrolled for the new year, paying $1.50 for membership including the Oregon Teachers Monthly for one year. Watch the list grow! Those enrolled to March 15 are as follows:

1 Belle Smith, Glide
2 Normal School, Emporia, Kans.
3 Margaret Thompson, Oregon City
4 Marion Mudgett, Hoff
5 Mary Vierhus, Oregon City
6 J. Q. Willits, Kerby
7 Herbert Blatchford, Waldport
8 Emma H. Murray, Klamath Falls
9 Marguerite Clark, Klamath Falls
10 M. Ethel Davey, Mill City
11 Ethel Shaffer, Lebanon
12 Julia Hamer, Lutgens
13 Hazel Hall, Turner
14 Hilda Muender, Butler
15 Bessie McFarland, Prineville
16 Emma Howard, Portland
17 Lillian Koeller, Peardale, Calif.

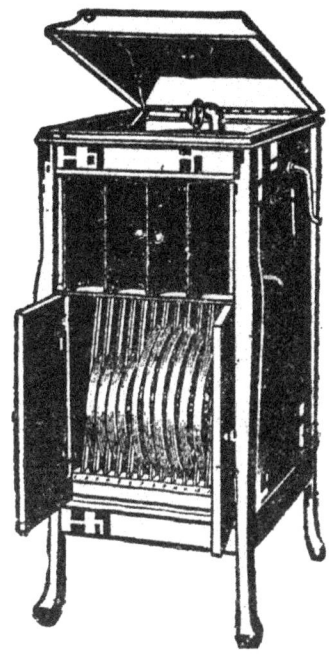

18 L. W. Riley, McMinnville
19 Verna G. Gardner, Amity
20 Ruth Chamberlain, Portland
21 Mildred N. Tilden, Nehalem
22 Annie Wickman, Marshfield
23 Laura Johanson, Cline Falls
24 Martha Skersies, Monmouth
25 Nell Moran, Portland
26 Bessie Parsons, Crawfordsville
27 Rae Langsworthy, Laurel
28 Lillian Loretz, Antone
29 W. T. Foster, Portland
30 Ruth Elkins, Canby
31 Cora E. Devor, Goshen
32 Jessie L. Turnidge, Sheridan
33 Edwin Woodworth, Molalla
34 H. Wayne Keesee, Klamath Falls
35 Buena S. Morganson, Scio
36 Alma L. Absten, Viento
37 Marguerita Andrews, Lostine
38 Mrs. M. E. Stockton, Freewater
39 G. H. Colvin, Haines
40 Sister M. Honorata, Tekoa, Wash.
41 Elsie Denson, Meacham
42 Mrs. M. E. Norton, Blachly
43 Frank J. O'Connor, Crescent
44 Guy E. Dyar, Eugene
45 Helen M. Crump, Airlie
46 Grace Snook, Alicel
47 Arlina A. Pickett, Lewiston, Ida.
48 Leona C. Jackson, Newberg
49 Nellie Herding, Astoria
50 Mrs. Joyce L. Hays, Cecil
51 P. C. Luh, Westerville, Ohio
52 Mrs. Helen Garey, Powell Butte
53 Anna V. Caldwell, Roseburg
54 Roberta Rippey, Portland
55 Mrs. Anna Barzee, Edenbower
56 Mrs. Daisy Short, Myrtle Point
57 Ruth Norton, Philomath
58 T. J. Means, The Dalles
59 F. H. Robinson, Port Orford
60 Mrs. Aurie Jewell, Portland
61 Herman Clark, Salem
62 Mrs. L. Allard, Woodburn
63 Leola Dunham, Cloverdale
64 Esther Suydam, Agness
65 Alice A. White, Chemawa
66 Will J. Roberts, Vale
67 Josephine O'Leary, Portland
68 Emily G. Forrester, Portland
69 Ebba Wiren, Astoria
70 Frances Gittens, Culver
71 Ethel A. Hopkins, Mikkalo
72 Margaret McCulloch, Jackson, Cal.
73 Anna Doyle Blackfoot, Idaho
74 Mrs. C. E. Goetz, Portland
75 Pres. W. J. Kerr, Corvallis
76 E. B. Lemon, Corvallis
77 C. J. McIntosh, Corvallis
78 Sister M. Guntilda, Tacoma
79 F. S. Gannett, Salem
80 Fred S Crowley, Dallas
81 Ruth E. Lutje, Enterprise
82 Mrs. N. A Springer, Aberdeen, Wn.
83 George E. Day, Yachats
84 Arleen E. Tilden, Barnesdale
85 Blanche Hubbs, Silverton
86 Mrs. Mae Anderson, Monmouth
87 Joyce Teeters, Monmouth
88 Bessie Williamson, Corvallis
89 May E. Reeves, Summer Lake
90 Chas. H. Jones, Salem
91 R. H. Powell, Prineville
92 Ava B Milam, Corvallis
93 N. H. Comish, Corvallis
94 Joyce Casteel, Flora
95 Adona Cochrane, Salem
96 Mary E. Fawcett Corvallis
97 E. S. Evenden Monmouth
98 Albert Carey, Nortons
99 E. D Ressler, Corvallis
100 Mrs. M. L. Fulkerson
101 Sherman Shoales, Hubbard
102 Clara I. Langdon. Carlton

103 Lelah Parks, Creswell
104 J. H. Tompkins, Amity
105 Norma Reid, Portland
106 Mary E. Good, Gresham
107 Lucile Clark, Rainier
108 Mrs. Clara Beach, Klamath Falls
109 C. Hansen, Cottage Grove
110 F. C. Fitzpatrick, Roseburg
111 Eva Trent, Dayton
112 Lottie Dimick, Salem
113 Clara L. Green, Denio
114 R. G. Dykstra, Independence
115 Abbie Coon, Philomath
116 H. F. Durham, Salem
117 J. E. Fulkerson, LaGrande
118 Eliza M. Pearson, Baker
119 O. C. Bennett, Sherwood
120 Mabel Barnes, Union
121 Gertrude Biever, LaGrande
122 Mrs. Chas. Ritchie, Lakeview
123 Minnie R. Allen, Monmouth
124 Belle Barker, Salem
125 Lane Morley, Talbot
126 Estella Criswell, Hubbard
127 W. A. Scott, Albany
128 D. J. Steiner, Colfax, Wash.
129 Ethel E. Miller, Post
130 F. D. Braly, Aurora
131 W. I. Reynolds, Dallas
132 Etta Stimpson, Acme
133 W. B. Young, Albany
134 A. B. Cordley, Corvallis
135 Mina B. Hubbs, Canby
136 Wm. A. Fletcher, Buell
137 Elizabeth Wirt, Willamette
138 B. S. Wakefield, Creswell
139 Agnes Hilary, McMinnville
140 Grace Hottinger, Stayton
141 Eunice Townsend, Molalla
142 Dominican Sisters, Portland
143 Rachel Maneman, Klamath Falls
144 Sara Mark McMinnville
145 Edith Sherwood, Mill City
146 Lelah Hevland, Newberg
147 Oliver Weesner, Newberg
148 John Gavin, The Dalles
149 F. Thordarson, Bend
150 Lexie Strahan, Joseph
151 Grace M. Reed, Milwaukie
152 Helene S. Biggs, Burns
153 G. A. Ruring, Vale
154 Mrs. Ada Burch, Berlin
155 Sabra L. Nason, Pendleton
156 B. E. Wick, Armington, Mont.
157 Lucy Kopan, Hood River
158 Martha M. Eddlemon, Flora
159 Myrtle E. Lay, Molalla
160 LaVine Sheridan, Canby
161 Isabella J. McCullogh, Astoria
162 E. B. Hughson, Portland
163 Clara Rutherford, Canby
164 Herbert W. Copeland, Pendleton
165 Sisters of St. Francis, Pendleton
166 Hazel Mulkey, Vale
167 Sisters of St. Mary, Sublimity
168 Belle Cologne, Wheeler
169 Carrie B. Adams, Elgin
170 Mrs. H. B. Brooks, Corvallis
171 H. T. Vance, Corvallis
172 J. F. Brumbaugh, Corvallis

Friendship is a plant of slow growth, and must undergo and withstand the shocks of adversity before it is entitled to the appelation.—Washington.

Oregon Congress of Mothers

By MRS. ELIZABETH HAYHURST, 1070 E. Burnside, Portland

Now that the legislature is over, we are rejoicing over the passage of several bills that the association was directly interested in, namely: The "Universal school suffrage" measure, introduced by Representative Sheldon; the "Eight months minimum school term" bill introduced by Mrs. Thompson; an enabling act that empowers school boards to establish parental schools when authorized to do so by the vote of the people, introduced by House Committee on Education; and a "substitute pension" bill introduced by Senator Huston.

The Congress of Mothers and Parent-Teachers' Association met with the representatives of the County Judges' Association and agreed to substitute rather than fight the bill to repeal the present law which had been introduced in the house at the solicitation of the county judges. In order to overcome the disastrous effect of the recent decisions of our supreme court which were responsible for much of the unpopular feeling toward the law, the word "pension" has been omitted and in the future it will be known as "Mothers Aid." The new law is largely composed of restrictions upon the recipient, and the mother who now receives the aid must be very worthy and needy indeed. The association accepted the compromise on the principle that it will be much easier to get more liberal amendments in the future than it would be to re-enact the law if the repeal bill had passed, and unfortunately, the law had been abused in a few cases which the officials seemed to keep uppermost in their minds rather than the great amount of good it was doing—so it is hoped that the new law will create a more popular public feeling.

As a tribute to their co-worker, the Oregon Congress of Mothers and Parent-Teachers' Associations, together with the Federated Clubs gave a banquet to Hon. Mrs. Thompson at the Multnomah Hotel, February 22, which was largely attended by representative men and women of the state. Mrs. F. S. Myers was the very capable chairman, and arranged an excellent program that was replete with surprises. Scores went from the banquet to the Grade Teacher's Colonial Party which was another success of the same evening.

Members of the state board will aid Supt. Churchill in preparing a new hand book on "Parent-Teacher Work" that is expected to be ready for distribution at the opening of the fall term. With this splendid co-operation it is hoped that Oregon will head the list in the states making the most progress in the Parent-Teachers' Association work.

The vacant lot movement that was started in the Portland Council of the Parent-Teachers' Association two years ago has grown to quite large proportions. The city government now recognizes the merit of it and is aiding to the extent of plowing the lots for the needy and will furnish 300 sacks of seed potatoes free as well as aid in the distribution of seeds that are coming from the government. Prof. Bouquet of O. A. C. and School Gardener L. A. Read will aid in the supervising. This is the highest type of charitable work as it helps the needy out of their poverty rather than help them in it.

The president, Mrs. Geo. McMath, and the treasurer, Mrs. A. Bonham, are planning to attend the National Convention of Congress of Mothers and Parent-Teachers' Association that meets in Washington, D. C., April 24 to May 4.

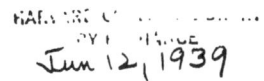

OREGON TEACHERS MONTHLY

The Official Journal of the State Teachers' Association

Vol. XXI	SALEM, OREGON, MAY, 1917	No. 9

Published Monthly Except July and August by the State
Teachers' Association

Entered at the Postoffice at Salem, Oregon, as second-class mail matter, April 1, 1898.

EDITORIAL BOARD

H. D. SHELDON, School of Education, University of Oregon, Eugene
E. F. CARLETON, Assistant Superintendent of Public Instruction, Salem
O. T. BONNEY, County School Superintendent, The Dalles
R. E. OHLOUPEK, Director Manual Training, Pendleton.
O. G. DONEY, President Willamette University, Salem
E. S. EVENDEN, Department of Education, Oregon Normal, Monmouth
MRS. M. L. FULKERSON, Institute Instructor, Salem
GEORGE W. HUG, City Superintendent, McMinnville
HOFKIN JENKINS, Principal Jefferson High School, Portland.
MISS VIOLA ORTSCHILD, President Grade Teachers' Association, Portland
E. D. RESSLER, Department of Education, Oregon Agricultural College, Corvallis
MISS LILLIAN TINGLE, Supervisor Domestic Science, Portland
CHAS. H. JONES, Business and Managing Editor, Salem

RULES OF PUBLICATION

1. The mailing label on the Oregon Teachers Monthly shows the date to which subscriptions are paid.
2. The Oregon Teachers Monthly will be sent to subscribers until ordered discontinued and all arrearages are paid.
3. Notice of change of address should be given at once, naming both old and new postoffice.
4. When renewing, always state that subscription is a renewal.
5. The subscription price, including membership in State Teachers' Association, is $1.50 a year in advance. Single copy, 20 cents.
6. Advertising rates will be furnished on application.
Address all communications to Oregon Teachers Monthly, Salem, Oregon.

Editorial Notes

We desire to call attention to the list of committees for investigations announced later in this issue. The personel of these bodies as well as the importance and scope of the subjects should arouse the interest of all members of the Association. This interest may well take practical form, in the shape of letters and suggestions to the chairmen of the various committees. With such a variety of subjects to choose from, including as it does minimum salaries, training of teachers, promotion of thrift, sex hygiene, retardation in rural districts, it should be possible for every member to contribute points of value from his experience.—S.

* * * *

One of the least satisfactory achievements of the last legislature was the enactment of the law reducing the term of school director in first class districts from five years to three. While on the surface this move was a cheap appeal to popular democracy, its real motivation was very different, being an attempt to score a point in a local feud agitating one of our leading communities. The administration of schools is a business and like every other business demands both experience and expert knowledge. Few men have enjoyed the advantage of this particular type of experience before election, at least one or two years must intervene before efficiency is reached. By the new law, a member is dropped from the board just after he has mastered the situation; it insures a majority of inexperienced members on the board. An appropriate title for this law would have been, "An act to secure inefficiency in the administration of the larger school systems in Oregon."—S.

*   *   *   *

The report of the Committee on Military Training of the Department of Superintendence is in many respects a timely and useful document. It contains a clear-cut account of the systems of military training now in use, a discussion of the physical values of military training and a warning against expecting very much in the way of real service from the training of boys under eighteen years of age. The last point mentioned is one of some importance as there seemed to be a tendency to overestimate the value of military training for school boys. Notwithstanding the serviceability of the report, one must confess to a disappointment at the tone of the committee. There is no bugle call to action, no recognition of the part which cadet corps play in arousing public opinion; the report is too predominantly negative. In fact it smacks of that invertebrate pacifism which for some years unfortunately characterized the public utterances of the National Education Association but which that organization repudiated last year in New York.—S.

*   *   *   *

This issue of the Oregon Teachers Monthly finds United States at war with the most aggressive and best organized nation of the old world. It must be remembered that this war has been forced on us against our will by tactics which no self-respecting nation could tolerate. Nor should it be forgotten, that the cause of political liberty and fair play is bound up with the outcome of this struggle; victory for the United States and its democratic allies in Western Europe means freedom throughout the civilized world, in Berlin and Vienna as well as in London, Paris and Petrograd. This being the case, we can cheerfully bear the privations and sufferings entailed by war. The unanimity with which the entire American people are supporting President Wilson shows how thoroughly our national ideals have permeated every class of society and every section of the country. In bringing about this desired result no element has been more influential than the public school system. This war with its quickening of the public pulse and its elevation of public opinion to a loftier plane of nationalism, is a great opportunity for the school teacher.—S.

*   *   *   *

Every teacher should make the most of the present opportunity to teach patriotism. Open every school day with the salute to the flag and the pledge of allegiance. There may be a question as to the ad-

visability of discussing the issues involved, particularly in the lower
grades. The writer believes that our government's position in this
war should be presented to the pupils of the junior and senior high
schools as a part of their civic education. If the presentation is made
without rancor and in the spirit of President Wilson's message, only
good can result. However that may be, all of us are Americans and owe
allegiance only to the Stars and Stripes. It is proper that teachers
and pupils should respond to the country's call with enthusiastic
loyalty. Our emotions are rightfully stirred with love of country and
we should be ashamed were it otherwise. But emotional response is
not enough. There must be action. Every teacher and every child
may "serve his country." Our government's program of preparedness
includes practically every activity, public and private. We may do
our teaching, our studying, our ordinary household, shop, store, field
and other daily duties for our country. Give every child something to
do. Let him feel the thrill of pride in loyal service. At the time this
is written, a great shortage in farm labor is foreseen, imperiling the
food supply through failure to get the crops planted. Here is an
opportunity for the larger and more mature boys in the upper grades
and high school to volunteer for service in our industrial army. Con-
scription may even be necessary. The production and conservation of
food is vital to both the combatant and non-combatant. The girls can
be used in harvesting and preserving fruit and other crops. It is
probable that this service may call out from school some of our pupils.
This may not be as heroic as the call to the front, but the service is
none the less vital and may be performed in the same spirit.—R.

* * * *

A resolution was adopted at the annual meeting of the Inland
Empire Teachers' Association in Spokane in which the teachers of the
four states accepted a special responsibility for the success of the N. E.
A. convention in Portland next July. In addition to urging the teachers of Idaho, Montana, Washington and Oregon to take out memberships and attend the convention, it was resolved that the teachers of
the Inland Empire accept the obligation of hosts to the teachers of the
other states. This is the first time in the sixty years' history of the
National Association that its annual convention has been scheduled
within the borders of the Inland Empire and Portland and Oregon's
invitation to make it a "family affair" was enthusiastically received.
Reports from Washington, Montana and Idaho indicate that Oregon
will be hard pushed in the race for advance memberships. There are
actually more teachers in Washington than in Oregon within a given
radius of Portland and our neighbors on the north are very much
awake. So far as the Executive Committee of the N. E. A. is concerned, Oregon's generosity in sharing the honors of host with her
neighbors will not relieve her of any responsibility in the matter of
memberships. State Superintendent Churchill is highly pleased with
the response to the campaign from his office and he is confidently

relying upon Oregon to equal or surpass the great record of Utah at the Salt Lake meeting of 1913 when 108 per cent of her teachers were enrolled. Only one other record above 50 per cent has been made and that was 86 per cent by California in 1888. Can we finish one, two, three?—R.

* * * *

"Fear, the great destroyer of standards," is one of the principal reasons for the unprofessional attitude which many teachers take toward their contracts. It is often the fear that no position will be secured for the next year which causes the premature signing of a contract and its subsequent breaking, when a more desirable opening may have come. It is often the fear of the teacher under contract for another year in a place where she does not wish to teach permanently, but where she is just beginning to be a constructive force, that if she does not accept the offer of another position, she may never get another opportunity to advance. These and other similar fears, engendered oftentimes by consciousness of inefficiency or lack of preparation have caused teachers to be very selfish in their attitude toward a contract. In no other business are so many contracts broken. In a great majority of cases this is done by the teacher, who goes unpunished because of a community's loathness to have enforced unwilling service. It stands to reason that school boards will be interested in the merited advance of teachers and will not only not hinder but will aid whenever they can without jeopardizing the best interests of those they serve. The state has put its endorsement on the effort to check this lack of conscience in regard to a signed contract by passing Senate Bill 270, which prevents any teacher, after signing a contract, from resigning within thirty days before the term of school begins or at any time during the year without the unanimous consent of the school board. Let Oregon's further professional growth in this matter be voluntary rather than law imposed.—E.

* * * *

In the great undeveloped West the promises of the future lie in the development of its natural resources, most of which are obviously in the thinly settled districts ministered to educationally by rural schools. It is therefore a source of gratification to those interested in the economic development of Oregon to realize that at last the rural schools are beginning to come into their heritage. The active interest of the State Department, the standardization of rural schools, the careful attention of most of the county superintendents to their rural problems, the additional supervision of the county supervisors, the work of the Extension Department of the Oregon Agricultural College, the emphasis placed on the preparation of rural teachers by the Oregon Normal School, the industrial club work, the increasing of the minimum school term to eight months, the raising of standards of preparation for teachers, and other similar movements are rapidly increasing the efficiency of these smaller schools. Now comes the additionally gratifying news that the Executive Committee of the State Teachers' Association at its recent meeting appointed as one of its research committees a committee to investigate rural school conditions, especially those pertaining to the very important factors of ventilation and minimum salary. The report of this committee promises to be of more than state-wide interest and of immense practical benefit. If this commitee should in any way give you the opportunity to aid it in its study of this problem, do so willingly and conscientiously, feeling that it is our problem.—E.

* * * *

Governor Withycombe's appointment of the Textbook Commission is most gratifying to the teachers of Oregon. He has recognized the value of professional and expert opinion in the selection of the books which form the basis of instruction in the public schools. The majority of the commission is composed of teachers who are now and for many years have been active in the work. All the members are entitled to the respect and confidence of the teachers and general public as well. The governor has exercised unusual care and discrimination, doubtless due to his own appreciation of the importance of the work based on his personal experience as a teacher. Speaking for our profession we express our heartiest appreciation of the service rendered the boys and gils and of the recognition accorded the teachers. The personnel of the commission is as follows: Miss Margaret J. Cosper, primary supervisor in Salem Public Schools; Mrs. A. E. Ivanhoe, superintendent Union County Schools; Mr. F. A. Tiedgen, superintendent Marshfield Public Schools; Mr. A. C. Schmitt, banker, Albany, also former teacher and college professor; Mr. Harrison G. Platt, attorney-at-law, Portland. —R.

Minutes of the Executive Committee

By E. D. RESSLER, Secretary-Treasurer

Pursuant to the call of the chairman, the first meeting of the Executive Committee of the Oregon Teachers' Association for 1917 was called to order in the office of the State Superintendent of Public Instruction, Salem, at 10:30 a. m., March 17, 1917, by the chairman, Supt. G. A. Briscoe of Ashland. Other members present were Supt. Mrs. A. E. Ivanhoe of Union county; Principal W. T. Fletcher, James John High School, Portland; Dean H. D. Sheldon, University of Oregon; State Superintendent J. A. Churchill, Salem; Assistant State Superintendent E. T. Carleton, Salem. Members absent were Mr. J. Percy Wells, Jacksonville, and Principal E. H. Whitney, Ockley-Green School, Portland. Acting Secretary E. D. Ressler was present by invitation of

Chairman Briscoe. Minutes of the last meeting of the Executive Committee for 1916 were read and approved.

Chairman Briscoe announced that he had appointed H. D. Sheldon as delegate and J. A. Churchill as alternate to the League of State Teachers' Associations at the annual meeting in Kansas City, Mo., February 26-March 3. Delegate Sheldon reported that he had attended the meeting and participated in the deliberations. Some of the state associations were organized along similar lines to that of the Oregon Association and others were planning re-organization. Valuable experiences in the operation of the various associations were exchanged and formal papers presented. The chairman continued Mr. Sheldon's appointment as delegate to represent the association at the next meeting to be held in connection with the N. E. A. convention in Portland July 7 to 14, 1917.

The question of State Headquarters for the N. E. A. convention in Portland was discussed at length. On motion of Mr. Churchill, it was ordered that an appropriation of $75 be made and a committee of three appointed to assist State Director Plummer in maintaining headquarters. Chair appointed Mr. Fletcher, Mrs. Ivanhoe, and Dr. Sheldon.

The next order was the discussion of the appointment of committees to make educational investigations and report at the annual convention of the State Association. On motion of Mr. Sheldon, chairman was authorized to appoint a committee of five to prepare a plan for School Credit for Private Music Study. On motion of Mr. Carleton, chairman was authorized to appoint a committee of nine on Standardization of Rural Schools. On motion of Mr. Carleton, chairman was authorized to appoint a committee of seven on Certification of Teachers for High School and Elementary Grades. On motion of Mr. Sheldon, chairman was authorized to appoint committee of nine on Thrift. On motion of Mr. Churchill, chairman was authorized to appoint committee of nine to continue work on Teachers' Retirement Fund. On motion of Mr. Sheldon, chairman was authorized to add to the committee on Retardation three members and to direct committee to consider also the problem in rural schools. On motion of Mr. Churchill, the chairman was authorized to appoint a committee of nine on Social Service.

On motion of Mr. Sheldon it was ordered that precedence be given to the committees on Standardization of Rural Schools and Certification of Teachers in the discussions of the Representative Council at the annual meeting. On motion of Mr. Sheldon, an appropriation of $50 was made to defray necessary expenses of all committees appointed, with the understanding that the respective chairmen secure authorization of the chairman of the Executive Committee before incurring any expense.

A recess for luncheon was taken at 12:15 p. m. Session resumed at 1:30 p. m., with Chairman Briscoe in the chair. On motion of Mr. Carleton, the hours of 9:30 to 12 m. were selected for the forenoon session of the department program of the annual convention of the

State Teachers' Association; for the afternoon session, 1:30 p. m. to 4 p. m. The motion also directed that the department programs be limited to three papers of 20 minutes each, with 30 minutes for discussion. On motion of Mrs. Ivanhoe, the dates December 27, 28, and 29, 1917, were selected for the annual convention. (The constitution fixes Portland as the place).

The chairman announced the appointment of Mr. Sheldon, Mr. Fletcher, and Mr. Carleton as the Finance Committee in accordance with the provisions of the constitution. On motion of Mr. Carleton, the expenses of this meeting of the Executive Committee were authorized.

After prolonged discussion of ways and means of increasing the membership and strengthening the work of the association, on motion of Mr. Sheldon an appropriation of $10 was voted for use of the president in organizing a campaign for memberships in the association. On nomination of Mr. Sheldon, E. D. Ressler, Corvallis, was elected Secretary-Treasurer, without salary. On motion of Mr. Churchill, the chairman was authorized to appoint an editorial board for the Oregon Teachers Monthly, official organ of the association.

On motion of Mr. Carleton, committee adjourned at 3:45 p. m.

REPRESENTATIVE COUNCIL COMMITTEES FOR 1917

1. **Social Service**—Supt. R. W. Kirk, Tillamook, chairman; Prof. B. W. DeBusk, University of Oregon; Supt. B. A. Adams, Lakeview; Supt. J. E. Dunton, Lebanon; Supt. Daniel Hull, Grants Pass; Rev. W. G. Elliot, Jr., Portland; Prin. S. F. Ball, Portland; Prin. H. K. Shirk, Burns; Supt. A. T. Park, Pendleton.

2. **School Credit for Private Music Study**—Supt. J. O. McLaughlin, Hood River, chairman; Mrs. Thomas Carrick Burke, Portland; Supt. L. B. Gibson, Hood River; Miss Mary Hohan, Oregon Normal School; Miss Jessie B. Miller, Salem; Prin. C. R. Bowman, Klamath Falls.

3. **Standardization of Rural Schools**—(This committee to make a study and report upon what has been accomplished in standardizing the rural schools in Oregon and what further requirements should be established along the following lines: (a) Qualification of teachers; (b) Minimum salary; and (c) Heating and Ventilation.)—Mrs. M. L. Fulkerson, Salem, chairman; Supt. W. W. Austen, Hamilton; Mr. R. P. Burkehead, Shaniko; Supervisor Floyd D. Moore, Dallas; Supt. W. M. Smith, Salem; Asst. State Supt. E. F. Carleton, Salem; Supt. Fay Clark, Vale; Miss Jean Byers, Macleay; Supt. J. E. Calavan, Oregon City.

4. **Thrift**—Supt. F. J. Tooze, Oregon City, chairman; Mr. J. W. McCoy, Ashland; Supt. C. T. Bonney, The Dalles; Mr. Thomas H. West, Ladd & Tilton Bank, Portland; Miss Gertrude Orth, Portland; Dean J. A. Bexell, Oregon Agricultural College; Mr. Luke Goodrich, First National Bank, Eugene; Supt. A. C. Strange, Baker; Mr. Jos. H. Albert, Capital National Bank, Salem.

5. **Certification of Teachers for High Schools and Grades**—(This committee to investigate certification laws in other states and make recommendations for Oregon certification, with a special reference to the question, "Should a standard university graduate be certified to teach in the grade schools, or should there be specific preparation for the sort of service a teacher is to render?")—Supt. F. A. Tiedgen, Marshfield, chairman; Supt. B. W. Barnes, Hillsboro; Miss Winifred Dennis, Portland; Miss Lucile Davis, Portland; Supt. Geo. W. Hug, McMinnville; Miss Gertrude Engle, Ashland; Prin. J. F. Elton, Astoria.

6. **Teachers' Retirement Fund**—Supt. R. L. Kirk, Springfield, chairman; Supt. Alfred Powers, Oakland; Miss Ida M. Smith, Eugene; Supt. I. E. Young, Pendleton; Supt. W. C. Alderson, Portland; Supt. John W. Todd, Salem; Miss Hallie Thomas, Portland; Supt. G. W. Ager, Jacksonville; Miss Margaret J. Cosper, Salem.

7. **Retardation**—Supt. C. W. Boetticher, Albany, chairman; Supt. V. Meldo Hillis, Medford; Supt. C. A. Rice, Portland; Supt. H. H. Hoffman, Heppner; Supt. R. E. Cannon, Corvallis; Supt. C. A. Howard, Coquille; Supt. F. Thordarson, Bend; Supervisor E. R. Peterson, Jacksonville; Supt. F. E. Fagan, Moro; Prof. F. L. Stetson, University of Oregon.

Some Stress Points in the Teaching of Arithmetic

By H. C. OSTIEN, Department of Mathematics, Monmouth

Why study arithmetic? The answer given to this question a generation ago differs materially from the answer we give to the same question today. I shall not stop to consider the answer of a generation ago; this is only interesting as history. But the answer we give to the question today is much to the point, because the content of that answer is the big factor in shaping and directing our teaching of the subject. A clearly defined and specific aim is a fundamental necessity in efficient teaching.

What then is our answer today to the question: Why teach arithmetic? What should be the dominant aim in teaching this subject in the elementary schools? Whether our aim is ultimately the best or not, I am not prepared to say, but at present we are answering the question after this fashion: Aim—To attain an accurate and ready knowledge of number and the number facts and processes and to apply this knowledge as an efficient business man does to the solution of such problems as one may meet in life. This aim, as you see, is strikingly utilitarian. But that is a quality that seems to mark most of our school work these days.

In analyzing this aim it is seen to be a dual one: First, gaining a knowledge of the number facts and processes, and second, making an application of this knowledge to the solution of problems. The logical relation of these two elements is that of a means to an end; the second, the end; the first, the means through which the end is attained. A knowledge of the number facts and processes has no value in itself; its value is found in its application.

Our best teaching today has this order of procedure: (1) Learn a number fact or process; (2) Follow this closely by applying the fact or process learned to the solution of such concrete problems as hold the interest of the pupil and are in content well within his mental grasp. In our State Course of Study the arithmetic work of the first five grades is given over very largely to a mastery of these number facts and processes in integers and fractions, the last three grades to an application of this knowledge to the solution of such classes of concrete problems as, in our judgment, have a maximum practical value.

The main task in the first five grades is that of mastering (1) the reading and writing of numbers, (2) the forty-five addition combinations with their corresponding substractions, (3) the multiplication tables with their corresponding divisions, (4) the four fundamental processes of addition, substraction, multiplication, and division, in both integers and fractions. Some additional work is provided, such as a study of the units of time, value, capacity, weight, length, area, and volume. But the main purpose of this provision is to supply problem material. These number facts and processes make up the pupil's kit of tools in arithmetic, for that is what they are, tools with which he does his work.

By constant and painstaking practice the apprentice learns to handle his tools with skill, ease, and certainty, and with the efficient workman, the movements in handling approach the automatic. In much the same way must the pupil master these number facts and processes. They must be so thoroughly learned that their handling will be with an ease and certainty that approaches the automatic. The result should be seen or the operation performed with a minimum of conscious effort.

The business world is prone to find fault with our school product for lack of accuracy and for failure to do work in a business-like way. Doubtless in many cases this charge is well grounded. Better work on our part will help to remove it. Much of the trouble is due to the failure of the pupil to master thoroughly the number facts and processes. Let us consider some of these causes of failure. The most prominent one is due to lack of proper drill. Drill work is usually the most difficult work the teacher meets in arithmetic, that is, efficient drill work. The very nature of drill makes it difficult to hold the interest of pupils, and listless drill accomplishes little. Pupils must be kept mentally alert. "Everyone on his toes" is the quality that should characterize drill. Switch frequently from individual to concert drill, but remember that individual drill alone will fasten individual responsibility. Drill on small units of work at a time: for example, take only three or four number combinations, and, by varied drill, see that they are mastered. And, above all, after intervening work, bring them up over and over again. Do not delude yourself with the notion that since a pupil knows a thing today that he will readily remember it tomorrow. The teacher's ingenuity and resourcefulness will be taxed to give variety to drill. Number games, devices, and individual and group contests are very helpful. Another cause of failure is due to a lack of neatness and order in doing work. From the start pupils should be taught to do their work in a neat and orderly manner. These qualities are matters of habit, therefore constant watchfulness, direction, and suggestion are necessary on the part of the teacher. To break up the habit of doing careless and disorderly work is one of the teacher's difficult tasks. It is often easier to form correct habits than to break up incorrect ones. See that figures are correctly formed and that work is put down with system and order. Try adding a zigzag column of figures in which you are not sure whether a certain figure is a 1 or a 7 and see how you lessen your chance for accuracy. Still another cause of failure is due to a lack of placing proper emphasis on accuracy. Some teachers are satisfied apparently with results nearly correct. They accept an answer correct within 2 cents, forgetting that the same error in computation in some other part of the work might have shown an error of $2000. Almost right in arithmetic is wrong. Also do not forget to have pupils form the valuable habit of checking their work; the business man always does this. Finally: In the work of the first five grades, the core of which is the mastery of the fundamental number facts and processes (the pupil learning to handle efficiently his kit of tools) the ever-present aim of the teacher should be to secure on the part of the pupils accuracy, speed, ease and skill, and neatness, order, and system in all written work.

If the pupil can handle efficiently his kit of tools of arithmetic, then his success in the solution of practical problems is fairly well assured. But at the best many difficulties arise, and, for one reason or another, pupils fail in the solution of concrete problems. Let us look at some of the causes of failure. Often pupils fail because of their inability to grasp the content of the problem. Problems should be such as hold the interest of the pupil; and also, as far as possible, such as can be brought within the pupil's experience. When a new topic is to be taken up for study every effort should be made to give the topic its proper business and social setting. For example: Before the problems in banking are worked, a study of banks should be made, a bank visited, if possible, and the nature and scope of its business learned; and the different blanks used should be shown and explained. In this way the content of problems may be brought within the experience of pupils.

More often pupils fail in the solution of problems because of their inability to discover relations. This is usually their stumbling block, and unfortunately, it is also the point on which it is most difficult to give instruction. These suggestions may help: (a) Problems in a new topic may be presented objectively, orally, reading by pupil. (b) Pupils must be led to discover the proper relations of the numbers in the problem by a logical sequence of questions asked an answered. Proper questioning in these cases is an art that many teachers have yet to learn. It is, in fact, the heart of this whole matter of leading pupils to discover the correct relations in a problem. Many times the questions asked by the teacher tend to confuse rather than to properly direct the thought of the pupil. (c) Time may be saved and more problems studied by giving the class period to an analysis (getting the "position") of problems, and having pupils make the computations outside class time. (d) Emphasize the oral solution of problems. (e) Train pupils in the separation of complex problems into their several simple problems. (f) Train pupils to do independent work. (g) Teachers should recognize that problem solving is a process of deductive reasoning and when explicitly stated takes the syllogistic form. For example—If one pencil costs 5 cents, what will three pencils cost? Major premise, 3 pencils cost 3 times as much as 1 pencil; minor premise, 1 pencil costs 5 cents; conclusion, therefore 3 pencils cost 3 times 5 cents, or 15 cents. Of course problems are not to be solved as above, but the principle on which the major premise depends should be understood. Pupils can be led to discover these principles by proper questioning. (h) Do not neglect this important rule of the business man: Estimate your answer; ask yourself the question, "From the conditions of the problem, is my answer a reasonable one?" (i) Lastly, put a premium on clear thinking. It doesn't hurt pupils to think; they enjoy it.

Cheerfulness And Mirth.

I have always preferred cheerfulness to mirth. The latter I consider as an act, the former as a habit of mind. Mirth is short and transient, cheerfulness fixed and permanent. Those are often raised into the greatest transports of mirth who are subject to the greatest depressions of melancholy. On the contrary, cheerfulness, though it does not give the mind such an exquisite gladness, prevents us from falling into any depths of sorrow. Mirth is like a flash of lightning, that breaks through a gloom of clouds and glitters for a moment; cheerfulness keeps up a kind of daylight in the mind, and fills it with a steady and perpetual serenity.—Addison.

Love Is Life's End.

Love is life's end; an end but never ending;
All joys, all sweets, all happiness awarding;
Love is life's wealth; ne'er spent but ever spending,
Love' life's reward, rewarded in rewarding.
Then from thy wretched heart fond care remove,
Ah! shouldst thou live but once love's sweet'st to prove,
Then wilt not love to live unless thou live to love.
—Edmund Spenser.

Educational Measurements

By O. A. GREGORY and F. C. AYER, University of Oregon

The following list of educational tests is here submitted to assist those teachers, who, in the past, have been unable to secure them because they did not know what tests were available and where they could be secured. The list is not complete but it is fairly representative of those tests that have been more or less standardized.

Perhaps a few words of caution will be appropriate at this time. (1) Educational tests are not a panacea for all educational ills. (2) They are used in diagnosis only. Just as a physician must, sometimes, make several tests before the real ailment is discovered, so it is, many times, necessary to give more than one educational test to discover the real school ailment. (3) When a test is made and a school is found to be below standard, a remedy should be applied and the school tested again to see if improvement has been made. Hence, at least two tests are necessary to discover progress. (4) Tests that are to be compared with standards must be done under standard conditions and unless they are done in that way, erroneous conclusions will be drawn. (5) Those unskilled in the use of tests should be careful and conservative in comparing the results of tests in their own schools with those in other schools.

Perhaps the best single book giving tests in the fundamentals with a discussion of them is "Educational Measurements" by Daniel Starch, published by the Macmillan Co., San Francisco, California, 1916 edition. This book gives from one to three tests in each of the following subjects: Reading, writing, spelling, grammar, arithmetic, composition, drawing, Latin, German, French, and physics. Two chapters of the book are devoted to "Marks as a Measure of School Work" which are very helpful and suggestive to teachers for grading examination papers.

Gray's Reading Tests—Address William B. Gray, School of Education, University of Chicago, Chicago, Ill. (oral-reading tests with directions and score sheets, $0.50 a hundred; silent-reading tests, $0.50 a hundred; state number wanted for each grade when ordering.) Read "Measuring the Work of the Public Schools," by Charles H. Judd, Cleveland Foundation, Cleveland, Ohio.

The Kansas Silent Reading Tests, Designed by F. J. Kelly—Address Bureau of Educational Measurements and Standards, Kansas State Normal School, Emporia, Kansas. Test 1 is for grades III, IV, and V; test II, for grades VI, VII, and VIII; test III, for grades IX, X, XI, and XII (price including directions and record sheets, $0.33 a hundred.) Read "The Kansas Silent Reading Test," by F. J. Kelly, Journal of Educational Psychology, February 1916.

Courtis Arithmetic Test, Series V—This test consists of a series of examples in each of the four fundamental operations. Address S. A. Courtis, 82 Eliot Street, Detroit, Michigan (price for tests, instructions and record sheets for a class of forty children, any grade from III to VIII, $0.35.) Read "A Manual of Instuctions for Giving and Scoring the Courtis Standard Tests" (price $0.75.)

Ayres' Handwriting Scale—Address Russell Sage Foundation, Division of Educational Research, New York City (scale, $0.05 a copy; descriptive bulletin, entitled "A Scale for Measuring the Quality of Handwriting of Children," $0.05 a copy.)

Thorndike's Handwriting Scale—Address Bureau of Publications, Teachers College, Columbia University, New York City, (handwriting scale, $0.08 a copy; handwriting scale with samples for practice and record sheet, $0.20 each.) Read "Handwriting," by E. L. Thorndike, Teachers College Record, March, 1910.

Ayres' Spelling Scale—Address Russell Sage Foundation, New York City (scale, $0.05 a copy.) Read "A Measuring Scale for ability in Spelling," by Leonard P. Ayres. Russell Sage Foundation, New York City.

Harvard-Newton Composition Scale—Address Frank W. Ballou, Department of Educational Investigations and Measurements, Boston, Mass. Read "Harvard-Newton Bulletin No. 2," September, 1914. Address Bureau of Educational measurements and Standards, Kansas State Normal School, Emporia, Kansas, and secure scale with directions for use and class record sheet (price $0.10.)

Hillegas' Composition Scale—Address Bureau of Publications, Teachers College, Columbia University, New York City (Hillegas' Composition Scale, $0.03. Hillegas-Thorndike Extension of Hillegas' Scale, $0.06.) Read "Hillegas Scale for Measurement of English Compositions," Teachers College Records, September, 1912.

Standard Research Tests in Algebra, By Walter S. Monroe—Address Walter S. Monroe, Bureau of Educational Measurements and Standards, Emporia State Normal School, Emporia, Kansas (price $1.25 per hundred.) Read "A Test of the Attainment of First-year High School Students in Algebra," by Walter S. Monroe. School Review, March, 1915.

If it is desired to test pupils in silent reading I would suggest the test designed by F. J. Kelly. Teachers should bear in mind that in silent reading an entire class can be tested at one time, while in oral reading but one can be tested at a time and it takes from two to four minutes to test each pupil. Test papers should be filed as a part of the permanent record of the school.

The New Committees for the 1917 Meeting

By G. A. BRISCOE, Ashland, Oregon

The committee on Social Service is to work out definitely as possible the question of sex hygiene as it is related to schools. Most school men, also many citizens, recognize it as a question of great importance in its bearing upon human welfare, yet no plan has been devised by which it may be safely and efficiently taught in the school room. The executive committee would be greatly pleased to have this committee make a full report of its investigations, findings and recommendations on December 27, 1917. If it is found that the subject can be properly handled in the school room, suggestions as to time and method should accompany the report. If it is found inadvisable to undertake the work in the school room, sufficient reasons should be assigned for the finding. In fact, school men being anxious to do the best for their communities and recognizing the importance and delicacy of this subject are awaiting with interest the finding of some impartial body on this question of sex hygiene. It is hoped that each member of this committee will feel the responsibility resting upon him and that no effort will be spared to obtain something definite and conclusive.

The committee on school cerdit for private music study has an important work to do. Many children in the public schools are giving time to the study of music out of school hours. Such study makes them valuable members of society. It is quite possible that ability to play a piano well, or any other musical instrument for that matter, may contribute more to the happiness and contentment of a people than the ability to read Latin or Greek. For that reason pupils who really accomplish something in music should be allowed high school credit to a certain amount. However, this does not mean that all who take music should have credit therefor. Nor does it mean that every person giving private music lessons should be accredited teachers of music. They may teach so far as the schools are concerned, but the high schools must not give credit for their work, unless the teachers have had a certain standard of training and their pupils reach a certain standard of accomplishment after a proper time under reasonable regulations as to practice and study. It is hoped this committee can work out standards of preparation for private teachers whose work high schools may accept; standards of accomplishment or attainment for which pupils may be given credit and how much credit may be allowed; blank forms for statement of hours of practice, credit, etc. The purpose of the whole movement is to put this question upon a satisfactory basis, both to the capable private teacher and to the school people. To do so would put this important question upon a higher plane and help all parties concerned—the worthy private teacher, the party paying for the lessons and the public school officials.

School people have the feeling that the rural school in Oregon has gone forward very rapidly in the past decade; however, a new era of progress is opening up at this time. Few states offer their children eight months of school each year. Fewer probably have laws guaranteeing to every rural child a high school education upon such favorable terms as Oregon. The executive committee thought it wise to have the recent progress made in the rural school tabulated and reported to the representative council in December, 1917. In this report it is hoped that the present standardization requirements will be set forth, showing what these requirements have accomplished throughout the state. In addition to a report upon what has been accomplished it is expected that the committee on standardization of rural schools will investigate as thoroughly as possible the most progressive rural schools throughout the states in order to suggest other improvements for the rural schools of Oregon. It is desired that the committee give especial attention to (a) qualifications of teachers for the rural schools; (b) minimum salary for rural teachers; and (c) standard heating and ventilation plants for rural schools.

In making up the committee on thrift it was thought desirable to enlist the sympathy and support of as many directly interested as possible. It is hoped that some plans may be worked out by which thrift will not only be taught but practiced by the pupils in the Oregon schools. It is not enough that our youth be taught to earn, they should be taught to save—saving should be a passion. They should be possessed with the idea so that money coming into their hands may be spent wisely or put to some investment. Many cities and some states have given much attention to this subject. So much, in fact, that it seems quite possible that a scheme may be worked out by this committee suitable to the conditions in Oregon. Much time, money and energy have been devoted to the organization and promotion of industrial clubs—corn clubs, canning clubs, etc. The federal government at the present time is emphasizing the home garden. The executive committee is expecting that this committee, by the study of all these plans, shall suggest something that will enlist the support of teachers and patrons alike. Probably the boys and girls are willing enough to undertake projects if proper means are provided and the probability of gain reasonable. The parent's and the community's support being necessary to any successful plan, it is expected that the committee's recommendations will include them.

It is desired that the committee on certification of teachers for high schools and grades go into its assignment most thoroughly. The present certification laws of Oregon have received much attention from many of the progressive educational centers and after investigation have been given the stamp of approval. So much is this true that recently the state of Washington adopted a certification law almost identical with that of Oregon. One of the Dakotas, at its recent legislature, also passed a law very much like Oregon's. Yet, the value of the Oregon law was attacked by a bill to repeal in the last legislature. If there is a better law, the welfare of the children in our schools considered, for the certification of teachers, Oregon should have it and the change should come at the suggestion and initiative of the teachers themselves. The executive committee expects the whole question to be investigated, but is especially desirous that the report covers the phase of the question, "Should a teacher teach the sort of work prepared for or should he, after a college course, be permitted to teach everything and anywhere?" In other words, should a college or university graduate be certificated to teach in the grammar grades as well as the high schools of Oregon and should a normal graduate receive a license to teach in four year high schools as he now does in the grades?

Last year the teachers' retirement fund committee did very valuable work. A plan, meeting the approval of the experts in the Carnegie Institute, was worked out and presented to the representative council in December, 1916. The council adopted the plan and referred it to the legislative committee with instructions for presentation, but on account of the lack of sufficient data for definite planning, legislative committees looked with disfavor upon the bill. As a result it was withheld. The executive committee believes it best to set about the collection of this necessary information at once. It was thought best to appoint a new committee (a) to relieve the members of the old committee from so much work, and (b) to get a new group of people interested in the subject. Some of the information needed is how much money the state would need to put the law into operation for the first biennium, and how many teachers would at once come under the terms of the law. Apparently, there is need of educating the teachers and public to the necessity as well as the advantages of such a law. If the committee can find and carry into operation such a plan, probably much good will result. It is to be hoped that a campaign of information may be carried on through the Oregon Teachers Monthly as the investigation proceeds.

In the main, the personnel of the committee on retardation is the same as the one reporting to the representative council in December; 1916. A few changes have been made in the interest of the rural schools so the problem of retardation as it exists in the rural schools, may be studied also. The executive committee believed the matter of sufficient importance to ask the special committee to take up the work just where last year's report left it and to continue the investigation, looking especially to causes and remedies for retardation.

The interest and the value of the next session of the Oregon State Teachers' Association depend, in a very large degree, upon the reports of these committees to the representative council on the first day of the annual meeting in December next. The chairman of each committee has been asked to notify his co-workers of their appointment and to set about the investigations immediately so that their findings may be published in the Oregon Teachers Monthly preceding the meeting of the 1917 representative council. In this way, not only the members of the representative council, but all the teachers of the state may be familiar with the work of the committees and each be prepared to do his part in promoting the welfare of the schools of this state.

Through the chairman, the executive committee sends greetings to these committees, offering to assist in every way possible and hoping that as a result of their labors the findings of the 1917 committees will mark a new era of progress for the schools and teachers of Oregon.

Rural School Department

Edited by MRS. M. L. FULKERSON, Salem, Oregon

THE OREGON NORMAL RURAL WEEK IN RETROSPECT.

Rural Week at the Oregon Normal was inspiring in prospect, thrilling in reality, and convincing in retrospect. As a dream, an untried experiment, it promised much. As an existing fact it was full of interest and new experiences. As a historical fact, it will bear examination.

It has been difficult to convince the rural people that the educational institutions are really interested in their problems. Only the agricultural colleges have been able to convince the populace that they are really practical and down to bed rock and even they find it necessary to revise their modes of service very often. The Rural Week in Oregon has been able to do this for the Normal School. Now the people of four counties in particular, and the entire state in general, believe that the Normal is really trying to serve the rural need.

To reveal to students the real rural need by a class discussion is practically impossible. Objective teaching is necessary in this as in the sciences. Observation and demonstration are far better than explanation. One week in a rural school and in a rural community is equivalent to many weeks reading about them. Both are necessary. They are supplementary. This one week clarified the entire year of study and class work in the minds of the students.

To keep teachers close to the real problem is quite difficult. There is a great danger that as a profession we will theorize, speculate, and dream. We too often systematize our knowledge to an extent that we make it impractical. This is an especial danger of the higher institutions. It becomes necessary for us to correct our readings, as the surveyors would say. We must square our theories by the real facts. In the efforts for rural betterment, laboratory facilities have been abundant but not always available. Towns readily submit to educational and other experiments, rural districts are far more wary. The problem has been to discover a scheme that would work. The Rural Week answers the need. Normal school instruction is brought back to earth when one hundred and fifty alert students return from the field filled with real problems, not hypothetical ones, and inject them into the class discussion of every department and ask for workable and satisfactory solutions. The rural people are not disturbed by visitors for ONE week. Thus the rural week does two things: Takes Normal views in to the country and brings rural views, red hot, back to the Normal.

To create a real true rural spirit among the students attending the Normal is quite difficult. The greater part of the students who go to the rural schools to teach do so not because of desire but necessity. This is due entirely to training. What is needed is a new vision, a new purpose. Rural Week helps to make this possible. When only one student is going out to perform a task he is likely to pity himself as an unfortunate, but when every body is doing it he becomes proud of himself. The man who thinks that he is to be murdered is horror stricken but let war occur and away we march to death with uplifted heads, joyous hearts and conscious pride. So with the work of the rural school. When an army attacks the problem, the problem vanishes; when only one attacks it the one flees as quickly as possible. This is the psychology of Rural Week.

At the Oregon Normal we are a unit in our belief that our Rural Week was a good thing—good for the country districts visited by the students, most beneficial to the visiting students, refreshing to the entire Normal School, and helpful to the educational tone of the entire state.

The observations of the students and the result of their investigations, aside from their class room practice, were interesting and profitable indeed. They studied and reported upon the social, religious, political, educational, and economic status of each community visited. They found out the value of school property, the rate of school taxes, the relative amount invested in education when compared to other interests, and evaluated the educational intelligence and spirit of the community. They studied the national composition of the citizenship and discovered to what extent it is now American or alien. They investigated the religious spirit of the community and ascertained whether it was Christian or just sectarian, divided or united, intelligent or ignorant. They searched out the causes of economic strength or weakness—land, buildings, stock, industries, marketing organizations, co-operative buying, agricultural college service, governmental aid, etc. They sought to find who were the social leaders of the community, where they were leading and how they were leading. They went with open eyes and note books, alert minds and tactful words. They returned informed but with new questions to propound and new concepts formulated. They left a rural people conscious that they were alive, truly interested, with vision guiding them and a real purpose to prepare themselves for rural service.

The Rural Week of the future will be slightly different but it will not likely be more interesting or, perhaps, profitable than the first—February 18-24, 1917.—M. S. Pittman, Head of Rural Department, Oregon Normal.

* * *

FOURTH GRADE GEOGRAPHY.

The three-fold need of man is food, clothing, and shelter. These are studied in the order named above because that was the order of their development. The following is a report of a series of lessons handled in the

fourth grade in geography by Agnes Carter and Margaret Tiffany, student
teachers in the Oregon Normal training school.

I.—The Evolution of Clothing.

Preparation—Children, what are some of the things we need most?
(Air, water, place to live, something to eat, clothes to wear.)   Next in
importance after food, comes clothing.   Today we are going to find out how
the clothing long ago differed from our clothing now.

Presentation—Did you ever notice the clothing of the humming bird?
He wears such a pretty suit of delicate green, red and gold.   And the polar
bear has such a nice warm coat; it is white and his enemies can's see him
easily.   Why?   God clothes the animals but people have to call upon the
world to clothe them.

When warm weather comes, what do we do.   (Put on lighter clothing.)
Also go to the coast or mountains.   What do animals do?   The animals
either migrate (go north) or shed their winter coat.   Examples given.

People live in warm countries.   What would you think about their
clothing?   (Would wear very little.)   A long time ago people were naked.
Then the people in the warm countries used grasses, bark, or feathers, and
the people in the cold countries used skins and furs.   Even yet there are
people who are half-naked living in different parts of the world such as the
southern part of South America and Central Africa.   (Point to map.)   Now,
people's clothes are a sign of civilization.   (Explain meaning of civilization.)
As people began to get more civilized they learned to make cloth of certain
kinds and they discovered how to color it.   They sewed their clothes with
needles made of sharpened bones of fish and thread made from the sinews of
animals.   The first clothes that were made were from the fibres of wool.
Savages of today own herds of sheep and have learned how to spin wool into
cloth for their needs.   As time went on man learned that there were other
animal fibres that could be woven.   For other animals besides sheep produce
excellent wool—camels, goats, alpacas, llamas, and yaks.

People knew how to weave some kinds of cloth thousands of years ago.
(Cotton weaving discovered much later.)   About the time your grandmother lived, the people who lived in the country raised their own sheep,
the men washed and sheared them and the women straightened out the wool
by means of cards.   (Describe.)   Every home had its spinning wheel (described later) and the yarn was sent to someone in the neighborhood who
had a loom and they would weave it into cloth.

We are going to learn how the materials are produced and how in
factories and work-shops they are changed into the clothing that you wear
now.   (Wool is taken up in detail next, as it was perhaps the first material
woven into cloth.)

II.—Sheep and Wool.

Preparation—You may all close your eyes and see if you can see a sheep.
Now you may all open them.   You may describe the coat that the sheep you
saw had on, Wilfred.   (A woolly coat.)   I wonder why it has a woolly coat?
(To keep it warm.)   You all know how warm one of your mother's cotton
quilts is.   Now wool is much warmer.   What color was the wool of the sheep
you saw, Hugh?   (Black.)   We do have a very few black sheep.   What is it
Wilfred?   (The sheep I saw was white.)   Was it as white as snow?   (No, it

was a gray or blackish color.) Can any one tell me why it is this color instead of white? You may tell me, Cecil. (They only wear it for about a year and it gets very dirty.)

Presentation—How do we feel when the warm spring days come, Wilfred? (We feel very warm.) Yes, we feel so uncomfortable when those first warm days do come in the spring. You have rather heavy coats on now. Do you wear those heavy coats in the summer? (No.) How do you think the sheep will feel when summer comes? (They will feel warm.) Now if you are too warm what can you do with those heavy coats, Cecil? '(Take them off.) When summer comes the sheep's coats are very heavy and they begin to get loose and some of the wool begins to fall off; we call this shedding. Now do you suppose the sheep would like to take their coats off, Hugh? (Yes.) Can they take them off? (No.) Who do you suppose could help them? (Men could shear it off.) What do you mean by shearing the wool off, Wilfred? (Cutting it off.) How can they cut it off, Hugh? (With shears.) Are they like your mother's scissors, Irving? (No.) What is it, Wilfred? (I can draw a sheep shears on the board.) Very well, you may draw it. Now, just how do the men use the shears, Hugh? (He holds them in hands and clips the wool off.) Do the men let the sheep run all around while they are cutting the wool off? (The men hold them.) How do the men hold them, May? (They put the sheep's head on their knee.) Do the sheep hold still? (No, not at first.) When the sheep find they cannot get away they lie quietly and the big shears says "snip, snip, snip." Then what happens to the coat, Hugh? (The coat falls off.) Then how do you suppose the sheep feel, May? (They feel cool.) They feel so cool and light that they frisk about and are very happy. I will show you a picture of a man shearing sheep. On ranches where they have thousands of sheep, how would they shear the sheep? Some might say by hand and I should say the following: When Lincoln was a little boy, how did his mother sew his clothes? (She sewed them all by hand.) How did your mother sew your dress, May? (On the machine.) Now how might they shear sheep, Hugh? (By a machine.) You listen while I tell you how a machine is used to shear sheep. You may all imagine you see a large room. We might let this school room be the sheep shearing room. Now there are many shearing machines arranged on each side of the room. There is a man at each machine. Each is shearing a sheep. The sheep is held down by the man while he runs over its body with a little clipper. This clipper is like that which the barber uses to clip the hair close to the scalp. As the clipper moves over the sheep's body, two sets of knives fly back and forth like those of a mowing machine. This clipper is attached to a tube and is run by steam or electricity. This clipper cuts the wool off very smoothly. (Many times some child can tell this, and I would not tell it if the child can tell it to the class.) Every man can shear 100 sheep a day. If they are paid 5 cents for shearing one sheep, how much can one man earn in a day, Hugh? (Hugh works it out on board.) Do you think it is better to shear by machinery, Wilfred? (Yes.) Why? (It doesn't take as long.) Why don't all farmers use shearing machines? (Too expensive if they only have a few sheep.) Sometimes a man who has a shearing machine will go from farm to farm and shear his neighbor's sheep. Now what have we found out today? We have found out how wool is taken from the sheep. You may tell us all about it, Hugh. (Hugh comes to front of class and tells all he can remember. The other pupils put in what Hugh leaves out.)

III.—Washing the Wool.

Preparation—What did we find out yesterday, Mary? (How the wool is taken from the sheep.) Now you remember I showed you a picture yesterday with the little track. What did we say the track was used for, Wilfred? (To carry out the wool.) What is done with the wool? (It is sent to the city.) What do they do with the wool in the city, Cecil? (They take it to the mill.) Now you remember we said they wore their coats a long time. What did we say about the condition of those coats? (We said they were dirty.) Today we are going to see how the wool is washed in Salem.

Presentation—We will go to Salem today and visit the woolen mill. How shall we go, Cecil? (We can go by train.) Can anyone tell me what route to take? You may, Hugh. (We can go over to Independence in the Peanut Roaster. Then we get on the steam train and ride as far as Gerlinger. We change trains there and get on the motor and go right into Salem.) (If the children mention any other way we will go that way.) You may all imagine you have your wraps on and we are now in the cars on our way to Salem. Now we can see Salem. Where will we get off of the cars, Irving? (At the depot.) We will get off on State street. Then we go down State street to the mill. Inside of the mill yard we cross a stream of water. What do you suppose they might use this water for, Eldon? (To run the mill.) Can we go through the mill alone, May? (No.) Why? (Because it isn't safe to let anyone go through alone.) Mr. Kay will take us through the mill. This man is also the state treasurer, one of the officers in our state. First he takes us into a large room where the wool is stored in large sacks. Where did the wool come from, Hugh? (The country.) Then we go into a small room and here we see two men who are sorting wool. What do we mean by sorting anything? (Picking out different sizes, shapes, etc.) Now these men are doing this very thing. Why, Hugh? (I don't know.) Does anyone know? Wool is not all the same length and some is fine while some is coarse. This is the reason they put it into different piles. After your mother has sorted her clothes, what does she do next? (She washes them.) Then what might be done with the wool, May? (Wash it.) What does your mother wash the clothes in, Wilfred? (In a tub.) Does your mother use anything else? (A machine.) Then what might they use in this mill? (A machine.) This machine looks very much like a huge tank. What does your mother use to wash the clothes with? (Soap and water.) Then what might they use to wash the wool? (Soap and water.) Why would they use soap? (To get the grease out.) Is there anything else we use in place of soap? (Gold dust.) Now this is what they use in this mill. They have large bins of gold dust and they shovel the gold dust into the huge tubs of water. Then what will they put in next? (The wool.) What does your mother do when the clothes water and soap are all in the washing machine? (She turns the machine.) Will these men do that? (No.) Why not? (Too large.) How did we say this mill was run? (By steam.) Then how might these machines be run? (By steam.) While it is in these machines, it has the oddest habit of moving about and rolling over and over as if it longed to get itself clean. In these tubs are many teeth, that tear the wool in small pieces. Then the wool is drawn out of this tub into another tub of clean water. Here it is rinsed and then it is taken out. It is pressed between rollers to get the water out. Then it is dried by huge fans which are whirling. Now what have we found out, Hugh? (How the wool is washed in Salem.) —Lillian Dinius, Critic Teacher, Oregon Normal School.

(To be continued.)

* * *

THE WIND SYSTEM.

The climate of the world can be nicely worked out through the study of the wind systems. Since industries are so dependent on climate the children should have a clear idea of the principles which control it so as the better to understand its relation to human conditions. With a knowledge of these principles as a starting point, children ought to be able to infer the products and industries of a given region. This article attempts to show how this may be done with upper grade children. Of course the outline embodies material sufficient for several lessons.

Children should be in possession of the following facts at the close of the lesson: (1) That the rising column of air over the heat equator area chills and drops its moisture. That as it rises, air rushes in from the northeast and south-east, resulting in the trade winds. That the heat equator area is a belt of calms several hundred miles in width. (2) That some of this air which rises at the heat equator area descends to the earth's surface between 28 degrees and 30 degrees N. and S. lattitudes depending upon the season of the year. That it becomes warmer as it nears the earth, and therefore increases its moisture holding power. That these regions are belts of calms and the one north of the equator is known as the "Horse Latitude." That the air which does not fall here continues to the poles and finally settles there to again sweep toward the heat equator. (3) That some of this air which settles at these calm belts turns eastward and becomes known as the westerlies. That these winds operate in the temperate zones. (4) That in the temperate zones there are also cyclonic and anti-cyclonic winds which are caused by high and low pressure areas. That the cyclonics whirl inward and upward bringing rain providing they pass over bodies of water. That anti-cyclonics whirl outward and down, usually bringing clear weather. That the westerlies push these winds in a northeasterly direction. (5) That these wind belt areas shift north and south with the heat equator.

Today class, I am going to test you out on some past lessons. Name the heat belts into which the earth is divided, and also give the degrees of their boundries. (Beginning at the north they are the North Frigid which extends from the north pole to 66 ½' degrees N. lattitude; the North Temperate, 66 ½ degrees N. to 23 ½ N.; the Torrid, 23 ½ degrees N. to 23 ½ degrees S.; etc.) Tell what you have learned, affects climate. (Latitude and altitude.) How? (The farther one goes from the direct rays of the sun the colder it becomes. The higher one ascends the greater the radiation and hence the colder the temperature.) When you warm your hands at the stove where do you place them to get the most heat? (Above the stove.) What is it that warms your hands? (The air.) In which direction does the heated air move? (Upward.) If you place a feather over the heated area what will it do? (It will rise.) What have you noticed about leaves in a bon-fire? (They fly upwards, also.) What did heated air do in each of these cases? (It rose.) What would it be safe to assume then about all heated air? (That it rises.) What might you say then about the weight of heated air as compared with the weight of an equal volume of cold air? (It is much lighter.) Where is the place on the earth's surface that is exceptionally hot? (On the heat equator area.) Where is it? (It shifts from 23½ degrees N. to 23½ degrees S. and even farther on land areas.) When is it directly over the Absolute Equator? (March 21 and September 22.) For this lesson let us assume that it is either of these dates. What will be happening to this highly-heated air? (It will be rising.) Correct, for today let us find out how the rising of the air over the heat equator affects the climate of the entire world.

The area affected by the heat equator is several hundred miles wide. What will happen when the heated air rises over this area? (Other air will come in.) From what directions? (From north and south of the equator.) Why? (Because when the air rises over the heat equator it would leave a space without any air unless some other rushed in, and the air just north and south of this rising air being the handiest, rushes in. Besides it is colder and heavier so it would naturally blow along toward the heated areas.) What is such a surface movement called? (Wind.) What will happen when these winds meet? (They will become heated and follow the warm air into higher altitudes.) Will there be any movement over the land or sea? (Not enough to notice.) What do we say about the atmosphere in such places? (We say it is calm.) Therefore we might call this belt what? (A belt of calms.) What happens to the temperature of this air as it rises? (It cools.) When air cools what happens? (It can not hold as much moisture as when it was warm.) If this air that is rising over the heat equator contains moisture, what will it do with it when it becomes cold? (It will drop it as rain.) Look at the map and see if there are chances for it to pick up moisture. (Yes, it passes over oceans.) What would you expect in this region, then? (Much rain.) That is just what happens. You said the winds moving toward the heat equator came from what directions? (North and south.) Which way does the earth turn? (Eastward.) Put your finger on the globe and move it southward while I spin the globe eastward. What direction did your finger move? (It went south-west.) Why? (It could not keep up with the whirl.) That is just what happens to the winds. We name winds from the direction from which they blow, so what would we call this one? (A northeast wind.) Now place your finger south of the equator and draw it northward while I spin the globe eastward, what direction does your finger move? (It comes from the south-east.) Therefore we would name the wind what? (South-east wind.) What may we say about the constancy of these winds? (They will always blow toward the heat equator.) That is right and because they could be depended upon during the days of sailing vessels, they became known as the North-east Trade Winds and the South-East Trades. Now let us recall our aim—to find out how the rising of the air over the heat equator affects the climate of the entire world. In what heat belt are these winds? (In the torrid zone.) What is the temperature there? (Hot.) What do these winds do as they blow over water? (Pick up moisture.) What will cause them to drop it? (Having to cross high mountains will chill them and cause them to drop their moisture.) Look at the map of the continents. Tell how the trade winds will effect South America. (Since they move over an ocean on the east they will carry moisture inland and precipitate it on the eastern slope of the highlands and mountains of eastern Brazil, Bolivia and the countries north.) What can you infer about the countries west of Brazil? (The mountains look as though they were high enough to prevent any moisture from getting over.) You are correct, then what will you say about Peru and Equador? (They would have little or no rainfall.) How about

Australia? (Her eastern coast would have plenty of rainfall because there is an ocean to the east. Mountains are running parallel to the coast and on those the moisture would be dropped.)

What have we found out so far? (How the rising air over the heat equator affects the climate of the torrid zone.) Make a full summary. (There is a belt of calms at the heat equator area caused by the rising of the air when the winds from the north-east and south-east meet over the heated area. As this air' rises it chills and loses its ability to carry so much moisture. Accordingly the air that has passed over water bodies on its way to this belt, being laden with moisture, drops it in the form of rain usually on the eastward side of the mountains. This accounts for the heavy rains in eastern Australia, eastern Brazil, etc.} (To be continued.)—Katharine Arbuthnot, Critic Teacher, Oregon Normal School.

* * *

TEACHING THE GARDEN PLAN.

We are just emerging from a winter of high prices, perhaps the highest the present generation of Americans has been forced to experience. Onions, potatoes, produce, everything has literally been out of sight. We are to pass through another winter a few months hence, which judging from present indications, promises to be even more severe upon the poorer people. With the war cloud hovering over our fair land the dire consequences of the above statement should be given the closest consideration. We must be prepared for war. Every man under arms adds one more to the already too large class of consumers and lessens the producers by that much. If all other conditions were to remain constant, the law of supply and demand will certainly operate to make high prices during the winter of 1917-18. Without enlarging, here lies the public school teachers' opportunity. If we actually want to be of real service to our patrons what better can we do than teach the necessity of agricultural preparedness and how can we accomplish this better than by stressing efficiency with the home garden. We can not hope in a day to rouse a sleeping people to the foolishness of paying three dollars a sack for potatoes when all about them lies untilled land, waiting for the plow. But we can hope to rouse the children by various devices to an active interest in vegetable gardening, the raising of potatoes, beans or some other foodstuffs. We can, and we owe it to the country to do this. Now how can it be done? Briefly, I shall attempt to outline a course.

When the subject of gardening comes up, enlarge upon the facts outlined above, point out how the German school children are helping to feed the German soldiers. If you wish, make the German plan of using every available spot for productive purposes, the basis of your lesson. By all means drive home the necessity of deriving the maximum returns from the ground. Let this form your approach to an aim something like this. Let us find out how the Germans are able to support so large an army, or, let us find out how we can obtain the highest returns from the family garden. Once you have the problem clear in your own mind you may state it in several ways.

You will not be able to find definite information in the text for such a lesson, so make use of the best gardens in the community, bulletins, and publications for the subject matter. After the aim has been stated develop the idea that to be efficient in any line, one must have a plan. Apply this to gardening. Develop separately these points, that any good garden plan rotates the crops, that it does not plant the same crop two years in succession on the same land; that to secure maximum returns the garden plan must embody a

scheme of companion cropping, that is the planting of such things as lettuce, radishes and other rapid maturing crops between potatoes, corn and
even tomatoes or other crops that are planted in rows far apart; that succession cropping should be practiced, that is the land should be made to yield
early and late, for instance after the radishes and lettuce are gone, celery and
even beans might follow; that the crops should be so arranged as to give the
maximum amount of sun, that is if the rows run east and west corn and
other high crops should be in the north half of the garden while low growing
crops should be to the south; that the rows should be figured out and a
sketch of the plan made before planting; that wherever necessary arrangements for irrigation should be made, etc.

Each of these points should be driven home and the children by way of
assignment required to bring to school a plan of the home garden for class
room criticism. In case the children do not have gardens at their homes,
have them study anothers. Prof. Bouquet, O. A. C., has some excellent
information on this in bulletin form.

Teach this as if you mean it, and perhaps your landlady will not have to
raise the board next year. Seriously teachers, we are facing a national
crisis, and the least we can do is to boost, beg, and even force each child
to do his "bit" toward feeding the American public at a reasonable price.—
L. P. Gilmore, Oregon Normal School.

*   *   *

SOME MODERN HEROINES.

We often read thrilling accounts of basketball and football teams. However, they are not the only kind of teams which arouse public interest. The
canning team of Yoncalla, Douglas county, Oregon, has a remarkable story.
It has demonstrated what team work can do in industrial work as well as in
sports.

When the Yoncalla Industrial Club received a letter from the state
leader, Miss Cowgill, asking if it were possible to organize a canning team,
the local leader immediately sent letters or phoned to all the canning
members. It was agreed to call a meeting and ask Miss Cowgill to be present
and tell them exactly what the work of such a team would be.

At the appointed date the canning girls met with Miss Cowgill. A team
was organized. They pledged themselves to carry out the instructions sent
out by the Oregon Agricultural College, in the canning work of their homes.
They also agreed to meet and learn to work together. This last was indeed a
hard proposition, for some of these girls lived three and one-half miles apart.
Then, too, the summer season is a busy one for farm girls; first harvest and
then prune and hop picking. These girls had to decide that there was no
time "under the sun" for them to work together.

As "fair" time approached their leader suggested that a night meeting
be called. The leader, who was two and one-half miles from town herding
turkeys, gave her turkeys a good chase in the morning and left them to rest
in the heat of the day, while she went to town. She secured a vacant shanty,
borrowed two small oil stoves, and a wash boiler; obtained jars and fruit
from neighbors, and made all necessary arrangements for a canning team
meeting after dark. She then went home and put the turkeys in safety for
the night.

That evening at 7:30, each girl with her lantern, stew pan, tea towel and
paring knife, trudged into town to the vacant shanty. Three of the team
lived at a distance of more than two miles from town. However, they seemed

to realize "that work is play, if you only take your work with a little song."
They hung up their lanterns, carried water from a neighbor's house, and set
busily to work. At 9 o'clock that evening several jars of fruit were canned
and the girls were beginning to get an idea of what it is to work together.
Two evenings were spent, in succession, in this way. The next evening two
of the girls who lived in town were missing. The three country girls and
their leader went in a body to inquire. These girls had decided to spend the
remaining part of the season in the hop fields. What was the team to do?
Give up? No, indeed, not for a while at any rate. They canvassed the town
and country that evening, and the next day. At last, two enthusiastic girls
were found.

About this time prune picking set in. Four out of the team had contracts as prune pickers. So they picked up prunes all day long and for two
weeks had evening sessions for canning apples, peaches, pears and tomatoes.

At the time of the local fair prune picking was still going on and the
girls were held by their contracts to the job. They managed to get the
canning exhibits arranged for the fair in the evening before. They then
succeeded in begging off for the afternoon to give their canning demonstrations before the public.

The occasion was a community and industrial fair combined. It was
interesting to compare the exhibits of the juvenile with those of the adult
department. The exhibits in canning made by the canning team proved that
girls from twelve to fifteen years of age can do just as good work as their
mothers. Leota Wilson exhibited 44 different kinds of fruits, vegetables,
jellies and meats. She canned by herself, during the summer, 480 pints;
Vivian Carr canned 300 pints and Rachel Huntington 280 pints. Josephine
McCourt and Thelma James were the two girls who came in during the prune
picking season. They were not industrial club members so they had not
canned during the summer at home. The team canned collectively 300 pints.
making a total of 1360 pints of fruit during the season.

Their demonstration at the local fair was so successful that the community sent them to the Roseburg county fair to compete against three other
teams. There the girls showed their skill and knowledge of the work in more
ways than one. While the fruit was cooking three of the girls gave short
talks about their work. Leota Wilson told the crowd how she canned all
kinds of meats. She took several jars of her meats and pointed out to the
audience the desirable qualities in each. Vivian Carr talked on the canning
of soft fruits. She showed the people jars of fruit which she had canned
according to the methods which she was giving them. Rachel Huntington
told how to make good jelly. She tipped a glass of her jelly out on a plate
and pointed out all the essential qualities for perfect jelly. The sight of her
jelly was enough ot convince the audience that she knew how to get the right
results.

The ability which all of these girls evidenced along canning lines was
remarkable. They carried off the first prize in Douglas county. They were
then urged to compete against the other counties at the state fair. Unfortunately one of the girls fell ill and a substitute had to be secured and
trained. The girls again held a few night sessions.

At the state fair they again gained the highest honors. Besides a
cash prize of $12.50 they were given a free trip to the Farmer's Week at the
Oregon Agricultural College. There they gave an interesting demonstration
in the Economics building. They worked in the college domestic science

kitchen. Form a mental picture of these girls working by lantern light in a deserted shanty, then look at them in a splendid white kitchen. It was like going from a "lowly log cabin to the White House."

Next year even greater things may be expected of these girls. They are so permanently interested in canning that they desire to utilize some of the fruit which wastes by the bushel in their community. Besides filling their own home shelves with canned fruit and vegetables, some of the market shelves will likely be selling their produce.

* * *

SUGGESTION FOR SCHOOL RALLIES.

Supt. S. S. Duncan, of Yamhill county, supplies his schools with a rally song each year; this is learned by every pupil and teacher in the county. When the parents are invited to a school rally, the song is sung, thus giving the visitors a gentle hint of the things needed in and about the school. Yamhill county's 1917 rally song is given here and it may be sung to the tune of "Tramp, Tramp, Tramp, the Boys Are Marching":

When the winter days have passed,
Bringing springtime here at last,
    And the birds and flowers and boys and girls are gay;
We will sing the cheerful song,
And with music all day long,
    Try to please our friends upon this holiday.

      Chorus—
Sing, O sing the song of progress,
Ring, O ring the bells of joy;
    For they're thinking one and all,
    How to answer to the call,
That is coming from the rural girl and boy.

Country schools deserve the best,
And we never mean to rest,
    Till our every just demand is well supplied;
Till our rooms are heated right,
And we have corrected light,
    And our playgrounds all are shady, smooth, and wide.

We must have our playground swings,
And our well suspended rings,
    Where the boys will make their muscle big and strong;
Then a place for basketball,
Out of doors or in the hall,
    And our shout of joy and gladness will be long.

Now in every modern school,
There is one established rule,
    That no luncheon served at noontime must be cold;
For all hygienic lore,
Teaches us that heretofore,
    Every child was injured thus in days of old.

Drinking fountains are the thing,
If we have a nearby spring,
And a playshed should be built on every ground;
And a place for patrons' teams,
For the day has come, it seems.
When the time to visit schools has now been found.

Now we thank you every one,
For the things that you have done,
And for every task we know you mean to do;
And we promise, one and all,
Who've responded to our call,
To repay in service everything to you.

Selections for Memorial Day

Arranged by MRS. M. L. FULKERSON, Salem, Oregon

Sleep, Soldier, Sleep.

Sleep, soldier, sleep! The clear notes
of the bugle
Call thee no more to the heat of the
fray.
Bright on thy resting place—grave of
the hero—
Bloom the fair wreaths of Memorial
Day.
Under the sod which thy life-blood has
hallowed—
Under the flag you so long fought to
save—
Sleep, soldier, sleep! God watches thy
slumber—
A nation pays homage today to the
brave.

Soldier in Blue who gave life for the
Union;
Soldier of Southland who fought in
the Gray—
God has decided the right of your
struggles—
Under one flag you are sleeping to-
day.
Garlands of laurel and garlands of
willow
Strew we today on the graves of our
dead—
Sleep, soldier, sleep! For thy warfare
is over—
Rest thee in peace in thy flower-
strewn bed.

Sleep, soldier, sleep! O'er thy grave in
the jungle
Love stands on guard through the
lone hours of night;
Honor stands guard through the heat
of the noonday—
You who have died for your God and
the right.
Millions will kneel in deep prayer for
the hero
Giving his life for humanity's sake.
Sleep, soldier, sleep! Thou hast died for
thy brother—
Sleep till God's reveille bids thee
awake.

Sleep, soldier, sleep! The bright flag of
the Union
Still proudly floats o'er the land and
the sea;
Beacon of hope to the world's toiling
peoples;
Banner of truth and the Flag of the
Free.
Sleep, soldier, sleep! The flowers of
springtime
Lay we today on thy low, narrow
bed.
Sleep, soldier, sleep! For the hands of
the living
Garland today all the nation's brave
dead.
—Will M. Maupin.

In Remembrance.

Tune.—Massa's in de Cold, Cold Ground.
In the North are soldiers sleeping
'Neath the violets fair.
In the South land, too, there's weeping,
• Soft magnolias blossoms there.

Chorus—
Fair blossoms bring,
In remembrance true
Of our soldiers who are sleeping
In their coats of gray and blue.

But for us the sun in shining
And our homes are bright,
Peace the motto we are twining,
Golden as the sun's pure light.

And where'er our flag is flying,
Red and White and Blue,
In war may soldiers ne'er be dying,
May we to our land be true.
—Primary Plans.

Memorial Day.

First Pupil—
Come let us twine together
These knots of fragrant flowers,
We'll bind them into garlands
To crown these graves of ours.
We'll deck them with bright blossoms,
And plant a flag to wave
Its colors, bright and loving,
Upon each humble grave.

Second Pupil—

Ah yes, we'll gladly twine them
    With wreaths of myrtle green,
Until each mound of earth here,
    A fairy bed would seem.
I think that war is cruel,
    But then it must be just
Brave soldiers' forms were given
    To moulder now to dust.

Third Pupil—

How many lonely, aching hearts,
    Throughout our land today,
Will grieve for many loved ones,
    But lately passed away;
In Cuba and the Phillipines,
    As well as here at home—
Our soldiers lie in peaceful sleep,
    And 'neath the ocean's foam.

Fourth Pupil—

I'm thinking of the heroes,
    Who went down with the Maine;
'Tho never killed in battle,
    We count them with the slain.
I'll wind a special wreath of flowers,
    And flags, and garlands bright,
And dedicate it to our boys
    Who perished that sad night.

Fifth Pupil—

I think that war is very sad,
    But yet it seems to me,
The cruel Boxers of the East,
    Were dreadful as could be.
Oh, think of all the Godly men
    Who gave their life for sin;
They're soldiers though they did not die
    Amid the battle's din.

All in Concert—

Yes, all the heroes we will crown
    With blossoms at their head;
Nor one of them will we forget,
    For they are honored dead.
We'll laud them in our hearts as well,
    And not forget to pray
That God will comfort saddened hearts,
    On this Memorial Day.
            —Nelle S. Mustain.

Offering of Flowers.

First Child—

A bunch of fragrant violets,
    As my offering I have brought,
True blue, as were the soldiers,
    When for the right they fought.

Second Child—

I bring the golden buttercups,
    So hardy and so brave,
What flower can be more fitting
    To deck a soldier's grave?

Third Child—

I bring a bunch of daisies,
    Some humble grave to crown,
As innocent as the pure young lives,
    So willingly laid down.

Fourth Child—

This bunch of purple lilac
    As my offering I bring;
'Tis fragrant as the memory
    Of those whose praise we sing.

All Together—

We'll never forget the soldiers,
    And when we've passed away,
May other hands the flowers bring
    Each Decoration Day.
            —Selected.

We Talk of the Flag.

"Tell me about the flag," he said,
As I was putting him to bed,
"And why men wave their hats and
        cheer
Whenever it is drawing near."
And so we stopped undressing then
To talk about the time when men
Were facing cannon shot and shell
To serve the flag we love so well.

I told him of the men who died
In frozen wood and countryside
Long years ago in battles grim
To keep a flag like that for him,
I told him all about the stars,
The spotless white and crimson bars,
And what they dreamed of and they
        sought
As bitterly they bled and fought.

"Let no one tell you as you grow
That nothing to the flag you owe.
Let no one whisper that it means
But pleasant days and peaceful scenes,
And merely calls to mind a land
Where wealth abounds on every hand,
Because no more that flag will fly
When men for it refuse to die.

"And it may be," said I, "that you
Must some day serve that banner too,
And then if such a day should come
That sounds again the stirring drum
And blows once more the martial fife
Be not a slave to peaceful life.
As they were men, you be a man
And give that flag the best you can."
            —Detroit Free Press.

Rest In Peace.

Laurels and roses,
Lilies and cypress,
Kissed by the starlight,
    Waked by the sun;
Lay them, O, tenderly,
Over the heroes
Of the cause that was lost
    And the cause that was won.

Better than laurels,
Sweeter than roses,
Whiter than lilies,
    Purer than dew,
Are the pledges of forgiveness,
The hands clasped in friendship,
The peace and the prayers
O'er the Gray and the Blue.
            —Selected.

To the Veterans.

Grizzled with years and bent with age,
The hoary headed veterans come,
No youth among them.

Once they were boys of the school yard;
    Now boys of '61,
They look to the boys of the present
        day,
To fill up the ranks as they pass away,
Midst the slanting light of their day's
        last ray,
And the sound of the sunset gun.

As school boys they studied the print-
        ed page
Of deeds that have lived in story;
And now as boys of the old brigade,
In the brilliant light of history made
By their valorous deeds and God's high
        aid,
They share in the selfsame glory.

Lie still in your graves, old soldiers;
God rest you forever more.
Listen and hear above your heads
The rising host from the cradle beds;
School boys next, then warriors dread
  To those who would try our land
    with war.

As the veterans creep into their tombs,
  A countless host succeeds them.
The same rich blood is in their veins,
That wakes at patriotic strain,
That from their bodies the steel shall
    drain,
  Whene'er Columbia needs them.

Our schools are bulwarks of freedom.
  And the boys that are taught therein,
American Guards of a future day,
Must learn with the aged sires to pray
That God may deliver this land alway
  From foreign foe and domestic sin.

Remorseless Time lays monarchs low;
  Tho soldier and the sage
In endless cavalcade pass by
'Neath triumphal arch of the Union sky,
Rendering thanks to God on high
  For America's golden age.

Then reverence the boys of '61,
  Those matchless boys in blue.
Who pointed the sword and gripped the
    gun
From early morn till day was done;
Who fought the fight, the victory won,
  To save this land for you.
                    —Selected.

The Palmetto and the Pine.

There grows a fair palmetto in the
    sunny southern lands;
Upon the stern New England hills a
    sombre pine tree stands;
And each towers like a monument
    above the perished brave;
A grave 'neath the palmetto—beneath
    the pine a grave.

The Carolina widow comes this bright
    May day to spread
Magnolia and jessamine above her sol-
    dier dead.
And the Northern mother violets strews
    upon her son below,—
Her only son, who fell so many weary
    years ago.

Tears for the gallant Yankee boy—one
    of Grant's heroes he;
Tears for the stalwart Southern man—
    the man who marched with Lee.
But love, and only love, between the
    lonely ones who twine
Their wreaths 'neath the palmetto—
    their chaplets 'neath the pine.

Oh, tried tree of the Southland' from
    out whose trunks were wrought
The ramparts of that glorious fort
    where Sergeant Jasper fought;
Oh, true tree of the Northland! whose
    pictured form supplied
The emblem of our earliest flag, that
    waved when Warren died—

Still watch the dead you've watched so
    long, the dead who died so well,
And matrons mourn, as mourn you
    must, your lost dear ones who fell,
But joy and peace and hope to all, now
    North and South combine
In one grand whole, as one soil bears
    the palmetto and the pine.
                    —Manley H. Pike.

The Man With the Musket.

Soldiers, pass on from this stage of re-
    nown,
  This ant-hill commotion and strife;
Pass by where the marbles and bronzes
    look down
  With their fast frozen gestures of
    life.
On out to the nameless, who lie 'neath
    the gloom
  Of the pitying cypress and pine.
Your man is the man of the sword and
    the plume,
  But the man of the musket is mine.

I knew him! By all that is noble I
    knew
  This commonplace hero I name!
I've camped with him, marched with
    him, fought with him, too,
  In the swirl of the fierce battle
    flame,—
Laughed with him, cried with him,
    taken a part
  Of his canteen and blanket, and
    known
That the throb of this chivalrous
    prairie-boy's heart
  Was an answering stroke of my own.

I knew him, I tell you, and also I knew
  When he fell on the battle-swept
    ridge
That the poor, battered boy that lay
    there in blue
  Was only a plank in the bridge
Over which some should pass to a fame
  That shall shine while the high stars
    shall shine.
Your hero is known by an echoing
    name,
  But the man with the musket is mine.

I knew him! All through him the good
    and the bad
  Ran together and equally free,
But I judged as I trust Christ will
    judge the brave lad,
  For death made him noble to me.
In the cyclone of war, in the battle's
    eclipse,
  Life shook out its lingering sands.
And he died with the names that he
    loved on his lips,
  His musket still grasped in his
    hands!
Up close to the flag my soldier went
    down
  In the salient front of the line.
You may take for your heroes the men
    of renown,
  But the man of the musket is mine.
                    —H. S. Taylor.

To the Unknown Dead.

Sleep well, O sad-browed city!
  Whatever may betide,
Not under a nation's pity,
  But mid a nation's pride.

The vines that round you clamber
  Brightest shall be and best;
You sleep in the honored chamber,
  Each one a royal guest.

And aye in realms of glory
  Shine bright your starry claims—
Angels have heard your story,
  And God knows all your names.
                    —Will Carleton.

Boys In Blue.

Tune.—Baby Mine.

We've a message for our soldiers,
  Boys in Blue, Boys in Blue,
With "Old Glory" we'll salute you,
  Boys in Blue, Boys in Blue,
As you pass in grand review,
With your hearts so brave and true,
We shall honor and revere you,
  Boys in Blue, Boys in Blue.

"When you heard your country calling,
  Boys in Blue, Boys in Blue,
Where the shot and shell were falling,
  Boys in Blue, Boys in Blue,
When the Southern host withdrew,
Pitting Gray against the Blue,
There were none more brave than you,
  Boys in Blue, Boys in Blue.

On Memorial Day you gather,
  Boys in Blue, Boys in Blue,
Paying tribute to your brothers,
  Boys in Blue, Boys in Blue,
On the graves of Blue and Gray
Earth's best garlands you will lay
One each Decoration Day,
  Boys in Blue, Boys in Blue.

Each Memorial Day we'll greet you
  Boys in Blue, Boys in Blue,
One by one we'll sadly miss you
  Boys in Blue, Boys in Blue,
In the Roll Call bye and bye
When your name is called on high
You will answer, "Here am I,"
  Boys in Blue, Boys in Blue.
                —Western Teacher.

Decoration Day.

Tune.—Red, White and Blue.

Let us march to the graves of the
  soldiers,
With flags and with flowers today:
And there let us tenderly place them,
  These blossoms so bright and so gay;
Let us think of the soldiers there sleep-
  ing,
  While our flag doth so proudly yet
    wave,
How they fought and fell in the battles
  These soldiers so true and so brave.

Chorus—

These soldiers so true and so brave,
These soldiers so true and so brave;
How they fought and fell in the battles,
These soldiers so true and so brave.

No flowers or garlands too precious,
  For the graves of our heroes so true;
We will deck them with fair, fragrant
    blossoms
  And colors of Red, White and Blue.
Far from home and from kindred and
    loved ones,
  Many heroes lie sleeping today;
We will keep green and tender their
    memory,
We will honor their valor alway.

Chorus—

We will honor their valor alway,
We will honor their valor alway;
We will keep green and tender their
    memory,
We will honor their valor alway.
                —Selected.

A New Memorial Day.

By the sob of the southern rivers,
  By the sigh of the northern hills,
To the tender tune of the soft tattoo,
  While the muffled drum-beat thrills
The heart of a common nation
  With a common sorrow today,
Let roses fall, for one and all,
  On the graves of the blue and the
    gray!

Clasp hands forever and ever—
  There are no sections now,
They are one and one in the new faith
    won
  From the faith of a patriot vow.
The wounds that were wide and bitter
  Are healed by the touch today
Of the tender fingers of love that press
  Rose-wreaths for the blue and the
    gray!

They are calling the veteran legions
  Who march from the fields of the
    past;
They are calling the brave young
    heroes
  Who are one with the old ones at
    last
And the flag they are marching under
  Is my flag and your flag today—
The stripes and the stars of old glory,
  The flag of the blue and the gray!

Bend down with your blossoms, ye liv-
    ing,
  Sleep on in your silence, ye dead!
The bugles are mute, the drums
    muffled,
  Tho columns swing slow in their
    tread;
But the north and the south march to-
    gether,
  They are under one banner today,
And they pluck the white rose of re-
    membrance
  Alike for the blue and the gray!

For the graves that are green with the
    verdure
  Of the years that have healed with
    their song;
The sting and the stain and the anger,
  The passion, the pride and the
    wrong;
For the graves with the fresh turf up-
    on them,
  Those young graves that call us to-
    day,
With the rose-wreaths of common af-
    fection
  Made one for the blue and the gray!
                —Baltimore News.

The June Number.

For fifteen years the June number
of the Oregon Teachers Monthly has
been devoted to songs suitable for
institute singing. The question now
arises, shall the next June number
be a song number? Teachers who
see this notice are invited to write,
giving their views on the question.
Anyone having suitable songs are requested to send them. Only uncopy-
righted songs can be used and it will
be useless to send copyrighted selections.—C. H. J.

Studies of Famous Pictures

These studies are used by permission of the C. M. Parker Estate, Taylorville, Illinois, who will furnish a complete list of other famous pictures free on application.

PILGRIM EXILES—BOUGHTON.

By L. Eveline Merritt

Pilgrim Exiles! What a pathos in the very name! But does this picture have to be given a name? Look at it. What do you see? Three lonely figures on the shore of the vast ocean. What are they doing? What are they gazing at? What are they thinking? Do they see anything on the distant horizon? Probably not, only in their loving memory do they see the vision of that distant home which their eyes will never again behold. Where are they? Why are they there? Why are they so sad?

Exiled from their native land by

ones; yet picture, if you will, in your imagination a comparatively small band of Pilgrims felling trees, breaking soil, building their own shelter, making their own implements, in a new territory with savage Indians as their only neighbors. We are led to believe that these Pilgrims were happy withal and contented, too, for they were living their lives according to the dictates of their own conscience. They never regretted the step they had taken and would never have returned had they been given the opportunity. However, we cannot but think that they must have had many a homesick moment. We can imagine that many, many times, especially during the melancholy twilight

royal decree unless they were willing to conform to the established church of England, they at first wandered to Holland, then to the new world, and, at the time of this picture, were well established in their new home in Plymouth, Massachusetts.

The first years were years of struggle against fearful odds. The strong and the brave survived the first frightful winter. The years that followed were somewhat brighter

period after the day's work was done, they must have wandered down singly or in family groups to the shore and there communed with the all pervading spirit with whom time and space are naught.

Such a moment is shown us in this picture. There are three figures. A young, manly looking fellow stands erect with a beautiful, sad-faced, young girl by his side, who may be his sister or his bride, while an older woman sits on a nearby rock. This perhaps is the mother. All are dressed in the simple, picturesque garb of the early Plymouth colonists. The dark dresses, white kerchiefs and dainty caps add so much of grace to the women of those times, whereas the broad-brimmed hats, wide white collars and flowing capes of the men add a picturesqueness that is most attractive.

The coast is rather bleak in its appearance. There are rocks scattered about, some grass has braved the elements, while marsh shrubbery is seen along the shore. It is a typical seashore of the country along the Cape Cod coast. But it is not the land or the sea that holds the attention, but those three figures gazing out into the distance. The young man is alert, venturesome, strong, brave, tender. He is ready to go on with his tasks in this new land come what may. The young woman is more fearful. She is slightly bent by the burdens that have been hers to bear while so young. She is almost afraid, she doesn't quite understand how it will work out. It seems very, very hard to her although she is willing to do any service, to undergo any hardship, for those she loves. She has one hand on the young man's shoulder recognizing that bond of sympathy which is necessary to a soul like hers. The older woman has lived through those years and has come out triumphant in self-forgetfulness. Perfect resignation is stamped on her face. Of course she would like to see the old home once more but it is not necessary. Life is a bigger thing to her than a particular home in a certain place.

Thus these three people have come down here at sunset as to a family altar. Each in his own individual way looks out across the deep and sees the comforts and friends that they have left. They are voluntary exiles—these Pilgrims—and in that moment these three reconsecrated their lives to high endeavor in their wilderness home.

George H. Boughton was a painter of many pictures, his subjects usually being taken from the early Puritan life of New England, the tales of the Canterbury Pilgrims, or the Breton peasant life of the present time. His pictures were popular and high prices were paid for them. They are now mostly to be found in private collections in England and America. There is in nearly all of his work a happy mingling of landscape and figures, the figures being a part of their environment.

Boughton entered into the lives of the early people so intimately and so sympathetically that he has interpreted that life for us, not correct merely in its outward forms, but in its feelings, its spirit, its soul. Through his pictures we can easily reconstruct those early times. we can understand better the lives of our forefathers, we can feel with them the pathos, the loneliness, the resignation, the trust and the faith in the all-pervading good. Those days are nearer to us because Mr. Boughton lived and interpreted them for us. He has thus done a great service for the country in perpetuating the lives of those pioneers in these Pilgrim pictures.

RETURN OF THE MAYFLOWER— BOUGHTON.

By L. Eveline Merritt

Meanwhile the Master alert but with
　dignified air and important,
Scanning with watchful eye the tide
　and the wind and the weather,
Walked about on the sands, and the
　people crowded around him
Saying a few last words, and enforcing
　his careful remembrance.
Then, taking each by the hand, as if he
　were grasping a tiller,
Into the boat he sprang, and in haste
　shoved off to his vessel,
Glad in his heart to get rid of all this
　worry and flurry,
Glad to be gone from a land of sand
　and sickness and sorrow,
Short allowance of victual, and plenty
　of nothing but Gospel!
Lost in the sound of the oars was the
　last farewell of the Pilgrims.
O strong hearts and true! not one went
　back in the Mayflower!
No, not one looked back, who had set
　his hand to this ploughing!

Soon were heard on board the shouts
　and songs of the sailors
Heaving the windlass round, and hoist-
　ing the ponderous anchor.
Then the yards were braced, and all
　sails set to the wind,
Blowing steady and strong; and the
　Mayflower sailed from the harbor,
Rounded the point of Gurnet, and leav-
　ing far to the southward
Island and cape of sand, and the Field
　of the First encounter,
Took the wind on her quarter, and
　stood for the open Atlantic,
Borne on the sand of the sea, and the
　swelling hearts of the Pilgrims.
Long in silence they watched the re-
　ceding sail of the vessel,
Much endeared to them all, as some-
　thing living and human;
Then as if filled with the spirit, and
　wrapt in a vision prophetic,

Baring his hoary head, the excellent
   Elder of Plymouth
Said, "Let us pray," and they prayed, and
   thanked the Lord and took courage.
Mournfully sobbed the waves at the
   base of the rock, and above them
Bowed and whispered the wheat on the
   hill of death, and their kindred
Seemed to awake in their graves, and to
   join in the prayer that they uttered.
Sun-illumined and white, on the eastern
   verge of the ocean
Gleamed the departing sail, like a
   marble slab in a graveyard;
Buried beneath it lay forever all the
   hope of escaping.
Lo! as they turned to depart, they saw
   the form of an Indian,
Watching them from the hill; but while
   they spoke with each other,
Pointing with outstretched hands and
   saying, "Look!" he had vanished.
So they returned to their homes; but
   Alden lingered a little,
Musing alone on the shore, and watch-
   ing the wash of the billows
Round the base of the rock, and the
   sparkle and flash of the sunshine,
Like the spirit of God, moving visibly
   over the waters.
Thus for a while he stood, and mused
   by the shore of the ocean,
Thinking of many things, and most of
   all of Priscilla;
And as if thought had the power to
   draw to itself, like the loadstone,
Whatever it touches, by subtile laws of
   its nature,
Lo! as he turned to depart, Priscilla
   was standing beside him.

Thus Longfellow has given us in
poetic form the story of the depart-

lurking dangers in the form of fam-
ine and the wild Indian, to the
humble acceptance of the stern realities, and to the deep reverence in-
born in these Pilgrims of Plymouth.

That was the word picture. Now
let us look at the pictorial representation of the same scene by the artist
George H. Boughton. It is all there
—the barren unfriendly shore, the
Mayflower as it is about to dip beneath the horizon, the groups of
sober devout Pilgrims as they are
about to turn from the farewell to
their homes of toil, and here in the
foreground are John Alden and Priscilla standing side by side.

Who can tell what is in their
minds as they gaze out over the
ocean at the retreating Mayflower?
Are they for one brief instant regret-
ting the departure and are they fearful of what the future may have in
store for them? We think it may be
true, but we know too that there is
a vigor, a strength, a will and a
power in them both that will face
anything and will dare anything that
is right. Both figures are true to
the times in the usual Pilgrim costumes But more than all else the
whole picture is true to the spirit of

ure of the Mayflower. Every line is
filled with significant references to
that hard first winter, to the stern
nature of the early settlers, to the

the times. The picture was first exhibited in 1868.

Since 1861 Boughton has been the
interpreter of life among the early

settlers of America. To quote from the New England Magazine, "Boughton has found a great deal that is lovely and attractive which even to those who know little and care less about the history of the New England founders, has under his interpretation become beauty and delight. Artistically he is better equipped for the work than were any of his predecessors. By his early education in early life and by the environment he has made for himself, having thoroughly studied the Pilgrims' three homes, England, Holland and America, he has a firmness of touch and warmth of coloring which make his pictures seem so natural."

Mr. Boughton's power lay in his ability to enter into the spirit of a scene or story. Some one has said, "Before a collection of his works it is an April day with us between his pathos and humor." This power

seems to be equally shown in nature or people. The latter are not portraits but are rather types of people. Though those types we are brought into close contact with the life depicted, whether it be Puritan days or Knickerbocker days or what not. In 1873 a contributor of the Art Journal wrote concerning Boughton's work, "As a whole his pictures are not of a character to attract the visitor or to a public gallery by striking effects of color or by the setting forth of subjects that would at once attract the attention. They are works to be looked into and studied for their negative rather than their positive qualities of excellence, for their simplicity of design, tenderness of emotion, felicitous expression, and charm of subdued, yet not weak coloring. He is steadily advancing to a high position among our genre painters."

Oregon Govermental Affairs

By ROBERT CARLTON CLARK, Eugene, Oregon

Special Election in June.

In a spasm of enthusiasm for road building the legislative assembly at its last session provided for a special election in June at which time opportunity might be given to sanction bonds for this purpose. At the same time the voter will be asked to pass judgment on some eight other measures and any other legislative acts upon which the referendum might be invoked. Such an election will cost the state and counties some $200,000. The county budgets have been made up for the year and could not anticipate this additional expense. It seems unfair to saddle it upon them upon such short notice. The county commissioners of Curry county are reported as having refused to order or provide for the election on the grounds that there are no funds available. At the time that the legislative assembly authorized this election it was anticipated that the United States would soon be drawn into the European war. With the whole energy and thought of the people turned towards doing their part in the prosecution of the war there is no time and should be no

time for these more or less petty state matters. Besides the steadily mounting cost of all the necessities of life calls for economy.

The Road Bonds.

During the last hours of the session some bright mind, or minds, within, or without the legislative assembly conceived the idea of securing the fund for a much needed system of good roads by means of a special issuance of bonds to the amount of $6,000,000. The interest and finally the principal on these bonds, we are told, can be paid by simply doubling the license tax on automobiles. The automobile owner will not object to this increase, in spite of the fact that now besides paying a personal property tax upon his machine he pays a license fee to the state, because improved roads means a decrease in the cost of operation of his car. Under the terms of the measure the counties must put the road in readiness to receive a hard surface. From this fund raised by means of the bonds the state is to put on the final hard surface. The act provides for a highway commission of three members.

appointed by the governor, whose duty it will be to supervise and authorize the expenditure of this fund..

Specific Repeal Amendment.

Some one with a passion for consistency and harmony and who thinks that constitutions should be beautiful as well as useful has persuaded the legislature to add another to the list of measures that go on the June ballot. The object of this amendment is to secure that "every provision of the constitution shall be consistent and harmonious with every other provision," and that any amendment that henceforth shall be made to the constitution to be effective must specifically repeal all other parts of the constitution that may conflict with it, otherwise the said amendment shall be void and of no effect. The purpose of this amendment would seem to be to relieve the labor of the supreme court whose duty it has been to harmonize the discords and render consistent the inconsistencies of the constitution. Should this amendment pass, hereafter that body would simply have to decide if an amendment be "consistent and harmonious." Should it clash or discord it plainly could not be allowed to stand. Then we would need to elect supreme justices with aesthetic faculties well developed and ears attuned to the harmonious.

Taxation Amendments.

It is not creditable to the intelligence of the voters of the state that they have repeatedly refused to pass amendments several times proposed by the state tax commission as necessary if Oregon ever expects to have anything like a just system of taxation. The object of these amendments is to do away with the present constitutional provisions that taxes on all classes of property shall be equal and uniform and make possible a different rate of taxation as between different classes of property. These amendments should be supported.

All Elections on Same Day.

Another amendment to the constitution requires that city elections be held upon the same days as state elections. In behalf of economy this measure is meritorious It overlooks, however, the object desired in sep-arating municipal from state and national elections. Questions upon which local elections hinge are distinctively different from those involved in state or national elections. There is danger if all come upon the same day that local interests may not receive the consideration they deserve. It is also possible that a keenly contested municipal election might obscure the state and national concerns.

Ship Subsidy.

This measure would authorize any city that is a port to raise money by taxation or sale of bonds to be used in the form of a bonus to aid in establishing water transportation between such port and any other domestic or foreign port. This involves the principle of ship subsidies as usually applied on a national scale. This measure would empower Portland, for instance, to subsidize lines of vessels plying between it and other parts of the world. It is not generally recognized as a good principle to tax the many for the benefit of the few. It seems bad enough for one nation to bid against another by means of ship subsidies. It is worse practice for city to bid against city. It means applying artificial stimulus where natural advantages have proved ineffective. The measure would be less objectionable if it authorized a city to purchase outright and operate its own ships. By this means such profits as accrue would be divided among all the residents and taxpayers of the city.

Primary School of Methods.

Have you yet written to Mrs. Ruby Shearer Brennan, 460 E. Burnside street, Portland, telling her that you mean to attend her primary school this summer? She needs to know about how many teachers wish to attend before she can announce the place for holding the school. Last year about one hundred teachers were in attendance. The teachers who have taken the course are highly pleased and have been able to secure better positions on account of having the certificate of attendance which Mrs. Brennan issues.

No really great man ever thought himself so.—Hazlett.

Oregon Tree Studies

By WM. E. LAWRENCE, Department of Botany, O. A. C.

XII.—The Western Yew.

In those who know the western yew, it inspires a feeling of renewing old acquaintance, because, although found over a wide geographic range, it is not frequently seen. It offers a gentle reminder of the sentiment associated with the yew of Europe,

Fig. 1.

which is frequently mentioned in literature. Its western relative is a larger and more handsome tree.

The western yew (Taxus brevifolia Nuttall) is little known except to the woodsman and botanist. It was first discovered by David Douglas in 1825, on the lower Columbia river and later found by Thomas Nuttall in the "dense maritime forests of Oregon." It may be most easily recognized by the reddish purple bark of the trunk and numerous short, soft and flatly disposed leaves (Fig. 3) and in season by the scattered red berry-like fruits. It is commonly called "yew," but should be given a more distinctive name, such as western yew, to distinguish it from the well-known yew of Europe. It is also called Oregon yew, Pacific yew, and other less desirable names.

The yews are set apart in a family by themselves, because they produce bony, one-seeded fruits in place of cones like the pine, firs, and other conifers, belonging to the pine family. Just as we find the members of the pine family particularly abundant in the northern hemisphere, so we find the members of the yew family widely distributed in the southern hemisphere. There are two genera of the yew family in North America, both of which are relatively unimportant economically, while in South America and Australia other members of this family constitute some of the most important timber trees.

Of the six species of yews north of the equator, four occur in North America, of which one is found in eastern United States, another in Florida, one in Mexico, and the "western yew" on the Pacific coast. The only near relative of the yew on the Pacific slope is the California nutmeg (Tumion Californicum), which does not occur north of California.

The western yew is a beautiful evergreen tree or shrub, occurring west of the Continental Divide from Alaska to Montana, Idaho and Oregon, thence southward, west of the Cascade and Sierra Nevada mountains, into California to Santa Cruz county, in the Coast Range and to Tulare county in the Sierra Nevada mountains. It may be found at various altitudes according to its latitudinal range. In Oregon it ranges between sea level and 6000 feet.

The western yew is a small tree, 15 to 30 feet, sometimes 35 to 50 feet, with diameters varying between 6 and 30 inches. The long, slender, horizontal or slightly drooping branches form a broad conical head, irregular in outline (Fig. 1). due to the unequal length and varying positions of the branches. The branches extend nearly or quite to the ground, except in the larger and older trees The western yew is slow growing, both in height and diameter, especially under the deep shade. It requires from 75 to 90 years to produce a trunk of six inches, while those varying between 12 and 20 inches are 140 to 245 years old. The largest trees are thought to be from 350 to 375 years old. It attains its largest size in Oregon, Washington, and British Columbia. The trunk is tall and straight, frequently unsymmetrical and irregularly ridged,

Fig. 2.

with broad, rounded lobes. (Fig. 2). The thin bark, the scales of which flake off, becoming shreddy, is smooth, red-brown to red-purple. The inner or new bark is a pale rose or purple-red.

The very slender leaf bearing branches hang down, giving the tree a weeping appearance, which is especially notable in trees growing partly or entirely in the open, where the leafy branches are most numerous. The leaves are a deep, yellowish green, shining above, paler below, with a prominent yellowish midrib, sharp pointed, thickish and leathery. The leaves are evergreen, persisting from 2 to 23 years, usually from 5 to 12 years. The flowers are bright yellow, minute, and usually occurring on different trees. The seeds are produced on the under side of the twig and when mature partly surrounded by a fleshy scarlet cup (Fig. 3) having the appearance of a brightly colored berry. The fleshy scarlet cup is often eaten by birds, but the hard-shelled seeds are unaffected by digestion. In this way the birds materially assist in seed dis-

posal. The fleshy cup is sweetish and edible, not poisonous.

The western yew is a prolific seeder, the seed having a persistent vitality and a moderately high percentage of germination. The seeds germinate in the wet moss and decaying wood in the deep shade of tall coniferous forests. The western yew is nowhere abundant but most frequently found near the margins of low mountain streams, deep gorges and damp ravines or on moist flats and benches, where it is found singly or in small groups. It is generally sparingly associated with the Douglas fir, grand fir, redwood, tanbark oak, vine and broadleaf maple.

The wood is very heavy, strong, hard, brittle, close-grained, elastic, and a clear rose-red color becoming gradually duller when exposed to light. The sap wood is thin and light yellow. It is durable and takes a fine polish. It is of little commercial importance on account of its scarcity. The attractive color, elasticity and durability renders it useful for such articles as canoe paddles, bows and small fancy cabinet work. Also used for pulleys, machine bearings, tool handles, wedges, mauls,

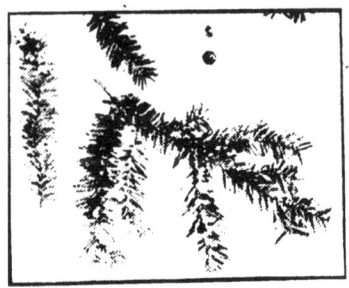

Fig. 3.

and fence posts. The ranchmen dress the wood green. It was used by the Indians of the Northwest for spear handles, fish hooks, bows and other small articles. It was at one time highly prized among the Indians of Southern Oregon and a product of barter and sale with the native tribes of California far southward.

The bark and leaves of the European yew have been used in medicine, the former also in dyeing. Its wood was highly prized by the ancients for making bows and even by modern archers. The leaves of the European yew have long been regarded as poisonous. It is also thought that the western yew is poisonous and it would be interesting to know to what extent.

Grade Teachers' Department

Edited by SABRA CONNER, 421 West Park Street, Portland, Oregon

Elementary teachers and elementary teachers' associations are cordially invited to send news items of their activities which would be of interest or value to other teachers to this department of the The Oregon Teachers Monthly. Address Editor of Grade Teachers' Department, Room 300, Court House, Portland, Oregon.

Miss Jessie McGregor was made the presiding officer over the largest organization of women in Portland, when she was elected president of the Portland Grade Teachers' Association, which has a membership of 600. Miss McGregor, who is a teacher in the Holladay school, has for the past year been the editor of the Bulletin, the official organ of the association, and of this she has made a notable success. She combines good business judgment with a deep interest in the organization and in the affairs of the day, with a winning personality, and thus is especially well fitted to hold this office. Other officers chosen are: Recording secretary, Miss Lutie Cake; corresponding secretary, Mrs. Laura Black; treasurer, Mrs. Jennie Richardson; first grade vice president, Miss Belle Joseph; fifth grade vice president, Miss Emma Dobie; seventh grade vice president, Miss Kate Cahalin; ninth grade vice president, Miss Julia Spooner. In her farewell address Miss Viola Ortschild, the retiring president, made a strong plea for individual thought and decision on the matters of the day, and urged that more women be sent to the state legislature, in the hope of securing better and more just legislation.

* * *

The co-operative luncheon given by the High School Teachers' Association on March 17 was a most enjoyable affair. It was well attended by members of the various educational associations of the city who listened with pleasure to Mme. Aino Malmberg, a native of Finland, whose talk on the present Russian situation was intensely interesting. Dr. E. H. Lindley took for his subject "From Plato to Henry Ford" and delighted his audience with the breadth and scope of his address. Mr. Koehn, president of the High School Teachers' Association, presided and introduced the speakers. This was the second in what is hoped will be a series of such luncheons, the first having been given under the auspices of the Grade Teachers' Association early in the winter. The spirit of acquaintance, of co-operation, of mutual understanding, and of unity of effort is worth cultivating and such gatherings as these luncheons have been will go far to accomplish it.

* * *

The Northwest Steel Company was visited on March 10 by a group of teachers who were shown through the shipbuilding plant by a capable guide. The four ships now under construction are for Norwegian owners and are freight carriers, built at the cost of over a million each. In less than a year the plant of the Northwest Steel Company has grown from a structural shop to a most modern and fully equipped ship building plant, now about ready for its first launching, which will be an event in Portland's industrial history.

For Primary Teachers.

No primary teacher who is not thoroughly up on primary methods can afford to miss attending Mrs. Ruby Shearer Brennan's school this summer, if it is possible for her to attend. You will find an advertisement of the summer school in this number. Remember that the dates are from June 25 to July 7, the two weeks immediately preceding the meeting of the National Education Association.

City Superintendents' Department

Edited by GEORGE W. HUG, McMinnville, Oregon

Supt. F. A. Tiedgen of Marshfield hopes to make his district one of the first class next year.

Mr. E. A. Thomas, of Spokane, Wash., has been re-elected secretary of the board, with a salary of $2400 per year.

Supt. J. M. Gwinn, of New Orleans, La., has been unanimously re-elected for a term of four years, beginning July, 1917.

Supt. L. W. Mayberry, of Wichita, Kansas, has been re-elected for a two-year-term, with an increased annual salary of $3800.

At Berkeley, California, a school for janitors has been opened to make possible a higher degree of efficiency on the part of these employes.

Supt. A. T. Park of Pendleton has been re-elected for another year. He has introduced departmental work in the 5th, 6th, 7th and 8th grades.

H. L. Hussong, principal of the Taylor school of Astoria, has been elected superintendent of the Astoria public schools for a period of three years.

Military training, with uniforms and rifles under the direction of United States army officers, has been made a part of the Chicago high school course.

Prof. E. A. Kirkpatrick, of the Fitchburg, Mass., State Normal School, is spending the year as exchange professor at the Bellingham State Normal.

At Cleveland, Ohio, the board has raised the pay of grade teachers $50 a year, making the maximum $1200. Principals have been given increases of $120 per year.

Supt. Ben Blewett of the St. Louis schools was stricken with apoplexy on January 26 while speaking before the Congress of Constructive Patriotism in Washington, D. C.

R. M. Himelick, principal of the Cleveland Normal School, who was offered $5000 in the State Department of Indiana, has declined the offer and will remain in Cleveland.

R. J. Cunningham, superintendent of Bozeman, Montana, for the past twelve years has been unanimously re-elected for a term of three years at $3000 salary, an increase of $500.

Supt. H. B. Wilson, of Topeka, Kansas, has been re-elected for a two-year term, with a salary of $4800. Mr. Wilson has served two terms as head of the Topeka schools.

The New York school board is looking for a $10,000 man to manage its business affairs. The essential qualifications, as announced, are successful business and educational experience.

Principal L. A. Wiley of the Montavilla school, Portland, has been transferred to the principalship of the Couch school. Jesse McCord will be Mr. Wiley's successor at the Montavilla school.

To. Supt. Daniel Hull of Grants Pass belongs the credit of leading all Oregon cities in aligning his school teachers for the convention of the National Education convention in Portland July 7 to 14.

Edward S. Quigley, of Seattle, Wash., has been elected assistant superintendent of Los Angeles. For several years Mr. Quigley was assistant superintendent in Seattle. He will receive an annual salary of $3000.

Supt. Francis, of Columbus, Ohio, has ordered the abolition of examinations. He argues that the teacher should know from day to day whether the child has learned what he has studied and whether he is ready to take up the work of the next grade.

Dr. John W. Withers, president of Harris Teachers College, St. Louis, Mo., has been appointed superintendent of schools for St. Louis to succeed the late Ben Blewett. Dr. Withers is a graduate of Yale University and holds two degrees. He has been head of the Teachers College since 1905.

Twelve school buildings are being used in Bend, Oregon to accommodate the school children, in addition to a store, a shop, a church and a tent which temporarily house the overflow. The board has appointed ten new teachers within eighteen weeks, to take charge of the increase of children.

Mrs. Leota Leever, principal of the Columbus school, McMinnville, died March 19 after an illness of about ten days. Her position is being filled by Miss Bess Shepherd. Mrs. Leever was a very efficient principal and was recognized as one of the strongest primary teachers in the state.

At Kansas City, Missouri, a plan whereby sick and disabled teachers may receive compensation for time lost has been put into execution by the teachers' club. All teachers who join receive, when disabled more than twenty days, $1.50 per day. The initial fee is $5, with annual fees of $3 per year, thereafter.

The average tenure of the office of high school principals in districts of first class in Oregon exclusive of Portland for the past four years shows a gradual decline. In 1913-14 the average was 3.8 years; 1914-15, 3.8 years; 1915-16, 2.5 years; and in 1916-17 it is 2 years. Including Portland the average would be increased from one to almost two years.

Dr. H. D. Sheldon, dean of the school of education of the state university, urges that all University of Oregon students seeking recommendations for teaching positions should have participated in at least two lines of activities before receiving endorsement for such activities as athletics, debating, music, dramatics and publication of school paper or magazine.

Under the direction of L. L. Summer, manual training supervisor in the Portland public schools, a citywide poultry contest has been launched. Manual training teachers and principals in the various schools will assist and an effort will be made to secure contestants in every school of the city. The boys or girls who enter the contest are supposed to make their own chicken houses in the manual training shops, along plans which have been provided by Supervisor Summer.

Supt. A. C. Barker, of Oakland, California, has resigned his position. Seven of the biggest educators in California have been selected to select his successor. The seven people are: Dr. Benjamin Ide Wheeler, president of the University of California; Dr. Ray Lyman Wilbur, president of Leland Stanford Junior University; Dr. Aurelia Henry Reinhardt, president of Mills College; Joseph H. King, president of the Oakland Chamber of Commerce; Reuben H. Wiand, labor representative; Geo. Randolph, manager of the Union Iron Works, and Rev. Albert W. Palmer, pastor of Plymouth Congregational Church of Oakland.

Dr. B. W. DeBusk of the University of Oregon estimates 10,000 school children in the state are adding $300,000 a year to the expense in the maintenance of the schools. These children are those who are one or more grades behind the standard for their age. Dr. DeBusk says the causes for the backwardness of these children are largely defective teeth, adenoids, diseased tonsils, defective vision and bad hearing. First grade students in the state show about 12½ per cent failures. The percentage decreases up to the sixth grade and then the failure curve ascends through the seventh, after which the survivors show an increating ratio of mental capacity.

The graduating class of the Salem High School, which this year numbers 133 members—the largest in the history of the school—has voted for a change in the form of the commencement exercises. Instead of having a speaker, as has been the custom in past years, the exercises will be conducted by the class themselves. Six representatives will be chosen—two by vote of the class, two by vote of the teachers, and two on the basis of highest scholarship for the last two years of the course. Each of these will be expected to contribute to the program, with a reading, an oration, or a musical number, according to their preference. The idea is to let the public see what the graduates themselves can do, instead of letting them sit passive while an outsider does it all. The class are very enthusiastic over the idea, and public sentiment seems to approve it.

The average number of years of experience in present positions of city superintendents of the nineteen first class districts of Oregon for the year 1916-17 is 4.4 years. For 1915-16 is 4.1 years; 1914-15 is 4.4 years; and for 1913-14 is 4 years. Supt. Dunbar, of Klamath Falls, is the oldest superintendent in point of service having held his present position for the last twelve years. Supt. Ford, of Dallas; Supt. Imel, of Astoria; Supt. Tooze, of Oregon City, and Supt. Stanbrough, of Newberg, are filling their respective positions for

eight successive years. The six year
incumbents are Supt. Boetticher, of
Albany, and Supt. Briscoe, of Ashland. The fourth year superintendents are Supt. Alderman, of Portland,
and Supt. Strange, of Baker. Supt.
Hamilton, of Medford; Supt. Hug, of
McMinnville, and Supt. Rutherford,
of Eugene, are in their second year.
Supt. McCulloch, of La Grande; Supt.
Park, of Pendleton; Supt. Powers, of
Corvallis, and Supt. Todd, of Salem,
are serving their first year. The
average number of years experience
in the state of Oregon for the nineteen city superintendents of the first
class districts is 10.5 years. The average number of years experience of
the nineteen superintendents is 20.4
years. The number of superintendents of the first class districts with
no experience outside of the state
totals six. The number of superintendents in first class districts with
experience in Oregon when taking
present positions totals eight. Eleven
of the nineteen superintendents re-
receive a salary of $2000 or more
and eight a salary under $2000.

Superintendent Simonds has carefully worked out a statement of comparative enrollments and teacher-
cost of the Lewiston Junior-Senior
High School at the close of first semester for four years. First half of
the school year 1913-14: Seventeen
teachers were employed in the seventh and eighth grades and high
school work at a salary of $6850,
teaching 327 pupils, or a teacher cost
of $21 per pupil. First half of school
year 1914-15: The first year under
the fully reorganized plan, eighteen
high school teachers were employed
in the junior and senior high schools
at a salary of $7788, teaching 422
pupils, or a teacher cost of $18 per
pupil. First half of the school year
of 1915-16: Eighteen high school
teachers were employed in the junior
and senior high school at a salary of
$8703, teaching 469 pupils, or a
teacher cost of $18.50 per pupil. First
half of the school year 1916-17: This
year nineteen school teachers are employed in the junior-senior high
school at a salary of $9219, teaching
537 students during the first semester, at a teacher cost of $17 per
pupil. This shows a salary increase
of over $2278 since reorganizing the
school on the present basis, including the employment of two extra
teachers, and yet the per capita cost

for teachers decreased from $21 to
$17 per pupil. The attendance has
increased from 327 to 537 in the
same period of time, representing an
increase of 64 per cent in three years,
with a comparatively stationary
school population. The census
enumeration of pupils during the
past four years is as follows: 1869,
2021, 1973, 1896.

Change of Address.

If your address is changed before
the June number is published (May
25), you should write giving your
new address. The June number will
be a good one and no teacher should
fail to receive it.—C. H. J.

An Error Corrected.

There was an error in the dates
given for Mrs. Ruby Shearer Brennan's summer school in the advertisement in the Oregon Teachers
Monthly for March. Instead of June
23 to July 4, it should have been
June 25 to July 7. Teachers who are
planning to attend this school should
bear in mind the correct dates.

Moving Picture Outfit.

J. P. Claybaugh of Vernonia, Oregon, has for sale a moving picture
outfit. Anyone who is interested in
this machine should read Mr. Claybaugh's advertisement on another
page of the Oregon Teachers Monthly.

High School Diplomas.

If you need high school diplomas,
write to the Oregon Teachers Monthly for prices and samples.

General State School News

Grant County.

Miss Zetta Mitchell of Eugene has been elected principal of the Austin schools which position she formerly held.

Miss Sarah Miller, of Sumpter, Or., is now teaching the Hamilton school which is progressing nicely under her able management.

Mrs. W. W. Slaughter of the Ritter school and her pupils some time since gave a school entertainment which netted $40.00 for school purposes.

Mrs. R. Robinson of Seneca and Mrs. W. W. Slaughter of Ritter, two among our most successful teachers, have been re-elected to teach their respective schools for the school year 1917-18.

In school district No. 36, Fern Creek, Mrs. Maude Cork, the teacher, and her pupils recently gave a basket social that netted $60 with which a new organ for the school will be purchased.

Miss Mary Viegas, who is now attending the State Normal School at Monmouth, has been engaged to teach the summer term of school in the Cross Hollows district between Long Creek and Galena.

New joint school district, No. 7-33, between Grant and Wheeler counties, has one of the best small rural school houses in the county and Miss Elsie Miller, of Spokane, Washington, has charge of this school.

The Carter school district, No. 26, where Mr. Wesley Harryman of Long Creek is teaching, has installed a new jacketed stove and about $60 worth of much needed equipment. This school has one of the best and most interesting literary societies in the county.

The Cottonwood school, in charge of Mr. Coleman H. Justice of Fox, recently gave a successful play to procure funds with which to install much needed jacketed stove. The directors of this school have purchased ample green hyloplate blackboard and provided proper lighting for their school. Other improvements are to be made.

Miss Winnie Roe, of Monument, has completed a successful term of school in district No. 48 near Hamilton. The directors of this school installed new up-to-date single adjustable desks during the fore part of this term of school; and the teacher and pupils gave a successful social which netted $22.75. This money was used to purchase a new green hyloplate blackboard and a set of maps for the school.

The Dayville schools are making substantial progress under the management of Mr. W. M. Bennett, Miss Gertrude Lyon and Mrs. Clara B. Carroll. During the past summer an additional room to the school house was erected and other improvements made. By means of a series of successful entertainments and school plays funds were raised with which one of the best school pianos in the state was purchased and installed.

The domestic science department of the Prairie City schools now serves hot lunches to sixty-five pupils who thereby are able to do much better school work. These schools are making remarkable progress under the able management of Prof. D. W. Boitnott and his able corps of efficient assistant teachers. Perhaps no other town of its size in the state has a better system of elementary and secondary schools than Prairie City. The work in all departments of the Prairie City schools is characterized by a high state of efficiency and the best possible scientific economization and utilization of energy and time based on thoroughness and practicability of all instruction.

Linn County.

A local teachers' institute was held at Scio on March 30. Besides music, recitations and dramatization by pupils, addresses were delivered by Earl Kilpatrick, University of Oregon, and E. T. Reed of the Oregon Agricultural College.

The third Local institute in Linn county was held at Mill City on March 31. At this institute there were plenty of good songs and instrumental selections. Miss Ethel Davey read a paper entitled "The Value of English," and W. A. Scott gave a paper on, "The Teacher and the

Pupil." Addresses were given by Mabel Albee and Dean Berchtold of O. A. C.

A local teachers' institute was held at Harrisburg on March 10. The program consisted of musical selections and some good dramatization work by primary pupils. Besides this, papers were read as follows: "One Way to Grade and Standardize a Rural School" by Mabel Haan; "School Courtesy" by Jennie Reed; "Preparation for High School English" by Marguerite Keefe; "Consolidation of School Districts" by George Schreiber; "New School Legislation" by L. L Gooding; "The Story Hour" by Mrs. Dr. Dale; "Play and Playtime" by Mrs. Cecil Wilhelm. Three addresses were also given as follows: "Professional Reading for Teachers" by Earl Kilpatrick; "The Parent, Teacher and Pupil" by F. M. Maxwell; "Preparation for Citizenship" by Judge Geo. G. Bingham. Miss Ambrosine Murphy gave instructions in Palmer writing.

- -- -

Jackson County.

Six boys have denoted their desire to enter the Jackson County Corn Acre project. Others may enter soon.

Quite a large number of contracts employing teachers for next year have been received at the superintendent's office recently for registering. All so far have been for full terms of nine months.

Applegate will have another rally this year. The various schools in Jackson and Josephine counties in the Applegate valley will join in an all-day celebration. The Valley Pride Creamery Association is back of the movement and will aid the schools in putting the event through. The date set is May 24 at Applegate.

Over one thousand letters are being sent by school children in this county to teachers in the east, especially in Massachusetts, calling their attention to the National Education Association in Portland, July 7 to 14, and incidentally extending an invitation to them to stop off in Jackson county to visit Crater Lake and other places of interest.

The teachers' institute at Ruch on March 24 was attended by about sixty in spite of threatening weather. The talks by Messrs. Sheldon, Frost, Nibert and Cramer were enjoyed by all. Miss Morrissey gave a demonstration in writing. Local music and an appropriate luncheon furnished by the ladies of the community aided materially in making the occasion enjoyable as well as profitable.

Talent will again hold the Southern Oregon Field and Track meet, May 4, at Talent, at which time Rogue River, Gold Hill, Central Point, Jacksonville, Phoenix, and Talent will compete in athletic events for the Olympic trophy. A separate list of events is being offered for rural schools. The Olympic Society, as has been customary, is taking the lead in an endeavor to make the day really worth while to every school in the county.

Field meets and community day rallies are now in season. West Side held a rousing rally on April 20. The day consisted of sports, singing, speaking together with an old-time picnic dinner and general good time. Seven near-by schools joined in the festivities. Eagle Point has set May 3 for a similar jollification. Principal W. O. Wheeler is working hard to enlist the interest of every teacher and pupil to join Eagle Point in making the day a success.

School District 24, Miss Alice Cromar, teacher, was recently added to the list of standard schools of Jackson county. The occasion was celebrated in a very appropriate manner by the Community club. After the entire neighborhood of about sixty had satisfied their appetites at dinner served by Mr. and Mrs. Sheets, all proceeded to the school house where a standard school certificate was presented the school by the county school superintendent. An interesting program followed, consisting of music, stereoptican talk and a short business session at which time it was decided to purchase a phonograph of Mr. Rose of Ashland who demonstrated the use of same in the rural school.

Before the close of the school last May, fourteen girls petitioned the Grants Pass Board of Education to open a class in carpentry for them. As an experiment the board granted the request and now the authorities are surprised and gratified by the progress made. Each girl makes little articles for personal use, such as glove boxes, rolling pins, card trays, picture frames; several of the more ambitious or skillful put together

dressing tables with mirrors, tea-wagons, while each girl is now working on a cedar chest (hope chest.) The construction work is alternated with lessons on the use and care of tools, on the making of stains, varnishes and other "finishes." They study the stock sizes of lumber, the nature of woods, distinguishing different varieties, imported oaks from native woods, walnuts from tropical woods, etc. No girl is allowed in this class unless she has first taken at least a year of sewing and a year of cooking. Some of the neighboring towns are following this example and Southern Oregon will be able to send skilled women workers to replace the men, if the international crisis demands it. An interesting sequel to this form of "preparedness" was quite natural. This semester sixteen boys asked for a course in camp cooking and for eighty minutes each day the school kitchen is about full of capped and aproned cooks preparing cereals or soups or milk and egg recipes, quick breads, corn bread, pancake, the doughs, pies, cakes, meats both wild and stall-fed, even ice creams and salads. Later on, as the weather permits, actual picnic lessons will be given on the use of camp utensils and emergency methods of preparing hearty meals from few and simple ingredients. Some of the boys are trying it on the home folks and the consequent symptoms surprise all concerned. Grants Pass is likely to make this a permanent feature of its high school course.

Yamhill County.

Fairview gave a splendid play to crowded houses on the evening of March 20, and also on March 21. The title of the play is "The Finger of Scorn," and it was so well rendered that the company has been asked to repeat it in other places. The net proceeds were $25 which will be used in erecting a stage in the school building, and in the purchase of an added supply of dishes needed in the various banquets held at various times by the people of the community.

On Thursday, March 22, the Grand Ronde school, Clover Leaf, Rogue River, and Valley Junction assembled in the Grand Ronde school, and filled the large school building to overflowing. The Grand Ronde band gave the first number on the program

after which the children sang "America First," in a manner which showed that patriotism is being instilled into the minds of American children today just as it ever has been. The demonstration which followed the song made it clear to every one that the song had struck a popular chord, and that America is first, not only with the children, but with every citizen of our commonwealth. The band furnished many selections throughout the program, both in the morning and in the afternoon, and accompanied the audience while they sang "America" as the closing number. A club will be organized in every district that was represented in the rally and the children will no doubt contribute largely to the success of the local fair that is being planned for Grand Ronde and vicinity for the coming autumn.

One of the most interesting and important meetings ever held among the schools of the county was the patriotic meeting held in the Moore's Valley school house, on Sunday, April 1. Almost every patron and citizen of the district, and many from adjoining districts were present and a very interesting and appropriate program was given. The teacher, Miss Ruth Westerman, gave the opening address and very clearly showed to every citizen his duty toward the flag and all that it represents, and urged upon all present those lessons in patriotism that every American citizen loves to hear. Other interesting and appropriate numbers followed, after which the county superintendent was accorded the privilege of addressing the meeting, and afterwards was given the honor of raising for the first time, their splendid new flag on the 75 foot flag pole recently provided by the district. As Old Glory reached the top of the staff, and her immense folds, 8x16 in dimensions, floated wide on the breeze, the audience sang "The Star Spangled Banner," and cheered loyally for the grandest flag of the greatest nation that has existed since the world began.

Kind Hearts.

If kind hearts are the gardens,
  We will plant kind seeds;
If kind words are the flowers,
  We will do kind deeds.
From an acorn small you know
  Some day a great oak will grow!
        —Selected.

Membership in the State Teachers' Association

Membership in the State Teachers' Association for 1917 began with January 1. Already a number of teachers have enrolled for the new year, paying $1.50 for membership including the Oregon Teachers Monthly for one year. Watch the list grow! Those enrolled to April 15 are as follows:

1. Belle Smith, Glide
2. Normal School, Emporia, Kans.
3. Margaret Thompson, Oregon City
4. Marion Mudgett, Hoff
5. Mary Vierhus, Oregon City
6. J. Q. Willits, Kerby
7. Herbert Blatchford, Waldport
8. Emma H. Murray, Klamath Falls
9. Marguerite Clark, Klamath Falls
10. M. Ethel Davey, Mill City
11. Ethel Shaffer, Lebanon
12. Julia Hamar, Lutgens
13. Hazel Hall, Turner
14. Hilda Muender, Butler
15. Bessie McFarland, Prineville
16. Emma Howard, Portland
17. Lillian Koeller, Peardale, Calif.
18. L. W. Riley, McMinnville
19. Verna G. Gardner, Amity
20. Ruth Chamberlain, Portland
21. Mildred N. Tilden, Portland
22. Annie Wickman, Marshfield
23. Laura Johanson, Cline Falls
24. Martha Skersies, Monmouth
25. Nell Moran, Portland
26. Bessie Parsons, Crawfordsville
27. Rae Langsworthy, Laurel
28. Lillian Loretz, Antone
29. W. T. Foster, Portland
30. Ruth Elkins, Canby
31. Cora E. Devor, Goshen
32. Jessie L. Turnidge, Sheridan
33. Edwin Woodworth, Molalla
34. H. Wayne Keesee, Klamath Falls
35. Buena S. Morganson, Scio
36. Alma L. Absten, Viento
37. Marguerita Andrews, Lostine
38. Mrs. M. E. Stockton, Freewater
39. G. H. Colvin, Haines
40. Sister M. Honorata, Tekoa, Wash.
41. Elsie Denson, Meacham
42. Mrs. M. E. Norton, Blachly
43. Frank J. O'Connor, Crescent City
44. Guy E. Dyar, Eugene
45. Helen M. Crump, Airlie
46. Grace Snook, Alicel
47. Arlina A. Pickett, Lewiston, Ida.
48. Leona C. Jackson, Newberg
49. Nellie Gerding, Astoria
50. Mrs. Joyce L. Hays, Cecil
51. P. C. Luh, Westerville, Ohio
52. Mrs. Helen Garey, Powell Butte
53. Anna V. Caldwell, Roseburg
54. Roberta Rippey, Portland
55. Mrs. Anna Barzee, Edenbower
56. Mrs. Daisy Short, Myrtle Point
57. Ruth Norton, Philomath
58. T. J. Means, The Dalles
59. F. H. Robinson, Port Orford
60. Mrs. Aurie Jewell, Portland
61. Herman Clark, Salem
62. Mrs. L. Allard, Woodburn
63. Leola Dunham, Cloverdale
64. Esther Suvdam, Agness
65. Alice A. White, Chemawa
66. Will J. Roberts, Vale
67. Josephine O'Leary, Portland
68. Emily G. Forrester, Portland
69. Ebba Wiren, Astoria
70. Frances Gittins, Culver
71. Ethel A. Hopkins, Mikkalo
72. Margaret McCulloch, Jackson, Cal.
73. Anna Doyle, Blackfoot, Idaho
74. Mrs. C. E. Goetz, Portland
75. Pres. W. J. Kerr, Corvallis
76. E. B. Lemon, Corvallis
77. C. J. McIntosh, Corvallis
78. Sister M. Guntilda, Tacoma
79. F. S. Gannett, Salem
80. Fred S. Crowley, Dallas
81. Ruth E. Lutje, Enterprise
82. Mrs. N. A. Springer, Aberdeen, Wa.
83. George E. Day, Yachats
84. Arleen E. Tilden, Barnesdale
85. Blanche Hubbs, Silverton
86. Mrs. Mae Anderson, Monmouth
87. Joyce Teeters, Monmouth
88. Bessie Williamson, Corvallis
89. May E. Reeves, Summer Lake
90. Chas. H. Jones, Salem
91. R. H. Powell, Prineville
92. Ava B. Milam, Corvallis
93. N. H. Comish, Corvallis
94. Joyce Casteel, Flora
95. Adona Cochrane, Salem
96. Mary E. Fawcett, Corvallis
97. E. S. Evenden, Monmouth
98. Albert Carey, Nortons
99. E. D. Ressler, Corvallis
100. Mrs. M. L. Fulkerson
101. Sherwin Shoales, Hubbard
102. Clara I. Langdon, Carlton
103. Lelah Parks, Creswell
104. J. H. Tompkins, Amity
105. Norma Reid, Portland
106. Mary E. Good, Gresham
107. Lucile Clark, Rainier
108. Mrs. Clara Beach, Klamath Falls
109. C. Hansen, Cottage Grove
110. F. C. Fitzpatrick, Roseburg
111. Eva Trent, Dayton
112. Lottie Dimick, Salem
113. Clara L. Green, Denio
114. R. G. Dykstra, Independence
115. Abbie Coon, Philomath
116. H. F. Durham, Salem
117. J. E. Fulkerson, LaGrande
118. Eliza M. Pearson, Baker
119. O. C. Bennett, Sherwood
120. Mabel Barnes, Union
121. Gertrude Biever, LaGrande
122. Mrs. Chas. Ritchie, Lakeview
123. Minnie R. Allen, Monmouth
124. Belle Barker, Salem
125. Lane Morley, Talbot
126. Estella Criswell, Hubbard
127. W. A. Scott, Albany
128. D. J. Steiner, Colfax, Wash.
129. Ethel E. Miller, Post
130. F. D. Braly, Aurora
131. W. I. Reynolds, Dallas
132. Etta Stimpson, Acme
133. W. B. Young, Albany
134. A. B. Cordley, Corvallis
135. Mina B. Hubbs, Canby
136. Wm. A. Fletcher, Buell
137. Elizabeth Wirt, Willamette
138. B. S. Wakefield, Creswell
139. Agnes Hilary, McMinnville
140. Grace Hottinger, Stayton
141. Eunice Townsend, Molalla
142. Dominican Sisters, Portland
143. Rachel Maneman, Klamath Falls
144. Sara Mark McMinnville
145. Edith Sherwood, Mill City
146. Lelah Hevland, Newberg
147. Oliver Weesner, Newberg
148. John Gavin, The Dalles
149. F. Thordarson, Bend
150. Lexie Strahan, Joseph
151. Grace M. Reed, Milwaukie

152 Helene S. Biggs, Burns
153 G. A. Ruring, Vale
154 Mrs. Ada Burch, Berlin
155 Sabra L. Nason, Pendleton
156 B. E. Wick, Armington, Mont.
157 Lucy Kopan, Hood River
158 Martha M. Eddlemon, Flora
159 Myrtle E. Lay, Molalla
160 LaVine Sheridan, Canby
161 Isabella J. McCulloch, Astoria
162 E. B. Hughson, Portland
163 Clara Rutherford, Canby
164 Herbert W. Copeland, Pendleton
165 Sisters of St. Francis, Pendleton
166 Hazel Mulkey, Vale
167 Sisters of St. Mary, Sublimity
168 Belle Conlogne, Wheeler
169 Carrie B. Adams, Elgin
170 Mrs. H. B. Brooks, Corvallis
171 H. T. Vance, Corvallis
172 J. F. Brumbaugh, Corvallis
173 W. S. Caverhill, Caverhill
174 Mrs. Lottie Tomlinson, Wauna
175 Veda E. Rhodes, Sheridan
176 R. J. Davis, Nyssa
177 Caroline Jokisch, Lawen
178 Edith Leep, Halfway
179 Helen Chadbourne, Park Place
180 Josephine Locher, Burns
181 Fay Goble, Lorane
182 Ernini Rathbun, Murphy
183 W. P. Matthews, Algona, Wash.
184 Hannah Mey, Alma, Mich.
185 Eugenia Morse, Portland
186 J. B. Rees, Roseburg
187 Belle B. Whitaker, Myrtle Point
188 Sisters of St. Francis, La Grande
189 T. O. Hutchinson, Divide
190 R. F. Robinson, Alsea
191 Alma Hoppe, Dallas
192 Mabel A. Thomas, Keno
193 Mabel Maginnis, Corvallis
194 Samuel W. Amey, Newberg
195 Mrs. M. W. Bullard, Harriman
196 J. M. Markel, St. Antony, Idaho
197 Minnetta R. Emmel, Milwaukie
198 Mary A. Sias, Forest Grove
199 Bertha M. McCallister, Grants Pass
200 Mrs. Pansy Davidson, Walterville

201 Florence Laufman, Ft. Rock
202 Mrs. W. Jamieson, Brogan
203 Margaret Aldrich, Algoma
204 J. J. Sturgill, Halfway
205 Mrs. Ada Sherman, Elkhead
206 Annie B. Romig, Camas
207 Alice M. Bacon, Grants Pass
208 D. W. Boltnott, Prairie City
209 Esther Krupke, Portland
210 E. Vera Powell, Rex
211 Mary A. Scott, Oregon City
212 Frances Murk, Portland
213 Edith Pechin, Orenco
214 Fred N. Fox, Union
215 Roxie Denny, Canyon City
216 B. H. Conkle, Silverton
217 W. A. Johnston, McCoy
218 Loraine Goehring, McCoy
219 Alta Linderman, Rufus
220 Clara E. Sterns, West Linn
221 Victoria L. Weber, Newberg
222 Bessie E. Knauff, Eddyville
223 Elva Conklin, Flora
224 A. C. Morrison, Marshfield
225 Blodwin Davies, Astoria
226 Mrs. Gertrude McElfresh, Corvallis
227 Bertha Stephens, Cottage Grove
228 Frieda Close, Clatskanie
229 P. O. Brainard, Nyssa
230 A. B. Owen, Thomas
231 Mrs. Nellie G. Tirrill, Prineville
232 Ethel A. Poland, North Bend
233 K. E. Wagner, Oak Grove
234 A L. Briggs, Watsonville, Calif.
235 Alvhied Romtvedt, Lakeview
236 Geo. D. Ingram, Hillsboro
237 Minerva Thrall, The Dalles
238 Lucy W Glass, Jeannette, Pa.
239 Beth Perry, Houlton
240 Susie Faith, Missouri Valley, Ia.
241 Lulu B. Montgomery, Ashwood
242 Winnifred Osten, Heppner
243 Carrie Eilertsen, Dairy
244 Fannie M. Fisher, Haines
245 Mrs. C. F. Yergen, Newberg
246 Geo. A. Hoover, McMinnville
247 Thelma Blair, Medford
248 Wm. A. Neumann, The Dalles
249 F. J. Tooze, Oregon City
250 Pearl E. Miller, Tillamook

The State Schools

Oregon Agricultural College.

The Oregon Agricultural College is preparing. At the first call to arms, which came at mid-night, March 27, nine cadets reported to the armory for service with Company K, and the next morning two more left for Portland to enlist with Company M of Salem. Twenty-seven others have enlisted since then, and there are 1050 men in the college taking military training who will throw down books and take up guns the moment they are needed. There is unusual activity in the military department; target practice is going on, trenches are being dug and bayonet drill is being carried on. Seniors who leave college to enter the United States military service will be given full credit for all work which was of passing grade at the time of enlistment; all others leaving to enter the service will be given credit for all work in which they had a passing grade when enlisting, excepting those subjects which are pre-requisites. These subjects will be marked "incomplete," and upon the student's return to college he will be given special instruction for the removal of these incompletes. The technical training in the regular college courses is being utilized for military purposes, since there is a place in the officers' reserve corps for every man

who is proficient in some one branch of work.

Several of the faculty have responded to the call. Dean H. M. Parks was the first faculty man to receive an appointment, which was a captaincy in the engineering corps. He is also a member of the examining board for recruits for the engineering officers' reserve corps. W. H. Peaslee, instructor in electrical engineering, has also received a captain's commission in the signal service. And the men are not alone in their desire to serve the country. Nearly one hundred girls have signed the pledge which admits them to membership in the Girls' National Honor Guard, and lessons in the different corps are going on daily. They have also cancelled all social functions and the money which would have been spent in entertainment will be given to the Honor Guard. A great many of the girls have joined the class in First Aid, organized by Dr. Browne, of the physical education department.

The Extension Service is also doing its share in preparing for the crisis by lecturing and demonstrating on the best and most efficient ways to produce and preserve the nation's food materials. Never in history has there been such a shortage of food all over the world as there is now, and with the entrance of the United States into the war, the situation becomes yet more tense, for thousands of men will be taken from the producers' class and put into the consumers' class. To aid the people in taking advantage of their resources in the best possible way, the Extension Service sent, in co-operation with the O-W. R. & N. railway, an exhibit car into Eastern Oregon with lectures and exhibits from the college. Poultry raising, vegetable gardening, and home canning were the subjects taken up, and experts will show the most approved methods of dealing with them. A. G. Bouquet, of the horticultural department, told how to convert the vacant lots and back yards into productive vegetable gardens, and Miss Cowgill, of the home economics work, showed by actual demonstration, the best way of canning these vegetables. Poultry raising was discussed by C. C. Lamb, of the poultry department, and Miss Johnson, of the domestic science staff, told of the best substitutions of

cheaper foods for the more expensive —food value being considered. The car was out two weeks, leaving Corvallis April 9, and visited all the larger towns of Eastern Oregon.

Correspondence regarding the summer school work is coming into the registrar's office very rapidly, says Mr. Hennant. Letters are received daily from all parts of Oregon and from central and southern California, as well as from the northern states, indicating that the registration will, in all probability, exceed that of last year.

A new constitution governing the college assembly was recently adopted by the student body. The desire of a change from the old system of government has long been felt, for due to the rapid growth of the student body, both in size and variety and extent of activity, the need for centralization of responsibility has become more and more evident. Two new offices have been created by the new construction, that of general manager and of board of control. The board of control, consisting of the student body officers and three faculty members, selects the general manager, who assumes control of all student body affairs. The new constitution has been in the hands of the executive committee and the advisory board since last fall, and they have worked out as nearly a perfect a plan as possible. It is hoped that by the new system there will be a centralization of authority and responsibility in student affairs that the old did not provide for.

Dean J. A. Bexell, of the School of Commerce, has been asked by the United States Office of Farm Management to investigate the business practice of some of the larger concerns throughout the country. If the plans materialize, he will leave Corvallis about the middle of June, and before returning in September, will have visited practically every state in the union. The results of the investigation will be published in bulletin form by the U. S. Department of Agriculture.

Oregon Normal School.

The faculty was represented by Miss Laura Kennon, of the English department on the morning of March 2. Miss Kennon took for her subject, "The Bible As Literature." This attitude toward the Bible, which Miss

Kennon so ably presented, was more or less new to her audience and was made more forceful by the judiciously selected illustrations of various kinds of literature to be found in this wonderful book. Miss Kennon's talk will cause many who heard her to look on the Bible from an entirely different point of view.

The outside speaker for the assembly period of March 9 was Superintendent Tooze of Oregon City. Mr. Tooze took for his subject "Some Phases of Education." He began with a comprehensive view of pioneer education and came on down to practical problems of the present day teacher whose characteristics he enumerated. The Normal School enjoyed Mr. Tooze's interesting address and was delighted to have him as a guest.

Nearly one hundred and fifty students from the Oregon Normal School on a special chartered train "stormed" the Oregon Agricultural College on March 9. The immediate cause of this "invasion" was the State Oratorical Contest in which Miss Mamie Radabaugh represented the Normal School. Miss Radabaugh gave a very creditable oration in a pleasing manner and the decision of the judges was entirely satisfactory to the Normal School delegation. In enthusiastic support of their representative the Normal School was voted the laurels of the occasion.

The week from March 16 to 23 was used by President Ackerman to visit the Normal Schools of Chico and San Jose, in California. President Ackerman made this visit with the intention of studying the plans of organization, arrangements of courses of study and the type of work done in each of these courses in order that a direct comparison might be made with the work done in the Oregon Normal School. This visit was the more timely considering the fact that the Oregon Normal School course will be re-arranged next year with the elimination of all work below graduation from a standard four-year high school. President Ackerman's report of his visit was enthusiastic in praise of the work done in these two schools, and very optimistic in regard to the work being done in Monmouth, considering the financial limitations and plant facilities.

Mr. M. S. Pittman, head of the rural department was the faculty representative March 19. Mr. Pittman read a very thoughtful and interesting paper on some phases of educational evolution. Mr. Pittman outlined the growth of our educational system and pointed out the mistakes of the past which would serve as a basis for lessons in the future. He made the prediction that the salvation of American education in the next few years will rest largely in the popularizing of industrial education, an industrial education that would be practicable in the efficient economic development of the country.

Superintendent George Hug of Mc-Minnville schools was the assembly speaker for March 16. Superintendent Hug gave a very interesting talk on the fundamentals of success in a teacher and outlined concretely many of the problems which confront the beginning teacher and the ways of successfully meeting these problems. Since he himself typifies a man who has carried out these ideas, his sincere advice was doubly appreciated by the student body. Mr. Hug's talk was an inspiration toward professionalism.

Mr. H. C. Ostien, of the department of mathematics, represented the faculty March 23 and chose for his topic "The Columbia River Highway." With beautifully colored photographic slides of the scenic beauty of this wonderful region Mr. Ostien made it possible for everyone to enjoy the splendid trip. Those who had made the trip enjoyed the pictures most of all. "Good Roads" and their relation to Oregon's development and particularly their relation to public schools of Oregon was the point of departure for the trip. The pictures were an interesting revelation to many of the students, made more so by the comments of Mr. Ostien as the pictures were shown.

Miss Mabel G. West, the librarian, has been in Los Angeles during the month where she has undergone two operations. Her many friends will be interested to know that she was recovering rapidly at last reports.

One of the biggest days of the semester was Junior Day, March 30. With the largest junior class in the history of the school, some 270 in number, the possibilities for the day were unlimited. The careful organization of the plan and the accurate carrying out of the work of the various committees made the day a mem-

orable one. The special theme was "See Oregon First." This started with a skit during chapel time depicting a varied lot of travelers who wished to visit Oregon. During the program in the afternoon these travelers were shown the state educational institutions, the Willamette Valley Cherry Fair and characteristic industries of the various parts of the state. The program was interspersed with delightful bits of costumed dancing, scenic pictures and original catchy music. After the main program in the chapel a side trip was taken to the summit of Mt. Hood along the Columbia Highway. After this climb, which was at the gymnasium, the climbers were rewarded by a generous helping of Mr. Hood ice cream and the pleased guests went home enthusiastic over Junior Day.

During the recent campaign for the Oregon militia a goodly number of the men from the Normal School stu-dent body responded to the call. This depletion from the small number of men in the student body makes their absence very noticeable.

Senator J. K. Gill of Portland was the assembly speaker for April 2 and spoke on the "Indians of the Columbia River Basin." He held the closest attention of his audience for an hour while, in his exceptionally pleasing way, he told of these people, so romantically interesting to all Americans. Senator Gill used interesting charts and drawings in tracing the development of the Indians from the crude Stone Age to the present. He told fact after fact about their life, religion, and customs as obtained from fossils and traditions and left in the minds of his hearers a permanent interest in this subject and a store of interesting information which will be passed on to many boys and girls of the state.

The Independent Colleges

Pacific College.

President Pennington gave the closing address at the Ministry and Missions Conference of the Y. M. and Y. W. C. A. at Salem, April 6-8.

Miss Norma Harvey, of the class of 1917, has been chosen by the student body as May Queen. The May Day celebration will be held on Saturday, May 6.

In accord with the discipline of the Friends Church (Quakers) Pacific College will officially center its efforts for service to the United States in the present war on the ambulance service, Red Cross work, etc. Friends are already in communication with President Wilson in regard to this work.

March 3 the faculty and student body of the college gave a unique "At Home" to the college board, alumni, woman's auxiliary, visiting committee and other friends. Members of the faculty and student body gave addresses of appreciation to their friends, which were responded to by representatives of each of the organizations honored.

Pacific College was this year the winner of the Willamette Valley Basketball championship, the league of the independent colleges of the state, playing through the season with the loss of only one league game. Only one game was lost outside the league, and that was with the O. A. C. team, which the Pacific College team defeated on the Newberg floor, losing, however, in the return game at Corvallis.

Through the instrumentality of the college, Newberg audiences had two opportunities to hear David Starr Jordan recently. With Portland, Chehalis, Vancouver and Seattle asking for his services on the evening of his address in Newberg, he came to the Quaker city and the Quaker college, because he had become acquainted with President Pennington in a contest in oratory which David Starr Jordan judged and President Pennington, then an undergraduate, won; and because Pacific College was the school attended by Herbert C. Hoover, head of the Belgian Relief Commission, before he went to Leland Stanford for his work in mining engineering.

Summer Session 1917

JUNE 11 to JULY 28

Oregon Agricultural College

COURSES OF INSTRUCTION

1. Courses for Teachers.
2. Courses for College Entrance and College Credit.
3. Boys and Girls Short Courses.
4. Preparation for Teachers Examinations.
5. Vocal and Instrumental Music.

SPECIAL INSTRUCTORS

1. Home Economics—Miss Alice Ravenhill, London, England; Mrs. Mary Schenck Woolman, Boston.
2. Manual Training—Mr. Geo. Fred Buxton, Stout Institute.
3. Additional Specialists—Will be announced in bulletin and subsequent advertisements.

REGULAR COLLEGE FACULTY

Instructors from the regular staff include specialists in Home Economics, Manual Training, Commerce, Agriculture, Art, Biology, Chemistry, Physics, Education, Economics, Political Science, Psychology, etc. In all, about one hundred courses will be offered.

CUT OUT AND MAIL COUPON BELOW

E. D. RESSLER, Director
     O. A. C. Summer School,
         Corvallis, Oregon.
    Please send copy of 1917 Summer School Bulletin to my address.

....

....

....

McMinnville College.

Beginning with the new year the faculty of McMinnville College prohibited the use of tobacco in all forms. As a result of this ruling the college lost only one or two students, all the others having accepted the situation. This is an example which every educational institution ought to follow in view of the deadly effect of nicotine upon students.

McMinnville College has lost about a dozen students from its ranks who have enlisted in Company A of McMinnville. A Cadet Corps has been organized in which very nearly one hundred students are now training daily. It is expected that a company A of McMinnville College will result from this movement. The company is being drilled by Mr. Leonard S. Hopfield who has had several years of service in the army. The faculty has agreed to give two credits to every student who drills regularly and faithfully.

The library of McMinnville College has just received a copy of a new book entitled "The Development of China" issued by Houghton-Mifflin Company. The author of this book is Prof. Kenneth Scott Latourette, Ph.D., who graduated from McMinnville College in 1904. He received his Ph.D. from Yale University and later taught for several years in the College of Yale in China. Mr. Latourette has in preparation a similar work on Japan.

Albany College.

Commencement day this year will be June 13, 1917, and the class has selected for its commencement orator, the Rev. George L. Clark, of La Grande, Oregon.

Francis W. Tolles, Kenneth Diven, David Martin, Thomas Kirkwood, Warren C. Hunter, Annie Watkins, and Prof. F. C. Kent represented Albany College at the Salem meeting of Ministry-Missions Conference.

For the May Day celebration, which will occur Tuesday, May 1, 1917, Miss Marion Stanford, May Festival Queen, has chosen Bertha McCormick, Margaret Gibson, Georgia Thompson, and Ibby Green as her maids of honor. Delmer Gildow will be master of ceremonies.

The Albany College Annual brought out by the student body is rapidly approaching completion, and copies are expected from the printer in a very few days. The Y. M. C. A., of Albany, is planning a circus, the proceeds of which will be used to help finance the Annual.

President Lee, chairman of the committee on co-operation, of the privately supported colleges of the state, is sending out a circular letter to all the accredited high schools of the state, making the same offer of an Oregon Conference Scholarship that the private colleges made last year. It is hoped that the high schools will respond promptly to this offer of a scholarship.

The student body of Albany College is showing its patriotism in a most emphatic and tangible manner, as shown by the fact that the following young men have enlisted in the service of their country, having joined the Coast Artillery Corps: Louis A. Jones, Paul C. Dawson, Charles D. Jones, Arthur R. Jones, Clifford F. Fairfax, Orville C. Smith, Francis W. Tolles, Forest S. Campbell, L. L. Myers, Alva Starr, Lewis R. Dougherty, C. K. Logan and J. C. Haberly. The young ladies of the Y. W. C. A. are working enthusiastically in connection with the Red Cross society, taking First Aid lessons.

Pacific University.

Pacific University at Forest Grove this year has finished its debate and oratorical contests with other colleges in a rather remarkable way. In its inter-colegiate debate with Willamette University on "The Literacy Test" for immigrants, we won both the negative at Forest Grove, and the affirmative held in Salem. A double headed victory of this sort is rather unusual in the history of state debates. To fill its cup of glory to overflowing, it also came out victor in the Oregon College's Inter-collegiate Oratorical Contest participated in by the colleges of this state including the State University and the Agricultural College at Corvallis. Here again its representative, Mr. Lester T. Jones, proved the thoroughness of his logic and delivery by ranking first in thought and composition as well as in delivery. This, too, is a rather remarkable performance. Pacific University rejoices in the campaign of a closer affiliation of its alumni and former students

and re-organized faculty and in its aggressive campaign to double its attendance next year. The faculty of the conservatory of music has been out on quite an extensive tour, giving concerts which have been received everywhere with very sincere appreciation. All the student body are at present interested in the proposed military drill which promises to enroll every young man in college.

Reed College.

Reed College will co-operate with other institutions in the work of the National Research Council, and, for that purpose, has appointed a committee consisting of the president, five other members of the faculty, one member of the board of trustees and one alumnus.

During the coming summer, Prof. Hudson B. Hastings will give courses in Commerce and Industries at the University of California, and Prof. William F. Ogburn will give courses in Sociology at the University of Washington.

Reed College has arranged, at the request of the colleges of the Northwest, for Dr. LeBaron Russell Briggs, president of Radcliffe College and dean of the Faculty of Arts and Science of Harvard University, to speak at various college commencements. He will give addresses at the University of Oregon on June 4, Reed College on June 5, the University of Idaho on June 8, the University of Washington on June 9, and the Washington State College on June 14.

Willamette University.

The response of the Willamette University men to the call for volunteers has been enthusiastic, and 43 have enlisted in the National Guard of Oregon up to the present time. Nearly half are sophomores. Among those who are now under arms are Raymond Attbery, president of the university Y. M. C. A., and Charles Randall, former president of the Y. M. C. A. Randall enlisted when he could not make immediate arrangements to go with the company as a Y. M. C. A. secretary. The enlistments were not secured through any pressure on the students, but seemed to be a spontaneous expression of the patriotic spirit in the school. Coach R. L. Mathews of Willamette University, graduate of a military school,

has organized a company of students for military drill on the campus. Nearly every male student remaining at the university has voluntarily joined this organization.

The faculty of Willamette University adopted resolutions at a recent meeting announcing that seniors who have enlisted will be graduated with their class in June, and that members of other classes will be aided in making up their work for the remainder of this semester and continuing with their courses in college without loss of time or credit.

A "jolly-up" farewell celebration was given in the gymnasium Thursday night, March 29, in honor of the Willamette students who were to depart the next day with Company M of the guard for Vancouver barracks. Games, refreshments and informal leave-takings made up the program. Friday morning classes were dismissed and the students marched in a body to the station to see the student soldiers entrain.

The enlistment of Errol Proctor and Harold Miller, editor-in-chief and manager, respectively, of the Wallulah, the university annual, has made a re-organization of the staff necessary. Miss Ruth Spoor, who was associate editor, has been chosen editor, and Harry Bowers has been elected manager.

Prof. Wm. E. Kirk, head of the department of Classical Languages, and librarian, gave his contribution to the faculty lecture course in a stimulating and valuable adress on "The Practcal Idealist" Monday evening, April 9, in Waller hall. Prof. Kirk indicated the position which the practical idealist will take on matters of present moment, economically, socially, religiously, and educationally. Prof. Kirk contended that the theory of formal discipline is far from dead, and that the evidence and authority in support of the belief that this educational doctrine is passe is insufficient and not well founded. The address included references to many authorities upholding the position taken by the speaker.

Miss Violet Maclean was chosen May Queen at a student election, Wednesday, March 28. Miss Lila Doughty and Miss Rosamond Gilbert will act as maids of honor. Plans for the May Day program are nearly completed.

Law Questions Answered

By ELMO S. WHITE, Salem, Oregon

Under this head Elmo S. White, of the Marion County Bar, will endeavor to answer such questions of law as our readers may care to ask. Conformably with the established policy of this magazine to be of the greatest usefulness possible, there will be no charge for this service. Questions will be answered in the next issue after receipt whenever possible. Every question must be accompanied by the name and address of the inquirer, but these will not be published unless the person so desires. Questions accompanied by a fee of one dollar will be answered by mail as quickly as possible and will not be published unless requested by sender. Address all communications to Attorney Elmo S. White, Masonic Temple, Salem, Oregon.

Attorney White: "What is the legal minimum school term in Oregon?" Under the present law, six months. The 1917 session of the legislature has changed this, however. The new law, which goes into effect May 21, next, provides for a minimum term of eight months.

Attorney Elmo S. White: "Who can vote for school director? Must a person to so vote be the owner of real estate in the district?" By the law which goes into effect May 21, 1917, any citizen of Oregon who is 21 years of age and who has resided in the school district 30 days immediately prior to such election is entitled to vote for director and clerk. Property qualifications are removed as regards voting for such offices.

Attorney Elmo S. White: "I understand that Arbor Day has been changed; also that a new holiday has been created in the public schools. If so, what are they?" The latest legislature has decreed that the second Friday in February shall hereafter be known in Western Oregon as Arbor Day, and in Eastern Oregon the second Friday in April, as it is now. The fourth Friday in October is to be known as Frances E. Willard Day. In the afternoon of such day exercises and instruction are to be given relating to her life.

"Attorney Elmo S. White—Did the supreme court hand down a decision that children born of alien parents were not citizens of the U. S.? If so, in what way will that affect the 14th amendment?" I do not find such a decision. In the case of the U. S. versus Wong Tim Ark, reported in the 169th U. S. on page 649, however, the supreme court has held, in substance, that children born of Chinese parents who at the time of the birth of the children are subjects of the emperor of China, but who have a permanent, residence in the U. S., and who are engaged in business here, and are not here merely as attaches of the Chinese government at Washington or elsewhere in the U. S., are citizens by virtue of the first clause of said 14th amendment.

Attorney Elmo S. White: "A former pupil of mine has just reached the age of 21 and may have the right to some property. The circumstances are these: His father had a deed to some property. He became insane. While insane and while my pupil was about 4 years of age, and before committal of the father to an asylum, the father deeded the property to a third party. Nothing was given him for the property. The deed was recorded, and this and all subsequent transfers appear on the records to be perfectly regular. The father died in the asylum several years ago. Can anything be done for the benefit of my pupil, since the different owners since the transfer from the father have expended considerable money on the land in improvements?" Yes, if their is sufficient proof of the facts you outline. The law allows six months after reaching the age of majority within which to begin an action of this kind. Ordinarily, of course, such a cause of action "outlaws" with a few years of the transaction, but as a minor cannot bring an action during the years of his minority, the statute of limitations is held in abeyance until his majority is reached, when it begins to run. The pupil, if sufficient proof can be had, can recover the land, but likely will have to allow a reasonable value for the improvements which have been made by the innocent purchaser.

Call no man happy until his death.
—Solon.

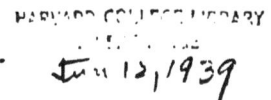
‘OREGON TEACHERS MONTHLY

The Official Journal of the State Teachers' Association

Vol. XXI	SALEM, OREGON, JUNE, 1917 .	No. 10

Published Monthly Except July and August by the State
Teachers' Association

Entered at the Postoffice at Salem, Oregon, as second-class mail matter, April 1, 1898.

EDITORIAL BOARD

H. D. SHELDON, School of Education, University of Oregon, Eugene
E. F. CARLETON, Assistant Superintendent of Public Instruction, Salem
C. T. BONNEY, County School Superintendent, The Dalles
R. K. OHLOUPEK, Director Manual Training, Pendleton.
C. G. DONEY, President Willamette University, Salem
E. S. EVENDEN, Department of Education, Oregon Normal, Monmouth
MRS. M. L. FULKERSON, Institute Instructor, Salem
GEORGE W. HUG, City Superintendent, McMinnville
HOPKIN JENKINS, Principal Jefferson High School, Portland.
MISS VIOLA ORTSCHILD, President Grade Teachers' Association, Portland
K. D. RESSLER, Department of Education, Oregon Agricultural College, Corvallis
MISS LILLIAN TINGLE, Supervisor Domestic Science, Portland
CHAS. H. JONES, Business and Managing Editor, Salem

· RULES OF PUBLICATION

1. The mailing label on the Oregon Teachers Monthly shows the date to which subscriptions are paid.
2. The Oregon Teachers Monthly will be sent to subscribers until ordered discontinued and all arrearages are paid.
3. Notice of change of address should be given at once, naming both old and new postoffice.
4. When renewing, always state that subscription is a renewal.
5. The subscription price, including membership in State Teachers' Association, is $1.50 a year in advance. Single copy, 20 cents.
6. Advertising rates will be furnished on application.
Address all communications to Oregon Teachers Monthly, Salem, Oregon.

Editorial Notes

Teachers should endeavor to be better informed during the coming year than ever before, which virtually obligates every teacher to spend more on magazines than at any other time, for in no other way can she know the events, happening daily, which are of great national importance and which the pupils should be told about. In no other way can she know the responsibilities and obligations which have been assumed by the teachers of the land and especially by the teachers of her own state. Some teachers are discontinuing their subscriptions to their magazines because of the increased cost of living, but that increased cost does not decrease a teacher's responsibilities, and "hysterical saving" is deplored by our federal and state authorities. One form of patriotic service is to "keep regular." Especially is this ex ́ected of the teacher and more especially of the teacher who is so successful in her work that she is a community leader, because as such she will have th moulding of much of the patriotic sentiment of her pupils and patrons. In order to perform our patriotic duty in this respect, our educational str ngth must be increased by an enlarged membership in the State Teachers' As ociation, insuring success to its undertakings which will be voiced through th ~~per, its official organ.—E.

President Wilson has given his official sanction to the decision of the Executive Committee to make the annual convention of the N. E. A. in Portland the occasion of a great conference on preparedness. The high schools, colleges and universities have contributed students and instructors to the army and navy and the elementary schools have joined the others in providing recruits to assist in the vital campaign for food production and preservation. Our participation in the war is bringing us to an earlier inventory of our national resources. Just as England, France and the other great nations discovered that some of their supposed greatest assets were dangerous liabilities, so we shall be compelled to readjust our institutions. Undoubtedly we shall receive some rude shocks as to our educational system. No Oregon teacher can afford to miss the great meeting in Portland July 7 to 14. Should serious illness or other misfortune prevent attendance, the volume of proceedings will compensate in a measure. Whether one is permitted to attend or not, he should take out an advance membership and secure the proceedings, not only for the intrinsic worth of the volume but for the honor of the state. Director Plummer and State Superintendent Churchill are much pleased with the fine response made to date but we are still a long way from the hundred per cent goal. Send the two dollars to you County or State Superintendent today.—R.

* * *

"The world faces the greatest food shortage of modern times. Fifty-six millions of the most able-bodied men have been taken from the ranks of producers since the beginning of the great war." These words are taken from a poster calling for volunteers for service in the production of food. The O-W. R. & N. Co. and the Southern Pacific Co. have equipped and sent over the state special trains in the interest of greater food production and conservation. The federal and state governments have made special appropriations and the Extension Service of the State Agricultural College is putting forth all its resources through county and district agents and special lecturers to arouse people to the dire need and to instruct them. Upon the teachers as the leaders of the youth rests a grave responsibility in this crisis. This is no idle alarm. Our experts have the facts and our government is appealing to our patriotism. If the war ends before this issue appears, the food shortage will not be lessened this year and will be serious for several years. There will be grave suffering in America and starvation in Europe under the most favorable circumstances. We teachers must promote the work of the Boys' and Girls' Clubs as never before and we must encourage them throughout the summer. Not alone by precept but by example as well must we preach preparedness. It's a crime against humanity to neglect any possible opportunity to plant, cultivate, harvest and conserve.—R.

* * *

In pursuance of the desire to have the Oregon Teachers Monthly . the sentiments of the teachers of Oregon as expressed in their Represents Council, we have tried to keep the "Teachers' Code of Ethics" before teachers of the state. Instances have come to our attention of teachers have followed the code and have failed to get places which were awarde teachers who used unprofessional methods in securing them. This is b natural situation when some people begin to control their conduct by his standards. We do not relinquish our ideals of honesty because a individuals handle the truth carelessly. Another point in the code should have the thoughtful attention and conscientious support of teacher is that she should "take an active part in all community activities of an educational nature." At the present time a most liberal interpretation must be placed upon "activities of an educational nature." The teachers who lives up to this point of our code will take an active part in the social life of the community and will help at the games and parties of the younger people. She will know her pupils individually. She will be interested in and sometimes a participant in the industrial life of the community. She will be active in the Parent-Teacher Association, Reading Club, Red Cross, and similar organizations. She will enthusiastically support the Boys' and Girls' Industrial Clubs. She will know how to profitably use the public and circulating libraries and the extension courses offered by the various state institutions. She will encourage joint and competitive meetings with nearby schools. She will do all these and many other things, and as each additional activity is entered the horizon will be extended to include a more efficient teaching vision and a greater field of social service.—E.

*   *   *

With the accusation that big business has gone to the extent of being unpatriotic to the equivalent of treason or insurrection one of the most radical resolutions that has as yet come forth from any body of Salem people against the ever increasing cost of living has been signed by a number of state officials and other prominent people and is now being circulated with a request that individuals and organizations pass and sign it and forward it to representatives and senators in congress. It was wired to the Oregon delegation in congress. The following is the text of the resolution: "Whereas, the prices of staples, the necessaries of life, have advanced to figures exceeding the cost of production to an extent far beyond the limits of conscience and any possible conception of human rights or reason, and are still advancing. Whereas, this condition is proof of the utter lack of humane consideration on the part of those responsible and indicates a frantic desire and effort to levy merciless war assessments in advance upon the public whereby the beneficiaries may later meet their own obligations without sacrifice if not at actual profit. Whereas, such business is unpatriotic to the equivalent of treason or insurrection. It proves its perpetrators to be limited only by the heartless principle of taking all the traffic will bear, or all an unprotected people can be forced to pay. Whereas, Congress has undisputed authority over every resource of the nation in the present crisis, which authority is being exercised in the taking of the bodies of our best young men for military service and the action is met with ready support in a spirit of glorious sacrifice by the people. But the flagrant abuses by the food speculators, pursued from palpable motives of greedy disregard of the great emergency that is upon us, goes unchecked and unchallenged except by ineffective and dilatory discussion. Therefore, be it resolved, that (insert name of organization or g up) does hereby most earnestly urge upon our national congress the great n d of immediate and effective action to relieve this most menacing situation w ch is rapidly contributing to the aid of the enemies of the nation and a ady amounts to one of the gravest obstacles to the success of our country i he great crisis that now confronts it."

t is time to face the fact that the world must patiently go to school until it learned the great lessons of justice, self-sacrifice and helpfulness which make wars and rumors of wars memories of "far-off, unhappy things tles long ago."—The Outlook.

Membership Campaign for State Association

By GEORGE A. BRISCOE, Ashland, President of the Association

The executive committee of the Oregon State Teachers' Association, after much consideration of ways and means to increase the subscription list of the Oregon Teachers Monthly, decided to appeal to the loyalty of the school force of the state. As president of the State Teachers' Association, the plan of organization was left to me. I have decided upon the following plan: (1) County superintendents to be responsible for teachers in all third class districts; (2) Superintendent, if there be one, otherwise the principal to be responsible for teachers in all second class districts; (3) City superintendents to be responsible for the teachers in the first class districts; (4) Head of educational departments in schools of higher education to be responsible for all teachers in the institution to which each belongs.

The county superintendent will appoint one or more teachers, especially qualified by nature and by professional standing, to work intensively during the county institute among teachers of the third class districts. Before and after the county institute, this person or persons will endeavor to enroll every teacher in this group. The superintendents in the first and second class districts will appoint one or more teachers to be responsible for securing subscriptions of all the teachers in these classes.

If this plan be adopted, the enthusiasm of superintendents and solicitors means everything. Without them, the plan must fail; with them, we may reasonably expect success. The county superintendents are asked at this time to set apart a period on the forenoon of the first day for a full presentation of this whole matter by themselves, some representative of one of the state schools or some other effective speaker. This means much; for this reason I am asking each county superintendent to give this his personal attention. Mr. Jones will be in attendance upon as many institutes as possible to take subscriptions singly or in combination with his special offers.

At the most, the teachers of Oregon can muster a strength of five or six thousand. From each subscription of $1.50, 50 cents goes to the fund of the Association. This money is used to defray expenses of the annual meeting, to pay the expenses of the investigations of special committees, printing reports, etc. At present, fewer than 3000 teachers have paid for the official organ. Our income from all sources scarcely pays the most meager expenditure of funds. Every department is handicapped and will be until some plan is put into operation that will produce more funds. No one is paid for the time and effort put into making both the official paper and the state meeting a success. For these reasons we appeal to you to lend a hand now that we may enroll most of our teachers as subscribers to the Oregon Teachers Monthly. All of us will have to work without pay and wit' thought of self if our profession means what it should to the teacher : the state.

The state association proposes, through its representative cu... initiate and solve questions that will benefit every member of the ---- —not only this but to promote the welfare of the people of this st.

May I count on you to carry out the part of this plan falling to all those who occupy positions of leadership will insist upon the teac this state supporting their official paper, not only the State Teachers' '' will be more effective and satisfactory, but the teach-- ----

assume a solidarity that will count for much. Can't we, by pulling together, create such sentiment of loyalty that teachers employed in any of our schools will not refuse to be one of us, counting it a privilege to help carry on the work the state association has undertaken? Are you willing to get under your part of the burden?

Supervision of Teachers in the Small High Schools

By H. K. SHIRK, Burns, Oregon

The principal of every school, whether it consists of two or fifty rooms, realizes the importance of keeping in touch with the work of his teachers. Without this supervision the situation soon gets beyond his control and his influence as a leader has become hopelessly lost. And, except for the fact that he signs the reports that are sent to the county superintendent and draws a somewhat larger pay check, or warrant as the case may be, he is of no more value to the school than any of his teachers. The district, too, is loser as it, and rightly, expects its principal to guide and direct the studies of the children entrusted to the care of the school so that they may get the best results from the years they spend in the school room.

The problem of keeping in touch with the work of the teacher in a small high school is a hard one. Oftentimes the principal, besides having to do the manifold duties that arise from his position, is called upon to teach almost, if not quite, as many classes as any of his teachers. Where this is the case it is out of the question for him to give the oversight to the work the teacher is doing by visiting the rooms. So it is necessary that some other plan be adopted. But what shall it be? A good and well arranged course of study is a big help and a necessity for every school; but it is inelastic. And if the average principal has learned one thing well, it is that classes vary through wide limits in their ability to apprehend the principles presented and in the amount of work they can cover in a given time. Besides, the too minutely divided course of study makes a machine of the teacher, deprives her of individuality and thus the incentive to good work.

A plan that gives good results and enables the principal to keep in daily touch with the work of each teacher has been tried out in the Harney County high school. It is a modification of the daily plans of the grade teacher which are so seldom used in the high school. The first day of each semester after the daily program has been made out, though the departmental system is used as far as possible, and the usual stray class or two has been assigned to some teacher who can do the work, the principal makes out a blank form fit the classes and needs of each of his teachers. These blank forms, en filled out, contain the necessary information to enable him to keep in ch with the work of each teacher without making their use burdensome he one who has to fill them out. A sufficient quantity is then printed to each teacher a supply to last throughout the semester or year. These ik plans properly filled out must be turned into the office every evening ore the teacher goes home. In this way the work is planned for the day before the teacher leaves the building. A glance through them les the principal to decide whether or not the work is being carried out ·· to the course of study and as it should be; if he thinks it is not, a word to the teacher the next morning before school straightens the matter out. It also enables the principal to decide whether or not the lessons are too long or short, whether they are adapted to the needs of the pupils. It is a real help to the young teacher and a steadying influence on the more experienced. These plans are punched to fit any good loose leaf note book cover and with such a cover for the plans of each teacher are reference books that are often invaluable in the future. Some might suggest that it was not necessary to have the forms printed, but if they are not the instructions about writing the lesson plans are soon forgotten and the value of the report is largely lost. The cost is not great as it is less than a cent apiece.

Now as to checking up on the daily plans of the teacher, for there are teachers who sometimes forget that they have made plans and wander off on some other subject. At the end of each week this school has a report on the work covered during this time. It need not be long. A paragraph on each subject taught is enough to show just what has been done. Two extracts from these weekly reports are quoted showing their nature:

"Ancient History, Botsford—Pages 1 to 21 were covered. (4 days' work). Special References—Maspero, Life in Egypt (Chapters 1 to 10); The Mentor, Egypt; Hales, The Flight Through Egypt (Chapters on the Pyramids.)" If these references were first looked up and then a paper written on them, as is generally done in this school as well as discussing them in class, the principal drops in after school sometimes and runs through a few of them. This enables him to judge of the amount and quality of the work. It is not necessary to read every paper or all of any paper to know what is being done. "Agriculture III—Laboratory work in testing cream, skim milk and causes of error in testing. Special reports on phases of the dairy industry."

This is the way one school keeps in touch with its teachers and their work. It is not claimed that it is original, or that it is a cureall for lack of time to properly supervise the work, for nothing can take the place of good, personal supervision; but it does enable one to keep properly in touch with the work of every day and of every lesson.

Living Statues.

An amusing game that can be played quite as well indoors as out is that of living statues. All the apparatus needed is a soft rubber ball. The players stand in a circle; one has the ball. This he throws to the next player, and then to the next, and so on, round and round the circle. Every player to whom a ball is thrown must catch it, and if it is missed the player who misses must stand for the rest of the game in exactly the position he was in when the ball was missed. First one then another will miss and these will be standing in all kinds of amusing positions and attitudes like grotesque statues.—Selected.

The value of all true education is in giving a man the ability to do the thing he ought to do when it ought to be done, regardless of whether he is like doing it or not.—Huxley.

The highest excellence is seldom attained in more than one voca n. The roads leading to distinction in separate pursuits diverge, and the r er we approach the one, the farther we recede from the other.—Bovee.

Advice is like snow; the softer it falls, the longer it dwells upon he deeper it sinks into the mind.—Coleridge.

Some Aspects of the Study of Geography

By WARREN D. SMITH, University of Oregon

"The sun and the moon, the right eye and left eye of all History, are Chronology and Georgraphy."—Hakluyt. Some of the readers of this article may have read the indictment of college students in the Nation of December 16, 1915. A freshman class was reading Marlowe's "Hero and Leander": "Hellespont suggested Gallipoli, and I (a professor in a Middle Western University) asked the class—it was quite a chance shot—where Gallipoli was. To my surprise, no one knew. I wrote the word on the blackboard, and was amazed when the class confessed that not one had ever seen the word before! Within the next twenty-six hours I had met three other sections of freshmen, and had placed 'Gallipoli' before them with the same result. A more advanced course yielded two men who had never heard the name—one of them was on the staff of the university daily paper."

The matter of Gallipoli is bad enough, but imagine the writer's chagrin on finding but one in a class of forty in geography who knew by name the scene of the greatest naval engagement in modern times. A junior in the university informs the class that the Danube is in India, while another one says that Babylon is one of the large trade emporia (at the present time, mind you) of the Mesopotamian region.

Let me say that this indictment must not be leveled at students alone. Some teachers and others the writer knows of, are avoiding the study of the geography of the war under the pretense of being absolutely neutral. This is as bad a confession of weakness as that of the man who has to take a pledge to keep decent. In the case of the war it is a pitiful excuse and nothing more. Laziness will explain a good deal of this. And so we'll give the poor much maligned student a rest and pass to bigger game. A New York business house instructs its Havana branch to settle a certain matter with some people in Manila (thinking the latter place somewhere in the Caribbean.) A wealthy woman of Fresno, California, is overheard on the S. S. "Manchuria" telling a friend that she and her husband are going "first to Manila and then take the train from there to Shanghai!" And so on ad nauseam.

How long are we going to "stand for" the implications in the nation? Just as long as we lay ourselves open to them. One fundamental difficulty in all our dealing with foreigners, whether Europeans, Mexicans, Japanese or Filipinos, can, in our opinion, be shown to be due to lack of knowledge of these peoples and therefore of geography. We do not seem to get their viewpoint at all. A world view point is needed. Now how can you expect the student to get it if many high officials of the land and the teachers haven't it? Our dealings with Japan, Mexico and Europe in general would be made vastly easier if we personally knew these countries and their peoples better than we now do. Most of the trouble in the world has come about through misundestanding, either intentional or unintentional. The first has usally to be overcome by force, the second by education.

When the writer came to the University of Oregon three years ago as professor of geology, he found that there were no courses in anthropology, ethnology or geography, and he has since found that there is little or no geography taught beyond the grades in Oregon schools save a little physical geography and that, through lack of inspiring and well trained teachers, is in its death throes. It is only fair to say that there are several schools where no fault could be found with the teaching of this subject.

Now geography is a great synthetic subject, a fine melting pot for so many interesting facts and principles culled from both the sciences and the humanities that it ought to be one of the most popular and profitable courses in the school or college curriculum. The writer, whose first love was geology (and for this subject he still feels a great attraction), finds himself in these times of momentous world changes irresistibly drawn into a deeper study of geography. He instituted a course in advanced economic geography at the State University three years ago with the following enrollment: The first year, 23; second year, 35; third year, 42. (Fifteen or 20 were turned away as the lecture room would only accommodate about 40.) He hopes in time to see courses in ethnology added. These are not theoretical studies; they are immensely practical. How can the American business man market his products abroad if he does not have salesmen who know thoroughly the countries in which they expect to travel, or if he himself does not know what those people want? Germany's success in foreign commerce has been due to this sort of training. Geogaphy must and will have its day, but some of us are still in a "Spanish doze," or have our attentions so diverted by educational experiments that we don't seem to see the real needs of the hour.

Having consumed some time in fault finding, let us proceed to something constructive. We wish to offer a few suggestions to the teacher of geography who may not have access to the best libraries or who has not seen much of the great world beyond the boundaries of his or her state. The writer makes no pretense at being an authority, but he has found that extensive travel in foreign lands and association with leading geographers at the headquarters of the Royal Geographic Society in London has furnished him with a perspective and a kind of information which he personally has found of the greatest help. His desire is to aid those less fortunate in this respect, as well as to criticize.

What are the qualifications for a successful teacher of this subject? We don't know positively, but we may venture to state some of them (if some of this is old matter and has been said before, it won't do any harm to repeat here): First, enthusiasm; second, wide reading in geographic literature; third, broad training in the fundamental sciences; fourth, ability to associate facts and to make deductions; fifth, (if possible) wide travel, and actual first-hand acquaintance with various peoples in other lands. There are many good books, but none can impart a knowledge of temperament, sympathy for strangers, etc. These can be gained only by personal contact. A speaking knowledge of a foreign language is of tremendous help.

Methods.—One word will convey most of what is essential in this paragraph: Visualize, and do this by means of (1) pictures, (2) maps. (3) graphs. A second point: Make the oceans and not the contin "turning points." Oceans unite instead of separate the continents days. There is more in common, in many ways, between the east coast and our west coast today than there is between the eastern and shores of our own continent, and this will be accentuated with the years.

A teacher cannot be the best teacher except he has done, or is engaged in, some sort of individual research. Only in that wa the feeling which actuated the early discoverers of new land

geography. The research men in our colleges and schools are our modern explorers. Exploration is intensive now, instead of being extensive, but it is exploration just the same.

O. Henry, in his inimitable way, has said that "all the world is divided into two parts: Men who wear rubbers and pay poll taxes and those who discover continents. There are no more continents to be discovered, but long before the supply of rubber has given out these same men will be paralleling the canals of Mars with radium railways." And we might add that although all the continents have been discovered, not all the valuable facts about these continents have been discovered. Are you, reader, going to be a mere "middle man" in the world or do you care to take a part in the gathering, at first hand, of knowledge?

Equipment.—Let it be said that expensive apparatus is not imperative. A good atlas, a daily metropolitan paper, maps which can be had for nominal prices, relief maps, which you can make yourself, a good collection of pictures (post cards if you can afford nothing better) and you have the essentials.

Socializing Education

By E. J. KLEMME, Ellensburg, Washington

"I would rather have an eighth grade graduate in my bank than a student that has completed the high school, and two-thirds of my associates here would agree with me," said a member of the Bankers' Association that met in Spokane recently. There were three hundred bankers at that meeting and from their silence they seemed to agree. The speaker continued by saying that the reason he made the statement was two-fold. His experience led him to the conclusion that a high school graduate had secured a great deal of knowledge but no ability to use it, and that when he entered a bank he wanted to be either manager or receiver.

It would be a difficult concession for us to admit that the banker's statement was true in total, but we are almost forced to conclude that there may be some truth in the statement. Many of our high schools have been acquiring knowledge rather than skill. Many of the tests are for knowing rather than for doing. To get facts is easy; to get accuracy in doing is quite different. To teach text books is occupying a position; to teach skill is filling it. Our problem is to make unresponsive plans responsive to the social life about us; to make inactive students active; to make indifferent teaching, different. Too many students and some teachers are after a situation with emphasis on the sit.

Many high school students are looking after the learned professions, or honorable career and they think this means the getting out of work, rather n success through it. Recently a Y. M. C. A. worker wanted a boy to ist in association work, and a bright high school student responded. He s asked to study the system of financing and to become thoroughly uainted with the books. He took the suggestion with indifference and or going to the secretary said, "This work is not in my line, I do not care do it. I thought you wanted an assistant, one who would meet people, nd conventions, make addresses, but this is too much like drudgery. I ⌐ ⌐it.'" Too many students leave school expecting to get a white collar position and are disappointed because they do not secure it. Nor are the students wholly to blame for this. The school system trains quite generally for the so-called learned professions, forgetting that learning may be used in digging alfalfa roots as well as Greek roots, and it may be as cultural, too. We need less of that culture that takes us from the activities of life, and more agriculture that connects us with life.

Our leisure class is still too large. This class is distributed as generally among the masses as among the classes. The pupils in our schools must be prepared for life's effort, not for life's ease. One-third of the people in this country are feeding the entire population.

Our schools are making many changes in harmony with the demands. Courses are working successfully, that a few years ago were not thought of by the most progressive school men. In most schools in our state courses are given in agriculture, commercial branches, manual training, domestic science and household economies. We are beginning to catch the vision of the future, but the light comes slowly.

Considerable change has come about in the teaching of the subjects in the cirriculum. Physics is now taught with a view to its use in the particular problems of the community. Botany is now a study of fruit pests and insect life in the local neighborhood. Geometry is not a repetition of theorems, but is an application of these to the necessities of life. This is socializing education. Let the good work go on.

Rural School Department

Edited by MRS. M. L. FULKERSON, Salem, Oregon

EFFECTIVE CLUB WORK.

No chain is stronger than its weakest link. Nor is any business enterprise stronger than its most vulnerable point. As a matter of good business industrial club work has been introduced into our schools. Its philosophy is admirable. Some of the results are excellent. But it has a weak link, sometimes due to the teacher herself, unsupervised summer work. It is needless for me to reiterate what is already too well known; how when there is no one to show an intelligent interest, the club boy or girl drops by the way. However, in the light of what is certain to be a severe winter in more ways than one, the writer feels justified in singing the old song. Patriotism demands it. This year, more than ever, there should be a black mark placed opposite the teacher's name for every child not finishing the project selected, unless of course there is some valid excuse. This is a strong statement ---- is made in spite of the fact that the writer has fifty projects being carrie in his club. If it were only possible for us to realize the significance of food drive, to grasp the quickened pulse of the community and turn it unified and consistent end; at this moment there would not be a club Oregon which has not been arranged for in the absence of the teacher. we feel the sacred obligation to our district, our state, our nation, and have not attended to this matter as yet, make haste to select some patr literally thrust the care of the district club upon that party. Thi eachers can appeal to patriotism as well as to the pocketbo-

years we have desired results, this season our country demands them. It is easy to give advice. The fact is it is so cheap that too much of it is foisted upon the public. It is not so much the fact that we do not know what to do as it is we lack the driving power to put through what our better judgment sometimes urges upon us. Obey that impulse and tell that board member you are up against it, that you need assistance in order to do the district justice in your absence. Tell him you expect him to either assist or secure assistance. Duty to his country demands it. It is surprising what one can do if he has the courage of his convictions. Then after you are on your vacation don't forget that postal you promised Lazy Willie or Fretful Sally. It is a good idea to get in touch with the next year's teacher and acquaint her with the facts. Encourage her to write by way of inquiry. Children like mail just as well as we. Then, too, an occasional letter to the parent counts. A visit is better. Arrange with the county agriculturist or the O. A. C. extension men to drop off at your district. The writer intends to continue his present policy of visiting with parent and pupil alike. The visits are for encouragement, not for the spreading of learning. Assume the farmer knows that end of the game. The coach pats his men on the back and says, use your head but get there. I say the same, anything that is fair, only make your club work effective.—L. P. Gilmore, Oregon Normal School.

* * *

PRIMARY NUMBERS.

We might treat this subject under the following subdivisions: (1) Number ideas, (2) number drills, (3) number habits.

1. Number ideas must be gained through counting objects, children in the class, objects in the room, collecting objects. The children enjoy being live counters. They will suggest what they would like to be—trees, birds, or flowers. The play spirit should enter into all of this. One may count while another writes the number on the blackboard. Count by 1's, 2's, 3's. What is 1 more than 6? What is 1 less than 6? Teach one combination a day, for example, 2 plus 3; 3 plus 2. Continue addition until the children understand the process, say up to and including 12; then it would be wise to introduce subtraction. Be sure the pupils are well drilled in addition. Review addition when presenting subtraction.

2. Number drills should be given through games. In the April number of this magazine you will find "A Dozen Number Games."

3. All combinations must be made automatic. If the pupil is allowed to count through the first two grades and not made to memorize each combination as it is presented, very careless habits will be formed, in fact, he will be sure to count on his fingers when required to add.

First Grade Numbers.

The following is a lesson plan used in our school:

Teacher's Aim.—To teach the following subtraction: 12 minus 5; 12 minus 7.

Preparation.—Write 7 plus 5; 5 plus 7 on the blackboard. Have some child write the answers. What is another name for 12? (A dozen.) What do we buy by the dozen? (Eggs, oranges.) What do we sell by the dozen? (Eggs. apples.) How many eggs should you get for one-half dozen? (Six.)

How many oranges? Have the children give oral number stories using these combinations. What did we do with these numbers? (Pointing to the board.) (Added them.) What other thing can we do with them?

Pupils' Aim.—Now, let us find out how to subtract them. (Our class numbers 12 so we use the children for live counters.) Count the children in the class. Take 5 away. How many have you left? How many did you have? Who can write it? Which number do you write at the top? Why? Which number at the bottom? Why? Now take 7 from your 12. How many have you left? The children may give oral number stories, using the subtraction.

Drill.—Send the class to the board to write the four combinations from memory.—Elizabeth C. Riecker, Training Department, Oregon Normal School.

* * *

FOURTH GRADE GEOGRAPHY.

(Concluded from May)

IV. Spinning and Dyeing.

Preparation.—Now children let us all think about what we found out yesterday. You may tell me, Cecil. (How wool is washed.) What color was it after it was washed? (White.) Now look at May's dress. What is it made of, Hugh? (Wool.) Oh, surely not, because you told me that wool was white after it was washed. What about it, Wilfred? (It has been dyed.) That is true, but it can't be wool for even then it doesn't look like the material in May's dress. (No it must first be made into thread.) Yes, we call this spinning. Then let us find out how wool is spun into thread in Salem.

Presentation.—How many of you have seen your mothers dye or color cloth? (Nearly all have.) You may tell us how she did it, Hugh. (Hugh tells.) If the children have never seen it, the teacher tells it and illustrates simply. Would the people in the mill do it the same way? (No.) Why? (Too much wool.) They use large tanks very much like the ones they washed wool in. Here is a picture of the dye tanks. These tanks are filled with dye. This dye is mixed by men who understand the process very well. We used to get these dyes from Europe. Why don't we now? (War.) We make it ourselves now. Is it as good as that which we got from Europe? (No.) Why not? (It fades.) Why can't we make it as good? (Because our men haven't worked at it as long as the men in Europe.) The men in Europe have made a study of it for years and years. Europe is much older than our country. Our men are getting so they can make the dyes better every day. Our own dyes are very expensive too; and for what we once had to pay a few cents, we must now pay a few dollars. Now after the wool is put into the tanks of dye, what is done? (It is boiled.) Does any one k how long your mother boils the cloth when she dyes it? (Two hours.) and so here it takes how long? (Two hours.) What does your mother after the cloth is dyed? (Dries it.) Do you suppose these people do same? (Yes.) What have we found out, Eldon? (How wool is dy that what we started to find out? (No.) What did we start to find (How the wool is spun into thread in Salem.) How did our great g mothers make the wool fibers into thread? (Spinning wheel.) picture of one. Would they use this in the mill at Salem? (I (It would take too long.) After the wool is dyed, it is fed (explain) where it is torn into small pieces. Then it is put through a scribbling machine. This changes the wool into a thin, flat fleece. It looks very much like a heavy wool blanket. Then this fleece is passed through the carding engine. This engine has teeth like a comb which tears the fleece into the form of slivers. What are slivers? (Small pieces of wool.) Then these slivers are changed into rovings which look like pieces of soft cord. (All of these various things can be shown to the children if you have a woolen exhibit.) Now the real spinning begins. There are a great many frames in the room. These are called mule frames. These frames move backward and forward and draw the thread from a long spool. Then back they glide and a thousand little spindles begin their whirling dance and wind the thread evenly on the spindles or bobbins. The bobbins look like this. (Draw picture.) As soon as the bobbins are filled, more bobbins are put on. Either a picture may be shown of the mule frame or better still draw one on the board as you tell about it. Now what have we found out? (How the wool is spun into thread in Salem.)

V. Weaving.

Preparation.—What did we find out yesterday? (How the wool is spun into thread.)? Yes. Did you ever weave a rug or a hammock? (Yes.) What did you use to weave it on? (Cardboard.) Do you suppose cloth is woven on cardboards? (No.) Well today let us find out how the thread is woven into cloth in Salem.

Presentation.—What did you call the cardboards that you wove your rug on? (A loom.) Then what might they call the machine that they weave cloth on? (A loom.) Yes, and when you did your weaving, how did you get your loom ready? (We cut little slits in both ends of the cardboard and then we strung twine back and forth across this space.) Does any one know what we call these threads? (The warp threads.) What did you do next? (We took the yarn and wove it back and forth between the warp threads.) What are these threads called? (The woof threads.) Yes. Did any of you see the loom they used in "Silas Marner"? (Several saw it. Have it described —show a picture of a loom.) What is the man doing? (He is putting in the warp thread.) He does it very much the same as you did it. He strings it from the thread on the bobbins we talked about yesterday. Now over here is a loom. What is this woman doing? (She is putting in the woof threads.) How does she put these in? (She slides a shuttle in and out between the warp threads. This shuttle is filled with thread.) Yes. This shuttle is very much like your mothers' tatting shuttle only of course it is larger. Now as these woof threads go over and under the warp threads they are pushed up close together by the machine. Then after a while the long piece of cloth is en. What colors are the woof threads? (Sometimes they are all one or and sometimes different colors are used.) How much do you suppose people who do the weaving get? (Pupils guess.) They get about 15 ts a yard. How many hours a day do they work? (About nine hours.) w many yards can they make in an hour? (Pupils guess.) About two ds. Now if they get 15 cents a yard and make two yards in an hour, how ch money will they get? (30 cents.) And if they work nine hours how h will they make? ($2.70.) Yes, that is about what most of them e. Now what have we found out? (How the thread is woven into cloth —Lillian Dinius, Critic Teacher, Oregon Normal School.

THE WIND SYSTEM.

(Continued from May)

Now let us follow the air after it has ascended over the heat equator. What of its temperature, moisture and weight? (It becomes cool, drops part of its moisture, condenses and becomes heavier.) What does it then tend to do? (Drop.) Where? (On either side of the heated area.) Since it is in motion above the earth it becomes what? (A wind.) Since this wind blows in a direction opposite to that of the trade winds, what might it be called? (Antitrade.) Because of the earth's rotation what would be the direction of the antitrades? (North of the equator; they will blow toward the right and south of the equator to the left.) That is correct. Lava and ashes from volcanoes in the torrid zone have been hurled in a direction opposite to the trades. Our army aviators who penetrated Mexico far enough to the south say the same thing about the antitrades. Some of these winds descend to the earth between 28 and 30 degrees north and south latitudes. What change will there be in their temperature as they near the earth? (They will become warmer.) What will they do as they settle over water? (Take up moisture and retain it.) Since the air is descending what might be said as to surface motion? (There would not be enough to notice.) Then we would call this what kind of an area? (Calm and dry.) North of the equator this region was once called the "horse latitudes." Would you like to know why? Well, it is said that during the days when most of the shipping was done in sailing vessels, sometimes boats carrying cargoes of horses and mules were unable to pass though these latitudes on account of there being no wind. Sometimes under such conditions a vessel would have to lie at anchor for days awaiting a favorable wind. During this time the horses would drink up the fresh water and eat the fodder so that to save their own lives the sailors had to throw the horses overboard. From this practice this lattiude drew its name. The like region south of the equator is also referred to by the same name. What would you say as to the climate in the regions or these latitudes? (It would be rainless, warm and calm.) Would a given region always be in this belt? (No, because of the shifting of the heat equator.) Name a region affected by the "horse latitudes." (Southern United States.) What have we found out now? (How the air which rose at the heat equator descends to the earth and affects the climate.)

Make a statement summing it up. (This upper air becomes chilled and so drops its moisture, after which it moves in an opposite direction from the trade winds, and drops to the earth about 28 and 30 degrees on either side of the equator. As this air drops to the earth it becomes warmer and takes up and retains moisture as it descends over water bodies. These regions are called the "horse latitudes" and the winds responsible for them are called the antitrades.) Now let us see what becomes of the air which is constantly descending. What is its temperature? (Warm.) In what direction wil move? (It will move toward the still warmer area.) Where then? (F to the heat equator.) Yes, part of it does and part of it goes in the direc of the earth's whirl. Then it would blow from which direction? (South in the northern hemisphere and northwest in the southern hemisph These winds blow as far north and south as the arctic and anarctic cir. Little is known concerning the winds in the frigid zones that would bear our aim. From the general direction of these winds what might t called? (Westerlies.) In what zones do they blow? (The temper As they blow over water what may we expect them to do retain moisture.) Under what conditions will they drop it? (When they are cooled by hitting mountains or some cold winds blowing in an opposite direction.) Would this be good for a country? (Yes.) Look on your maps and see which continents would be favorably affected by the westerlies. (Western United States, Europe and southwestern South America.) Why? (There are oceans in the paths of the westerlies from which to take the water, and high mountains or rising slopes to force the rainfall.) What season would have the heaviest rain? (Winter.) Why? (Because in winter the land is cooler than the water so the moisture laden winds blowing from the oceans would become chilled and drop their moisture when passing over the land.) Is this the best season for rain? (No, the growing season is the best.) Now what have we discovered? (What becomes of the air in the descending column.)

Sum up this unit. (Some of the descending air returns to the heat equator while the rest is caught in the earth's whirl and becomes known as the westerlies. These winds blow in the temperate zones. Providing they blow over bodies of water and are obstructed by mountains or other adverse conditions on land, they drop their moisture as rain.) Look at the map of the United States. What winds operate here? (Westerlies.) Why have we found winds important? (They carry moisture.) How far across the United States will they be able to carry it? (To the west side of the Sierra Nevadas and Cascades.) What would that indicate for the land east of this? (It would be dry.) Look at your maps. Do you see indications of such dryness? (Yes, there are some rivers that empty into lakes which have no outlets. There are also stretches of land without any rivers.) Look farther east. What do you see? (Large rivers and a number of towns and cities, also the great lakes.) What does this indicate? (That central United States must secure its rainfall from some source other than the westerlies.) Quite right. Do you see any large bodies of water from which this moisture might come? (The Gulf of Mexico and the Atlantic.) Very well, we shall see some of this moisture is precipitated over central United States. Sometimes there are portions of the interior of the United States that become heated to higher temperatures than other portions. For instance Arizona and New Mexico are quite dry and hot. What will the air do in such localities when it becomes heated? (It will rise.) Then what will happen? (Air will rush in from all sides to fill up the place of the heated air rising.) If the earth were standing still and if there were no westerlies blowing what course would this air that rushes in likely take? (The shortest or easiest course.) Correct, but the westerlies are blowing from the southwest, so what effect will they likely have upon this rising air. (They will tend to blow it in a northeasterly direction.) Correct, and in addition the earth is rotating so it will tend to do what? (Make it whirl like a dust funnel such as we can see form on the heated pavement or road during the hot summer days.) You are right, now here will this whirling wind likely go? Look at your maps. (It can't go aight toward the Atlantic because the mountains would offer too much istance. It would likely follow some river like the St. Lawrence.) Yes, quently these winds strike across the Great Lakes down the St. Lawrence l cross the Atlantic before stopping. You told me a while ago that this air hes into the whirl from all directions. Some of it must come from what ies of water then? (The Gulf of Mexico and Atlantic.) That is true. you see any reason why during the growing season there should be an dance of air sweep inland from the gulf? (The growing season is our hot season. During our hot season the land is warmer than the water, so the air over the land should be warmer and lighter than that over the ocean. That makes the air from over the gulf and ocean displace the warmer air over the land so it rushes into this whirl.) Very good. Once the air gets into this whirl in what direction does it move? (Upward.) As it goes up it becomes how? (Cooler.) And does what? (Drops its moisture if it has enough.) Very well, then in the vicinity of such whirls we may expect what? (Rainfall.) That is correct. I am wondering whether you could reason out how fast this whirl must move? (Well as the ground is fairly level it ought to pick up speed.) Yes, it moves at the rate of fifty to sixty miles an hour on land and as fast as eighty miles on sea. Of course if it travels that fast would you expect it to cover a large territory? (Yes, it must be many miles wide.) As a matter of fact, sometimes these storms cover a territory the shape of a large circle, one thousand miles in diameter. I am wondering what effect these large storms will have on the climate of the place after they pass over. (They will make it clear and colder.) Why? (Because the moisture has been dropped from the winds and only dry winds remain and because water requires about five times as much heat to make it rise as much in temperature as soil. Everybody knows how damp soil is cold because of the water it contains.) Now children, do any of you know the name of this kind of storm we have been talking about? (None do.) Look on your maps and see what states are apt to be crossed by these storms. (Kansas.) Yes, have you ever heard of the severe storms which that state has? Perhaps some of you have relatives living there. (My uncle lives there and he says those storms are so severe that sometimes people build sod dugouts to crawl into when they see the storm coming.) How can they tell when such a storm is approaching? (He says they usually come from the southwest and the clouds are black. He calls them cyclones.) Yes children, they are called cyclones or cyclonics.

Of course this air that goes up in the cyclone and precipitates its moisture must drop. When it comes down what will it be like? (It will be dry and cool and instead of whirling in will spread out just like the air does in the horse latitudes.) Yes. Then in comparing it with the cyclone what may we say? (It is just the opposite.) What would be a good name for such winds then? (Anticyclonics.) These whirling winds are apt to be in all temperate zones where there is a sufficient difference in altitude, kind and lay of the land. Name another place affected by them. (Western Europe.) Have we worked out our problem?

You may sum up. Recall the aim. Now briefly summarize the entire topic. (Because of the rising air at the heat equator many winds are set in motion all over the earth. Since they operate in regular order we might call them wind systems. Because of the shifting of the heat equator these wind systems also shift. As winds are rain bearers, most regions, other cond" being favorable, are at some season visited by rain.)

How will being able to figure out this feature of the climate of a co. help us in our study of geography? (It will help us to infer the pro. of a country and the industries growing out of them.) Illustrat natural vegetation of a mountain district in the path of the wester" be timber and plenty of pasture grasses. Lumbering and da'— follow.—Katherine Arbuthnot, Critic Teacher, Oregon Nor

INSTRUCTIONS FOR CLUB ADVISORS OF OREGON.

The boys' and girls' club work in Oregon is progressing so well that we do not need to say much regarding it at this time, but just a word as to the work for the summer and the preparation of the exhibits for the many local, county and state fairs to be held in the state this fall, may be profitable. By advisors we refer to county superintendents, county agents, local county leaders, teachers, and those loyal men and women in different communities who are giving of their valuable time in order to help the children of their respective communities in this great work. We know that you have carefully gone over the different instructions sent to the club members and are prepared to help them interpret the instructions, lessons, etc., that they receive from time to time.

Meet with the club members in their meetings once or twice a month, and at these meetings have the members tell of their successes or failures, praise their good work, suggest to others, who have troubles, that they may be able to secure some help from what some member has just said regarding his or her work, offer a suggestion to other members who may be having some trouble, and check up on all reports that should be sent to the state club leader. By reports we mean the report cards following each lesson on the sewing, canning and baking projects, also the cards on all other projects that are to be filled out on May 10 and July 10.

The lessons for sewing, canning and baking cannot be sent to a club member until the member has completed the previous lesson and sent in the report card for the same. Instructions cannot be sent to members in other projects until the cards for May 10 and July 10 have been received by the state club leader. As soon as the members have completed their lessons on sewing, canning and baking the final report blank and instructions for preparing the exhibit will be sent to them. This report should be carefully filled out at once and mailed to the state leader in order to have it graded and the grade will be reported to the county superintendent immediately.

Division 1 in poultry and also the dairy herd record keeping projects should be completed at the duration of six months' work, the final report filled out at that time and mailed to the state club leader. The handicraft project may be finished and report mailed just as soon as the required number of enterprises are prepared. The reports on all other projects will be mailed to all club members sending in their report cards for July 10. These reports may then be filled out just as soon as the projects are completed. All advisors should go over these reports with the club members in the meetings as soon as your members receive their blanks.

You can do much during the year by taking or having some one take pictures of the club members at work, or pictures of the completed projects. These pictures will be of much help in creating interest among clu ⸱ members and also the general public. They may be used in the local, cou ⸱ty, and state fairs, also in the local newspapers, and if sent to the state lea ⸱⸱r, they will be used in many ways.

⸱ust before the local, county, or state fairs are held, a meeting of the clu _members may be held and at this meeting the preparation of the exhibits shc uld be carefully discussed. Also the instructions on the preparation of ⸱exl ibits for each project, as prepared by the Oregon Agricultural College, shc uld be carefully studied. If possible, have some of the field workers meet wit⸱ ⸱ʰᵃ club and give specific instructions.

⸱⸱riotic spirit this year will mean that all of us want to do all possible to aid our government in the war in which we are now engaged. The food problem is one of the greatest, if not the greatest, and every boy and girl in the state can do much to help in this work. Advisors, by encouraging the members to produce and then conserve all possible, will be doing a great and patriotic service for the country. We must not only feed our own people but the starving millions across the water.

President Wilson is asking for an army of 2,000,000 boys and girls to help in the great drive on the food campaign, and you, as advisors, will be real officers of this great army and will be doing a noble work by directing these willing young people in their part of the struggle.

If any instructions or help is needed in any way pertaining to the work, write, telephone, or call on the state club leader or his assistants.—Article prepared by H. C. Seymour, state club leader, Oregon Agricultural College, United States Department of Agriculture, and State Department of Education, co-operating.

The Inland Empire Teachers' Association

By E. D. RESSLER, Corvallis, Oregon

The nineteenth annual session of the Inland Empire Teachers' Association met in Spokane April 4 to 6. It was a well-attended meeting, ably-officered and hospitably entertained. The speakers on the general program were President Suzzallo of the University of Washington, who took the subject "American School and National Character" for his presidential address; Professor David Snedden of Teachers' College, Columbia University, who spoke three times on various phases of Vocational Education; Dr. E. A. Kirkpatrick of the State Normal School, Fitchburg, Mass., on "Democracy and Efficiency" and "Formal and Incidental Education"; Professor E. H. Lindley of Indiana University, on "The Psychology of Leadership" and "The New Pioneers"; Chancellor E. C. Elliott of the University of Montana, on "Crux Criticorum."

Five general sessions were held during the three forenoons, the second evening and the third afternoon. Twenty-seven departmental programs were scheduled, fourteen the first afternoon and thirteen the second. The banquet at 6:30 the first evening and the reception following at 9 o'clock were well attended and much enjoyed. The social feature of the meeting is noteworthy. While it interfered seriously with the attendance at the departmental meetings and to a degree at the general sessions, the value of making acquaintances and exchanging experiences with fellow workers in four states alone justifies the expense of attendance. In the opinion of the writer, however, it should be possible to combine both experiences, greatly to the advantage of the formal programs at least.

State Superintendent Churchill was elected president for next year; J. A. Burke of Spokane, secretary; J. E. Buchanan of Cheney, treasurer; E. D. Ressler is the Oregon member of the Executive Committee. Among Oregon teachers in attendance, most of whom participated in the program, were J. A. Churchill, O. M. Plummer, Mrs. George McMath, W. R. Rutherford, P. L. Campbell, Mrs. M. L. Fulkerson, A. T. Park, E. F. Carleton, Mrs. Hallie C. Thomas, E. D. Ressler, H. C. Drill, G. W. Hug, Miss Anna Johnson, L. McCullough, J. H. Ackerman, H. C. Seymour, J. W. Todd, G. F. Sykes. Spokane is the permanent place of meeting and the time fixed is the Wednesday to Friday preceding Easter. While the meeting is chiefly for the Inland Empire, which includes parts of the four states, Idaho, Montana, Oregon and Washington, supervisory officers and other teachers who can get away should plan to attend in larger number from the more remote parts of the su[...]

states. Such a sectional meeting should answer the need for a broader conception of the problems of education than can be gained by teachers who confine their attendance to their own state meetings. It would give in some measure the inspiration of the great national meeting of the N. E. A., which most of us cannot hope to attend regularly or even occasionally.

The reading by Chairman Churchill of the resolutions committee of the "patriotic resolution" was greeted with great applause, the audience rising and singing the national anthem, while Superintendent Frazier of Everett and Superintendent Rose of Boise stood on the platform waving the two large flags used in decoration. The resolution closes this brief report: "Whereas, the American flag is the emblem of freedom, of equality and of justice for all, is the symbol of the brotherhood of man, and stands for courage, for chivalry, for generosity and for honor; Resolved, that the first duty of the American school is to teach reverence for our national colors, the Star-Spangled Banner. It should be displayed in accordance with the United States army rules. Its slight-

est abuse must never be tolerated. The pledge of allegiance should be taught to every child and frequent opportunity be given for repeating its sacred words. Our national anthem and patriotic songs should be memorized and sung on frequent occasions. That finally, in view of America's entrance into the great world war with all its unprecedented possibilities for national weal or woe, we hereby pledge our unswerving fidelity to, and faith in, our national ideals and our national leaders. We believe that these ideals are worth whatever sacrifices may be necessary to uphold them. We believe that the schools, at a time like this, should teach the childen that the essence of true patriotism in self-sacrifice and should imbue them with the willingness and desire to subordinate their personal welfare to the infinitely more important welfare of that great social group—our beloved republic. One and all, we will stand solidly behind President Wilson. He is our leader, and we will follow the appointed path to the end. There is now no thought of divided opinion, no word of censure, no hesitation or flinching. Onward is our only word henceforth."

The Northwest and the National Education Association

By C. C. THOMASON, Secretary of the Portland General Committee

Add the year of your birth, the year of your marriage, your age at your 1917 birthday, and the number of years since you were married (or minus the number of years since you were married if you are single), and divide the total by 2, and you will have the year of opportunity for the teachers of the Pacific Northwest. Every teacher should be able to point to at least one National Education c vention that he has attended. The t chers of Oregon, being acquainted v h Portland and the vicinity, s uld be able to get the most out of t 1917 convention.

he rumor, that the convention r ght be called off on account of the v , has been definitely set at rest t President Wilson, who has sent v d that he can see no reason why t convention should not be held. 1 N E. A. represents one of the

vital and constructive forces of the nation in the education of the people for preparedness and true conservation. President Robert J. Aley, Secretary D. W. Springer, and the Portland general committee are unanimously of the opinion that the 1917 convention will be one of the most important meetings in the history of the association.

The program in full is to be printed in the June N. E. A. Bulletin issued from Ann Arbor, Michigan, by Secretary Durand W. Springer. The general plan is to have the meetings of the various departments both forenoons and afternoons from 9 to 12 o'clock and from 2 to 4 o'clock respectively. The evenings will be given over to general sessions. The department meetings will be held in the auditorium, Y. M. C. A., White Temple, First Presbyterian church,

First Methodist church, First Congregational church, Ladd School, Lincoln High School, Shattuck School, Commercial High School, Beth Israel Temple, St. James Lutheran church, First Christian church, Public Library, and Unitarian church.

Some features of special interest already fixed are the naturalization of 100 applicants Thursday evening, the general reception Tuesday evening, the opening meeting Monday afternoon, the "Plummer Luncheon" to N. E. A. officials Wednesday noon, an open air reception in the City Park featured by the State Societies on Wednesday, and the Oriental Tea Thursday afternoon. A community sing will be held one evening after the program. Each evening at the headquarters hotel tea will be served. Arrangements will probably be made by the Portland school board to have

the Couch and Shattuck swimming tanks open during the entire week with swimming exhibitions at certain hours.

John H. Finley, state commissioner of education of New York, has recently left for France on a mission for President Wilson. He expects to be back in time to attend the N. E. A. in Portland and to bring to the teachers a live message direct from America's ally. Ella Flagg Young will be prominent in many of the programs. The representative men and women from all sections will be present. Memberships from the teachers of the Northwest may be sent directly to R. H. Thomas, clerk of district No. 1, Portland, Oregon, at any time prior to the convention. Attendance will be limited to those having membership badges unless there is found to be room to spare in some of the meetings.

Oregon Govermental Affairs

By ROBERT CARLTON CLARK, Eugene, Oregon

Oregon and California Land Grant. The fortunes of the Oregon and California Railway land grant have been recorded in these columns from time to time. Another chapter has been added to this history. It is to be hoped that its legislative and judicial history is now at an end. The supreme court of the United States has at last upheld the so-called Chamberlain-Ferris act by which provision for the disposition of these lands was made last year. Under the terms of this act the government reserves the timber, minerals, etc., and sells such lands as may be suitable for agriculture under the usual homestead regulations. The Southern Pacific railway is to receive its equity of $2.50 an acre and no more. The more specific terms of this act were given in a previous number of the Oregon Teachers Monthly. It would seem that the Railway has used its last means of delaying the carrying out of the provisions of this law and that it must now go into effect as rapidly as necessary surveys may be made.

The Voters Pamphlet.

The pamphlet describing the proposed constitutional amendments

and measures, with arguments supporting or opposing them, which are to be voted upon at the special election, June 4, next, has been sent out by the secretary of state. It shows eight proposals submitted by the legislative assembly. These may be increased by four or five more if all the petitions in course of circulation that invoke the referendum on other legislative acts secure the necessary 14,000 signatures. Referendum petitions may be filed as late as May 21. The time between last date for filing and the election would seem to be almost too short for proper printing of the ballot. Effort is being made by appeal to the courts to keep one of the measures off the ballot on the ground that it did not receive a majority of the votes in the l-- :r house of the legislative assemb

Taxing Oregon and California ' id Grant.

Last month five of the measu. to appear on the June ballot were e- scribed. Another, the second in r- der of appearance on ballot, prop es to place the lands known a- ie Oregon and California railv id grant on the tax rolls. ° he government filed suit against the Southern Pacific railway for the recovery of these lands on the ground of failure to carry out the terms of sale under the original granting act the railway has refused to pay any taxes on the land. Large tracts of this land lie in certain counties and within certain port districts and the revenue from taxing same has constituted a large proportion of taxes of such counties and districts. To be deprived of such revenues is a real hardship upon other property owners as the burden of taxation is fixed and the amount collected from year to year is not inclined to decrease. The government in the Ferris-Chamberlain Act proposes to pay back taxes up to the date when the measure became law. But for 1916 and ensuing years no taxes will be collected from these lands, or at least until they pass into private ownership. Interested sections of the state persuaded the legislative assembly to enact a law for submission to vote of the people to determine if these lands shall be placed on the tax rolls. If title to the lands has reverted to the federal government such land is not subject to taxation by the state. It is contended by those who defend this act that the railway has retained a share of $2.50 an acre in the lands and that this share justly should be taxed. This seems much too technical a matter for submission to the people. Whichever way the majority vote may be given the courts will ultimately have to determine whether the state has the right to tax the land. If the measure is defeated the county tax assessors may put the land on tax rolls and if there is refusal to pay the tax who would be made the defendant in a suit, the federal government or the railway? One real objection to the measure is that if passed it may add a cloud to the title. The burden of paying taxes in arrears might fall upon the purchaser. The voter is likely to vote no on this measure simply because no one seems to understand its possible effect.

Increasing Pay of Legislators.

The third measure on the ballot purports to have for its intention the laudable object of limiting the number of bills that may be introduced in the legislative assembly and in addition the perhaps no less praiseworthy effect of increasing the pay of the legislators from $3 to $6 per day. The wildest imagination would find trouble in detecting the least connection between these proposals. If either be desirable they should have been submitted in separate bills. I may believe that the individual members of the legislature are unnecessarily productive in inventing laws and that the allowance of four as proposed in this measure is ample and more than generous and at the same time feel that the present honorium of $3 per diem is all and more than any legislature deserves. Yet the method of submitting these two very distinct proposals in the same measure prohibits my voting my honest convictions on each. It is hard to escape the conviction that the legislative assembly hoped to secure a raise in pay by holding out what was hoped might prove the attractive bate of fewer laws. It seems to say to the voter: "Pay me more and I will ease up on making laws."

The Year's Volume.

The present issue brings the year's volume to a close. The results are before the teachers of the state. The editors desire the frank opinions of the members of the association as to matters of policy in order that the paper may be more effective. If you believe that too much space is given to news, to general articles, to discussions on method, to any particular feature, write in and say so. If you believe that important interests are neglected, do not hesitate to express yourself. It is your paper, you have a right to make your influence felt. But remember that it represents all the teachers of the state, rural as well as city, primary as well as high school and vocational, so that it is necessary to publish material which does not always appeal to everyone with equal force. The editors have done their best, but realize keenly their limitations as regards time and materials and welcome criticism, either sympathetic or unsympathetic.—S.

Oregon State Library

By CORNELIA MARVIN, Librarian, Oregon State Library

The commissioner of education in his report for 1916 has the following review of recent significant educational literature: "It was noted in the last previous report on the subject that much of the significant contribution to current educational literature is in the form of reports of surveys and investigations. Especially important as contributions to educational literature are the volumes of the Cleveland survey. Well written and attractively printed, these books may well serve as an example to other makers of educational reports. Public Education in Maryland, by the general educational Board, and Higher Educational Institutions of Iowa, by the bureau of education, are among other reports issued during the year that appear to have elements of permanence as educational documents. A large part of the material compiled in the survey work is later being issued in book form. This procedure, begun in the case of the New York school inquiry, has become fairly well established; witness Professor Cubberly's recent books on school administration. The educational survey, after all, represents largely the application of accumulated theory and practice; it should therefore be a valuable medium for the formulation of educational doctrine.

"In addition to the report of the Maryland survey, the general education board published during the year two pamphlets in its Occasional Papers series that have already caused widespread discussion—Flexner's A Modern School and Eliot's Needed Changes in Secondary Education. A controversial literature of no mean dimensions threatens to develop from Dr. Flexner's concrete statement of certain advanced demands. The annual reports and bulletins of the Carnegie Foundation for the Advancement of Teaching have a deserved reputation for scholarly handling of important problems in education. Teachers' pensions and law schools are the two subjects which material has recently been published.

"Among general educational writings should be mentioned John Dewey's Democracy and Education, the author's most complete formulation of the ideas implied in a democratic society and the means of applying these ideas to the enterprise of education; and E. C. Moore's What Is Education. In the field of educational psychology, Judd's The Psychology of the High School Subjects, Miss C. M. Meredith's The Educational Bearings of Modern Psychology, and Freeman's Experimental Education, may be noted.

"The literature of standards and tests has to its credit for the year the important papers in the Fifteenth Yearbook of the Society for the Study of Education; Starch, Educational Measurements; and Terman, The Measure of Intelligence, besides numerous articles on tests for the various school subjects in educational periodicals and survey reports. Rapeer's Educational Hygiene from the Public School Period to the University contains chapters by leading specialists and is therefore a convenient summary of this important phase of education. Two books of widely differing scope in the general subject of play are to be recorded—Henry S. Curtis, The Practical Conduct of Play, and Joseph Lee, Play in Education. The kindergarten is treated from opposite angles in Nora Atwood's Kindergarten Theory and Practice and Kilpatrick's Froebel's Kindergarten Theories Critically Examined. The Gary experiment, besides calling forth a large amount of pamphlet and periodical material, has produced at least one new book —Randolph S. Bourne's The Gary Schools. Of special interest is Hall-Quest's Supervised Study." Any of these books may be borrowed from the state library.

* * *

The new edition of the list of books for high school libraries has been distributed by the state library. It should be used in making the choice of books for school libraries for 1917. Copies may be had upon application to the county school superintendents or to the state library.

Supplement to the list of books for elementary schools has also been issued containing notes of titles of all the attractive new books. The corrected price list for this year's orders about seven hundred changes necessitated by the increased prices of books which, the publishers say, is due to the additional cost of materials and manufacture.

* * *

Junior high school students and others more mature may well have some suggestions for summer reading. The following American biographies are suggested, as interesting, attractive, and well worth while: Adams, Familiar Letters; Alcott, Louise May Alcott, Her Life, Letters and Journals; Antin, The Promised Land; Boone, Gulliver, Lucile, Daniel Boone; Clemens, Boy's Life of Mark Twain; Moores, Life of Christopher Columbus for Boys and Girls; Sprague, Davy Crockett; Eastman, From the Deep Woods to Civilization; Meadowcroft, Boy's Life of Edison; Franklin, Autobiography; Nicolay, The Boy's Life of Ulysses S. Grant; Goodwin, Dolly Madison; Keller, Story of My Life; Crow, Lafayette; Larcom, A New England Girlhood Outlined From Memory; Hasbrouck, LaSalle; Gillman, Robert E. Lee; Schurz, Abraham Lincoln; Nicolay, The Boy's Life of Abraham Lincoln; Goodwin, Dolly Madison; Muir, Story of My Boyhood and Youth; Holland, William Pen; Riis, Making of An American; Roosevelt, Autobiography; Crowe, Harriet Beecher Stowe; Wade, Pilgrims of Today; Washington, Up From Slavery; Scudder, George Washington.

* * *

Teachers who are planning for summer reading should write to the library for suggestive list. One of the most attractive groups of books which might be suggested would be Fabre's works with the wonderful [ ] of the author by Legros. This is [ ] of the most inspiring books ever [wr]itten. "One need not be familiar [wit]h his writing to find in the pages [t]his biography a wonderful inspir[ati]on for greater achievement in any [kin]d of endeavor. Those who already [sit] at the feet of the aged naturalist [wil]l hail this volume with delight, [whi]le those who have yet in store the [plea]sure of meeting the man through [his] own pen can have no happier in[troduc]tion than this."

The state library has a list of commencement parts and will send package libraries for any of the parts in this list or for any good subject chosen by school and teachers. It is hardly worth while to get together a collection of literature on such a subject as "If" or "Ambition" or "Woman's Part in the Present Crisis." Teachers may well suggest to students that if they wish to write upon abstract subjects it would be well for them to outline their work before they rush to the library for literature.

* * *

Some school may wish an old edition of the International Encyclopedia; it is quite old but good for the standad articles on history and literature; it will be sent free, except for transportation, to anyone who wishes it. The state library also has more primers and readers to give away; they are not complete, but may serve for schools which would put them in order and which has no other books.

* * *

The following books by Fabre may be borrowed from the Oregon state library: The Hunting Wasps, The Life of the Fly, The Life of the Spider, The Mason-Bees, Social Life in the Insect World.

* * *

Members of President's Cabinet.— Robert Lansing, secretary of state; Williams Gibbs McAdoo, secretary of the treasury; Newton Diehl Baker, secretary of war; Thomas Watt Gregory, attorney general; Albert Sidney Burleson, postmaster general; Josephus Daniels, secretary of the navy; Franklin Knight Lane, secretary of the interior; David Franklin Houston, secretary of agriculture; William Cox Redfield, secretary of commerce; William Bauchop Wilson, secretary of labor.

Bureau of Education.—Commissioner, Philander P. Claxton; chief clerk, Lewis A. Kalbach.

Supreme Court of the United States.—Edward Douglas White, chief justice, Joseph McKenna, Oliver Wendall Holmes, William R. Day, Willis Van Devanter, Mahlon Pitney, James Clark McReynolds, Louis Dembitz Brandeis, John Hessin Clarke.

State Elective Officials.— Governor, James Withycombe; secretary of state, Ben W. Olcott; state treasurer,

Thos. B. Kay; supreme justices, Frank A. Moore, Thomas A. McBride, Henry J. Bean, Geo. H. Burnett, Wallace McCamant, Henry L. Benson, Lawrence T. Harris; attorney general, Geo. M. Brown; superintendent of public instruction, J. A. Churchill; dairy and food commissioner, John D. Mickle; state engineer, John H. Lewis; labor commissioner, O. P. Hoff; public service commission, Fred Buchtel, H. H. Corey, Frank J. Miller.

Oregon Senators.—Geo. E. Chamberlain, Harry Lane.

House of Representatives.—Willis C. Hawley, Nicholas J. Sinnott, C. N. McArthur.

Oregon Tree Studies

By WM. B. LAWRENCE, Department of Botany, O. A. C.

XIII—Red Alder.

The red alder is familiar to all who have an acquaintance with the lower mountain streams, and will be pleasantly recalled by others upon mention of the conspicuous white bark and delicate branching of the tree as seen in winter or by the short, hard, ever present cone-like fruits. The red alder, known also as Oregon alder, was first discovered by a Russian botanist in 1827 and a few years later by Thomas Nuttall at the mouth of the Willamette river. It fringes the streams from Sitka, Alaska, through the many islands and coast ranges of British Columbia, western Washington and Oregon to the Santa Inez Mountains of California near Santa Barbara. It may also be found on the western slopes of the Cascades of Washington and Oregon to the Siskiyou mountains. This readily shows that the red alder is a tree of the moist regions and situations. It is found chiefly along streams, near springs ,in river bottoms and on the well-watered slopes. The rainfall of this distribution varies between 40 and 100 inches. It will not endure severe cold for it is found mostly below 2000 and 3000 feet in elevation, generally much lower.

The roots of some species of alder produce small nodules in which numerous nitrogen-fixing bacteria grow. These bacteria bear the same relation to the alder that is found in clover, alfalfa, etc.

The red alder reaches its maximum size in the humid regions of Puget Sound. It is a rapid grower when young (between 20 to 30 years), but short lived and may be soon overtopped by certain of its associates. It is mature in about 50 years and has attained an old age at 75 years. Trees between 10 and 18 inches in diameter are from 28 to 55 years old. The red alder is the larger of the two largest alders on the Pacific Slope and the six tree alders of the United States. It is usually between 35 and 40 feet high, and 10 to 15 inches in diameter but may become 60 to 90 feet high and 18 to 30 inches through. In pure stand the trunk may be free of branches for 25 to 30 feet, while those occurring in the open are apt to fork early, producing a short trunk. The straight trunk gives off numerous somewhat slender branches which droop into a rather narrow, long, dome-like crown.

The bark is thin and smoothish. The younger bark is smooth and has a decided greenish cast. The bark of alder trees is white because it is covered by confluent patches of several different kinds of lichens, so that the true color of the bark is seldom seen. The bark of old trees becomes broken into shallow grooves and narrow flat ridges. The young twigs are a clear, shiny, mahogany-red with many light-colored dots, or lenticels. The twigs are sometimes hairy near the ends. The deep red buds are long and covered with a light-colored scale-like down.

The mature leaves are 3 to 5½ inches long, smooth and deep yellow-green above. They are paler beneath and covered with very short rust-colored hairs. The margins are toothed.

The flowers of alder are borne in two catkins. The staminate catkins may be 5 or 6 inches long and ¼ inch thick. Pollen is produced abundance and blown by the wind to the very much smaller pistillate catkins which soon mature into a thick short cone-like fruit. The seeds are produced in moderate abundance and ripen and fall in autumn. When shed they are contained within the dry papery ovule-cases, which are the only fruits of most plants. These miniature fruits have winged margins that greatly assist in seed dispersal. The conditions of germination are imperfectly known, but the seedlings are abundant in rather dense and partial shade and in the litter of exposed soils.

The alder sprouts freely, but this method of reproduction is more common in Oregon and Washington than in California. Along with the alder may be found the willows, black cottonwood, grand fir, broadleaf and vine maples, western dogwood, chittim, and Oregon ash. The red alder sometimes occurs in pure stands over large areas in the coast mountains of Oregon and Washington. Pure stands are usually on burned-over areas which have been slow to reforest, but ultimately the alder will give way to conifers according to the region.

The wood is pale reddish brown, brittle, and light when dry. Fresh cut surfaces of the whitish sapwood soon become stained a red brown. The wood is fine grained, cherry-like and suitable for cabinet work. The wood is of minor importance because it furnishes only a little more than one-tenth of 1 per cent of the wood used in Oregon, yet nevertheless it is an important factor when the deficiency of hardwoods in the Northwest is considered.

More than nine-tenths of the alder wood is used for furniture, and the remainder for saddles, handles, pulleys, interior work, and piling. The ability of the wood to resist marine bores makes it very suitable for piling although the available amount is limited. It is also valuable for fuel and for smoking salmon. The Alaska Indians use the alder for making canoes.

Some Oregon Weeds and Seeds

By A. R. SWEETSER, University of Oregon

Filaree or Alfilaria.

This immigrant plant has made itself thoroughly at home and quietly taken possession of the soil wherever it could find a piece of unused ground. Many look upon it as a troublesome interloper and class it without hesitation as a weed. But observant ones have noticed that in many places it is eaten with avidity, and even sought by the stock. Its scientific name is Erodium cicutarium, erodium being the Greek for Heron, hence this may be called Heron's Bill. It belongs to the geranium family and geranium is from the Greek meaning Crane, so the whole family is commonly called the Crane's Bill family. The cultivated, so called, geraniums belong also to this group but should be named Pelargoniums, which, being interpreted, Stork's Bill.

The drawing shows flower and and leaves. The plant has a spreading habit and the stem is often more or less purple. The blossoms are pink or light purple, have five sepals, five petals, five stamens with anthers, alternating with five without anthers. The pistil consists in reality of five parts but so closely united that they may be regarded as forming one. The ovary may be regarded compound, of five cells the styles united together around a central axis. As the fruit develops this axis and the styles elongate forming the crane's bill stage; as it ripens and dries the styles twist into spirals separating the parts of the ovary with a jerk, and if the seeds are ripe, throws them as from a sling. Or the force may be so great as to separate the whole seed case with its spiral tip from the axis allowing it to fall to the ground or become attached to some grazing animal. Upon the ground the tips uncoil when moist and coil again upon drying, imparting a twisting motion to the seed case, thus boring it into the ground and planting it.

It will be an interesting study for

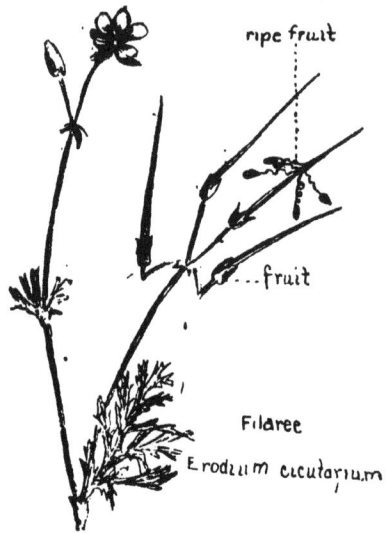

ripe fruit

fruit

Filaree
Erodium cicutarium

the children to make out for themselves the elongation of the parts in the ripening fruit and the method of seed dissemination rather than explaining it in advance. This may

also be used as a theme for their language work.

Since it is an annual or biennial and disseminated by seed, it may be exterminated by cultivation if so desired but it may be that it could even be cultivated as a stock food with advantage.

To Be an Instructor at Syracuse.

C. W. Tenney, a graduate of the law department of the University of Oregon, who has been state inspector of rural schools in Montana, has been selected as one of the instructors during the summer school to be held at Syracuse University, Syracuse, New York, June 25 to August 17. Mr. Tenney will have charge of the classes in rural school administration, rural school inspection, and rural leadership. On his way to Syracuse, Mr. Tenney will deliver a series of lectures on history and rural problems at the summer school of the Dakota Wesleyan University at Belle Foursche, South Dakota.

Teachers' Training School.

A teachers' training school will be held at Vale beginning June 4 and ending June 26. The instructors are G. A. Ruring and R. J. Davis.

Studies of Famous Pictures

These studies are used by permission of the O. M. Parker Estate, Taylorville, Illinois, who will furnish a complete list of other famous pictures free on application.

Distinguished Member of the Humane Society.

By L. Eveline Merritt.

"The Distinguished Member of the Humane Society" is a portrait of a great big noble Newfoundland dog. Look at it. The dog is lying there— not asleep—no, rather alert in mind although the body is relaxed. It is resting with its magnificent head erect, mouth open with tongue out in the usual way. Look closely. See the great knowing eyes uplifted. Ah, there is the secret. Here is a dog which will romp and play with the children and will be their faithful

friend to the very end. There is almost human intelligence in that face.

Look at Landseer's other pictures of dogs. See the agony in the attitude and expression of the dog in "Suspense," join in the sorrow of the "Chief Mourner," smile at the sa mischievous expression on the fa of the "King Charles Spaniel," c sider the delightful playfulness comradeship between the "T Dogs," the aristocratic gentlema ness in "High Life," the vulgar loc ness in "Low Life" and we have secret. Here are dogs, every on them common ordinary dogs dogs that are kin to human bei

But why is this de—

studying named as it is? Where is the dog lying? It is very evidently out of doors and in the full sunlight. There is a great expanse of sky which is somewhat threatening in appearance toward the horizon. What are the birds which are flying about so gracefully on either side? They are the birds of the sea, the gulls, that sail through the air as calmly and peacefully as doves and add to the feeling of assurance that all is well. The dog is plainly lying on the last stone of a quay, the front face of the water is gently lapping. A mooring ring is visible. There the dog lies looking out over the water. The ears are lifted almost imperceptibly to catch the slightest sound. It is a

all—the Scotch collie, the terrier, the hound, the little spaniels and all the others. Any lover of dogs must find enjoyment in his pictures.

Although Landseer was perhaps happiest in his portrayal of dogs, he did not limit his work to those. His deer pictures are almost as familiar as those of dogs, while every child knows his squirrels in the "Piper and the Nutcracker," and the monkeys in his "Sick Monkey," and almost his last work was the modeling of the lions placed at the base of the Nelson monument in Trafalgar Square in London. He was a painter of animals in the broadest sense. He knew all animals intimately and had the power to so picture them that

wonderful dog portrait. Notice the fore-shortening of the paws, the representation of the hair in various parts of the body, the knowing look of the face, the semi-human pathos of the eyes. Landseer certainly understood and loved this friend of man, and knew how to paint it.

No one can see that handsome Newfoundland dog lying on the quay without a sense of safety for all concerned in that harbor. This friend , humanity will guard the waters 'ell. The picture is well named. his fine specimen of the dog world indeed a distinguished member of ie humane society.

This dog that Landseer knew so 1ll and painted so well was a Newndland as were also "Saved,' y Dog," and some others. Howr, Landseer was not limited in his ʳˡᵃdge of dogs; he knew them

others less fortunate could also enjoy that intimacy.

Who was Edwin Landseer and what was his training? The story of Edwin's childhood is a most interesting one. There are few families in which the father personally guides his son in his work and his play. The Landseer family was such an one. The father was an engraver and lecturer upon art. We are told that he often took his three sons, Thomas, Charles, and Edwin to the open country, where they spent the day in sketching the animals as they grazed in the fields—this, too, when the youngest, Edwin, was hardly old enough to hold a pencil in his little fingers. Often it would be Edwin alone who would be lifted over the stile and stationed in some shady spot. There the father would leave him, returning later in the day to sit beside the lad, draw with him, correct the work done, and talk with him. Do you get the picture?

The father was not only the first teacher but the first to inspire the love for animal life and the desire to picture that life. This is the simple story of a beautiful relationship that lasted as long as there was life. His father fondly kept the sketches that Edwin made at this early time. Some of these can be seen now in the collection in the South Kensington Museum in London. From notes upon them made by the father at the time it is learned that some were sketched when Edwin was only 5 years of age. Think of it! He was sketching at 7 years of age and painting in oils at 12! He won a prize form the Society of Arts for his animal drawings when he was 11 and medals during each of the succeeding years!

Whenever and wherever animals were to be seen, Edwin was sure to be there with his sketch book. His father had early led him to nature, his great teacher throughout his life. Edwin knew that there was nothing that could teach a person how to draw better than to be continually drawing. Thus the young Landseer

sketched and sketched again until he knew the animals in their every phase.

One other influence was felt in his early tutors. This was the painter, Benjamin R. Haydon, who became his teacher for a time. Mr. Haydon urged him to dissect animals. By this he became familiar with their anatomical structures, this made his drawing more sure. Mr. Haydon also urged a study of the Greek marbles from the Parthenon and the cartoons made by Raphael for tapestry designs. This study produced a' certain breadth of feeling and spirit of repose, balance, and freedom that he might not otherwise have attained.

From Landseer's eleventh year, when he became an exhibitor at the Royal Academy, London, under the name of "Master E. Landseer, H." (the "H" meaning that he was an honorary exhibitor since he was too young to be accepted as a full artist) his story reads as a triumphal march. At 14 he entered the schools of the Royal Academy where the head master used to call him "his little dog boy." From that time on he painted much, he exhibited year after year, his pictures were popular and found a ready sale.

Oregon Congress of Mothers

By MRS. ELIZABETH HAYHURST, 1070 E. Burnside, Portland

Preparations for the National Education Association are well under way. Just what part the Parent-Teacher Associations will be given to do is not definitely settled yet, but one way in which we at one time can both be helpful and be helped is suggested in the following excerpt from a letter sent by our president, Mrs. Geo. McMath to all local and state presidents in United States—two thousand in all: "Have you considered the matter of the new provision for institutional memberships in the National Education Association? This provides that the school districts, or any other organizations interested in education, may become associate members upon payment of the regular associate membership fee of $2.00. This institutional member-

ship is taken out in the name of the organization, and entitles the organization taking such a membership to the volume of printed proceedings. Every school house should have a copy of the proceedings of the National Education Association. These reports will be of great value to the parent-teacher association and to the teacher. The lectures of the t educators in the country are prin therein in full, and I know of better way to spend an afterno than by taking up for discuss some of these lectures. The t dollar membership fee may be s directly to the chairman of the vance Membership Committee Oregon, 405 Court House, Portla Or. Will you not take up the ter with your district, and,

through your own association or
through your school board, secure
the privileges of membership for
your district?"

* * *

Among the Oregon people who
took part in the program of the Inland Empire Educational Association
at Spokane, April 4, 5, and 6. was
our state president, Mrs. Geo.
McMath.

* * *

One of the easiest and most delightful methods, of raising funds
ever experienced by the writer was
"The Mock Trial" recently given at
the Kerns School of Portland, under
the capable management of Mrs.
William Davis. One hundred twenty
dollars was netted, which was expended for a victrola and standard
records for the school. Whenever a
definite appeal is made for funds it
will be found always to bring forth
a more generous response from the
public, and in this instance the committee showed excellent judgment in
making the definite appeal for the
victrola. Incidentally, this would be
a splendid work for the larger parent-teacher associations in general,
as a victrola not only aids the pupils
in appreciation of good music, but
becomes a source of pleasure at all
the parent-teacher association meetings.

* * *

The Molalla Parent-Teacher Association recently netted $60 at a
bazaar and .cafeteria supper, with
which it is proposed to aid in establishing a course in domestic science
in the high school. The Clackamas
County Council Parent-Teacher Associations will be entertained at Mol-
lala in May.

* * *

The following message has been
sent by the president, Mrs. George
McMath, to all the parent-teacher
associations: "Our year's work is
rapidly drawing to a close and I be-
ve we may say that in most in-
ances it has been a very success-
year. There are a few matters
would like to call your attention
before you disband for the sum-
r. (1) Our next convention will
et in Eugene October of this year.
 are entitled to one delegate for
ry ten members besides your pres-
nt. Won't you make an effort to
e money during the summer to
+h- --'lroad fare of your presi-

dent to this convention? She will
bring back to your circle such an inspiration and so many new ideas that
you will feel it was money well spent.
The Eugene people will provide the
rooms. (2) Have you sent in the
name, initial and addresses of your
president and secretary just as you
want it printed in the new year book
we will get out in August? (3) If
your school is not standardized will
you not make an effort to have it so
by next year? (4) If you have any
suggestions you would like to have
taken up at the convention will you
not make an effort to inform us by
July 1 as we ·are already preparing
the program? (5) Would it not be a
very wise act to appoint a committee
to assist the teachers who return to
you next fall,· some perhaps strangers
in your country, in securing boarding
places and to greet them on their
arrival in your district? (6) Are the
children of your district all properly
fed and clothed? It is a terrible
thing to let little children go to
school cold or hungry and every
parent-teacher association should
know that there are none in their
school. When the delegates meet
next October in Eugene it will be
their duty to elect a new group of
officers to carry on the work of the
state association and you should give
this matter some consideration as we
are now one of the largest and most
powerful agencies in the state and
the questions that come before the
state board are often quite wide in
their effect and need serious consideration before action is recommended
to you. We must try to confine ourselves as nearly as ·possible to the
uplift of the school and the home."

* * *

The legislative committee has sent
a condensed report of the legislation
passed at the last session, which is
of interest to all our members, to
every circle, and the committee will
ask Superintendent Churchill to send
each circle a copy of the small
pamphlet issued by his office which
contains a digest of all the new
school legislation.

* * *

Molalla entertained the Clackamas
county parent-teacher council May 5
in a splendid manner. An interesting program was given under direction of Supt. Calavan and Pres. Mrs

J. L. Waldson. A delicious chicken dinner was served to teachers and parents by the Molalla parent-teacher association.

* * *

On May 5 the Marion county parent-teacher council met at Salem. Forty-one associations were represented and much enthusiasm shown. Mrs. Geo. McMath addressed the gathering. The Marion county parent-teacher council has lately affiliated with the state organization. Yamhill county parent-teacher council will meet next at McMinnville, and Multnomah county parent-teacher council at Troutdale. Multnomah county parent-teacher association has set out to standardize every school in Multnomah county within a year.

* * *

At the annual election of the Portland parent-teacher association held May 4 Mrs. W. I. Swank was unanimously elected president. Mrs. Swank is especially fitted for the important position as she has served most successfully as president of the Holliday parent-teacher association and as chairman of the social service and program committees, as well as a vice president of the Portland parent-teacher council and is the possessor of a most pleasing personality. Other officers elected are: First vice president, Mrs. Archibald McIntyre; second vice president, Mrs. J. D. Zurcher; third vice president, Miss Alice Joyce; recording secretary, Mrs. Percy Stowell; corresponding secretary, Mrs. E. W. Finzer; treasurer, Mrs. W. L. Bloch; auditor, Robt. R. Steele.

Nature Study Instruction.

Miss Alice Joyce will assist Mrs. Brennan in her Primary Methods School, beginning June 25. She will have charge of the nature study work. Miss Joyce has recently been appointed garden supervisor of all the West Side in Portland.

High School Teachers' Department

Edited by HOPKIN JENKINS, Portland, Oregon

High School Composition.

Last year one of the largest of the American universities sent out a questionaire on high school English asking, among other things, this: Which is a more important aim of high school English, arousing appreciation of good literature or developing facility in expression in the mother tongue?

When the query came to me I unhesitatingly decided for the second. But my colleague in the small high school where I was teaching was as certain that the first aim should be considered more important. Her belief is shared by many English teachers. In my opinion this accounts for the poorly balanced English courses in some high schools. The classes are over-crowded with book material and the written work is almost exclusively second-hand reproduction of literary criticism based on aesthetic canons too mature for the high school age. However, our quarrel is not with the champions of literature. We are inquiring, "How may be vitalize the English composition?"

The teacher who has learned that the only composition that really makes the student grow—in both enthusiasm and power of expression —is based upon the student's own experience and observation, has gone far towards a solution of the question.

The scope of this paper will not admit of the laying out of a detailed plan for a course of composition founded on experience and observation. It is meant to be suggestive only. As a matter of fact, such detailed planning is not necessary desirable. Once the redeeming po er of this idea of constructive rath than reproductive composition is f the minutiae will take care of the selves. The stereotyped plan is (pressing. Each new group of si dents should help the teacher pl for the individual needs of their p ticular class. Community inter helps.

Don't try to do too much. 1

yourself to a few big objectives. Following are five guiding principles, which, insisted on, will get results: (1) Using realistic details.—This idea originated with Daniel Defoe and is the secret of his popularity. It can easily be taught to high school students. (2) Employing the specific in place of the general.—Most books of rhetoric treat of this but many teachers neglect to emphasize it. (3) Training the five senses.—Martha Hale Shackford and Margaret Judson of Wellesley and Vassar have show the possibility of this. It has a natural appeal for the adolescent age. (4) Composing with the audience in mind.—When students once grasp the necessity of this, most of the troubles of exposition and argument are smoothed over. (5) Being intellectually honest. There is too much attitudinizing and affectation in high school English. Once the student begins to compose he ceases to be natural. Destroy this insidious feeling.

Let us be specific. You make a general assignment: "I want you for your first theme to write about something from your own experience or observation. What was the most exciting thing that ever happened to you? Tell us about it. Have you seen anything lately that is still vivid like a picture in your mind? Describe it for us." Some days later the papers come in. Some are fair, some are indifferent, but there is a discouraging number of colorless "Best-Day-in-Vacations." From the lot you winnow out one splendid idea. A member of the class has written an account of an afternoon canoe ride in which two girls, absorbed in reading, drift with the current, oblivious, until they are caught in the rapids. But there is no artistry to the composition. It has no beginning. The sentence structure toward the end, as the rapids are approached, is the me as at the beginning, where the irrent is lazy. The rescue is commonplace. There is no suspense. Here is your chance for commun- effort. Let the whole class take a germ idea and try to improve the pression of it. Show the students at you mean by realistic details. hat was the name of the stream? at kind of trees grew along it? m what kind of landing place did mbark? What was the name

of the fascinating book that beguiled you from the realization of your peril? How many sofa pillows did you carry along? The student probably said the stream flowed. Make him see the difference between this general term and the specific glided, swirled, eddied, churned, plunged, raced.

The hypothetical theme discussed above was primarily narration, with incidental description. Suppose you wish to reverse the emphasis and have the class write primarily description, with incidental narration. Try this laboratory plan: "For our next theme we will take a walk through the woods. Remember that you have five senses. You will not only see the trees and the ferns, but you will hear the birds and insects and smell the leaf mold and flowers. The fir needles will feel smooth beneath your feet and if you walk on moss it will be soft like a plush carpet. Perhaps you will sample the taste of some wild berries or break a twig and chew it. Try to get sense appeals." Simple and obvious as this sounds it will often produce astonishing results. It is even conceivable that after a little preparatory work along these lines students may be able to comprehend the sensuousness of Keats.

Obviously such a course will consist largely of narration and description at first. But it leads naturally into exposition and will surely ultimately provoke argument. Every boy is a specialist. One collects stamps. Another is an amateur zoologist. Still another is skilled in the use of tools. Girls, too, have their hobbies which you can utilize. Let them write of the things they really know at first hand. Insist that they make things clear enough for anybody to understand. In the arguments—which are always evoked when people become interested and aroused—let the students talk in favor of the side they really believe in. This is intellectual honesty.—Thomas M. Henley, Jefferson High School, Portland.

Are School Athletics Safe and Sane?

By athletics we mean strenuous competitive physical exercise, such as ball games, field and track work, not the training offered by Turn Hall gymnastics. Regarding the mild benefits of the latter there is little difference of opinion, but there is considerable discussion waging around these highly competitive games.

If we go back far enough we shall find the American love of competitive sport deeply rooted in those anti-Colonial British customs, which have yielded us equal rights, true democracy, and bulldog courage. The Asquiths and Kitcheners were trained upon the cricket fields of Eton and Rugby. In our new world eagerness to absorb without full time to assimilate we magnify the competitive side of British sport, and in our enthusiasm we often overlook their fair play traditions.

Competitive sport—play, is a natural manifestation common among healthy lambs, kittens, boys and girls. Muscular exercise falls short of its complete benefit unless performed in a spirit of play. Not only are ward children fond of play, but high school and college students give it considerable attention, as we well know.

Our newspaper sporting columns daily display generous paragraphs in praise of this or that college or high school team of victorious athletes, embellished with pictures of the star performers, while the brilliant academic student receives little notice and less praise. It has come to pass that a winning team advertises an institution favorably, and coaches search the accredited schools and the woods for strong muscles—mentality to be developed later. Some time ago I noticed in the "Harvard Crimson" that the lecture by Prof. Peabody on "The Political and Social Significance of the Life of Jesus Christ" was postponed because of the football mass meeting on that date. At one time in Kansas City we offered the high school boys a chance to compete in a "cross country run" and the reporters gave the event several columns on the first page where we expect to find news of grave international importance involving the fate of nations.

Are we giving too much attention to competitive sports in our schools? The old Greeks believed in a sound mind in a sound body; so do we. All contests of physical prowess interest us. Our school games attract crowds of all classes, mostly cultured. Since we fully believe in a sound mind in a sound body, so strong has the rivalry become in this muscle-tearing, bone-breaking business of preparing a home for a sound mind, that the enthusiasm breaks its banks and much physical disability results.

The British school boy, through centuries of adaptation, enjoys his cricket, tennis or football, with a more amateurish relish than ours do. He plays for the pure joy of motion. It is a common spectacle on English and Canadian school grounds to see a couple of fellows batting and bowling for hours. Just for the fun of it, "don't you know," but we time and tone our practice so as to get into the best possible condition to beat the others.

As it now stands we put up the very best trained athletes to represent the school. The rank and file of the student body seems content to root—one form of lung development. Those individuals who need physical training the least get all of it. If the body must be trained as well as the mind, what would we think of a system of class instruction for the few best scholars and absolutely nothing for others. This is precisely our procedure in athletics. Through centuries of monastic training we have developed a science of education, education of the mental faculties, but our science of play is in its infancy. In congested centers of population we are laying out play grounds, recognizing at last that a child has as much right to play as to breathe. Wisely directed play has as much educational value as manual training or physical science. Give it a place in all curricula, but soften down the fierceness of competition.—Daniel Hull, Superintendent of Schools, Grants Pass, Or.

Course in Nature Study.

Miss Alice Joyce will give a practical course in nature study and g dening at the Primary Meth School conducted by Mrs. R Shearer Brennan. The fundamer principles of agriculture and the p sibility of its co-ordination with r ular school studies will be prepa in outline forms to assist the prim teacher. Please write to Mrs. Br nan at 460 E. Burnside street, P land, and tell her if you plan tend this school.

Vocational Education Department

Edited by R. B. CHLOUPEK, Pendleton, Oregon

The manufacturer, the wage-earner, the artist, the psychologist, the practical man of affairs, and the educator, all have different reasons for advocating industrial arts in our public and high schools. The manufacturer hopes for mechanical skill, skilled workmen for his manufacturing plant; the wage-earner sees in it free training for better wages; the artist hopes for the development of the esthetic and artistic nature and hopes for the awekening of, and development of appreciation of proper proportion, good construction and good finish in architecture and cabinet work, and in all things mechanical. From his standpoint, "a thing of beauty," in things mechanical, "is a joy forever," and the awakening of the artist in the mechanic is an important and legitimate function of the school.

The psychologist sees in industrial training the development of an entirely different mental fibre. He looks upon a saw, a square, a marking gauge, a plane, as new intellectual dumb-bells. He sees in industrial training approach to undiscovered and unexplored intellectual possibilities. The practical man of affairs sees in an industrial arts course the acquisition of useful information and the development of skill that will just fit the need of the rancher, the agriculturist, or the machinist.. And doubtless any one of these men see enough in an industrial arts course to justify its place in our educational system; but the educator's viewpoint must be more comprehensive than any one of these. He must see more than mechanical skill; more than advanced wages; more than artistic reciation in things mechanical; re than psychological opportunity; re than mere utility.

he industrial arts course is pri-.ily a means of salvation for our and girl. It offers a new means developing our boy into a man; girl into a woman. The concern educators is not the problem of .king a living," but the problem "making a life worth living." -- -- a possibility in this extreme-ly progressive and practical age to overwork the work utility. Grant there is satisfaction in the consciousness that what you teach is practical; that your pupils can go out and build a shed ,or run an engine or build a brick chimney, yet if such skill is obtained at the sacrifice of a taste for the political, the sociological, moral and religious, then that satisfaction is tempered with failure so far as the real education of these pupils is concerned. If the state educates the young people, the state has a right to demand a culture that will make them public servants. The business of the educator is to stimulate and unfold all of the dormant powers of the pupil and educate him until he becomes an all-round man; a man with memory, imagination, judgment, reasoning power; a man with social instincts, with political interests, with esthetic and artistic tastes, with moral and religious convictions and interests. A trained mechanic who has no use for newspapers, magazines, libraries, lectures, fireside association with wife and children, and neighborhood life in general is not an educated man.

Industrial arts in our public schools must never be made an end in themselves. The object and aim in the shop must remain the same as in history or literature, or Latin or science—broad-minded, scholarly, altruistic, ambitious lives worth living. There is real culture of this type in the carpenter shop and in the forge room, but any course that makes these a substitute for poetry, music, language, history and public speaking misses the mark. Let every school have a modern, well-equipped shop, with the best of tools and machines; but never at the expense of a well-equipped historical reference library; or a library of the world's best literature. Put the best trained man in the state at the head of the industrial arts department, but at the same time put a Van Dyke at the head of the department of literature.

Our public schools and high schools can not be held responsible for the technical training of our youth in the arts and industries only so far as the teaching of these subjects may serve the educator in gaining and maintaining the boys's or girl's interest in his own development and education. The time allotted to industrial work in our high schools is too limited to make good mechanics. The average high school graduate can not possibly be prepared to compete with skilled carpenters and mechanics. Such training is rather the province of trades schools.

So far as the old fashion trades are concerned, the machine has quite eliminated the skilled workman anyway. In the Pullman shops there are single machines, run by one man, that do the work formerly done by hundreds of men. The simple care and operation of these machines can be learned by a green hand in three or four days. One single riveting machine fed by a boy or girl does the work formerly done by one hundred men. One-tenth of the world's working men equipped with modern machinery, could do all the work of the world. It goes without saying that mechanical efficiency of the type that does the world's work, is quite outside the province of the public or high school.

The future of the industrial movement in our public and high schools depends upon its effectualness, directly or indirectly, as a cultural salvation; as a means of intellectual interests and enthusiasms, rather than upon any assurance of turning out trained, efficient workmen. It serves a good purpose in satisfying the natural longing of the boy for hand activity. It gives opportunity for the "hand-minded" boy to discover himself. It keeps many a boy from dropping out of our school system and allowing his intellectual, his esthetic, his artistic, his moral faculties to hibernate.—I. B. Sevy, Stanfield, Ore.

Industrial Educational Meeting.

The convention for the promotion of industrial education was held at Indianapolis, February 21 to 24, and was attended by D. A. Grout, assistant superintendent of the Portland schools, as a delegate from Portland. Mr. Grout makes the following brief report of the convention:

Keynote of Meeting—The keynote of the convention was to emphasize to states and communities the fact and warning that the reconstruction of the old educational plant should not be undertaken until there has been a careful and penetrative investigation of the needs of the boys and girls, and of the community and the state, along vocational lines. A careful and complete study of present day industries should be made to determine just what sort of training is required. The recently completed survey for vocational education in Indiana was the text of a majority of the speakers, although many held lightly to the text. Prominent representatives of labor, capital, and education were on the program.

The Triangle—It early developed that each of these forces held tenaciously to its own angle and that the harmonizing of these is a necessary preliminary to any successful scheme of industrial education. Even should a plan meet their approval, popular endorsement is still to be won, a fact which no speaker seemed to take into account.

Labor—Representatives of labor insisted that the present cultural studies be not reduced and that, what they termed a "reconstructed apprenticeship" system be established. In this reconstructed apprenticeship they ask that the whole of a trade be taught and not just a specialized part of it. They object to intellects being made stolid in the monotonous piece-work of large scale industry.

Capital—The representatives of capital who addressed the convention were some of those who recently made, with the approval of local labor unions, trade and industrial agreements with the schools of Indianapolis. They approved and commended these agreements. By these agreements pupils spend two days per week in trade or industry, working under actual business conditions. They do not play at the occupation but actually work at it and they must accomplish satisfactory results, o- be discontinued. Upon their retur. to school, studies related to these c a-pations are taken up.

Education—The educators a-tended that there was a much hi er goal than just industrial efficie y, however desirable that may be. 1 ey held that boys and girls are ill American citizens, human units, nd not primarily industrial or milit r units. They said that neith nor labor was inclined to be ideal-istic or self-sacrificing. For these reasons, they urged that the state must always be the supreme party to these agreements and must have par-amount in mind the economic and in-dustrial welfare of the people of a whole, and the welfare of the child and then the welfare of the man or woman that it has directed toward industry. While not entirely satis-fied with the Indianapolis agree-ments, they were accepted as a for-ward step in industrial education.

The Smith-Hughes Law—For the ten years of its existence the Society for the Promotion of Industrial Edu-cation, worked for the passage of a law of this kind. Some members thought there was no further need of the society. It was decided, how-ever, to continue it, that it might be a directive force and an open forum for the benefit of industrial educa-tion. The Smith-Hughes law makes continuing appropriations for voca-tional education, the first year $1,-700,000, and increasing each year until 1924 when $7,200,000 will be available. These amounts will be distributed to state boards by a fed-eral board. The Portland schools are, no doubt, entitled to and will receive fair consideration in the distribution of the funds in this state.

High School Agriculture.

A brief survey of the high schools of Oregon will reveal the fact that a full four year course in agriculture is offered by only a very few and that in most schools that make any at-tempt to teach agriculture, the sub-ject is merely skimmed over. When we stop to consider that Oregon is pre-eminently an agricultural state, and no doubt always will be, this con-dition of affairs seems to be inexcus-able.

There appears to be some good rea-sons why agricultural instruction in a high schools of this state has not en successful. The first of these, the lack of a standard prescribed urse that is in any sense adequate the needs of farming communities. neral agriculture should not be erated in any high school curricu-n. What we need is an agricul-al course that deals separately l thoroughly with each of the im-tant branches of agriculture, giv-nrominence to the branches that

are practical in the section where the high school is located.

In high schools where agriculture is now taught in this state, it is us-ually left to the instructor to formu-late his own course. As a result, with every change of instructors there is usually a change in the course. Is it any wonder that no two courses in the state are alike. There can be no progress as long as this condition exists.

Someone will say that because ag-ricultural practice differs so widely in different sections of Oregon, it would be impossible to prescribe a standard course in agriculture for high schools throughout the state. It is true that a single prescribed course for the whole state could not me made to fit in with the agricul-ture in all the different sections. But the sections of the state in which different systems of agriculture pre-vail are more or less clearly defined. It would be difficult to formulate a course for each section that would meet the requirements of agricul-tural practice in that section.

Again it might be argued, this plan would create such a variety of agricultural courses in the state that we would be no nearer a standard than we are at present. But there are certain fundamental subjects in agriculture that should be included in any high school agricultural course, so the different courses would differ only in details that would adapt them to the section of the state for which they were intended. Some of these fundamental subjects are farm management, soils, crop production, animal husbandry, farm buildings and farm sanitation, vege-table gardening and poultry keeping. A knowledge of these subjects will make life on the farm more worth living.

The educational department of our state agricultural college, in co-oper-ation with the agricultural depart-ments of the college could prescribe a standard course in agriculture for the entire state. All the various kinds of agriculture practiced in the state are represented in these depart-ments. The instructors in each of these departments are thoroughly fa-miliar with the agriculture in the sections of the state where their line of agriculture predominates. Anoth-er thing that has discouraged high school agriculture in this state is the fact that when a student who has done agricultural work in high school takes an agricultural course in our state college, he is required to duplicate much of his high school work. This is true not only of agriculture but of manual training subjects as well.

Much of our high school agriculture has been of such character that college credit could not well be given for it. But standardization would improve the work to a point where it would be equal to much of the work of a similar nature that is given in college during the freshman and sophomore years. A high school semester credit in agriculture given on the basis of five periods per week often represents more and better work than a two credit college course in the same subject given on the basis of two hours work per week.

With the high school work standardized it would not be difficult for some authority from our agricultural college to inspect the schools in the various districts and determine exactly how much of the work was of such nature that it could be credited in college. And the same thing ought to be done with high school manual training.

Another handicap to high school agriculture in the past has been the lack of good text books. Teachers have been forced to depend upon lecture methods or upon text books on general agriculture that are worse than useless. We do not attempt to teach other subjects in high school without good text books. But we have no authorized test books on agriculture for high school use in this state that are worthy to be called text books.

There are many good agricultural books published today that deal thoroughly with one subject and are especially written for use for high school text books. The selection of these would not be difficult, but it is a part of the problem of standardization.—Virgil Fendall, Pendleton, Oregon.

The State Schools

Oregon Normal School.

The building committee of the board, Supt. J. A. Churchill, Miss Cornelia Marvin, Mr. H. G. Starkweather and Mr. C. L. Starr, met in Monmouth April 16 and approved the plan of Mr. Bennes for the addition to the main normal school building provided by the last legislature. This addition, to be completed during the summer, will increase the capacity of the assembly room to nearly 1000, provide two additional class rooms and more extensive locker facilities for the women students. These improvements will materially advance the efficiency of the normal school.

"Some Things Gleaned from Print" was the interesting title of a most helpful talk given by Miss Parrott in chapel April 13. Some of the finest thoughts of the world's philosophers, from Epictetus to Elbert Hubbard, were included in this splendidly worked out talk. The senior class was represented during the month by Miss Wolfer on "Success in Choosing One's Life Work"; Miss Ellsworth on "The Boy and His Gang"; Miss Esther Anderson on "We Are Only Human After All"; and Miss Anna Kleinwachter on "Supervised Play."

An enthusiastic chapter of the National Honor Guard was organized among the Normal students, with Ella Dixon as leader. The membership of nearly 200 was divided into classes studying First Aid, automobile management and agricultural pursuits.

Because of the state of war and the fact that a good many of the Normal school boys have enlisted, the student body voted not to hold the annual May Day celebration. Instead of this, special exercises were held on Patriot's Day with a patriotic program of music, readings and pantomimes. Attorney General Geo. M. Brown of Salem gave one of strongest addresses that has been heard in the chapel. Especial mention should also be given to number, "The Growth of Democracy," given by the girls' National Honor Guard, which traced interesting and instructive way the four great epochs in the development of American democracy.

Supt. Churchill spoke to the student body April 20, taking for his subject "The By-product in Education," and discussing the numerous incidental ways in which a teacher's influence may make itself felt in the education of boys and girls. He mentioned the many present-day changes in educational methods and the distribution of students in high school courses, but showed that it is not the subjects studied that are in the end most important, but rather the by-products in the form of character, patriotism, life's ideals and the ability to accomplish a useful piece of the world's werk.

The Summer School Bulletin has been published and will be sent to any one interested. The session begins June 18, and arrangements will be made by which teachers so desiring will have an opportunity to visit the N. E. A. during its session. Miss Butler, Miss Hoham, Miss Kennon and Miss Dinius of the regular faculty will spend the summer elsewhere, and among those who will take their places are Miss Nell Sullivan, director of music in the Eugene schools, Mrs. Jean McCracken of Portland, and Mr. W. H. Burton, who returns from a year at Columbia to become a member of the faculty.

Miss McIntosh represented the faculty April 27 by having her eighth grade girls present Kate Douglas Wiggin's "The Old Peabody Pew." This was extremely well done and was especially interesting after Miss McIntosh's explanation that the preparation for it had all been done as a part of the regular reading work.

The program for commencement week is as follows: Saturday, June 9, President's breakfast; Junior prom. Sunday, June 10, Baccalaureate sermon to be preached by Rev. V. Poling, of Dallas. Monday, June 11, Faculty reception; class y. Tuesday, June 12, Last chapel class day; alumni picnic; alumni quet. Wednesday, June 13, Commencement. The commencement address is to be given by Prof. Norman eman, of Reed College. It may interesting for graduates of the ool to know that special reunions he classes of '72, '77, '82, '89, '92, '07, and '12 will be held. All

graduates, however, are cordially invited to come back and help make this commencement week one of the best in the school's history.

University of Oregon.

War conditions at the University of Oregon have resulted in the postponement of the Oregon historical pageant which was to have been given on Kincaid field as a feature of commencement week. The decision to give up the pageant for this year was made by President Campbell after a thorough study and discussion of the situation caused by the participation of a great body of university men and women in various activities connected with military affairs. In place of the pageant Professor Reddie will produce " A Midsummer Night's Dream." This bright little comedy of Shakespeare's will require only a fraction of the immense cast which would be needed for the pageant and, altogether, will be a much less ambitious and taxing affair. Prof. Reddie has begun the work of preparing for this production and nothing will be left undone to make the play successful from an artistic standpoint.

For the convenience of Portland teachers who can not leave the city this summer on account of the National Education Association meeting there, courses for university credit in at least four departments will be offered by the Portland center of the extension division of the university at the Portland Central Library during the time that the regular summer school is in session at Eugene. A uniform fee of $10 paid by each person enrolled as at the regular summer school, will cover the registration cost, and this entrance fee will be payable at 451 Courthouse office of the University of Oregon on on any of the following registration days: May 19, 26, 31, and June 9, 15, 16, and 18. Arrangements for instruction will depend to a large extent on the number of registrations and those registering first will receive first consideration if it should become necessary to limit the number of students in any course. Entrance requirements are the same as for admission to the summer school at Eugene except that registration in the Portland department will be limited to Portland residents whose duties keep them in the city. Six semester hours credit may be earned in these classes. Special faculty ruling puts teachers taking this summer work on the same basis with those in resident summer school. There will be a general assembly on Friday evenings throughout the entire session, to which the general public will be invited. Probable speakers at these meetings are G. Stanley Hall, president of Clark University; Henry Churchill King, president of Oberlin College; Norman F. Coleman, professor of English in Reed College; George Rebec, resident director of the Portland summer extension classes. The following are the courses to be offered: Philosophy, Psychology, English, Education, History, Recent American History.

The University Summer School bulletin is now ready for distribution and fifty-five hundred copies are to be mailed over the state. The opening pages are devoted to general information—date of opening and closing, purpose of the session, its benefits for different classes of people, all new requirements, terms of admission, information for those wishing to communicate with the heads of the school, a list of required fees, credits given, residence and registration requirements, information as to available room and board and a general description of the advantages of Eugene and the university as places of summer residence and work. An important feature is the plan for reduced railroad rates, one and one-third fares on the certificate plan have been granted the university from June 1 to August 5. These rates are good for all campus events coming between the two dates, including commencement exercises on May 31 to June 4, summer school June 18 to August 3, and any convention which may be announced.

Have you a specimen of a flower which you want classified as to species or variety? The University of Oregon botany department will be glad to perform such service gratis. Many persons already are taking advantage of the offer of A. R. Sweetser, professor of botany, who welcomes the opportunity to receive specimens of uncommon varieties and learn their habitat. Queries come to the department continually concerning plant life. It is the work of the instructors to receive, identify, classify and make a report of the samples accompanying the letters. Many simply send a leaf of a petal and it is impossible for the department to tell the classification unless the stalk or the entire flower is included.

The following is an outline of Red Cross work to be given by Miss Lulu Geil at the summer school: (1) First Aid Materials—Bandages, compresses, splints, torniquets, heat, cold, stiumlants, emetics; demonstrations as to uses of materials. (2) Injuries in which the skin is not pierced or broken—Bruises, strains, sprains, and fractures; demonstration of first aid treatment. (3) Injuries in which the skin is pierced or broken—Varieties of wounds; first aid treatment. (4) Practical Points on Home Nursing—Demonstration in bed making. (5) General considerations of the care of the sick in their own homes. (6) General Care of Patients—Demonstration of bed baths.

Oregon Agricultural College.

When summer school opens at the O. A. C., June 11, it is expected that the enrollment will be even larger than last year. Letters are received daily in the registrar's office from all parts of the Northwest and from California, indicating that a large number are planning to attend. The faculty will include prominent educators from various parts of the United States, among them being R. J. Aley, of the University of Maine and president of the Educational Association, who will lecture July 2; Mrs. H. W. Calvin, former dean of the school of home economics at O. A. C., and now a member of the United States Bureau of Education; Mrs. Max West, of the Childrens' Bureau in the department of labor, and Miss Edith Parrott, state agent of home economics in South Carolina. Three supervisors of the Portland schools also visit the college during the session, addressing the students. They are Miss Lillian Tingle, principal the girls' polytechnic school; L. Summers, supervisor of manual training; and Miss Edna Groves, supervisor of domestic science.

At a recent convocation in of the 200 students who left to the reserve officers' training the Presidio, President Kerr delivered the farewell address with an earnestness that impressed the students as perhaps they had never been impressed before. He said: "When you arrive at your destination, study the situation, absorb the spirit of this conflict, and whatever comes, you men, do your duty, not only as officers but as men. We have no doubt as to your valor, nor do we question your integrity, but you will be confronted with temptations to which you have not been subjected; you will be placed in trying positions. And when the critical moment comes, with a silent prayer to God, be true to yourself, true to your parents, true to your college, true to your nation, and true to your God." The president concluded his address by stating that, contrary to rumor, the college would open as scheduled next September, and that instead of a decrease, in enrollment, there should be a large increase. "Right now, if ever, are trained agriculturists, engineers, and indeed, trained men of every profession in demand, and the longer this war lasts the greater will be the demand. For that reason the attendance next fall should reach three thousand."

The entire senior year class in logging engineering at O. A. C. reported at the armory en masse and offered their services to the government with in 15 minutes after the notice of the opening of the training camp at the Presidio. This class of 13 men is the only senior class in logging engineering in the world. Since the enlistment the men have specialized in military engineering, military work having been substituted for the regular classes in logging engineering. They will endeavor to get into the engineering corps. The members of the class are: C. R. Hazeltine, L. R. Woods, C. A. Fertig, E. M. Paulse i, W. J. Wakeman, W. J. O'Neil, J. A. Crawford, H. P. Thomas, C. C. J oby, H. G. Patton, T. C. Van Orsd .,Olaf Jonasen and C. J. Budelier.

f the ten members of the senior cl s in farm crops, nine have withd wn from college to enter into agri ltural work. J. D. McKay, R. J. W ner, W. A. Bailey and T. D. Case h e become assistant county agents i arious parts of the state. Harri s Fisher has a position with the C on Milk Company of Forest

Grove and R. M. Pavey with the William Hanley Company of Burns. V. M. Haywood is employed on a stock ranch in Wyoming and Arthur Ferguson is now manager of a wheat farm in Gilliam county, W. W. Johnson is doing investigational work in irrigation in Harney county.

Statistics recently compiled on the alumni association by one of their number show that there are 1970 graduates in the association. Of this number 1305 are men and 665 are women. Classified according to occupation they are: Agriculturists, 327; engineering (civil, mining, electrical, etc.), 194; professional (doctors, lawyers, etc.), 157; housewives, 280; industrial (those owning their business), 641; teachers, 333; merchants (those owning their business), 31; army (before the present situation), 12; government (forestry, etc.), 54; general (unclassified, or those living at home or doing graduate work), 200; unknown(present address unknown), 66; deceased, 87. Classified as to location they are: Those connected with O. A. C. as instructors or doing graduate work, 59; residents of Corvallis not in the above, 149; graduates living in Portland, 245; others living in Oregon, 673; graduates living in California, 136; in Washington, 122; in Idaho, 43;; in Montana, 20; in Nevada, 16; in New York, 35; in Illinois, 18; in Arizona, 14; in Wisconsin, 12; in Washington, D. C., 11; in Ohio, 10; scattered over other states, 94; in outlying possessions, 25; in foreign countries, 18. Number of states in which graduates are located, 39.

Mrs. Ruby Shearer Brennan.

Mrs. Brennan will hold her third session of Primary Methods School, beginning June 25, and ending July 6—full two weeks immediately preceding the National Education Association. Mrs. Brennan is so well known throughout the state that she needs no further recommendation. She has done institute work in almost every county in the state. A course in her school will certainly lead to a better position at higher salary. If you are planning to attend, write to her today at 460 E. Burnside street, Portland, Oregon.

No Land Like Oregon

Words and Music by C. R. MOORE.

1. Where the rest-less Pa-cif-ic beats ev-er and aye, On the sands and the
2. When the peo-ples of East call this "Set-ting-sun Land," It's be-cause they do

rocks we know well,_____ Where the fir and the ce-dar loom tall on the
not yet sur-mise_____ That in spite of this nick-name, our State is the

hill, And the brooks wend their way thru the dell._____ Where the ring of th
place, Where the sun has just start-ed to rise._____ We've no an-cient tn

No Land Like Oregon. Concluded.

ax and the low-ing of herds, Are the heralds of e - ras to come, That's the
di - tions on i - vy-clad tow'rs, We've no cas - tles made fa-mous in song, But if

land that to us is most wondrous and dear, It's the land that we love to call "Home."——
ev - er you come here you'll find that our land, Is the land where you feel you be - long. ——

con. deliberato.

There is no land like Or-e-gon, The land of the Western sea; In East or West it

is the best, It's where you like to be; Though you wan-der on and on, No

matter where you may roam, Your heart still clings to Oregon, Because it's home, home, home.

THE BATTLE-CRY OF FREEDOM.

1. Yes, we'll ral - ly 'round the flag, boys, we'll ral - ly once a - gain,
2. We are spring-ing to the call of our Broth-ers gone be - fore,

Shout-ing the bat - tle - cry of Free - dom; We will ral - ly from the hill - side, we'll
Shout-ing the bat - tle - cry of Free - dom; And we'll fill the va - cant ranks with a

gath - er from the plain, Shout - ing the bat - tle - cry of Free - dom.
mil - lion free - men more, Shout - ing the bat - tle - cry of Free - dom.

CHORUS.

The Un - ion for - ev - er, Hur-rah! boys, Hurrah! Down with the traitor, Up with the star; While we

ral - ly 'round the flag, boys, Ral - ly once a - gain, Shout-ing the bat - tle - cry of Free - do

OREGON'S SCHOOL

for

OREGON'S TEACHERS

Oregon Normal School
Monmouth, Oregon

PURPOSE:—
The training of teachers for professional work.

FACULTY:—
Every member professionally trained.

DEPARTMENTS:—
For fitting elementary teachers for city and rural schools.

COURSES:—
Professional, Supervisors, Rural, Primary.

ENTRANCE REQUIREMENTS:—
Beginning with September 1, 1917, the minimum requirements for entrance to the Oregon Normal' School shall be the completion of the fourth year of a standard four-year high school, or the equivalent.

GRADUATION:—
Completion of Elementary or Standard Courses leads to State Certificate without examination.

TERMS BEGIN:—
Summer, June 18; Regular, September 10.

INFORMATION:—
For further information write to the Registrar.

THE STAR SPANGLED BANNER.

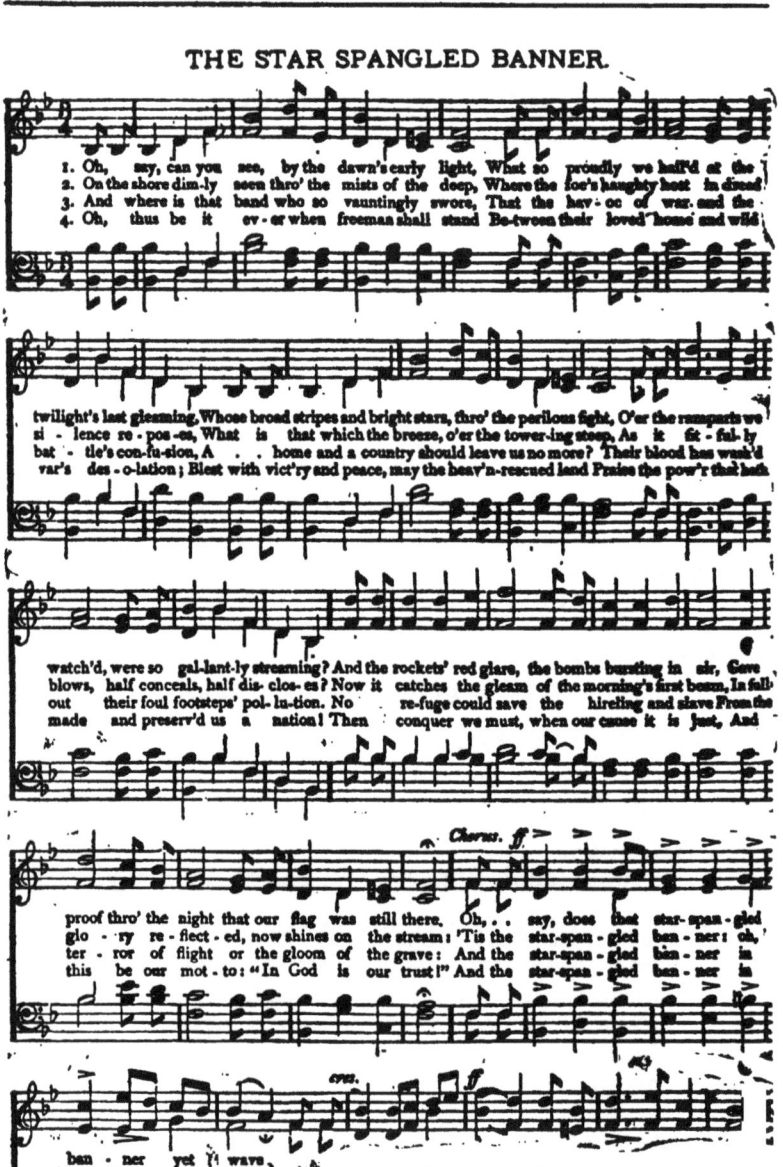

AMERICA THE BEAUTIFUL

* Words by
KATHARINE LEE BATES

Music by
WILL C. MACFARLANE
Municipal Organist, Portland, Maine

Battle Hymn of the Republic.

JULIA WARD HOWE.

1. Mine eyes have seen the glo-ry of the coming of the Lord; He is
2. I have seen Him in the watch-fires of a hundred circling camps; They have
3. He has sounded forth the trumpet that shall never call re-treat; He is
4. In the beau-ty of the lil-ies Christ was born a-cross the sea With a

tramp-ing out the vin-tage where the grapes of wrath are stored; He hath
build-ed Him an al-tar in the ev'-ning dews and damps; I have
sift-ing out the hearts of men be-fore his judgment seat: O, be
glo-ry in His bo-som that trans-fig-ures you and me; As He

loosed the fateful lightning of his terri-ble quick sword: His truth is marching on.
read his righteous sentence by the dim and flaring lamps: His day is marching on.
swift, my soul, to answer Him! be jubi-lant, my feet: Our God is marching on.
died to make men holy, let us die to make men free, While God is marching on.

CHORUS.

Glo-ry, glo-ry, hal-le-lu-jah! Glo-ry, glo-ry, hal-le-lu-jah!

Glo-ry, glo-ry, hal-le-lu-jah! His truth is marching on.

MARCH OF THE MEN OF HARLECH.

THE SOLDIER'S FAREWELL.

(MALE QUARTETTE.)

J. KINKEL.

1. Ah, love, how can I leave thee? The sad thought deep doth
2. No more shall I be - hold thee, Or fo my heart en-
3. I'll think of thee with long - ing, When thoughts with tears come

grieve me; But know what - e'er be - falls me I
fold thee; In war's ar - ray ap - pear - ing, The
throng-ing; And on the field, if ly - ing, I'll

go where hon - or calls me.
foe's stern hosts are near - ing   Fare-well, fare - well   My
breathe thy dear name, dying

own true love! Fare-well, fare - well   My own true love!

HOLY, HOLY, HOLY.

AMERICA.

OREGON LIBRARY LIST

OVER EIGHTY OF

Houghton Mifflin Company's

Books were added during 1917. Among these:

List price.

For the Grades.

131a A Course in Citizenship (Cabot, et al) $1.35
200a Civics for New Americans (Hill and Davis) .... .80
276a Opera Stories from Wagner (Akin) .... .45
348b The Story of a Thousand-Year Pine, etc. (Mills) .... .28
348c Boyhood of a Naturalist (Muir) .... .28
351b The Year Out-of-Doors (Sharp) .... .36
416a The Cave Twins (Perkins) .... .56
463a Little Bird Blue (Finley) .... .45
732a Dramatized Scenes from American History (Stevenson) .. .60

The Industrial Readers.

1106a The Farmer and His Friends .... .50
1106b Diggers in the Earth .... .50
1106c Makers of Many Things .... .50
1106d Travelers and Traveling .... .50
1278a At School in the Promised Land (Antin) .... .28

High School Books.

2245   The Business Letter (Dwyer) .... .85
2541   (Minimum) College Requirements in English. One volume .80
2545   The High School Prize Speaker (Snow) .... .90
2435   A Handbook of Oral Reading (Bassett) 1.60
3165   A History of Mediaeval and Modern Europe (Davis) 1.60

Teachers Books. Reading Circle.

Public School Administraion (Cubberley) 1.75
Types of Teaching (Earhart) 1.25
The Social Emergency (Foster) 1.35
How to Teach the Fundamental Subjects (Kendall and
        Mirick) 1.25
The Hygiene of the School Child (Terman) 1.65

For Sale by The J. K. Gill Company, .
Portland, Oregon

HOUGHTON   MIFFLIN   COMPANY, Boston, New York, Chicago

Tenting on the Old Camp Ground

Walter Kittredge.

1. We're tent-ing to-night on the old camp ground, Give us a song to cheer
2. We've been tent-ing to-night on the old camp ground, Thinking of days gone by,
3. We are tired of war on the old camp ground, Ma-ny are dead and gone,

Our wea-ry hearts, a song of home, And friends we love so dear.
Of the lov'd ones at home that gave us the hand, And the tear that said "good-bye!"
Of the brave and true who've left their homes, —— Others been wound-ed long.

Chorus

Ma-ny are the hearts that are wea-ry to-night, Wish-ing for the war to cease;

Ma-ny are the hearts look-ing for the right, To see the dawn of peace.

Tent-ing to-night, Tent-ing to-night, Tent-ing on the old camp ground.

Summer Session 1917

JUNE 11 to JULY 28

Oregon Agricultural College

COURSES OF INSTRUCTION

1. Courses for Teachers.
2. Courses for College Entrance and College Credit.
3. Boys and Girls Short Courses.
4. Preparation for Teachers Examinations.
5. Vocal and Instrumental Music.

SPECIAL INSTRUCTORS

1. Home Economics—Miss Alice Ravenhill, London, England; Mrs. Mary Schenck Woolman, Boston.
2. Manual Training—Mr. Geo. Fred Buxton, Stout Institute.
3. Additional Specialists—Will be announced in bulletin and subsequent advertisements.

REGULAR COLLEGE FACULTY

Instructors from the regular staff include specialists in Home Economics, Manual Training, Commerce, Agriculture, Art, Biology, Chemistry, Physics, Education, Economics, Political Science, Psychology, etc. In all, about one hundred courses will be offered.

CUT OUT AND MAIL COUPON BELOW

E. D. RESSLER, Director
O. A. C. Summer School,
Corvallis, Oregon.
Please send copy of 1917 Summer School Bulletin to my address.

....

....

....

Flag of the Free.

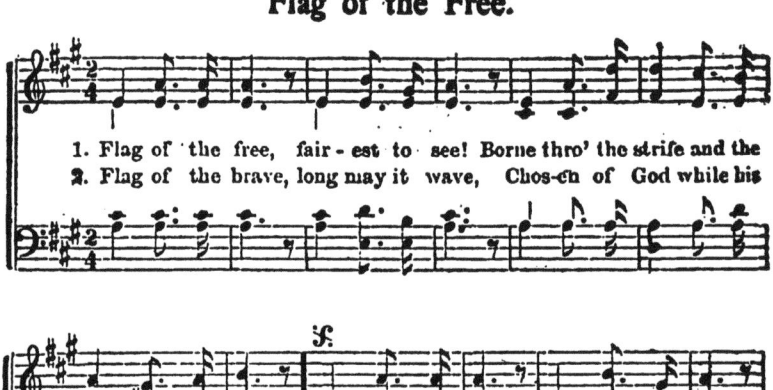

1. Flag of the free, fair-est to see! Borne thro' the strife and the
2. Flag of the brave, long may it wave, Chos-en of God while his

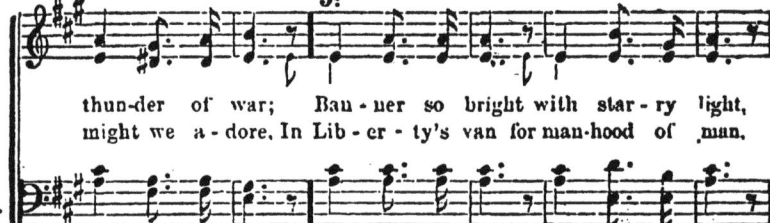

thun-der of war; Ban-ner so bright with star-ry light,
might we a-dore, In Lib-er-ty's van for man-hood of man.

D. S. While thro' the sky loud rings the cry,

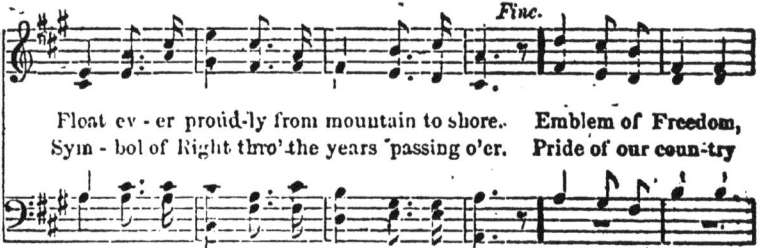

Float ev-er proud-ly from mountain to shore.   Emblem of Freedom,
Sym-bol of Right thro' the years passing o'er.   Pride of our coun-try

Un-ion and lib-er-ty! one ev-er-more!

hope to the slave, Spread thy fair folds but to shield and to save.
hon-ored a-far, Scat-ter each cloud that would darken a star.

BEAUTIFUL BELLS.

Come to the Greenwood.

J. W. STEWART.

1. Come to the greenwood, come, come a - way, Come where the rip - plin
2. Come from the mountain, come from the sea, While sounds of mu - sic
3. Come to the greenwood, come with us now, Where hide the fai - ries

wa - ters play; Where gentle zephyrs danc-ing a-long, There we will blithe
float o'er the lea; While shine the moonbeams bright o'er the dew, We'll sing to measu
'neath the green bough; There thro' the noon-tide we'll gaily stray, While ring the echo

CHORUS.

sing our sweet song. Sing - ing, we're mer-ri - ly sing ing. We'
joy - ous and true.
to our sweet lay. Come, come, come, come, come, come, come, come,

happy, light and free, our hearts are full of glee, Sing - ing, we're cheeri-l₇
Come, come, come, come,

sing - ing, We're hap-py, light and free, happy are we, are we.
come, come, come, come,

Repeat

HEAR DEM BELLS.

1. We goes to church in de ear - ly morn, When de birds am a-sing-in' on de trees,
2. De church am old, and de bench-es worn, De Bible am a-git-tin' hard to read,
3. All day we work in de cott'n and de corn, Wid feet and hands so sore.

Some - times dese cloe's am wer-ry much worn, But we wears dem out at de knees.
But de Spir - it am dare, as sure as you're born, Which is all de com-fort we need;
A pray-in' for Ga - briel to blow his horn, So we don't hab to work an - y more.

At night when de moon am a-shin-in' bright, And de clouds hab pass'd a - way, Dem
We sing and shout wid all our might, To keep a - way de cold; Dem
I hear dem char - iots comin' dis way, And I know dey's comin' for me, So.

bells keep a-ring - in' for de Gos-pel fight, Dat will last till de judg-ment day.
bells keep a-ring - in' out de Gos-pel light, Till de story ob de Lamb is told.
ring dem bells till de judgment day, And de land dat I'se gwine for to see.

CHORUS.

Hear dem bells, don't you hear dem bells? Dey's a - ring - in' out de

glo - ry ob de Lamb;................ Hear dem bells, don't you
Lamb; Dey's ringin', don't you hear dem?

Repeat 40.

hear dem bells? Dey's a - ring - in' out de glo - ry ob de Lamb.

THE CHURCH IN THE WILDWOOD.

Dr. WM. S. PITTS.

1. There's a church in the val - ley by the wild-wood, No love - li - er
2. O come to the church in the wild-wood, To the tree where the

spot in the dale; No spot is so dear to my child - hood,
wild flow - ers bloom; Where the part - ing hymn will be chant - ed,

As the lit - tle brown church in the vale.
We will weep by the side of the tomb.

CHORUS.

O come, come, come; come,

Come to the church in the wild - wood, O come to the church in the dale;
wild-wood, come,

come, come;

No spot is so dear to my child - hood, As the lit - tle brown church in the vale.
child-hood, come,

Men are often capable of greater things than they perform. They are sent into the world with bills of credit and seldom draw to their full extent.

Wisdom is knowing what to do next, skill is knowing how to do it and virtue is doing it.—David Starr Jordan.

Give to a gracious message a host of tongues, but let ill tiding themselves.—Shakespeare.

With God go over the sea; without him not over the thresh Russian Proverb.

LONG LIVE AMERICA

1. No - ble Re - pub - lic! hap - piest of lands! Fore - most of na - tions
2. Should ev - er trai - tor rise in the land, Cursed be his home - stead,
3. To all her heroes jus - tice and fame; To all her foes, a

Co - lum - bia stands; Freedom's proud ban - ner floats in the skies,
with - er'd his hand! Shame be his mem - 'ry, scorn be his lot, —
trai - tor's foul name; Our stripes and stars still proud - ly shall wave,

CHORUS.

Where shouts of lib - er - ty dai - ly a - rise. "U - ni - ted we stand, di
Ex - ile his her - i - tage, his name a blot! "U - ni - ted we stand, di
Em - blem of lib - er - ty, flag of the brave. "U - ni - ted we stand, di

SOLO.

vid - ed we fall; "U - nion for - ev - er, free - dom to all; Throughout the
vid - ed we fall," Granting a home and free - dom to all; Throughout, etc.
vid - ed we fall," Glad - ly we'll die at our country's call; Throughout, etc.

world our mot - to shall be, Long live A - me - ri - ca, home of the f

General State School News

Clackamas County.

Of more than usual interest have been the programs of the local institutes during the year. Meetings were held at Estacada, Milwaukie, Oregon City ,Willamette, Wilsonville, Sandy, and Molalla. The Clackamas County Teachers' Association has held three meetings, one at Milwaukie ,and two at Oregon City. The attendance at these locals has shown that our teachers are loyal to their chosen profession and have the interest of their pupils at heart.

The results of the contests in arithmetic and spelling in Clackamas county this year have been highly gratifying. The work was carried on in grades four to eight inclusive, under the direction of Supt. J. E. Calavan and Supervisor Brenton Vedder. In arithmetic, five tests were sent out to the schools during the year, the teachers giving the tests. The questions were based on the state course of study and the state text. Each class making an average of 80 per cent in the year's work has the privilege of electing one of their number as class representative to take part in the sixth and final contest. These finals were held in conjunction with the spelling tests and each class whose representative made a grade of 95 per cent was given a diploma, over 100 of these being granted.

In spelling, the plan of the state text was followed carefully, and the tests were given by the teachers at stated times, four in all. The words were taken from Lesons 40, 80, 120, and 160, and many teachers gave all the words in these lessons. Pupils who made an average of 98 per cent or better were given diplomas for excellent work. More than 1300 of these diplomas were issued. Eighth grade pupils who averaged 98 per cent were granted exemptions in spelling. The ones earning diplomas for excellent work were eligible to take part in the fifth and final contest,at which the fourth and fifth grades were given 50 words each om Lessons 120 and 160, while the h. seventh, and eighth grades led 100 words each from Lessons

120 and 160. For convenience in conducting the finals the county was divided into twenty-two units or zones, and pupils and teachers gathered at these various central places. At eighteen of these meetings the tests were conducted by the superintendent and supervisor, the remaining four being looked after by teachers appointed by the superintendent. All pupils who made .100 per cent at this test were given championship diplomas, and over 750 pupils handed in perfect papers.

Coos County.

The Coos River consolidated district will probably annex another district at the time of the next annual meeting.

Victor P. Morris, superintendent of the Myrtle Point schools, has resigned his position for next year and will probably continue his post graduate work at the University of Oregon next year.

The Lakeside school district on Tenmile Lake has voted bonds for the purpose of constructing a $5000 school house. There is a prospect that the district will be enlarged by consolidation with one or two other districts.

Coos county boys will do their share toward raising an adequate food supply and reducing the high cost of living this year, but none will be excused from school attendance until individual contracts for employment have been made. It is believed that to turn loose a large number of boys because they say they are willing to work on farms but who have no definite employment secured would demoralize both the schools and the labor situation.

A series of local insti ls
held in Marshfield, North p o-
quille, Bandon, and Myr at
during the week of April : y
4 inclusive, State Supt. e-
ing the principal spea 0
teachers attended th a,
and much good was acco l.
On Saturday, May 5, a d
convention was held l.
Banquets given of
Myrtle Point, le
science depar d

high school to the visiting teachers and school board members were pleasant features of the series of meetings.

Crook County.

A very successful local institute was held at Prineville May 5. Dean Earl Kilpatrick was the principal speaker morning and afternoon.

Most of the children are planting "war" gardens of the hardy varieties—potatoes and onions predominating. Clubs have been organized and are doing effective work. The four ministers in Prineville are acting as general club leaders. At the same time the local parent-teacher association has appointed an adult commission to take charge of the grade work in gardening.

After one year's experience, it can safely be said that the military drill in the Crook county high has been a decided success. Regular school periods are devoted to this three times each week. Every boy in school has his suit and gun. In keeping with this, the military band has advanced so fast in their work that they are able to play creditably at all school functions, as well as those for the town.

On account of the very heavy war enlistment in this county the high school is closing two weeks earlier than at first scheduled so that the boys can take the places of those enlisting. The dearth of laborers seems to demand it. April 11, the public and high school combined in calling a mass meeting of the citizens to discuss our relations to the war situation. On account of the many patriotic and practical addresses the spirit of preparedness was appreciably enhanced.

Columbia County.

Columbia county will produce bigger and better crops—more and better gardens than ever before, the weather permitting. N. C. Maris, of the extension department, is conducting the food drive in Columbia county, assisted by D. C. Howard, county agent, and J. W. Allen, county superintendent.

The schools of Columbia county have taken a commercial course in business and letter writing. Special forms, strictly in accordance with the best business practice, have been adopted and much benefit has been derived. The school children of Columbia county, especially those in the upper grades, know how to write a good business letter.

E. E. Ralston of North Bend, has been elected principal of the Clatskanie school; W. C. Gauntt of Stayton has been elected principal of the Rainier school; Mrs. Bird B. Clarke has been re-elected at Chapman; Kenneth Blakeslee has been elected principal at Deer Island; J. B. Wilkerson will be at the head of the Vernonia school; L. L. Baker will retain his position at St. Helens; and Miss Marguerite Kearns has been elected principal at Goble.

The annual county spelling contest was held in the high school auditorium at St. Helens on the evening of May 5. Three delegates, selected from the seventh and eighth grades of the various schools of the county, were entitled to spell. The schools of the county were well represented and the spelling match was the best ever held in the county. Corinne Hill of the St. Helens school, was the champion speller of Columbia county. Spelling booklets containing two thousand select words, were sent out some time ago to all the schools in the county and the contest was based on the words thus listed.

Certificates of perfect attendance are being issued for the first time this year, to all pupils who have been neither absent nor tardy during the year. The results are quite gratifying. The Mist school is erecting a modern, two-room schoolhouse, and have acquired more ground. When completed, this will be a very nicely equipped and modern building, and much to the credit of the district. District No. 35 will erect a new schoolhouse this summer. Oak Grove and Natal schools will vote on consolidation on June 18. Lost Creek and Delena schools will also vote the same proposition. Goble has best equipped playshed in Colum county. They have all the appar that could be desired. Miss Kete. principal. Columbia county ne sixteen schoolhouses to be buil sixteen districts which are e able to build them. School bo are quite generally requiring t teachers who are not normal ates to attend the sum

Our teachers and pupils are more interested in Palmer writing than ever before. Many Palmer certificates are being obtained.

Douglas County.

J. Percy Wells, former county superintendent of Jackson county, now a member of the emergency force of the food campaign being conducted by the O. A. C., spent the second week of May among our schools.

Geo. M. Murphy, supervisor of District No. 2, has purchased a car for use in his school work. He finds this somewhat more expensive than his former method of travel but much more convenient and satisfactory.

The single session plan has been inaugurated in the Roseburg high school. This is in compliance with the popular demand that boys and girls be given every possible opportunity to do garden work and work for the Red Cross.

Much work has been done during the past month along industrial lines. H. C. Seymour, state club leader, from the O. A. C., passed through the county and stopped off for a brief conference with Supt. Brown and others on the food preparedness campaign.

Many young men of this county are enlisting in the army or navy. Our high schools have already lost heavily from this source. Fifteen or twenty more high school boys belong to the coast artillery and the sanitary corps and are daily expecting a call.

Commencement exercises of the Roseburg high school will be held this year in the assembly hall of the new high school building, on June 1. Dr. Schafer of the U. of O. will deliver the class address. His subject is, "The United States in War." Forty-one students will graduate.

State Supt. Churchill, accompanied by County Supt. Brown, recently spent a day at Wilbur and Sutherlin. The Wilbur high school was standardized as a four-year high school and the Sutherlin public schools were inspected and found to be fully up to the standards established by the state, and were standardized.

N. C. Maris, field worker of the state department, spent the third week of April in the schools of the county, beginning at Drain and stop-

ping at the principal schools along the line as far south as Glendale, where a local teachers' institute was held on Saturday, April 21. He was accompanied by Supt. Brown; also, in the northern end of the county by Supervisor H. M. Cross, and in the southern end of the county by Supervisor Geo. W. Murphy.

Mrs. Inez Miller of Wilbur is arranging a "Home Coming" in honor of former students and graduates of the old Umpqua Academy, one of the oldest educational institutions in the state. Among those who will attend and take part in the program are: Hon. R. A. Booth, Hon. H. L. Benson, Hon. Geo. M. Brown, and Hon. James Hamilton. Many other prominent men and women received their early education here and are looking forward with a great deal of pleasure to this reunion.

An effort is being made to form a consolidation of school districts No. 12, 65, and 68, all near Glide, with good prospects of success. These include property assessed at approximately $1,500,000. A union high school effecting these same districts is already in operation. Similar projects are being agitated at several points in the county among them being one in the Smith River country, one to include two schools on the Calapooia, one at Elkhead, one to unite Wilbur and Winchester, and one to unite seven districts in the vicinity of Elkton.

Jackson County.

Indications seem to point to a large attendance at the N. E. A. in Portland, from this county.

Supervisor E. R. Peterson has informed the county board of education that he will not be an applicant for reappointment at the expiration of his present contract.

State Supt. Churchill ma.   personal inspection of most of th   igh
schools of Jackson county   ing
April. He will be back to '   the
others during the latter part c   lay,
at which time he will also d   r a
number of commencement - '   ses.

Principal Leonard M. F   the
Butte Falls school has '   lled
into service in the offic   rve
corps. For the present   he
located at the Presid' '   ...

cisco, where he will receive training for duty as an officer in the army.

Consolidation will be voted on in June in Gold Hill, Dardanelle, Galls Creek and Rock Point, it being proposed to join these into one district, with Gold Hill as the place for the central school. It is to be hoped that the proposition carries, for conditions there are almost ideal for such a plan.

The following teachers have met all the requirements for a state professional certificate: W. W. Smith, Central Point; Mrs. Harriet Minthorn, Rogue River; Miss Minnie B. Taylor, Eagle Point; Evangeline Poley, Ashland. Many others are expected to qualify during the coming month.

Under the direction of Principal Peter Spencer, the Talent boys and girls have been gathering up old paper, rags, rubber, copper, iron and other junk. The original purpose was to meet the expense of the annual field and track meet. However, the returns far exceeded the necessary funds for that event. One shipment of junk netted the school the sum of $132.65.

Considerable interest is being shown among the schools in industrial work, with special emphasis upon agricultural preparedness. Mr. Maris, of the state department, spent several days in the county in the interests of the work. State Club Leader H. C. Seymour also has been looking after his line of work here. Up to the present time, twenty-five boys and one girl have enrolled in the Jackson County Corn-Acre Army. Many of them are planning to go to Corvallis for the two-weeks' course in June.

In the writing contest, which has extended throughout the year, and was based upon the highest average improvement made by each school in penmanship, closed with the following results: First, 7th grade, Central Point; second, Persist school; third, Oak Grove school, upper grades. Many other schools showed a great deal of progress, and honorable mention is given to the following: Long Mountain, Pinehurst, Central Point, Gold Hill, Talent, Eagle Point, Oak Grove, and the Dewey school.

Jackson county held a number of very successful local institutes during the past winter. Several track and field meets have been held this spring in connection with community gatherings. The first of the season was held at the Westside school, where the honors were won by the Griffin Creek school. The afternoon was devoted to speaking and free-for-all sports. The principal speakers of the day were Mr. Earl Kilpatrick, of the University of Oregon, and Mr. H. C. Seymour, state club leader. The second and one of the largest meets occurred at Eagle Point, where the honors went to the local school. A feature in the afternoon was the famous bird and animal pictures by our state biologist, W. L. Finley. The principal address of the day was made by M. S. Pittman of the Oregon Normal School. The Talent meet entered the largest number of contestants of any in the county so far, the number being more than 200. The indoor baseball outfit, which was offered to the rural school making the highest number of points, was won by Applegate. At Soda Springs the field meet was combined with contests in arithmetic and in spelling. The honors were carried off by the Pilot Rock school. Probably the last event of the kind to be held in the county this season will occur at Applegate on May 24, where all the schools of the Applegate valley, in both Jackson and Josephine counties, will compete for the cup. Applegate has won the cup two years in succession and if it wins this year, it becomes the permanent owner. It is expected, however, that some of the other schools will see that the winner works hard for it.

Linn County.

A parent-teacher institute was held at Shedd recently. F. M. Maxwell of the Halsey school delivered an excellent address on "The Teacher." "Teachers' Training Course for High School," by L. L. Gooding of Harrisburg schools. "Vocatic Training in Our Rural Schools," G. R. Schreiber of the Shedd sch "The Ideal Parent," H. L. Rob, the Tangent school. "Back to Farm Movement," by C. W. B ticher of the Albany schools. Comparison of the Oregon and S Dakota Courses of Study," by F Shedd of Shedd. "Our Opportun by Mrs. G. W. Hawthorne,

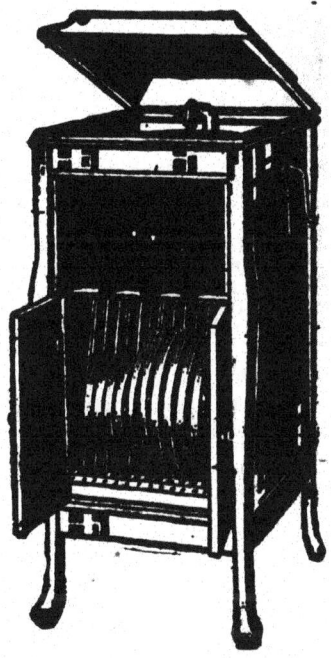 

of the Shedd parent-teacher association. "The School and the Community," by Fred D. Merritt, of the University of Oregon. Besides the several musical selections, seven schools competed in a contest, Tangent received first prize, Plainview second prize.

Lincoln County.

The annual institute for Lincoln county was held at Newport, April 25, 26, and 27. About 85 teachers were present. It was said by everybody to have been a very interesting and successful institute. The instructors were: J. A. Churchill, Salem; M. S. Pittman, Monmouth; Prof. Allen, Corvallis; E. J. Ortman, Newport; John Blough, Toledo; P. L. Coleman, Newport; Chas. H. Jones, Salem. A vote for the place of holding the meeting next year resulted in a majority for Newport.

Morrow County.

Heppner has two industrial clubs, one in the high school and one in the grades. They are doing all they can to help the food supply in Morrow county.

Districts 4, 9, and 11 are contemplating building new school houses. District No. 4 is a new district and expects to have school this fall.

District No. 27 has petitioned for enlargement of their district and if successful will build a modern two-room school with a hall above for social center. Mrs. Jessie Hineline is the teacher and much praise is given her for her work.

Sixteen of our schools have closed. The entertainments given by some of these schools on the last day were considered successful both from a social and financial standpoint. One school, district No. 31, took in $108. This money will go towards buying new seats and other equipment as well as buying books for the library.

In February C. C. Lamb gave Morrow county three days service in the interest of poultry husbandry. Short programs were arranged and at each of the meetings Mr. Lamb took up the various lines of industrial club work and assisted the county school superintendent in explaining this work. Heppner, Lexington, Ione, Boardman and Irrigon were visited.

An appreciative audience attended each meeting.

Boardman is scheduled to become one of the leading districts in Morrow county. They have been granted a deed to six acres of land and have a perpetual water right. This means free water for a life time. They are contemplating the erection of a three-room modern school building and expect to maintain a standard high school. Miss Clara Voyen is the teacher, and has done splendid work. Her school room is one of the surprises, on account of its cheerfulness and homelikeness.

Wallowa County.

"Our youngest child," District No. 87, has just begun a spring term of school in their splendid new building with Ruth Baker as teacher.

Enterprise is to have a new $60,-000 school building this year. The plan is to have the building ready for occupancy by the 1st of September.

A splendid local institute was held at Lostine Saturday, May 5, with about thirty teachers present. J. J. Beatty, of the Lostine schools, was elected president of the association for the coming year, and Miss Lexie Strachan, superintendent of the Joseph schools, was re-elected secretary. It was voted to have the next meeting at Flora early in September. All teachers who can possibly do so should attend as a trip to Flora at this time of years is a delight within itself.

Polk County.

Patriotism is at high tide in Polk county. The flag salute is given every day and flags are floating at all times.

Supt. Fred S. Crowley expects to attend the summer school at the U. of O., leaving Supervisor Floyd D. Moore in charge during his absence.

Fifteen out of the twenty teachers in Dallas schools have membership in the N. E shows the excellent spirit

A large rally was held dale May 11. Teach surrounding schools most of all the excelle served by the lad preciated.

Club work is

Supt. Crowley and Supervisor Moore on their last circuit of the county. Polk county has over 500 boys and girls working earnestly on club projects of various kinds and they expect to make a good showing at the state fair as usual.

The last local institute was held at Falls City April 14, 1917, and was attended by a large number of teachers. Among the instructors were Mrs. M. L. Fulkerson, Mr. Dunton, formerly superintendent of the Falls City schools, and J. B. V. Butler of the Oregon Normal.

The principals club held its last meeting and banquet at the Dallas high school on the evening of May 5. The domestic science class served a delicious banquet ,after which Assistant State Supt. Carleton gave an inspiring address, and Supervisor Floyd D. Moore entertained with several readings.

Union County.

A. C. Hampton, principal of the La Grande high school, has been elected principal of the Eugene high school. Mr. Hampton's many friends regret to see him leave us but feel that his promotion is a deserved and fitting recognition of his worth and work.

L. P. Harrington industrial field worker from the state superintendent's office, visited the county from April 14 to 21, and put in a strenuous week's work, visiting La Grande, Union, Cove, Elgin, Island City and Fruitdale schools, enrolling many club members and doing great work in the Agriculture Preparedness movement. He also spoke at the business men's luncheon at the Foley hotel to a large and appreciative assembly. During his first visit to Union county he made many friends and he will always find the latch string hanging out whenever he comes this way.

A splendid local institute was held at Elgin, Saturday, April 21, The program was as follows: The Teachers' Memorandum, P. E. Christenson, Alicel; History, W. V. Connor, Imbler; Some Helps to Professional Training, Mrs. Grace Fine, Elgin; Chautauqua as an Aid to Teachers, Mrs. W. R. Underwood, Elgin; Military Training in High School, H. E. Dixon, La Grande; The Playground, Ivan D. Wood, Union; Function of

the School Library, Flora M. Koch, La Grande; Industrial Club Work, L. P. Harrington, Salem. Music was furnished by Elgin local people and all pronounced the day one of the best of school gatherings.

Washington County.

The teachers of this county have faithfully worked for standardization this year. About half of the schools have now reached the standard mark. The re-arrangements of windows has been required only in very bad cases of cross light.

The sixth annual spelling contest has closed. It was the largest and most successful contest ever held in this county. More than 2000 pupils were in the contest for four months. About 1500 pupils made an average of 98 per cent during the contest period and have received certificates. One thousand ninety-six wrote on the 100-word tests at Hillsboro April 28. Three hundred and thirty nine made a perfect grade and have received diplomas. In the afternoon 3000 people watched the May Day exercises. Supt. J. A. Churchill crowned the May queen.

The Independent Colleges

Albany College.

Albany College claims to be at the head of the list of Oregon Colleges in patriotism, if its patriotism is measured by the percentage of boys enlisted in the service of their country. Over 70 per cent of the male students of Albany College have enlisted and some of them have already gone into service in the navy in various capacities and one in the aviation corps. Two of the faculty also have signified their willingness to listen to the call of their country.

Albany College celebrated May Day with the regular May queen, folk dances, and other festivities incident to the day. On account of the weather, which was not particularly bad, but threatening, it was decided to hold the exercises in the armory. There was a large enthusiastic crowd present and everything went off with snap and success. It was followed by a cafeteria supper served by the young ladies of the college, with other refreshments.

Albany College this year has been next to the top in the list of colleges represented at the San Francisco Theological Seminary. Four students from Albany College have been attending that Seminary this year, and two of them were graduated the last week in April. They are both of them bright young men, and are entering their chosen profession with great promise and success.

A music team consisting of Miss Clement, pianist, and Mr. South, violinist, conducted a tour of concerts the first week in May in Wasco county, and were everywhere greeted with large houses and great enthusiasm.

Commencement exercises occupy the four days, June 10 to 13. On S day, June 10, will occur the usual B calaureate services; Monday, J e 11, will be devoted to the pres- i it's reception and the senior class d exercise; Tuesday will be marked b ocial events and the annual com- n icement concert of the depart- n nt of music; Wednesday will close t year with the graduation of a f class of nine young people, who h e completed their course with h or and credit to themselves and t ......

Pacific College.

This college which is under the control of the Friends Church (Quakers) has a larger number of students than any other in the state who are forbidden both by church discipline and conscientious convictions from participating in warfare. The men of the student body have, however, taken up strenuous physical training, looking toward the possibility of ambulance work along the line of the Friends Ambulance Units that have done such splendid work for England, and are also doing what they can to aid in the increase of crop production in Oregon. A "First Aid" class has also been formed, and the students are seeking to know every way in which they can serve their country without violating their consciences. The ladies of the college are also co-operating in this work.

May Day was celebrated with all the usual features and some unusual ones, by Pacific College, Saturday, May 5. Miss Norma Harvey, of the senior class, a leader in scholarship as well as in popularity, was May Queen. A May Day breakfast, parade, drills, a big basket picnic dinner, a tennis match with Pacific University and a baseball game with the Chemawa Indian School were features of the day's celebration.

Miss Addie Emlin Wright has been elected to head the department of history and political science at Pacific College for the coming year. She is a graduate of Earlham College, with post-graduate in the University of Wisconsin and Columbia University, and a Master's degree from the latter, and has had eight years of successful experience as a teacher.

Philomath College.

The year which is closing at Philomath College has been one of increased enrollment and advancement in many lines. New equipment has been added to the library and laboratory.

A number of our boys have heard their country's call and have enlisted. Others have heard the call to the land and have gone back to the farm for the season. Prospects are excellent for a good enrollment next year.

By the terms of the will of Sarah A. Baker, deceased, Philomath College will receive a bequest in a short time which will net nearly $30,000. This will be a great encouragement in our work.

The school of music has been crowded this year and plans are being made for increased facilities and teaching forces for another year.

We are planning a celebration of the 50th Commencement Anniversary, June 8 to 13. At that time many alumni and former students will be present for reunion and enjoyment. Any former student seeing this item will confer a favor by writing President Epley at Philomath, giving notice of his intention to be present.

Willamette University.

May Day at Willamette was a success in every way this year, and for the first time in several seasons was unspoiled by rain. Miss Violet Maclean was crowned Violet I, Queen of May, at 1:30 o'clock Saturday afternoon, May 5, and sitting in state watched the winding of the May-pole on the campus. Among the features of the May Day festivities were the Willamette Glee Club concert in the armory Friday evening, a May morning breakfast Saturday morning, the funeral of the freshman green caps, tennis and baseball games, and the Junior Prom Saturday evening. The hearse which carried the coffin filled with green caps was an old motor truck drawn by a horse.

President Carl Gregg Doney is in much demand as a commencement speaker. He will give high school commencement adddesses as follows: Imbler, May 17; Joseph, May 18; Lostine, May 19; Enterprise, May 21; Goldendale, Wash., May 25; Myrtle Creek, May 31; Albany, June 1; Drain, June 6; Jefferson, June 7; and Independence, June 8. He also will give sermons and addresses as follows: Monitor, Association of Congregational Churches in Oregon, May 9; Redmond, sermon in the morning, and address in the afternoon at the Union Army Y. M. C. A. campaign meeting, May 13; Prineville, sermon in the evening, May 13; Prineville, Parent-Teacher Association, May 14; Joseph, sermon, May 20; Goldendale, Wash., sermon, May 27. President Doney also will give the baccalaureate sermon at Willamette University, June 10. From June 24 to 31 he will attend the Epworth League Institute at Lake Chelan, and from July 12 to 15, the Epworth League Institute at Cour d'Alene.

The Rev. Dr. Joshua Stanfield, pastor of the First Methodist Episcopal church of Portland, will give the commencement address at Willamette University, June 13.

Dr. and Mrs. F. W. Chace, of Willamette University School of Music, will conduct a summer school of music beginning June 15 and continuing for six weeks.

Professor Gustav Ebsen, head of the Modern Languages department, will conduct summer school classes this summer in German, French, and Spanish.

The work of the College of Music is being well represented in a series of student recitals being held at the University. Two recitals were given in April, and a number are planned for May. The concert to be given by the advanced pupils May 29 will be held in the First Methodist Episcopal church. Other recitals will be held May 8, May 22, and June 5.

A recital was given by the Public Speaking department in Waller Hall, May 7, which reflected much credit on the work of Professor Helen Miller Senn.

Harry Bowers was chosen president of the Willamette University student body at the recent student election. Other officers elected were Miss Lola Cooley, vice-president; Miss Helen Goltra, secretary; Harold Nichols, treasurer; Donald Matthews, editor, and Lyle Bartholomew, manager of the Willamette Collegian.

The Willamette student body has sent a resolution to President Wilson asking the president to propose national prohibition to congress. "Inasmuch as we have given one out of three of the young men of our student body," the resolution read, "to the army of the United States, and since we desire the condition in which they are placed to be of the cleanest possible, we consider th[illegible] a just request."

H. R. Winslow, of Salem, a [illegible]shman in the School of Law, [illegible]as drowned in Willamette river [illegible]ril 26, when he fell from the [illegible]rry while attempting to prevent the launch from drifting into a pie[illegible] of the Southern Pacific railroad br[illegible]ge.

Miss Margaret Garrison, repre[illegible]ating Willamette University, won [illegible]rst place in the state Intercollegi[illegible] rohibition Association contest held at McMinnville, April 21. Miss Garrison will represent the state in the inter-state contest in Los Angeles soon. Her oration is entitled, "A New Con-struction."

Chief Justice McBride, of Oregon, gave an address to the students at the chapel April 17. He was intro-duced as the Nestor of the supreme court. City Superintendent John N. Todd, of the Salem schools, spoke on "The Difficulty of Getting Start-ed" at the chapel service April 19.

Heldover Material.

Quite a lot of very excellent ma-terial had to be omitted this time be-cause there was not room for it. Much of the omitted material will appear in later numbers.

13	Hazel Hall, Turner	
14	Hilda Muender, Butler	8
15	Bessie McFarland, Prineville	9
16	Emma Howard, Portland	9
17	Lillian Koeller, Peardale, Calif.	9
18	L. W. Riley, McMinnville	9
19	Verna G. Gardner, Amity	9
20	Ruth Chamberlain, Portland	10
21	Mildred N. Tilden, Nehalem	10
22	Annie Wickman, Marshfield	10
23	Laura Johanson, Cline Falls	10
24	Martha Skersies, Monmouth	10
25	Nell Moran, Portland	10
26	Bessie Parsons, Crawfordsville	10
27	Rae Langsworthy, Laurel	10
28	Lillian Loretz, Antone	10
29	W. T. Foster, Portland	10
30	Ruth Elkins, Canby	11
31	Cora E. Devor, Goshen	11
32	Jessie L. Turnidge, Sheridan	11
33	Edwin Woodworth, Molalla	11
34	H. Wayne Keesee, Klamath Falls	11
35	Buena S. Morganson, Scio	11
36	Alma L. Absten, Viento	11
37	Marguerita Andrews, Lostine	11
38	Mrs. M. E. Stockton, Freewater	11
39	G. H. Colvin, Haines	11
40	Sister M. Honorata, Tekoa, Wash.	12
41	Elsie Denson, Meacham	12
42	Mrs. M. E. Norton, Blachly	12
43	Frank J. O'Connor, Crescent City	12
44	Guy E. Dyar, Eugene	12
45	Helen M. Crump, Airlie	12
46	Grace Snook, Alicel	12
47	Arlina A. Pickett, Lewiston, Ida.	12
48	Leona C. Jackson, Newberg	12
49	Nellie Gerding, Astoria	12
50	Mrs. Joyce L. Hays, Cecil	13
51	P. C. Luh, Westerville, Ohio	13
52	Mrs. Helen Garey, Powell Butte	13
53	Anna V. Caldwell, Roseburg	13
54	Roberta Rippey, Portland	13
55	Mrs. Anna Barzee, Edenbower	13
56	Mrs. Daisy Short, Myrtle Point	13
57	Ruth Norton, Philomath	13
58	T. J. Means, The Dalles	13
59	F. H. Robinson, Port Orford	13
60	Mrs. Aurie Jewell, Portland	14
61	Herman Clark, Salem	14
62	Mrs. L. Allard, Woodburn	14
63	Leola Dunham, Cloverdale	14.

153 G. A. Ruring, Vale
154 Mrs. Ada Burch, Berlin
155 Sabra L. Nason, Pendleton
156 B. E. Wick, Armington, Mont.
157 Lucy Kopan, Hood River
158 Martha M. Eddlemon, Flora
159 Myrtle E. Lay, Molalla
160 LaVine Sheridan, Canby
161 Isabella J. McCulloch, Astoria
162 E. B. Hughson, Portland
163 Clara Rutherford, Canby
164 Herbert W. Copeland, Pendleton
165 Sisters of St. Francis, Pendleton
166 Hazel Mulkey, Vale
167 Sisters of St. Mary, Sublimity
168 Belle Conlogne, Wheeler
169 Carrie B. Adams, Elgin
170 Mrs. H. B. Brooks, Corvallis
171 H. T. Vance, Corvallis
172 J. F. Brumbaugh, Corvallis
173 W. S. Caverhill, Caverhill
174 Mrs. Lottie Tomlinson, Wauna
175 Veda E. Rhodes, Sheridan
176 R. J. Davis, Nyssa
177 Caroline Jokisch, Lawen
178 Edith Leep, Halfway
179 Helen Chadbourne, Park Place
180 Josephine Locher, Burns
181 Fay Goble, Lorane
182 Ernini Rathbun, Murphy
183 W. P. Matthews, Algona, Wash.
184 Hannah Mey, Alma, Mich.
185 Eugenia Morse, Portland
186 J. B. Rees, Roseburg
187 Belle B. Whitaker, Myrtle Point
188 Sisters of St. Francis, La Grande
189 T. O. Hutchinson, Divide
190 R. F. Robinson, Alsea
191 Alma Hoppe, Dallas
192 Mabel A. Thomas, Keno
193 Mabel Maginnis, Corvallis
194 Samuel W. Amey, Newberg
195 Mrs. M. W. Bullard, Harriman
196 J. M. Markel, St. Antony, Idaho
197 Minnetta R. Emmel, Milwaukie
198 Mary A. Sias, Portland
199 Bertha M. McCallister, Grants Pass
200 Mrs. Pansy Davidson, Walterville
201 Florence Laufman, Ft. Rock
202 Mrs. W. Jamieson, Brogan
203 Margaret Aldrich, Algoma
204 J. J. Sturgill, Halfway
205 Mrs. Ada Sherman, Elkhead
206 Annie B. Romig, Camas
207 Alice M. Bacon, Grants Pass
208 D. W. Boitnott, Prairie City
209 Esther Krupke, Portland
210 E. Vera Powell, Rex
211 Mary A. Scott, Oregon City
212 Frances Murk, Portland
213 Edith Pechin, Orenco
214 Fred N. Fox, Union
215 Roxie Denny, Canyon City
216 B. H. Conkle, Silverton
217 W. A. Johnston, McCoy
218 Loraine Goehring, McCoy
219 Alta Linderman, Rufus
220 Clara E. Sterns, West Linn
221 Victoria L. Weber, Newberg
222 Bessie E. Knauff, Eddyville
Elva Conklin, Flora
A. C. Morrison, Marshfield
Blodwin Davies, Astoria
Mrs. Gertrude McElfresh, Corvallis
Bertha Stephens, Cottage Grove
Frieda Close, Clatskanie
P. O. Brainard, Nyssa
A. B. Owen, Thomas
Mrs. Nellie G. Tirrill, Prineville
Ethel A. Poland, North Bend
K. E. Wagner, Oak Grove
A. L. Briggs, Watsonville, Calif.
Alvhied Romtvedt, Lakeview
Geo. D. Ingram, Hillsboro
Minerva Thrall, The Dalles

238 Lucy W. Glass, Jeannette, Pa.
239 Beth Perry, Houlton
240 Susie Faith, Missouri Valley, Ia.
241 Lulu B. Montgomery, Ashwood
242 Winnifred Osten, Heppner
243 Carrie Eilertsen, Dairy
244 Fannie M. Fisher, Haines
245 Mrs. C. F. Yergen, Newberg
246 Geo. A. Hoover, McMinnville
247 Thelma Blair, Medford
248 Wm. A. Neumann, The Dalles
249 F. J. Tooze, Oregon City
250 Pearl E. Miller, Tillamook
251 M. B. Estes, Scotts Mills
252 J. H. Dickinson, Paulina
253 Vivian Brinker, Freewater.
254 G. N. Anderson, Falfuririas, Tex.
255 J. W. De Priest, Friend
156 Eva Rocheford, Troy
257 W. Eugene Smith, Pasadena, Cal.
258 Hazel Fawcett, Coquille
259 Pearl Applegate, Salem
260 Ivy Williams, Cove
261 Mrs. Birdeen Myers, Medford
262 Myrtle Witcher, Saginaw
263 Elmetta Bailey, Baker
264 Mrs. F. E. Musick, Grants Pass
265 Laura Harvey, Buell
266 Olive M. Doak, Dayton
267 Grace Shields, Scotts Mills
268 C. Pearl Yoder, Hubbard
269 Kathryn Ward Edmonds, Oretown
270 Agnes Grimsted, Roseburg
271 Father Dommico, Mt. Angel
272 Louise K. Weniger, Salem
273 Nellie Davis, Salem
274 J. B. Wilkerson, St. Helens
275 S. B. Port, Toledo
276 W. C. Fischer, Yaquina
277 Helen N. E. Ogden, Tidewater
278 A. L. Stephens, Taft
279 John Blough, Toledo
280 Della Trapp, Chitwood
281 James H. Bohle, Orton
282 R. P. Goin, Toledo
283 Retta E. Joseph, Philomath
284 Chester H. Coovert, Ona
285 Vernie Ross, Toledo
286 Nellie King, Winant
287 Dr. F. M. Carter, Newport
288 J. S. Goin, Siletz
289 Eliza Bruseth, Elk City
290 John Miller, Newport
291 Mary E. Whitney, Newport
292 Rachel Bradbury, Toledo
293 Mrs. Daisy Halleck, Newport
294 Clara I. Thompson, Waldport
295 Maggie L. Hampton, Toledo
296 Leland Sebring, The Dalles
297 Hazel A. Ellsworth, Monmouth
298 Mrs. Ethel L. Stow, Dallas
299 Cassie A. Bell, Wallowa
300 J. A. Churchill, Salem
301 J. A. Briggs, Greeley, Colo.
302 Theresa Dehler, Albany
303 Delia Ahlsen Yoncalla
304 Imogene Jewell, Portland
305 Daniel Hull, Grants Pass
306 E. L. Coe, North Bend
307 Elizabeth Bogard, Laurel
308 Sister Superior, Beaverton
309 Minnie B. Taylor, Eagle Point
310 Ina Elmund, Hood River
311 H. W. Herron, Portland
312 Hulda Parr, Fossil
313 Mary E. Thompson, Marshfield
314 Edith A. Irish, Marshfield
315 Mrs Florence Aldous, Walton
316 Marion C. Bliven, Salem
317 G. E. Richards, Forest Grove
318 Stella Barklow, Myrtle Point
319 Edna Wells Klamath Falls
320 Mrs. Amy McDaniel, Weston
321 Mrs. R E Reid, Sumpter
322 Mrs. Ethel F. Parent, Gold Hill

No Numbers for July and August.

There will be no issue of the Oregon Teachers Monthly for July and August. Teachers should bear this in mind and not write for the copies for those months. The September number will be issued about August 25. If your address has been changed before that date, please let us know.

Moving Office.

As this number of the Oregon Teachers Monthly goes to press we are moving our whole printing establishment, and that is the reason we are late in getting out the June number.

INDEX OF SONGS.

Science and Mathematics Teachers.

School Science and Mathematics the official professional magazine of the Science and Mathematics division of the Oregon State Teachers' Association, may be subscribed for through the division at the rate of $2. By special arrangement 50 cents of the subscription will go into the treasury of the division. Send money orders or checks to E. L. Keezel, Sec.-Treas., Eugene, Oregon.

Place for Primary School.

Teachers who attend Mrs. F. Shearer Brennan's Primary Methods School should report at the Y. M. C. A. building at Sixth and Taylor streets, Portland, Oregon, on J 25. You had better write to M Brennan at 460 E. Burnside str and tell her you are expecting to tend.

Sea Pictures.

The song, "I Love the Sea" is the first number in the 16-page booklet, "Sea Pictures," recently published by Carrie S. M. Henderson, of Newport, Oregon. The ocean is shown in all its moods, poems of love, beauty, majesty, tragedy, each a gem of literature. The author's own pen contributes the song, also an intoduction which is an epic in prose. From Byron, Poe, Taylor, Longfellow, Tennyson and others of yesterday, to Simpson, Higginson, VanDyke, Ina Coolbrith, Robert Diven, George Sterling, the little book will be an inspiration to lovers of the sea, equally valued for the library, as a beach companion, as as a souvenir of the West. It is worth many times its price of 25 cents.

National Education Association.

C. C. Thomason, who has been handling the publicity for the National Education Association convention from the offices of Superintendent Alderman, head of the N. E. A. committee, has transferred his office to that of Mark Woodruff, secretary of the publicity and conventions bureau of the Chamber of Commerce, in the Oregon building. Mr. Thomason will take over the N. E. A. work of the Chamber beginning at once, as Mr. Woodruff will leave the city June 1 to become the Chicago representative of the Northwest Tourist Association. He has a six months' leave of absence from the Chamber. Mr. Thomason will take over much of the work of the office until the N. E. A. convention is held.

Reprint of Songs.

Most of the songs used in this number of the Oregon Teachers' Monthly are patriotic. If anyone should want additional copies of these songs, we will print them at the rate of $1.25 per hundred, or if 200 are wanted, the price will be $1.75. Orders should be sent to the Oregon Teachers Monthly.

If you attend Mrs. Brennan'- Primary Methods School in Portland beginning June 25, inquire at Y. M. C. A. for the room where the school is held.

Sixteenth Annual Institute Number

Teacher's Name ....

Address ....

At the close of the institute fill out the blank below, cut it out and hand to the secretary of the meeting.

Record of Institute Attendance

Upon my honor as a teacher, I most truthfully affirm that I have attended the County Institute.

held at ....

n .... 19....

or....................hours.

....

Teacher.

FAREWELL TO MY HOME.

Words by CHAS. H. JONES.   *Tune—Aloha.*   Arr. by DR. Z. M. PARVIN.

1. My child-hood home so dear to me, My pret-ty home down by the
2. Mem-o-ries sweet will come to me And bring re-membran-ces of
3. I'll ev-er long and wish for thee, My dear old home down by the

sea! I bid thee now a last fare-well, And go to dist-ant
thee— Of thee, old home down by the sea, Where once I lived so
sea; And there my thoughts will ev-er dwell, Though now I say a

REFRAIN.

lands to dwell. Fare-well old home so dear to me, One
safe and free.
last fare-well.

last fare-well to thee dear home oi mine; My

fond-est mem-o-ries around thee twine, Old home so dear to me.